DICTIONARY *of* VIRGINIA BIOGRAPHY

VOLUME 1
Aaroe–Blanchfield

DICTIONARY *of* VIRGINIA BIOGRAPHY

VOLUME 1
Aaroe–Blanchfield

EDITORS
John T. Kneebone, J. Jefferson Looney,
Brent Tarter, and Sandra Gioia Treadway

ASSISTANT EDITORS
Daphne Gentry and Donald W. Gunter

THE LIBRARY OF VIRGINIA
RICHMOND • 1998

Library of Congress Cataloging-in-Publication Data will be found on the last printed page of this book.

Standard Book Number: ISBN 0-88490-189-0

Library of Virginia, Richmond, Virginia.

Printed in the United States of America.

This book is printed on acid-free paper meeting the requirements of the American Standard for Permanence of Paper for Printed Library Materials.

Jacket illustrations, from back left: Maria Blair (Virginia Historical Society); James Blair, by John Hargrave (Muscarelle Museum of Art, College of William and Mary); Beverly Allen (courtesy of Alice L. Reid and John H. Lee); Edwin Anderson Alderman (Library of Virginia); Turner Ashby (Library of Virginia); William Segar Archer, by George Peter Alexander Healy (Library of Virginia); Hazel Kathleen Doss Barger (*Roanoke Times*); Sir William Berkeley, by Sir Peter Lely (photograph courtesy of Virginia Historical Society); and Janie Porter Barrett (Hampton University Archives).

Jacket design: Sara Daniels Bowersox, *Graphic Designer,* Library of Virginia.

INTRODUCTION

Biography is one of the oldest literary and historical forms. Since ancient times, chroniclers have used the lives of important and interesting people to tell the history of major events, societies, or nations. While modern critics periodically debate the merit and methodology of biographical study and disagree on whether it is more art than science or history, biography has continued to endure as a popular and useful genre. Most people find it easier to relate to the past through the life stories of individuals viewed within the context of their time and place. Historians rely heavily on biography, finding themselves unable to interpret and analyze important episodes and developments without knowing something about the men and women involved in shaping them.

Those who study Virginia's past have long been hampered by a dearth of easily accessible and reliable biographical information. Helpful collective biographies have been published in the past half century, but most of these works have focused on particular professions, organizations, or sections of the state. The only comprehensive work, now long out of print, is Lyon Gardiner Tyler's five-volume *Encyclopedia of Virginia Biography*. Published in 1915 (with a supplementary volume in 1929), the *Encyclopedia* undertook to present the lives of Virginia's most important political, military, business, and social leaders primarily in the seventeenth, eighteenth, and early nineteenth centuries. Reflecting the time in which it was written, the *Encyclopedia*'s pages fail to mention virtually all notable or accomplished Virginia women, Native Americans, African Americans, and, of course, twentieth-century figures. In 1940 the staff of the Virginia Writers' Project began extensive research in the collections of the Virginia State Library (now the Library of Virginia), hoping to produce a more inclusive statewide reference work. This New Deal venture ended before the research could be completed, but the need for a modern biographical series persisted. The new social history pioneered in the 1960s further increased the need for an updated biographical work. Community-based studies illuminated the lives of many Virginians unknown to previous scholars, and researchers showed that so-called "ordinary" people sometimes had an extraordinary impact on larger historical events and trends.

The Library of Virginia established the *Dictionary of Virginia Biography* project to help fill this gap in the historical literature as well as to foster greater awareness of the richness and variety of Virginia's past. The *DVB* also represents one of the Library's most important scholarly contributions to the commemoration of the four-hundredth anniversary of Virginia's founding in 2007.

Criteria for Inclusion

The *Dictionary of Virginia Biography*, or *DVB*, is a multivolume historical reference work intended for teachers, students, librarians, historians, journalists, genealogists, museum professionals, and other researchers who have a need for biographical information about those Virginians who, regardless of place of birth or death, made significant contributions to the history or culture of their locality, state, or nation. From the late sixteenth through the eighteenth centuries, the term *Virginia* has been applied to territory much farther north, south, and west on the North American continent than the state's modern-day borders. For purposes of the *DVB*, Virginia is defined by the state's current geographic boundaries, plus Kentucky prior to statehood in 1792 and West Virginia prior to statehood in 1863. With a few exceptions, no person is included who did not live a significant portion of his or her life in Virginia.

A biographical reference work such as the *DVB* cannot possibly include every interesting or successful person who lived in the past, but it should encompass all those who had an important impact on their communities or who achieved extraordinary recognition from their contemporaries or from posterity. The definition of significance necessarily varies from century to century, from one geographic region to another, and from one field of endeavor to another.

Certain categories of people, most of whom were involved in public life, are included automatically because their participation in events of great consequence has made them frequent subjects of requests for biographical information. The categories of automatic inclusion are: Virginia-born presidents of the United States; governors and lieutenant governors of Virginia (including absentee royal governors); members of the governor's Council during the colonial period and of the Council of State between 1776 and its abolition in 1851; Speakers of the House of Burgesses, the House of Delegates, and the Senate of Virginia; African American and female members of the General Assembly; Virginia members of the Continental Congress, the Confederation Congress, the United States Congress, and the Confederate States Congress; cabinet officers of the United States and the Confederate States governments resident in Virginia when appointed; justices of the United States Supreme Court and judges of the United States appellate and district courts resident in Virginia when appointed; judges of the highest appellate court in Virginia; attorneys general of Virginia; members of all Virginia constitutional conventions from 1776 through 1902 and of the federal constitutional convention of 1787; members of the Virginia Ratification Convention of 1788 and of the Secession Convention of 1861; members of the Virginia State Corporation Commission; general officers from Virginia in the American Revolution, the War of 1812, and the Civil War; winners of major national or international awards, such as Pulitzer and Nobel Prizes; presidents of important national or international organizations; and presidents of the major institutions of higher education in Virginia.

Most of the persons who are included in the *Dictionary of Virginia Biography* do not fall into one of these automatic categories. Rather, they are Virginians whose lives and careers made them exceptional in their communities and professions. Some are associated with unusually important or notorious events, such as Floyd Allen, principal in the 1912 gunfight in the Carroll County courthouse, and the slave Mary Aggie, defendant in a precedent-setting court case. Others, such as frontierswoman Anne Hennis Trotter "Mad Anne" Bailey, are included because they became legendary figures and require a reliable biographical entry that separates fact from fiction.

As a historical reference work, the *Dictionary of Virginia Biography* does not include persons living at the time of publication. Military and naval officers temporarily residing in Virginia also fall outside the selection criteria. As a general rule, persons who moved to Virginia to take employment with the United States government and whose distinction in their professional or political careers was entirely associated with United States government service are not included.

The many native Virginians who have left the state in pursuit of fame, fortune, or professional success pose more complicated questions of inclusion. Many expatriates achieved significant national or international success in fields that they could not pursue at the highest levels in Virginia, such as diplomacy, military service, the theater, or sports. In the process many of them have ceased to be identified in the public eye as Virginians, and their limited contributions to Virginia's history and culture do not justify including entries on them in the *Dictionary of Virginia Biography*. One such person is the singer Pearl Bailey who, though born in Virginia, did not pursue her career in the state and instead became a truly national figure. The lives and careers of many other people became inextricably linked with other places, such as Great Britain (Nancy Langhorne Astor, viscountess Astor), Kentucky (Henry Clay), or Texas (Sam Houston), and they are not included because their lives are not normally regarded as integral parts of Virginia's history and culture.

Some native Virginians who left the state will be included if they continued to identify themselves as Virginians, if their contemporaries regarded them as Virginians, or if they left such convincing evidence of their permanent attachment to Virginia that their lives and their careers elsewhere cannot be separated from the Virginia context. Public administrator Robert Franklin Bane and illustrator Walter Joseph Biggs are examples. The editors have considered each of these cases individually and have tried to keep the focus on the history and culture of Virginia.

Family history research has played an important part in the production of the *Dictionary of Virginia Biography,* although the biographies do not contain a full genealogical record of Virginia's most influential families. Authors have noted family relationships, as needed, to find, verify, and correct dates of birth, death, and marriage; to identify or enumerate parents, children, siblings, and spouses; to evaluate the role of important family members in a subject's life; and to take notice of other family members whose lives a subject strongly influenced.

In the process of conducting research in original records, *DVB* contributors have discovered many new sources of information, verified or corrected many dates, and overturned several old assumptions. An example is the biography of David Bell, who died in December 1799, eleven years after he represented Buckingham County in the ratification convention of 1788. The few references to Bell in secondary sources identify him as an aging brother-in-law of Revolutionary statesman Archibald Cary. During the research on Bell's life, the contributor discovered that Cary's brother-in-law David Bell had actually died in 1770 and that the convention delegate from Buckingham County was that man's second son of the same name. Another instance involves Edward Bennett, one of the great seventeenth-century merchants of England and the Netherlands. He was the head of a large and far-flung trading family, and several of his close relatives rose to economic and political prominence in Virginia. The name Edward Bennett appears on the list of burgesses for the General Assembly session in the spring of 1628. If this burgess had been Edward Bennett the famous merchant, he certainly would have warranted inclusion in the *DVB*. Careful research, however, revealed that the merchant Bennett was residing at that same time in Hamburg, where he was serving as deputy governor of the English merchant community in that German city. Since he could not have been in Jamestown and Hamburg simultaneously, clearly it was one of his namesake kinsmen who served in the General Assembly in 1628. The famous merchant and paterfamilias may never have resided in Virginia at all, or if he did it was for so brief a time as to place him outside the criteria for the *DVB*.

Search for Subjects

The editors realized from the outset that the task of identifying all the Virginians who ought to be included in the *Dictionary of Virginia Biography* was a daunting one. The project's inception in the mid-1980s enabled the *DVB* staff and contributors to benefit from many technological advances. The advent of desktop computers equipped with sophisticated word-processing and data-management programs made an ambitious project such as the *DVB* much more feasible and manageable. Research across four centuries of Virginia history has also been facilitated tremendously in recent years by the nationwide conversion of paper-based library and manuscript catalogs to online, searchable databases. In addition, there has been tremendous growth in the number of collection analyses, finding aids, and indexes to original source material appearing in published, microfilm, and electronic formats. The development of Internet technology has further revolutionized traditional research methodologies, particularly in the area of biography. Only a few keystrokes are now necessary to search for personal names in the Virginia Colonial Records Project, Virginia's Revolutionary and Civil War Pension Records, or the Research Libraries Information Network (RLIN) database of manuscript holdings, to name only a few of the thousands of resources to which researchers can gain access by computer in their libraries, offices, and homes.

The wonders of technology have transformed the way historians practice their craft and enhanced their ability to ferret out new information, but they cannot overcome the many frustrating realities that continue to plague students of Virginia history. It is difficult, and occasionally impossible, to research particular periods and topics comprehensively because of the loss of many of the state's records to war, fire, natural disaster, and neglect. And despite the recent surge of innovative scholarship ranging from early Chesapeake settlement to the twentieth-century political arena, for a myriad of important Virginia subjects too little is still known because the topics have yet to be explored seriously. The editors of the *DVB* have striven since the beginning of the project to surmount these obstacles, to the extent possible, through creative and careful research, understanding that the quality and usefulness of the project would depend in large part on the thoroughness of the quest for potential *DVB* subjects.

The editors began the search for *Dictionary of Virginia Biography* candidates by surveying all existing nineteenth- and twentieth-century reference works, encyclopedias, directories, and historical journals containing biographical information on Virginians. Once this task was completed, they spent several years reading the extensive printed literature in the Library's vast collection relating to Virginia's towns, cities, counties, churches, schools, businesses, professions, industries, social and cultural organizations, political institutions, military units, and reform societies. Much of this material consisted of books and articles written by modern-day historians, but a large proportion of the Library's collection also comprises annual reports, yearbooks, catalogs, promotional brochures, and commemorative publications issued through time by community organizations across the state. These works in particular proved to be gold mines for biographical information about Virginians whose stories have not yet been adequately told elsewhere. For example, a systematic survey of the surviving records of women's voluntary associations and the extant issues of nineteenth- and twentieth-century African American newspapers helped to fill important gaps in the existing historiography. *DVB* staff members traveled to the state's leading public libraries and historical repositories to study their rich printed and manuscript resources and regularly sought the advice of local historians, genealogists, subject specialists, and scholars whose collective expertise extended well beyond the available published sources.

When the initial search for *DVB* candidates concluded, the editorial staff had compiled a list of 18,500 possible subjects. Further research to assess and substantiate each potential subject's significance within the project's selection criteria substantially pared down this list. The final number of biographies to be published in the completed *DVB* series is expected to be about 6,000.

The Biographies

The entries in the *Dictionary of Virginia Biography* appear in alphabetical order. Where two or more subjects share the same name, they appear in chronological order by date of birth. Insofar as possible, persons of the same name are distinguished by their dates, not by the confusing and changing use of appellations such as *Jr.* and *Sr.*, or by Roman numerals, unless the subjects always identified themselves in that way. Subjects holding titles of nobility will appear under the title in its proper alphabetical order. Thus the biography of Governor Norborne Berkeley, baron de Botetourt, will appear under Botetourt with a cross-reference at Norborne Berkeley. When a woman had more than one surname during her lifetime, the biography will be included under the name by which she became famous or under which she is most likely to be looked up, usually but not always the last surname. For example, Frances Culpeper married three times—to Samuel Stephens, Sir William Berkeley, and Philip Ludwell. She is best known to students of Virginia's colonial history as Lady Frances Berkeley, and the biography of Frances Culpeper Stephens Berkeley Ludwell will consequently appear under Frances Berkeley, with a cross-reference under her last married surname, Ludwell.

Some people who spent all or parts of their lives as slaves and left no recoverable surname will be listed under the name they used. For example, Gabriel, who was hanged in October 1800 for organizing an antislavery conspiracy, is identified in some older reference works as Gabriel Prosser, but the surname belonged to his owner and was not applied to him at the time of his sudden fame. His entry will be given under the single name of Gabriel, rather than Gabriel Prosser. By the same line of reasoning the slave named James, who gained his freedom for his meritorious services during the American Revolution and subsequently took the surname Lafayette, will be listed as James Lafayette, the appellation that he chose, and not as James Armistead (Armistead being the surname of his owner), although some subsequent accounts refer to him as James Armistead or James Armistead Lafayette.

The biographies of Native American Virginians will also be listed under the name that each person used during his or her lifetime, when that can be determined accurately. It is often impossible to know precisely which name (or spelling of a name) sixteenth- or seventeenth-century Native Americans preferred, for the evidence documenting their lives is commonly derived from accounts written by English and other European explorers and settlers. When it is not possible to determine the authentic rendering of a Native American name, or when a Native American became widely known by another name in the surviving records, the name that can best be documented will be used. The biography of Powhatan's famous daughter, therefore, will appear under Pocahontas, the name by which she was known to the Jamestown settlers and to history ever since, with cross-references for her given Indian name, Matoaka, and for the English name by which she was known after her marriage, Rebecca Rolfe.

All dates before Parliament's adoption of the Gregorian, or New Style, calendar for Great Britain and its colonies in 1752 are rendered in the *DVB* in the way that modern scholarship treats them. The new year is understood to begin on 1 January rather than on 25 March, which had been the case with the Julian, or Old Style, calendar. Colonial Virginians were accustomed to the two calendar systems and often combined them to avoid confusion. A date could, for example, be rendered as February 1714/5—that is, February 1714 by the Julian calendar, February 1715 by the Gregorian calendar. In the *Dictionary of Virginia Biography*, the date will be given in the modern form according to the Gregorian calendar.

Names of Virginia counties, cities, and towns ordinarily appear without additional identification, unless they are too obscure to be familiar to a general reader. Counties, cities, and towns outside Virginia are normally followed by the name of the colony, state, or nation in which they are found unless there is no possibility of confusion. Spellings of place-names follow the latest edition of *Merriam Webster's Geographical Dictionary* supplemented by Thomas H. Biggs, *Geographic and Cultural Names in Virginia* (1974).

A concise bibliographical source note follows each *DVB* entry. The source notes are not comprehensive lists of all materials used in preparing the biographies. They are intended rather as references to the most important primary and secondary sources for further research on each subject, including citations of obituaries and, if known, the location of at least one formal portrait or other likeness. The bibliographical notes do not contain references to the archival location of original county and municipal government records and record groups because many of these records are readily available elsewhere in other formats, such as microforms, and also because, as the state's archives and the localities' records and archival programs change and expand, many classes of local records are being moved from courthouses to other record centers. Researchers should consult the bibliographies and other archival finding aids at the Library of Virginia to ascertain the location of original records and to learn whether they may also be available elsewhere or in an alternative microform or electronic format.

Entries in the *DVB* vary greatly in length. The length of each entry depends in part on the significance of the subject but also on the complexity of the subject's career, the breadth of source material documenting his or her life, and whether it is possible to find information about the subject handily in other secondary accounts. As the editors of the *Dictionary of American Biography* advised readers when their first volume was published in 1928, a biographical reference work is not a suitable place to supply complete, detailed accounts of the subjects' lives, indulge in elegant prose, or unveil and defend controversial interpretations of historic events. A biographical dictionary should instead provide reliable facts and an informed assessment of the significance of the subjects' lives and careers, and the editors of the *DVB* have endeavored to follow this model.

Many of the entries in the *Dictionary of Virginia Biography* have been prepared by members of the Library's staff, but the editors have also invited distinguished outside experts to contribute biographies based on their own research. Volume one of the *DVB* contains 477 biographies researched and written by 262 contributors from three countries on two continents. The subject who was probably born the earliest is John Berkeley, believed to have been born about 1560; the subject with the most recent birth date is Arthur Robert Ashe, born on 10 July 1943. The subject who probably died the earliest is Gabriel Archer, who perished in or near Jamestown during the starving winter of 1609–1610; the subject who died the latest is Odessa Pittard Bailey, who died on 8 January 1994. Each volume of the *DVB* will have a cutoff date for inclusion, determined well in advance of publication. No person who died after 31 December 1995 is included in volume one. An index to the contents of volume one will be issued separately at the time the volume is published. At the conclusion of the project a comprehensive index to the *DVB* will be published as the final volume.

The *Dictionary of Virginia Biography* project has been from the start a fully cooperative and collaborative effort, relying on the interest, support, and expertise of a worldwide community of archivists, historians, librarians, genealogists, and other researchers who are committed to preserving and interpreting Virginia's past. The project's many strengths flow from the collective talents and energy of this vast assemblage, as well as from the contributions of generations of researchers and writers whose work has provided the critical foundation on which all contemporary historians must rely.

Acknowledgments

The editors of the *Dictionary of Virginia Biography* are deeply grateful to all those associated with the Library of Virginia who have worked long and hard to make this project a reality. They are especially grateful to former State Librarian Donald R. Haynes, who enthusiastically endorsed the idea and secured the Library Board's staunch commitment, and to current Librarian of Virginia Nolan T. Yelich for his unwavering support and for understanding that anything worth doing takes time.

The talented and dedicated historians, editors, archivists, librarians, and other specialists on the Library of Virginia's staff have provided valuable assistance to the project at every stage of the work, and more than a dozen present and former staff members contributed biographies to the first volume. Many colleagues deserve special mention. Jon Kukla, former director of the Library's publications program, successfully transformed the *DVB* project from idea into reality and launched the project on a sound footing. He established an effective organizational structure, allocated fiscal and human resources to the endeavor, sought the advice and won the endorsement of the scholarly community, and appointed the project's first editors, Brent Tarter and Sandra Gioia Treadway. John T. Kneebone became an editor of the project in 1986 and J. Jefferson Looney joined the enterprise in 1996. The *DVB* has also benefited immeasurably from the skill and dedication of assistant editors Daphne Gentry and Donald W. Gunter, and from the tenacity and attention to detail of copy editor Emily J. Salmon. Their editorial contributions, and those of Antoinette G. van Zelm, whose assistance in the year prior to the appearance of this volume was invaluable, have improved every entry and every page. Other Library staff members who have offered indispensable advice, conducted specialized research, checked facts, entered data, read proof, and done whatever else has been necessary to move the project forward are Barbara C. Batson, Sara Daniels Bowersox, Mary F. Brame, Edward D. C. Campbell, Jr., Julie A. Campbell, Mary Carroll Johansen, Gregg D. Kimball, Patricia A. Kloke, Jennifer Davis McDaid, Stacy Gibbons Moore, Sandra Roger Peterkin, W. Donald Rhinesmith, Billilyn Savage, Susan Bracey Sheppard, Cynthia Spindle, and Brenda M. White. The editors are also grateful to numerous research assistants, interns, and volunteers who have devoted time and energy to the *DVB*, particularly John Alley, Mary Pat Buckenmeyer, Carl Childs, Lucy Colebaugh, Glenn Courson, Sarah Shields Driggs, Rick Golumbeski, Kelly Henderson Hayes, Elizabeth Herbener Mansfield, Caroline Mabry, Susan Y. Miller, Emily Ray, Grace Robinson, Carol Rowley, Gina Sauceda, Karen Sisco, Bonnie Spiers, Robert J. Vejnar, and Roger Ward.

The editors, staff, research assistants, and contributors have visited virtually all of the major research libraries containing materials relating to Virginia history as well as many specialized repositories, historical societies, and research centers across Virginia and the South. Without exception, the staffs of these institutions have offered gracious assistance and encouragement for the *Dictionary of Virginia Biography* project, for which the Library of Virginia is deeply grateful. In particular, the *DVB* staff members wish to thank their colleagues in the library, manuscript, and special collections areas of the Colonial Williamsburg Foundation, the College of William and Mary, Duke University, the Library of Congress, the National Archives and Records Administration, Randolph-Macon College, the University of Virginia, the Virginia Baptist Historical Society, the Virginia Historical Society, and Washington and Lee University. Several Virginia public library systems with large and valuable local or regional history collections hosted the editors for extended research visits. The editors deeply appreciate the efforts on the project's behalf made by the talented librarians at the Arlington Public Library, the Fairfax County Public Library, the Handley Library in Winchester, the Jones Memorial Library in Lynchburg, the Lloyd House Library in Alexandria, the Norfolk Public Library, the Richmond Public Library, and the Roanoke City Public Library. Members of local historical societies (most notably in Albemarle, Chesterfield, and Fairfax Counties) also contributed lists of names and assisted the editors in evaluating the accomplishments of potential subjects for inclusion.

It is impossible to thank individually each of the hundreds of researchers who have advised the editors along the way and generously shared their scholarly insights and expertise. Several men and women devoted an extraordinary amount of time to this effort during the critical early work and deserve special mention, among them Fred Anderson, Frederick W. Bell, Warren M. Billings, Charles E. Brownell, J. Frederick Fausz, Christian F. Feest, James J. Holmberg, Barbara J. Howe, Robert K. Krick, Dumas Malone, F. Thornton Miller, Roddy Moore, Nan Netherton, Ross Netherton, Helen C. Rountree, Darrett B. Rutman, John E. Stealey III, Lee A. Wallace, Jr., Vaughan Webb, John Wells, and Richard Guy Wilson.

Sadly, the editors will not have the privilege of working again with several contributors to volume one of the *Dictionary of Virginia Biography,* as they have died since completing their biographical entries. The editors wish to pay tribute to the memories of these departed colleagues and friends: Evelyn Crary Bacon, Martha H. Brown, Alonzo Thomas Dill, Cheryl Yielding Fales, Sarah A. Hickson, Frank L. Klement, Carolyn H. Leatherman, L. Floyd Nock III, Anita H. Rutman, Darrett B. Rutman, Virginia W. Sherman, George J. Stevenson, E. Dolores Swanson, Lee A. Wallace, Jr., Lib Wiley, and Waverly K. Winfree.

Abbreviations and Short Titles Frequently Used

Acts of Assembly	*Acts of the General Assembly of Virginia, Passed at the Session of . . .* (1730–). Title varies over time.
Adm	Admiralty Papers (PRO).
Adventurers of Purse and Person	Virginia M. Meyer and John Frederick Dorman, eds., *Adventurers of Purse and Person, Virginia, 1607–1624/5*, 3d ed. (1987).
AHR	*American Historical Review.*
Annals of Congress	*Debates and Proceedings in the Congress of the United States* (1st–18th Congresses, 1789–1824, published 1834–1856), also known as *Annals of Congress of the United States.*
AO	Exchequer and Audit Department Papers (PRO).
bap.	Baptized.
Billings, *Effingham Papers*	Warren M. Billings, ed., *The Papers of Francis Howard, Baron Howard of Effingham, 1643–1695* (1989).
Bruce, *Rhetoric of Conservatism*	Dickson D. Bruce Jr., *The Rhetoric of Conservatism: The Virginia Convention of 1829–30 and the Conservative Tradition in the South* (1982).
Bruce, *University of Virginia*	Philip Alexander Bruce, *History of the University of Virginia, 1819–1919: The Lengthened Shadow of One Man* (1920–1922).
Bruce, Tyler, and Morton, *History of Virginia*	Philip Alexander Bruce, Lyon Gardiner Tyler, and Richard L. Morton, *History of Virginia* (1924).
BT	Board of Trade Papers (PRO).
BVS	Bureau of Vital Statistics, Commonwealth of Virginia.
BW	Bounty Warrants, 1779–1860, Office of the Governor, RG 3, LVA.
C	Chancery Papers (PRO).
Caldwell, *History of the American Negro*	Arthur B. Caldwell, ed., *History of the American Negro*, vol. 5: *Virginia Edition* (1921).

Calendar of Virginia State Papers	William P. Palmer et al., eds., *Calendar of Virginia State Papers and Other Manuscripts, 1652–1869*. (1875–1893).
Catlin, *Convention of 1829–30*	George Catlin, *The Convention of 1829–30*, VHS, painting reproduced in Hall, *Portraits*, 271–274.
Cavaliers and Pioneers	Nell Marion Nugent, *Cavaliers and Pioneers: Abstracts of Virginia Land Patents and Grants, 1623–1732* (1934–1979).
Census	United States Census Schedules, RG 29, NARA. References are to Lists of Inhabitants unless otherwise indicated.
Charter Book	State Corporation Commission Charter Book, RG 112, LVA.
Circuit Court Ended Cases	United States Circuit Court, Virginia District, Ended Cases, LVA.
CO	Colonial Office Papers (PRO).
Compiled Service Records	Compiled Service Records of Confederate Soldiers Who Served in Organizations from the State of Virginia, 1861–1865, War Department Collection of Confederate Records, RG 109, NARA.
Convention of 1901–1902 Photographs	Virginia Convention of 1901–1902, [*Photographs of Members*], unpublished bound photograph album of convention members [1902], copies at LVA and UVA.
CW	Colonial Williamsburg Foundation Library, Williamsburg.
Debates and Proceedings of 1867–1868 Convention	*Debates and Proceedings of the Constitutional Convention of the State of Virginia* (1867).
Documents of 1867–1868 Convention	*Documents of the Constitutional Convention of the State of Virginia* (1868).
Draper MSS	Lyman C. Draper Papers, State Historical Society of Wisconsin, Madison, Wis.
Duke	Duke University Library, Durham, N.C.
DVB Files	Dictionary of Virginia Biography Editorial Files, LVA.
E	Exchequer Papers (PRO).
Evans, *Confederate Military History*	Clement A. Evans, ed., *Confederate Military History Extended Edition* (1899; repr. 1987–1989).

Executive Journals of Council	Henry R. McIlwaine, Wilmer L. Hall, and Benjamin J. Hillman, eds., *Executive Journals of the Council of Colonial Virginia* (1925–1966).
Foote, *Sketches of Virginia*	William Henry Foote, *Sketches of Virginia, Historical and Biographical* (1850–1856).
Freedmen's Bank Records	Registers of Signatures of Depositors, Freedmen's Savings and Trust Company, RG 101, NARA.
Freedmen's Bureau Records	Records of the Assistant Commissioner for the State of Virginia, 1865–1869, Bureau of Refugees, Freedmen, and Abandoned Lands, RG 105, NARA.
French Biographies	S. Bassett French MS Biographical Sketches, Personal Papers Collection, LVA.
Glass and Glass, *Virginia Democracy*	Robert C. Glass and Carter Glass Jr., eds., *Virginia Democracy* (1937).
Hall, *Portraits*	Virginius Cornick Hall Jr., *Portraits in the Collection of the Virginia Historical Society: A Catalogue* (1981).
Hampton	Hampton University Library, Hampton.
HCA	High Court of Admiralty Papers (PRO).
Hening, *Statutes*	William Waller Hening, ed., *The Statutes at Large: Being a Collection of All the Laws of Virginia, from the First Session of the Legislature, in the Year 1619 . . .* (1809–1823).
Hummel and Smith, *Portraits and Statuary*	Ray O. Hummel Jr. and Katherine M. Smith, *Portraits and Statuary of Virginians Owned by The Virginia State Library, The Medical College of Virginia, The Virginia Museum of Fine Arts, and Other State Agencies: An Illustrated Catalog* (1977).
Jackson, *Free Negro Labor*	Luther Porter Jackson, *Free Negro Labor and Property Holding in Virginia, 1830–1860* (1942).
Jackson, *Negro Office-Holders*	Luther Porter Jackson, *Negro Office-Holders in Virginia, 1865–1895* (1945).
JAH	*Journal of American History*.
Jamerson, *Speakers and Clerks, 1776–1996*	Bruce F. Jamerson, ed., *Speakers and Clerks of the Virginia House of Delegates, 1776–1996* (1996).

Jefferson Papers	Julian P. Boyd et al., eds., *The Papers of Thomas Jefferson* (1950–).
JHD	Virginia General Assembly, House of Delegates, *Journal of the House of Delegates of the Commonwealth of Virginia* (1776–).
JNH	*Journal of Negro History*.
Journal of 1829–1830 Convention	*Journal, Acts, and Proceedings of a General Convention of the Commonwealth of Virginia* (1829).
Journal of 1850 Convention	*Journal, Acts, and Proceedings of a General Convention of the State of Virginia* (1850).
Journal of 1867–1868 Convention	*Journal of the Constitutional Convention of the State of Virginia* [1868].
Journal of 1901–1902 Convention	*Journal of the Constitutional Convention of Virginia* (1901).
Journals of Council of State	Henry R. McIlwaine et al., eds., *Journals of the Council of State of the State of Virginia, 1776–1791* (1931–1982).
Journals of House of Burgesses	Henry R. McIlwaine and John Pendleton Kennedy, eds., *Journals of the House of Burgesses of Virginia, 1619–1776* (1905–1915).
JSH	*Journal of Southern History*.
JSV	Virginia General Assembly, Senate, *Journal of the Senate of Virginia* (1776–).
Kaminski, *Ratification*	John P. Kaminski et al., eds., *The Documentary History of the Ratification of the Constitution: Ratification of the Constitution by the States, Virginia*, vols. 8–10 (1988–1993).
Kingsbury, *Virginia Company*	Susan Myra Kingsbury, ed., *The Records of the Virginia Company of London* (1906–1935).
Kukla, *Speakers and Clerks, 1643–1776*	Jon Kukla, *Speakers and Clerks of the Virginia House of Burgesses, 1643–1776* (1981).
LC	Library of Congress, Washington, D.C.
Legislative Journals of Council	Henry R. McIlwaine, ed., *Legislative Journals of the Council of Colonial Virginia* (1918–1919; 2d ed., 1979).
LOMC	Land Office Military Certificates, 1782–1876, Virginia Land Office, RG 4, LVA.

LVA	The Library of Virginia, Richmond.
Madison, *Congressional Series*	William T. Hutchinson et al., eds., *The Papers of James Madison* (1962–1991).
Madison, *Presidential Series*	Robert A. Rutland et al., eds., *The Papers of James Madison: Presidential Series* (1984–).
Madison, *Secretary of State Series*	Robert J. Brugger et al., eds., *The Papers of James Madison: Secretary of State Series* (1986–).
Manarin, *Senate Officers*	Louis H. Manarin, *Officers of the Senate of Virginia, 1776–1996* (1997).
Marshall Papers	Herbert A. Johnson et al., eds., *The Papers of John Marshall* (1974–).
MCV	Medical College of Virginia Library, Virginia Commonwealth University, Richmond.
Meade, *Old Churches*	William Meade, *Old Churches, Ministers, and Families of Virginia* (1861).
Military Service Records	Military Service Records, World War I History Commission Records, RG 66, LVA.
Minutes of Council and General Court	Henry R. McIlwaine, ed., *Minutes of the Council and General Court of Colonial Virginia*, 2d ed. (1979).
MOC	Museum of the Confederacy, Richmond.
MVHR	*Mississippi Valley Historical Review*.
NARA	National Archives and Records Administration, Washington, D.C.
NCAB	*National Cyclopædia of American Biography* (1892–1984).
OR	United States War Department, *The War of the Rebellion: A Compilation of the Official Records of the Union and Confederate Armies* (1880–1901).
Pecquet du Bellet, *Virginia Families*	Louise Pecquet du Bellet, *Some Prominent Virginia Families* (1907; repr. 1976).
por.	Portrait, for location of an original or a source reproducing a photograph, painting, engraving, drawing, or sculpture of the subject.

Presidential Pardons	Virginia Case Files for United States Pardons, 1865–1867, United States Office of the Adjutant General, RG 94, NARA.
PRO	Public Record Office, London.
Proceedings and Debates of 1829–1830 Convention	*Proceedings and Debates of the Virginia State Convention of 1829–1830* (1830).
Proceedings and Debates of 1901–1902 Convention	*Report of the Proceedings and Debates of the Constitutional Convention, State of Virginia* (1906).
Quarles, *Worthy Lives*	Garland R. Quarles, *Some Worthy Lives: Mini-Biographies, Winchester and Frederick County* (1988).
Reese, *Journals and Papers of 1861 Convention*	George H. Reese, ed., *Journals and Papers of the Virginia State Convention of 1861* (1966).
Reese and Gaines, *Proceedings of 1861 Convention*	George H. Reese and William H. Gaines Jr., eds., *Proceedings of the Virginia State Convention of 1861* (1965).
Resolutions of 1901–1902 Convention	[*Resolutions of the Constitutional Convention of 1901–1902*] [1901–1902].
Revolutionary Virginia	William J. Van Schreeven, Robert L. Scribner, and Brent Tarter, eds., *Revolutionary Virginia, the Road to Independence: A Documentary Record* (1973–1983).
RG	Record Group.
Slemp and Preston, *Addresses*	C. Bascom Slemp and Thomas W. Preston, eds., *Addresses of Famous Southwest Virginians* [1939].
Smith, *Complete Works*	Philip L. Barbour, ed., *The Complete Works of Captain John Smith (1580–1631)* (1986).
Smith, *Letters of Delegates*	Paul H. Smith et al., eds., *Letters of Delegates to Congress, 1774–1789* (1976–).
Southern Claims Commission	Records of the Commissioners of Claims (Southern Claims Commission), 1871–1880, Department of the Treasury, RG 56, NARA.
SP	State Paper Office (PRO).
Sprague, *American Pulpit*	William B. Sprague, *Annals of the American Pulpit* (1857–1869).

Stoner, *Seed-Bed*	Robert Douthat Stoner, *A Seed-Bed of the Republic: A Study of the Pioneers in the Upper (Southern) Valley of Virginia* (1962).
T	Treasury Office Papers (PRO).
Tyler, *Encyclopedia*	Lyon Gardiner Tyler, ed., *Encyclopedia of Virginia Biography* (1915).
Tyler, *Men of Mark*	Lyon Gardiner Tyler, ed., *Men of Mark in Virginia* (1906–1909); 2d ser. (1936; anonymously edited). References are to original series unless otherwise indicated.
UNC	Southern Historical Collection, Library, University of North Carolina at Chapel Hill, N.C.
United States Reports	*Cases Argued and Decided in the Supreme Court of the United States* (title varies; first ninety volumes originally issued in seven distinct editions of separately numbered volumes with *United States Reports* volume numbers retroactively assigned; original volume numbers here given parenthetically; citations are to original pagination).
UVA	University of Virginia Library, Charlottesville.
VBHS	Virginia Baptist Historical Society, University of Richmond, Richmond.
VCU	Virginia Commonwealth University Library, Richmond.
VHS	Virginia Historical Society, Richmond.
Virginia Reports	*Cases Decided in the Supreme Court of Appeals of Virginia* (title varies; issued consecutively for the highest appellate court of Virginia under its variant names of Court of Appeals of Virginia [to 1851], Supreme Court of Appeals of Virginia [1852–1971], and the Supreme Court of Virginia [since 1971]; first seventy-four volumes originally issued in ten distinct editions of separately numbered volumes with *Virginia Reports* volume numbers retroactively assigned; original volume numbers here given parenthetically; citations are to original pagination).
Virginia State Bar Association Proceedings	*Proceedings of the Annual Meeting of the Virginia State Bar Association*; variant titles include *Report of the Annual Meeting*.
VM	Valentine Museum, Richmond.

VMHB	*Virginia Magazine of History and Biography.*
VMI	Virginia Military Institute Library, Lexington.
VPI	Virginia Polytechnic Institute and State University Library, Blacksburg.
W&L	Washington and Lee University Library, Lexington.
W&M	College of William and Mary Library, Williamsburg.
Washington, *Colonial Series*	William W. Abbot et al., eds., *The Papers of George Washington: Colonial Series* (1983–1995).
Washington, *Confederation Series*	William W. Abbot, Dorothy Twohig, et al., eds., *The Papers of George Washington: Confederation Series* (1992–1997).
Washington, *Presidential Series*	Dorothy Twohig, William W. Abbot, et al., eds., *The Papers of George Washington: Presidential Series* (1987–).
Washington, *Revolutionary War Series*	Philander D. Chase, William W. Abbot, et al., eds., *The Papers of George Washington: Revolutionary War Series* (1985–).
Wells and Dalton, *Virginia Architects*	John E. Wells and Robert E. Dalton, *The Virginia Architects, 1835–1955: A Biographical Dictionary* (1997).
Winfree, *Laws of Virginia*	Waverly K. Winfree, comp., *The Laws of Virginia: Being a Supplement to Hening's The Statutes at Large, 1700–1750* (1971).
WMQ	*William and Mary Quarterly.*
WPA Biographies	Biographical Files, Virginia Writers' Project, Work Projects Administration Papers, LVA.
WVU	West Virginia University Library, Morgantown, W.Va.

DICTIONARY *of* VIRGINIA BIOGRAPHY

VOLUME 1
Aaroe–Blanchfield

AAROE, Alden Petersen (5 May 1918–7 July 1993), radio broadcaster, was born in Washington, D.C., the only child of George Aaroe, an army officer, and Anna Petersen Aaroe, a teacher. When he was very young his parents separated, and he went to live with his maternal grandparents in Oxford, Warren County, New Jersey. His mother, who taught school in Summit, a New Jersey suburb of New York City, traveled to Oxford on weekends to be with her son. At six years of age Aaroe went to live with his mother and was enrolled in the public schools. As he grew up he often returned to his grandparents' farm on weekends and during summers.

In 1936 Aaroe entered the University of Virginia, where he majored in economics and minored in dramatics but did not graduate. During his fourth year he worked as a part-time announcer for Charlottesville radio station WCHV, and after he left school he became its full-time program director. On 5 February 1942 he married Edna Louise Kirby, and they had one daughter. Three days before his wedding he enlisted in the aviation cadet program of the United States Army Air Corps and in January 1943 was commissioned a second lieutenant. While stationed at U.S. bases in Cairo, Egypt, and Tehran, Iran, he logged more than two thousand hours as a pilot of transport planes. At the end of the war he held the rank of captain.

On 1 February 1946 Aaroe joined the staff of radio station WRVA in Richmond, where he worked for the remainder of his career. His early assignments included serving as master of ceremonies for the station's popular Saturday night music program, the *Old Dominion Barn Dance*, and broadcasting a downtown morning segment called *The Street Man*, sponsored by the Strietmann Biscuit Company, in which he conducted on-the-street interviews and passed out orchids. In 1956 he launched the *Alden Aaroe Morning Program*. His informal, conversational style soon attracted a large audience, and the show became one of the longest-running radio programs of its kind in the country. Because the station broadcast with a very powerful signal, Aaroe's program gained a loyal following throughout much of central and eastern Virginia and in parts of North Carolina and West Virginia as well. In 1967 he became program director of WRVA, and the following year he was named the station's vice president.

For thirty-seven years Aaroe's morning show was the centerpiece of WRVA's programming, and trade magazines ranked him as one of the most popular morning-show announcers in the business. His enduring appeal derived from a relaxed and personal broadcast style and his deep, well-modulated voice. He mixed informal, neighborly discussions of gardening and fishing with news, weather, and agricultural reports, reaching across social and demographic boundaries. For many years he sprinkled his commentary with anecdotes about suburban life at his Henrico County house, located on what he called "Mad Mountain." Aaroe gave time on the air and in person to a number of service organizations and received numerous honors, including election to the Virginia Communications Hall of Fame in 1989 and an honorary doctor of humanities degree from the University of Richmond in 1990.

In November 1985 Tim Timberlake joined Aaroe's popular morning show in order to take some of the burden of a one-man show off of the sixty-seven-year-old broadcaster and thereby extend Aaroe's career. In 1986 the station staged an anniversary commemoration of Aaroe's forty years with WRVA, and on his seventy-fifth birthday in May 1993 the station's Shoe Fund for the Salvation Army was named in his honor. Aaroe had been a founder of the fund, which during its annual Christmas campaigns had raised more than $3.5 million to provide shoes for needy children.

After his first marriage ended in divorce, Aaroe married Frances Perry on 29 August 1975 and moved to Hanover County. He underwent surgery for lung cancer in the winter of 1992, but it recurred in the spring of 1993, and on 23 June he announced his retirement from broadcasting. Alden Petersen Aaroe died at his residence in Hanover County on 7 July 1993 and was buried in Hollywood Cemetery in Richmond.

Steve Clark, *Alden Aaroe: Voice of the Morning* (1994); family information verified by Frances Perry Aaroe and daughter, Anna Louise Aaroe Schaberg; obituary file, WRVA News, Richmond; biography files, Richmond Public Library; feature articles in *Richmond Magazine*, Nov. 1974, 26–28, 52, and *Richmond Style Weekly*, 25 Feb. 1986, 22–25; obituary in *Richmond Times-Dispatch*, 8 July 1993 (por.).

DONALD W. GUNTER

ABADY, Nina Babette Friedman (16 May 1924–5 November 1993), civic leader, was born in Steubenville, Ohio, the daughter of Sydney Loth Friedman, a clothier, and Josephine Schuster Friedman, and grew up in Macon, Georgia, and Selma, Alabama. She received a B.A. from Goucher College in Baltimore in 1944 and pursued graduate studies in social work that autumn at the University of Pittsburgh and from 1947 to 1948 at Richmond Professional Institute (subsequently combined with the Medical College of Virginia to form Virginia Commonwealth University). In Selma on 12 September 1949 she married Abraham Aaron Abady, a businessman, with whom she had two daughters and a son before his death on 11 July 1965. Early in the 1960s Abady studied law at the University of Richmond. She was an adjunct instructor in sociology at the Richmond Professional Institute from 1963 to 1966 and also at the Medical College of Virginia from 1965 to 1966. From 1966 to 1971 she served as an assistant professor of sociology at Virginia Union University, a predominantly black liberal-arts college in Richmond. In 1973 the university's administration asked her to head the school's fund drive, and between then and 1977 Abady raised $7.5 million, an infusion of money that was crucial to its survival and that helped Abady achieve her broader goal of making the city as a whole aware of Virginia Union's importance.

Abady continued her successful career as a fund-raiser and promoter with service from 1977 to 1980 as development director for Virginia State College, in Ettrick near Petersburg, a historically black, state-supported institution that changed its name to Virginia State University in 1979. During her tenure she raised $1 million in private donations for the school. In 1980 Abady applied her fund-raising talent to the task of providing a permanent home for Richmond's performing arts. Despite discouragement from consultants, she managed to raise $8 million to transform Loew's Theater at Sixth and Grace Streets into the Virginia Center for the Performing Arts, later renamed the Carpenter Center for the Performing Arts. During three years as director of development, she saw the building, an atmospheric theater designed by John Eberson, restored to the Moorish-Rococo glory it enjoyed at its opening in 1928. That challenge met, she served as executive director of the Virginia Opera Association from 1983 until 1985. Abady defined her fund-raising activities in terms of accountability. She believed in what she worked for and had a strong business sense. In one interview Abady said of investors that "I've got to look them in the eye and be damn sure I can say what happens to the money. . . . They have to believe the money is going to be well shepherded."

In 1985 Abady helped found Downtown Presents, a nonprofit organization designed to bring events and people to downtown Richmond. During service as its executive director that continued until her death eight years later, she made herself "synonymous with downtown Richmond," as one memorialist put it. Abady estimated in 1987 that her organization sponsored nearly five events per week in the city, including New Year's Eve celebrations in Festival Park; Hoop It Up, a citywide basketball tournament; and the Big Gig, a series of summer concerts. Two years earlier she had observed that growing up as a white Jewish girl in the segregated South had shaped her life and its work. "I care about creating the opportunity for diverse people to get together in a non-confrontational situation," she said. "To rub shoulders. To shake hands." She believed that Virginia's capital city was the ideal place for this to happen and dedicated her formidable talents to bringing events and people together.

Abady served on the state's Equal Employment Opportunity Committee and the boards of directors of several Richmond concerns, including Emergency Shelter Inc., the Richmond Urban League, the Richmond Children's Museum, Theatre IV, and Virginia Commonwealth University. She was named "Outstanding Woman of the Year in the Arts" by the Young Women's Christian Association in 1983 and received an honorary doctorate from Virginia Union University in 1989.

Nina Friedman Abady died of cardiac arrest in her Henrico County home on 5 November 1993. A member of Congregation Beth Ahabah, she was buried in Hebrew Cemetery. Downtown Presents survived her, the Virginia Association of Fundraising Executives named its development recognition award after her, and on 16 May 1995 Festival Park, located in downtown Richmond between the Sixth Street Marketplace and the Coliseum, was renamed Nina F. Abady Festival Park in her honor. Early in 1998 her daughter Josephine Abady released *To Catch a Tiger*, a thirty-minute film crafted to spread her mother's message of racial tolerance among young people.

Husband's obituary and articles on Abady and renaming of park in *Richmond Times-Dispatch*, 12 July 1965, 30 Nov. 1980, 6 Jan., 7 Sept. 1985, and 17 May 1995; film featured in *Richmond Style Weekly*, 3 Mar. 1998; obituaries in *Richmond Times-Dispatch*, 6 Nov. 1993, and *Richmond Style Weekly*, 9 Nov. 1993 (por.); amateur videotape of memorial service, 7 Nov. 1993, Virginia Union University Archives.

JENNIFER DAVIS MCDAID

ABBOT, Scaisbrooke Langhorne (16 January 1908–29 July 1985), painter, was born in Lynchburg and lived his entire professional life there. He was the youngest of four sons and fourth of six children of William Richardson Abbot, a Bedford attorney, and Lucy Lewis Abbot. From childhood Brooke Abbot, as he preferred to be known, wanted to be an artist and to work in Lynchburg. His first instructors in drawing were the noted Lynchburg art teachers, Sallie Lee Hunt Mahood and her daughter Carrie Mahood. Abbot's grandmother Elizabeth Langhorne Lewis and his aunt Elizabeth Lewis Otey encouraged him in his ambition and enabled him to tour the major museums and galleries in Europe. After attending the Virginia Episcopal School in Lynchburg, Abbot went to Paris when he was fifteen to study art under André Victor Edouard Devambez. At age seventeen Abbot entered the Pennsylvania Academy of Fine Arts in Philadelphia.

Abbot returned to Lynchburg and worked there as an artist until World War II. He served in the United States Army from 1942 to 1945, originally with the 89th Field Artillery. Wounded on Guadalcanal, he was sent to New Zealand for hospitalization. He spent part of the war as a medical illustrator for the 39th General Hospital. When he returned to Lynchburg, Abbot resumed his artistic career, and he became the most popular portrait painter in the area. He went elsewhere when commissions required but continued to live and work in Lynchburg, where he specialized in painting portraits of local citizens. His likenesses of children were especially sought after. He worked in a contemporary, Postimpressionist style that employed bright colors to produce paintings radiating great warmth. For his own pleasure he frequently sketched relatives and friends and painted floral still lifes. His works included murals, perhaps the most notable being one for the old post office in Lynchburg, and he painted theater scenery for the local little theater, in which he sometimes acted. A gregarious man, he was known also for his wit and humor.

Many of Abbot's paintings are privately owned, and some are unsigned. Others belong to the Virginia Historical Society, the American Philosophical Society, the University of Virginia, Washington and Lee University, and the Albemarle County courthouse, for which he did a notable set of portraits of Thomas Jefferson, James Madison, and James Monroe. Abbot painted on private commission and never entered any competitions or mounted any special exhibitions, so that he was not widely known outside of the Virginia Piedmont or the large circle of his family and friends. Although he was demanding of his subjects during the many hours of posing required for portraits, he often developed a special rapport with children, whom he permitted to call him "Brookie." Some of his young subjects returned to visit so often that Abbot, a bachelor who enjoyed the company of the youngsters, eventually established

Thursday afternoon "at homes" for children. Brooke Abbot painted until the day that he died of cancer on 29 July 1985. He was buried in Saint Stephen's Episcopal Church Cemetery in Forest, Bedford County.

Biographical and family history information in archives of Lynchburg Historical Foundation, corroborated by sister Catherine Abbot Johnson and cousin Elizabeth O. Watson; feature article in *Lynchburg News*, 26 Sept. 1982 (por.); *Magazine of Albemarle County History* 12 (1951–1952): 46; two self-portraits in possession of Catherine Abbot Johnson, Lynchburg; obituaries in *Lynchburg News* and *Lynchburg Daily Advance*, both 31 July 1985.

R. LEWIS WRIGHT

ABBOTT, Charles Cortez (30 October 1906–8 May 1986), educator, was born in Lawrence, Kansas, the only son and one of two children of Wilbur Cortez Abbott, a professor of history at the University of Kansas, and Margaret Ellen Smith Abbott. Abbott grew up in New England, where his father taught at Yale from 1908 to 1920 and at Harvard from 1920 to 1937. Abbott attended Harvard and earned an A.B. in 1928, an M.A. in 1930, and a Ph.D. in business administration in 1933. On 31 August 1934 he married Louise Slocum, a Phi Beta Kappa, cum laude graduate of Vassar. Between 1936 and 1947 they had three sons and two daughters.

Abbott taught at Harvard from 1932 to 1954, rising by 1952 to become Edmund Cogswell Converse Professor of Banking and Finance. His publications, in addition to numerous articles and reviews, included *The Rise of the Business Corporation* (1936), *The New York Bond Market, 1920–1930* (1937), *Financing Business during the Transition* (1946), *Managing the Federal Debt* (1946), and *The Federal Debt: Structure and Impact* (1953). During World War II he worked for the War Shipping Administration and taught at the Naval Midshipmen Officers Training School at Harvard.

In 1954 President Colgate Whitehead Darden Jr. of the University of Virginia lured Abbott from Harvard to become the first dean of what later became known as the Colgate Darden Graduate School of Business Administration. Abbott oversaw the development of the school from its inception with only thirty-three graduates in its first class of 1955 until by 1972 it had become the outstanding graduate school of business in the South, with 275 candidates for graduation. Abbott attracted distinguished academicians as well as business executives to the faculty. He also created outreach and service agencies, such as the Executive Program, the Tayloe Murphy Institute, the Center for the Study of Applied Ethics, and the affiliated Institute of Chartered Financial Analysts.

Laconic in speech, Socratic in teaching style, and wry in wit, Abbott was a popular but demanding professor as well as a skilled administrator. Accustomed to the orderly style at Harvard, he once complained that the evolving policies at the University of Virginia were too much like the British constitution in that "they were not written down anywhere." He frequently made his own policies, putting the needs of the students above all other considerations. While serving as dean, he edited and published *Basic Research in Finance: Needs and Prospects* (1966). Although a New Englander and a Republican, Abbott adapted well to life in Virginia. At the time of his retirement in the spring of 1972 he received many accolades, but one, from a member of the board of directors of the Chesapeake Corporation, was especially gratifying: "He has all the dignity and charm of a true Virginia Gentleman—no one would ever know he wasn't born in Virginia." During his retirement he lived in Pomfret Center, Connecticut, where he had owned and managed a dairy farm for many years. Charles Cortez Abbott died there on 8 May 1986 following a stroke and was buried in Pomfret Center.

Biographies in *University of Virginia Alumni News* 42 (Apr. 1954): 7–8 and 60 (May–June 1972): 11–13; family history verified by Louise Slocum Abbott; portrait in Darden Graduate Business School, UVA; obituaries in *Richmond Times-Dispatch* (por.) and *Richmond News Leader*, both 9 May 1986.

C. STEWART SHEPPARD

ABBOTT, Earl Leighton (20 February 1905–25 May 1973), circuit court judge, was the fourth of five sons and fifth of seven children of Francis Leighton Abbott and Lillian Mae Britts Abbott and was born in New Castle, Craig County, where his father practiced law. Abbott began his education in New Castle and then moved to Roanoke, where he worked at odd jobs while attending Jefferson High School. He graduated in 1923 and then matriculated at the University of Virginia, where he earned an LL.B. in 1928. He began the practice of law in the Roanoke firm of James C. Martin and Gustave A. Wingfield. After he married Flora Elizabeth Coleman on 30 June 1931, they had two daughters and two sons.

Confirming service that had begun some months previously, on 4 September 1929 Abbott was appointed commonwealth's attorney of Craig County, an office his father had once held. He served until the end of 1931, when he resumed the full-time practice of law in Roanoke, again in partnership with Martin. The practice was successful, and by the time he was thirty-five Abbott had appeared before the Virginia Supreme Court of Appeals, the United States Fourth Circuit Court of Appeals, and the U.S. Supreme Court. In June 1940 the governor appointed Abbott judge of the Nineteenth Circuit, which included the counties of Alleghany, Bath, Botetourt, and Craig, and the city of Clifton Forge. Abbott moved to Clifton Forge and lived there for the remainder of his life. The General Assembly continuously reelected him until he died. Abbott began his career on the bench as one of the youngest judges in Virginia; when he died he was the senior circuit court judge in the state.

Abbott became widely regarded in legal and legislative circles for his knowledge of juvenile court law and annexation law as well as judicial procedure. In 1947 he served on the judicial council that revised the state's juvenile court laws. Two years later the General Assembly appointed Abbott chair of a committee to study the state's annexation laws. In 1950, while still on the judicial council, Abbott helped formulate new rules of judicial procedure, and he and Erwin S. Solomon later prepared a revised, three-volume edition of the manual for instructions to juries, *Instructions for Virginia and West Virginia* (1962).

Abbott was a colorful judge, well-known for his extemporaneous comments from the bench and his assistance to journalists in preparing accurate reports of trials. He also insisted on proper decorum in court. In 1963 he banned George Lincoln Rockwell, the leader of the American Nazi Party, from his courtroom for interrupting the proceedings. The most important case of Abbott's career was the contentious annexation suit between the city of Richmond and Chesterfield County. The Richmond City Council attempted to annex a large suburban portion of the county in order to increase its tax base and to add a large number of white voters to the city's population so that African Americans would not become a voting majority in the city. Early in 1969 the Supreme Court of Appeals named Abbott chief judge of a special three-judge tribunal to hear the case. In an unorthodox private meeting, Abbott helped promulgate a compromise agreement that enabled the city to annex twenty-three square miles of the county with a population of about 47,000 people, most of whom were white. The compromise was challenged in the federal courts, where the city officials were shown to have been racially motivated in part, a violation of the Voting Rights Act of 1965. Further judicial proceedings, in which Abbott played no part, were necessary to resolve all the financial, political, and legal difficulties.

Abbott was a community leader in Clifton Forge and an active advocate of the area's economic development. In 1950 he helped found the Clifton Forge Development Corporation to buy real estate and attract industry, the first such organization of its kind in Virginia. Earl Leighton Abbott died on 25 May 1973 in Emmett Memorial Hospital in Clifton Forge and was buried in Mountain View Cemetery.

Family history supplied by Flora Elizabeth Coleman Abbott, Richmond; Elizabeth Hicks Corron, *Clifton Forge, Virginia: Scenic, Busy, Friendly*, revised ed. (1971), 148–149; John V. Moeser and Rutledge M. Dennis, *The Politics of Annexation: Oligarchic Power in a Southern City* (1982), 97–123; obituaries in *Covington Virginian* (por.) and *Richmond News Leader*, both 25 May 1973, *Lynchburg Daily Advance*, *Lynchburg News*, *Roanoke Times*, and *Richmond Times-Dispatch*, all 26 May 1973; memorial in *Virginia Bar Association Proceedings* (1973): 291–292.

JOHN V. MOESER

ABBOTT, Stanley William (13 March 1908–23 May 1975), landscape architect, was born in Yonkers, New York, the middle child of two sons and a daughter of Edward Thomas Abbott, owner of a construction business, and Eva Charlotte Sturges Abbott. As a student at Yonkers High School, Abbott became attracted to landscape architecture, which combined the skills of artist, ecologist, and engineer. In 1926 he enrolled in the professional degree program in landscape architecture at Cornell University. He was an excellent student with a broad range of intellectual interests, including poetry and literature. He became a facile writer and was also a fine athlete who earned a varsity letter as captain of the five-man rowing shell. He graduated in 1930.

Abbott first found work as a writer and designer for the Finger Lakes State Park Commission in Ithaca, New York. In 1931 he became public information officer for New York's Westchester County Park Commission, in charge of photography and of preparing annual reports. Westchester had one of the nation's most elaborate and sophisticated park systems. Abbott's colleagues included two pioneers of parkway design, Jay Downer and Gilmore D. Clarke. In their view, a "parkway" was essentially a linear park traversed by an automobile road designed solely for recreational use. No commercial traffic was allowed, and the road's perimeters were carefully designed as an extensive landscape park that shielded from the driver's view all industrial and commercial development. Thus, a parkway provided the pleasurable and restful experience of driving through an uninterrupted sequence of park scenery. Parkways were primarily used to connect larger recreational areas such as forest preserves and lakes in a regional park system.

On 27 December 1933 Abbott joined the National Park Service and was placed in charge of designing the nation's most extensive parkway project, the Blue Ridge Parkway in Virginia and North Carolina, to link the Shenandoah and Great Smoky Mountains National Parks. Abbott's mentors, Downer and Clarke, had been appointed consultants to the project and insisted on having Abbott represent them on the site, but they soon resigned over a fee dispute, and Abbott was left to design the parkway on his own. He married Helen Constance Schanck, of Yonkers, on 10 February 1934, and settled with her in Salem. They had two daughters and one son. Abbott prepared some of the parkway's early designs on his dining-room table in Salem before he could secure adequate office space in Roanoke. He had the formidable task of selecting 469 miles of rights-of-way through difficult mountainous terrain for which accurate maps were not always available.

Abbott took as his point of departure the basic concept of a parkway learned from Clarke and Downer. He viewed his task as the design of a 469-mile linear park traversed by a road. In meeting the unique challenges of his duties, Abbott refined and enlarged the parkway concept in three decisive ways and profoundly influenced all subsequent parkway design by the National Park Service. First, he immediately grasped that to preserve the scenery of the parkway corridor much larger rights-of-way than the meager 500 feet that Downer and Clarke recommended were needed. Abbott called for the outright purchase of 100 acres per mile of roadway, with an additional 50 acres per mile in scenic easements. Secondly, he routed the parkway through diverse scenery, including forests, farmsteads, and stream valleys, thus avoiding the monotony of continuous panoramic views, which he considered to be a major fault in the recently constructed Skyline Drive. Thirdly, Abbott envisioned the parkway as a "museum of the managed American countryside," featuring the regional cultural landscape of cropland and farms as well as attractive natural scenery. Whereas the Skyline Drive had focused almost exclusively on the natural landscape, Abbott and his staff took great pains to preserve representative vernacular buildings along the route as important artifacts of Appalachian rural culture. They also restored derelict farmland in order to use the parkway corridor as an example of enlightened agricultural practice. The parkway was to be more than a recreational corridor, functioning also as an instrument of historic preservation and of agricultural conservation.

Abbott based his decisions throughout the project on a design philosophy of elegant restraint and the combining of beauty with function. He maintained the safety of the parkway but minimized its impact on the land through careful grading and alignment as well as the use of native plants and high-quality construction materials. Abbott wanted the roadway to "fit the land like a glove." He designed visitor facilities to reflect the scale, form, materials of the local vernacular architecture. Carefully planned wayside recreational areas, which Abbott called "gems for the necklace," provided respite along the route, although his superiors in the National Park Service vetoed some of his more expensive and visionary schemes, such as the purchase and inclusion of Natural Bridge in the right of way. Nevertheless, he worked enthusiastically, as he put it, "with a ten league canvas and a brush of a comet's tail." In addition to his formal design work, he had to deal with political issues, such as bureaucratic rivalries and the suspicions of the local population. He met frequently with individual landowners, held public meetings, and published a newsletter, the *Blue Ridge Parkway News*, which was distributed in country stores and post offices along the parkway. Through such measures, Abbott quickly won the trust and respect of locals, which greatly expedited the completion of the project.

In 1937 Abbott became acting superintendent of the parkway without relinquishing his responsibility as chief design coordinator. In 1943, when the work was about two-thirds completed, Abbott was drafted into the United States Army. He spent the remainder of World War II as a corporal in the Corps of Engineers at Fort Lewis, Washington. In 1946 Abbott returned to the National Park Service and worked on a number of important projects, including the design for the Mississippi River Parkway, North Cascades National Park, and the Colonial Parkway linking Jamestown, Williamsburg, and Yorktown. He concluded his career with the Park Service as superintendent of Colonial National Historical Park from 1953 to 1965. While there, he participated in planning the 1957 festivities for the 350th anniversary of the founding of Jamestown.

Abbott retired from the Park Service in 1965 and lived in Williamsburg for the next ten years. With his son Carlton S. Abbott he formed a private practice as Abbott Associates, landscape architects. Abbott worked on a wide range of significant projects in Virginia, including the redesign of the gardens of the Executive Mansion in Richmond and major site-planning for Virginia Military Institute, Hollins College, Virginia Polytechnic Institute, Radford College, Mary Baldwin College, and Roanoke College. He also served as a consultant for design of the interstate highway system and planned several state and local parks in Virginia, among them Seashore, Chippokes Plantation, York River, and False Cape State Parks, James River Park in Richmond, and Waller Mill Park in Williamsburg. In addition, he designed gardens for numerous private residences in the vicinity of Roanoke.

Abbott received many honors, including the Department of the Interior's distinguished service award, a citation for his work in historic preservation and design from the Virginia Chapter of the American Institute of Architects, and induction as a fellow of the American Society of Landscape Architects and the American Institute of Park Executives. He served on many planning commissions and civic organizations and acted as president of the Yorktown Day Association throughout his tenure as superintendent of Colonial National Historical Park. The highest award for graduating students in landscape architecture at the University of Virginia is named in his honor, as are Virginia Tech's awards for the best senior project and best master's thesis. Lake Abbott on the Blue Ridge Parkway at the base of the Peaks of Otter also honors him. Stanley William Abbott died suddenly of a heart attack in Williamsburg on 23 May 1975, and his body was cremated.

Blue Ridge Parkway Archives, Asheville, N.C.; Stanley William Abbott Papers, in possession of Carlton S. Abbott, Williamsburg; interview with Carlton S. Abbott, 15 Oct. 1990; Harley E. Jolley, *Painting with a Comet's Tail: The Touch of the Landscape Architect on the Blue Ridge Parkway* (1987); S. Herbert Evison, "Designing and Building the Blue Ridge Parkway: Oral History Interview with Stanley W. Abbott, 1958," tape and transcription at National Park Service History Collection, Harpers Ferry Center; Barry M. Buxton and Stephen M. Beatty, eds., *Blue Ridge Parkway: Proceedings of the Blue Ridge Parkway Golden Anniversary Conference* (1986); Abbott's publications include his annual reports to the chief architect of the

National Park Service's Branch of Designs and Plans for the years 1937 through 1942 and *Blue Ridge Parkway News* (copies in Blue Ridge Parkway Archives), "Parkways—Past, Present and Future," *Parks and Recreation* 31 (1948): 681–691, and "Historic Preservation: Perpetuation of Scenes Where History Becomes Real" and "Parks and Parkways: A Creative Field Even When the Task is to Avoid Creation," *Landscape Architecture* 40 (1950): 153–157 and 44 (1953): 22–24; obituaries in *Richmond Times-Dispatch* (por.) and *Richmond News Leader*, both 24 May 1975, and *Williamsburg Virginia Gazette*, 30 May 1975.

REUBEN M. RAINEY

ABELL, George Washington (11 December 1818–27 December 1874), Disciples of Christ minister, was born in Charlottesville, the second of three children, all sons, of John S. Abell and Lydia Ralls Abell. His father was a slaveholding landowner of modest means who became a Baptist minister about 1830. Abell attended country schools for approximately six years then enrolled in a classical school in Charlottesville. In his late teens he decided to follow his father into the Baptist ministry and in 1839 he entered the University of Virginia, where he studied for three years and excelled in mathematics, moral and natural philosophy, Greek, and Latin.

In about 1840 or 1841, after hearing a sermon by Reuben Lindsay Coleman, Abell joined the Disciples of Christ, the loosely organized denomination founded by Barton Warren Stone, Walter Scott, Thomas Campbell, and Alexander Campbell that was then experiencing rapid growth in Virginia and the neighboring states. Encouraged by his friend James W. Goss, Abell traveled the evangelistic circuit during school vacations. He lived in Charlottesville and preached occasionally while teaching school until 1848, when he moved to Barboursville to teach in a classical school. With the assistance of Coleman, Goss, and others, Abell became state evangelist of the Disciples on 1 February 1850. His statewide preaching campaigns usually involved a series of protracted meetings lasting from five to twelve days. Despite denominational competition, he frequently preached in Baptist and Methodist churches, as well as at schools and courthouses.

Abell continued to preach during the Civil War and often ministered to Confederate soldiers. For a short time in 1863 he acted as chaplain to a North Carolina regiment encamped near the Rapidan River. After the war he resumed his work as state evangelist and served from 1866 through 23 May 1868. Abell stimulated the institutional development of the Disciples in Virginia by organizing congregations, raising funds for church buildings, endorsing the endowment of a professorial chair at Alexander Campbell's Bethany College, and encouraging the establishment of a Disciples newspaper. As the most prominent and successful Disciples evangelist in the 1850s and 1860s in eastern Virginia, he probably did more than any other man of his generation to establish Disciples churches and baptize new members. Following the Civil War he also ministered to freedpeople and attempted to link their aspirations with the Disciples and to counter perceived competition from the Catholic Church. In 1868 he moved to Christiansburg to undertake a mission in southwestern Virginia and in Tennessee, and in 1873 he assumed a settled pastorate in Murfreesboro, Tennessee.

On 30 May 1845 Abell married Mary Ann Nalley, daughter of Dennis Nalley, in Nelson County. They had two sons and six daughters. Abell was away from his family as an itinerant minister so often that his wife once asked one of his colleagues to try to persuade him to spend more time at home. In his will the hard-driving evangelist admitted that he had neglected to provide for the financial future of his wife and children and commended them to the care of the Virginia Disciples of Christ. George Washington Abell contracted pneumonia while on a brief trip to Alabama and died a few days later, on 27 December 1874. His body was buried at the Stone graveyard, Montgomery County, Virginia, but was subsequently moved twice, first to the Laurel Hill Church in Montgomery County and later to the Snowville Church at Hiwassee in Pulaski County.

Peter Ainslie, *Life and Writings of George W. Abell* (1875); Horace Abell and Lewis P. Abell, *The Abell Family in America* (1940), 264–266; Edgar Woods, *Albemarle County in Virginia* (1901), 137; Nelson Co. Marriage Bonds; Joseph Zachary Tyler, ed., *The Disciples of Christ in Virginia* (1879); numerous contemporary accounts of his ministry in *Millennial Harbinger* and *Christian Standard* (Disciples journals); biographical file, including photograph of gravestone, at Disciples of Christ Historical Society, Nashville, Tenn.

DAVID A. JONES

ABERNETHY, Thomas Perkins (25 August 1890–12 November 1975), historian, was born at Collirene, Lowndes County, Alabama, the eldest of five sons and two daughters of William Hines Abernethy and Annie Pierce Rast Abernethy. His mother's family had moved from South Carolina to Alabama before the Civil War and succeeded as large-scale cotton planters, but the Civil War almost wiped them out financially. Abernethy's father, the son and grandson of Methodist ministers, moved the family to Birmingham in 1893 and worked thereafter in a variety of brokerage positions. Perkins Abernethy, as he was known as an adult, was educated in a succession of schools, eventually completing high school at the Marion Military Institute in Marion, Alabama. While he was there the family moved briefly to Charleston, South Carolina. Rejoining them there, Abernethy received B.A. and M.A. degrees from the College of Charleston in 1911 and 1912.

Abernethy's father wanted him to go to medical school, but Abernethy leaned toward biology or English. One of his professors dissuaded him from the first, and he dissuaded himself from the second. He became a historian, he later wrote, "by a process of elimination." After spending two years teaching at the Marion Institute and two years in residence at Harvard, where he took a second M.A. in 1916, he returned to Alabama to research his doctoral dissertation, supporting himself in a variety of teaching positions and through a personal loan. On 6 December 1917, shortly before entering the army as a second lieutenant, he married Ida Erckman Robertson, whom he had first met in Charleston but who was then working as secretary at the Marion Institute. Abernethy returned to teach at the Institute after service in the army. He spent much of the academic year 1921–1922 as acting assistant professor at Vanderbilt University, received his Ph.D. from Harvard in 1922, and taught at the University of Chattanooga from 1922 to 1928 and at the University of Alabama from 1928 to 1930. In 1930 he moved to Charlottesville to begin a long association with the University of Virginia, initially as associate professor, and from 1937 to his retirement in 1961 as Richmond Alumni Professor.

Abernethy's tenure was not always pleasant. He no sooner assumed the professorship than the Great Depression ended the ability of the alumni to support it, and at the same time the university's ability to help finance research time was reduced. Administrative duties chafed him; he served as chairman of the Corcoran Department of History from 1946 through 1955. The need to join with his brothers to support his widowed mother kept his finances straitened until her death in 1960. The years at the University of Virginia were nevertheless productive. His mother's antebellum Alabama, only a generation or two removed from its frontier stage, was undoubtedly the greatest single influence on him. Abernethy had sought out Harvard's Frederick Jackson Turner, the preeminent historian of the American frontier, as his teacher. In contrast to Turner, who studied the midwestern frontier, Abernethy was interested in the Old South and throughout his life was very consciously a southerner. During his career he published a remarkable sequence of studies of the development of the southern frontier: *The Formative Period in Alabama* (1922), his doctoral dissertation; *From Frontier to Plantation in Tennessee: A Study in Frontier Democracy* (1932); *Western Lands and the American Revolution* (1937); *Three Virginia Frontiers* (1940); *The Burr Conspiracy* (1954); and *The South in the New Nation, 1789–1819* (1961).

Abernethy cherished the Old South that was for him the genteel, cultured, aristocratic society of Thomas Jefferson, which was destroyed in the course of the making of modern America. For its part, the frontier embodied America's future—crass, market-oriented, opportunistic, anti-intellectual, parvenu—not at all the egalitarian Elysium his mentor had posited. In terms of scholarship, Abernethy's work significantly amended that of his teacher. In personal terms, however, it bore all the marks of tragedy. The very thing he studied for most of his life was antagonistic to the ideal he most loved. In the late 1950s and 1960s, years of social and political turmoil, the very nation itself began to seem alien to him. Abernethy came to feel ill-used by his profession. He completed a seventh book, on the southern frontier during the War of 1812, but could not place it with a publisher. In 1966 he wrote to a brother that, having wandered into history and made some contributions during a career spanning almost fifty years, he found the nation and its historians enamored of principles alien to his own.

Active in all the major historical associations, Abernethy was a founding member of the Southern Historical Association and served in 1937–1938 as its third president. He was one of thirteen founders of the Institute of Early American History and Culture at Williamsburg and a member of its first council from 1946 to 1950. Three years after his retirement, eleven of his former students presented him with a Festschrift aptly centered on *The Old Dominion* (1964). He received honorary degrees from Washington and Lee in 1947 and from the College of Charleston in 1972. Four of his works were selected for the White House Library in 1963, and the whole body of his scholarship was honored in 1967 by an award of merit from the American Association for State and Local History, which commended Abernethy for "writing state history with insight and distinction."

Abernethy's wife died in 1969. They had no offspring, but numbered some thirty "academic children" in the doctoral students that he had trained. Thomas Perkins Abernethy died at his Charlottesville home on 12 November 1975 and was buried in the University of Virginia Cemetery in Charlottesville.

Fred Arthur Bailey, "Thomas Perkins Abernethy: Defender of Aristocratic Virtue," *Alabama Review* 45 (1992): 83-102; David Alan Williams, "Thomas Perkins Abernethy," *The University of Virginia Magazine* (Easter 1961): 8–9 (por.); Thomas Perkins Abernethy Papers, UVA; Faculty Record forms, University News Service, UVA; Thomas P. Abernethy, *The Antecedents of the Abernethy Family in Scotland, Virginia and Alabama* (ca. 1966); obituary in *Charlottesville Daily Progress*, 13 Nov. 1975.

DARRETT B. RUTMAN

ABRAHALL, Robert (fl. 1620s–1680s), merchant, was probably born in Herefordshire, England, sometime before 1624. Some Virginia documents record his name as Abrall, but he used the spelling Abrahall on several extant papers, including a 19 October 1668 deed to which he affixed a wax seal bearing the arms of the Abrahall family of Herefordshire. The Abrahalls were deeply engaged in English colonial commerce. Members of the family resided in London and the Bahamas and had connections with mercantile houses in the Netherlands. It was undoubtedly for the purpose of looking after or expanding the family business that Abrahall settled in Virginia sometime before 23 March 1646, when he witnessed a document in York County.

For almost forty years he was involved in extensive and lucrative commerce. He lived in the upper part of York County on the banks of the Mattaponi River. He eventually built or bought a house on the north side of the river in Saint Stephen's Parish, which in 1654 became part of the new county of New Kent and today is in King and Queen County. His near neighbors included such important colonists as William Claiborne, Edward Diggs, and John West. On 3 April 1651 Abrahall obtained a patent for 300 acres on the west side of the river, the first of twenty-one land grants he received during the next thirty-two years that totaled about 14,000 acres. More than eighty percent of the grants were issued on the basis of headrights, the fifty acres of land to which the person who paid the transportation cost of an immigrant to Virginia was entitled. Abrahall became one of the largest landowners in the area and consequently one of its most important and influential men.

In May 1648 Abrahall was appointed undersheriff of York County, but during the summer another undersheriff accused him of forging the signature of Nicholas Martiau, and although the charge was not proved, Abrahall was removed from office in September. He became the first burgess to represent New Kent County with his election to the 1654–1655 session of the General Assembly, a position to which he was returned for the session of 1660. Thereafter he remained constantly engaged in conducting his business, patenting and buying and selling land, and managing the public affairs of New Kent. He became an officer in the militia as early as 1653 and rose to lieutenant colonel by 1655 and colonel by 1662. In 1672 he was sheriff of the county and two years later he and John West took charge of raising men for its defense.

Because of the loss of most of the records of New Kent County, it is not known whether or when Robert Abrahall married or had children or when or where he died. His death occurred after 20 September 1683, the date of his last recorded land patent, which was for 600 acres on the branches of the Chickahominy River. The surname Abrahall, or Abrall, does not appear in the 1704 Virginia quitrent roll.

Petitions of 1662 and 19 June 1675, Colonial Papers, RG 1, LVA; signed and sealed 19 Oct. 1668 deed, Bassett Family Papers, VHS; numerous references to Abrahall's land- and officeholding in records of York Co., *Cavaliers and Pioneers*, *Journals of House of Burgesses*, and *Minutes of Council and General Court.*

DAPHNE GENTRY

ABRAMS, Joseph (1791–4 June 1854), Baptist minister, was a slave for fifty-three of the sixty-three years of his life. He married Sarah and had two daughters, Emily and Frances. Manumitted on 8 November 1844 by Richmond commission merchant Joshua J. Fry, Abrams soon gained ownership of his wife, daughters, and six grandchildren, whom he freed on 13 October 1851. Although listed in the 1850 census as an unskilled laborer, Abrams commanded sufficient resources to free himself and his immediate relatives, purchase two building lots in Richmond's Madison Ward from Fry in 1845, erect a comfortable house for his family, and leave an estate valued at nearly $1,500 when he died. His journey from bondage to respectability in but a few years marked Abrams as a person of rare abilities and good fortune.

Abrams was best known as a man of faith. For most of his adult life he enjoyed an enviable reputation as a religious leader and gifted preacher among Richmond's numerous African American Christians. He joined the First Baptist Church in 1817, served as its deacon for many years, and functioned as an ordained Baptist minister until legally silenced by the ban on black preachers in the wake of Nat Turner's Rebellion. White Richmonders regarded him highly and permitted him to officiate at funerals and deliver informal exhortations. In 1841 Abrams became a founding member and pioneer deacon of the First African Baptist Church. As a religious leader he deftly ministered to his people's need for affirmation and self-respect without arousing the enmity of the authorities. When discoursing on the trials that early Christians faced, for example, he reminded listeners that suffering persecution for doing the Lord's work was not confined to the apostolic age and recalled a brutal whipping he had received for preaching the Gospel. Testifying to Abrams's effectiveness, Robert Ryland, the white pastor of the African Church, remarked that Abrams "was heard with far more interest than I was, and on this account, I should have often requested him to speak, but for fear of involving him and the church in legal trouble."

Joseph Abrams's death on 4 June 1854 was an ordinary event in the life of the city, but the African American community responded to it in extraordinary fashion. Black Baptists in Richmond, Manchester, Petersburg, and Fredericksburg raised money for a tombstone, fellow deacons inscribed it with an eloquent memorial, and a massive crowd attended his funeral. The outpouring illuminated the man and his community. His funeral, which attracted eight thousand mourners of both races, was one of the largest held in the city to that time, and it dwarfed those usually accorded public officials and business leaders. In death Abrams's importance to his fellow free blacks and slaves was fully manifested. By turning out in record numbers to honor one of their own, black Richmonders honored each other. By paying homage to an exemplary man who had been a slave for most of his life, they publicly repudiated racial mores and slave codes that crimped their lives and burdened their spirits.

Robert Ryland, "Reminiscences of the First African Church, Richmond, Virginia," *American Baptist Memorial* 14 (1855): 354, quotes gravestone giving year of birth and date of death; deed of manumission in Henrico Co. Deed Book, 48:214; deed of manumission for family in Richmond City Hustings Court Deed Book, 60:543; property ownership recorded in ibid., 56:521, 70B:687–689, and 72B:582–583; Richmond City Hustings Court Minute Book, 21:209; Land Tax Returns, Richmond City, 1850, and Personal Property Tax Returns, Richmond City, 1849–1852,

RG 48, LVA; Census, Richmond City, 1850; minutes of First Baptist Church, 1825–1830, photostat of typescript in LVA; minutes of First African Baptist Church of Richmond, LVA microfilm; funeral reported in *Richmond Dispatch*, 7 June 1854.

JOHN T. O'BRIEN

ACKISS, Amos Johnston (30 August 1871–30 November 1928), attorney and civic leader, was born near Blackwater Station in Princess Anne County, the second of five children, all sons, of John B. Ackiss and Virginia Whitehead Ackiss. His father was a farmer who served as commissioner of revenue for the county before his death in 1880. Ackiss attended the county's public schools and worked at various odd jobs around the county courthouse to earn money for further education. He studied at the College of William and Mary during the 1889–1890 academic year on a form of scholarship by which recipients attended free of tuition in exchange for pledges to teach for two years in their local school district. He accordingly taught in his native county and attended the summer law school at the University of Virginia between 1892 and 1894 before being admitted to the bar in the latter year. On 7 November 1894 he married Bessie Sheild Kempshall. They had one daughter.

Ackiss served in several minor Princess Anne County offices before being appointed commonwealth's attorney in 1897 to fill out an unexpired term. He was unopposed in the election of 1899 and served nearly a full term of four years before being appointed judge of the county circuit court in 1903. He served in that capacity until 1908, when he resigned to become commonwealth's attorney again. He was reelected in 1911 without opposition and completed the term in 1915.

A well-respected lawyer and businessman, Ackiss maintained a law office in Norfolk from 1900 to 1925, and he actively promoted the development of the town of Virginia Beach as a vacation resort. Following the erection of the first cottages and hotels by the beach and the construction of the Norfolk and Virginia Beach Railway early in the 1880s, the town had become a popular oceanfront summer resort. Waterfowl shooting at nearby Back Bay gave the area a winter resort reputation as well. Many of the promoters of Virginia Beach lived elsewhere and encouraged the growth of the town to enhance their investments in its hotels and railroads. Ackiss, however, was a local resident who witnessed the transformation of the small town into a major vacation area, with the construction of many hotels, new roads, and the extension of a commuter rail line all the way from downtown Norfolk. He contributed to the development of the resort as an investor and booster. The owner of a number of lots, he touted the town as the "Garden Spot of the World," a "Mid-Atlantic Playground North of South and South of North," and during his life Virginia Beach blossomed and greatly expanded. Ackiss served on the town council and in 1925 started its first newspaper, the *Virginia Beach Weekly*, forerunner of the *Virginia Beach News*.

A series of strokes forced Ackiss to turn the paper's editorial duties over to his son-in-law, John B. Taliaferro. Following a third and especially severe stroke, Amos Johnston Ackiss died at his Linkhorn Park home on 30 November 1928. Originally buried in the family plot in Princess Anne County, his remains were later moved to the Eastern Shore Chapel cemetery in Virginia Beach.

William Stewart, *History of Norfolk County, Virginia and Representative Citizens* (1902), 1016; College of William and Mary, *Catalogue* (1890/1891): 8; *Norfolk Landmark*, 26 May 1899; *Norfolk Virginian-Pilot*, 10 Nov. 1911; obituaries in *Norfolk Virginian-Pilot* and *Norfolk Ledger-Dispatch*, both 1 Dec. 1928, and *Virginia Beach Weekly*, 7 Dec. 1928; memorial in *Virginia State Bar Association Proceedings* (1929): 244–247 (por.).

PETER C. STEWART

ACRILL, William (d. by 2 April 1783), member of the Convention of 1776, was a son of William Acrill and Anne Cocke Acrill, of Charles City County. Because of the destruction of most of the county's records, little is known about the family, but the younger William Acrill was related through his mother to two influential families, the Cockes, of Bremo, in Henrico County, and the Carters, of Shirley, in Charles City County. His father, who served his county as a justice of the peace, sheriff, king's attorney, and member of the House of Burgesses for the brief session of August–September 1736, died in March 1738. His mother's death occurred about 1755.

Acrill may have studied law, but he owned a small mercantile house from which he earned his living. He and a partner William Edlow imported a variety of merchandise in 1772 and 1773, but his firm usually conducted business under the name of William Acrill and Company. He owned the hundred-ton brigantine *America* by 1770, when he engaged Thomas Adams (whose mother was a half sister of Acrill's mother) to insure it in London for £400. In 1776 Acrill sold military supplies to the Virginia army.

Acrill was presumably at least twenty-one years old when he was appointed a justice of the peace on 30 April 1752. He probably served in that capacity until his death. He became a colonel in the militia by the mid-1770s and was most likely a vestryman of one of the parishes in the lower part of the county. He represented Charles City County in the House of Burgesses from 1766 to 1776 and in the House of Delegates from 1776 to 1778. He was usually appointed to one or two of the major committees (courts of justice, propositions and grievances, religion, or trade), but he was not among the leaders in the assembly. Acrill attended all the recorded protest meetings and signed all the recorded associations against British policies before the Revolution, and he also attended all five of the Revolutionary Conventions held between August 1774 and July 1776. He was present throughout the fifth convention, which unanimously voted for independence and adopted the Virginia Declaration of Rights and the first constitution of the commonwealth, but the records show only that Acrill received a routine appointment to the very large Committee on Propositions and Grievances.

William Acrill died, probably unmarried and childless, before 2 April 1783. On that date his nephew Acrill Cocke posted a bond of £7,000 to administer his estate, which judging by the amount of money involved must have been substantial.

James Cocke Southall, "The Cocke Family of Virginia," *VMHB* 4 (1897): 326; Acrill's name appears frequently in the *Williamsburg Virginia Gazette* during the 1770s, in *Journals of House of Burgesses, 1766–1776*, and in *Revolutionary Virginia*; bond of 2 Apr. 1783, Charles City Co. Papers, W&M; fragments of estate debt suits, 1785–1794, Charles City Co. County and Superior Court Cases.

BRENT TARTER

ADAIR, Cornelia Storrs (9 November 1884–14 April 1962), president of the National Education Association, was born at Red Sulphur Springs in Monroe County, West Virginia. She was the second of three daughters and fifth of eight children of Lewis Cass Adair and Rebecca Sidney Taylor Adair. The family moved to Richmond, where Adair attended Richmond Female Seminary and graduated from Richmond High School. At age seventeen she took a clerical job at an insurance company and enrolled in a course for teachers at Richmond High School. Adair and her sisters, who also became teachers, probably chose careers in education in emulation of other family members.

Adair began her career teaching at Elba Elementary School in Richmond in 1904. During the next fifteen years she taught at Nicholson, Robert Fulton, and Bellevue Elementary Schools and took summer courses at Columbia University, Richmond Normal School, and New York University. In 1921 she enrolled as a full-time student at the College of William and Mary, and two years later she received her A.B. degree. Adair joined the faculty of Bainbridge Junior High School in 1924 and in 1931 became principal of Franklin Elementary School, where she remained until she retired in 1954.

Adair attributed her passion for education to the influence of her aunt and namesake, Cornelia Storrs Taylor, one of the pioneer public school teachers in Richmond. Taylor taught Adair to be concerned not only about the welfare of her pupils, but also about the salaries, working conditions, and retirement benefits of teachers. Adair succeeded Taylor in leading the campaign for a retirement plan for Virginia's public school teachers, presiding for twenty-five years over the Virginia Education Association's committee on teacher retirement. She was an ardent supporter of women's rights and opposed discriminatory practices such as the exclusion of married women from the classroom and unequal pay scales for male and female teachers.

Adair was an active member of the Teachers' Co-operative Association, and in 1925 the Richmond School Board sent her as a delegate to the first biennial conference of the World Federation of Education Associations in Edinburgh, Scotland. Adair served as president of the Richmond League of Teachers Associations for ten years, and she also headed the National League of Teachers Associations in 1919 and the National League of Classroom Teachers in 1927. After five years as treasurer of the National Education Association, in 1927 she became the first classroom teacher ever elected to its presidency. School administrators and college professors had dominated the organization before the mid-1920s, but Adair's election as president symbolized the growing importance and influence of teachers in national educational organizations. The Richmond School Board gave her a year's leave of absence with pay in order to travel on behalf of the national organization. The theme of her presidency was education for citizenship. At the end of her one-year term she refused other job offers and returned to her Richmond classroom.

Although Adair opposed some of the progressive educational theories of the early twentieth century and emphasized traditional drilling in basic skills in the classroom, she also insisted that the artistic and spiritual side of children must be stimulated. In defense of symphony concerts for children she argued that children, no matter how poor, should be fed cake in addition to oatmeal. Adair strongly supported universal education but recognized that the brightest children should be given opportunities to develop their talents by furthering their education. She did not limit her concern to intellectually gifted children, but also worked with mentally and physically handicapped students and was instrumental in founding the Virginia Society for Crippled Children and Adults.

Adair was a diligent clubwoman and community volunteer for various causes relating to education, health, and public welfare. During the Great Depression, she served as Richmond director of the federal government's Works Progress Administration Emergency Education Program, and from 1935 to 1937 she directed the National Youth Administration's Out-of-School Youth Program in Virginia. She was a founder of the Virginia chapter of Delta Kappa Gamma, an honorary society for teachers, and of the Virginia Federation of Business and Professional Women's Clubs. She served as president of the Richmond League of Women Voters and sat on the boards of the National Education Association, the National Council for the Study of Education, and the Consultation and Evaluation Clinic of the State Health Department. Her wide-ranging activities also included involvement in Goodwill Industries, the Virginia League for Planned Parenthood, the Virginia Cancer Society, the American Association of University Women, the Presbyterian Church, the Democratic Party, and numerous other organizations.

During her term as National Education Association president, Adair received the degree of doctor of pedagogy from New York State Teacher's College. In 1934 she became the first woman to receive the Alumni Medallion from the College of William and Mary, and in 1963 the college named its women's gymnasium in her honor. In 1952 the Swansboro Citizens Association and the Franklin Parent Teacher Association commissioned Richmond artist David Silvette to paint an oil portrait of Adair for presentation to Franklin Elementary School. She retired two years later but remained active in many organizations until shortly before her death. Cornelia Storrs Adair died in the University of Virginia Hospital in Charlottesville on 14 April 1962 and was buried in Hollywood Cemetery in Richmond.

Virginia Iota State Organization of Delta Kappa Gamma Society, *Adventures in Teaching: Pioneer Women Educators and Influential Teachers* (1963), 22–26 (por.); Elizabeth Copeland Norfleet, "Cornelia Storrs Adair: 'Good in Every Significant Way,'" *Richmond Quarterly* 7 (Fall 1984): 33–37; birth date in Adair family Bible in possession of niece Cornelia Adair Green, Bristol, Tenn., 1998; election to NEA presidency documented in *Richmond Times-Dispatch*, 30 July 1927; feature article in *Richmond News Leader*, 21 Dec. 1936; Glass and Glass, *Virginia Democracy*, 2:303–305; family history information furnished by Margaret Adair Atmar, Cornelia Adair Green, Rebecca Adair Narnow, and Katharine Adair Woods; Biographical Files, Richmond Public Library; Silvette portrait, depicted in *Richmond News Leader*, 17 May 1952, now in family possession; obituaries in *Richmond News Leader*, 14 Apr. 1962, and *Richmond Times-Dispatch*, 15 Apr. 1962; editorial tribute, *Richmond News Leader*, 17 Apr. 1962; memorial in *Virginia Journal of Education* 55 (May 1962): 44.

JOHN CARROLL PRESLEY

ADAIR, Douglass Greybill (5 March 1912–2 May 1968), historian and editor, was born in New York City, the second of three sons and third of four children of Douglass Greybill Adair and Lilian Hunt Augustine Adair, both of whom were natives of Richmond. When Adair was seven his father moved the family from New York to Birmingham and later to Mobile, Alabama, where Adair attended public schools. After studying for the academic year 1928–1929 at Sewanee Military Academy in Tennessee and graduating as salutatorian, in September of the latter year he entered the University of the South in Sewanee. In 1933 he received a B.A. with a major in European history and a minor in English literature. He studied law at Harvard University in 1933–1934 at the insistence of his family, but in the following academic year he registered for graduate study in history and received an M.A. from Harvard in 1935.

Unable to obtain a fellowship for further study at Harvard, Adair worked in Washington, D.C., from 1936 to 1938 as a research assistant at the Social Security Administration. With the director of its Research Bureau, Walton H. Hamilton, he collaborated on a study of the commerce clause of the Constitution, *The Power to Govern: The Constitution—Then and Now* (1937), that was cited as authoritative in later Supreme Court decisions. In 1937 Adair married Virginia Hamilton, a promising poet whom he had met when she was pursuing graduate study in English at Harvard. They had two sons and one daughter.

Adair resumed graduate study at Yale University from 1938 to 1941, teaching as a part-time instructor from 1939 to 1940. He then held an instructorship at Princeton University from 1941 to 1943 before receiving his doctorate from Yale in the latter year. Although never published, his dissertation, "The Intellectual Origins of Jeffersonian Democracy," attracted much scholarly attention and went far to establish Adair's reputation as a historian.

In 1943 Adair joined the faculty of the College of William and Mary. The Institute of Early American History and Culture, a collaborative effort of William and Mary and the Colonial Williamsburg Foundation, was founded in December of that year and took over the editing of the *William and Mary Quarterly.* Adair served for a year as the quarterly's book review editor and succeeded Richard L. Morton as managing editor with the first issue of 1947. In the years following World War II the somewhat-neglected field of early American history experienced a renaissance, and under Adair's guidance the journal achieved wide recognition as the publisher of much of the new scholarship. The fifteen articles, reviews, and edited documents that he contributed, sometimes with collaborators, provided one strand of that new work. Many of the pieces addressed his lifelong concern with the political thought and influence of the Founding Fathers, including influential works on the *Federalist Papers*. The appearance in the *Quarterly* in 1948 and 1952 of his editions of *The Candidates*, a play by Robert Munford that satirized colonial Virginia elections, and the autobiography of a Virginia evangelical Anglican minister, Devereux Jarratt, brought important documentary sources to light. Adair was also a coinvestigator in a classic example of historical detective work that proved that the Horn Papers, allegedly a newly discovered source on eighteenth-century western Pennsylvania, were a forgery.

For all his success and promise, Adair sometimes found the dozen years he spent in Virginia frustrating. Although a consummate teacher, the combination of a heavy teaching load with the equally exacting work of an editor placed heavy demands on him without corresponding material reward. He was also characteristically generous with his advice and time to other scholars. Perhaps, too, his penetrating intellect and responsiveness to new ideas were balanced by an aversion to finality that added to the difficulty he found in turning his research and insights into an even more substantial body of published work. For whatever reason, in a letter written some years later to a close friend and colleague, he referred to Williamsburg as "the shining city of my manhood's grief."

In 1955 Adair accepted a professorship in California on the faculty of Claremont College (later named the Claremont Graduate School), where he spent the remainder of his career, apart from an occasional visiting appointment. For the most part these appeared to be happy years for Adair and his family. His wife taught in the English department at California State Polytechnic School in Pomona. Long after her husband's death she won wide recognition with the publication of a volume of her collected poems, *Ants on the Melon* (1996), a number of which reached back to the Adairs' years in Virginia for their subjects.

Claremont afforded Adair his first opportunity to teach doctoral students, many of whom commented on his enthusiasm for his subject and the generous encouragement that he gave them. From the mid-1950s to the mid-1960s, he continued to produce, as he did in Virginia, a number of shorter writings and edited documentary volumes. A term on the Council of the Institute of Early American History and Culture from 1963 to 1966 brought him back to Williamsburg to attend its annual meetings. Apparently as a result of his continuing distress at his failure to produce the larger works of history of which he knew he was capable, Douglass Greybill Adair committed suicide in Claremont on 2 May 1968.

In 1972 friends, colleagues, and family members established in his memory the Douglass G. Adair Memorial Award, administered jointly by the Institute of Early American History and Culture and the Claremont Graduate School and presented quadrennially (biennially since 1982) to the author of the most significant article published in the *William and Mary Quarterly*. A posthumous volume, *Fame and the Founding Fathers* (1974), edited by one of his students, brought together his most important published essays and added one that had not previously appeared in print, a study of the Thomas Jefferson–Sally Hemings relationship that argued against Jefferson's paternity of her children and anticipated the later preoccupation of numerous historians with that issue.

Biographies by Trevor Colbourn and Caroline Robbins and bibliography by Robert E. Shalhope in *Fame and the Founding Fathers: Essays By Douglass Adair*, ed. Colbourn (1974), ix–xxiii (por.), 307–308; autobiographical statement, papers, and related Adair materials in Omohundro Institute of Early American History and Culture, Williamsburg; teaching style described in Daniel Sisson, *The American Revolution of 1800* (1974), 12–17; family history in Augustine Family Genealogical Notes, LVA, confirmed by Douglass Greybill Adair III; Keith B. Berwick, "A Peculiar Monument: The Third Series of the *William and Mary Quarterly*," *WMQ*, 3d ser., 21 (1964): 6–8; memorial in *WMQ*, 3d ser., 25 (1968): 518–520.

THAD W. TATE

ADAM, John (1 August 1774–4 August 1848), silversmith, was probably born in Alexandria. His mother's name is not known. His father, James Adam, was a silversmith who worked in Alexandria from about 1771 until his death in 1798, but little is known of him other than what can be deduced from a few surviving samples of his work. John Adam may have learned the craft from his father or from another Alexandria silversmith, Mordecai Miller, to whom he was apprenticed in December 1791. By 1800 he had completed his apprenticeship and married Mary Hayes. They had three sons and three daughters.

The earliest evidence of John Adam's work as an independent silversmith dates from 1801. Neither he nor his father used stamps that included a first name, choosing instead to use a variety of marks that defy positive identification. Though many of the surviving pieces have been attributed stylistically to one or the other, some of the most interesting work dates from the late eighteenth century, when either man could have been the creator. John Adam's advertisements appeared regularly in the Alexandria newspapers between 1803 and 1846, announcing the availability of his own work and also frequently offering for sale items imported from Philadelphia and New York, as was common at the time. Over the years he sold a range of goods, including percussion pistols, tortoiseshell combs, and Britannia ware. He was reported to have made a significant amount of money selling silver gambling boxes, but he did not specifically advertise them. He produced spectacle frames, silver spectacle cases, thimbles, chatelaines, and lancets. A pair of sunglasses in the collection at Mount Vernon bearing his mark evidences the wide variety of goods that metalsmiths produced in early America.

Adam's surviving works are rendered in a simple, classical style relying on broad, plain surfaces, gently curving shapes, elegant proportions, and delicate beading. Although stylish, the designs were not unusual for the period, and it is for skilled craftsmanship that the Adam name is remembered. A portrait of a man said to be one of his sons and a self-portrait in which he holds a portcrayon of his own making demonstrate his skill as a painter. He was allegedly a friend of the artist Thomas Sully and of Elizabeth Arnold Poe, the actress and mother of Edgar Allan Poe, but these relationships have not been confirmed.

Adam's career spanned important changes in American silversmithing, starting in an era that relied heavily on imported British goods, continuing through a period that fostered the growth of domestic design and skilled craftsmanship, and concluding in an era of mechanization that transformed the trade. As early as 1801 Adam produced silver spoons using new techniques of rolling and stamping silver sheets. By the time of his death, large New England manufacturing firms were producing silverware at prices within the means of the growing middle class and thus practically eliminated work for creative local silversmiths. Many of them instead became watchmakers or jewelers. As early as 1846 John Adam's son William Wallace Adam (1817–1878) filled that position in the Alexandria shop and went on to take over the family business after his father's death. He adapted to the new market and specialized in watchmaking. Two of his sons, Robert L. Adam (1846–1898) and Charles Frederick Adam (1848–1925), inherited the family watchmaking and jewelry business, with the latter working as a watchmaker as late as 1917.

John Adam died in Alexandria on 4 August 1848 and was buried in the cemetery of Alexandria Presbyterian Church.

Catherine B. Hollan, *In the Neatest, Most Fashionable Manner: Three Centuries of Alexandria Silver* (1994), 7–8, 10, 13, 89–120, reproduces self-portrait and photographs of most of Adam's known extant pieces; George Barton Cutten, *The Silversmiths of Virginia (Together with Watchmakers and Jewelers) from 1694 to 1850* (1952), 3–4, 22; birth date in apprenticeship record in Alexandria City Hustings Court Minute Book for 1791–1796 (LVA microfilm filed with Arlington Co. records), 6; death date on gravestone in Alexandria Presbyterian Church graveyard; Alexandria City Will Book, 5:79–82.

SARAH SHIELDS DRIGGS

ADAM, Robert (4 May 1731–27 March 1789), merchant, was born in West Kilbride, Ayrshire, Scotland, the youngest of five brothers and ninth of ten children of John Adam, a Presbyterian minister, and Janet Campbell Adam. He immigrated to Alexandria in 1752. From 1753 to 1756 he acted as local agent for the mercantile firm of John Kirkpatrick, John Pagan, William Wallace, and Company. In 1758 he established a tanyard of his own, and in 1762 he set up a new tannery with the brothers Peter and John Weis.

Although tobacco seemed king in northern Virginia, Adam was one of the first merchants to perceive the potential in the exportation of cereals and foodstuffs to the Caribbean. In 1763 he and John Carlyle combined as Carlyle and Adam and purchased George Washington's wheat and flour for export. They erected two gristmills on Four Mile Run north of Alexandria, and during the years 1769–1771 they continued their joint ventures and set up James Muir in an Alexandria retail store. Between 1767 and the outbreak of the American Revolution, Adam formed partnerships with James Adam and Matthew Campbell (probably his cousins) in another new business, Robert Adam and Company, which contracted with Washington for grain and milled flour and for the use of his herring and shad fisheries in the Potomac River. In 1772 the firm built another mill on Four Mile Run and opened a large store in Alexandria stocked with consumer goods that Adam had selected on a 1771 trip to London. Owner in whole or in part of three ships, the company exported flour, fish, and other foodstuffs to the West Indies, sent tobacco and Caribbean products to England, and imported wine, spirits, and sugar on the return voyages. Adam dissolved his partnerships in 1776 and conducted his affairs until 1788 as Robert Adam and Company.

In addition to becoming one of the leading merchants in the Potomac River boomtown of Alexandria, Adam served as a trustee for the town and became a justice of the peace for Fairfax County in 1758, a position he held for the remainder of his life. He was sheriff of the county in 1765 and also became a captain in the militia. In 1782 he was instrumental in founding Alexandria's first Masonic lodge, and in 1783 he became its first worshipful master. He also supported the protests against British policies that led up to the American Revolution. He subscribed to the Association of 1770, served on the Alexandria and Fairfax committees, and signed the Fairfax Resolves of 1774. His support for his adopted country did not come cheap. In 1777 the British captured a cargo en route to him from Boston, and in 1782 he lost the *Saint Patrick*, a brand new vessel, and its cargo of flour that he and Alexandria residents Richard Conway and Valentine Peers had purchased. His interest in commerce prompted him in 1785 to sign a petition to increase the power of Congress over international trade.

Robert Adam died at his residence in Fairfax County on 27 March 1789. He left a widow, Anne Adam (maiden name unknown), two sons and two daughters (all minors), and a "valuable estate real and Personal."

Birth recorded in West Kilbride Parish records; scattered details about business and political affairs in Prince William Co. Land Causes, 1789; Fairfax Co. Court minutes, deeds, wills, and land records; Ramsay-Dixon account book, 1753–1756, Smithsonian Institution; account books of Glassford and Henderson's store in Alexandria, 1765–1768, LC; George Washington Papers, LC; Harry Piper Letter Book, UVA; Alexandria Board of Trustees Minutes, Alexandria Public Library; various sources in PRO, the *Williamsburg Virginia Gazettes*, and *Annapolis Maryland Gazette*; death recorded in Masonic records (Franklin L. Brockett, *The Lodge of Washington* [1876], 93).

JAMES D. MUNSON

ADAMS, Andrew Washington (21 July 1905–10 September 1985), Upper Mattaponi chief, was born in King William County, the second of six sons and fourth of twelve children of Jasper Lewis Adams and Mollie Wade Holmes Adams. He began his education in a private school and in 1919 was one of the first students to attend the tribe's new Sharon Indian School. He worked on his father's farm before going into the timber industry, cutting wood for the Chesapeake Corporation, one of the largest pulp mills in the Southeast. In 1941 he was drafted into the United States Army. Adams was stationed at Fort Benning, Georgia, and at Camp Blanding, Florida, before his discharge on 2 September 1945.

On 13 October 1945 Adams married Ocie Allmond, the daughter of Caroline Adams Allmond and William Thomas Allmond, a widow who lived on the Pamunkey reservation with her three-year-old son. Adams moved his new family to Philadelphia, Pennsylvania, where he worked as a mechanic until he retired in 1973. Both of his parents died that year, and Adams returned to Virginia. He was elected leader of the Upper Mattaponi in 1974, the office his father had held from 1923 until his death. Adams reformed the tribe's governmental organization and on 14 June 1976 obtained a charter incorporating the Upper Mattaponi Indian Tribal Association. With the tribe's legal ability to manage its affairs secured, he worked to improve educational opportunities for the children. Adams was also very active in the campaign to obtain formal recognition of the Upper Mattaponi as a distinct Virginia Indian tribe in order to enable it to participate in more federal Indian programs. The Virginia General Assembly adopted a joint resolution in February 1983 recognizing the Upper Mattaponi as a Virginia tribe. Unfortunately, Adams's poor health kept him from the ceremony in the governor's office in Richmond in March 1983 at which Governor Charles S. Robb signed the recognition papers.

Andrew Washington Adams died in a Richmond nursing home on 10 September 1985 and was buried in the churchyard of Indian View Baptist Church in King William County.

The contributor is a sister of Adams; Malcolm Tuppance, *History of Upper Mattaponi* (n.d.); Helen C. Rountree, *Pocahontas's People: The Powhatan Indians of Virginia Through Four Centuries* (1990), 252 (por.); obituary in *Richmond News Leader*, 11 Sept. 1985.

EUNICE A. ADAMS

ADAMS, Berkley Dickenson (2 January 1875–10 November 1945), member of the State Corporation Commission, was born on his father's farm near Chatham, the eldest of six sons and one daughter of Samuel Chaplin Adams and

Christiana Wade Dickenson Adams. He attended local schools, an academy in Patrick County, Emory and Henry College, and Roanoke College before graduating from Southern Business College in Lynchburg in 1893. He went to work as a bookkeeper at the Alberene Stone Company's quarry in Albemarle County, and on 24 October 1897 he married the superintendent's daughter, Marie Angelina Pruneau. The following year he moved to Red Oak in Charlotte County, where he acquired a large farm. Except for the decade from 1919 to 1928, Adams lived the remainder of his life at Red Oak, where he managed his farm and a number of other family businesses, including a soft drink–bottling plant. Berkley and Marie Adams had four sons and three daughters before her death on 17 January 1915. On 22 January 1917 he married Beatrice Sackett in New Jersey, and they had three sons but divorced during the 1920s.

In 1903 Adams was elected to the House of Delegates as a Democrat. Although he did not run for office in 1905, between 1907 and 1917 Adams won six consecutive terms to the House. He became an influential delegate and served as chairman of the Committee on Agriculture and Mining from 1914 to 1918. In 1916 he was appointed to a joint committee that, under the guidance of first-term state senator Harry Flood Byrd prepared the first comprehensive plan for a statewide system of public highways. Adams also served on the State Board of Agriculture from 1907 until 1919, the last nine years as chairman.

Adams resigned after the first session of the 1918–1919 General Assembly following his gubernatorial appointment in June 1919 to a vacancy on the three-member State Corporation Commission. In November 1919 Adams was elected to serve the remainder of the term, and three years later he captured a full six-year term. Each member of the commission had primary responsibility for a portion of the commission's extensive operations. Adams's responsibilities included oversight of public utilities and telephone, telegraph, and express companies, as well as supervision of the state's bank examiners. He became chairman of the commission in November 1925. Meanwhile, a constitutional amendment extended the governor's patronage power to include the State Corporation Commission. A month before Adams's term expired at the end of January 1928, Governor Byrd appointed William Meade Fletcher to replace him. Adams probably owed his ouster to his associations with the Democratic Party's prohibitionists, especially G. Walter Mapp, Byrd's opponent in the 1925 Democratic Party primary, and his ties to Westmoreland Davis and other opponents of the Byrd wing of the party.

Adams quickly emerged as a critic of Byrd's administrative reforms of the state government as well as his new state tax structure. During the gubernatorial primary campaign of 1929, Adams managed the campaign of Mapp, who unsuccessfully challenged Byrd's hand-picked candidate, John Garland Pollard. Despite this setback, Adams served four more terms in the House of Delegates, representing Charlotte County in the assemblies of 1932 through 1938. Berkley Dickenson Adams died at his home in Red Oak on 10 November 1945 and was buried nearby.

Gerald Tate Gilliam, "Berkley Dickenson Adams: Farmer and Politician," *Southsider* 7 (1988): 63–69 (por.); Duval Porter, *Official Virginia: A Composition of Sketches of the Public Men of Virginia at the Present Time* (1920), 31–33; Tyler, Bruce, and Morton, *History of Virginia*, 4:98–99; birth, marriage, and death dates in Bible records printed in *Southsider* 7 (1988): 60–62; other family history information furnished by son Gordon S. Adams; Adams letters in Harry Flood Byrd Papers, UVA; obituaries in *Richmond News Leader*, 10 Nov. 1945, *Richmond Times-Dispatch* and *Roanoke Times*, both 11 Nov. 1945, and *Charlotte Gazette*, 15 Nov. 1945.

BRENT TARTER

ADAMS, Emma (21 July 1875–23 August 1959), musician and concert manager, was born just outside Lynchburg in Campbell County, the only daughter and fourth of six children of Emma Camm Saunders Adams and Stephen Adams, a local attorney, judge, and sometime member of the General Assembly. She received a private education and from 1894 to 1897 attended Randolph-Macon Woman's College in Lynchburg in the class of 1898. She grew up in a musical household and lived all her adult life in Lynchburg, where prosperous business leaders and their families prized music and the arts. Her father played the violin and her brothers sang in local choral groups. One of them,

William S. Adams, became a professor of music at Randolph-Macon Woman's College.

Emma Adams also played and taught the piano in her home for many years and served as organist at the First Presbyterian Church for twenty-six years. In middle age she also discovered a talent for organization, which she used with enthusiasm and skill during the second half of her adult life to enrich the cultural life of Lynchburg. In 1925, after a Richmond friend told her that operatic soprano Alma Gluck was scheduled to sing in Richmond and suggested that she also be invited to Lynchburg, Adams wrote to Gluck's manager and arranged to have the latter city added to the tour. Gluck's successful appearance in Lynchburg launched Adams on her career as a concert manager. For the next twenty years she produced concerts and recitals featuring some of the world's most distinguished musicians and entertainers. First at the Academy of Music and later at the Municipal Auditorium, she provided the citizens of Lynchburg and its surrounding counties with as fine and varied an artistic fare as could be had in any comparable city in the South.

Among the famous singers Adams brought to Lynchburg were the operatic sopranos Geraldine Farrar, Amelita Galli-Curci, Mary Garden, Lily Pons, and Rosa Ponselle; tenors Richard Crooks and John McCormack; and renowned baritone Lawrence Tibbett. She also attracted some of the world's greatest violinists, including both Jascha Heifetz and Fritz Kreisler. Among the pianists, she arranged appearances by Josef Hofmann, Ignacy Paderewski, and Sergei Rachmaninoff. Several major orchestras also performed in Lynchburg, including the Philadelphia Orchestra, under the baton of Eugene Ormandy. In addition, Adams presented the talented actress Cornelia Otis Skinner, popular entertainers Jeanette MacDonald and Nelson Eddy, and many other entertainers and lecturers, among whom were humorist Will Rogers and aviator Richard Evelyn Byrd. So central did Adams become to the cultural life of Lynchburg that at the time of her death an editorial in the *Lynchburg Daily News* compared her local influence with that of the great New York impresario, Sol Hurok, and recommended that if ever the city of Lynchburg erected a proper concert hall, it should be named for her.

After her retirement in 1945, Adams continued to teach piano in her home. Two days after suffering an acute cerebral thrombosis, Emma Adams died on 23 August 1959 and was buried in Spring Hill Cemetery in Lynchburg.

Emma Adams prepared a partial list of artists for her entry in the 1947 edition of *Who's Who in the South and Southwest*; feature articles in *Lynchburg Daily Advance*, 10 Nov. 1949, and *Lynchburg News*, 1 Apr. 1956; obituaries in *Lynchburg News* and *Lynchburg Daily Advance* (por.), both 24 Aug. 1959, and editorial tributes in both papers, 25 Aug. 1959.

SARAH A. HICKSON
E. DOLORES SWANSON

ADAMS, George Frederick (3 October 1802–16 April 1877), Baptist minister, was born in Dorchester, Massachusetts, the fourth of six sons and one of nine children of Seth Adams and Elizabeth Apthorp Adams. The family moved to Marietta, Ohio, about 1805 and a few years later to Zanesville, Ohio, where he grew up. He joined a Baptist church there and in 1822 was licensed to preach. Realizing that he was insufficiently prepared for the ministry, in 1824 Adams enrolled in the preparatory school of Columbian College (now George Washington University) in Washington, D.C. He was ordained at a Baptist church in Washington on 22 April 1827. He received his B.A. from Columbian in 1829 and served as the principal of its preparatory school from 1829 to 1830.

While he was in college Adams worked with Robert Ryland during the summer as a missionary in eastern Virginia. Adams moved to Falmouth in 1830 to teach in a school for girls and to serve as assistant to Robert B. Semple, pastor of the Fredericksburg Baptist Church. In 1831 Adams succeeded Semple as pastor and for five years taught and preached in Falmouth and Fredericksburg. On 1 January 1830 Adams married Mary Marvin, who died, possibly in childbirth, on 15 March 1834. On 28 December 1835 he married Sarah L. Bayly, of Stafford County. They had at least three daughters.

In 1836 Adams became pastor of the Calvary Baptist Church in Baltimore, Maryland, where he served until 1842. While there he helped to organize the Maryland Baptist Union

Association to promote that state's mission program. He served as corresponding secretary for the association and was its moderator for thirteen years. In 1842 he resigned his pastorate to become a general missionary for the Baptists in the state of Maryland. The following year he moved to Hereford, Baltimore County, Maryland, and served as pastor of three small congregations, returning to Baltimore in 1846. For the next two years Adams operated a bookstore and served as a supply pastor for Baptist congregations in the area. From 1847 to 1869 he sat on the board of trustees of Columbian College, and he received the college's M.A. in 1866 and its D.D. in 1874. In 1848 Adams had accepted the pastorate of the Second Baptist Church in Baltimore. He became one of the editors of the *True Union*, the weekly newspaper for Maryland Baptists, when it was established in 1849. Adams's second wife having died on 24 December 1850, he married Catherine E. White in October 1854. They had one son.

Adams left Baltimore and returned to Virginia in December 1860 to become pastor of the Hampton Baptist Church, and he was elected moderator of the Dover Baptist Association in 1861. His congregation had almost 200 white members and nearly 950 African American members. Starting on 24 June 1861 Adams served as chaplain to a regiment of Confederate troops stationed on the Peninsula during the first months of the Civil War. He moved his family to a safe place in the country during the summer but remained in Hampton himself, ministering to his parishioners and also preaching to the soldiers. Adams was arrested and briefly imprisoned when the Union army occupied Hampton. After his release in 1862 he and his family returned to Baltimore, where he again served as state missionary for the Baptists of Maryland. He also prepared his posthumously published *History of Baptist Churches in Maryland Connected with the Maryland Baptist Union Association* (1885).

In 1865 Adams again returned to Virginia as principal of the Atlantic Female College at Onancock in Accomack County. Two of his daughters taught at the college while he was principal. He also preached for several months at the Pungoteague Baptist Church. In October 1866 he was called back to resume his former ministry in Hampton. The Hampton Baptist Church had been burned during the war, and Adams raised money in Baltimore to erect a new building, which he opened in March 1869. The new congregation was small and racially segregated. It had fewer than 60 members when he resumed his pastorate but increased to almost 150 during his nine years there. George Frederick Adams resigned on 26 April 1876, suffering from cancer of the throat, and moved back to Baltimore, where he served as city missionary until he died on 16 April 1877.

Biography by Charles C. Bitting and editorial tribute in *Religious Herald*, 26 Apr. 1877; Oscar H. Darter, *History of Fredericksburg Baptist Church, Fredericksburg, Virginia* (1959), 62–64; Compiled Service Records; Blanche Sydnor White and Emily Lewelling Hogg, *History of the Hampton Baptist Church, 1791–1966* (1966), 24–33; death notice in *Baltimore Sun*, 17 Apr. 1877.

W. Harrison Daniel

ADAMS, Horace (24 May 1884–26 October 1964), clerk of court, was born in Charlotte County, the only son and elder of two children of John James Adams and Evelyn Ermina Adams Adams. His parents moved to Farmville when he was three years old, and he attended the public schools of Prince Edward County. At age eighteen he took a job in the office of the clerk of the local circuit court. In 1905 he became deputy clerk and on 11 May 1907 Judge George J. Hundley named Adams clerk of court. He held the position without interruption for the next fifty-three years and lived the remainder of his life in Farmville.

Adams faced opposition for reelection only once, defeating a fellow Democrat in the primary election in 1911. Thereafter he was virtually a nonpolitical officeholder. During Adams's long tenure the profession of clerk of court gradually became professional rather than political, and unlike most earlier clerks and many of his contemporaries, he did not use his office to exercise backroom political influence. He took no part in local politics and even managed to avoid disclosing his personal opinion on the most controversial political event in Prince Edward County during his lifetime, the struggle over the desegregation of the public schools. Adams was one of the founding members in 1910 of the Virginia Court Clerks' Association and was the only charter member still in office when he retired on 1 September 1960. Although not widely known outside the central Virginia counties, he was popular with local attorneys. On the occasion of Adams's fiftieth anniversary in office, Judge Joel W. Flood convened a special session of court and ordered his own personal words of praise "spread on the county records."

On 1 October 1918 Adams married Mattie Lucile Nichols, and they had one son. Adams served on the board of directors of the First National Bank of Farmville from 1933 to 1957, when he was elected vice president. He was also an active Mason, Shriner, Odd Fellow, and Lion, and he was an elder for many years of the Farmville Presbyterian Church. Horace Adams died of a heart attack on 26 October 1964 while visiting his son in Asheville, North Carolina, and was buried in Westview Cemetery in Farmville.

BVS Birth Register, Charlotte Co.; dates of service established from Prince Edward Co. Common Law Order Book, 4:233, 12:154; feature articles in *Farmville Herald*, 3 Oct. 1930, 29 Dec. 1944, 17 May 1957, 5, 9 Aug. 1960, and *Richmond Times-Dispatch*, 3 Aug. 1960 (por.); family and political information obtained from interviews and correspondence with Horace Adams Jr., John C. Spencer, and Vernon C. Womack; portrait of Adams in Prince Edward Co. Circuit Court; obituaries in *Richmond News Leader*, 27 Oct. 1964, and *Farmville Herald*, 27, 30 Oct. 1964.

KATHERINE M. SMITH

ADAMS, Howard Hanson (18 December 1891–3 December 1971), member of the House of Delegates, was born at Harborton, Accomack County, the eldest of two sons and one daughter of William Lawrence Adams and Effie Lee Evans Adams. His father was chief engineer on a steamboat in the Chesapeake Bay menhaden fishery. Adams served a short time as a teacher and principal in the Accomack County public schools after graduating from high school. In the summer of 1911 he worked in a general store in Cheriton and there favorably impressed George T. Tyson, who was campaigning for clerk of the circuit court of Northampton County. After he won the election Tyson offered Adams the job of deputy clerk.

Adams accepted and began a career of public service that spanned more than half a century. He brushed up his typewriting and other clerical skills with courses at Beacom Business College in Salisbury, Maryland, and in his spare hours he read law, took correspondence courses, and served from 1926 to 1931 as clerk and treasurer of Eastville, the county seat. Adams passed the state bar examination in July 1931 and opened a law office near the courthouse in Eastville while continuing to act as deputy county clerk until 1934. His wife, Mabel Edith Pruitt Adams, whom he had married on 20 July 1916, was his secretary. She also performed so efficiently as office manager and paralegal aide that he often later introduced her simply as "my partner." They had no children.

In 1933 Adams was elected to the Virginia House of Delegates from the district encompassing Accomack and Northampton Counties. He won the 1 August Democratic Party primary with 64 percent of the votes and was unopposed in the November general election. Thereafter he never again faced opposition in fifteen campaigns for reelection. At the opening of the 1934 General Assembly, Adams was appointed to the Committee on Appropriations, a plum rarely given to a freshman delegate. Seniority raised Adams in 1950 to the chairmanship of the committee, the assembly's most important committee in charge of the state's biennial budget bill and all other spending measures. During the administrations of four governors over the ensuing sixteen years, longer to date than any other chairman of the committee, Adams served effectively as legislative spokesman on budget matters.

Adams's time in the assembly overlapped the peak years of political power of the conservative state Democratic Party organization of Harry Flood Byrd. Democratic majorities from rural districts controlled both houses, and Adams was one of the reliably conservative country delegates dedicated to the organization's pay-as-you-go orthodoxy of austere frugality. Just five feet five inches tall, Adams was also one of the shortest of Byrd's legislative leaders. When Chairman Adams "took the center aisle" —i.e., spoke from the lectern in front of the

Speaker's dais—to present the budget bill, he stood on a box so that he could see over the mahogany fixture. When required to answer challenging questions or fend off hostile amendments, he did so calmly and courteously, often drily, rarely raising his voice, secure in the knowledge that the organization's substantial majority of House votes would sustain him. His spunky performances on the House floor and in presiding over committee hearings inspired someone to dub him "The Little Colonel." The sobriquet stuck, and in later years colleagues often addressed him simply as "Colonel."

Adams's devotion to his budget-shaping chores left him little opportunity for exercising leadership on other legislative matters, but he later cited two actions that had given him the most satisfaction. He served on the commission that produced the Potomac River Compact of 1958 by which fishing-law quarrels with Maryland were resolved, and he was one of the patrons of the legislation that authorized construction of the Chesapeake Bay Bridge-Tunnel in the 1960s. Adams went along with, but sometimes questioned, the hard line of Massive Resistance that Byrd laid down in the hope of thwarting the Supreme Court's school desegregation decisions of the 1950s, but on a few occasions the Little Colonel transcended the conservative political orthodoxy. In the 1959–1960 session of the assembly Byrd and Governor J. Lindsay Almond Jr. clashed over the school desegregation issue and fiscal policy during legislative agonies that were sometimes known as the Byrd organization's Götterdämmerung. Adams sided with the Massive Resisters on most racially tinged issues, but he supported Almond's efforts to raise new revenues with a state sales tax in order to increase appropriations for all levels of education.

After court-ordered reapportionment reduced the Eastern Shore's representation in the House of Delegates from two members to one, two younger men declared their candidacies, and Adams announced in March 1965 that he had reluctantly decided not to run for reelection. He had served longer in the General Assembly than any other Eastern Shore delegate or senator since the Revolution. Howard Hanson Adams died at the Hermitage retirement home in Onancock on 3 December 1971, just two weeks before his eightieth birthday, and was buried in the cemetery of Saint George's Episcopal Church between Harborton and Pungoteague. Mabel Adams died less than a year later.

Adams always used the birth date 18 Dec. 1891, but his birth was recorded in BVS Birth Register, Accomack Co., on 10 July 1892; Glass and Glass, *Virginia Democracy*, 2:413–414; scrapbooks of James E. Mears, Eastern Shore Public Library, Accomac (microfilm in LVA); the author covered the General Assembly for the *Richmond Times-Dispatch* during most of Adams's career in state politics; interviews with John Warren Cooke, Joseph H. Holleman Jr., Ruth Kelly, George N. McMath, A. L. Philpott, Baxley Tankard, Nora Miller Turman, and George A. Williams; feature articles in *Richmond Times-Dispatch*, 20 Jan. 1952 (por.), *Richmond News Leader*, 5 Mar. 1954, and *Onancock Eastern Shore News*, 15 Apr. 1965; obituaries in *Richmond Times-Dispatch*, *Richmond News Leader*, and *Norfolk Virginian-Pilot*, all 4 Dec. 1971, and *Onancock Eastern Shore News*, 9 Dec. 1971.

JAMES H. LATIMER

ADAMS, Isaac Holcombe (12 August 1837–9 February 1911), businessman, was born in Lynchburg, the second of three sons and third of five children of Isaac Adams and Susan Elizabeth Duval Adams. His father was a Lynchburg merchant until the 1840s, when he moved to Poplar Spring, a farm in the portion of Buckingham County that in 1845 became part of Appomattox County. Following his death in 1857, the family moved back to Lynchburg, where Isaac Holcombe Adams became a merchant. He married Mary Ann Patteson on 1 December 1859, and they had seven sons and five daughters. During the Civil War, Adams served first as a mail agent and later went to Montgomery County, where he and his older brother, William Duval Adams (10 July 1835–26 August 1906), operated a coal mine that supplied fuel to the Confederate navy.

By July 1865 I. H. Adams had taken the lead on behalf of himself, his older brother, and their younger brother, Richard Henry Toler Adams (6 November 1839–14 November 1900), in the purchase of a Lynchburg coal and lumber business, and he became president of the new company, I. H. Adams and Brothers. The company grew and diversified, adding a brickmaking plant, among other things, and taking on additional partners in the 1870s. On 29 April 1897 it was chartered as Adams Brothers and Paynes with I. H. Adams as president. The three brothers formed several other joint ventures in which all held offices, including a wholesale leaf tobacco dealership begun by 1876 and called R. H. T. Adams and Company (later Adams, Chambers, and Company) that annually exported thousands of pounds of tobacco to Europe and Australia.

The Adams brothers were leaders in the rapid commercial and industrial development that made Lynchburg one of the most prosperous cities in Virginia by 1900. That affluence enabled the city to become a cultural center where literature, the arts, music, and stylish residential architecture flourished. The brothers were active in the Court Street Methodist Church, and each had several sons and daughters who contributed to the commercial and cultural life of Lynchburg during the first half of the twentieth century.

W. Duval Adams was a deputy postmaster in Lynchburg before the Civil War and had a brief stint as a railroad agent for the Confederate post office before going to Montgomery County about 1862 to work at the coal mine. In addition to his participation in the family businesses after the war, he served as a director of the local Rivermont Investment and Construction Company from 1894 to 1896 and a member of the Lynchburg City Council from 1889 to 1895. He married Elizabeth Victorine Mullan on 18 July 1865, and they had five daughters and six sons. Duval Adams died 26 August 1906 and was buried in Spring Hill Cemetery in Lynchburg.

R. H. T. Adams clerked in a Richmond mercantile house from 1857 to 1861, and during the Civil War he served in the Confederate States Signal Corps on the staff of General A. P. Hill. Captain Adams, as he was called thereafter, became president of the family tobacco company and was also a successful businessman on his own. He invested wisely in several coal-mining companies, became secretary-treasurer of the Virginia Slate Mining Company, and served as a director of the West Lynchburg Land Company and as an executive of the Virginia Paving and Brick Company, which succeeded the family's brickmaking operation. He was also a founder of the Lynchburg Construction Company and president of the First National Bank of Lynchburg from 1892 to about 1896. In the 1870s and again in the 1880s he unsuccessfully attempted to raise capital to construct a cotton mill in Lynchburg. He was a member of the city council from 1881 to 1883. On 10 September 1868 he married Susan Leigh Scott, and they had three daughters and five sons. R. H. T. Adams died 14 November 1900 and was buried in Spring Hill Cemetery.

I. H. Adams was the financial head of the family, but like his brothers he also had other business interests. He served as a director of the National Exchange Bank of Lynchburg from 1881 to 1896 and as its vice president from 1888 until 1891. In 1896 he became president of the Citizens' Building and Banking Company. Adams was also an officer of the Glamorgan Pipe Foundry and of the Virginia Slate Mining Company, a founder of the Adams-Thornhill Manufacturing Company (which produced windows, doors, and other building supplies), and a director of the Eureka Coal and Coke Company and of the Lynchburg Coal and Coke Company. He retired from the family businesses about 1903 and died on 9 February 1911. He was buried in Spring Hill Cemetery where his wife, who died on 30 April 1902, was also buried.

The brothers' careers are discussed in "Lynchburg at the 20th Century!," special ed. of *Lynchburg News*, Oct. 1900; family history detailed in Richard L. Guild, *Mt. Comfort Plantation: A History and Description of an Authentic Colonial Virginia Home* (1983), 59–69 (with pors. of all three brothers), in Tyler, *Men of Mark,* 5:3–5, and in records of Court Street Methodist Church, Lynchburg; *Journal of the Congress of the Confederate States of America, 1861–1865* (1904–1905), 2:357, 3:97; Robert T. Bell, *11th Virginia Infantry* (1985), 63; advertisement in *Daily Lynchburg Virginian*, 10 July 1865; Lynchburg city directories, 1873–1899; Charter Book, 28:168–170, 33:392–396, obituaries of brothers and wife in *Lynchburg News*, 15 Nov. 1900, 1 May 1902, 28 Aug. 1906; obituary in *Lynchburg News*, 10 Feb. 1911.

PHILLIP WAYNE RHODES
BRENT TARTER

ADAMS, James Taylor (3 February 1892–3 September 1954), writer and folklore collector, was born in Letcher County, Kentucky, the only son and second of two children of Joseph Adams, a farmer and Baptist minister, and Mary Jane Short Adams. Although he read widely and continued to educate himself for the rest of his life, his formal education consisted of only a few months in the first four grades of school and some tutoring by his father, who died when James Adams was eight years old. The family then moved to Wise County, and at age thirteen Adams went to work in a coke yard in Glamorgan.

On 16 December 1908 he married his cousin Dicy Roberts. He was not quite seventeen, and she was fifteen. Their three sons and five daughters included a girl who died in infancy. For the first fifteen years of Adams's married life his restless energy and intellectual curiosity kept him moving and working at various jobs while he sought a profitable way to combine his curiosity about people, places, and events with his developing interest in writing. During those years the Adamses lived in Arkansas, Kentucky, Missouri, West Virginia, and Virginia. He farmed, sold nursery stock and insurance, dug coal, wrote for magazines and newspapers, ran a country store and a post office, and operated a subscription library by mail.

In 1923 Adams settled in Big Laurel, Wise County. For four years he wrote articles on local history and the regional lore of the Cumberland Mountains for *Crawford's Weekly*, edited and published in Norton by a man with interests similar to his own. Bruce Crawford was a skillful editor and writer who promoted industrial development but also championed working people, especially coal miners. The *Weekly* was much more than just another country newspaper. For five months in 1926 Crawford also published a literary journal, *The Virginia Digest*, and he encouraged Adams to do likewise. Adams accordingly traded some of the books of his large library for a small printing plant and began a series of periodicals, but he could not replicate Crawford's success at remaining solvent while producing entertaining and instructive columns for the limited local market. Adams's short-lived ventures in newspaper and magazine publishing included *The Wise Gazette* (1927), the *Vagabond Gazette* (1928–1930), the *Adams Weekly* (1929), the *Liberal* (1929), the *Neon (Ky.) News* (1932), and the *Cumberland Empire* (1932–1933), a magazine of regional history and folklore.

Adams also took an interest in his family history, establishing a library and genealogical research center near his home, and beginning a journal, *Adams Family Records* (1929), that survived for only two issues. The only book by Adams to appear in his lifetime was his self-published *Death in the Dark: A Collection of Factual Ballads of American Mine Disasters, with Historical Notes* (1941). This pioneering collection of American folk songs included a plea for the welfare of coal miners, one of many reform causes he espoused.

By late in 1935 Adams had registered for relief. He soon joined the Works Progress Administration's Virginia Historical Inventory Project, one of several New Deal cultural programs designed to aid unemployed professional men and women. He documented places, events, and objects of historical interest in Wise County. On 29 March 1938 he was assigned to the WPA's Virginia Writers' Project and began officially collecting folklore in Wise County. Initially the Writers' Project focused on publishing *Virginia: A Guide to the Old Dominion* (1940), but as the book neared completion the WPA turned its attention to other subjects, including the collection of folklore. By the time the Virginia Writers' Project ended in June 1942, it had amassed eleven file boxes of prose material and 2,732 songs. Adams turned in about one-third of all the folklore material. His longstanding familiarity with and interest in his native region's culture made the quality and authenticity of his material superior to most of that collected in other parts of Virginia.

On 22 September 1953 Adams began an "Outline for my Memories." He wrote, "I think I will call it 'I've Struggled Along.'" He listed fifteen books that he wished to write and four others that he had written and wished to publish. None was printed while he was alive, although his memoir of his childhood, *Grandpap Told Me Tales*, was finally published in 1993. At another time or, perhaps, in another place, Adams might have been a successful writer and publisher, but during his lifetime in Big Laurel, Virginia, it was not to be. However, for thirty years he documented the history and culture of the people of his native Cumberland Mountains. More than his numerous small publications, his legacy is his contribution to the WPA's folklore collection and the 137 boxes of invaluable material in his collected papers. James Taylor Adams died of cancer on 3 September 1954. At the time of his death he was trying to dictate a story, but he was too weak to make himself understood. He was buried near his home.

James Taylor Adams Papers, Clinch Valley College Library, Wise; biographical treatments include Frederic D. Vanover, *James Taylor Adams: A Brief Biography* (1937), Patsy Mellon and Edward L. Henson Jr., "James Taylor Adams, 1893–1954: Mountain Scholar," *Virginia Cavalcade* 21 (spring 1972): 12–17 (por.), and Charles L. Perdue Jr., *Outwitting the Devil: Jack Tales from Wise County, Virginia* (1987), 80–119; the WPA folklore collection is at UVA; obituaries in *Norton Coalfield Progress* and *Big Stone Gap Post*, both 9 Sept. 1954.

CHARLES L. PERDUE JR.

ADAMS, Jasper Lewis (27 October 1879–31 January 1973), Upper Mattaponi chief, was born in King William County, the only child of Millard Adams and Catherine Wala Forten Adams. His mother died when he was two years old. His father then remarried and had two more sons and one daughter before dying when Adams was twelve years old. Adams attended a one-room Indian school for a short time before it closed because there were too few pupils to keep it open. His father and stepmother taught him all they could, but his formal education stopped early and he was essentially self-educated.

On 14 November 1900 Adams married Mollie Wade Holmes. They had six sons and six daughters. He worked as a farmer and hunted and fished in his spare time. In later years he became a truck driver and a salesman and held a variety of temporary jobs. He did not retire until he was eighty years old.

For most of his adult life Adams was a leader of the Upper Mattaponi community known during his youth as the Adamstown tribe. With links to the Mattaponi and the Pamunkey who occupied two historic reservations southeast of Adamstown, the Upper Mattaponi had never held reservation lands but lived on their own property or, like many other Tidewater Virginians, rented farmland or worked on timber farms. Adams assisted in the purchase of the property on which the Upper Mattaponi constructed the Sharon Indian School in 1919. He also helped build Indian View Baptist Church in King William County in 1942, served as its senior deacon for more than thirty years, and became a trustee of the church and its cemetery. On 4 July 1923 the Adamstown tribe officially organized itself as the Upper Mattaponi and appointed Adams its chief. He held the office until his death almost fifty years later. A year after he died, his son Andrew Washington Adams was elected chief of the Upper Mattaponi.

Adams lived to be ninety-three years old and had a very large family. His wife and nine of his twelve children were living at the time of his death, and he then had thirty-six grandchildren, fifty-one great-grandchildren, and three great-great-grandchildren. Jasper Lewis Adams died in King William County on 31 January 1973 and was buried in the churchyard at Indian View Baptist Church.

The contributor is a daughter of Adams; photograph in *Upper Mattaponi Tribal Spring Festival & Pow-Wow, May 27, 1989* (1989); obituaries in *Richmond News Leader*, 2 Feb. 1973, and *Richmond Times-Dispatch*, 3 Feb. 1973.

EUNICE A. ADAMS

ADAMS, John (14 July 1773–23 June 1825), physician, merchant, and Richmond City mayor, was born in Richmond. He was the fifth of six sons and tenth of eleven children of Richard Adams (1726–1800) and Elizabeth Griffin Adams. His brothers Richard Adams and Samuel Adams were both men of consequence in the social, economic, and political affairs of Richmond after the death of their wealthy and distinguished father, but John Adams was the most prominent of Richard Adams's sons.

Adams studied medicine with Richmond physician John Cringan before going to Edinburgh, where he earned an M.D. in 1796 with a thesis entitled *De Suspensa Respiratione*. He returned to Richmond and began his practice in partnership with Cringan. Adams was later an original member of the first Medical Society of

Virginia, organized in 1821 and chartered in 1824. Sometime before 1800 he married Margaret Winston, daughter of Geddes Winston, one of the wealthiest men in Richmond. They had six daughters and two sons. In 1801, near his father's commodious frame house on Church Hill, Adams built an imposing brick residence that later became the Van Lew family mansion.

Adams was a busy public man. He was a Federalist member of the House of Delegates from 1802 to 1804, a Richmond alderman in 1808, 1809, and 1817, and a member of the Richmond Common Council, 1810–1812, 1814–1817, and 1818–1819. On 15 April 1819 he was elected mayor of Richmond and remained in the office until his death. The General Assembly having given additional powers to the office of mayor and to the mayor's court early in 1819, Adams was the first mayor of Richmond with these expanded duties. He was most remembered for improving the roads, completing the naming of streets and numbering of houses, and being "the terror of evil-doers in the mayor's court."

Adams became one of the most important investors and builders in Richmond. By 1818 only four men owned more real estate in the city than he did, and only seven paid taxes on more personal property, slaves excepted. On his own or with any of several business partners, he built warehouses, commercial property, and large residential buildings. With Benjamin Mosby he laid off and developed Union Hill and the adjacent Venable Street neighborhoods. Adams built and owned several buildings on E Street, later Main Street, including the Union Hotel (1817), the city's first large, modern hotel. He also acquired much of Church Hill's best real estate, and he owned farmland and coal-mine interests as well. The panic of 1819 and the depression that followed severely reduced the value of Adams's property, and he lost a great deal of money, which prevented him for making any more large investments thereafter. John Adams died in Richmond on 23 June 1825 and was probably buried in the family cemetery at what is now the corner of Marshall and Twenty-third Streets. The graves were moved to Hollywood Cemetery in 1892.

C. W. Coleman, "Genealogy of the Adams Family of New Kent and Henrico Counties, Va.," *WMQ*, 1st ser., 5 (1897): 163; Wyndham B. Blanton, *Medicine in Virginia in the Eighteenth Century* (1931), 80, 87, 151, 287; Blanton, *Medicine in Virginia in the Nineteenth Century* (1933), 76, 319; George Wythe Munford, *The Two Parsons* (1884), 76; W. Asbury Christian, *Richmond, Her Past and Present* (1912), 58, 72, 79, 102–103, 105; Mary Wingfield Scott, *Houses of Old Richmond* (1941), 12, 57, 68–69, 73, 92–93, 143; Scott, *Old Richmond Neighborhoods* (1950), 31, 51, 59, 71–72, 139; Marianne Patricia Buroff Sheldon, "Richmond, Virginia: The Town and Henrico County to 1820" (Ph.D. diss., University of Michigan, 1975), 81–82, 120, 298, 353; obituaries in *Richmond Whig*, 24 June 1825, and *Richmond Enquirer*, 28 June 1825.

Brent Tarter

ADAMS, John Henry (ca. January 1848–5 March 1934), Richmond City alderman, was born at 227 West Leigh Street in Richmond, the younger of two sons and second of four children of John Adams and Octavia Jackson Adams. His father was a contractor and plasterer, one of fifteen free blacks in Virginia who had accumulated at least $4,000 in property by 1860. The senior Adams owned thirteen houses and lots in that year and bought eight more by 1871, making him Richmond's leading African American real estate holder. When he died in 1873 his estate was reportedly worth about $40,000. Adams's father had at least a basic education and an excellent reputation. He took a leading role in the First African and Ebenezer Baptist Churches in Richmond, interested himself in the colonization movement, and served after the war as an officer in black labor unions.

John H. Adams matriculated in 1869 at Lincoln University in Chester County, Pennsylvania, and received an A.B. in 1873. He became a plasterer and was active in several of Richmond's black organizations. On 26 July 1876 he married Anna Boyd. Their two sons both died in infancy and she died on 29 May 1879.

Adams is best known for his involvement in the politics of Richmond's Jackson Ward, gerrymandered by conservative whites in 1871 so as to concentrate African American voters into one district and thereby limit the number of city council members they could elect at one time. Adams was one of thirty-three African American Republicans who represented the ward on the Richmond City Council between 1871 and 1898. His tenure in office coincided with the peak of black political power in post-Reconstruction Richmond. Elected to the common council for a two-year term in 1882, Adams was one of only six blacks appointed to the school committee during this period. With his colleagues, as a councillor and subsequently as an alderman (1884–1888), he won improvements in neighborhood schools, streets, and lighting, but he failed to gain a park, an armory, and other goals of ward residents.

Adams's photograph depicts a man of unmistakable dignity, with a long, heavy moustache and the clothing of a prominent citizen. He was part of the city's black elite and one of the pioneer political leaders whose successes and failures epitomized the biracial politics of the late nineteenth century and anticipated the political struggles of African Americans in the twentieth century. Like his father, Adams was active in the Ebenezer Church and was one of five delegates from the congregation to a council of Richmond's black Baptist churches that met in 1881 to settle a controversy within the First African Baptist Church. Adams was also a trustee of the city's Friends' Asylum for Colored Orphans.

On 19 November 1895 Adams married a young widow, Letitia Banister, of Danville. The register described him as a resident of New Haven, Connecticut, and they may have resided there for a time before settling in Danville, where Adams worked as a plasterer for the Charles Orchard Company. Of their two children, only a son survived childhood. John Henry Adams retired around 1930 and returned to Richmond. He died in the Richmond home of a niece on 5 March 1934 and was buried in Richmond's Evergreen Cemetery.

Census, Danville City, 1900, gives Jan. 1858 birth date, but other census, marriage, and death records give ages indicating birth as early as 1845 and as late as 1861, although generally clustered in 1847–1849; obituary of father in *Washington New National Era*, 27 Feb. 1873; *Lincoln University College and Theological Seminary Biographical Catalogue* (1918), 11; BVS Marriage Registers, Richmond and Danville Cities; *Richmond Planet*, 30 Nov. 1895; Richmond and Danville city directories; Richmond City Common Council Records, 1882–1884, and Board of Aldermen Journal, 1884–1888; Michael B. Chesson, "Richmond's Black Councilmen, 1871–1896," in *Southern Black Leaders of the Reconstruction Era*, ed. Howard N. Rabinowitz (1982), 200; Jackson, *Free Negro Labor*, 151, 157–158, 161–162; Jackson, *Negro Office-Holders*, 11 (por.), 57; John T. O'Brien, "Factory, Church, and Community: Blacks in Antebellum Richmond," *JSH* 44 (1978): 509–536; Peter J. Rachleff, *Black Labor in the South: Richmond, Virginia, 1865–1890* (1984), 56–57, 162, 243; Mary Wingfield Scott, *Old Richmond Neighborhoods* (1950), 231, 245–246, 250, 291; BVS Death Register, Richmond City.

MICHAEL B. CHESSON

ADAMS, Martha Rivers (10 November 1882–29 June 1959), journalist, was born on a plantation in Giles County, Tennessee, the youngest of four daughters and three sons of James William Rivers, a Confederate veteran, and Mary Flournoy Rivers. Martha Rivers attended Athens Female College in Athens, Alabama, and Martin Female College in Pulaski, Tennessee, before enrolling in 1900 at Randolph-Macon Woman's College in Lynchburg, where she studied for two years but did not take a degree. On 12 January 1904 she married William Duval Adams Jr., son of a prominent Lynchburg businessman. During the ensuing thirteen years they had eight children, two of whom died at birth.

In 1917, after serving occasionally as a substitute for the society editor of the *Lynchburg News*, Adams became a full-time reporter on the newspaper's staff. She was one of the first generation of Virginia women to take up journalism as a career. In her case, her husband's profession as a civil engineer was punctuated by periods of unemployment and absence from home, and she needed an additional and reliable income to support her children long before he died in June 1936. She had gotten her start reporting on cultural events and women's activities, which were considered proper subjects for a woman's pen, but she almost immediately began covering the local courts, reporting city government news and local politics, writing about the city's servicemen, and contributing to every portion of the newspaper except the sports pages. An avid reader, she wrote book reviews and music reviews throughout her long career, and in 1950, assisted by her namesake daughter, she began a weekly column called "Browsings," which treated a wide variety of cultural subjects. In the newsroom Adams had the reputation of a skilled professional who was good at covering a story, writing, editing, and training young reporters.

Adams also participated in local arts organizations and served as a director of the Travelers' Aid Society from 1914 to 1950. Her one brief period of public service occurred in June 1926, when Governor Harry Flood Byrd appointed her to the large citizens' advisory committee he created during his reorganization of the state government. Martha Rivers Adams died in Virginia Baptist Hospital in Lynchburg on 29 June 1959 and was buried in Spring Hill Cemetery.

Biographical files, Jones Memorial Library, Lynchburg; death notices of husband in *Lynchburg Daily Advance*, 10 June 1936, and *Lynchburg News*, 11 June 1936; some family history provided by William Duval Adams III; obituaries in *Lynchburg News* (por.), *Lynchburg Daily Advance*, *Washington Post*, and *New York Times*, all 29 June 1959; editorial tributes in *Lynchburg Daily Advance*, 29 June 1959, and *Lynchburg News*, 30 June 1959.

LIB WILEY

ADAMS, Pauline Forstall Colclough (29 June 1874–10 September 1957), woman suffrage activist, was born in Dublin, Ireland, to Henry Vesey Colclough and Catherine Forstall Colclough. Sometime in her youth, perhaps in 1890, she immigrated to America with her family. By 1898 she was living in Brunswick County, North Carolina, where she married Norfolk physician Walter J. Adams on 18 April. The couple moved to Norfolk and there he established a medical practice and she gave birth to their two sons. Unlike many women of her era, however, Adams's life reached far beyond her household and into the community.

When the Woman's Jamestown Association was formed in 1903 in preparation for the 1907 Jamestown Ter-Centennial Exposition, Adams joined, had a brief stint as associate editor of its publication, the *Jamestown Bulletin*, and served as treasurer from 1905 until the exposition ended. In 1906 she was elected head of Norfolk's Jamestown Esperanto Club. She also belonged to the Housewives' League. Of the many meetings that undoubtedly took place at Adams's house, located in the Ghent area of the city, the most influential occurred on 18 November 1910, when the Norfolk Equal Suffrage League was organized there.

Adams served as the first president of the Norfolk league (a National American Woman Suffrage Association affiliate) and was reelected in 1911 and 1912 before declining to run again. During her last year as president the Equal Suffrage League held its state convention in Norfolk. She invented two popular suffrage games (now lost), Politics and Political Auction, which were sold in Virginia and Maryland in 1913 to raise funds for suffrage work. Adams advocated a more militant approach to winning the vote for women than her fellow Virginia suffragists, shunning the primarily educational activities of the Norfolk league in favor of speaking in the city's streets and marching in Washington during President Woodrow Wilson's 1913 inaugural parade. Her opinions and actions prompted a serious rift in the conservative Norfolk league and brought a reprimand from state league headquarters in Richmond. Before her decisive move toward militancy, Adams had been a rising star in the Virginia league, serving as one of its five vice presidents.

Despite the Equal Suffrage League's censure, the Congressional Union for Woman Suffrage organized a Virginia chapter at a June 1915 meeting in Richmond. Founded in April 1913, the Congressional Union was originally formed as a section of NAWSA dedicated to the passage of a federal amendment. Serious differences soon divided the two groups. While the parent organization was committed to winning the vote through state campaigns, the CU demanded an exclusive campaign for a federal amendment. Techniques also differed, with NAWSA favoring an educational approach while the CU advocated more militant means, including picketing. When the CU campaigned against the Democratic Party in 1914 despite NAWSA's nonpartisan stance, the latter expelled the CU. In 1916 the militants renamed themselves the National Woman's Party. Adams—who had retained her membership while other members of the Equal Suffrage League withdrew—was elected a CU vice chairman at the 1915 meeting and later served as president of the Norfolk NWP branch from 1917 to 1920. Her NWP membership placed her in the minority among southern suffragists.

With the outbreak of World War I, Adams sprang into action, calling for the formation of a Women's Home Guard in Norfolk in April 1917. She was sure that women would join, and planned to volunteer herself. Sixty women enlisted and were trained to guard the city's bridges. Unlike the Equal Suffrage League, which suspended political activities in favor of charitable work, the National Woman's Party continued the fight for suffrage during the war while also doing its part for America's troops. As local NWP president, Adams led the women's section of Norfolk's Preparedness Parade and sold war bonds and stamps at local hotels. Other members volunteered for the Red Cross, entertained sailors with coffee and home-cooked meals, and chaperoned dances.

The war escalated the fight for suffrage. In the summer of 1917 the Virginia Equal Suffrage League joined NAWSA in condemning women who picketed the White House. On 4 September 1917 Adams was one of thirteen picketers arrested for "flaunting their banners" in front of President Wilson's reviewing stand before a selective service parade. Similar charges were already pending against her for other actions. Along with some of her fellow protesters, Adams addressed the court in her own defense. When given a choice between sixty days in jail or a $25 fine, the suffragists as a whole chose prison and were sent to the workhouse at Occoquan, in Prince William County.

Not long after Adams was imprisoned, the Occoquan workhouse was investigated, at the prompting of the National Woman's Party, for mistreatment of its inmates. Adams complained, along with other prisoners, that the food was infested with worms and that women were deprived of blankets, combs, eyeglasses, soap, and (most offensive to her) toothbrushes.

After the Nineteenth Amendment was passed in August 1920, Adams looked for new challenges. In 1921 she passed the bar exam and became the second woman lawyer in Norfolk. She remained involved in politics, running unsuccessfully for city council and campaigning in November 1923 for Sarah Lee Fain, one of the first two women ever elected to the House of Delegates. A member of Christ and Saint Luke's Episcopal Church, Pauline Colclough Adams died of myocardial failure on 10 September 1957 and was buried in Elmwood Cemetery in Norfolk.

Equal Suffrage League Papers, LVA; Marjorie Spruill Wheeler, *New Women of the New South: The Leaders of the Woman Suffrage Movement in the Southern States* (1993), 28, 76–77, 151–152, 174; Christine A. Lunardini, *From Equal Suffrage to Equal Rights: Alice Paul and the National Woman's Party, 1910–1928* (1986), 32–49, 111–113, 131; *Virginian-Pilot and the Norfolk Landmark*, 7, 17 Apr. 1917; *Washington Post*, 5, 6 Sept. 1917; jail letters to sons Edward Forstall Adams, 30 Sept. 1917, and Walter P. Adams, 23 Oct. 1917, Norfolk Public Library; affidavit by Adams on Occoquan workhouse conditions, 8 Nov. 1917, National Woman's Party Papers, LC; *Norfolk Ledger Dispatch*, 16 Dec. 1921 (por.); obituary in *Norfolk Virginian Pilot*, 11 Sept. 1957; editorial tributes in *Norfolk Virginian Pilot* and *Norfolk Ledger-Dispatch*, both 12 Sept. 1957.

JENNIFER DAVIS MCDAID

ADAMS, Richard (17 May 1726–1 or 2 August 1800), merchant and member of the Convention of 1776, was born in New Kent County, the fourth of five sons and fourth of eight children of Ebenezer Adams and Tabitha Cocke Adams, daughter of Richard Cocke, of Bremo, Henrico County. His eldest brother, also named Richard, died in infancy. Ebenezer Adams emigrated before 1714 from Essex County, England, to New Kent County, where he was probably a merchant factor.

On 10 April 1755 Richard Adams married Elizabeth Griffin, daughter of Leroy Griffin and Mary Anne Bertrand Griffin, of Richmond County, and sister of Cyrus Griffin, later the last president of the Confederation Congress and a federal district court judge. Of their six sons and five daughters, all but one son lived to maturity and several achieved prominence in early-ninteenth-century Richmond, the most notable being the physician John Adams. Early histories sometimes confuse Richard Adams with his namesake son, who lived from 1760 to 1817.

Adams lived at Cumberland Town in New Kent County and later at Richmond in Henrico County. He served as a trustee of Richmond before the Revolutionary War, operated a mercantile house there in partnership with his brother Thomas Adams, and engaged in lucrative land speculation. By the 1770s he was probably Richmond's wealthiest citizen and well on his way to being one of the richest men in central Virginia. When he died he owned at least

16,761 acres of land, including valuable lots near his residence on Church Hill (also called Adams Hill or Richmond Hill) in Richmond, a plantation at White Oak Swamp in Henrico County, his father's lot in Cumberland Town, and property in the counties of Augusta, Botetourt, Essex, Fluvanna, Goochland, and Patrick. He also owned a coal mine in Goochland County and a half-interest in 3,000 acres in Fayette County, Kentucky. He lived in one of the largest houses in Virginia's capital and owned four carriages.

Adams wielded extensive commercial and political influence. His firm's many business clients included Thomas Jefferson, who ordered some of the first furnishings for his mansion at Monticello through the Adams brothers. Adams was elected to the Henrico Parish vestry on 3 October 1761 and was still serving in 1773 when the extant records end. A justice of the peace for New Kent County from before 1752 until about 1774 and for Henrico County from 15 December 1766 until his death, he also served as a burgess for New Kent from 1752 to 1765 and for Henrico from 1769 to 1776, attended all five of the conventions between 1774 and 1776, and in May and June 1776 was a member of the committee that reported the draft Virginia Declaration of Rights and the state's first constitution. He supplied foodstuffs and military equipment to the Virginia army beginning in 1775 and became chairman in 1776 of a three-member board charged with erecting a public foundry at Westham near Richmond.

Adams represented Henrico in the House of Delegates from 1776 to 1778, and he sat in the Senate of Virginia for the district comprising Henrico, Goochland, and Louisa Counties from 1778 to 1782, when he concluded a legislative career interrupted only once in thirty years. In May 1780 the General Assembly named him one of the directors of public buildings in charge of overseeing the erection of the new Capitol. He offered to give the state some of his choice Church Hill lots (the acceptance of which would certainly have increased the value of his other lots) but, according to persistent legend, Thomas Jefferson persuaded the other directors to select a site on nearby Shockoe Hill. Adams allegedly broke off his friendship with Jefferson as a result.

When the municipal government of Richmond was organized on 2–3 July 1782, Adams gained a seat on the common council but resigned two weeks later, perhaps because he was not among those chosen as aldermen. He did subsequently become an alderman on 5 January 1784, and he was elected mayor on 11 December 1786. Adams held the office until he resigned on 21 February 1788.

Almost no public function or civic improvement took place in Richmond without Adams's prominent participation, beginning with his subscription of £8 in 1762 to a fund for the encouragement of arts and manufactures and his participation three years later in the first canal company to attempt improvement of the navigation of the James River. His letters to his brother Thomas Adams contain informative accounts of business and political conditions in Richmond from the 1760s to the 1780s.

Richard Adams died during the night of 1–2 August 1800 and was buried in the family cemetery, located near what is now the corner of Marshall and Twenty-third Streets. He was reinterred in Hollywood Cemetery in 1892.

Adams Family Papers, VHS; birth recorded in Churchill G. Chamberlayne, ed., *The Vestry Book and Register of St. Peter's Parish, New Kent and James City Counties, Virginia, 1706–1786* (1937), 451; letters to brother in *VMHB* 5 (1897–1898): 132–138, 290–297; 22 (1914): 379–395; C. W. Coleman, "Genealogy of the Adams Family of New Kent and Henrico Counties, Va.," *WMQ*, 1st ser., 5 (1897): 160–163; George H. S. King, ed., *Marriages of Richmond County, Virginia, 1668–1853* (1964), 1; death reported with variant dates in *Richmond Virginia Argus* and *Richmond Virginia Gazette, and General Advertiser*, both 5 Aug. 1800; transcript of will in Kentucky Court of Appeals Deed Book, Y:84–89 (photocopy in Adams Family Papers, VHS).

Brent Tarter

ADAMS, Samuel Chaplin (14 March 1853–23 November 1926), president of the Inter-State Tobacco Growers' Protective Association of Virginia and North Carolina, was born in Halifax County, the eldest of two sons and two daughters of William Wilson Adams and his first wife, Susan A. Wilson Adams. Nothing is known of Adams's education. He was working as a conductor on a railroad in Pittsylvania County when he married Christiana Wade Dickenson on 28 October 1873. They had one daughter and six sons, the eldest of whom, Berkley Dickenson Adams, became chairman of the State Corporation Commission.

Adams was a farmer in Pittsylvania County during the 1870s and 1880s. Perhaps through his membership in the Baptist Church, he became a well-known advocate of Prohibition in Southside Virginia. He also joined the Farmers' Alliance. His advocacy of Prohibition and his participation in the alliance taught him public speaking and organizational skills and enlarged his ambitions. In 1890 he ran for Congress as an independent from the Fifth Congressional District. He evidently hoped to capitalize on dissatisfaction with the political parties and on his connections with the Farmers' Alliance and the Prohibition movement. Even though he did little campaigning, he garnered almost 10 percent of the vote.

In about 1894 Adams moved to Red Hill in Charlotte County, where he farmed and operated a sawmill and a spoke factory. He soon became active on behalf of tobacco farmers. On 17 November 1903 delegates from eleven counties along the Virginia–North Carolina border meeting in Danville elected Adams president of the Tobacco Growers' Protective Association of Virginia and North Carolina. The organization changed its name in 1904 to the Inter-State Tobacco Growers' Protective Association of Virginia and North Carolina. Until he relinquished the presidency in 1909, Adams played a leading role in organizing tobacco farmers in what was known as the Old Belt growing area, which produced tobacco for the rapidly expanding cigarette-manufacturing industry. The association sought to curtail the influence of tobacco warehouse owners, who often set the prices tobacco farmers received and kept large proportions of the sums manufacturers paid for leaf tobacco. Adams advocated establishing cooperative storage facilities to enable farmers to sell their tobacco directly to manufacturers. He did not, in the tradition of the trustbusters, attack the largest manufacturer, the American Tobacco Company. Rather, he tried to negotiate contracts with it to cut out the middlemen. The association enjoyed only limited success. Rising prices and the breakup of the American Tobacco Company in 1911 increased competition in the tobacco auction warehouses but reduced the influence of the association and its cooperative schemes.

Christiana Adams died on 18 December 1910. The following year Adams married a widow, Jenny Wellbrook, of South Carolina. He lived in Charleston, South Carolina, for most of the remainder of his life and operated a soft-drink bottling plant, which his sons later purchased. They moved the equipment to Red Oak after his death and the family operated it for more than thirty years as one of its many business enterprises in that part of Charlotte County. Samuel Chaplin Adams died at Red Oak on 23 November 1926 and was buried in the family cemetery.

Lona Odell Adams Fletcher Seitz and Gordon S. Adams, eds., *An Adams Family of Virginia, 1800 to Present* (1990), 7–19; family records in Samuel C. Adams Bible printed in *Southsider* 7 (1988): 60–62 (por.); first marriage also recorded in Pittsylvania Co. Marriage Register; other family history verified by grandson Gordon S. Adams; Census, Agriculture Schedule, Pittsylvania Co., 1880; Election Records, vol. 92, RG 13, LVA; Nannie May Tilley, *Bright-Tobacco Industry, 1860–1929* (1948), 428–442, contains a history of the Inter-State Tobacco Growers' Protective Association and cites the Samuel C. Adams Papers, which can no longer be located; the association's activities received extensive coverage in its paper, the *Southern Tobacconist and Modern Farmer*, and some coverage in the *Progressive Farmer*; Gerald T. Gilliam, "Red Oak Bottling Company," *Southsider* 8 (1989): 42–47; obituaries in *Danville Register*, 24 Nov. 1926, and *Drakes Branch Charlotte Gazette*, 25 Nov. 1926.

CHRISTOPHER E. ALLEN

ADAMS, Theodore Floyd (26 September 1898–27 February 1980), president of the World Baptist Alliance, was born in Palmyra, New York, the eldest of three sons and one daughter of Floyd Holden Adams and Evelyn Emma Sarah Parks Adams. His father was a Baptist minister, and the family moved frequently. Young Adams lived in McMinnville, Oregon, in Lebanon and Hammond, Indiana, and in Brooklyn, New York. Following his graduation from high school in Hammond he spent a year studying English and grammar before enrolling in the National College of Chiropractic in Chicago. With a chiropractic degree in hand and contemplating a career in the ministry, he and his brother Earl Adams enrolled as freshmen together at Denison University in Granville, Ohio. Adams graduated Phi Beta Kappa in 1921, then entered Rochester Theological Seminary in New York. He took his bachelor of theology degree and was ordained at the Baptist Temple in Rochester on 22 May 1924.

At Denison, Adams had met Esther Josephine Jillson, whom he married on 26 February 1925 in Beaver Dam, Wisconsin. They had one daughter and two sons. Adams began his ministerial career at the Cleveland Heights Baptist Church in Cleveland in 1924. In 1928 he moved to the Ashland Avenue Baptist Church in Toledo, where he remained for eight years and served as president of the Toledo Council of Churches, an indication of his emerging ecumenical spirit. Although Adams belonged to the Northern Baptist Convention, in December 1936 the First Baptist Church of Richmond, a historic Southern Baptist congregation, invited him to become its pastor.

Adams began his ministry in Richmond in February 1937 and was an immediate success. During his first two years, the congregation increased from fourteen hundred to nineteen hundred members. The church soon overcame the financial difficulties of the Great Depression and eventually grew to include about four thousand members. Adams was essentially a conservative theologian and minister, although clearly not an inerrantist fundamentalist. He was a popular preacher whose sermons tended to be practical in nature. Among his best-received sermon topics was an annual series on marriage and the Christian family. The first and most popular of his four books published during his lifetime, *Making Your Marriage Succeed: The Christian Basis for Love and Marriage* (1953), featured several of these sermons. Another collection of his sermons, *The Windowsill of Heaven* (1992), saw print a dozen years after his death. In addition to his ministry at the church, he also delivered sermons and short daily messages on Richmond radio and television stations.

First Baptist Church remained Adams's chief responsibility and concern, but he devoted significant time and energy to other causes. From 1941 to 1956 he served as president of the board of trustees of Virginia Union University, a historically black Richmond college, and was honorary president thereafter until his death. From 1942 until his retirement he also sat on the board of the University of Richmond. In addition, Adams was a member of the Southern Baptist Convention's Foreign Mission Board, which had its headquarters in Richmond. He helped found Richmond Memorial Hospital, which he described as a living memorial to the men and women killed in World War II, and was the president of its board from 1946 to 1960 and again from 1977 to 1980. In 1981 the trustees named a new wing of the hospital the Theodore Floyd Adams Emergency Medical Center. The international relief organization, CARE, also benefited from his attention, through both the financial support of the First Baptist Church and Adams's service as its vice president. He was also president of the board of the Baptist Children's Home in Salem for more than a decade and was founding president of the Virginia Institute of Pastoral Care, established in 1967.

Adams served the Baptist World Alliance continuously throughout his career. Appointed to its youth committee as early as 1928, he served on the executive committee from 1934 until his retirement. The crowning achievement of his career came on 20 July 1955, when the Ninth Congress in London elected him to a five-year term as president. His travels in the service of the alliance took him to Europe, Asia, Africa, and South America. In the Soviet Union he became the first American Protestant clergyman since 1917 to administer communion. His term ended in 1960 at the Tenth Congress in Rio de Janeiro.

Adams was deeply involved in international ecumenical affairs. He attended the first meeting of the World Council of Churches in Amsterdam in 1946, even though the Southern Baptist Convention was not an affiliate. His commitment to the ecumenical movement assured that he would never attain the national presidency of the conservative Southern Baptist Convention. A man of northern birth in a city of southern traditions, Adams occasionally faced disagreements with his views. In 1965 two Virginia Union University students, both sons of

Nigerian Baptist ministers, applied for membership in the church. Integration of the congregation was a highly charged emotional issue, which Adams settled for the moment by a compromise. The students were allowed to participate in church affairs under what was called the "watchcare" of the church but were not accepted as full voting members. When he retired three years later, the *Richmond Times-Dispatch* editorially remarked that it was a tribute to Adams and to Richmond that he had become one of the most important clergymen in its history: "The fact that 'Ted' Adams was quickly accepted in Richmond just about as wholeheartedly as if he had been a direct descendent of Robert E. Lee testifies to his exceptional qualities."

Following Adams's retirement from the ministry on 23 June 1968, he began a second career as a professor at the Southeastern Baptist Theological Seminary in Wake Forest, North Carolina. Until his second retirement in 1978 he drew on his own rich experience to help prepare young men and women for the ministry. Widely regarded as one of the most able and prominent Baptist ministers in the country, he received honorary degrees from ten colleges and universities. The 5 December 1955 issue of *Time* magazine featured Adams on its cover. In 1960 the *Upper Room*, a devotional magazine issued by the Board of Evangelism of the Methodist Church, awarded him its annual citation for accomplishment in worldwide Christian fellowship, and he also received a National Brotherhood Award from the National Conference of Christians and Jews in 1964. Theodore Floyd Adams suffered a stroke on 24 February 1980 and died in Richmond three days later. He was buried in Westhampton Memorial Park.

Theodore Floyd Adams, "Why I Became a Minister," *Richmond Times-Dispatch*, 5 July 1955; *Time*, 5 Dec. 1955, 66–74 (por.); obituaries in *Richmond News Leader* and *Richmond Times-Dispatch*, both 28 Feb. 1980, *New York Times*, 29 Feb. 1980, *Washington Post*, 3 Mar. 1980, and *Religious Herald*, 6 Mar. 1980.

BERNARD H. COCHRAN

ADAMS, Thomas (ca. 1730–July 1788), merchant and member of the Continental Congress, was probably born in Cumberland Town in New Kent County. He was the youngest of five sons and sixth of eight children of Ebenezer Adams and Tabitha Cocke Adams. About 1775 he married Elizabeth Fauntleroy Cocke, widow of his cousin Bowler Cocke (1726–1772). They had no children.

Adams was a justice of the New Kent County Court for many years before his removal from the court on 6 February 1773 because of his long absences. Probably through the influence of his uncle Bowler Cocke (1696–1771), Adams was appointed clerk of Henrico County and served from 5 February 1753 until 1778 or 1779. He belonged to the vestry of Henrico Parish from 5 December 1757 until 1761.

From 1762 to 1772 Adams resided in London, where he conducted business for the family mercantile firm that his brother Richard Adams directed from Richmond. In 1772 Patrick Henry proposed that the House of Burgesses appoint Thomas Adams to succeed its London agent, Edward Montague, but supporters of Adams, Montague, and Arthur Lee could not agree, and no agent was named. Before returning to the colony, Adams persuaded the Florentine merchant Philip Mazzei to immigrate there, and he later introduced Mazzei, who served during the American Revolution as a European agent of Virginia, to the most important men in the colony.

Adams supported American protests against British policies before the Revolution but seldom took a public part in politics. On 28 June 1777 the General Assembly elected him to the Council of State, but he did not serve because his clerkship of Henrico County disqualified him.

On 9 December 1777 the General Assembly named Adams to succeed Joseph Jones in Congress. He took his seat in York, Pennsylvania, on 16 April 1778 and served on the Committees on Commerce, Marine Affairs, and Indian Affairs. On several occasions Adams voted against the Lee family in its prolonged and ultimately successful effort to discredit Silas Deane, American commissioner to France. When the assembly elected a new delegation on 29 May 1778, Adams received the most votes, and he signed the Articles of Confederation on

9 July 1778 as head of the state delegation. Adams was absent on a trip to Virginia from 28 August 1778 to 7 January 1779 but then served until he resigned from Congress on 28 April 1779, citing personal reasons.

Adams retired to his plantation on the Calfpasture River in Augusta County. He had been appointed presiding justice of Augusta County on 24 March 1778, but he did not take the qualifying oath until 21 March 1780 and was removed on 13 June 1786 for infrequent attendance. In April 1783 he was elected to the Senate of Virginia, and he represented the district comprising Augusta, Rockbridge, Rockingham, and Shenandoah Counties for three years.

Adams was wealthy in spite of large domestic and foreign debts remaining from his days in commerce. In the 1780s he owned more than two thousand acres of land in Augusta, Amherst, and Buckingham Counties worth more than £950 and a partial interest in several thousand acres in the Ohio Valley. His thirty-seven slaves were valued at nearly £2,000 and his other personal property was worth almost £800. Adams directed his executors to treat his slaves with "that kindness and humanity to which they have been Accustomed and not sell or barter them away as Cattle," and he emancipated his slave Joe, stating that there was "no man to whom I Consider myself under Greater Obligations." Thomas Adams died at his home about the middle of July 1788.

Adams Family Papers, VHS; C. W. Coleman, "Genealogy of the Adams Family of New Kent and Henrico Counties, Va.," *WMQ*, 1st ser., 5 (1897):163–164; Worthington C. Ford, ed., *Journals of the Continental Congress, 1774–1789* (1904–1937), vols. 10, 11, 13; Smith, *Letters of Delegates*, vols. 10–12 (por., 12:88); will and estate inventory in Augusta Co. Will Book, 7:99–100, 312–317; will printed with John Marshall's legal opinion in *Marshall Papers*, 2:112–116; two of Adams's account books are at Duke, with one containing records of the sale of his personal estate in Augusta Co. on 7 Nov. 1788 and 12 Jan. 1789 and in Amherst Co. on 1 Jan. 1789; death notice in *Virginia Centinel: or, the Winchester Mercury*, 6 Aug. 1788.

BRENT TARTER

ADAMS, William Henry (23 March 1872–24 September 1958), businessman and member of the House of Delegates, was born in Richmond, the eldest of two sons and one daughter of Henry C. Adams, a grocer, and Emma F. Haynes Adams. After graduating from Central High School, Adams learned bookbinding and the stationery business in a Richmond shop, then went into business for himself. In 1900 he purchased the Simmons Blank Book Company, which in 1909 he enlarged and renamed the Virginia Stationery Company. On 11 April 1905 he married Ivy Nelson Longworth, of Richmond, and they had one daughter. Adams was the president of Virginia Stationery Company until the autumn of 1953, when he retired and his daughter took over.

Adams had one of the longest careers in public affairs of any citizen in Richmond's history. In 1894 he won election to the local Democratic Party committee and served on it until 1900, when he was elected to the Richmond City Council from Jefferson Ward. In 1902 Adams was elected to the Board of Aldermen. During his tenure on the board he was its president from 1912 until 1925, frequently served as acting mayor, and took a leading role in pushing through the annexation of the city of Manchester. He served continuously as an alderman until 1925, when he retired after moving from Jefferson Ward to the city's West End. Adams also sat on the boards of several Richmond corporations and civic organizations, including that of the Richmond Chamber of Commerce during the 1920s and 1930s.

In 1929 Adams won election to the House of Delegates as one of the six members from Richmond. Until the end of the 1940s he regularly led the ticket in Democratic primaries and in general elections. With his background in business and municipal government, Adams served on the Committee on Finance and Public Properties and on the Committee on Insurance and Banking. He was chairman of the latter for his last eight years in the assembly. Although not a House floor leader, Adams was a respected and popular delegate whose colleagues called him "Uncle Billy." In 1952 the lifelong Democrat joined many other conservative Democrats in supporting the presidential candidacy of Republican Dwight D. Eisenhower.

Adams was reelected to the General Assembly without interruption until 1953, when he retired, having completed sixty years of public service. He was the oldest member of the House and the most senior in years of service. William Henry Adams died in a Richmond hospital on 24 September 1958 and was buried in Oakwood Cemetery.

BVS Birth Register, Richmond City; BVS Marriage Register, Richmond City; Glass and Glass, *Virginia Democracy*, 2:119–120; feature articles in *Richmond* 1 (Mar. 1915): 9 (por.), and *Richmond News Leader*, 8 June 1945, 12 Apr. 1951; obituaries in *Richmond News Leader* and *Richmond Times-Dispatch*, both 25 Sept. 1958.

BRENT TARTER

ADAMSON, Arthur Learoyd (30 May 1856–1 April 1944), businessman, was born at Stockton-on-Tees, Durham County, England, the youngest of three sons and one daughter of Martha Learoyd Adamson and William Adamson, a chemist and wholesaler and retailer of chemical products. Adamson attended a local boarding school and passed entrance examinations at Cambridge University before he and his brother William R. Adamson immigrated to the United States in July 1873. After a brief stint in Kansas they began farming in Lunenburg County. In 1874 the brothers moved to Nottoway County and two years later to Chesterfield County, where their parents had recently settled. In 1882 Adamson moved to the city of Manchester, across the James River from Richmond.

Adamson returned to England several times during his first decades in the United States. On one such trip on 24 February 1880 he married Sarah Barningham, the daughter of Thomas Barningham, a wealthy coal-and-iron merchant of Manchester, England. They had two daughters and two sons. The financial resources of his wife helped Adamson launch his long and successful career in real estate development, banking, and insurance. For the next sixty years he was intimately involved with the business and commercial development of Manchester before and after its annexation by Richmond in 1910.

In 1882 Adamson and Frank Sampson started a real estate business, Sampson and Adamson, which lasted until Adamson went into business under his own name in 1888. Adamson bought, sold, rented, and developed commercial properties. In addition to his own firm, he was a director of the West Manchester Land Company, the Mason Park Land Company, the Richmond and Manchester Land Company, and almost every other development enterprise of note in South Richmond. Adamson organized the Mechanics and Merchants Bank of Manchester in 1885 and served as its president for the remainder of his life. His investments in other area businesses included the Leader Publishing Company, which issued the *Manchester Evening Leader* from 1890 to 1903, but he did not take an active role in its editorial operations.

Adamson moved to Bon Air in suburban Chesterfield County in 1888 and commuted to his office on Hull Street. He later moved into Richmond, but his business interests continued to be centered in the old Manchester neighborhood. He was a founder and steward of the Centenary Methodist Church in Richmond and from 1917 to 1934 was superintendent of its Sunday school. Adamson also served as president of the Richmond YMCA.

Adamson formed a partnership with his son Thomas Darnley Adamson and about 1941 he retired from the daily conduct of most of his businesses. When Arthur Learoyd Adamson died on 1 April 1944 at his home on West Franklin Street in Richmond, his half interest in the partnership and his other holdings amounted to more than half a million dollars. He was buried at Hollywood Cemetery.

Eminent and Representative Men of Virginia and the District of Columbia (1893), 391; Bruce, Tyler, and Morton, *History of Virginia*, 4:115–116 (por.), with birth date confirmed on gravestone; Arthur Learoyd Adamson Papers and Business Records, LVA; estimation of estate value in *Richmond News Leader*, 6 Apr. 1944; obituaries in *Richmond Times-Dispatch*, 2 Apr. 1944, and *Richmond News Leader*, 3 Apr. 1944.

WILLIAM B. OBROCHTA

ADDISON, Lucy (8 December 1861–13 November 1937), educator, was born at Upperville in Fauquier County, the third of six children and second of four daughters of Charles Addison and Elizabeth Anderson Addison. After freedom, her father purchased land there and farmed. Addison acquired some schooling locally before going to Philadelphia to attend the Institute for Colored Youth, a private school with a talented black faculty, from which she graduated with a teacher's diploma in 1882.

Addison began teaching in Loudoun County but moved to the First Ward Colored School in Roanoke in 1886. In January 1887, after the principal died, Addison took his place as the interim head of a school with 217 enrolled students and only two teachers. A larger school building was ready for occupancy in 1888, but by then a male principal had been found and Addison was demoted to assistant principal and teacher. Thirty years passed before she became a principal once again.

Inadequate facilities and barriers to her advancement must have frustrated her at times, but Addison dedicated her life to education in Roanoke. The name of the First Ward Colored School was changed to the Gainsboro School, and principals came and went, but Miss Lucy Addison, as she was known, remained a constant for generations of students. She periodically refreshed her classroom experience with summer courses at Howard University, the University of Pennsylvania, Hampton Institute, and other schools, even though the travel must have strained her finances. Black teachers earned less than white teachers, and women pedagogues of both races earned less than their male counterparts.

In 1918 Addison became principal of the new Harrison School. One of the students recalled that she was prim and proper in appearance, but all considered her fair and approachable. The Harrison School officially offered course work only through grade eight, but Addison arranged for high school classes to be taught as well. She gradually added all the elements of a full high-school curriculum, and in 1924 the State Board of Education accredited the Harrison School as a secondary school. Until then, African Americans of Roanoke who desired a high school diploma had to go elsewhere to earn one.

Addison retired at the end of the 1926–1927 school year and moved to Washington, D.C., but she returned at the beginning of the next session to assist her successor. By then construction was underway on a new high school for blacks. In January 1928 the city school board announced that the school would be named Lucy Addison High School, Roanoke's first public building named after one of its own citizens. Addison proudly attended the school's formal opening on 19 April 1929.

In Roanoke, Addison resided in the household of physician Isaac David Burrell, for whom Burrell Memorial Hospital was named. She was a member of the hospital's board of trustees and chaired its Woman's Auxiliary. She also served on the board of the Industrial Home School for Colored Girls at Peaks, in Hanover County, from 1915 to 1927, and for twenty-seven years as superintendent of the Sunday school of the Fifth Avenue Presbyterian Church. Lucy Addison never married and in retirement lived with a sister. Chronic nephritis made her a near-invalid, and she died in Washington, D.C., on 13 November 1937. She was buried in Harmony Cemetery in Washington.

Caldwell, *History of the American Negro*, 195–197 (por.); no known source states whether Addison was born a slave, but no free blacks with the surname of Addison appear in Census, 1850 or 1860, for Fairfax, Fauquier, or Loudoun Cos.; *Roanoke World-News*, 27 Jan. 1928, 18 Apr. 1929; *Roanoke Times*, 19 Apr. 1929; *Roanoke Times and World-News*, 13 Feb. 1987; Virginia Writers' Program, *Roanoke: Story of County and City* (1942), 283–289; interview with Oliver W. Hill, 15 May 1989; employment history confirmed by Frank P. Tota, superintendent of Roanoke Public Schools, 28 June 1989; obituaries in *Roanoke World-News*, 13 Nov. 1937, *Roanoke Times*, 14 Nov. 1937, and *Richmond Afro-American* (D.C. edition), 20 Nov. 1937.

JOHN T. KNEEBONE

ADKERSON, Joseph Carson (10 February 1892–15 March 1985), president of the American Manganese Producers Association, was born in Lynchburg, one of four sons and a daughter of Alonzo Thomas Adkerson and Lizzie Lillian Carson Adkerson. He was educated in the local public schools and Lynchburg High School.

Shortly after his high school graduation, J. Carson Adkerson went to work in 1912 as an assistant mining engineer for the Piedmont Manganese Corporation, of Lynchburg. He subsequently became chief engineer at Oxford Mining and Manganese Corporation, also based in Lynchburg. In 1915 he became manager and engineer of the Powell's Fort Manganese Mines, near Woodstock, and helped develop it into one of the largest ore-mining operations for high-grade manganese in the United States. He served between 1916 and 1919 as engineer and manager in charge of the Stockwood Realty Corporation, Incorporated, a subsidiary of the National Carbon Company. In 1919 he became vice president and general manager of the Hy-Grade Manganese Company, of Woodstock, and National Metals Corporation, of Damascus in Washington County. Adkerson also served as the consulting engineer for the Cuban and American Manganese Corporation, of New York, as well as for other manganese interests. He maintained a home in Woodstock from 1915 until his death, although he lived in Washington, D.C., from the mid-1930s until the early 1960s.

Adkerson married Anne Winfield Clower, an antiques dealer in Woodstock, on 11 March 1961. They had no children, and she died in 1974. He was a Presbyterian, a Mason, a Shriner, a Democrat, a student of astrology, and for many years a member of both the Woodstock Chamber of Commerce, which he had helped to establish and from which he received the Outstanding Citizen Award in 1979, and the Woodstock Rotary Club, by which he was also honored. He lived to be the Woodstock Rotary's last-surviving founder.

A prominent member of the American Institute of Mining and Metallurgical Engineers, Adkerson was instrumental in the 2 August 1927 founding of the American Manganese Producers Association, a small organization of mine owners and mining engineers. He was the association's only president and its principal lobbyist and spokesman from 1927 until 1969. In 1930 he urged the United States government to prohibit the importation of low-priced ore from the Soviet Union, arguing that Russian mines used slave labor. During World War II he advised the government unofficially on the production of steel and nonferrous metals, and after the war he advocated building public stockpiles from domestic manganese production.

Discoveries of manganese ore multiplied throughout the world after World War II, and American producers lost much of the rapidly expanding market to foreign competition. Early in the 1960s Adkerson moved the association's headquarters from Washington to Woodstock, and he and the organization went into what amounted to retirement. J. Carson Adkerson died in Woodstock on 15 March 1985 and was buried there in Massanutten Cemetery.

J. Carson Adkerson Papers, including records of American Manganese Producers Association, UVA; biography in Bruce, Tyler, and Morton, *History of Virginia*, 4:373–374; *Engineering and Mining Journal* 124 (1927): 924 (por.); manganese lobbying documented in *New York Times*, 20 Apr. 1927, 26 July, 23 Aug. 1930, 16 Aug. 1936, 16 Oct. 1941, 2 July 1950; obituaries of Adkerson and wife in *Woodstock Shenandoah Valley-Herald*, 21 Aug. 1974, 21 Mar. 1985.

BRENT TARTER

ADKINS, Ozias Oliver (24 May 1911–23 October 1987), Chickahominy chief, was born in Charles City County, one of three sons and a daughter of Ozias Westmore Adkins and Susan Henry Adkins. His parents were members of the Chickahominy Indian tribe when the tribal organization was revived in 1908, and from 1918 to 1939 his father served as the second chief of the Chickahominy. Adkins grew up in Charles City County and attended the Samaria Indian School. He married Juliet Oleta, a member of the Chickahominy tribe, whose maiden name has not been discovered. Like many other Virginia Indians, the couple married outside the state to avoid discriminatory racial classifications assigned in its vital records. The chaplain of the House of Representatives performed the ceremony in Washington, D.C., on 1 April 1937. They had three daughters and also raised a nephew in their home.

O. Oliver Adkins worked with heavy machinery in his father's Charles City County lumber business and as a cabinetmaker in Richmond. He also had a long career as a historical interpreter, beginning at the Syms-Eaton Museum in Hampton and continuing for many years as an interpreter at the Jamestown Festival Park, where he was popular with visitors. He particularly enjoyed teaching visitors about the resiliency of the native culture of Virginia.

Known as Lone Eagle within the tribe, Adkins succeeded his father as chief of the

Chickahominy in 1940 and was reelected without interruption until 1986. He worked to improve educational opportunities for the children of the tribe but was best known for his work on behalf of Indian rights at the state and national levels. He attended out-of-state meetings of Indians while his father was chief, and he continued to travel throughout his own terms as chief. In 1972 Governor Abner Linwood Holton Jr. appointed him to the Virginia Minority Economic Development Commission to serve as a consultant on economic problems facing the state's native population and to act as a liaison between the Indian community and the state government. In 1983 Adkins became a member of the State Commission on Indians. He wholeheartedly supported the commission's efforts to encourage research about Virginia Indian history and culture in order to increase public awareness of Indian contributions to Virginia's heritage and to dispel misunderstandings about Native American cultures. His efforts culminated in February 1983 when the General Assembly granted official recognition to the modern Chickahominy Indian tribe. He retired in 1986 and became chief emeritus.

O. Oliver Adkins, Chief Lone Eagle, died at his home in Charles City County on 23 October 1987 and was buried in the cemetery at Samaria Indian Baptist Church, to which he had belonged for most of his life.

Family records and papers in possession of Brenda Kay Adkins Montez; interviews with Adkins, Jan., May, Aug. 1984; tribal registers in possession of Adkins, 1984; other data provided by Claude Evans, Charles City Co.; gravestone inscriptions, Samaria Indian Baptist Church, Charles City Co.; obituaries in *Richmond Times-Dispatch*, 25, 26 Oct. 1987, *Richmond News Leader* (por.), 26 Oct. 1987, and *Williamsburg Virginia Gazette*, 28 Oct. 1987.

MICHAEL J. PUGLISI

AERY, William Anthony (24 September 1882–16 October 1963), educator and writer, was born in New York City, the son of Charles H. Aery and Catherine Geib Aery. After graduating from a local high school in 1900, he entered Columbia University and received a bachelor's degree in 1904 and a master's degree from Teachers College in 1906.

In the autumn of 1906 Aery became an instructor of sociology, history, and economics at Hampton Normal and Agricultural Institute. Although hired to teach, he took on numerous administrative duties. He served as Hampton's publicity officer, director of the School of Education, director of the Academy and Normal School, and superintendent of French. He wrote frequently for the *Southern Workman*, the Institute's monthly magazine, and was its business manager from April 1908 to December 1917 and a contributing editor from January 1918 to July 1939. Aery was involved in much of the planning and implementation of educational policies at Hampton, where he sought to develop an educational program that would satisfy both the proponents of industrial education, as advocated by Booker T. Washington, and the need for a more rigorous liberal arts education and the training of teachers.

Aery was a friend and adviser to Booker T. Washington and accompanied him as a publicist on several of Washington's southern tours. Aery tirelessly promoted education for African Americans in the pages of the *Southern Workman*, as Hampton correspondent for the *New York Times*, and as a contributor of articles to a wide variety of other publications. He was one of the white members of the Virginia Commission on Interracial Cooperation and of the Negro Country Life Commission.

On 1 September 1910 Aery married Clara Thompson Chase, the daughter of a Methodist minister, who grew up in upstate New York and studied in Germany before joining Hampton Institute as a secretary at the same time as Aery. They had one daughter. Aery continued to teach and write and contribute to the educational evolution of Hampton until he retired in 1939. From 1942 to 1948 he worked as an administrative assistant to the personnel officer for the National Advisory Committee for Aeronautics at Langley Field. He also contributed his time to many community organizations, including the Red Cross, the Girl Scouts, and the Peninsula Catholic Scholarship Fund.

William Anthony Aery died of lymphatic leukemia in Dixie Hospital in Hampton on 16 October 1963 and was buried in Hampton Institute Cemetery beside his wife, who had died in August 1934.

William A. Aery Papers, Hampton; marriage reported in *Southern Workman* 39 (1910): 571; wife's death reported in *Newport News Daily Press*, 12 Aug. 1934; indexes to *Southern Workman* contain several pages of references to his articles in that journal; William A. Aery, "How to Teach High School Pupils a Proper Regard for Constituted Authority," *Virginia Journal of Education* 18 (Nov. 1924): 94, 97, 102; obituaries in *Newport News Daily Press* (por.) and *New York Times*, both 17 Oct. 1963, and *Norfolk Journal and Guide* (home edition), 19 Oct. 1963.

MICHAEL E. HUCLES

AGGIE, Mary (fl. 1728–1731), principal in a court case, like the much better known Dred Scott of the next century, was an otherwise obscure African American who earned a place in history as the central figure in an important legal case. The place and date of her birth and the names of her parents are not recorded. She was probably the adult slave named Mary Aggy who was living in Williamsburg in 1717 as the property of Susanna Allen, but all that is known with certainty about the court principal named Mary Aggie relates to two cases heard in Virginia courts between 1728 and 1731 and to a law the General Assembly enacted in 1732. The paucity of personal data about Mary Aggie stands in sharp contrast to her significant role in changing Virginia's statute law with respect to the rights of convicted felons, including women and all African Americans, Indians, and persons of mixed ancestry.

Of Aggie's first case in the General Court late in the 1720s, by which time she was at least twenty-one years old, we know only that she sued for her freedom from slavery, that "she was examined touching her Faith of which she gave a tolerable Account," in the words of Lieutenant Governor William Gooch, and that her bid for freedom failed. She had, however, established her belief in Christianity to the satisfaction of Gooch, the presiding judge at the trial.

The other case involving Aggie is better documented and had further-reaching significance. On 7 November 1730 Aggie was indicted, tried, and convicted by a court of oyer and terminer in York County for stealing three sheets valued at forty shillings from the house of her owner Annie Sullivan, a Williamsburg tavern keeper. Ordinarily the court would have sentenced Aggie to death or some severe corporal punishment, but Aggie's was not a routine case. Gooch had sent an attorney to observe the trial and to secure for her, if she were convicted, the benefit of clergy to which Gooch thought she would have been entitled if she had not been a slave. Under English law dating from the Middle Ages, benefit of clergy was a privilege entitling ostensibly literate persons to escape death or the most serious penalty of the law on a first conviction for all but a specified few of the many capital offenses. Learning from the attending lawyer that the York County justices might deny Aggie's plea for benefit of clergy, Gooch arranged for her case to be called up to the General Court. As Gooch explained to the bishop of London, he had resolved "to have this Matter argued in the most public manner by our best Lawyers, as a thing of great consequence, by which all the Courts in the Country for the Future should govern themselves, not doubting but it would be carried in favour of the Christian though a black one." Four of the five attorneys whom Gooch asked to prepare legal briefs later argued that Mary Aggie had the right to plead benefit of clergy, but when the lieutenant governor, as presiding judge of the General Court, put the question in April 1731, the bench was divided, six to six.

Gooch ordered the case referred to the attorney general and solicitor general in England for a final ruling, but on 6 May 1731 Gooch and the Council, sitting in executive session, pardoned Mary Aggie "upon condition that she be transported out of this Colony to Some other of his Majesties plantations there to be sold as a Slave." Gooch had saved Aggie's life, but the deadlock in the General Court left unanswered the question of whether women and slaves were entitled in Virginia to plead benefit of clergy in mitigation of a first capital conviction. To settle that question, the General Assembly, making circumstantial but unmistakable references to both of Aggie's cases in the General Court, passed a sweeping law on 1 July 1732 that allowed virtually everyone to plead benefit of clergy except in certain cases in which such pleas were not allowed under English or Virginia statutes. Although the act explicitly extended benefit of clergy "to any Negro, mulatto or

Indian whatsoever," it added to the number of felonies for which those persons could not plead benefit of clergy. The new law also allowed courts to inflict other corporal punishments, and it denied to all Indians and persons of African descent the right to give testimony in court except "upon the trial of a slave, for a capital offence." What the statute granted in some clauses in the names of mercy and justice, it took away in others for the protection of the institution of slavery and the property of slaveholders. Nonetheless, as a result of the actions of Mary Aggie, William Gooch, and the General Assembly, for more than sixty years all Virginians enjoyed the right to plead benefit of clergy on first conviction. Even after benefit of clergy began to disappear from Virginia law in 1796, Virginia slaves retained some limited rights to make the plea until its use was abolished in 1849.

No known source indicates whether Mary Aggie learned of the important consequences of her trials, nor does the record disclose to which colony she was sent to be sold or tell when or where she died.

Draft of unrealized 1717 marriage contract of Jos. Seward and Susanna Allen, Godfrey Pole Papers, Northampton Co. Courthouse, Eastville; William Gooch to bishop of London, 28 May 1731, Fulham Palace Papers, Lambeth Palace Library, England; York Co. Records, Orders, and Wills, 17:113, 114, 123–124; *Executive Journals of Council*, 4:243; Hening, *Statutes*, 4:325–327.

JOHN M. HEMPHILL II

AGNEW, Ella Graham (18 March 1871–5 February 1958), educator and public administrator, was born at Roseland in Prince Edward County, the ninth of ten children and fifth of six daughters of James Anderson Agnew and Martha Chaffin Scott Agnew. Her mother died in 1872, and her father moved to Burkeville in neighboring Nottoway County, where he practiced medicine and in 1877 married Elizabeth Jane McLean. Agnew grew up and attended school in Burkeville and lived there with her stepmother after her father died in 1879.

Inspired by the independence of her stepmother and older sisters, Agnew enrolled in a stenographic course at Smithdeal Business College in Richmond. In 1892 she moved to Abingdon to take charge of the commercial department at the Stonewall Jackson Institute and to be secretary to the principal. Two years later she moved to New York to work as a secretary in a Long Island publishing firm. Her employer there recommended her to a recruiter seeking a business teacher and secretary for Huguenot Seminary at Paarl, Cape Colony, South Africa. Agnew accepted the job offer and in June 1895 sailed for South Africa. She taught stenography at the seminary for three years and attended classes in other subjects. She became an active leader of the student Christian movement in South Africa and met a number of notable people, among them Cecil John Rhodes and Olive Schreiner. In 1897 Agnew accepted the invitation of Piet Joubert, vice president of the Transvaal, to become the principal of Amajuba Seminary, a boarding school for Boer girls at the village of Wakkerstroom. During her second year at Amajuba the school closed because of the Boer War. Unable to leave until 1900, Agnew spent the interval performing clerical, administrative, and nursing work for the Boers and the American consulate.

After returning to the United States, Agnew taught school near Burkeville and continued her education through correspondence courses and private tutors at Richmond College. For a brief time she worked in New York City as an office manager for the Men's Forward Movement of the Presbyterian Board of Foreign Missions. Then she began a long, but not continuous affiliation with the Young Women's Christian Association, which included service as the general secretary of chapters in Greensboro, North Carolina, and Toledo, Ohio. While in Ohio she became interested in practical and vocational education for rural girls. When she inquired in November 1909 about vocational education plans in Virginia, Joseph D. Eggleston, the state superintendent of public instruction, invited her to return to Virginia and create a program.

Agnew began work in Nansemond County in February 1910. In May of that year she met Seaman A. Knapp, known as the founder of home demonstration work, who instructed her in starting a girls' tomato-raising club to be financed by the General Education Board in New York and supervised by the United States

Department of Agriculture. Agnew became the first woman field service home demonstration agent in the United States, work corresponding to that of the county agricultural extension agents. By the time the Virginia Agricultural and Mechanical College and Polytechnic Institute in Blacksburg took over administration of home demonstration work, Agnew had expanded her program to include poultry husbandry, sewing, and other aspects of home economics.

Agnew was the founding president of the Virginia Federation of Business and Professional Women's Clubs in 1919, and she was also active in the League of Women Voters in Virginia. In 1920 she rejoined the YWCA as a secretary in the Finance Department of the National Board, located in New York. Traveling to rural YWCAs throughout the country, she gathered information about how to finance these chapters and in 1923 completed instructional materials based on her findings. She then carried out work in Oklahoma and Texas for the National Board. In 1927 Agnew again returned to Virginia as the first woman editor at the *Southern Planter*, the oldest and one of the most influential southern agricultural periodicals. She edited "The Woman's Department" until 1931.

Agnew became an extremely able administrator as a result of her experiences in the YWCA and in home demonstration work. Her comprehensive knowledge of women's work, both in rural Virginia and in the increasingly industrialized cities, made her the ideal person to become the Virginia director in 1933 of work relief activities for women with the New Deal's Federal Emergency Relief Administration and its mammoth successor, the Works Progress Administration (later the Work Projects Administration). She appointed associates from her work in other women's organizations to direct the programs in Virginia, among them Eudora Ramsay Richardson to head the Virginia Writers' Project and Adèle Clark to direct the Virginia Art Project, both of which won national acclaim. Agnew was the senior state director in the country, and her work programs became models for other states. She was one of the few state directors who remained on the job throughout the lives of the FERA and the WPA.

When the WPA was liquidated in 1943, Agnew was seventy-two years old and in frail health after decades of arduous work. She retired to the Home for Needy Confederate Women in Richmond but remained active in civic affairs. Known nationwide as Miss Ella, she was the first woman to receive a certificate of merit from the Virginia Agricultural and Mechanical College for a career devoted to rural women and girls. In addition, the campus home economics building was named in her honor. In 1952 the College of William and Mary awarded her an honorary doctorate of laws in recognition of her lifelong initiatives to improve the lives of all Virginians and to make more professional and personal choices available to women. She gradually lost her eyesight and in 1957 broke her hip. Ella Graham Agnew died in Richmond on 5 February 1958 and was buried in Sunset Cemetery in Burkeville.

Autobiography in Virginia Iota State Organization of Delta Kappa Gamma Society, *Adventures in Teaching: Pioneer Women Educators and Influential Teachers* (1963), 113–126; Helen Wolfe Evans, "Ella Graham Agnew" (paper for graduate program in liberal studies, Duke, 1989); feature article in *Richmond Times-Dispatch*, 20 Oct. 1944; Ronald L. Heinemann, *Depression and New Deal in Virginia: The Enduring Dominion* (1983); Ella Graham Agnew File Papers, VPI; Virginia Series, Work Projects Administration Papers, RG 69, NARA; portraits in Agnew Hall, VPI, and in residence of Helen Wolfe Evans, Raleigh, N.C.; obituaries in *Richmond News Leader*, 5 Feb. 1958 (por.), and *Richmond Times-Dispatch*, 6 Feb. 1958.

MARTHA H. SWAIN
HELEN WOLFE EVANS

AHALT, Clarence Randolph (28 May 1888–15 October 1962), real estate developer and Republican Party leader, was born into a comfortable, middle-class family in Rockville, Maryland, the eldest of three sons and six daughters of Charles R. Ahalt and Lilly Main Ahalt. After graduating from Rockville Academy in 1906 he went to work for N. L. Sansbury and Company, a real estate firm in Washington, D.C. He attended night classes at the National University Law School and by 1912 received both LL.B. and LL.M. degrees. By then he was manager of the company's rental department, and on 19 June 1912 he married Tillie Alice Pilmer, of Carlisle, Indiana. During the next five years they had two daughters.

Rapid growth of Arlington County in the 1920s attracted Ahalt's attention, and he and another attorney, Frank Campbell, began their long careers as real estate developers. In 1923 they platted the subdivision of Oakcrest. Ahalt also invested in and developed a number of other neighborhoods, including Overlee Knolls and Aurora Heights. In 1930 he moved his law practice from the District of Columbia to Arlington. Although he retired from active practice in 1942, he remained the head of the firm until his death. Ahalt and Campbell established the Virginia Title Insurance Company in Arlington in 1933, and the same year Ahalt helped found the Metropolitan Savings and Loan Association of Northern Virginia. He was president of the Metropolitan from 1942 until his death.

Ahalt also became active in politics during the 1930s. Although he was a newcomer to statewide politics, in 1933 the Republican Party nominated him for attorney general of Virginia. He lost his lopsided contest with Democratic Party nominee John Richard Saunders by a margin of about three to one. In 1936 Ahalt directed the Virginia campaign of Republican presidential candidate Alfred M. Landon, and in March 1937 he was elected state party chairman, serving for seven years.

After his retirement in 1942 Ahalt moved to his country estate, Ketocktin, near Leesburg. There he managed his Arlington business interests and invested in land and businesses in Loudoun County. He participated in many community organizations and projects and donated sixteen acres to the Loudoun County 4-H Club for use as a fairground. Ahalt retained his interest in politics and from 1944 to 1962 was Republican Party chairman of Loudoun County. He also served on several local boards and chaired the Loudoun County Board of Zoning Appeals from 1945 to 1962. Clarence Randolph Ahalt died in Leesburg Memorial Hospital on 15 October 1962 and was buried in Union Cemetery in Leesburg.

Family records in possession of daughters, Katherine Burdell Ahalt Kimble and Alice Pilmer Ahalt Hayes of Arlington; other professional and business collections of Montgomery Co., Md., Historical Society, Loudoun Co. Historical Society, and Arlington Historical Society; Arlington Co. Bar Association Papers, Woodmont Center, Arlington; obituaries in *Washington Post*, 16 Oct. 1962 (por.), *Richmond Times-Dispatch*, 17 Oct. 1962, and *Loudoun Times-Mirror*, 18 Oct. 1962.

KATHRYN HOLT-SPRINGSTON

AIKEN, Archibald Murphey (12 February 1888–27 November 1971), corporation court judge, was born in Danville, the only child of Judge Archibald Murphey Aiken and Mary Ella Yates Aiken. He attended Danville Military Institute and the Virginia Military Institute before matriculating in the 1905–1906 academic year at the University of Virginia, where he earned B.A. and LL.B. degrees in 1910 and 1913 respectively. In 1922 Aiken married Corinne Conway, of Danville, and they had one son. They were divorced in 1942, and Aiken later married Mary Mickley.

Aiken served in France as a captain in the United States Army during World War I. He subsequently returned to Danville, where he was city attorney from 1919 to 1939, interrupted by interim service in 1921 and 1922 as circuit court judge, the office his father had once held. Aiken practiced law from 1939 to 1950. From the latter year until his death he was judge of the Danville Corporation Court.

Aiken was an outspoken supporter of the state's policy of Massive Resistance to court-ordered desegregation of the public schools. In 1963 he gained national notoriety for his handling of civil rights demonstrations in Danville, which were inspired by the protests then occurring in Birmingham, Alabama, under the leadership of local African American ministers and the Southern Christian Leadership Conference. Beginning early in June, Danville ministers led daily marches protesting segregation in public facilities and racial discrimination in hiring practices. Judge Aiken personally confronted the demonstrators on 5 June with an order to disperse. When they refused, he ordered them arrested. The following day he issued a sweeping injunction banning most forms of public protest. Danville police used clubs and fire hoses to assault demonstrators who violated the injunction, resulting in forty-eight injuries and numerous arrests. Aiken convened a special grand jury and had the demonstrators indicted under what was called "John Brown's Law," a slavery-era statute that made "inciting the colored population against the white population" a felony. On 16 June, acting in concert with Aiken's response to the protests, the city council adopted an ordinance essentially codifying the judge's antidemonstration injunction.

Young civil-rights activists sponsored by the Student Non-Violent Coordinating Committee converged on Danville from other places in the South, and by mid-July more than two hundred fifty people had been arrested on various charges stemming from the marches. Judge Aiken established remarkable rules for the trials of those arrested. He excluded virtually the entire public, kept a large force of armed police present, required all defendants to attend roll calls every day, subjected the defendants and their attorneys to daily searches for weapons, and banned discussion of the constitutionality of the injunction or the city ordinance. Defense lawyers sought to remove the cases from state jurisdiction into federal court, an effort the United States Department of Justice supported with a brief criticizing Aiken's conduct and noting that he carried a gun into the courtroom. Aiken acknowledged that on police advice he carried a firearm to the courthouse, but he denied carrying arms into the courtroom. The U.S. district courts refused to take over the trials, and after a long series of state and federal appeals Aiken's injunction and most of his actions were deemed constitutional, though only by close votes and over strong dissents in the U.S. Fourth Circuit Court of Appeals and the U.S. Supreme Court.

Controversy followed Aiken into the later years of his life. In December 1966, as he continued to try the cases from the 1963 arrests and to hand down fairly harsh sentences, W. Leigh Taylor, an executive of a large textile manufacturer based in Danville, wrote a letter to Aiken criticizing his judgment. Aiken cited him for contempt and sentenced him to ten days in jail, with eight suspended. This action drew strong protest in Virginia, including a fruitless call for Aiken's impeachment from James Jackson Kilpatrick, editor of the *Richmond News Leader*. On 30 July 1969 Aiken gained more national attention when he sentenced twenty-year-old Frank Provost Lavarre to twenty-five years in prison (five years conditionally suspended) and a $500 fine for possession of a small amount of marijuana. Governor Mills E. Godwin later reduced the sentence.

Although events singled Aiken out for national attention, many political leaders of his generation in Virginia's Southside shared his views on social change. Throughout the civil rights controversy and after his death, the all-white Danville Bar Association passed resolutions supporting Aiken and praising his integrity and devotion to duty. The Danville City Council named a bridge for him in 1970. Judge Archibald Murphey Aiken died of a heart attack in Danville on 27 November 1971 and was buried in Green Hill Cemetery in that city.

James W. Ely Jr., "Negro Demonstrations and the Law: Danville as a Test Case," *Vanderbilt Law Review* 27 (1974): 927–968; Simon E. Sobeloff Papers, LC; Len Holt, *An Act of Conscience* (1965); Arthur Kinoy, *Rights on Trial: The Odyssey of a People's Lawyer* (1983), 181–208; William M. Kunstler, *Deep in My Heart* (1966), 211–232; *Richmond News Leader*, 21, 23 Dec. 1966, 31 July 1969; obituaries in *Danville Register* and *Richmond Times-Dispatch*, both 28 Nov. 1971, and *Washington Post*, 30 Nov. 1971; memorial in *Virginia Bar Association Proceedings* (1973): 298–300 (por).

JAMES H. HERSHMAN JR.

AINSLIE, George (10 October 1868–18 July 1931), Richmond City mayor, was the youngest of four children, all sons, of Janet Currie Ainslie and George Alexander Ainslie, who for several years headed Richmond's fire department. He was educated in the city's public schools and entered the Virginia Military Institute in August 1886. During his final year he was first captain of the corps, the highest-ranking cadet. He graduated with distinction and a B.S. in 1890. After working for a year, Ainslie entered the University of Virginia and received an LL.B. in 1893. He began his law practice in Richmond later that year and on 2 September 1893 married Marie Antoinette Burthe. They had two daughters.

Ainslie's career in public service began in 1903 when he was appointed to Richmond's Board of Police Commissioners. The next year he ran unsuccessfully for a circuit court judgeship. He resigned from the Board of Police Commissioners on 5 January 1905 to campaign for the seat in the Senate of Virginia being vacated by his brother-in-law George Wayne Anderson. Defeated in the Democratic primary, Ainslie continued to practice law and take part in Democratic Party politics. His law partner Miles M. Martin became chairman of the city Democratic committee.

On 4 September 1912 the Common Council and Board of Aldermen elected Ainslie to a two-year term as mayor of Richmond after the previous mayor, David Crockett Richardson, resigned to accept a judicial appointment. Legislation adopted by the General Assembly in 1912 established a new city Administrative Board that reduced the administrative responsibilities of the councilmen, and in 1919 amendments to the city charter abolished the board and further strengthened the office of mayor. First as an appointed mayor and later as an elected one, Ainslie served for twelve years. During that time the city changed rapidly as it responded to the service demands of an expanding metropolis. Ainslie contributed significantly to the successful implementation of an agenda of urban improvements that made Richmond an exemplary city of the New South.

During Ainslie's first administration, the city nearly doubled in size through the annexation of several large residential neighborhoods. He was one of the most vocal advocates of government planning to manage Richmond's expanding area, and he pushed through the charter amendments that strengthened the mayor's office in 1919 and that also authorized creation of the city's first planning commission. With Ainslie's support, Director of Public Works Allen J. Saville drew up a temporary zoning ordinance and secured an amendment to the state's Plat Act that empowered the city to regulate all subdivision growth within five miles of its boundaries.

Ainslie used the expanded powers of his office to begin an ambitious public improvements program for the annexed areas and to upgrade services in the older sections of the city. He oversaw street construction to connect the city's center to the suburbs, completion of a new waterworks, installation of a conduit in Shockoe Creek to carry away sewage and reduce flooding, establishment of a fully motorized fire department, and improvements in the health department and the school system. Ainslie attempted to manage Richmond's growing financial responsibilities by cutting costs, but he also had to press for an increase in taxes. By 1920 he could report that the debt had been brought under control and that the city's financial position would enable it to complete his aggressive public improvements program.

When Ainslie ran for reelection in 1924, he discovered that his brand of urban progressivism was no longer a salable political commodity. Although he won business support for his development program, he encountered intense disapproval from many of his constituents, particularly among the laboring classes, and a formidable challenge for the mayor's office from J. Fulmer Bright, a local physician who advocated government retrenchment. Bright portrayed Ainslie as a big spender, attacking him for using borrowed money to finance public improvements. Ainslie countered that Bright was opposed to the city's achieving its full potential. Ainslie lost the 1 April 1924 primary by almost 1,300 votes, largely because of the substantial majorities Bright received in working-class neighborhoods.

In 1928 Ainslie opposed Bright's bid for reelection by proposing another ambitious program of public improvements requiring the expenditure of $11 million. He contended that Bright had failed to live up to his 1924 campaign pledge of "better government for the same money." However, the voters once again rejected expensive urban progressivism. Bright won a second term handily, with the key being his continued strength among working-class voters.

After his service as mayor, Ainslie joined the local insurance company of Diggs and Cary as a special agent. George Ainslie died at his home in Richmond on 18 July 1931 and was buried in the family plot in Hollywood Cemetery.

Autobiographical letter to Joseph R. Anderson, 14 Nov. 1908, VMI Archives; *Richmond News Leader*, 4 Sept. 1912 (por.); political career documented in numerous articles in *Richmond News Leader* and *Richmond Times-Dispatch*; George Ainslie, "Local Assessments for Abutting Improvements," *Virginia Municipal Review* 3 (1926): 58–59; Christopher Silver, *Twentieth-Century Richmond: Planning, Politics, and Race* (1984), 61, 90–93; Bureau of Municipal

Research of New York City, *Richmond, Virginia: Report on a Survey of the City Government* (1917); G. M. Bowers, "Richmond's Experience in City Planning," in *Planning for City, State, Region and Nation: Proceedings of the Joint Conference on Planning* (1936), 47–50; obituaries and editorial tributes in *Richmond News Leader*, 18 July 1931, and *Richmond Times-Dispatch*, 18, 19 July 1931.

CHRISTOPHER SILVER

ALBEMARLE, William Anne Keppel, second earl of (5 June 1702–22 December 1754), governor of Virginia, was born at Whitehall Palace, London, the only son and one of two children of Arnold Joost van Keppel, first earl of Albemarle, and Geertruid Johanna Quirina van der Duyn Keppel, countess of Albemarle. He was baptized in the royal chapel in the presence of his namesake and godmother, Queen Anne. His father, a member of a noble family of Holland and a friend and confidant of William of Orange, accompanied his patron to England when the latter assumed the British throne in 1689. He became a general and a diplomat, and in 1696 King William created him first earl of Albemarle.

William Anne Keppel was educated in the Netherlands but returned to England to become a soldier. In 1718 he succeeded to his father's titles and estates and in 1723 married Lady Anne Lennox. They had seven daughters and eight sons, one of whom became a general, one an admiral, and one a bishop. Albemarle began his distinguished military career in 1717 as a captain in the Coldstream Guards, an appointment that carried with it the equivalent army rank of lieutenant colonel. He was promoted to brigadier general in 1739 and to major general in 1742. His service at the Battles of Dettingen and Fontenoy in the War of the Austrian Succession won him promotion to lieutenant general. During the Jacobite Rebellion of 1745 he fought under the duke of Cumberland at Culloden and was later named commander in chief of the forces in Scotland. He led the British infantry at Laffeldt in 1747 and in the Low Countries the following year. Military successes led to political and diplomatic appointments. In 1748 Albemarle became ambassador to France, a post he held the rest of his life. He became a knight of the garter in 1749, a groom of the stole in 1750, and a member of the Privy Council the same year.

In the meantime, on the recommendation of Sir Robert Walpole, George II commissioned Albemarle governor of Virginia on 4 November 1737. Albemarle never went to America but employed lieutenant governors (William Gooch until 1749 and Robert Dinwiddie after 1751) to administer the government in Williamsburg. Relations between Albemarle and his lieutenant governors were often strained because the former attempted to exercise certain appointive powers that Gooch and Dinwiddie, in order to preserve their political influence, were reluctant to relinquish. Albemarle arranged with a succession of political leaders in London to outmaneuver the lieutenant governors in the appointment of some of the most important officers in the colony's government. Ironically, even as the king's ministers were attempting to increase the London bureaucracy's control over the colonies, their patronage policies were undermining the lieutenant governors and contributing to their inability to withstand or curtail the rising political importance of the colonial assemblies and politicians. Albemarle's place in Virginia history rests in part on the role he played in the unintentional weakening of imperial ties between the colony and England.

The earl of Albemarle died in Paris on 22 December 1754 and was buried in a Church of England chapel in South Audley Street, London.

George Thomas Keppel, sixth earl of Albemarle, *Fifty Years of My Life* (1876), 303–375; Albemarle's Papers, Add. MSS 32687–33066, British Library; commission as governor, PRO CO 66/3598, entry 38; Randall Shrock, "Maintaining the Prerogative: Three Royal Governors in Virginia as a Case Study, 1710–1758" (Ph.D. diss., UNC, 1980); Andrew Karl Prinz, "Sir William Gooch in Virginia: The King's Good Servant" (Ph.D. diss., Northwestern University, 1963); portrait by Jean Fournier owned by the Coldstream Guards, with copy in Albemarle Co. courthouse.

DONALD W. GUNTER

ALBURTIS, John Van Meter (23 August 1778–6 May 1827), printer and publisher, was born in Baltimore, Maryland, the youngest of two sons and three daughters of John Alburtis and Ann Amo Van Meter Alburtis. He served an apprenticeship with the printer Nathaniel Willis, who had founded the *Potowmac Guardian, and Berkeley Advertiser*, later renamed the *Potomak Guardian*, at Shepherdstown in 1790 but moved it to Martinsburg in 1791. Alburtis left the employ of Willis, an ardent and contentious Jeffersonian Republican, and on 3 April 1799 founded a rival Federalist newspaper, the *Berkeley Intelligencer*, at Martinsburg. In May 1810, following a number of name changes, his newspaper became the *Martinsburgh Gazette*.

In an era of bitterly partisan journalism, the *Martinsburgh Gazette* was generally restrained in tone. On 1 February 1811, however, Alburtis severely criticized the administration of President James Madison, declaring that ever since Thomas Jefferson had become president in 1801, the country had "contrived to get, and are now, in the wrong on every difference with England." Nevertheless, Alburtis volunteered for service in an infantry company organized at Martinsburg during the War of 1812.

Alburtis also printed books and pamphlets while at Martinsburg, including many sermons and religious treatises by Episcopal ministers. Among his publications were *Interesting Account of the Project of France Respecting Louisiana* (1803), an abridgement of *An Address to the United States, on the Cession of Louisiana to the French*, attributed to Charles Brockden Brown and originally published in Philadelphia earlier the same year; William Huntington, *The Arminian Skeleton; or, The Arminian Dissected and Anatomised* (1810); *On Intemperance* (1818), a pamphlet for the Presbyterian Church; and the Reverend Benjamin Allen's Episcopal weekly, the *Lay-Man's Magazine* (1815–1816).

In 1822 Alburtis sold the *Martinsburg Gazette*, as it was then styled. He declared in his farewell address on 9 January 1823 that he had "pursued it with a fond assiduity, and had it not been for untoward circumstances, perhaps he might have lived and died the Editor of the Gazette." He then moved to Shepherdstown, where he published the *Shepherdstown Journal* from 8 December 1824 until 1 April 1827. Suffering from a "protracted illness," he sold the *Journal* and returned to Martinsburg about a month before his death.

Alburtis married Catherine Elizabeth Taylor on 31 December 1805. She died on 18 April 1807. Their only child, a daughter, died in 1812. On 7 February 1809 Alburtis married fifteen-year-old Nancy Van Meter. They had six sons and two daughters. After Alburtis's death, his widow attempted to carry on her husband's work. The first woman to publish a newspaper in what would become West Virginia, Nancy Alburtis established the *Farmer's Museum and Berkeley and Jefferson Advertiser* in Martinsburg and published six issues between 26 July 1827 and 30 August 1827, after which it failed for lack of support. Later, sons Samuel Alburtis and Ephraim Gaither Alburtis collectively or individually published the *Virginia Republican* at Martinsburg from 1841 to 1855 and again from 1857 to 1862.

Alburtis was a man of modest means and acquired part of his real property through an inheritance of his second wife. At the time of his death he had five slaves, four of whom were under eight years of age; he gave directions in his will that they and their increase were to be manumitted on reaching the age of twenty-eight years. When he died in Martinsburg on 6 May 1827, Alburtis was well-known and respected as "much the oldest Printer and Publisher of a newspaper in this Valley." He was buried in Old Norborne Cemetery, Martinsburg. His wife, who survived him by more than a quarter century, died 14 December 1852. John Van Meter Alburtis was inducted into the West Virginia Press Association Hall of Fame in 1959.

Otis K. Rice, "West Virginia Printers and Their Work, 1730–1830," *West Virginia History* 14 (1953): 297–338; Bette Delfs Alburtis, *Families of Alburtis* . . . (ca. 1986); Berkeley Co. Marriage Bonds, 3:7, 107; transcription of family Bible at Martinsburg-Berkeley Co. Public Library; *Martinsburg Gazette*, 1, 8 Feb. 1811, 9 Jan., 18 Sept. 1823, 18 Mar., 2 Dec. 1824, 2, 30 Aug. 1827, 28 Oct. 1828; check-list of Alburtis imprints in Delf Norona and Charles Shetler, *West Virginia Imprints, 1790–1863* (1958); Berkeley Co. Will Book, 9:32–33; *Martinsburg Journal*, 12 Nov. 1959; obituary in *Martinsburg Gazette*, 10 May 1827.

OTIS K. RICE

ALDEN, Harold Lee (10 January 1890–3 February 1964), astronomer, was born in Chicago, the younger of two children, both sons, of David Adonijah Alden, a Congregational minister, and Emily Worcester Alden. He received his A.B. at Wheaton College in 1912 and his M.S. from the University of Chicago the following year. From 1912 to 1914 he was an assistant at the University of Chicago's Yerkes Observatory, using photography to determine the brightness of stars. In the autumn of 1914 he went to the University of Virginia, where he became one of the first members of a research group that eventually included such notable members as Peter van de Kamp, Alexander N. Vyssotsky, and Emma T. R. Williams.

Alden earned his Ph.D. from the University of Virginia in 1917 and became an expert in parallax determinations, an aspect of astrometry. During that period refracting telescopes using lenses for objectives (as opposed to reflecting telescopes using mirrors) were in vogue. They were used like cameras to produce film images of bright and faint stellar and nonstellar objects. Over time, nearby stars may show a change of position as a result of the earth's motion about the sun. Those changes, when disentangled from other effects, lead to a means of determining a star's distance from the earth. By the end of Alden's long and distinguished career, he was responsible for every stage in the determination of the parallaxes of some five hundred fifty stars.

Alden served as assistant professor and then as associate professor of astronomy at the University of Virginia until 1925, when he was appointed astronomer in charge of Yale University's southern station at Witwatersrand, South Africa. There, his first responsibility was to oversee the erection of a large refractor that, during the following seventeen years, produced some forty thousand photographs, most of them the work of Alden himself.

In 1945 Alden returned to the University of Virginia and following the resignation of Samuel Alfred Mitchell became professor of astronomy and director of the Leander McCormick Observatory, positions he held until he retired in 1960. He continued the parallax program, began the long process of modernizing the observatory's equipment, and served on the site-selection committee of the National Radio Astronomy Observatory. He published more than seventy-five scientific papers, including work on orbits and mass ratios of double stars, on unseen companions of stars, on brightness variations of several stars, and on the determination of the mass of a moon of Neptune. Alden's work on parallaxes gained him his greatest recognition, including a vice presidency of the American Association for the Advancement of Science in 1951 and the chairmanship of the Commission of Twenty-Four of the International Astronomical Union from 1952 to 1955. The International Astronomical Union recognized his contributions to astronomy in 1971 by designating a crater on the far side of the moon Alden Crater.

Alden served as an elder of the Westminster Presbyterian Church in Charlottesville after his return to the University of Virginia. On 25 December 1917 he had married Mildred Viola Davidson. They had two daughters and one son. Harold Lee Alden died at his home in Charlottesville on 3 February 1964 and was buried in the University of Virginia Cemetery.

American Men of Science, 10th ed. (1960), 1:30; *Astronomical Journal* and *Publications of the Leander McCormick Observatory* for the vast majority of his published papers; family and professional information provided and verified by Harold Lee Alden Jr., Peter van de Kamp, and Heinrich Eichhorn; portrait by Walter Barrett at McCormick Observatory, UVA; obituary in *Charlottesville Daily Progress*, 4 Feb. 1964.

GEORGE S. MUMFORD

ALDERMAN, Edwin Anderson (15 May 1861–29 April 1931), president of the University of Virginia, was born in Wilmington, North Carolina, the only son and third of four children of James Alderman and Susan Jane Corbett Alderman. He grew up in a home that was serious, thrifty, and religious. His father was a timber inspector and Presbyterian lay leader. Alderman attended several private schools, including the Bethel Military Academy near Warrenton, Virginia. Four years after entering the University of North Carolina in Chapel Hill in 1878, he received a Ph.B., with honors in English and Latin, as well as the coveted Mangum Medal for oratory.

Alderman intended to become a lawyer, but soon after accepting a teaching position in 1882 in the public schools of Goldsboro, North

Carolina, the strong influence of Superintendent Edward Pearson Moses made him a zealous advocate of public education. In 1885 Alderman succeeded Moses as superintendent of schools in Goldsboro, and in 1889 he left that post to join Charles Duncan McIver in a three-year program conducting weeklong institutes for teachers in every county of the state.

Alderman taught at the new State Normal and Industrial School for Women in Greensboro during the 1892–1893 academic year and then became a professor in the Department of History and Philosophy of Education at the University of North Carolina. In 1896 he became president of the university, which he hoped to make the capstone of a broad educational system for North Carolina. During Alderman's tenure as president, the university grew in size and in public esteem, but a penurious legislature was in no mood to give it the financial support it needed, in part because of powerful opposition from the state's denominational colleges.

Discouraged, Alderman accepted the presidency of Tulane University in New Orleans in 1900. Under his leadership Tulane expanded its course offerings and gained greater public visibility. Alderman also took a prominent part in the campaign to develop the public schools of Louisiana. By then he had emerged as a leading spokesman for the movement to create a genuine system of public education in the South. Alderman was a charter member of the Southern Education Board, which was founded in 1901, and he contributed in many ways to the ongoing campaign waged by southern reformers in collaboration with northern philanthropists. His growing reputation owed much to his accomplishments as a public speaker. Handsome, urbane, and a bit imperious, he had a golden voice that could charm the ear of high and low alike.

As one of the South's preeminent educators, Alderman was a natural choice to become the first president of the University of Virginia in 1904. Until then, a committee under the chairman of the faculty had administered the university. Alderman assumed office on 15 September 1904 and immediately became a vital member of the Southern Education Board team that was leading a campaign for educational reform in Virginia. His desire to make the university the locus of educational expansion in Virginia was ultimately undermined by the trend toward state control over public education. In his broader plans for the university, too, he was hampered by the school's dependence on the General Assembly for financial support and by the fiscal conservatism of the state's leading politicians. Nevertheless, Alderman attracted large private donations, and during his administration he strengthened the faculty, increased student enrollment, reorganized the undergraduate curriculum, and presided over notable advances in the schools of engineering, law, and medicine.

Alderman had traditional as well as progressive views. His advocacy of a new public spirit that would back expansion and improvement of the public schools and an enlarged leadership role for the university did not prevent him from supporting, as did many other southern progressives, the disfranchisement of African Americans. Like many other educational reformers, he spoke of educating all of the people and of dealing fairly with black southerners, but he also evidently shared a widespread perception that improvement of the conditions of African Americans could not take place without a greater emphasis on the education of white southerners. In keeping with the spirit of the times during World War I, Alderman refused to support journalism professor Leonidas Rutledge Whipple, who had delivered an address on pacifism at the university that embroiled the school in controversy, and as a consequence Whipple lost his job.

Alderman was not at heart a scholar, although he and Armistead Churchill Gordon wrote and published a biography of the great southern educator J. L. M. Curry in 1911, and Alderman participated with Joel Chandler Harris in the publication between 1909 and 1923 of the seventeen-volume *Library of Southern Literature*. Alderman was essentially a propagandist for popular education and a constructive administrator who brought a more democratic spirit to higher education in the South. He was effective in both roles and was a popular and persuasive lecturer. Dignified and magisterial in public, Alderman had a genial and attractive personality. Among friends he was a debonair and witty companion who liked to travel and to fish.

Alderman was careful to avoid the hurly-burly of politics, but he became an ardent supporter of the 1912 presidential candidacy of his fellow educator Woodrow Wilson. Soon after Wilson's victory, Alderman entered a sanatorium at Saranac Lake, New York, suffering from tuberculosis of the larynx and complications in both lungs. He stayed there until April 1914 and was never again the buoyant campaigner of earlier days. During his absence from Charlottesville the deans and faculty council administered the university. After his return, a member of the faculty usually served as assistant to the president to relieve Alderman of some of the strain of his work. The University of Virginia continued to prosper under his leadership, even during prolonged public controversies over proposals that he advocated to establish a coordinate college for women, which failed, and to allow women to attend the university's graduate and professional schools, which was implemented. He won applause in 1922 for his part in preventing the removal of the medical school to Richmond. Alderman's stature as a national education leader was reinforced in 1924 when he delivered a widely acclaimed memorial address on Woodrow Wilson before a joint session of Congress.

Alderman married twice. On 29 December 1885 he wed Emma Graves in Chapel Hill, North Carolina. They had three children, all of whom died in childhood, and Emma Graves Alderman died in 1896. On 10 February 1904 he married Bessie Green Hearn in New Orleans. They had one son. Edwin Anderson Alderman suffered a stroke while en route to deliver an address at the inauguration of the president of the University of Illinois and died on 29 April 1931 in Connellsville, Pennsylvania. He was buried in the University of Virginia Cemetery in Charlottesville.

Dumas Malone, *Edwin A. Alderman: A Biography* (1940) (por. opp. 328); Clement Eaton, "Edwin A. Alderman—Liberal of the New South," *North Carolina Historical Review* 23 (1946): 206–221; Edwin Anderson Alderman Papers, UVA; W. Conard Gass, "Kemp Plummer Battle and the Development of Historical Instruction at the University of North Carolina," *North Carolina Historical Review* 45 (1968): 1–22; Charles William Dabney, *Universal Education in the South* (1936), esp. 1:45–46, 195–199, 204–214, 2:53–64, 298; Rose Howell Holder, *McIver of North Carolina* (1957); Louis R. Harlan, *Separate and Unequal: Public School Campaigns and Racism in the Southern Seaboard States, 1901–1915* (1958); Dewey W. Grantham, *Southern Progressivism: The Reconciliation of Progress and Tradition* (1983), esp. 234, 249–250, 259; William A. Link, *A Hard Country and a Lonely Place: Schooling, Society, and Reform in Rural Virginia, 1870–1920* (1986), esp. 91–92, 106–107, 118–123; Alan B. Bromberg, "Free Speech at Mr. Jefferson's University: The Case of Professor Leon Whipple," *VMHB* 88 (1980): 3–20; obituaries in *Charlottesville Daily Progress* and *Richmond Times-Dispatch*, both 30 Apr. 1931, and *New York Times* and University of Virginia, *College Topics*, both 1 May 1931; numerous tributes in *University of Virginia Alumni News* 19 (1931): 228–255.

DEWEY W. GRANTHAM

ALDERSON, John (5 March 1738–3 March 1821), Baptist minister, was one of five sons and a daughter of John Alderson and Jane Curtis Alderson, and was probably born in Bethlehem Township, Hunterdon County, New Jersey. His father was a Baptist minister who emigrated from England as a young man and lived first in New Jersey and then in Pennsylvania before moving his family to Frederick County, Virginia. In 1756 he led in organizing Smith's and Linnville's Creek Baptist Church, which was formed to serve the portions of Augusta County that became respectively Rockingham and Shenandoah Counties, and he subsequently helped establish other churches in the Shenandoah Valley. In 1776 he was briefly imprisoned in Botetourt County for performing marriages as a dissenting clergyman.

The younger John Alderson married Mary Carroll about 1759 and had three sons. Although he earned his living as a farmer, Alderson also became a clergyman after his father baptized him in March 1769 and supervised his ministerial instruction. In 1773 he preached a trial sermon at the meetinghouse at Linnville's Creek, and when the Smith's and Linnville's Creek Church split into separate congregations he became pastor of the Linnville's Creek Church in October 1775. Alderson received little or no income from his preaching or from performing marriages, even though his marriage register indicates that he performed 408 marriages between 1776 and 1798. He was usually known as John Alderson Jr. to distinguish him from his father, but some early writers have attributed some of Alderson's missionary work to his father and some of his father's to him. Some local histories have also confused the elder Alderson with his namesake son and perpetuated errors about their respective places of residence.

Between 1775 and 1777 Alderson made several trips to the frontier, including the area that became Greenbrier County in 1778. He braved unfriendly Indians in order to reach the isolated forts and settlements where he preached to the soldiers and settlers. He was not always gladly received; the occupants of one fort closed the gates in his face. In 1777 he settled near the Greenbrier River to farm and minister to the few settlers in the area. Although his initial successes were only modest, he baptized a few converts and in time other people from the Linnville's Creek Church migrated into the area. At first they considered themselves a branch of the former church, but in 1781 Alderson led in the constitution of the new Greenbrier Church with twenty-four members. It was one of the first Baptist churches—maybe the very first—west of the Allegheny Mountains and only the fourth Baptist church to be established in what became West Virginia.

Alderson traveled in a wide area around Greenbrier and founded Baptist churches in at least eight communities. In the autumn of 1805, following the death of his wife, he made an extended preaching journey to Pennsylvania. He also ventured into eastern Virginia, and on one such trip he distributed copies of his friend Josiah Osborne's book, *David and Goliath: or, A Treatise on Water Baptism* (1807). At about eighty years of age, Alderson ceased to travel and preach, and so the Greenbrier Baptist Association, which he and Osborne had helped found in 1807, chose to schedule its meetings at the Greenbrier Church for his accommodation. A Methodist attending the meeting in 1820 announced that, under Alderson's tutelage, he wished to be baptized by immersion. At that, Alderson "became overcome by ecstasy of feelings so that he broke out in a most impassioned exhortation," which made a lasting impression on the assemblage. It was his last sermon. John Alderson died on 3 March 1821 and was buried in Greenbrier Church cemetery. The inscription on his gravestone reads, "To a vigorous mind was united eminent piety."

Biographies in James B. Taylor, *Virginia Baptist Ministers*, ser. 1 (1859), 156–160, Robert B. Semple and George W. Beale, *A History of the Rise and Progress of the Baptists in Virginia*, rev. ed. (1894), 423–429, and Ralph C. McDanel, "Elder John Alderson, Jr., and the Greenbrier Church," *Virginia Baptist Register* 7 (1968): 307–319; Alderson's diary and marriage register and typed transcripts of Smith's and Linnville's Creek Baptist Church minute books in VBHS.

FRED ANDERSON

ALDHIZER, George Statton (15 June 1907–20 May 1986), member of the Senate of Virginia, was born in Broadway, a small town in Rockingham County, the only son and third of four children of Henry Hamilton Aldhizer, a pharmacist and businessman, and Sidney McNeill Pugh Aldhizer. He was usually known as George Statton Aldhizer II to distinguish him from his namesake grandfather, who was a pharmacist, banker, businessman, and civic leader in Broadway from the 1880s until his death in 1941. The younger Aldhizer grew up in Broadway. He graduated from Broadway High School in 1923 and from the University of Virginia, Phi Beta Kappa, in 1930. In 1932 he received his law degree from the University of Virginia.

Aldhizer practiced law in Harrisonburg. Over the years he was in partnership with some of the most prominent local attorneys, including John T. Harris, who died in 1936, William W. Wharton, and Russell M. Weaver. The firm, which eventually became Wharton, Aldhizer, and Weaver, had a general practice and also served a number of large corporate clients. In addition to his share of the law practice and his investments, Aldhizer owned and operated a farm in Rockingham County. He was active in various civic groups, including the Boy Scouts, and during the 1930s he sat on the Rockingham County School Board. He never married.

Aldhizer was a Democrat, and in 1949 he was elected to the House of Delegates. He was reelected in 1951, then in 1953 won election to the Senate of Virginia, where he served for twenty-two years. Aldhizer eventually acquired considerable influence. He became chairman of the Committee on Commerce and Labor and ranking member of the Committee on Finance and the Committee on Insurance and Banking. He also served on a number of special study commissions and on the State Crime Commission. During the school desegregation crisis of the 1950s, Aldhizer parted company with some of the Senate's Democratic leaders when it became clear to him that the Byrd organization's policy of Massive Resistance to court-ordered desegregation would close the state's public schools.

In 1968 Aldhizer chaired a special commission to recommend a method of securing the financial future of the city of Richmond, which was losing population and its tax base to the neighboring counties of Chesterfield and Henrico. In an attempt to increase the city's white population so as to offset the growing number of African Americans, the city tried to annex a large portion of suburban Chesterfield County. A lengthy and acrimonious litigation ensued. Aldhizer proposed a constitutional amendment granting the General Assembly authority to alter the political boundaries of the capital city every ten years to secure its revenue base. The proposal was opposed because it would enable the assembly to perpetuate white political domination in the city. Aldhizer's proposal failed.

Aldhizer was continuously reelected to the Senate until 1975, when Republican Nathan Miller defeated him. Aldhizer continued his practice of law in Harrisonburg and his involvement with other local businesses. He served as a trustee of the Virginia Museum of Fine Arts and encouraged public support for the arts. For his contributions to education, James Madison University gave Aldhizer a distinguished service award in 1976. He endowed the George S. Aldhizer II Business Department at Bridgewater College, which granted him an honorary LL.D. in 1980. George Statton Aldhizer died of cancer at Rockingham Memorial Hospital on 20 May 1986 and was buried in the cemetery at Broadway Presbyterian Church.

Biographies in William Cowper, ed., *History of the Shenandoah Valley* (1952), 3:323, and Glass and Glass, *Virginia Democracy*, 2:673–674; family history information confirmed by sister Mary Moore Aldhizer, 26 Sept. 1989; interviews with Harry F. Byrd Jr., 10 Oct. 1989, and Phillip C. Stone, 14 July 1989; Herbert Lundy Garris, "Constitutional Revision in Virginia: An Evolution of the Democratic Process, 1968–1970" (Ph.D. diss., University of Maryland, 1973), 120, 148–160; Murel M. Jones Jr., "The Impact of Annexation-Related City Council Reapportionment on Black Political Influence: The Cities of Richmond and Petersburg, Virginia" (Ph.D. diss., Howard University, 1977), 195–198; obituaries in *Harrisonburg Daily News-Record* and *Richmond Times-Dispatch* (por.), both 21 May 1986.

CLIVE R. HALLMAN

ALEXANDER, Archibald (17 April 1772–22 October 1851), president of Hampden-Sydney College, was born seven miles east of what soon became Lexington, the second of three sons and third of nine surviving children of William Alexander and Agnes Ann Reid Alexander. His grandparents were Ulster Scots, his father a respected farmer, merchant, and Presbyterian elder in what is now Rockbridge County. Alexander studied with several tutors, the most influential of whom was William Graham, principal of Liberty Hall in Lexington. Graham, a 1773 graduate of the College of New Jersey (now Princeton University), taught the combination of personal piety, moderate Calvinism, and Scottish common sense philosophy that he had learned from Princeton's John Witherspoon and that Alexander in turn promoted throughout his life.

At about age seventeen, Alexander served briefly as a tutor in the home of General John Posey in Spotsylvania County. During a period of religious doubt and confusion about the claims of competing Protestant sects, Alexander read the works of John Flavel, a seventeenth-century exponent of practical Puritan divinity, under whose influence he made a profession of faith. The Lexington Presbytery took him under its care on 20 October 1790 and licensed him on 1 October 1791. He preached first as an itinerant around Winchester and then as a missionary to southern Virginia and the borders of North Carolina. From the first, Alexander was an effective communicator, zealous yet not overbearing, affective while still intellectual. He was ordained by the Presbytery of Hanover on 7 June 1794 and then called as pastor of two churches, Cub Creek in Charlotte County and Briery in Prince Edward County.

In August 1796 Alexander was asked to assume the presidency of nearby Hampden-Sydney College. He accepted the post in November, was installed on 31 May 1797, and served in this position for the next decade, with the exception of a one-year absence (1801–1802) spent traveling in New England. When Alexander arrived at Hampden-Sydney, the college had been governed by an acting president since 1789. Alexander's direct forceful manner, combined with his obvious piety and considerable learning, hastened its recovery from the difficulties remaining from the Revolutionary War. During his tenure the student body at Hampden-Sydney seems to have ranged between twenty and thirty, an increasing number of whom actually finished the three-year degree program. Included among Alexander's students were the sons of several prominent Virginia families, especially the Cabells. Following the example of the College of New Jersey, Alexander gave greater attention to the teaching of science and secured new laboratory equipment. Less propitiously, Hampden-Sydney also followed Princeton and other colleges of the era in witnessing scenes of student unrest. Problems of discipline increased after the turn of the century and climaxed at Hampden-Sydney with a night of wild disorder on a Sunday in July 1805. Alexander and the trustees succeeded in restoring calm by suspending all but six of the student body, but the bloom of college teaching was fading fast for Alexander. In 1820 trustees would ask him to come back to the college as well as to take up duties at the Hampden-Sydney (later Union) Theological Seminary. But by that time he had more than enough to do in a new setting.

In the fall of 1806, after another summer of student unrest, Alexander accepted the call of the Pine Street (or Third) Presbyterian Church in Philadelphia. The next year he was elected moderator of the Presbyterian General Assembly. His sermon in 1808 as retiring moderator included a moving appeal for more-thorough ministerial training. The Presbyterian Church remembered this appeal on 2 June 1812, when it named Alexander the first professor at its new theological seminary in Princeton. Alexander served there with distinction for almost exactly half of his long life, teaching until the month before he died. His students included many future luminaries, among them the Presbyterian Charles Hodge, the Lutheran Samuel Simon Schmucker, and the German Reformed John Williamson Nevin. Although Alexander did not publish his first book until after he was fifty, he was an indefatigable writer whose many articles, pamphlets, and books included a sympathetic account of religious experience, a defense of the Bible, popular histories on biblical and Presbyterian themes, and even an unpublished novel. For nearly twenty-five years he was also a mainstay of the seminary's theological quarterly, *The Biblical Repertory and Princeton Review*, to which he contributed essay-reviews on an impressive range of subjects. At Princeton, students came to cherish the kindness of heart joined to fidelity of doctrine that had earlier earned Alexander wide regard in Virginia.

Alexander married Janetta Waddel, daughter of the eminent Presbyterian minister, James Waddel, on 5 April 1802. They were the parents of one daughter and six sons, three of whom (James Waddel Alexander, Joseph Addison Alexander, and Samuel Davies Alexander) also became prominent pastors, authors, and educators. Archibald Alexander died at his home in Princeton on 22 October 1851 and was buried in Princeton.

James Waddel Alexander, *The Life of Archibald Alexander, D.D., First Professor in the Theological Seminary, at Princeton, New Jersey* (1854), contains a bibliography of Alexander's works; Charles Hodge, "Memoir of Archibald Alexander," *Biblical Repertory and Princeton Review* 27 (1855): 133–159; John Oliver Nelson, "Archibald Alexander, Winsome Conservative (1772–1851)," *Journal of the Presbyterian Historical Society* 35 (1957): 15–32; books by Alexander still in print include *Evidences of the Authenticity, Inspiration and Canonical Authority of the Holy Scriptures* (1826), *Thoughts on Religious Experience* (1841), and *A History of Colonization of the Western Coast of Africa* (1846); John Luster Brinkley, *On This Hill: A Narrative History of Hampden-Sydney College, 1774–1994* (1994) (por., 38); Hanover and Lexington Presbytery Papers, Union Theological Seminary in Virginia; Hodge Family Papers, Princeton University Library; Alexander's academic papers, Princeton Theological Seminary Library; Alexander Brown, *The Cabells and Their Kin*, 2d ed. (1939), 647–649; Lefferts A. Loetscher, *Facing the Enlightenment and Pietism: Archibald Alexander and the Founding of*

Princeton Theological Seminary (1983); portrait by John Neagle at Princeton Theological Seminary.

MARK A. NOLL

ALEXANDER, Catherine Lucille Churchill Burgess (28 February 1888–5 September 1974), civic leader, was born in Warren County, the youngest of three children, all daughters, of Sarah Margaret McIntire Churchill and William A. Churchill. Raised on a small farm outside Front Royal in a home that she later remembered as always having music, love, and books in it, but very little money, she attended public schools and Eastern College, a local four-year coeducational institution. On 21 April 1906 she married Harrie A. Burgess, a widowed mining engineer almost twice her age. They separated soon after the marriage.

Lucille Churchill Burgess, who never used her first name as an adult, taught school in the Fork District of Warren County from about January 1909 until she moved to Charlottesville, where she taught from the autumn of 1910 through 1917. She took courses at the University of Virginia during the summers and in 1916 served on the faculty of the university's summer school program, where she met another educator, Frederick Milton Alexander. They married in Albemarle County on 28 July 1917 and moved to Newport News, where he had just been appointed principal of the city high school. The Alexanders had one son and one daughter.

Alexander stopped teaching to care for her young family, but she joined the Newport News Woman's Club and quickly became one of its most prominent members. During the 1920s she held important offices in the local Associated Charities, in the Young Women's Christian Association, and in patrons' leagues, associations of parents formed to improve local schools. She was also active in the Daughters of the American Revolution and the Red Cross.

Alexander's enthusiasm and efficiency as president of the Newport News Woman's Club from 1930 to 1932 was recognized in the autumn of 1932 when she was asked to edit the *Virginia Club Woman*, the official publication of the Virginia Federation of Women's Clubs. In May 1935 she was elected the fifteenth president of the federation, which then had nearly nine thousand members. She pledged to support a revision of the Virginia public school curriculum, modernization of the federation's bureaucracy, and active recruitment of younger federation members. Alexander promoted responsible citizenship as one of her administration's themes, encouraging Virginia's clubwomen to participate in the University of Virginia's Institute of Public Affairs and to formulate creative responses to the problems posed by economic depression at home and threats of war overseas.

Stepping down as president of the VFWC in 1938, Alexander turned her interests increasingly toward the field of public health and welfare. When the American Society for the Control of Cancer appealed to the General Federation of Women's Clubs in 1936 for help in establishing state branches of the new Women's Field Army, a lay organization raising funds and promoting education to fight cancer, she had enthusiastically committed the VFWC. In February 1940 she became the first paid state commander and education director of the Field Army's Virginia Division. Operating from the Virginia Cancer Foundation's office in Richmond, where her family had moved in 1936, Alexander was responsible for the organization of local cancer society units, public education, and fund-raising for the entire state. Under her direction the Field Army helped the foundation raise almost $15,000 in 1940, and by 1947 it was raising more than $189,000 annually. Alexander continued her work despite the deaths of her son in 1946 and her husband in 1948, and from 1944 to 1948 she edited the Field Army's bimonthly *Messenger*.

Early in 1948 Alexander resigned from the Field Army to become a national field representative for the recently renamed American Cancer Society, a position she held until she retired in 1953. In 1949 she won the J. Shelton Horsley Memorial Award for her outstanding contribution to the fight against cancer in Virginia. Her other health-related activities included service on the board of the Virginia League for Planned Parenthood and the Richmond Area Heart Association. She was also an active member of Richmond's Episcopal Church of the Good Shepherd. Lucille Churchill

Alexander died at the Protestant Episcopal Church Home in Richmond on 5 September 1974 and was buried in Hollywood Cemetery.

Etta Belle Walker Northington, *A History of The Virginia Federation of Women's Clubs, 1907–1957* [1958], 73–76; Richard Lee Morton, *Virginia Lives: The Old Dominion Who's Who* (1964), 10; feature article in *Richmond Times-Dispatch*, 12 May 1935 (por.); Alexander family Bible in possession of James Craig, of Manassas; Warren and Albemarle Co. Marriage Registers; *Commonwealth* 11 (July 1935): 19; her activities are documented extensively in *Virginia Club Woman*, 1931–1940, and *Annual Report of the Virginia Cancer Foundation, Inc.* (title varies), 1942–1950; obituaries in *Richmond News Leader* and *Richmond Times-Dispatch*, both 6 Sept. 1974.

Sandra Gioia Treadway

ALEXANDER, Fleming Emory (14 April 1888–13 December 1980), journalist and Baptist minister, was born Fleming Pore in Christiansburg. His mother died when he was an infant, and he and his eight brothers and sisters were separated. When he entered school, he assumed the surname of his foster father, Robert Alexander, and he chose for himself the middle name Emory. Badly treated as a child, he left Christiansburg as a teenager, walking across the mountains into West Virginia to join an older brother who worked in the coalfields. His formal education ended at about the fifth grade.

The details of the next decades of his life are obscure. Somewhere in Kentucky he learned the printing trade, and he is said to have worked for newspapers in Georgia, Kentucky, and Virginia. At one time he owned a movie theater and a taxi company in West Virginia. During World War I he served in France with the 802d Pioneer Infantry.

By the mid-1920s Alexander had moved to Lynchburg, where he taught printing at the Virginia Theological Seminary and College while operating a private printing business. There he came under the influence of Vernon Johns, the pastor at Court Street Baptist Church and a brilliant preacher-scholar who inspired a generation of southern civil rights leaders. Ordained to the ministry in Lynchburg, Alexander served from 1930 to 1935 as pastor of Rustburg Baptist Church in Campbell County. In 1935 he was called to the pastorate of First Memorial Baptist Church in Christiansburg with Johns preaching his installation sermon. Alexander later renamed the church Schaeffer Memorial Baptist Church in honor of the church's founder, Captain Charles S. Schaeffer of the Freedmen's Bureau. Alexander left the Christiansburg church early in 1951 to become pastor of the First Baptist Church of Buchanan, in Botetourt County, a position he held for almost twenty years.

In February 1941 Alexander founded the *Roanoke Tribune*, a weekly newspaper serving the African American community. Like most black publishers, he struggled financially. He augmented his income with job printing, borrowed funds to keep the paper afloat, often set the type himself, and by necessity relied on white businesses for most of his advertising. During the 1950s Sarah Patton Boyle, of Charlottesville, wrote a regular column for the *Tribune* entitled "By a White Southerner." At the same time Alexander had an office in Charlottesville with Thomas Jefferson Sellers as his agent. He also had reporters in several other towns in southwestern Virginia, and in 1961 he opened an office in Martinsville.

Alexander was a fervent Democrat and even supported candidates of Harry F. Byrd's organization during the 1940s and early 1950s. In October 1953 he became Negro Democratic campaign manager in the Sixth Congressional District, the first black campaign manager ever, for the statewide ticket of Thomas Bahnson Stanley, Allie Edward Stokes Stephens, and J. Lindsay Almond. In 1954 he advised Stanley to call together leaders of both races in order to find a peaceful means to desegregate the public schools. When Stanley and Almond instead joined Byrd and leaders in the General Assembly in support of Massive Resistance, Alexander criticized them strongly in the *Tribune*. His stance was still too mild for some of the Roanoke ministers, and tensions between them ensued. In 1956, when Alexander and another black minister both ran for the Roanoke city council after each understood that the other would not and then publicly traded insults, the Roanoke Baptist Ministers' Association publicly rebuked Alexander for his conservatism. Alexander countered by suing several prominent civic and religious leaders for libel. Although the suit was eventually settled out of court, it soured his relations with his fellow African American clergymen. Alexander ran again for city council without success in 1966 and 1968, when it was widely believed that his campaigns were encouraged by white business leaders who considered him a safe and acceptable candidate.

Alexander's first marriage, to Huzella Walker, ended in divorce after the birth of a daughter. In 1923 he married Sedonia Rotan, a graduate of Ohio State University and a teacher of English and French. They had two daughters and a son. After her death in 1973, Alexander married Florence Fields Wood, a retired music teacher. In 1971, after an automobile accident forced his retirement, Alexander sold the *Tribune* to his daughter Claudia Sedonia Alexander Whitworth. Fleming Emory Alexander died while on a visit to another daughter in New York on 13 December 1980. His funeral was held at Schaeffer Memorial Baptist Church in Christiansburg, and he was buried at Roselawn Memorial Gardens in Blacksburg.

Family history information provided by Claudia Sedonia Alexander Whitworth and Mary Ann Elizabeth Gayles; LVA has 266 issues of the *Roanoke Tribune* for the years 1951–1957; the clipping file on Alexander at the *Roanoke Times and World News* contains numerous useful items, especially for the dates 15 Sept. 1952, 26, 31 July, 18 Sept. 1956, and 25 Apr. 1982; the *Tribune*'s anniversary issue of 11 May 1989 also contains useful information; other information about Alexander and Roanoke politics provided by Melville Carico; obituary in *Roanoke Times and World News*, 14 Dec. 1980 (por.).

ANN FIELD ALEXANDER

ALEXANDER, Frederick Milton (7 February 1888–13 December 1948), educator, was born on a farm in Clarke County, the only child of Henry Milton Alexander and Minnie Lee Grubbs Alexander. Around the beginning of 1897 the impoverished family moved to Frederick County. Alexander attended the small rural schools that, typical of the time, were underfunded, often understaffed, and usually pedagogically backward. Nevertheless, he developed a love of books and a commitment to education by the time he had completed the course of study at the Shenandoah Valley Academy and in the secondary schools of nearby Winchester.

Fred M. Alexander, as he was always professionally known, began his teaching career at age nineteen with only a high school diploma. He served as principal of the little school at Morrisville in Fauquier County from 1907 to 1910, principal at Orange from 1910 to 1913, and principal at Cape Charles High School at the southern end of Virginia's Eastern Shore from 1913 to 1917. While at Cape Charles he began studying at the College of William and Mary, from which he received an A.B. in 1921. In the meantime, he moved to Newport News in 1917 to become principal of the public high school. Just prior to assuming his duties there, on 28 July 1917 he married Catherine Lucille Churchill Burgess near Charlottesville, where the two had met while taking classes in a summer institute at the University of Virginia. They had one son and one daughter. Lucille Alexander had a distinguished career of her own promoting good citizenship and public health.

When Alexander took over the Newport News High School, it had fewer than four hundred students. During the following two decades he transformed it into one of the best and largest secondary schools in Virginia, marking him as one of the state's outstanding public school administrators. Alexander was a disciple of philosopher and educational reformer John Dewey, whose theories of education Alexander studied at Teachers College, Columbia University, where he earned an M.A. in educational administration in 1929. During his time in Newport News, Alexander insisted on excellence and attempted to move all the students toward graduation. Imbued with democratic values, he was an innovative and sometimes controversial administrator. His plans worked, however, and not only did the Newport News school system improve, but Alexander conducted seminars on school administration at the University of Virginia during a number of summer sessions. During the 1930s he frequently wrote articles on school administration for the *Virginia Journal of Education*.

Alexander became a respected leader in the Virginia educational community while at Newport News and was elected president of the

Virginia State Teachers Association in 1924. He presided over its reorganization and enlargement to include administrators and school trustees as the Virginia Education Association in 1925 and served as the first president of the new body. In 1932 Alexander chaired the Committee on Educational Aims of the Virginia Curriculum Revision Project, a comprehensive review by Virginia educators that produced some of the most progressive curricular reform proposals ever written for America's schools. Undaunted by criticism and resistance, Alexander was convinced and continued to argue that democratic society required a democratic education and democratic action along the lines he had instituted in Newport News. During the 1930s teachers and students in more than five hundred Virginia classrooms experimented with the revised curriculum based on Alexander's vision.

In 1936 Alexander moved to Richmond to become the supervisor of Negro education for Virginia. Although an officer of the state Department of Education, he was paid with funds from the Rockefeller General Education Fund. His interest in the educational problems confronting African American students was of long standing. Alexander's thesis at Teachers College, which he revised and published in 1943, was *Education for the Needs of the Negro in Virginia*, the most important study of the subject ever made to that time. An editorial in the influential *Norfolk Journal and Guide* called it "The Book of the Century." Alexander argued that the welfare of Virginia required improved schooling for black students. He explained that African American families were poor "not because of low intelligence. Rather they have low intelligence because they are poor . . . and because cultural, educative, and economic opportunities have been denied them." When Alexander began his new job only 58 percent of black school-aged children were in school, and the schools were distinctly inferior to those provided for white children. He sought to reduce the inequities resulting from the formula for distributing state aid to localities that permitted some local administrators to divert money intended for the black schools to other uses.

Alexander's conspicuous role as an educational reformer resulted in his appointment in 1943 to the United States Commission on Secondary Education, and in the same year he became Supervisor of Secondary Education for the state of Virginia. During the 1940s he worked on a master plan for the consolidation of rural southern schools and their replacement with larger, more-comprehensive secondary schools. Convinced that excellence of secondary school education was the key to making important contributions to southern culture, Alexander worked closely with the Southern Association of Colleges and Secondary Schools. In 1947 he was elected a vice president of the association, which put him in line for its presidency. On 13 December 1948, however, just after returning to Virginia from the annual meeting of the association, Fred M. Alexander suffered an aneurysm of the heart and died in Richmond. He was buried in Hollywood Cemetery in that city.

Earl B. Broadwater, "Dr. Fred M. Alexander, Memorial Address," *Virginia Journal of Education* 49 (Apr. 1956): 30–32; Alexander family Bible in possession of James Craig, of Manassas; variant birth date of 24 Jan. 1888 and given name of Thomas in BVS Birth Register, Clarke Co.; Alexander's educational philosophy is clearly laid out in his *Education for the Needs of the Negro in Virginia* (1943) and in his articles on educational administration in the *Virginia Journal of Education*, 1930–1937; family history information verified by daughter, Margaret Lee Craig, and other information by Ethel M. Guildersleeve, a colleague at Newport News High School; obituaries and editorial tributes in *Newport News Daily Press*, *Richmond News Leader*, and *Richmond Times-Dispatch*, all 14 and 15 Dec. 1948, *Norfolk Journal and Guide*, 18 Dec. 1948, and *Virginia Journal of Education* 43 (Sept. 1949): 24 (por.).

MICHAEL E. JAMES

ALEXANDER, George Murrell (1 August 1889–3 March 1961), National Guard officer, was born in Lynchburg, the only son and elder of two children of Frank Alexander and Fanny Murrell Alexander. After the death of his father, his mother married attorney James Emory Hughes on 12 February 1896. Alexander was educated in the Lynchburg public schools and graduated twelfth in his class of thirty-nine at Virginia Military Institute in 1909, after which he attended classes at the law school of

Washington and Lee in 1910. During the academic year 1909–1910 he also served as assistant professor of English and director of physics at VMI. On 30 June 1910 Alexander resigned his position at the institute and relinquished his commission as a captain in the Virginia Volunteers to return to Lynchburg.

George "Hack" Alexander did not reenter the state militia until 6 June 1916, when he was invited to stand for election as captain of the Lynchburg Musketeers, Company L, 1st Infantry, Virginia National Guard. On 30 June the unit was mustered into national service for duty on the Texas-Mexico border as part of General John J. Pershing's expedition against Francisco "Pancho" Villa. Alexander and his company remained on active duty until 16 January 1917.

In July 1917 Alexander's company, redesignated part of the 116th Infantry, was again mustered into national service. After training in Alabama and New Jersey, the regiment arrived in Europe on 15 June 1918. Alexander was promoted to major and commander of the 116th's 1st Battalion on 28 September, and he was severely wounded by a sniper on 11 October during the Meuse-Argonne offensive, for which he received the Purple Heart. He was unable to rejoin his unit until 3 January 1919. In the spring of that year, as one of a select group of officers chosen from the American Expeditionary Force, he attended Magdalen College, Oxford University. Back in the United States, Alexander was discharged from national service on 30 July 1919.

He returned to Lynchburg in 1919 and entered business. Within several years he had acquired the insurance firm of Ivey and Kirkpatrick. On 8 November 1921 he married Margaret Elizabeth Kinner, of Lynchburg. They had one son and one daughter. One of the few field officers of the Virginia National Guard who served throughout the period between the world wars, Alexander was named major of the reconstituted 1st Infantry in November 1920. The following year he was transferred to the state's 2d Infantry, renumbered the 116th Infantry in March 1922. He was promoted to lieutenant colonel on 6 May 1929, to colonel on 26 June 1933, and to brigadier general on 16 October 1940, when he was reassigned to the command of the 91st Infantry Brigade, Virginia National Guard, part of the 29th Infantry Division commanded by Major General Milton A. Reckord, of Baltimore.

Alexander was one of three general officers in the Virginia National Guard when on 3 February 1941 his brigade, renumbered the 88th Brigade of the 29th Division, was inducted into the United States Army. Alexander served as brigade commanding general and later assistant division commander. After training at Fort George Gordon Meade in Maryland, the 29th arrived in England in October 1942. In 1943 Reckord was reassigned as provost marshal, European Theater of Operations, and kept Alexander as his assistant. For his World War II service, Alexander received the Bronze Star and the Croix de Guerre, with Palm. He was retired in May 1946 with the rank of major general, Virginia Militia, Unorganized, and in 1948 was awarded the Virginia National Guard's Distinguished Service Medal in recognition of his service in both world wars.

In addition to his insurance business in Lynchburg, Alexander was active in civic affairs and served as a member of the Lynchburg Hospital Authority, a vestryman of Saint Paul's Episcopal Church, chairman of the city's Red Cross disaster committee, and a director of the First National Trust and Savings Bank. George Murrell Alexander died in Lynchburg of a heart attack on 3 March 1961 and was buried in Spring Hill Cemetery.

Brief biographies in *Report of the Adjutant General of the State of Virginia* for 1940 (1941), 3, and *Commonwealth* 7 (Nov. 1940): 17 (por.); Edley Craighill, *The Musketeers* (1931), 61–62, 291; Francis E. Lutz, *The 29th Infantry Division and Fort George G. Meade* (1941), 54–55; Joseph H. Ewing, *29 Let's Go! A History of the 29th Infantry Division in World War II* (1948), 1, 21; *Richmond News Leader*, 28 June 1933, 20 Sept., 16 Oct. 1940, *Richmond Times-Dispatch*, 20 Sept. 1940, and *Lynchburg News*, 3 May 1946; Distinguished Service Medal citation printed in *Report of the Adjutant General of the State of Virginia* for 1948 (1950), 18; obituaries in *Lynchburg News*, *Lynchburg Daily Advance*, and *Richmond Times-Dispatch*, all 4 Mar. 1961; editorial tribute in *Lynchburg Daily Advance*, 6 Mar. 1961.

EDWARD D. C. CAMPBELL, JR.

ALEXANDER, James (4 March 1804–20 October 1887), journalist, was born in Boston,

Massachusetts, the eldest of three children, all sons, of James Alexander, a prominent cabinetmaker, and Elizabeth Williston Alexander. He attended public school until the age of thirteen, when he went to work in the first of several Boston shops where he learned the trade of printing. In 1820 he began an apprenticeship with the Boston firm of Wells and Lilly and completed his service on 4 March 1825. In December 1826 he accepted a position as superintendent in the offices of the *Brooklyn Journal and Windham County Advertiser* in Brooklyn, Connecticut.

Alexander moved to Charlottesville in November 1828 and began work as one of the printers of Thomas Jefferson Randolph's pioneering edition of the *Memoir, Correspondence, and Miscellanies, From the Papers of Thomas Jefferson*, which Charlottesville publisher Frank Carr issued in four volumes in 1829. Jefferson's political views profoundly influenced Alexander, and except for the years 1830 to 1835, when he edited and published the *Virginia Republican* in Abingdon, he lived the remainder of his life in Jefferson's hometown of Charlottesville. On 20 December 1832 he married Rebecca Ann Wills, of Albemarle County. They had three sons and three daughters.

Alexander returned to Charlottesville in May 1835 and started the *Jeffersonian Republican* in opposition to Charlottesville's Whig newspaper, the *Advocate*. Solidly Democratic from the beginning, Alexander's paper frequently included articles by such party supporters as Thomas Jefferson Randolph, Frank G. Ruffin, Shelton F. Leake, and William Henry Brockenbrough. It just as often attacked the rival *Advocate* and local Whig politicians, most notably Alexander Rives. The *Jeffersonian Republican* was a highly partisan newspaper that increasingly took a strong position in favor of southern rights during the antebellum years.

In 1860 Alexander served as secretary of the local Breckenridge Club in support of the southern Democratic Party presidential nominee, John C. Breckenridge. Alexander supported secession in 1861 and championed the Confederacy during the Civil War. The war forced him to suspend publication of the *Jeffersonian Republican* in 1862. He may have written subsequently for other newspapers. Dispatches about Charlottesville published in the *Lynchburg Daily Republican* over the pseudonym "Monticello" have been convincingly attributed to him. He continued to work as a job printer during the war and also served from 1862 to 1866 as an alderman of Charlottesville and as an overseer of the poor. In his capacity as alderman, Alexander was one of the city officials who surrendered Charlottesville to the Union army on 3 March 1865. Although he took great pride in his New England ancestry, he was not easily reconciled to the Union. When news of the assassination of Abraham Lincoln reached Charlottesville, Alexander expressed his delight to a celebrating crowd, jumping up and down with excitement and repeating John Wilkes Booth's words (and Virginia's motto) "*sic semper tyrannis*."

Following the Civil War, Alexander continued printing for local businesses and for the University of Virginia, but he sold the *Jeffersonian Republican* before it resumed publication in 1873. He was editor of the paper in 1873 and 1874 and later contributed occasional articles, including a series of personal recollections of life in Charlottesville during his early years there that are a rich source of local color and anecdote. James Alexander died in Charlottesville on 20 October 1887 and was buried in Maplewood Cemetery.

Family Bible record and Alexander's MS family genealogy, "Ancestors," both in UVA and printed in Mary Catherine Murphy, ed., *Writings of James Alexander Concerning His Ancestors* (1966); Mary Rawlings, ed., *Early Charlottesville: Recollections of James Alexander 1828–1874*, 2d ed., ed. Velora Carter Thomson (1963; frontispiece por.); some Alexander letters in UVA; Lincoln assassination anecdote in Helen R. Duke, ed., "Recollections of Judge R. T. W. Duke, Jr.," *Papers of the Albemarle County Historical Society* 3 (1942–1943): 49; obituaries in *Charlottesville Chronicle*, 21 Oct. 1887, and *Charlottesville Jeffersonian Republican*, 26 Oct. 1887.

R. H. F. LINDEMANN

ALEXANDER, Mark (7 February 1792–5 or 6 July 1883), member of the House of Representatives and member of the Convention of 1829–1830, the only child of Mark Alexander and his first wife, Lucy Bugg Alexander, was born at his father's house, Salem, on the

Roanoke River in eastern Mecklenburg County. During the 1790s Alexander's father, a member of a prominent North Carolina family, served in the Virginia House of Delegates. He remarried twice and had two more sons and four daughters. After his father's death in 1824, Alexander became the guardian for his underage siblings.

Alexander attended a local school and then entered an academy in Louisburg, North Carolina. He matriculated at the University of North Carolina in 1807 and remained there for three years without graduating. In 1813 Alexander obtained his license to practice law in Mecklenburg County, and in 1815 he was elected to the House of Delegates, serving until his election in 1819 to the United States House of Representatives from the district composed of Brunswick, Lunenburg, and Mecklenburg Counties. He was reelected, apparently without serious opposition, until 1833, when he declined to seek another term. While in Congress he served on the Committee on Ways and Means and was chairman of the Committee on the District of Columbia for several sessions. His friends and allies in politics included John Randolph of Roanoke, Littleton Waller Tazewell, and North Carolina congressman Nathaniel Macon. He joined them in supporting strict construction of the Constitution, states' rights, and limited federal involvement in the economy and internal improvements.

Alexander was one of four delegates to the Virginia Convention of 1829–1830 from the district comprising Brunswick, Dinwiddie, Lunenburg, and Mecklenburg Counties. His name does not figure prominently in its recorded proceedings, but in one speech he expressed his continuing concern lest the governor be given too much power and criticized his fellow delegates for valuing party interest above principle at the convention. Nevertheless, he voted for adoption of the constitution in its final form. Alexander served one more term in the House of Delegates in 1845, and in 1850 he was nominated against his wishes for one of six seats allotted to the Halifax, Pittsylvania, and Mecklenburg district in the Convention of 1850. He was not elected.

On 1 June 1831 Alexander married Sally Park Turner, nineteen years his junior and daughter of his friend James Turner, a former North Carolina governor and U.S. senator. They lived at Salem until 1845, when Alexander built a new brick house just to the west on an estate that he called Park Forest. They had four sons and four daughters, of whom three sons and two daughters lived to adulthood. Alexander continued to practice law and operate his plantation and became one of the wealthiest men in the county. On the eve of the Civil War he owned more than four thousand acres of land and 105 slaves in Mecklenburg County, as well as a plantation in Mississippi.

Hugh Blair Grigsby described Alexander as "one of the most graceful men of his generation," and a portrait by Chester Harding, probably executed during the Convention of 1829–1830, shows a handsome man with a kindly face. The Civil War ruined him financially. He had accumulated substantial debts before the war and also lent money to neighbors who later could not repay him. He eventually lost all his property, including Park Forest, in 1880. About 1882, after a period in which they rented Park Forest from its new owners, he and his wife moved in with their daughter Rebecca and her husband, Norfleet Smith, in Scotland Neck, North Carolina. There, on either 5 or 6 July 1883, Mark Alexander, reportedly the country's oldest living former congressman, died, probably of complications resulting from a broken hip. He was buried in the Trinity Episcopal Church cemetery at Scotland Neck.

Hugh Blair Grigsby Diary (1876–1877), 349, 350, VHS; Alexander letters in VHS; Alexander's license to practice law and Sally Park Alexander Diary in Baskervill Papers, VHS; election to convention reported in *Richmond Enquirer*, 2 June 1829; *Proceedings and Debates of 1829–30 Convention*, 715, 882; Catlin, *Convention of 1829–30* (por.); public letter by Alexander published in *Richmond Semi-Weekly Examiner*, 26 July 1850; interview with Alexander described in *Richmond Daily Dispatch*, 2 June 1881; portrait by Chester Harding and a silhouette, ca. 1818, owned by E. Hatcher Crenshaw, Richmond; gravestone, Trinity Episcopal Church cemetery, gives death date of 5 July 1883, but it is a day later in obituary in *Richmond Daily Dispatch*, 11 July 1883.

SUSAN BRACEY SHEPPARD

ALEXANDER, Mary C. (2 March 1893–16 April 1955), aviator, was probably born

Mary C. White in Loudoun County. Information about her early life is not available, and some statements about her career that were published during her lifetime and that she did not contradict are demonstrably inaccurate or cannot be proved. She later identified her parents as William White and Ella White and stated that she had attended Immaculata Seminary in Washington, D.C., but neither assertion can be verified. When she married John Ira Alexander in Baltimore, Maryland, on 28 November 1911, she listed her address as Arlington.

Mary C. Alexander and John Alexander had one son and one daughter before they moved to Lynchburg about 1917 or 1918. John Alexander worked first as a traveling salesman and then as a salesman for a local automobile dealership. In April 1924 they founded the J. I. Alexander Motor Company, a Studebaker dealership, with Mary C. Alexander as president and treasurer and John Alexander as general manager and salesman. She was one of the earliest women to be president of an automobile dealership in Virginia, though perhaps not the very first, as was later asserted. Within two years John Alexander deserted Mary Alexander, and she subsequently filed for a full divorce, which was granted in the Circuit Court of Campbell County in January 1929. She did not take pains to dispel among her later acquaintances an impression that she was a widow. She may have believed that she could pursue her professional interests with fewer difficulties as a widow than as a divorcée.

In July 1929 Alexander went to Roosevelt Field on Long Island in New York to take flying lessons, and later that year she graduated from the Curtiss Wright Flying School in Baltimore. She told a journalist who wrote a story about women who were learning to fly that she wanted to be able to add sales of airplanes to her Lynchburg automobile dealership, but that business had closed by 1929. Clearly what she really wanted to do was fly. Alexander became a charter member of the first association of women aviators, called the Ninety-Nines, and she knew most of the first generation of women pilots. Amelia Earhart referred to Alexander in 1932 as the "flying grandmother," although Alexander may not yet have become a grandmother for the first time.

Alexander lived in Lynchburg until about 1935 and listed herself in the city directory as an "aviatrix." She was an advocate of women in aviation when flying was still a glamorous and dangerous pursuit. In an article for the magazine *Southern Aviation*, Alexander stated in 1932 that she saw no conflicts among her roles as a woman, mother, business executive, and aviator. One of only a very few licensed women pilots in Virginia early in the 1930s, she flew at air shows in Virginia and elsewhere during the decade but avoided the stunt flying and high-risk flamboyance of barnstorming. About 1932 she acquired a transport pilot's license and obtained permission to use a Virginia National Guard airfield in Virginia Beach to begin a scheduled air service between Washington, D.C., and Norfolk, but in August 1934 the National Guard canceled her permit to use the airfield after one of her pilots violated the field's regulations.

Alexander continued to fly until the end of the decade, after which she took a desk job with Pan American Airways. Following her second marriage, to Emil Charles Held, of Washington, D.C., she lived in Washington or its Maryland suburbs and pursued a new interest in art. Mary C. Alexander Held died in Georgetown Hospital in Washington on 16 April 1955. Emil Held's service in World War I having entitled her to the privilege, she was buried in Arlington National Cemetery.

Birth date in records of Arlington National Cemetery; first marriage reported in *Baltimore Morning Sun*, 29 Nov. 1911; divorce recorded in Ended Chancery File 1120, Campbell Co. Circuit Court; issuance and revocation of charter of J. I. Alexander Motor Co. recorded in Charter Book, 127:145–147; Lynchburg city directories, 1918–1934; "Why Do Women Fly?," *Southern Aviation* 3 (May 1932): 15–16 (por.); letters respecting Washington-Norfolk air route in correspondence of Adjutant General's Office, RG 46, LVA; obituaries in *Lynchburg Daily Advance*, *Lynchburg News*, *Washington Post*, and *Washington Star*, all 18 Apr. 1955.

BRENT TARTER

ALEXANDER, Robert (ca. 1750–by 11 December 1820), member of the Convention of 1788, was born in the southern part of Augusta County, one of six sons and four daughters of Robert Alexander and Esther Alexander. The elder Robert Alexander immigrated to Pennsylvania from Ulster in 1737 and to the Valley of Virginia about nine years later. In 1749 he established an academy that some regard as the predecessor of Washington and Lee University. The schoolmaster gave his son a good education, but little else is known about Robert Alexander's youth.

On 25 January 1773 Alexander became deputy to the clerk of Bedford County, James Steptoe. Alexander later served as clerk of the Bedford County Committee formed on 23 May 1775. He was commissioned a lieutenant in the county militia on 26 May 1778 and promoted to captain on 29 June 1779 but never went on active duty during the Revolutionary War. In 1781 the General Assembly formed Campbell County out of Bedford County, and at the first meeting of the new county court on 7 February 1782 the justices of the peace appointed Robert Alexander clerk. Alexander remained clerk of Campbell County until his death, when he was succeeded by his son John, who had been clerk of the Superior Court of Law in Campbell County since 1809.

Robert Alexander married Anne Austin about 10 March 1774. They had two sons and eight daughters. She probably brought some property to the marriage and with this, together with Alexander's fees from the clerkship and what he earned by serving as administrator of estates, he gradually prospered. By 1782 he owned 565 acres of land in Bedford County, and he acquired almost 1,750 acres in Campbell County by 1789. When he composed his will on 4 February 1814 he owned a thousand-acre plantation and eighteen slaves, and he lived in Rock Castle, one of the largest houses in the county.

On 6 March 1788 Robert Alexander and Edmund Winston were elected to represent Campbell County in the convention called to consider the proposed constitution of the United States. Alexander was so little known outside his region that Richmond newspapers misidentified him as John Alexander. Alexander attended the convention but took no recorded part in its debates. On 25 June 1788 he voted for amendments before ratification, then voted to reject the Constitution.

Captain Alexander, as he was usually called, was a respected gentleman, but he was also eccentric and violently opinionated. He figures in some of the most colorful anecdotes of Campbell County's early history. His habit of carrying a large musket frightened his neighbors because he was prone to wild behavior when he had too much to drink. Robert Alexander died between adjournment of the county court on 17 November 1820 and the next session on 11 December.

Alexander Brown, "Archibald Alexander, of Scotland, and His Descendants in Ireland and America," *Richmond Standard*, 11 Sept. 1880; Ollinger Crenshaw, *General Lee's College* (1969), 4–5, 10; Bedford Co. Order Book, 5A:37; 6:141, 157, 236, 360; Campbell Co. Order Book, 1:2, 3, 13:163; Bedford Co. marriage bonds; will, dated 4 Feb. 1814 and proved 14 May 1821, and estate inventory in Campbell Co. Will Book, 4:307–308, 316–317; Kaminski, *Ratification*, 10:1538, 1541, 1565; anecdotes in memoirs of grandson Robert Enoch Withers, *Autobiography of an Octogenarian* (1907), 11–12, 14–18.

BRENT TARTER

ALFRIEND, Edward Morrison (25 October 1837–24 October 1901), playwright, was born in Richmond, the eldest of three sons and a daughter of Thomas Morrison Alfriend and Mary Jane Eger Alfriend. His father was a prominent Richmond businessman, president of the Virginia Fire and Marine Insurance Company, and founder of his own insurance company, Thomas M. Alfriend and Son.

Ned Alfriend, as he was known to his family and friends, was educated in Richmond and joined his father's insurance business late in the 1850s. On 10 June 1861 he enlisted in the Richmond Zouaves, Company E, 44th Regiment Virginia Infantry, and served as first lieutenant and as captain of the company. He had a checkered career in the Confederate army. On 24 May 1864 he was fined twenty-five days' pay for being absent without leave. He returned to the company but then contracted typhoid fever in June 1864 during the Shenandoah Valley campaign and went to Richmond to recuperate. Alfriend was arrested on 4 January 1865 and charged with being absent without leave and disobeying orders. On 13 February 1865 a court-martial convicted him on both charges and cashiered him from the army. Several officers from the brigade supported his appeal to President Jefferson Davis in March, but the war ended before any action was taken on his case.

After the war Alfriend resumed his work in the family insurance company with his father and youngest brother, Thomas Lee Alfriend. He quickly won wide recognition in the business. In 1871 Governor Gilbert Carlton Walker named him a delegate to the National Insurance Convention, and Alfriend later testified before a committee of the House of Delegates about a general insurance bill that the convention had proposed.

Perhaps drawn by the example of his younger brother, Frank Heath Alfriend, he began to write. He published several articles in the *Old Dominion Magazine* and wrote at least one play while still living in Richmond. In the autumn of 1889 he left the insurance business in Thomas Lee Alfriend's hands and moved to New York to devote his full attention to his literary work. He contributed occasionally to magazines, writing articles for such journals as *Cosmopolitan* and *Lippincott's*. By the time of his death he had also written at least fourteen plays, several of which were produced in New York. His first staged play, *A Foregone Conclusion*, an adaptation of William Dean Howells's novel of the same name, opened at Palmer's Theatre in June 1890. Other openings included *The Louisianian* at Madison Square Theatre in June 1891; *Across the Potomac* (written with Augustus Pitou) at Proctor's Theatre in April 1892; *The Great Diamond Robbery* (written with noted critic Andrew Carpenter Wheeler) at the American Theatre in September 1895; *New York* (also written with Wheeler) at the American Theatre in February 1897; and *The Magdalene* at Murray Hill Theatre in November 1897. Reviewers dismissed both *A Foregone Conclusion* and *The Louisianian*, but Alfriend's plays were popular with the public. Most of his work has not stood the test of time, and several of his plays have been lost. *The Great Diamond Robbery*, which was still being produced in 1905, was his most successful effort and has been included in two anthologies of popular nineteenth-century plays.

In 1891 Alfriend and Henrietta Lander, a New York actress who appeared in several of his plays, became engaged, but they never married. Edward Morrison Alfriend died unexpectedly of kidney failure at his residence, Ashland House, in New York on 24 October 1901 and was buried in Hollywood Cemetery in Richmond.

Brief biography with Alfriend's "Social Life in Richmond During the War," *Cosmopolitan* 12 (1891): 229–233 (por.); Compiled Service Records, with transcript of court-martial proceedings; Kevin C. Ruffner, *44th Virginia Infantry* (1987), 27–28, 53, 57, 73; *Insurance Advocate* 2 (1871): 114; 3 (1872): 34–35; his other publications include "Unpublished Recollections of Edgar Allan Poe," *Literary Era* 8 (1901): 489–491, and the posthumous "Recollections of Stonewall Jackson," *Lippincott's Magazine* 69 (1902): 582–588; his other known plays are *A Woman's Ordeal* (1877), *Eugene Aubrey* (pre-1891), *Old Memories* (pre-1891), *Phillippe de Loro* (pre-1891), *Wanda* (pre-1891), *The Diplomats* (1894), *His Double Life* (1896), and *Mrs. Stuyvesant of New York* (1901); the plays are documented in George C. D. Odell, *Annals of the New York Stage* (1945), vol. 14, and in play memorabilia and typescripts at the Museum of the City of New York and the William Seymour Theatre Collection at Princeton University Library; *The Great Diamond Robbery* is reprinted in *The Great Diamond Robbery and Other Recent Melodramas,* ed. Garrett H. Leverton (1940, repr. 1963), and Barrett Harper Clark, ed., *Favorite American Plays of the Nineteenth Century* (1943); obituaries in *Richmond Evening Leader*, 24 Oct. 1901, and *Richmond Times*, 25 Oct. 1901.

PATRICIA C. CLICK

ALFRIEND, Frank Heath (10 January 1841–3 May 1887), writer and journalist, was born in Richmond, the second of three sons and second of four children of Richmond insurance underwriter Thomas Morrison Alfriend and Mary Jane Eger Alfriend. His elder brother was the playwright Edward Morrison Alfriend. After obtaining his early education in Richmond, Alfriend attended the College of William and Mary from 1858 to 1860 and had just begun a career as a journalist in Richmond when the Civil War began. His first important publications were two articles for the *Southern Literary Messenger* early in 1863 defending the cause of the Confederacy. He asserted that the Civil War was in essence a contest pitting true republicanism in the South in defense of the "benign institution of slavery" against a "Consolidated Democracy" in the North that he likened to plebeian mob rule in ancient Rome.

Late in December 1863 Alfriend and George C. Wedderburn purchased the *Southern Literary Messenger*. Wedderburn intended to manage the business end of the enterprise, with Alfriend to assume the editorial work. It was not a propitious time, and Alfriend was the last editor of the most distinguished magazine of its kind in the old South. Through no fault of Alfriend it failed, and no issues appeared after June 1864. On 20 December 1864 Alfriend married Sarah Alice Womble, of Richmond. They had no children. Despite frequent illness, Alfriend supported himself by teaching school in Richmond during the remaining bleak months of the war.

During the war Alfriend had formed an adulatory friendship with Jefferson Davis, and he visited Davis in his Canadian exile in the autumn of 1867. By the end of that year Alfriend had completed the manuscript of the first full biography of the former president of the Confederacy. Alfriend stated that it had been "prepared under the personal supervision of Mr. Davis" and therefore assumed something of an authorized character. *The Life of Jefferson Davis*, published early in 1868 by the Caxton Publishing House in Cincinnati, was an able political and military biography, unabashedly pro-Southern. As Alfriend stated in the preface, he wrote it in order to vindicate "the motives and conduct of the South and its late leader." An unflinching and admiring defender of Davis, Alfriend produced an intensely partisan volume. His "leading object" in the composition of the manuscript, he wrote James A. Seddon on 31 March 1868, was to "write a book which should affront the sensibilities of no true son of the South."

Alfriend wrote for various southern newspapers during the next five years, including the *Wilmington Star*, the *Louisville Courier-Journal*, and the *Atlanta Constitution*. While in Atlanta he formed a close friendship with John Brown Gordon, a former Confederate brigadier general. When Gordon became a United States Senator in 1873, Alfriend went with him to Washington and divided his time between journalism and patronage appointments. His gentle and attractive personality, fluent and entertaining speaking and writing style, and storehouse of information on southern politics made him a popular and respected member of the fourth estate.

Alfriend never lost his interest in Virginia politics. When the heterogeneous Readjuster movement emerged during the 1870s, Alfriend threw his considerable talents behind it, in part because he believed that the state needed new leaders who combined practical experience with innovative ideas. By the early 1880s he achieved his greatest influence. He penned editorials and articles for the *Washington National Republican* and the *Richmond Whig*, briefly edited the *Woodstock Virginian*, and played political troubleshooter. His ability to win friends for the Readjusters among the press corps in Washington was especially noteworthy. Characteristic of the strong friendships he was able to form was one with the leader of the Readjusters, William Mahone, a former Confederate general from Petersburg and from 1881 to 1887 one of Virginia's U.S. senators. When Mahone became a Republican, Alfriend switched parties with him but later supported Readjuster Governor William Evelyn Cameron in his rift with Mahone. Despite his varying political alliances, Alfriend remained friendly enough with southern Democrats that early in 1887 they secured him his last federal patronage appointment, a post as assistant librarian of the Senate.

During the spring of 1886 Alfriend accompanied Jefferson Davis on his triumphal tour in Georgia. He had begun to collect materials for a revision of his biography of the aging leader when his own ill health intervened. Alfriend died of acute gastritis at his home in Washington, D.C., on 3 May 1887. A colleague penned a tribute for the *New York Times* that summed up his career: Alfriend had a "taste for journalism" but "a distaste for continuous application to routine newspaper work," and he had been gifted with "a memory of events and their significance so keen and tenacious that he could at any moment write fully, freely, and brightly, about the men and measures that have interested the country for twenty-five years." Frank Heath Alfriend's funeral service was conducted in Monumental Church in Richmond, and he was buried in Hollywood Cemetery.

Monumental Church parish register, VHS, and College Archives, W&M, contain personal information; Alfriend defended the Confederacy in "The Great Danger of the

Confederacy" and "A Southern Republic and a Northern Democracy," *Southern Literary Messenger* 35 (1863): 39–43 and 37 (1863): 283–290; the Jan.–June 1864 issues of *Southern Literary Messenger* list Alfriend as editor; Alfriend's letters to William Mahone in the Mahone papers at Duke are especially valuable; a few Alfriend letters are in VHS, including a photocopy of the 1868 letter to Seddon; obituaries in *Washington Post* (por.) and *Richmond Whig*, both 4 May 1887, and *New York Times*, 8 May 1887.

TERRY ALFORD

ALFRIEND, John Samuel (6 July 1897–8 July 1974), banker and civic leader, was born in Norfolk, the second of three sons and fifth of eight children of businessman Richard Jeffery Alfriend and Mary Emily Hume Alfriend. He attended public schools in Norfolk and entered Norfolk Academy in 1911, but he withdrew in 1914 without graduating to become a messenger for the National Bank of Commerce of Norfolk. During World War I he served with a machine-gun company in the United States Marine Corps and received the Purple Heart for wounds received in France nine days before the 1918 armistice.

After the war Alfriend joined the Marine Bank of Norfolk, but by 1923 he was back with his first employer. Instrumental in establishing a Norfolk chapter of the American Institute of Banking in 1919, he took its courses for more than a decade. In 1931 he was promoted to cashier of the National Bank of Commerce, in 1942 he was elected president, and in 1956 he became chairman of the board, by which time it was one of the leading banks in southeastern Virginia. His greatest contribution to the development of the banking industry came in 1963, when he initiated the first large merger in Virginia to create a statewide bank. Following passage in 1962 of a state law allowing banks to establish branches in more than one community, Alfriend engineered the merger of his Norfolk bank with the People's National Bank of Central Virginia, headquartered in Charlottesville, to create the Virginia National Bank. He served as the chairman of the board of the new company. For a time the biggest bank in the state, the Virginia National Bank was the first to open offices in a large number of towns.

Alfriend achieved significant professional recognition long before the creation of the Virginia National Bank. He was elected to the executive council of the American Bankers Association in 1944 and 1952, served as president of the Virginia Bankers Association in 1949–1950, and in 1957 became only the third Virginian since 1914 to serve on the Advisory Council to the Federal Reserve Board. Alfriend also sat on the boards of many of the most important corporations in Virginia, including the Norfolk and Western Railway Company and the Chesapeake and Potomac Telephone Company.

Alfriend's personal concern for his associates and employees was well-known and was reflected in his service to the city of Norfolk. The list of community organizations and service groups to which he belonged, often as a responsible officer, filled two-and-a-half tightly spaced pages and earned him virtually every civic award given in Norfolk. He served terms as president of the Norfolk Chamber of Commerce and of the Norfolk Community Chest; sat on the boards of the College of William and Mary, the Virginia Military Institute, the Norfolk Academy, and the Norfolk General Hospital; and chaired the regional war finance committee during World War II. In the 1950s Alfriend supported regional governmental cooperation and stimulated discussion of a merger of all the south Hampton Roads cities and counties into a new municipal government. He also played a leading role in transforming the Norfolk division of the College of William and Mary into an independent four-year college. In recognition of his contributions to the new school, including raising funds on its behalf, Old Dominion College named its chemistry building after Alfriend in 1967.

On 17 June 1922 Alfriend married Harriet Lucille Sanderlin, who was then also employed by the National Bank of Commerce, and they had two daughters. Alfriend was a lifelong member of the Episcopal Church and senior warden of the Church of the Good Shepherd. Dignified but unpretentious, gentle and patient, John Samuel Alfriend was one of the most innovative and influential citizens in Norfolk during the middle decades of the twentieth century. Following his death from an acute cerebral thrombosis on 8 July 1974, a writer for the *Norfolk Virginian-Pilot* stated that "he was the last to squeeze, however imperfectly, into the Horatio Alger mold." Alfriend was buried in Elmwood Cemetery in Norfolk.

Biographies in Rogers Dey Whichard, ed., *History of Lower Tidewater Virginia* (1959), 3:1, in *Old Dominion University Bulletin* (summer 1973), 16–18, and in a special 30 July 1962 issue of the National Bank of Commerce's "Commerce Gleanings" devoted to his career; some Alfriend letters are in the archives at Old Dominion University and at Virginia Wesleyan College; family and business history facts verified by Harriet Lucille Sanderlin Alfriend, Ann Bolling Abbitt, Richard Jeffery Alfriend III, Henry Clay Hofheimer II, Patricia Hollingsworth, and Mary Wilson Vellines; Military Service Records; obituaries and editorial tributes in *Norfolk Ledger-Star*, 8, 9 July 1974, *Norfolk Virginian-Pilot*, 9 July 1974 (por.), and *Richmond Times-Dispatch*, 9 July 1974.

STEPHEN S. MANSFIELD

ALLAN, Edgar (26 February 1842–28 October 1904), attorney, Republican Party leader, and member of the Convention of 1867–1868, was a son of John Allan and Ann Allan. He was born in Birmingham, England, where he attended parochial schools and received training as a typesetter. In 1863 he immigrated to the United States and on 17 June, just six weeks after his arrival, enlisted as a private in George A. Custer's 7th Michigan Cavalry. He was wounded at Shepherdstown on 24 August 1864 and discharged from the army in Washington, D.C., in the summer of 1865.

Allan bought a small farm in Prince Edward County, where he studied law by himself. In December 1867 he was admitted to the bar and afterward moved to Farmville. He unsuccessfully applied for a position with the Freedmen's Bureau and soon became active in the local Republican Party and as a statewide leader of the Union League of Virginia. On 22 October 1867 Allan and James W. D. Bland were elected to represent Appomattox and Prince Edward Counties in the constitutional convention that met in Richmond from 3 December 1867 to 17 April 1868. Of the 2,306 votes Allan received, only one was cast by a white man, the rest by African Americans, many of whom had recently been slaves. Allan served on the Committee on County and Corporation Courts and County Organizations and chaired the Committee on Printing and was prominent at the convention despite his youth, the brevity of his residence in Virginia, and his inexperience in politics. He criticized the constitution that the convention produced because he feared that it would not sufficiently protect the rights of the former slaves and would prolong hard feelings by virtue of its clauses imposing political restrictions on former Confederates. Out of party loyalty, he nevertheless supported the constitution at the referendum that ratified it in 1869.

Allan backed the conservative Republican, Gilbert Carlton Walker, in the 1869 campaign for governor. Although called a carpetbagger and nicknamed "Yankee" Allan because of his Union Army service, he became a popular and effective campaigner and was one of the best-known Republicans in Virginia for the next three and a half decades. From 1871 to 1883 he was commonwealth's attorney of Prince Edward County, and he also served as clerk of the Farmville Town Council. From 1874 to 1877 he represented the district of Amelia, Cumberland, and Prince Edward Counties in the Senate of Virginia, and he allied himself with the Readjusters during the long and bitter political conflict over the payment of the state's debt.

In 1883 Allan moved to Richmond, where he enlarged his increasingly lucrative law practice and continued his political career. He seldom missed a Republican state convention or failed to make a speaking tour during campaign season and perennially sat on the city, county, and district Republican executive committees. He was also active in the Grand Army of the Republic. He served as commander of the Philip Kearney Post in Richmond in 1885–1886, was junior vice-commander of the national GAR in 1886, and was commander-in-chief of the GAR Constitutional Centennial in 1887. Thereafter he was more often referred to as General Allan than as Yankee Allan.

Allan married Mary Edna Land, a native Kentuckian, in Prince Edward County on 6 February 1867. They had three daughters and a son, Edgar Allan Jr., who eventually joined his father in the Richmond law firm of Allan and Allan. In 1892 Allan added to his stature among the state's African American population by serving as one of the attorneys for Bettie Thomas Lewis, a young Richmond woman. She was the daughter of William A. Thomas, a wealthy and reclusive white man, and one of his former slaves.

Thomas had frequently declared his intention to leave the bulk of his fortune of about $220,000 to Lewis, but he never executed a valid will. Lewis's attorneys persuaded the Virginia Supreme Court of Appeals to honor Thomas's often-stated intention, making Bettie Lewis one of the wealthiest women in Richmond.

In 1900 Allan ran for the House of Representatives from the Third Congressional District but lost to the incumbent Democrat, John Lamb. In 1901 President William McKinley appointed Allan United States attorney for the Eastern District of Virginia, but the following year President Theodore Roosevelt, siding with a segment of the Virginia Republican Party that opposed Allan's faction, failed to reappoint him. Suffering from Bright's disease and a chronic back condition resulting from his Civil War wound, and bitter with disappointment at this withdrawal of recognition to which he believed his long service to the Republican Party entitled him, Edgar Allan wrote a short suicide note, purchased a pistol and one cartridge, and shot himself to death in Richmond on 28 October 1904. He was buried in Glenwood Cemetery, Washington, D.C.

Brief biography in *Norfolk Virginian-Pilot*, Twentieth-Century Edition, June 1900; Allan's compiled military service and pension records, NARA, contain important information about his early years; a few Allan letters are in VHS and in William Mahone Papers, Duke; Hamilton J. Eckenrode, *Political History of Virginia During the Reconstruction* (1904), 60–61; vote tally in 1867 documented in Election Records, no. 427, RG 13, LVA; *Journal of 1867–1868 Convention*; *Debates and Proceedings of 1867–1868 Convention*; speech denouncing constitution printed in *Richmond Whig*, 21 Apr. 1868, and excerpted in *New York Times*, 20 Apr. 1868; *Address of the Hon. Edgar Allan, Republican Candidate for Congress* (1900); in an exchange of campaign pamphlets Democrats assaulted Allan's past cooperation with African Americans, Readjusters, and Republicans in *The True Record of Edgar Allan* (1900), and he defended himself in *Edgar Allan's Reply* (1900), which recapitulates his early political career; *Thomas's Administrator* v. *Bettie Thomas Lewis* (1892), *Virginia Reports*, 89:1; *Richmond Planet*, 25 June 1892; obituaries in *Richmond News Leader*, 28 Oct. 1904, and *Richmond Times-Dispatch*, 29 Oct. 1904 (por.).

TED TUNNELL

ALLAN, John (10 September 1779–27 March 1834), merchant, was born in Irvine, Ayrshire, Scotland, the son of William Allan, a ship's master and customs officer, and Elizabeth Galt Allan. Nothing is known about Allan's education, but his adult letters disclose a wide acquaintance with English literature. He immigrated to Richmond in 1795, leaving behind four sisters, and went to work in the mercantile house of his wealthy bachelor uncle, William Galt. In 1800 he and another Galt employee, Charles Ellis, formed their own import-export business, Ellis and Allan. On 9 February 1803 Allan married Frances Keeling Valentine, of Richmond. They had no children, but with her husband's approval Frances Allan took custody of two-year-old Edgar Poe after the death of his actress mother, Elizabeth Arnold Poe, in Richmond on 11 December 1811.

The family, which included Frances Allan's sister Anne Moore Valentine, lived above the Ellis and Allan store at Main and Thirteenth Streets in Richmond. Allan sent Edgar Poe to local schools in Richmond and placed him in schools in England from 1815 to 1820, when the family lived in London while Allan attempted to improve the firm's business there following the War of 1812. The small firm, "hobbled" by creditors, was dissolved in 1824, but in January 1825 Allan joined William Galt on the board of directors of the Richmond branch of the Bank of Virginia. Allan inherited a considerable fortune following Galt's death on 24 March 1825. With his inheritance Allan purchased Moldavia, a prestigious mansion at Fifth and Main Streets in Richmond. He evidently did not promptly convey to his sisters in Scotland their portions of the inheritance, disclosing a selfish side of his character that contributed to the deterioration of his relationship with Edgar Poe, who had taken Allan as his middle name.

Allan was a man of shifting passions, alternately indulgent and demanding, as his relationship with the sensitive young Poe amply demonstrated. In 1826 Allan sent Poe to the University of Virginia but provided him with insufficient funds, and after Poe accumulated gambling debts Allan refused to supply additional money. The resulting conflict caused Poe to withdraw from the university at the end of 1826 and leave Virginia in March 1827. Frances Allan died on 28 February 1829. Later that spring Poe, who had been very fond of her, returned to Richmond, where he and Allan were temporarily reconciled. Allan later helped Poe enter the United States Military Academy at West Point and during the next two years reluctantly sent him small amounts of money.

After his wife's death Allan formed a liaison with Elizabeth Wills. Twin boys, whom she identified as Allan's sons, were born in July 1830. On 5 October 1830 Allan married Louisa Gabriella Patterson in New York, and during the next three years they had three sons. Probably as a result of his changing family circumstances, Allan wrote and twice amended his will in 1832. It provided for his three young sons by Louisa Allan and his two illegitimate sons by Elizabeth Wills, one of whom died in 1832, but it made no provision at all for another illegitimate son, Edwin Collier, whose education he had financed from 1812 to 1817, or for Edgar Allan Poe. John Allan was still one of the wealthiest men in Richmond when he died suddenly at his home on 27 March 1834. He was buried in Shockoe Cemetery.

Agnes M. Bondurant, *Poe's Richmond* (1942); Dwight Thomas and David K. Jackson, *The Poe Log* (1987); transcript of Allan family Bible record, VM; business and family letters in Ellis and Allan Papers, LC, William Galt Jr. Papers, Duke, and VM; Allan's General Notebook, Humanities Research Center Library, University of Texas at Austin; Poe's letters to him in John Ward Ostrom, ed., *The Letters of Edgar Allan Poe* (1948); portrait of Allan in Poe Museum, Richmond, and of Frances Allan in VM; Richmond City Circuit Court Will Book, 2:457–462; death notice in *Richmond Enquirer*, 1 Apr. 1834.

AGNES BONDURANT MARCUSON

ALLAN, William (12 November 1837–17 September 1889), educator, writer, and Confederate army officer, was born at Winchester Gardens, near Winchester, one of two children, both sons, of Thomas Allan and Jane Dowdell George Allan. After being educated in a local private school, he taught in Jefferson County and in Winchester to earn enough money to enroll in the University of Virginia in 1857. Allan excelled at debate and graduated with honors in 1860 with an M.A. in applied arithmetic. He moved to Loudoun County where he was assistant to the principal of Bloomfield Academy when the Civil War began.

Allan enlisted in the Confederate army and served as a clerk in the quartermaster department under Thomas J. "Stonewall" Jackson. In 1862, sponsored by University of Virginia classmate Alexander "Sandie" Pendleton, Allan took the ordnance officer examination. He passed with the highest score and on 27 December 1862 became a captain of artillery. On 19 January 1863 he was appointed to Jackson's staff as chief of ordnance of the Second Corps, Army of Northern Virginia. He served throughout the war, advancing to the rank of major on 25 April 1863 and lieutenant colonel on 28 March 1864. He was assigned to Jubal A. Early's Shenandoah Valley command on 1 March 1865.

After the war Allan took a job as cashier of the National Valley Bank in Staunton. In 1866 he accepted an invitation from Robert E. Lee, then president of Washington College in Lexington, to join the faculty as professor of applied mathematics. For almost eight years he taught there and published three books on applied mechanics between 1873 and 1875, all of which were reprinted shortly after his death.

While at Washington College, Allan wrote the first of many articles and books on the Civil War. He collaborated with Jedediah Hotchkiss on *The Battle-fields of Virginia: Chancellorsville* (1867) and also wrote a long unsigned article on the Battle of Gettysburg that appeared in the *Southern Review* in 1869. The piece on Gettysburg benefited from his interviews with Lee and was the first of a great many articles Allan wrote, so many that altogether they probably contained more words than his books. He became a popular figure on the lecture circuit and at commemorative ceremonies, and he published articles and speeches in *Century*, the *Nation*, and the *Magazine of American History*, but most of his articles, reviews, and commemorative pieces appeared in the *Southern Historical Society Papers*. His 1866 memoir of his own field ordnance service has been pronounced "priceless." Allan's published work on the causes, conduct, and significance of the Civil War not only placed a substantial body of reliable information on the record, but also helped establish the literary genre of the Lost Cause. Allan's most enduring and useful volumes on the Civil War were the *History of the Campaign of Gen. T. J. (Stonewall) Jackson in the Shenandoah Valley of Virginia* (1880), which was reprinted several times with variant titles and reissued in 1974, and *The Army of Northern Virginia in 1862* (1892), published posthumously, the first part of an intended complete wartime history of Lee's army.

On 21 November 1873 Allan was elected the first principal of McDonogh Institute, an endowed private school for poor boys at Owings Mills, near Baltimore, Maryland. He married Elizabeth Randolph Preston, daughter of a professor at the Virginia Military Institute, John Thomas Lewis Preston, on 14 May 1874, and they had two daughters and three sons. She was active for many years in the Presbyterian Church, in promoting Sunday schools, and in founding chapters of the Young Women's Christian Association. She also became a successful author after her husband's death, writing a novel published by the Congregational Sunday-School and Publishing Society, a biography of Margaret Junkin Preston, and her own posthumously published memoirs.

Under Allan's leadership McDonogh Institute flourished. In 1885 he published a biographical tribute to the philanthropy of the institute's founder, John McDonogh. In Maryland Allan remained active in organizations as diverse as the Society of the Army and Navy of the Confederate States, the Southern Historical Society, and the Military History Society of Massachusetts. From 1873 until his death he was a trustee of Washington and Lee University (as Washington College had become in 1871). He also served on the board of the Lee Memorial Association and prepared the historical sketch that the association used when raising money to build the Lee Mausoleum at Washington and Lee. William Allan died at his home at McDonogh School on 17 September 1889 and was buried in Garrison Forest Cemetery.

Biographies in John Randolph Tucker, *Life and Character of Col. William Allan, Late Principal of McDonogh School* (1889), and Robert K. Krick's introduction to the reprint of *The Army of Northern Virginia in 1862* (1984), xi–xxi (por.); his papers, including memorandums of his conversations with Robert E. Lee, are in UNC; Compiled Service Records; in *Southern Historical Society Papers* 4 (1877): 77, Allan asserted his authorship but misstated the publication date of the article on Gettysburg that had appeared in *Southern Review* 5 (1869): 419–445; Allan, "Reminiscences of Field Ordnance Service with the Army of Northern Virginia, 1863–'5," *Southern Historical Society Papers* 14 (1886): 137–146; Janet Allan Bryan, ed., *A March Past: Reminiscences of Elizabeth Randolph Preston Allan* (1938); obituaries in *Baltimore Sun*, 18 Sept. 1889, and *Richmond Dispatch* and *Lexington Gazette*, both 19 Sept. 1889.

DONALD W. GUNTER

ALLASON, William (d. 30 or 31 January 1800), merchant, was born in Glasgow, Scotland, one of five or six sons and three daughters of Zacharius Allason and his second wife, Isobel Hall Allason. As a boy he apprenticed as a baker, the trade of his father and of one of his three elder half-brothers, and he attended the Glasgow Grammar School, although the dates of his attendance are unknown. His half brother Robert Allason was a rising international merchant in Glasgow from the 1740s to the 1770s. In 1748 and again during the years 1750–1752 William Allason traveled to Virginia as a supercargo and merchant's factor, or agent, and in 1755 and 1756 he made two similar voyages to Antigua and Saint Kitts in the West Indies.

In 1757 Allason returned to Virginia on another trading voyage and remained. Although he never did business on a very large scale, the stages through which his career passed symbolized the metamorphosis of foreign traders into American businessmen. From 1757 until 1759 he served as an itinerant factor for Baird and Walker, of Glasgow, in what was known as the "lumping trade," in which packaged assortments of merchandise were sold rather than retailed as individual items from a store or on a circuit. He took tobacco in payment and shipped it back to Scotland on ships that Baird and Walker chartered.

The second phase of Allason's Virginia business career began in 1760, when he opened his own store in Falmouth, Stafford County, in partnership with John Mitchell, of Fredericksburg, and John Gray, of Port Royal, Caroline County, with Robert Allason acting as their agent in Scotland. The firm operated exclusively in Falmouth until 1770, except for a brief interval early in the 1760s when his brother David Allason conducted an outlet in Winchester. William Allason did not engage in the traditional consignment system, under which local merchants took orders for merchandise from Virginia planters, imported these goods from a single British source, and then paid for the merchandise with tobacco received from the planter. Allason instead dealt with many specialty suppliers in Glasgow, Whitehaven, Liverpool, Leeds, Bristol, and London, obtaining the best prices wherever he could. He sold the tobacco that he received from his customers to other Virginia merchants and paid his British suppliers in cash or bills of exchange. This system reduced his profit margin on each transaction, but he rarely had quantities of his own tobacco at risk on the high sea, and he was shielded to some extent from the volatile European tobacco trade. So energetically did Allason strive to open markets in the northern Virginia Piedmont and in the Shenandoah Valley that by the end of the decade nearly 20 percent of his customers lived west of the Blue Ridge. During the 1760s Allason's annual profits increased substantially, from £492 to £3,243.

From 1770 until the American Revolution, Allason conducted his business without any partners. He expanded his markets in the Shenandoah Valley and dealt in agricultural commodities such as wheat, milled flour, and hemp, rather than tobacco. The subsequent wartime shutdown of the tobacco trade consequently produced relatively little financial hardship for Allason. By October 1775 his only British creditor was Robert Allason, and he was able to turn his energies to the erection of a gristmill and a sawmill and to other interests. During the 1770s and 1780s he purchased about four thousand acres of land in the Piedmont and in the Shenandoah Valley and acquired a labor force of fifty-seven slaves. As a planter he concentrated on producing corn and wheat. Although he reopened his Falmouth store in 1783, he placed it under the management of David Allason and worked on expanding his trade in flour and timber products. By the end of that decade the Scottish factor had become an American planter and businessman and a prosperous, though perhaps not wealthy, gentleman. His land and taxable slaves were worth more than £11,000 altogether.

Allason married Anne Hooe on 26 June 1772. Their only son and one of their two daughters died in infancy. Allason was a founding member of the Masonic lodge in Falmouth. His role in the American Revolution might best be described as observer rather than rebel or loyalist before 1776, while he supported independence during the conflict. William Allason died during the night of 30–31 January 1800 and was buried with full Masonic rites in Saint Paul's cemetery in Falmouth.

Robert William Spoede, "William Allason: Merchant in an Emerging Nation" (Ph.D. diss., W&M, 1973); Edith E. B. Thomson, "A Scottish Merchant in Falmouth in the Eighteenth Century," *VMHB* 39 (1931): 108–117, 230–238; birth not recorded in largely complete Scottish parish registers and evidence on its date conflicts: Allason twice gave an age pointing to a Dec. 1731 birth date, but he became a Glasgow burgess on 23 July 1747, a dignity not bestowed on fifteen-year-olds, and he may actually have been the son baptized James on 29 Sept. 1728, with a subsequent name change (Stuart M. Nisbet and Thomas C. Welsh, *Robert Allason and Greenbank* [1992], esp. 14, 25–27, 35–37, 40, 60–63, and letter from Nisbet to editors, 8 Mar. 1994); Allason's business ledgers and papers in LVA form one of the largest and best collections of their kind and contain many biographical facts; marriage recorded in George H. S. King, ed., *Register of St. Paul's Parish, King George County, Virginia* (1960), 66; David D. Plater, "Building the North Wales Mill of William Allason," *VMHB* 85 (1977): 45–50; Ronald E. Heaton and James Royal Case, eds., *The Lodge at Fredericksburgh: A Digest of the Early Records* (1975), 32–33; Fauquier Co. Will Book, 2:249–251; death date and description of funeral in Walter Colquhoun to David Grinnan, 2 Feb. 1800, Grinnan Papers, UVA.

PETER V. BERGSTROM

ALLEN, Arthur (ca. 1608–May or June 1669), merchant and planter, was born in England, but the date and place of his birth and the names of his parents are not known. He probably arrived in Virginia during the 1640s as an agent for tobacco merchants trading out of Bristol, in which capacity he made at least one return trip to Bristol. He also dealt with several leading London merchants, among them Micajah and Phillip Perry and also Thomas Lane. By 1649 Allen had settled between Lawnes Creek and Chippokes Creek in the southern part of James City County. When that area became Surry County in 1652, Allen was appointed to the court, and by 1661 he was a member of the quorum. He also served on the vestry of Lawnes Creek Parish.

By the 1660s Allen had acquired more than two thousand acres of land, making him one of the wealthiest men in the county. As a reflection of his status, he built a large new residence, a three-story Jacobean-style edifice that is thought to be the oldest brick house still standing in the former British colonies of North America. It was probably erected by local craftsmen using local materials and was much less polished in its workmanship than contemporary English country houses, but it made the same kind of statement about its owner's standing in the community. It was called Allen's Brick House during the lifetimes of its first two owners. Early in the nineteenth century it became known as Bacon's Castle because about seventy followers of Nathaniel Bacon (1647–1676) occupied it between 18 September and 28 December 1676.

Arthur Allen may have married twice, not once about 1650 as stated in early histories of Surry County and Bacon's Castle; and he probably had at least seven children, not the two or three who are mentioned in some accounts of the family. His first son, Humphrey Allen, was probably born in England early in the 1630s and died in Virginia in 1666. Arthur Allen (ca. 1652–1710) inherited Allen's Brick House, carried on the family name, and had a long and varied political career. Allen's four daughters all married well, with the result that some of the area's most notable persons were descended from him. Mary Long, the wife of the Arthur Long who commanded the company of Bacon's men who occupied Allen's Brick House, was probably yet another of Arthur Allen's daughters.

Arthur Allen died late in May or early in June 1669. On 15 May he sat with the county court, but by the middle of June, when the tax list was compiled, his widow, Alice Tucker Allen, was charged with the eleven tithables resident at Allen's plantation. She later married a widower, John Hardy, of Isle of Wight County.

A 3 Mar. 1668 deposition gives age as sixty years (Surry Co. Deeds, Wills, Etc., 1:307); a number of documents involving him are recorded in Surry Co. Deeds, Wills, Etc., vol. 1, most signed with his distinctive mark; will and landholdings mentioned in Winfree, *Laws of Virginia*, 364–367; Stephenson B. Andrews, ed., *Bacon's Castle* (1984); numerous descendants are traced in Eddis Johnson and Hugh Buckner Johnston, *The Johnsons and Johnstons of Corrowaugh in Isle of Wight County, Virginia* (1979).

DAPHNE GENTRY

ALLEN, Arthur (ca. 1652–15 June 1710), merchant, planter, and Speaker of the House of Burgesses, was probably the youngest of two sons and five daughters of Arthur Allen (ca. 1608–1669) and was probably born at his father's estate in what became Surry County in 1652. After his father died, his mother, Alice Tucker Allen, administered his inheritance until her remarriage. By 1681 Allen had married Katherine Baker, daughter of Lawrence Baker. They had four sons and four daughters.

Like his father, Allen engaged in trade and also occasionally went to England on business. He gradually increased his landholdings until, at the time of his death, he owned almost ten thousand acres in Surry and Isle of Wight Counties. Like some of his fellow planters, Allen gradually shifted from the use of indentured English servants on his plantations to the acquisition of lifetime slaves of African origin or descent.

Indicative of his status in the county, Allen served on the Lawnes Creek Parish vestry by age twenty-one. At age twenty-four he became a member of the Surry County Court, and he was appointed surveyor of both Surry and Isle of Wight Counties. A friend and ally of Governor Sir William Berkeley, Allen was with the governor at Jamestown on 18 September 1676 when a group of about seventy followers of Nathaniel Bacon (1647–1676) seized his residence, then known as Allen's Brick House but later as Bacon's Castle. By the time they were driven out on 28 December, the rebels had destroyed, damaged, or carried away property that royal commissioners later valued at more than £1,000 sterling. Allen's close association with Berkeley and with his followers, who came to be called the Green Spring faction, led to his appointment in May 1677 to the quorum of the Surry County court, but Lieutenant Governor Herbert Jeffreys, who replaced Berkeley, had Allen deprived of his offices later in the year. Following Jeffreys's death in December 1678, Allen was reappointed to the court.

In 1682 Allen won election to the House of Burgesses and was promptly placed on the important Committee on Propositions and Grievances. The session was ridden with conflict following the plant-cutting riots in several counties north of the James River, and Allen joined Robert Beverley (1635–1687) and Philip Ludwell of the old Green Spring faction in opposing Governor Thomas Culpeper's attempts to punish the rioters. Allen was reelected and served in the House with growing distinction during the spring of 1684 and the autumn of 1685.

Allen soon crossed swords with another governor, Francis Howard, baron Howard of Effingham, who removed Allen from the county court in the spring of 1686 for objecting to Effingham's choice of a sheriff for Surry County. On 21 October 1686, following the death of Speaker William Kendall between sessions, the House of Burgesses elected Allen its Speaker. Allen led the fight against Effingham's policies, among them the governor's attempts to use the royal negative to retain laws that the House insisted be repealed. Effingham regarded Allen as one of the three most influential burgesses obstructing his political program. As a sign of his displeasure Effingham dissolved the assembly.

The voters in Surry County returned Allen to the House again on 17 February 1688, and his fellow burgesses reelected him Speaker. Allen again led the opposition to Effingham. When the governor learned that the House had petitioned the king with twelve grievances against him, he angrily dissolved the assembly and removed Allen from his county surveying posts as punishment for leading the opposition.

Allen was reelected to the next assembly, called in the spring of 1691. However, he and one other burgess-elect, James Bray, did not take their seats. With William and Mary on the English throne following the Glorious Revolution, Parliament rewrote the oaths of allegiance and supremacy and required all officials to subscribe to them. Arthur Allen, "through Scruple of Conscience," declined to do so. Never giving any other reason, Allen likely refused to renounce his oath of allegiance to James II, and he consequently held no offices in Virginia for fourteen years. In 1697 the Surry County court ordered Allen to subscribe to the oaths, but he again refused. Not until April 1702, after James's death, did Allen willingly take the new oaths, after which he was almost immediately sworn in as one of the visitors of the College of William and Mary. In September of that year he was returned to the county court as its senior member. In the spring of 1703 he again stood for election to the House of Burgesses, but he was defeated despite Governor Francis Nicholson's efforts on his behalf. In a rage Allen ordered the sheriff not to confirm Major Thomas Swan's election, claiming that in so doing he had Nicholson's sanction. This action resulted in an investigation of Allen's conduct by the House and his appearance before it. The burgesses forced him to admit that he had not intended to show disrespect to the members. In April 1703 Nicholson appointed Allen naval officer for the Upper District of James River, a customs post he held until his death. In 1704 he was once again named surveyor for the counties of Surry and Isle of Wight, a position he relinquished to his son John in 1707.

In 1708 Council President Edmund Jenings recommended Allen to the Board of Trade for a position on the Council, but he did not receive the appointment. By then Allen was at odds with his old political allies, and Philip Ludwell Jr. went so far as to refer to Allen in a letter to his father as a "meddlesome old fool" and criticize his actions as naval officer. Despite his frequent troubles, Allen remained influential in Surry County. Made a captain of the militia in 1677 and a major between October 1680 and May 1681, he was usually referred to as Major Allen.

Aged and weakened after a long winter that "helped his distemper," Arthur Allen died on 15 June 1710. His estate was valued at £838, not counting twenty-eight slaves worth more than £682, enormous landholdings, and his Brick House. His third son, Arthur Allen (ca. 1689–1727), inherited the Brick House.

A deposition recorded in Mar. 1695 in Surry Co. Deeds, Wills, Etc., 5:33, gives age as about forty-three; testimony about 1676 property losses in ibid., 2:145, and in the report of the royal commissioners in PRO CO 5/1371, fols. 179–181; conflicts with Jeffreys documented in Surry Co. Deeds, Wills, Etc., 2:202, 205, 206, and with Effingham in *Journals of House of Burgesses*, *Legislative Journals of Council*, and Billings, *Effingham Papers*; dispute with Swan documented in PRO CO 5/1314, fols. 56–62; will, inventory, and account current recorded in Surry Co. Deeds, Wills, Etc., 6:84–88, 120–121; death date in Louis B. Wright and Marion Tinling, eds., *The Secret Diary of William Byrd of Westover, 1709–1712* (1941), 193.

DAPHNE GENTRY

ALLEN, Benjamin (29 September 1789–13 January 1829), Episcopal minister, was born in Hudson, New York, the eldest of two sons and two daughters of Benjamin Allen and Mary Allen. Leaving school in his eleventh year, he worked as a clerk in his father's store until it closed in 1802. For the next decade he mixed stretches of employment in commercial establishments with periodic returns to formal schooling and a growing interest in literature and religion. He studied privately with Dr. Samuel Blatchford, a Presbyterian minister in Lansingburg, Rensselaer County, New York.

Allen also composed poetry, publishing his first volume, *Miscellaneous Poems on Moral and Religious Subjects* (1811) under the pseudonym Osander and dedicating it to Blatchford. The well received volume came out in a second edition in 1812. In his early writings Allen invoked conventional images of nature when describing intense religious feelings, but his voice was engagingly fresh and youthful and his verse had an attractive musical quality. He also experimented with a variety of constructions for his poems and enlivened his message with humor. In 1812 he produced a second work, *United We Stand, Divided We Fall: A Poem*. Three more pieces followed in quick succession: *Uranie, or The True Use of Poesy: A Poem* (1814); *The Phoenix, or The Battle of Valparaiso: A Poem* (1814); and *The Death of Abdallah: An Eastern Tale* (1814).

On 6 August 1812 Allen married Harriet Swift, also of Hudson. They had four sons and two daughters. He decided on a career in the church at about the time that he married, studying at the Theological Seminary of the Associated Reformed Church in New York City. In 1814 he traveled to Virginia, where under the influence of Bishop Richard Channing Moore he became a member of the Episcopal Church. Licensed as a lay reader in November of that year, Allen served the various Episcopal congregations in Charles Town and Shepherdstown and also attended to the spiritual needs of the African Americans in those localities and the surrounding countryside. He was ordained in 1818. William Meade, who often traveled with him, recalled that Allen's pulpit style had been "of the moderate order," but Allen was a learned man and an influential minister. After seven years in Virginia his parishioners certified that no man had done more for the church in that part of Virginia than he.

Allen's ministry left him time for study and writing, and from 1815 to 1816 he published the weekly *Layman's Magazine*, one of the first religious magazines published in the Shenandoah Valley. In 1820 he printed two of his sermons, *The Duty of Spreading the Gospel* and *The Gospel an Antidote to Affliction and Death*, as well as *History of the Reformation*, an abridged edition of Gilbert Burnet's *History of the Reformation of the Church of England*. The work for which Allen became best known, the history appeared in a second edition in 1823.

In 1821 Allen moved his family to Philadelphia, where he joined Saint Paul's Church as an assistant rector. He became rector of this church two years later, and when not absorbed with his congregational duties he ministered to members of the black community and developed Sunday school and Bible class programs for their use. He also composed a number of religious tracts and scholarly studies, including *Jesus Christ, and Him Crucified* (1822), a two-volume *History of the Church of Christ* (1823–1824), *The Parent's Counsellor, or The Dangers of Moroseness: A Narrative of the Newton Family* (1825), and *The Christian Warrior* (1826). In 1827 he established his own publishing house, the Prayer Book or Church Missionary House, but his health began to fail, and the publishing venture did not long survive.

In an attempt to regain his vigor, Benjamin Allen went to England in March 1828. While there he preached on behalf of the British and Foreign Bible Society. Severely weakened, he sailed for Philadelphia in November but died en route on 13 January 1829 and was buried at sea.

Thomas G. Allen, *Memoir of the Rev. Benjamin Allen* (1832; frontispiece por.); Meade, *Old Churches*, 2:304–307; Sprague, *American Pulpit*, 5:589–596; *Magazine of the Jefferson County (W.Va.) Historical Society* 26 (1960): 17; publications listed in John McClintock and James Strong, *Cyclopædia of Biblical, Theological, and Ecclesiastical Literature* (1867–1881), 1:163.

WARREN R. HOFSTRA

ALLEN, Beverly (August 1859–1918), educator, was born a slave in King and Queen County, the youngest of two sons and a daughter of Beverly Allen and Harriet White Allen, a midwife. According to family tradition, Allen's father worked as a slave on one of the Robinson tracts in lower King and Queen County near Gressitt. After emancipation, he became a hired farmhand in New Kent County before moving his family across the Mattaponi River to West Point. There he worked as a fisherman and oysterman. On 11 January 1870, the year of the town's incorporation, Allen paid the West Point Land Company $130 for a lot at the intersection of what are now Lee and Third Streets. The house that he erected there, no longer standing, was probably the first one owned by a former slave in that community. The Allen house soon sheltered a school for blacks, taught by two white women from Boston who resided with the family. Children attended school during the day, and adults attended at night. In 1872 the elder Beverly Allen won election to the newly established town council and helped the school obtain an appropriation of $55. In 1874, after his single term as a councilman ended, the council reimbursed him $2.50 a month for the use of his residence as a school during the previous winter.

Beverly Allen assimilated his father's devotion to education. According to family legend, the elder Allen stitched up his savings under patches on an old coat, which he presented to his son in 1879 to help finance his education at Hampton Institute. Beverly Allen graduated from Hampton in 1881 and returned to West Point to become the second principal of the public school for blacks.

Public education developed slowly in West Point, and the school for blacks received less support than schools for whites. Always crowded, it was moved a number of times to ever-larger buildings, settling early in the twentieth century at a site on Thirteenth Street. During Allen's thirty-five years as principal and teacher, the school offered classwork only through the sixth grade, and when the school was not in session Allen worked on the river with his father to supplement his meager salary. A dedicated and inspiring educator, Allen wrote to a former teacher at Hampton Institute in 1906 that "the occupation has a hold on me." Alumni who continued their educations elsewhere demonstrated that Allen's school had prepared them well.

In 1893 Allen married Alice Burns, a native of Augusta County, who had been adopted by a family named Cochran and had also become a teacher. They had eleven children, of whom five sons and five daughters were alive in 1910. Allen's father resided with them in the house that he had erected years before until his death in 1910. Beverly Allen died sometime in 1918, probably before the school term began in the autumn. He was buried in Memorial Garden in West Point.

Alice Allen continued to teach at the West Point Colored School until her retirement in 1939. In that year the school graduated its first high school class, an act that represented the culmination of seven decades of dedication by the Allen family and others to education for blacks in West Point. Two years later a new, brick school building replaced the aged frame structure where the Allens had taught. In 1942 it was named the Beverly Allen School in tribute to the pioneer principal and, perhaps, to his father as well. It became an elementary school in 1954 and was closed when the city's schools were desegregated in 1966.

Alice L. Reid, comp., *Negro Leadership, 1870–1970* [1970], 4–17 (por.); Beverly Allen File, Hampton; household and family data compiled from Census, King William Co., 1870, 1880, 1900 (which gives month and year of birth), and 1910, and verified by Allen's granddaughter Alice L. Reid; King William Co. Deed Book, 4:420–421, 10:367, and 11:34; West Point Town Council Minutes; Alonzo Thomas Dill, *York River Yesterdays: A Pictorial History* (1984), 72, 82, 113, 175; Charles A. Loving, *History of West Point United Methodist Church, 1869–1989* (1989), 10; King William Co. Release Deed Book, 1:402; year of death inferred from Personal Property Tax Returns, King William Co., RG 48, LVA.

ALONZO THOMAS DILL

ALLEN, Elizabeth Bray (ca.1692–by 22 February 1774), planter, was christened Elizabeth Bray. She was one of two daughters and at least four children of Mourning Burgh Pettus Bray and her second husband, James Bray, who were married about 1691. She was probably born at the Bray family estate at Middle Plantation, where Williamsburg was founded during her childhood, or at the nearby plantation of Littleton in James City County.

On 27 November 1711 Elizabeth Bray married Arthur Allen, the owner of a large plantation and resident of the brick house in Surry County that became known as Bacon's Castle early in the nineteenth century. They had one son and one daughter. Arthur Allen died intestate in 1727, leaving an estate valued at about £900, including twenty-three slaves on two large properties. Elizabeth Allen took over management of the extensive Allen estate, and she augmented her own wealth by the sale of some of the valuable James City County lands and Williamsburg town lots that she inherited from her father, who died in 1725. On 28 February 1728 William Byrd (1674–1744) stopped at "the Widdow Allen's" house in Surry County on his way to survey the boundary between North Carolina and Virginia, noting with approval her elegant entertainment and well-ordered household.

On 17 February 1729 she executed a marriage contract with Arthur Smith, a prosperous Isle of Wight County planter and proprietor of much of the town of Smithfield. By the marriage contract she secured for herself and her children the property that she owned and had inherited. Even though Allen owned more property than Smith, the contract bound Smith to pay each of her children the £300 that was their share of their father's estate and Elizabeth Allen was to receive £300 as compensation for her dower claim to Allen's estate. Thus the marriage contract converted property in which she had a life interest to ready money over which she retained full control. Their one son drowned in a swimming accident in 1743, and the following year her son by Arthur Allen also died.

Elizabeth Bray Allen Smith established a £140 trust fund in 1753 to create a free school for poor boys and girls in Smithfield. She reserved to herself the right to name the trustees, and she gave precise directions for the building that the trustees erected. She specified that the boys were to study reading, writing, and arithmetic for three years, and the girls were to study reading and writing for two years. The boys were then to be bound out as apprentices to learn a trade or craft, and the girls were to be bound "to some Honest Woman to be taught Household affairs."

After Arthur Smith died in 1754, his widow undertook to administer his large estate in addition to managing her own property. Sometime between September 1761 and April 1763 she married a third time. If she executed a marriage contract before her third wedding as she had done before her second, no record of it has been found, but none of the relevant family records and only some of the pertinent county records survive. Her third husband was surnamed Stith, but his first name is not known. Her failure to mention her third husband when she wrote her will sometime before 1769 suggests that by then she was a widow for the third time. In her will she set aside money for the education of several grandchildren and godchildren, gave valuable personal property to her granddaughters, and provided for the purchase of portraits of Moses and Aaron to be donated to the church she attended in Southwark Parish. She also left £120 and the residue of her estate to her Smithfield school.

Although the date and place of her death are not precisely known, Elizabeth Bray Allen Smith Stith probably died at her home in Surry County about the middle of February 1774. Her will was proved in the Surry County Court on 22 February 1774, and a brief report of her death appeared two days later in a Williamsburg newspaper.

Stephenson B. Andrews, ed., *Bacon's Castle* (1984), 7–8, contains several errors; family relationships in Winfree, *Laws of Virginia*, 381–384; first marriage in Louis B. Wright and Marion Tinling, eds., *The Secret Diary of William Byrd of Westover, 1709–1712* (1941), 444; marriage contract with second husband and first husband's estate records in Surry Co. Deeds, Wills, Etc., 5:396-400, 7:807–810, 841; Louis B. Wright, ed., *The Prose Works of William Byrd of Westover:*

Narratives of a Colonial Virginian (1966), 49–50; founding of school in Isle of Wight Co. Deed Book, 9:78–84, and Segar Cofer Dashiell, *Smithfield: A Pictorial History* (1977), 66; second husband's estate papers in Isle of Wight Co. Will Book, 6:108–109, 144–154, 235A–240, 526–528; misdated copy of her will and estate inventory in Surry Co. Wills and Deeds, 10A:361–372; will printed in *WMQ*, 1st ser., 5 (1896), 114–117; undated death notice in *Williamsburg Virginia Gazette* (Purdie and Dixon) 24 Feb. 1774.

JOAN R. GUNDERSEN

ALLEN, Floyd (5 July 1856–28 March 1913), principal in the 1912 gunfight in the Carroll County Courthouse, was the fourth of seven sons and fifth of eleven children of Jeremiah Allen and Nancy Combs Allen. He was born in Carroll County, where members of his father's family had lived as farmers, stockmen, and distillers for decades prior to the county's formation in 1842. Jacksonian Democrats in politics before the Civil War and Primitive Baptists in religion, the Allens at the time of Floyd Allen's birth shared in the nonslaveholding, egalitarian culture of their time and locale. His father and eldest brother served in the Confederate army, and the family experienced the deprivations common to the Civil War period.

After Appomattox the family improved its economic and social standing. Jeremiah Allen served for a time as a township supervisor, and his sons flourished as farmers, lumbermen, gristmill operators, distillers, storekeepers, real-estate speculators, and part-time preachers and teachers. One of the boys, Sidna, even ventured north to the Klondike in 1898 in an unsuccessful quest for gold. Enterprising and hardworking, several family members became what mountaineers called "high livers," residing in modern houses with telephones and other conveniences, owning and riding fine horses, and educating their sons for business or professional careers.

Floyd Allen was one of those who aspired to the high life. Although he had almost no formal schooling, he accumulated an estate worth between $10,000 and $20,000 by farming, keeping a store, and dealing in real estate. An ardent Democrat, he was elected or appointed to stints as deputy sheriff, constable, and county supervisor. On 9 August 1877 he married Cornelia Frances Edwards, of Carroll County, who was described in contemporary sources as a devoutly religious woman and a gracious hostess. Of their three children, one boy died in childhood. The elder surviving son, Victor Allen, seems to have enjoyed few advantages and became a rural mail carrier. Floyd Allen Jr. later changed his name to Claude Swanson Allen, after a Pittsylvania County Democrat who served successively as congressman and governor. Thanks to his father's increasing wealth, the younger Allen attended a private boarding school near Hillsville and enrolled for a time at a business college in Raleigh, North Carolina.

Although contemporary accounts characterize Floyd Allen as well-dressed, courteous in his routine business and personal contacts, and better informed about current events than most of his neighbors, his personality also had a darker, more ominous aspect, with a propensity for violent rage arising from an uncontrollable temper. According to family sources he was so unmanageable during his youth that his mother sometimes restrained him with ropes. As an adult he occasionally came to blows with other Carroll County residents over politics, clashed with federal revenue agents about insults they had allegedly made while visiting his home, was fined for shooting a neighbor in the leg during a 1904 land dispute, and even engaged in a pistol duel with his equally pugnacious brother Jasper "Jack" Allen, in a confrontation that left both men badly wounded. Rumors also circulated that Floyd Allen had killed a black man for hunting on his property, an accusation that Allen vehemently denied.

Although they persistently denied any wrongdoing, Allen and several of his brothers probably combined their hot tempers with a willingness to stray occasionally beyond the strict confines of the law. Jack Allen and Floyd Allen were widely reputed to have sold moonshine liquor, and in 1910 federal authorities in North Carolina charged Sidna Allen with counterfeiting. He was acquitted but subsequently indicted for perjury.

Family proclivities for personal violence exposed the Allens to the attentions and arrest warrants of hostile law-enforcement officers. Political trends in Carroll County eventually augmented this vulnerability, setting the stage for the disaster that was to come. Led by Dexter Goad, a strikingly adept and somewhat unscrupulous organizer, the county's Republicans captured the major local offices between 1904 and 1911, installing William M. Foster as commonwealth's attorney, Lewis F. Webb as sheriff, and Goad himself as clerk of court. Firm in their traditional Democratic allegiance, Floyd Allen and most of his relatives opposed these Republican inroads, but Jack Allen temporarily collaborated with the new courthouse incumbents, allegedly because of promises that his illicit liquor business would receive official toleration. When the Republicans refused to nominate one of his sons for commonwealth's attorney, however, Jack Allen rejoined his brothers in opposition to, and increasingly embittered isolation from, the dominant elements at the county seat of Hillsville. From the Allens' perspective, the increased surveillance of their activities by federal revenue agents and the United States Secret Service's abortive prosecution of Sidna Allen for counterfeiting were not accidental. Instead, in the view of the Allens, Republican spoilsmen in Carroll County were cooperating with a Republican-controlled federal bureaucracy in a politically motivated campaign to harass and intimidate them.

The chain of events leading to the courthouse shooting began in March 1911 when two of Floyd Allen's nephews, Wesley Edwards and Sidna Edwards, became embroiled in a fistfight with four neighborhood boys during worship services conducted by their uncle Garland Allen, a Primitive Baptist preacher. Authorities in Hillsville issued arrest warrants charging the pair with disturbing a religious gathering. On advice from Floyd Allen, the young men fled to Mount Airy, North Carolina, in order to allow the situation to cool and to give Allen time to arrange for bail and to employ lawyers for their defense.

On 20 April 1911 Allen went to Hillsville, made the necessary arrangements, and agreed to bring his nephews to court for trial. As he was returning to his home in the southern part of the county, Allen met two deputy sheriffs who had already gone to Mount Airy and apprehended the fugitives without obtaining the necessary extradition papers. The officers were driving buggies and had the Edwards men in custody, their hands and feet secured with handcuffs and ropes. Enraged by what he regarded as a calculated insult to his family, Allen disarmed the deputies, assaulted one of them, released his nephews, and shortly thereafter turned them over to lawmen in Hillsville as he had earlier pledged to do.

The Edwards boys were convicted of the charges against them and served brief sentences in the county jail, but Floyd Allen's legal troubles had only begun. He was indicted for attacking the deputies and, after various delays, brought to trial in the March 1912 term of the circuit court. In the year that had passed between the incident and the trial, Circuit Court Judge Thornton Lemmon Massie, the lone Democrat in the law-enforcement bureaucracy at Hillsville, signaled his own good opinion of Allen by appointing him to a special police force.

The case was heard on 13 March 1912. The jury's verdict, however, was delayed until the next morning, when the little courtroom was packed with more than a hundred people, an astonishing number of whom were armed with revolvers or automatic pistols. Among those thus equipped were the defendant himself, his brother Sidna Allen, his son Claude Allen, his nephews Wesley Edwards and Sidna Edwards, and Jack Allen's son Friel Allen. Victor Allen was also in attendance, although apparently without a gun. Anticipating trouble, a large contingent of the county's Republican officials (the sheriff, four deputies, the commonwealth's attorney, the clerk of court, and the deputy clerk) were all armed as well.

The 14 March court session began in a routine way, with the consideration of various procedural matters. The jury then reported that it found Floyd Allen guilty and recommended a one-year term in the state penitentiary. His lawyers immediately requested that the verdict be overturned. Judge Massie rejected the appeal, but he agreed to conduct a hearing the next day at which additional witnesses would be interviewed and a final decision rendered on the motion for a new trial. Refusing a further plea that Allen be permitted to remain at large on bond until that time, Massie instructed the sheriff to take charge of the prisoner and escort him to jail. Sheriff Webb and Clerk Goad apparently made no secret of their satisfaction at the course of events, and Allen's notorious temper erupted. Declaring, "Gentlemen, I ain't a-goin'!" (or words to that effect), he began to search inside his coat and sweater for what he subsequently testified were subpoenas and what others claimed was a pistol.

What happened next has been the subject of endless debate. According to the Allens, several court officers opened fire on Floyd Allen, but other witnesses maintained that his son Claude Allen started the shooting, supported almost instantly by his uncle Sidna Allen. The consequences were horrible. The combatants exchanged approximately sixty shots in the crowded courtroom and more on the steps and in the yard outside. Killed immediately or mortally wounded were Judge Massie, Sheriff Webb, Commonwealth's Attorney Foster, juror Augustus C. Fowler, and a young spectator, Bettie Ayers. Clerk Goad was wounded in the face and a bullet fractured Floyd Allen's leg, while Sidna Allen suffered comparatively minor wounds.

Regardless of who started the battle, the Allens and their Edwards allies won it. Most of their surviving opponents fled the scene. It was then the Allens' turn to flee Hillsville, with the exception of Floyd Allen, who was too seriously injured to make the attempt, and Victor Allen, who remained to care for his father. The rest of the men took refuge in the Blue Ridge Mountains. Militiamen, bloodhounds, and posses organized and directed by the Baldwin-Felts Detective Agency of Roanoke scoured the hills for them. Governor William Hodges Mann offered rewards for the capture of the fugitives, dead or alive, and threatened to prosecute anyone who aided their escape.

Discovered in a Hillsville hotel on 15 March 1912, Floyd Allen and Victor Allen were the first to be taken into custody. They offered no resistance, although Floyd Allen tried unsuccessfully to cut his own throat with a penknife. Various friends of the Allens who had been present in the courtroom were also temporarily placed under arrest. Between 22 and 29 March the pursuit turned up three more men: Claude Allen, Sidna Edwards, and Friel Allen, the last two of whom, according to some accounts, surrendered voluntarily. Sidna Allen and Wesley Edwards proved more difficult to capture. After eluding the dogs and posses for several weeks, they left the Blue Ridge on foot and then escaped by train from Asheville, North Carolina. Six months later Baldwin-Felts agents finally apprehended them in Des Moines on 14 September 1912.

Meanwhile, the commonwealth had begun to prosecute Floyd Allen and his kinsmen for the courthouse killings. The trials took place at Wytheville from April until December 1912. Juries empaneled for the successive cases from Virginia's southwestern and northern counties heard wildly inconsistent testimony. The prosecution made little or no effort to use ballistics tests or autopsy findings to demonstrate that a particular Allen or Edwards was individually and definitively responsible for any particular death. Instead, the state attempted to prove the existence of a premeditated conspiracy on the part of the defendants to murder the court officers, an approach that would make each of them equally liable for all of the deaths. Jurors generally resisted the tactic. On 16 May they convicted Floyd Allen of the first-degree murder of Commonwealth's Attorney Foster, but a prosecution of Claude Allen for the death of Judge Massie resulted in a jury finding of second-degree murder on the grounds that premeditation had not been proved. Claude Allen was then tried twice for murdering Foster, with one trial culminating in a hung jury and the second, after prolonged deliberations, ending with a first-degree verdict. In subsequent cases confessions to lesser offenses, plea bargains, and convictions for manslaughter or second-degree murder prevailed. Friel Allen and Sidna Edwards each received eighteen-year penitentiary terms, while Wesley Edwards was sentenced to twenty-seven and Sidna Allen to thirty-five years in prison. Victor Allen was the only defendant acquitted.

In September 1912 Judge Waller R. Staples, who presided at all of the trials, sentenced Claude Allen and Floyd Allen to die in Virginia's electric chair on 22 November. Governor Mann was unsympathetic to the Allens and a staunch advocate of capital punishment, but he nevertheless stayed the execution of both men on four occasions between November 1912 and March 1913 in order to permit them to exhaust their opportunities for appeal. Meanwhile, a dramatic shift of public opinion took place in their favor. Many people believed that the two men were no more deserving of the death penalty than their kinsmen who, in later trials, had received lesser sentences. Furthermore, defense attorneys in subsequent cases had shown that Dexter Goad and other officeholders were partially responsible for the courthouse tragedy. Reflecting these developments, petitions bearing tens of thousands of signatures urging executive clemency were submitted to the governor. Such prominent Virginians as Richard Evelyn Byrd, the Speaker of the House of Delegates; the Reverend George W. McDaniel, of Richmond's First Baptist Church; and U.S. Senator Claude A. Swanson exerted their influence to save the pair.

The Allens' public support became increasingly fervent, but their prospects for legal relief continually diminished. The Virginia Supreme Court of Appeals twice rejected their appeals, and the U.S. Supreme Court declined to review the convictions. Satisfied that further delay would be pointless, the governor reiterated his belief in the justice of the sentences and set 28 March 1913 as the execution date. On 27 March the campaign to save the two Allens took a final and particularly bizarre turn. With Governor Mann en route to New Jersey for a speaking engagement, lawyers for the condemned men approached Lieutenant Governor J. Taylor Ellyson with the suggestion that during the governor's absence from Virginia Ellyson had the right as acting chief executive to commute the death sentences. On the night of 27 March Ellyson asked Attorney General Samuel W. Williams to rule on the constitutionality of this proposal, and the penitentiary warden accordingly postponed the executions, originally scheduled for the next morning, until the legal question could be resolved. Informed of these intrigues by a late-night telephone call, Mann hastened back to Richmond by train early on 28 March and ordered that the executions be carried out.

At 1:30 P.M. on 28 March 1913 Floyd Allen was electrocuted in the penitentiary in Richmond. A few minutes later Claude Allen was put to death. Both men reportedly died bravely and without complaint. Over the protests of Victor Allen, the bodies of his father and brother were placed on public view at Bliley's Funeral Home in Richmond, where more than twelve thousand mourners and curiosity seekers viewed them. Transported back to Carroll County by train and wagon, Floyd Allen and Claude Allen were buried on 30 March 1913 in a cemetery near the Blue Ridge. A crowd estimated at five thousand persons attended the service.

Victor Allen and Cornelia Frances Allen eventually moved out of Virginia. Governor E. Lee Trinkle pardoned Sidna Edwards and Friel Allen in October 1922, and Governor Harry F. Byrd did the same for Sidna Allen and Wesley Edwards in April 1926. There were no pardons, of course, for those who died in the courtroom or for Claude Allen and Floyd Allen. Considered villains by some and martyrs by others, the Allens left their mark on the history and folklore of twentieth-century Virginia. Variously known as the "Hillsville Massacre" and the "Courthouse Tragedy," the violent episode left seven people shot dead or executed and four more serving long prison terms. It sparked controversies that simmered for generations. An array of newspaper accounts, magazine articles, and books have analyzed the much-disputed facts of the case, and mountain poets and balladeers have commemorated its tragic features, but many questions about the Hillsville gunfight and its participants remain unanswered.

M. Clifford Harrison "Murder in the Courtroom," *Virginia Cavalcade* 17 (summer 1967): 43–47; Seth Williamson, "Hillsville Massacre," *Roanoker* 9 (Nov. 1982): 28–29, 44–51; Allen Clemency Papers and Allen-Edwards Case Papers, both RG 13, LVA; Elmer J. Cooley Papers, UVA; Etta Donnan Mann, *Four Years in the Governor's Mansion of Virginia, 1910–1914* (1937); books reflecting an anti-Allen bias include Edgar James, *The Allen Outlaws* (1912), Edwin Chancellor Payne, *The Hillsville Tragedy* (1913), J. J. Reynolds, *The Allen Gang* (1912), and George M. N. Parker, *The Mountain Massacre* (1930); favorable books include J. Sidna Allen, *Memoirs* (1929), Elmer J. Cooley, *The Inside Story of the World Famous Courtroom Tragedy* [ca. 1961], and Rufus L. Gardner, *The Courthouse Tragedy, Hillsville, Va.* [ca. 1968]; also pertinent are Ethel Park Richardson and Sigmund Spaeth, eds., *American Mountain Songs* (1927), 34, Mellinger Edward Henry, ed., *Folk-Songs From the Southern Highlands* (1938), 317–320, and an account in verse by Samuel S. Hurt, *"Gentlemen, I Ain't A-Goin"* (1913).

JAMES TICE MOORE

ALLEN, George Edward (31 March 1885–21 July 1972), attorney, the youngest of two sons and a daughter of George Thomas Allen and Mary Irby Burke Allen, was born at Woodstock, his father's farm in Lunenburg County. His brother did not survive infancy. When Allen was eighteen months old his mother died. He spent the remainder of his childhood in the Amelia County home of his maternal aunt and uncle Lula Burke Coleman and William O. Coleman. Allen attended the public schools of Amelia County, spent one year at the Virginia Agricultural and Mechanical College and Polytechnic Institute, and in 1907 entered the University of Virginia. He received an LL.B. in 1910 and returned to Lunenburg County to begin the practice of law. He married Susie Lee Jones on 20 May 1913, and they had one son and one daughter before her death on 14 October 1918. On 22 April 1920 he married Mary Lee Bridgeforth. They had two daughters and two sons.

Allen served as mayor of Victoria in Lunenburg County from 1914 to 1915 and sat for one term, from 1916 to 1920, in the Senate of Virginia from the district composed of the counties of Amelia, Cumberland, Lunenburg, Nottoway, and Prince Edward. His most significant accomplishment as a senator, according to his later recollection, was securing in 1919 the requirement that railroads rather than local governments pay for the elimination of dangerous grade crossings. A conservative Democrat all his life, Allen occasionally broke with Virginia's party leaders to support some aspects of the New Deal, and he approved of President Franklin D. Roosevelt's attempt in 1937 to enlarge the number of judges on the United States Supreme Court after it struck down a number of New Deal programs.

In 1931 Allen moved to Richmond, where he practiced law for the remainder of his life. He and his eldest son, George Edward Allen Jr., established their own firm in 1935. The younger George Allen later represented Richmond in the House of Delegates from 1954 until 1982. Allen's other sons also eventually joined the firm, which, as Allen, Allen, Allen, and Allen developed into one of the most successful firms of trial lawyers in Virginia. The partnership became known for representing clients in personal injury cases, and George Allen was recognized as a pioneer in the field. His advocacy resulted in new legal doctrines, case law, and investigative and trial procedures in cases involving product liability and commercial and industrial accidents. Automobile mishaps were one of the firm's early specialties. Allen's practice often placed him on the side of those who had traditionally been powerless against large corporations and insurance companies. He developed a reputation as a careful attorney, but one who stretched the bounds of settled law in pursuit of compensation for his clients.

Although Allen practiced law until his death, he took enough time off late in life to compose a short autobiography, *The Law as a Way of Life: Memoirs of George E. Allen, 1910–1970.* In it he recounted his involvement in some of his pathbreaking cases and thereby risked overstepping the bar's code of ethics by revealing details of suits in which he had acted as counsel. After the volume had been printed in 1969, Allen sought an informal ruling from his district bar association's ethics committee, which advised in the autumn of 1970 that publication and distribution of the book would indeed violate one or more provisions of the ethics code. Allen nevertheless distributed some copies, and after the volume had been reviewed in the press and in at least one law journal, he went ahead with a wider distribution. In the autumn of 1971 he was brought up on charges of violating the code of ethics, not for revealing secrets but for publishing memoirs so self-congratulatory that they could be construed as advertising, which the code then strictly forbade. In March 1972 a Richmond judge ruled that the book had just escaped the rules that were in force when it was written but that it would not have been acceptable under rules subsequently adopted.

Allen played an active role in the American Bar Association, the Virginia State Bar Association, and the Richmond Bar Association, serving as president of the last in 1959–1960. He was a founding member of the International Academy of Trial Lawyers and a fellow of the American College of Trial Lawyers. In 1960 he was a founder and the first president of the Virginia Trial Lawyers Association. During Allen's lifetime he lectured at law schools in at least four states, and he received awards from the Law Science Institute in 1953, the American College of Trial Lawyers in 1965, and the American Trial Lawyers Association in 1972. He received a special citation in 1965 from fellow Richmond attorney Lewis F. Powell Jr., then-president of the American Bar Association, in recognition of Allen's pro bono representation of Fred Wallace, an African American law student who was arrested in the courthouse of Prince Edward County while attempting to deliver legal papers for a Richmond law firm for which he was working during summer recess.

An avid tennis player, Allen also played often in amateur golf tournaments. In addition, he actively supported the World Peace Through Law Center in Washington, D.C., and served as a delegate to its international conference in Belgrade, Yugoslavia, in 1971. George Edward Allen died in Richmond on 21 July 1972 and was buried in Kenbridge in Lunenburg County.

Family history in *The Law as a Way of Life: Memoirs of George E. Allen, 1910–1970* (1969 [i.e., 1971]; frontispiece por.); George Edward Allen Papers, UVA; BVS Birth Register, Lunenburg Co.; Lunenburg Co. Marriage Register; Allen's principal professional publications were "Some Defects in Virginia Practice and Procedure" and "The Role of a Plaintiff Lawyer in Personal Injury Litigation," *Virginia Law Review* 32 (1946): 429–442 and 41 (1955): 827–842, "Automobile Negligence: Entrustment Doctrine" in *Automobile Negligence: A Compilation of the Original Dicta Published by the Virginia Law Weekly, 1955–56*, ed. Richard S. Harrell (1956), 43–48, and "Evaluation and Settlement of a Personal Injury Claim for Damages," *Washington and Lee Law Review* 14 (1957): 1–28, which is very similar to "The Role of a Plaintiff Lawyer in Personal Injury Litigation"; proceedings on memoirs documented in *Richmond Times-Dispatch*, 16 Sept. 1971, 27 Feb., 25 Mar. 1972, and in Richmond Law and Equity Court judgment of 24 Mar. 1972, *Third District Committee of the Virginia State Bar* v. *George E. Allen* (photocopy in DVB Files); obituaries in *Richmond News Leader*, 22 July 1972, and *Richmond Times-Dispatch*, 23 July 1972; memorial in *Virginia Bar Association Proceedings* (1973): 302–305.

BRENT TARTER

ALLEN, Guy Richard Champlain (18 August 1803–4 December 1856), attorney and member of the Council, was born in Wood County, the youngest of three sons and one of six children of Samuel Allen and Mary Allen. By 1823 he was living in Preston County, where he was admitted to the bar, and in April 1825 he was admitted to the bar in Monongalia County. He married Delia Lowry on 20 November 1834 and had a son and three daughters.

In 1828 and 1829 Allen was elected to the House of Delegates from Preston County. His political views are not well known, but in February 1829 he made a speech in the House of Delegates recommending that if a constitutional convention met as anticipated, its seats should be apportioned on the basis of white population only, a position he reiterated in 1850 prior to the next convention. Allen's service in the House of Delegates was otherwise uneventful until 20 January 1830, when the General Assembly elected him to the Council of State, the governor's advisory board. The Council was often thought of as a way-stop for rising public figures.

Allen took his seat on the Council on 19 June 1830. He attended eighty-four of ninety-two recorded meetings of the Council held in Richmond between then and 30 March 1831. Except for one dissent, Allen concurred with the Council's majority in disposing of the usually routine business. The Constitution of 1831 reduced the number of councillors from eight to three, and Allen's service terminated with the final Council meeting under the old Constitution on 30 March 1831.

Allen returned to Morgantown, where he lost a bid to return to the House of Delegates in 1832. He served as prosecuting attorney of Monongalia County from May to September 1831 and of Preston County from 1832 to 1852. Contemporaries regarded Allen as a learned and able attorney. A number of young men read law in his office and later had important careers at the local bar, including Ralph Lazier Berkshire and Edward C. Bunker. Allen served as a trustee of the Morgantown Female Academy, joined the Sons of Temperance, and was an original member of the board of the Morgantown Bridge Company, which in 1854 built a suspension bridge across the Monongahela River. He failed in efforts to organize an Episcopal parish in Morgantown early in the 1850s, but after his death when one began to function in October 1860 it was named Allen Parish. Guy Richard Champlain Allen died of apoplexy at his home in Morgantown on 4 December 1856.

Brief biography in Samuel T. Wiley, *History of Monongalia County, West Virginia* (1883), 342, which contains a number of other useful references, as does James Morton Callahan, *History of the Making of Morgantown, West Virginia* (1926); father's will in Wood Co. Will Book, 3:43; *Richmond Enquirer*, 12 Feb. 1829; Census, Monongalia Co., 1850, 1860; Monongalia Co. Will Book, 2:1; BVS Death Register, Monongalia Co.; obituary in *Morgantown American Union*, 6 Dec. 1856.

JOHN E. STEALEY III

ALLEN, Henry Clay (19 March 1838–31 October 1889), Speaker of the House of Delegates, was born at Beaverdam, the house of his paternal grandfather in Botetourt County. He was the fourth of seven sons and sixth of nine children of John James Allen and Mary Elizabeth Payne Jackson Allen. He attended the University of Virginia between 1854 and 1857, read law in his father's office, and by 1860 was a practicing attorney in Fincastle.

Allen entered the Confederate army on 1 July 1861 and was promoted to lieutenant on 1 May 1862, serving as adjutant of the 28th Regiment Virginia Infantry. The regiment participated in both Battles of Manassas (Bull Run), the Peninsula campaign, the Seven Days' Battles, and the Battles of Sharpsburg (Antietam Creek) and Gettysburg, where Allen's cousin Robert Clotworthy Allen, the colonel in command of the regiment, was killed. Allen was also present at Cold Harbor and at Petersburg. He had been captured during the Battle of Williamsburg on 5 May 1862, paroled on 12 May at Fort Monroe, and exchanged on 13 August. He was captured again on 6 April 1865 at Saylers Creek, imprisoned at Johnson's Island near Sandusky, Ohio, and released after taking the oath of allegiance on 18 June 1865.

Allen returned to Fincastle and resumed his law practice. On 24 January 1867 he married Julia McKay Gatewood. They had six daughters and seven sons. He moved to Woodstock in 1868 and opened a law office there. In April 1870 the General Assembly unanimously elected him a county court judge, an office he held until March 1873. As both his father and his uncle Robert Allen had served in the Senate of Virginia and in Congress, Allen's decision to enter politics is unsurprising. In 1873 he ran for the House of Delegates but was defeated by twenty-nine votes. Two years later he did win a seat in the House. Allen was a busy freshmen delegate, sponsoring thirteen bills, five of which were enacted into law. During his second year in the House he served on the influential Committees on Courts of Justice and on Propositions and Grievances.

In 1877 Allen won reelection to the General Assembly and was elected Speaker of the House, defeating longtime Speaker Marshall Hanger by a large margin. The majority group in the assembly that first met in December 1877 was committed to reducing the state's large public debt by adjusting downward the proportion of the public debt to be paid. The Readjusters, as they were called, were a loose coalition that cut across party and racial lines and included Democrats, Conservatives, Republicans, and African Americans. Allen was in sympathy with the Readjusters, to whom he owed his election as Speaker, and he presided over the hot debates on the two debt payment bills that the assembly passed. The governor vetoed both of them.

In the autumn of 1878 Allen sought election to the House of Representatives, but he was opposed both by enemies of the Readjuster movement and by some of its more radical proponents, and he failed to get on the ballot. During the 1879 assembly session he supported the debt payment bill that the Funders, the Readjusters' opponents, introduced, and he opposed a move by the Readjusters' leader, William Mahone, to establish a formal Readjuster Party. Allen was one of many political leaders who were willing to support some readjustment of the debt but would not go so far as to ally formally with the Republicans and the state's African American political leaders against the Conservatives and the Democratic Party.

Although Allen had not intended to run for reelection to the House of Delegates in 1879, in

September he was persuaded to do so. He lost. In 1880 he accepted the Democratic Party nomination for Congress, but the popular Readjuster, John Paul, defeated him by a wide margin. Thereafter, Allen campaigned only on behalf of other candidates. In 1885 President Grover Cleveland rewarded Allen's services to the Democratic Party by appointing him United States attorney for the western district of Virginia.

Henry Clay Allen died on 31 October 1889, probably from a massive stroke, during a visit to Roanoke to give an address on behalf of Democratic gubernatorial nominee Philip Watkins McKinney. He was buried in Massanutten Cemetery at Woodstock.

Jamerson, *Speakers and Clerks, 1776–1976*, 94–95 (por.); Compiled Service Records; Frank E. Fields Jr., *28th Virginia Infantry*, 2d ed. (1985), 47; BVS Marriage Register, Shenandoah Co.; House of Delegates Election Records, 1871–1879, RG 13, LVA; James Tice Moore, *Two Paths to the New South: The Virginia Debt Controversy, 1870–1883* (1974), 131; *Staunton Vindicator*, 21 Dec. 1877, 26 July, 8 Nov. 1878; *Richmond Dispatch*, 5, 6 Dec. 1877; *Richmond Whig*, 5, 6 Dec. 1877; *New Market Shenandoah Valley*, 12 Sept. 1879; Memorandum Regarding the Defection of Delegates Samuel H. Moffett, Isaac C. Fowler, and H. C. Allen from the Readjusters in January 1879, Abram Fulkerson Papers, LVA; obituaries in *Richmond Dispatch*, 2 Nov. 1889, *New Market Shenandoah Valley*, 7 Nov. 1889, and *Staunton Vindicator*, 8 Nov. 1889.

EMILY J. SALMON

ALLEN, James (6 December 1762–26 September 1844), General Court judge, was born in Ireland, the second son and third child of Robert Allan and Mary Walkinshaw Allan. In 1763 the family immigrated to Cumberland County, Pennsylvania, where he grew up and where his younger brother and three more sisters were born. He served in the Pennsylvania militia during the American Revolution and studied law after the war. During the late 1780s—by which time he had altered the spelling of his surname—Allen moved to Virginia and settled by 1788 in Woodstock. In April 1791 he married Jane Steele. Her child, Edwin Steele Duncan, was raised in their household along with their four sons, two of whom died in infancy, and one daughter. Allen may also have had two sons and two daughters with a woman named Elizabeth Smiley.

Allen qualified to practice law in Shenandoah County in 1790. The friendship he formed with Gabriel Jones, one of the most influential lawyers in the region, probably helped advance his legal career. In 1800 Allen was elected to the first of two consecutive terms in the House of Delegates, where he served on the powerful Committee for Courts of Justice. In 1802 Allen won election as a Jeffersonian Republican to a four-year term in the Senate of Virginia representing the district composed of the counties of Augusta, Bath, Pendleton, Rockbridge, Rockingham, and Shenandoah. In 1808 the voters elected him to the House of Delegates for one more term, during which he was the ranking member of the Committee for Courts of Justice and chairman of the Committee on Claims. While in the assembly, Allen played a key legislative role in the reform of the state court system and supported unsuccessful efforts to call a state convention to revise the constitution.

On 30 March 1811 the governor and Council appointed Allen to the General Court to fill a vacancy in one of the districts in western Virginia. Allen declined the post because he did not want to be required to preside over circuit superior courts of law in each county in such a distant district as well as have to travel to Richmond twice a year when the General Court judges met there to hear appeals. On 20 June 1811 the governor named Allen the General Court judge for the circuit comprising the counties of Botetourt, Cabell, Greenbrier, Kanawha, Mason, and Monroe. This time Allen accepted the appointment and moved to Botetourt County, where he eventually acquired almost 650 acres of land and in 1820 built a large house near Fincastle called Beaverdam.

Allen served as judge of the district for almost twenty years. Unfortunately, none of his written opinions was published in the reports of the General Court from this significant era in the development of Virginia jurisprudence. Surviving correspondence reveals that Allen was an outspoken advocate of judicial independence and a champion of procedural simplification. Following adoption of the new state constitution in 1830, the assembly again reorganized the state's court system and merged the county superior courts of law with the district superior courts of chancery and directed the district court judges to preside over them. Allen disapproved of the new system and feared that it would produce an increase in litigation. Nearly seventy years old, he retired from the bench when the new system went into operation.

Allen spent the rest of his life as a gentleman farmer at Beaverdam. His surviving letters reveal a careworn public servant, distrustful of Jacksonian Democrats, disappointed by the unrealized promise of the republicanism of the American Revolution, and wary of antebellum political and judicial reforms. Allen's two surviving sons and his stepson all followed him into the law. His stepson became a judge in Virginia. Robert Allen and John James Allen both served in the House of Representatives, and the latter also served on the Virginia Supreme Court of Appeals. James Allen died at his home on 26 September 1844 and was buried at Lauderdale Cemetery near Beaverdam.

Birth and death dates on gravestone, Lauderdale Cemetery, Botetourt Co.; Allen Family Papers, LVA; Allen Family Papers, VHS; other Allen records and genealogical notes in possession of Jean Showalter, of Lynchburg, and William Watts, of Roanoke; Stoner, *Seed-Bed*, 265; John Allen to governor, 4 Apr., 2 July 1811, Governor's Office, Letters Received, RG 3, LVA; Botetourt Co. Deed Book, 23:231; Botetourt Co. Will Book, G:104–105; obituary giving wrong place of death in *Richmond Enquirer*, 22 Oct. 1844.

E. LEE SHEPARD

ALLEN, James Henry (1828 or 1829–28 April 1898), educator, was born in York County, the younger of two sons and third of four children of Benjamin Allen, a moderately prosperous planter, and Frances Maria Brown Coke Allen. During the 1830s the fortunes of the Allens declined, and in about 1843 they moved to James City County, where Allen attended subscription schools and paid part of his tuition by working as a teacher's assistant. He received a bachelor's degree after attending one term at Columbian College (now George Washington University) in Washington, D.C. Allen then taught school in New Kent County and moved a few years later to James City County.

Allen's father died in September 1853, leaving him a small inheritance. In 1860 the census enumerator identified him as a classical teacher and evaluated his personal estate at $2,510. When the Civil War began, Allen joined the James City Cavalry, which was mustered in as Company H of the 5th Regiment Virginia Cavalry on 22 May 1861. The regiment was consolidated with the 15th Virginia Cavalry in November 1864. During the war Allen was wounded at least once. He rose from private in May 1861 to lieutenant colonel as of 6 June 1864.

Allen never married, and after the war he lived with his unmarried sister Fannie Allen, who kept house for him. The war also left him with little property and no income, but the high reputation of his school enabled him to reopen it and receive paying students soon afterward. On 18 September 1870 the new State Board of Education appointed Allen superintendent of the new system of public schools for the district comprising York and James City Counties and the city of Williamsburg. He faced daunting prospects. His district had no money and no school building, state aid was inadequate at the outset and was soon sharply reduced, and many white Virginians were suspicious of the new public schools. Despite the obstacles, Allen and the public school system survived. By the late 1870s he was describing local sentiment about public education as gradually improving, and the schools had become so popular "that no public officer opposed to them could live for a day in the hearts of his countrymen."

In 1881 Allen's district was divided and he became superintendent of schools for James City County. Except for the period from 1882 to 1886, when the Readjusters replaced almost all Democratic officeholders in the state, Allen held office in James City County for twenty-seven years, a record exceeded by only one other of the original superintendents appointed in 1870. Allen's long tenure reflected a discreet but impressive leadership. His firmness, decisiveness, and striking appearance enabled him to succeed and survive where others might have faltered or failed.

Allen was a political realist who accommodated himself to the limited available resources, worked within the constraints of local control, and avoided controversy. James City County had a small population, with only 721 students of both races enrolled in its public schools in 1900.

Allen stressed in his annual reports that he rarely intervened in local matters. He permitted each of the three-member district boards within the county to operate autonomously, a policy that resulted in little change. The number of schools, for example, remained roughly constant between 1881 and 1900, rising from ten white and eight black schools to twelve for whites and nine for blacks. When the state superintendent of public instruction asked all of the county superintendents in 1891 what improvements their educational systems had achieved, Allen's reply for James City was "only that which comes from having more experienced and better teachers."

Financially, Allen never recovered from the Civil War. His salary as superintendent declined from $466 in 1872 to $156 in 1881 after his district was reduced in size. During the 1880s and 1890s, when urban superintendents often received more than $2,000, his salary remained at about $200, the lowest in the state. Allen had to sustain himself and his sister by working on his small farm. Early in 1898 he suffered a severe attack of malaria that confined him to his bed. On 27 April he experienced what was described as an episode of apoplexy. James Henry Allen died at his home in James City County the following day, 28 April 1898.

Brief biography in *Virginia School Journal* 2 (1893): 116 (por.); birth date inferred from ages given in memorial in *Virginia School Journal* 7 (1898): 160, and in Census, James City Co., 1850, 1860; Compiled Service Records; James H. Allen, "The James City Cavalry: Its Organization and Its First Service," *Richmond Dispatch*, 16 June 1896, reprinted in *Southern Historical Society Papers* 24 (1896): 353–358; service as superintendent documented in annual published reports of the state Superintendent of Public Instruction, 1871–1881 and 1886–1899, and records of the Board of Education and Superintendent of Public Instruction, RG 27, LVA; Martha W. McCartney, *James City County: Keystone of the Commonwealth* (1997), 330–331, 516–517; Rawls Byrd, *History of Public Schools in Williamsburg* (1968), 3, 21–22; obituary in *Richmond Dispatch*, 30 Apr. 1898.

WILLIAM A. LINK

ALLEN, James Walkinshaw (2 July 1829–27 June 1862), Confederate army officer, was born in Shenandoah County, the eldest of five sons and third of ten children of Robert Allen and Frances K. Harvey Allen. He was named in honor of his Scottish ancestor James Walkinshaw. In 1839 the family moved to Bedford County, where Allen attended local schools and the New London Academy. He graduated with distinction from the Virginia Military Institute in 1849 and taught at the Piedmont Institute in Liberty, Bedford County, prior to his appointment as an assistant professor of mathematics at VMI in 1852. On 13 February 1856 he married Julia Pendleton, of Jefferson County. They had one son. Allen farmed near Summit Point in Jefferson County from 1857 until the Civil War began.

In 1859 Allen had been elected colonel of a regiment of volunteers formed in Berkeley, Clarke, and Jefferson Counties, and although he had opposed secession, he led his militia contingent to Harpers Ferry on 18 April 1861 and proclaimed the arsenal the property of Virginia. His unit was organized as the 2d Regiment Virginia Infantry under Brigadier General Thomas J. Jackson. Allen's regiment was conspicuous as one of the best-drilled regiments in what soon came to be known as the Stonewall Brigade. As the result of a childhood injury Allen had lost the sight in one of his eyes, and in the fighting at Manassas (Bull Run) on 21 July 1861 he was wounded in the other eye and temporarily blinded.

When Jackson was promoted to major general in October 1861, Allen was appointed acting brigadier general, but the promotion was never made permanent. His decision to keep the brigade in training when he returned to duty paid off during the strenuous marching and fighting that Jackson directed in the Shenandoah Valley in 1862. The 2d Regiment charged into the thick of the fighting at the Battle of Kernstown on 23 March, and although not engaged at Jackson's victories at McDowell and Front Royal in May, Allen's regiment joined in the rout of the Union army at Winchester on 25 May 1862, pursuing Union troops through the streets of the city. At Port Republic on 9 June 1862 Allen led the 2d Regiment in a direct frontal attack and a daring but unsuccessful flanking maneuver against superior artillery and infantry forces.

The Stonewall Brigade was transferred eastward to participate in the defense of Richmond. During the Seven Days' Battles, Allen's 2d Regiment fought at Gaines's Mill on 27 June 1862. On another part of the field, his younger brother, Colonel Robert Clotworthy Allen, was wounded. During the afternoon attack on McGehee's Hill, the 2d and 5th Regiments charged ahead of the rest of the Stonewall Brigade and came under concentrated fire. The 2d Regiment carried the hilltop, but James Walkinshaw Allen, while rallying his men for a final charge against the wavering Union line, was shot and killed instantly. He was buried in Hollywood Cemetery in Richmond but later reinterred near the family residence at Liberty.

Charles D. Walker, *Biographical Sketches of the Graduates and Elèves of the Virginia Military Institute Who Fell During the War Between the States* (1875), 21–25; James Walkinshaw Allen Notebook, 1848–1864, Duke; Jefferson Co. Marriage Register; Compiled Service Records; Allen's account of Manassas, *Richmond Times-Dispatch*, 4 June 1905, reprinted in *Southern Historical Society Papers* 34 (1906): 365–367; James I. Robertson Jr., *The Stonewall Brigade* (1963); Dennis Frye, *2nd Virginia Infantry* (1984); Ethelbert Nelson Ott, "William D. Washington (1833–1870), Artist of the South" (master's thesis, University of Delaware, 1968), 183 (por.).

DONALD W. GUNTER

ALLEN, John (ca. 1684–by 21 April 1742), planter, was the eldest of four sons and second of eight children of Arthur Allen (ca. 1652–1710) and Katherine Baker Allen. He was probably born at his father's plantation, now called Bacon's Castle, in Surry County. He attended the College of William and Mary and in 1702 and 1705 served there as an usher, or teaching assistant. In 1707 Arthur Allen relinquished to his son his position as surveyor for Surry and Isle of Wight Counties, and in 1708 John Allen became clerk of Surry County. Allen retained both lucrative and influential offices until shortly before his death. By 1711 he was a captain in the militia and within a few years more he had become the colonel for his county. Among other valuable properties, Allen inherited a plantation at the mouth of Upper Chippokes Creek, where he resided for most of his adult life.

Soon after taking up residence there Allen began making extensive improvements. He also added greatly to his landholdings during his lifetime, acquiring more than 24,000 acres in the counties of Isle of Wight, Nansemond, and Surry, including the area that became Brunswick County in 1720. He became one of the wealthiest planters south of the James River, and at the time of his death owned more than 200 slaves. The 1743 inventory of Allen's estate includes costly luxury items such as nearly four dozen silver spoons, many silver serving dishes, and twenty-eight wine glasses, indicating that he was not only wealthy, but living in splendid elegance.

Like his father and grandfather before him, Allen probably engaged in commerce in addition to planting and investing in land, and he may have sold merchandise from a warehouse at Upper Chippokes. Judging by the record-keeping he supervised as county clerk, Allen was probably a wise and careful businessman. He caused the young men who worked for him to prepare detailed and thorough indexes to the court orders and to the deed and will books, which were kept in excellent and businesslike order.

In October 1720 Allen married Elizabeth Bassett, daughter of Councillor William Bassett, of Eltham, New Kent County, one of the wealthiest planters north of the James River. The marriage probably made Allen even more prosperous. When William Byrd (1674–1744) visited the Allen household on 27 February 1728 on his way to survey the dividing line between Virginia and North Carolina, he described Allen's residence as an "elegant seat." Byrd's visit gives the only glimpse we have into John Allen's personality. He implied that Allen, "Capricorn," lived very well but that his hospitality was disappointingly frugal, though Allen could be congenial and was very talkative over the punch bowl. Byrd also suggested that Allen may have used his wife's ill health to decline his arduous and possibly dangerous appointment as one of the surveyors on the boundary commission. Allen did not shirk other responsibilities, though. He advised his younger brothers and sisters after their father's death, and in 1718 he made his youngest brother, Joseph Allen, deputy surveyor of Surry County. Allen also represented Surry County in the House of Burgesses from 1736 to 1740.

John Allen's children died young, and his wife died on 14 October 1738. Allen ordered from England an expensive and elaborate tomb for her that combines the arms of the Bassetts and the Allens. Allen also outlived his three brothers, and so his principal heir became Joseph Allen's son William Allen (1734–1793). In his will John Allen directed that William Allen be maintained at the College of William and Mary until he came of age. William Allen moved to Upper Chippokes Creek following his marriage in the mid-1750s and probably soon afterward employed some of the enormous wealth he had inherited from John Allen to begin construction of the stylish house that he later named Claremont. John Allen resigned his clerkship of Surry County in December 1741. He died between 5 March 1742, when he made his will, and 21 April 1742, when it was proved. Allen was undoubtedly buried near his wife in the family cemetery, but no stone marks his grave.

Eve S. Gregory, *Claremont Manor: A History* (1990), 33–44; Winfree, *Laws of Virginia*, 364–367; *Executive Journals of Council*, 4:149, 167; Louis B. Wright, ed., *The Prose Works of William Byrd of Westover: Narratives of a Colonial Virginian* (1966), 48–49, 172; because of imprecision in the records of the House of Burgesses, when John Allen, of Surry Co., and Edward Allen, of Accomack Co., were both eligible to attend, details of John Allen's service in the General Assembly cannot be accurately documented, but he was clearly identified by name as a member on 2 Sept. 1736 and on 8 and 16 Nov. 1738 (*Journals of House of Burgesses, 1727–1740*, 285, 329, 343); will, dated 5 Mar. 1741, but actually 1741/1742, and estate inventory in Surry Co. Deeds, Wills, Etc., 9:400–402, 434–442.

EVE S. GREGORY

ALLEN, John (ca. 1756–May 1793), member of the Convention of 1788, was the only recorded child of William Allen (1734–1793) and his first wife, Clara Walker Allen. He was probably born in the northwestern part of Surry County, where his father had inherited extensive land and personal property from his own uncle John Allen (ca. 1684–1742). Allen's mother died when he was a boy. His father married Mary Lightfoot on 9 November 1765, and they had eight children, four of whom died in infancy. As the eldest son of William Allen, of Claremont, John Allen grew up a privileged young man. His father was an extremely successful planter who held the usual succession of offices for a leading man in the county, serving as a vestryman of Southwark Parish, militia colonel, justice of the peace, and member for one term of the House of Burgesses. William Allen had been educated at the College of William and Mary, and his son may have been the John Allen who joined Phi Beta Kappa while attending that institution.

At a special election held in Surry County between 18 November and 12 December 1783, John Allen was elected to the House of Delegates to succeed James Kee. Allen won additional terms in 1784, 1786, and 1792. He received appointments to important committees but did not become one of the influential members of the House. In July 1786 he was commissioned a justice of the peace in Surry County, but there is no record that he ever served as a militia officer.

On 25 March 1788 Allen was elected one of the delegates from Surry County to the convention called to consider the proposed constitution of the United States. He attended the convention but did not speak, so far as the records show. He voted for ratification on 25 June 1788 and supported the federalist position again two days later by opposing a move to restrict the taxing power of Congress.

Allen never married but lived with his father at Claremont. He wrote his will in May 1783 and devised his entire estate to his father. John Allen died ten years later, sometime in May 1793, just before his father's death in July. At the time of John Allen's death his estate consisted of ten slaves and two hundred acres of land in Surry County that he had purchased from his father in April 1783, two thousand acres in James City County that he had purchased in 1784 and 1785, nine horses, and twenty-five more slaves. He was probably buried at or near Claremont. Two years after his death, his half brother and executor, William Allen (1768–1831), complied with his wishes by emancipating five of the thirty-five slaves. Disposition of the estate went into the courts and was not finally settled until October 1802.

Eve S. Gregory, *Claremont Manor: A History* (1990), 45–47, 124; father's will, Surry Co. Will Book, 1:49–52; financial information in Land and Personal Property Tax Returns, Surry and James City Cos., RG 48, LVA, and in

Surry, Sussex, and James City Co. Deed Books; approximate dates for unlocated will and for death are in *Harrison et al.* v. *Allen* (1802) (3 Call) *Virginia Reports*, 7:289–306; Kaminski, *Ratification*, 10:1540, 1557, 1565.

DAPHNE GENTRY

ALLEN, John (d. 13 May 1799), member of the Council, was probably a son of Jones Allen, of James City County, but no extant records verify any details of his family history. At least six other men named John Allen lived in Tidewater Virginia during the latter years of the eighteenth century, not counting John Allen, of Surry County (ca. 1756–1793), with whom the councillor has often been confused.

John Allen is first unambiguously mentioned in the land tax books for James City County in 1795 as proprietor of one hundred acres of land, formerly the property of Jones Allen. In the same year the county's personal property tax list identifies John Allen as an attorney. A court case begun in 1800 in neighboring Charles City County mentions a gambling debt that he owed to William F. Allen and identifies William O. Allen as his executor.

John Allen was elected to the House of Delegates from James City County in 1796 and was reelected in 1797 and 1798. On 14 December 1798 the assembly elected him to the Council of State to fill the vacancy created when Meriwether Jones resigned to become public printer. Allen waited until the adjournment of the assembly before taking his seat on the Council and was present in the House of Delegates on 21 December 1798 to vote for the Virginia Resolutions that James Madison wrote condemning the Alien and Sedition Acts. On 23 January 1799 Allen took the oath of office as a councillor, but he fell ill shortly thereafter, attended only four other meetings of the Council, between then and 2 February, and died in Richmond on 13 May 1799 following what a local printer called "a tedious indisposition with which Mr. Allen had been harrassed for several years."

Land Tax Returns, James City Co., 1795–1805, and Personal Property Tax Returns, James City Co., 1794–1798, RG 48, LVA; the debt suit is *William F. Allen* v. *William O. Allen, executor of John Allen*, Charles City Co. County and Superior Court Cases; election to Council and vote on Virginia Resolutions in *JHD*, 1798–1799 sess., 23, 32; obituary in *Richmond Virginia Argus*, 21 May 1799.

DAPHNE GENTRY

ALLEN, John Christopher (25 December 1876–26 December 1953), civic leader, was born in Charles City County, the eldest son and second of eight children of Graham Allen and Mary Brown Allen. His father was a literate farmer who owned his own house. Nothing is known about the extent of Allen's education. In 1899 he moved to Newport News, and on 24 December 1900 he married Mary A. Holmes in Charles City County. They had three daughters and two sons, and they adopted a boy as well.

Allen worked on the docks at Hampton Roads before being employed by the Newport News Shipbuilding and Dry Dock Company for nearly ten years. Later he worked as a stevedore for the Chesapeake and Ohio Railway Company. Allen was secretary of Local 846 of the International Longshoremen's Association, the preeminent labor organization in the area. He also became a director of the Crown Savings Bank, a deacon and treasurer of Zion Baptist Church, and a member of several fraternal organizations. But Allen was best remembered by the African American community in the Newport News area for serving for about thirty-five years on the board of directors of Whittaker Memorial Hospital, much of the time as chairman.

When Allen first arrived in Newport News, the infirmary of the city jail was the only place where blacks who could not afford health care could obtain medical services. In 1908 four black physicians rented a four-room flat for a hospital, but it closed soon thereafter due to a lack of funds. Four years later Dr. William Tecumseh Foreman established a two-room facility where blacks could receive medical treatment. An African American woman's club in Newport News led by Carrie J. Clarke Bolden soon conducted an intensive campaign to raise money for a new and better hospital. On 27 May 1914 a group of community leaders received a certificate of incorporation for Whittaker Memorial Hospital, named for deceased black physician Robert L. Whittaker. In March 1915 the hospital received a donation from George Benjamin West, the white president of a local bank, of two lots between Roanoke and Orcutt Streets on Twenty-ninth Street, where the new hospital was erected and opened to the public on 14 March 1917. The new facility was paid for without any help from the city of Newport News.

The medical complex also included a tuberculosis sanatorium and a training school for nurses. In 1943 the hospital moved to a new thirty-five-bed building at the intersection of Twenty-eighth Street and Orcutt Avenue. Its staff then consisted of seven physicians and thirty-two nurses. Guided by Allen's vision, the hospital continued to grow and provide improved services. By the time of his death the hospital had expanded to a modern fifty-three-bed facility. Twenty-five years later Whittaker Memorial Hospital moved to 5100 Marshall Avenue, and the name was changed to Newport News General Hospital.

John Christopher Allen died at his home in Newport News on 26 December 1953 and was buried in Holly Grove Cemetery in Hampton.

Charles City Co. Marriage Register; Charter Book, 85:15; Alexander Crosby Brown, *Newport News' 325 Years: A Record of the Progress of a Virginia Community* (1946), 229; service on hospital board characterized by chairman emeritus Bernard Howard, Newport News, 1996; obituaries in *Newport News Daily Press* and *Norfolk Virginian-Pilot*, both 28 Dec. 1953, and *Norfolk Journal and Guide*, 2 Jan. 1954.

EARL LEWIS

ALLEN, John F. (1814–23 August 1890), tobacco manufacturer, was born in Wexford, Ireland, the only son and second of four children of John Allen and Ann Allen. The family moved to Richmond in about 1819. Very little is known about Allen's childhood and education. From 1834 to 1841 he was a manager of John Allen and Company, his father's tobacco-trading firm that also manufactured tobacco boxes and other items.

Following the death of his father in 1841, Allen went to work as a supervisor of production for William Barret, who owned one of the largest chewing-tobacco factories in Richmond. According to the narrative that the escaped slave Henry "Box" Brown published in 1849, Allen surreptitiously took between a thousand and fifteen hundred dollars more out of Barret's factory each year than he earned in salary. Brown also described Allen as a "low, miserable, cruel, barbarous" overseer of Barret's factory slaves. Neither charge can be independently corroborated, but Brown's characterization of Allen formed the heart of a criticism of industrial slavery that was well publicized in the northern states.

Allen began investing in other businesses about 1853, and by the end of the decade he had become a successful independent tobacco manufacturer. In 1860 he employed forty workers and produced tobacco products worth about $40,000. The Civil War set him back but did not destroy his business. In 1870 his workforce consisted of eleven employees who processed smoking tobacco worth about $25,500. Allen's fortunes improved dramatically after Lewis Ginter, a Richmond entrepreneur and stockbroker, joined him in the renamed John F. Allen and Company. Allen managed the Richmond factory, and Ginter traveled to develop new markets. They were pioneers in the mass production of hand-rolled cigarettes during the years when cigarette smoking rapidly increased in popularity. From a total cigarette production of 3.1 million in 1875, the city's output grew to 65 million by 1881. John F. Allen and Company expanded rapidly and employed about 350 people by 1880, and the annual value of their factory's production rose to about $200,000. The company's tobacco brands won prizes at the fair the Virginia State Agricultural Society held in Richmond in 1873 and at the New South Wales Agricultural Society's exposition held in Sydney, Australia, in 1877, and its products also won a bronze medal at the centennial exposition in Philadelphia in 1876.

Allen retired around the end of 1880 and sold his share of the firm to Ginter for a sum that was variously reported at between $65,000 and $100,000. Ginter renamed the tobacco company Allen and Ginter. The decision to retain Allen's name reflected his importance to the development of the company and took advantage of his excellent reputation among Virginia and North Carolina tobacco dealers. During the next decade Allen and Ginter grew rapidly until it employed a thousand people, and its purchase in 1890 by the American Tobacco Company made Ginter a multimillionaire.

Allen spent his leisure time and his retirement years indulging his love of literature, music, and painting. He lined the walls of the house that he shared with his sisters with works of art, and he painted the scenery for an amateur production of *HMS Pinafore*. He was a founding member of the Mozart Society in 1876, served on its board of governors for several years, and seldom missed one of its concerts. At the time of his death Allen was reported to be worth about $120,000. John F. Allen died at his home in Richmond on 23 August 1890 and was buried in Shockoe Cemetery in Richmond.

Edward Alvey Jr., "John F. Allen and Lewis Ginter: Richmond Cigarette Pioneers," *Richmond Quarterly* 7 (1984): 38–41; Charles Stearns, ed., *Narrative of Henry Box Brown* (1849), 40–46; numerous references in Land Tax Returns, Richmond City, RG 48, LVA, and Census, Industrial Schedule, Richmond City; Benjamin W. Arnold Jr., *History of the Tobacco Industry in Virginia from 1860 to 1894* (1897), 36; John F. Allen & Co., *What Do We Smoke* [ca. 1878], 28, lists awards; estimates of estate in *Richmond Daily Dispatch* and *Richmond Times*, both 9 Oct. 1890; obituaries in *Richmond State*, 23 Aug. 1890, in *Richmond Daily Dispatch* and *Richmond Times*, both 24 Aug. 1890, and in weekly trade journal, *Tobacco*, 29 Aug. 1890 (por.), which gives year of birth.

EMILY J. SALMON

ALLEN, John James (26 September 1797–18 September 1871), member of the House of Representatives and Virginia Supreme Court of Appeals judge, was the youngest of four sons and fourth of five children of James Allen and Jane Steele Allen. He was born in Woodstock, where his father was practicing law. Robert Allen, the only other son to survive early childhood, served in the House of Representatives.

Allen entered Dickinson College in Carlisle, Pennsylvania, in 1811 and Washington College in Lexington in 1814 but graduated from neither. He then began studying law under his father, who had taken up residence at Beaverdam, his estate in Botetourt County. Allen was admitted to the bar in 1818, and in 1819 he moved to Clarksburg and practiced law there for seventeen years. On 11 November 1824 he married Mary Elizabeth Payne Jackson, daughter of John George Jackson, a United States District Court judge and former congressman. They had two girls and seven boys, one of whom, Henry Clay Allen, became Speaker of the House of Delegates.

Allen represented the large district composed of the counties of Cabell, Harrison, Kanawha, Lewis, Logan, Mason, Randolph, and Wood in the Senate of Virginia from 1828 to 1830. In April 1833 he ran for Congress with the support of the new Whig Party and defeated Lewis Maxwell, the incumbent Democrat, in the Twentieth Congressional District. Allen lost his bid for reelection to Democrat Joseph Johnson by a very narrow margin in 1835. While he was a member of Congress, Allen also served as commonwealth's attorney for Harrison, Lewis, and Preston Counties.

On 26 July 1836 the governor and Council gave Allen an interim appointment as judge of the circuit court over which his father had once presided. The General Assembly subsequently elected him to a full term as judge, and he moved to his father's Beaverdam estate in Botetourt County. Allen's reputation at the bar and his brief career in politics almost led him into the U.S. Senate. In January 1840 the General Assembly took five ballots attempting to elect a senator but ended deadlocked. On the fourth and fifth ballots, Allen received eighty votes and Democrat John Y. Mason eighty-one, with four votes for other candidates. Later in the year the assembly settled on William Cabell Rives.

On 12 December 1840 the General Assembly selected Allen over John F. May to fill a vacancy on the Virginia Court of Appeals. By nature a quiet, reserved man of dignified bearing, Allen was better suited to serving on the bench than engaging in elective politics, and he became a highly respected judge, though not a brilliant or innovative jurist. Because the senior judges, Francis T. Brooke and William H. Cabell, were quite old and wrote only a few opinions, Allen and the other younger justices had to take on a large workload. The Constitution of 1851 transferred to the court all of the criminal appellate jurisdiction that the discontinued General Court had exercised, renamed the court the Supreme Court of Appeals, and required the judges to be elected by the voters. In 1852 Allen was elected to a twelve-year term. He served as president of the court from the spring of 1853 until 8 February 1865, the last meeting of the court under the authority of the

Constitution of 1851. During the 1850s the workload of the judges was more evenly distributed than it had been during the 1840s, but as Allen aged, his share of the written opinions declined. Throughout his tenure the other judges relied heavily on Allen's expertise in the common law and in appeals from chancery proceedings. He seldom indulged in conspicuous displays of legal erudition, nor did he often file separate dissenting opinions. Few of the cases that Allen heard attracted significant public attention or involved issues that aroused political controversy.

Allen's possession of twenty-two slaves and real estate worth almost $52,000 in 1850 made him one of the wealthiest men in Botetourt County. He had admired Henry Clay, whose compromises preserved the Union during several sectional crises, but Allen took strong prosouthern positions on national political issues during the 1850s. On 10 December 1860, after the election of Abraham Lincoln but before the secession of South Carolina, Allen addressed a mass meeting in Botetourt County and presented resolutions advocating the secession of Virginia. He called for a state convention that could act independently or in conjunction with other southern states. The meeting adopted Allen's resolutions almost unanimously.

After voting for secession, the Convention of 1861 created a three-member advisory council on 20 April 1861 to assist the governor in preparing the state for war. Governor John Letcher appointed Francis Henney Smith, the superintendent of the Virginia Military Institute; Matthew Fontaine Maury, the renowned naval officer; and Allen, who became president of what became known as the Council of Three until it was enlarged to include former congressman Thomas S. Haymond and Lieutenant Governor Robert L. Montague. As its most important responsibility the council advised the governor on the appointment of military officers to defend the commonwealth. Its first recommendation on 21 April 1861 was that Robert E. Lee be named commander of the military and naval forces of Virginia. After two months of intense activity the council disbanded on 19 June 1861, and Allen resumed his less hectic duties on the Supreme Court of Appeals.

John James Allen lived in quiet retirement after the war and died at his home in Botetourt County on 18 September 1871. He was buried in nearby Lauderdale Cemetery.

Birth date and other family information in Allen family Bible, photocopy in Allen Family Papers, LVA; biographies by Seargent S. P. Patteson in *Green Bag* 5 (1893): 363–364, by Dorothy Davis in *History of Harrison County, West Virginia*, ed. Elizabeth Sloan (1970), 159–160, and in Stoner, *Seed-Bed*, 265–266, 401–402; *Richmond Daily Enquirer*, 17 Dec. 1860; James I. Robertson Jr., ed., *Proceedings of the Advisory Council of the State of Virginia, April 21–June 19, 1861* (1977); Hummel and Smith, *Portraits and Statuary*, 1 (por.); obituaries in *Richmond Whig*, 22 Sept. 1871, and *Richmond Dispatch*, 25 Sept. 1871.

F. N. BONEY

ALLEN, Joseph (ca.1836–after 1905), Richmond City Council member, was born in Richmond, the son of Lewis Allen and Emily Allen, but whether he was freeborn or later manumitted is not known. His father, a bricklayer, was free and living on Fifteenth Street between Marshall and Clay Streets in 1852. Eight years later Joseph Allen lived in the same general area, a racially mixed neighborhood in the valley of Shockoe Creek. Literate and single, he resided with Effy Allen, a seventy-year-old black washerwoman who headed the household and was probably his grandmother. Other family members included Emily Allen, age thirty, Harriet Allen, age nineteen, Mary F. Allen, age sixteen, and Ida V. Allen, an infant of two. All natives of Virginia, they shared a house with another family. Joseph Allen plied his father's craft, joining many other Richmond free blacks who worked in the building trades.

Joseph Allen married Rebecca Gardner on 4 March 1869. She was born into a Richmond family that had been free before the Civil War. Their son and daughter both died young. The Allens moved westward and upward to a house at Ninth and Marshall Streets. Near the Virginia State Capitol and city offices, he worked in nearly all the construction trades, with sources variously describing him as a plasterer, carpenter, bricklayer, and whitewasher. In the early 1880s he became a grocer, operating a store at

206 North Fourth Street. The family also moved to 1006 North Sixth Street, in the second precinct of Jackson Ward, Allen's residence for the rest of his life.

Allen was one of thirty-three black Republicans that Jackson Ward's predominantly African American electorate sent to the Richmond City Council between 1871 and 1898. The famous political district was created by conservative whites in 1871 through a classic gerrymandering of black neighborhoods in order to concentrate them in one ward, nullifying their political strength in five others, thus reducing the overall impact of their votes in city elections. One of the more obscure of these political newcomers, Allen served only one term on the common council, 1882–1884. He was appointed to the moderately important committee on lunatics, where he worked to improve conditions in the segregated black asylum, and to the second market committee, which was less prestigious but still significant to Allen in that many of his own constituents were hucksters. He either did not seek reelection or failed to win renomination by ward Republicans.

Allen was again working as a plasterer by the late 1880s and owned the house on Sixth Street free of mortgage. Rebecca Allen contributed to the family's income by taking in laundry. Joseph Allen last appeared in city directories in 1905. He probably died not long thereafter, but he left no will, and the passing of one of the city's pioneer black councilmen apparently went unnoticed by the Richmond press.

Birth year between 1835 and 1837 inferred from ages given on Richmond City Marriage Register and Census, Richmond City, 1860, 1870, 1880; Census, Richmond City, 1900, gives variant birth date of Nov. 1845; professions and addresses from census and Richmond city directories, 1852, 1869–1905; wife's account information in Freedmen's Bank Records, Richmond branch, account 4544; children documented in Richmond City Birth Register, 16 May 1869, 25 Aug. 1875, and Richmond City Death Register, 24 Nov. 1873; Richmond Common Council Records, 1882–1884; Michael B. Chesson, "Richmond's Black Councilmen, 1871–1896," in *Southern Black Leaders of the Reconstruction Era*, ed. Howard N. Rabinowitz (1982), 201.

MICHAEL B. CHESSON

ALLEN, Madison Crencha (24 June 1890–31 March 1968), president of Virginia Theological Seminary and College, was born in Buckingham County, the second of five sons and third of nine children of Cary Allen and Cornelia Winston Allen. He grew up on a farm that his father, a former slave, had purchased from his former owner. At an early age, Allen recognized the importance of education to rural African Americans, and he made the most of the limited opportunities available to him. From 1908 to 1910 he worked his way through the Boydton Academic and Bible Institute, a school founded in 1871 to educate freedpeople. In 1910 he began studying for the Baptist ministry at Virginia Theological Seminary and College in Lynchburg.

Allen's ministerial career started in 1913 with service as pastor of Mount Ararat Baptist Church in Middlebrook and Cedar Grove Baptist Church, both in Augusta County. He was ordained at the latter church on 14 July 1914. In 1916 he earned a B.A. from the seminary, became minister of Shiloh Baptist Church near Danville, and was elected moderator of the Smith River Baptist Association. Two years later he received the seminary's B.D.

While at Shiloh Baptist Church, Allen inspired his congregation to build the County Training School, a combined grammar and high school that became the first accredited black school in Pittsylvania County. Allen served as its principal for six years. He helped establish Green Valley School in Halifax County and was its principal for two years. He also conducted a four-week summer teacher-training institute in 1921. Although he devoted much of his time to the improvement of educational facilities in the Danville area, Allen also was instrumental in obtaining better streets, lights, and water service for the black community from the city.

During World War I, Allen served as a United States Army chaplain, and afterward he continued his education by taking summer courses at the University of Chicago, Virginia Normal and Industrial Institute (now Virginia State University), and Hampton Institute. He married Wilhelmina Leona Yarborough Cunningham on 23 April 1919. They had one daughter and two sons.

In February 1925 Allen became minister of Cool Spring Baptist Church, which he renamed First Baptist Church, in Franklin. During his ten years there Allen struggled constantly to improve Southampton County's segregated schools. The county school board spent most of its revenue on the schools for white children. After the board refused to provide buses to transport black pupils to their schools, Allen organized the effort by which parents purchased and operated their own buses. He became a member of the board of directors of the Hayden High School in Franklin and despite strenuous opposition he helped make it a part of the public school system, became its principal in 1930, and enabled it to become accredited in 1934. He taught at the Franklin Normal School when it opened in 1930, and in 1928 he founded a monthly journal, the *Expected*, to promote self-help efforts and educate African Americans about black history. He edited the journal for almost forty years.

In 1935 Allen moved to Knoxville, Tennessee, where he served as pastor of Rogers Memorial Baptist Church. The following year he moved to Baltimore to become pastor of Leadenhall Baptist Church. While there he also taught classes in theology. In 1938 he received an honorary D.D. from Virginia Theological Seminary and College. He also served on its board, and early in the 1940s he took a fifteen-month leave of absence from his pulpit to conduct a fund-raising drive to keep the seminary solvent.

In 1946 Allen was named president of Virginia Theological Seminary and College, which was renamed Virginia Seminary and College in 1963. During his successful twenty-year administration, he improved the curriculum, the faculty, and the campus. The school won accreditation in 1950, and he organized the annual Hayes Day celebration, named for Gregory W. Hayes, a former seminary president, to raise money for its endowment. Allen's principal accomplishment was keeping the small black seminary alive during difficult times. An active member of the Virginia Baptist State Convention, the parent organization of the seminary, he served as the convention's corresponding secretary for ten years, superintendent of education for three years, chairman of the finance committee for eight years, and campaign director for six years.

Allen was also an auditor of the National Baptist Convention for thirty years. Before and after his service as president of the seminary, Allen published several sermons and articles and also edited the *National Baptist Union Review*, a weekly newspaper. He served on the curriculum committee for the Virginia State Board of Education and from 1959 to 1967 was a member of the Interracial Council of the city of Lynchburg.

Madison Crencha Allen retired in 1966 and died in a hospital in Baltimore, Maryland, on 31 March 1968. A funeral ceremony was conducted in the chapel of Virginia Seminary and College, and he was buried in Buckingham County.

Biographies in *NCAB*, 55:7–8 (por.), *Richmond Planet*, 9 Sept. 1916, *Norfolk Journal and Guide*, 4 Nov. 1950, and Charles W. White, *The Hidden and Forgotten: Buckingham County* (1985), 243–245, 287; author's interview with Allen, 12 May 1964; G. James Fleming and Christian E. Burckel, *Who's Who in Colored America*, 7th ed. (1950), 6–7; *The 96th Anniversary, First Baptist Church . . . Franklin, Virginia* (1962), 20–21; *Norfolk Journal and Guide*, 29 Dec. 1934; obituaries in *Baltimore Sun*, 1 Apr. 1968, *Lynchburg Advance* and *Lynchburg News*, both 3 Apr. 1968, and *Norfolk Journal and Guide* and *Richmond Afro-American*, both 6 Apr. 1968.

RALPH REAVIS

ALLEN, Mary Magdalene Rice Hayes. See **HAYES, Mary Magdalene Rice**.

ALLEN, Oscar James (4 March 1889–1 July 1942), Baptist minister, was born in Gastonia, North Carolina, the only known son and youngest of four known children of Victor Allen, a stonemason, and Ellen White Allen. He also had one younger brother or half brother. His father died when Allen was young. Early in life he decided on a career in the ministry and began preaching when he was only sixteen years old. He was ordained a year later, in 1906. Later that year he became pastor of the Washington Baptist Church in Waco, Cleveland County, North Carolina, and began his formal religious education as a student at nearby Biddle University, from which he received an A.B. in 1910. On 9 June 1909 he married Ella Mae Christian. They had two daughters and one son.

Allen received a call in 1911 from the Shiloh Baptist Church in Shelby, North Carolina. In

March 1914 he moved to the First Baptist Church of Statesville, North Carolina, where he remained for ten years. Allen became widely known both as an evangelical minister and for the quality of his voice. He often sang while preaching and led the congregation in song during the service. He also worked as an educator early in his career. He served as principal of a public school in Waco for two years and as principal of the Belmont Rosenwald School at Statesville. In 1923 he received an honorary D.D. from Friendship College in Rock Hill, South Carolina. That same year he became a member of the influential Baptist World Alliance and made the first of four evangelical and educational trips abroad. During the 1920s and 1930s he preached in Germany, Bermuda, and the Bahamas, toured the Holy Land, and led revivals in Canada.

On 24 May 1924 Allen was installed as pastor of First Calvary Baptist Church in Norfolk. By then he was recognized as one of the most scholarly and progressive ministers in the Baptist Church and held in high esteem throughout the country. During Allen's eighteen-year pastorate in Norfolk, 1,500 people joined the church, and they generously supported him and his new programs. A popular minister, his inspired preaching and singing filled the church day and night, and First Calvary became known as "Holy Ghost Headquarters." Allen became one of the most successful revivalists in the country. In addition to overseas trips and evangelical work in Canada, he visited forty-five states and was credited with converting more than 38,000 people.

Allen served as president of the Baptist General Association of Virginia from 1937 until shortly before his death. He remained active in the Baptist World Alliance, became corresponding secretary of the Evangelical Board of the National Baptist Convention, and was elected president of the Hampton Ministers Conference of Hampton Institute. Two volumes of his writings, *Allen's Sensational Sermons* (1938) and *Allen's Inspirational Sermons* (1940), were published. He also took part in civic activities and encouraged his parishioners to do likewise. He worked on behalf of Community Chest Fund campaigns, served as a trustee of Norfolk Community Hospital and of the Independent Order of Saint Luke, and became a Mason. Of special concern to Allen were the young people of Norfolk. About one hundred boys regularly attended youth services at which he preached sermons prepared especially for them. Allen tried to impress young minds with the true spirit of religion by precept and by his own example. He supported the Norfolk unit of Virginia Union University before it became the independent Norfolk State University, and he financed the studies of twelve students at the college.

Oscar James Allen suffered a stroke in the spring of 1942 and died in Norfolk Community Hospital on 1 July 1942. Many of the leading black Baptist ministers in eastern Virginia attended or took part in his funeral service. He was buried in Calvary Cemetery in Norfolk.

Arthur B. Caldwell, ed., *History of the American Negro*, vol. 4: *North Carolina Edition* (1921), 104–107 (por.); family information verified by granddaughter Ruth Allen Hardy; *First Calvary Baptist Church, Norfolk, Virginia, 1880–1980* (1980), 13; *Norfolk Journal and Guide*, 23 Feb., 24 May 1924; obituary and account of funeral in *Norfolk Journal and Guide*, 4, 11 July 1942 (por.).

TOMMY L. BOGGER

ALLEN, Otway Slaughter (8 April 1851–17 February 1911), real estate developer and member of the Convention of 1901–1902, was born in Richmond, the youngest of three daughters and two sons of William C. Allen and Allaville Slaughter Allen. His father had begun his career as an apprentice bricklayer, but during the accelerated growth of Richmond in the 1830s and 1840s he became one of the city's most prosperous building contractors and developers. Before retiring from business in the 1850s William Allen had amassed many lots, including the fifty-eight-acre site that later became known as the Allen Addition, from which Monument Avenue developed. His landholdings, valued at $275,000 in 1860, constituted much of the substantial inheritance he left his children.

Otway Allen graduated from Virginia Military Institute in 1873 and returned to Richmond. His brother had not survived childhood, and after his father died in 1874 Allen devoted much of his attention to a model farm in the Allen Addition. In 1881 he joined with Charles G. Shafer to form Allen and Shafer Commission Merchants. That partnership was evidently amicably dissolved in 1888, and Allen continued thereafter as a successful investor who was described as a "capitalist" in city directories. He served as president of the Richmond Standard Spike and Iron Company in 1895 and 1896 but retired from business about 1900. Allen also belonged to Saint Paul's Episcopal Church, the Commonwealth Club, the Westmoreland Club, the Deep Run Hunt Club, the Richmond Boat Club, the Richmond German Club, and the Richmond Chamber of Commerce. He served as captain of the Stuart Horse Guards, a Richmond militia company, from 25 February 1885 to 15 April 1886 and major of the 1st Cavalry Battalion until November 1888.

On 1 February 1888 Allen married Mary McDonald, the daughter of James McDonald, the adjutant general of Virginia. They had no children and lived in the fashionable house Allen's father had built at 17 North Sixth Street. In an 1886 newspaper article, Allen became the first to suggest that a boulevard modeled on Baltimore's Mount Vernon Place be developed as the setting for an equestrian monument to Robert E. Lee, using the Allen Addition lot as a starting point. A year later he and his sisters donated to the city the land on which the Lee statue was unveiled in May 1890 at what is now in the intersection of Monument and Allen Avenues. His family's contribution of land for the Lee statue helped Allen cement his ties to the city and become a suburban developer. Entering local politics early in the 1890s, Allen was elected an alderman from Madison Ward in 1892 and held the office until 1904 and again in 1906, sitting on the important committees of finance and streets and serving as chairman of the latter.

After Virginius Newton resigned midway through the Convention of 1901–1902, Allen concluded a lackluster campaign to succeed him by easily defeating fellow Democrat A. Sidney Lanier on 3 December 1901. Allen was sworn in two days later and was appointed to the Committees on the Organization and Government of Cities and Towns, on Agricultural, Manufacturing, and Industrial Interests, and on Immigration. He did not participate in debates so far as the convention records show, and his committee work is not documented. On 4 April 1902 he voted with the majority in favor of restrictive voter registration requirements designed to reduce the number of black voters, and on 29 May he again sided with the majority against submitting the constitution to the electorate.

Otway Slaughter Allen died from complications of Bright's disease on 17 February 1911 and was buried in Hollywood Cemetery.

Birth date in Jacob N. Brenaman, *A History of Virginia Conventions* (1902), 96, and confirmed in Hollywood Cemetery interment records, although it is given as Apr. 1852 in Census, Richmond City, 1900; the assertion by Brenaman that Allen served as a private in the Confederate army has not been confirmed; Richmond city directories, 1879–1911; wills of father, mother, and Allen, Richmond City Chancery Court Will Book, 1:419–421, 3:325–326, 11:457–460; father's obituary in *Richmond Daily Dispatch*, 8 Sept. 1874; "Report before Tuckahoe Farmer's Club on Otway S. Allen's Farm," *Southern Planter* 44 (1883): 273–276; BVS Marriage Register, Richmond City; *Richmond Elite Directory* (1893), 25, 229, 235, 249; Kathy Edwards, Esme Howard, and Toni Prawl, *Monument Avenue: History and Architecture* (1992), 12–17, 28–33, 57–61, 147; Drew St. J. Carneal, *Richmond's Fan District* (1996), 41–43, 80–81, 125; *Richmond Dispatch*, 28 Mar. 1886, 1 Dec. 1901 (por.); *Journal of 1901–1902 Convention*, 260, 264, 486, 487, 501–504; *Convention of 1901–1902 Photographs* (por.); obituaries and descriptions of funeral in *Richmond News Leader* and *Richmond Times-Dispatch*, both 18, 20 Feb. 1911.

BRENT TARTER

ALLEN, Robert (30 July 1794–30 December 1859), member of the House of Representatives, was the third of four sons and third of five children of James Allen and Jane Steele Allen. He was born in Woodstock, where his father practiced law before becoming a judge of the General Court. Both of his elder brothers died in early childhood, and his younger brother, John James Allen, served in the House of Representatives and on the Virginia Supreme Court of Appeals.

Allen was educated in a small academy in Shenandoah County and enrolled in 1811 in Dickinson College in Carlisle, Pennsylvania, for one year. During the War of 1812 he served in the field for three months when the volunteer artillery company of Woodstock was ordered to Norfolk. Allen attended Washington College in Lexington during the 1814–1815 school year and then studied law under the tutelage of his father, who had moved to Botetourt County. Allen married Frances K. Harvey, of Botetourt County, on 17 October 1822. They had five daughters and five sons. Two of the sons, James Walkinshaw Allen and Robert Clotworthy Allen, died while serving as officers in the Confederate army.

Allen was admitted to the bar in January 1817 and opened a law office in Woodstock. He soon began taking part in local politics and became commonwealth's attorney of Shenandoah County. Late in December 1821 he was elected to a vacant seat in the Senate of Virginia for the district of Rockingham and Shenandoah Counties. He served the remainder of the term, through the session in the winter of 1825–1826. He did not run for reelection, but in the spring of 1827, at the urging of his friends, he became a Democratic-Republican candidate for Congress. He was elected to three consecutive terms, serving until 1833, when he declined to stand for reelection. Allen appears to have been a passive congressman, never serving on a committee or uttering a word in debate. He later cited illness and a desire not to be separated from his family as his reasons for not seeking a fourth term in Congress.

From 1833 until his death Allen was a gentleman planter and attorney. He lived on his Shenandoah County farm until 1839, when he sold it and bought a large farm in Bedford County, five miles north of Liberty, near the base of the Peaks of Otter. His new estate, known as Mount Prospect, consisted of 1,580 acres, of which more than half was in cultivation, and was valued for tax purposes in 1850 at $21,640. Allen also owned thirty-two slaves in 1850. He practiced diversified commercial farming and unlike many of his neighbors grew no tobacco. His main crops consisted of peas, beans, potatoes, and small grains, and he kept a few cattle, two yoke of oxen, a herd of swine, and after 1848 a large flock of sheep. Allen was one of an increasing number of Bedford landowners who raised sheep for their wool, and his annual production of wool was approximately one thousand pounds. At the time of his death his estate, which included household finery, silverware, and musical instruments, was appraised at more than $32,500. Robert Allen died at his home in Bedford County on 30 December 1859 and was buried in Longwood Cemetery in the town of Liberty.

Autobiographical letter to Charles Lanman, 19 May 1858, Lanman Papers, VHS; Botetourt Co. Marriage Register; will and estate inventory in Bedford Co. Will Book, 17:398–400, 18:27–32; death notice in *Lynchburg Daily Virginian*, 3 Jan. 1860.

W. Harrison Daniel

ALLEN, Robert Clotworthy (22 June 1834–3 July 1863), Confederate army officer, was born in Shenandoah County, the second of five sons and fifth of ten children of Robert Allen and Frances K. Harvey Allen. He was named in honor of his Irish ancestor Hugh Clotworthy. In 1839 the Allen family moved to Bedford County, where Allen received his early education. He then entered the Virginia Military Institute and graduated in 1855. After studying law he formed a partnership with William Watts, of Roanoke County. In 1857 Allen moved to the town of Salem and on 6 February 1861 married Mary E. Wingfield.

In April 1861 Allen was elected captain of a volunteer company, the Roanoke Grays, which was reorganized a month later into the 28th Regiment Virginia Infantry and ordered to Manassas Junction, where he was commissioned a major on 1 July 1861. Allen gained a reputation as an exacting drill officer, and his regiment performed well at the First Battle of Manassas (Bull Run) on 21 July 1861. On 28 February 1862 Allen's regiment, part of the 5th Brigade, was assigned to Major General James Longstreet's division and subsequently ordered to defensive positions at Yorktown. During the Peninsula campaign between March and July 1862, Allen was captured but escaped, and on 2 April he was promoted to colonel. Allen's brigade suffered heavy losses at the Battle of Seven Pines on 1 June 1862. A few weeks later at Gaines's Mill during the Seven Days' Battles, Allen was disabled by a shell fragment, and elsewhere on the field his elder brother, Colonel James Walkinshaw Allen, was killed.

Allen was wounded again at the Second Battle of Manassas (29–30 August 1862). He missed the campaign in Maryland that September but rejoined the army on its return from Sharpsburg (Antietam). After a foray into North Carolina for supplies, the 28th Virginia reunited with the Army of Northern Virginia in the spring of 1863 in time for the second invasion of the North. Allen's men were held in reserve until the third day of the Battle of Gettysburg. Before dawn on 3 July 1863 his regiment joined General George E. Pickett's division southwest of town. In the afternoon, following a tremendous artillery bombardment, the brigade advanced on the center of the Union lines. Allen led the 28th Virginia across the Emmitsburg Road and charged the Union positions on Cemetery Ridge. He stopped to retrieve the regimental battle flag from a fallen color-bearer and passed it on to a lieutenant. Moments later Robert Clotworthy Allen was shot in the head and died instantly. His body was buried in an unmarked grave on the Gettysburg battlefield.

Charles D. Walker, *Biographical Sketches of the Graduates and Elèves of the Virginia Military Institute Who Fell During the War Between the States* (1875), 26–29; BVS Marriage Register, Bedford Co.; Compiled Service Records; Frank E. Fields Jr., *28th Virginia Infantry* (1985); Kathleen R. Georg and John W. Busey, *Nothing But Glory: Pickett's Division at Gettysburg* (1987); death described in E. P. Allen to Judge Camden, 12 Sept. 1863, Dabney-Jackson Papers, LVA.

DONALD W. GUNTER

ALLEN, Robert McClanahan (31 August 1889–6 November 1931), architect, was born in Roanoke, the only child of Frank W. Allen and Sara McClanahan Allen. He was educated in the Roanoke public schools and at the University of Virginia, from which he received a B.S. degree in 1912. Allen then studied architecture as a special student at the Massachusetts Institute of Technology from September 1912 to May 1916. He returned to Roanoke and began his career in the office of architect Homer M. Miller.

Allen attempted to join the army when the United States entered World War I in April 1917, but he was rejected because of a heart problem. He sailed for France the following month to serve in the ambulance corps of the American Field Service. His heart condition was serious, however, and he was discharged. Allen then joined the French Foreign Legion, attended its officers' training school, and was commissioned a sous-lieutenant. He saw action with the 40th Battery Field Artillery and received the Croix de Guerre.

After the war Allen returned to Roanoke and on 16 December 1920 married Augusta Christian Glass, of Lynchburg, daughter of United States Senator Carter Glass. They had one son and one daughter, both of whom died in childhood. Allen was suffering from tuberculosis, which he probably contracted while in France, but he resumed his career as an architect. An attractive and popular young man, he quickly earned the professional respect of experienced architects and later acted as a mentor to some younger ones. Early in his career, when he was an assistant in the firm of Smithey and Tardy in 1923, Allen worked on the plans for the Roanoke Country Club. On his own, he also designed a number of private residences in a variety of revival styles. The most notable include a French Provincial house for Junius P. Fishburn in 1924, a Georgian Revival house in 1925 for John B. Newton that later became known as Neuhoff House, and a Tudor Revival house for John W. Waynick in 1930.

Allen's most significant and recognized designs were for two important commercial buildings. In 1929 he designed a new downtown Roanoke headquarters for Jefferson Electric Company. The building is vaguely reminiscent of the Spanish Colonial Revival style, but it combines elements from other styles in a successful eclectic design. A large arch on the front recalls Norman-Moorish forms, and it has a bronze facade and massive bronze hanging lamps. In front of the second-floor window, a bronze three-masted sailing ship floats in a sea of bronze. The other design was for a new facility for the two Lynchburg newspapers, the *News* and the *Daily Advance*. Completed after his death, in 1931, the Art Deco building featured a monumental semiclassical motif and received an award from the Virginia chapter of the American Institute of Architects.

Allen's promising architectural career was cut short when he was forty-two years old. His tuberculosis grew worse, and even removal of one of his lungs failed to cure the disease. Robert McClanahan Allen died on 6 November 1931 at the Glass family's summer house, Montview Farms, near Lynchburg. He was buried in Fairview Cemetery in Roanoke.

Norma Lugar, "The Tragic Genius of Robert Allen," *Roanoker* 5 (Jan.–Feb. 1978): 30–33, 60–63 (por.); marriage reported in *Lynchburg News*, 16 Dec. 1920; information furnished by Evelyn Fishburn James, Lynchburg; Raymond P. Barnes, *History of Roanoke* (1968), 722; Wells and Dalton, *Virginia Architects*, 4; S. Allen Chambers, *Lynchburg: An Architectural History* (1981), 465; William L. Whitwell and Lee W. Winborne, *The Architectural Heritage of the Roanoke Valley* (1982), 146; descriptions of newspaper building in *Lynchburg News*, 2 Jan. 1932, and of Jefferson Electric Building in *Roanoke Times and World News*, 19 Mar. 1982; obituaries in *Roanoke Times* and *Lynchburg News*, both 7 Nov. 1931.

WILLIAM L. WHITWELL
LEE W. WINBORNE

ALLEN, William (7 March 1768–29 November 1831), planter and businessman, was the elder of two sons and second of eight children of William Allen (1734–1793) and his second wife, Mary Lightfoot Allen. He was born at his father's plantation on Upper Chippokes Creek in Surry County. Although his father had been educated at the College of William and Mary and his only half brother, John Allen (ca. 1756–1793), may have studied there too, William Allen undoubtedly studied under private tutors but probably did not attend college. He achieved his later success in life through good fortune and good business judgment. The author of an obituary wrote that Allen was "gifted with a very shrewd mind and possessed a vast deal of strong common sense, though he was little indebted to books."

The deaths of his mother in January 1789 and his father and half brother in 1793 made Allen the head of the family and heir to Claremont plantation and the bulk of the vast wealth of the Surry County Allens when he was twenty-five years old. Allen acquitted himself extremely well in the management of his inheritance. He lived luxuriously and added to his estate in 1808 the large and valuable Wakefield plantation adjacent to Claremont. He also joined the other wealthy local landowners in breeding and racing prime horses and in keeping a fine table and liquor cabinet. He was a justice of the peace for most of his adult life and served in a number of other local capacities. In addition, he served in the House of Delegates from 1802 to 1810. Allen was a lieutenant colonel in the militia by 1809 and commanded the county regiment when it took the field during the British invasions of 1813 and 1814.

Following in the footsteps of his ancestors, Allen devoted his talents to the acquisition of wealth. Adding to what he had inherited, he purchased other plantations and by 1831 owned more than 26,000 acres and more than 700 slaves. He invested wisely in saw- and gristmills and in a number of other business ventures, among them a spinning and weaving factory in Southampton County, a freight-hauling schooner, the *Claremont*, that plied the James River, and a drawbridge company in Norfolk. He also owned valuable shares in the Farmer's Bank of Virginia in Richmond and in the Petersburg Railroad Company. Allen became, next to James Bruce, of Charlotte County, one of the wealthiest men in Virginia during the first third of the nineteenth century.

Allen never married and left the largest portion of his estate, which was valued at more than $360,000, to William Griffin Orgain, the young grandson of his sister Ann Armistead Allen Edloe, with the stipulation that he take the surname of Allen. William Allen died at the Union Hotel in Richmond on 29 November 1831, several days after suffering what was probably a heart attack. He was buried in a vault at the family cemetery at Claremont.

Eve S. Gregory, *Claremont Manor: A History* (1990), 51–58, 124–126, 129–130, includes a transcription of family Bible (in possession of Mrs. Walter Hughes, Albuquerque, N.M., 1990) showing birth date; additional information about inheritance in *Harrison et al.* v. *Allen* (1802) (3 Call) *Virginia Reports*, 7:289–306; will and estate inventory in Surry Co. Will Book, 6:218–223, 341–368; obituaries in *American Beacon and Norfolk and Portsmouth Daily Advertiser*, 1 Dec. 1831, and *Richmond Enquirer*, 2 Dec. 1831.

EVE S. GREGORY

ALLEN, William (29 July 1828–19 May 1875), entrepreneur, was born in Petersburg as William Griffin Organ, the younger of two sons and third of four children of Richard Griffin Organ, a businessman, and Martha Armistead Edloe Organ. His brother died in infancy, and when he was three years old his mother's uncle, the wealthy bachelor, William Allen, of Claremont in Surry County, died and left the bulk of his very large estate to William Griffin Organ, on the condition that the boy take the name William Allen. The General Assembly passed a bill in 1832 to change the name of William Griffin Organ to William Allen.

The estate was appraised in 1832 at more than $360,000 and included Claremont, Kingsmill in James City County, and Curles Neck in Henrico County, plus properties in Brunswick and Southampton Counties. Allen's father served as his guardian and administered the estate until he died in 1837, after which his mother served as Allen's guardian. From the revenue that the estate earned, she increased his holdings with the purchase of additional land. He was educated by tutors at Claremont and attended Amelia Academy from 1844 until June 1847. In the summer of 1847 he accompanied an Episcopal clergyman, Philip Slaughter, on a tour of the northern and eastern states, and the following year they toured Europe together. On 1 January 1850 Allen received his estate, which then consisted of nearly 23,000 acres in five counties and more than $52,000 in cash. He married Frances Augusta Jessup at her Brockville, Canada, home on 22 December 1852. They had three daughters and three sons.

With his inheritance and successful business ventures, Allen was generally regarded as one of the wealthiest men in Virginia. He raised livestock and produced a wide variety of crops on his several plantations. Contemporaries estimated that he owned as many as eight hundred or a thousand slaves, but tax and census records indicate that the number varied between three hundred and five hundred. In 1854 Allen formed a partnership with John A. Selden and Augustus Hopkins. Allen supplied the capital and bought the land, and Selden and Hopkins built a railroad, established a sawmill, and sold timber from a wharf they constructed near Claremont. After the partnership was dissolved by mutual consent in 1857, Allen gained sole ownership of all the property. In 1858 he contracted to deliver wood to the wharf by railroad car and sell it to William A. Allen, of Baltimore, an agreement that lasted until 1860, when Allen foreclosed on the Marylander. He then operated the railroad and lumber business on his own. He also invested in a Richmond mercantile firm and in the operation of schooners that carried freight on the James River. By 1860 his landholdings were valued at about $250,000 and his personal estate at about $1 million.

A lavish entertainer, Allen freely indulged himself in cigars and wine, and he enjoyed hunting and cruising aboard his yacht. In 1857 he permitted free access to Jamestown Island, which he then owned, for the celebration of the 250th anniversary of Jamestown's founding. Allen gained brief military experience as a lieutenant in a militia regiment after John Brown's raid on Harpers Ferry and he answered the call to arms when Virginia seceded from the Union. On 21 April 1861 he assembled volunteers at Brandon Church in Prince George County and organized the Brandon Heavy Artillery. With Allen as the captain, the company was designated Company E, 1st Virginia Artillery as of 10 May 1861. Tradition holds that he fully equipped the company himself. The battery was stationed on Jamestown Island to guard the James River route to Richmond. Allen's slaves assisted in the construction of fortifications, and it was reported that he permitted the rails from his railroad to be taken up and used for artillery demonstrations to test the armor for the CSS *Virginia.* On 25 March 1862 Allen's battery was reorganized and called the Jamestown Heavy Artillery, and on 4 April 1862 it was designated Company D, 10th Battalion Virginia Heavy Artillery, with Allen promoted to major and battalion commander. When besieged Yorktown fell, Jamestown Island was abandoned on 4 May 1862 and Allen's men were assigned to the defenses of Richmond.

On 19 August 1862 Allen resigned from the army to attempt to salvage the remainder of his property. His losses already neared $500,000, and most of his land was in Union possession. Murders committed at Jamestown by his former slaves demonstrated their hostility toward the chattel system. He nonetheless continued to support the war effort with the resources at his disposal. When the Confederacy collapsed his personal fortune went with it. His schooners, railroad, and other business ventures were gone, and his lands were desolate. From 1862 to 1874 he lived in Richmond and at Curles Neck, then returned to Claremont. Beleaguered by debts dating to the 1850s, he sold or mortgaged as much property as he could, but he could not dispose of lands from his inheritance because his granduncle's will had directed that the property be bequeathed to Allen's eldest son. On 18 June 1872 Allen consolidated his debts in a mortgage on property he owned in Surry County.

William Allen died suddenly on 19 May 1875 of a chill that he caught during a boat trip. He was buried in the graveyard at Claremont.

Eve S. Gregory, *Claremont Manor: A History* (1990), 57–69; Surry Co. Will Book, 6:218–222, 341–368; petitions of Griffin Organ, 8 Feb. 1832, and Martha A. Organ, 21 Dec. 1842, Legislative Petitions, Surry Co., RG 78, LVA; *Acts of Assembly*, 1831–1832 sess., 305; Surry Co. Fiduciary Account Books; agricultural and business history documented in John A. Selden Diary, VHS, and in Surry, Henrico, and James City Co. records, Richmond City records, and U.S. census returns; David F. Riggs, *Embattled Shrine: Jamestown in the Civil War* (1997); Compiled Service Records; Presidential Pardons; Hall, *Portraits*, 12 (por.); debt consolidation in Surry Co. Deed Book, 15:587–589; postwar business, death, and funeral described in James Nathaniel Dunlop Papers, VHS; Surry Co. Wills, Etc., 11:341–342; obituaries in *Richmond Daily Dispatch*, 20 May 1875, *Richmond Enquirer*, 20, 23 May 1875, and *Petersburg Index and Appeal*, 21 May 1875.

DAVID F. RIGGS

ALLERTON, Isaac (ca. 1630–by 30 December 1702), member of the House of Burgesses and member of the Council, was born in Plymouth, Massachusetts, the only son and younger of two children of Isaac Allerton, a tailor, and the second of his three wives, Fear Brewster Allerton. Allerton's mother died in the mid-1630s, after which he lived and received his early education in the household of his maternal grandfather, William Brewster, who had immigrated to Massachusetts in the *Mayflower* along with Allerton's father and his father's first wife. Brewster was a learned and religious man who had been one of the leaders of the separatists long before the Pilgrims had left England and the Netherlands for the New World.

Following Brewster's death in 1644, Isaac Allerton moved to New Haven to join his father, who had remarried and become a merchant engaged in extensive commerce with several colonies, including New Netherland, the West Indies, and Virginia. Allerton graduated from Harvard College in 1650 and then returned to New Haven to work in his father's business. He married a woman named Elizabeth, surname unknown, and they had one daughter and one son. Allerton's wife and son died about 1655, and his father died early in 1659.

In about 1660 Allerton left his young daughter in New England and moved to Virginia, where he owned land that his father had acquired. Unlike many immigrants for whom marriage into an influential Virginia family was a vehicle to prosperity and power, Allerton was already a man of substance and culture before he married twice-widowed Elizabeth Willoughby Overzee Colclough in about 1662. They had at least three daughters and one son. Over the next twenty years Allerton acquired more than five thousand additional acres of land along the Rappahannock River. In August 1662 he was commissioned a justice of the peace in Westmoreland County, and not long thereafter he became an officer in the county militia. Although he had been brought up by New England separatists, he easily embraced Virginia's Anglican establishment. The loss of the parish records makes it impossible to know whether he served on his local vestry, but in his will he left £10 to ornament the Cople Parish Church.

Allerton steadily ascended the military and civil ranks. Although surviving records reveal periods when he was an absentee officeholder, he was often exceptionally active in public life. If consistency of effort is a reliable measure, he was most committed to his work in the General Assembly. He represented Westmoreland County in the House of Burgesses in 1667, from 1680 to 1682, and in 1684, and sat for Northumberland County from 1668 to 1674 and 1676 to 1677. He was a leading man of business from the beginning and usually served on or chaired the main standing and ad hoc committees. He often conferred with the governor and Council, and he reported to the House on a range of critical issues, including the revenue bill of 1680, apportionment of the levy, the appellate jurisdiction of the burgesses, Indian affairs, the creation of towns, and the records of the House. Allerton was nominated for Speaker in 1680 but was not elected. Instead, he became chairman of the powerful Committee of Propositions and Grievances.

In August 1675 Governor Sir William Berkeley and the Council appointed Allerton, then a militia major, second in command to Colonel John Washington in a contingent cooperating with Maryland militiamen to protect the northern frontier from Indian attacks. Soon after the Virginians joined the Marylanders, five Susquehannock Indian leaders came out of their stronghold to confer and were killed at the direction of the Maryland commander. The complicity of the Virginia commanders was at worst passive. An eyewitness later testified that Allerton had objected to the executions, and in June 1677 a formal inquiry exonerated him.

The incident inflamed a crisis that in turn fueled Bacon's Rebellion. Allerton served in the dramatic June 1676 session of the General Assembly before which Bacon's men appeared in arms. Allerton remained loyal to Berkeley during the rebellion and was one of twenty men whom Nathaniel Bacon denounced by name for sustaining Berkeley. After the rebellion Allerton moved from loyalty to Berkeley to support for the new regime of Governor Culpeper. Not everyone made that transition, but Allerton's contemporaries evidently did not fault him for continuing to support the government of the colony. He was one of the men who attempted to settle the complicated estate claim of the widow of a leading member of the rebellion, Giles Bland. Culpeper promoted Allerton to lieutenant colonel in 1680 and named him escheator of one or more of the counties in the Rappahannock River valley.

Culpeper also recommended Allerton for appointment to the Council. Charles II and James II both approved, but the Council had no vacancy until early in 1687. Allerton was sworn in as a councillor on 21 April 1687. Surviving records confirm his attendance at only eight of twenty-five sessions held during his tenure of exactly four years. On 26 April 1689 the governor and Council proclaimed William and Mary the monarchs of England and ordered a day of celebration. Allerton was present when the Council issued the order, but two years later, after Parliament required that the members of the Council take new oaths of allegiance, he and two other members refused "thro Scruple of Conscience," believing that their oaths to James II still bound them. Allerton attended his last meeting as a member of the Council on 21 April 1691.

Allerton served one more term in the House of Burgesses. He represented Westmoreland County in the session of September 1696 and again served as chairman of the Committee of Propositions and Grievances. In October 1697 he wrote the burgesses that illness prevented him from attending the session of the assembly that had just begun, and with this notification he concluded a twenty-five-year career in the colony's government. In the summer of 1699 the Council appointed him naval officer and receiver of Virginia duties in Westmoreland County, but he probably hired a deputy to perform most of the work.

Allerton wrote his will and dated it on 25 October 1702. He provided for his children and grandchildren in Virginia as well as the children of his first daughter, who had remained in New England. Isaac Allerton died between then and 30 December 1702, when his will was proved in Westmoreland County Court.

Newman A. Hall, "Allerton of Virginia," *Virginia Genealogist* 32 (1988): 83–92, 171–178; Mary-Agnes Brown Groover, "Mayflower Heritage Brought to Northern Neck by Isaac Allerton, Jr.," *Northern Neck of Virginia Historical Magazine* 31 (1981): 3497–3499; Allerton to Thomas Ludwell, 4 Aug. 1676, Marquis of Bath, Coventry Papers, Longleat, Warminster, Eng.; Billings, *Effingham Papers*, 42, 281, 297, 309–310; *Executive Journals of Council*, 1:80–81, 172, 450, 526; will in Westmoreland Co. Deeds and Wills, 3:115–116, printed in *Mayflower Descendant* 7 (1905): 173–176.

MARTIN H. QUITT

ALLEY, Reuben Edward (9 July 1896–19 September 1983), Baptist minister and journalist, was born in Petersburg, the third of four sons and fourth of six children of Robert L. Alley and Katherine Elvira Friend Alley. He graduated from Petersburg High School in 1914 and attended Randolph-Macon College during the following academic year. From 1915 to 1919 he worked in a chemical factory in Hopewell. He married Mary Elizabeth Sutherland on 1 August 1917. They had two sons.

Alley had grown up as a Methodist, but he joined the Baptist Church and in 1919 entered Richmond College as a ministerial student. He served as the pastor for Mountain View and Oakland Baptist Churches in King George County while he was a student and received a B.A. in 1922. Alley taught physics at Bluefield College for one year, then enrolled in the Southern Baptist Theological Seminary in Louisville, Kentucky. He received a master of theology degree in 1926 and a Ph.D. in 1929. During his years in the seminary, Alley was part-time pastor of a church in Indiana and of two churches in Kentucky. He returned to Virginia and served as the pastor of Blackstone Baptist Church from 1930 to 1935 and as minister of the Irvington and Claybrook Baptist Churches in Lancaster County from 1935 to 1937.

In the summer of 1937 Alley purchased the *Religious Herald*, the weekly journal that served as the organ of the Baptist General Association of Virginia. He moved to Richmond and edited the paper and remained its sole owner until he sold it to the Baptist General Association in 1950. He continued to edit the *Religious Herald* until he retired in 1970. His thirty-three-year tenure was the longest in the history of the paper, and through his editorials he became one of the most influential Baptists in Virginia. He addressed many broad themes, such as his concern for public morality and his opposition to pari-mutuel betting and the manufacture and consumption of alcohol. During the Civil Rights movement he argued for calm tolerance and acceptance of change. Alley's passionate dedication to causes was well known. He was a plainspoken, earnest, and resolute man who never shrank from an argument either in conversation or in print.

Few American Baptists have been more devoted than Alley to the classic Baptist conviction that religious faith is a matter of personal choice and practice and that government has no right to intrude or dictate. He opposed federal grants and loans to religious institutions, although late in his career he tolerated federal loans to students, and he criticized the Southern Baptist Convention's Christian Life Commission in the 1950s for accepting money from a controversial political organization called the Fund for the Republic. During the 1960 presidential campaign Alley publicly expressed his concern over the election of a Catholic to the presidency. He published editorials on the history and beliefs of the Catholic Church and attempted to demonstrate that it did not support the separation of church and state. Although Alley's convictions regarding religious liberty defined him as a classic Baptist, in reality he did not fit neatly within either the evangelistic or pietist camps of the Southern Baptist Convention. He vigorously opposed requiring theological educators to conform to any stated orthodoxies when the issue arose at Southern Baptist Theological Seminary in 1958 and at Midwestern Baptist Theological Seminary in 1962.

As an active member of the Baptist community, Alley served on the Foreign Mission Board from 1938 to 1954 and as a trustee of the University of Richmond from 1947 to 1969, the Crozer Theological Seminary in Chester, Pennsylvania, from 1948 to 1956, and the Midwestern Baptist Theological Seminary in Kansas City, Missouri, from 1962 to 1970. The University of Richmond conferred an honorary D.D. on him in 1941. After he retired from editing the *Religious Herald* in 1970, Alley researched and wrote three substantial books, *Frederic W. Boatwright* (1973), a biography of his friend and longtime president of the University of Richmond; *History of Baptists in Virginia* (1974), in which he emphasized the role of Virginia Baptists in the struggle for religious freedom; and *History of the University of Richmond* (1977).

Reuben Edward Alley suffered a stroke in August 1983. He died in a Richmond hospital on 19 September 1983 and was buried in Blandford Cemetery in Petersburg.

Julian H. Pentecost, "Reuben Edward Alley," *Religious Herald*, 22 Sept. 1983, 4–5; family history provided by Robert S. Alley; Reuben E. Alley Papers in family possession; Mark Newman, "The Baptist General Association of Virginia and Desegregation, 1931–1980," *VMHB* 105 (1997): 257–286 (por., 261); obituaries in *Richmond News Leader* and *Richmond Times-Dispatch*, both 20 Sept. 1983, and *Religious Herald*, 22 Sept. 1983, 3; memorial in *Virginia Baptist Annual* (1983): 149–150.

SAMUEL S. HILL

ALLIN, Thomas (14 May 1757–26 June 1833), member of the Convention of 1788, was born in Hanover County, one of three sons and five daughters of William Allin and his second wife, Frances Grant Allin. In 1758 the family moved to a farm in Granville County, North Carolina, where Allin grew up. Very little is known about his youth. That he received a thorough English education, including mathematics, is clearly evident in his careers as a clerk of court and surveyor. The Allins were of Scots-Irish descent and probably Presbyterians, but early in the nineteenth century Thomas Allin joined the Christian Church.

During the American Revolution Allin served in the field with the North Carolina militia on several occasions in 1776 and from 1779 to 1781, as a soldier and as an issuing commissary, forage master, express rider, and on the staff of General Nathanael Greene. After a brief visit to Kentucky in the spring of 1780, Allin moved to Lincoln County early in the fall of 1781 and settled near Harrodsburg. In August 1782 he joined the militia and served as a commissary and quartermaster during the ensuing campaign against the Indians. He was on active duty for approximately twenty-two months during the Revolutionary War years and apparently rose to the rank of major.

Allin served as deputy surveyor of Lincoln County from 20 November 1781 until 1786 and as deputy sheriff from 18 June 1782 to 1784. He worked as a surveyor for the Transylvania Company, laid out Henderson, Kentucky, in 1797, and was credited with laying out Harrodsburg, Danville, and several other Kentucky towns as well. On 24 September 1785 Allin was appointed deputy clerk of the Kentucky District Court and served for about seven years. When Mercer County was formed out of Lincoln County, he was appointed county court clerk and remained in office from 1 August 1786 until he resigned on 7 February 1831. He also served as clerk of the Mercer County Court of Quarter Sessions, later called the Circuit Court, from its establishment on 25 September 1792 until 1825. From 24 March 1786 to 4 May 1816 he was a member of the Harrodsburg Board of Trustees, and in 1811 he was elected town surveyor. In addition to his income from clerkships and surveying, he owned a farm, a mill, a distillery, and several slaves. He was also a member of the Kentucky Society for the Promotion of Useful Knowledge in 1787 and 1788.

Allin belonged to the influential Danville Political Club from 1786 to 1790 and served as treasurer, secretary pro tempore, and president. In March 1788 Allin and Alexander Robertson won election to represent Mercer County in the Virginia convention called to consider ratification of the proposed constitution of the United States. Allin was present when the convention opened on 2 June 1788 and attended seventeen of the twenty-three sessions, but he did not speak during the debates, insofar as the extant records show. He voted with the majority of the western delegates in favor of requiring substantial amendments to the Constitution prior to ratification. After the convention voted against prior amendments, Allin voted against ratification.

Allin represented Mercer County in the second Kentucky Constitutional Convention in August 1799. He was probably a Jeffersonian Republican early in the nineteenth century and a Democrat later in his life. He married Mary Jouett in Mercer County on 13 February 1789. They had eight sons and two daughters. Thomas Allin died of cholera at Harrodsburg on 26 June 1833, and his wife died two days later. He was buried on his farm, but his body was later reinterred in Springhill Cemetery in Harrodsburg.

Benjamin Casey Allin, *Some Notes Regarding Thomas Allin, Surveyor of the Transylvania Company* (1945), 5–6; John Bennett Boddie, ed., *Historical Southern Families* (1959), 3:4–8; Allin letters in Kentucky Papers and George Rogers Clark Papers, Draper MSS; Michael Cook, ed., *Lincoln County, Kentucky, Records* (1988); numerous references in Mercer Co. records, Harrodsburg, Ky.; Kaminski, *Ratification*, 1539, 1541, 1557, 1565; Mercer Co. Marriage Register; Danville Political Club Records, 1786–1790, Filson

Club, Louisville, Ky.; *Cemetery Records, Mercer County, Kentucky* (1969): 2:121.

JAMES J. HOLMBERG

ALLISON, Fred (4 July 1882–2 August 1974), physicist and educator, was born in Glade Spring, Washington County, the youngest of three sons and three daughters of Robert Clark Allison and Rebecca Jane Clark Allison. His father was a mathematician, teacher, and surveyor, and his mother, a Wythe County native, was a teacher as well. Allison was educated in public and private schools before matriculating at age seventeen at nearby Emory and Henry College, his father's alma mater, where he concentrated on classical languages and mathematics. Curriculum standards also required that he enroll for a year in both chemistry and physics. After graduating first in his class in 1904, Allison remained at Emory and Henry and taught history, English, and mathematics while pursuing his own studies in French and German so that he would be able to pass the modern-language requirement associated with advanced graduate study. He also coached the school's first basketball team.

Between 1906 and 1920 Allison pursued graduate work in physics, largely during the summer, at Johns Hopkins University, the University of Virginia, and the University of Chicago. At Chicago he studied with Albert Abraham Michelson, winner of the Nobel Prize in physics in 1907, and Robert Andrews Millikan, the 1923 recipient. In 1909 Allison was appointed professor of physics and biology at Emory and Henry. He was both a mentor to his students and a force for progressive change at the college. Determined to develop its physics department, Allison launched a campaign in 1912 to raise money for a modern physics building to replace the one-room lecture hall then in use. His efforts brought the new building to fruition by February 1914. The project was crowned with an eighteen-foot observatory featuring a six-inch, clock-driven, refracting telescope that had been delivered on Allison's personal guarantee that its cost would be fully paid within two years. When funds became scarce Allison persuaded Secretary of State William Jennings Bryan to give a series of speeches in Virginia during a trip south. The college's share of the proceeds canceled the debt on the telescope.

On 24 August 1915 Allison married one of his former Emory and Henry students, Washington County native Elizabeth Harriet Kelly, and they had one son and one daughter. In 1920 the couple moved to Charlottesville, where Allison entered the graduate program at the University of Virginia, concentrating on the field of optics. He received an M.A. in 1921 and a Ph.D. in 1922, winning the President and Visitors' Scientific Research Prize for his dissertation on light wavelength. He then accepted an invitation to chair the Department of Physics at Alabama Polytechnic Institute, in Auburn, renamed Auburn University in 1960. When Allison arrived at the school in 1922, he found conditions much like those that he had encountered at Emory and Henry, and he went to work building a physics department with a reputation for solid academic credentials.

As at Emory and Henry, Allison served both his students and Auburn University with distinction. He wrote a laboratory manual, *College Physics: Laboratory Instructions* (1930), which was reprinted several times. In addition to his teaching responsibilities and his duties as chairman of the physics department, Allison accepted an appointment in 1949 as dean of the graduate school and presided over the development of the university's doctoral programs. From 1949 until 1951 he was director of Alabama Polytechnic's Research Foundation. An inspiring classroom teacher, he also sent an impressive number of physics majors on to graduate schools elsewhere.

Allison's research efforts progressed less smoothly than his teaching and administrative duties. In January 1927 the scientific journal *Physical Review* published a paper that Allison coauthored with his former colleague in Auburn Jesse Wakefield Beams, which introduced the magneto-optic apparatus, an experimental device Allison had developed to measure the time taken by polarized light to "twist" as it passed through liquids in a magnetic field. This process, initially only of theoretical interest, proved to have far wider applications. During the early 1930s Allison and his fellow researchers in Auburn announced that they had used the magneto-optic method of chemical analysis to identify two new elements, numbers 85 and 87, which Allison named respectively alabamine and virginium after the states in which he had lived. He also astonished the scientific community by proclaiming the discovery of deuterium, the heavy isotope of hydrogen that became a basic ingredient of the atomic bomb. He published his findings in the *Physical Review*, the *Journal of the American Chemical Society*, and the *Journal of Chemical Education*.

Allison's discoveries initially won him wide acclaim. Alabama Polytechnic awarded him an honorary doctor of science degree in 1931, and eminent Princeton physicist John Archibald Wheeler later described the "Allison Effect" (the magneto-optic method) as one of the two most important scientific developments of the 1930s. But Allison's method required a level of subjective judgment and skill that caused it to fail the key test of scientific progress when researchers were unable to use it to replicate his findings consistently. Ultimately other methods were used to confirm the existence of deuterium and elements 85 and 87 (renamed astatine and francium), and other scientists were formally credited with their discovery. By the late 1930s scientific journals had stopped publishing papers based on the Allison Effect, although Allison continued attempting to perfect the technique until his death.

Despite the controversy over his method, Allison remained an active physicist. During World War II he served as an advisor on the production of proximity fuses for artillery. After the war he helped to found the Oak Ridge Associated Universities, an organization devoted to converting nuclear physics from military to peacetime use. Allison's involvement in these activities contributed to the choice of Alabama Polytechnic by the Atomic Energy Commission as a site for a proposed Nuclear Sciences Center.

Having reached the age of mandatory retirement, the seventy-year-old professor emeritus left Alabama Polytechnic in 1953 and returned to his alma mater for two years as a professor of physics and mathematics. He had already been honored with Emory and Henry's LL.D. degree in 1932 and its establishment of an isotopes laboratory bearing his name. In 1955, while a visiting professor of physics at the University of Texas, he traveled to Bangkok, Thailand, on behalf of a United States government-sponsored program at the school to serve as a physics and engineering advisor at Chulalongkorn University. From 1956 until 1968 he taught at Huntingdon College in Montgomery, Alabama, and he also worked as a consultant for the U.S. Air Force. In 1964 Auburn University dedicated in his honor the Allison Laboratory, a four-story research facility housing the physics department and forty-eight laboratories.

Allison finally quit the classroom in 1968. In 1971 he was awarded the George B. Pegram Award by the Southeastern Section of the American Physical Society for outstanding contributions to the teaching of physics. Fred Allison worked on research projects in his laboratory on the Auburn University campus until just a month before his death at the age of ninety-two at his home in Auburn on 2 August 1974. He was buried at Pine Hill Cemetery, in Auburn.

Feature articles and memorials in *Auburn Alumnews* (Apr. 1960): 3 and (Sept.–Oct. 1974): 4–8 (por.), and *Physics Today* 28 (Jan. 1975): 107–109; George J. Stevenson, *Increase in Excellence: A History of Emory and Henry College* (1963), 113–114, 120, 183; Allen G. Debus et al., eds., *World Who's Who in Science* (1968), 36; Fred Allison Papers and alumnus file, Emory and Henry College; Fred Allison Papers and Oral History Collection, Auburn University; BVS Marriage Register, Washington Co.; obituaries in *Montgomery Advertiser* and *Richmond News Leader*, both 3 Aug. 1974, and *New York Times*, 8 Aug. 1974.

GEORGE J. STEVENSON

ALMOND, James Lindsay (15 June 1898–14 April 1986), governor of Virginia, was born in Charlottesville, the elder of two sons and second of three children of James Lindsay Almond and Edmonia Nicholas Burgess Almond. He grew up in rural middle class circumstances on his family's farm in Orange County. His father was a locomotive engineer and farmer, and both of his grandfathers and numerous other relatives were Confederate army veterans. Almond began his education in a one-room county public school. After graduating from high school in 1917, he entered the Student Army Training Corps at the University of Virginia. Almond completed his collegiate education, raising tuition by working at various jobs, including a stint as a rural high school principal. He entered the University of Virginia's law school in 1920, received his law degree in 1923, and joined a law firm in Roanoke. Though raised a Baptist, Almond became a lifelong and active member of the Lutheran church in 1925 after marrying Josephine Katherine Minter. They had no children, but they raised her nephew Lewis Minter as a son.

J. Lindsay Almond Jr., as he identified himself throughout his life, entered politics in 1925 and campaigned for the Democratic Party's gubernatorial candidate, Harry Flood Byrd. His political work soon brought rewards. In 1930 Almond was appointed an assistant commonwealth's attorney, and two years later the General Assembly elected him judge of the Roanoke Hustings Court, ending the tenure of an incumbent and evidently making Almond the youngest person to that time to occupy the bench in a Virginia court of record.

In a 1946 special election, Almond won a seat in the House of Representatives. Although his congressional post earned him a higher salary, in 1948 leaders of Byrd's Democratic Party organization asked him to give it up to fill out the remaining term of the recently deceased state attorney general. In exchange for doing so, Almond expected to receive the organization's nod for the 1953 gubernatorial nomination. By the early 1950s, however, Almond was no longer fully trusted at the highest levels of the Byrd organization. He had advocated stronger loyalty to the national Democratic Party than the organization's leadership thought proper, and he had written a letter to President Harry S. Truman endorsing an antiorganization Democrat for appointment to a federal office. When 1953 arrived, the organization passed him over in favor of Congressman Thomas Bahnson Stanley. Almond ran for and won reelection as attorney general.

Almond found himself almost constantly occupied in defending Virginia's practice of racial segregation in public schools, then under attack by black citizens legally represented by the National Association for the Advancement of Colored People. The Virginia segregation case, *Davis* v. *County School Board of Prince Edward County, Virginia*, along with cases from three other states and the District of Columbia, came before the United States Supreme Court in 1952. Disputing all aspects of the NAACP case, Almond made the most thorough defense of any of the attorneys of the states' position that they had a right to keep their schools segregated. Despite his efforts, in its 1954 decision on *Brown* v. *Board of Education of Topeka, Kansas*, the Supreme Court ruled unanimously that racial segregation in public education was unconstitutional.

Initially Almond and Governor Stanley responded to the decision with statements of reluctant acceptance, urging compliance with the law. Within weeks, however, their stand began hardening into defiance. By early in 1956 Almond stood behind Senator Harry Byrd's call for Massive Resistance to public school desegregation. In February the General Assembly adopted a resolution "interposing" its authority between Virginia and the *Brown* decision, and in September it adopted a multifaceted Massive Resistance program. The plan mandated that the governor close any public school that was subjected to a federal desegregation order. The community could then substitute a publicly subsidized, private segregated system. Because he was serving as defense counsel in the school cases, Almond did not advise the legislators drafting the Massive Resistance statutes, though privately he expressed doubts as to their constitutionality.

By assiduously building support throughout 1956 at the Byrd organization's courthouse level, Almond was able to edge out his chief rival, ardently pro–Massive Resistance state senator Garland Gray, for the organization's backing in the 1957 gubernatorial race. From the beginning of the campaign Almond staked out strong positions on two issues of great concern to a majority of Virginia voters: the desire to maintain racial segregation in the public schools, and the need to improve and strengthen public education coupled with a program of economic development. Skillfully employing his gift for oratory, Almond emphasized one or the other goal depending on which section of Virginia he was addressing. Before Southside audiences, his Massive Resistance rhetoric could be extravagant. The Republican candidate, state senator Theodore Roosevelt Dalton, stated that the all-out defiance demanded by Massive Resistance would be futile and advocated instead a pupil placement plan to limit and control desegregation. Public opinion surged in Almond's favor a month before the election when President Dwight David Eisenhower dispatched federal troops to Little Rock, Arkansas, to enforce a federal judge's school desegregation order. Almond won the election with 63.2 percent of the votes cast.

In his inaugural address in January 1958, Almond restated the two themes of his campaign, stridently denouncing the *Brown* decision and proposing significant improvements in public education. He asked Virginians to carry out Massive Resistance firmly but to protest legally and not violently. In September 1958, when federal judges issued desegregation decrees for schools in Front Royal, Charlottesville, and Norfolk, Almond obeyed the Massive Resistance laws and closed the schools, shutting nearly thirteen thousand students out of their classrooms. Although he fulminated against the federal courts, Almond presented no alternative education plan. With pressures mounting, Almond found the state far from united behind him. Virginia's major business leaders expressed concern over the economic impact of the school closings, and middle-class citizens in several cities began organizing to save the public schools. Publicly urging defiance, Byrd refused to return Almond's telephone calls for advice. The governor bided his time, awaiting the outcome of challenges to the school closings then being heard in state and federal courts.

On 19 January 1959 the Virginia Supreme Court of Appeals and the United States District Court in Norfolk both struck down the school closing law as unconstitutional. That evening Almond made a fiery radio and television address denouncing federal usurpation of Virginia's rights. He added comments with clearly racial overtones regarding the potential effects of desegregation. A week later, when he convened a special session of the General Assembly, hard-line segregationists anticipated an uncompromising defense of the color line. To their surprise, Almond declared that Massive Resistance was no longer tenable and that it was time to retreat to a program of restricting desegregation. The governor appointed a commission to prepare a containment plan for consideration at a special session scheduled for April. With the resistance barrier gone, the first desegregation was carried out on 2 February 1959 in Arlington and Norfolk.

Supporters of Massive Resistance thought Almond had betrayed them. Thousands rallied in Capitol Square calling for continued defiance, angry protest letters poured into the governor's office, and someone even fired a shot at Almond as he walked in front of the Executive Mansion. The break between Almond and Byrd, who remained adamant in his support of Massive Resistance, was irrevocable.

In April 1959, when the special commission presented the assembly with its proposals to permit limited desegregation, the lines of division between Almond's moderates and the supporters of Massive Resistance were bitterly and closely drawn. The moderate measures narrowly passed the House of Delegates and cleared the Senate of Virginia by only one vote. The fight persisted into the regular General Assembly session in 1960. Almond proposed a 3 percent sales tax to finance increased funding for education and other state services. The Massive Resisters defeated the sales tax but passed the governor's budget recommending increases in funds for education to be paid for by higher alcohol and tobacco taxes.

Almond's travail reflected the ambivalence and turbulence felt by Virginia's white majority during the years of Massive Resistance. When forced to choose between maintaining public education with the least possible disruption and continuing the struggle to preserve racial separation, the majority of white Virginians and their governor grudgingly placed the future of public education and the goal of economic development ahead of the defense of racial segregation. In 1980 the General Assembly passed a resolution praising Almond for the courage of his stand in 1959.

Constitutionally prohibited from succeeding himself, Almond hoped for a federal judicial appointment. In 1960 he had warmly supported the presidential candidacy of John Fitzgerald Kennedy, a friend since their service together in Congress. Most of the Byrd organization's leaders tacitly or openly opposed Kennedy's election. After Kennedy won, Almond got his chance for a postgubernatorial appointment. Faced with opposition from Senator Byrd, Kennedy decided against appointing Almond to a district court judgeship and instead nominated him to the Court of Customs and Patent Appeals. Byrd still vented his displeasure by keeping the Almond nomination from coming before the Senate for more than fourteen months, finally allowing it to pass in June 1963.

In 1973 Almond took senior status as a patent court judge, a kind of semiretirement. J. Lindsay Almond Jr. died in Richmond of heart failure on 14 April 1986 and was buried in Evergreen Burial Park in Roanoke.

Ben Beagle and Ozzie Osborne, *J. Lindsay Almond: Virginia's Reluctant Rebel* (1984; pors.); James W. Ely Jr., "J. Lindsay Almond, Jr.," in *The Governors of Virginia: 1860–1978*, eds. Edward Younger and James T. Moore (1982), 349–359; James Lindsay Almond Jr. Papers, VHS; James Lindsay Almond Jr. Executive Papers, RG 3, LVA; Benjamin Muse, *Virginia's Massive Resistance* (1961); J. Harvie Wilkinson III, *Harry Byrd and The Changing Face of Virginia Politics, 1945–1966* (1968); James H. Hershman Jr., "A Rumbling in the Museum: The Opponents of Virginia's Massive Resistance" (Ph.D. diss., UVA, 1978); Richard Kluger, *Simple Justice* (1976), 480–507; Hummel and Smith, *Portraits and Statuary*, 2 (por.); obituaries in *Richmond News Leader*, *Richmond Times-Dispatch*, and *Roanoke Times and World News*, all 15 Apr. 1986; editorial tribute in *Roanoke Times and World News*, 16 Apr. 1986.

JAMES H. HERSHMAN JR.

ALSTON, David Daniel (13 February 1891–8 November 1974), labor leader, was born in Wilson County, North Carolina, the eldest of fifteen children of Henry Alston and Mary Jane Taylor Alston. He acquired his respect for work at an early age. Like many children in black sharecropping families, his labor was indispensable to the family. Even before he could fully reach the handles of a plow, he joined his parents in the fields, removing worms from tobacco leaves. He subsequently helped plant, cultivate, and harvest tobacco, cotton, and corn. Soon after Alston left home in 1910 to work as a farm laborer in Halifax County, North Carolina, he met a young woman whom he liked. His friends told him that he would like her sister, a resident of Richmond, even better. Alston accordingly came to Virginia, where he soon met the sister, Irene C. Johnson, and married her in Richmond on 9 July 1911.

Late in 1912, seeking better employment opportunities, Alston moved to Norfolk, where he first worked for Lamberts Point Dredging Company dismantling old streetcar tracks for twenty-five cents an hour. He changed jobs, eventually went to Baltimore in 1917 to secure a better-paying position as a longshoreman, and joined the International Longshoremen's Association the same year. After a difficult interval commuting between the two Chesapeake Bay cities, Alston obtained employment in 1918 as a coal trimmer at the Norfolk and Western Railway Company's piers in Norfolk and held the job for the next twenty-eight years. Trimmers worked in gangs of forty at the backbreaking task of spreading crane-loaded coal evenly in the cargo holds of ships.

When Alston returned to Norfolk in 1918, the city and its workers were familiar with unions and labor activism. As blacks had flocked into Norfolk during World War I, the discrepancies between expectations and conditions produced explosive results. At least eight strikes occurred during the war years, several engineered and orchestrated by blacks, especially longshoremen belonging to the Coal Trimmers Union, an affiliate of the American Federation of Labor, and the Transportation Workers Association. Following the war the International Longshoremen's Association gained control over unionized workers at the ports. Alston began his climb up its leadership ladder in 1921, when he became timekeeper for a crew of coal trimmers. During the early years of the Great Depression when many black workers questioned old approaches and old leaders, however, Alston and other local officers were expelled by the membership of Local 978. The rank-and-file members challenged what they deemed too conservative an approach, forcing Alston and his associates to form a new local. He subsequently served as president of ILA Locals 1248 and 1379, as vice president at large of the Virginia State Federation of Labor in 1939, and as the first full-time black organizer for the latter organization in 1945. When a group of white delegates to the annual Virginia State Federation of Labor convention tried to persuade the body's sixty-three black delegates to help vote out the incumbent officers in May 1939, Alston blocked the move. In 1946 he became president of the district council of the ILA, and from 1947 until his death he served as an ILA international vice president and general vice president of its Atlantic Coast District, with primary responsibility for the Hampton Roads area.

Alston became involved in many civic ventures through his membership in religious, social, and fraternal organizations. He served as chairman of the board of deacons of the First Baptist Church of Lamberts Point for thirty-nine years, as a scoutmaster for the Boy Scouts of America, and as a board member for the Norfolk chapter of the National Association for the Advancement of Colored People. He also held high offices as an Elk, Mason, Oddfellow, and Shriner. Alston occasionally found himself in the middle of community controversies as well. In 1935 he took the lead in opposing communist participation in the annual Emancipation Proclamation celebration. This stance put him in opposition to several people who had worked assiduously to improve the lot of black workers. As a community leader of undoubted ability and dedication, he was one of two African Americans appointed to the Norfolk Civilian Defense Council in 1942.

The labor movement was central to Alston's life, and his commitment to it brought him the respect of colleagues and adversaries. Alston often told union members that "whether you're right or wrong, I'll be with you all the way." Appropriately, he was in the middle of many key labor changes, including the guarantee of a minimum wage for ILA members and establishment of a union pension and welfare fund. Colleagues recognized Alston's efforts with at least five testimonial dinners between 1961 and 1972, and in the latter year the Hampton Roads Foreign Commerce Club named him its first black Commerce Builder of the Year.

Late in life Alston summarized his career and in effect penned his own epitaph: "I never worry about the texture of a man's hair or the color of his skin, but I worry about the conditions he works in." He labored much of his life to improve those conditions, served on the Virginia State Port Authority and the National Labor Relations Board, and counted politicians, shipping-line executives, labor leaders, and the rank and file as friends. David Daniel Alston died of a heart attack on 8 November 1974 in a Norfolk hospital, two months after the death of his wife on 10 September. He was buried in Roosevelt Memorial Park in Chesapeake.

Feature articles in *Norfolk Journal and Guide*, 25 Apr. 1959 (por.), *Norfolk Virginian Pilot*, 19 June 1967, and *Norfolk Ledger Star*, 7 Nov. 1972; vertical files, Norfolk Public Library; BVS Marriage Register, Richmond City; Earl Lewis, *In Their Own Interests: Race, Class, and Power in Twentieth-Century Norfolk, Virginia* (1991), 29–65, 150, 184, 188, 197; labor convention documented in *Norfolk Journal and Guide*, 27 May 1939 (por.); obituaries in *Norfolk Ledger Star*, 8 Nov. 1974, *Norfolk Virginian Pilot*, 9 Nov. 1974, and *Norfolk Journal and Guide*, 16 Nov. 1974.

EARL LEWIS

ALWOOD, William Bradford (11 August 1859–13 April 1946), horticulturist, was born in Fulton County, Ohio, the son of David William Alwood and Ann Eliza Bradley Alwood, and grew up on the family farm near Delta, Ohio. At age nineteen, before he completed high school, he began teaching in the local schools, but he continued to work on the farm until 1882. He then became the superintendent of field experiments at the new Ohio Agricultural Experiment Station in Columbus, the fourth such station in the United States. In part because of the quality of Alwood's work, its appropriations were more than doubled during his four-year tenure there. Simultaneously, he resumed his education and studied agriculture, botany, chemistry, and horticulture at Ohio State University from 1882 to 1885.

Alwood married Seffie Stanley Gantz on 6 March 1884. They had four sons and four daughters. In 1886 he moved to Washington, D.C., to work as an assistant entomologist for the United States Department of Agriculture. He directed a study on farm and orchard insects and at the same time studied at Columbian University (now George Washington University).

In 1888 Alwood was appointed vice director of the new Virginia Agricultural Experiment Station at Virginia Agricultural and Mechanical College in Blacksburg, and in 1891 he became the college's professor of horticulture, entomology, and mycology. He successfully combined teaching, administrative, and research duties. The experiment station attracted national attention by participating in cooperative studies on Irish potatoes, a long-term investigation of the San Jose scale, and innovative research in forestry. Alwood published leading papers on all three programs, prepared draft legislation to control the San Jose scale, and integrated the station's work into new ideas of scientific organization and methodology.

Alwood's best-known research was on fruit orchards and treatments for insects and fungi. He developed a spray pump, standard spray mixtures, and other orchard treatments to improve fruit production. Because of the limited budget at the station, he often used his own money for necessary supplies, and he never patented any of his devices or procedures or earned any personal profit from them. He was one of the creators of the twentieth-century Virginia apple industry and a founding member of the Virginia Horticultural Society, which promoted commercial fruit production. Alwood's work became the basis for teaching pomology in Virginia and earned him international recognition. Some of his publications on fruit growing and orchard management were collected in a small handbook, *Series of Bulletins on Orchard Technique* (1900). He was elected vice president of the International Congress on Agricultural Education that met in Paris in 1900, and he attended the Royal Pomological School in Germany in 1900 and 1901.

Alwood resigned from the Virginia Agricultural Experiment Station in 1904 following a misunderstanding with the president of Virginia Agricultural and Mechanical College and Polytechnic Institute, who appointed someone else to direct the station and serve as dean of the agriculture department because he mistakenly believed that Alwood did not want the posts. Alwood then moved to Charlottesville. He divided his time during the next decade between his Albemarle County farm and Washington, D.C., where as director of a laboratory in the United States Department of Agriculture he investigated the fermentation of fruit products and conducted a series of chemical studies on wine making. During his career Alwood published more than sixty papers, pamphlets, reports, and bulletins dealing with the cultivation, marketing, and processing of apples, bush fruits, cherries, grapes, pears, plums, potatoes, strawberries, and tomatoes, with fruit and forest tree seedlings, and with plant diseases, insects, and insecticides. After he retired from scientific research in 1915, Alwood established his own commercial fruit orchards at Mountain Hollow, near Greenwood in Albemarle County.

Alwood received many honors and awards from national, foreign, and international professional and learned societies, including memberships or fellowships from the American Association for the Advancement of Science, the National Council of Horticulture, the Royal Horticultural Society of Great Britain, the Société des Chimistes Experts de France, and the Permanent International Commission on Viticulture; election as president of the International Congress on Viticulture held in San Francisco in 1915; two medals awarded at the 1904 Louisiana Purchase Exposition in Saint Louis, a silver medal and diploma from the Société Nationale d'Agriculture de France, and a Certificate of Meritorious Services to Agriculture from Virginia Tech in 1923. In 1938, at its fiftieth anniversary, the Virginia Tech Department of Horticulture that he had helped establish unveiled an oil portrait of him.

William Bradford Alwood died at his home in Albemarle County on 13 April 1946 and was buried in Riverview Cemetery in Charlottesville. As he had requested, a bugler from the Virginia Tech corps of cadets sounded "Taps" at the service.

Feature articles in *Virginia Fruit* 23 (June 1935): 22–23, *Commonwealth* 3 (Dec. 1936): 20, and *Charlottesville Daily Progress*, 12 Aug. 1940; photocopy of unpublished biography by Harvey Lee Price (ca. 1908), VPI; William B. Alwood Papers and Virginia Experiment Station letter books, VPI; Harold N. Young, *Virginia Agricultural Experiment Station 1886–1966* (1975), 2–5, 12–13, 42, 84–87, 111–112; Duncan Lyle Kinnear, *First 100 Years: A History of Virginia Polytechnic Institute and State University* (1972), 155, 167; bibliography of publications in *Dictionary Catalog of the National Agricultural Library, 1862–1965* (1967), 4:184–186; portrait by Mary W. Rasche at VPI; obituaries in *Charlottesville Daily Progress*, 13 Apr. 1946, and *New York Times* and *Richmond Times-Dispatch*, both 14 Apr. 1946; memorial in *Virginia Fruit* 34 (May 1946): 14–20.

GLEN ELLEN ALDERTON

AMBLER, Gordon Barbour (14 May 1896–1 December 1951), Richmond city mayor, was born in Winston-Salem, North Carolina, the elder of two sons and second of five children of John Nicholas Ambler and Anna Rockwell Neal Ambler. By 1897 the family had moved to Salem, Virginia, where his father, an engineer, taught mathematics at Roanoke College. Ambler attended schools there and in Winston-Salem, to which the family returned about 1906. He entered the University of Virginia in 1916 but left the next year to enlist in the United States Navy for service in World War I. After his discharge in April 1919 Ambler returned to the university, won honors as a debater and a law student, and graduated with the law class of 1921. A year earlier, on 1 July 1920, he had been admitted to the bar of Virginia.

Ambler moved to Richmond, where his family now lived, and alternated between public service in the city's justice system and private practice as a lawyer. On 19 June 1923 he married Nancy Holmes Harrison Payne. They had one son. Ambler served as a probation officer for the juvenile and domestic relations court from 1922 to 1925, when he resigned as its chief officer in order to work under Harry Marston Smith Jr., a noted criminal lawyer. Ambler became a judge of the civil justice court in October 1931, after serving as a substitute justice for the previous six years. He made his reputation as a lawyer by defending Garland Smith, who was indicted for killing two law-enforcement officers in Mecklenburg County in 1929 and sentenced to die a year later for one of the murders. Ambler represented Smith through three trials before finally winning his acquittal and pardon in 1932. The next year Ambler ran unsuccessfully for commonwealth's attorney and in 1934 resigned his judgeship to return to private practice.

By the mid-1930s Ambler had gained a citywide reputation as a talented lawyer and effective government official. In January and November 1935 he declined proposals that he run for mayor of Richmond, but during the intervening August he won election to the Senate of Virginia. He managed the reelection campaign of Congressman Andrew Jackson Montague in 1936, and after Montague's death on 24 January 1937 ran for the seat himself. Ambler declared himself a liberal and associated his campaign with President Franklin D. Roosevelt but lost to the more conservative David Edward Satterfield, who had the support of Senator Harry Flood Byrd's political organization.

Ambler's political philosophy and his independence from the Byrd machine blocked any future in state politics, and he left the Senate after the 1938 legislative session. To the delight of his supporters Ambler announced in August 1939 that he would finally run for mayor of Richmond. His opponent, J. Fulmer Bright, had served as mayor for sixteen years. Bright's opposition to increasing taxes in order to improve city services and his bitter refusal to modernize the administration of city government brought together a coalition of liberals and businessmen who saw the new candidate as their best hope for change. Ambler promised to reorganize the police department, fire department, and social services bureau. He proposed to create a centralized purchasing agency for the city and establish a housing authority to clear slums and construct low-cost housing. He also supported a referendum on changing the bicameral city council to a smaller unicameral body. Ambler won the election easily, carrying all four city wards.

Richmond's mayor wielded great power under the city charter then in force, and Ambler fulfilled all of his major campaign promises except for the referendum on a unicameral city council, which incumbent members blocked. World War II added civil defense to his responsibilities but enabled him to fulfill another campaign pledge by balancing the city's budget. Full employment had increased tax revenues while wartime restrictions on materials delayed expenditures on promised improvements to sections of the city recently annexed from Chesterfield and Henrico Counties. Ambler's support for urban planning also invigorated the moribund City Planning Commission, which began work on a master plan for the city's future development.

An advocate of good government rather than a spokesman for any particular class, Ambler disliked the rough-and-tumble of politics, and newspapermen considered him excessively sensitive to criticism. Conflicts with allies of former mayor Bright and some of his own erstwhile supporters occupied his last years in office, and Ambler seemed relieved to announce that he would not seek reelection in 1944. Nonetheless, even his critics acknowledged that he had effectively reorganized and modernized the city's government during his four tumultuous years in office. He returned to private practice as a lawyer and in 1950 opened a firm with his namesake son. Gordon Barbour Ambler died of a sudden heart attack at his home in Richmond on 1 December 1951 and was buried in Hollywood Cemetery.

Virginius Dabney, *Richmond: The Story of a City* (1976), 320–321; Christopher Silver, *Twentieth-Century Richmond: Planning, Politics, and Race* (1984), 150–159; *Record and Platform: Gordon B. Ambler for Mayor, City of Richmond* (1940), pamphlet in Biographical Files, LVA; *Richmond Times-Dispatch*, 16 Aug. 1939, 23 Mar., 1 Sept. 1941, 30 Aug. 1942; *Richmond News Leader*, 26 Aug. 1944; obituaries and editorial tributes in *Richmond Times-Dispatch*, 2, 3 Dec. 1951, and *Richmond News Leader*, 3 Dec. 1951; memorial in *Virginia State Bar Association Proceedings* (1952): 121–123 (por.).

JOHN T. KNEEBONE

AMBLER, James Markham Marshall (30 December 1848–ca. 30 October 1881), United States Navy surgeon, was born at the Dell in Fauquier County, the second of four sons and second of five children of Richard Cary Ambler, a physician, and Susan Marshall Ambler. At age sixteen Ambler joined the 12th Regiment Virginia Cavalry and served during the closing months of the Civil War. He attended Washington College in Lexington from 1865 to 1867 and the University of Maryland School of Medicine in Baltimore, from which he graduated in 1870.

Ambler practiced medicine for four years before joining the U.S. Navy in 1874 as an assistant surgeon. His duty assignments included service aboard the screw tug USS *Mayflower*, the gunboat USS *Kansas*, and the steam frigate USS *Minnesota*. While Ambler was serving at the Norfolk Naval Hospital with the rank of passed assistant surgeon (one qualified by examination) in 1878, his superiors suggested that he volunteer to serve as medical officer of an Arctic expedition then in preparation. Although he was not eager to go, he felt duty-bound to sign on after few responded to the call for volunteers. The expedition was undertaken with some support from newspaper publisher James Gordon Bennett, who provided a 142-foot ship, the *Jeannette*, which became a naval vessel by special legislation. The expedition's commander, George Washington De Long, planned to take advantage of what was believed to be a warm-water Japanese current and approach the North Pole via the Bering Strait.

On 8 July 1879 the USS *Jeannette* steamed out of San Francisco with a crew of thirty-three. The ship was slow and was delayed several times. It entered the Arctic Ocean late in the season and became icebound on 6 September, far south of where De Long had hoped to encounter the polar ice cap. Imprisoned in the ice pack, the *Jeannette* drifted in the polar currents for the next twenty-one months. Ambler's skillful practice of preventive medicine preserved the crew's health. A daily ration of lime juice prevented scurvy, and Ambler rigged a distillery to produce potable water from the salty sea ice. He also established rigorous standards of sanitation and hygiene. Except for an outbreak of lead poisoning caused by badly soldered food cans, everyone stayed remarkably healthy by the standards of nineteenth-century polar exploration. The only exception was the ship's navigator, who suffered an acute eye affliction, syphilitic iritis, which required constant attention. Ambler operated on him fifteen times under primitive conditions, yet the patient survived the painful surgeries and the ensuing hardships.

On 11 June 1881 ice crushed the *Jeannette*'s wooden hull. The men left the sinking ship and began a long trek over the ice, dragging small boats and tons of supplies. Ambler tended the sick and part of the time commanded the crew opening the way through crevasses in search of stretches of open water. After an ordeal of nearly three months, the sailors reached the edge of the pack ice. By then bad weather, soaked bedding, short rations, and physical exertion had taken their toll. Three boatloads of weakened men set out for Siberia's northern shore, where their inaccurate charts showed nonexistent settlements along the Lena River. On 12 September a fierce gale sank one of the boats, drowning its crew, and separated the other two. Siberians rescued one contingent, but De Long, Ambler, and twelve other men became hopelessly lost in the Lena Delta's maze of channels and inlets.

On 9 October 1881, with food supplies exhausted, De Long offered Ambler a chance to join the two strongest crewmen as they departed to seek help. The pair eventually reached safety, but Ambler chose instead to remain with the sick. The starving men gnawed strips of leather from their boots, and one by one they died. Ambler closed his journal with a farewell letter to his family on 20 October. The last entry in De Long's journal was dated 30 October 1881. It recorded the deaths of several men. Ambler was still alive then and was probably the last of the party to die.

Late in March 1882 Chief Engineer George Wallace Melville, leader of the expedition's survivors, found the frozen bodies of De Long's team members. In 1883 another U.S. Navy party went to Siberia to retrieve the remains, returning them to New York in February 1884. The body of James Markham Marshall Ambler was buried in the Leeds Episcopal Church cemetery near Markham in Fauquier County.

Robert B. Houston Jr., "'If it had been God's Will'; Dr. James M. M. Ambler and the *Jeannette* Expedition," *Virginia Cavalcade* 36 (1986): 16–29 (por., 18); Ambler Family Genealogical Records, VHS; Compiled Service Records; James M. M. Ambler Medical Logbook, 1879–1881, Medical Journals of Ships, Records of Bureau of Medicine and Surgery, RG 52, NARA; James M. M. Ambler Journal, 11 Sept.–20 Oct. 1881, Archives of Navy Bureau of Medicine and Surgery, Wash., D.C.; James M. M. Ambler Diary, 1881, VHS; Raymond Lee Newcomb, *Our Lost Explorers: The Narrative of the Jeannette Arctic Expedition* (1882); Emma J. De Long, ed., *The Voyage of the Jeannette: The Ship and Ice Journals of George W. De Long* (1884); George Wallace Melville, *In the Lena Delta: A Narrative of the Search for Lieut.-Commander De Long and His Companions* (1884); Leonard F. Guttridge, *Icebound: The Jeannette Expedition's Quest for the North Pole* (1986).

JAN K. HERMAN

AMBLER, Jaquelin (9 August 1742–10 January 1798), member of the Council and treasurer of Virginia, was born in Yorktown, the fourth of six sons and seventh of nine children of Richard Ambler and Elizabeth Jaquelin Ambler. He was the youngest of the four children who survived childhood. Unlike his two older brothers who were educated in England, he attended the grammar school at the College of William and Mary from 1752 to 1756 and the College of Philadelphia, from which he graduated in 1761. Following two years of training in his father's Yorktown mercantile house, he became a partner in the family business. He married Rebecca Burwell on 24 May 1764. They had one son and seven daughters. Four of the daughters survived to maturity, and they all married into prominent Virginia families.

Ambler's father died in 1766, and his elder brothers died of consumption in 1766 and 1768. Ambler and the young sons of his brother Edward were the heirs to his father's extensive property and thriving commercial business. Ambler moved into the family residence and took charge of the store and lots in Yorktown, together with lands in the vicinity and a plantation in Warwick County. He was also heir to the family's political and social prominence in York County. He succeeded his father as collector of customs at Yorktown from 1766 to 1776, sat on the vestry of Yorkhampton Parish, became a justice of the peace in 1767, and served as sheriff of York County from 1771 to 1773.

The American Revolution disrupted Ambler's life as a prosperous merchant and planter. He left Yorktown and moved his family several times, going as far inland as Winchester, before relocating in the autumn of 1777 in Hanover County. The family did not return to Yorktown until 1778 or 1779, and then to a small tenement, not to the spacious old family residence. One of his neighbors in Yorktown in 1780 was Colonel Thomas Marshall, the commanding officer of a state artillery regiment. Captain John Marshall, the colonel's son, fell in love with Ambler's daughter Mary Willis "Polly" Ambler while on leave from the Continental army and later married her.

Ambler served on the Virginia Navy Board during the last three months of its existence in the spring of 1779. From June 1779 to April 1780 he served on the Virginia Board of Trade, which oversaw the importation, domestic manufacture, and allocation of military supplies and necessities such as salt, cotton, and woolens. Ambler's experience as a merchant served him well in that important office. In the spring of 1780 the General Assembly elected him to the Council of State. He served from 21 June 1780 until 12 April 1782, during two British invasions and the most trying months of the war in Virginia. The capital moved from Williamsburg to Richmond while Ambler was a member of the Council, and he left Yorktown and took up permanent residence in the new capital.

On 13 April 1782 the Council appointed Ambler treasurer of Virginia. The assembly annually reelected him, and he served as treasurer until his death. His official letters and reports attest to a diligent, methodical, and efficient administrator. Along with his treasury post, Ambler served from 1784 to 1791 as one of the directors of the public buildings and helped supervise construction of the new Capitol. A dedicated public servant and administrator, Ambler remained above the fray of partisan politics, though his sympathies during the 1790s were undoubtedly with the Federalists.

From July 1782 to May 1783 Ambler served as an alderman of Richmond. He purchased several lots on Shockoe Hill and built a new house there. Over the years Ambler gathered about him all his daughters and their families, forming a close-knit society. A deeply religious man, he began and ended each day with prayer and regularly attended services of the Episcopal Church. For several years the rector of Henrico Parish, John Buchanan, lived in the Ambler household. Ambler was serious and reserved, ever attentive to his duties and obligations as husband, parent, and public gentleman. He was not inclined to participate in society and appeared to some people to be reclusive. Because of his wife's frail health, he assumed principal responsibility for the care and instruction of his daughters. As a parent, he was a strict disciplinarian who did not spare the rod. Only a few beneficiaries were aware of his many acts of charity and benevolence.

Jaquelin Ambler suffered from a painful inflammation of the kidneys and died in his Richmond home on 10 January 1798. The General Assembly adjourned for his funeral the following day. He was buried in the yard of Saint John's Church in Richmond.

Hope Mary Hockenberry, "The Amblers of Virginia: A Family's Rise to Prominence" (master's thesis, W&M, 1973); George D. Fisher, *Descendants of Jaquelin Ambler, with Letters from his Daughter, Mrs. Col. Ed. Carrington, and Extract from his Funeral Sermon Delivered by Rev. John Buchanan* (1890); Pecquet du Bellet, *Virginia Families*, 1:30–33, 2:18–22; Elizabeth Jaquelin Ambler Brent Carrington Papers, LC; Ambler letters in *Calendar of Virginia State Papers* and Madison, *Congressional Series*; death notice in *Richmond Virginia Argus*, 12 Jan. 1798; obituary in *Richmond Virginia Gazette, and General Advertiser*, 17 Jan. 1798.

CHARLES F. HOBSON

AMBLER, Richard (24 December 1690–ca. February 1766), merchant, was born in the city of York, England, the seventh of eleven children of John Ambler and Elizabeth Bickerdike Ambler. He was one of only three who lived to maturity. He received little formal education and probably went to work as a young man for his uncle Arthur Bickerdike, a merchant with business connections in London. Bickerdike took Ambler to Virginia in 1716 and established a trading house in Yorktown.

Bickerdike died in 1720, leaving Ambler to operate the business under his own name. Ambler prospered during the 1720s and in 1728 petitioned the Council for permission to build a wharf and erect a storehouse on the waterfront. In 1729 he married Elizabeth Jaquelin, the daughter of Edward Jaquelin, a wealthy merchant who owned half of Jamestown Island. At Jaquelin's death in 1739, Ambler and his wife inherited his property, and between 1744 and 1765 Ambler acquired the remainder of the island through a combination of purchases and lease agreements. As his prosperity mounted,

Ambler also purchased land and slaves in Hanover, James City, Louisa, and Warwick Counties. Altogether by the time of his death he had accumulated almost two thousand acres of land and probably a hundred or more slaves.

Throughout his life Ambler occupied himself principally as a merchant. He lived in Yorktown and traded in tobacco on his own account or in association with his Yorktown neighbors and fellow merchants, John Norton and his son John Hatley Norton, Philip Lightfoot, and Thomas Nelson and his sons William Nelson and Thomas Nelson. Ambler's principal London connections were the great mercantile houses of Micajah Perry and Company, Edward and Samuel Athawes, and Edward Hunt and Company. He also traded with Bowden, Farquahar and Kinlock, of London and Edinburgh, and with Farrell and Jones, of Bristol. None of Ambler's business records survive, but the extent of his trade is evident in the appraisals of his estate following his death. His property, including merchandise on hand and outstanding debts, amounted to about £15,000.

Ambler served as a justice of the peace for York County from November 1724 until November 1737 and as the enumerator of tithables in the county in 1727, 1728, and 1731. The surviving records of Yorkhampton Parish show that he was a vestryman as early as January 1732 and as late as January 1753, and he probably served until his death. He was also collector of the York River customs district for thirty-five years under an appointment made on 29 April 1724. He took the oaths of office in December 1724 and relinquished the office to his son John Ambler in 1759. Richard Ambler had six sons and three daughters, but only three children, all sons, were still alive when he dated his will on 31 August 1765. The date of his death is not known, but family history records suggest that he died about February 1766. His will was proved in York County court on 21 July 1766.

Birth recorded in the register of Parish of St. Michael-le-Belfry, city of York, abstracted by Louis Ambler and included in his memorandum, "Notes Concerning the Origin of the Ambler Names and Family," VHS; Elizabeth Ambler Brent Carrington to Anne Ambler Fisher, 10 Oct. 1796, CW; J. J. Ambler Manuscript, microfilm in LVA, published serially in *WMQ*, 1st ser., 4 (1895–1896): 46–52, 95–103, 183–187; 5 (1896): 50–53; Meade, *Old Churches*, 1:97–110; Lucille Griffith, ed., "English Education for Virginia Youth: Some Eighteenth-Century Ambler Family Letters," *VMHB* 69 (1961): 7–27; petition of 1728 in *Executive Journals of Council*, 4:183–184; appointment as collector of York River in PRO T 11/18, 437; will and estate valuations in York Co. Wills and Inventories, 21:278–282, 386–396.

Peter V. Bergstrom

AMBLER, William Marshall (13 July 1813–25 August 1896), member of the Convention of 1861, was born either in the city of Richmond or in Hanover County, the youngest of four sons and seventh of eight children of John Ambler and his third wife, Catherine Norton Bush Ambler. He had several half brothers and half sisters from previous marriages of his father and his mother. Ambler attended school in Richmond, where his father had helped finance construction of Monumental Episcopal Church. After taking classes at the College of William and Mary for the academic year 1830–1831 and at the University of Virginia for the years 1831–1833, he studied law under John Tayloe Lomax in Fredericksburg.

Ambler returned to live in Richmond, but in 1837, a year after his father's death, he moved to Louisa County in order to practice law and take possession of some 2,000 inherited acres known as Lakeland. In 1850 his property holdings included real estate valued at $18,676 and fifty-one slaves. Ten years later he had eighty-one slaves, including some acquired by way of his 20 June 1855 marriage to Martha Elizabeth Coleman. Of their three sons and two daughters, two boys and one girl died in infancy.

Ambler was a Democrat and in 1846 was elected to the Senate of Virginia from the district consisting of Fluvanna, Goochland, Hanover, and Louisa Counties. He quickly became a leader in that body. In December 1848 the Senate appointed him to the joint legislative committee to revise the code of Virginia, and in 1849 he became chairman of the influential Committee on General Laws. From 1852 through the end of his tenure in 1858 he served as chairman of the Committee on Courts of Justice. In January 1858 the Senate unanimously elected him president pro tempore.

In February 1861 Ambler was elected to represent Louisa County in the Virginia convention. He believed that Virginia and the South had compromised enough on sectional issues and in his speech on 8 March 1861 declared that further compromise with the Northern states was undesirable and impossible. Ambler was one of the minority of delegates who voted for secession when the motion was defeated on 4 April 1861. He voted for secession again on 17 April when the motion passed, and his was the first signature on the formal parchment of the Ordinance of Secession.

Ambler wrote his will in June 1861. He did not take an active role in the army during the Civil War and continued to farm and practice law. His house had burned in 1860, and he lived throughout the war in a small cabin on his property in Louisa County. He applied for and received a presidential pardon in August 1865. His militia title of major remained with him after the war. Ambler bitterly opposed the reforms that followed in the war's wake, supporting the Conservatives during the late 1860s and the Funders during the later controversies over the settlement of the antebellum state debt. He employed tenant farmers to raise tobacco and during the 1870s became an avid member of the Virginia State Grange of the Patrons of Husbandry.

William Marshall Ambler died of pneumonia on 25 August 1896 at his house in Louisa County and was buried near his daughter's Hanover County residence in what came to be known as Chantilly Cemetery.

Birth and death dates on gravestone, printed in *Louisa County Historical Magazine* 7 (summer 1975): 15; birth date of 26 June 1813 given in French Biographies and repeated elsewhere; Pecquet du Bellet, *Virginia Families*, 1:42, 74–76 (por.), gives birth date of 25 July 1813; biographies in Manarin, *Senate Officers*, 199–200, and John Jaquelin Ambler IV, *The Amblers of Virginia* (1972), 3–5; Reese and Gaines, *Proceedings of 1861 Convention*, 1:518–522; Presidential Pardons; Malcom H. Harris, *History of Louisa County, Virginia* (1936), 107, 132; postwar letters of Martha Elizabeth Coleman Ambler to Phoebe Howson Clark Bailey, Bailey Family Papers, VHS; *Gordonsville Gazette*, 4 Sept. 1873; articles by Ambler in *Southern Planter and Farmer* 36 (1875): 66–70, 294–297; death notice in *Fredericksburg Daily Star*, 27 Aug. 1896.

SHEARER DAVIS BOWMAN

AMES, Adeline Sarah (6 October 1879–11 February 1976), botanist, was the eldest of one son and three daughters of Elwyn Ames and Hettie Owen Ames. She was born near Henderson, York County, Nebraska, and attended high school and Lincoln Normal Academy in Lincoln, Nebraska, before matriculating at the University of Nebraska, from which she received a B.S. in 1903 and an A.M. a year later. While attending the university she worked as an assistant botanist there.

In January 1905 Ames went to work for the United States Department of Agriculture in Washington, D.C. She conducted research on diseases of several classes of plants, including cotton and fungi, until late in 1909, when she entered graduate school at Cornell University. In 1913 she received her doctorate in botany from Cornell for a dissertation entitled "Studies in the Polyporaceae: A Consideration of Structure in Relation to Genera of the Polyporaceae." Ames was one of only a handful of women who earned doctorates in botany at Cornell during the early decades of the twentieth century and one of an even smaller number to be actively engaged in professional scientific research. During summer vacations she worked for the Department of Agriculture, and in December 1912 she returned to the agency full time to investigate illnesses of chestnut bark and other forest diseases. From July 1914 to June 1916 she was an assistant pathologist and one of the coordinators of a research project on plant sickness in the western United States. During World War I she lived in Normal, Nebraska, and did additional research on the pathology of forest plants.

In 1920 Ames became assistant professor of botany and bacteriology at Sweet Briar College, a small school that was distinguished for the number of women with doctorates on its faculty. Ames was promoted to full professor and named chairman of the department of biology in 1922. She taught and chaired the department until June 1945. She and her students often collected specimens of fungi and other plants on field trips, and her collection formed the bases for Sweet Briar's arboretum and herbarium, which were named for her. At the time of her retirement the college began raising funds to erect a greenhouse, and when it was dedicated in

1951 it was named for Ames. She was a fellow of the American Association for the Advancement of Science and a member of the Botanical Society of America, the American Phytopathological Society, the Virginia Academy of Science, Phi Beta Kappa, and Sigma Xi scientific honor society. She listed her specialties in books of scientific reference as systematic mycology and plant pathology.

After Ames retired from teaching in 1945, she moved to California, where she was active in Democratic Party politics and lived with one of her sisters. Adeline Sarah Ames died of heart disease on 11 February 1976 at Bixby Knolls Hospital in Long Beach, California. After cremation, her ashes were buried in Wyuka Cemetery in Lincoln, Nebraska.

Biography in Jane C. Belcher, "Both Cactus and Violet," *Sweet Briar Alumnae Magazine* 16 (winter 1977): 16 (por.); Personnel File, Office of Personnel Management, U.S. Department of Agriculture, Saint Louis, Mo.; Deceased Alumnae Records, Cornell University Archives, Ithaca, N.Y.; death date verified by Department of Health Services, Sacramento, Calif.

ELIZABETH HERBENER MANSFIELD

AMES, Susie May (10 January 1888–30 July 1969), historian, was born at Pungoteague, Accomack County, the eldest of five daughters and second of seven children of Samuel William Ames, a businessman, and Sarah Anne Edmonds Mears Ames. She attended local schools and graduated in 1908 from Randolph-Macon Woman's College in Lynchburg, with a major in English and minor in Latin. Her extracurricular activities included terms as president of the Franklin Literary Society and the Eastern Shore of Virginia Club and editor-in-chief of the *Tattler*, the monthly student magazine.

After graduation Ames began teaching at Crewe High School in Nottoway County and then served as principal of Harborton High School in Accomack County from 1909 to 1911. During the next five years she taught at high schools in Maryland and Indiana and at Eastern Kentucky State Normal School (now Eastern Kentucky University) in Richmond, Kentucky. Returning to the Eastern Shore to teach at Franktown-Nassawadox High School in 1916, Ames became principal of Pungoteague High School in 1917 and then served on the faculty of E. C. Glass High School in Lynchburg from 1920 to 1923.

While teaching at levels then commonly open to women, Ames set her sights on graduate study and attended summer sessions in English at the University of Chicago in 1915 and history at the University of California in 1923. That autumn she was appointed instructor in history at Randolph-Macon Woman's College, one of the dozen institutions in the country that offered serious educational opportunities for women. From 1923 to 1955 Ames devoted her life to the college and its students, accepting promotions to adjunct professor in 1926, associate professor in 1940, and professor in 1954.

Fewer than 3,000 American women a year received master's degrees in any field when Ames joined her alma mater's faculty. She promptly enrolled at Columbia University, where she earned an A.M. in 1926 and a Ph.D. in 1940. A scholarship in 1927 enabled her to attend the European Summer School of the Bureau of University Travel. During a leave of absence for her doctoral residence from 1929 to 1931, Ames was a member of Evarts B. Greene's seminar and studied with Robert Livingston Schuyler, William L. Langer, Dixon Ryan Fox, and Allan Nevins. A manuscript she discovered at the New York Public Library became the basis of her first major article: "A Typical Virginia Business Man of the Revolutionary Era: Nathaniel Littleton Savage and His Account Book," *Journal of Economic and Business History* 3 (1931): 407–423. She also indulged an interest in the Civil War on the Eastern Shore, gathering the recollections of area residents by interview and letter.

Ames was one of fewer than 500 women to earn a doctorate in history between 1920 and the completion of her graduate work in 1940. Her dissertation, published as *Studies of the Virginia Eastern Shore in the Seventeenth Century* (1940; reprinted 1973), was a pioneering investigation of social and economic history based on thorough analysis of the earliest county court records in the nation. Some reviewers mistakenly dismissed the Eastern Shore as atypical of the early colony, but Ames's scholarship anticipated by three decades many methodological concerns and findings of subsequent Chesapeake historians.

Ames never married, taught a heavy course load, and took care of her aging mother. Although a member of many professional associations (and a contributor or reviewer for many journals) she, like many other female academicians in the South, was often unable to attend their meetings. Her interest in social history found expression in polished essays first presented, as often as not, as talks to women's clubs. Ames interacted with leaders of the historical profession at Columbia and elsewhere but had little contact with historians at Virginia's colleges and universities, which offered fewer opportunities for female scholars than did some of their northern counterparts.

After publishing her dissertation Ames reacted to European dictatorships and World War II with an investigation of the flagrant aggression of one of Accomack County's early chief magistrates, Edmund Scarburgh. Jamestown authorities merged Northampton and Accomack Counties in 1670 to reduce his influence and separated the counties again two and a half years after his death in 1671. In a draft Ames mentioned parallels with "the emergency of today," but she deleted the section before publishing "The Reunion of Two Virginia Counties" in the *Journal of Southern History* 8 (1942): 536–548. Similarly, issues of civil rights and Massive Resistance in the 1950s prompted her inquiry into "Federal Policy Toward the Eastern Shore of Virginia in 1861," *Virginia Magazine of History and Biography* 69 (1961): 432–459. Ames believed that "the basic character of a nation or people is largely determined by its early years," but her lectures and publications taught people to draw their own lessons from history.

By February 1941 Ames had begun work on her edition of *County Court Records of Accomack-Northampton, Virginia, 1632–1640*, which the American Historical Association published in 1954 as volume 7 of the American Legal Records series sponsored by the Littleton-Griswold Fund. Ames saw the Eastern Shore as "a small laboratory in which to study the transit of civilization from the Old World to the New." Her interests transcended the preoccupation of the series editors with legal records that showed "adherence to and adoption of English law and forms." Ames cared more for "Law-in-Action," as she explained in an article of that title about Eastern Shore court records that appeared in the *William and Mary Quarterly*, 3d ser., 4 (1947): 177–191. On 2 October 1944 she was appointed to the Virginia World War II History Commission, which was charged with documenting the state's involvement in that conflict. Ames also wrote two long chapters on the Eastern Shore during the colonial period for Charles B. Clark, ed., *The Eastern Shore of Maryland and Virginia* (1950).

After twenty-five years at Randolph-Macon Woman's College, Ames took a leave of absence for the 1948–1949 academic year to care for her mother, and she moved back to Pungoteague for the same reason when she retired in June 1955. Still an active scholar, after giving up teaching Ames edited a second volume of Eastern Shore legal records covering the years 1640–1645. The Virginia Historical Society published it posthumously in 1973. As part of the celebration of the 350th anniversary of the Jamestown settlement, Earl Gregg Swem commissioned her to write *Reading, Writing and Arithmetic in Virginia, 1607–1699* (1957), and in 1965 she published *"The Bear and the Cub": The Site Of The First English Theatrical Performance in America.* Ames was admitted to Phi Beta Kappa in 1943 and awarded a certificate of commendation from the American Association for State and Local History in 1964. She was a founder and president of the Eastern Shore of Virginia Historical Society and was active in many patriotic organizations, local women's and garden clubs, and the Pungoteague Methodist Church.

Susie May Ames died on 30 July 1969 at the Hermitage in Onancock, Accomack County, and was buried in the cemetery of Saint George's Episcopal Church near Pungoteague.

Brief biography by John Melville Jennings in Susie M. Ames, ed., *County Court Records of Accomack-Northampton, Virginia 1640–1645* (1973), vii–viii; birth date in Ames family Bible records, LVA, and Onancock newspaper obituary; BVS Birth Register, Accomack Co., gives incorrect birth date of 10 June 1888; Susie M. Ames Papers, VHS;

autobiographical questionnaire of 18 July 1937 and newspaper clippings in alumna file, Randolph-Macon Woman's College, Lynchburg; *Helianthus* (college yearbook) (1908): 17 (por.), 38; early teaching career summarized in Randolph-Macon Woman's College, *Catalogue* (1933/1934): 13; other publications include "Colonel Edmund Scarborough," Randolph-Macon Woman's College, *Alumnae Bulletin* 26 (Nov. 1932): 16–23, and *A Calendar Of The Early History Of Virginia's Eastern Shore* (1959); obituaries in *Lynchburg Daily Advance* and *Lynchburg News* (por.), both 1 Aug. 1969, *Onancock Eastern Shore News*, 7 Aug. 1969, and *Randolph-Macon Alumnae Bulletin* 63 (fall 1969): 20.

JON KUKLA
J. JEFFERSON LOONEY

AMHERST, Sir Jeffery (29 January 1717–3 August 1797), governor of Virginia, was the second of four sons and third of five children of Jeffery Amherst and Elizabeth Kerril Amherst, of Riverhead, Sevenoaks Parish, Kent County, England. In 1735 he entered the army as an ensign in the 1st Regiment of Foot Guards. He rose rapidly through the service as an aide-de-camp to General John Ligonier during the War of the Austrian Succession and during the Jacobite Rebellion of 1745. In 1746 he was reassigned to the Netherlands and the following year became aide-de-camp to the Duke of Cumberland, in whose household he later resided.

On 3 May 1753 Amherst married Jane Dalyson, who died in November 1763. Four years later he married Elizabeth Cary. He had no children by either marriage. By 1756 Amherst had become a colonel, but his ascendancy truly began in January 1758 when William Pitt elevated him to the rank of major general and named him to command the British forces that took the French stronghold at Louisbourg on Cape Breton Island on 27 June of that year. In 1759 Amherst succeeded Ligonier as commander in chief in North America and directed the British and colonial forces that took control of the strategic forts at Ticonderoga, Niagara, and Quebec, and in 1760 brought about the collapse of New France by capturing Montreal. For these successes, Amherst was rewarded with the office of governor of Virginia on 25 September 1759, and in 1761 he was named a knight of the bath, but his unwillingness to provision Indians in the Northwest, one of many instances of his antipathy toward Native Americans, helped provoke Pontiac's Uprising in 1763 and led to Amherst's recall as commander in chief.

Amherst remained royal governor of Virginia, although he never visited the colony. He left the administration of the government to the lieutenant governor, Francis Fauquier. They corresponded frequently about military affairs but less often about other political matters in Virginia. During the war with France the General Assembly was reluctant to appropriate large sums of money to keep soldiers in the field, and following the Peace of Paris in 1763 Amherst and Fauquier tried without much success to maintain a large military force on the Virginia frontiers to prevent conflicts between settlers and Indians. In spite of Amherst's efforts to stabilize Virginia's western borders, officials in London found Virginia's contributions to the military effort disappointing and, after the death of Francis Fauquier in the spring of 1768, the British ministry decided that the royal governor should reside in Williamsburg and no longer entrust the government of the colony to a lieutenant governor. As anticipated, Amherst refused to live in Virginia, and in July 1768 he was dismissed from office.

Amherst angrily resigned his commission in the army following his dismissal, but, as he was hugely popular with the public, he was soon persuaded to resume it. In 1770 he was appointed governor of Guernsey, in 1772 he became a member of the king's Privy Council, and in 1776 he was created baron Amherst. He was appointed to the rank of full general in 1778 and given command of all British forces in England, but he saw no action during the American Revolution and the resultant conflict with France. In 1796 George III awarded Amherst the rank of field marshal. Lord Amherst died on 3 August 1797 at Montreal, his estate in Kent County, and was buried in the family vault at Sevenoaks.

John C. Long, *Lord Jeffery Amherst: A Soldier of the King* (1933); Amherst's papers in the Kent Archives Office, Maidstone, Eng. (issued in microform in 1983), are described in F. Hull, *Catalogue of the Amherst Mss, Kent County Council, Archives Office* (1968); J. Clarence Webster, ed., *The Journal of Jeffery Amherst, Recording the Military Career of General Amherst in America from 1758 to 1763* (1931); George Reese, ed., *Official Papers of Francis Fauquier, Lieutenant Governor of Virginia, 1758–1768* (1980–1983);

Nellie Norkus, "Francis Fauquier, Lieutenant-Governor of Virginia, 1758–1768: A Study in Colonial Problems" (Ph.D. diss., University of Pittsburgh, 1954); portrait by Joshua Reynolds in possession of Amherst family, and portrait by Thomas Gainsborough in National Portrait Gallery, London.

DONALD W. GUNTER

AMISS, Thomas Benjamin (4 July 1839–9 November 1913), Confederate army surgeon, was born at Amissville, the Rappahannock County residence of his parents, Elijah Amiss and his third wife, Eliza Ann Leavell Amiss. He was the fourth of Elijah Amiss's five sons and eighth of eleven children. He attended Virginia Military Institute, where he studied under Thomas J. Jackson, and the medical school of the University of Pennsylvania, from which his elder brother William Henry Amiss (1829–1903) had graduated in 1853. Thomas B. Amiss received his medical degree in March 1861 and returned to Virginia in time to vote for the Ordinance of Secession at the referendum in May 1861. He married Mary Elizabeth Miller on 16 July 1861. They had two sons and one daughter.

Amiss taught military drill to Confederate volunteer companies in Rappahannock and Culpeper Counties and then enlisted as a private in the 6th Virginia Cavalry. He participated in the First Battle of Manassas (Bull Run) and in September 1861 was commissioned an assistant surgeon and posted to Bailey's Factory Hospital in Richmond. After the Peninsula campaign he requested field duty and was assigned to the 31st Georgia Infantry. He served in the field until after the Battle of Chancellorsville. In the spring of 1863 he requested hospital duty because he suffered from piles (hemorrhoids), which made riding difficult, and he had also developed severe dysentery. For the rest of the war Amiss served in prison hospitals in Salisbury and Weldon, both in North Carolina.

After the Battle of Cedar Mountain on 9 August 1862, Thomas Amiss and his brother William, then a surgeon with the 60th Georgia Infantry, performed a remarkable feat of surgery on Confederate major Richard Snowden Andrews of the 1st Maryland Artillery. Andrews had been struck by a shell fragment that tore away part of his abdominal wall, allowing his intestines to protrude from his body, a wound uniformly considered fatal. Amiss and his brother treated Andrews by washing away the dirt and weeds with salt solution, removing portions of a fractured hipbone, and sewing him up. Andrews not only survived but returned to duty eight months later and lived to a ripe old age in Baltimore. After the operation was described in an unidentified British medical text, Andrews and his recovery from the wound became better known than the surgeons who had saved his life. The lessons learned from the procedure were reportedly influential in treating similar wounds during the Franco-Prussian War. Hunter Holmes McGuire described the operation, by "Drs. Amus and Walls, of Virginia," in the chapter on abdominal wounds that he wrote for the first American edition of Timothy Holmes's classic *System of Surgery, Theoretical and Practical* (1882), 3:499–500. A few years before his death Amiss related the story of the operation at a meeting of the Association of Medical Officers of the Army and Navy of the Confederacy, and it was printed in the *Southern Practitioner* in 1907.

Amiss returned to Rappahannock County after the war and quietly practiced medicine in Slate Mills until 1874, when he moved to Alma in Page County, followed by relocation in 1889 to Luray, where he practiced for the remainder of his life. He was a member of the Medical Society of Virginia and an assistant surgeon for the Norfolk and Western Railway. He was also a Mason and a charter member of the Rosser-Gibbons Camp of the United Confederate Veterans. Thomas Benjamin Amiss died in Luray on 9 November 1913 and was buried in his gray veteran's uniform in Green Hill Cemetery in Luray.

Harry J. Warthen Jr., "The Doctors Amiss of Luray," *Virginia Medical Monthly* 89 (1962): 552–53; unpublished letters, genealogy, and por. in possession of Amiss's great-granddaughter Ruth Ann Moore, of Arlington; family history in Mary Elizabeth Hite, *My Rappahannock Story Book* (1950), 208–209; and in Bruce, Tyler, and Morton, *History of Virginia*, 5:217–219; Compiled Service Records; Thomas B. Amiss, "Experiences as Soldier and Surgeon," *Southern Practitioner* 29 (1907): 599–603; Amos R. Koontz, "Disembowelment in the Field with Cure: The Amazing Feat of a Confederate Surgeon," *Current Medical Digest* 28 (May 1961): 50–52; obituary in *Luray Page News and Courier*, 14 Nov. 1913; memorial in *Virginia Medical Semi-Monthly* 18 (1913): 444.

E. RANDOLPH TRICE

ANDERSON, Abner (2 December 1832–3 August 1906), journalist, was born at Spring Garden in Pittsylvania County, the eldest of four sons and second of six children of Joseph Eggleston Anderson and Minerva Caroline Terry Anderson. His father was a prosperous merchant as well as a justice of the peace. Anderson grew up at Spring Garden and was educated at a private school in Botetourt County. In 1852 he entered the University of Virginia, where he studied for two years, taking general courses in ancient and modern languages, natural philosophy, and mathematics. He taught one session at Chatham Academy in Pittsylvania County after leaving the university.

In 1856 Anderson purchased the *Danville Register* in partnership with Lindsay M. Shumaker. They edited and published the weekly paper until 1857, when Anderson took sole control of it. Like most civic and business leaders in Danville, Anderson probably opposed secession during the winter of 1860–1861, but when the Civil War began, his Danville Blues militia company became part of the 18th Regiment Virginia Infantry. With the rank of captain, Anderson served as quartermaster from 24 April 1861 until 3 September 1862, when he resigned due to ill health. Thereafter he concentrated on his printing business and on publishing his newspaper. He even converted the *Register* to a daily in 1864. According to his brother Joseph Anderson, who served as a printer's apprentice at the time, the *Danville Register* published Jefferson Davis's last proclamation to the Confederacy, for which Secretary of State Judah P. Benjamin read the proof sheet in the newspaper office.

On 5 April 1865 Anderson's paper was the first in the South to publish the story of the fall of Richmond two days earlier. On 27 April several Union army regiments entered Danville. Union officers used the *Register*'s printing press to publish a newspaper, the *Sixth Corps*, which printed the first account of the occupation of Danville. The army published sixteen issues of the *Sixth Corps* on the presses of the *Danville Register*. Anderson resumed publishing weekly and semiweekly editions of the *Danville Register* in May 1865, and in February 1882 he again transformed it into a daily newspaper.

In 1869, as Reconstruction was coming to an end in Virginia, Anderson was elected to represent Pittsylvania County in the Senate of Virginia. He usually voted with the Conservatives in opposition to the Republicans, and he was appointed to the influential Committees on Finance and Federal Relations as well as the Joint Committee on the Library. He served one four-year term and declined to run for reelection in 1873.

In September 1884 Anderson relinquished control of the *Danville Register* to Abner Wentworth Clopton Nowlin. He did not immediately end his career in journalism but for a short time was a co-owner of the *Richmond Whig*. He served on a committee of local leaders who investigated the race riot that took place just before election day in Danville in 1883. Anderson also served as superintendent of schools in Danville from 1891 until 1905. He was a member of the First Presbyterian Church in Danville, of the Cabell-Graves Camp of the United Confederate Veterans, and of the Roman Eagle Lodge of Ancient Free and Accepted Masons. At the time of his death he was president of the Danville Perpetual Building Loan and Savings Company.

On 26 November 1862 Anderson married Maria Louise Dupuy. They had no children. Abner Anderson died of a heart attack at his home in Danville on 3 August 1906 and was buried in Green Hill Cemetery in Danville.

William Pope Anderson, *Anderson Family Records* (1936), 123–124; French Biographies; Compiled Service Records; James I. Robertson Jr., *18th Virginia Infantry* (1984), 39; Benjamin Simpson [Duval Porter], *Men, Places and Things* (1891), 295–296; Jane Gray Hagan, *The Story of Danville* (1950), 105–106, 156; obituary and account of funeral in *Danville Register*, 4, 5 Aug. 1906, and *Richmond Times-Dispatch*, 4 Aug. 1906.

CAROLYN SPARKS WHITTENBURG

ANDERSON, Archer (15 October 1838–4 January 1918), industrialist, was born at Old Point Comfort, the eldest of five sons and seven daughters of Sarah Eliza Archer Anderson and Joseph Reid Anderson, a United States Military Academy graduate then stationed at Fort Monroe. The birth took place in the home of maternal grandfather Robert Archer, a surgeon also serving at the fort. In 1841 the Andersons moved to Richmond, which remained their permanent home. Joseph Reid Anderson first managed, then leased, and finally purchased a controlling interest in the Tredegar ironworks, which developed into one of the South's major industrial complexes under his leadership and subsequently played an important role in the Confederate war effort.

Supervised early on by two "cultivated gentlewomen," the Misses Myers, Anderson later attended Turner's Classical School. Though fond of sports, he was also devoted to books. By the time he entered the University of Virginia at the age of fifteen he was fluent in French, Italian, and German, and could read and write Latin and some Greek. Until his death he continued to enjoy the classics in their original languages. Completing his M.A. in two rather than the usual three years, after graduation in June 1856 Anderson traveled in Europe for two years, studying briefly at the University of Berlin before returning to study law at the University of Virginia for the 1858–1859 school year.

In the summer of 1859 Anderson returned to Europe and on 9 August married Mary Anne Mason, the daughter of U.S. minister to France John Young Mason, a Virginian, in an Episcopal ceremony at the American legation in Paris. After a tour of Switzerland and Germany the newlyweds returned to Virginia and Archer entered the employ of his father at the Tredegar ironworks. The Andersons had four sons and three daughters, of whom the eldest son died young.

Anderson belonged to Company F, 1st Regiment Virginia Volunteers, a militia unit of prominent Richmond men. On 28 June 1861 he and his comrades were mustered into Confederate service as Company F of the 21st Regiment Virginia Infantry. In September he was appointed assistant adjutant general, 1st Brigade, Aquia District, with the rank of captain. Anderson fought in the Seven Days' Battles in 1862 and later that year, in a skirmish before the Battle of Sharpsburg (Antietam), had his horse shot from under him and was rendered unconscious for nearly ten hours. After his transfer to the Army of Tennessee, he lost another horse in the same manner at the Battle of Chickamauga. On 19 March 1865 Lieutenant Colonel Anderson participated as assistant adjutant general in that army's last major battle, at Bentonville, North Carolina.

Soon thereafter Anderson rejoined his father at the Tredegar Company and, along with other Tredegar officials, received a pardon from President Andrew Johnson in the fall of 1865 that enabled them to regain possession of the ironworks from the Union army. In 1866 and early in 1867 the General Assembly allowed the reincorporation of the Tredegar Company. Ten thousand shares were issued at $100 per share. Joseph Reid Anderson held 6,950 shares, while Archer Anderson had 500.

Early in 1867 Anderson was elected to the company's board and appointed its secretary and treasurer at an annual salary of $3,000. Only he and his father were empowered to sign contracts for the reorganized company, which prospered until the depression of 1873, when the failure of the New York and Oswego Midland Railroad and other companies indebted to Tredegar ultimately forced the ironwork's officers to declare it insolvent in 1876.

The corporation remained in receivership until 1879, but Joseph Reid Anderson had himself named receiver and led Tredegar out of bankruptcy, although he incurred a $1 million debt in the process. The debt was gradually reduced to $294,000 by January 1884. Dividend payments were reinstated in 1882 and maintained throughout the depression of 1893, though usually at only 2 percent.

A week after his father's death on 7 September 1892, Archer Anderson was elected Tredegar's president. Under his leadership the firm did not try to compete in steel but concentrated largely on proven iron products, such as spikes, rail fastenings, railroad-car wheels, and horseshoes. By 1903 artillery-shell production had been resumed, and in 1910 the stock dividend was increased from 5 to 7 percent. The outbreak of war in Europe in 1914 brought an even-bigger increase in profits, to nearly $300,000 in 1916, with the corporation declaring a 17 percent dividend. The next year total assets exceeded $2 million. While the corporation modernized by producing steel shells for the military and constructing a large shell foundry, it was in general conservatively operated in Anderson's last years. The bulk of the profits were used to pay down the small debt, to purchase other securities, and to increase the stockholders' dividends.

The company's profits also directly supported the Anderson children. Three sons held managerial positions at Tredegar, with Archer Anderson Jr. following his father as president of the firm. Sarah "Sally" Archer Anderson, one of the three daughters, played a prominent role in the Confederate Museum in Richmond. Her parents provided the inspiration, as both participated in Confederate memorial activities. Archer Anderson sponsored and attended veterans' reunions and delivered several orations on Confederate themes, the most notable being the principal address at the dedication of the Lee statue in Richmond on 29 May 1890. He encouraged remembrance of Confederate sacrifice and heroes, but he also looked forward to economic and industrial progress. Anderson was active in a variety of civic and veterans' organizations, including the Southern Historical Society, the Virginia Historical Society, and R. E. Lee Camp Number 1 of the United Confederate Veterans.

Archer Anderson died at his house in Richmond on 4 January 1918 after a short illness. Funeral services were held at Saint Paul's Episcopal Church, to which he had belonged for many years, and he was buried in the family plot at Hollywood Cemetery in Richmond.

Firm's history extensively documented in Tredegar Company Records, LVA, including typescript biography in Minutes of Directors and Stockholders, 2:256–266; family information in Anne Hobson Freeman, "A Cool Head in a Warm Climate," *Virginia Cavalcade* 12 (winter 1962–1963): 9–17, and Mason Family Papers, VHS; marriage reported in *Richmond Enquirer*, 2 Sept. 1859; Compiled Service Records; Susan A. Riggs, *21st Virginia Infantry* (1991), 59; Charles B. Dew, *Ironmaker to the Confederacy: Joseph R. Anderson and the Tredegar Iron Works* (1966); on Confederate memorialization see Archer Anderson Papers, MOC, and Anderson's addresses, most notably *Robert Edward Lee: An Address Delivered at the Dedication of the Monument to General Robert Edward Lee at Richmond, Virginia, May 29, 1890* (1890); obituaries and funeral notice in *Richmond News Leader*, 5, 7 Jan. 1918, and *Richmond Times-Dispatch*, 5 (por.), 6 Jan. 1918.

R. BARRY WESTIN

ANDERSON, Charles Rhodes (27 November 1877–24 October 1953), Winchester mayor, was born in Rock Enon Springs, Frederick County, the only son and elder of two children of Meredith Anderson and Susannah McCoy Anderson. Anderson was educated in a private school in Rock Enon Springs and in the public schools of Frederick County. He taught school at Gore in that county for several terms before attending Maryland Medical College in Baltimore and transferring to the University of Maryland School of Medicine in Baltimore, from which he received an M.D. in 1908 with a special interest in X-ray technology. Anderson practiced medicine in Gore from 1908 to 1916, when he moved to Winchester. In 1917–1918 he served in the Army Medical Corps, retiring with the rank of captain.

After his return to Winchester in 1918, Anderson maintained a private practice, was associated with Winchester Memorial Hospital, and served on the Frederick County Board of Health from 1918 until 1951. He invested wisely in real estate and was an active and prosperous member of the local business community. He served on the boards of the Northwestern Turnpike Company and the Commercial and Savings Bank and as a one-term president of the Winchester Chamber of Commerce. He was also an elder for many years and chairman of the board of the Cork Street Christian Church, which he had helped to build. Anderson's other activities included membership in veterans' and fraternal organizations and the American Medical Association, Southern Medical Association, and Medical Society of Virginia.

Anderson won election to the Winchester City Council for the first time in 1920 and served until 1928. In 1932 he was elected mayor of the city and was reelected without opposition three times. His sixteen years as mayor spanned depression and world war and were a period of population growth and an expanding economic base. On 8 June 1948 he lost his fifth race for mayor to a young veteran of World War II, but he won a seat on the council again in 1951 and served until he died.

Anderson married Ida Xanthippe Pugh, of Gore, on 23 October 1897. She died on

16 January 1929, and he married Lena Riley on 1 August 1930. He had no children with either wife, but adopted a son and a daughter. From his medical student days, his army service, and the use of his office X-ray machine, Anderson received or aggravated severe radiation burns on his hands and especially on his left arm. In 1952 a malignancy attributed to the burns necessitated the amputation of his left arm and eventually led to his death. Charles Rhodes Anderson died at his house in Winchester on 24 October 1953 and was buried in Mount Hebron Cemetery. By his will he created a scholarship fund for graduates of Frederick County's James Wood High School who wished to study agriculture at Virginia Polytechnic Institute.

Quarles, *Worthy Lives*, 3–4 (por.); Ralph T. Triplett, *A History of Upper Back Creek Valley* (1983), 24–25; other family information in obituaries of Ida X. Anderson, Charles R. Anderson Jr., and Lena R. Anderson, given respectively in *Winchester Evening Star*, 17 Jan. 1929, 6 Sept. 1930, and 9 Aug. 1971; Winchester City Circuit Court Will Book, 22:286–290; obituary in *Winchester Evening Star*, 24 Oct. 1953; memorial in *Virginia Medical Monthly* 80 (1953): 705.

BRENT TARTER

ANDERSON, Conwell Axel (24 May 1926–4 June 1986), president of Averett College, was born in Sister Bay, Door County, Wisconsin, the only son and youngest of three children of Arthur John Anderson and Amy Maria Seaquist Anderson. He grew up on his father's dairy farm and graduated from high school in 1943. After one year at Bethel Junior College in Saint Paul, Minnesota, he enlisted in the United States Navy. While serving on a minesweeper, he was wounded on 6 April 1945 during the battle for Okinawa. In 1946 he returned to Bethel Junior College and after completing his second year married Marjorie Jean Erickson on 29 August 1947. They had two daughters and one son.

Anderson then entered the University of Alabama in Tuscaloosa, where he received a B.A. in 1949, an M.A. in 1950, and a Ph.D in Latin American history in 1954. The same year that he completed his doctorate he joined the faculty of Mary Hardin-Baylor College, a small Baptist college for women in Belton, Texas. He was appointed academic dean in 1955 and devoted the remainder of his career to church college administration instead of scholarly research and teaching. He did, however, publish two articles on history as well as several short pieces about education.

In 1960 Anderson became president of Judson College in Marion, Alabama. During his years as its head, Anderson persuaded the college's trustees to desegregate Judson, but local tensions over race relations made Anderson uncomfortable, and in 1965 he accepted an offer to become president of Maryland Baptist College, which was still in the planning stages. The board of trustees, however, voted to make the new school a junior college instead of the four-year institution originally planned, and Anderson immediately resigned. In January 1966 he became associate director of the Institute of Higher Education at the University of Georgia in Athens.

On 1 September 1966 Anderson assumed the presidency of Averett College, a two-year Baptist college for women in Danville. During the next thirteen years he completely transformed Averett. It became a four-year institution in 1969 and coeducational in September 1970, and it won accreditation from the Southern Association of Colleges and Secondary Schools in December 1971. The student population more than doubled, and the number of faculty members with doctorates grew from less than 1 percent to 50 percent by 1979. Under Anderson the operating budget increased fivefold and salaries rose above the average for southern Baptist colleges. Averett acquired or constructed several new buildings, including a library, which increased its holdings 500 percent. Late in the 1960s the college began accepting federal student-aid money and enrolled its first minority students. Approximately one-fourth of the 1,993 students who graduated during Anderson's tenure at Averett College became teachers in Virginia schools.

Anderson steered a delicate course with the board of the Virginia Baptist General Association. The board allowed him to retain some Baptist funding as he increased revenue from state and other sources, and it also allowed him to relax some of the traditional strict requirements for student behavior. Anderson was not able to bring about a merger with neighboring Stratford College, which soon closed, and he also failed in a bid to move Averett College to a larger site several miles from the campus. Nevertheless, Anderson's achievements during his thirteen years as president can be considered among the most significant in the college's history. He served on the boards of several Danville cultural and charitable organizations, on an advisory committee of the State Council of Higher Education in Virginia, and on the board of the Council of Independent Colleges in Virginia and as its president in 1976–1977. Anderson suffered a heart attack in the autumn of 1975, and he underwent bypass surgery in March 1976. His recovery was not complete, and in the spring of 1978 he resigned effective 30 June 1979, after which he retired to Sister Bay.

Conwell Axel Anderson died on 4 June 1986 of a heart attack suffered on the golf course in Sister Bay. He was buried in that town's Little Sister Cemetery.

Birth and death dates courtesy Wisconsin Department of Health and Social Services, Madison; Jack Irby Hayes Jr., *History of Averett College* (1984), 151–193 (por., 157); Anderson's publications include "Spanish Caribbean and Gulf Defense, 1763–1783" (Ph.D. diss., University of Alabama, 1954), "Gibraltar: Fortress or Pawn?," *Southwestern Social Science Quarterly* 39 (1958): 224–231, "Quality Instruction: A Sine Qua Non for the Christian College" and "What About Year-Round Operation?," *Southern Baptist Educator* 24 (Jan. 1960): 12–13 and 30 (Nov. 1965): 3–5, *The Idea of a Judson Education* (1964), and "Anglo-Spanish Negotiations Involving Central America in 1783," in *Militarists, Merchants, and Missionaries: United States Expansion in Middle America*, ed. Eugene R. Huck and Edward H. Moseley (1970), 23–37; *Religious Herald*, 25 Aug. 1966, 1 Apr. 1976, 3 May 1979; *Virginia Baptist Annual* (1973): 164; (1976): 210; (1986): 148; obituary in *Danville Register*, 6 June 1986.

EMILY J. SALMON

ANDERSON, David (ca. 1760–18 June 1812), merchant and philanthropist, was born in Scotland. He arrived in Petersburg about 1782 and belonged for the next three decades to the town's thriving community of merchants. He probably acquired land in Prince George County, and in 1801 he purchased half of lot number 44 on the south side of Old Street in Petersburg. Almost nothing else is known of his background or personal life.

Anderson was one of many Scottish merchants who played important roles in Petersburg's economy both before and after the Revolution. They directed the shipment of tobacco to British ports and imported manufactured goods to Virginia. Some of them directed country agents who sold merchandise to farmers and bought tobacco for export. Anderson's name frequently appeared in the Petersburg city deed book in the capacity of surety and court-appointed appraiser of estates, evidence that he was regarded as solvent and reliable. His high standing in the community is affirmed by a tombstone that the city ordered erected over his grave twenty years after his death, with an inscription praising Anderson, "long a member of the Common Hall and Chamberlain of the Town of Petersburg," as "upright, honorable, kind, and benevolent."

Anderson is best remembered for providing funds from his estate for the first free school in Petersburg, the origin of the city's public school system. He made the bequest in his will, which he signed two days before his death. The document also provided small bequests for Nancy Hall, a free black woman, and Richard, a slave. He named his executors as guardians for Jingo, his slave and "dutiful servant" for twenty years, and directed the guardians to let Jingo "enjoy the fruits of his labor" and to pay him $300 annually from the estate. After Jingo's death, the city of Petersburg was to receive the residue of the estate with the "stipulation that the interest shall be applied and expended in the education of Poor Boys and Girls (white children)," whose parents could not otherwise afford to educate them. Each child was to receive three years of schooling. As his executors Anderson named fellow merchants Alexander Brown, Joel Hammon, Archibald Baugh, who was a recent mayor of Petersburg, and Robert Ritchie, who succeeded Anderson as town chamberlain, or treasurer.

Petersburg did not wait for Jingo's death to press its claim to Anderson's estate. Jingo was still alive in February 1821, when the Superior Court of Chancery for the Richmond district ordered Anderson's executors to turn over the estate's assets of $10,027.56 to the town chamberlain. The school, named the Anderson Seminary, then opened in May 1821. Its curriculum of reading, writing, and basic arithmetic was conducted on the innovative Lancasterian plan, under which advanced students taught the beginners. The school had enrolled more than four hundred students by 1830, and in 1835 it occupied the building of the defunct Petersburg Academy. During the following years principals of the Anderson Seminary included two clergymen, Minton Thrift and John D. Keiley, as well as noted Virginia historian Charles Campbell. By the time of the Civil War the Anderson Seminary was one of three free schools operated by the town for the benefit of children whose parents could not afford to pay for tutors or to send them to private academies.

In 1868, with help from the Peabody Education Fund, Petersburg established its first board of education to oversee a new public school system consisting of the Anderson Seminary, the two other existing free schools, and a new high school, as well as four elementary schools for African American students. This system antedated the state public school system by two years. A large brick structure was built for the Anderson School on its property on West Washington Street in the 1870s, and soon afterward the Petersburg High School was merged with the Anderson School.

David Anderson died in Petersburg on 18 June 1812 and was buried in Blandford Cemetery near the southeast corner of Blandford Church.

James G. Scott and Edward A. Wyatt IV, *Petersburg's Story: A History* (1960), 117–119, 261–266; William D. Henderson, *The Unredeemed City: Reconstruction in Petersburg, Virginia, 1865–1874* (1977), 74, 158, 183–188, 280; Petersburg Hustings Court Deed Book, 3:21–22, 6:301; will dated 16 June 1812 and proved 6 July 1812, Petersburg Hustings Court Will Book, 2:69–70; gravestone inscription, Blandford Cemetery, Petersburg, records date of death at age fifty-two.

J. MARSHALL BULLOCK

ANDERSON, David Wesley (22 September 1828–30 April 1903), Confederate army officer, was born in Louisa County, the sixth of seven sons and tenth of eleven children of John B. Anderson and Nancy Lasley Anderson. Nothing is known about his education, but he was a well-read man and also a devout Methodist. He moved to Fluvanna County while young and lived on a farm near the confluence of the Hardware and James Rivers. The 1860 census recorded his possession of six slaves. He married Ann Roberta Williams on 23 November 1853. Their daughter and son both died in infancy.

When the Civil War broke out Anderson organized and was elected captain of the Fluvanna Guard, which became Company K of the 44th Regiment Virginia Infantry. The regiment fought in western Virginia during 1861 and in 1862 in the Valley campaign, in the Seven Days' Battles, and at the Second Battle of Manassas (Bull Run). Anderson was severely wounded at the Battle of Sharpsburg (Antietam) on 17 September 1862 and recuperated for several months at home before rejoining his company early in 1863. He participated in the Battle of Chancellorsville, was promoted to major effective 16 June 1863, and served with the regiment on Culp's Hill at Gettysburg. On 12 May 1864 he was field officer of the day during the Battle of Spotsylvania Court House and was captured along with many of the regiment's other officers when the Union army overran his position, the so-called Bloody Angle. Anderson was imprisoned in Delaware, but in June he and about fifty other Confederate officers were sent by ship to Charleston, South Carolina, where they were placed in the line of fire in retaliation for Confederate guns having fired on Union prisoners.

Anderson was exchanged in August 1864 and after a brief furlough returned to the 44th Virginia Infantry. He was wounded a second time at Cedar Creek on 19 October 1864 and convalesced in a Charlottesville hospital and at home before he rejoined the regiment for the last time early in 1865. Anderson was in command of the remaining seventeen officers and men of the 44th Virginia Infantry when it surrendered at Appomattox Court House on 9 April 1865.

Anderson returned to his farm in Fluvanna County after the war. His wife died on 25 November 1869, and on 5 July 1871 he married her sister Abigail Elizabeth Williams. They had one daughter and one son, both of whom lived until the 1950s. In addition to farming and teaching in the Methodist Sunday school, he was active in Fluvanna County Democratic Party politics and served in the House of Delegates in the session of 1887–1888. At the time of his death he was chairman of the Fluvanna County Board of Supervisors. David Wesley Anderson died of a stroke at his home on 30 April 1903 and was buried in the Champion family cemetery in Fluvanna County.

Family Bible records, with 30 Apr. 1903 death date, in private possession, 1989; Kevin C. Ruffner, *44th Virginia Infantry* (1987; por., 64); Compiled Service Records; death notices with date of 1 May 1903 in *Richmond Times-Dispatch*, 3 May 1903, and *Richmond News Leader*, 4 May 1903; obituary with 30 Apr. 1903 death date in *Confederate Veteran* 12 (1903): 236–237 (por.).

KEVIN CONLEY RUFFNER

ANDERSON, David Wiley (20 August 1864–7 April 1940), architect, was born in Albemarle County, the youngest of six sons and four daughters of John Bledsoe Anderson and Mary Morris Anderson. He attended public schools, where he excelled in drawing and mathematics. During holidays he worked for his father, a respected contractor, and became interested in architecture, although he never had any formal architectural training. He moved to Richmond about 1889 and worked for George Parsons, a builder-designer who had himself learned the craft as an apprentice to another builder-designer. Anderson worked with Parsons for six years and learned not only how to design and erect buildings, but also how to advertise his services and promote himself.

D. Wiley Anderson established his own architectural practice in 1895. Throughout his career he listed the names of important clients and identified his projects on the back of his office stationery, and early in the twentieth century he distributed an illustrated promotional booklet to advertise his achievements. More than sixty buildings in central and eastern Virginia are known to have been done to his specifications, but that is probably only a fraction of his entire body of work. Anderson designed churches, apartment and office buildings, warehouses, schools, theaters and auditoriums, recreational buildings, at least one courthouse, and many residences. Several of his earliest houses were for the new suburban development on the north side of Richmond in the vicinity of Lewis Ginter's Westbrook estate. He prepared plans for spacious and sometimes luxurious houses appropriate for country estates, and by engaging manufacturers and retailers of building supplies to participate in the design and construction of these buildings, he sought to tie his work to theirs and thereby promote his career further. Anderson also designed a number of residences in each of the principal new developments in Richmond during the first third of the twentieth century, including the Fan District and neighborhoods west of the Boulevard, on Monument Avenue, and near Ginter Park. One of his best-known residential commissions outside Richmond was for Ednam, a spectacularly ambitious white-columned mansion in Albemarle County.

Anderson's residential designs, even more than his commercial and public projects, reflected his individualism and proclaimed the lack of academic training that might have confined his work to one or a few of the styles then currently popular. His work was bold and sure with lively elevations. It featured Romanesque, Gothic, and other Romantic styles and often displayed an eccentric use of detail. He enlivened the Colonial Revival style with a love of surprise and asymmetry, and he juggled styles and changed and resold variations on previous designs with the energy of a creator and the instincts of an entrepreneur.

In 1902 Anderson entered the design competition for enlarging and renovating the Capitol in Richmond. He recommended adding a portico like that on the south front to the north end, placing shallow porticoes on the east and west sides, extending interior offices out onto part of the main porticoes, and placing a cupola on a drum on top of the roof. The judges of the contest rejected Anderson's design, but his somewhat-cluttered adaptation of Colonial Revival elements to the classical temple-form structure evidently gained Anderson a degree of local publicity and probably brought him additional commissions as well.

Anderson married Cora B. Marshall on 23 May 1888. They had two daughters and three sons before she died on 20 February 1896. On 30 June 1897 he married Sarah Wilkinson. They had five daughters and three sons. In his spare time Anderson continually worked on inventions. He designed a heating stove with a temperature regulator, bricks molded for specific architectural purposes, and an ingenious bathtub-shower combination that could be folded into the wall of a small apartment like a Murphy bed. With the income from his professional work and his inventions he purchased a farm on the line between Albemarle and Fluvanna Counties in 1915 and named it Albevanna Farm. He installed his family there and lived at the farm on weekends before he retired and moved there for good in 1919. The property had a spring on it, and Anderson made ambitious plans to develop it into a spa, but he never completed the work necessary to attract paying customers.

D. Wiley Anderson died of bronchitis at Albevanna Farm on 7 April 1940 and was buried nearby in the cemetery at Scottsville Presbyterian Church.

D. Wiley Anderson Papers, VHS; Wells and Dalton, *Virginia Architects*, 6–8; early work documented in advertising pamphlet, *Short Reviews: A Few Recent Designs* [ca. 1904], photocopy in Virginia Department of Historic Resources, Richmond; obituaries in *Richmond News Leader* and *Richmond Times-Dispatch*, both 8 Apr. 1940.

SARAH SHIELDS DRIGGS

ANDERSON, Dice Robins (18 April 1880–23 October 1942), president of Randolph-Macon Woman's College, was born in Charlottesville, the only son and one of three children of Methodist minister James Madison Anderson and Margaret Olivia Robins Anderson. He attended Hoge Academy (later called Blackstone Military Academy) in Blackstone, and Randolph-Macon College in Ashland. He graduated with a B.A. in 1900 and the next year received his M.A. in history.

Anderson taught mathematics at Central Female College in Lexington, Missouri, during the academic year 1901–1902. He returned to Virginia to teach history at Randolph-Macon Academy in Bedford in 1902–1903, and was principal of Chesapeake Academy at Irvington, Lancaster County, from 1903 to 1906. In 1906–1907 he served as president of Willie Halsell College in Vinita, Oklahoma. He married a music teacher, Ada James Ash, on 24 June 1903. They had two sons.

Anderson published "Robert Mercer Taliaferro Hunter" in the *John P. Branch Historical Papers of Randolph-Macon College* 2 (1906): 4–77, which his mentor at Randolph-Macon, William E. Dodd, edited. After Dodd joined the faculty of the University of Chicago, Anderson entered the university in 1907 as a graduate student. Anderson's 1912 doctoral dissertation on William Branch Giles was enlarged and published two years later as *William Branch Giles: A Study in the Politics of Virginia and the Nation from 1790 to 1830*, and he also produced an article on "The Insurgents of 1811," *American Historical Association Annual Report for 1911* (1913): 1:165–176.

After he completed his course work and while he was researching and writing his dissertation, Anderson taught history at Richmond College. He served as professor of history and political science from 1909 to 1919 and in 1919–1920 became professor of economics and political science and director of the college's School of Business Administration. In 1915 he founded the *Richmond College Historical Papers* in imitation of Dodd's *John P. Branch Historical Papers*. In this venue he published a number of previously unknown Revolutionary War and early national period letters and documents that he identified in the Virginia State Library, but the college suspended financial support for the journal after only three issues. Anderson's scholarship on Virginians of the early national period culminated in his essay on Edmund Randolph's term as secretary of state in a distinguished biographical reference work edited by Samuel Flagg Bemiss, *American Secretaries of State and Their Diplomacy* (1927), 2:97–159.

Richmond College granted Anderson leaves of absence twice between 1916 and 1918 to serve as executive secretary of the Richmond Civic Association and to participate in a major reorganization of the Richmond city government. Anderson was a founder of the Richmond First Club, which campaigned for adoption of a new city charter.

Anderson was elected president of Randolph-Macon Woman's College in Lynchburg early in 1920 and took office on 1 April of that year. His foremost challenge was to raise funds to pay off the school's debts. During the next eight years he obtained more than $1.25 million from the General Education Board of the Methodist Church, alumnae, and other sources. He raised additional money to construct a new library and a new music building, and he presided over the founding of a distinguished permanent art collection. He also moved to end the rigidity of the curriculum by proposing a radical change in the college's degree requirements. In September 1930, after two years of heated debate, the faculty and the board adopted a new curriculum that allowed up to sixty hours of elective courses.

Anderson served as president of the Department of Colleges of the Virginia Education Conference and as president of the Virginia Association of Colleges in 1923. In 1924 the College of William and Mary awarded him an LL.D. degree. He was an active Methodist layman and served as a delegate to seven Virginia conferences of the Methodist Episcopal Church South.

In the spring of 1931 Anderson resigned from Randolph-Macon Woman's College to become president of another Methodist-affiliated college for women, Wesleyan College in Macon, Georgia. His wife died on 17 May 1931, a few days before he left Lynchburg. Anderson faced even more severe financial problems in Macon than when he had moved to Lynchburg. Wesleyan College had recently relocated to a new campus and owed its creditors a million dollars. The Great Depression made raising funds extremely difficult, and in 1938 the college was sold at auction. Wesleyan continued to operate, however, and Anderson and the board undertook the massive task of buying back the college. The Wesleyan Corporation acquired title to the school in March 1939, but it remained in precarious financial condition, and in December 1941 the Southern Association of Colleges and Secondary Schools placed it on probation.

Anderson married Martha Crumpton Hardy on 24 December 1932. As he had in Virginia, he participated in education and church affairs while he lived in Georgia. He served as president of the Georgia Assembly of Colleges in 1936 and from 1933 through 1938 on the South Georgia Conference of the Methodist Episcopal Church South. He was also a delegate to two national church conferences.

In 1941 Anderson retired as president of Wesleyan College and returned to Virginia to become professor of history and government at Mary Washington College. Dice Robins Anderson died of a heart attack on 23 October 1942 at his home in Fredericksburg and was buried in Spring Hill Cemetery in Lynchburg.

Dice Robins Anderson Papers, Randolph-Macon Woman's College Library; W. Harrison Daniel, *History at the University of Richmond* (1991), 54–63, 71–74, 100–107; Roberta D. Cornelius, *History of Randolph-Macon Woman's College* (1951), 207–261; F. N. Boney, "'The Pioneer College for Women': Wesleyan Over a Century and a Half," *Georgia Historical Quarterly* 72 (1988): 523; obituaries in *Fredericksburg Free Lance-Star*, 23 Oct. 1942, and *Lynchburg Daily Advance*, *Lynchburg News* (por.), *New York Times*, and *Richmond News Leader*, all 24 Oct. 1942.

ROBERT S. ALLEY

ANDERSON, Edward Clifford (26 November 1893–25 July 1985), banker, was born in Richmond, one of four children of Estelle Marguerite Burthe Anderson and George Wayne Anderson, who later became Richmond's city attorney. Anderson attended Woodberry Forest School near Orange from 1906 to 1913 and the University of Virginia, where he studied engineering and played varsity football, from 1913 to 1916. He then transferred to the Massachusetts Institute of Technology. Anderson interrupted his education in 1917 to enter the United States Army. He served in the artillery in France and received the Silver Star and French Croix de Guerre. He returned to MIT and received his bachelor's degree in engineering in 1919.

After two years as a traveling agent for a tobacco company, Anderson joined the Richmond brokerage and investment banking firm of Scott and Stringfellow. He became a general partner there in 1927, and by World War II, when he directed several drives to sell war bonds, he was one of the leading investment bankers in Richmond. He also served on the board of visitors of the University of Virginia from 1942 to 1952. He married Isabel Walker Scott, daughter of one of the firm's founders, on 12 January 1922. They had two daughters and one son.

In January 1948 a reorganization of Scott and Stringfellow took place, in which several new partners joined the firm and Anderson and another partner, Edmund Strudwick Jr., left it to form their own small investment-banking business, Anderson and Strudwick. In one early venture, the new firm promoted Eastern Natural Gas, a company that intended to bring natural gas service to Richmond. Scott and Stringfellow was handling a public offering of stock by a competitor, Commonwealth Natural Gas Corporation, in 1950. In the end, the two gas companies merged under the latter name, and Anderson and Strudwick together with Scott and Stringfellow jointly managed the underwriting of the stock in the new corporation. By 1957 Anderson and Strudwick had become a member firm of the New York Stock Exchange and an associate member of the American Stock Exchange. Anderson served as vice president of the Richmond Stock Exchange and as a vice chairman of the Southeast Group of the Investment Bankers Association of America. In addition to underwriting stocks and bonds, Anderson and Strudwick invested in real estate and other businesses in Richmond. Anderson also owned Bushy Park Farm, a dairy near Deltaville in Middlesex County, and was a member of the Virginia State Dairymen's Association and the American Dairy Association.

Anderson and his wife were active in many civic and educational organizations from the 1930s into the 1970s. After World War II he served on the finance committee of the Children's Home Society of Virginia and chaired the American Red Cross blood drive in Richmond. He had grown up as a Presbyterian, but after he married he joined the Episcopal Church and served as a vestryman of Richmond's Saint Paul's Church. He was also on the vestry of Saint Ann's Parish in Kennebunkport, Maine, where he owned a summer house and indulged his love of golf and sailing. He withdrew from the daily management of the firm after suffering a heart attack. Edward Clifford Anderson died in Saint Mary's Hospital in Richmond on 25 July 1985 and was buried in Hollywood Cemetery.

Family history in Tyler, *Men of Mark*, 4:10–12; other family and professional history courtesy of son, George Wayne Anderson, of Richmond; formation of Anderson and Strudwick announced in *Richmond News Leader*, 2 Jan. 1948; obituaries in *Richmond News Leader* (por.) and *Richmond Times-Dispatch*, both 26 July 1985.

Martha L. Reiner

ANDERSON, Eleanor Gladys Copenhaver (15 June 1896–12 September 1985), women's organization leader, was born in Marion, the eldest of one son and four daughters of Laura Lu Scherer Copenhaver and Bascom Eugene Copenhaver. Her mother was an accomplished author, leader in the Lutheran Church, and founder of Rosemont Industries in Marion. Her father was a teacher and for thirty-six years superintendent of Smyth County schools. She grew up in Rosemont, one of the oldest houses in town, next door to Marion College, which her maternal grandfather, John Jacob Scherer, had founded in 1873. She attended the public schools in Marion and graduated from Westhampton College in Richmond in 1917. After teaching for one year in Marion, she entered Bryn Mawr College and in 1920 received a certificate in social economy from the Department of Social Economy and Social Research. She received a master's degree in political economy from Columbia University in 1933.

In 1920 Copenhaver joined the national staff of the Young Women's Christian Association. She worked in Florida as a county and district secretary until 1923, when she transferred to the central region as a staff member of the YWCA's new industrial department. In 1925 she moved to New York to work at the national headquarters of the industrial department, overseeing organizations of factory workers and serving as a liaison officer with trade unions, women's clubs, businesses, and government agencies. She traveled extensively to attend conferences, visit local YWCA offices, serve as a counselor at camps, and conduct major field studies in Chicago, Kansas City, and San Francisco. From 1938 to 1946 she was director of the YWCA national industrial staff.

While visiting Marion in 1928, she met the writer Sherwood Anderson, who had moved to Virginia two years earlier and become editor of the local newspapers. They were married in Marion on 6 July 1933. For the first five years of their marriage she spent half her time working for the YWCA and half her time in Marion or on the road with Anderson. She used the Copenhaver name for several years but gradually became known as Eleanor Copenhaver Anderson. As a result of her influence, he committed himself to studying and writing about industry in the South. Sherwood Anderson died in Panama on 8 March 1941 while they were on a trip to South America.

Anderson's responsibilities at the YWCA increased when she became head of the industrial staff in 1938. She worked on problems of women in industry, such as poor working environments, inadequate child care, and crowded housing. She also kept up a demanding schedule of nationwide speaking engagements, tours, conferences, and workshops, and spent five months on the West Coast in 1942 studying wartime working conditions. In 1946 the YWCA abolished its industrial division, which had become one of its most controversial programs. In 1947 Anderson joined the foreign division of the YWCA and spent two years in Italy coordinating relief programs. Afterward, she worked with the United Community Defense Service and with the American Labor Education Service, and before she retired in 1961 she conducted an investigation of working conditions in South America for the YWCA.

Anderson also managed her husband's literary estate. In 1947 she deposited his manuscripts in the Newberry Library in Chicago and helped organize the collection. She assisted Paul Rosenfeld, who edited *The Sherwood Anderson Reader* (1947), and she encouraged the production of a stage version of Anderson's *Winesburg, Ohio* on Broadway in 1958. She also helped scholars who were studying her husband's literary career, and she maintained Ripshin, his house near Trout Dale, Grayson County, much as he had left it. After her retirement Anderson spent the winters in her YWCA apartment in New York and the remainder of the year at Rosemont in Marion. From 1967 to 1985 she helped run Rosemont Industries and renamed it Laura Copenhaver Industries.

Eleanor Copenhaver Anderson died of pneumonia in Marion on 12 September 1985, and her ashes were buried next to Sherwood Anderson's body in Round Hill Cemetery in Marion.

Margaret Ripley Wolfe, "Eleanor Copenhaver Anderson of the National Board of the YWCA: Appalachian Feminist and Author's Wife," *Winesburg Eagle* 18 (summer 1993): 2–9 (por.); oral history interview in "Southern Women After Suffrage," Southern Oral History Program, UNC; "An Interview with Mrs. Sherwood Anderson" in *Sherwood Anderson: Centennial Studies*, ed. Hilbert H. Campbell and Charles E. Modlin (1976), 67–82; Sherwood Anderson Papers, Newberry Library, Chicago, Ill.; Charles E. Modlin, ed., *Sherwood Anderson's Love Letters to Eleanor Copenhaver Anderson* (1989); Ray Lewis White, ed., *Sherwood Anderson's Secret Love Letters* (1991); Hilbert H. Campbell, ed., *The Sherwood Anderson Diaries* (1987); Margaret Ripley Wolfe, "Sherwood Anderson and the Southern Highlands: A Sense of Place and the Sustenance of Women," *Southern Studies* 3 (1992): 253–275; obituaries in *Richmond News Leader*, 12 Sept. 1985, *Bristol Herald Courier* and *Richmond Times-Dispatch*, both 13 Sept. 1985, and *Winesburg Eagle* 11 (Nov. 1985): 11.

CHARLES E. MODLIN

ANDERSON, Francis Thomas (11 December 1808–30 November 1887), Supreme Court of Appeals judge, was born at Walnut Hill in Botetourt County, the fourth of six sons and seventh of ten children of William Anderson and Anna Thomas Anderson. His brothers John Thomas Anderson and Joseph Reid Anderson became prominent iron manufacturers and politicians.

Francis Thomas Anderson studied with a series of local schoolmasters before matriculating at Washington College in Lexington. He graduated in 1827, read law in the offices of Fleming B. Miller and Allen Taylor, and was admitted to the bar in Botetourt County on 8 February 1830. On 8 December of the latter year he married Mary Ann Alexander, of Rockbridge County. The most notable of their three sons and six daughters was William Alexander Anderson, attorney general of Virginia from 1902 to 1910.

Anderson practiced law and lived in a house called Montrose near Fincastle in Botetourt County until about 1856. He then moved to

Rockbridge County, where he spent most of his time for the next twelve years operating a large iron foundry at Glenwood. Anderson admired Henry Clay and belonged to the Whig Party. Local party leaders frequently mentioned him as a possible candidate for the General Assembly or for Congress, but he held no political office until 1860, when he served as a presidential elector for John Bell, the Constitutional Union Party candidate. Anderson opposed secession until after the firing on Fort Sumter, then represented Rockbridge County in the House of Delegates during the wartime sessions from December 1861 through March 1863.

About 1869 Anderson resumed practicing law in Lexington. On 23 March 1870 the General Assembly elected him one of the five justices of the Supreme Court of Appeals under the new constitution that went into effect that year. He served for one twelve-year term. Anderson dealt with a broad range of subjects, with cases involving the settlement of Virginia's public debt coming up several times. He usually found reasons to uphold statutes enacted by the conservative Funders, who were resisting public pressure either to repudiate some of the principal of the public debt or to invalidate the controversial provisions of the Funding Act of 1871 that permitted bondholders to pay taxes and other public dues with coupons. In two cases, adopting the extreme view of the most adamant Funders, Anderson ruled that the contract clause of the United States Constitution gave the state's creditors precedence over schools and other state institutions in the appropriation of public money. Unsurprisingly, Anderson was not reelected in 1882, when the Readjuster Party controlled the assembly and replaced all the members of the Supreme Court of Appeals.

Anderson returned to Lexington and lived there for the remainder of his life. He had been elected to the board of Washington College in 1853 and was rector of the renamed Washington and Lee University from 1879 until his death. He had participated in inviting Robert E. Lee to assume the presidency of the college in 1865, and he was a pallbearer at Lee's funeral in 1870. Francis Thomas Anderson died in his sleep early in the morning of 30 November 1887 and was buried in Lexington.

Biography with extracts from memorial addresses by judges and attorneys in Seargent S. P. Patteson, "The Supreme Court of Appeals of Virginia," *Green Bag* 5 (1893): 407–415 (por.); Anderson Family Papers, UVA, contain Anderson's handwritten memoir of his parents, legal papers, and William A. Anderson's draft for the biography that appeared in *Green Bag*; letters from Anderson in Bruce Family Papers, UVA; Ellen Graham Anderson, "The Four Anderson Brothers," *Journal of the Roanoke Historical Society* 6 (summer 1969): 15–27; Anderson's comments on public debt cases in *Antoni* v. *Wright* (1872) (22 Grattan), *Virginia Reports*, 63:833, at 874, and *Clarke* v. *Tyler* (1878) (30 Grattan), *Virginia Reports*, 71:134, at 162; Hummel and Smith, *Portraits and Statuary*, 2 (por.); obituaries in *Lexington Gazette*, 1, 8 Dec. 1887, and *Richmond Dispatch*, 1 Dec. 1887.

BRENT TARTER

ANDERSON, George Kimbrough (6 March 1860–3 February 1930), member of the Convention of 1901–1902, was born at Old Hickory, the family residence in Louisa County on the Hanover County line, the second of three sons and third of six children of Matthew A. Anderson, a physician, and Ella Kimbrough Anderson. By the time Anderson was thirteen both of his parents had died, and he spent the next few years in the Louisa County home of his aunt and uncle Maria Louise Kimbrough Sims and Dr. Frederick H. Sims. He attended local schools including Harmony Academy and later read law in the offices of Edward W. Morris, of Hanover County, and Henry W. Murray, of Louisa County.

Anderson was admitted to the bar in Louisa County on 11 July 1881 and practiced there for nine years. On 22 October 1884 he married Susie L. Gooch, sister of his law partner, William S. Gooch. They had three daughters and one son. On 26 May 1887 Anderson defeated fellow Democrat William E. Bibb in the election for commonwealth's attorney of Louisa County and served from 1 July 1887 until he resigned effective 15 April 1890.

Anderson then moved to Clifton Forge, opened a law office, and for the next forty years was a leading citizen of Alleghany County. On 11 December 1895 the General Assembly elected him judge of Alleghany and Craig Counties. It reelected him in 1897 and added Bath County to his district.

On 23 May 1901 Anderson defeated a former member of the House of Delegates, John T.

Byrd, of Highland County, 1,696 to 507 in the election to represent the counties of Alleghany, Bath, and Highland in a state constitutional convention. Anderson was appointed to the Committees on the Organization and Government of Cities and Towns and on Privileges and Elections. He introduced three resolutions: to hold quadrennial sessions of the General Assembly, to abolish the county court system and provide for the popular election of some magistrates, and to disfranchise as many black voters as possible without reducing the number of white voters. Anderson opposed literacy tests as a prerequisite for voting because many of his constituents were nonliterate white Democrats. Nevertheless, he voted for the restrictive suffrage provisions that the convention adopted on 4 April 1902. Anderson participated in the debates on several occasions and argued for retention of twelve-member juries and against proposals to allow majority verdicts in some civil cases. He also advocated stricter regulation of railroads in the interest of safety. In a key vote taken on 29 May, he unsuccessfully opposed proclaiming the new constitution in effect without obtaining the approval of voters in a referendum.

Following reorganization of the state's court system under the new constitution, the General Assembly in February 1903 elected Anderson judge of the Nineteenth Judicial Circuit, which included the counties of Alleghany, Bath, Botetourt, Craig, and Highland, and after 1906 the city of Clifton Forge as well. He was reelected three times, serving until his death and acquiring a reputation for carefully reasoned and just decisions that were seldom overturned on appeal. George Kimbrough Anderson died at his home in Clifton Forge on 3 February 1930 and was buried in Crown Hill Cemetery there.

Richmond Daily Times, 12 June 1901 (por.); *Clifton Forge Daily Review*, 3, 5 Feb. 1930; Malcolm H. Harris, *History of Louisa County, Virginia* (1936), 240; *Journal of 1901–1902 Convention*; *Convention of 1901–1902 Photographs* (por.); *Proceedings and Debates of 1901–1902 Convention*; obituaries in *Clifton Forge Daily Review*, 3 Feb. 1930, and *Lexington Gazette*, 4 Feb. 1930; tributes in *Clifton Forge Daily Review*, 5, 6 Feb. 1930; memorial in *Virginia State Bar Association Proceedings* (1930): 180–183 (por.).

BRENT TARTER

ANDERSON, George Wayne (10 July 1863–30 December 1922), attorney, was born at Edgehill in Albemarle County, one of two sons and two daughters of Edward Clifford Anderson, a colonel in the Confederate army, and Jane Margaret Randolph Anderson, a granddaughter of Thomas Jefferson. He grew up in Savannah, Georgia, where his father became a banker, and was educated at Hanover Academy and at the University of Virginia, from which he received a law degree in 1888. That same year he began the practice of law in Richmond.

Anderson joined the Virginia militia as a second lieutenant in the cavalry on 25 September 1890. After several changes of duty and promotions he retired with a rank of colonel on 20 November 1906. He played a key role in one of the most controversial assignments that the militia undertook during those years. In the summer of 1903 he commanded the thirteen hundred men Governor Andrew Jackson Montague called out during a strike by underpaid and overworked Richmond streetcar operators. The strikers had the support of much of the public, many businessmen, and Richmond mayor Richard M. Taylor, and after the company brought in outsiders to replace the striking streetcar workers, several violent incidents took place. Virginia militiamen under Anderson's command rode the streetcars for a month to protect the nonunion employees. During the unpopular operation, militiamen shot and killed a man who attempted to escape after being arrested.

Anderson also commanded a unit of militiamen who in February 1904 transported an accused rapist from Richmond to Roanoke to stand trial because Governor Montague and Roanoke authorities feared that without the presence of the militia a riot or lynching might ensue. On both occasions Anderson's performance received the approbation of the adjutant general of Virginia, but his participation in putting down the streetcar strike may have shortened his promising political career.

Anderson won election to the House of Delegates in 1899 as one of the five members from the city of Richmond. Two years later he was elected to the Senate of Virginia as one of two members for the district composed of

Richmond and Henrico County. His term included service on the legislative commission that oversaw the renovation and enlargement of the Capitol, but his principal achievement was sponsorship of a bill that reformed the procedure by which cities annexed territory from neighboring counties. Anderson's bill was enacted early in 1904 and ended the cumbersome and politically charged process requiring cities to obtain special legislation for each municipal boundary alteration. The new law substituted a judicial proceeding intended to remove political considerations from the process of city expansion.

In the spring of 1904 Anderson entered the race for mayor of Richmond, but he withdrew before the election, and later in the year he decided not to seek reelection to the Senate in 1905. He ran for commonwealth's attorney of Richmond but lost the nomination in the 1905 primary election. He served as assistant city attorney from 1907 to 1921 and as city attorney in 1921 and 1922.

On 21 December 1889 Anderson married Estelle Marguerite Burthe, who for many years was a leader in charitable and musical organizations in Richmond, a founder of the Instructive Visiting Nurse Association, an officer of the Association for the Preservation of Virginia Antiquities, president of the Richmond women's auxiliary of the American Legion, and a founder of Richmond's Riverview Cemetery. One of their four children was Edward Clifford Anderson, who became a leading banker and stockbroker in Richmond. George Wayne Anderson died of cancer in Richmond on 30 December 1922 and was buried in Hollywood Cemetery in Richmond.

Tyler, *Men of Mark*, 4:10–12; family history verified by grandson George Anderson, of Richmond; feature article on wife in *Richmond Times-Dispatch*, 30 Nov. 1952; Jo Lane Stern, *Roster, Commissioned Officers, Virginia Volunteers, 1871–1920* (1921), 6–7; Adjutant General of Virginia, *Report* (1903): 25–54; (1904): 44–51, 71–78; Thomas J. Headlee Jr., "The Richmond Streetcar Strike of 1903," *Virginia Cavalcade* 25 (1976): 176–183; Chester W. Bain, *Annexation in Virginia* (1966), 8–10; *Richmond Times-Dispatch*, 9, 10, 15 Apr. 1904, 22 June 1905; obituaries in *Richmond News Leader*, 30 Dec. 1922 (por.), and *Richmond Times-Dispatch*, 31 Dec. 1922.

W. H. BRYSON

ANDERSON, Henry Watkins (20 December 1870–7 January 1954), attorney and Republican Party leader, was born at Hampstead, the Dinwiddie County estate of his father, William Watkins Anderson, a doctor and farmer, and Laura Elizabeth Marks Anderson. He was the younger of two sons, and he and his twin sister were the third and fourth of five children. Although once prosperous, the Anderson family had lost much of its property and standing as a result of the Civil War. Anderson attended public schools in Dinwiddie County and had a succession of private tutors. After a brief stint at a business college, he worked for four years as a stenographer with the Richmond and Danville Railroad, then moved to Roanoke to take a similar position with the Norfolk and Western Railway.

In the summer of 1897 Anderson began to study law and work as a clerk for the law firm of Staples and Munford in Richmond. Later that year he became the secretary of William L. Wilson, president of Washington and Lee University, a position that enabled him to attend law school. He received an LL.B. in 1898 and returned to Richmond. He was admitted to the bar and on 1 October 1899 formed a partnership with his former employer, Beverley Bland Munford. Two years later Anderson persuaded Munford, Edmund Randolph Williams, and Eppa Hunton to form a new firm, which evolved into Hunton Williams, one of the largest and most prestigious law firms in the South.

Anderson soon demonstrated that he was a brilliant corporate lawyer. After a lengthy litigation he reorganized several Richmond companies and helped put together the Virginia Railway and Power Company. He served as vice president and general counsel of the company from 1909 to 1916, and he was also the general counsel of the International and Great Northern Railway from 1912 to 1914.

In 1916 Anderson met and fell in love with the novelist Ellen Glasgow. The two brilliant eccentrics, who did not easily fit into Richmond society, began to write a political novel together, for which Anderson supplied copies of his speeches. As a result, the character David Blackburn in Glasgow's *The Builders* (1919) strongly resembles Anderson. When World War I broke out Anderson immediately lent his talents to the Virginia war relief effort. His attempt to enlist in the army once the United States entered the conflict was rebuffed because of age. When offered the opportunity to command the 150-person American Red Cross Commission to Romania, with the rank of lieutenant colonel, Anderson jumped at the chance. On the eve of his departure, on 19 July 1917, he and Glasgow became secretly engaged.

Anderson remained at his post in Romania until March 1918, when Romania's surrender to Germany forced the Red Cross mission to flee the country. He led a dramatic escape by train across Russia, risking falling into the hands of the equally unfriendly Bolsheviks and Mensheviks. He returned to Richmond but after the Armistice went back to Europe as Red Cross commissioner for the entire Balkans. His untiring efforts to secure and distribute twelve thousand tons of food and medical supplies during the next six months earned him the gratitude of the Balkan States and an unprecedented series of medals: the War Cross (Czechoslovakia); the War Medal (France); Commander of the Royal Order of the Saviour (Greece); the War Medal (Italy); Commander of the Order of Prince Danilo I (Montenegro); Grand Officer of the Star of Romania and Commander of the Order of the Crown and the Order of Regina Maria, First and Second Classes (Romania); Commander of the Order of Saint Anne, with swords (Russia); and Grand Cross of Grand Commander, Order of Saint Sava, First and Second Classes, and the Serbian Red Cross (Serbia).

While in the Balkans Anderson became infatuated with Queen Marie of Romania. Her feelings for him are more difficult to gauge, but she certainly viewed him as a sympathetic confidant and as one in a string of knights errant she attracted. As early as 1918 she and Anderson began a daily exchange of letters and presents similar to that Anderson had undertaken with Glasgow. The rumors surrounding the relationship between Anderson and the queen and his blatant exploitation of their friendship caused his engagement with Glasgow to disintegrate. Glasgow was eventually reconciled to Anderson and remained close to him until her death in 1945, but she obtained some measure of revenge by grafting recognizable details of his life onto her weak-willed and faithless heroes in various novels, particularly *Barren Ground* (1925), *Vein of Iron* (1935), and—probably the most hurtful—*The Romantic Comedians* (1926). Another Richmond writer, Emily Clark, included a caricature of Anderson as John Sylvester in her *Stuffed Peacocks* (1927).

On his return from Europe, Anderson found himself in great demand politically. Although he came from a staunchly Democratic family, during the presidential campaign of 1896 he had served as secretary of the Virginia Sound Money Convention and vehemently opposed the election of William Jennings Bryan. By 1908 Anderson considered himself a Taft Democrat and not long thereafter moved from a vague association to formal identification with the Republican Party. In 1920 he received the unanimous endorsement of the state Republican convention for the vice presidency and at the national convention placed fourth in the initial balloting, but Calvin Coolidge received the nomination. Anderson was chairman of the Republican state convention in 1921 and was nominated for governor of Virginia. He ran on a platform advocating abolition of the poll tax, improvement of highways, reform of the educational system, and greater fiscal responsibility on the part of state government. Underlying all his proposed reforms was an insistence on the necessity of dismantling the state Democratic Party machine and making the South into a competitive two-party region. After Anderson remarked that the Republican Party in Virginia should be a party of white men, African American Republicans bolted the party and nominated their own slate, headed by John Mitchell Jr. In the November general election, Anderson won only about 35 percent of the vote and lost to E. Lee Trinkle. Anderson failed to carry his home district, and even his mother and brother refused to vote for him.

Four years later the Virginia Republican Party chose Anderson to run for governor against Harry Flood Byrd, but he declined the nomination. Anderson was mentioned for the vice presidency in 1928 and again in 1931. Presidents Warren G. Harding and Herbert Hoover considered nominating him to the United States Supreme Court in 1924 and 1931 respectively, but on both occasions opposition from Virginia Republican leader Campbell Bascom Slemp and a lack of support from Virginia's Democratic senators led to early abandonment of the idea.

In the strictest sense, Anderson's political career was a series of near-misses and might-have-beens. His lack of broad-based support in his own state and his inability to deliver votes made him seem politically ineffective. In another sense, however, Anderson's political career was influential. The Byrd organization implemented many of his suggestions for fiscal responsibility, governmental reorganization, road improvement, and educational reform once the perceived challenge from the Republican Party had been put down.

Anderson served with distinction in a number of appointive national offices. Coolidge chose him in 1924 as the agent to settle the Mexican claims resulting from retaliatory raids against Pancho Villa in 1916. For two years Anderson shuttled between Richmond, Washington, and Mexico City before withdrawing on 30 June 1926, ostensibly to resume private practice but actually because of dissatisfaction with the way the claims were being decided. In May 1929 Hoover appointed him to the National Committee on Law Observance and Enforcement, under the chairmanship of George W. Wickersham. Anderson headed the subcommittee on the causes of crime, but his most lasting contribution to the commission was his minority report, written after a research trip to Sweden at his own expense, urging the repeal of Prohibition and recommending the establishment of a system of liquor sales under government licensing similar to the Alcoholic Beverage Control Board that Virginia adopted in 1933.

Throughout two decades of political ambitions, appointments, and disappointments, Anderson continued to practice law with lucrative success. The Great Depression provided an unprecedented opportunity for his creative administrative and organizational strengths. He was a pioneer in corporate reorganization, especially for railroads and transportation companies. He became counsel for the Seaboard Air Line Railway, the Saint Louis–San Francisco Railway, the Denver and Rio Grande Western, and the Baltimore and Ohio. Anderson took a major part in developing what became Chapter XV of the 1939 Bankruptcy Act.

Anderson was unquestionably a brilliant, widely read, and attractive person, and he was a compelling orator. He was also one of the most flamboyant and controversial personalities in Richmond society, and his extravagant lifestyle provided grist for Richmond gossipmongers for half a century. He had always been active in support of the artistic and literary life of Richmond, and in the twilight of his career he found an outlet for his interest in the visual and decorative arts by serving as one of the original trustees of the Virginia Museum of Fine Arts in 1934 and as its president from 1947 until his death.

Anderson was stricken with colon cancer late in the 1940s, and he was eventually confined to bed. Henry Watkins Anderson died at his home on 7 January 1954 and was buried in Hollywood Cemetery. His estate, valued at nearly $1,000,000, was divided among his twin sister, eight nieces and nephews, and one grandniece.

NCAB, 44:10–11; Sara B. Bearss, "Queen Marie of Rumania and Colonel Henry Anderson of Virginia," *Virginia Country* 10 (Apr. 1987): 20–28 (por.); Henry Watkins Anderson Papers, VHS; Ellen Glasgow Papers, UVA; Thomas B. Gay, *The Hunton Williams Firm and Its Predecessors, 1877–1954* (1971), 36–46; Anne Hobson Freeman, *The Style of a Law Firm: Eight Gentlemen from Virginia* (1989), 76–103; Hummel and Smith, *Portraits and Statuary*, 3 (por.); Hall, *Portraits*, 14; obituaries in *Richmond News Leader*, 7, 8 Jan. 1954, *New York Times*, 8 Jan. 1954, and *Richmond Times-Dispatch*, 8, 9 Jan. 1954; memorial in *Virginia State Bar Association Proceedings* (1954): 115–117.

SARA B. BEARSS

ANDERSON, James (17 November 1678–16 July 1740), Presbyterian minister, was born in Edinburgh, Scotland. He may have been one of the children of George Anderson and Mary Matthews Anderson, and he may also have been a younger brother of John Anderson, president of the Executive Council in New Jersey at the time of the latter's death in 1738. James Anderson received his education in Edinburgh under John Stirling, who later served as principal of Glasgow University, and on 17 November 1708 the Irvine Presbytery ordained him in preparation for a missionary sojourn in Virginia.

Anderson arrived at the Rappahannock River on 22 April 1709, but after staying in Virginia only six months he judged the religious climate unsuited to Presbyterianism and moved to New Castle, Delaware. He joined the Presbytery of Philadelphia, which later reorganized as the Synod of Philadelphia, and remained an active member of the synod for the rest of his life. Anderson was a staunch supporter of Old Style Presbyterianism who extolled the virtues of order, discipline, and a university education for ministers. He married Suit Garland on 2 February 1713. They had seven sons and four daughters before she died on 24 December 1736. One year later, on 27 December 1737, Anderson married Rebecca Crawford, who has also been identified as Rebecca Wilson. Anderson's second marriage was childless.

In 1717 Anderson left Delaware to accept a call in New York City. His tenure there was difficult because the congregation was divided between adherents of New England Congregationalism and supporters of the Church of Scotland. In 1726, after an acrimonious dispute concerning the funding of the debt incurred to build the church's meetinghouse, Anderson asked the synod for permission to leave New York. In September of that year he accepted a call to Donegal Church in Lancaster County, Pennsylvania.

Anderson's second and more significant involvement with Virginia Presbyterianism stemmed from his position at Donegal. In 1732 he became a founding member of the Donegal Presbytery, which encompassed most of the Pennsylvania backcountry and the Valley of Virginia. Many Pennsylvanians moved to western Virginia, and Anderson and the Donegal Presbytery actively supported their attempts to secure ministers. As early as 1735 he asked the presbytery to send an itinerant minister to Virginia. In 1738 he carried a letter from the synod to Lieutenant Governor William Gooch in Williamsburg requesting permission for Presbyterians in backcountry Virginia to practice their own brand of Protestantism. In compliance with the Act of Toleration, Gooch granted the Presbyterians living west of the Blue Ridge the same privilege of worshiping under their own ministers that he soon thereafter granted to the German Lutherans. While in Virginia, Anderson may have preached at several backcountry settlements and probably assisted the Presbyterians at Beverley Manor in Augusta County in formally organizing a religious society.

In conjunction with other members of the Donegal Presbytery, Anderson was instrumental in securing ministers for and encouraging active lay Presbyterians in the Valley of Virginia. Surviving Virginia church records and traditions do not indicate how often he personally ministered to the settlers, but his work prepared the way for the full institutionalization of Presbyterianism in western Virginia between 1740 and 1755. James Anderson died at his home in Lancaster County, Pennsylvania, on 16 July 1740 and was buried next to his first wife in Donegal churchyard.

Biographies in Richard Webster, *A History of the Presbyterian Church in America, From Its Origin Until the Year 1760* (1857), 326–332, in Franklin Ellis and Samuel Evans, *History of Lancaster County, Pennsylvania* (1883), 774–775, and in Robert Stewart, *Col. George Stewart and His Wife Margaret Harris* (1907), 26–29; correspondence with John Stirling, 1716–1726, in National Library of Scotland, Edinburgh (microfilm, Union Theological Seminary, Richmond); Minutes of Donegal Presbytery, Presbyterian Historical Society, Philadelphia (microfilm, Union Theological Seminary); Guy S. Klett, ed., *Minutes of the Presbyterian Church in America 1706–1788* (1976), 8, 113, 154, 158, 159, 163, 165; Samuel Miller, *Memoirs of the Rev. James Rodgers, D.D.* (1813), 133–139; Jacob L. Ziegler, *An Authentic History of the Donegal Presbyterian Church* (1902), 22–24, 127; Robert F. Scott, "Colonial Presbyterianism in the Valley of Virginia, 1727–1775," *Journal of the Presbyterian Historical Society* 35 (1957): 71–92.

GAIL S. TERRY

ANDERSON, James (24 January 1740–8 September 1798), armorer, was born in Gloucester County, the eldest of three sons and second of seven children of William Anderson, a schoolmaster, and Sarah Pate Anderson. His early life is undocumented, although he was probably the James Anderson, of Gloucester County, whose height is given as five feet two inches on the size roll of Captain Robert McKenzie's company of volunteers during the French and Indian War.

James Anderson and his brother Matthew Anderson were probably apprenticed to master craftsmen to learn trades. Matthew Anderson later becamc public shoemaker to supply the needs of the Virginia soldiers during the American Revolution and managed a staff of workmen and apprentices. James Anderson became a blacksmith and in November 1762, in the earliest-known business transaction of his career, purchased some hides from a Williamsburg harnessmaker in order to construct bellows for his shop. Anderson became armorer for the colony's arms magazine in April 1766, and like his brother employed a number of skilled and unskilled workmen, displaying managerial competence and business acumen in addition to a mastery of his craft. He owned a workshop "in the Back Street" in Williamsburg until the autumn of 1770, when he moved into new and larger buildings on Duke of Gloucester Street in the center of the little city. Anderson contracted for work on the public buildings, including the jail and the Capitol, and for the stage line, and he did work for private individuals and local businesses. Besides shoeing horses, his smiths repaired tools and wagons and occasionally repaired and cleaned firearms. On 8 February 1766 Anderson married Hannah Tyler. Between 1767 and 1781 they had six sons and two daughters.

On 20 March 1776 the Virginia Committee of Safety hired Anderson as public armorer and blacksmith for one year to put into working order the firearms being collected to fight the British. The government renewed his contract for six months in March 1777 and every six months thereafter until March 1780, when he was hired "for five years or the end of the war if it shall sooner happen." Judging by the amount of work he completed during 1776, Anderson already maintained a sizable staff of workmen able to perform a considerable variety of specialized tasks, but during the war years he repeatedly advertised for journeymen gunsmiths and blacksmiths as well as for "healthy boys as apprentices" in order to keep up with the work. In 1779 the government rented a building in Williamsburg for Anderson's workmen, who were busily engaged in cleaning and repairing public arms, manufacturing nails, mounting cannon, and preparing ironwork for warships. By then Anderson already had two buildings of his own and at least three forges in operation and had enlarged his original blacksmith shop into a small, but busy industrial complex.

Anderson left his Williamsburg shops under the direction of a foreman and shifted most of his government work to Richmond shortly after the capital was moved from Williamsburg to that city. He continued to work as public armorer, but he suffered financially. Benedict Arnold's raid on Richmond in January 1781 resulted in the destruction of most of Anderson's tools and all eight pairs of his bellows. Anderson then moved his workshops to the Point of Fork in Fluvanna County, where his workers repaired as many as 150 muskets each week. During the transfer of his equipment, Anderson was captured by a detachment of British cavalry and detained for several weeks before being paroled on 11 June 1781. In August of that year he was appointed captain of a newly created Corps of Artificers, but placing his shops and workers under military discipline did not solve his major problems. He did not receive adequate compensation from the state for his equipment lost in January 1781; he had no money with which to purchase needed supplies; he received minimal provisions from the public to support his family and his workmen; and the demands of the state for skilled metalwork did not abate. By March 1782 Anderson was employing two gunsmiths, nine blacksmiths, nine nailers, and one gun cleaner at Point of Fork to work on repairing more than two thousand stand of arms. In July of that year, after eight months of complaints and increasing frustration and personal financial hardship, Anderson refused to do any more work for the state.

Anderson operated a blacksmith shop in Richmond near the temporary capitol from the summer of 1782 until January 1794, when he turned that operation over to his namesake son and moved back to Williamsburg. Anderson's business never recovered from the losses it sustained during the American Revolution, although he had materially assisted in the winning of the war and at the same time had successfully raised his children and seen them into promising careers. His youngest son, Robert Anderson, became a prominent merchant and attorney who served as mayor of Williamsburg and made repeated, but unsuccessful attempts to gain compensation for his father's wartime losses. James Anderson died at his home in Williamsburg on 8 September 1798 and was buried in the churchyard of Bruton Parish Church.

Genealogical information recorded in son's account book at VHS is in *WMQ*, 1st ser. 12 (1903–1904): 116–118, 201–205; size roll in *VMHB* 1 (1894): 379; Williamsburg property and operations documented in research reports and archaeological investigations prepared and conducted by the Colonial Williamsburg Foundation between 1932 and 1993; two account books in VHS; records of service as public armorer for colony in PRO T 1/461 and Robert A. Brock Collection, Henry E. Huntington Library, San Marino, Calif.; service during American Revolution documented in minute and account books of Committee of Safety and letter book of War Office, RG 2, journal of Council of State, RG 75, and Governor's Office, Letters Received, RG 3, all in LVA; financial losses documented in Robert Anderson's 1839 claim for compensation, Rejected Claims, RG 3, LVA, and in papers accompanying his 1849 petition to General Assembly, Legislative Petitions, James City Co., 11 Dec. 1849, RG 78, LVA; refusal of further government work in William Davies to governor, 17 July 1782, Governor's Office, Letters Received, RG 3, LVA; transcript of estate inventory taken after death of widow in 1803 in Robert Anderson's account book, VHS; death notice in *Norfolk Herald*, 13 Sept. 1798.

DAPHNE GENTRY

ANDERSON, James Aylor (26 December 1892–16 November 1964), educator and civil engineer, was born in Linden, Warren County, the only son and second of four children of Conway Marion Anderson and his first wife, Anna Lou Walter Anderson. Conway Anderson was a surveyor, teacher, farmer, and justice of the peace, whose commitment to education influenced his son to follow in his footsteps. James A. Anderson attended local public schools and then matriculated at the Virginia Military Institute in 1909. His four years there ingrained in him a sense of service to the community and personal integrity that became the hallmarks of his career; and VMI, next to his family, was the love of his life.

Anderson graduated with a B.S. in 1913 and was awarded the Jackson-Hope Medal as the institute's top scholar. He taught at Shenandoah Valley Academy in Winchester for a year and then returned to VMI as assistant professor of engineering prior to taking a civil engineering degree at Cornell University in 1917. Already a member of the Virginia National Guard before World War I, Anderson served in France with the American Expeditionary Force in 1918. He rose from captain to lieutenant colonel and was on the staff of George C. Marshall, another VMI alumnus.

For the next twenty years Anderson taught civil engineering at his alma mater. He also served as town engineer for Lexington and did summer work with several railroads and with the United States Bureau of Public Roads. In August 1933 Governor John Garland Pollard selected him to be state engineer and director of the Virginia branch of the new Public Works Administration, the federal agency created to fund major construction projects such as libraries, college dormitories, and hospitals as a means of reducing unemployment resulting from the Great Depression. During the next three years Anderson supervised the expenditure of more than $30 million on public works projects in Virginia.

In 1936 Anderson returned to VMI and a year later became dean of the faculty, but his reputation as an expert highway engineer and innovative, no-nonsense administrator caused his state to call him back into service. Governor James H. Price appointed Anderson coordinator and executive secretary of the State Council of Defense in December 1940 to prepare for the war that seemed imminent. Eight months later, after the death of Henry G. Shirley, Price named Anderson state commissioner of highways.

Anderson was in the unenviable position of succeeding a legend. During his twenty-year tenure, Shirley had overseen the development of a 45,000-mile road network employing some 10,000 people. Shirley was one of the great "road" men in the country and had enjoyed the lasting respect of the leaders of the Virginia Democratic Party who were committed to the construction of highways on a pay-as-you-go system of state financing. Anderson was not daunted, however, and during the next sixteen years established his own reputation as a great "road" man, an achievement recognized in 1955 when he received the George S. Bartlett Award from the American Association of State Highway Officials for outstanding service to the highway systems of the nation.

During his tenure as highway commissioner, Anderson supervised the improvement of 12,000 additional miles of highway and the construction of the Hampton Roads Bridge-Tunnel. Faced with the obsolescence of many roads, he created a twenty-year development plan with the goal of making Virginia's highways the best in the nation. He established an urban roads division, a cost analysis office, a public relations section, and an electrical cost-accounting system. Insisting on first-rate quality construction utilizing the latest designs and techniques, he instituted an in-service training program that brought in dozens of recent engineering graduates to work for the department. His major accomplishments included helping to lay out the new federal interstate highway system.

One of Anderson's strengths was his ability to remain above politics in a department that was a source of state jobs and local construction projects involving millions of dollars a year. Although friendly with leading members of Harry F. Byrd's Democratic organization, Anderson never let that friendship or partisan considerations interfere with the operation of his department. He fought against political allotments of road-building money, and he refused to succumb to pressure to lower safety standards.

Anderson became a brigadier general in the Virginia State Guard and was usually referred to as "the General" and addressed as "General Anderson." His short, stocky stature belied an energetic, commanding personality. A perfectionist who did not tolerate anything less than a best effort, he had a booming voice that could be heard down the hallways of the department's headquarters in Richmond, but it could not entirely conceal a jovial good nature and sense of humor.

Anderson married Isabella Bronson Webster, of Norfolk, on 23 June 1917. They had two sons and two daughters and lived in Lexington. Anderson purchased a farm called Sunnyside near Lexington, to which he retired from state service in 1958. He was an avid hunter, great fan of VMI football, and active in a number of professional civil engineering organizations. In 1951 he served as president of the American Association of State Highway Officials, and in 1960 he received the distinguished service award of the Virginia Citizens' Planning Association for his contributions to the creation of a state planning board in 1933 and his fifteen years of service thereon. James Aylor Anderson died of a heart attack at Sunnyside on 16 November 1964 and was buried in Stonewall Jackson Memorial Cemetery in Lexington. In honor of his longtime service to the state, U.S. Highway 60 between Richmond and Lexington was named the James A. Anderson Highway.

Family records, papers, and newspaper clippings in possession of James A. Anderson Jr., Thomasville, Ga.; family history information verified by James A. Anderson Jr., 16 July 1989; *NCAB*, 50:447; Virginius Dabney, "General James A. Anderson," *Virginia and the Virginia County* 5 (Apr. 1951): 11–12 (por.); *Commonwealth* 22 (Mar. 1955): 37–38; *V.M.I. Alumni Review* (Finals 1955): 12; obituaries in *Richmond News Leader* and *Richmond Times-Dispatch*, both 17 Nov. 1964, and *Roanoke World-News*, 18 Nov. 1964; memorial in *Richmond News Leader*, 19 Nov. 1964.

RONALD L. HEINEMANN

ANDERSON, John (6 May 1750–13 October 1817), frontier innkeeper, was born in Augusta County, but the exact place of his birth and the names of his parents are not known. Early in the 1770s he married Rebecca Maxwell, probably also of Augusta County. They had four sons and four daughters. In the spring of 1774 Anderson sought to acquire a tract of land in the Clinch River valley from the Loyal Land Company, and in 1775 he moved to what is now Scott County. On 24 August 1781 he obtained title to 200 acres of land on the south side of the Clinch River, in Elk's Garden, where he had been living for several years and had made substantial improvements. As one of the early settlers in that portion of the frontier, Anderson became one of the first justices of the peace for Washington County in January 1777 and received a commission as a captain in the militia in May of that year.

The area in which Anderson lived was between two survey lines that had been run to define the border between Virginia and North Carolina, and he and his neighbors, according to a later recollection, "sometimes adhered to one state and sometimes to the other." He served as a justice of the peace of North Carolina and in October 1784 received a commission as a lieutenant colonel in the militia. Anderson also played a role in attempting to create a new state of Franklin in 1785, but it is uncertain whether it was he or another man of the same name who was appointed a judge of one of Franklin's courts. William Blount, governor of the Southwest Territory (the predecessor of the state of Tennessee), commissioned Anderson a justice of the peace in 1790. John Anderson had never moved, though, and when Scott County, Virginia, was created in February 1815, he was its first sheriff.

Colonel Anderson, as he was usually referred to later in life, was well known in the West as the builder and proprietor of the Blockhouse at the eastern end of the Wilderness Road that thousands of travelers took en route from Virginia and North Carolina through the Cumberland Gap into Kentucky. Anderson erected the Blockhouse about 1777 in Carter's Valley, six miles east of Moccasin Gap and about six or seven miles northeast of the mouth of the North Fork of the Holston River. An early traveler described it as a "log house with the upper part built wider than the under." It contained two large rooms, and the upper story had portholes from which the inhabitants could shoot at attacking Indians, which happened at least twice. Anderson later constructed a larger, two-story house with a log kitchen and converted the original Blockhouse into a loom house. The Blockhouse remained in the Anderson family's possession until it burned in September 1876. A plaque was placed near the site about 1921.

John Anderson never became wealthy. After his death he was described as a plain farmer and innkeeper and a man of "good sense" who was "fond of society." He was reputed to have become a hard drinker in old age. On the day of his death at the new Blockhouse on 13 October 1817, he made a will mentioning several hundred acres of land in Scott County, a warrant for 500 acres pending in North Carolina's land office, and some land in Grainger County, Tennessee, title to which was then being contested in a court in Knoxville. Anderson's personal estate, including six slaves, was valued in April 1818 at more than $2,800.

Robert M. Addington, *History of Scott County, Virginia* (1932), 301–302, cites a family Bible for birth and death dates and digests early accounts of the Blockhouse; other information in David Campbell to Lyman C. Draper, 11 July 1845 (Draper's source for a 17 Oct. 1817 death date), and in a letter from son Isaac C. Anderson to David Campbell, 11 Apr. 1846 (with an undated memorandum from Campbell to Draper), Draper MSS, 10DD52, 15DD27; will and estate inventory in Scott Co. Will Book, 1:80–83, 110–111.

MARY B. KEGLEY

ANDERSON, John Thomas (5 April 1804–27 August 1879), iron manufacturer and member of the Convention of 1850–1851, was born at Walnut Hill in Botetourt County, the second of six sons and fifth of ten children of William Anderson and Anna Thomas Anderson. His father was a surveyor, a farmer, a justice of the county court, and an administrator of several ventures to build or improve canals, rivers, and turnpikes.

Anderson established a law practice and entered politics while still a very young man. He was elected to the House of Delegates in 1827, at age twenty-three, and served two one-year terms. In 1834 he won election to the Senate of Virginia for the first of two consecutive four-year terms. He supported legislation for road construction and for improvement of the navigation of the tributaries of the James River. He also advocated the establishment of branch banks, particularly in Botetourt County, and encouraged the development of cotton, woolen, and iron manufacturing in the county. Anderson placed a high value on education. Between 1833 and 1846 he signed several petitions to the General Assembly dealing with educational reform and internal improvements projects. He supported the Botetourt Seminary for boys, and after his purchase on 20 December 1845 of Mount Joy, an estate near Buchanan that featured a magnificent twenty-four-room brick mansion, he deeded part of his previous estate to the new Fincastle Female Seminary. He also served on the board of trustees of Washington College in Lexington from 1845 to 1853.

Botetourt County possessed some of the richest deposits of iron ore in the state, and Anderson, alert to the profits to be made, formed the Catawba Iron Company with two other men in January 1833. One of them, Thomas Shanks, had served with him in the legislature, and their ties grew stronger when Anderson married Shanks's twenty-six-year-old widowed sister, Cassandra Morrison Shanks Patton, on 27 May 1834. She had three sons from her first marriage, and they added a daughter and another son.

Anderson and Shanks established a dry goods store and mercantile business in the town of Fincastle, and Anderson also speculated in real estate and opened the Cassandra Iron Furnace in Rockbridge County. He later purchased the Grace and Cloverdale Furnaces in Botetourt County, the latter famed for producing superior pig iron that was ideal for the manufacture of heavy guns. By 1850 he claimed real estate holdings valued at more than $50,000. In 1843 he had lent his youngest surviving brother, Joseph Reid Anderson, money to lease the Tredegar ironworks in Richmond, and for the next two decades the brothers enjoyed a close business relationship.

Anderson remained involved in the principal political issue of his day, the sectional struggle between the eastern and western regions of Virginia. In August 1843 he attended a meeting at Lewisburg to protest the legislature's failure to reapportion the General Assembly, and he was among the delegates at a Staunton meeting in December 1846 that called for a constitutional convention. After the legislature refused in 1847 to pass a bill extending the Kanawha Canal from Lynchburg to Buchanan, Anderson angrily organized meetings at Fincastle that persuaded the legislature to reverse itself and fund the project.

In 1850 the General Assembly finally provided for a constitutional convention. Anderson was one of three delegates elected to represent the district composed of Alleghany, Bath, Botetourt, and Roanoke Counties. He played a minor role on the convention floor, rising only to comment on procedural questions, but served on the Committee on the Executive Department and Ministerial Officers that provided for a significant strengthening of the office of governor and the abolition of the Council of State.

During the 1850s iron production at Anderson's furnaces declined and his financial condition deteriorated. In 1853 he sold his interest in Cassandra Furnace, by 1858 he had sold his Fincastle properties, and in 1860 he converted Cloverdale Furnace to production of cheaper grades of iron.

Anderson returned to politics and in 1859 was elected to the House of Delegates. A reluctant secessionist, he nonetheless helped Virginia prepare for war after the state left the Union and served as chairman of the House Committee on Military Affairs. In her historical novel, *The Long Roll* (1911), Mary Johnston portrayed him as an advocate of gradual manumission and colonization, and as such at odds with eastern slave owners. Anderson leased his Cloverdale and Grace Furnaces in 1861 and a year later sold them to Tredegar for $94,500. Anderson was reelected to the assembly in 1863. His son, Joseph Washington Anderson, was wounded near Vicksburg and died on 17 May 1863, and Anderson traveled to Mississippi in November to bring the body back to Fincastle for burial. In June 1864 the Union army destroyed Anderson's elegant house and his barn, shops, and mills, as well as the Cloverdale Furnace. He estimated his financial losses at about $70,000, a blow from which he never recovered.

John Thomas Anderson died in Botetourt County on 27 August 1879 and was buried in the Fincastle Presbyterian Church cemetery.

Anderson Papers, UVA, including transcript of William Anderson family Bible records; Ellen Graham Anderson, "Civil War Comes to Buchanan: II, The Burning of Mount Joy" and "The Four Anderson Brothers," *Journal of the Roanoke Historical Society* 1 (winter 1964–1965): 19–21 and 6 (summer 1969): 18–20 (por.); Botetourt Co. Marriage Register; Charles B. Dew, *Ironmaker to the Confederacy: Joseph R. Anderson and the Tredegar Iron Works* (1966), 4, 11, 12, 48–49, 78, 100–102, 149; Kathleen Bruce, *Virginia Iron Manufacture in the Slave Era* (1931), 181, 182 , 212, 272–274; Robert P. Sutton, *Revolution to Secession: Constitution Making in the Old Dominion* (1989), 220; *Journal of 1850 Convention*, 59; Presidential Pardons; obituary in *Richmond Dispatch*, 6 Sept. 1879.

PATRICIA P. HICKIN

ANDERSON, Joseph Reid (16 February 1813–7 September 1892), iron manufacturer, member of the Convention of 1861, and Confederate army officer, was born at Walnut Hill in Botetourt County, the fifth of six sons and ninth of ten children of William Anderson and Anna Thomas Anderson. He attended a school in nearby Fincastle and received an appointment to the United States Military Academy at West Point, from which he graduated in 1836, fourth in a class of forty-nine. He served briefly in the 3d Artillery, U.S. Army, before being assigned to engineering duties and was later transferred to the Corps of Engineers. He served in Washington, D.C., at Fort Monroe in Virginia, and at Fort Pulaski in Georgia, but he lost interest in a military career soon after he married Sarah Eliza Archer, of Norfolk, in May 1837, and in September 1837 he resigned his commission. The Andersons had five sons and seven daughters, of whom three sons and four daughters reached adulthood.

In the autumn of 1837 Anderson became an assistant state engineer in the construction of the Valley Turnpike between Staunton and Winchester, service that stimulated his interest in Virginia's economic development. He promoted the construction of canals and railroads to connect the Valley of Virginia to Tidewater Virginia, and his concern for internal improvements led him into the southern commercial convention movement and into the Whig Party. Those activities brought him to the attention of the owners of Richmond's Tredegar Iron Company. He became the company's commercial agent in March 1841 and remained associated with Tredegar until his death.

At the time Anderson joined Tredegar, the four-year-old company was in financial difficulty. He actively sought and obtained contracts with the federal government to manufacture munitions and other supplies for the army and navy and rapidly brought about an improvement in the company's fortunes. During the next two decades Tredegar produced 881 cannon for the armed forces, an iron revenue cutter for the Treasury Department, and engines and boilers for two navy frigates. As Tredegar became profitable, Anderson tired of the board of directors' meddling in technical matters, and in November 1843 he leased the entire ironworks for five years. Anderson prospered as superintendent of Tredegar and also from 1846 to 1848 as president of the Armory Iron Company. In April 1848 he purchased the Tredegar Iron Company and assumed complete control over all phases of the work.

One of Anderson's most notable innovations was the introduction of slaves in skilled industrial work. He began using bondsmen in unskilled jobs in 1842, and in 1847 he proposed using them in skilled work at the Armory rolling mill. When the skilled white workers, many of whom were northern-or foreign-born, responded with strikes at both the Armory and Tredegar rolling mills, Anderson fired the strikers and put slaves in skilled jobs at both establishments. The replacements successfully demonstrated their ability to perform such labor, but before the Civil War slaves were given skilled work largely in the rolling mill and the blacksmith shop. The company owned many of them and hired others from local owners, but despite Anderson's determination to employ skilled slaves, he continued to rely heavily on northern and European immigrant workers, with whites constituting the vast majority of his workforce in 1860.

Through his success in making Tredegar the largest ironworks in the South and one of the largest in the United States, Anderson became one of the region's leading industrialists. Although Tredegar produced a substantial amount of armaments for the government, the largest part of its production was railroad iron. Tredegar also turned out a wide variety of finished iron products, including steam engines for gristmills, sawmills, and sugar mills, and iron for bridges. By 1860 the Tredegar workforce of about eight hundred was the fourth largest of any American ironworks. In the face of competition from northern mills and from England, Anderson entered into a series of partnerships that permitted him to complete the payments on the purchase of Tredegar in 1856, and in 1859 he formed Joseph R. Anderson and Company, combining Tredegar with Archer and Company, a rolling mill that Anderson's father-in-law and brother-in-law owned.

Anderson was elected to the Richmond City Council in 1847 and served five terms before the Civil War. In 1852 he was elected to a vacant seat in the House of Delegates and was reelected in 1853. He served on the Committee on Roads and Internal Navigation and promoted state support for the construction of railroads and canals. Following the collapse of the Whig Party, Anderson became a Democrat. He was elected to the House of Delegates again in 1857, but he was defeated in 1859. After Abraham Lincoln was elected president in November 1860, Anderson advocated secession and actively promoted the sale of arms to the Southern states. Tredegar sold munitions to South Carolina during the Fort Sumter crisis and geared up to increase arms production. Anderson also negotiated arms contracts with the provisional government of the Confederacy. He was elected to the Virginia convention that met in Richmond in February 1861, and in April he voted for secession. When Virginia left the Union, Anderson offered to turn Tredegar over to the Confederate government by lease or purchase, but the government declined the offer.

In May 1861 Anderson organized 350 of his white workmen into a home defense unit known as the Tredegar Battalion, which he commanded with the rank of major. On 21 August he requested a commission in the Confederate army and on 3 September 1861 was appointed a brigadier general. He commanded the District of Cape Fear, North Carolina, from 30 September 1861 to 19 March 1862 and the Department of North Carolina from 19 to 24 March 1862. He led a brigade at Fredericksburg in April and May and a brigade in A. P. Hill's division during the Seven Days' Battles. Anderson was slightly wounded in the face on 30 June 1862. He temporarily commanded Hill's division from 13 July to 19 July 1862, when he resigned his commission to resume management of the Tredegar ironworks.

Tredegar was the largest supplier of arms and other iron products to the Confederate government and produced 1,099 cannon during the war. Tredegar also produced armor plate and machinery for Confederate warships, including the CSS *Virginia*; artillery shot and shells; machinery and tools for the production of small arms by other armories and for the powder mill at Augusta, Georgia, and for the naval ordnance plant at Charlotte, North Carolina; and an armor-plated railroad car mounting a heavy cannon. Tredegar was also a major supplier of iron for Southern railroads. The company grew enormously during the war. It expanded the Richmond plant, acquired blast furnaces to produce pig iron, and purchased coal mines to supply the furnaces. The total workforce rose as high as 2,500 men, and Anderson increased the use of slave labor after many of the white workers entered military service or fled the Confederacy. By 1864 more than half of the workers were slaves, many filling skilled positions. Even though shortages of food became widespread in the Confederacy, Tredegar fed not only its slaves, but also its white employees and their families, to whom it sold food at cost.

Anderson and his partners also purchased large quantities of cotton during the war and shipped them to European markets on blockade runners, including a ship called the *Coquette* that they purchased from the Confederate navy in 1864. Anderson insisted that the cotton sales were used to finance greater production of military and railroad supplies at Tredegar, but most of the money went into a sterling account in London, and Anderson used those funds to keep control of Tredegar after the war.

Following the fall of Richmond on 3 April 1865, Anderson became a strong peace advocate. With other Richmond leaders he met with Abraham Lincoln in the city on 4 April to discuss how to end the war, and Anderson headed a citizens' commission to call the General Assembly into session to take Virginia out of the Confederacy. By taking part in the peace movement, Anderson hoped to keep the Union army from taking possession of the ironworks, but he was unsuccessful even though the surrender of the Confederate army brought a speedy end to the war. Anderson enlisted the aid of many prominent southern Unionists, Virginia railroad executives, and even some northern businessmen and Richmond African Americans, and obtained a pardon from President Andrew Johnson on 21 September 1865.

Anderson regained control of Tredegar after being pardoned, but the company remained in financial difficulty, and he had trouble attracting new capital. In February 1867 he and his son Archer Anderson and three other partners reorganized the venture as Tredegar Company, with Joseph Reid Anderson as the majority stockholder. The reorganization enabled Tredegar to attract northern capital and expand its operations. By 1873 Anderson had doubled the factory's prewar capacity, and its labor force exceeded 1,000 men, many of them black laborers and skilled workmen who received equal pay with the whites. The panic of 1873 and the resulting depression forced Tredegar into receivership in 1876. Anderson served as receiver of the company until September 1879, when the company successfully funded its debt, but Tredegar failed to make the transition from iron to steel production late in the nineteenth century and lost its position as one of the premier southern industrial enterprises, although the Richmond plant continued in operation until the 1950s and the company survived as a manufacturing entity into the 1980s.

Anderson remained one of Richmond's most successful and famous citizens. He returned to public life in the 1870s and served in the House of Delegates in 1874 and 1875 and again from 1877 to 1879. He was president of the Richmond Chamber of Commerce from 1874 to 1876, when he resigned to become president of the Richmond City Council. Anderson served on the vestry of Saint Paul's Episcopal Church from 1844 until his death and was a senior warden for twenty-one years. Following the death of Sarah Eliza Archer Anderson in 1881, he married Mary E. Pegram of Richmond in November 1882. After a period of poor health, Joseph Reid Anderson died on 7 September 1892 while visiting Isles of Shoals, New Hampshire. He was buried in Hollywood Cemetery in Richmond.

Charles B. Dew, *Ironmaker to the Confederacy: Joseph R. Anderson and the Tredegar Iron Works* (1966); Anne Hobson Freeman, "A Cool Head in a Warm Climate," *Virginia Cavalcade* 12 (winter 1962–1963): 9–17 (por.); Anderson Family Papers, UVA; Joseph Reid Anderson Papers, MOC; other Anderson family and business papers in records of Tredegar Iron Company, LVA; Bruce, Tyler, and Morton, *History of Virginia*, 6:634–636; Ellen Graham Anderson, "The Four Anderson Brothers," *Journal of the Roanoke Historical Society* 6 (summer 1969): 24–26; Lawrence Buckley Thomas, *The Thomas Book* (1896), 556; Kathleen Bruce, *Virginia Iron Manufacture in the Slave Era* (1931), including an African American's memorial tribute, 258; Patricia A. Schechter, "Free and Slave Labor in the Old South: The Tredegar Ironworkers' Strike of 1847," *Labor History* 35 (1995): 165–186; George H. Daniels, "The Confederate Government and Industrialization: Joseph R. Anderson and the Tredegar Iron Works," in *Divided We Fall: Essays on Confederate Nation Building*, eds. John M. Belohlavek and Lewis N. Wynne (1991), 129–150; Compiled Service Records; Presidential Pardons; Dennis Maher Hallerman, "The Tredegar Iron Works, 1865–1876" (master's thesis, University of Richmond, 1978); obituaries in *Richmond State*, 7 Sept. 1892, and *Richmond Dispatch* and *Richmond Times*, both 8 Sept. 1892.

ALAN B. BROMBERG

ANDERSON, Matthew Garland (28 June 1904–7 May 1981), businessman and Democratic Party leader, was born in Louisa County, the eldest of three sons and second of seven children of Erle Purrington Anderson and Daisy Riddell Anderson. In 1919 his father, a farmer and county supervisor, died of pneumonia and the family was forced to separate, with some of the children moving to Hanover and others remaining in Louisa with their mother. Anderson moved to Goochland County, lived with his cousin, and graduated from the local high school.

Matt G. Anderson eloped to New York with his childhood sweetheart, Frederica Mitchell, and married her on 27 March 1924. They had one son. After living in Buffalo for approximately five years they returned to Goochland, where Anderson worked in Wendall Watkins's grocery store, became a partner, and eventually bought the business. Renamed Anderson's Grocery, the store doubled as a post office, with Frederica Anderson as postmaster.

Anderson's business interests soon diversified to include a sawmill and a cattle farm. He also served as a director of the Henrico Mutual Fire Insurance Company. In 1947 he was elected to the Bank of Goochland's board of directors, rising to vice president the following year and part-time president in 1955. In 1959 he became the bank's first full-time president. It prospered steadily under Anderson's direction. He was elected to the board of Southern Bankshares, Incorporated, after that company acquired the Goochland bank in 1972.

Anderson's success extended beyond the business world into the political arena. In 1939 he was elected to the Goochland County Board of Supervisors, a post that he held for eleven years. In 1946 the governor appointed Anderson to a six-month term on the newly formed State Board of Elections, and he was elected chairman. Reappointed in February 1947, he served two consecutive four-year terms as the board's chairman and began a third in January 1955 but resigned in June to accept an interim appointment as Goochland County treasurer. He was elected permanent treasurer later in 1955, resigning to run unopposed in a special election held on 6 January 1959 for a vacated seat in the House of Delegates. During twelve years as the delegate from the district comprising Fluvanna, Goochland, Louisa, and (starting in 1966) Powhatan Counties, Anderson served on key committees on appropriations, insurance and banking, and agriculture.

A conservative, Anderson was a staunch Democrat. From 1937 until the early 1970s he served as the Goochland County Democratic Party chairman. In 1962 he began a ten-year tenure as the state party treasurer. During the years following the breakup of the Byrd machine, Anderson felt increasingly out of step with the party's new direction. He resigned as treasurer in July 1972, citing his disenchantment with the takeover of the party leadership by liberal Democrats at the Roanoke state convention.

Matt G. Anderson died at his house in Oilville on 7 May 1981 and was buried in Westhampton Memorial Park in Richmond.

William P. Anderson, *Anderson-Overton* (1945), 212; feature article in *Richmond Times-Dispatch*, 23 June 1972; author's interviews with daughter-in-law Evelyn Anderson, 9 Aug. 1989, and Clopton Knibb, 19 Sept. 1989; Bank of Goochland documented in *Goochland Gazette*, 22 Feb. 1962, 8 June 1972; Minute Book, 1946–1956, State Board of Elections, Richmond; *JHD*, 1982 sess., 1:649; obituaries in *Richmond Times-Dispatch*, 8 May 1981 (por.), and *Goochland Gazette*, 14 May 1981.

ELIZABETH HERBENER MANSFIELD

ANDERSON, Paul Vernon (24 November 1874–3 July 1961), psychiatrist, was born at Black Creek, Wilson County, North Carolina, the eldest of three children, all sons, of William Staton Anderson and his first wife, Mary Virginia Woodard Anderson. Anderson also had three half brothers from his father's second marriage. After obtaining an A.B. from Trinity College (now Duke University) in 1897, he served as principal of a school in Wilson. He received an A.M. from Trinity in 1901, while teaching English at a Durham high school. That same year, he entered the University of Virginia's medical school, graduating in 1904. Anderson spent the following two years as an intern at the Polyclinic Hospital in Philadelphia, where he met James King Hall, another young physician from North Carolina.

In 1906 Anderson and Hall became assistant physicians at the State Hospital for the Insane in Morganton, North Carolina. A highly regarded institution, the hospital employed the colony method of treatment, with groups of patients living in separate quarters and performing farm labor as therapy and a means to reduce costs. The young physicians carried heavy caseloads but learned hospital administration and gained experience treating the mentally ill.

Hall and Anderson eventually decided to open a private psychopathic hospital. On 24 April 1911, along with Edward Maupin Gayle, an associate from the Philadelphia Polyclinic, they purchased the Westbrook estate in northern Richmond that had once belonged to tobacco magnate Lewis Ginter. The partners subdivided the parcel and sold thirty-four lots while retaining the main estate as Westbrook Sanatorium, one of the first such hospitals in Virginia. Unlike state hospitals, which were usually located in rural areas, private psychopathic hospitals treated patients who entered voluntarily and also served as training centers for medical schools, thus making an urban location preferable. The partners also chose a Richmond site because of the presence there of Beverley Randolph Tucker, professor of nervous and mental diseases at the Medical College of Virginia and a former colleague from Philadelphia. Hall and Anderson also joined the faculty of MCV, with Anderson serving as an associate professor of neurology and psychiatry from 1915 to 1937.

Offering treatment to persons with drug and alcohol dependencies as well as those suffering from nervous disorders, Westbrook Sanatorium grew swiftly. Following the example of the Morganton hospital, patients lived in separate facilities and helped grow food on the grounds. In the early years the proprietors resided at the sanatorium and sometimes worked as farmers and maintenance men as well as physicians and managers. By 1916 the sanatorium was flourishing, with a patient population of about 130.

In July 1917 Anderson was commissioned a first lieutenant in the United States Army Medical Corps. Promoted to captain that December, he served at several domestic bases before embarking for France in July 1918. In his absence, and with Gayle disabled by diabetes, Hall operated the sanatorium alone through the war. Anderson obtained his discharge in February 1919, and by early in the 1920s the Westbrook Sanatorium was again a secure and lucrative institution. Anderson, like Hall and Tucker, believed that mental disorders derived from both hereditary and environmental factors and that expert intervention might alleviate a sufferer's symptoms. After the war Anderson and Hall incorporated insights from Sigmund Freud's system of psychoanalysis into their thinking and the treatment offered at Westbrook.

Anderson devoted his later years to teaching and treating patients at the sanatorium. He also participated in professional societies and served a term as president of the Tri-State Medical Association. On 23 August 1924, in Richmond, he married Alice V. Boatwright Anderson, a widow eighteen years his junior. They had no children. Anderson, hitherto vice president and treasurer, served as president, treasurer, and medical director of Westbrook from Hall's death in 1948 until January 1961. Paul Vernon Anderson died on 3 July 1961 and was buried at Forest Lawn Cemetery in Richmond. In 1971 Westbrook Sanatorium became part of the Charter Medical Corporation and its name was changed to Charter Westbrook Hospital.

William E. Wingfield, "The Emergence of American Psychiatry in the Twentieth Century: James King Hall, 1905–1921" (Ph.D. diss., Duke, 1987); Anderson's articles include "Importance of Mental Hygiene in the Young" and "Fallacies Concerning Insanity," in Medical Society of Virginia, *Transactions of the Annual Session* 43 (1912): 213–221 and 44 (1913): 196–201, and "Dementia Praecox With Special Reference to the Predementia Stage," *Charlotte Medical Journal* 66 (1912): 36–39; Rex Blankinship, "Private Psychiatric Hospitals in Virginia," *Mental Health in Virginia* 9 (spring 1959): 17–22 (por.), 25, 27; Military Service Records; obituaries in *Richmond News Leader*, 3 July 1961, and *Virginia Medical Monthly* 88 (1961): 689–690.

WILLIAM E. WINGFIELD

ANDERSON, Peyton Everett (ca. 1857–24 December 1950), educator and Baptist minister, was born near Farmville, the eldest of three sons and third of eight children of Paschal Anderson, a laborer, and Martha Dupuy Anderson, a seamstress. His parents were among the forty or more slaves owned by Joseph Dupuy, a prosperous Prince Edward County farmer. Anderson's exact date of birth is disputed, but he was old enough to remember occasions during the Civil War when Union troops stopped by the Dupuy farm for food. One of his brothers died during the war while acting as a bodyguard for Joseph Dupuy's son William P. Dupuy.

Although opportunities in postwar Virginia were few, Anderson was ambitious to educate himself for the ministry. William Dupuy paid for his schooling, a kindness that Anderson repaid by working as Dupuy's bookkeeper. In 1876, after Anderson completed the seventh grade, he was inspired to become an educator by the attentive instruction of his white teacher. Because half of Farmville's black youth worked seasonally in tobacco factories, Anderson taught in Prince Edward County at the one-room Virso School between October and February and at nearby Burkeville in Nottoway County from March to July. In his spare time during the years between 1876 and 1880, he studied for the ministry at Richmond Theological Institute. During the 1880s he attended summer sessions at Hampton Institute, at which he came to know and admire James S. Russell, who founded Saint Paul's College in Lawrenceville, and Booker T. Washington, who founded Tuskegee Institute in Alabama. Anderson also attended the Virginia Normal and Collegiate Institute (now Virginia State University) in Ettrick, near Petersburg.

During the 1880s, when land acquisition among blacks rose sharply, Anderson was able to buy seventy-nine acres adjacent to the Dupuy farm. On 2 May 1892 he married Pattie E. Price, of Meherrin, a village on the border of Prince Edward and Lunenburg Counties. They had four daughters and five sons. Shortly after the birth of their last child in 1909, Pattie Anderson died.

In 1910 Anderson became the first African American superintendent of black rural schools in Prince Edward County, a post he held until 1915. One of his most important accomplishments was the establishment of forty school patron leagues, which were instrumental in building twenty-three rural schoolhouses. Promoting the value of economic self-sufficiency, he introduced industrial education classes into these schools. About 1913 Anderson returned to Virso, where he worked as principal until he retired from education in 1938. One county superintendent described him as the most versatile schoolteacher he had ever seen.

Throughout his career Anderson typified the many former slaves who benefited from, and advocated, Booker T. Washington's doctrine of racial progress and independence through industrial education, the teaching of trades and technical skills. Anderson found strength in his associations with like-minded African Americans in fraternal orders such as the Knights of Pythias, the United Order of Moses, and the Independent Order of Saint Luke. Although a Republican, he retained close postwar ties with the politically active Dupuy family. To the consternation of some other African Americans, Anderson's father voted for William Dupuy in the 1880s, when Dupuy was a Democratic candidate for the General Assembly. Anderson's continuing postwar ties with the Dupuys may have reflected in part his desire to work with political opponents when feasible in hopes of softening opposition to black progress. During his career in education, Anderson remained devoted to his ministerial duties, serving as pastor of New Bethel and Shiloh churches and as president of the Bluestone Sunday School Convention. His retirement from teaching when he was in his eighties did not prompt him to retire from the ministry. At the time of his death he was acting pastor of Mount Zion Baptist Church in Green Bay, Prince Edward County.

Peyton Everett Anderson died in Meherrin on 24 December 1950, when he was approximately ninety-three years old, and was buried in the cemetery of Mount Zion Church.

Birth year of 1857 in obituary corroborated by ages of twelve and twenty-two given respectively in Census, Prince Edward Co., 1870 and 1880; variant birth date of Aug. 1860 in 1900 census with that year repeated in 1910 census; Frank Lincoln Mather, ed., *Who's Who of the Colored Race, 1915* (1915), 1:19 (gives birth date of 3 Aug. 1861); feature articles in *Richmond Times-Dispatch*, 3 Oct. 1949 (por.), and *Norfolk Journal and Guide*, 5 Sept. 1970; Charles H. Corey, *A History of the Richmond Theological Seminary, with Reminiscences of Thirty Years' Work Among the Colored People of the South* (1895), 151; W. E. B. Du Bois, "The Negroes of Farmville, Virginia: A Social Study," *U.S. Bureau of Labor Statistics Bulletin* 14 (1898): 12–13; obituary in *Norfolk Journal and Guide*, 6 Jan. 1951.

LYNDA J. MORGAN

ANDERSON, Pressley Warren (4 May 1887–7 May 1962), banker, was born near Amissville in Rappahannock County. He was the youngest of three sons and third of seven children of Norval Peyton Anderson and his wife, Lou Thomas Lewis Anderson. He grew up on his father's cattle farm, Bleakland, and attended the public school in Amissville. After working in John Martin Ramey's general store in Marshall, Fauquier County, Anderson attended Massey Business College in Richmond for the 1907–1908 session.

In 1909 Anderson took a position as assistant cashier of the Rappahannock National Bank in Washington, Rappahannock County. In 1915 he became the auditor of the Farmer's and Merchant's Bank of Staunton, and two years later he was one of the founders of the Fauquier-Loudoun Bank in Upperville, Fauquier County. In 1919 Anderson moved back to Marshall to become cashier of the Marshall National Bank, of which his first employer, John Martin Ramey, had been a founding director. Anderson took an active part in the business affairs of the community. He helped found the Marshall Chamber of Commerce in 1924, and he also developed real estate and owned a share of a canning factory in addition to operating Bleakland farm after his father's death. When the town of

Marshall was incorporated, Anderson served on its first town council. He was active in the Marshall Baptist Church and served as treasurer of the Potomac Baptist Association. He married Stewart Elizabeth Trainham, the daughter of a Baptist minister, in 1923. They had one daughter and one son.

Anderson was one of the leading businessmen in Fauquier County for more than thirty-five years. During the Great Depression the Marshall National Bank remained solvent. It closed for only one day during the National Bank Holiday of March 1933, and Anderson was credited with keeping the bank financially sound. On 27 April 1948 he became its president. Anderson served on the executive committee of the American Bankers Association and throughout his career was active in the Virginia Bankers Association. In 1946–1947 he served as president of the latter, a recognition of his standing as one of the most successful small-town bankers in the state.

Anderson was accustomed to being in charge, was sometimes reluctant to delegate responsibility, and occasionally alienated some associates. As a result, in spite of his years of successful work as cashier and president, he resigned from the Marshall National Bank in 1954 under pressure from the board of directors. The following year he became senior vice president of the National Bank of Manassas, where he remained until he retired in 1960. In his second retirement he formed the Anderson Investment Corporation. Pressley Warren Anderson died of cancer at the Medical College of Virginia Hospital in Richmond on 7 May 1962 and was buried in Stonewall Memorial Gardens in Manassas.

Feature article in *Warrenton Fauquier Democrat*, 1 Jan. 1953 (por.); BVS Birth Register, Rappahannock Co.; family history information confirmed in interviews with Pressley Warren Anderson Jr., Stewart Elizabeth McKee, and Genevieve Trainham; T. Triplett Russell and John K. Gott, *The Marshall National Bank and Trust Company: A History* (1980), 15–27; Gott, *High in Old Virginia's Piedmont: A History of Marshall (formerly Salem), Fauquier County, Virginia* (1987), 115–127; obituaries in *Richmond Times-Dispatch*, 9 May 1962, and *Manassas Journal Messenger* and *Warrenton Fauquier Democrat*, both 10 May 1962.

MARIANN LYNCH
AVA LEE

ANDERSON, Richard Clough (12 January 1750–16 October 1826), Continental army officer and surveyor, was born at Gold Mine plantation in Hanover County, the fourth of seven sons and sixth of eleven children of Robert Anderson and Elizabeth Clough Anderson. He learned the rudiments of surveying from his father and grandfather, but when he was about sixteen years old he went to sea as supercargo on a trading vessel for Richmond merchant Patrick Coutts. On one of his voyages he witnessed the Boston Tea Party in December 1773.

Anderson was back in Virginia in 1775 and served as quartermaster of the Hanover Minute Men. On 7 March 1776 he received a captain's commission in the 5th Virginia Regiment and went on active duty in the Continental army. He fought at the Battle of White Plains on 28 October 1776, and on Christmas Day of that year, on the eve of the Battle of Trenton, Anderson led a reconnaissance across the Delaware River into New Jersey and clashed with a Hessian patrol. The skirmish with Anderson's small unit reinforced British commander Johann Gottlieb Rall's belief that no large force of Americans was in New Jersey and contributed to his leaving his encampment unprepared for George Washington's surprise attack the following morning.

Anderson was wounded the day before the Battle of Princeton in the delaying action at Assumpink Bridge near Trenton on 2 January 1777. While recuperating in Philadelphia from his injuries he contracted smallpox, which kept him from returning to active duty until May. Anderson served under General Nathanael Greene during the Battles of Brandywine and Germantown and spent the winter of 1777–1778 at Valley Forge with Washington's army. He was assigned to the 6th Virginia Regiment on 10 February 1778, fought at Monmouth in June, and on 14 September 1778 transferred to the 1st Virginia Regiment, in which on 20 March 1779 he received a retroactive promotion to major, dating from 10 February 1778. Ordered to the Southern Department, Anderson was seriously injured on 9 October 1779 during the assault on Savannah, Georgia. On 12 May 1780, while in the military hospital at Fort Moultrie, he was captured and imprisoned. After his release Anderson returned to Virginia and during the spring and summer of 1781 served on the staff of General Lafayette. In late summer, probably in September, he was detached from regular army duties to assist Governor Thomas Nelson with organizing the Virginia militia. Sometime during this period, Anderson was assigned to the 3d Virginia Regiment. Later, possibly after the British surrender at Yorktown, he was promoted to lieutenant colonel.

On 15 January 1784 Governor Benjamin Harrison commissioned Anderson as principal surveyor of the western bounty lands, two tracts of land together covering about ten million acres on either side of the Ohio River that the state had set aside for Virginia officers, soldiers, sailors, and marines whose service during the Revolutionary War entitled them to grants of western land as bounties for their enlistments or service. Anderson took the oath of office in Richmond on 2 February 1784 and moved to Kentucky, where he opened an office near Louisville before the end of March. Until his death more than forty-two years later, Anderson supervised the locating, surveying, and patenting of land in the two reserves, dealing with county and state officials of Virginia, Kentucky, and Ohio, with the commissioner of the United States General Land Office, and with the secretary of war, who issued the titles.

Problems inherent in the office soon threatened to overwhelm Anderson. Congress, land speculators, officials at the federal, state, and local level, and private citizens all made competing demands on the principal surveyor. Federal and state bureaucracies both claimed jurisdiction over the office, and its regulations and policies were further muddled by obstructive congressional legislation and the vagaries of the Virginia land system that, among other things, allowed "indiscriminate location," the practice of surveying irregularly shaped tracts to acquire only the best lands. Anderson's office in Louisville was convenient to neither reserve, and complaints about his failure to keep up with his correspondence and the way in which his agents conducted surveys became so numerous that on 25 February 1818 the General Assembly passed a law requiring Anderson to move his office to Chillicothe, Ohio. When Anderson refused, on 18 February 1819 Governor James Preston issued orders to remove him from office. Anderson declined to relinquish his office to his newly appointed successor, Cadwallader Wallace, arguing that although he had been appointed by Virginia, his work made him an agent of the United States government and therefore not liable to removal by the state. The United States Supreme Court agreed, and on 5 April 1820 the commissioner of the General Land Office informed Wallace that Anderson was the sole legal occupant of the office of principal surveyor of the Virginia bounty lands.

Anderson had prevailed, but he and his staff remained unequal to the administrative burden of his office. While the demands were formidable, he made matters worse by disregarding state and federal regulations when they did not suit him or advance the interests of land speculators with whom he was friendly. He also neglected the Ohio reserve in favor of Kentucky lands in which he had a personal interest and failed to publicize his office's policies and procedures, leading to improperly patented claims. The resulting charges of corruption and favoritism may not have been entirely justified, and the most enterprising and diligent public servant could have failed under similar circumstances, but frustration and Anderson's own poor administrative abilities certainly undercut all his efforts save for his tenacious defense of his own appointment.

During the 1790s Anderson had built a schooner called the *Caroline*, which was reported to have made the first round-trip commercial voyage from Louisville to London. He also took some part in Kentucky politics. He was a delegate to the Kentucky convention of 1788 and served as a presidential elector in 1792, and he was a justice of the peace for Jefferson County and a trustee of the Jefferson County Seminary. In November 1787 Anderson married Elizabeth Clark. They had three daughters and one son, whom he raised at Soldier's Retreat, the house he built on property he purchased in Jefferson County in April 1789. After the death of his first wife, he married

Sarah Marshall and had five daughters and seven sons, including Richard Clough Anderson Jr., who served as a congressman from Kentucky and a diplomat, and Robert Anderson, the United States Army major who defended and surrendered Fort Sumter in April 1861. Richard Clough Anderson died at Soldier's Retreat on 16 October 1826 and was buried in the family cemetery there.

Edward L. Anderson, *Soldier and Pioneer: A Biographical Sketch of Lt.-Col. Richard C. Anderson of the Continental Army* (1879); family history data, including a photograph of the grave monument giving birth date, in William P. Anderson, *Anderson Family Records* (1936), 43–49 (por.); Edward L. Anderson, *The Andersons of Gold Mine, Hanover County* (n.d.); Lawrence A. Barr, *A New Look at the Soldiers Retreat* [1978]; Richard Clough Anderson Papers, University of Illinois at Urbana-Champaign Library; Anderson-Latham Papers, LVA; *Jefferson Papers*, 3:651–652; Louis Gottschalk, *Lafayette and the Close of the American Revolution* (1942), 220, 243; Asa Lee Rubenstein, "Richard Clough Anderson, Nathaniel Massie, and the Impact of Government on Western Land Speculation and Settlement, 1774–1830" (Ph.D. diss., University of Illinois at Urbana-Champaign, 1986); obituaries in *Lexington Reporter*, 23 Oct. 1826, *Richmond Enquirer*, 7 Nov. 1826, and *Niles' Weekly Register*, 11 Nov. 1826.

DONALD W. GUNTER

ANDERSON, Robert Alexander (24 January 1864–16 August 1938), journalist and Republican Party leader, was born at Adwolf in Smyth County, the eldest of three sons and two daughters of Isaac Campbell Anderson and Eliza Jane Anderson. He attended local schools before entering Emory and Henry College, where he graduated with a B.A. in 1888, after which he began to teach school. On 25 December 1889 he married Cora Evelyn Wolfe. They had two sons and six daughters.

In 1893 Anderson's increasing interest in state and local politics inspired him to run as the Republican candidate for the Senate of Virginia against Benjamin Franklin Buchanan, a popular Democrat. Anderson lost the election. Rebuffed by the voters, he enrolled in Richmond College and graduated with a law degree in 1895. He returned to Smyth County and opened a law office in Marion. On 15 May 1896 he purchased a part interest in one of the Marion newspapers, the *Southwestern News*, which he and his partner renamed the *Marion News*. Two years later he became the sole owner and editor and made the *Marion News* an influential Republican journal. Anderson served as the party's county chairman and was a delegate to its 1916 national convention. He was an ally and supporter of Campbell Bascom Slemp, a longtime member of the House of Representatives and the party's leader in southwestern Virginia. Anderson's party loyalty earned him two appointments as postmaster of Marion, from 1903 to 1915 and from 1927 to 1934. His avid support of Prohibition helped him to a post as assistant regional administrator of the Department of the Treasury's Bureau of Prohibition from 1921 to 1927.

In 1915 Anderson once again ran for the Senate, but even with Slemp's support he lost to John Preston Buchanan. In March 1917 Anderson transferred management of the *Marion News* to his son and business manager, Marvin J. Anderson, perhaps so that he could concentrate on his political aspirations. On 3 September 1917 Anderson won the Republican nomination for the Smyth County seat in the House of Delegates. His campaign platform called for election law reform, abolition of the poll tax, extension of the public school system, and admission of women to the University of Virginia. Without serious opposition from the other five candidates, he captured nearly all of the 1,305 votes cast. He served one two-year term in the General Assembly.

Anderson purchased the rival local newspaper, the *Marion Democrat*. The Marion Publishing Company, managed by his son, published this paper as well as the Republican *Marion News*. On 1 January 1921 the Andersons sold their newspapers to a Lawrenceville businessman. The new owner changed the name of the *Marion News* to the *Smyth County News* and Robert A. Anderson contributed to it as political editor and columnist until his death.

Anderson served as a director of the Marion National Bank for twenty-five years. He was a member of the board of trustees of Marion College from 1915 to 1938 and president of the board from 1933 until early in 1938, when he became the school's vice president. A lifelong farmer, he raised livestock on his 400-acre farm southwest of Marion. He was deacon in the Marion Baptist Church, clerk of the Lebanon Baptist Association, and served for ten years on the association's executive committee. On 14 June 1938 he was elected to the Marion Town Council.

Robert Alexander Anderson was critically injured in an automobile accident near Marion on 5 August 1938 and as a result died in Homeland Hospital in Marion on 16 August 1938. He was buried in Round Hill Cemetery in Marion.

Goodrich Wilson, *Smyth County History and Traditions* (1932), 111–112, 168; Election Records, vols. 33, 71, 72, RG 13, LVA; public life documented in editorial and news columns in *Marion News*, *Marion Democrat*, and *Marion Smyth County News*; obituaries in *Roanoke World-News*, 17 Aug. 1938, *Roanoke Times*, 18 Aug. 1938, and *Marion Democrat*, 23 Aug. 1938 (por.).

JOAN TRACY ARMSTRONG

ANDERSON, Robert Homer (29 October 1888–2 April 1977), Lutheran minister, was born in Marion, the eldest of seven sons and one daughter of John Robert Anderson, an inspector of buildings and bridges for the Norfolk and Western Railway, and Laura Hash Anderson. After attending public schools, he earned a bachelor's degree at Roanoke College in 1910 and a master's degree there in 1911. He lettered in baseball, basketball, and football. His aggressive play on the football field together with his stocky build and deep voice earned him the nickname "Bulldog," which stuck with him for life.

Anderson studied at Mount Airy Lutheran Seminary in Philadelphia and received a B.D. in 1914. He was ordained that same year and between then and 1928 served as pastor of Lutheran churches at Pomaria, Newberry County, South Carolina, at Burkes Garden in Tazewell County, at Toms Brook and Strasburg, both in Shenandoah County, and in the city of Lynchburg. In 1928 he was appointed superintendent of the Virginia Synod, the second-ranking position under the president. The synod extended from Norfolk into eastern Tennessee, and as the synod's only full-time officer for the next thirty years, Anderson traveled frequently throughout its bounds with responsibility for field administration and internal development of congregations. Establishing new churches was difficult during the 1930s, but in the decade following the creation of the Home Missions Committee in 1945, Anderson was able to assist in the founding of about twenty-five new churches. He also served long terms as a trustee of both Roanoke and Marion Colleges.

In 1929 Anderson created the synod's Summer Assembly program of inspirational and educational talks, classes, and events that drew hundreds of Lutherans to weeklong meetings at Massanetta Springs in Rockingham County. For twenty years Anderson also edited the *Virginia Lutheran*, the synod's monthly newsletter, and wrote a column called "Siftings" that contained news of interest from the synod's churches and of its grassroots activities. He was a delegate to almost every biennial convention of the United Lutheran Church in America for forty-five years and served as president of the denomination's Parish Education Board from 1937 to 1938 and as a member of its Board of American Missions from 1949 to 1960. Among other honors, he received a D.D. from Roanoke College in 1935 and was named to the school's athletic hall of fame in 1971.

On 13 June 1914 Anderson married Helen Atkins Morrissette. They had two sons and two daughters. He retired in 1958 and remained in Roanoke. Robert Homer Anderson died of emphysema at his home on 2 April 1977 and was buried at Blue Ridge Memorial Gardens in Roanoke.

Family history information verified by sister, Lena Mae Anderson Ayers, and daughter, Garnett Celeste Anderson Secrist; BVS Birth Register, Smyth Co.; William Edward Eisenberg, *The Lutheran Church in Virginia, 1717–1962* (1967); records of Roanoke College; Virginia Lutheran Synod Archives, Roanoke; obituary in *Roanoke Times and World News*, 3 Apr. 1977; memorial in Virginia Synod of the Lutheran Church in America, *Minutes of the Annual Convention* (1977): 112–113 (por.).

GEORGE A. KEGLEY

ANDERSON, Robert Lane (16 August 1907–7 June 1951), journalist, was born in Cleveland, Ohio, the eldest of two sons and one daughter of Sherwood Anderson, the novelist, and Cornelia Platt Lane Anderson, his first wife. As a boy he lived in Elyria, Ohio, and Union Pier, Illinois, near Chicago, before his parents divorced in July 1916. The next year his mother moved the family to Michigan City, Indiana, where she resumed teaching. Anderson graduated from high school in 1924 and gained some journalistic experience covering high school sports for the *Michigan City Evening Dispatch*.

During the next few years Anderson worked as a reporter and rewrite man for a variety of newspapers, including the *Item-Tribune* and *Times-Picayune* in New Orleans, the *Indianapolis News*, and the *Charlottesville Daily Progress*. He attended the University of Virginia for the academic year 1927–1928 and worked briefly for the *Roanoke Times*. He was writing for the *Philadelphia Evening Bulletin* in 1928 when he accepted his father's invitation to settle in Marion and assist him in publishing two weekly newspapers he had acquired the previous year.

On 18 December 1931 Anderson married Mary Leigh Chryst, an English teacher at Marion Junior College. They had two daughters. Anderson had arranged to purchase his father's business, and on 1 January 1932 he officially took control of the *Marion Democrat* and the *Smyth County News*, a Republican paper. An active Democrat, Anderson was the youngest member of the Convention of 1933, which met in Richmond on 25 October to consider ratification of the Twenty-First Amendment to the United States Constitution. He joined in the convention's unanimous vote for an end to Prohibition.

In April 1935 Anderson added a third newspaper to his holdings when he established the *Washington County Forum*, a nonpartisan paper located in Abingdon. He served as president of the Young Democratic Club of Smyth County from 1936 to 1937, became chairman of the organization's Ninth District in 1937, and in 1938 assumed the presidency of the Young Democratic Club of Virginia at its annual convention.

After the bombing of Pearl Harbor Anderson volunteered for duty in the U.S. Navy and received a commission as lieutenant in June 1942. He served as an intelligence officer on the USS *Wake Island*, a small aircraft carrier, for most of the war. While he was away his wife edited the *Smyth County News*, which had absorbed the *Marion Democrat* before Anderson left.

After the war Anderson returned to his journalistic duties and civic activities in Smyth County. He resumed his involvement in the Marion Chamber of Commerce, serving as secretary for many years and later as president. He directed the Community Chest, served on the Electoral Board of Smyth County and the Marion Public Library Board, and became the first president of the Mountain Empire Broadcasting Corporation, which operated radio station WMEV. He was elected mayor of Marion twice, serving from September 1948 to June 1951.

A skillful journalist, Anderson garnered awards for both news and feature writing in 1940, 1941, 1947, and 1950. His article "Chicken Fight" appeared in the *American Mercury* in September 1933, and he published two pamphlets, *Thwarted Ambitions* (1935), an account of an unusual court case, and *A Long Letter to Mary* (ca. 1948), a narration of his experiences during the invasion of the Philippines in January 1945.

Robert Lane Anderson enjoyed training horses, handling dogs, and hunting birds. He expressed the hope that he would die at age seventy while jumping a horse over a fence. His death at the age of forty-four was caused instead by a heart attack suffered while playing golf in Marion on 7 June 1951. He was buried in Roselawn Cemetery in Marion.

Interview with daughter Elizabeth Chryst Anderson; Glass and Glass, *Virginia Democracy*, 3:36–37; BVS Marriage Register, Smyth Co.; *Journal of the Convention Called in Pursuance of an Act of the General Assembly to Ratify or Reject an Amendment to the Constitution of the United States . . . October 25, 1933* (1934), 8, 30; *Time*, 20 Feb. 1939, 49–50 (por.); Kim Townsend, *Sherwood Anderson* (1987), 215, 251; obituaries in *Richmond Times-Dispatch*, 8 June 1951, *New York Times*, 9 June 1951, and *Marion Smyth County News*, 14 June 1951.

JOAN TRACY ARMSTRONG

ANDERSON, Robert Nelson (6 May 1899–27 April 1976), attorney, was born in Roanoke, the second of three sons and third of five children of Thomas Gerald Anderson and Lena Stuart Nelson Anderson. When he was six years old the family moved to Washington, D.C. Anderson graduated from McKinley High School and received a scholarship to Harvard, but he enrolled instead at George Washington University. He served as president of the student council, won the Davis Prize for debate, and graduated cum laude in 1921. Anderson then enrolled in the George Washington University Law School and received his law degree in 1923. On 24 March 1924 he married Agnes Mary Rogers. They had one daughter and two sons.

After graduating from law school and passing the bar examinations for Virginia and the District of Columbia, Anderson worked in the solicitor's office of the Bureau of Internal Revenue in Washington. In 1925 he left government service and was a member of the Washington law firm of Humphreys and Day until 1932, when he formed his own partnership, Anderson, Lawrence, and Anderson. He moved from Washington to Lyon Village in Arlington County in 1926 and lived there the remainder of his life. Anderson participated in many community and regional organizations. In 1930 he served as chairman of the Arlington County Better Government League, a committee composed of representatives of several leading civic organizations that successfully campaigned to have the county manager form of government adopted for Arlington County, making it one of the first in Virginia to adopt the manager form that was rapidly transforming city governments nationwide.

Anderson was one of the first northern Virginia Democrats to endorse Franklin D. Roosevelt for president in 1932, and he was a delegate to the Democratic National Convention that year. In 1934 Anderson rejoined government service as a special assistant for tax policy to the attorney general of the United States. He spent the next thirty-five years in the Department of Justice, with a transfer in 1957 to a post as the reviewing officer under the legal coordinating counsel. During his long tenure with the department Anderson argued cases before the United States Supreme Court and every one of the United States circuit courts of appeal. He served on the attorney general's advisory committee on citizenship from 1949 to 1954 and in 1966 became president of the Friends of the Law Library of Congress. Anderson also belonged to the Arlington County Bar Association, the Bar Association of the District of Columbia, and the Virginia State Bar Association. He was president of the Federal Bar Association in 1942–1943 and a member of the House of Delegates of the American Bar Association in 1944–1945. He was a delegate to the first convention of the Inter-American Bar Association in Havana, Cuba, in 1941, and during the years 1944–1946 played a leading role in the founding of the International Bar Association.

Anderson retired from the Department of Justice in 1969 and joined a Washington law firm, but in 1971 he opened his own law offices in Washington and Arlington, specializing in corporate, tax, and international law and representing clients before federal government departments and in the federal courts. He remained active in the International Bar Association. On his way home from a meeting of its executive council in Geneva, Switzerland, Robert Nelson Anderson died of a heart attack in London, England, on 27 April 1976. He was buried in Warrenton Cemetery in Warrenton.

Glass and Glass, *Virginia Democracy*, 2:594–598; Robert Nelson Anderson, "Arlington Adopts the County Manager Form of Government," *Arlington Historical Magazine* 1 (Oct. 1958): 52–67; obituary in *Washington Post*, 30 Apr. 1976 (por.).

PETER R. HENRIQUES

ANDERSON, Sarah Archer (8 November 1862–20 October 1954), preservationist, was born in Richmond, the eldest of three daughters and second of seven children of Archer Anderson and Mary Anne Mason Anderson. Her elder brother died young. She was born and lived the first years of her life in the residence of her grandfather Joseph Reid Anderson, president of the Tredegar ironworks, the major producer of Confederate ordnance during the Civil War. Her father went to work at Tredegar just before the Civil War and in 1881 moved his family into a remodeled residence a block away from his eldest daughter's birthplace. She resided there, at 103 West Franklin Street in Richmond, for the remainder of her long life.

Anderson was christened on 25 December 1862 at Saint Paul's Episcopal Church, to which she belonged until her death. She grew up in a family dedicated to preserving the memory of the Civil War. The Anderson family regularly hosted former Confederate officers who visited Richmond, and during reunions the Anderson house became one of the social centers of the city. She listened to her father and his friends talk about the war while she entertained them, and at the dramatic unveiling of Richmond's Lee statue on 29 May 1890 she heard her father deliver the principal address.

Miss Sally Anderson, as she was known, accepted and propagated the Lost Cause interpretation of the Civil War, which celebrated the heroism of the Confederate armies and extolled the Old South. She believed that the women of her generation had a "sacred duty" to "gather and to preserve the things which would keep alive the memory of the men who had died." Anderson first took an active part in the work of historic preservation through the Confederate Museum, which was located in the old White House of the Confederacy. Anderson's mother belonged as early as 1897 to the Confederate Memorial Literary Society that saved the house from destruction, and she served as a vice president in 1899. Sally Anderson joined the society in 1903 and in 1907 became chairman of the Life Membership Committee. In 1909 she was elected a society vice president, and in 1912 she became president.

Anderson led the society for forty years, working tirelessly to expand the collections and improve the library. Deeply committed to the mission of the museum and determined to succeed, she acted as spokeswoman for the institution, appearing at countless society-sponsored events, raising money, hosting dignitaries, guiding the development of the collections, and working with other women across the South to create an attractive facility of historic importance. When she retired as president in November 1952, the Museum of the Confederacy boasted one of the largest collections of Confederate items in the world, and its library's valuable research collection of rare books, personal papers, and other manuscripts pertaining to the war enjoyed a national reputation.

Anderson also helped found Richmond's Sheltering Arms Hospital, which opened in February 1889. She belonged to the Woman's Auxiliary of Saint Paul's Church and the Association for the Preservation of Virginia Antiquities, and for the last twelve years of her life she was an honorary president of the Virginia Division of the United Daughters of the Confederacy. She was fondly remembered for continuing to use her horse-drawn carriage in the streets of Richmond long after automobiles and traffic lights had become the norm. Sally Archer Anderson died at her house in Richmond on 20 October 1954 and was buried in Hollywood Cemetery.

Feature articles with portraits in *Richmond Times-Dispatch*, 4 Mar. 1946 and 16 Nov. 1952; Saint Paul's Church Registry, Richmond; Sally Archer Anderson Papers and Minute Book of Confederate Memorial Literary Society, MOC; presidential reports in Confederate Memorial Literary Society, *Year Books*, 1912–1952; Michael I. Shoop, "A History of the Museum of the Confederacy, Richmond, Virginia, and Its Library" (master's thesis, UNC, 1983); obituaries in *Richmond News Leader*, 20 Oct. 1954, and *Richmond Times-Dispatch*, 21 Oct. 1954; editorial tribute in *Richmond Times-Dispatch*, 23 Oct. 1954.

MALINDA WYATT COLLIER
TUCKER H. HILL

ANDERSON, Sherwood (13 September 1876–8 March 1941), writer, was born in Camden, Preble County, Ohio, the second of five sons and third of seven children of Irwin McLain Anderson and Emma Smith Anderson. His father was a restless man who moved the family from one Ohio town to another before settling down in 1883 in Clyde, where he worked improvidently in the saddlery and harness business. His mother took in washing to supplement the family's income.

Outwardly, young Sherwood Anderson was determined to escape the stigma of being poor by achieving material success and becoming respectable. Inwardly, he was a dreamy boy who sought refuge in reading. His mother nurtured his imagination, and her insightful observations awakened within him a curiosity about the human drama lying below the surface of everyday life. She died in 1895, and the next year Anderson left home for Chicago where he worked in a warehouse and took a business course at night at the Lewis Institute. In 1898, as war loomed between Spain and America, he enlisted in the army, but his company arrived in Cuba after the fighting ended.

Anderson returned to Clyde and in 1900 earned the equivalent of a high school diploma from Wittenberg Academy in nearby Springfield. He then moved back to Chicago and wrote copy for an advertising agency. In 1904 he married Cornelia Platt Lane, the cultivated daughter of a successful businessman and a graduate of the College of Women of Western Reserve University in Cleveland. They had two sons and a daughter. In 1906 they moved to Cleveland, where Anderson became president of the United Factories Company, a mail-order business that he hoped to expand using his considerable advertising skills. After the company suffered financial reverses, Anderson moved in 1907 to nearby Elyria and there established a different mail-order firm that gradually diversified and prospered.

About 1909 dormant tensions began to surface within Anderson. Increasingly unhappy with his career, his vague socialistic ideas at odds with the business ethic, he began to imagine another life for himself as a writer, and at nights he experimented with autobiographical fiction. Financial worries and growing marital problems added to his woes. The crisis finally occurred in November 1912. Suffering from what was later characterized as a mental breakdown, Anderson walked out of his office in a disoriented state and wandered about the city for several days. Early in 1913 Anderson left his family and returned to Chicago, where he resumed his advertising work and met Theodore Dreiser, Floyd Dell, and others associated with the Chicago Renaissance.

On 27 July 1916 Anderson divorced his wife and four days later married Tennessee Mitchell, a dance and piano teacher and a sculptor. With the help of Dreiser and Dell, Anderson published two autobiographical novels, *Windy McPherson's Son* (1917) and *Marching Men* (1918), and the tales that collectively became his best-known work, *Winesburg, Ohio* (1919). To many eastern critics, Anderson came to symbolize the possibility of America's literary rejuvenation, and in the 1920s he tried to live up to that promise. Between 1921 and 1925 he published the novels *Poor White*, *Many Marriages*, and *Dark Laughter*, stories collected as *The Triumph of the Egg* and *Horses and Men*, and an autobiography, *A Story-Teller's Tale*. He spent some time in Alabama and New Orleans, and in 1921 he visited London and Paris. In the latter city he met Gertrude Stein, whom he acknowledged as a major influence on his writing. Anderson also helped William Faulkner and Ernest Hemingway launch their careers.

In 1924 Anderson divorced Tennessee Mitchell and married Elizabeth Prall, a graduate of the University of Michigan and a bookseller. Although in 1925 *Vanity Fair* described him as the country's most distinctive novelist, and in the same article H. L. Mencken was quoted as praising *Dark Laughter* as a profound novel, Anderson artistically had reached a dead end. His reputation as a writer declined precipitously, and he was soon eclipsed by the next generation of writers, particularly by Hemingway (who parodied Anderson's style in *The Torrents of Spring*) and F. Scott Fitzgerald.

Anderson withdrew from his old life and started over. He had vacationed in southwestern Virginia, and in 1926, with the proceeds of *Dark Laughter*, his one best-seller, Anderson began building a house that he called Ripshin, after the creek that ran through his property near Trout Dale in Grayson County. In 1927 he dissolved his contract with his publisher and purchased the two weekly papers published in nearby Marion, the Republican *Smyth County News* and the *Marion Democrat*. Employing his writing skills as a journalist, he produced enough editorials, personal columns, and pieces by a character he named Buck Fever to fill a sizable volume, and in 1929 he published *Hello Towns!*

Anderson immersed himself in the life around him, writing about the natural beauty of the area and the ways of its mountain communities. Inspired by Eleanor Gladys Copenhaver, a native of Marion who worked in the industrial department of the Young Women's Christian

Association, Anderson also became interested in the social and economic conditions of the region. In November 1930 he introduced Stringfellow Barr and John Crowe Ransom at a Richmond debate on "Industrialism versus Agrarianism." In lengthy opening remarks Anderson practically stole the show as he commented on the predatory nature of the machine age that was transforming the lives and landscapes of rural and small-town America.

Anderson had become the advocate of a disadvantaged people and strove to become one of them. His office became a kind of town library and art gallery. He was the local celebrity, but he was down-to-earth and often traded stories on the courthouse steps. "Here," he wrote, "I am closer to life than I have ever been." Having divorced Elizabeth Prall in 1932, Anderson married Eleanor Gladys Copenhaver on 6 July 1933 at her parents' house in Marion. He then began in earnest an examination of labor conditions in other parts of the country, touring the mills and mines of Virginia, the Carolinas, Georgia, and Tennessee in an effort to understand labor problems. By 1937 he had published two collections of essays, *Perhaps Women* and *Puzzled America*, a novel dealing with labor issues, *Beyond Desire*, which he dedicated to Eleanor Copenhaver Anderson, and a play based on *Winesburg, Ohio*. A long illustrated essay, *Home Town*, came out in 1940.

Early in 1941 Sherwood Anderson set out for South America to write on labor conditions there, but on the voyage he accidentally swallowed a toothpick, contracted peritonitis, and died on 8 March 1941 at Colón, Panama. He was buried in Round Hill Cemetery in Marion.

James Schevill, *Sherwood Anderson: His Life and Work* (1951); William A. Sutton, *The Road to Winesburg* (1972); Kim Townsend, *Sherwood Anderson* (1987; por.); Sherwood Anderson Collection, Newberry Library, Chicago; Eugene P. Sheehy and Kenneth A. Lohf, *Sherwood Anderson: A Bibliography* (1960); Charles E. Modlin, ed., *Sherwood Anderson, Selected Letters* (1984); William A. Sutton, ed., *Letters to Bab: Sherwood Anderson to Marietta D. Finley, 1916–33* (1985); Hilbert H. Campbell, ed., *The Sherwood Anderson Diaries* (1987); Charles E. Modlin, ed., *Sherwood Anderson's Love Letters to Eleanor Copenhaver Anderson* (1989); Ray Lewis White, ed., *Sherwood Anderson's Secret Love Letters* (1991); Charles E. Modlin, ed., *Certain Things Last: The Selected Short Stories of Sherwood Anderson* (1992); Welford D. Taylor, ed., *Buck Fever Papers* (1971); obituaries in *New York Times*, 9 Mar. 1941, and *Marion Smyth County News*, 13, 27 Mar. 1941.

KIM TOWNSEND

ANDERSON, William (2 June 1764–13 September 1839), surveyor, was born in Delaware, the eldest child of Robert Anderson, an immigrant from Ulster, Ireland, and Margaret Neely Anderson. In 1770 the family moved to Virginia, where Anderson's father purchased 500 acres of land on the Catawba River in Botetourt County. Little is known about Anderson until he enrolled in the Virginia militia at age sixteen. He served with Colonel William Campbell's regiment at the Battle of King's Mountain and fought under General Nathanael Greene at the Cowpens and at Guilford Courthouse during the final years of the American Revolution.

Anderson returned to Botetourt County and in 1782 became deputy county surveyor. Ten years later he was appointed surveyor for the county, a position he held until his death. On 15 May 1796 he married Anna Thomas in Frederick County, Maryland. Following his marriage, he resided at Walnut Hill near Fincastle, where his six sons and four daughters were born. Three of his four sons who lived to maturity, John Thomas Anderson, Francis Thomas Anderson, and Joseph Reid Anderson, had distinguished legal, industrial, or political careers in Virginia.

A militia officer since 1795, in 1811 Anderson was commissioned lieutenant colonel of the 48th Regiment, one of two Botetourt militia regiments. During the War of 1812 he remained commander of the 48th but also served as a staff officer with the 4th Virginia Regiment at Norfolk from April to August 1813 and in August 1814. Later accounts of Anderson's having served as inspector general of the Eastern Shore, raised a regiment, and marched it to Norfolk are unsupported by contemporary archival records.

In addition to farming and working as a surveyor, Anderson served as a deputy sheriff of Botetourt County from 1793 to 1799, as a justice of the peace beginning in 1806, as county sheriff in 1828, and as a member of the House of Delegates for the 1831–1832 session. As a surveyor, he did much to expand Virginia's links with its western lands during an era of intense internal improvements. Anderson served as construction superintendent of the Kanawha Road for the James River Company from June 1822 to January 1823. In April of the latter year he became commissioner of the company's Kanawha River navigation and road, a position he held until March 1826. In these capacities he surveyed routes, contracted for assistants and road engineers, maintained accounts, provided overall supervision in constructing the turnpike from Covington to the Kanawha River, and oversaw improvements to the river for better navigation. Anderson also supervised the construction of the Blue Ridge Canal from the mouth of the North River to Irish Falls. In 1833 he surveyed the route for the Fincastle and Blue Ridge Turnpike, and four years later he did the same for the New Market and Sperryville Turnpike. A largely self-taught surveyor, he was able through hard work on important public projects to become perhaps the most-respected man in the county.

On 13 September 1839 William Anderson died in Botetourt County at Montrose, the house of his son Francis Thomas Anderson. He was buried in the cemetery of the Fincastle Presbyterian Church, of which he had long been an elder.

Ellen Graham Anderson, "The Four Anderson Brothers," *Journal of the Roanoke Historical Society* 6 (summer 1969): 15–19; abstract of family Bible records in Anderson Papers, UVA; Frederick Co., Md., Marriage Register; Foote, *Sketches of Virginia*, 2:584–586; Stoner, *Seed-Bed*, 270–271; *Organization of the Militia of the State of Virginia* (1814); Compiled Military Service Record, 4th Virginia Regiment, War of 1812, Adjutant General's Office, RG 94, NARA; Anderson letters and surveys in files of Special Engineers and in records of James River Company, Fincastle and Blue Ridge Turnpike, and New Market and Sperryville Turnpike, all in Board of Public Works, RG 57, LVA; Hall, *Portraits*, 16 (por.); Stephen F. Cocke, *A Funeral Sermon on The Death of Col. William Anderson, Late of Botetourt County, Virginia, Preached at the Presbyterian Church at Fincastle, September 15, 1839* (1840); obituary in *Richmond Enquirer*, 13 Oct. 1839.

STUART LEE BUTLER

ANDERSON, William (1788–by 3 April 1856), member of the Convention of 1829–1830, was born in Shenandoah County in the latter part of 1788, the youngest of at least three sons and three daughters of John Anderson and Mary Black Anderson. His father, a cattle dealer who saw service both on the county court and as coroner, was reportedly murdered late in 1797. Nothing is known of Anderson's early years. By 1820 he and David Crawford had formed the mercantile firm of Crawford and Anderson in Woodstock. When Isaac Trout joined the firm in 1829, the name was changed to Crawford, Trout, and Company. Anderson probably withdrew from the firm shortly after Trout's arrival.

Anderson received a commission as Shenandoah County's deputy sheriff in 1821 and served until 1828. He represented his county in the House of Delegates for three consecutive sessions beginning in November 1824. In addition to service on the Committee of Propositions and Grievances in all three sessions, he sat on the Committee for Examining Enrolled Bills during the first two and on the Committee on Finance during the session that first met in December 1826. In that same month he became a member of the Shenandoah County Court.

In the spring of 1829 Anderson led nine candidates in a district consisting of Rockingham and Shenandoah Counties for four seats in the Convention of 1829–1830. He served on the Committee on the Legislative Department of Government. Although he did not take an active role in the debates, he voted regularly with other delegates from the western counties in favor of such proposals as extending the franchise to nonfreeholders, abolishing the governor's Council, democratizing the county court system, and mandating the popular election of the governor. Because none of these reforms was included in the constitution that the convention submitted to a public referendum, he voted against its adoption.

Anderson married Rachel Cameron Eliza White, of Bath County, on 26 November 1818 in Shenandoah County. They had five sons and one daughter before her death on 19 July 1831. By April 1834 he had married her sister, twice-widowed Alice M. White Fravel Hupp. They had one son. Late in 1833 or early in 1834, Anderson moved to the Fort Seybert area of Pendleton County, where he purchased tracts of land that together encompassed more than 2,500 acres of farmland and were valued at $20,000 in 1850. There he farmed and raised livestock.

He also owned slaves, the number fluctuating between six when he left Shenandoah County and twenty-one at his death. A well-read man, he owned a library that was reportedly the best in Pendleton County.

William Anderson had died by 3 April 1856, on which date his widow relinquished her right to the administration of his estate. He was buried in Cedar Hill Cemetery in Franklin, Pendleton County.

Oren F. Morton, *A History of Pendleton County, West Virginia* (1910), 174, gives year of birth confirmed by Census, Pendleton Co., record compiled 29 July 1850, which lists age as sixty-one; family connections in Pendleton Co. Will Book, 4:296–297; Registers of Justices and County Officers, RG 13, LVA; Shenandoah Co. Marriage Bonds, 26 Nov. 1818; Land and Personal Property Tax Returns, Shenandoah Co., 1817–1834, and Pendleton Co., 1834–1859, RG 48, LVA; *Richmond Enquirer*, 19 May 1829; Records of Convention of 1829–1830, RG 91, LVA; Bruce, *Rhetoric of Conservatism*, 36–37; Catlin, *Convention of 1829–30* (por); Pendleton Co. Order Book (1850–1856), 318.

ROBERT P. SUTTON

ANDERSON, William Alexander (11 May 1842–21 June 1930), member of the Convention of 1901–1902 and attorney general of Virginia, was born at Montrose, near Fincastle in Botetourt County, the eldest of three sons and sixth of nine children of Francis Thomas Anderson, later a justice of the Virginia Supreme Court of Appeals, and Mary Ann Alexander Anderson. He was educated at home and also attended the Fincastle Academy. Anderson enrolled at Washington College in Lexington in 1857 but did not graduate. In April 1861 he left school to join the Liberty Hall Volunteers, which he and his classmates had just formed. He enlisted on 2 June and became orderly sergeant of Company I, 4th Regiment Virginia Infantry. Anderson was shot in the left kneecap at the First Battle of Manassas (Bull Run) on 21 July 1861, spent several months recuperating at the Richmond home of his uncle Joseph Reid Anderson, a prominent industrialist, and was discharged on 14 December. In 1863 he entered the University of Virginia, from which he received an LL.B. on 20 June 1866.

Anderson returned to Lexington and began a long and successful career as an attorney and important conservative Democratic politician. By acting as counsel for a number of mining and other business firms, he became relatively affluent. Between 1889 and 1891 Anderson won praise for helping to attract foreign investment to turn the Rockbridge town of Glasgow into a major industrial center, but the boom collapsed in 1893. Unlike many other investors, Anderson apparently made money out of the Glasgow bubble. He married Ellen Graham Anderson, daughter of his uncle Joseph Reid Anderson, in Richmond on 19 July 1871, but she died on 25 January 1872. He then married Mary Louisa "Maza" Blair, of Lexington, on 9 August 1875, and they had four daughters and one son.

In 1868 Anderson first ran for elective office and was nominated to the House of Delegates, but the state's military commander postponed the election. The next year Anderson ran successfully for the Senate of Virginia and represented Alleghany, Bath, and Rockbridge Counties from 1869 to 1873. He was deeply committed to returning the antebellum patrician oligarchy to power and spent the next thirty years working toward that goal. In a legislative session known later for passing the two ill-considered bills, Anderson voted both for the controversial 1871 Funding Bill to repay in full Virginia's $37 million antebellum internal improvements debt and for the act to dispose of the state's railroad holdings at bargain rates. At the same time, as a lifelong advocate of education, he also sponsored and helped pass William Henry Ruffner's 1870 act to establish the public school system that the Funding Act was soon to deprive of state aid.

Anderson did not seek elective office again until 1879, when he campaigned unsuccessfully for the House of Delegates as a Funder (who favored full funding of the state's debt) against a pair of Readjuster candidates who had initially been elected two years earlier. The Readjusters, who wanted the state's debt readjusted downward, first won a majority in the General Assembly in 1879. By 1883 the Conservative Party, renamed the Democratic Party, had learned from its losses and revised its platform in order to wrest control of Virginia's government from the Readjusters. Anderson benefited from the change by winning election to the

House of Delegates, defeating the three-term Readjuster candidates to whom he had lost in 1879. Anderson served as chairman of the Committee on Schools and Colleges, and in spite of his earlier vote on the Funding Bill he introduced the resolution by which the Democrats accepted the Riddleberger Act of 1882 as the final downward readjustment of the public debt. With Delegate J. Marshall McCormick, Anderson also sponsored what became the Anderson-McCormick Election Law of 1884, which was designed to give control of elections to the Democratic Party and thereby cripple the Readjuster and Republican Parties. The result was widespread voter fraud.

Anderson did not seek reelection in 1885 but did serve for the 1887–1888 term and again chaired the Committee on Schools and Colleges. Elected a trustee of Washington and Lee University in 1885, he served on the board until he died forty-five years later. He was rector from 1913 until 1924 and supported breaking the school's ties to the Presbyterian Church as a prerequisite for making it a major national university.

In 1885 Anderson became a member of the Democratic State Central Committee, serving until 1900. He also served on the Democratic Executive Committee from 1885 to 1890. Jeopardizing his party standing, he was one of many conservative Democrats who resented the ascendancy within the party of Thomas Staples Martin who had used railroad money and influence to become United States senator in 1893. Anderson joined a splinter movement to break Martin's power, curb widespread voting fraud, and lobby for the direct election of U.S. senators. He served as permanent chairman of the conference and made the principal speech in Richmond on 10 May 1899 at the meeting of the disaffected Democrats to decide a course of action. However, Martin crushed the May Movement, as it was called, and retained his Senate seat. Nevertheless, election reform remained an issue that ultimately had to be addressed.

Many Democrats believed that voter fraud could be eliminated by disfranchising the black electorate. Chosen president of the Virginia State Bar Association on 30 April 1900, Anderson used his 17 July 1900 presidential address to explain how the forthcoming constitutional convention could disfranchise black voters without violating the letter of the Fifteenth Amendment to the U.S. Constitution. In fact, his speech formed the basis of the suffrage provisions of the Constitution of 1902. Anderson and James William Gilmore easily defeated two Republicans on 23 May 1901 to represent Rockbridge County in the convention. Anderson was elected president pro tempore and chaired the Committees on the Elective Franchise and on Final Revision. He voted with the majority for the restrictive suffrage provisions adopted on 4 April 1902 but sided with the minority that favored submitting the constitution to a ratification referendum.

In the meantime, on 15 August 1901 the Democratic state convention nominated Anderson for attorney general of Virginia, and he easily defeated Republican D. Lawrence Groner on 5 November 1901 with 61 percent of the vote. On 7 November 1905 he won election to a second term, defeating Republican candidate George A. Revercomb with 66 percent of votes cast in an election that saw a one-third decrease in total votes from the 1901 figure.

Anderson served as attorney general from 1 January 1902 until 1 January 1910. The years were unusually busy ones for the office because of questions that arose under the new constitution, its requirement that the attorney general represent the interests of the state before the new State Corporation Commission, and Anderson's defense of its controversial suffrage provisions and the decision to put the constitution into effect without voter approval. His most important achievement was instituting the *Virginia* v. *West Virginia* suit in the U.S. Supreme Court that in 1915 resulted in a final settlement of the longstanding disagreement between those states over debts incurred for internal improvements prior to the Civil War. Anderson served as paid counsel for Virginia in the case after leaving office as attorney general.

At the age of seventy-six Anderson served one more term in the House of Delegates session of 1918–1919 and supported the better roads movement. He was one of the last Civil

War veterans active in politics and because of the pronounced stiff-legged limp that had resulted from his war wound became known as the "Lame Lion of the Confederacy." The sobriquet "Lame Lion of Lynchburg" had originally been applied to railroad executive and U.S. senator John Warwick Daniel, who had rebuilt the Democratic Party in the 1880s, but after Daniel's death Anderson received the honorific title in appreciation of his lifelong commitment to the Democratic Party. William Alexander Anderson died at his house in Lexington on 21 June 1930 and was buried in Lexington Cemetery.

Anderson Family Papers and Rockbridge Historical Society Papers, W&L; Anderson Papers, UVA; birth date on tombstone and corroborated by most published sources; Lois G. Moore, "William Alexander Anderson, Attorney General of Virginia, 1902–1910" (master's thesis, UVA, 1959), summarized in *Proceedings of the Rockbridge Historical Society* 5 (1954/1960): 79–87; articles by daughter Ellen G. Anderson are "W. A. Anderson, Leader in Public Life of County," *Lexington Gazette* bicentennial edition, 1938, and "The Wounding and Hospital Care of William A. Anderson," *VMHB* 62 (1954): 205–207; Compiled Service Records; Raymond H. Pulley, "The May Movement of 1899," *VMHB* 75 (1967): 186–201; Anderson's most important publications include "Virginia Constitutions," presidential address, *Virginia State Bar Association Proceedings* (1900): 145–178 (por.), and "Increase of Federal Power Under the Commerce Clause of the Federal Constitution," American Political Science Association, *Proceedings of the Annual Meeting* 5 (1909): 74–82; *Convention of 1901–1902 Photographs* (por.); reports as attorney general published in pamphlet form; records pertaining to *Virginia* v. *West Virginia* include 17 linear feet of correspondence and papers for the years 1899–1920 in Department of Law, RG 5, LVA, about 1,000 pages of correspondence and draft material in Anderson Papers, UVA, and 9 bound volumes of printed briefs, exhibits, and arguments in LVA; obituary in *Lexington Gazette*, 24 June 1930 (with incorrect 10 May 1842 birth date); memorial by Greenlee D. Letcher in *Virginia State Bar Association Proceedings* (1930): 184–191.

BRENT TARTER

ANDREWS, Charles Wesley (27 July 1807–24 May 1875), Episcopal minister, was born in Pittsford, Vermont, the son of Zelotus Andrews and Betsy Andrews. His father died when he was six, and the austere piety of his Congregationalist mother had an important influence on him. Andrews was educated at Castleberry Academy in Rutland and at Middlebury College. There he may have developed symptoms of the tubercular condition he suffered from later, and in June 1827 he moved to Virginia for his health. He served as a tutor for the families of Richard Kidder Meade and William Strother Jones in Frederick County.

Andrews was drawn to the Episcopal Church under the influence of William Meade, who later served as bishop of Virginia, and his sister Ann Randolph Meade Page. Andrews's temperament and training were well suited to Meade's evangelical approach, which stressed a conversion experience followed by a personal relationship with God, a life of moral discipline, identification with the evangelical community, missionary enterprise, and religious reform. Andrews was ordained into the Episcopal ministry at Alexandria on 20 May 1832.

On 28 February 1833 Andrews married Ann Page's daughter Sarah Walker Page, who manumitted her slaves on the day of the marriage. They had one son and two daughters, and they also raised two of her nieces. Andrews soon became active in the American Colonization Society, which promoted the immigration of free African Americans to the colony of Liberia. The society was suited particularly well to the concerns of Andrews and other evangelical Episcopalians, as it combined their zeal to convert Africans with their desire to end slavery in Virginia. Evangelicals also sought to revitalize the Episcopal Church by infusing it with the energy of personal conviction and righteous living. Andrews and Meade were part of a national Episcopal evangelical movement critical of rigid church doctrine and high church ritual.

Andrews's reform work illustrates the intersection of evangelicalism and moral issues with nineteenth-century American politics. He regarded slavery as an individual sin and believed that slaveholders could be persuaded to emancipate their slaves once they saw the system as evil. With his fellow evangelical colonizationists Andrews was unshaken by arguments that sending all black Virginians to Africa was a practical impossibility. He was also a leader in the temperance movement and preached against dancing, the theater, and the use of tobacco. The self-discipline that Andrews championed reflected an evangelical world view that accorded well with the Whig Party's campaigns for order and commercial development.

Andrews was Meade's assistant from 1832 to 1835 in Millwood Parish in the part of Frederick County that soon became Clarke County. From 1835 to 1837 he served as general agent for the American Colonization Society, and from 1838 to 1841 he was pastor of Saint Andrew's Parish in Pittsburgh. His health once again failing, Andrews took a yearlong tour of Europe and the Near East, returning to Virginia in 1842 to become rector of Trinity Church in Shepherdstown. He supervised the erection of a new church at the end of the 1850s and later deeded the old church to the local African Methodist Episcopal church. Andrews served as president of the Episcopal church's Convocation of the Valley of Virginia from 1850 to 1875. He was also an officer of the Evangelical Knowledge Society and before the Civil War an editor of the *Parish Visitor*.

Although a product of New England and a leader of a moral crusade in harmony with northern-style industrialization, Andrews feared that both massive immigration to the northern states and slavery in the southern states threatened American order. He opposed secession in 1861 but remained loyal to Virginia during the Civil War, believing that the old union had been corrupted by foreigners who had been given citizenship but who had not yet learned self-restraint through religion. He expressed this opinion forcefully in a 1 August 1861 letter to Charles P. McIlvaine, bishop of Ohio, that appeared as a pamphlet the same year.

The Civil War strained but did not break ties between northern and southern evangelicals in the Episcopal Church. Andrews and others resumed attacks on high church doctrine and ritual after the war. Continued doctrinal disputes over communion and baptism, the hymnal, and temperance led to the division of the church and the formation of the Reformed Episcopal Church in the year of Andrews's death.

Besides sermons, tracts, pamphlets, and essays, Andrews's major publications were *Memoir of Mrs. Anne R. Page* (1844), which extolled her antislavery views; *Historic Notes of Protestant Missions to the Oriental Churches* (1866); *The Relationship of Christianity to Education* (1867); *The Remembrance Which the Christian People Owe to Their Ministers* (1868); *"Baptismal Regeneration": A Review of the Controversy, With Thoughts on the Duty of the Evangelical Portion of the Episcopal Church at the Present Time, Touching the Toleration of Ritualism* (1869); *On the Incompatibility of Theatre-Going and Dancing with Membership in the Christian Church* (1871); and *Notes on the State of the Church. Also on the Question of Revision* (1874).

Sarah Page Andrews died on 30 January 1863, and Andrews married Nannie Boteler, the widow of Charles Boteler, on 12 March 1865. Charles Wesley Andrews died on 24 May 1875 at Fredericksburg while on his way to attend a church convention in Richmond. He was buried in Elmwood Cemetery in Shepherdstown.

Cornelius Walker, *Memoir of Rev. C. W. Andrews, D.D.* (1877); Alva D. Kenamond, *Prominent Men of Shepherdstown During Its First Two Hundred Years* (1963), 18–20 (por.); Charles Wesley Andrews Papers, Duke; American Colonization Society Papers, LC; Donald G. Mathews, *Religion in the Old South* (1977), 117, 129–131; Patricia P. Hickin, "Antislavery in Virginia, 1831–1861" (Ph.D. diss., UVA, 1968), 284–286, 290–296, 381; obituary in *Richmond Dispatch*, 25 May 1875.

MARIE TYLER-MCGRAW

ANDREWS, Jeremiah (d. 14 Feb. 1817), silversmith, was probably born in England. Nothing is known of his life before he came to the colonies from London except that he had been trained in his craft in that city. By 15 September 1774 he was working in New York City, where he published his earliest-known trade advertisements. Like his contemporaries, Andrews created and repaired silverware as well as selling imported silver goods from London. Because most silver was shipped from England, Andrews's London background, his knowledge of the latest styles, and his relationships with the city's merchants facilitated his business, despite his frequent relocations.

By 1776 Andrews had moved to Philadelphia and was advertising his services there. In 1784 he notified members of the Society of the Cincinnati in Baltimore that medals he was manufacturing for the society in his shop in Philadelphia could be purchased at a colleague's shop in Baltimore. He continued selling these medals when he moved to Savannah, where he resided from at least 1788 until 1790. Andrews led a rather nomadic life, but like his fellow craftsmen he used his travels to establish a network of associates who would display his goods in their shops, hold his mail, run local advertisements, and even provide him with lodging when he was in town. He advertised in newspapers in Georgia, South Carolina, Baltimore, and Richmond.

By September 1791 Andrews had settled in Norfolk, where he soon established a successful trade. As was the standard practice at the time, he bought old silver, sold both imported and domestic dry goods, and produced his own jewelry and other creations. Patrons often traded older pieces to silversmiths for more fashionable pieces, and Andrews used either a client's old hollowware or silver he had purchased elsewhere for his commission work. He continued to import from London and went to England in 1801 and 1802. He also allowed other artisans to advertise their services through his shop, including Monsieur Christopher, a portrait painter from Paris, as well as a clockmaker who took nine years to repay Andrews a $300 debt.

The modern reputation of regional silversmiths frequently depends on the evaluation of their surviving works, but since most of Andrews's pieces remain in private collections in Virginia his work has not become widely known. Although his mark is frequently identified in collectors' books on silver, his work is rarely described. Known pieces make it clear that his hollowware was well crafted and gracefully executed in the latest styles, a testimony to his early training in London. Andrews also adapted his designs to the taste of his clientele, as evidenced by his use of the urn form, much in vogue for tea services in America, and his preference for galleried rims, common in Philadelphia during his stay there. In his advertisements he proudly compared his work to imported silver. The shapes of his stamps vary, but he marked his silver "J. Andrews" and sometimes included "Norfolk." Some lists of early American silversmiths include a Joseph Andrews from Norfolk, but early researchers probably assumed mistakenly that the *J* in Jeremiah stood for Joseph.

Andrews owned considerable property in Norfolk, including his dwelling and shop on Main Street, as well as a farm in Ridley, Pennsylvania. He and his wife, Catherine Andrews, maiden name and marriage date unknown, had one daughter, who married in 1806, and three sons. Jeremiah Andrews died on 14 February 1817 after a brief illness.

George Barton Cutten, *The Silversmiths of Virginia (Together with Watchmakers and Jewelers) from 1694 to 1850* (1952), 84–86, including a photograph of his work; advertisements in *Rivington's New-York Gazetteer*, 15 Sept. 1774, and *Norfolk and Portsmouth Chronicle*, 10 Sept. 1791; Louise Conway Belden, *Marks of American Silversmiths in the Ineson-Bissell Collection* (1980), 32; craftsman files, Museum of Early Southern Decorative Arts, Winston-Salem, N.C.; Kathryn C. Buhler, *Masterpieces of American Silver* (1960), 28, 96; Mutual Assurance Society Declarations, nos. 268 (1799), 889 (1807), 3134 (1822), LVA; Norfolk City Will Book, 3:308–309; Norfolk City Order Book, 22:46, 81; Norfolk City Deed Book, 18:205–206; obituary in *Norfolk and Portsmouth Herald*, 17 Feb. 1817.

SARAH SHIELDS DRIGGS

ANDREWS, Marietta Minnigerode (11 December 1869–7 August 1931), painter and writer, was born in Richmond, the eldest of five boys and four girls of Virginia Cuthbert Powell Minnigerode and Charles Minnigerode, a broker of railroad equipment. Although they were related to several of Virginia's best-known families, during her childhood years her parents often had financial difficulties. Her father moved several times, and she spent part of her childhood at Oakley, the Fauquier County house of her maternal grandmother Marietta Turner Powell and her maternal aunt and uncle Ida Powell Dulany and Henry Grafton Dulany. In 1879 the Minnigerode family moved to New Orleans, but the mother and children still spent their summers in Virginia. While in New Orleans, Marietta Minnigerode began decorating small items for sale in a local department store, augmenting in this small way the family's meager and uncertain income.

In 1884 Charles Minnigerode's business failed, and the family moved back to Virginia. He committed suicide four years later, leaving his wife and children dependent on the generosity of relatives and friends. Marietta Minnigerode had by then begun taking art classes at the Corcoran Gallery of Art in Washington, D.C., where she studied with Eliphalet Fraser Andrews, a well-known artist and teacher. The classes were free and offered one of the few opportunities for formal artistic training available to women. Minnigerode soon began to offer art lessons and classes herself and to write sketches for newspapers, although she declined to publish under her own name. The income was small, and she devoted it to the support of her brothers and sisters. She was able, though, with funds provided through the gallery, to visit and study in the principal galleries of Europe.

On 7 September 1895 Minnigerode married Andrews, who had become the first director of the Corcoran School of Art in 1890, in London. He was thirty-four years her senior, a widower with two children and a comfortable inheritance. They had one daughter and one son and kept a house in Washington and a country residence, Vaucluse, near Alexandria, where they entertained and taught art classes in the summer. She continued to paint, specializing in still life, and to teach, and the Andrews family became a fixture of the capital city's artistic world. Her watercolors and other paintings now hang in the Corcoran Gallery in Washington, D.C., at the Virginia Historical Society in Richmond, and at Ash Lawn, the house of James Monroe, near Charlottesville.

Andrews turned from painting to writing after the death of her husband on 19 March 1915. Writing enabled her to deal with her emotions as well as earn money. In 1917 she published *Songs of a Mother: A Book of Verses*, for which she prepared her own illustrations, and she followed this with a second volume of poetry, *Out of the Dust* (1920), and *The Darker Drink* (1922), a book on spiritualism. Among her most interesting works is *Memoirs of a Poor Relation: Being the Story of a Post-War Southern Girl and Her Battle with Destiny* (1927). In this autobiography she recounted her own experiences and acutely analyzed the values and attitudes that shaped the lives of Virginians of her class during the final years of the nineteenth century, noting, for example, that "the public school was impossible for folks with pedigrees" and lamenting the poor quality of the education that she and her brothers and sisters received in the small private schools they attended. In 1929 she published *Scraps of Paper*, a collection of family letters and diaries describing experiences during the Civil War and during World War I, with the latter drawn in part on the service in France in 1918 of her son, Eliphalet Fraser Andrews Jr.

Andrews's final published works included *My Studio Window: Sketches of the Pageant of Washington Life* (1928), which she illustrated with her silhouettes of Washington and other Virginians, *George Washington's Country* (1930), a volume describing the houses where Washington lived, and her one novel, *The Seventh Wave* (1930). She also collaborated on a musical celebration of the bicentennial of George Washington's birth by supplying the text for *Many Waters: A George Washington Pageant* (1931).

Marietta Minnigerode Andrews had successful careers as an artist, art teacher, and writer. By age fifty-seven she had become diabetic and was restricted in her ability to travel, but she continued to write. Her last large project, with the working title of "Black Brother," was an attempt to understand the history of former slaves in the South after the Civil War. She had completed most of it before she died at her son's house near Alexandria on 7 August 1931. She was buried in the family graveyard in Middleburg, Loudoun County.

Barbara J. Griffin, "The Life of a Poor Relation: The Art and Artistry of Marietta Minnigerode Andrews," *Virginia Cavalcade* 40 (1991): 148–159 (por., 159); 41 (1991): 20–33; Marietta Minnigerode Andrews Papers, including unfinished and unpublished writings, VCU; Andrew J. Cosentino and Henry H. Glassie, *The Capital Image: Painters in Washington, 1800–1915* (1983), 132–135, 142–143, 170; drawings in National Woman's Party Papers, LC; *Washington Post*, 10 Sept. 1895, 20 Mar. 1915; obituaries in *New York Times*, *Richmond Times-Dispatch*, and *Washington Post*, all 8 Aug. 1931.

BARBARA J. GRIFFIN

ANDREWS, Orianna Russell Moon. See **MOON, Orianna Russell**.

ANDREWS, Robert (ca. 1748–28 January 1804), mathematician, educator, and member of the Convention of 1788, was probably born in Cecil County, Maryland, the fourth of five children, four sons and a daughter, of Moses Andrews and Letitia Cooke Andrews. His older brother John Andrews became a noted classical scholar at the University of Pennsylvania. On 20 May 1766 Robert Andrews received a B.A. from the College of Philadelphia. About three years later he became a tutor in the family of Mann Page, of Rosewell, in Gloucester County. In September 1772 he went to England for ordination as a minister of the Church of England, and on his return to Virginia in January 1773 he served as a curate under the Reverend James Maury Fontaine at Ware Parish in Gloucester County. He later officiated at Yorkhampton Parish in James City County.

Andrews helped enforce the nonimportation agreement in 1775 by serving on the York County Committee and the Williamsburg City Committee. In January 1777 he became chaplain of the 2d Virginia Regiment, Continental Line. He was with the regiment in the campaigns in New Jersey but returned to Virginia at midyear. He later served as chaplain to the regiment of state artillery that was formed in the spring of 1778. Andrews left the service in January 1780 but acted as private secretary to General Thomas Nelson in 1781.

Andrews began his long association with the College of William and Mary in 1777, first as professor of moral and intellectual philosophy and later also as professor of fine arts after the reorganization of the faculty in 1779. He became bursar of the college on 4 December 1779 and professor of mathematics in 1784. Andrews remained active in church affairs, but in 1785, as a friend explained it, he "quitted his Gown to avoid starving." He served as Bruton Parish's lay deputy to the Virginia Episcopal conventions from 1787 through 1799, was secretary of the conventions from 1789 through 1796, and was Virginia's single lay deputy to the General Conventions of the national Episcopal Church in 1789, 1792, 1795, and 1799.

Andrews was a member of the Virginia Society for the Advancement of Useful Knowledge in 1774, a Williamsburg alderman in 1779, sheriff of James City County between 1786 and 1790, worshipful master of Williamsburg's Masonic lodge and deputy grand master of the Grand Lodge of Virginia, and from 1787 until his death served on the board of directors of the Public Hospital in Williamsburg. As early as 1776 Andrews was employed to prepare maps for the government of Virginia, and in 1779 he and the Reverend James Madison were appointed Virginia's commissioners for determining the boundary between Virginia and Pennsylvania. Andrews served on a similar commission to settle the boundary with Kentucky in 1797. He also advised the surveyors for the Dismal Swamp Canal Company in 1785 and later owned stock in the company and was its president during the last two or three years of his life. Andrews also served as "philomath" (presumably the astronomy expert) for thirty-six editions of almanacs issued by various American publishers between 1781 and 1796.

On 14 April 1788 Andrews and Nathaniel Burwell were elected to represent James City County in the convention called to consider ratification of the proposed constitution of the United States. Andrews voted for ratification, but he did not speak during the debates. Subsequently he represented Williamsburg in the House of Delegates from 1790 until he lost a close election to Benjamin C. Waller in 1799. Andrews aligned himself with the emerging Federalist Party, and although he denounced the Jay Treaty in 1795, he voted against the Virginia Resolutions in December 1798. In 1800 he opposed the election of Thomas Jefferson to the presidency.

Andrews married Elizabeth Ballard, daughter of Robert Ballard, the clerk of Princess Anne County, in January 1775. They had two sons and three daughters before she died about 1794. On 24 March 1795 he married Mary Blair, daughter of John Blair (1731–1800). They had no children. Robert Andrews died in Williamsburg on 28 January 1804 and was buried either in Bruton Parish Church graveyard or at the chapel of the College of William and Mary. His friend St. George Tucker composed an inscription for the gravestone, but no stone was ever erected, and the site of Andrews's grave is now unknown. The Robert Andrews Hall of Fine Arts was dedicated at the College of William and Mary in February 1967.

Robert Andrews Papers, W&M; Andrews letters are also in W&M Archives and Tucker-Coleman Papers, W&M, the latter also containing Tucker's draft epitaph, giving Andrews's place of birth as Pennsylvania and no date; family genealogy in *WMQ*, 1st ser., 3 (1895): 277–278; ordination documented in Fulham Palace Papers, Lambeth Palace Library, Eng.; Kaminski, *Ratification*, 10:1539, 1540, 1557, 1565; copy of will, dated 17 July 1803, together with much documentation of family history, in LOMC; silhouette reproduced in Wilford Kale, *Hark Upon The Gale: An Illustrated History of the College of William and Mary* (1985), 60; obituary in *Richmond Virginia Gazette, and General Advertiser*, 4 Feb. 1804.

DAPHNE GENTRY

ANDREWS, Thomas Coleman (19 February 1899–15 October 1983), businessman and public administrator, was born in Richmond, the eldest of two boys and one girl of Cheatham William Andrews and Dora Lee Pittman Andrews. He also had an adopted older brother. Andrews's father was a maintenance man and streetcar motorman for the city of Richmond before joining the security division of Liggett and Myers Tobacco Company. As a youth Andrews worked at various part-time jobs, including a stint in the mail room of the *Richmond Virginian*. He graduated from John Marshall High School in 1916.

T. Coleman Andrews, as he was known throughout his career, then worked as a bookkeeper and office manager until enrolling in Richmond College in September 1918. He was a sergeant major in the Student Army Training Corps when, determined to put his younger brother through the College of William and Mary, he left school later that autumn to become a junior accountant at the American Audit Company in Richmond. Andrews was confident that he could educate himself by reading comprehensively and enrolling in extension courses. On 19 October 1919 he married Rae Wilson Reams. They had two sons and their long marriage ended with his death.

Andrews passed the certified public accountant examination in 1921 and was promoted to chief accountant the next year. Later in 1922 he founded T. Coleman Andrews and Company, an accounting firm that was his principal business interest until the 1950s. He also taught accounting and business administration at the Virginia Mechanics' Institute in Richmond from 1922 to 1925.

Governor John Garland Pollard appointed Andrews auditor of public accounts on 1 February 1931. Audits soon disclosed that more than forty county treasurers and several other local offices had shortages totaling more than $1.1 million. Through Andrews's efforts most of the shortfall was recovered and some local officials were prosecuted. Andrews then instituted a uniform system of strict accounting standards for all Virginia counties. Having improved accounting procedures statewide, he resigned his post on 25 February 1933 to end a controversy over the apparent conflict of interest inherent in his accounting firm's negotiation with the State Corporation Commission for a contract to study power rates. Andrews had taken a leave of absence from the firm but had continued to advise in its contract work.

After his return to private life Andrews remained involved in public affairs. His audit of Richmond finances from 1935 to 1936 resulted in twenty-four recommendations for modernizing the management of municipal funds. As the city's comptroller and director of finance from 1938 to 1940 he acquired a reputation for efficiency by enforcing collection of delinquent taxes, saving hundreds of thousands of dollars by revising the procedures for city bond issues, exposing waste in the Social Service Bureau, cutting salaries, eliminating positions within his own office, and refusing to release public funds to pay for a $2,250 trip by city councillors to Philadelphia.

In 1941 Andrews took a temporary leave from his firm to work in the fiscal division directed by the United States undersecretary of war, and the next year he worked in the Contract Renegotiation Division headed by the undersecretary of the navy. In 1943 he joined the Marine Corps and was assigned to the Department of State as chief accountant and director of transportation of the North African Economic Board in Algiers. Andrews became a member of the general staff of the Fourth Marine Aircraft Wing in 1944 and was later awarded the Bronze Star for meritorious action during the fighting in the Marshall and Gilbert Islands in the Pacific theater. He was discharged from the Marine Corps as a major in 1945.

After the war Andrews directed the Corporation Audits Division of the U.S. General Accounting Office in Washington, D.C. In 1948 he was appointed to a task force assisting the Commission on Organization of the Executive Branch of Government, also known as the Hoover Commission. That year Andrews cofounded Bowles, Andrews, and Townes, actuaries and pension-fund consultants, and four years later he helped establish Andrews and Howell, management and engineering consultants, which operated out of Washington, D.C., New York, and Richmond. He served as president of the American Institute of Accountants from 1950 to 1951 and was inducted into the Accounting Hall of Fame in 1953.

In January 1953 President Dwight David Eisenhower appointed Andrews, a self-described "independent Democrat," to head the Bureau of Internal Revenue. Andrews went to work with customary vigor at the bureau, renamed the Internal Revenue Service during his term. He reduced the number of regional commissioners to improve efficiency, expanded the application of the merit system, and established an advanced agency-training center. Andrews encouraged forceful prosecutions of tax-fraud cases, but he also responded to harassment complaints by eliminating incentives that spurred agents to seek additional collections during audits. In 1955 he left the IRS and became chairman and later president of two Richmond firms, the American Fidelity and Casualty Company, Incorporated, and its subsidiary, the Fidelity Fire Insurance Company. He was a visiting lecturer at the University of Virginia's Graduate School of Business Administration during the academic year 1955–1956.

After leaving the IRS, Andrews attracted national attention by attacking the federal income tax. Condemning the steeply graduated tax, which then rose to a marginal rate of 91 percent, as "legalized confiscation" destructive of both the middle class and individual initiative, he called for Congress to create a commission to evaluate the tax system and either overhaul it or develop an entirely different method of collecting revenues.

On 29 August 1956 Andrews received the presidential nomination of the new Constitution Party, an organization comprised of the States' Rights Party in Virginia and small conservative parties in fourteen other states. In his acceptance speech on 15 October at the party's convention in Richmond, Andrews called for sharp reductions in federal spending, major reform of the income tax, a restoration of states' rights, and cuts in foreign aid. He viewed the Eisenhower administration's refusal to block the Supreme Court's desegregation rulings as an attempt by the federal government to usurp local control of public school systems and aligned himself with the supporters of Massive Resistance. Poorly funded and on the ballot in only about a fourth of the states, Andrews and his Californian running mate, Thomas Werdel, garnered 110,000 votes nationwide, approximately 43,000 of which were cast in Virginia. In 1960 Andrews drew nearly 15,000 write-in votes (22 percent) in an unsuccessful bid to become U.S. Representative from Virginia's Third District.

In December 1958 Andrews's public life had taken another turn when he attended the formative meeting of the John Birch Society. A year later he accepted Robert Welch's invitation to join the executive council of the society after receiving assurances that he would neither be expected to make major financial contributions nor be subjected to costly lawsuits over statements made by the organization. A confidential manuscript in which Welch labeled as "conscious communist agents" Presidents Franklin D. Roosevelt, Harry S. Truman, and Eisenhower became public in 1960, in response to which a spate of newspaper articles assailed the society. While Andrews was committed to the John Birch Society's stringent anticommunism, he objected to Welch's excesses and believed that he should step down as head of the organization. Yet Andrews himself generated a storm of protest late in 1964 when he announced at a Barry Goldwater campaign rally in Hanover

County that President Lyndon B. Johnson supported "people who want America to become a satellite" of the Soviet Union. Such episodes called his judgment into question and overshadowed his professional and civic accomplishments. Andrews resigned from the society's executive council late in 1965.

In 1963 Andrews relinquished his corporate offices except for the chairmanship of Fidelity Bankers Life Insurance Company, which he retained for two more years. In 1965 he accepted the chairmanship of the National Liberty Life Insurance Company, of Valley Forge, Pennsylvania, a position he held until he retired in 1967. Andrews received numerous honors during his career, including an outstanding service award from the American Institute of Accountants in 1947, the Alexander Hamilton Award from the U.S. Treasury Department in 1955, and honorary degrees from Pace College in New York City, the University of Michigan, the University of Richmond, and Grove City College, Grove City, Pennsylvania. He was a student of religion, a horseman, a marksman, and an accomplished gardener. By the time of his retirement he had mastered six languages and long since overcome the lack of a college education. After a long illness T. Coleman Andrews died in Richmond on 15 October 1983 and was buried in Hollywood Cemetery.

Biographies in Edward N. Coffman and Daniel L. Jensen, eds., *T. Coleman Andrews: A Collection of His Writings* (1996), xv–xxiv (frontispiece por.), and *Commonwealth* 17 (Dec. 1950): 45; T. Coleman Andrews Papers, University of Oregon, Eugene; T. Coleman Andrews III to Timothy G. O'Rourke, 31 Jan. 1994, DVB Files; *Richmond Times-Dispatch*, 14 Jan. 1953; interviews in *U.S. News and World Report*, 8 May 1953, 28–42, and 25 May 1956, 62–73; obituaries in *Richmond Times-Dispatch*, 17 Oct. 1983, and *Washington Post*, 18 Oct. 1983.

TIMOTHY G. O'ROURKE

ANDREWS, Virginia Cleo (6 June 1923–19 December 1986), author, was born in Portsmouth, the only daughter and youngest of three children of William Henry Andrews, a tool-and-die maker, and Lillian Lilnora Parker Andrews, a telephone operator. She attended Woodrow Wilson High School in Portsmouth until 7 October 1940 and then studied art for four years. Crippled by rheumatoid arthritis as a young woman, she underwent several painful operations but had to use crutches and later a wheelchair for the rest of her life. Andrews never married and always lived with her mother.

Secretive about the details of her life, particularly her age, Andrews related little about her early adult years. She resided in Manchester, Missouri, and Apache Junction, Arizona, but had returned to Portsmouth by the time she began earning professional acclaim late in the 1970s. Later she moved to Virginia Beach. Andrews worked as a portraitist, commercial artist, and fashion illustrator, but she eventually tired of these vocations and turned to writing. Often typing in bed or propped up in an awkward body brace, she wrote thirty to forty pages a night for years with but little success in placing her work. Her only publications before 1979 were short pieces for confession magazines.

Andrews eventually completed a 290,000-word novel, *The Obsessed*, which attracted some interest from publishers despite its great length. Retitling the work *Flowers in the Attic*, she shortened it to ninety-eight pages, only about one-tenth of its original length, but was again told to revise it. As Andrews later recalled, she then added "all those unspeakable things my mother didn't want me to write about." She dedicated the new version to her mother and sold it for $7,500 to Pocket Books, a division of Simon and Schuster. The company invested in extensive print and broadcast advertising for the novel. Published under the name V. C. Andrews in 1979, *Flowers in the Attic*, the first of the Dollanganger trilogy, told the story of four children born of an incestuous union and imprisoned in an attic by their sadistic grandmother.

Many critics dismissed Andrews's novel and one described it as "deranged swill," but it was an immediate success. The book remained on the paperback best-seller list for fourteen weeks and prompted the early release of a sequel, *Petals on the Wind* (1980), in which the children escaped and exacted their revenge. Both novels were book-club selections and together sold more than six million copies. The final installment, *If There Be Thorns*, appeared the following year with an initial printing of 2.5 million copies.

Still working primarily at night, Andrews empathized greatly with her characters. While writing of the imprisoned children in *Flowers in the Attic*, for example, she reportedly lost twenty pounds. Her novels of terror, sadism, and suspense also reflected a strong belief in extrasensory perception and reincarnation. During bouts of composition Andrews often glanced into a mirror behind her typewriter so that she could "project better." She told an interviewer that her stories were "based on dreams, and situations taken from my own life, in which I changed the pattern so that what might have happened actually does happen."

Andrews followed her first successes with *My Sweet Audrina* (1982), *Seeds of Yesterday* (1984), *Heaven* (1985), and *Dark Angel* (1986). Together, the seven novels sold more than thirty million copies and consistently reached best-seller lists. They were particularly popular with adolescents and young women. At her publisher's behest Andrews always used her initials rather than her given name so as "to add a sense of mystery" and to avoid being "slotted as just a writer of 'women's books,'" according to her editor. All of the novels were originally issued as paperbacks, although each was simultaneously or subsequently released in a hardcover edition for collectors and libraries.

Critics placed V. C. Andrews in a genre first explored by Mary Wollstonecraft Shelley and Bram Stoker and more recently popularized by Stephen King, Ira Levin, and Tom Tryon. Like them, she attracted an international audience. Her works were translated into eight other languages, including Hebrew and Turkish. In 1984 the city of Norfolk named her Professional Woman of the Year.

On 19 December 1986 Virginia Cleo Andrews died in Virginia Beach of breast cancer and was buried in Olive Branch Cemetery in Portsmouth. A movie adaptation of her first novel was completed in 1987. Well before her death Andrews had reportedly already completed synopses for another sixty-three story lines, as well as several more novels. Four Andrews novels published posthumously may have been completed by Andrew Niederman, who also wrote many additional novels under her name.

Biographies and bibliographies in E. D. Huntley, *V. C. Andrews: A Critical Companion* (1996), 1–15, 143–148, and *Contemporary Authors*, New Revision Series, 21 (1987): 23–25; V. C. Andrews, "Turning a Profit from Memories," *Writer* 95 (Nov. 1982), 7–8, 46; reviews, features, and interviews in *Washington Post Book World*, 4 Nov. 1979, *New York Times Book Review*, 6 July 1980, 14 June 1981, 3 Oct. 1982, *Richmond Times-Dispatch*, 6 June 1981 (por.), 10, 24 Nov. 1985, *Washington Post*, 20 Sept. 1981, *Publishers Weekly*, 14 Nov. 1986, *Richmond News Leader*, 19 Dec. 1986, *USA Today*, 7 July 1989; obituaries in *Norfolk Virginian-Pilot and Ledger-Star*, *Richmond News Leader* (por.), and *Richmond Times-Dispatch*, all 20 Dec. 1986, *New York Times* and *Washington Post*, both 21 Dec. 1986, and *Time*, 5 Jan. 1987.

EDWARD D. C. CAMPBELL, JR.

ANDREWS, William H. (b. ca. 1839), member of the Convention of 1867–1868, reportedly had been a schoolteacher in New Jersey before he came to Virginia. Newspaper accounts described him as a mulatto. No other evidence has come to light on his origins or activities prior to 22 October 1867, when he easily defeated George T. Clarke in racially polarized voting to choose a delegate to a state constitutional convention from Isle of Wight and Surry Counties. Clarke won the votes of only four blacks in the two counties, while Andrews received a single white vote in each county. In the convention Andrews served on the Committee on the Pardoning Power but otherwise did not play a significant role, although he rarely missed a session. After voting generally with the Radicals, he shifted his stance and became the only African American delegate to vote against the new constitution, an erratic and unexplained course that prefigured his disastrous term in the legislature.

Whatever his constituents thought of his convention votes, Andrews remained prominent in Surry County, where he was one of several men appointed on 4 June 1869 as registrars for the coming statewide election. Soon thereafter he received the Republican Party's nomination to the lower house of the General Assembly and defeated William Dillard by seventy-eight votes on 6 July.

In the House of Delegates, Andrews was appointed to the standing Committees on Propositions and Grievances and on Manufactures and Mechanic Arts, and political observers no doubt expected him to serve quietly and vote with the

Republican minority. Andrews was an alcoholic, however, and Richmond provided far more opportunities for dissipation than did Surry County. He took advantage of them and soon showed himself to be dangerous when drunk. On 5 March 1870 city policemen arrested him on charges of drunk and disorderly conduct and assault. Two days later the House assigned a committee to investigate the charges, and after reporting that Andrews had admitted his guilt it recommended a reprimand from the Speaker. After some debate, the House tabled the committee's report.

Less than two weeks later William Henry Brisby and other African American delegates charged that Andrews had struck a House page with a whip and called for his expulsion. After other delegates questioned the severity of the punishment, on 22 March Andrews made a public apology to the House and accepted a reprimand from the Speaker. One newspaper reporter stated that he immediately left the chamber, drew his pay, and departed for the saloons.

Andrews conclusively burned his political bridges on 25 March 1870 by calling for the expulsion of two of his accusers. One of them, George Fayerman, of Petersburg, reported to the House on 23 April that Andrews had been jailed in that city four days earlier for drunkenness and for firing a pistol in a public place. Despite seemingly universal agreement about Andrews's incapacity while under the influence of alcohol, Fayerman's proposal that he be expelled was tabled.

Andrews apparently then hired William Grey to accompany him on his nightly rounds and to bring him home safely, but Grey soon tired of his unpleasant duty. In mid-June Andrews charged him with theft. Testimony given later suggested that he intended the accusation to scare Grey into remaining in his employ. In quick succession Andrews dropped the charge, brought and dropped it a second time, and then made the charge yet again. His patience finally gone, the justice of the peace accused Andrews of perjury. On 30 June 1870 the Richmond mayor's court agreed and sent him to jail without bail.

In response Andrews hired G. D. Wootton, an attorney who petitioned the legislature about this outrage against a sitting member (although, in fact, legislators could be jailed on felony charges). Perhaps in response, the judge then set bail at $500. Thoroughly discredited, Andrews returned to the legislature and to his wastrel ways while his case hung fire. In January 1871, as the legislature settled into protracted debate over bills presented by competing railroad interests, members objected to Andrews's equally protracted absence from the House. When he offered a physician's note certifying his ill health, they dropped the inquiry.

One month later, on 21 February 1871, Wootton finally obtained a nolle prosequi judgment on the perjury charge. The attorney later testified that he did so in return for a promise by Andrews to vote in favor of the construction of a railroad from Washington to Richmond, a measure favored by the Pennsylvania Central Railroad and opposed by William Mahone's Atlantic, Mississippi, and Ohio Railroad. Lobbyists for the contending interests swarmed the halls of the Virginia State Capitol, and rumors of bribery circulated widely enough that the House appointed a committee to investigate them.

N. J. Hinton, an Irish-born Radical and formerly a doorkeeper at the constitutional convention, saw an opportunity to make money as a broker of bribes on behalf of the Pennsylvania interests and approached several legislators. Some of them, he testified, had already sold their votes, others said that they could obtain more money elsewhere, and some refused a bribe entirely. Only Andrews accepted his offer (never mentioning that he had already pledged to vote for the bill). After Andrews failed to supply Hinton's fee for brokering the bribe, he went to Andrews, whom he believed had already been paid. Andrews denied that he had received his bribe money and, foolishly, wrote a letter of complaint for Hinton to carry back to his employers. The legislative committee investigating rumors of corruption called Hinton to testify, and he gave it Andrews's letter.

The latter indiscretion, not corruption, distinguished Andrews from his peers. Observers then and now agree that the assorted railroad interests distributed vast quantities of alcohol, cash, and other favors to corral legislators. The newspapers predicted that under the circumstances nothing would come of the legislative inquiry, but Andrews's letter, coupled with his weak defense that he had viewed the offered cash merely as a generous gift, made his action impossible to ignore. On 29 March 1871, the final day of the session, legislators once again introduced a resolution calling for his expulsion, and once again the House voted to table it.

From the beginning of his troubles with the law, Andrews's fellow African American legislators were his most outspoken critics and as a group would have readily voted to expel him. The white Conservative majority obviously preferred the erratic and often absent Andrews to a more competent Radical legislator who might have taken his place, and it therefore voted to protect him from punishment. William H. Andrews disappears from the records after 1871. Perhaps he went elsewhere, reformed, and led a productive life. Given his past, it seems likelier that he went swiftly to a bad end.

Approximate birth date inferred from age in Census, Richmond City, 1870; Richard G. Lowe, "Virginia's Reconstruction Convention: General Schofield Rates the Delegates," *VMHB* 80 (1972): 358; Richard L. Hume, "The Membership of the Virginia Constitutional Convention of 1867–1868: A Study of the Beginnings of Congressional Reconstruction in the Upper South," *VMHB* 86 (1978): 481; *Documents of 1867–1868 Convention*, 129; *Journal of 1867–1868 Convention*; *JHD*, 1869–1870 and 1870–1871 sess.; Allen W. Moger, "Railroad Practices and Politics in Virginia after the Civil War," *VMHB* 59 (1951): 438–441; Jack P. Maddex Jr., *The Virginia Conservatives, 1867–1879: A Study in Reconstruction Politics* (1970), 150–155; scrapes with law and legislature documented in *Richmond Dispatch*, *Richmond Whig*, and *Petersburg Daily Index*.

JOHN T. KNEEBONE

ANDROS, Sir Edmund (6 December 1637–by 27 February 1714), governor of Virginia, was born in London, the second of four sons and third of seven children of Amice (or Amias) Andros and Elizabeth Stone Andros. His great-great-grandfather John Andros, "alias Andrews," migrated from Northamptonshire, England, to Guernsey in the Channel Islands and in 1543 married Judeth de Sausmarez, heiress to the Seigneurie of Sausmarez. John Andros's descendants inherited the lordship. During the English Civil Wars the Andros family adhered to the Royalists, and following the Restoration in 1660 young Edmund Andros was made gentleman in ordinary to the queen of Bohemia, a sister of King Charles II. Andros was commissioned an ensign in the Regiment of Guards in 1662, a captain in the Barbados Regiment in 1667, and a major in the Barbados Regiment of Dragoons in 1672. At the death of his father in 1674 Andros received the office of bailiff of Guernsey and held it for life. In 1685 he was elevated to captain in the Regiment of Horse of Princess Anne of Denmark, an office that carried with it the equivalent army rank of lieutenant colonel. The unit was one of the first to abandon James II in 1688 and support William of Orange at the beginning of the Glorious Revolution.

Andros's military career earned him important political appointments. The duke of York appointed him governor of his proprietary province of New York in 1674 and had him knighted in the winter of 1677–1678, but he had to recall Andros in 1680 because of colonial grumbling and disgruntled merchants in London. Andros received an even more important post in 1686, a year after the duke became King James II. He appointed Andros governor of the new Dominion of New England, which stretched from New Jersey to Maine. Three years later, the autocratic and unpopular dominion was overturned, and Andros was imprisoned at Castle Island in Boston Harbor before returning to England.

In spite of Andros's close association with James II and his unpopular administration of two colonies, William and Mary appointed him governor of Virginia. He received his commission on 1 March 1692. The goals of the monarchs in sending Andros to Virginia included persuading the Virginians to live in cities (a perennial hope); sending men and money from Virginia to aid the colony of New York, which was under attack during King William's War; raising the salaries of the Anglican clergy; creating a fleet of small boats to patrol the Chesapeake to prevent violations of the Navigation Acts; paying for soldiers to guard the frontier; and levying a tax on the importation of spirits to help pay for it all.

Andros arrived in Virginia on 13 September 1692 and took charge of a colony reeling from the effects of King William's War on its economy, which was almost entirely dependent on tobacco. The temporary interruption of shipping prevented the sale of Virginia's crop in England, and the disruption of trade reduced the principal source of revenue for the royal government—an export duty on tobacco. The inability of the planters to sell their tobacco drove down its price and in effect reduced the value of the clergymen's salaries, which were paid in tobacco. Exacerbating that problem was a general dissatisfaction of the planters with the clergymen in the colony, many of whom were Scots. The discontented clergymen found an able leader in James Blair, commissary in Virginia for the bishop of London, and matters were worsened by the inability of Andros and Blair to work together harmoniously.

Andros had learned his lessons from New York and New England and often deferred to the powerful Virginia planters who dominated the governor's Council, but he succeeded only partially in implementing his instructions. In 1693 he sent £600 from the royal revenue to New York, but not until 1695 did the House of Burgesses finally agree to send £500 from the colonial treasury. In 1696 the burgesses agreed to raise the salary for a clergyman to 16,000 pounds of tobacco. That was then equivalent to about £64 sterling, an amount considerably below the Crown's expectation. Andros had to pay for the guard boats from royal quitrent revenue, and he completely failed to convince the Virginians, many of whom had never seen a city and none of whom needed one, to create and live in them.

Andros's efforts to expand royal power were subtle. Despite formal complaints from the burgesses, he continued the precedent established in 1688 of appointing the clerk of the House of Burgesses, and he extended his appointing power to the burgesses' messenger. He allowed British laws passed after the last charter to apply to Virginia, binding Virginia more closely than ever to English statutes. Andros was favorably remembered for putting the government's papers in order after his arrival and again after the fire that destroyed the State House on 20 October 1698.

James Blair was Andros's biggest problem. In April 1695 they quarreled and the Council expelled Blair from its membership, but he was restored in November. In April 1697 the Council suspended Blair from sitting as a judge since, as a Scot, he was excluded by the Navigation Act of 1696. Blair posed a far greater threat during his visits to England than when he was in Virginia. On 27 December 1697 he seized the opportunity to complain to the highest ecclesiastical authorities in England that Andros did not sufficiently support either the new College of William and Mary or the Anglican Church, even though Andros had donated a large silver paten to the church in Jamestown. Blair blamed Andros for every failure of the Virginians to give the clergymen what they wished. Andros's chief defender was young William Byrd (1674-1744), but Byrd was badly outnumbered. In addition to influential enemies in the church, Maryland governor Francis Nicholson supported Blair's effort to have Andros removed. The powerful Board of Trade also displayed hostility to Andros as part of its effort to wrest control of colonial information from the hands of Andros's ally in London, the wily bureaucrat William Blaythwayt. The board clearly disliked Andros's terse and lackadaisical correspondence and sent him a stiff reprimand in September 1697. Despite the power of such a combination of antagonists, Andros's friends in England, including Blaythwayt, were able to keep him in office.

Andros's most powerful enemy of all was the Virginia climate. In March 1694 he complained of being "Incomoded By the Excessive Heats" and was granted permission to leave the colony for two months every year. In March 1698 Andros asked permission to resign his office because of his poor health. He met with the Council a third less frequently that year than previously. By October 1698 he learned that his request had been granted. His replacement was Francis Nicholson, who took office in December of the same year.

Andros left Virginia early in 1699. He served as lieutenant governor of Guernsey from 1704 to 1706, after which he retired from public life.

Andros married three times and was twice a widower. In February 1671 he married Marie Craven, and sometime after 1688 he married Elizabeth Crispe Clapham. She died in August 1703. His third wife was Elizabeth Fitzherbert, whom he married on 27 April 1707. He had no children. Sir Edmund Andros died in London and was buried in Saint Anne's Church in Soho, Westminster, on 27 February 1714.

Biography, family history, and will in William Henry Whitmore, *The Andros Tracts* (1868–1874), 1:v–xlix; Edith F. Carey, "Amias Andros and Sir Edmund His Son," *Transactions of the Guernsey Society of Natural Science and Local Research* 7 (1913–1916): 38-66; Charles Dalton, *English Army Lists and Commission Registers, 1661–1714* (1892–1904), 1:28, 37, 75, 115, 119, 168, 174, 2:9, 14, 82, 5:157; Andros letters in PRO CO 5/1306–1307, 1309, 1358–1359; William Blaythwayt Papers, CW; *Executive Journals of Council*, vols. 1–2; *Journals of House of Burgesses, 1659/60–1693, 1695–1702*; William Stevens Perry, *Papers Relating to the History of the Church in Virginia* (1870), 9, 10–29, 32–36, 76; contrasting interpretations in Robert Beverley, *The History and Present State of Virginia* (1705; repr. 1947, ed. Louis B. Wright), 100–103, 255–256, and Stephen Saunders Webb, *The Governors-General: The English Army and the Definition of the Empire, 1569–1681* (1979), 96, 104, 218, 475, and Webb, *1676: The End of American Independence* (1984), 303–403; Hall, *Portraits*, 16–17 (por.).

JAMES EDWARD SCANLON

ANDRUS, Caroline W. (25 December 1875–13 November 1961), educator, was born in Saratoga Springs, New York, to Davis W. Andrus and Mary Fish Andrus. In November 1886 she traveled with her mother to Hampton to attend to her ill sister, Jessie F. Andrus, a new instructor at Hampton Normal and Agricultural Institute. Founded by Samuel Chapman Armstrong, an agent of the Freedmen's Bureau, Hampton Institute had opened in 1868 as a private school for the industrial education of African Americans and in 1878, with federal funding, added a program for Native American students.

After her sister's recovery Caroline Andrus remained in Virginia, attended the Tileston Hall School in Hampton, and in 1895 began working in Hampton Institute's Indian Records Office. Her involvement with the school was part of an unusual family effort. Her sister taught there for nine years, and her mother was matron of the Teacher's Home for four. The origin of their motivation for this dedication to Hampton Institute and to Indian education remains unknown.

Initially an assistant to Cora Mae Folsom, Andrus took over the operations of the Indian department about 1910, keeping copious records on students and graduates. She was later also part of the editorial staff of the school's monthly *Southern Workman*. As Indian correspondent she worked to ease the students' difficult transition from reservation to academic life and coordinated summer work programs in which students practiced farming and trades. This work was of special importance, since "labor as a moral force" was, in the words of President Hollis B. Frissell, "the keynote of the school." Andrus was of necessity a prolific correspondent, keeping up with former students, answering queries from those interested in the Indian program, and calming the fears of worried parents. She believed that her most important duty was to act as each Indian student's advocate and "special friend, . . . someone who knows their homes and their people."

In May 1912 the United States House Committee on Indian Affairs eliminated the federal funding for Hampton Institute's Indian program after concluding that the school could not meet the government quota of 120 students per year, that comparable facilities for Indian education were available in the West, and that the biracial student body was unacceptable. Even without federal support, Hampton continued to admit Indians, although it could no longer offer them a free education. The number of Indian students declined steadily, and special classes for them were discontinued in the face of mounting administrative pressure for integration. In 1918 Andrus commented on the low morale of the few remaining Indians, who felt submerged in the largely black student population. Always comparatively few in number, Indian students had become tangential to the school's mission, a condition that prompted Andrus's resignation in April 1922 after twenty-seven years of service. The following year the last Indian student graduated, by which time nearly 1,400 members of sixty-five western tribes had traveled to Virginia for an education in traditional academic subjects as well as practical trades.

At various times after her resignation Andrus managed a boardinghouse, a tearoom, and a bookstore in Hampton. Caroline W. Andrus died on 13 November 1961 and was buried in Greenridge Cemetery in Saratoga Springs. Her will established a scholarship at Harvard University named for her fiancé, William Jones, a member of the Sac-and-Fox tribe and graduate of Hampton, Harvard, and Columbia, who was killed by Illgonot tribesmen in March 1909 while doing fieldwork in the Philippines for Chicago's Field Museum of Natural History. Andrus never married.

Caroline W. Andrus Papers, including annual reports of the Indian Records Office, 1911–1921, Hampton; feature article in *Newport News Daily Press*, 14 Sept. 1958; Caroline W. Andrus, "Education of Indians," in *Hampton Normal and Agricultural Institute: Its Evolution and Contribution to Education as a Federal Land-Grant College*, ed. Walton C. John (1923), 89–93; Donal F. Lindsey, *Indians at Hampton Institute, 1877–1923* (1995), 165, 258–262 (por. opp. 90); obituaries in *Newport News Daily Press*, 14 Nov. 1961, and *Saratogian*, 18 Nov. 1961.

JENNIFER DAVIS MCDAID

ANGELL, Robert Henderson (25 January 1868–12 November 1933), businessman, was born in a log house near Callaway in Franklin County, the fourth of five sons and fourth of six children of Marshall Jefferson Angell and Ida (or Emma) Noell Angell. His mother died when he was four, and as a youngster Angell helped around the family farm and with the cooking for workers at his father's small brickyard. He was spared from chores to attend the local county school during the three-month winter session, but this introduction to schooling merely whetted his appetite for more education. Only sixteen but already possessed of ambition and a restless energy, Angell ran away from home in May 1884 to the recently incorporated city of Roanoke. The various jobs he held during the next two years included work at one point as a farm laborer while attending school during the winter, followed by service as a janitor for the public school at Salem, where he also attended classes. Several years older than his classmates, he hoped to save enough money to attend Roanoke College.

In the mid-1880s Angell secured a position at Waller P. Huff's brickyard in Roanoke. Huff was so impressed by him that he made the young man a junior partner within two months. Angell abandoned his plans for college and for two years managed Huff's lumber, brick, and cement business. In 1888 the operation was renamed Huff and Angell, with Angell piloting the business successfully through the panic of 1892–1893. Sometime later he bought out his partner and incorporated the firm as the Central Manufacturing Company.

In 1897 Angell married Mary J. Barlow, a Pennsylvania native, and the couple had eight sons and one daughter. In 1901 Angell's growing reputation as a businessman helped him win election to the House of Delegates as the first Republican to represent the district composed of Roanoke City, Roanoke County, and Craig County. He served only one term, finding the pressures of business too demanding to remain in politics at that time.

Angell's career took root during the ten-year period when Roanoke evolved from the village of Big Lick to a city of 25,000, acquiring along the way the appellation the "Magic City" as a result of its rapid growth. By nature a builder, Angell personified this phenomenon, directing his abundant energies toward fostering economic growth through the development of various enterprises, large and small. His steadily multiplying financial interests won him a reputation as one of the Roanoke Valley's premier businessmen. At one time or another between 1902 and his death, Angell was president of the Colonial Bank and Trust Company, Diamond Orchard Company, Liberty Trust Company, Roanoke Glass Company, and Virginia Lumber Manufacturing Company. When Colonial Bank merged with American National Bank in 1928, he became board chairman. He also was vice president of the Keyser Chemical Company, Old Dominion Fire Insurance Company, Roanoke and Bent Mountain Railway Company, Roanoke Cotton Mills, and Roanoke Iron and Bridge Works. Even this impressive résumé is by no means complete. Angell seemed to have a hand in everything, and it is little wonder that his contemporaries admired his prodigious efforts.

Angell's most significant contribution, however, was the establishment of the Shenandoah

Life Insurance Company, which he helped charter on 23 December 1914. The company officially started business on 1 February 1916 with Angell as president, a position he held until his death. His business acumen helped Shenandoah Life grow into a community and industry giant. Fifty years later the mature corporation ranked in the top 10 percent of insurance businesses in America, and late in the 1990s it remains a competitive and financially healthy midsize corporation.

Angell was also devoted to the community. He succeeded Harry Flood Byrd as state fuel commissioner in 1918 and served on the Roanoke City Council from September 1918 until July 1922. Angell also started the Merchants Association and joined the Chamber of Commerce. Throughout the 1890s he worked with local organizations such as the Baptist Orphanage of Virginia, the Salvation Army, and the Young Men's Christian Association. In 1917 Angell founded and became president of the original Ground Hog Club, a men's organization the annual ceremonies of which featured earthy skits and satirical comments about politicians and prominent citizens that attracted thousands to the old Roanoke Auditorium during the 1920s. He was also active in fraternal organizations, including the Elks, the Kazim Temple, the Odd Fellows, the Scottish Rite Masons, and the Shenandoah Club.

Poor health finally slowed Angell early in the 1930s, but he still managed to chair the Republican State Committee from 1929 until his death. Robert Henderson Angell died of a stroke on 12 November 1933 at his house and was buried in Roanoke's Fairview Cemetery.

"Our President" (biography with some reminiscences by Angell) in *Shenandoah* (house organ of Shenandoah Life Insurance Co.), Nov. 1927, copy in Roanoke Public Library; Hiram H. Herbert, *Shenandoah Life: The First Fifty Years* (1966); William McCauley, ed., *History of Roanoke County, Salem, Roanoke City, Virginia* (1902), 403–404; George S. Jack and Edward B. Jacobs, *History of Roanoke County and History of Roanoke City* (1912), 173; Raymond Barnes, *A History of Roanoke* (1968); Roanoke city directories; obituary and related articles in *Roanoke Times*, 13 Nov. 1933 (por).

JAMES E. SARGENT

ANGLE, Nathaniel Peter (16 September 1861–23 December 1936), businessman, was born near Ferrum in southwestern Franklin County, the third of six sons and fifth of ten children of Nathaniel Angle, a farmer, and Sarah Frances Wills Angle. While still in their teens, both he and a brother taught in the same public schools in which they had been educated. Subsequently, he attended National Normal University in Lebanon, Ohio, in 1882.

On his return to Franklin County, Angle worked in the leaf tobacco and sawmilling industries, prospered, settled in Rocky Mount, and extended his business interests into various other fields. In the latter half of the 1880s, with Halifax W. Peak, Angle established the mercantile store of Peak and Angle, which soon restricted its stock to furniture. He followed this business with Angle and Company, a store devoted to ladies' and gentlemen's clothing, dry goods, and notions, and in 1887 he opened the Angle Hardware Company. With a department store, a hardware store, a furniture store, and a grocery store in a single complex on Rocky Mount's Franklin Street, by the turn of the century Angle had given a town of fewer than one thousand inhabitants an early version of the modern shopping center. On 19 November 1891 he married Mary Elizabeth Shearer, who died on 14 September 1926. They had no children.

In 1903 Angle organized what became his largest business enterprise, the Bald Knob Furniture Company. By 1910 it had a work force of sixty-five, a number that rose steadily until it reached six hundred in 1927. Using local poplar and chestnut, the company manufactured a superior line of bedroom furniture. Although it suffered during the Great Depression and lost one of its favored materials to the chestnut blight, the company recovered, continued operations, and was purchased in 1957 by the Lane Furniture Manufacturing Company.

From its incorporation in June 1929 until his death, Angle served as president and treasurer of the Angle Silk Mills, which manufactured silk and rayon fabric for use in women's clothing. J. P. Stevens Company purchased the firm some years later. Angle's varied holdings also included the Rocky Mount Motor Company,

Peoples National Bank, and Bankers' Trust Company, of all of which he was president when he died; Franklin Printing and Publishing Company, which began the weekly *County News* in September 1923; and the Rocky Mount Hotel. Perhaps his only major business failure was the Franklin and Pittsylvania Railroad Company (known locally as the "Fast and Perfect") which he purchased in 1922 and closed after a decade of loss.

Angle was a civic leader as well as a businessman. His forty years of service on Rocky Mount's city council ended only with his death. Also a longtime member of the Rocky Mount Masonic Lodge No. 201, he was instrumental in the construction of its Masonic temple as well as of a local public school. He headed the Liberty War Bond efforts during World War I, chaired the executive committee of the Franklin County Chapter of the American Red Cross, and contributed with his wife to the building of a new structure as well as the refurbishing of Scott Memorial Methodist Church, afterwards renamed Rocky Mount Methodist Episcopal Church South.

After a yearlong illness, Nathaniel Peter Angle died at his house in Rocky Mount on 23 December 1936. Hundreds attended his funeral on Christmas Day, after which he was buried beside his wife in High Street Cemetery, Rocky Mount.

John S. Salmon and Emily J. Salmon, *Franklin County, Virginia, 1786–1986: A Bicentennial History* (1993), esp. 341–342; family Bible records in Eula Ferguson Angle, *Peter Angle, 1754–1968, and Related Families* [1969]: 65–66, 97–99; WPA Biographies; obituary and editorial tributes in *Roanoke Times*, 24 (por.), 26 Dec. 1936.

JOHN S. SALMON

ANN (fl. 1706–1712), Pamunkey chief, was a successor to the most famous Pamunkey queen, Cockacoeske, who led the Pamunkey for thirty years until her death in 1686. Cockacoeske was succeeded by an unidentified niece, perhaps the leader whose mark and the name "Mrs. Betty, the Queen," appear on a petition requesting the confirmation of a sale of Pamunkey land to English subjects that was submitted to the General Court on 22 October 1701. Sparse documentation and the Powhatan Indians' practice of changing their names on important occasions have led to confusion in identifying the principal leaders of the Pamunkey. It has been conjectured that the niece who succeeded Cockacoeske, Mrs. Betty, and Ann were the same woman and that she changed her name to Ann after Queen Anne ascended the English throne in 1702.

Ann's parentage, the times and places of her birth and death, and other important information about her life are not known. She had at least one son, whom she sent to the Indian school at the College of William and Mary in November 1711 as a hostage for the tribe's good behavior and to receive the rudiments of education. Although not required to do so, she also sent the sons of two of the Pamunkey "Greatmen."

Ann's name and mark appear on three extant documents submitted to the colonial government, one by August 1706 and the others about 1710 and 1712. Several other eighteenth-century records, the latest dated in June 1723, refer to the Pamunkey leaders in similar words, "the Queen and Great Men of the Pamunkey Indians," but do not name the queen. The three petitions on which Ann's name appears, together with the others that do not name her, all eloquently document important events in the history of her people. Despite provisions of the 1677 peace treaty that Cockacoeske had signed that forbade English settlement within three miles of any Indian town, settlers gradually encroached on the Pamunkey lands. With less land on which to hunt and fish, younger members left the lands. This reduction in population left the Pamunkey in a "distressed & miserable state & condicion," unable to pay the tribute required by the treaty. At the same time unscrupulous colonists were selling liquor to Indians, getting them into debt, and then taking their possessions. In the petitions that Ann and the great men of the Pamunkey submitted to the government, she firmly requested that squatters on Indian land be removed, that ownership of tribal lands be confirmed, and that the annual tribute be reduced. In records not bearing her actual mark but obviously reflecting the queen's beliefs, she asked that young Indians employed away from the reserved lands be returned to their people and that strong liquor be kept out of Native American towns. Despite the survival of only a few records, Ann is known as an Indian leader who fought for the rights of her people.

Ann's name does not appear on any known documents after the petition of about 1712. She probably died in or not long after 1723, the last year in which reference to a hereditary ruler of the Pamunkey appears in extant records.

Helen C. Rountree, *Pocahontas's People: The Powhatan Indians of Virginia Through Four Centuries* (1990), 112–113, 163–164, 168–169; Mrs. Betty's petition is in PRO CO 5/1312, pt. 1, fols. 318–319; *Executive Journals of Council*, 3:290–291; Ann's mark is on item 27 of folder 17, item 18 of folder 22, and item 12 of folder 29, Colonial Papers, RG 1, LVA; Winfree, *Laws of Virginia*, 263–265.

HELEN C. ROUNTREE

ANTHONY, Katy Viola (1 August 1873–25 September 1962), educator, was born in Harrisonburg, the daughter of George Dean Anthony and Emma Theresa Miller Anthony. In 1882 the family moved to Staunton, where her father worked as a stonecutter while Anthony distinguished herself in the public schools. She graduated from Staunton High School in June 1889 at the age of fifteen.

Instead of entering teaching immediately after graduating from high school as many young women did in her day, Anthony accepted a four-year scholarship to Wesleyan Female Institute in Staunton. After graduating from Wesleyan and studying music at Staunton's Mary Baldwin Seminary, she began her teaching career in the rural schools of Augusta County in 1893. Anthony served as principal of West End School in Staunton from 1900 to 1904, when she transferred to Staunton High School to teach. In September 1919 Anthony moved to Richmond to teach English at Robert E. Lee Junior High School. In midyear she transferred to the city's Binford Junior High School, where she served as a teacher and later as head of the English Department until she retired in 1944. Anthony took summer courses at the College of William and Mary, receiving her A.B. in 1921 and her A.M. in 1923.

Armed with good humor, a keen mind, and a forceful yet gracious manner, Anthony became a state and national leader in two major movements in education during the first half of the twentieth century. One was the struggle of women to participate equitably in leadership roles in professional education organizations. The other was the emergence of classroom teachers as a major force in the National Education Association. During the decades after the Civil War, women outnumbered men in the teaching profession, but men outnumbered women in administrative positions and in offices held in professional organizations. Until well into the twentieth century, school administrators and male college professors dominated policy-making committees and offices in the NEA. Anthony was one of the educational leaders who changed that. She was active in the League of Teachers and was elected eastern director in 1928. Later she became a leader of the NEA's Department of Classroom Teachers, serving as its secretary in 1938, southeastern regional director in 1939 and 1940, and national president in 1941. The classroom teachers' department was the largest in the NEA. Its state and regional branches trained classroom teachers for positions of leadership and responsibility in the profession. During Anthony's years of active leadership, the department led in the transformation of the NEA into a more democratic organization and witnessed the emergence of women from passive roles into active participants and leaders in all aspects of its work.

In recognition of her pioneering contributions, Anthony received the Alumni Medallion of the College of William and Mary in 1937. In November 1941 she was one of the first women elected to William and Mary's chapter of Phi Beta Kappa, and she was a founder of Virginia's Iota Chapter of Delta Kappa Gamma, an international honorary society for women educators. On the completion of her one-year term as national president of the Department of Classroom Teachers, Anthony received a lifetime membership in the NEA. Katy Viola Anthony lived in Richmond until her death on 25 September 1962. She was buried in Thornrose Cemetery in Staunton.

Virginia Iota State Organization of Delta Kappa Gamma Society, *Adventures in Teaching: Pioneer Women*

Educators and Influential Teachers (1963), 27–31 (por.); correspondence and biographical material at Delta Kappa Gamma state headquarters, Richmond; occupational and professional organization history verified by National Education Association publications and material in its archives in Washington, D.C., annual reports of the Virginia Superintendent of Public Instruction, RG 27, LVA, and records of Staunton City School Board and Richmond City Office of Superintendent of Schools; transformation of women's roles in national educational organizations discussed in Edgar B. Wesley, *NEA, The First Hundred Years: The Building of the Teaching Profession* (1957), and Joel H. Spring, *American Education: An Introduction to Social and Political Aspects*, 3d ed. (1985); obituaries in *Richmond Times-Dispatch* and *Staunton Leader*, both 26 Sept. 1962.

MARTIN A. TARTER JR.

APPERLY, Frank Longstaff (26 July 1888–24 October 1961), physician and educator, was born in Shepparton, Victoria, Australia, the son of William B. Apperly and Pauline Longstaff Apperly. He attended Wesley College and Queen's College in Melbourne before beginning his medical studies at the University of Melbourne in 1907. Apperly was awarded a Rhodes Scholarship in 1910 to further his study of medicine at Oxford University. He subsequently earned a B.A. in 1912 and the M.A., M.B., and B.Ch. degrees in 1916. While studying at the Rotunda Lying-In Hospital in Dublin, Ireland, he met Elizabeth "Bess" Mary Foley, a talented young actress who performed in Dublin and London under the stage name of Ann Coppinger. They were married in Oxford on 26 June 1915 and had two daughters, one born in London and the other in Melbourne.

Following his graduation Apperly joined the British Royal Army Medical Corps and served until the conclusion of World War I, attaining the rank of captain. He received an advanced medical degree from Oxford in 1920 and returned to Australia to begin a medical practice, fulfilling the obligations of his scholarship. He joined the staff of the Royal Melbourne Hospital and became junior lecturer in the Department of Pathology at the University of Melbourne. The university awarded him an M.D. in 1923 and a doctorate in science in 1924. To supplement his salary and support his family, Apperly became the outpatient physician at Saint Vincent's Hospital in 1926. He also served as secretary of the Australian Society for Combating Venereal Diseases from 1922 to 1925. Apperly continued his scientific research and published almost two dozen papers on the pathological physiology of the stomach. He received two prestigious awards, the Armytage Prize for Medical Research in Australia in 1922 and the David Syme Research Prize for Australian Scientific Work in 1923.

In October 1931 William T. Sanger, president of the Medical College of Virginia, offered Apperly the chairmanship of the Department of Pathology. Apperly accepted, moved to Richmond in July 1932, and immediately began to rebuild the department. He was disappointed with the teaching, laboratory, and clinical facilities, but he strengthened the instructional program in pathology, which had been severely criticized during his predecessor's tenure, and he also began to rebuild the college's pathological museum.

The first ten years posed problems for Apperly. He had difficulty managing a staff of diverse personalities and maintaining the hospital's autopsy and surgical pathology services. Sanger eventually helped to resolve Apperly's administrative troubles. The surgical pathology section was moved to the Department of Surgery, and the hospital autopsy service was assigned to another professor. Apperly could then concentrate on teaching and research. He successfully built a department committed to biomedical research and recruited able assistants, including M. Katherine Cary. With her he collaborated on a number of research projects and published several scientific papers focused on the development of a muscle pump used to prevent shock and blood clotting after surgery and on the effects of ultraviolet light on cancer. During his twenty-six years at the Medical College of Virginia, Apperly published, frequently in cooperation with his colleagues, more than fifty papers in the medical and scientific literature, and he wrote more than forty articles for nonmedical magazines. His stature in the field earned him election as a fellow of the Royal College of Physicians in 1942.

Apperly also belonged to the British Medical Association, the Medical Society of Virginia, the Richmond Academy of Medicine, the American Association of Pathologists and Bacteriologists, the American Society for Experimental Pathology, and the Virginia Academy of Science, but he still devoted considerable energy to his teaching. He approached the subject of pathology from the perspective of a physiologist, teaching his students about the body's aggressiveness in responding to illness. He passed along his love for the subject to his students through a series of well-organized and stimulating lectures illustrated with specimens from the pathological museum. The lectures formed the nucleus of his only book, *Patterns of Disease on a Basis of Physiologic Pathology* (1951), which became and for many years remained a leading text in the field.

In 1958 Apperly reached the mandatory retirement age of seventy. The Medical College of Virginia recognized his achievements by electing him emeritus professor of pathology and naming the pathological museum in his honor. After his retirement Apperly and his wife traveled and enjoyed entertaining guests at their house in Henrico County. In addition to a passion for crew, a sport in which he had excelled as a student in Australia and England, he shared his wife's interest in the stage. She worked with the Richmond Children's Theater, the Barksdale Theater, and the Virginia Museum Theatre and remained active in the Richmond theater community until 1968.

Three years after he retired, Frank Longstaff Apperly died in Richmond of prostate cancer on 24 October 1961.

Who's Important in Medicine (1945): 6; (1952): 48; Apperly correspondence, including bibliography of professional publications, MCV; feature articles in *Richmond News Leader*, 10 June 1942, and *Richmond Times-Dispatch*, 17 Apr. 1951, 25 May 1958 (por.); reminiscence by niece Grace Lane Mullinax, "Around the World in Eighty Years," *Richmond Quarterly* 9 (spring 1987): 1–7; Hummel and Smith, *Portraits and Statuary*, 3 (por.); obituaries in *Richmond News Leader* and *Richmond Times-Dispatch*, both 25 Oct. 1961, and *Virginia Medical Monthly* 89 (1962): 71–72.

JODI L. KOSTE

APPERSON, Harvey Black (28 June 1890–2 February 1948), member of the State Corporation Commission and attorney general of Virginia, was born in Marion, the eldest of three sons and one daughter of John Samuel Apperson and his second wife, Elizabeth A. Black Apperson. He was named for his maternal grandfather, Harvey Black, under whom his father had served as a hospital steward in the Army of Northern Virginia. Apperson attended the public schools of Marion and after graduating from high school in 1909 enrolled in Virginia Agricultural and Mechanical College and Polytechnic Institute. After one year he transferred to Washington and Lee University, where he studied from 1910 to 1913, the last two years as a law student. Although he obtained neither an undergraduate nor a law degree, Apperson passed the bar examination in 1913 and began practicing law in Marion. He moved to Roanoke County shortly thereafter and joined a law firm in the city of Roanoke. On 28 July 1920 he married Louise Logan Hansbrough. They had two sons and also raised her three sons and one daughter by her earlier marriage.

For thirty years Apperson lived in Salem and practiced law in Roanoke. In 1931 he served as president of the Roanoke Bar Association. He became involved in Democratic Party politics in the 1920s and sought public office for the first time in 1933, running for a vacant seat in the Senate of Virginia. Campaigning on a platform that advocated repeal of prohibition, Apperson won a special election held on 10 August 1933 to represent the district consisting of Floyd, Franklin, Montgomery, and Roanoke Counties and the cities of Radford and Roanoke. He was elected to a full four-year term in the general election in November 1935 and successfully sought reelection twice more.

In the Senate Apperson served on the Committees on Finance, Privileges and Elections, Public Institutions and Education, and Roads and Internal Navigation. He also belonged to the Governor's Advisory Legislative Council in 1935 and 1936 and its successor, the Virginia Advisory Legislative Council, from 1936 to 1938 and as chairman from 1942 to 1944. In 1935 he chaired a special council committee to study the Alcoholic Beverages Control Act and recommend comprehensive legislation for amending it. Three years later he played a key role in legislation to create a retirement system for state judges and to simplify the practice of law before the Supreme Court of Appeals.

Although reelected to the Senate in 1943, Apperson did not serve. Instead, he sought a vacant seat on the Virginia State Corporation

Commission. The General Assembly unanimously elected Apperson, and he took his place on the three-person regulatory body on 25 January 1944. When the chairman of the commission died in June of that year, Apperson filled the remaining months of the chairman's term and was then elected to a full one-year term as chairman on 31 January 1945. The General Assembly reelected him to a full six-year term on the commission starting 1 February 1946.

On 29 August 1947 Governor William M. Tuck appointed Apperson attorney general of Virginia. He took the oath of office on 7 October 1947, but his tenure as attorney general was brief. Four months later, on 2 February 1948, Harvey Black Apperson died suddenly of a heart attack in his home in Richmond. His funeral was held at Saint Paul's Episcopal Church in Salem. Governor Tuck and a delegation from the General Assembly, which went into recess in his memory, attended the service. Apperson was buried at East Hill Cemetery in Salem.

Glass and Glass, *Virginia Democracy*, 2:175–176; *Commonwealth* 5 (Mar. 1944): 17; Apperson Family Papers, including political scrapbooks, 1933–1948, family Bible records, and other genealogical information, VPI; obituaries in *Richmond News Leader* and *Roanoke World-News*, both 2 Feb. 1948, and *Richmond Times-Dispatch*, *Roanoke Times*, and *New York Times*, all 3 Feb. 1948; memorial in *Virginia State Bar Association Proceedings* (1948): 141–143 (por.).

GLENN L. MCMULLEN

APPERSON, John Samuel (21 August 1837–9 August 1908), physician and businessman, was born near Locust Grove in Orange County, the eldest of three boys and three girls of Alfred Apperson and Malinda Jones Apperson. Like many sons of Virginia farmers, he had little formal education and did not attend school at all until the age of twelve. He worked on his father's farm and at age seventeen became a clerk in a store, but his lack of education held him back. Foreseeing little opportunity in his native county, he decided to make a new start with relatives in Georgia.

On his way to Georgia, Apperson stopped briefly in Lynchburg, where he met a man from Smyth County who assured him that he could find work there. Penniless, he arrived in Smyth County on 11 February 1859 and found a job cutting cordwood and railroad ties for $8 a month. He also met William Faris, a physician who advised Apperson to take up the study of medicine. Although Apperson had never considered becoming a doctor, he began to study under Faris and worked for him two days a week to pay for room and board.

The Civil War interrupted Apperson's formal study but further stimulated his interest in medicine. He approved of secession as early as January 1861, and on 18 April he enlisted in the Smyth Blues, later designated Company D of the 4th Regiment Virginia Infantry in the Stonewall Brigade. Thanks to influential friends he was appointed a hospital steward on 12 March 1862 and ordered to report to a field infirmary under the command of surgeon Harvey Black. In this capacity he was present at most of the major engagements of the Army of Northern Virginia.

After the war Apperson returned to Smyth County and began to practice medicine. Within a year he enrolled at the University of Virginia and received an M.D. in 1867. He then moved to Chilhowie in Smyth County to practice medicine and to farm. On 20 February 1868 he married Ellen Victoria Hull, who had achieved distinction by heroically preventing a troop train from crashing into a wrecked train during the war. They had two boys and five girls. Apperson continued to practice as a country doctor, visiting his patients on horseback, until Black asked him to become an assistant physician at the new Southwestern Lunatic Asylum in Marion, of which he was the superintendent. Apperson, who had served on both the site selection and building committees for the institution, began his duties on 1 March 1887. Later that year his wife and eldest daughter died, and Black died the following year. Unwilling to work for the new superintendent, Apperson resigned his position with the asylum on 30 November 1888 and established a private medical practice in Marion.

On 5 February 1889 Apperson married Elizabeth A. Black, daughter of his old friend and superior. Their three sons and one daughter included Harvey Black Apperson, who became attorney general of Virginia. Following

Apperson's remarriage he began a second career in business. Along with seven other local men he organized the Staley's Creek Manganese and Iron Company, of which he was secretary and treasurer. By 1890 Apperson had ceased actively practicing medicine in order to concentrate on his business career. In 1906 he expanded the operations of the Marion Foundry and Milling Company into the Marion Foundry and Machine Works and was elected treasurer of the reorganized company. Hoping that it would help him to exploit his mineral holdings, he also promoted the building of the Marion and Rye Valley Railroad.

As the four-hundredth anniversary of the first voyage of discovery of Christopher Columbus approached, Apperson began advocating state action and the appropriation of money to celebrate the event. In the spring of 1892 the Virginia Board of World's Fair Managers employed him as business executive commissioner to collect items and transport Virginia exhibits to the 1893 World's Columbian Exposition in Chicago. Apperson later served on the Smyth County commission for the Jamestown Ter-Centennial Exposition in 1907. He also served on the board of Emory and Henry College from about 1890 until his death.

John Samuel Apperson died at his home in Marion on 9 August 1908 and was buried in Round Hill Cemetery in Marion.

Tyler, *Men of Mark*, 3:6–9; Apperson Family Papers, including Civil War diary, family Bible records, other genealogical data, and unpublished biographical notes, VPI; Compiled Service Records; James I. Robertson Jr., *4th Virginia Infantry* (1982), 37–38; Joan Tracy Armstrong, ed., *History of Smyth County, Virginia* (1983–1986), vol. 2 (por., 81); obituaries in *Roanoke Times*, 12 Aug. 1908, and *Virginia Medical Semi-Monthly* 13 (1908): 240; memorial in Medical Society of Virginia, *Transactions* 39 (1908): 232–233.

CRANDALL A. SHIFFLETT

APPERSON, Richard Duncan (16 August 1863–6 October 1913), businessman, was born in Mount Sterling, Kentucky, the youngest of two sons and two daughters of Richard Apperson, a prominent local politician and railroad president, and his third wife, Margaret Izora Marshall Apperson. His father, who died three months before his son's birth, was a Union sympathizer and at the time of his death was collector of internal revenue for the Ninth Kentucky District. While not impoverished, the family had limited income. Years later Apperson stated that he started life without capital and had to depend on "honesty, energy and the determination to succeed."

After some formal education, in public schools and with a private tutor, Apperson found it necessary to seek work at the age of twelve. His first job was in the New Orleans office of the Pullman Palace Car Company. There he began to develop skills that proved invaluable as electric power changed the shape of the nation's economy late in the nineteenth century. From New Orleans he went to Kansas City, Missouri, where he managed the local office of the Bell Telephone Company from 1879, when he was still only sixteen, until 1881. On 7 September 1886 Apperson married Lola L. Garrett, of Lexington, Kentucky. They had two sons and two daughters. By 1887 he had relocated to Little Rock and worked as cashier and supervisor for two local streetcar companies. When new owners took over the companies in 1890, Apperson resigned and moved to Virginia to become general manager of the City Street Car Company, of Staunton.

In Staunton, Apperson extended the rails to residential sections and supervised the transition from horsepower to electricity. To attract customers in off-peak hours, he established a small zoo and theater at Gypsy Hill Park and a Ferris wheel and merry-go-round at adjacent Highland Park. In 1897 he organized and served as first president of the Virginia Street Railway and Electric Association, an organization to encourage cooperation and communication between managers of such companies. Despite his efforts, the City Street Car Company declared bankruptcy in 1902.

By then Apperson, backed by a group of Philadelphia capitalists, had purchased and consolidated the Lynchburg Gas Company and the city's two competing street railway companies. On 6 July 1901 the Lynchburg City Council granted the new company a thirty-three-year franchise. During his years as president and general manager of the Lynchburg Traction and Light Company, Apperson replaced the old fleet of streetcars with the newest and best cars available. His labor policies—clubrooms for workers, a pension plan, and regular raises—avoided the strikes that plagued other companies. Lynchburg Traction and Light turned a profit more often than not and always returned generous dividends to its stockholders. In association with his satisfied backers, Apperson purchased other properties: the Petersburg Gas Company in 1901 (sold in 1909); the Roanoke Railway and Electric Company in 1903; and the Montgomery Traction Company, of Montgomery, Alabama, in 1905.

Apperson had other interests as well. A music lover, he was a leader in the construction of Lynchburg's Academy of Music, a luxurious theater for the performing arts, which opened in February 1905. He advocated outdoor sports, enjoying camping, hunting, and fishing. He was also an automobile enthusiast, competing in 1909 in a road race from Atlanta to New York. Perhaps recognizing that the automobile would eventually supersede street railways, Apperson became a partner in a Lynchburg auto dealership.

In 1910 Apperson began to suffer from the symptoms of tuberculosis. The illness led him to resign his company positions in 1913 and seek a healthier climate in Santa Monica, California. Richard Duncan Apperson died in that city on 6 October 1913. His funeral was held on 12 October at Lynchburg's Saint Paul's Episcopal Church, where he had served as a vestryman, with burial following in Spring Hill Cemetery. During the service the cars of the Lynchburg Traction and Light Company halted for five minutes in tribute to his management and his contributions to the city's economic development.

Tyler, *Men of Mark*, 4:15–18; Richard K. McMaster, *Augusta County History, 1865–1950* (1987), 81–82; Harold E. Cox, *Hill City Trolleys: Street Railways of Lynchburg, Va.* (1977), 25–32, 50–55; State Corporation Commission of Virginia, *Annual Report* (1903–1913); obituaries in *Lynchburg News*, 7 Oct. 1913 (por.), and *Roanoke Times*, 8 Oct. 1913.

JOHN T. KNEEBONE

APPLEWHAITE, Henry (ca. 1643–before 9 May 1704), merchant, was probably born in England, possibly at Stoke Ash in Suffolk County, although the parish register, which records the baptisms of many members of the Applewhaite family, does not mention him. The Applewhaites were a large family of Suffolk and London merchants with numerous overseas investments. The 1674 will of a Barbados merchant named Thomas Applewhaite mentions "my loving cousin Henry Applewhaite now resident in Virginia," but other contemporary and later references confuse Henry Applewhaite of Virginia with Thomas Applewhaite's son Henry, also of Barbados, who died in 1705.

Henry Applewhaite came to Virginia as a merchant, arriving in Surry County by May 1667. He resided at Smith's Fort Plantation in Surry County in June 1668, but after purchasing three hundred acres of land in Isle of Wight County in January 1668, he moved to that county by 1670 and lived there for the remainder of his life. During his first decades in Virginia, Applewhaite made at least five trips to England, probably while conducting his mercantile business. Between 1674 and 1683 Applewhaite patented almost five thousand acres of land in Isle of Wight County under the headright system that provided fifty acres for each person whose passage into the colony was proven. Whether Applewhaite actually paid the transportation costs of almost one hundred settlers or simply purchased certificates proving their importation cannot be determined. This land, combined with what he purchased outright, made him one of the largest landowners in that part of the colony.

As Applewhaite's fortunes increased, so did his standing in the community. By June 1678 he was a justice of the peace and by 1679 a captain of militia, and in 1682 he was sheriff of the county. Applewhaite was elected to the House of Burgesses on 16 April 1684 and was reelected to the sessions of 1685–1686, 1688, and 1691–1692. Though not one of the more influential burgesses, he held positions on the important Committees on Elections and Privileges and on Public Claims. He or his namesake son also served in the House in 1700–1702.

Applewhaite had at least four sons and one daughter, all of whom, along with his wife and several grandchildren, were alive when he dated his will on 26 August 1703. His eldest son,

Henry, who received a disproportionate share of the estate, succeeded him as a merchant, justice of the peace, and militia officer, and he also later served as a burgess for Isle of Wight County. Applewhaite's other sons received approximately equal portions of his remaining land and of his personal property, which included such emblems of prosperity and gentility as a silver-headed cane, a silver-hilted rapier and belt, a signet ring, a "great Bible," and his "Book Dalton," which was probably either a copy of Michael Dalton's *The Countrey Justice* or of his *Officium Vicecomitum: The Office and Authoritie of Sherifs*, both of which had gone through numerous editions by 1703 and were often in the libraries of influential public gentlemen in Virginia. Henry Applewhaite's will was proved on 9 May 1704, but the date, place, and cause of his death are unknown.

Age given as about twenty-five in 5 May 1668 deposition (Surry Co. Deeds, Wills, Etc., 1:308); his name in many different spellings appears frequently in records of Council, General Court, and House of Burgesses, RG 1, LVA, in Virginia Miscellany, Foreign Business and Inquisitions, 1665–1676, LC, and in deed and order books of Isle of Wight and Surry Cos.; headrights recorded in Patent Book, vols. 6, 7, 9, RG 4, LVA, abstracted in *Cavaliers and Pioneers*, vols. 2–3; James C. Brandow, *Genealogies of Barbados Families* (1983), 109–123; will, signed with mark, in Isle of Wight Co. Wills and Deeds: 2:462–463.

DAPHNE GENTRY

ARBOGAST, Benjamin (13 November 1825–31 March 1881), educator, was born in Pocahontas County, the youngest of five sons and seven daughters of Benjamin Arbogast, a farmer, and Frances Mullens Arbogast. Facing the prospect of an onerous agricultural life, Arbogast as a young man apparently moved to Huntersville, then the Pocahontas County seat, where he may have served as a constable but definitely made himself part of thc town's political and social life, partly by indulging in alcohol and gambling. About 1847 he converted to Methodism and met Charles See, a tutor in a local family who became his teacher and mentor. Arbogast briefly attended the Huntersville Academy before entering Dickinson College in Carlisle, Pennsylvania, in 1848. After graduating in 1854, he remained at Dickinson as a tutor until 1856. In 1857 Arbogast entered the ministry on trial in the Baltimore Conference of the Methodist Episcopal Church and was appointed an assistant in the Rockingham District in Virginia. He became the principal of the Wesleyan Female Institute in Staunton in 1858, beginning twenty-three years as a leading Methodist educator. On 2 February of the same year Arbogast married Frances Carnelia Gibbons in Rockingham County. They had seven sons and four daughters, of whom four sons and one daughter died in childhood.

During the summer of 1860 Arbogast was elected president of Cassville Female College in what soon became Bartow County, Georgia, a school with an enrollment of about fifty young women operated under the auspices of the Georgia Conference. He closed the college after the 1863 fall term because of the rigors of the Civil War. Cassville was occupied by the Union army in May 1864, and in October of that year Northern soldiers burned the college and its library in retaliation for a Confederate guerrilla attack. Arbogast was then given a pastorate within the Rome District.

In spring of 1866 Arbogast transferred to the Holston Conference as president of Martha Washington College in Abingdon. In the war's aftermath Martha Washington, like other schools, faced nearly overwhelming financial difficulties. During his five years at the college, however, Arbogast succeeded in improving its buildings and reducing its debt. In 1871 he was appointed president of Kentucky Wesleyan University in Millersburg (now Kentucky Wesleyan College in Owensboro).

Although the faculty later attested to his scholarly insight and boundless energy on behalf of the school, Arbogast quickly became embroiled in a financial scandal at Kentucky Wesleyan. He borrowed $16,500 from one of the school's trustees, in the name of the Kentucky Conference, to purchase a farm adjacent to the university. Arbogast intended to sell part of the farm to Kentucky Wesleyan as a president's house and offer the rest of the land for sale in lots. The plan failed, and he also ran up debts with local merchants to supply the boarding-house that he and his wife ran at the farm. By

May 1873 he had returned to Virginia, and in 1875 the Kentucky Conference dropped charges of immorality and falsehood against him in connection with the debt scandal but still suspended him from the ministry for one year. When he violated the suspension by continuing to preach, the conference removed him from the itinerant ranks.

Arbogast's case had become moot, however, because by 1874 he had accepted leadership of the newly established Valley Female College in Winchester, within the bounds of the Baltimore Conference, Methodist Episcopal Church South. In his address to the graduating class of 1876, he challenged the conventional view that hard study impaired the health and beauty of young women, excoriated the legislature for failing to fund women's education, and encouraged his students so to emulate Lady Jane Grey as to "read Plato while others attend the theatre or hunt in the park." Benjamin Arbogast served Valley Female College until his sudden death on the afternoon of 31 March 1881. He was buried in Winchester's Mount Hebron Cemetery.

Birth and death dates on tombstone in Mount Hebron Cemetery; William T. Price, *Historical Sketches of Pocahontas County, West Virginia* (1901), 134–135; George Leffingwell Reed, ed., *Dickinson College Alumni Record* (1905), 154; Harold Lawrence, *Methodist Preachers in Georgia, 1783–1900* (1984), 20, *Supplement* (1995), 8; Claude D. Curtis, *Three Quarters of a Century at Martha Washington College* (1928), 41–51; Lee A. Dew and Richard A. Weiss, *In Pursuit of the Dream: A History of Kentucky Wesleyan College* (1992), 40–44, 335; por. in Kentucky Wesleyan College Archives; Valley Female College, *Catalogue* (1875): 11–13, 16–17; (1876): 11–31; memoir in Baltimore Annual Conference of Methodist Episcopal Church South, *Minutes of the Annual Conference* (1882): 36–37.

GEORGE J. STEVENSON

ARBUCKLE, Matthew (ca. 1741–27 June 1781), frontier militia officer, was probably born in Cambusland, near Glasgow, Scotland, the oldest of at least four sons of James Arbuckle and his first wife, Margaret Arbuckle. On 5 September 1749 James Arbuckle received a grant of four hundred acres on the north side of the James River in what was then Augusta County but is now Alleghany County. Matthew Arbuckle served in the Augusta County militia as early as 1758 and qualified as a lieutenant on 20 May 1767. On 10 March 1770 he was commissioned a captain in the militia of newly created Botetourt County. He was also a justice of the peace until the commission issued by the Council on 11 June 1773 excluded him and two others "who appear not to be fit persons for the office." Nonetheless, he sat at the court held on 16 September 1773.

Arbuckle married Jane Lockhart in about 1767, and they had two sons before her death. In December 1774 he married a widow, Frances Hunter Lawrence, and they had four sons. The second child, his namesake Matthew (1778–1851), served at the Battle of New Orleans in the War of 1812 and founded Fort Gibson, Oklahoma, while commanding the 7th United States Infantry. The Arbuckle Mountains in Oklahoma were named for him.

Arbuckle made his living as a fur trapper. To sell his pelts he traveled a number of times from his hunting camp, situated north of the settlement that became Lewisburg in 1782, along the Kanawha River valley to a French-established trading post at its mouth. Begun in 1764, these trips through lands inhabited almost exclusively by Indians and into what is today the state of Ohio brought him recognition as a fearless woodsman. During the spring of 1774 at the mouth of Mill Creek in the Muddy Creek Valley, Arbuckle built a stockade that came to be known as Arbuckle's Old Fort.

On 6 September 1774 Arbuckle led a seventy-member company of the Botetourt County militia when it set out as part of Colonel Andrew Lewis's southern division of Lord Dunmore's forces to rendezvous with Dunmore and the northern division. Dunmore intended to invade the Shawnee country in the present state of Ohio. Covering about one hundred sixty miles in thirty days, the southern forces arrived at the Ohio River on 6 October and established a camp on the north side of the Kanawha, at Point Pleasant. On the morning of 10 October a Shawnee force numbering about one thousand warriors under the command of Cornstalk attacked Dunmore's combined forces. Arbuckle's company suffered casualties of about 50 percent and most likely participated in a flank attack that contributed to the defeat of the Shawnee and their subsequent agreement to a peace treaty. In the autumn of 1775 Arbuckle built Fort Randolph at the site of the battle.

In September 1775 the Botetourt County Committee appointed Arbuckle to a captaincy as part of a force to defend the western frontiers. Incorporated into the 12th Virginia Regiment on the Continental Establishment, his company of one hundred men was stationed on the Ohio until 10 October 1778. He was thus in command on 10 November 1777 when a mob of newly arrived and undisciplined militiamen responded to an Indian war party's killing and scalping of one of their number by ignoring their higher officers and murdering Cornstalk, his son Elinipsico, and several other Indians whom Arbuckle had detained as hostages in an attempt to prevent the Shawnee from allying with Great Britain. The failure of Arbuckle's efforts to maintain order and prevent the killing of the Indian leaders resulted in almost two more decades of Shawnee enmity toward the United States.

After his active military service ended, Arbuckle lived in Fort Savannah, the site of Lewisburg, where he farmed and occasionally undertook public duties. At the time of his death he owned three slaves. In March 1781 the Greenbrier County Court had commissioned him to lay out a route from the courthouse to the Warm Springs. On 27 June of that year, returning from Williamsburg where he had successfully sought "substantial aid to settle and defend the county," Matthew Arbuckle was caught in a violent storm near the banks of the Jackson River and killed instantly by a falling tree. He was evidently buried on a bluff near the river.

Joseph C. Jefferds Jr., *Captain Matthew Arbuckle: A Documentary Biography* (1981), contains Arbuckle letters from Draper MSS and estate inventory from Greenbrier Co. Will Book, 1:3; *Revolutionary Virginia*, 4:205, 314, 7:136.

JOSEPH C. JEFFERDS JR.

ARCHER, Edinboro (July 1849?–3 December 1907), member of the Richmond City Council, was probably born in Amelia County, the son of a slave woman named Ammy who was owned by Robert P. Archer, a wealthy planter. Edinboro Archer may have grown up on his owner's Powhatan County plantation, where he learned carpentry. By 1869 Archer had moved to Richmond, where he obtained work as a carpenter. He ran a wine and liquor store for a year before settling into his profession as a wheelwright.

About the time he moved to Richmond, Archer married a woman named Amanda, whose last name is not recorded. Between 1869 and 1887 they had seven sons and two daughters. By 1880 they had moved to 1006 North Eighth Street in Richmond, where he lived the rest of his life. Other members of his family also lived in Richmond, and his mother, a sister, and two brothers shared his home. Another sister, Kate, married Albert V. Norrell, a Richmond educator after whom a school was later named.

Archer was one of four dozen members expelled from the First African Baptist Church in 1880 after an unsuccessful protest over the pastorate of the Reverend James H. Holmes and his deacons. Such was his standing in the community that Archer was chosen as one of four delegates from his new church, the Fifth Street Baptist, to a council of black Baptist churches called to investigate First African in 1881.

In 1882 Archer was elected to one of the Richmond City Council's two boards, the common council, from the largely black Jackson Ward. The ward had been created by an 1871 gerrymander that put most African Americans into one district. While this redistricting lessened their overall political power, it guaranteed the election of a few black councilmen. Between 1871 and 1898 thirty-three African Americans were elected either to the common council or the board of aldermen. Archer served for six years. The first year he was appointed to the committees on elections and lunatics. In 1884 he was put on the committee on the first market and the retrenchment and reform committee, one of only five blacks ever to serve on the latter, an important body. In his final two years he was appointed to four committees: elections, police, first market, and lunatics. He was also one of six blacks admitted to the Knights of Labor reform caucus on the council in1886. Archer fought hard to gain needed improvements, such as a city park, for Jackson Ward. His efforts on behalf of his constituents were not always successful, but Archer certainly was not the buffoon portrayed by a white reporter who used dialect to ridicule Archer's speech opposing a one-third pay increase for Dr. Thomas E. Stratton, president of the city's Board of Health.

After leaving the council, Archer continued to work as a wheelwright for Reliance Wagon Works and was promoted to foreman about 1894. By 1903 he held a similar position for Pioneer Transfer Company, but a year later his occupation was listed as carpenter. In 1906 Edinboro Archer was employed by Evergreen Cemetery, and when he died on 3 December 1907, he was its superintendent. He was probably buried either there or at Union Sycamore Cemetery in Barton Heights, Richmond, in which he owned lot 207.

Census, Richmond City, 1880 (gives age as forty-seven), 1900 (gives month of birth as July 1849), 1910; First African Baptist Church Minute Book, 27 June 1880, LVA microfilm; *Richmond Daily Dispatch*, 14 Jan. 1881; Richmond Common Council Records, 1882–1888; Richmond city directories, 1869–1908; Herbert T. Ezekiel, *The Recollections of a Virginia Newspaper Man* (1920), 86–87; Michael B. Chesson, "Richmond's Black Councilmen, 1871–1896," in *Southern Black Leaders in the Reconstruction Era*, ed. Howard N. Rabinowitz (1982), 201; Rabinowitz, "From Exclusion to Segregation: Health and Welfare Services for Southern Blacks, 1865–1890," *Social Science Review* 48 (1974): 327–354; Peter J. Rachleff, *Black Labor in the South: Richmond, Virginia, 1865–1890* (1984), 97, 154, 162; obituary in *Richmond Times-Dispatch*, 4 Dec. 1907.

MICHAEL B. CHESSON

ARCHER, Edmund Minor (28 September 1904–13 July 1986), painter, was born in Richmond, the youngest of three children, all sons, of William Wharton Archer, sometime editor of the *Richmond State*, and Rosalie Harrison Pleasants Archer, both members of families long associated with the cultural life of the city. His oldest brother, Adair Pleasants Archer, founded the Little Theater League of Richmond, and after his death from influenza in 1918, their mother served as president of the theater group for many years.

Ned Archer, as he was known, began studying art at the age of eight under Nora Houston at the Richmond Art Club's Saturday morning school. After the club closed its doors in 1916, Archer continued to study with Houston and with Adèle Clark, another distinguished Richmond art teacher, in a Saturday class sponsored by the Virginia League of Fine Arts. Houston later recalled that Archer possessed a natural artistic talent but was more interested in the study of humanity than of formal composition. He remained a pupil of Houston and Clark until 1918. After graduating in 1921 from Saint Christopher's School in Richmond, he spent the summer studying with Charles W. Hawthorne at Provincetown, Massachusetts. Archer attended the University of Virginia for the 1921–1922 academic year and studied art history under Fiske Kimball.

Thus prepared, Archer entered the Art Students League in New York City, where his teachers included Kenneth Hayes Miller, Allen Tucker, and Boardman Robinson. In 1923 and 1924 the league purchased paintings by Archer of a nude and of three heads for its permanent collection. In the summer of 1924, while copying from works at the Metropolitan Museum of Art, Archer received his first portrait commission from a stranger who had seen and admired his work. He served on the board of the Art Students League in 1924 and 1925. In the latter year he traveled to Paris, where he maintained a studio and attended the Academie Colarossi, and to Italy, where he made a special study of the frescoes of Raphael at the Vatican and of Piero della Francesca in Arezzo.

In 1926 Archer returned to Richmond and devoted the next four years to painting. For part of that time he occupied the studio of sculptor Edward Virginius Valentine. While in Richmond he completed a number of portraits and other studies of African Americans. For his *Colored Cellist Practicing*, he persuaded the sexton at Grace and Holy Trinity Episcopal Church to pose.

Archer held his first one-man show in 1929 at the Pancoast Gallery in Boston, which helped establish him in the art world. Among the fifteen paintings of African Americans that comprised the exhibition, *Show Girl*, depicting a dancer from a musical revue standing before a curtain, received the third William A. Clarke Prize of $1,000 and the 1930 bronze medal in the Corcoran Gallery of Art's biennial exhibition. In 1930 Archer was appointed assistant curator of the new Whitney Museum of

American Art in New York, which opened in April 1931. His arrangement with the museum allowed him time to paint, which he always considered his major pursuit in life. During the ensuing three decades his works appeared in exhibitions at major American galleries and were also purchased by many private collectors.

Archer often returned to Richmond in the summers to paint, and his work received appreciative recognition in Virginia. His *Brick Carrier* won second prize in 1936 at the fifth annual exhibition of Work of Virginia Artists at the Virginia Museum of Fine Arts, and Archer served as a juror for the following year's show. In 1938 the Virginia Museum included his *Groundsmen and Linemen* in its first biennial exhibition of contemporary American painters. Later that year, from 13 November through 3 December, the museum honored him with a one-man show in its Virginia Artist Series. Notable among the fifteen works exhibited was *Waiting for the Departure*, a study of three African American women at an open window, used as the cover illustration for the show's catalog. Neither obvious nor sentimental, the painting is an authoritatively composed dramatization of black life as the artist saw it.

Dwarfing in size the other works in the show was Archer's *Captain Francis Eppes Making Friends with the Appomattox Indians*, a mural commissioned by the United States Department of the Treasury's Section of Fine Arts for the post office in Hopewell. The mural features Eppes, who patented the land that became Hopewell, and a representative Native American leader, each reclining and stretching out his hand towards the other. Although well received by the citizens of Hopewell when installed in 1939, some later critics found Archer's combination of fifteenth-century Italian motifs and figures resembling twentieth-century motion picture idols humorously incongruous.

Archer exhibited at the Golden Gate International Exposition in San Francisco in 1939 and at the New York World's Fair the following year. His *Maggie*, a straightforward portrait of a black woman wearing a maid's uniform, received a purchase award at the Virginia Museum's 1941 exhibition of the Works of Virginia Artists. The following year he was commissioned to paint the portrait of former governor John Garland Pollard for display in the Virginia State Capitol.

In 1940 Archer left the staff of the Whitney Museum, of which he had by then become associate curator. During World War II he served in the 603d Engineers, United States Army, in Washington, D.C., and he subsequently worked on maps for the U.S. Coast and Geodetic Survey. In 1944 he became an instructor of painting, drawing, and composition at the Corcoran School of Art and also taught at George Washington University. After the war Archer executed a number of commissioned portraits, including one of Charles Cortez Abbott, of the University of Virginia's Graduate School of Business Administration. In 1961 he was elected a fellow of the International Institute of Arts and Letters in Switzerland.

Archer retired from the Corcoran School of Art in 1968 and returned to Richmond. One of the most-respected Virginia artists of his generation, his work was on display in many of the country's leading galleries, including the Virginia Museum of Fine Arts and the Whitney Museum of American Art. Edmund Minor Archer died in Richmond from complications of anemia on 13 July 1986 and was buried in Hollywood Cemetery.

L. Moody Simms Jr., "Edmund Minor Archer: Virginia Painter," *Richmond Literature and History Quarterly* 2 (winter 1979): 41–43; two feature articles in *Richmond Times-Dispatch*, 13 Nov. 1938 (por.); Thomas C. Colt Jr., *Edmund Minor Archer* (1938), Virginia Museum of Fine Arts exhibition catalog; Vertical Files, VM; Karal Ann Marling, *Wall-to-Wall America: A Cultural History of Post-Office Murals in the Great Depression* (1982), 309–310; Sue Bridwell Beckham, *Depression Post Office Murals and Southern Culture: A Gentle Reconstruction* (1989), 256–257; obituaries in *Richmond News Leader* and *Richmond Times-Dispatch*, both 14 July 1986.

L. Moody Simms Jr.

ARCHER, Fletcher Harris (6 February 1817–21 August 1902), Confederate army officer and Petersburg mayor, was born in Petersburg, one of the youngest of five sons and four daughters of Allen Archer, a prosperous miller, and Prudence Whitworth Archer. He attended school in Petersburg before entering the University of

Virginia, where he received his bachelor of law degree on 3 July 1841. He then returned to his native city and established his practice.

On 2 April 1842 Archer was elected captain of the 7th Company, 39th Regiment Virginia Militia. He held that rank in December 1846, when he raised the Petersburg Mexican Volunteers, which became Company E of the 1st Regiment Virginia Volunteers. His was one of the few Virginia units that saw active military service during the Mexican War. The regiment reached Mexico early in 1847 and served on General Zachary Taylor's line until the end of the war. By 1 August 1848 the company was back in Petersburg, where Archer resumed his law practice. He married Eliza Ann Eppes Allen and they had one daughter, born shortly before her mother's death in April 1851.

Within two days of Virginia's secession from the Union, Archer raised a company of one hundred men that was designated Company K, "Archer Rifles," 12th Regiment Virginia Infantry. He was elected its captain. Shortly thereafter, on 5 May 1861, he was appointed lieutenant colonel in the 3d Regiment Virginia Infantry. After brief intervals of service in command of the Naval Hospital in Norfolk, as lieutenant colonel of the 5th Battalion Virginia Infantry, and as commander of the 1st Brigade, Department of Norfolk, Archer retired in May 1862 to civilian life in Petersburg. On 31 March 1863 he married Martha Georgianna Morton Barksdale, a widow with three sons and one daughter.

As the armies moved ever closer to the Richmond-Petersburg front, Archer again offered his military expertise to the Confederacy. On 4 May 1864 he was commissioned a major commanding the 3d, or "Archer's Battalion," Virginia Reserves. Composed of men between the ages of sixteen and eighteen and between forty-five and fifty-five from Petersburg and the counties of Dinwiddie and Prince George, the reserves were to be used for state defense and detail duty. They participated in Archer's greatest military accomplishment, his defense of Petersburg on 9 June 1864 in what has come to be called the "Battle of Old Men and Young Boys." As more than 1,300 Union cavalry troops led by Brigadier General August Kautz attempted to ride into Petersburg from the south and Union infantry threatened the defenses east of the city, 125 members of Archer's unit and 5 men and one gun from an artillery unit answered a call for reserves and militia to assemble at Battery 29 on the Jerusalem Plank Road. Later Archer recalled that details for special service and guard duty in Richmond had left him with barely a company of inadequately armed men in civilian clothes, combining those "with head silvered o'er with the frosts of advancing years" and others who "could scarcely boast of the down upon the cheek." His command repelled the first attack by the Northern troops but a second assault forced him back into the city. The arrival of Confederate cavalry and artillery put a check to further Union movement, but at the cost of 76 casualties to the reserves, more than half of those who had gone into action.

Promoted to lieutenant colonel, Archer led his unit in the defense of Petersburg during the subsequent Union attack of 15–18 June and throughout the nine-and-one-half-month siege of the city. Wounded in the arm at Petersburg, he was hit again during the retreat to Appomattox, where his combined force of the 3d and 44th Battalions of Virginia Reserves surrendered sixty-five men.

After the war ended Archer returned to Petersburg and began to rebuild his law practice. Active in the local Conservative Party, he eventually became its chairman. He sought the party's nomination for mayor in 1876 and 1878 but lost both times to William E. Cameron, who had aligned himself with the Readjuster movement before the second campaign. In 1879 Archer and tobacconist Charles A. Jackson were the Conservative nominees for seats in the House of Delegates, but both lost as the Readjusters carried the city with 55 percent of the vote.

Following this defeat Archer was elected to the Petersburg City Council and his fellow councillors elected him president of that body. By virtue of this position Archer became mayor on 2 January 1882 when Cameron was sworn in as governor. At this point the council still had a Conservative majority, but the Readjusters controlled all of the elective executive offices in

Petersburg except the mayor's office and vowed to oust Archer in the May 1882 election.

To counter a Readjuster–Fusionist Republican coalition, the Conservatives formed an alliance with the Straightout Republicans and ran as the Citizens' Party. Archer received their nomination for mayor but lost to Thomas J. Jarratt, and the Readjusters won a narrow majority on the city council. The Conservatives then tried to keep the Readjusters from taking their seats by alleging a violation of the city charter, and on 1 July Archer refused to vacate his office at the end of his term. He did not finally step down as mayor until a lawsuit confirmed Jarratt in the office on 23 March 1883.

In 1884 Archer was a delegate to the state Democratic convention in Richmond and tried to encourage dissident white Readjusters to rejoin the Democratic Party. He did not run for another public office thereafter. Fletcher Harris Archer died at his home on High Street on 21 August 1902 after having been in "feeble health by reason of his advanced age for some months." He was interred in Petersburg's Blandford Cemetery.

Fletcher Harris Archer Papers and Notebooks, Duke; reminiscences by Archer in George S. Bernard, *War Talks of Confederate Veterans* (1892), 107–148 (por. opp. 107); Militia Commission Papers, RG 3, LVA; Compiled Service Records; John F. Glenn, "Brave Defence of the Cockade City," *Southern Historical Society Papers* 25 (1907): 1–24; William G. Robertson, *The Battle of Old Men and Young Boys, June 9, 1864* (1989); William D. Henderson, *Gilded Age City: Politics, Life and Labor in Petersburg, Virginia, 1874–1889* (1980), 111–120; obituary in *Petersburg Daily Index-Appeal*, 21 Aug. 1902.

CHRISTOPHER M. CALKINS

ARCHER, Gabriel (ca. 1574–ca. 1610), colonist, was probably the elder of two known sons of Christopher Archer and Mary Archer, of Mountnessing, Essex County, England. He matriculated as a pensioner of Saint John's College, Cambridge University, about 1591 and entered Gray's Inn on 15 March 1593. Very little else is known about his life in England.

Archer's name first appears in association with the New World as a member of Captain Bartholomew Gosnold's 1602 exploring expedition to New England, which at that point was still part of Virginia. Archer wrote an important account of the expedition, "The Relation of Captaine Gosnols Voyage to the North Part of Virginia," which was first published by Samuel Purchas in 1625. Archer gave an accurate account of the voyage between its departure on 26 March 1602 and its New England landfall on 14 May, and he recorded much detail about the exploration of Cape Cod Bay and the offshore islands, including Martha's Vineyard. Though he joined one expedition into Buzzards Bay, he was primarily engaged in dealing with Wampanoag Indians and supervising the construction of a trading post at Cuttyhunk Island. His narrative contains useful information on the Indians and valuable accounts of fauna and flora gained from a commonsense comparison with English examples. After the expedition's leaders decided to abandon the trading post, Archer left America on 18 June 1602 to return to England. How far his narrative circulated in manuscript is not known, but it is the first detailed English account of any part of New England.

Late in 1606, in close association with Gosnold, Archer enrolled in the expedition of the Virginia Company of London to establish a colony in what was then known as South Virginia. Safely entering Chesapeake Bay in the spring of 1607, Captain Archer, as he is referred to in the records, suffered an injury to both hands during an Indian attack on the night of 26 April. On the journey up the James River he selected a settlement site, thereafter named Archers Hope, which Captain Christopher Newport rejected in favor of the deeper water a few miles away at Jamestown Island. He accompanied Newport in his exploration of the James River as far as the fall line at what became the city of Richmond. Archer's primary function was to maintain a journal of the expedition's progress. An unsigned document in the Public Record Office in London contains his narrative of events between 21 May and 21 June. A parallel document in a different handwriting, also unsigned but plausibly attributed to Archer on stylistic grounds, gives a useful but superficial account of the topography and Indians encountered in the initial exploration. Both manuscripts have always remained in official custody and were probably sent to Robert Cecil, earl of

Salisbury, the most prominent official supporter of the Virginia venture. Archer's reports are among the most informative eyewitness accounts of the first weeks of the Jamestown colony.

Archer's subsequent activities in Virginia are difficult to document thoroughly. He survived the sickness that killed more than half the colonists during the summer and autumn of 1607, and he was nominated recorder of the colony, effectively a magistrate. As such he participated with several councillors in the political trial at which the president, Edward Maria Wingfield, was convicted of a string of minor offenses and deprived of his office on 10 September. Wingfield was confined to the pinnace, where he continued to inveigh against Archer throughout the following months.

Captain John Smith, having been captured by the Pamunkey Indians and handed over to Powhatan, the paramount chief, was returned to Jamestown on 2 January 1608. According to Wingfield, Archer then charged Smith with responsibility for the death of two of his men, who had been killed by the Indians. On the strength of a text in Leviticus, Archer sought the death penalty. Smith was on the verge of being hanged when Newport appeared in the river with supplies and reinforcements. Smith's version of events merely stated that Archer and his friends had attempted to exclude him from the Council. Newport eventually dealt with the squabbling handful of survivors by leaving for home on 10 April 1608 with Wingfield and Archer on board, much to Smith's relief.

While in England in the summer of 1608, Archer probably supplied the Virginia Company with copies of his reports. Although he made some unrealistic recommendations for crops that could be profitably cultivated in Virginia, including pineapples, sugar, and olives, he did think that tobacco had export potential. During Archer's 1608–1609 English sojourn he apparently came to terms with Wingfield. Some of the evidence of Archer's intrigues must also have come to light, but his defects were overlooked because of his experience and his skill as a reporter. When a great national effort was mounted to put the Virginia colony on a sounder footing with a relief fleet of nine vessels, Captain Archer was placed in command of the *Blessing*. His ship survived the storm that scattered the flotilla, reaching Jamestown on 11 August 1609.

Archer found Captain John Smith installed as president until his one-year term expired on 10 September. Because the documents conveying authority to Sir Thomas Gates had gone astray during the stormy Atlantic crossing, Smith refused to surrender his presidency to the newcomers and endeavored to distribute the 300 to 400 arrivals at new settlements up and down the river. Using a legalistic ruse that Archer probably devised, the newly arrived councillors announced that they would formally take over when Smith's term ended. After Smith was injured in an explosion, he finally agreed to leave with one of the departing vessels.

Archer's last surviving letter, dated 31 August 1609 and sent to a friend via one of the ships returning to England, included a brief but lucid account of the voyage as well as an attack on Smith for not showing "due respect to many worthy Gentlemen that came in our ships." Archer reported on the beginnings of the new administration, admitting that Smith would "have it blazoned a mutenie." One final record of this antagonism is a series of trivial charges against Smith by Archer that were later forwarded to England.

Gabriel Archer died in Virginia on an unrecorded date during the "Starving Time" in the winter of 1609–1610.

William S. Simpson Jr., "The Parentage of Gabriel Archer," *Virginia Genealogist* 41 (1997): 15–17, which infers approximate year of birth from date of college matriculation; John Venn and John A. Venn, *Alumni Cantabrigienses* (1922–1954), pt. 1, 1:37; Joseph Foster, *The Register of Admissions to Gray's Inn, 1521–1889* (1889), 83, 504; Smith, *Complete Works*, vols. 1–2; Archer's principal writings are in Samuel Purchas, *Hakluytus Posthumus, or Purchas His Pilgrimes* (1625), 4:1647–1651, Philip L. Barbour, ed., *The Jamestown Voyages Under the First Charter, 1606–1609* (1969), 1:80–104, 2:279–283, and David B. Quinn and Alison M. Quinn, eds., *The English New England Voyages, 1602–1608* (1983), 112-138.

DAVID B. QUINN

ARCHER, Robert (28 August 1794–19 May 1877), iron manufacturer, was born in Norfolk, the oldest of two boys and two girls of Edward

Archer, a merchant, and his second wife, Mary Silvester Wormington Archer. The family included four children from his father's first marriage and at least one of his father's sisters, under whom he received his early education. As a boy Archer showed an interest in mechanics by making and selling wooden tops to neighborhood children and trying unsuccessfully to duplicate a perpetual-motion machine he saw exhibited in Norfolk. In 1810 he began four years of medical training with John Francis Oliveira, a former physician to the Portuguese royal court who assumed the surname Fernandes while in Norfolk. Recalled to his homeland about 1818, Oliveira subsequently served as a leading Portuguese diplomat.

Although Archer enlisted in a local artillery company in 1813, his medical knowledge caused him to be granted an unsolicited commission as a lieutenant and surgeon's mate. He spent the next twenty-five years as an army physician, stationed at Fort Monroe and, for a short while, at Fort King, Florida. On 28 March 1816 he married Frances Williamson in Norfolk. They had five sons and seven daughters, of whom one boy and three girls died young. When a request for a leave of absence for family reasons was not granted in 1839, Archer retired from the army and took up farming near Fort Monroe. During the next nine years he contributed ten articles to Edmund Ruffin's *Farmers' Register* and served as president of the local agricultural society.

In January 1848 Joseph Reid Anderson, Archer's son-in-law and head of the Tredegar Iron Company, persuaded Archer to move to Richmond to become superintendent of the Armory Iron Company, a firm formed five years earlier to produce rails for a rapidly expanding railroad network by using excess waterpower from the state armory. By May Archer had risen to the presidency of the company. A drop in iron prices caused the rolling mill to shut down during the summer of 1850. The company reorganized as a private corporation and then reincorporated in 1852 as R. Archer and Company with Archer and his son Robert Samuel Archer as two of the three leading stockholders. Decreased demand for rails led Archer to begin the production of bar iron and axes. In 1853 Archer and Anderson combined to recommence the rolling of rails and two years later were showing a profit at the rolling mill, which then consisted of nine puddling furnaces, four heating furnaces, and two trains of rolls driven by waterpower with the capability of producing up to six thousand long tons of rails and bar iron annually. By 1858 depressed economic conditions and British competition had again caused a sharp drop in sales. As he had done before, Anderson provided the financial aid necessary to allow Archer's mill to weather the slack. In 1859 Anderson and Archer formally joined forces and the physically contiguous Armory mill and Tredegar works merged into the newly formed Joseph R. Anderson and Company. From its inception the new firm was heavily involved in the production of cannons and shells.

By 1860 the charcoal blast-furnaces of the state's iron industry could no longer compete with the anthracite furnaces of Pennsylvania. Joseph R. Anderson and Company found itself importing four tons of Northern pig iron for every ton it bought from within the state. With Virginia's secession in 1861 the company again had to rely on the state's charcoal furnaces for pig iron. Though gun-quality metal was hard to obtain, the firm produced most of the heavy ordnance made in the Confederacy. While Anderson served in the army during the first year of the war, Archer and John F. Tanner ran the company. During the war, Archer developed a method of producing rifled shot for cannons and a device to prevent the premature explosion of cannon shells, and he or his nephew Robert Archer Talley also invented an automatic machine for the production of railway chairs, the pieces of iron used to connect rails and secure them to ties.

On 3 April 1865 the United States Army occupied the company property, and all work stopped. The owners regained possession in September after obtaining presidential pardons. The inability of most of its prewar railroad customers to pay their debts to the firm exacerbated financial problems caused by the war and its aftermath, but these losses were offset by profits made through cotton speculation and the sale of a portion of its interest in the Dover coal mines in Goochland County. Early in 1867 Joseph R. Anderson and Company was reorganized as the Tredegar Company with a capitalization of $1 million. Robert Archer and his son Robert Samuel Archer both sat on the six-member board of directors. Tredegar doubled its antebellum capacity by 1873, but during the ensuing depression the failure of northern railroads with which Tredegar had enormous contracts swept the company into receivership just three years later.

Robert Archer died on 19 May 1877 at his residence on the corner of Franklin and Madison Streets in Richmond, two months after celebrating his sixtieth wedding anniversary. Funeral services were held at Saint Paul's Episcopal Church, of which he had been a member, and he was buried in Hollywood Cemetery in Richmond.

Robert Archer, *Archer and Silvester Families: A History Written in 1870*, ed. Edward L. Goodwin (1937; frontispiece por.); Charles B. Dew, *Ironmaker to the Confederacy: Joseph R. Anderson and the Tredegar Iron Works* (1966); Joynes Family Papers, Mason Family Papers, and Watson-Archer Papers, all in VHS; Kathleen Bruce, *Virginia Iron Manufacture in the Slave Era* (1931); Tredegar Iron Company Records, LVA; *The Night After Christmas*, a parody on *The Night Before Christmas* written by Archer in 1866, was privately printed in miniature format in a limited edition of sixty copies in 1975; obituary in *Richmond State*, 21 May 1877.

R. BARRY WESTIN

ARCHER, Vincent William (3 August 1895–31 July 1968), radiologist, the only son and eldest of three children of Isaac James Archer and Cornelia Salineaux (also given as Saleno) Archer, was born in Berwyn, Illinois, while his father was a student at Northwestern University's medical school. The elder Archer practiced in Chicago after his graduation in 1896, but moved to Black Mountain, North Carolina, early in the twentieth century to become superintendent of the Cragmont Sanatorium and of the Royal League Sanatorium, two small institutions that treated pulmonary tuberculosis.

Vincent Archer attended Guilford College and Davidson College in North Carolina before transferring to the University of Virginia in 1915. During World War I he served as a second lieutenant in the Sanitary Corps. On 10 January 1918 he wed Kate Eleazer, of Newberry, South Carolina. They were married for fifty years and had a son and daughter who survived him. After the war Archer resumed his studies at the University of Virginia and graduated with a B.S. in 1920 and an M.D. in 1923. His academic records do not show any formal course work in roentgenology (named for Wilhelm Conrad Roentgen, the discoverer of X rays). However, Archer must have taken a special interest in the lectures and demonstrations that Dr. Robert Graham Wiatt, assistant professor of roentgenology there since 1919, offered to third-year students, because the medical school hired Archer as an instructor of roentgenology after his graduation. When Wiatt died in an automobile accident on 2 November 1923, the young physician shouldered full responsibility for the school's training in the comparatively new medical specialty. Thirty-eight years later he finally retired as chairman of the Department of Radiology, the term used after the medical applications of radium and other radioactive substances were joined with those of the X ray. By then, his one-man department had expanded to a staff of one hundred. In addition to teaching, Archer served on the staffs of the University Hospital and Charlottesville's Martha Jefferson Hospital.

Archer published more than forty scientific papers, including investigations into both the diagnostic and therapeutic applications of radiant energy. Two of his articles won the American Medical Association's Bronze Medal and Certificate of Merit in 1930 and 1934, respectively. His primer for physicians, *The Osseous System: A Handbook of Roentgen Diagnosis* (1945), emphasized the need for careful study when making medical diagnoses from radiographic images. Unprotected exposure to X rays took a fearful toll among the pioneer generation of roentgenologists, and the profession remained alert to the dangers of radioactivity. Archer himself developed a lead-glass fabric that protected against beta and X rays and was used for gowns worn during fluoroscopic examinations.

In addition to his research, teaching, and administrative duties, Archer was active in professional societies. He was chairman of the Board of Chancellors of the American College of

Radiology (1940–1943), chairman of the Executive Committee of the American Roentgen Ray Society (1946–1947), president of the Medical Society of Virginia (1954), and from 1952 to 1966 represented Virginia in the House of Delegates of the American Medical Association. Archer was also a cofounder in 1945 and later chairman of the board of the Virginia Medical Service Association, which became Blue Shield of Virginia. He received a silver medal from the American Roentgen Ray Society in 1949.

Archer stepped down as chairman of the Department of Radiology in 1961 but continued to teach until 1966, when he was named emeritus professor. In 1967 he received the Distinguished Service Award of the Medical Society of Virginia. Vincent William Archer died on 31 July 1968 in Charlottesville and was buried in the University of Virginia Cemetery.

Vincent William Archer Jr. to author, 20 Dec. 1989, DVB Files; Archer alumnus file, Office of University Registrar, UVA; *Who's Who Among Physicians and Surgeons* (1938): 26; *Who's Important in Medicine* (1952): 49; "Our New President—Dr. Archer," *Virginia Medical Monthly* 80 (1953): 642–643 (por.); obituaries in *Charlottesville Daily Progress*, 1 July 1968, and *Virginia Medical Monthly* 95 (1968): 594.

John T. Kneebone

ARCHER, William Segar (5 March 1789–28 March 1855), member of the House of Representatives and member of the United States Senate, was born in Amelia County, the eldest of at least five sons and four daughters of John Archer and Elizabeth Eggleston Archer. He attended the College of William and Mary in the class of 1806, studied law, and practiced in Amelia County for the rest of his life.

Archer represented Amelia County in the House of Delegates from 1812 to 1814 and again in 1818 and 1819. Late in December 1819 he was elected to the House of Representatives to succeed James Pleasants, who had resigned to become a U.S. senator. Archer took his seat on 3 January 1820. He was a conservative, states' rights Republican who shortly before being elected to Congress had introduced a lengthy resolution in the House of Delegates denying that Congress had constitutional authority to charter the new Bank of the United States. In 1824 he supported the presidential candidacy of Virginia native William H. Crawford, and four years later he favored Andrew Jackson. Archer served in the House for sixteen years. From 1829 until 1835 he was chairman of the Committee on Foreign Affairs.

Archer and other southern states' rights supporters broke with the president early in his second term after Jackson denounced nullification. Archer also criticized as high-handed the president's removal of government deposits from the Bank of the United States. As a result, Archer joined the new Whig Party, a disparate group of politicians opposed to Jackson's policies, albeit often for contrary reasons. Although never an advocate of Henry Clay's American System, which became the cornerstone of the Whigs' national appeal, Archer remained allied with the Whigs for the remainder of his life. He lost his seat in Congress to Democrat John Winston Jones in the election of April 1835.

On 3 March 1841 the General Assembly, which had a small Whig majority, chose Archer on the second ballot over the Democratic U.S. Senate incumbent, William H. Roane, for the six-year term that began the next day. Archer's Senate service plunged him into controversies over slavery, territorial expansion, the annexation of Texas, bank policy, and the disruption of the Whig Party during the administration of President John Tyler. Archer chaired the Committee on Foreign Relations from 1841 to 1845 and later supported President James K. Polk's attempts to end British claims to the Oregon territory. He opposed the annexation of Texas, in part because he feared it would lead to war with Mexico, even though he evidently favored it in principle in order to permit the expansion of slavery to the Southwest. Archer had a reputation for long and rambling speeches that one critic stated made as much sense when read backward as forward. Before his term concluded, the Democrats had regained control of the General Assembly. Archer therefore had no real chance of reelection, in spite of the hope of some Whigs that factionalism among the Democrats would let him slip into a second term. On the sixth ballot on 15 January

1847 the assembly chose Robert Mercer Taliaferro Hunter over Archer and Governor William "Extra Billy" Smith.

Archer served as a trustee of Hampden-Sydney College from 1820 to 1839 and campaigned unsuccessfully for seats in the 1829 and 1850 state constitutional conventions. His published opinions on the latter convention clearly placed him in agreement with conservative leaders in eastern Virginia who resisted all efforts to broaden the franchise, introduce more democratic election practices, dilute the influence in the General Assembly of the slaveholding eastern counties, or accede to any political or economic demands that originated in western Virginia.

William Segar Archer died on 28 March 1855 at his Amelia County house, the Lodge, and was buried nearby. He was a wealthy man, with nearly 2,000 acres of land and eighty-eight slaves in Amelia County, a large and valuable estate in Mississippi, and a library of more than 2,500 volumes. Never married, he willed all of his property to his three sisters, with whom he had lived. They then divided it into four equal portions, with the fourth, according to a later report, set aside to provide for Archer's illegitimate son, William Segar Archer Work.

Birth and death recorded in Archer Eggleston family Bible, VHS; gravestone inscription and identification of son in Walter A. Watson, *Notes on Southside Virginia* (1925), 147, 155; no large collection of Archer papers is known, but letters from him can be found in most collections of the politicians of his time, and his speeches in Congress appear in its published debates and were frequently printed or excerpted in newspapers or published as pamphlets; Senate elections described in *Richmond Whig and Public Advertiser*, 5 Mar. 1841, and *Richmond Semi-Weekly Whig*, 19 Jan. 1847; public letter in *Richmond Whig and Public Advertiser*, 23 July 1850; Sandra Gioia Treadway and Edward D. C. Campbell, Jr., eds., *The Common Wealth: Treasures from the Collections of the Library of Virginia* (1997), 269 (por.); will, estate inventory, and estate division in Amelia Co. Will Book, 17:378, 421–422, 423, 18:67–70; obituaries in *Richmond Enquirer*, 29 Mar. 1855, and *Richmond Whig and Public Advertiser*, 3 Apr. 1855.

BRENT TARTER

ARENTS, Grace Evelyn (1848–20 June 1926), philanthropist, was born in New York City, the youngest of three sons and three daughters of Stephen Arents and Jane Swain Ginter Arents. Her father, a cedar cooper, died in January 1855. Jane Arents's unmarried younger brother Lewis Ginter, who had been in the mercantile business in Richmond between 1842 and the outbreak of the Civil War, returned to that city from New York in 1873. By 1879 Jane Arents and Grace Arents were living with him in an affluent and fashionable Richmond neighborhood. At his death in 1897 Ginter was one of the wealthiest tobacco manufacturers in Virginia and one of Richmond's greatest benefactors. He left his estate to his nieces and nephews, among whom Grace was often said to have been his favorite.

Shy by nature, Grace Arents carefully guarded her privacy throughout her life. However, her charitable generosity, which followed the example set by both her uncle and her mother, brought her much public notoriety. She developed a special concern for the plight of the local poor and on their behalf unselfishly made donations that were often unsolicited and anonymous. Joining Saint Paul's Episcopal Church after moving to Richmond, Arents was introduced to its mission offshoot, Saint Andrew's Church in the Oregon Hill community, by her friend Annie Woodlief Jeffery, with whom she had run the short-lived Richmond Circulating Library in 1879 and 1880. After her mother's death in July 1890 Arents took Saint Andrew's under her protective wing. Beginning with her donation of a pipe organ for the church in 1890, Arents acted to meet nearly all of its financial needs by donating property, financing the construction and maintenance of a number of new church buildings, and contributing $70,000 for the erection of an impressive Gothic Revival church that was dedicated in 1903.

The church became a social center in its working-class neighborhood, due largely to Arents's philanthropic efforts. She also built a public bath close to the church and began a library nearby, which in 1899 became the first free circulating-library in Richmond. In her will she provided funds to guarantee the library's continued operation after her death under the guidance of the Saint Andrew's Association, of which she was a founding member and director. The library subsequently became part of the William Byrd Community Center. Ginter's Franklin Street mansion, which Arents had coinherited with an older sister and then acquired in her sole right as her own residence in 1900, later housed the Richmond Public Library for several years.

Recognizing a need for educational and social improvement programs in the neighborhood, Arents instituted a church sewing school in 1894 and a kindergarten in 1895. The success of the kindergarten program persuaded Arents to underwrite the building of Saint Andrew's School in 1901. To finance the tuition-free institution, she built several comfortable houses in the vicinity and endowed the school with the proceeds from the rents. The buildings were the city's first subsidized housing units. Saint Andrew's School educated boys and girls in both trade and academic subjects and offered evening classes for working adults. Arents went on to donate funds and a city lot for the construction of an elementary school for basic public education in Oregon Hill. Completed in 1912, the Grace Arents School (now Open High School) stands at the corner of Pine and China Streets.

Arents funded similar improvements in Ginter Park, the area that her uncle had developed in the city's Northside. She had in fact supported so many charities and institutions in Richmond by the time of her death that the author of her front-page obituary in the *Richmond News Leader* wrote that it would be impossible to list all of the libraries, recreational centers, schools, churches, hospitals, and similar institutions that she had aided. She gave personally to many of the city's clergymen, whether Protestant, Catholic, or Jewish, for programs to care for the poor and sick and to educate children. She also established a hospital for poor children at Bloemendaal, a property in the Lakeside neighborhood of Henrico County, near Richmond, originally acquired by Lewis Ginter to house the Lakeside Wheel Club. The Instructive Visiting Nurse Association, of which Arents was a strong supporter, began its home-care program in the city in the 1910s and thereby reduced the need for institutional care for sick children. She then moved to Bloemendaal herself and lived the final decade of her life there in quiet seclusion, continuing her philanthropic work.

Arents's greatest personal pleasures were reading (despite her extremely poor eyesight), gardening, and travel. Although few of her papers survive to shed light on her deliberately private life, two extant foreign travel diaries reveal a hunger for knowledge. She indulged her love of gardening during her residence at Bloemendaal. By developing the property as an ideal small farm of approximately seventy-two acres, she made it a model of land use to Virginia farmers and gardeners. In her will, which she wrote and dated on 26 July 1925, she granted her friend Mary Garland Smith a life interest in Bloemendaal, after which it was to become the property of the city of Richmond. By 1981 the trust that she created for the farm amounted to $2.6 million, and the Lewis Ginter Botanical Gardens at Bloemendaal subsequently became a major horticultural center in Virginia.

For much of her life Arents refused to be photographed, never had a portrait painted, and seldom appeared in public, even in association with one of the many charitable institutions she had founded or endowed. Grace Evelyn Arents died of a heart attack at Bloemendaal on 20 June 1926 and was buried in Hollywood Cemetery in Richmond.

Mary Holt Carlton, "Grace Evelyn Arents: Child of Light," *Richmond Quarterly* 4 (fall 1981): 49–51; feature articles in *Richmond News Leader*, 19 Dec. 1946, *Richmond Times-Dispatch*, 30 Aug. 1970, and *Richmond Style Weekly*, 24 Feb. 1998 (por.); year of birth on gravestone corroborated by age given in Census, New York City, 1850; Arents's commonplace book, 1868–ca. 1876, and her travel journals, 1888 and 1896, both in Lewis Ginter Papers, and some Arents letters in Bagby Family Papers, VHS; William N. Glenn, *St. Andrew's Episcopal Church and Its Environs* (1978); Mary H. Mitchell and Robert S. Hebb, "A History of Bloemendaal," *Bloemendaal: The Newsletter of the Lewis Ginter Botanical Gardens* 1 (autumn 1986), 3–18; vertical files, Lewis Ginter Botanical Center, Richmond; vertical files, Richmond Public Library; obituaries in *Richmond News Leader* and *Richmond Times-Dispatch*, both 21 June 1926, and *New York Times*, 22 June 1926.

GEORGE C. LONGEST

ARGALL, Samuel (bap. 4 December 1580–24 January 1626), deputy governor of Virginia, was born in England at the manor of East Sutton in the county of Kent, the fifth son and last of eleven children to survive infancy of Richard Argall, a gentleman with extensive properties in Kent, Essex, and London, and Mary Scott Argall, daughter of Sir Reginald Scott, of Scots Hall, Kent. Richard Argall died when his youngest child was eight years of age, and Mary Scott Argall remarried. The single clue to Samuel Argall's early education is John Pory's remark that Argall was "a soldier truly bred in that university of warre the lowe Countries." In 1606 Argall was working in the transatlantic fishing trade between Newfoundland, Spain, and England, experience that proved useful three years later when he was placed in command of a small ship and charged with discovering a shorter route to the Virginia colony, fishing for sturgeon, and selling provisions.

Argall left England on 15 May 1609 and reached the colony on 23 July 1609. By following the 30th parallel, which took him north of the Caribbean route, he trimmed the voyage from the twelve to eighteen weeks it had taken previously to just nine weeks and six days. Argall returned to England that fall and in March 1610 set sail again, this time transporting Thomas West, baron De La Warr, the new governor. Traveling the northern route resulted in his entering the James River on 10 June 1610—just in time to prevent Sir Thomas Gates and those sixty-five colonists who had survived the "Starving Time" of 1609–1610 from abandoning the colony for Newfoundland.

Determined to relieve and reform the distressed colony, which had suffered 350 deaths and cost the company some £20,000 since 1607, De La Warr appointed Argall captain of a fifty-man company of musketeers and ordered him to seek provisions on Bermuda. Argall left Jamestown on 19 June 1610 but encountered violent storms and wound up off Cape Cod, where he loaded his pinnace with fish before sailing down the coast and reaching the Chesapeake on 31 August. In the interim the colonists had initiated retaliatory raids against the Algonquians under Powhatan. Argall joined the effort early in September 1610 by attacking and burning the Warraskoyack village.

When the Jamestown garrison again required provisions in December, Argall was dispatched to the Potomac River and procured maize and furs there from Iopassus (Japazaws), the weroance of Passapatanzy, a Patawomeck town. On 28 March 1611 Argall sailed for England, accompanied by the malaria-ridden De La Warr. He remained there until 23 July 1612, when he commanded Sir Robert Rich's 130-ton ship, *Treasurer*, which reached Virginia on 17 September after a fifty-seven-day voyage that was the fastest then recorded.

Between December 1612 and May 1613 Argall sailed the Potomac River and northern Chesapeake, reaching the falls near modern Washington, D.C. During this time he observed bison, investigated minerals and water thought to have medicinal purposes, explored much of the Eastern Shore, and traded with Iopassus. Early in April 1613 Argall used his extensive knowledge of the area and its Indian population to kidnap Pocahontas while she was with the Patawomecks—an event that ultimately helped bring the devastating Anglo-Powhatan War of 1609–1614 to a conclusion. Argall obtained Iopassus's complicity in the kidnapping by threatening that they would otherwise "be no longer brothers nor friends," but he also rewarded him for his assistance and established an alliance to protect the Patawomecks from Powhatan's wrath. This diplomacy proved as damaging to the paramount chief as had the English raids, for Eastern Shore tribes also repudiated domination by the Powhatan chiefdom after they learned from the Patawomecks of Argall's "courteous usage of them."

Between July and November 1613 Argall routed a French outpost on what is now Mount Desert Island in Maine, claimed it for James I, devastated two other French settlements on the coast of Nova Scotia, and paid a hostile visit to the "pretended Dutch governor" at Manhattan. Having thus rendered inestimable service for England's future colonization of New England, Argall assisted Sir Thomas Dale, the deputy governor of Virginia, in negotiating a peace with the Pamunkey and Chickahominy in March and April 1614. That England's first Indian war ended diplomatically, with the John Rolfe–Pocahontas marriage, and not as a bloody Armageddon, owed more to Argall's strategic alliances with friendly Indians than to Dale's terroristic tactics against hostile ones. Returning to

London late in the spring of 1614, Argall was exonerated of charges that he had encroached on French rights in Canada. He returned to Virginia during the summer of 1615, having again traveled the northern route but inexplicably taken almost five months for the journey. Argall again commanded a ship returning to England when Pocahontas, her husband, and their young son took passage in the spring of 1616. He also commanded the Virginia-bound *George* from which Pocahontas came ashore, ill and dying, at Gravesend, Kent, late in March 1617.

Argall finally left Plymouth on 10 April and arrived in Virginia about 15 May 1617, when he assumed the office of deputy governor to the absent De La Warr. His administration during this key transitional period between the martial law invoked by Dale and Sir Thomas Smythe, Virginia Company treasurer, and the representative government initiated by subsequent leaders remains controversial thanks to sparse and contradictory records. Although feuding factions in the Virginia Company and changing conditions in the colony made Governor Argall a universal scapegoat, he successfully administered Virginia by balancing old and new policies. He improved military preparedness and cautiously restricted the colonists' contacts with Indians, much as had John Smith. He continued to invoke articles of Dale's *Lawes Divine, Morall and Martiall* but rarely enforced the harshest of its provisions. He was troubled over the colonists' growing dependence on tobacco to the neglect of foodstuffs, but by promoting private settlements, of which Argall's Gift (1617) was probably the first, he helped erode the Virginia Company's power, which rested on public landownership.

In effect, Argall's administration anticipated the collapse of the company. His promotion of a self-sufficient, militarily and economically strong colony governed by an experienced leader who merged public policy with private profits served as the model for Virginia's ruling oligarchy in the 1620s and 1630s. When other Kentishmen established an Anglo-Indian entrepreneurial empire in the northern Chesapeake, they followed Argall's precedents in fur trading, exploration, native diplomacy, and relations with London merchants and imperialistic noblemen. After enduring considerable criticism from both sides of the Atlantic, Deputy Governor Argall turned the government over to Nathaniel Powell on 9 April 1619 and left Jamestown within the next few days. Sir George Yeardley arrived on 18 April and assumed the position of deputy governor.

Successfully defending himself against new charges leveled against him in London, Argall refurbished his reputation by commanding a ship in a 1620 attack on Algiers and being appointed admiral of New England and a member of the Council for New England. James I knighted him on 26 June 1622. On 15 July 1624 Argall was appointed to the Mandeville Commission, which oversaw the reorganization of Virginia following the demise of the Virginia Company. He voted to surrender the company's charter but was defeated in his bid for election as the royal colony's governor. After commanding a large English fleet in an abortive attack on Cádiz in the fall of 1625, Sir Samuel Argall, of the manor of Lowhall, Walthamstow, Essex, died at sea aboard the *Swiftsure* on 24 January 1626. He was survived by one daughter, Ann Argall Percivall.

Seymour V. Connor, "Sir Samuel Argall: A Biographical Sketch," *VMHB* 59 (1951): 162–175; James D. Alsop, "Sir Samuel Argall's Family, 1560–1620," *VMHB* 90 (1982): 472–484; Kingsbury, *Virginia Company*, 2:55, 3:80, 92–99, 219–222, 247; Samuel Purchas, *Purchas his Pilgrimes* (1625; repr. 1905–1907), 19:90–95, 106, 120, 213–216; Smith, *Complete Works*, 2:215–217, 232–234, 236–237, 242–249, 261–268; Philip L. Barbour, *Pocahontas and Her World* (1970), passim, including endpaper map showing voyages; Leo Francis Stock, *Proceedings and Debates of the British Parliaments Respecting North America* (1924), 1:117–119; Wesley Frank Craven, *Dissolution of the Virginia Company* (1932), 36–39, 58, 65, 121–124, 197, 328; will in Hele 69, Prerogative Court of Canterbury, Eng.

J. FREDERICK FAUSZ

ARISS, John (ca. 1729–November 1799), builder, was born in Cople Parish, Westmoreland County, the youngest of five children of John Ariss and Frances Spencer Ariss. His mother was the granddaughter of Nicholas Spencer, a member of the Council in the 1680s and a sizable landowner in the parish. Within the space of two months in the winter of 1730, one sibling whose sex is unknown died and the already-widowed father drowned. John Footman became the guardian of the two boys and two girls who had been orphaned and of their considerable estate, valued at more than £350. At Footman's death in 1739, Wharton Ransdall assumed the guardianship of the three younger children. In November 1743 Ariss chose his older brother Spencer Ariss as his guardian. He was probably apprenticed to a local carpenter from whom he could learn the intricacies of the building process and gain practical experience in the use of tools and techniques practiced by builders.

On the strength of his financial resources and familial connections, Ariss by 1749 had moved into an entrepreneurial role as an undertaker of buildings in the region. To add to his professional prestige, he may have obtained several architectural books, including James Gibbs's *Book of Architecture* (1728), on a trip to England about this time. Ariss sought to extend his business by advertising his design, drafting, and contracting skills in the *Annapolis Maryland Gazette* on 15 May 1751. His early work most likely consisted of overseeing the construction and repair of farm buildings on local plantations. Documentary evidence of his private commissions does not exist, but he may have been among those few craftsmen who translated the desires for elegant and commodious dwellings and well-constructed public buildings into the colonial Chesapeake architecture that has been the source of pride and speculation ever since. From 1755 through 1761 Ariss owned a plantation next to Stratford and may have been involved in the renovations to the main house and the construction of outbuildings undertaken by Philip Ludwell Lee during those years. His work rapidly expanded in the 1750s as he began taking on apprentices to perform the drudgery of planing and sawing. For a few years he supervised a number of unspecified repairs to the Westmoreland County public buildings on the courthouse grounds.

Ariss could have integrated novel English design concepts in his private work in the Northern Neck and southern Maryland, but what little is known of his skills as an architect and contractor shows up in his public commissions. In 1751 he won the contract to build a brick church for Trinity Parish in Charles County, Maryland, and in 1766 he supplied the plan for Payne's, or the Upper Church, in Truro Parish in Fairfax County. Ariss's last known architectural commission was a design for a new chapel for Frederick Parish in Frederick County that was accepted on 31 May 1773. He was involved in the construction of this edifice until at least September 1774. The Maryland church was severely altered in the nineteenth century and neither of the Virginia structures survives, but the specifications for the three buildings drawn up by Ariss in consultation with each vestry suggest a competent but traditional handling of Chesapeake church forms.

Ariss married Rebecca Eskridge by October 1754, and she died before July 1757. He married again before September 1762, but the surname of his wife Elizabeth is unknown. He evidently had no children. By 1773 he was living in Norborne Parish, Berkeley County, where he was named to the court on 14 April 1773 and again on 9 December 1776. In August 1784 Ariss asked his distant kinsman George Washington to lease him land on Bullskin Creek where he might spend his remaining years and commented that his "Infirm Crazy Indisposition" prevented his moving far from his current residence. Ariss leased a small tract from Washington in 1786 and there built a house called Locust Hill. He probably continued to design and build houses until his death, using skilled slave laborers. After John Ariss died early in November 1799 his personal estate, including forty-seven slaves, drawing instruments, livestock, and household furniture, was appraised at more than $8,500. He asked that he be buried at Fairfield, the Warner Washington estate attributed to his design in what is now Clarke County.

Year of birth inferred from ability to choose own guardian in Nov. 1743 in Westmoreland Co. Order Book (1743–1747), 6; Ariss to George Washington, 5 Aug. 1784, in Washington, *Confederation Series*, 2:24–25; Frederick Parish Vestry Book, 13 Apr. 1773–6 Sept. 1774, LVA; Thomas T. Waterman, *The Mansions of Virginia, 1706–1776* (1946), gives an exaggerated assessment of his work that is tempered in Richard Beale Davis, *Intellectual Life in the Colonial South, 1585–1763* (1978), 3:1203–1204;

Westmoreland Co. records contain references to Ariss and family; ownership of plantation next to Stratford in Westmoreland Co. Deed and Will Book, 12:266–271, 14:191–196; month of death inferred from bill for coffin presented in Jefferson Co. Will Book, 2:41; will and estate inventory in Berkeley Co. Will Book, 3:315, 475.

CARL LOUNSBURY

ARMISTEAD, Anthony (d. by 2 May 1705), member of the House of Burgesses, was the youngest of three sons and one of at least four children of William Armistead and Anne Armistead. He was probably born in Elizabeth City County a few years after his parents moved there in the mid-1630s from Kirk Deighton, Yorkshire, England. Like other settlers who were adroit in taking wealth and power where they were to be had, Armistead's father quickly amassed a significant amount of land that, coupled with the strategic marriages of three of his children, enabled him to make the family an integral part of Virginia's planter aristocracy. Armistead's brother John Armistead eventually served on the governor's Council, the highest position to which a Virginian could reasonably aspire.

Armistead married Hannah Ellyson and had at least three sons and one daughter. His wife's father was Robert Ellyson, who had close ties to Governor Sir William Berkeley and was a member of the James City County Court and the House of Burgesses. Armistead became a member of the Elizabeth City County Court and a captain of the militia by the mid-1670s. During Bacon's Rebellion he supported Berkeley, and the governor afterward appointed him to a court-martial that condemned one of the rebels to death by hanging. Armistead served his first term in the House of Burgesses during the third session of the General Assembly of 1680–1682. Speaker Thomas Ballard named him to the Committee on Public Claims, one of three standing committees of the House.

Armistead returned to the assembly in October 1693. At that time he helped draft a bill regulating tanners, but the bill was not passed. He served in every General Assembly but one during the next decade and became prominent in the House. He was usually assigned to the influential Committee on Propositions and Grievances, which often recommended changes in existing statutes and also received and considered petitions requesting changes in the law. The assignment thus enabled Armistead to influence most of the legislation that came before the House. He frequently participated in conference committees that negotiated with the governor and the Council on the passage of bills and other legislative matters. He also sat on a joint committee of burgesses and councillors who laid the groundwork for the revised legal code of 1705, but he did not live to see the work completed.

Armistead ran afoul of House procedure at times, and he was not immune to opposition in Elizabeth City County. His legislative attendance was less than faithful and earned him a number of reprimands from his colleagues. The absences may have encouraged competition at the polls. In 1699 several constituents challenged his reelection, but the Committee on Elections and Privileges discovered no improprieties. He may have learned his lesson and was never again disciplined for absences.

Armistead's career mirrored those of other men like him, the grasping, ambitious colonists who gave pattern and substance to Virginia's evolving political fabric, even if he did not rank in the first echelon of the colony's rulers. His three sons, Anthony Armistead, Robert Armistead, and William Armistead, helped set him apart from many of his more successful and more powerful contemporaries by sustaining the family's place at the head of Virginia society. The Armisteads remained a part of the planter elite for the rest of the colonial era and beyond.

Anthony Armistead died while attending a session of the House of Burgesses. The exact date is not recorded, but he was evidently present in the House on the opening day of a new session, 19 April 1705, after which his name next appeared in the journals on 2 May, when the House asked the governor to issue a warrant for the election of a new burgess from Elizabeth City County "in the Room of Mr *Anthony Armistead* Decd."

"Armistead Family," *WMQ*, 1st ser., 6 (1897–1898): 31, 226–227; *Minutes of Council and General Court*, 454, 527; *Journals of House of Burgesses, 1695–1702*, 134, 139, 141; *1702/3–1712*, 88–89, 102.

WARREN M. BILLINGS

ARMISTEAD, John (fl. 1650s–1690s), member of the Council, was the second of three sons and one of at least four children of William Armistead and Anne Armistead, of Kirk Deighton, Yorkshire, England. He may have been born in Virginia, his parents having settled in Elizabeth City County in the mid-1630s, which is the most likely approximate time of his birth. When he reached adulthood he moved to Gloucester County, where he lived and farmed for the rest of his life. His father had prospered so rapidly after immigrating to Virginia that both of his surviving sons began their adult lives as substantial planters. He may have sent John Armistead to Gloucester County in the 1650s to manage the properties he acquired after that section of the colony was first opened to English settlement.

Sometime in the 1660s Armistead became associated with Robert Beverley (1635–1687), an association that led to several profitable joint business ventures. The relationship grew even closer when Armistead married Beverley's sister-in-law Judith Hone. Armistead had two sons and two daughters, and he acquired even more influential family connections later, when one of his daughters married Ralph Wormeley and the other married Robert "King" Carter.

Destruction of most of the records of Gloucester County has obscured the details of Armistead's participation in politics. He probably became a vestryman of Kingston Parish within a few years of moving to the county, and by 1670 he was a member of the county court as well as a colonel in the county militia. He became sheriff in 1676 and again in 1680. In 1682 he arrested several local women who were destroying tobacco plants. This put him in opposition to Robert Beverley, the putative instigator of the plant-cutting riots, by which the perpetrators hoped to reduce the supply of tobacco and thereby raise its price. Armistead differed from Beverley on political issues, too. Beverley grew increasingly outspoken in his opposition to English policies designed to control Virginia after Bacon's Rebellion, while Armistead inclined favorably toward the new order.

Armistead served in the House of Burgesses twice. Elected in 1680, he sat at the first meeting of the General Assembly of 1680–1682. His part in suppressing the plant cutters may explain his absence at the second session, and he did not return to the House until 1685. By the mid-1680s he was on friendly terms with Governor Francis Howard, baron Howard of Effingham, who resided at times with Armistead's son-in-law Ralph Wormeley. The association with Effingham proved beneficial, and in 1688 Effingham appointed Armistead to a vacancy on the governor's Council. He was sworn in on 18 October 1688, but his tenure lasted only two and a half years. In April 1691, following the Glorious Revolution, Armistead refused "Thro Scruple of Conscience" to swear allegiance to the new monarchs, William and Mary. He consequently lost his seat on the Council. Seven years later the Crown ordered him restored to his place, but Armistead did not take the oaths after the commission was presented to the Council on 9 December 1698.

John Armistead may have been dead by that date, but he could also have been alive and in political retirement in Gloucester County while continuing his refusal to forswear his oath to James II. The date and place of his death are not recorded.

"Armistead Family," *WMQ*, 1st ser., 6 (1897): 31–33, 97–99; *Executive Journals of Council*, 1:10, 23–24, 89, 172, 398; Billings, *Effingham Papers*, 355, 373, 386.

WARREN M. BILLINGS

ARMISTEAD, John Maurice (1 March 1852–3 December 1929), Baptist minister, was born in Lynchburg, the only son and one of two children of Frank B. Armistead and Eliza Maxey Armistead, mulatto slaves. His father was a shoemaker, and after emancipation Armistead was working in that trade when, during services at Court Street Baptist Church in Lynchburg, he was so deeply moved as the congregation sang "Come Holy Spirit Heavenly Dove" that he joined the church and devoted his life to Christianity.

Armistead enrolled at Richmond Theological School for Freedmen (now Virginia Union University) in 1868. He studied for the ministry there until 1873 and then at Roger Williams College in Nashville, Tennessee, where he completed his course work in 1879. In the latter year the General Association of East Tennessee ordained him and he accepted a call from the First Baptist Church of Knoxville. During his several years there the congregation flourished. While in Knoxville he also founded and edited the *Baptist Companion*, the major news organ for the black Baptists of Tennessee.

On 6 November 1880 Armistead married Emma J. Niles, with whom he had two daughters. Soon after, he traveled to Montgomery, Alabama, to attend a convention of more than 150 black Baptists gathered from at least ten states to promote the establishment of foreign missions in Africa. At the initial meeting on 24 November 1880 he was elected one of two secretaries of what was known first as the Baptist Foreign Mission Convention and evolved into the National Baptist Convention, one of the largest black organizations in the world. Armistead, a member of the new group of African American leaders who were born slaves but grew to maturity in freedom, played an important role in the organization for many years.

In 1882 Armistead returned to Virginia to become the pastor of Zion Baptist Church in Portsmouth. He continued to publish the *Baptist Companion*, which he renamed the *Virginia Baptist*, and he built Zion into one of the state's leading black Baptist congregations. During his forty-three-year pastorate there, his congregation's membership grew from 900 to more than 2,600. To accommodate this growth an impressive new house of worship was erected under his leadership and dedicated in 1895. Five new congregations, Olive Branch Baptist Church, Little Zion Baptist Church, New Hope Baptist Church of Saint Julian Creek, First Baptist Church of Sherwood Place, and First Baptist Church, Truxton, grew out of Armistead's ministry at Zion Baptist. His natural drive and intelligence complemented his mastery of the spoken word. With a voice of tremendous power and range, Armistead became one of the most inspiring pulpit orators of his time, lauded as a "powerful and persuasive" speaker possessed of "originality, apt in illustration, [and] logical and systematic."

Armistead was chairman of the State Mission Board for a number of years, and he served the Virginia Baptist State Convention as second vice president from 1882 to 1884 and president from 1884 to 1890. Founded 9 May 1867 in Portsmouth, the Baptist State Convention grew out of an effort by black churchmen to establish institutions independent of the paternalistic support of white Baptist churches in the North. The needs of African Americans for autonomy, or at least greater participation in church organizations, was evident in the controversy surrounding the American Baptist Publication Society, when white leaders refused to permit blacks to contribute written articles to Sunday school publications. Such behavior drew a rebuke from Armistead at the 1890 Virginia Baptist State Convention, and his comments helped persuade whites to grant concessions to black Baptists.

Armistead also helped establish the Virginia Seminary and College at Lynchburg. He was named a trustee in its original acts of incorporation as the Lynchburg Baptist Seminary on 24 February 1888 and as the Virginia Seminary on 4 February 1890 and 20 March 1895. The school opened early in 1890 but later that year construction came to a halt for lack of money. Despite the urging of black Baptist leaders, their average parishioner was not sufficiently committed to the idea of a school owned and controlled by African Americans. Faced with a crisis, Armistead and two other black churchmen persuaded the American Baptist Home Mission Society to accept the school as an affiliate in an agreement reached before the Virginia Baptist State Convention's annual session in May 1891. Some thought that this arrangement undercut black independence, but the alternative was an early death for the institution. Armistead later served as president of the school's board of trustees.

Armistead was also active in Portsmouth's political and civic life. A member of the city council, he attended its meetings from February 1890 into 1891 and participated in community organizations such as the Masons, the Good Samaritans, and the Pythians. Armistead was a widower by June 1895 and later married Martha

Bridson, who also predeceased him. Despite a heavy workload and personal losses, he remained committed to his ministry, and his work was recognized in 1906 when he received an honorary D.D. from Virginia Union University.

After serving Zion Baptist Church faithfully for forty-three years, Armistead retired on 22 March 1925 and was unanimously named pastor emeritus by the congregation. John Maurice Armistead died at his house in Portsmouth on 3 December 1929.

Caldwell, *History of the American Negro*, 89–92 (por.); "Zion Baptist Church: An Authentic History, 1865–1949" (photocopy of typescript in Norfolk State University Archives), 14; Virginia Baptist State Convention, *Minutes of the Annual Session* 18 (1885): 2; James Melvin Washington, *Frustrated Fellowship: The Black Baptist Quest for Social Power* (1986), 169, 193; Ralph Reavis, *Virginia Seminary: A Journey of Black Independence* (1990), 57–59; *Acts of Assembly*, 1887–1888 sess., 291–292; 1889–1890 sess., 236–237; Charter Book, 27:477–481; feature article in *Norfolk Journal and Guide*, 18 Oct. 1958; obituaries in *Portsmouth Star*, 6 Dec. 1929, and *Norfolk Journal and Guide*, 7 Dec. 1929.

TOMMY L. BOGGER

ARMISTEAD, Lewis Addison (18 February 1817–5 July 1863), Confederate army officer, was born in New Bern, North Carolina, the eldest of four sons and second of nine children of Walker Keith Armistead and Elizabeth Stanly Armistead. He lived with his maternal grandparents in New Bern for a year, then joined his family at Ben Lomond, a 300-acre farm located near Upperville, in Fauquier County, where he grew up. His father was a graduate of the United States Military Academy and a colonel of the U.S. Army who fought, along with four brothers, in the War of 1812. One of these uncles, George Armistead, commanded Fort McHenry near Baltimore during the British bombardment that inspired Francis Scott Key's "Star Spangled Banner."

Almost by birthright, therefore, sixteen-year-old Lewis Armistead entered the U.S. Military Academy in 1833, but an illness early in his first semester put him behind in algebra, and he resigned effective in November. He returned the next year, but he proved to be anything but a model cadet. On 29 November 1834 Armistead faced a general court-martial for taking another cadet's guard duty. He was found guilty of this offense, although cleared of the more serious charge that he had answered for the cadet at roll call, and sentenced to four extra tours of Sunday guard duty. At the close of the academic year in June 1835, Armistead was found deficient in French and ordered to recommence his studies. On 30 June he was arrested for talking with a civilian while on post and was sentenced to an extra tour of guard duty. He managed to complete the following semester satisfactorily, but after he became involved in a fracas in the mess hall on 16 January 1836 he submitted his final resignation effective 15 February of that year. The records state only that the charge was "disorderly conduct," but Armistead reportedly hit fellow cadet and future Confederate general Jubal A. Early over the head with a mess-hall plate after a quarrel on the parade ground.

Despite this inauspicious beginning, on 10 July 1839 Armistead entered the U.S. Army as a second lieutenant in the 6th Infantry. He saw action against the Seminole Indians in Florida under the command of Zachary Taylor and his own father. In the Mexican War he earned two brevet promotions for gallantry in the campaign that captured Mexico City. The next dozen years brought gradual promotion to captain during the typical succession of tours of duty on the frontier. He married Cecilia Lee Love, of Fairfax County, in February 1844, and they had one son and one daughter. The daughter died in April 1850, and after the death of Armistead's wife on 12 December 1850 he cared for their son, who later became his aide during the Civil War. At Christ Church in Alexandria on 17 March 1853 Armistead married Cornelia L. Taliaferro Jamesson, a naval officer's widow with one daughter. The Armisteads probably had one child, a son who died young. Cornelia Armistead's own death followed on 2 August 1855.

While assigned to the garrison of Fort Towson in present-day Oklahoma, Armistead had struck up a close friendship with Winfield Scott Hancock, a Pennsylvanian. Three days after Virginia officially seceded from the Union on 23 May 1861, Armistead resigned his commission. In a tearful farewell he told his friend,

"Hancock, good-by—you can never know what this has cost me."

After returning to Richmond by way of Texas, Armistead was appointed a major in the Confederate army on 14 September 1861 and made a colonel in charge of the 57th Regiment Virginia Infantry later that month. He was promoted to brigadier general on 1 April 1862 and given command of a brigade of five Virginia regiments. During the bungled Confederate attack at Seven Pines (31 May–1 June 1862) Armistead was unable to rally his fleeing troops, but he and his brigade distinguished themselves by hard fighting at Malvern Hill (1 July 1862). The unit was only lightly engaged at Second Manassas (Bull Run) on 29–30 August 1862 and at Sharpsburg (Antietam) on 17 September 1862, though Armistead was slightly wounded there. Incorporated into George E. Pickett's all-Virginia division after Sharpsburg, Armistead's brigade also saw little action at Fredericksburg (13 December 1862) and was on detached service with the rest of Pickett's division during the Battle of Chancellorsville (1–4 May 1863).

Pickett's division served as rear guard of General James Longstreet's corps when the Army of Northern Virginia invaded Pennsylvania in June 1863. Armistead did not participate in the first two days of fighting at Gettysburg. But for Armistead and the rest of the division, this inaction ended abruptly and violently on 3 July 1863.

At 3:00 P.M., Armistead took his place at the head of his brigade to lead it in the assault on Cemetery Ridge, where the Union Second Corps was under the command of his friend Hancock. Four Confederate divisions, exposed to cannon and musket fire, advanced across nearly a mile of open plain and approached the stone wall atop Cemetery Ridge. Armistead, using the point of his sword to hold his black hat aloft as a guidon, called to his men to follow him over the wall and into the Union lines. He was wounded, and about half of the 150 men still with him were killed. Removed to the rear of the Union position, he requested that Hancock see that his family receive his spurs and pocket watch. Lewis Addison Armistead died in a Union field hospital on 5 July 1863 and was buried at the battlefield. He was subsequently reinterred at Saint Paul's Church in Baltimore. A monument commemorates the spot where Armistead's shattered brigade penetrated to the farthest point on Cemetery Ridge, which is often referred to as the "high water mark of the Confederacy."

Wayne E. Motts, *"Trust in God and Fear Nothing": Gen. Lewis A. Armistead, CSA* (1994; por., 16); James E. Poindexter, *Address on the Life and Services of Gen. Lewis A. Armistead* (1909); William S. Appleton, *The Family of Armistead of Virginia* (1899), 14–17; Virginia Armistead Garber, *The Armistead Family, 1635–1910* (1910), 66–68; Military Academy Orders, and Correspondence Relating to Military Academy, both in Records of Adjutant General's Office, RG 94, NARA; Alexandria Co. Marriage Register (LVA microfilm filed with Arlington Co. Records); Compiled Service Records; Kathleen R. Georg and John W. Busey, *Nothing But Glory: Pickett's Division at Gettysburg* (1987); Carol Reardon, *Pickett's Charge in History and Memory* (1997), 6, 24–26, 53–56, 88, 183.

JAMES M. MCPHERSON

ARMSTRONG, Edward Jones (29 March 1808–1 August 1877), merchant and member of the Convention of 1850–1851, was born in Frederick County, the younger of two children, both sons, of George Armstrong and Susannah Armstrong. His family moved to Harrison County about 1815, and his father died early in 1821. By the age of twenty-three he had established himself as a merchant in Williamsport, which changed its name to Pruntytown in 1845. He married Sophia Rightmire on 19 January 1826, and they had at least three daughters and two sons before her death early in the 1850s. He married Catharine Martz sometime before 1854, and they had two sons.

By the 1830s Armstrong had become a prominent local merchant, and in 1837 he was appointed a justice of the peace in Harrison County. From 1839 to 1844 he served in the House of Delegates as a Democrat and was instrumental in enacting the law that created Taylor County in 1844. Armstrong was elected first clerk of the Taylor County Court and held the office from 1844 to 1848.

In September 1850 Armstrong was one of four men elected to represent the district of Marion, Monongalia, Preston, and Taylor Counties in the Convention of 1850–1851. He was appointed to the Committee on Executive

Departments and Ministerial Officers but did not play an influential role. Armstrong voted with the other western delegates in favor of virtually unrestricted white manhood suffrage and for apportionment of seats in the assembly entirely on the basis of the adult white population.

The Constitution of 1851 provided for the popular election of three commissioners of the Board of Public Works, which had been created in 1816 to oversee the expenditure of public funds to aid in the construction of internal improvements. Armstrong, clearly an advocate of western economic interests, was unopposed in his 1853 bid to represent the forty-county Third District. He served one four-year term, the last two years as president of the board.

Armstrong owned seven slaves in 1860, and during the secession crisis he sided with the South. His name headed the six subscribers to a letter to Governor John Letcher on 24 April 1861 requesting arms for the volunteer company being organized as part of a home guard. On 7 May Armstrong was appointed assistant quartermaster at Taylor County with the rank of captain of volunteers, and in August he became a captain and assistant quartermaster in the Confederate army. By October 1863 he had left the service and purchased a house and business in Bridgewater. For the next fourteen years he ran a general store and participated in local civic affairs. He served as a town trustee until the military authorities removed him from office in October 1869. He was also a trustee of the Bridgewater Graded School, a patron of the Valley Normal School and Summer Institute in Bridgewater, a charter member of the local Masonic lodge, and a member of the Baptist Church.

On 27 February 1869 Armstrong shot and killed Martin L. Shank, a neighbor and plasterer, in a scuffle concerning Shank's purchase of a sieve at Armstrong's store. The justices of the peace judged that Armstrong had acted in self-defense. The county grand jury indicted him, nonetheless, but his plea of self-defense was sustained, and when he was charged yet again at the insistence of the Reconstruction military government, he was again acquitted on 20 November 1869.

In 1873 Armstrong was returned to the House of Delegates, and he won reelection in 1875. He supported the Conservatives in opposition to the Republicans. On 1 July 1874 he was elected to a three-year term as mayor of Bridgewater. Edward Jones Armstrong died of heart disease at Rawley Springs in Rockingham County on 1 August 1877 and was buried in Greenwood Cemetery in Bridgewater.

Details of family and professional life pieced together from 1840–1870 Census returns, deed books and land and personal property tax records of Harrison, Taylor, and Rockingham Cos., records of General Assembly and Board of Public Works at LVA, and numerous references in Clarence E. May, *Life Under Four Flags in North River Basin of Virginia*, 2d ed. (1982); *Journal of 1850 Convention*; Shank's death and aftermath in *Staunton Vindicator*, 5 Mar., 26 Nov., 3 Dec. 1869, *Luray Page Valley Courier*, 12 Mar. 1869, and *Harrisonburg Rockingham Register*, 25 Nov. 1869; BVS Death Register, Rockingham Co.; obituary in *Harrisonburg Rockingham Register*, 2, 9 Aug. 1877.

DAPHNE GENTRY

ARMSTRONG, Edward McCarty (18 October 1816–1 April 1890), merchant and member of the Convention of 1861, was born in Romney, Hampshire County, the second of three sons and third of four children of William Armstrong and Elizabeth McCarty Armstrong. His father was an attorney, tavernkeeper, and member of Congress, and his younger brother became a judge, but Edward M. Armstrong earned his living as a merchant and a dealer in land. He held the usual local offices of a gentleman of prominence: justice of the peace for Hampshire County from 1849 to 1861, postmaster during the 1840s, and militia officer. By 1860 he was colonel commandant of the Hampshire County militia. On 3 September 1837 he married Hannah Angeline Pancake in Cumberland, Maryland. Before her death on 3 August 1854 they had six sons and one daughter. About 1857 or 1858 he married Louisa Tapscott White, a local woman twenty years his junior. They had three sons and four daughters.

Armstrong owned nine slaves and property worth about $6,000 in 1850. During the next decade he moved to New Creek Station (now Keyser) and purchased coal lands and other real estate along the Baltimore and Ohio Railroad line in Virginia and Maryland. By 1860 his real estate was worth more than $24,000, his coal holdings about $20,000, his personal property, including eighteen slaves, almost $40,000.

The secession crisis propelled Armstrong briefly into political turmoil and altered his life forever. As one of the most prosperous businessmen and respected local Democratic leaders in Hampshire County, he was elected as a Unionist by a margin of more than five hundred votes over secessionist candidates to represent Hampshire County in the convention that met in Richmond in February 1861. Armstrong attended regularly, missing only a few minor votes, but spoke only twice. He voted against secession on 4 April 1861 and against it again when it passed on 17 April. He later signed the ordinance of secession and made a trip home to Hampshire County at the end of April to look after his personal affairs. At least three of Armstrong's sons served in the Confederate army, and Governor John Letcher stated that Armstrong was "entirely loyal and reliable."

A local historian has asserted without citing reliable evidence that Armstrong was among sixty people whom the United States Army took prisoner when it occupied Romney on 27 October 1861, but by the middle of November Armstrong was back in Richmond attending the short final session of the convention. For the remainder of the war, as far as records show, Armstrong and his family lived quietly in the remote Cacapon River valley of Hampshire County. The war seriously reduced the value of his property, but he sold his New Creek Station land to Henry Gassaway Davis in the mid-1860s and relocated in March 1866 to Salem, Roanoke County, where he operated a dry goods dealership for several years before retiring sometime during the 1870s. Edward McCarty Armstrong died, probably of a heart attack, while reading his mail on 1 April 1890. He, his second wife, and several of his children are buried in East Hill Cemetery in Salem.

Birth date on gravestone, East Hill Cemetery, Salem; one Armstrong letter in West Virginia and Regional History Collection, WVU; family and wealth documented in Census, Hampshire Co., 1850, 1860, and Roanoke Co., 1870; information on business affairs in deed books of Hampshire and Mineral Counties, W.Va., and on political affiliation in Hu Maxwell and Howard L. Swisher, *History of Hampshire County, West Virginia* (1897); Reese, *Journals and Papers of 1861 Convention*; Reese and Gaines, *Proceedings of 1861 Convention*; Roanoke Co. Will Book, 1:363–364; obituaries in *Roanoke Daily Times*, 3 Apr. 1890, and *Romney Hampshire Review*, 10 Apr. 1890, quoting *Salem Times Register*.

JOHN E. STEALEY III

ARMSTRONG, Frank (26 October 1871–7 May 1954), apple product manufacturer, was born at Central Station, Doddridge County, West Virginia, the younger of two sons and second of four children of William Armstrong, a Baltimore and Ohio Railroad employee, and Emily Shannon Armstrong. After attending public schools in Central Station and Parkersburg, West Virginia, Armstrong went to work at age seventeen as a clerk for Shattuck and Jackson, a Parkersburg wholesale grocer. On 17 November 1897 he married Nellie Steel, daughter of the mayor of Clarksburg, West Virginia. They had a son and a daughter.

After eighteen years in the wholesale business, Armstrong sought to start his own company. Interested in the cider and vinegar industry, he toured the area around Winchester and learned of the large yields expected from the apple orchards being planted in the Shenandoah Valley. Through business contacts in Washington, D.C., Armstrong met B. Fleet Board, a partner in a cider and vinegar concern. In 1908 the two men organized Board, Armstrong, and Company, took over Board's former business, and began production at a factory on Alexandria's Potomac River waterfront. Board died in 1911, and on 1 March 1913 Armstrong changed the business's name to the National Fruit Product Company. He began marketing products under the White House brand, named after the American presidential mansion.

An industry innovator, Armstrong pioneered the four-cup apple peeler and developed new strategies for marketing apple products. Initially the company made cider vinegar almost exclusively, distributing the vinegar in large wooden kegs to grocers, who dispensed it to their customers. Armstrong developed glass containers with wide mouths to market vinegar in retail packages directly to consumers. The company grew dramatically because of the success of the jars, and Armstrong varied the size and shape of the glass containers to maintain consumer interest. In 1915 the National Fruit Product Company took advantage of apple production in the Shenandoah Valley by building its second vinegar plant in Winchester. Three years later Armstrong opened a canning plant nearby and developed a process to put sliced apples in a vacuum-packed can, an improvement that revitalized the canned-apple business. The company purchased a vinegar distillery in 1919 in Martinsburg, West Virginia, and a short time later it began producing sweet cider and apple juice. Armstrong also experimented with pineapples, but the hard winter of 1918–1919 ruined his Florida crop and convinced him to confine his energies to packaging and promoting the apple.

Early in the 1920s Armstrong's company began commercial production of applesauce, a product virtually unknown at the time, and then expanded the Winchester cannery to handle consumer demand for the popular new item. After the Alexandria plant burned down in 1925, the company developed new manufacturing sites in the Shenandoah Valley, New Jersey, Pennsylvania, and Georgia. By the time its corporate headquarters moved from Washington to Winchester in 1938, the National Fruit Product Company employed about 1,500 people to make apple juice, cider, vinegar, apple butter, applesauce, and canned apples.

Armstrong belonged to the New York Avenue Presbyterian Church in Washington, where he continued to maintain a residence after the executive offices moved to Winchester. In 1942 he canceled the church's indebtedness with a cash gift of $39,000. When his active service in the church ended he was named honorary chairman of the church's board of trustees, a unique distinction. Armstrong later joined and contributed $100,000 to construct Mount Carmel Baptist Church in Haywood in Madison County, close to his farm called Gilnockie, where he raised Aberdeen Angus cattle for twenty years.

Frank Armstrong remained active in the company he founded until shortly before he died at his farm on 7 May 1954. He was buried at Mount Carmel Cemetery. His namesake son, elected company president in 1950, served until 1971, when Frank Armstrong III took the helm. In 1986 the National Fruit Product Company was the fourth-largest apple processor in the United States and the largest in the Southeast.

NCAB, 43:59 (por.); National Fruit Product Company archives, Winchester; company brochures (copies in DVB Files), including *A Brief History of National Fruit Product Company, Inc.* [ca. 1960s], and 75th and 85th anniversary brochures, both entitled *National Fruit Product Company, Inc.*, and issued in 1983 and 1993; *Commonwealth* 38 (May 1971), 40; obituaries in *Winchester Star*, 8 May 1954, and *Richmond Times-Dispatch*, 9 May 1954.

RAYMOND M. HYSER

ARMSTRONG, George Dod (15 September 1813–11 May 1899), Presbyterian minister and writer, was born in Mendham, New Jersey, the youngest of three sons and ninth of ten children of Amzi Armstrong and Mary "Polly" Dod Armstrong. His father served as pastor of the Presbyterian church in Mendham from 1796 to 1816, when he assumed charge of the Bloomfield Academy in Bloomfield, New Jersey, at which young men studied for the ministry. George Armstrong was raised at the academy until 1826, when his mother died and his father retired.

Armstrong entered the College of New Jersey (now Princeton University) on 11 June 1830 and received an A.B. in September 1832. He then traveled to Virginia to visit relatives, including his eldest brother, William Jessup Armstrong, pastor of First Presbyterian Church in Richmond. Instead of returning to New Jersey, Armstrong taught school in Virginia for three years and entered Union Theological Seminary in Farmville in 1836. The next year Washington College (now Washington and Lee University) in Lexington made him Robinson Professor of Physical Science. From 1839 to 1845 he was also professor of natural philosophy and chemistry at the Virginia Military Institute. About 1840 he married Mehitabel H. Porter, and by 1850 they had four daughters.

Fearing that science might distract him from his interest in preaching, Armstrong announced his intent to remain at Washington College only until he received "the call of the Lord." He prepared for that call through constant religious activity. He was licensed to preach in 1838 and ordained an evangelist in 1843. From 1839 to 1851 Armstrong served as part-time pastor of the Timber Ridge Church in Rockbridge County. He resigned his teaching post in April 1851 to become pastor of First Presbyterian Church in Norfolk. Armstrong received a D.D. from the College of William and Mary in 1854, and from that year until about 1861 he served on the board of trustees of Hampden-Sydney College in Farmville.

Disaster struck Armstrong's family when yellow fever ravaged Norfolk and Portsmouth during the summer of 1855. Like most clergymen who remained in the city to minister to the sick, he was stricken by the fever, and his wife and all but one of his children died. Subsequently Armstrong published a highly acclaimed history of the epidemic, *The Summer of the Pestilence: A History of the Ravages of the Yellow Fever in Norfolk, Va., A.D. 1855* (1856). On 6 October 1857 he married Lucretia N. Reid, daughter of his parishioner, Charles Reid, a prominent Norfolk businessman and fellow temperance advocate and Whig. They had one daughter.

Armstrong courted controversy throughout his life. During his tenure in Lexington he and some of the trustees of Washington College charged that the leaders of the Virginia Military Institute were exceeding their legislative mandate by making their school a rival of the college. He published letters in the newspapers, testified on the subject to the legislature in August 1844, and helped fuel a dispute that resulted in the termination in February 1846 of the schools' 1839 cooperative agreement. Like many other Princeton graduates, Armstrong became an advocate of the "positive good" theory of slavery, publishing *Politics and the Pulpit* (1856), *The Christian Doctrine of Slavery* (1857), and *A Discussion of Slaveholding: Three Letters to a Conservative, by George D. Armstrong, D. D., of Virginia, and Three Conservative Replies by C. Van Rensselaer, D. D., of New Jersey* (1858). Having demonstrated to his own satisfaction that the Scriptures sanctioned slavery, he insisted that ministers keep the subject out of the pulpit. Armstrong's major theological publications included *The Doctrine of Baptisms* (1857), *The Theology of Christian Experience* (1858), and *The Sacraments of the New Testament as Instituted by Christ* (1880).

As a supporter of the Confederacy during the Civil War, Armstrong became embroiled in a controversy with Union general Benjamin F. Butler. Armstrong's sermon, *"The Good Hand of Our God Upon Us": A Thanksgiving Sermon Preached on Occasion of the Victory of Manassas, July 21st, 1861 (1861)*, and his criticism from the pulpit of Northern occupation forces in Norfolk antagonized Butler, commander of the Department of Virginia and North Carolina for a year beginning late in 1863. Early in 1864 Butler had Armstrong arrested and interrogated him concerning his loyalties. When Armstrong confessed that the loyalty oath he had taken to the United States covered his actions rather than his thoughts, Butler ordered him jailed at Fort Hatteras and later assigned him to labor on street repair. Armstrong, in effect, became a prisoner of conscience before he was exiled to the Confederacy in September 1864. He spent the remaining months of the war as a chaplain and traveled with the Army of Northern Virginia from Petersburg to Appomattox.

During the 1880s Armstrong staunchly advocated a literal interpretation of the Bible and opposed the theory of evolution. Generally recognized as the most articulate southern Presbyterian to explore the relationship between science and theology, he attacked evolution in such church journals as the *Presbyterian Quarterly*, *Southern Presbyterian Review*, and *North Carolina Presbyterian*, as well as in *The Two Books of Nature and Revelation Collated* (1886). His strong background in science as well as religion added to the potency of his assault on evolution and led him to become the foremost proponent within the Presbyterian General Assembly of the biblical version of creation. In 1886 Washington and Lee University granted him an honorary LL.D.

After forty years in the Norfolk pulpit, Armstrong retired from active service. No other contemporary minister had even approached his long period of service to a Tidewater congregation. In a retirement ceremony at First Presbyterian Church on 2 July 1891, his congregation and the citizens of Norfolk celebrated his dedication to the community and presented him with a gift of gold valued at $1,150.

After giving up his pulpit Armstrong still served First Presbyterian Church of Norfolk as pastor emeritus and occasionally delivered sermons at the nine Presbyterian churches that he had helped to establish in the city. Infirmity limited his activity during the final two years of his life. On 11 May 1899, in the company of his wife and his two surviving daughters, George Dod Armstrong died in his Norfolk home. He was buried in Elmwood Cemetery in Norfolk.

Biographies in *The Church on the Elizabeth River* [1892?], 35–38 (por.), Alfred Nevin, ed., *Encyclopedia of the Presbyterian Church in the United States of America* (1884), 33–34, and Sally Harbaugh, "Rev. George Dod Armstrong," 1940 typescript, WPA Biographies; letter of acceptance to Washington College and receipts and expense vouchers, Trustees Papers, W&L; William Couper, *One Hundred Years at VMI* (1939), 1:63, 108, 139–143, 149; BVS Marriage Register, Norfolk City; letter of resignation from First Presbyterian Church, Norfolk, in Vertical File, Union Theological Seminary, Richmond; *Norfolk Landmark*, 3 July 1891; obituaries and memorials in *Norfolk Public Ledger* and *Norfolk Virginian-Pilot*, both 12 May 1899, and *Norfolk Landmark*, 15 May 1900.

R. LYN RAINARD

ARMSTRONG, James Edward (15 October 1830–7 April 1908), Methodist minister, was born in Alexandria, the eldest of three sons and four daughters of James Lamb Armstrong and Mary Jane Smith Armstrong, both of whom were Methodists. When he was two years old the family moved to Baltimore, a center of the rapidly expanding Methodist movement. The city offered a vibrant congregational life of revivals, love feasts, and temperance meetings. Baptized as a young boy at Wesley Chapel, Armstrong attended Sunday schools from age five and later noted their influence on his calling to preach. In 1845 he experienced conversion at a large Methodist revival in the city.

In 1846 Armstrong graduated from Baltimore's male high school, which he had attended since 1843. Six of the thirteen graduates in his class later became pastors. Armstrong returned to teach and receive advanced instruction at the school for a year. He then worked as a clerk in a Baltimore countinghouse for five years.

Armstrong's preaching career began in 1852, when Light Street Methodist Church licensed him as an exhorter, or assistant lay preacher. As was typical for the time, the congregation groomed him for the pulpit. In March 1853 Armstrong was licensed as a lay preacher and recommended for full-time preaching. Later that same year the Baltimore Conference received him as a circuit preacher. Following three years as a junior preacher on northern Virginia circuits, he became senior pastor on the Fincastle Circuit in 1856. In Woodstock on 1 November 1855, while still a junior preacher, Armstrong married Margaret Hickman, of Shenandoah County. Of their seven children, three sons and two daughters survived to maturity. After passing examination by his elders, Armstrong was ordained deacon in 1855 and elder in 1857.

Throughout his life Armstrong experienced sectional tensions within the Methodist Episcopal Church. During the denominational schism in 1844, the Baltimore Conference, which included counties north of the Rappahannock River and in the Shenandoah Valley, joined the northern branch of the church. During the Civil War two rival Baltimore Conferences developed, one independent and the other associated with northern Methodism. Affiliating with the independent Baltimore Conference, Armstrong preached on circuits in the war-torn Shenandoah Valley, where many congregations were rent by sectional loyalties. In 1866 the independent Baltimore Conference became part of the Methodist Episcopal Church South. That same year Armstrong took his first "station," or town church, at Staunton. He later served stations in Winchester, Fredericksburg, Harrisonburg, and Salem. In 1872 he became presiding elder, or overseer, in the Roanoke District. He served as presiding elder again from 1893 to his retirement in 1906 in the East Baltimore, Rockingham, and Roanoke Districts.

In 1858 Armstrong had been elected assistant secretary to the Baltimore Conference, and he served in the same capacity for the Baltimore Conference, Methodist Episcopal Church South, until he became secretary in 1889. He earned a reputation for diligence and thoroughness. During the annual conference of April 1895, his colleagues unanimously requested that he write a history of the original Baltimore Conference from its eighteenth-century beginnings to its development into the largest of the church's forty-six conferences by 1857, when it was divided into the Baltimore and East Baltimore Conferences. Published in 1907, the book dealt with both the turmoil over episcopal reform during the 1820s and the dissension over slavery that resulted in the schism of 1844. The illustrated history also included an extensive selection of clerical biographies. According to Armstrong's memorialist, he handled divisive issues so diplomatically that the book received praise from both branches of the church. In 1895 Armstrong became a trustee of Randolph-Macon College in Ashland, and the school awarded him an honorary D.D. in 1901.

James Edward Armstrong died of pneumonia in Roanoke on 7 April 1908, one week after attending the Baltimore Conference's annual meeting in that city. He was buried in East Hill Cemetery in Salem.

Biographies in Nolan B. Harmon, Albea Godbold, and Louise L. Queen, eds., *The Encyclopedia of World Methodism* (1974), 1:143–144, and James Edward Armstrong, *History of the Old Baltimore Conference from the Planting of Methodism in 1773 to the Division of the Conference in 1857* (1907), 496–506 (frontispiece por.); Census, Baltimore City, 1850; Shenandoah Co. Marriage Register; East Hill Cemetery Records, LVA typescript; obituary in *Roanoke Evening News*, 7 Apr. 1908; memorial by J. S. Hutchinson in Baltimore Annual Conference, Methodist Episcopal Church South, *Minutes of the Session* 125 (1909): 80–84.

BETH BARTON SCHWEIGER

ARMSTRONG, Richard (16 July 1873–4 August 1938), head of the State Commission of Fisheries, was born in Saybrook, Connecticut, the second of three sons and second of four children of William Nevin Armstrong and Mary Frances Morgan Armstrong. Armstrong could claim a distinguished, albeit somewhat exotic, family background. His paternal grandfather, for whom he was named, was a Pennsylvania-born, Princeton-educated missionary who became the superintendent of public instruction in Hawaii by appointment of King Kamehameha III. Armstrong's father was born on Maui in 1835, practiced law in New York City, served as attorney general of Hawaii in 1881–1882, and became involved in agriculture and oyster cultivation in the vicinity of Hampton, Virginia. His mother was a Connecticut native whose father had owned a line of clipper ships involved in the China trade. Further reflecting his activist-reformist heritage, Armstrong's uncle General Samuel Chapman Armstrong had founded Hampton Institute as a vocational school for blacks in the post–Civil War years.

From about the age of ten Armstrong lived near Hampton and attended a local private school followed by Phillips Academy in Andover, Massachusetts. He received a B.A. in engineering from Yale University in 1895, compiling an impressive record as a member of the football and rowing teams. Thereafter, maintaining a lifelong enthusiasm for sports, he coached football and crew at the United States Naval Academy in Annapolis late in the 1890s, coached crew at Yale in 1914, played football for the Hampton Athletic Club, and was an avid yachtsman and golfer.

By 1900 Armstrong had returned to Hampton, where he spent four years as surveyor of Elizabeth City County. On 21 April 1906 he married Rosa Fairfax Lee in Hampton. They had no children. An Episcopalian in religion and a Democrat in politics, Armstrong participated in an array of public service activities, including overseas work with the Red Cross during World War I and membership in the Peninsula Chamber of Commerce. He also took over and expanded his family's oyster-planting operations in the Tidewater and Eastern Shore. In 1930 Armstrong retired from the oystering business but retained the presidencies of the Armstrong Land and Improvement Company, a Hampton-based real estate firm that he ran with his brother Matthew C. Armstrong, and the Security Storage and Safe Deposit Company in Norfolk.

His background in the oystering industry made Armstrong an obvious choice for his appointment by Governor John Garland Pollard to the State Commission of Fisheries, which took effect on 1 July 1930. In December 1931 Pollard named Armstrong the agency's commissioner, or head, an appointment reconfirmed in 1934 by George C. Peery, the new governor. Victimized by overfishing and increasingly threatened by pollution, Virginia's oyster industry had entered a period of prolonged decline by the 1930s. Since the 1890s regulatory policies had been based on the Baylor Survey, which had divided the underwater terrain of the state's coastal areas into "natural" oyster beds, open to all watermen who purchased state licenses, and previously "barren" areas that could be leased and planted with oysters by entrepreneurs who paid an annual rent to the commonwealth. With time the productivity of the natural beds had waned because of excessive exploitation, while the privately managed planting grounds had generated an ever increasing share of the output. This disparity produced so much ill will that by the 1920s it had erupted into the "oyster wars," sporadic outbursts of violence between planters and their "natural rock" or "public ground" competitors. Championing not only the planters' interest, but also a conservation ethic, Armstrong opposed continued reliance on the Baylor Survey and argued that more of the oyster beds should be subject to lease and private management.

Despite Armstrong's managerial expertise and firsthand knowledge of conservation issues, continuation of the status quo more than reform characterized his tenure as commissioner of fisheries. The Great Depression reduced demand for seafood, impoverishing the state's watermen and cutting into commission revenues from taxes, licenses, and rents. Preoccupied with the economic crisis, the General Assembly paid scant heed to appeals by Armstrong and Governor Pollard for alterations in the Baylor Survey and also ignored a prescient report by Armstrong urging establishment of a state agency for pollution control. Armstrong could point to successes, but they were of a limited nature: passage of an omnibus fisheries act in 1936 that consolidated and updated previous legislation without substantially altering policies; ongoing efforts to replenish the natural oyster beds using shells and seed oysters; cooperative research work with Maryland scientists on the life cycle of Chesapeake crabs; acquisition of an oceangoing patrol boat to prevent illegal trawling; improved auditing and record-keeping procedures; purchase of new surveying equipment; collaboration with federal agencies to develop fish hatcheries and expand stocks of clams, oysters, and terrapins; and implementation of new marketing programs to enhance sales of shad and salt herring. Inadequate funding limited the effectiveness of most of these initiatives.

Administrative frustration ultimately culminated in political humiliation. Governor James H. Price, an ardent New Dealer, took office early in 1938 and, as part of an abortive revolt against the Byrd organization, fired Armstrong and three of his associates from the State Commission of Fisheries, replacing them with insurgent Democrats of a more liberal stripe. Richard Armstrong suffered a paralytic stroke soon afterward and, following treatment at Johns Hopkins Hospital in Baltimore, died on 4 August 1938 of cirrhosis of the liver and ascites at his home near Hampton. He was buried in Saybrook, Connecticut.

Biography in Glass and Glass, *Virginia Democracy*, 2:178–181 (por.); Census, Elizabeth City Co., 1900; BVS Marriage Register, Elizabeth City Co.; *Report of the Commission of Fisheries on the Subject of Pollution of the Tidal Waters of the Commonwealth*, Doc. 8 appended to *JSV*, 1932 sess.; State Commission of Fisheries, *Annual Report*, 1930/1931–1937/1938; obituaries and editorial tributes in *Norfolk Virginian-Pilot*, 5, 6 Aug. 1938, *Portsmouth Star* and *Richmond News Leader*, both 5 Aug. 1938, and *Richmond Times-Dispatch*, 6 Aug. 1938.

JAMES TICE MOORE

ARMSTRONG, Samuel Chapman (30 January 1839–11 May 1893), educator, was born on the island of Maui in the kingdom of Hawaii, where his parents were missionaries. Of the family's ten children, he was the youngest of three sons and fifth of eight children to survive infancy. His father, Richard Armstrong, was a Presbyterian from Northumberland County, Pennsylvania, and his mother, Clarissa Chapman Armstrong, came from a Congregationalist family from Stockbridge, Massachusetts.

As a youngster Sam Armstrong exulted in the outdoor life that the Hawaiian Islands provided. A serious student first at the Punahou School and then at its collegiate branch, Oahu College, he was also a prankster who secretly lowered the flag of the American Consulate in tribute to the death of a family pet and hanged his sisters' dolls to thwart their "i-doll-try."

Armstrong's most important model in shaping his own life was his father, who had become a government servant as well as minister of the largest native church in Honolulu by the time Armstrong was an adolescent. Richard Armstrong was a member of the king's Privy Council, minister of education and, ultimately, superintendent of public instruction. In the schools that the senior Armstrong created for the people of Hawaii, he inculcated the principle of manual labor whereby students helped support the cost of their education and acquired useful skills by farming or practicing crafts such as blacksmithing, carpentry, and barrel making. For most of his teenage years Armstrong was his father's secretary, and the experience influenced his own approach to education.

Richard Armstrong was killed in a horseback-riding accident in 1860. His bereaved son followed his father's last wishes and journeyed to the United States for the first time to attend Williams College in Williamstown, Massachusetts. There he completed his last two years of college education. He was housed and given special training by the college president, Mark Hopkins, who became the second-most-important influence in Armstrong's life and career. Under Hopkins's tutelage he refined his concept of practical or useful education, which played down the academic benchmarks of a classical education in favor of teaching students how to make a living and be good Christians.

The Civil War did not initially concern Armstrong, who still identified Hawaii as his homeland. His parents had opposed slavery, but Armstrong had met few African Americans before coming to the United States. After graduation, however, many of his schoolmates, including future president James A. Garfield, enlisted in the Union army, and Armstrong soon followed. He wrote a friend that the war should not end until "every slave . . . can call himself his own, and his wife and children his own." He joined the 125th New York Infantry and was commissioned a captain. The regiment fought at Gettysburg, where Armstrong earned a promotion to major. By April 1864, he was a lieutenant colonel in command of the 9th Regiment United States Colored Troops, then stationed in South Carolina and subsequently transferred to the Army of the James. By 11 October he had been promoted to colonel of the 8th Regiment U.S. Colored Troops, Twenty-Fifth Corps. At some point he was breveted brigadier general. During the final assault on Petersburg on 3 April 1865, Armstrong's troops were among the first to enter the city after it was abandoned by the Confederate army. The 9th Regiment received, in Armstrong's words, "a most cheering and hearty welcome from the colored inhabitants of the city, whom their presence had made free." In the aftermath of the war he commanded black troops in Virginia and Texas.

From 1866 to 1868 Armstrong served as assistant subcommissioner of the Bureau of Refugees, Freedmen, and Abandoned Lands (the Freedmen's Bureau) for the district covering the lower peninsula between the James and York Rivers as well as Surry and Isle of Wight Counties and portions of the Eastern Shore. He strove to reduce the huge population of homeless refugees by pressing former slaves to accept employment as farm laborers. As a result some blacks felt that Armstrong and his associates at the bureau sympathized more with the defeated white landowners than with the freed African Americans they were charged with aiding. Armstrong was himself deeply committed to assisting the black population, but he also believed in the superiority of the white race. He sought to train the freed people so that they might better compete within the constraints of their circumstances.

Even before the Freedmen's Bureau closed down at the end of 1868, Armstrong had acted to create a school to train black teachers who would in turn educate other African Americans. Hampton Normal and Agricultural Institute accordingly opened in April 1868. It was not to be an ordinary school. Armstrong incorporated many of the lessons about education he had learned from his father and from Hopkins but also introduced ideas of his own. For example, he believed that the future for African Americans depended on the strength of their families. Thus, Hampton was coeducational in order that future married partners could be educated together.

Hampton Institute emphasized practical knowledge. Students took courses in English, arithmetic, basic science, geography, and history, including what was then known of African history. In addition, all students were required to work in the school shops or on the school farm. Many critics have charged that Armstrong's program mirrored and even reinforced convictions that blacks were suited only for manual labor. Whereas some of this criticism of Hampton is justified, especially in Armstrong's last years and after his death, his initial design was strictly practical. Hampton had no endowment, and most of its early students were impoverished. Manual labor in the school's fields and shops subsidized their education. Furthermore, most graduates expected to go into teaching, and because most southern schools for blacks remained open for fewer than six months a year, teachers needed supplemental skills to support themselves and their families.

Armstrong's design succeeded. Within a decade graduates of Hampton were teaching thousands of black children all over the South. Alumni were also entering professional fields such as medicine and law and participating in politics. In fact, Armstrong not only helped many of them to obtain advanced educations, but he also depended on black members of the Virginia legislature to assist him in securing additional funding for the institute.

In 1878 Armstrong initiated a program for Native American students at Hampton. Many of the Indian students distinguished themselves, but with that program the nature of the school began to change. As the institute grew, so did its need for donors. Armstrong increasingly gave up supervision of day-to-day operations in order to raise funds to keep the school going. By the 1880s he was much celebrated among Northern philanthropists. In 1887 his alma mater, Williams College, and in 1889 Harvard University each honored him with an LL.D.

Hampton grew more and more dependent on major benefactors who set restrictions on how their contributions could be used. A rising national tide of racism made it easier to rationalize industrial education and manual labor than to advocate genuine black advancement, and Armstrong eventually succumbed to those pressures. Academics at Hampton were publicly deemphasized in favor of its trade-school programs. Coping with new pressures, raising money, and overseeing the school took their toll. After suffering one stroke in 1891, Samuel Chapman Armstrong died of a second one on 11 May 1893. As he had requested, he was buried in the student cemetery on Hampton's campus.

Armstrong's life and legacy have been subjected to much criticism, partly because he may have inspired Hampton's most famous graduate, Booker T. Washington, to advocate a philosophy of accommodation to racial segregation. Such criticism has some validity, but it also distorts by oversimplifying Armstrong's design for Hampton. Moreover, he laid down a solid foundation, and the school survived. A century later Hampton is a respected small university with an honored past. This achievement is, in part, also a result of the continued dedication of Armstrong's descendants to the school he founded.

Armstrong married his first wife, Emma Dean Walker, of Stockbridge, on 13 October 1869. She died on 10 November 1878 after many long illnesses. Their two daughters, Louise H. Armstrong and Edith E. Armstrong, both taught briefly at Hampton Institute as adults, and the former married William Scoville, who served as secretary of Hampton's administrative board from 1918 to 1935 and as an institute trustee from 1941 until his death in 1943.

Armstrong did not remarry until 10 September 1890, when he wed Mary Alice Ford in Montpelier, Vermont. A teacher at Hampton Institute at the time of their marriage, she briefly resumed work as an educator at Hampton after the general's death and then returned to her native New England, where she directed summer camps. They had two children. Their son, Daniel Armstrong, graduated from the U.S. Naval Academy and commanded the Negro Recruit Training Program at the Great Lakes Naval Training Center near Waukegan, Illinois, during World War II. Their daughter, Margaret Armstrong, married Arthur Howe, president of Hampton Institute from 1931 to 1940, and their sons in turn served on the school's board of trustees from the 1950s into the 1970s.

Edith Armstrong Talbot, *Samuel Chapman Armstrong: A Biographical Study* (1904); Suzanne Catherine Carson, "Samuel Chapman Armstrong: Missionary to the South" (Ph.D. diss., Johns Hopkins University, 1952); Samuel Chapman Armstrong Papers, Hampton; American Missionary Association Archives, Amistad Research Center, Tulane University, New Orleans; Hawaiian Missionary Children's Society Library, Honolulu; Armstrong Papers, Williams College; *OR*, 35, pt. 2, 79; 42, pt. 3, 174; 46, pt. 2, 1237; Freedmen's Bureau Records; James D. Anderson, *The Education of Blacks in the South, 1860–1935* (1988); Robert Francis Engs, *Freedom's First Generation: Black Hampton, Virginia, 1861–1890* (1979) (pors., 127, 152); Louis R. Harlan, *Booker T. Washington: The Making of a Black Leader, 1856–1901* (1972); Francis Greenwood Peabody, *Education for Life: The Story of Hampton Institute* (1918); Robert F. Schriever, "Samuel Chapman Armstrong and the Founding of Hampton Institute" (senior thesis, Williams College, 1973); Donald Spivey, *Schooling for the New Slavery: Black Industrial Education, 1865–1915* (1978); second marriage documented in *Southern Workman* 19 (1890): 104; obituaries in *Norfolk Virginian*, 12 May 1893, and *Norfolk Landmark*, 13 May 1893, correctly give death date as 11 May 1893, as opposed to 12 May 1893 in BVS Death Register, Elizabeth City Co.

ROBERT FRANCIS ENGS

ARMSTRONG, William (23 December 1782–10 May 1865), member of the House of Representatives, was born in Lisburn, County Antrim, Ireland, the only son and one of three children of James Armstrong and Elizabeth Dillon Armstrong. His family immigrated to Philadelphia, and after the death of his father and sisters, Armstrong and his mother settled in Hampshire County in the mid-1790s. Armstrong studied law while working as a clerk in Winchester. In 1810 he married Elizabeth McCarty, with whom he had three sons and one daughter before she died on 4 July 1843. He subsequently wed Jane Baxter Armstrong, his first cousin, in 1844. They had no children.

Armstrong entered politics in 1811, running as a Jeffersonian Republican for a seat in the House of Delegates. Hampshire County was staunchly Federalist, and he lost. He was defeated again in 1812. Perhaps as a result of his opposition to the Federalists, he received a presidential appointment in 1813 as a tax collector for the United States government. In 1818 and 1819, after the influence of the Federalists had waned, he was twice elected to the House of Delegates. He served first on the Committee of Claims and then on the Committee for Courts of Justice, voted to establish the University of Virginia, and evidently favored using money from the Literary Fund to aid the new school. In 1822–1823 he served a one-year term on the state Board of Public Works.

Armstrong's political base rested securely on county politics. On 19 May 1817 the Hampshire County Court granted him a license to operate an ordinary in Romney, which became an important way station on the Northwestern Turnpike. The tavern remained a significant source of livelihood for Armstrong until he sold it in 1848. In 1824 he had become a justice of the peace for the Romney District of Hampshire County. On 27 February 1843 the county court elected him sheriff. He served as a presidential elector for James Monroe in 1820 and for William H. Crawford in 1824.

Armstrong's political career peaked with his election to four consecutive terms in the House of Representatives from the district comprising Berkeley, Hampshire, Hardy, Jefferson, and Morgan Counties. Serving from 1825 until 1833, he sat on the committees on private lands, territories, and the District of Columbia. With interests centered chiefly on local and regional matters, Armstrong may have been a competent legislator, but he made no recorded speeches and did not become prominent. On three of the most important votes taken while he was a member of Congress, he opposed President Andrew Jackson and the most doctrinaire states' rights Democrats. Armstrong supported the tariff bill of 1828, the so-called Tariff of Abominations. On 27 May 1830 he opposed Jackson's veto of the Maysville Road Bill, and he voted on 3 July 1832 for the bill to recharter the Second Bank of the United States.

After leaving Congress, Armstrong continued to operate his tavern in Hampshire County. Members of his family owned a few slaves, and they supported the Confederacy. Armstrong's son Edward McCarty Armstrong represented Hampshire County in the Virginia Convention of 1861. William Armstrong moved in 1862 to what is now Keyser, West Virginia, and died there on 10 May 1865. He was buried in Indian Mound Cemetery at Romney.

Armstrong Family Genealogical Notes, Acc. 35829, LVA, including obituary from unidentified newspaper; Mary K. Ashbrook, comp., "Hampshire County, West Virginia, Cemetery Records," typescript in Hampshire Co. Public Library, Romney, W.Va.; *Martinsburg Gazette*, 13 July 1843; Hu Maxwell and H. L. Swisher, *History of Hampshire County, West Virginia* (1897); other local information in Hampshire Co. Minute Book, 1817–1828, and Hampshire Co. Court Records, box 2, envelope 16A, and box 14, envelope 82, West Virginia and Regional History Collection, WVU.

STEPHEN W. BROWN

ARNOLD, Remmie LeRoy (25 January 1894–23 June 1971), businessman and civic association leader, was born in Petersburg, the second of three sons and second of four children of Andrew Alexander Arnold and Mary Virginia Arnold. His father was an unskilled laborer, and Remmie Arnold grew up with few advantages. After attending public schools, he went to work at a planing mill in 1907 for three dollars a week. Intelligent and resourceful, willing and able to take responsibility, Arnold subsequently worked for a number of other local businesses before becoming general manager of the Edison Pen Company in Petersburg in 1915. He eventually rose to the firm's presidency and in 1935 established his own R. L. Arnold Pen Company, where he served as president for the rest of his life. It became one of the largest manufacturers of fountain pens and mechanical pencils in the world.

On 27 April 1918 Arnold married Charlia Lawrence Sears, originally of Charleston, South Carolina, at her parents' home in Middlesex, Nash County, North Carolina. They had one son and one daughter. As Arnold's business became more successful, he became more active in civic affairs. He served on the Petersburg City Council from 1936 to 1944 and advocated better housing and recreational facilities for both races in Petersburg. He was one of the first to call attention to the pollution of the Appomattox River, chaired a committee that built an airport for Petersburg, and helped convince the army to reopen Camp Lee in 1940. A dynamic extrovert, Arnold enjoyed the conviviality of fraternal organizations. He served as national president of the Circus Saints and Sinners in 1938–1939, district deputy exalted ruler of the Elks in Virginia in 1944, and national imperial potentate of the Ancient Arabic Order, Nobles of the Mystic Shrine in 1953–1954. He also sat on the Crippled Children Hospitals Board of the Shriners Hospitals of North America.

Arnold's involvement in such organizations led naturally to another public service during World War II. He founded a Petersburg chapter of the National War Dads, an organization established in 1942 to help servicemen keep in touch with their parents and to press the government for better medical treatment in the military and to prepare for postwar medical care, insurance, job training, and education for veterans. Arnold attended the first national convention of the War Dads in 1943 and was elected national president. Reelected in 1944, he personally delivered thousands of pieces of mail from servicemen to their families during extensive travels in England and France as well as in the United States.

In 1949 Arnold campaigned for the Democratic Party nomination for governor of Virginia. His platform was an unusual mixture of pleas for increased public services and criticism of big government. He advocated repealing the poll tax as well as increasing salaries and pensions for public school teachers. He proposed issuing bonds for school construction and argued for additional improvements of the Hampton Roads ports. As a newcomer to elective politics, Arnold had no chance against experienced politicians with extensive networks of supporters. He placed fourth among the four candidates, receiving only about seven percent of the vote.

In spite of the apparently progressive nature of portions of his campaign platform, Arnold was in many other ways a typical conservative southern businessman. As a self-made man he was critical of the welfare state, and as a businessman he disliked governmental intervention in the economy. He was a well-known and highly vocal critic of labor unions. From 1946 to 1947 he served as president of the Southern States Industrial Council, one of the most conservative organizations of southern businessmen, which worked to keep labor unions out of the South and adopted a strong anticommunist stance that appealed to conservative politicians and reinforced opponents of some of the progressive policies Arnold was to advocate in 1949. In spite of his earlier pleas for better schools for African American children, Arnold was allied in the Southern States Industrial Council with many of the business leaders of the South who staunchly defended racial segregation.

During the 1950s and 1960s Arnold withdrew from leadership in partisan organizations to concentrate on his business and fraternal affairs and his Arnolda Ranch in Prince George County. The R. L. Arnold Pen Company remained a family business, and his son, Remmie LeRoy Arnold Jr., succeeded his father as president in 1971 and in 1974 won election to the Petersburg City Council. Remmie LeRoy Arnold died of heart failure on 23 June 1971 and was buried in Blandford Cemetery in Petersburg.

William Moseley Brown, *From These Beginnings: The Life of Remmie LeRoy Arnold* (1953); family history information verified by granddaughter Alexa Arnold Ricketts; *Virginia Journal of Education* 42 (May 1949): 14, 26; Peter R. Henriques, "The Organization Challenged: John S. Battle, Francis P. Miller, and Horace Edwards Run for Governor in 1949," *VMHB* 82 (1974): 372–406; portrait in possession of Mildred Spain Arnold, Petersburg; obituaries in *Richmond Times-Dispatch*, 24 June 1971, and *Petersburg Progress-Index*, 24 (por.), 25 June 1971.

JAMES R. SWEENEY

ARNOLD, Richard Watson (14 February 1843–27 September 1911), attorney, businessman, and politician, was born in Berlin, Southampton County, the eldest of two sons and three daughters of Isaac M. Arnold, a Methodist minister, and his second wife, Margaret Ann Anderson Arnold. Arnold was a private in Company D, 3d Virginia Infantry, from May 1861 until his capture in Richmond on 3 April 1865. From June 1863 to February 1864 he was detached to the provost guard of George E. Pickett's division. Arnold served in the Peninsula campaign, at the Second Battle of Manassas (Bull Run), at Fredericksburg, at Gettysburg, and during the siege of Petersburg. After the war Arnold read law in Petersburg and was admitted to the bar. He settled in Waverly in Sussex County and began his law practice. He also operated a livery stable and drayage company and a hotel, and as the founder of the Old Dominion Peanut Company he was credited with introducing the first peanut-cleaning machines and pioneering in large-scale peanut warehousing and marketing. On 14 January 1871 he married Ida Prince, of Sussex County. They had eight sons and four daughters.

Arnold entered public life as commonwealth's attorney for Sussex County from May 1870 through December 1873. When Waverly was incorporated in 1879, he was one of the five trustees who composed the town council until the first regular election. From January 1880 to December 1885 Arnold served as judge of the county courts of Sussex and Greensville Counties. Judge Arnold, as he was thereafter known, was a close political ally of his former commander, General William Mahone. He followed Mahone into the Readjuster Party and then into the Republican Party, campaigned vigorously in many counties in each election, advised Mahone on political strategy and patronage, and soon established himself as one of the leading Readjusters, and later one of the leading Republicans, in the Fourth Congressional District.

Arnold considered running for Congress in 1880 and in 1886, but his business interests and the needs of his large family prevented him from doing so. In 1888, however, when John Mercer Langston, the superintendent of the Virginia Normal and Collegiate Institute, ran for the Republican nomination, Arnold strongly opposed nominating an African American and, with Mahone's support, became a candidate himself. After a bitter contest in which Arnold's supporters used the party machinery against Langston, Arnold won the nomination at the district convention in Farmville. Langston promptly bolted the party and ran as an independent against Arnold and the Democratic Party nominee, Edward Carrington Venable. Langston received solid support from the district's African Americans, who formed the backbone of the Republican Party. Arnold canvassed the district tirelessly, but he received only eleven percent of the vote. Venable narrowly defeated Langston, although the Republican majority in the House of Representatives seated Langston because of widespread electoral fraud by the Democrats.

Following his defeat Arnold resumed his law practice and business interests. In 1889 he moved his peanut factory, by then named the Standard Peanut Company, to Portsmouth and then in 1892 to Norfolk. He resided in Norfolk from 1892 until the peanut company failed in 1898, after which he returned to Waverly and resumed the practice of law. Richard Watson Arnold was elected mayor of Waverly in June 1900, took office on 1 July, and was still serving when he died while on a visit to Norfolk on 27 September 1911. He was buried in Waverly.

Birth date on gravestone and in Thomas St. John Arnold, *The Arnold Family of Waverly, Virginia* (1981; por., 6); variant birth date of Feb. 1845 in Census, Sussex Co., 1900; Compiled Service Records; BVS Marriage Register, Sussex Co.; numerous Arnold letters in William Mahone Papers, Duke; Committee on Elections, *John M. Langston* v. *E. C. Venable*, 51st Cong., 1st sess., 1890, House Rept. 2462, serial 2814; Norfolk Chamber of Commerce, *Norfolk, Va.: Port and City* (1893), 108–109; obituaries in *Petersburg Daily Progress*, 27 Sept. 1911, and *Norfolk Virginian-Pilot* and *Petersburg Daily Index-Appeal*, both 28 Sept. 1911.

ALAN B. BROMBERG

ARTHUR, Charles Ralph (5 August 1917–13 October 1970), educator, was the second of three sons and second of four children of Davis Allen Arthur and Mary Esther Fitzpatrick Arthur, of Bedford County. In 1919 the family moved from Roanoke to Richmond, where Davis Arthur started an automobile service business. Ralph Arthur, as he came to be known, attended public schools and the University of Richmond, where he earned a B.S. in 1938. He went on to Duke University and in 1941 received its M.Div. After graduation he returned to Virginia, served as a trial Methodist deacon, and became an elder in 1943. On 22 January 1944 he married Mary Parker, and they had four boys. In 1947 Arthur was assigned to Mount Pleasant, a small rural charge in the Lynchburg District of the Methodist Church. He quickly developed a love for rural people and a sympathetic understanding of their needs.

Arthur's work with rural congregations and his advocacy of church outreach led to his appointment in 1948 to the Virginia Annual Conference's Town and Country Commission. He served as executive secretary and treasurer, organized the conference's first credit union, and helped launch the Methodist Rural Fellowship. When he was asked to evaluate Ferrum Junior College and the Highland region that it served, he proposed that resources be found to make the school a provider of educational services to students from middle- and lower-income families who might otherwise lack the opportunity to attend college. After Ferrum's leader unexpectedly stepped down in 1954, Arthur was named to succeed him as the college's seventh president. The appointment dramatically altered the course of his career and carried with it a distinct challenge, since the editor of the influential *Richmond Christian Advocate* had questioned whether the conference should continue to support the struggling Franklin County facility, a combined high school and junior college that it had founded in 1913.

Arthur moved quickly to terminate Ferrum's secondary school, raise $1 million to enlarge the institution's physical plant, and win accreditation from the Southern Association of Colleges and Secondary Schools. In October 1955 the board approved an ambitious but crucial million-dollar capital construction effort. The master plan called for a science and agriculture building, a gymnasium and athletic field, a new dining hall and kitchen, a men's dormitory, housing for faculty and married students, and a student center. Arthur worked vigorously to raise funds from alumni, the Virginia Annual Conference, the Woman's Missionary Society, businesses, and the local community. He also negotiated a loan from area banks to build additional residential facilities.

An extraordinary community response from Franklin County residents resulted in a new cafeteria and a new student activities facility, Franklin Hall. Private donations paid for a new stadium and helped Ferrum build an enviable athletic program with teams that competed for national titles in football and basketball and won regional distinction in baseball, tennis, and track. Federal funds made available to postsecondary institutions after 1957 were used in the construction of four new dormitory buildings, and enrollment swelled from approximately 500 when Arthur arrived on campus to more than

1,200 by 1968. The increase was made possible in part by Arthur's success in winning accreditation for the school in December 1960. The University of Richmond recognized his efforts with an honorary LL.D. in 1962.

Thanks to Ferrum's reputation for strong academic programs and steadily improving admissions standards, transfer arrangements from the two-year school were worked out with some of the state's finest colleges and universities. Moreover, during Arthur's presidency Ferrum boasted that no deserving student would be denied admission for want of financial resources. Various work-study plans reduced both operating costs to the college and tuition costs to needy students. His administration also reformed the school's admission-and-hiring practices to protect the rights of all ethnic and religious groups.

Arthur's last achievements for the school included the construction of the Vaughan Memorial Chapel and its adjoining bell tower. One of the area's commanding architectural features, this tower encompassed the burial site of Ralph Arthur, who died in office on 13 October 1970. The next year the board of trustees renamed the institution Ferrum College, and it became a four-year institution in 1976, acts that symbolized the strength and maturity that the school had attained during the sixteen years of Arthur's leadership.

Frank Benjamin Hurt, *A History of Ferrum College: An Uncommon Challenge, 1914–1974* (1977); Deroy Campbell, "History of Ferrum College" (master's thesis, Randolph-Macon College, 1951); interview with Mary Parker Arthur; obituary in *Richmond Times-Dispatch*, 14 Oct. 1970 (por.); memorial in Virginia Annual Conference of United Methodist Church, *Annual* (1971): 158–160.

DOUGLAS W. FOARD

ARTHUR, Gabriel (fl. 1673–1693), explorer, earned a place in history with his travels into unmapped areas of the southern colonies. The place and date of his birth and the names of his parents are not known. It has been conjectured that he arrived in Virginia as an indentured servant or that he bore some relation to James Arthur who, as early as 1642, lived in Nansemond County opposite the Indian Town.

On 10 April 1673 Gabriel Arthur, in the company of James Needham and eight Appomattox Indians, left Fort Henry (at what is now Petersburg) under the sponsorship of frontier entrepreneur and explorer Abraham Wood in search of a passage through the southern Appalachians to the sea that was believed to be not far distant to the south or southwest. Because Wood referred to Needham as "Mr. James Needham," to Gabriel Arthur as "my man" or "Gabriell," and to himself as Arthur's "Master," Arthur may have been indentured to Wood, who considered Arthur an intelligent and reliable observer.

Near what is today Morganton, North Carolina, the expedition encountered a party of the Tomahitan branch of the Yuchi Indians that had just crossed the mountains to confer with the Occaneechi. After the Tomahitan delegation visited Fort Henry, the combined groups set their course for a mountain passage known to the natives. Crossing the Blue Ridge at what is now Asheville, North Carolina, they passed south of the Great Smoky Mountains, eventually arriving at Tomahitan Town near the site of the modern town of Rome, Georgia. Needham left Arthur with the Tomahitan to return to Fort Henry, but Occaneechi Indians killed him on the return journey. When word of Needham's death reached the Tomahitans, several warriors sympathetic to the Occaneechi seized Arthur. Only the intervention of the Tomahitan king saved his life.

During the next year Arthur participated in four Tomahitan excursions designed "to forage, robb and spoyle other nations." In October 1673 Arthur joined a war party of fifty on an eight-day, 240-mile march to the Apalachicola River, where the Tomahitans stole weapons from a Spanish mission. In December another war party crossed northern Georgia, took its canoes down the Savannah River, and attacked a native village near Port Royal Sound, South Carolina. In the spring of 1674 Arthur, who by this time was dressed, painted, and equipped so as to be almost indistinguishable from a Tomahitan, accompanied a third war party northward along the Warriors' Path to Kentucky. He was captured during a Tomahitan attack on a Shawnee village, and only the whiteness of his skin induced his captors to release him. After making his way back to Georgia, Arthur participated in a fourth, more peaceful 325-mile canoe trip along the Coosa and Alabama Rivers, ending at Mobile Bay.

In May 1674 the Tomahitan king decided to return Arthur to his own nation. Near what is now Durham, North Carolina, several Occaneechi ambushed and dispersed the party and attempted to kill the Englishman. Escaping the trap, Arthur arrived in Fort Henry on 20 July 1674 and reported his adventures to Abraham Wood. The account of the continent's interior that Arthur gave Wood helped make Virginians aware of the spaciousness of North America. By virtue of his journeys, Arthur had acquired more personal knowledge of the southeastern portion of the continent than any other Englishman of the seventeenth century.

Arthur's whereabouts for the next decade are unknown. In September 1684 he purchased one hundred acres on the north side of the Appomattox River in Henrico County from Thomas Batte, who had participated in an exploratory expedition that Wood sponsored in 1671. Arthur apparently found himself considerably in debt, and a little more than two years later he assigned that same property to William Byrd (1652–1704), retaining an option to redeem the property within a year. At that time Arthur was identified as being of Bristol Parish in Henrico County. His personal property then consisted of nine cattle, two horses, and thirty hogs. Arthur was called on to answer indebtedness charges seven more times between 1686 and April 1693, his last-known presence in the colony. The date and place of Gabriel Arthur's death and burial are not known.

Abraham Wood to John Richards, 22 Aug. 1674, in Shaftesbury Papers, PRO 30/24/48, printed in Clarence W. Alvord and Lee Bidgood, *The First Explorations of the Trans-Allegheny Region by the Virginians, 1650–1674* (1912), 210–226; Alan Vance Briceland, *Westward From Virginia: The Exploration of the Virginia-Carolina Frontier 1650–1710* (1987), 147–170; Henrico Co. Records, Deeds and Wills (1677–1692), 290, 398; Henrico Co. Order Book (1678–1693), 159, 219, 409, 416; Henrico Co. Deeds and Wills (1688–1697), 407–408.

ALAN VANCE BRICELAND

ARTHUR, Lewis Crawford (ca. 1795–by 23 October 1866), member of the Convention of 1850–1851, was born in Bedford County, the son of Lewis Arthur and Sarah Hatcher Arthur. Surviving records disclose little about his early life. On 16 December 1817 he married Nancy R. Jones. They had three sons and four daughters. He was a successful Bedford County planter and by 1850 owned forty slaves and about two thousand acres of land, on which he raised grains, vegetables, tobacco, and livestock. He also owned land in Amherst and Franklin Counties.

Arthur took no recorded part in public life until 1840, when he became a member of the Bedford County Court and ran as the Democratic Party candidate for one of the county's two seats in the House of Delegates. Bedford's voters were overwhelmingly Whig, and Arthur was not elected. In 1850, however, he was one of four men elected to represent Bedford and Campbell Counties in the constitutional convention that met between 14 October 1850 and 1 August 1851. He did not participate actively in the floor debates and was the fourteenth member of the fifteen-member Committee on the Bill of Rights. On the principal votes on the main issues that had brought the convention into existence, Arthur voted most of the time with the reformers from the western counties. They favored an expanded suffrage, representation in the General Assembly based on the white population only, and popular election of the governor and of county court members and other local government officials.

In 1852 Arthur was elected a justice of the peace when the first court was chosen by the voters of Bedford County under the provisions of the new constitution. He declined to run for reelection in 1856. Arthur's real estate and personal property holdings had grown to more than $75,000 by 1860, but the Civil War exacted a great personal toll. One of his sons died from battlefield wounds in December 1864, and with the emancipation of Arthur's slaves and the distribution of portions of his land to his other children, his estate at the time of his death was valued at less than $1,500.

Lewis Crawford Arthur wrote a new will on 17 October 1866 and died between that date and 23 October 1866, when the Bedford County Court adopted a resolution in his memory.

Year of birth inferred from age in Census, Bedford Co., 1850; Bedford Co. Marriage Bonds; land and slave ownership compiled from Land and Personal Property Tax Returns, Bedford Co., RG 48, LVA, and Census, Bedford Co.; agricultural achievements detailed in *Lynchburg Daily Virginian*, 25 Sept., 14, 22 Oct. 1858; W. Harrison Daniel, *Bedford County, Virginia, 1840–1860: The History of An Upper Piedmont County in the Late Antebellum Era* (1985), 53–54; *Journal of 1850 Convention*, 59; Robert P. Sutton, *Revolution to Secession: Constitution Making in the Old Dominion* (1989), 134, 213; Bedford Co. Will Book, 21:138–139, 290, 366, 432, 22:204–206, 284; Bedford Co. Order Book, 35:158–159; *Lynchburg Daily Virginian*, 26 Oct. 1866.

W. HARRISON DANIEL

ARTHUR, Thomas (25 July 1749–8 September 1833), member of the Convention of 1788, was probably born in the part of Lunenburg County that in 1753 became Bedford County. He may have been one of the sons of the John Arthur whose will was proved in Bedford County in January 1793. Thomas Arthur married Sarah Dickson on 29 November 1782, but whether this was his first marriage and whether he had any children are not known.

Arthur lived between the Staunton and Blackwater Rivers in the southern part of Bedford County. He held only the lowly office of road surveyor early in the 1770s before he became a justice of the peace on 26 October 1778. With his neighbors he signed a petition to the General Assembly on 9 November 1779 that asked for the formation of a new county from parts of Henry and Bedford Counties. Although that attempt failed, Arthur's group persisted, and the legislature created the new county of Franklin in 1785. He was in the upper 10 percent of the taxpayers in the new county, and he was one of three men named to oversee the surveying of the boundary line between Franklin and Henry Counties.

Arthur was appointed one of the first justices of the peace for Franklin County. The men with whom he served were a contentious lot, and Arthur was the chief gadfly. In May 1786 he protested to the governor against the appointment of another justice, Hugh Innes, as colonel in the county militia, but the governor issued the commission nonetheless. In August 1787, just two months after he had been considered for the office of sheriff, Arthur was accused of refusing to pay his taxes and advising others to refuse, too. The Franklin County Court acquitted him, perhaps because the jurors and many of the county's citizens shared his presumed antipathy to the payment of taxes during a time of inflation and a shortage of cash. In the following year the justices of the peace successfully recommended that Arthur be appointed the county's militia colonel.

In 1787 Arthur was elected to a one-year term in the House of Delegates, and on 3 March 1788 he was elected to the convention called to consider ratification of the proposed constitution of the United States. Arthur did not take his seat in Richmond until 9 June, a full week after the other delegates had begun the debates. He did not speak during the convention. On the critical vote on 25 June 1788 he joined Patrick Henry and other antifederalists in voting for amendments to the constitution prior to ratification. When that motion was defeated, Arthur voted against ratification.

Arthur either did not seek or did not gain reelection to the House of Delegates. Early in 1791 his increasingly troubled relationship with his fellow justices in Franklin County came to a head. On 25 February 1791 the county lieutenant suspended Arthur from his duties as colonel because of accusations that he had committed forgery four times since 1788. He was also accused of perjury, lying, and knowingly receiving more money than he was entitled to for his assembly service. One of Arthur's alleged forgery victims was Thomas Prunty, a former deputy sheriff, who on 8 December 1789 swore that he went in fear of his life from Arthur. Early in January 1790 Arthur was forced to take out a bond to keep the peace, but he violated the bond by going about the county armed. Early in March 1791 the other justices refused to hold court if Arthur was present and petitioned Governor Beverley Randolph to remove him from the bench. Randolph was hesitant to interfere in local matters and took no action, but by August 1791 Arthur had ended the controversy himself by moving from Franklin County.

Arthur went west to Kentucky and was living on the Wilderness Road, in an area that had become Knox County in 1799, when he offered a saltworks for sale or rent in 1803. He probably farmed and may also have engaged in other businesses. Thomas Arthur died in Knox County, Kentucky, on 8 September 1833 and was buried in the family graveyard near Barbourville.

John S. Salmon and Emily J. Salmon, *Franklin County, Virginia, 1786–1986: A Bicentennial History* (1993), 66–68, 78–79, 81–83, 216; Bedford Co. Will Book, 2:100–101; marriage recorded in Bedford County Deed Book, 7:343; Kaminski, *Ratification*, 9:588, 10:1538–1541, 1557, 1565; *Lexington Kentucky Gazette*, 31 May 1803; Malle B. Coyle and Irene B. Gaines, *Kentucky Cemetery Records* (1972), 4:69, gives birth and death dates from gravestone.

JOHN S. SALMON

ASH, William Horace (15 May 1859–14 February 1908), educator and member of the House of Delegates, was born a slave in Loudoun County, the son of William H. Ash and Martha A. Ash. In 1880, calling himself Horace Ash, of Leesburg, he entered Hampton Institute. He had already attended a school operated by a Mrs. Martha C. Reed under the auspices of the Pennsylvania Abolition Society. He graduated from Hampton in 1882.

Ash taught for one term in Southampton County before moving to Nottoway County to teach at Ingleside Seminary at Burkeville, a school for African American girls supported by the Presbyterian Church, U.S.A. He was a successful teacher and regularly petitioned friends at Hampton for donations of reading matter and other classroom materials. At a summer institute at Farmville in 1884, Ash participated in founding the Teachers Reading Circle, the first statewide organization of African American educators, and he was elected president of the short-lived group.

By then Ash was involved in politics. Interested in the local Republican Party from the time of his arrival in Nottoway, he served as a county delegate to the state party convention in 1884. Three years later the party nominated him for the House of Delegates from the district comprising Amelia and Nottoway Counties. The Democrats offered only token opposition, but divisions within the Republican Party forced him to act cautiously, for Ash supported the party's powerful leader, William Mahone, who had alienated many other Republicans. In the senatorial district that included Amelia County, Samuel P. Bolling, of Cumberland County, ran as an independent candidate against Nathaniel M. Griggs, a Mahonite. Ash explained to Mahone that he had refrained from campaigning in Amelia in order to avoid publicizing his support for Griggs and thereby possibly losing votes. His caution proved excessive, for he carried both counties by wide margins.

In the legislature Ash voted with the Republican minority and served on the standing Committees on Propositions and Grievances and on Printing. He remained concerned with education, proposing an investigation of student complaints at Virginia Normal and Collegiate Institute (which became Virginia Normal and Industrial Institute in 1902, and is now Virginia State University), in Ettrick, near Petersburg, and introducing an unsuccessful bill concerning appointments of teachers in the public schools. He also began to study law and later identified himself as a lawyer, although he is not known to have practiced.

Meanwhile, Ash's political career came to a sudden end. In 1888 John Mercer Langston ran against Mahone's handpicked candidate for Congress. Ash warned Mahone of Langston's popularity in his district but stood by his leader. After the bitter election, another black Republican, Henry Johnson, of Amelia County, replaced him in the General Assembly. Ash returned to teaching.

On 29 May 1889 Ash married Sallie B. Miller, a native of Nottoway County and a fellow teacher. They had no children. In 1891 they moved to Leesburg in Ash's native Loudoun County and taught there, although he owned twenty acres of land in Nottoway County. They had returned to Nottoway by the beginning of 1904, when Ash tried to purchase a defunct school for young white women. He intended to turn it into a school for African American boys, modeled after Ingleside Seminary. That venture fell through, and in September 1904 Ash accepted a post at Swift Memorial Institute in Rogersville, Tennessee, where he taught nine classes ranging from Latin to beekeeping.

In 1907 Ash accepted an offer to teach agriculture and oversee the farm at the Virginia Normal and Industrial Institute in Ettrick. On

14 February 1908, after six days of illness, William Horace Ash died at the college from kidney failure. Funeral services took place at his home in Burkeville.

Feature article in *Petersburg Lancet*, 23 Aug. 1884; Hampton Institute catalogs, 1880/1881–1881/1882; Ash's correspondence with Hampton Institute, 23 Nov. 1885–1 Oct. 1907, alumnus file, Hampton; *Twenty-Two Years' Work of the Hampton Normal and Agricultural Institute* (1893), 180; Jackson, *Negro Office-Holders*, 1 (frontispiece por.); *JHD*, 1887–1888 sess., 56, 58, 103, 337; nine letters from Ash to William Mahone, 31 Oct. 1887–22 Oct. 1888, Mahone Papers, Duke; BVS Marriage Register, Nottoway Co.; obituaries in *Petersburg Daily Index-Appeal*, 15 Feb. 1908, and Virginia Normal and Industrial Institute, *V. N. & I. I. Gazette* 14 (Apr. 1908): 3.

JOHN T. KNEEBONE

ASHBURNER, Charles Edward (9 May 1870–26 October 1932), Staunton and Norfolk city manager, was born in Bombay, India, the son of Charles Edward Ashburner, a British army officer, and Annie Barber Ashburner. He had at least one brother and one sister. Ashburner studied at Cheltenham College in England and Heidelberg University in Germany, where he received training in civil engineering. In 1889 he moved to the United States and embarked on a successful engineering career, working initially for the Army Corps of Engineers on the James River and later serving as staff engineer for Richmond real estate developer Lewis Ginter, doing much of the technical work for laying out Ginter Park. Ashburner also helped construct Richmond's Jefferson Hotel. On 1 October 1896 he married Virginia native Cora Michaux Hobson, with whom he had three daughters and one son. Between 1896 and 1901 Ashburner operated his own construction business, worked for a New York building contractor, and spent two years in the West Indies engaged in harbor improvements and railroad surveys. After returning to Virginia in 1901 he supervised the maintenance of rights-of-way for the Chesapeake and Ohio Railway Company.

While Ashburner was with the Chesapeake and Ohio, the city of Staunton consulted him on a construction project, and his advice saved the municipality 80 percent on the cost of repairs to a leaky dam. When city officials decided to create the post of "general manager" for city affairs, Ashburner was a leading candidate, and in April 1908 he was appointed to the position. Other towns had already initiated similar sorts of administrative arrangements, but Staunton has long been regarded as the first city with a fully defined city manager system, and the experiment attracted national attention at the time. For more than three years Ashburner worked to upgrade Staunton's primitive infrastructure, pave streets, lay sidewalks, and improve the water supply and sewage and garbage-disposal systems, all at a low cost to the city treasury. He expressed his responsibilities in simple democratic terms: "I am hired by everybody in this town. I am working for everybody in it, rich and poor, black and white. Every citizen is a shareholder in this corporation, and every one of them is entitled to a shareholder's full privileges."

Ashburner left Staunton in July 1911 to work as a special engineer for American Railways of Philadelphia. On 1 January 1914 he became the city manager of Springfield, Ohio, where he again concentrated on upgrading the city's physical facilities. During his first year in Springfield he hosted the inaugural meeting of the City Managers' Association (later the International City Managers' Association) and served as the organization's first president.

Ashburner became Norfolk's first city manager on 1 September 1918, the effective date of the city's new charter adopting a commission-manager system of government. The wartime boom had boosted Norfolk's population from 67,000 in 1910 to 116,000 by 1920, placing a tremendous strain on public works. Ashburner embarked on a program of major expansion, developing new projects and improving existing facilities. He rebuilt the municipal water system to increase daily capacity from 7 million to 30 million gallons, laid out more streets and built the city's principal boulevards, constructed a municipal grain elevator and marine terminal, and extended municipal services to 30,000 new residents the city had obtained by annexing twenty-three square miles of Norfolk County.

In 1923 Ashburner became city manager for Stockton, California, assuming the responsibility for transforming that city into a deepwater port. The ambitious undertaking gained him some criticism and won him the nickname "cashburner." Although an attempt to reduce his salary failed, his political support eroded. Disheartened, he resigned in November 1928 and returned to Norfolk to enter the investment banking and insurance business. During his last years he was active in various business, civic, and fraternal associations, and was a member of the Freemason Street Baptist Church.

City managers during the 1910s and 1920s often possessed engineering backgrounds, and many shared Ashburner's belief that the office's primary responsibility was the construction and maintenance of a city's infrastructure. Ashburner also thought that city managers needed to be apolitical. Although active earlier in the Virginia Municipal League, of which he was president in 1909, and the City Managers' Association, he lost interest in professional organizations by the 1920s. He valued on-the-job experience and had little regard for public administration as an academic discipline. Impatient with obstructions, he attracted controversy with his decisive manner and straightforward style. As a pioneering city manager he personified the initial stage of strong individual leadership in municipal affairs that was later superseded during an era in which city management became a self-conscious profession. Charles Edward Ashburner died at Saint Vincent's Hospital in Norfolk on 26 October 1932 from a heart ailment complicated by pneumonia.

William M. E. Rachal, "Staunton Steps Out of the Mud," *Virginia Cavalcade* 1 (spring 1952): 9–11 (por.); Henry Oyen, "A City with a General Manager," *World's Work* 23 (1911): 220–228; Louis Brownlow, "The First City Manager," *City Manager Magazine* 5 (July 1923): 7–8; Leonard D. White, *The City Manager* (1927), 90–97; Ernest S. Bradford, "Manager Cities in Action: IV. The Virginia Cities," *National Municipal Review* 19 (1930): 297–299; *Stockton Record*, 20 Sept. 1928, 23 June, 1 Sept. 1933; obituary in *Norfolk Virginian-Pilot*, 26 Oct. 1932; memorial in *Virginia Municipal Review* 9 (1932): 220–221.

CARL ABBOTT

ASHBY, John (ca. 1719-by 13 May 1789), frontiersman and militia officer, was probably born near Ashby's Gap in what is now Fauquier County, one of six sons and four daughters of Rosa Ashby and Thomas Ashby, the pioneer settler for whom Ashby's Gap in the Blue Ridge Mountains was named. Ashby grew up on what was then the northwestern frontier of Virginia and may have participated in skirmishes with the Indians. At about the time of his marriage to Jean Combs, of Stafford County, on 11 May 1741, he settled on the banks of the Shenandoah River in what is now Clarke County.

Even during his life more unverified legends than established facts circulated about Ashby. He was a captain in the militia during the French and Indian War and served in the 2d Virginia Rangers. From 1752 to 1754 he commanded Fort Ashby at the confluence of the Potomac River and Patterson Creek. According to an early-nineteenth-century writer, Captain "Jack" Ashby was once almost captured by Indians but escaped by outrunning them, a fairly common legend that has also been attached to other pioneers. In the summer of 1755 Captain Ashby and his company marched westward in General Edward Braddock's ill-fated expedition. Ashby was present at Braddock's defeat and probably at his death. Another persistent legend is that Colonel George Washington selected him to carry the news to Williamsburg and that Ashby rode 210 miles from Winchester to Williamsburg in thirteen hours, riding thirteen horses in relay. The facts can no longer be ascertained, but the feat, or the legend, quickly gained currency. In an erroneous report that Ashby had been killed in Fincastle County, the *Virginia Gazette* for 2 June 1774 identified him as the "noted" officer who had carried the news of Braddock's defeat "with amazing Expedition."

Ashby was not a professional soldier and like other militia officers under Washington's command occasionally felt the sting of his commander's displeasure. On 28 December 1755 Washington wrote him concerning a charge that Ashby had illegally permitted one of his wife's relatives to sell alcohol from Ashby's private stock to his men. Washington also took the opportunity to admonish the captain about his wife, "who I am told sows sedition among the men, and is chief of every mutiny. If she is not immediately sent from the camp, or I hear any more complaints of such irregular Behaviour upon my arrival there; I shall take care to drive her out myself, and suspend *you*."

Jean Combs Ashby and John Ashby had at least three sons and three daughters before she died about 1770. On 3 November 1783 John Ashby signed a marriage contract with Catherine Huffman. They had one daughter. Ashby accumulated several thousand acres of land, most of it in the West, as a result of his military services and of timely purchases, and by the time he wrote his will in October 1788 he owned about fifty slaves. His will was proved in Prince William County Court on 13 May 1789.

Birth and death dates not known and the subject of much debate, with some writers assigning a birth date as early as 1707 and some a death date as late as 1797; the leading assessments, which also present virtually all the biographical and genealogical information, are H. C. Groome, "General Turner Ashby and His Ancestry," *Fauquier County Historical Society Bulletin* (1922): 150–154, George Harrison Sanford King, ed., "Will of Captain John Ashby," *Virginia Genealogist* 9 (1965): 147–153, and Lee Fleming Reese, ed., *The Ashby Book: Descendants of Captain Thomas Ashby of Virginia*, rev. ed. (1982), 12–35; escape story in Samuel Kercheval, *A History of the Valley of Virginia* (1833; 4th ed., 1925), 96; Washington, *Colonial Series*, 2:241–242.

William H. B. Thomas

ASHBY, Turner (23 October 1828–6 June 1862), Confederate cavalry officer, was born at Rose Bank, his family's farm in Fauquier County. He was the third of five sons and fifth of nine children of Turner Ashby and Dorothea Farrar Green Ashby, of Rappahannock County. Ashby traced his lineage to England from Thomas Ashby, who came to Virginia early in the 1700s. His grandfather John Ashby was wounded twice as a captain during the American Revolution, and his namesake father served as a colonel in the War of 1812. After his father's death in June 1834 Ashby was educated at home and at a nearby private school. In 1853 his mother sold their farm and Ashby acquired a house and a few acres at nearby Markham, where he ran a mercantile business. He named his new residence Wolf's Crag.

Angered by John Brown's raid on Harpers Ferry in 1859, Ashby raised a company of cavalry, the Mountain Rangers, and became its captain. A slight, wiry man and a superb horseman, he supported slavery but opposed secession. When Virginia left the Union in April 1861, however, he and the Mountain Rangers reported for duty at Harpers Ferry, and he was soon conducting picket and scouting operations along the upper Potomac River. On 17 July 1861 his command became part of the 7th Virginia Cavalry, with Ashby as lieutenant colonel. Just two weeks earlier his brother Richard, a captain in the regiment, died from wounds suffered during a reconnaissance mission. On the eve of the first major battle of the war, the 7th Virginia conducted screening operations for General Joseph E. Johnston's army during its July 1861 march from the Shenandoah Valley to fight at Manassas Junction (Bull Run).

In October 1861 Ashby became commander of the 7th Virginia. Two months later Thomas J. "Stonewall" Jackson took charge of Confederate forces in the valley. Jackson depended on his cavalry for more than picket and escort duty. He wanted it to penetrate Union lines and bring back information on enemy strength and movements. Ashby was an ideal light-horse commander in this kind of partisan warfare, combining the instincts of a gifted cavalryman with a bent for daring exploits. Promoted to colonel on 12 February 1862, he became the idol of the army, leading his troops more by force of personality than by military discipline, a situation made more unmanageable when Secretary of War Judah P. Benjamin accorded Ashby's command semi-independent status, allowing his ranks to swell with inspired but largely untrained recruits.

Even after Jackson's defeat at Kernstown on 23 March 1862, Union authorities remained obsessed with destroying his small army. In the drama that unfolded in May and June, Ashby played an invaluable role in the famed Shenandoah Valley campaign, in which Jackson crushed the pursuing Union commands. However, the two men had clashed earlier. Jackson thought Ashby a poor disciplinarian and attempted to reorganize his command late in April, but relented to prevent his resignation. On 23 May Ashby was promoted to brigadier general. When he was killed on 6 June while fighting a rear-guard action south of Harrisonburg, he was already a legendary figure. He was buried in the University of Virginia Cemetery in Charlottesville. On 25 October 1866 Turner Ashby was reinterred with Richard Ashby in Stonewall Cemetery in Winchester under a single gravestone inscribed "The Brothers Ashby."

Thomas A. Ashby, *Life of Turner Ashby* (1914; frontispiece por.); John R. Kerwood, "Turner Ashby: Partisan in Gray" (master's thesis, Pennsylvania State University, 1967); Compiled Service Records; Quarles, *Worthy Lives*, 4–6; Millard K. Bushong, *General Turner Ashby and Stonewall's Valley Campaign* (1980); Lenoir Chambers, *Stonewall Jackson* (1959), 1:489–490; James I. Robertson Jr., *Stonewall Jackson: The Man, The Soldier, The Legend* (1997), 235–236, 355, 361, 362, 371, 423.

JEFFRY D. WERT

ASHE, Arthur Robert (10 July 1943–6 February 1993), athlete and writer, was born in Richmond, the elder of two sons of Arthur Robert Ashe and Mattie Cordell Cunningham Ashe. When he was four, the family moved to a house at the Brook Field playground, Richmond's largest recreational facility for African Americans. Ashe's father was the playground's supervisor, and his mother worked as a waitress. Ashe was only six years old when his mother died at the age of twenty-eight from a stroke caused by undiagnosed hypertensive vascular disease. Ashe's father took primary responsibility for raising the boys and taught them to value dignity, hard work, and self-discipline. In 1955 the elder Ashe married Lorene Kimbrough, who had a son and a daughter.

About a year after his mother's death, Ashe was at the Brook Field tennis courts watching Ronald Charity, a student at nearby Virginia Union University, practice his serve. Charity offered to teach Ashe to play tennis. When Ashe displayed an innate talent for the game, Charity began coaching him in earnest. In 1953, with the endorsement of Ashe's father, Charity arranged for him to spend the summer at the Lynchburg home of Robert Walter Johnson, a physician and famed tennis coach. Johnson was a leader in the American Tennis Association, the African American counterpart of the all-white United States Lawn Tennis Association, but by early in the 1950s his students were competing successfully with whites in tournaments outside the South. Johnson drilled his charges in tennis techniques but also taught them to be unfailingly polite and to play without betraying their emotions, qualities that he considered necessary to overcome the prejudices of whites. Ashe thrived under his tutelage.

In 1955 Ashe won the ATA championship for boys under thirteen, the first of his eleven ATA titles. Gaining entrance to USLTA tournaments was often difficult, but in 1958 he entered and won the Maryland state tournament and was runner-up in the New Jersey and the national boys' championships. Highly ranked nationally among junior players, Ashe was not ranked at all in the Mid-Atlantic Region because he was not permitted to play the region's top white competitors. The regional championship in 1958 was held at the Country Club of Virginia in Richmond, and his entry was rejected, as was the case the following year at the Congressional Country Club in Washington, D.C. In 1960, when the tournament was held in Wheeling, West Virginia, Ashe was allowed to enter and became the first black to win.

Ashe attended Richmond public schools, but in 1960, after three years of high school, he accepted the offer of Richard Hudlin, a tennis coach in Saint Louis, Missouri, to move there for his senior year. In Saint Louis no color line was enforced for local tennis play, the competition was excellent, and indoor courts with fast hardwood surfaces helped Ashe develop a more aggressive game. In November 1960 he became the first African American to win the National Junior Indoor Tennis Tournament. He won his second national title in May 1961 at the National Interscholastic Tournament held at the University of Virginia and then graduated with the highest grades in his high school class. That summer Ashe won the ATA's men's singles championship and teamed with Charity to win the ATA's men's doubles title.

Ashe accepted an athletic scholarship from the University of California at Los Angeles, which had one of the country's top collegiate tennis programs. In 1963 he became the first African American named to the U.S. Davis Cup team. He played on the team through 1970 and again in 1975, 1976, and 1978. Ashe capped his senior year by winning both the singles and doubles intercollegiate championships, as UCLA went on to win the 1965 national collegiate title. When he graduated in June 1966 he was ranked as one of the top amateur players in the world.

Ashe entered the Army as a second lieutenant for a two-year tour of duty early in 1967. He worked as a systems analyst and assistant tennis coach at the U.S. Military Academy at West Point, New York, jobs that afforded him the time to compete in tournaments and Davis Cup matches. Ashe initially saw his pioneering rise in the tennis world primarily as a benefit for himself, earning him the same opportunities as white players to sign lucrative contracts for endorsements and make useful business connections. That viewpoint changed after Jefferson Paramore Rogers, a black clergyman and activist, challenged him to speak at his Church of the Redeemer in Washington. Despite army regulations against political oratory, Ashe addressed the congregation in March 1968 on the responsibility of blacks to defend the cause of justice. Afterward he felt a deep satisfaction, realizing that his talent and fame now enabled him to be heard and to act effectively. Less than a week after he won the first U.S. Open on 9 September 1968, Ashe appeared on the CBS television program *Face the Nation*. Black athletes, he told the interviewers, must champion the causes of their race.

Ashe turned professional in January 1969 after his military service ended. He played an important role in the sometimes-rocky transition to the open era of professional tennis, as the traditional amateur associations, such as the USLTA, reluctantly handed over control of the sport to promoters, agents, and players. As an officer of the Association of Tennis Professionals, he helped organize the professional players' boycott of the Wimbledon championships in 1973. As one of the world's best players, he also contributed significantly to the swift expansion of the game's popularity. Ashe won thirty-three major titles, including the 1970 Australian Open. In 1975 he was the year's top-ranked male player and won the men's singles championship at Wimbledon.

Tennis enabled Ashe to travel the world, and he pondered all that he observed and experienced. He took a special interest in Africa and traveled there both on his own and under the sponsorship of the State Department early in the 1970s. In 1970 he had applied for a visa to compete in the South African Open, a direct challenge to that nation's racial apartheid policies. When the application was rejected, he led a campaign to ban teams representing South Africa from international competition. He finally received a visa in 1973 and promptly won the men's doubles title and advanced to the men's singles final. Afterward he called for greater efforts to assist nonwhite tennis players in South Africa. A year later he started a foundation to train African players, simultaneously declaring that action by African Americans was legitimate and effective in helping to speed the transition from apartheid. In 1977 Ashe announced that he would not play in South Africa again until apartheid was abolished.

Ashe met Jeanne-Marie Moutoussamy, a professional photographer, in 1976. They married on 20 February 1977 and had one daughter, Camera Elizabeth Ashe, who was born on 21 December 1986. Ashe suffered a heart attack on 31 July 1979. He had surgery for a quadruple heart bypass in December and talked optimistically about returning to the tennis tour. Chest pains developed again during a training run, and he announced his retirement from competition on 16 April 1980. In September he was named captain of the Davis Cup team, a post that he held until 1985, the year that he was inducted into the International Tennis Hall of Fame.

Asked in 1983 to teach a college class on the history of African American athletes, Ashe discovered that no single source covered the topic. Setting out to remedy that lack, he invested his own money, time, and talent in a massive research project that resulted in an encyclopedic, three-volume compendium entitled *A Hard Road to Glory: A History of the African-American Athlete* (1988). Ashe received an Emmy award for a television documentary based on the book.

In 1981 Ashe served as national chairman of the American Heart Association. Two years later he had another heart-bypass operation, which involved a blood transfusion. In 1988 numbness in his hand and a brain infection sent him again to the hospital, where tests showed that due to the transfusion he had acquired HIV, the virus that causes AIDS. Ashe and his family kept his illness a secret, and he continued his busy pace of travel and activism.

Ashe developed closer connections with Virginia and with his hometown during the final years of his life. Despite an official Arthur Ashe Day on 4 February 1966, the prejudice that he had experienced as a youngster had estranged him from Richmond. With the passage of time, however, appreciation for the people and place that had nurtured him overcame the antipathy. Virginia Union University awarded him an honorary degree in 1976, and the Virginia Press Association named him Virginian of the Year in 1982, the same year that the city of Richmond named a new athletic center in his honor. Ashe accepted an honorary doctorate from Virginia Commonwealth University in 1989 and the next year conceived of Virginia Heroes, a program in which successful Virginians served as mentors to troubled schoolchildren.

Early in April 1992 Ashe learned that a national newspaper was planning to reveal that he had AIDS. He immediately called a press conference and announced his illness himself. Although angry at the disrespect for his privacy, Ashe used the event to educate people about the disease. He became an advocate for those suffering from AIDS and established the Arthur Ashe Foundation for the Defeat of AIDS to advance medical research about the disease.

Arthur Robert Ashe died of AIDS-related pneumonia in a hospital in New York City on 6 February 1993. Governor L. Douglas Wilder ordered state flags to fly at half-mast, and thousands of people filed past Ashe's open casket as it lay in state in the Executive Mansion in Richmond. On the day of his funeral, 10 February 1993, the International Olympic Committee posthumously awarded him the Olympic Order. His funeral took place at the Arthur Ashe, Jr., Athletic Center, and he was buried next to his mother's grave in Woodland Cemetery. The board of Virginia Heroes, Incorporated, commissioned a statue designed by sculptor Paul DiPasquale to honor Ashe in his hometown. The city council's decision to place it on Monument Avenue, hitherto confined to celebrations of eminent Confederates, was so controversial that the statue's unveiling on 10 July 1996 attracted national news coverage. In 1997 the U.S. Tennis Association named its new venue for the U.S. Open in New York the Arthur Ashe Stadium. The continued operation of the numerous organizations that he founded or inspired, such as the Arthur Ashe Institute for Urban Health, the Arthur Ashe Athletic Association, the Arthur Ashe Program in AIDS Care, and Virginia Heroes, suggests that Ashe will be remembered for the content of his character and for his service to society as well as for his athletic prowess.

Arthur Ashe with Arnold Rampersad, *Days of Grace: A Memoir* (1993); *Current Biography Yearbook* (1966): 10–12; Ashe with Clifford George Gewecke Jr., *Advantage Ashe* (1967); Ashe with Frank Deford, *Arthur Ashe: Portrait in Motion* (1973); Ashe with Neil Amdur, *Off the Court* (1981); *Sports Illustrated*, 16 Sept. 1968, 26–29; *Time*, 20 Sept. 1968, 82–83; John McPhee, *Levels of the Game* (1969); *Sports Illustrated*, 1 Mar. 1971, 62–75; *USA Today*, 11 July 1996; *Richmond Times-Dispatch*, 26 Aug. 1997; Richmond newspaper stories and portraits compiled in Brooke Taylor, ed., *Arthur Ashe, 1943–1993* (1993); obituaries in *Richmond Times-Dispatch*, 7, 10, 11 Feb. 1993, *New York Times*, 8 Feb. 1993, *Richmond Free Press*, 11–13 Feb. 1993, and *Sports Illustrated*, 15 Feb. 1993, 12–15.

JOHN T. KNEEBONE

ASHE, Victor Joseph (4 February 1915–9 March 1974), civil rights attorney, was born in Norfolk, the youngest of three boys and two girls of Alonzo Ashe and Sadie Freeman Ashe. He grew up in the Atlantic City section of Norfolk, a racially mixed working-class community located on the waterfront. His father, who packed oysters at a nearby plant, instilled a strong work ethic in his son, and while growing up Ashe held a variety of odd jobs. Raised a Catholic, he attended Saint Joseph's High School, where he was captain of the city championship football team in 1932 and won top honors in his graduating class the following year. Declining football scholarships, he accepted an academic scholarship and enrolled at Villanova College in Pennsylvania in 1933.

After graduating from Villanova in 1937 with a bachelor of science degree in education, Ashe entered the Howard University Law

School. In 1940 he received a law degree and returned to Norfolk, where he held various jobs while studying for the state bar examination. He passed the examination in 1942 and began to practice law in Norfolk in September of that year. On 9 October 1943 in Washington, D.C., he married Sarah J. Wyche, whom he had met while she was a student at Howard University. His son also became an attorney.

Ashe was exempted from the draft for physical reasons, but in January 1944 he entered the United States Navy as an apprentice seaman. Although he was an attorney, he was not given the opportunity to obtain an officer's commission but was sent instead to petty officers' school and subsequently served as an instructor at the School of Military Proficiency at the Great Lakes Naval Training Station in Chicago. Exposed to new political and social viewpoints while living in Chicago, Ashe awakened to some of the deeper contradictions in American society and returned to Norfolk after the war determined to fight at home for the fulfillment of the same democratic ideals for which American armies and navies had fought overseas.

Ashe received a medical discharge from the service on 28 June 1945. Soon after he returned to Norfolk, a group of local African American community leaders chose him to run for the city council in the June 1946 election. Ashe was the first black candidate for the Norfolk City Council in the twentieth century and the youngest of nine candidates in the hotly contested race. He campaigned intensely and received reasonably fair treatment from the local white newspapers, but he lost with a disappointing seventh-place finish. His campaign awakened the political consciousness of the African American community and featured what the *Norfolk Virginian-Pilot* described as the largest parade of African Americans in Norfolk's history.

In 1947 Ashe unsuccessfully sought the Democratic Party nomination for a seat in the House of Delegates. In June 1948 he ran again for the city council, but because he missed the filing deadline his name was left off of the ballot. Nonetheless, he waged another vigorous but unsuccessful campaign as a write-in candidate. His three campaigns attracted wide attention because he was one of the first blacks in Virginia to mount competitive campaigns for office after World War II. Ashe presented himself not as a representative of a particular group but as a candidate whose interests genuinely encompassed the entire city, and he received the support of a number of white voters. His campaigns and example energized the African American population and produced an increase in black voter registration.

Late in the 1940s Ashe became an attorney for the National Association for the Advancement of Colored People. His most important achievements were in that capacity, and his most significant case concerned school desegregation. On 10 May 1956 he filed suit in the U.S. District Court on behalf of black pupils who sought admission to previously all-white Norfolk schools. The litigation directly challenged the General Assembly's program of Massive Resistance to court-ordered public school desegregation. The assembly had established the State Pupil Placement Board to take the power to assign students to specific schools out of the hands of local school districts. On 11 January 1957 the federal district judge declared the Pupil Placement Board unconstitutional. In defiance of the state's policy but in compliance with the court's order, the city school board decided to follow the district court's order to desegregate the city's public schools.

The General Assembly had also enacted a statute that required the governor to close any public school that desegregated its student body, and in September 1958 Governor James Lindsay Almond Jr. ordered that the schools in Norfolk be closed. During the winter the governor abandoned the policy of Massive Resistance and reconciled himself to the supremacy of federal law. In February 1959 the Norfolk schools reopened, and the process of peaceful desegregation of the city's school system began. Ashe continued to represent the NAACP during the ensuing years of negotiation and litigation until Norfolk's public school system was finally desegregated. In the opinion of many of his admirers, this was Ashe's finest single achievement, and for it he received the National Bar Association's C. Francis Stradford Award.

Ashe believed that the best opportunities for fighting injustice came through the courts and the ballot box. He never again ran for political office, nor did he play so prominent a public role in the civil rights movement as many other African American leaders. His stature as an attorney and civic leader, however, led Governor Mills E. Godwin Jr. to appoint Ashe the first black member of the State Board of Welfare and Institutions in 1968. After Governor Abner Linwood Holton Jr. reappointed him in July 1972, Ashe's fellow board members elected him chairman. Ashe was also the first African American appointed to the board of directors of the Norfolk Chamber of Commerce. He sat on the board of directors of the Better Business Bureau of Norfolk and belonged to Kappa Alpha Psi fraternity, numerous other social and civic groups, and Saint Mary's Catholic Church in Norfolk.

Victor Joseph Ashe died on 9 March 1974 at Virginia Beach General Hospital following a heart seizure. He was buried in Calvary Cemetery in Norfolk.

Feature articles in *Norfolk Ledger-Dispatch*, 3 May 1946, and *Norfolk Virginian-Pilot*, 11 Feb. 1990; Victor Ashe papers in possession of sister-in-law Mabel Von Dickersohn, Virginia Beach; family history information verified by Mabel Von Dickersohn; desegregation litigation covered in detail in Norfolk and Richmond newspapers beginning with *Norfolk Virginian-Pilot*, 11 May 1956, and in brief in Jane Reif, *Crisis in Norfolk* (1960); obituaries with portraits in *Norfolk Virginian-Pilot*, 10 Mar. 1974, and *Norfolk Journal and Guide*, 16 Mar. 1974.

TOMMY L. BOGGER

ASHTON, Burditt (24 November 1747–8 March 1814), member of the Convention of 1788, was one of three children, all sons, of Charles Ashton and Sarah Butler Ashton. He was probably born at the family home in Westmoreland County. In the spring of 1761 Ashton inherited the entire estate of his namesake uncle. The property, which fell into King George County when the boundaries between Westmoreland and King George were adjusted in 1778, was probably administered by his father until Ashton came of age. Two other substantial inheritances received in 1780 and 1783 made Ashton the fourth-highest-taxed person in his district of the county, with some three dozen slaves composing most of his wealth.

Ashton's brother John Ashton signed the Westmoreland Association against the Stamp Act in 1766, and on 31 January 1775 both brothers were elected to the Westmoreland County Committee that was formed to carry out the provisions of the nonimportation association that the Continental Congress had adopted. They were reelected in November and served through the dissolution of the committee at the end of the summer of 1776. Although Burditt Ashton provided supplies for the Virginia and Continental armies during the Revolutionary War, he did not perform military service. He was commissioned a member of the King George County Court on 13 November 1784 and served nearly nine years. He also received commissions as county coroner on 23 February 1791 and as sheriff on 14 March 1794.

On 6 March 1788 Burditt Ashton and William Thornton were elected to represent King George County in the convention called to consider ratification of the proposed United States constitution. Ashton was present from the opening of the convention on 2 June through the conclusion on 27 June, but he apparently took no active part in the debates. On 25 June 1788 he voted to ratify the new plan of government.

On 19 December 1768 Ashton married Anne Washington, a daughter of Augustine Washington. They had two sons and two daughters before her death on 3 June 1777 at the age of twenty-five. On 3 December 1778 Ashton married Sarah Blair, and they had two daughters before her death on 11 November 1780, possibly from complications of childbirth. On 18 February 1783 Ashton married Mary Keene, with whom he had a son and two daughters.

A Burditt Ashton represented King George County in the House of Delegates between 2 December 1799 and 28 January 1800, and a man of that name was a county magistrate in 1803. The Burditt Ashton who had been a member of the ratification convention may have held either of those positions, or one or both may have been held by his namesake son who died in 1812 or by a nephew who died in 1826. Burditt Ashton, the former member of the Convention of 1788, died on 8 March 1814, probably in King George County.

Ashton family Bible records, LVA; "Ashton Family," *WMQ*, 1st ser., 7 (1899): 115–119, 174–178; List of County Officers, RG 13, LVA; Land and Personal Property Tax Returns, King George Co., 1782–1814, RG 48, LVA; *Revolutionary Virginia*, 2:272, 3:183–184, 4:492–493, 6:59–61, 196–197, 7:485–487; Kaminski, *Ratification*, 10:1539–1540, 1557, 1565; King George Co. Will Book, 3:137–138.

STACY GIBBONS MOORE

ASHTON, Henry (30 July 1671–3 November 1731), planter, was the only son of John Ashton and Grace Ashton, of Westmoreland County. His father, who had a total of two sons and four daughters by this and an earlier marriage, had purchased 600 acres of land in 1663 and received more than 1,300 acres in headrights the following year. He became a justice of the peace and died before 25 June 1677. Within a year Grace Ashton remarried. Henry Ashton probably grew up in the household of Charles Ashton, his elder half brother, who most likely continued his father's practice of employing a tutor for the children's education. Ashton received a bequest of 2,000 acres from William Frizer in 1677 and his mother subsequently gave him 500 acres more, making him a significant landowner in a colony and county where landownership was the basis of wealth and respectability.

In about 1698 Ashton married Elizabeth Hardidge, daughter and sole heir of William Hardidge, a wealthy planter and burgess. The marriage even more firmly established Ashton's standing among the elite group of families who owned large plantations along the Potomac River. Ashton and his wife resided on land that William Hardidge had originally acquired at Currioman Bay. They named the place Nominy Plantation after the adjacent Nomini Creek and lived in a two-story cross-shaped mansion. The couple had four daughters who reached adulthood. Elizabeth Ashton died on 25 February 1722, and Ashton subsequently married Mary Watts. They had one daughter and two sons.

As was typical for a man of his class, Ashton played a large and continuing role in local governance. He served as a vestryman for Cople Parish and in 1701 joined Charles Ashton as a justice of the peace, a post he held until his death. Both Ashtons represented Westmoreland County in the General Assembly of 1703–1705, and Henry Ashton also served in the assembly of 1715. He was the county's sheriff in 1718, a post that his half brother and his nephew Burditt Ashton had held before him, and was an officer of the county militia, rising to colonel in 1727.

Archaeological excavations of the foundations of Ashton's house and a nearby refuse pit together with his estate inventory indicate that the house's seven rooms contained furnishings appropriate for a gentleman of his station. The excavation uncovered thousands of fragments of porcelain and other fine tableware, the remains of imported clay pipes, a brick-lined wine cellar, and fifteen glass bottle seals, two of which bear the date 1686, the oldest such seals yet found in the county.

Henry Ashton died on 3 November 1731 from a cancer in his chest and was buried at Nominy Plantation. His gravestone inscription gives the dates of his birth and death, names his wives and children, and describes him as "a Good husband, a tender Father, a kind Neighbour, a most Compassionate Master, and an honest man."

Gravestone inscription in *WMQ*, 1st ser., 7 (1898): 94; Norman S. Fitzhugh, "Captain John Ashton of Westmoreland County, Virginia, and Some of His Descendants," *WMQ*, 2d ser., 14 (1934): 151–164; Westmoreland Co. Deeds, Patents, Etc. (1665–1667), 346; Vivienne Mitchell, "Glass Bottle Seals Found at Nominy Plantation," *Northern Neck of Virginia Historical Magazine* 25 (1975): 2759–2764; Virginia W. Sherman and Vivienne Mitchell, "Nominy Plantation," in *Westmoreland County, Virginia: 1653–1983*, ed. Walter Biscoe Norris Jr. (1983), 105–109; will in Westmoreland Co. Deeds and Wills, 8:159–162; estate inventory in Westmoreland Co. Records, Inventories, 1:110–112.

VIRGINIA W. SHERMAN

ASHUAQUID (fl. 1607), Arrohateck chief, was also known by the name of his tribe and is mentioned in extant records in 1607 and again about 1609. He was the head of a tribe consisting of about sixty warriors who resided in a town on the north bank of the James River about thirteen miles below the fall line, well within the territory that was part of Powhatan's original inheritance. Powhatan frequently placed a close relative, such as a son, brother, or sister, in such leadership positions, but evidence of Ashuaquid's relationship to Powhatan is lacking.

Ashuaquid was one of the first Native American leaders with whom the colonists had important dealings. On 21 May 1607 Christopher Newport set out from Jamestown with a small company of men to explore the upper reaches of the James River. Two days later they arrived at Arrohateck. Ashuaquid gave them a lavish entertainment, complete with ceremonious hospitality. When the expedition resumed its westward journey, five members of the tribe accompanied it as guides. The expedition stopped at the next village upriver, where Parahunt, one of Powhatan's sons, was the king. There the explorers were again treated with great hospitality. When the expedition returned to Ashuaquid's village on 25 May, yet another feast took place.

When the English departed Arrohateck town the second time, Navirans, Ashuaquid's young brother-in-law, accompanied them as a guide. Newport's party reached Jamestown on 27 May and found that more than 200 members of the Paspahegh tribe had attacked it the previous day, killing one man and wounding twelve others, one of them fatally. During the next few days the Indians made several small assaults on the colonists. Told of this attack by Navirans, Ashuaquid sent messengers to inform the Englishmen who their enemies were and to advise them to cut down the high weeds around the fort so that the attackers could be seen more easily. In the early months of the English colonizing effort Ashuaquid thus proved a firm, though perhaps not very important, friend.

By the autumn of 1609, perhaps due to attempts to establish a fort upriver, the Arrohatecks had become less friendly toward the English and were no longer willing to trade with them. Crowded by new English settlements and perhaps already weakened by exposure to European diseases, the Arrohateck population began to dwindle. The tribe is last mentioned in William Strachey's record of his visit to Virginia in 1609. By September 1611, when Sir Thomas Dale undertook to found the town of Henricus near the falls of the James, the Arrohateck town site had been deserted. The surviving Arrohatecks were probably assimilated into another tribe, perhaps that headed by Parahunt closer to the fall line. The personal fate of Ashuaquid is unknown. He may have fallen victim to a disease caught from, or died in a skirmish with, the Englishmen he had once welcomed to his town.

Gabriel Archer's and George Percy's accounts in Philip L. Barbour, ed., *The Jamestown Voyages Under the First Charter, 1606–1609* (1969), 1:81, 84–98, 171–172, 2:472; Smith, *Complete Works*, 1:146, 147, 173, 2:239–241; William Strachey, *The Historie of Travell into Virginia Britania (1612)*, ed. Louis B. Wright and Virginia Freund (1953), 43, 44, 64.

HELEN C. ROUNTREE

ASPLUND, John (d. 1807), Baptist minister, was born in Sweden and trained as a mercantile clerk. While in England on business in 1775, he was impressed into the British navy, but he later deserted and settled in North Carolina. There he experienced a religious conversion and was baptized about 1782 by David Welch, the Baptist minister for Ballard's Bridge Church in Chowan County. Asplund was licensed as an unordained preacher by that church and retained his membership there after he moved to Southampton County, Virginia.

In 1785 Asplund returned to Europe and then toured New England. Although not a particularly inspiring preacher, he enjoyed traveling and decided in 1790 to combine an itinerant ministry with a visitation of Baptists throughout the United States. His objective was to promote closer church cooperation by producing a register identifying the names, associations, and locations of all Baptist churches and ministers together with membership figures. Over a period of eighteen months in 1790 and 1791 Asplund covered approximately 7,000 miles, mainly on foot, and visited about 215 churches in fifteen associations. He published the results in Richmond in 1791 in *The Annual Register of the Baptist Denomination in North-America, to the First of November, 1790*. Unhappy with defects and inaccuracies in his first register, between then and September 1792 he corrected and reprinted it in two more editions and two other variant printings in Richmond and Philadelphia.

Asplund went back on the road while the first edition of his register was still in press, remaining active in Baptist affairs and participating in associational meetings in Southside Virginia. For two years between 1792 and 1794 Asplund resumed his travels, covering by his own estimate 10,000 miles, visiting about 550 churches, and meeting 700 Baptist preachers. Two additional revised and expanded editions of his register, now called *The Universal Register of the Baptist Denomination in North-America*, followed in 1794, one printed in Richmond and the other in Boston. With the assistance of Baptist leaders John Rippon in London and Isaac Backus and Morgan Edwards in America, he sought to collect and list all associational minutes and circular letters. Asplund's registers were and remain among the most important sources of information about the formation of new churches and the spread of the Baptist denomination throughout the United States late in the eighteenth century.

Meanwhile, Asplund had moved from Virginia to New England. His departure may have been related to his determined opposition to slavery. The first of his "remarks on practical religion" published in most editions of his *Register* attacked "Keeping our fellow-creatures in bondage" as "contrary to the doctrine of our Master Jesus, and to our holy profession." Asplund continued to preach and to collect data for his compilations. The final edition, *The Universal Annual Register of the Baptist Denomination in North America, for the Years 1794 and 1795*, was published in 1796 at Hanover, New Hampshire, where he had gone to improve his education at Dartmouth College.

Little is known of Asplund's later life, though he married and had one child. His plans to continue issuing annual registers and to write religious tracts failed to develop. He became embroiled in land speculation, and his Baptist brethren censured him for other unnamed faults. John Asplund's last home was on Maryland's Eastern Shore, but he died in Virginia, drowning in a canoe accident on Fishing Creek in Accomack County sometime in 1807.

Year of death in James B. Taylor, *Lives of Virginia Baptist Ministers*, 2d ed. (1836), 242–244; Charles Evans, *American Bibliography* (1903–1959), 9:214–218, 10:270; Roanoke District Association, Minutes, 12 June 1791, VBHS; Strawberry Association Minute Book, 26 May 1793, VBHS; Asplund to Isaac Backus, 2 July 1795, Backus Papers, Andover New Theological School Library, Newton Centre, Mass.

THOMAS E. BUCKLEY, S.J.

AST, William Frederick (ca. 1767–20 September 1807), entrepreneur, was probably born in Hesse-Cassel, but almost nothing is known of his early years or how he became involved in commerce. By the summer of 1787 he had emigrated from Germany to France and was acting as secretary to Thomas Barclay, consul general of the United States there. Ast opened a mercantile house in L'Orient, eventually forming a partnership with an Englishman and an American. In November 1792 he left France after a merchant neighbor who engaged in trade with England, as he did, nearly had his house burned and was himself decapitated during a riot that Ast blamed on French revolutionaries.

Ast arrived in Norfolk in January 1793 and with John Bingham formed a new mercantile partnership with stores in Norfolk, Petersburg, and Richmond. Ast moved to Richmond and became a citizen in January 1794. Richmond historian Samuel Mordecai later described Ast as "a small, shrivelled, wizen-faced man, who looked as if he was a descendant of the mother of vinegar; but although his aspect was sour, he was a man of considerable talent." Ast was an astute and careful businessman. Soon after forming his Virginia partnership, he sought fire insurance for his business from an established London insurance company, but that firm's rate was so high that Ast undertook to form his own insurance companies instead. He planned to offer fire insurance, insurance on ships, and insurance on business merchandise.

Ast initially approached Secretary of State Thomas Jefferson, with whom he had corresponded on consulate business when both men lived in France, with an offer to make the secret of his innovative insurance plan available to the public. He hoped to exchange this information for the guarantee of a modest annuity to himself and his wife, but Congress tabled the proposal. Ast then turned to Richmond attorney John Marshall, who signed and may have drafted a petition to the General Assembly in support of Ast's plan. On 22 December 1794 the assembly duly chartered the Mutual Assurance Society, against Fire on Buildings, of the State of Virginia. The directors of the company raised the required $3 million subscription during the ensuing year, and on 24 December 1795 put the company into operation with Ast in charge as its principal agent, a post he held until his death.

In 1794 only five other chartered fire insurance companies were doing business in the United States, three of them in Philadelphia, one in New York, and one in Baltimore. The germ of Ast's idea may have grown out of regulations attributed to Frederick the Great requiring that all residences be insured against fire. The Mutual Assurance Society operated on the principle of shared responsibility by all policyholders for losses suffered by any of them. They were all required to take precautions against fires, and the society welcomed the formation of fire departments in Virginia's towns. The Mutual Assurance Society gradually withdrew from insuring rural buildings, and in 1821 it canceled its remaining policies on property outside towns and concentrated exclusively on urban property, whose owners were better able than cash-poor farmers to make regular payments on their policies. With claims against its resources thereby reduced, the society enjoyed long-term financial success, and by the twentieth century it had become one of the oldest American insurance companies.

Little personal information is available about Ast's years in Richmond. Tax and insurance company records indicate that he owned two slaves, two horses, and two carriages, and that he also owned some rental property in the city. He apparently outlived his wife, whose name has not been determined, and was evidently childless. When he moved to Virginia he imported a large quantity of merchandise, but by the time of his death his estate was very modest. William Frederick Ast was only forty years old when he died suddenly in Richmond on 20 September 1807.

John B. Danforth and Herbert A. Claiborne, *Historical Sketch of the Mutual Assurance Society of Virginia* (1879), 1–3, 29, 126; Richard Love, *Founded Upon Benevolence: A Bicentennial History of the Mutual Assurance Society of Virginia* (1994), 3–12; Mutual Assurance Society Records, LVA; some Ast letters in VHS; account of John Bingham, 22 Apr. 1794, Matthew Boulton Correspondence, Birmingham Assay Office, Birmingham, Eng.; citizenship recorded in Henrico Co. Order Book, 5:680; family history information in Ruth Putney Coghill, *Carry Me Back* (1961), 17; Samuel Mordecai, *Richmond in By-Gone Days* (1856), 253–257; *Jefferson Papers*, esp. 12:371–372, 378, 573, 674, 13: 168, 14:279, 27:306–309, 359–360, 591–592; *Marshall Papers*, 2:296–297, 3:43–44, 4:137–138; estate inventory in Richmond City Hustings Court Deed Book, 5:114–115; death notice in *Richmond Virginia Argus*, 23 Sept. 1807; obituaries giving age at death in *Richmond Enquirer* and *Richmond Virginia Gazette, and General Advertiser*, both 26 Sept. 1807.

MARGARET T. PETERS

ASTON, Walter (ca. 1607–6 April 1656), merchant and planter, was the youngest of four children, all sons, of Walter Aston and Joyce Nason Aston, of Longdon, Staffordshire, England. Either Aston's father or his granduncle of the same name was a member of the Virginia Company of London by 1612, and the latter, created baron Aston of Forfar in 1627, was a patron of the poet Michael Drayton and an ambassador to Spain.

Aston settled at Causey's Care on the north bank of the James River about 1628 and by the 1640s had amassed 1,040 acres on present-day Eppes Island. His plantation was the Virginia terminus of his family's transatlantic commercial network. In London his three brothers, citizens and grocers, were importing Virginia tobacco in the 1630s and 1640s, and his granduncle Lord Aston held a royal license for its retail sale. Archaeological work at Aston's plantation has revealed a barn and dairy, a tiled-floor warehouse, a manufacturing site, trade goods, and such domestic items as brass candlesticks, gilded spurs, ceramic dolls, and special irons for pressing ruffles, the accoutrements of a comfortable provincial merchant and planter.

Little is known about Aston's first wife. Even her given name, Warbow, is uncertain. They had one daughter who was probably born early in the 1630s. After 1638 Aston married Hannah Jordan. Their two daughters and one of their two sons grew to maturity. Aston served Charles City County as a justice of the peace, lieutenant colonel of militia, and sheriff, and he was elected as a burgess to the General Assemblies of 1630 through 1633 and of 1642 through 1643. Complete membership lists do not survive for the intervening years. In 1639 the assembly appointed Aston a tobacco inspector for his neighborhood, and in 1641 it gave him and others a fourteen-year monopoly for exploration and trade to the "Unknowne land bearing west southerlye from Appomattock River." Apparently allied politically with Sir Francis Wyatt, after 1643 Aston did not serve in the General Assembly while Sir William Berkeley was governor. Except that he never sat on the governor's Council, Aston was typical of the merchant and planter elite who dominated Virginia during the second quarter of the seventeenth century.

Walter Aston died, probably at his house, on 6 April 1656. He was buried in the graveyard of old Westover Church, where his headstone bears the family arms. Events after his death subsumed his Virginia estate and his surname into the histories of other prominent Virginia families. His daughters married into the Major, Cocke, and Binns families, and his widow sold her part of Causey's Care to Edward Hill and later married him. Walter Aston's namesake son, then a minor, sold another part of the property before he died without issue on 29 January 1667, whereupon a parcel of his land called the Level went to his mother. The remaining acreage, called High Hills, passed through several hands before William Byrd (1652–1704) acquired it in February 1684.

Charles City Co. Records (1655–1665), 2, 17, 20, 22, 31, 38, 47, 59, 63, 71, 78, 111, 127; Joseph Jackson Howard and Joseph Lemuel Chester, eds., *The Visitation of London, Anno Domini 1633, 1634, and 1635* (1880), 1:29; Hening, *Statues*, 1:262, 376–377; Charles City Co. Records, 1642–1842, item 26, VHS; James Branch Cabell, *The Majors and Their Marriages* (1915), 18–28; excavation reported in *Richmond Times-Dispatch*, 23 Apr. 1984; plat of Aston property and will of namesake son in William Byrd Title Book, 270–283, VHS; gravestone inscription giving death date and age at death at Westover Church.

JON KUKLA

ASTON, William Ballarde (22 December 1817–18 December 1886), attorney and member of the Convention of 1861, was born at his father's farm on Copper Creek in Russell County, the youngest of five sons and ninth of ten children of Samuel Aston and his first wife, Sarah White Aston. His brothers all became successful merchants, but Aston studied law and qualified as an attorney in Russell County on 8 October 1839. In partnership with John Franklin McElhenney, he achieved some prominence in the civil courts and was also local agent for the Warder lands, a tract of almost 350,000 acres in the Clinch and Holston River valleys that a Philadelphia mercantile family had acquired in 1806. Aston served as commonwealth's attorney in Russell County from 6 July 1852 through the spring of 1856, when Wise County was formed. He was elected the first commonwealth's attorney for Wise County on 26 May and served for three years. On 26 May 1859 he was again elected commonwealth's attorney for Russell County, where he had continued to reside, and served through May 1874, except for a period between 1869 and 1871. Aston gained a regional notoriety in 1861 as prosecuting attorney in the murder trial of Alexander Carico.

Aston represented Russell County as a Democrat in the House of Delegates during the 1848–1849 assembly session. In February 1861 he defeated Thaddeus P. Thomas, a wealthy farmer and minister, 739 to 557 in the election to represent Russell and Wise Counties in the convention called during the secession crisis. Aston attended all three sessions and voted against secession on 4 April 1861. By the time of the second vote on 17 April, Aston had come to believe that preservation of the Union had become impossible and explained in his only important speech during the convention that he had been elected by a Unionist constituency and had hoped for a peaceful resolution of the crisis. Fearing that "war, destruction and utter ruin" would follow, he reluctantly voted for secession. During the war Aston remained in Russell County and continued to practice law while serving on several local war-related boards.

Aston had married Margaret C. Alderson, a native of Greenbrier County, on 18 August 1846. Their three children all died young. The Astons were early proponents of prohibition and signed separate petitions to the General Assembly in 1852 calling for prohibition of the manufacture and sale of alcohol. Aston was also prominent in the Methodist Episcopal Church

South. He was among the first lay delegates elected to represent the Holston Conference in the church's General Convention of 1870.

Aston was comparatively wealthy by the 1880s. He owned more than nine hundred acres of land, many cattle and sheep, and more than $11,000 in personal property, about $9,500 of which was in bonds. In 1875 a tornado destroyed Aston's house and seriously injured his wife. She remained an invalid until her death on 24 January 1885. William Ballarde Aston died on 18 December 1886 and was buried on his own property.

Biography in Charles A. Johnson, *A Narrative History of Wise County, Virginia* (1938), 144–147 (por.); H. Arthur Phillips, "A Great Forgotten Holston Layman," unpublished memorandum in archives of Holston Conference of United Methodist Church, Emory and Henry College; birth and death dates from gravestone and from family records compiled by Vera Duff Gilmer and furnished by Turner Ashby Gilmer Jr.; H. W. Bays, *A Tribute to the Memory of Mrs. Margaret C. Aston* (n.d.); court order books of Russell and Wise Cos. document law practice and service as commonwealth's attorney; prohibition petitions, 29 May 1852, 7 June 1857 [i.e., 1852], Legislative Petitions, Russell Co., RG 78, LVA; Election Records, Convention of 1861 Papers, RG 93, LVA; Reese and Gaines, *Proceedings of 1861 Convention*, 4:132–133; posthumous por. by Anne C. Fletcher in Russell County courthouse courtroom; papers relating to settlement of estate in Russell Co. Wills and List of Heirs.

DAPHNE GENTRY

ATKINS, James (18 April 1850–5 December 1923), president of Emory and Henry College, was born in Knoxville, Tennessee, one of four sons and a daughter of James Atkins, a Methodist minister, and Mary Jackson Crawford Atkins. He grew up in Riceville in McMinn County, Tennessee, and attended Riceville Academy until the outbreak of the Civil War. In 1866 his family moved to Virginia, and Atkins entered Emory and Henry College. After three years his money ran out, and he left college to teach in rural eastern Tennessee and to prepare for the ministry. After he was licensed to preach on 31 October 1870, Atkins divided his time between teaching and making rounds as a circuit minister. By the fall of 1871 he had earned enough to return to Emory and Henry. He graduated the following spring.

In the autumn of 1872 Atkins was admitted into the Holston Conference on a trial basis. He served initially as an apprentice preacher and then garnered appointments in Tennessee, North Carolina, and Virginia. On 14 September 1876, while serving at Asheville, North Carolina, he married Ella M. Branner, with whom he had two daughters and two sons. In 1879 Atkins gave up a congregation in Abingdon, Virginia, to become president of the Asheville Female College, where he acquired a reputation as an effective administrator. In September 1889 he was elected to the presidency of Emory and Henry College and took office about the beginning of 1890. He received a D.D. from Trinity College, now Duke University, at about the same time.

Atkins maintained that Emory and Henry, like other Holston Conference schools, received insufficient support from the Methodist constituency. He complained that educators touted the virtues of their own schools rather than urging the value of education in general, that pastors failed to encourage their congregations to use conference educational facilities, and that too often parents did not make education a priority or sent their children to mere finishing schools. Erratic income and a debilitating debt increased Emory and Henry's woes. Faculty salaries were raised when Atkins arrived, but the increase could not be sustained. Loans were sometimes needed to meet the payroll until, on his insistence, incomes were allowed to float based on the college's gross income. The school owed the commonwealth alone more than $62,000 on an 1843 loan. Atkins negotiated a major reduction of the debt. When the college's bank of deposit failed, Virginia again granted relief to the school.

Burdened with full-time teaching, the administration of the college, and a growing deficit, Atkins decided to leave. Reelected president in 1892, he resigned sometime before 6 June 1893, when the trustees named his successor. Atkins transferred to the new Western North Carolina Conference and returned to Asheville Female College for the next three years.

In June 1896 Atkins was elected editor of the General Conference's Sunday School Board and served until 1906, when he became a bishop. During the next seventeen years he presided over annual conferences in Asia, on the Pacific Coast, in Arkansas, and in Texas. He helped found Southern Methodist University in Dallas and regional Methodist camp and assembly grounds at Lake Junaluska, Haywood County, North Carolina, and Mount Sequoyah near Fayetteville, Arkansas. Atkins also chaired the commission through which the Missionary Centenary Campaign united both wings of American Methodism in support of domestic and foreign missions. Through this agency southern Methodists established missions in Belgium, Czechoslovakia, and Poland, with Atkins presiding over the first sessions in each of these countries. He wrote numerous tracts and monographs, including *The Kingdom in the Cradle* (1905), which examined educational policy issues.

His first wife having died on 3 August 1916, Atkins married Eva Rhodes on 7 June 1921. Despite deteriorating health, he presided over a meeting of the North Arkansas Conference in Little Rock on 2 December 1923 but suffered a stroke the following night. James Atkins died on 5 December 1923 and was buried in Waynesville, North Carolina.

W. W. Bays, "Rev. James Atkins," *Nashville Christian Advocate*, 24 Nov. 1881; James Atkins Papers, including brief diaries, UNC; Richard N. Price, *Holston Methodism: From Its Origins to the Present Time* (1903–1914), 5:255, 281, 476, 481; George J. Stevenson, *Increase in Excellence: A History of Emory and Henry College* (1963), 104, 106–109; Nolan B. Harmon, Albea Godbold, and Louise L. Queen, eds., *The Encyclopedia of World Methodism* (1974), 1:170–171 (por.), 2:1370; memorials in Western North Carolina Annual Conference of Methodist Episcopal Church South, *Minutes of Session* 35 (1924): 156–160, and *Southern Methodist Yearbook, 1924* (1925), 303–304.

GEORGE J. STEVENSON

ATKINSON, Adeline Detroit Wood (30 July 1841–11 December 1916), hotelier and businesswoman, was born Adeline Detroit Wood in Bedford County, probably the eldest of at least one son and two daughters of William Wood and Sarah Ann White Wood. On 17 September 1860, at the age of nineteen, she married thirty-two-year-old John M. Atkinson and eleven months later gave birth to the first of their three sons and three daughters. When the Civil War began John Atkinson enlisted in Company E of the 11th Virginia Infantry in Lynchburg, and the young couple settled there following his parole at Appomattox in April 1865. By the mid-1870s his income as a bricklayer was insufficient for the growing family and she began taking in boarders. By 1881 her business had become so successful that she opened the Warwick House hotel at a rented twenty-two-room building on Main Street.

The sole support of her family by the 1880s due to her husband's declining health, Atkinson decided to relocate in Richmond, where in 1884 she undertook the management of the financially troubled Saint James Hotel. She soon placed the Saint James on solid footing and in 1889 assumed proprietorship of the American Hotel, which she renamed the Lexington in 1894. Located at Twelfth and Main Streets in the heart of Richmond's financial district, the Lexington Hotel prospered, and within ten years Atkinson had saved enough money to build her own establishment. She purchased and demolished the Saint Clair Hotel, at the corner of Ninth and Grace Streets, and in its place built the Hotel Richmond, a 140-room structure. After it opened in 1904 a contemporary guidebook described it as "one of the most elegantly situated hotels in the city." Located at the western edge of Capitol Square and equipped with the latest conveniences, the Hotel Richmond ranked just below the famous Jefferson in reputation and popularity. The hotel did so well that in 1912 Atkinson doubled its capacity with a $400,000 addition, and four years later her property was estimated to be worth almost $1,000,000.

Atkinson brought her sons into the management but remained in charge of the Hotel Richmond until her health failed in the fall of 1916. Observers credited her success to the close personal attention she gave to all aspects of her business, including shopping in person at local markets for hotel supplies. She was one of Richmond's most prominent and visible businesswomen, and many community and women's organizations sought her advice and support. She declined active membership in any clubs or associations, however, and affiliated formally only with the Second Presbyterian Church. A. D. Atkinson, as she was professionally known, died in Richmond on 11 December 1916 at the age of seventy-five, following a two-month illness, and was buried in the family plot in Hollywood Cemetery.

Birth and death dates of Atkinson and husband on their gravestone; parents identified in Tyler, *Encyclopedia*, 5:886; Amherst Co. Marriage Register; business career documented in Census, Lynchburg, 1880, in Lynchburg and Richmond city directories, in feature article on Richmond businesswomen in *Richmond Times-Dispatch*, 21 July 1912, and in *Pen and Sunlight Sketches of Richmond* [ca. 1910], 70–72; Richmond City Chancery Court Will Book, 15:84–91; obituaries in *Richmond News Leader* and *Richmond Times-Dispatch* (por.), both 12 Dec. 1916.

SANDRA GIOIA TREADWAY

ATKINSON, Archibald (13 September 1792–7 January 1872), member of the House of Representatives, was born in Isle of Wight County to James Atkinson and Mary Atkinson. The father's occupation is not known, but the family's modest resources provided for only a limited primary education for young Atkinson. When he was about eighteen he secured a job copying documents for the county clerk. Through this employment Atkinson became interested in the law and in October 1812 he enrolled at the College of William and Mary. When fighting broke out during the War of 1812, he interrupted his studies to join a volunteer militia company and in June 1813 he helped repel an amphibious British assault at Craney Island near Norfolk. By the end of 1813 he was back home, where he opened a law practice.

His ambition fueled by a growing interest in politics, Atkinson ran successfully for the House of Delegates in April 1815 and was reelected the next year. In December 1828 he returned to the House of Delegates for the first of three successive terms. In 1839 he won a seat in the Senate of Virginia and served until 1843, when he was elected to the United States House of Representatives from the first congressional district, comprising the counties of Isle of Wight, Prince George, Southampton, Surry, and Sussex. During his first term he served on the Committee on Naval Affairs. He was reelected twice to Congress, serving during his second term on the Committees on Commerce and Revolutionary Pensions, and during his last term, ending in March 1849, on the Committee on Commerce.

An uncompromising conservative Democrat, Atkinson routinely baited the Whig opposition. He opposed internal improvements, tariffs, and taxes, insisting that ordinary people were the best judges of how to spend their own money. He even regarded with suspicion public expenditures on education.

At the same time Atkinson championed territorial expansion. On 7 February 1846 he defended the U.S. claim to the Oregon territory and maintained that war was not a certain or even a probable consequence of the dispute with Great Britain. In any event, he reasoned that the best way to confront danger was to "meet it fully in the face—to insist upon your smallest rights." Atkinson commended attempts by President John Tyler to annex Texas, and when the dispute over the Texas boundary led to war with Mexico in May 1846, Atkinson warmly supported both President James K. Polk and the war effort.

Atkinson outlined his beliefs passionately in his valedictory congressional speech on 1 March 1849. He warned northerners against supporting the "*hateful, detestable*, destructive" Wilmot Proviso, a provision restricting slavery in newly acquired territories that was attached to a bill seeking funds for purchasing lands from Mexico. Atkinson blasted critics of slavery who insisted that the system was evil and degraded, instead portraying bondage as a condition wherein Africans could evolve morally and intellectually. The "well-fed, well-clad, contented negro of Virginia asks not your sympathy for him," Atkinson admonished his fellow legislators. He cautioned that southerners would not submit to northern attempts to subvert their property rights, adding that such efforts forced southern states to reconsider their membership in the Union. A year earlier, on 11 April 1848, Atkinson had announced on the House floor that the contented slaves in his district would rise up against any abolitionists who went among them.

Atkinson discontinued his law practice after his congressional tenure ended, turning instead to agriculture, but he remained active in public affairs in Isle of Wight County. Since 1831 he had been a county justice, and he was periodically recommissioned in that office through July 1856. From 1852 to 1855 he served as mayor of Smithfield. He was married twice, first to Frances Day on 8 April 1815 and then, following her death, to Elizabeth Ann Chilton, on 24 April 1829. He had a daughter by his first wife and his second marriage produced at least two sons and five daughters. Archibald Atkinson died at his home in Smithfield on 7 January 1872 and was buried at the Old Brick Church (Saint Luke's Episcopal), four miles south of town.

Autobiographical letter of 2 Sept. 1858 in Charles Lanman Papers, VHS; Segar Cofer Dashiell, *Smithfield: A Pictorial History* (1977), 81–82 (por.); Register of Justices and Other County Officials, Isle of Wight Co., RG 13, LVA; *Congressional Globe*; Isle of Wight Co. Marriage and Death Registers; obituary in *Daily Richmond Enquirer*, 15 Jan. 1872.

DANIEL W. CROFTS

ATKINSON, John H. (7 January 1820–3 January 1906), manufacturer and member of the Wheeling Convention of 1861, was born in Licking County, Ohio, the eldest of three sons and one daughter of Thomas Atkinson, a farmer and brickmaker, and Malinda Adams Atkinson. His middle name may have been Henry. When he was seven his family moved to Brooke County in the northern panhandle of Virginia, where Atkinson attended a local school and also acquired some knowledge of carpentry. He later studied surveying at Grove Academy in Steubenville, Ohio.

Atkinson taught school for one year in Washington County, Pennsylvania, and on 8 November 1841 married Melissa Gilbert Haigh in the First Presbyterian Church of Pittsburgh. They had no children. He moved to Holliday's Cove in Brooke County, where he taught for five years. In 1841 he also became surveyor of Brooke County and held the office until the formation of Hancock County in 1848. Atkinson was the first clerk of both the county and circuit courts of Hancock County and served from 1848 to 1852. At the same time he became a commissioner of accounts and held that post for more than fifty years. He was also active in the temperance movement and on 7 May 1851 became a charter member of the Presbyterian Church of New Cumberland.

The development during the 1830s of the firebrick industry in the New Cumberland area attracted the attention of many enterprising men and created the basis for Atkinson's financial security. A talented and practical man of affairs, he and his brother Alexander Atkinson joined their father in a brickmaking establishment in Hancock County. Atkinson moved to New Cumberland about 1845. His father died in 1850, and in 1854 Atkinson bought out the other owners and ran the business until 1869. In 1856 he and Thomas Garlick opened a second brickyard, which Atkinson operated until 1867. That year his two brick factories were the largest in the county, with an annual production of 1.5 million bricks.

Atkinson's manufacturing interests led him into a wider political arena. The market for brick depended on the prosperity of the growing iron industry in Wheeling and Pittsburgh, but it expanded to include Louisiana sugar planters, too. The importation of English firebrick into New Orleans and the effects of English iron imports made domestic tariff policies of paramount interest to Atkinson. He also held strong opinions against slavery. In 1854 he attended a convention of the Free-Soil Party, and during the following years the emerging Republican Party attracted him because it advocated a protective tariff and opposed the extension of slavery into the western territories. In August 1856 Atkinson presided over the first state convention of the Republican Party of Virginia, which met in Wheeling. He was also a delegate to the 1860 state Republican Party convention in Wheeling.

Following the secession of Virginia in the spring of 1861, a majority in the western counties acted to create the new state of West Virginia. Atkinson participated in the movement from the beginning. He was part of a large contingent from Hancock County at the First Wheeling Convention on 13 May 1861, and he has been credited with suggesting that the convention call for a full meeting of duly elected delegates from all the western counties in June 1861. Atkinson represented Hancock County in all the sessions of the Second Wheeling Convention that led to the constitutional organization of the new state. He represented the first senatorial district in the Legislature of West Virginia from 1863 to 1869 and was chairman of the Committee on Education that drafted the first free school laws for the new state. His name was mentioned at least once as a possible candidate for the United States Senate.

After his term in the West Virginia Senate was over and he had sold his brickmaking business, Atkinson made a radical career change by serving briefly as a captain of the Mississippi River steamboat *Great Republic* running between Saint Louis and New Orleans. He soon returned to Hancock County and was admitted to the bar. By the time he attended the West Virginia Constitutional Convention of 1872 as one of only twelve Republicans among seventy-eight members, Atkinson was a practicing attorney. He remained a prominent citizen of the little town of New Cumberland for the rest of his life. John H. Atkinson died at his home on 3 January 1906 and was probably buried in New Cumberland Cemetery.

Biographies in *History of the Upper Ohio Valley* (1890), 1:645–646, which gives birth date, and in George W. Atkinson and Alvaro F. Gibbens, *Prominent Men of West Virginia* (1890), 378–381 (por.); undated clippings from *New Cumberland Independent* in possession of Preston Evans of New Cumberland; Atkinson wrote "The Fire-Brick Business of Hancock County," in *History of the Pan-Handle*, ed. J. H. Newton (1879), 422–424; Hancock Co. Will Book, B:192–193; obituary, with incorrect birth date, in *Wheeling Register*, 5 Jan. 1906.

JOHN E. STEALEY III

ATKINSON, John Mayo Pleasants (10 January 1817–28 August 1883), president of Hampden-Sydney College, was the fifth of six sons and tenth of eleven children of Robert Atkinson and Mary Tabb Mayo Atkinson, of Mansfield, the family estate in Dinwiddie County. Both parents died before he was seven years old. Thereafter kinfolk, including his uncle Thomas Atkinson and his much-older eldest brother, William Mayo Atkinson, then a lawyer practicing in Petersburg, looked after the youngest children.

John Atkinson, like his brothers Thomas Atkinson and Joseph Mayo Atkinson, attended Hampden-Sydney College, and the trio followed into the ministry William Mayo Atkinson, who gave up his legal career and became a clergyman in 1833. John Atkinson graduated in 1835 and spent the following three years at the Union Theological Seminary (then located at Hampden-Sydney). Licensed to preach in 1838, he then attended Princeton Theological Seminary in New Jersey for two years of further study.

Atkinson returned to Virginia in 1840, preached at his brother William Mayo Atkinson's church in Winchester, and served as a supply pastor at Lebanon Church in Albemarle County, which was part of the West Hanover Presbytery. On 5 May 1841 the East Hanover Presbytery ordained him an evangelist, and he went to the Republic of Texas. There Atkinson established the first Presbyterian church in Houston, but ill health caused him to return to Virginia. In 1843 he became pastor of the church at Warrenton, and on 15 September 1844 his brother William Mayo Atkinson preached the sermon at his formal installation. In 1850 Atkinson moved to the Bridge Street Presbyterian Church in Georgetown, District of Columbia, and served there for seven years.

On 1 May 1857 Atkinson was inaugurated as president of Hampden-Sydney College. He was not the first choice to follow Lewis Warner Green as president, although he was an alumnus and his eldest brother had served on the board of trustees. Albert Lewis Holladay, the board's first choice, died before he could take office and the board's next selection, Moses Drury Hoge, declined. Atkinson's nomination finally came after four ballots. Nonetheless, Atkinson served the school for twenty-six years, longer than any of his predecessors. In 1857 he also received an honorary D.D. from Washington College in Lexington.

Despite creation of a scholarship fund and an increase in the number of students during Green's administration, the college's actual income remained paltry. Unsuccessful efforts to obtain aid from the state and the Presbyterian Church occupied Atkinson's attention at first, but soon the Civil War created larger problems.

In March 1861 Atkinson signed a Prince Edward County petition favoring secession. He then organized and became captain of the Hampden-Sidney Boys, a volunteer unit that became Company G of the 20th Regiment Virginia Infantry. With the rest of the regiment Atkinson and his troops marched to Randolph County, where they suffered defeat at Rich Mountain in July 1861, and he was one of more than 600 Confederates captured. On 16 July the prisoners were paroled after agreeing not to bear arms against the United States again. The parolees were exchanged for captured Union troops in 1862, thus rescinding the conditions of their parole, but Atkinson had resigned from the army and had collected his back pay on 11 September 1861.

No one graduated from Hampden-Sydney during the war. When the few students who were there came of age, they departed for military service. Atkinson finally petitioned the secretary of war for an exemption from immediate service for those students who turned seventeen in the midst of a school session, but he apparently received no response.

From the Civil War until after Atkinson's presidency ended, the number of students never returned to the levels of the 1850s. The college regularly commissioned agents to raise funds for the school. As late as 1868 it had to secure loans to ensure payment of the salaries of faculty members. Finally, in 1875 the board appointed Atkinson himself general agent to increase the endowment. His successor as president credited him with adding some $45,000 to the endowment, but the college remained impoverished through his tenure.

Nonetheless, Atkinson did manage to expand the curriculum and even added a sixth faculty member, an English professor. Hampden-Sydney College offered a traditional curriculum of Greek, Latin, mathematics, physical science, moral philosophy, and political economy, with the last two courses taught by Atkinson. Elective courses in French, German, and civil engineering, for which students paid additional tuition, were added early in the 1870s. The compulsory curriculum was expanded in 1882, with new courses in English literature, rhetoric, history, and Biblical studies. In addition the college reinstituted the master of arts degree for those who continued their studies beyond the undergraduate level.

Former students and colleagues agreed that Atkinson was a man of deep faith and the utmost integrity. Several suggested, however, that as a speaker he lacked talent and as a teacher he depended too much on his textbooks. Atkinson certainly had no fear of controversy. Early in 1867 he argued in the *Central Presbyterian* that blacks should be granted full rights as members of the Presbyterian Church. Nonetheless, he wrote little and won no reputation as a pulpit exhorter. Instead, he gave his talents and energies to Hampden-Sydney College, guiding it safely through the Civil War and the hard years that followed. No other president surpassed Atkinson's overall contribution to the school.

In 1873, pleading ill health, Atkinson offered to step down as president of Hampden-Sydney while remaining a professor, if his fellow clergyman Richard McIlwaine would agree to replace him. McIlwaine could not do so then but became his successor when Atkinson resigned effective June 1883 because of ill health.

Atkinson married three times, first on 10 May 1843 to Elizabeth Carr Harrison, who died on 27 April 1847, shortly after giving birth to a son who died young. He wed Mary Briscoe Baldwin on 1 July 1852, and they had one son and four daughters, of whom only two daughters lived to maturity. Mary Atkinson died on 13 May 1867, and on 17 June 1869 he married Frances Peyton Stuart, the daughter of Alexander Hugh Holmes Stuart, of Staunton. They had no children, and she died on 5 January 1875. After suffering for several years from tuberculosis, John Mayo Pleasants Atkinson died on 28 August 1883 and was buried next to his second wife in the Hampden-Sydney College cemetery.

William M. Thornton, *John Mayo Pleasants Atkinson, D.D.: A Memorial Address* (1900); Alfred Nevin, ed., *Encyclopedia of the Presbyterian Church in the United States of America* (1884), 42–43; French Biographies; Henry C. Lay Jr., comp., Atkinson family history, 1901 typescript of 1883 MS, 33–34, Genealogical Notes, LVA; Compiled Service Records; John Luster Brinkley, *On This Hill: A Narrative History of Hampden-Sydney College, 1774–1994* (1994; por., 260); Richard McIlwaine, *Memories of Three Score Years and Ten* (1908), 336–338 (por.); *NCAB*, 2:26; William H. Whiting Jr., *The Professors at Hampden-Sydney College, 1877–1880: The Recollections of One of Their Students* [ca. 1934], 7–14; Quarles, *Worthy Lives*, 6–8; Alfred J. Morrison, ed., *The College of Hampden-Sidney: Calendar of Board Minutes 1776–1876* (1912); annual *Catalogue of the Officers and Students of Hampden-Sidney College*, 1871–1883.

JOHN T. KNEEBONE

ATKINSON, Roger (bap. 25 June 1725–by 21 July 1800), merchant and land speculator, was christened in the parish of Holy Trinity, Whitehaven, England, on 25 June 1725, the son of Roger Atkinson and Jane Benson Atkinson. He had at least two brothers and two sisters and at least one half sister. By 19 December 1746 he was residing in Virginia. On 21 April 1753 he married Ann Pleasants, daughter of John Pleasants, one of Virginia's leading Quaker merchants. Atkinson was an Anglican, and the marriage was performed by a minister of that faith. Ann Pleasants Atkinson was not reconciled with the Society of Friends until June 1755. Atkinson later served on the vestry of Bristol Parish, but the Weyanoke Monthly Meeting duly recorded the births of his three daughters and four sons in its register.

Atkinson became one of the most prominent and wealthy merchants in Virginia. He resided initially in Petersburg, which he served as a trustee from 1752 until 1762, but he also acquired a plantation called Mansfield in Dinwiddie County where he lived in his later years. Unlike many of his contemporaries, Atkinson was an independent operative in the tobacco trade and not a Virginia agent for a specific British firm. He traded heavily with the Whitehaven mercantile houses of Dixon and Littledale, John Ponsonby, and Samuel Martin, but he also did business with Farrell and Jones, of Bristol, and with John Backhouse and Dobson, Daltera, and Walker, of Liverpool. Atkinson shifted the bulk of his business to London-based firms during the 1760s, first to John Lidderdale and Company and after 1766 to Lyonel and Samuel Lyde and Company. Atkinson frequently dealt with Richard Hanson, of London and Petersburg, who may have served as his link to the London house of Gale and Fearon.

Atkinson operated on a very large scale, importing and retailing merchandise in Virginia and exporting tobacco. With his earnings he speculated in land in Virginia and North Carolina. By 1772 he estimated that his holdings in land and slaves in Virginia alone were worth £42,000. Like many other merchants and land speculators, Atkinson appeared to be wealthier than he was and sometimes had difficulty meeting large obligations if he could not speedily convert land to cash or collect from his own creditors. When the death of Mathias Gale in London led to a call for payment of £3,500 on trading balances due in 1772, Atkinson had to borrow £1,500 from his brother-in-law, Philadelphia merchant Samuel Pleasants. Unable to meet all of his obligations, Atkinson's debt to various London merchants probably totaled as much as £10,000 when the American Revolution broke out. His support for the American cause before and during the war should not be simplistically linked to the burden of his debts, but he did sign associations and participate in trade embargoes early in the 1770s, and he took full advantage of wartime and postwar Virginia statutes to try to keep his creditors at arm's length and pay off his debts in inflated currency.

After the Revolution Atkinson disposed of much of his land and had large tracts transferred to the ownership of his three adult sons. In so doing he obtained cash to buy land and pay debts and shielded part of his property from creditors. Atkinson wrote and dated his will on 16 November 1782, but he continued actively to manage his complicated affairs for another ten years or more. Sometime during the 1790s, however, his mental faculties began to deteriorate, and trustees evidently transacted his business for him after the middle of the decade. The date of Roger Atkinson's death is not known. He was certainly alive in December 1798, and probably died at Mansfield shortly before his will was proved in Dinwiddie County Court on 21 July 1800.

Christening recorded in register of Holy Trinity Parish, Whitehaven, Eng.; earliest record of Virginia residence in Henrico Co. Deed Book (1744–1748), 306; marriage date in Henry C. Lay Jr., comp., Atkinson family history, 1901 typescript of 1883 MS, 1–2, Genealogical Notes, LVA; wife's reconciliation with Quakers recorded in Record Book, Weyanoke Monthly Meeting, LVA, with births of children recorded in the meetings's Register of Births and Deaths, LVA; Roger Atkinson letter book, UVA, extracted in Alfred J. Morrison, ed., "Letters of Roger Atkinson, 1769–1776," *VMHB* 15 (1908): 345–359; business affairs documented in files on debts owed to British merchants, especially Richard Hanson, PRO T 79/17 (which contains a memorandum on Atkinson's "state of derangement of mind" and a copy of his will), Mathias Gale's estate, PRO T 79/21, Benson Fearon, PRO T 79/26, and Samuel Lyde, PRO T 79/31; *Revolutionary Virginia*, 1:79–84; Virginia land transactions documented in deed books of Brunswick, Chesterfield, Halifax, Lunenburg, Mecklenburg, and Pittsylvania

Counties, and in Virginia Land Office records, RG 4, LVA; case file of *Richard Hanson* v. *Atkinson's Executors et al.*, 1804, Circuit Court Ended Cases (unrestored), Box 63.

PETER V. BERGSTROM

ATKINSON, Thomas Pleasants (17 March 1797–30 August 1874), physician, was born in Chesterfield County, the second of four sons and sixth of twelve children of Roger Atkinson and Agnes Poythress Atkinson. Atkinson's grandfather Roger Atkinson emigrated from England about 1746, married Ann Pleasants, patented large tracts of land in Virginia and North Carolina, and built Mansfield, the family estate five miles west of Petersburg. Thomas Atkinson's parents lived at a house called Olive Hill in Chesterfield County. An influential clan, the Atkinsons married into the leading families of Virginia and during the 1800s became lawyers, clergymen, planters, journalists, and politicians.

Atkinson studied medicine at the University of Pennsylvania, where he wrote a thesis on hepatitis and received an M.D. in 1817. On 27 January 1820 he married Mary Harrison Baird, the daughter of William Baird, of Castleton, an estate in Person County, North Carolina. Of their two sons and two daughters, only one daughter lived to adulthood. The couple made their home in Halifax County, where Atkinson's father owned property on the Hyco and Dan Rivers.

Although active in the medical profession throughout his life, Atkinson soon branched out into politics and business. He represented Halifax County in the House of Delegates from 1827 until 1830 and Halifax and Mecklenburg Counties in the Senate of Virginia from 1832 until 1834. From 1827 to 1828 and again from 1832 to 1834 he served on the board of Union Theological Seminary at Hampden-Sydney College. The Atkinsons were intimately connected with the history of the school, with other family members also serving on the seminary board and cousin John Mayo Pleasants Atkinson becoming president of the college in 1857.

Early in the 1830s Atkinson moved to Danville as president of a manufacturing firm, but the state legislature's insistence on retaining the power to revoke the company's charter at will caused the dissolution of the business. He then became president of the Danville branch of the Bank of Virginia. He also served one-year terms as Danville's mayor in 1838–1839, 1851–1852, and 1861–1862, promoting internal improvements including a plank road to Wythe County. Atkinson acquired the *Danville Reporter* in 1840 and published it until 1846, with E. A. Howard joining him in 1843. The newspaper eventually became the *Danville Register*. Early in the 1840s Atkinson joined the Roman Eagle Lodge of Masons in Danville and served as senior warden from 1848 to 1851.

In 1852 Atkinson won offices in two statewide medical organizations when he was elected president of the General Convention of the Physicians of Virginia and vice president at the annual meeting of the Medical Society of Virginia. In the same year he helped the Pittsylvania Medical Society draft a constitution, bylaws, and code of ethics.

Atkinson was elected president of the Medical Society of Virginia in 1853 and immediately urged the organization to begin publishing its own medical journal. In accordance with his proposal the society purchased the *Stethoscope and Virginia Medical Gazette* in 1854 and shortened its name to *Stethoscope*. Atkinson became an editor and contributed an article of advice for beginning doctors. He represented the society as a delegate to the American Medical Association in 1853 and 1854, having already served the Pittsylvania Medical Society in this capacity in 1852.

In 1871 Atkinson was unanimously elected an honorary fellow of the Medical Society of Virginia. At this meeting he chaired a committee that recommended the establishment of a state board of health and drafted a legislative bill setting out rules and regulations for such a new state agency. The attempt failed.

Atkinson was active in the First Presbyterian Church of Danville, of which he became a ruling elder in 1866. He also served as delegate to the synod of the Presbyterian Church held in Fredericksburg in 1870. About this time, however, Atkinson began to suffer financial hardships, and from 1870 until after his death his wife was obliged to appeal to her brother Benjamin Baird for assistance. When Atkinson's health declined, the couple moved to Amelia

County to live with their daughter Agnes Poythress Atkinson Jones and her second husband, Benjamin M. Jones. Despite his illness, early in the 1870s Atkinson completed two articles comparing the anatomy, physiology, and pathology of whites and blacks for the Medical Society of Virginia's annual meetings.

Thomas Pleasants Atkinson was preparing historical sketches of men of medicine in Virginia and North Carolina when he died of apoplexy on 30 August 1874 while at Buffalo Springs in Mecklenburg County, where he had gone to try to restore his failing health. He was buried in Danville. Years later his Masonic lodge placed a headstone on his grave in Green Hill Cemetery in Danville.

Henry C. Lay Jr., comp., Atkinson family history, 1901 typescript of 1883 MS, 8–10, Genealogical Notes, LVA; graduation record and undated alumni questionnaire, University of Pennsylvania Archives, Philadelphia; activity in medical organizations documented in *Stethoscope*, vols. 2–5 (1852–1855), esp. 3 (1853): 285–290; 4 (1854): 306–314; 5 (1855): frontispiece to Apr. issue (por.); Thomas P. Atkinson, "Practical Suggestions to Young Physicians," *Stethoscope* 4 (1854): 211–218, and "Report on the Anatomical, Physiological and Pathological Differences Between the White and the Black Races, and on the Modifications of the Treatment of the Diseases of the Latter Rendered Necessary Thereby" and "Supplemental Report," in Medical Society of Virginia, *Transactions of the Annual Session* 3 (1873): 105–114 and 4 (1874): 65–71; Wyndham B. Blanton, *Medicine in Virginia in the Nineteenth Century* (1933); obituaries in *Richmond Dispatch* and *Richmond Whig*, both 1 Sept. 1874, *Petersburg Index and Appeal*, 2 Sept. 1874, and *Virginia Medical Monthly* 1 (1874): 449–451.

CAROLYN SPARKS WHITTENBURG

ATKINSON, William Mayo (22 April 1796–24 February 1849), Presbyterian minister, was born in Chesterfield County, the eldest of six sons and five daughters of Robert Atkinson and Mary Tabb Mayo Atkinson, and one of four brothers who became clergymen. He spent his youth at Mansfield, his parents' estate in Dinwiddie County. At sixteen Atkinson entered the junior class at the College of New Jersey (now Princeton University) and graduated in 1814. Of Quaker descent on his father's side but baptized in the Episcopal Church, Atkinson held strong religious feelings from an early age. A college classmate recalled that for a time he slept on the rounded top of a trunk as a penance. He also introduced works on religion into the library of his college literary club, the American Whig Society.

On his return to Virginia, Atkinson studied law under David Robertson in Petersburg and, after admission to the bar, established a practice in that city. On 10 July 1821 he married Rebecca Bassett Marsden, of Norfolk. One of their four sons and five of their eight daughters survived him. On 3 May 1821 Atkinson's father died, followed by his mother in March 1823. With his uncle Thomas Atkinson he looked after his younger siblings.

During a religious revival in the summer of 1822, Atkinson joined the Tabb Street Presbyterian Church and was elected an elder two years later. His combination of legal skill, courtesy, and piety soon made him one of the leading Presbyterian laymen in Virginia. In 1824 Hampden-Sydney College awarded him an honorary A.M. He served on the board of trustees of Union Theological Seminary from 1827 to 1829 and from 1840 to 1842 and on the board of trustees of the adjacent Hampden-Sydney College from 1830 until 1847.

The death of two of Atkinson's children within two weeks in June and July 1832 resolved his decade-long struggle to determine his proper calling: he closed his law practice and prepared for the ministry. On 23 April 1833 Atkinson was appointed general agent of the Bible Society of Virginia, a branch of the American Bible Society, which distributed Bibles and religious tracts to the unchurched. Although dominated by Presbyterians, the society included representatives from the other major Protestant denominations in Virginia, and Atkinson proved an excellent choice as agent. Widely known through his law practice, church activities, and family connections, he also expressed an evangelical devotion to spreading the Christian message without the doctrinal narrowness of a sectarian. He remained close to his younger brother Thomas Atkinson, later the Episcopal bishop of North Carolina, despite the latter's decision not to follow him into the Presbyterian Church. The East Hanover Presbytery, of which Atkinson was a ruling elder, recognized the importance of his new duties on 17 June 1833 by licensing him to preach.

Atkinson left his family in Petersburg and traveled throughout Virginia and into adjoining states, organizing Bible societies and women's auxiliaries, collecting contributions, and speaking at any church that would have him. The East Hanover Presbytery ordained him as a minister on 26 April 1834, but he continued to serve the Bible Society. Late in the summer of 1835 Atkinson was one of several prominent Virginia Presbyterian clergymen suspected of harboring abolitionist sentiments. From Lunenburg County he responded with a letter that the *Southern Religious Telegraph* reprinted on 11 September 1835 under the supportive headline, "Rev. Atkinson An Abolitionist?!!" Atkinson explained that he and his siblings owned slaves. He regarded slavery as "a great evil" that held back Virginia's progress, but he considered the abolitionists' remedy "a still greater" one. Atkinson seemed especially concerned that the charges might interfere with his work for the Bible Society.

Slavery was only one of a complex set of issues—also including matters of theology, church governance, relations with other denominations, and ecclesiastical control over voluntary societies—that divided Presbyterians into what became known as the "Old School" and "New School" factions and led in 1837–1838 to schism. Like most Virginia clergymen, Atkinson tried to maintain a neutral position, although he was closer to the more conservative Old School in his own views. As moderator of the Synod of Virginia in 1838, Atkinson preached the opening sermon at the annual meeting on 4 October from the text: "Let your moderation be known unto all men" (Philippians 4:5).

Following the meeting Atkinson took up his new duties as pastor of the Presbyterian church in Winchester. He had resigned as general agent of the Bible Society earlier that year, no doubt tired of constant travel and anxious to spend more time with his family. Formally installed as pastor on 2 February 1839, Atkinson soon faced schism in his own church. The Winchester Presbytery met in April, and Atkinson voted with the scant majority that approved a resolution endorsing Old School doctrines. The ministers and elders in the minority then withdrew from the Presbytery. On 17 June the elders and thirty-six members of Atkinson's congregation informed him of their decision to separate. He met with the remaining members, emphasized that the separation was not by his choice or acts, and counseled tolerance toward those of different opinions. Contemporaries credited him with easing a potentially divisive situation and ultimately limiting the effects of the schism in his own presbytery. In 1843 he received an honorary D.D. from Jefferson College in Canonsburg, Pennsylvania.

Atkinson preferred to preach without a written text, although when he gave his younger brother's installation sermon he did arrange for its publication as *A Sermon Delivered at the Installation of the Rev. John M. P. Atkinson as Pastor of the Church at Warrenton, Fauquier County, September 15, 1844* (1844). He spoke with a pronounced lisp, which contemporaries said actually drew attention to his words.

Atkinson's first wife died on 11 August 1844. On 6 January 1846 he married Elizabeth J. White, of Winchester, and they had one daughter and a son, William Mayo Atkinson, who later became a lawyer and mayor of Winchester.

In the spring of 1846 Atkinson resigned his pastorate to become a traveling agent in the southern states for the Presbyterian Board of Education. He apparently felt that he could be of greater usefulness in this capacity and that his church would be better off with a minister unconnected to the schism of 1839. Once again Atkinson traveled from church to church to collect funds, this time for the education of ministers. In 1848 he began to suffer from chronic respiratory ailments, and rest failed to restore his health. William Mayo Atkinson died on 24 February 1849 in Winchester and was buried in Mount Hebron Cemetery in that city.

Foote, *Sketches of Virginia*, 2:552–556; Sprague, *American Pulpit*, 4:777–782; Henry C. Lay Jr., comp., Atkinson family history, 1901 typescript of 1883 MS, 17–19, Genealogical Notes, LVA; J. E. Norris, ed., *History of the Lower Shenandoah Valley* (1890), 559–565; Quarles, *Worthy Lives*, 7–8; religious activities documented in *Southern Religious Telegraph*, 1833–1835, and *Watchman of the South*, 1838–1839; Ernest Trice Thompson, *Presbyterians in the South* (1963–1973), 1:344, 381; Robert Bell Woodworth, *A History of the Presbyterian Church in Winchester, Virginia,*

1780–1949 (1950), 34–37 (por.), 88, 112–113; memorial in *Minutes of the Synod of Virginia at Their Recent Sessions in Petersburg, October 1849* (1850), 14.

JOHN T. KNEEBONE

ATWELL, Joseph Sandiford (1 July 1831–8 October 1881), Episcopal clergyman, was born in Barbados. After completing his education at Codrington College, an Anglican school on that island, he moved to the United States in 1863 and attended Divinity Hall, forerunner of the Philadelphia Divinity School, from which he graduated in 1866. He also raised funds to help residents of Barbados immigrate to Liberia.

The emancipation of four million people from slavery drew Atwell to the southern states to participate in the Episcopal Church's efforts to evangelize the freedpeople. The church's American Missionary Society sent him first to Louisville, Kentucky, to serve a newly organized church and school for African Americans. While there, he met and married Cordelia A. Jennings, a graduate of the Institute for Colored Youth in Philadelphia and one of the school's teachers. They had three sons. Bishop Benjamin Smith ordained Atwell as the first black deacon in the Diocese of Kentucky and in 1867 received Atwell's parish of Saint Mark's as the first black Episcopal congregation in the state.

In 1868 the Diocese of Virginia persuaded Atwell to move to Petersburg to serve as minister of Saint Stephen's Church. On 7 May 1869 Bishop Coadjutor Francis Whittle ordained him to the priesthood, making Atwell the first black priest in the diocese. Atwell's parish, though dedicated in 1868, operated under a diocesan Committee on Colored Congregations. Despite this administrative restriction, Atwell helped the church grow toward self-sufficiency, and he raised funds to improve the interior of the wooden structure in which the members worshiped. His ministry was successful. In 1869 he baptized thirty-six people, presented twelve for confirmation, and enrolled more than one hundred students in the church school. He also served in 1870 as pastor of Saint Philip's Episcopal Church in Richmond, where he conducted services twice a month. Atwell actively participated in diocesan meetings and, according to one contemporary, "was treated precisely like all of the other clergy," but he continued to be dissatisfied with the subordinate status of his Petersburg parish, which remained subject to a special diocesan committee.

In part as a consequence of his disappointment at this ongoing snub to his parish, Atwell left Virginia in 1873 to accept the pastorate of Saint Stephen's Church in Savannah, Georgia, a parish established in 1856. He won wide recognition from his contemporaries for bringing some of the first black Episcopal churches in the South from infancy to maturity and for pioneering in the full acceptance of black clergymen in the southern Episcopal Church. In 1875 he moved to Saint Philip's Church in New York City, one of the oldest African American Episcopal congregations in the nation. Joseph Sandiford Atwell served that church until his death from typhoid fever at his home in New York on 8 October 1881.

George F. Bragg, *The Story of Old St. Stephen's, Petersburg, Va.* [1906], 31–40 (por.); Monroe N. Work, comp., *Negro Year Book and Annual Encyclopedia of the Negro* (1912–1913), 83–84; Bragg, *History of the Afro-American Group of the Episcopal Church* (1922), 87–88; G. Maclaren Brydon, *The Episcopal Church Among the Negroes of Virginia* (1937), 9–10; *American Church Missionary Register* 4 (1867): 52–53, 133–134; 5 (1868): 70–71, 233–235; 6 (1869): 114, 282–283; Episcopal Diocese of Kentucky, *Journal of the Proceedings of the Annual Convention* 39 (1867): 23; Episcopal Diocese of Virginia, *Journal of the Annual Council* 74 (1869): 28; vestry book of Saint Philip's Parish, Richmond, LVA photocopy; obituaries in *New York Times*, 10 Oct. 1881, *Alexandria People's Advocate*, 15 Oct. 1881, and *Protestant Episcopal Almanac and Parochial List* (1882): 181.

DENNIS C. DICKERSON

AUGUST, Thomas Pearson (October 1821–31 July 1869), attorney, was born in Fredericksburg, the fourth of five sons and fifth of six children of Philip August and Catherine Pearson August. His French-born father moved to Fredericksburg from Guadeloupe in 1812 and established himself as a merchant. The family moved to Richmond in 1827, where August's father engaged in the mercantile trade with varying degrees of success for the next forty years.

Tom August, as he was usually known, worked as a clerk in a Richmond store while he educated himself. He studied law with Richmond attorney James Lyons and qualified for the bar in 1842. His legal career was interrupted briefly by service as a volunteer in the Richmond Grays during the Mexican War. He became regimental adjutant to Colonel John F. Hamtramck of the 1st Virginia Volunteers.

In 1849 August resumed the practice of law in Richmond in partnership with Isaac R. Watkins and George Wythe Randolph. August specialized in commercial law and criminal advocacy and built up an extensive and successful practice. Like many fellow attorneys, he was a Freemason, serving as worshipful master of Dove Lodge Number 51 at its formation in the summer of 1850. August was a charming and gregarious man, much loved by his fellow attorneys and the citizens of Richmond. Even beyond the borders of Virginia he became well known as a punster and humorist of sharp and cynical wit. He may also have had a drinking problem, which could explain why, with all his talents and charm, he did not rise even higher in Richmond's distinguished legal community.

August remained active in the Virginia militia and in 1851 became a major in the new 1st Regiment Virginia Volunteer Infantry. He rose to colonel in 1853 and served until 1860, when he was appointed general of the 2d Brigade, 4th Division of the Virginia Militia.

In 1850 August ran for election to the House of Delegates from Richmond and defeated James C. Crane in one of the closest elections in the city's antebellum history. Crane contested the election, and the House did not resolve the question in August's favor until the final day of the session. August nevertheless served on the Committees on Finance and on Banks, and he proposed a number of reforms in Virginia commercial law and several amendments to the code. On behalf of the Central Southern Rights Association of Virginia he introduced a resolution that imports from northern states be taxed by Virginia in order to protect its "agricultural, manufacturing, mineral and commercial community."

August also served on a special legislative committee appointed to consider the governor's call for a convention of southern states to respond to the sectional crisis and northern criticism of slavery. The committee's resolutions, which the assembly adopted, cautioned against disrupting the Union over the issue of slavery but also warned "the non-slaveholding states" against interference with the "common institutions" of the slaveholding states. In the debates August endorsed the Compromise of 1850, but he favored announcing that a congressional repeal of the fugitive slave law would endanger the Union.

August returned to the General Assembly in 1857 as a member of the Senate of Virginia. In the midst of a severe money crisis during the first session, he served on the Committees on Banks and on Finance and Claims. The session of 1859–1860 was a tense and belligerent meeting in the immediate aftermath of John Brown's raid on Harpers Ferry. August chaired the powerful and important Committee on Military Affairs. In response to a request from South Carolina that Virginia send delegates to a convention of Southern states, August moved that Virginia both accept the invitation and recommend to "each of our Southern sister States that they proceed at once to organize, arm and equip their militia for active and efficient service." When a joint legislative committee to which he belonged recommended that the invitation be declined, August led the minority in filing a strongly worded report reviewing the "long course of aggression, outrage and injustice perpetrated by the non-slaveholding States upon the South." The minority report likened the condition of the Southern states early in 1860 to that of the American colonies in 1776.

During the early days of the Civil War August commanded a volunteer militia force. In May 1861 he was commissioned a colonel and his unit entered active state service as the 15th Regiment Virginia Infantry. On 1 July 1861 the regiment entered Confederate service. August served as a regimental commander under Major General John Bankhead Magruder at the Battle of Big Bethel on 10 June 1861 and saw action during the Peninsula campaign and the Seven Days' Battles. After he was severely wounded at Malvern Hill on 1 July 1862, he retired from active service. His old law partner, Secretary of War George Wythe Randolph, engaged him to work in the War Department, where he assisted General Samuel Cooper in the Conscription Bureau and commanded a conscription camp in North Carolina from January 1863 to the end of 1864. August finally retired on disability on 31 December 1864.

Following the war, August resumed his law practice. He was elected to the Richmond City Common Council in the spring of 1866. He served on the council's committee on finance and chaired the committees on claims and salaries and on poor relief. In the latter capacity he reported to the council on the great influx of free blacks into the city. Because the army and other federal authorities were feeding and caring for many of the recently freed slaves, August's committee opposed adding their names to the city's relief rolls. His report clearly summarized the plight of free blacks, the frustration of the defeated southern population, and the relative political and financial helplessness of the city government. In March 1869 General George Stoneman removed August and several other members of the council for failure to subscribe to the so-called test oath.

Thomas Pearson August contracted typhoid fever and died in Richmond on 31 July 1869. He was buried with full Masonic honors in Hollywood Cemetery.

E. Lee Shepard, "Sketches of the Old Richmond Bar: Thomas P. August," *Richmond Quarterly* 6 (spring 1984): 48–51; George L. Christian, "Reminiscences of Some of the Dead of the Bench and Bar of Richmond," *Virginia Law Register* 14 (1909): 743–744; father's obituary in *Fredericksburg Ledger*, 3 Oct. 1873; *Historical Sketch and By-Laws of Dove Lodge No. 51* (1891), 7, 12–13, 20 (frontispiece por.); George Green Shackelford, *George Wythe Randolph and the Confederate Elite* (1988), 24–27, 37, 51–52, 96, 101, 159; *JHD*, 1850–1851 sess., 3, 101, 209, 474–507; *Report of the Select Committee on the Compromise Measures*, Doc. 74, supplement to *JHD*, 1850–1851 sess.; *JSV*, 1859–1860 sess., 209–211; *Minority Report of the Joint Committee on the Subject of a Proper Response to be Made by the Commonwealth of Virginia to South Carolina*, Doc. 43, appended to *JSV*, 1859–1860 sess.; Louis H. Manarin and Lee A. Wallace Jr., *Richmond Volunteers: The Volunteer Companies of the City of Richmond and Henrico County, Virginia, 1861–1865* (1969), 151–154, 203, 205, 211 (por.), 250; Compiled Service Records; Richmond City Common Council Record Book, vols. 15–16; Richmond City Hustings Court Will Book, 26:358; obituaries in *Richmond Dispatch*, 2, 3 Aug. 1869, with month and year of birth in former.

E. LEE SHEPARD

AUGUSTINE, Harry Hamill (14 November 1892–17 September 1959), banker, was born in Richmond, the youngest of three sons and three daughters of John Anthony Augustine and Elizabeth Olivia Hamill Augustine. His paternal grandfather came to Richmond from the island of Corsica about 1835, and his mother, a native of Baltimore, was of Irish descent. Augustine left the public schools at fifteen to work as a runner, or messenger, for the First National Bank of Richmond. He acquired his business education through the American Institute of Banking, created by the American Bankers Association in 1901 to train bank employees for advancement. In the Richmond chapter of the AIB Augustine joined a cohort of ambitious young men who filled executive positions in the city's banks for the next half century, among them his elder brother William Franklin Augustine, who achieved success first in Richmond and after 1926 in Boston.

By 1917 Augustine was manager of the First National Bank's transit department, which processed records of transactions. In August of that year he joined the United States Army as a first lieutenant, serving initially in Company A of the 311th Machine Gun Battalion and transferring in February 1918 to Company D of the 2d Pioneer Infantry Regiment. He reached France in July 1918 and served there for a year.

After his discharge from the service on 29 July 1919, Augustine returned to the bank as assistant cashier. Three years later he joined the National State and City Bank as vice president for correspondent banking, in charge of transactions with other banks. That same year he married Fannie Carter Scott, of Richmond, on 10 June 1922. They had one son and one daughter. In 1926 National State and City Bank merged with the Planters National Bank to form the State-Planters Bank and Trust Company. Augustine became vice president and cashier of the new institution's commercial, or business banking, department. The State-Planters Bank was large enough and strong enough financially to weather the hard times of the Great Depression. In 1936 Augustine became executive vice president of the bank, and two years later he was placed on its board of directors.

On 26 June 1941 Augustine assumed the presidency of the State-Planters Bank and Trust Company. He guided it successfully through the chaotic years of World War II, when institutions just emerging from the depression suddenly had to help finance the nation's war effort. A conservative man with a background in commercial banking, Augustine nonetheless endorsed the bank's decision to expand lending to consumers as Richmond's economy continued to grow after the war. Third in size among Virginia banks, State-Planters served more Richmonders than any other. Until 1962 the state's banking laws strictly limited bank mergers and branch banking, but Augustine negotiated a merger with the Richmond-based Bank of Commerce and Trusts on 12 December 1955. The resulting institution was named the State-Planters Bank of Commerce and Trusts, and Augustine served as the its chief executive officer until 9 January 1958, when failing health required him to take the less-taxing post of chairman of the board. During his tenure the number of employees at the bank nearly doubled, capital grew from $4.1 million to $16 million, and assets increased from $79 million to more than $200 million. Augustine also attracted and retained a talented set of younger bank officers, a contribution that contemporaries considered his most important legacy to the institution known today as Crestar Bank.

As befitted a bank president, Augustine served on the boards of directors of several Virginia firms, the board of regents of the Rutgers University Graduate School of Banking, and the board of visitors of the Medical College of Virginia. He was also a trustee and treasurer of Richmond Memorial Hospital. Born into a Catholic family, he eventually became a vestryman of Saint Paul's Episcopal Church. Harry Hamill Augustine waged a courageous struggle against the cancer that took his life on 17 September 1959. He was buried in Hollywood Cemetery.

Augustine Family Genealogical Notes, LVA; *NCAB*, 48:351–352; feature article in *Richmond News Leader*, 3 Jan. 1955 (por.); Military Service Records; *Richmond Times-Dispatch*, 11 June 1922; Frances Leigh Williams, *They Faced the Future: A Saga of Growth* (1951), 92–94; Williams, *They Faced the Future II: A History of United Virginia Bank 1951 to 1980 and of United Virginia Bankshares Incorporated 1962 to 1980* (1982), 7–26; David C. Parcell, *State Banks and the State Corporation Commission: A Historical Review* (1974), 37–86; obituaries in *Richmond News Leader*, 17 Sept. 1959, and *Richmond Times-Dispatch*, 18 Sept. 1959.

JOHN T. KNEEBONE

AULICK, John Henry (ca. 1791–27 April 1873), United States Navy officer, was born in Winchester, the second of five sons and one of ten children of Charles Aulick and Ann Mary (or Maria) Aulick. He entered the navy as a midshipman in November 1809 and took his first extended cruise in 1811 aboard the schooner *Enterprise*. During the War of 1812 he commanded the forecastle on the *Enterprise* and later was aboard the brig *Rattlesnake* when it surrendered to the British in June 1814. After eight months in captivity, he returned to duty in March 1815 aboard the frigate *United States*. His war service earned him a medal with the thanks of Congress, a lieutenancy, and recognition as a young naval officer of talent and promise.

After the war Aulick served at sea aboard the brig *Saranac*, the sloop *Ontario*, and the frigates *Constitution* and *Brandywine*, and onshore on recruiting and ordnance duty. In 1831 he was promoted to master commandant (later redesignated commander) and was assigned to ordnance duty at the Washington Navy Yard, in Washington, D.C., where he and his wife, Mary Conover Aulick, established their permanent residence. The first of their three sons and three daughters was born about 1824. In 1834 Aulick received command of his first ship, the sloop *Vincennes*, which was stationed in the Pacific. From July 1835 to June 1836 he cruised around the world investigating trade conditions and the treatment of American citizens abroad. He came back to Washington in May 1838, on a posting as second officer of the navy yard and acting commandant that lasted until September 1842.

Aulick returned to the Washington Navy Yard a third time, taking charge as commandant on 7 March 1843. During his tenure the yard undertook increasingly advanced ordnance experiments, particularly Samuel Colt's research with controlled sea mines. Aulick was detached from the navy yard in February 1846 to command the frigate *Potomac* on Caribbean patrol. During the Mexican War the *Potomac* participated in the March 1847 siege of Vera Cruz, where Aulick used his ordnance experience to assist naval shore batteries.

On 7 December 1850 Aulick received orders to command the East India Squadron and later that month was assigned as his flagship the new side-wheel steamer *Susquehanna*. Before leaving for his new posting, Aulick suggested a plan to Secretary of State Daniel Webster to open trade negotiations with Japan. Webster presented Aulick's proposal to President Millard Fillmore, who designated Aulick as his envoy to negotiate a treaty of amity and commerce with the Japanese government. Aulick received his official orders to command the squadron on 11 February 1851 and sailed in June on the *Susquehanna*.

En route to Brazil, on the first leg of the voyage, Aulick quarreled with the *Susquehanna*'s new captain, William Inman, over their respective command responsibilities, and both officers irritated Secretary of the Navy William A. Graham by preferring charges against each other. Aulick removed Inman from command on reaching Brazil, and other misunderstandings of a more trivial nature developed into official charges that one of the diplomatic passengers filed against Aulick with the Department of State. To quiet the diplomats Fillmore ordered Aulick removed from command of the squadron. Aulick left the East India Squadron on 8 February 1853 at Hong Kong and returned to the United States. His successor, Commodore Matthew C. Perry, with a larger fleet, completed Aulick's mission and became famous for opening Japan to the West, one of the major American diplomatic achievements of the nineteenth century.

Despite the Navy Department's official acceptance of Aulick's denial of the charges against him, his long career effectively ended with his removal from command of the East India Squadron, a blow that devastated him. He remained on active duty as a senior captain awaiting orders until placed on the retired list on 21 December 1861. He spent much of the Civil War years touring Europe and was promoted to commodore on the retired list on 4 April 1867, after more than fifty-seven years in the navy and twenty-three years and nine months of sea duty.

John Henry Aulick died in Washington on 27 April 1873 of softening of the brain and was buried in Congressional Cemetery in that city.

Gravestone records death date and age at death of eighty-one, but obituaries, official naval records, and other contemporary documents imply a birth date as early as 1787; father's will in Winchester City Will Book, 1:128–139; Lewis R. Hamersly, *The Records of Living Officers of the U.S. Navy and Marine Corps* (1870), 42–43; John H. Aulick "Z" file, Operational Archives, Naval Historical Center, Washington, D.C.; Alberta Aulick Papers, Duke; Aulick Expedition Papers, Maryland Historical Society, Baltimore; duty assignments verified from official U.S. Navy *Registers*; Charles Oscar Paullin, "Early Voyages of American Naval Vessels to the Orient," in United States Naval Institute, *Proceedings* 36 (1910): 725–734; 37 (1911): 255–259; Kenneth E. Shewmaker et al., eds., *The Papers of Daniel Webster*, ser. 3, *Diplomatic Papers* (1983–1987), 2:212, 220, 226, 228–230, 253–256, 288–292, 298; will in Washington, D.C., Archives, copy in Winchester City Will Book, 2:325–333; cause of death in D.C. Interment Register, District of Columbia Vital Records Division; obituaries in *New York Times*, 28 Apr. 1873, *Washington Evening Star*, 28, 29 Apr. 1873, and *Army and Navy Journal* 10 (1873): 601.

TAMARA MOSER MELIA

AUSTIN, Archibald (11 August 1772–by 11 September 1837), member of the House of Representatives, was a lifelong resident of his native Buckingham County. He was one of three or more sons of Archelaus Austin, a farmer who owned thirteen slaves in 1782. The name of his mother is not known. In September 1808 he married Grace R. Booker. They lived at an estate called Westfield and had five sons and two daughters. For more than thirty years, according to his obituary, Austin was "a worthy member of the Anabaptist Church."

Austin practiced law and farmed in Buckingham County. He paid taxes on more than 1,100 acres of land, nineteen slaves, and nine horses late in the 1810s. His investments included land in Franklin and Kanawha Counties. A Jeffersonian Republican who became a Jacksonian Democrat, Austin served on the Buckingham County Court and represented the county in the House of Delegates from 1815 to 1817.

In the spring of 1817 Austin defeated John Randolph of Roanoke in the election for the seat in the United States House of Representatives from the district composed of the counties of Buckingham, Charlotte, Cumberland, and Prince Edward. Even though Randolph was not a candidate, he received many votes. Austin left little mark in the halls of Congress aside from a lengthy speech on 9 March 1818 against the constitutionality of federally funded internal improvements. He also steadfastly opposed the Second Bank of the United States and protective tariffs. In 1819 Randolph thwarted Austin's bid for reelection by a majority of about 490 votes. Two years later Randolph easily defeated Austin who, like Randolph in 1817, was not a candidate, but nonetheless received a majority of the votes cast in his native county.

After more than a decade out of elective office, Austin was chosen as a Democratic presidential elector in 1832 and 1836. From 1835 to 1837 he returned to the House of Delegates as Buckingham County's representative. During this second period of assembly service he was a member of the Committee for Courts of Justice, but he was essentially a backbencher without much influence. Austin's brief ventures into elective politics showed him to be a rather typical Virginia political leader, intent on preserving old Virginia's economic and social order with a comparatively narrow, doctrinaire political creed.

Archibald Austin died, probably at his home in Buckingham County, early in September 1837. The Buckingham County Court received news of his death on 11 September, and had a resolution in his honor published. He was buried in a family cemetery in Buckingham County, but no stone marks his grave.

Short biography in Jeanne Stinson, *Early Buckingham County, Virginia, Legal Papers, 1765–1806* (1993), v–vi; family papers and Austin letters and legal papers in Austin-Twyman Papers, W&M, and Fontaine Family Papers, VHS; undated marriage notice in *Richmond Virginia Argus*, 23 Sept. 1808; *Annals of Congress*, 15th Cong., 1st sess., 1201–1217; John Randolph of Roanoke, diary, 1817–1819, VHS; death notice and obituary in *Richmond Enquirer*, 3, 6 Oct. 1837.

DANIEL P. JORDAN

AUSTIN, Moses (4 October 1761–10 June 1821), merchant and mine operator, was born in Durham, Connecticut, the youngest of six sons and three daughters of Elias Austin and Eunice Phelps Austin. His mother died when he was about ten years old, and his father when he was about fifteen. Austin attended school in Durham and after he came of age in 1782 formed with his brother-in-law Moses Bates the first of a series of dry goods partnerships with close relatives. In 1783 Austin joined his elder brother Stephen in Philadelphia, and in 1784 he moved to Richmond and there opened a branch of the family business. On 28 September 1785 he married Mary, or Maria, Brown, of Sharpsburg Furnace, Sussex County, New Jersey. They had two sons and three daughters. Austin prospered in Richmond and was one of the city's most successful merchants by the time he erected a large, elegant new house in 1788.

In May 1789 Stephen Austin and Moses Austin leased from the commonwealth of Virginia the right to operate the lead mine on the banks of the New River in the part of southern Montgomery County that became Wythe County the following year. John Chiswell had discovered the mine during the 1750s, and Charles Lynch, who operated the mine for the state during the Revolutionary War, had extracted a great quantity of lead for the Virginia and Continental armies. The Austins hired men to reopen and operate the mine, began smelting, established a lead-shot plant in Richmond, and contracted to furnish lead for roofing the new Capitol. They also persuaded Congress to impose a protective tariff on lead. With the aid of a large loan, they purchased the mine property for £6,505 in 1792.

Moses Austin moved to Wythe County to direct the concern. He improved the smelting operation; established shops for potters, blacksmiths, and hatters; and created the new community of Austinville. Altogether the Austins invested more than $100,000 in the enterprise during a period of about seven years, making it probably the largest mining and smelting operation on the frontier. Moses Austin became a leading citizen of Wythe County and by 1796 was a justice of the peace and militia captain.

By the mid-1790s the Austin brothers faced serious financial problems. They were heavily in debt and unable to offset the high cost of transporting lead to eastern markets. Stephen Austin faced bankruptcy, and in the summer of 1797 the brothers dissolved their partnership. During the winter of 1796–1797 Moses Austin had visited the West, and in June 1798 he left Virginia and moved to Mine à Breton, in what is now Missouri. There he acquired a new mine and established an industrial colony. Austin had again become wealthy by 1819, when the failure of a bank in Saint Louis wiped out his fortune. Attempting to start again on yet another frontier, he traveled to San Antonio in December 1820 and made the initial proposals for the colonization of Texas to the government of the Spanish colony of Mexico. Moses Austin returned to Missouri and died at his home in Saint Francois County on 10 June 1821, leaving his son Stephen Fuller Austin, who had been born in Wythe County in 1793, to organize the first large-scale emigration from the United States into Texas.

David B. Gracy II, *Moses Austin: His Life* (1987); Austin Papers, Eugene C. Barker Texas History Center, University of Texas at Austin, contain the bulk of his business records, some of which Barker edited and published in the *Annual Report of the American Historical Association for the Year 1919*, vol. 2 in 2 parts (1924); George P. Garrison, ed., "A Memorandum of M. Austin's Journey from the Lead Mines in the County of Wythe in the State of Virginia to the Lead Mines in the Province of Louisiana West of the Mississippi, 1796–1797," *AHR* 5 (1900): 518–542; Mary B. Kegley, *Wythe County, Virginia: A Bicentennial History* (1989), 327–335; por. at Missouri Historical Society (Gracy, 229) once identified as Moses Austin is of doubtful authenticity; obituary in *Saint Louis Missouri Gazette and Public Advertiser*, 19 June 1821.

MARY B. KEGLEY

AVERETT, John Taylor (24 December 1827–23 February 1898), educator, was born at Halifax Court House, the fourth of six sons and fourth of ten children of Martha Coleman Wootton Averett and Thomas Hamlett Averett, a respected Halifax physician and planter who served in the House of Representatives from 1849 to 1853.

Averett completed his preparatory schooling in the private Male Academy in Halifax Court House and graduated with honors from Emory and Henry College in 1848. An episode of poor health caused him to abandon plans to study law, and he chose education as his profession. After service early in the 1850s as principal of a private school in Whitesville in Halifax County, he became headmaster of the prestigious Ringgold Military Academy in Pittsylvania County. On 5 September 1852 he married Louisa Frances Penick, of Halifax County. They had at least three sons and three daughters before she died in 1872.

At the end of May 1861 Averett joined the 38th Regiment Virginia Infantry as a second lieutenant. He was promoted to captain and regimental quartermaster and served in the latter capacity from the summer of 1861 until 15 September 1864, when he became assistant brigade quartermaster of Barton's Brigade, Third Corps. He surrendered with the remnants of the Army of Northern Virginia at Appomattox Court House at the end of the war and then returned briefly to the Ringgold school before becoming principal of the Danville Male Academy in 1867 and superintendent of the Danville public schools in 1872.

In 1873 Averett joined his brother Samuel Wootton Averett (1838–1896) as coprincipal of the Roanoke Female College in Danville. John Averett, who had served as a founding trustee of the school in 1859, taught ancient languages, English, history, and moral philosophy, while his brother led classes in modern languages, mathematics, and natural sciences. The curriculum also featured music and art. Under the guidance of the Averett brothers the college prospered. They oversaw an increase in enrollment, put the school on a sound financial footing, enlarged course offerings, expanded and modernized degree programs, and improved the faculty in various ways, such as adding to it the musician and aspiring composer Frederick Delius. After Samuel Averett left in 1887 to become president of Judson Institute in Marion, Alabama, John Averett's title was changed from principal to president.

The Averett family's contributions to the success of the Roanoke Female College during trying years guaranteed its survival into the twentieth century. Two of Averett's daughters taught at the school and a son sat on the board of trustees from 1898 to 1910. On 27 May 1917 the board of trustees renamed the school Averett College to honor the numerous family members who had served the school.

Averett also found time to participate in many civic activities. He served as the first lay moderator of the Roanoke Baptist Association from 1874 to 1881 and again from 1883 to 1887. A prominent Mason, he served as district deputy grand master in 1885 after stints as junior warden, senior warden, and (from 1881 to 1883) worshipful master of Danville's Roman Eagle Lodge. He was a leader among local Democrats and served from 1 July 1884 to 1 July 1886 and from 9 March 1887 to 2 July 1888 on the Danville City Council after publicly defending the actions of white Democrats who had battled African Americans and Republicans in the Danville Riot of 3–5 November 1883. A popular journalist, Averett reported as the local correspondent for the *Lynchburg News* and the *Norfolk Virginian*, contributed regularly to the *Richmond Dispatch*, and edited the *Tobacco Leaf*, a trade journal for the local tobacco industry. He also belonged to Danville's Cabell-Graves Camp, United Confederate Veterans.

A stroke confined Averett to a wheelchair in 1889 and finally forced his retirement in 1892. John Taylor Averett died in Danville on 23 February 1898 and was buried in Green Hill Cemetery there.

Kenneth H. Cook's lengthy article on Averett family, *South Boston News and Record*, 6 Oct. 1977, reprints obituary from *Danville Weekly Register*, 24 Feb. 1898; Compiled Service Records; G. Howard Gregory, *38th Virginia Infantry*, 2d ed. (1988); Jack Irby Hayes Jr., *A History of Averett College* (1984), 31–34 (por.), 45–46, 73; David W. Gray, "A History of Averett College" (master's thesis, University of Richmond, 1960); John Taylor Averett scrapbooks and vertical files, Danville Public Library; Danville City Council Proceedings, 1884–1888.

JACK IRBY HAYES JR.

AVERETT, Thomas Hamlett (20 July 1800–29 June 1855), member of the House of Representatives, was born near Halifax Court House, the oldest of at least three sons and one daughter of William Averett and Elizabeth Hamlett Averett. Little is known of his early life and education. At fourteen he substituted for his ill father in the War of 1812, serving for nearly three months as a drummer in the 4th Regiment Virginia Militia. He probably served a medical apprenticeship under Granville Craddock, whose will, dated 9 December 1819, and proved a decade later, left him half of Craddock's medical books and equipment. In 1820–1821 Averett completed one year of study at the University of Pennsylvania Medical School in Philadelphia, reportedly funded by friends who recognized his talent, but he evidently received no medical degree.

On 3 January 1822 Averett married Martha Coleman Wootton, of Prince Edward County. They settled at Halifax Court House and had six sons and four daughters, including the educator John Taylor Averett, one of several family members for whom Averett College in Danville was named. Averett gradually built his medical practice and became involved in public affairs, including the Baptist Church and the local Masonic lodge, in which he held office from 1824 to 1839. He began purchasing land in 1822 and eventually divided 914 acres among his heirs. In 1839 he was appointed county physician. By then his practice was said to extend into neighboring counties and North Carolina.

On 24 January 1848 Averett announced his candidacy to represent Halifax and Mecklenburg Counties in the Senate of Virginia. Halifax was strongly Democratic, and he had been active in the local party. The incumbent was a Democrat from Mecklenburg, but Halifax Democrats favored Averett as being more likely to resist state spending on internal improvements. Bad weather on election day contributed to low voter turnout in Mecklenburg, and Averett won easily. Less than a year later he resigned from the Senate to run for Congress in the district comprising Franklin, Halifax, Henry, Patrick, and Pittsylvania Counties. The voting after a quiet campaign was close everywhere except in Halifax, which gave Averett 352 more votes than his opponent and overall victory by a scant 8 votes.

In Congress, Averett served on the Committee on Invalid Pensions but gave most of his attention to the Compromise of 1850. A crisis had arisen over proposals to prohibit slavery in the new territories acquired in the war with Mexico. The compromise was actually a package of legislation designed to resolve the crisis by giving some satisfaction to all sections. Averett, a slaveholder himself, declared on 27 March 1850 that Congress had no authority to interfere with slavery anywhere, and he voted with the majority of Virginia's congressmen against admission of California as a free state and restriction of the slave trade in the District of Columbia. A newspaper report described his overall position on the compromise as "sullen acquiescence."

Averett won reelection in 1851 and served on the Committee for the District of Columbia. In that election voters also ratified a new state constitution. Reapportionment of the state's congressional districts had been postponed until the following election while the constitution went before the voters, and with its passage the Democrats controlling the General Assembly set out to create districts that would return only party members to Congress. After months of debate the reapportionment bill finally passed on 6 April 1853, and Averett became one of its first victims. His new congressional district included Campbell, Franklin, Halifax, Henry, Patrick, and Pittsylvania Counties, as well as Appomattox County, home of Congressman Thomas S. Bocock. Before Averett could mobilize his forces, Bocock obtained endorsements from county conventions that effectively locked up the Democratic nomination. Averett angrily announced that he would stay in the race, but ill health limited his active campaigning and guaranteed Bocock's victory.

Failing eyesight probably prevented Averett from continuing his medical practice after his return to Halifax Court House. No likeness of him is known to exist, but his wife described him in an 1878 pension application as "about five feet eight inches high, brown hair, fair complection." Thomas Hamlett Averett burned to death on 29 June 1855 when his pipe set his clothes on fire. He was buried in the Averett Square in the Halifax Town Cemetery.

Kenneth H. Cook, "Dr. Thomas Hamlett Averett: Physician, Mason, Legislator," *South Boston News and Record*, 6 Oct. 1977; French Biographies; Craddock will in Halifax Co. Will Book, 15:117–120; War of 1812 pension case files, Veterans Administration Records, RG 15, NARA; Lynwood Miller Dent Jr., "The Virginia Democratic Party, 1824–1847" (Ph.D. diss., Louisiana State University, 1974), 357–398; Henry T. Shanks, *The Secession Movement in Virginia* (1934), 18–45; *Congressional Globe*, 35th Cong., 1st sess., Appendix, 392–396; political campaigns documented in *Lynchburg Virginian* and *Richmond Enquirer*; will, estate inventory, and account of estate sale in Halifax Co. Will Book, A1:222–225, 243–253; obituary in *Richmond Enquirer*, 10 July 1855.

JOHN T. KNEEBONE

AVERY, Nina Belle Horton (4 September 1898–30 October 1980), women's organization leader, was born in Farmville, North Carolina, the second of six daughters and second of eight children of Albert Horton and Susan Narcissus Smith Horton. After graduating from high school she received a B.A. in 1917 from the State Normal and Industrial College (now the University of North Carolina at Greensboro) and then taught French and English for three years at the high school in Salisbury, North Carolina.

In 1920 Nina Belle Horton moved to Richmond, where she enrolled in and completed the secretarial course at Massey Business College. She then began a long and successful career with the Chesapeake and Ohio Railway Company, eventually becoming supervisor of contracts for the division that governed relations with the companies that strung telephone and electrical wires across railroad lines. In Richmond on 29 April 1925 she married Robert L. Avery, a chief clerk for the railway. The couple had no children.

Success in her career did not prevent Avery from fulfilling her childhood ambition to become a lawyer. She studied privately and enrolled in the night school at the Virginia College of Law in Richmond. She graduated in 1953 and was admitted to the Virginia bar four years later. She remained with the Chesapeake and Ohio Railway until she retired and opened her own law office in Richmond in 1963 at the age of sixty-five.

Avery's legal education served her reform interests. A speech by one of the pioneer suffragists that she heard as a college student inspired her to devote her energies to issues relating to the legal status of women. During the 1930s she emerged as a critic of institutionalized discrimination against women and joined the National Woman's Party and the National Federation of Business and Professional Women's Clubs. Avery achieved prominence in the latter organization, serving as president of the Richmond chapter from 1938 to 1940 and as president of the Virginia Federation of Business and Professional Women's Clubs for the 1942–1944 term. She became third vice president of the national organization in 1946 but was defeated in her bid for the presidency in 1948. Three years later she was the national representative to the International Federation of Business and Professional Women's Clubs.

Avery investigated allegations of discrimination against married female employees in the state government and persistently lobbied for passage of the 1950 Virginia law that first permitted women to serve on juries. Because federal court jurors were selected from lists of people eligible to serve on juries in the states, no Virginia women had hitherto been able to serve on a federal jury. Fittingly, Avery was one of the first women in Virginia to serve as a federal grand juror.

Avery supported the proposed Equal Rights Amendment during the 1940s as the optimal remedy for women's disadvantaged legal status. In 1944 the national president of the BPW appointed Avery to the Women's Joint Legislative Committee for Equal Rights, a national coalition of women's organizations formed a year earlier to secure congressional approval of the ERA. Avery soon became head of the committee, a position that put her at the center of disputes within the pro-ERA coalition.

Some BPW leaders viewed the Joint Legislative Committee as a tool of the NWP, which carefully guarded its longtime leadership of the ERA movement. Avery's close association with the NWP and service on its national council exposed her to criticism, and some BPW members accused her of compromising her loyalty to their organization. A split within the NWP in 1947 also contributed to conflict on the Joint Legislative Committee and further reduced the coalition's effectiveness. The NWP subsequently differed with the BPW over the latter organization's acceptance of the Hayden rider to the ERA, which mandated that protective legislation passed on behalf of women workers would not be affected by the amendment. The rifts within the proamendment ranks and the personal attacks distressed Avery, who bravely retained her membership in both organizations. In September 1954 the BPW withdrew from the Joint Legislative Committee and disavowed Avery as its representative.

Many feminists of Avery's generation greeted the resurgent activism for women's rights in the 1960s and 1970s with ambivalence, fueled in part by detachment from, and sometimes by hostility toward, the civil rights movement. In 1964, in hopes of bringing about more moderate race provisions in the civil rights bill pending before Congress, Avery actively supported the NWP's successful effort to add the prohibition of sex discrimination to the bill. Despite these ulterior motives, Title VII of the 1964 Civil Rights Act became one of the most significant achievements of the modern women's rights movement. Avery's distrust of the liberal politics of many younger feminists did not, however, disrupt her work for passage of the ERA.

Nina Belle Horton Avery died in retirement at a nursing home in Richmond on 30 October 1980, six months after her husband's death. They were buried in Oakwood Cemetery in Richmond.

Family history information provided by sister Kathleen Horton Moore, 25 Mar. 1990, and nephew Donald Gurley, 18 Apr. 1990; BVS Marriage Register, Richmond City; National Woman's Party Papers, LC; Richmond chapter of National Federation of Business and Professional Women's Clubs, scrapbooks, LVA; *Virginia Business and Professional Woman* 5 (June 1942): 1–4; 7 (Dec. 1944): 1–2; 10 (Apr. 1948): 1 (por.), 21, 37, 42; House Committee on the Judiciary, *Equal Rights Amendment to the Constitution and Commission on the Legal Status of Women: Hearings before the Committee on the Judiciary*, 80th Cong., 2d sess., 10, 12 Mar. 1948, 23–26; Senate Committee on the Judiciary, "Stenographic Transcript of Hearings before the Committee on the Judiciary" (unpublished hearing), 80th Cong., 2d sess., 17 Apr. 1948, 2:351–374; Leila J. Rupp and Verta Taylor, *Survival in the Doldrums: The American Women's Rights Movement, 1945 to the 1960s* (1987), 74, 75–76; *Richmond News Leader*, 13 July 1946, 3 Jan. 1951; *New York Times*, 18 May 1947; letter to editor and feature articles in *Richmond Times-Dispatch*, 6 Feb. 1948, 31 Aug. 1955,

14 Sept. 1973 (por.); Carl M. Brauer, "Women Activists, Southern Conservatives, and the Prohibition of Sex Discrimination in Title VII of the 1964 Civil Rights Act," *JSH* 49 (1983): 37–43; obituary in *Richmond Times-Dispatch*, 31 Oct. 1980.

CANDICE D. BREDBENNER

AWBREY, Henry (d. by 10 September 1694), planter, was probably born during the 1620s at Tredomen, in Brecon, Brecknockshire, Wales. He was a younger son of the seven sons and three daughters of Sir William Awbrey and Elizabeth Jones Awbrey. The family's fortunes were depleted by the time of Sir William Awbrey's death in 1631, and Henry Awbrey, lacking an inheritance, moved to Virginia about 1660. Two of his brothers joined him by 1664. On 7 October 1663 Awbrey witnessed a deed in Rappahannock County, and the following year he registered his cattle mark, a poplar leaf. He married at least twice and probably three times. References to his wife Sarah in the county records between 1664 and 1672 include one of 30 April 1670 alluding to her as his "now wife," which suggests that she was not his first spouse. By the time Awbrey wrote his will in the summer of 1694, he had married a woman named Mary, to whom he left a life interest in his residence. He bequeathed most of his property to his only known child, a son probably born early in the 1660s.

Awbrey became a large landowner in the vicinity of the port town of Tappahannock, which he served as a founding trustee in 1682. He received his first land patent on 9 April 1664 for a tract of 1,050 acres on Hoskins Creek and five years later added 480 acres of land adjoining his original grant. During the subsequent decade he patented additional land that brought his total holdings to almost 8,000 acres. Awbrey also bought and sold other properties, increasing his wealth in the process. He engaged in trade as well.

With prosperity came prominence and public responsibilities. Awbrey was one of five men who signed a 13 March 1677 list of Rappahannock County grievances after Bacon's Rebellion. As early as February 1683 he had become a justice of the peace, a position he held until May 1692, when the county was divided into Essex and Richmond Counties. He was the presiding justice and the first sheriff of the new county of Essex. Awbrey represented Rappahannock County in the House of Burgesses in the assemblies of November 1682, 1684, 1688, and 1691–1692. He did not become a leader in the assembly, but during his first session he served on the Committee on Public Claims, and during his last he sat on the Committee on Elections and Privileges.

In 1684 Awbrey had a role in the transportation of the Rappahannock Indians and their possessions thirty-five miles upriver to a site on Portobago Bay on the current Essex-Caroline border. The politics of this relocation are unclear, but the county may have acted to move the Native Americans beyond the edge of the rapidly expanding English settlements. Like other Tidewater Indians, the Rappahannocks' numbers diminished and their culture faded after they left their traditional lands late in the seventeenth century.

Awbrey was evidently a typical successful planter of the period, active in both politics and commerce. He left a large estate that included land, livestock, household goods, and prized personal possessions, including a silver tankard, a pendulum watch, and a collection of books. His will also disposed of two servants and ten enslaved "Negroes," exemplifying the transformation of the labor force in Virginia from British servants to slaves of African descent. Henry Awbrey dated his will on 1 August 1694 and died sometime between then and 10 September 1694, when the will was proved in the Essex County Court.

Theophilus Jones, *A History of the County of Brecknock* (1909–1930), 2:7–9; John Aubrey, *"Brief Lives," Chiefly of Contemporaries, Set Down by John Aubrey, Between the Years 1669 & 1696*, ed. Andrew Clark (1898), 1:59; Walton L. Aubrey, *Aubrey-Awbrey of Virginia and Kentucky* (1987), 3–14; Thomas Hoskins Warner, *History of Old Rappahannock County, Virginia, 1656–1692* (1965), 176; first record of presence in Virginia in old Rappahannock Co. Records (1656–1664), 309; land transactions, public officeholding, and trusteeship detailed in Patent Book, RG 4, LVA, and in deed and order books of Essex Co. and old Rappahannock Co.; county grievances in PRO CO 1/39, 197–198; will in Essex Co. Order Book (1692–1695), 311–313.

JAMES B. SLAUGHTER

AXTELL, Almon Decatur (8 February 1848–27 November 1922), railroad executive, was born in Elyria, Ohio, the elder of two sons and fourth of five children of Almon Axtell, a carpenter, and Sophronia Boynton Axtell. He worked on the construction of the first Union Pacific rail lines in western Missouri and eastern Kansas in 1864 and 1865 before matriculating in 1866 at Illinois College in Jacksonville, where he remained until late in 1867. From November 1867 until July 1880 he was employed by the Saint Louis, Iron Mountain, and Southern Railway. He began as a construction engineer in the tunnel division. From 1869 to 1880 he was an assistant civil engineer for the company, combined with the additional post of division superintendent as of 1875. He was also an assistant civil engineer for the Cairo and Fulton Railroad from 1869 to 1872, and chief engineer of the Cairo, Arkansas, and Texas Railroad from 1872 to 1875. Axtell married Ellen May Cantrell, of Little Rock, on 13 October 1875. They had no children.

In July 1880 Decatur Axtell, as he was known in adulthood, moved to Richmond to become general manager of the newly constituted Richmond and Alleghany Railroad, the name taken by the Richmond and Lynchburg Railroad in 1878. In March 1880 the General Assembly authorized the Richmond and Alleghany to acquire the property of the defunct James River and Kanawha Company. Soon thereafter the Richmond and Alleghany began constructing a line from Richmond to Clifton Forge using the towpath of the old James River and Kanawha Canal. The line formally opened in October 1881, but during the panic of 1883, brought on in part by a glut in railroad building throughout the United States, the Richmond and Alleghany defaulted on its loans and went into receivership. Axtell and New Yorker Lawrence Myers served as receivers of the line, and Axtell remained the railroad's general manager.

In January 1890 the Chesapeake and Ohio Railway Company purchased the Richmond and Alleghany, and Axtell became an assistant to the president of the Chesapeake and Ohio. He served as second vice president from 1891 until 1899, when he became the sole vice president, a position he held until he retired on his seventieth birthday in 1918. Axtell also sat on the board of directors from 1891 until 1918. The 1890s were a period of growth and prosperity for the railroad, and he worked closely with its two influential presidents, Melville Ezra Ingalls until 1900 and George Walter Stevens thereafter. Axtell earned a reputation as a skillful administrator as well as a fine civil engineer, and after 1900 his responsibilities grew to encompass the railroad's treasury, accounting, and construction divisions as well. Axtell also held offices in several other railroads that the Chesapeake and Ohio completely or partially controlled. He served as president of the Toledo and Ohio Central Railway from 1899 to 1901 and as chairman of its board from 1901 to 1908. In addition, he was vice president of the Kanawha and Michigan Railway from 1900 to 1901 and chairman of its board from 1902 to 1910. Both of these roads were controlled for a time by the Hocking Valley Railroad, over which the Chesapeake and Ohio gained sole control in 1910, with Axtell serving as vice president from 1910 to 1918.

During Axtell's long tenure the Chesapeake and Ohio also invested in two of the most famous resorts in the Allegheny Mountains. The railroad purchased and operated both the Homestead in Hot Springs, and the Greenbrier just across the border in White Sulphur Springs, West Virginia. Axtell was president of the Virginia Hot Springs Company, which Ingalls controlled, from 1891 to 1911, and president of White Sulphur Springs, Incorporated, which operated the Greenbrier, from 1911 until his retirement. The two venerable resorts had fallen on hard times after the Civil War, but the railroad invested heavily in improving them and promoting them as a destination for its passengers. At both resorts Axtell and the resident managers oversaw the construction of large new hotels, as well as the development of golf, tennis, and bathing facilities.

After Axtell retired from active business he began researching and writing a history of the Chesapeake and Ohio Railway. He expected to produce a major reference work covering the story of Virginia's internal improvements over the previous 125 years, but he died of a heart attack on 27 November 1922 at his home in

Richmond after a day spent working on his manuscript. Decatur Axtell was buried in Richmond's Hollywood Cemetery.

Tyler, *Encyclopedia*, 4:40–42 (por.); *NCAB*, 20:74; Census, Lorain Co., Ohio, 1850; Joseph T. McAllister, *Historical Sketch of Virginia Hot Springs, Bath County, Virginia* (1902), 29–35; obituaries in *Richmond News Leader* and *Richmond Times-Dispatch*, both 28 Nov. 1922, with editorial tribute in former.

ROBERT S. CONTE

AYER, Richard Small (9 October 1829–14 December 1896), member of the Convention of 1867–1868 and member of the House of Representatives, was born in Montville, Waldo County, Maine, the second of four sons and second of eight children of Caroline Small Ayer and William Ayer, a successful farmer, postmaster, and state senator. Ayer attended local schools and Kents Hill Seminary in Kennebec County, Maine, and then engaged in farming and the merchandising business. On 27 April 1861 he enlisted in Company A, 4th Regiment Maine Infantry. Promoted to captain on 15 December 1861 Ayer fought with the 4th Maine in the First Battle of Manassas (Bull Run) and in the Peninsula campaign early in 1862. Disabled by dysentery contracted in Hampton in April, he left Virginia for Maine on 29 July 1862. He was assigned to the recruiting service in October 1862. Shortly after being ordered to rejoin his regiment he obtained an honorable discharge on 22 March 1863 due to his disability and went home.

After the war Ayer returned to Virginia, settling by 1866 at Warsaw. In the Northern Neck, as elsewhere in the rural South, the freedpeople had turned to politics to gain the full fruits of emancipation. Ayer's service as a district registering officer had made him known to the new black voters. On 31 August 1867 a convention of Union Republican Clubs, commonly called the Union League, met at Warsaw and nominated him to represent Lancaster, Northumberland, Richmond, and Westmoreland Counties in a convention that had been called to write a new state constitution. More whites than blacks had actually registered in the four-county area, but more blacks than whites turned out to vote, and the results—almost completely divided along racial lines—gave the election to Ayer.

In the Convention of 1867–1868 Ayer served on the Committee on the Basis of Representation and Apportionment but did not otherwise play a significant role. He voted consistently with the Radical majority, even though he had been a Douglas Democrat in 1860. When the convention adjourned on 17 April 1868 politicians began to prepare for the statewide election scheduled for 2 June. The state Republican Party convention nominated Ayer for Congress from the First District, even though Daniel M. Norton, a black physician and delegate to the constitutional convention from James City and York Counties, had previously declared his candidacy.

Ayer and Norton remained candidates for more than a year, however, as the election was postponed twice and finally scheduled for 6 July 1869. By then the Republican Party had fallen apart, and the rival Conservative Party had abandoned its nominated candidates in order to make common cause with the moderate Republican faction against the Radicals. On 27 April 1869 Ayer announced that he still remained in the race, and shortly afterward Norton did the same. The Conservatives encouraged Norton's candidacy in order to divide the Radical vote, but the First District also had two Conservative candidates.

Norton was strongest in the Peninsula near his Yorktown home, while Ayer had the most support in the less-populous Northern Neck. Most observers therefore predicted a Norton victory. Ayer won the black vote in his home region and carried both Elizabeth City County and the Eastern Shore counties. When the Conservative candidates divided the white vote, he won the congressional seat by a small margin.

Congress did not readmit Virginia to the Union until 26 January 1870, after which Ayer was sworn in on the last day of January, in the midst of the second session of the Forty-First Congress. In a ceremony conducted on 9 February 1870 in the city of Richmond by Moses Drury Hoge, an eminent Presbyterian clergyman, Ayer married Ellen Frances Stevens, of Newton, Massachusetts. They had no children. Four days later, back in Washington, Ayer applied for an increase in his federal pension for invalids since he still suffered from chronic diarrhea. In Congress he served on the Committee of Claims and presented petitions from his constituents, but seldom spoke.

Ayer did not stand for reelection in 1870. At the expiration of his term on 3 March 1871, he and his wife returned to Maine. Ayer's father had died in 1867. The couple lived with his mother and Ayer farmed when his health permitted. He had inherited enough property to live comfortably but despite periods of improved health, including 1887–1888 when he served a term in the state legislature representing his hometown of Montville, he never recovered fully from the aftereffects of the dysentery that he had contracted in 1862. Richard Small Ayer died on 14 December 1896 at his home in Liberty, Maine, all but forgotten in Virginia. He was buried in Mount Repose Cemetery in Montville. The attending physician attributed Ayer's death to neuralgia resulting from his chronic diarrhea.

Biographical Sketches of the Members of the Senate and of the House of Representatives of Maine 13 (1887): 7; Regular Army Personnel Records, Records of Adjutant General's Office, RG 94, and Civil War Pension Case Files, Records of Veterans Administration, RG 15, NARA; Richard Lowe, *Republicans and Reconstruction in Virginia, 1856–1870* (1991), 177; Richard L. Hume, "The Membership of the Virginia Constitutional Convention of 1867–1868: A Study of the Beginnings of Congressional Reconstruction in the Upper South," *VMHB* 86 (1978): 481; *Debates and Proceedings of 1868–1869 Convention*, 60, 400; Report on Prominent Whites and Freedmen by Henry K. W. Ayres, 9 Apr. 1867, Freedmen's Bureau Records; *Williamsburg Virginia Gazette*, 6 May 1869; obituaries in *Augusta Daily Kennebec Journal* and *Lewiston Evening Journal*, both 16 Dec. 1896; no Virginia newspaper obituary has been located.

FRANCIS REXFORD COOLEY
JOHN T. KNEEBONE

AYER, Thomas Parker (3 April 1886–4 January 1962), librarian, was born in Merrimack, New Hampshire, the youngest of two sons and three daughters of Joseph Warren Ayer and Harriet Philbrick Ayer. He developed an interest in libraries while attending Manchester High School and served as a page in the Manchester City Library from 1902 to 1905. After he graduated from high school he attended Brown University, where he was a student assistant in the university library from 1905 to 1910 and evening reference assistant at the Providence Athenaeum from 1905 to 1909. Ayer received his A.B. from Brown in 1909.

Remaining in Providence for a year after he completed college, Ayer served as auditor of the Providence Public Library and as a reference librarian at the university library. From 1910 to 1913 he was supervisor of the binding and exchange departments at the Columbia University Library in New York. He spent the academic year 1913–1914 as a student at the University of Illinois Library School in Urbana and was shelf inspector in the university library there. Leaving before completing a degree, Ayer spent several months without employment before returning to Brown University in 1915 as a reference librarian. In 1916 he joined the Library of Congress as a reference assistant, and a year later he became the librarian for the Federal Trade Commission, where he remained until 1924. On 4 September 1920 Ayer married Leta Frances Tucker, of Waco, Texas. They had no children.

In 1924 Ayer became the first librarian of Richmond's newly established public library system. Except for a brief interval in 1927 and 1928 when he directed the public library in Reading, Pennsylvania, he spent the remainder of his career in Richmond. The opening of the library in July 1924 marked the advent of free public library service in the city, and in August 1925 Ayer provided the first public library service to Richmond's African Americans by inaugurating the city's first branch library. In 1947 black Richmonders began using the main library as well.

Ayer supervised construction of the city's new $543,000 library building, funding for which had been given to the city by Sallie May Dooley as a memorial to her husband, James H. Dooley. The facility opened in 1930. During his thirty-year career Ayer presided over expansion of the collections to almost a quarter-million items, opened five part-time lending stations, mostly in schools, and began systematic clippings files of regional news and feature items from local newspapers. He considered the music department that debuted in 1945 "the greatest single achievement of the library since we came into this building." During his tenure the collection grew to almost 12,000 music recordings. The realization of a career-long goal came as Ayer was retiring in 1955, when he learned that Richmond had bought land in the West End to build the city's second branch library, the Belmont Branch.

In the 1930s Ayer joined with other members of the Virginia Library Association to campaign for passage of a state law for the certification of librarians, enacted in 1936. At the same time the General Assembly established the State Board for the Certification of Librarians, on which Ayer served from its establishment in 1936 until 1949. He also completed two terms as president of the Virginia Library Association, in 1930 and again in 1940, and belonged to the Southeastern Library Association and the American Library Association. Ayer completed or contributed to several publications during his career, among them *Duplication of Titles for Required Undergraduate Reading* (1917) and *The Price of Coal* (1924), a bibliography he prepared with Clyde L. King for the American Academy of Political and Social Science. In addition, he wrote articles for the *Library Journal*.

Thomas Parker Ayer retired on 30 June 1955 after more than thirty years of almost continuous service at the Richmond Public Library. He resided for a time in New Mexico before moving to Sarasota, Florida, where he died on 4 January 1962. His remains were cremated.

Biography in Glass and Glass, *Virginia Democracy*, 2:752–753; feature articles in *Richmond Magazine* 16 (Aug. 1929): 11–12 (por.), 42; *Richmond News Leader*, 18 Sept. 1930, 5 Jan. 1955, *Richmond Times-Dispatch*, 24 Mar. 1937, 5 Jan. 1955 (por.), and *Virginia Librarian* 2 (Apr. 1955): 1–2; Ayer's journal articles include "The New Public Library in Richmond" and "A Schedule For Binding and Rebinding Magazines," *Library Journal* 56 (1931): 111–115 and 62 (1937): 856–857; obituaries in *Richmond News Leader*, 5 Jan. 1962, *Richmond Times-Dispatch*, 6 Jan. 1962, and *Southeastern Librarian* 12 (1962): 58.

CAROLYN H. LEATHERMAN

AYERS, Rufus Adolphus (20 May 1849–14 May 1926), attorney general of Virginia and member of the Convention of 1901–1902, was born in Bedford County, the elder of two sons and third of five children of Maston Jackson Ayers, a farmer and teacher, and Susan Lewis Wingfield Ayers. He grew up in Goodson (now Bristol). The family had stopped in Goodson on the way to Texas in 1856 so that Susan Ayers could visit relatives and decided to stay in the small town in southwestern Virginia, where Maston Ayers died in 1858. Although money for schooling was scarce thereafter, Ayers attended Goodson Academy until it closed at the outbreak of the Civil War. He went to war himself at the age of fifteen, joining a group of Confederate scouts in eastern Tennessee in April 1864.

After returning to southwestern Virginia, Ayers tried farming, working as a salesman, and running a store of his own, but none of his enterprises flourished. Throughout this period he also read law in books borrowed from his uncle Gustavus A. Wingfield, a judge in Lynchburg. On 8 June 1870 Ayers married Victoria Louisa Morison in Scott County. Of their six children, two sons and a daughter survived infancy. After studying under Henry S. Kane, his wife's uncle and a prominent local lawyer, Ayers was admitted to the bar in Estillville (now Gate City) in 1872. From that point on he rose rapidly. Attaching himself to the Conservative Party, Ayers was elected commonwealth's attorney of Scott County in 1875 and served for six years. He also made connections during these years in Richmond, where he worked as the reading clerk for the House of Delegates from 1875 to 1879. Ayers remained a staunch and effective loyalist in the Conservative Party as it evolved into the Democratic Party and fought against the Readjusters. He owned and edited a Democratic newspaper, the *Estillville Scott Banner*, and helped build up the party in southwestern Virginia even as many other men in the area felt the pull of the Republicans and the Readjusters. Ayers was soon to be rewarded for his efforts.

Even as Ayers became a leading figure in the Democratic Party in the 1870s and early part of the 1880s, he also achieved prominence in the new industrial enterprises of the Virginia Highlands. Moving forward on several fronts at once, he sometimes started companies himself—such as a railroad between Bristol and Big Stone Gap, where other capitalists were endeavoring to build a center of industry in the mountains—

and sometimes acted as an agent for large outside investors. He combined both roles in his work with the most important enterprise in Big Stone Gap, the Virginia Coal and Iron Company, which he served as director and vice president from its beginning in 1881.

In 1884 party leaders chose Ayers as vice president of Virginia's delegation to the Democratic National Convention. His increasing visibility in business and politics made him a logical choice for statewide office. The Democrats freely admitted that they needed greater strength in southwestern Virginia and considered several men from the area for the position of attorney general in the election of 1885. Ayers proved especially attractive to the party because he was only thirty-six at a time when the Democrats were purposely seeking young candidates in order to counter charges that they were merely an old guard holding on to power through inertia and privilege. Although the Richmond newspapers knew little of Ayers when he was nominated, they quickly endorsed the party's choice, commended his character, and publicized his political views. Opposition papers sought to label him a swindler for some of his earlier business dealings, but he refuted the charges to the satisfaction of the state's voters and won along with the rest of the Democratic ticket against the weakening Readjuster Party.

The Readjusters took their name from their position on the debt controversy that had divided the state for nearly a decade. They may have lost in 1885, but at least they had the satisfaction of watching Ayers wrestle with the legal implications of the debt in a highly personalized way when the new attorney general briefly went to jail during his four-year term. The debt had been incurred during the antebellum era, and the interest had increased dramatically during the Civil War and Reconstruction when few payments were made. The state struggled with the debt, as some called for its downward readjustment or repudiation and others insisted on repayment in full. One especially troublesome facet of the controversy came in a debate over bond coupons with which Virginia residents could pay state taxes. Speculators purchased unmatured coupons at a discount and sold them at a profit to those who owed the state money, thereby undercutting its revenue.

The General Assembly passed a law in 1887 that prevented county governments from accepting coupons that appeared to have passed through the hands of speculators, and one group of London investors challenged the state in the federal circuit courts. Ayers, who had been nominated partly because he was known to be a firm supporter of paying back the debt, argued that the United States courts lacked jurisdiction in the case. He therefore ignored a restraining order. Hugh L. Bond, the judge who had issued the order, then cited Ayers for contempt and levied a fine of $500 on the attorney general, who chose to test the case by going to jail with his two fellow defendants, commonwealth's attorneys from Virginia counties. During six days of incarceration in Richmond, from 8 to 14 October 1887, Ayers received fine food, bedding, and luxuries from the nearby Exchange Hotel and hosted prominent visitors, including U.S. senator John W. Daniel. The state hired former U.S. senator Roscoe Conkling, a Republican from New York, and Virginia Democrat John Randolph Tucker to defend Ayers, and they ultimately prevailed in the U.S. Supreme Court on the question of jurisdiction. Virginia leaders saw the victory as one for states' rights and celebrated Ayers's role in the battle. The rest of his term passed uneventfully, and he returned to Bristol at its completion.

Ayers received the 1889 Democratic gubernatorial nomination but dropped out of the race to devote his considerable energies to business endeavors in southwestern Virginia, especially at Big Stone Gap. He moved his family there in 1890, built an impressive house, and helped begin twelve businesses during the next fifteen years.

Ayers came back into statewide prominence briefly in 1901, when he was elected to represent his district at a state constitutional convention. He addressed the Convention of 1901–1902 on two of the most important political issues of the day, the restriction of the suffrage and the power of corporations. At the opening of the assemblage a newspaper reported that Ayers was "opposed to disenfranchising a single white man." During the convention he proposed establishing county boards to examine and qualify voters rather than imposing tax, property, or educational requirements. He predicted that such a system would enfranchise almost all the white men in the state and many, but considerably less than a majority, of the black men. Many white voters in the politically competitive mountain districts feared losing the ballot through constitutional restrictions, and Ayers obviously had some sympathy for their concerns. Nonetheless, he voted for the restrictive suffrage provisions that won approval on 4 April 1902. He defended the interests of railroads operating in his region during debate on the report of the Committee on Corporations. Ayers served on the Committee on the Judiciary and chaired the Committee on Public Institutions and Prisons. He spoke at length on the convention's right to put a constitution into effect without a referendum and voted with the majority that did just that on 29 May 1902.

Ayers's final political campaign was an unsuccessful bid for a congressional seat in 1912. Rufus Adolphus Ayers died on 14 May 1926 in Saint Alban's Sanatorium, East Radford, and was buried in Estill Cemetery, Gate City. His house in Big Stone Gap, now the Southwest Virginia Museum, remains as a symbol of the local brokers who played a large role in the history of the region.

William R. Dunn, "An Attorney General Goes to Jail," *Virginia Cavalcade* 21 (autumn 1971): 28–39 (por.); Pat Jones, "Career of a Southwest Virginian," *Richmond Times-Dispatch Magazine*, 30 Apr. 1939, 8–10; BVS Marriage Register, Scott Co.; contemporary descriptions in *Richmond Dispatch*, 31 July, 1, 7 Aug., 14 Oct. 1885, and *Richmond Daily Times*, 12 June 1901; *Journal of 1901–1902 Convention*, 49, 50, 486–487, 504; *Proceedings and Debates of 1901–1902 Convention*, 1:243–255, 2:2810–2813, 2830–2832; *Resolutions of 1901–1902 Convention*, nos. 129, 161; *Convention of 1901–1902 Photographs* (por.); obituaries in *Roanoke World-News*, 14 May 1926, *Richmond Times-Dispatch*, 15 May 1926, and *Big Stone Gap Post*, 19 May 1926; memorial in *Virginia State Bar Association Proceedings* (1926): 241–243.

EDWARD L. AYERS

AYLETT, Philip (31 October 1791–11 September 1848), militia officer, was the third of six sons and third of thirteen children of Philip Aylett and Elizabeth Henry Aylett. He was born at his father's plantation, Fairfield, in King William County. Aylett's well-connected family included his grandfathers Patrick Henry and William Aylett, Virginia's commissary of purchases during the American Revolution. He was probably educated privately and may also have attended nearby Rumford Academy. He was apparently a young member of the county militia during the War of 1812, and although his unit was not called into the field, he evidently served in some military capacity at Norfolk at the time of the British invasion of the Chesapeake in June 1813.

On 20 February 1823 Aylett married Judith Page Waller, the only daughter of Benjamin Waller, a prominent King William County planter. The best known of their three sons and four daughters were their first son, Patrick Henry Aylett, an attorney and political insider who was killed in the collapse of the courtroom in the Virginia State Capitol on 27 April 1870, and their third son, William Roane Aylett, longtime commonwealth's attorney for King William County and a colonel in George Pickett's division who was severely wounded at the Battle of Gettysburg.

Like his father and paternal grandfather before him, Aylett became a justice of the peace and a legislator. He was commissioned a justice in King William County on 16 August 1817 and held that office until his death. From 1817 to 1824 and again from 1826 to 1827, Aylett served in the House of Delegates. He was regularly appointed to the Committee for Courts of Justice and in 1822 gained a seat on the prestigious Committee of Privileges and Elections. From time to time he also sat on committees to examine the treasurer's accounts and those of the land office register. He remained in the King William County militia and in 1819 attained the rank of lieutenant colonel of the 87th Regiment. At the same time Aylett was appointed to a special legislative committee to recommend changes in the recruiting and training of the militia in response to Governor Thomas Mann Randolph's request for a revision of the state's militia laws. On 31 January 1834 the General Assembly elected Aylett brigadier general of the 14th

Brigade Virginia Militia and he held that rank until his resignation in January 1843.

In 1832 Aylett won election to the Senate of Virginia to complete an unexpired term, serving until 1834. While in the Senate he left the Democratic Party because he opposed President Andrew Jackson's handling of the Nullification Crisis and his removal of the nation's funds from the Second Bank of the United States. Aylett supported Benjamin Watkins Leigh and William Cabell Rives, both opponents of Jackson, for seats in the United States Senate, and he also voted for another Jackson critic, Littleton Waller Tazewell, for Virginia governor. When Aylett campaigned in 1837 for election to a full term in Virginia's Senate, he was defeated. During that campaign he reminded his constituents that he had opposed holding the Convention of 1829–1830, at which western delegates had tried unsuccessfully to introduce democratic reforms in a new state constitution.

During the last decade of his life Aylett lived in political retirement at Montville, his house in King William County. On his return from a trip to the mountains, which he had hoped would restore his health, Philip Aylett died at the City Hotel in Richmond on 11 September 1848. He was buried in the family cemetery at Fairfield.

Birth date and other family information in Aylett Family Genealogical Notes, esp. Acc. 20300, LVA; year of birth of 1787 on gravestone at Fairfield; despite a garbled assertion to this effect in Tyler, *Encyclopedia*, 5:1089, neither Aylett nor his father was a general in the War of 1812; marriage reported in *Richmond Enquirer*, 7 Mar. 1823; Aylett Family Papers, including 28 Mar. 1837 campaign broadside, VHS; Militia Commission Papers, RG 3 LVA; death reported in *Richmond Enquirer*, 15 Sept., 13 Oct. 1848.

STUART LEE BUTLER

AYLETT, William (1743–by 15 June 1780), member of the Convention of 1776 and commissary of purchases, was born at the family estate of Fairfield in King William County, the elder of two sons and second of four children of Philip Aylett, wealthy planter and merchant, and Martha Dandridge Aylett. His mother died when he was about four years old, and his father married for the second time in 1749. Nothing is known of his early education. In 1766 Aylett married Mary Macon, daughter of James Macon, of King William County. They had two sons and four daughters.

Aylett had powerful political connections through ties of kinship to the Dandridge, Lee, and Washington families. He followed relatives into the House of Burgesses, winning elections to represent King William County in 1771 and 1774. He was also elected to all five Revolutionary Conventions. Meeting on 26 August 1775, a Committee of Safety established by the Convention of July–August 1775 called for the appointment of a contractor, or commissary, with authority to obtain supplies on the best terms. Although he was not confirmed in the position until 18 September, Aylett was understood to hold the position of state agent and commissary of purchases by the first of that month. Quickly gathering as much as he could for immediate needs from merchants around the colony, he opened a supply depot, or "Public Store," in Williamsburg in October and over the winter procured additional supplies from Philadelphia and the Caribbean.

On 27 April 1776, shortly after the Virginia regiments entered the Continental army, the Continental Congress appointed Aylett the deputy Continental commissary general for Virginia. Because of the appointment the Convention of 1776 declared Aylett's seat vacant on 22 May 1776, after it unanimously voted in favor of independence but before it adopted the first state constitution and the Virginia Declaration of Rights. He retained his other state positions. Aylett expanded operations over the next year, managing a fleet of small coastal craft that brought French and Dutch supplies from the West Indies.

After reorganizing the Continental supply system into issuing and purchasing divisions, Congress appointed Aylett deputy Continental commissary general for purchases in the Southern Department on 18 June 1777. Shortly after his appointment, on 22 June Aylett described himself to Joseph Trumbull, the Continental commissary general for purchases, as "for some years . . . in the Commercial Circle & in the Wheat Affair business, having Mills of my own, and a moderate independent Estate." Aylett resigned his state positions on 3 December 1777 but continued his Continental service.

Criticism of Aylett's administration was inevitable for, on one hand, he was expected "to secure the country from loss, by a moderate profit" and, on the other, to "furnish the troops lower than they could supply themselves elsewhere." Wide fluctuations in his prices at the Public Store reflected the loss of cargoes to the British blockade or the difference in cost when he had to transport commodities overland. When the Continental supply system began to break down later in the war, he again came in for his share of criticism. Governor Patrick Henry embarrassed him by appointing special agents who found cattle and grain when Aylett reported that none was to be had, and once a congressional auditor who quizzed him "in the street" made him feel "a little awkward." He had repeated confrontations with private merchants who forced up prices, provided inferior merchandise, or reneged on government contracts for higher returns elsewhere. Toward the end of his public tenure, Aylett vigorously defended his policies against charges of impropriety in a spirited exchange with "Agricola" in the *Williamsburg Virginia Gazette* in December 1779 and February 1780.

Failing health led Aylett to attempt to resign his Continental post on several occasions during 1779, but his superiors postponed his departure on each occasion—a sign that they, at least, approved of his work—by permitting him to move his office from Williamsburg to King William. With the appointment of a new Continental commissary general in November 1779, however, Aylett finally resigned on the first of that month. Robert Forsythe succeeded him in the Southern Department on 2 December. William Aylett fell acutely ill while in Yorktown the next spring, wrote his will on 12 April 1780, and died between then and 15 June 1780, when his will was proved in court.

Charles E. Hatch, "Colonel William Aylett, A Revolutionary Merchant of Virginia" (master's thesis, UVA, 1936); *Revolutionary Virginia*; year of birth in Aylett-West-Dandridge-Moore-Macon Genealogical Notes, LVA; records of State Agent and of Public Store, RG 2, LVA; "Correspondence of Col. William Aylett, Commissary General of Virginia," *Tyler's Quarterly Historical and Genealogical Magazine* 1 (1919): 87–110, 145–161; Harold B. Gill Jr., "Williamsburg's Publick Store," *Colonial Williamsburg* 19 (winter 1996–1997): 58–63; Aylett papers, including letter to Trumbull, in Papers of the Continental Congress, RG 360, NARA; one letter each from Agricola to General Assembly, Aylett to Agricola, and Agricola to Aylett in *Williamsburg Virginia Gazette* (Dixon and Nicholson), 13 Nov., 11 Dec. 1779, 5 Feb. 1780; will in BW.

JOHN E. SELBY

AYLETT, William (26 July 1775–18 August 1847), member of the Council, was born at Fairfield in King William County, the younger of two sons and fourth of six children of Mary Macon Aylett and William Aylett, a planter, member of the House of Burgesses, and state and Continental commissary of purchases who died in 1780. Aylett's mother married Callohill Minnis by 1785, and he probably lived with his mother and stepfather in York County for a few years, but in 1788 his brother, Philip Aylett, reached legal age and became William Aylett's guardian.

Aylett became active in local politics as a Jeffersonian Republican in 1800, and on 22 April 1801 he was elected to represent King William County in the House of Delegates. Aylett served in the next five assemblies, representing King William through February 1806. During that time he commanded a company of King William County light infantry in the 87th Regiment Virginia Militia. Aylett married Martha A. Posey, also of King William County, on 29 April 1802. They had nine daughters and four sons.

In the assembly on 21 December 1805 Aylett was one of thirteen nominees to fill three vacant seats on the Council of State. Although defeated in the contest to fill the first vacancy, Aylett was elected on the fourth ballot to fill the second vacancy. He took the oath of office as a councillor on 31 May 1806, almost four months after the assembly session ended. At first he regularly attended Council meetings, including the emergency deliberations in June and July 1807 following the British attack on the American frigate *Chesapeake* off the Norfolk coast. By the end of the year, however, pressing family and business matters caused his attendance to slip. In 1808 he attended only about a third of the Council's meetings, and at least twice Governor William H. Cabell wrote to remind him of his duty. On 9 December 1808 Aylett resigned from the Council because he had decided to leave Virginia for "the Western country," where he believed that he could better provide for his growing family.

Sometime in 1809 Aylett moved to the section of the Mississippi Territory that ten years later became the state of Alabama. He settled first in what became Dallas County, where in 1820 he was a local judge and had slaveholdings large enough to rank in the county's top twenty. In 1832 he sold his Dallas County property and moved his family to a cotton plantation in Tuscaloosa County near the town of Tuscaloosa, the state's bustling new capital. Aylett retained close ties to his Virginia relatives, particularly to his nephew Philip Aylett, but he never returned to his native state. William Aylett died in Tuscaloosa County on 18 August 1847.

Aylett-West-Dandridge-Moore-Macon Genealogical Notes, LVA; some Aylett letters in Aylett Family Papers, VHS; *Calendar of Virginia State Papers*, 9:81, 227, 449–450, 486; *Richmond Enquirer*, 21, 24 Dec. 1805, 10 Dec. 1808; *JHD*, 1805–1806 sess., 40, and 1808–1809 sess., 11.

SANDRA GIOIA TREADWAY

AYLETT, William Roane (14 May 1833–6 August 1900), Confederate army officer, was the youngest of three sons and fourth of seven children of Philip Aylett and Judith Page Waller Aylett. He was born at Montville, his family's estate in King William County. His father was a planter prosperous enough to educate his children well. Aylett attended Rumford Academy in King William County and the University of Virginia, from which he graduated in 1854 with diplomas in French language and literature and in moral philosophy.

Aylett returned to his birthplace in King William County and was admitted to the bar in August 1854. A controversial case in 1858, in which he represented Maria Gregg in proceedings against her husband, Daniel H. Gregg, on grounds of mistreatment and abuse, won Aylett a wide reputation, and his practice eventually spread across five counties. By 1860 he listed his net worth from his law practice and his plantation at $60,000. On 31 July of that year he married Alice R. Brockenbrough. They had three sons and four daughters.

Aylett was commissioned a lieutenant in the Virginia militia in 1858. With the onset of the Civil War, he was chosen captain on 13 May 1861 of a company that became part of the 53d Regiment Virginia Infantry. He was a capable officer who earned the respect of his superiors. Aylett took part in the Battles of Seven Pines and Malvern Hill and was commissioned major on 29 August 1862 during the Second Battle of Manassas (Bull Run). He was promoted to lieutenant colonel on 2 February 1863 after participating in the fighting at Sharpsburg (Antietam) and Fredericksburg, and on 5 March 1863 he rose to colonel of the regiment. At Gettysburg, Aylett was wounded when a fragment of a spent shell struck him in the chest, giving him what he called "an awful lick." Bleeding from his nose and mouth, Aylett turned command of the regiment over to a subordinate, who led the 53d Virginia during Pickett's Charge.

After recuperating with his regiment in North Carolina, Aylett commanded a five-regiment brigade of which his 53d Virginia was a part. He fought at Cold Harbor and in the operations around Bermuda Hundred, but to his dismay he was never promoted to general. Letters of recommendation from Generals George E. Pickett and John D. Imboden, among others, left the Confederate War Department unimpressed. As a result Aylett submitted his resignation in September 1864, but it was not accepted, and he remained on duty until the end of the war. He was taken prisoner at Saylers Creek on 6 April 1865 and sent to the prison at Johnson's Island, where he remained until paroled in July of that year. One of the officers who shared a prison room with Aylett recalled him as "bright and smart and a good fellow." His parole described him as five feet, nine inches tall, with brown eyes and light hair.

Aylett returned home to a devastated plantation and a family in deep distress. He resumed his law practice and steadily rebuilt his professional reputation and his fortune. In April 1870 he became commonwealth's attorney for King William County, a post he held for sixteen years. He was one of the prosecutors in the sensational 1885 Richmond murder trial of Thomas J. Cluverius.

William Roane Aylett lived in the same King William County house for his entire life except when at school or in the army. He died at Montville on 6 August 1900, ten days after suffering the second of two paralytic strokes, and was buried in the family cemetery there.

Aylett Family Papers, VHS; Compiled Service Records; MS memoir of Theophilus G. Barham, in possession of Barham's descendants; obituary in *Richmond Dispatch*, 7 Aug. 1900 (por.).

ROBERT K. KRICK

AYRES, Blackstone Drummond (1 August 1896–8 January 1984), attorney, was born in Accomac, the eldest of two sons and two daughters of John Hack Ayres, a physician, and Mary C. Derby Ayres. He graduated from Accomac High School in 1912 and then received a civil engineering degree in 1916 from the Virginia Military Institute, where he was captain of the school's first track team.

B. Drummond Ayres, or B. D. as he was familiarly known, spent the 1916–1917 school year as principal of Wachapreague High School in Accomack County. In 1917 he became an assistant professor of military science and tactics at VMI and was assigned to duty at John Marshall High School in Richmond as commandant of the corps of cadets. After the United States entered World War I Ayres joined the Regular Army as a second lieutenant in the artillery. He was promoted to first lieutenant and sent to France in October 1918, but saw no action. After his resignation on 22 August 1919 he attended law school at the University of Virginia and graduated Phi Beta Kappa in 1922.

Ayres returned to Accomac to practice law. During a career of more than sixty years he became the dean of the Eastern Shore bar. Although his was a general law practice, he specialized in trial work. His outstanding record of winning appeals in the Virginia Supreme Court of Appeals was recognized in 1952 when Ayres was elected to a one-year term as president of the Virginia State Bar, after having served a year as vice president. In 1975 he established the law firm of Ayres, Hartnett, and Custis.

Ayres also participated in several Eastern Shore business enterprises. He served on the board of the Citizens Saving Bank from 1928 until 1933, when the bank merged with the Eastern Shore Banking Company to become the Eastern Shore Citizens Bank. He was elected to the board of the new institution, held various offices in the bank, and assumed its presidency in 1959. Under Ayres's leadership the Eastern Shore Citizens Bank grew into one of the leading rural banks in the state. He eventually guided its successful merger with the United Virginia Bank in 1971 and served as a regional director until his death. Ayres also operated several farms on the Eastern Shore, and during the 1940s and 1950s he served as a director and from 1942 to 1953 as president of the Eastern Shore Produce Exchange, one of the nation's leading truck-crop exchanges. Its Red Star Brand was known throughout much of the eastern and central United States.

Ayres was active in local Democratic Party politics but held public office only once. In 1927 he was elected to a two-year term in the House of Delegates. During World War II he was director of civil defense for Accomack County. A lifelong member of Saint James Episcopal Church in Accomac, he served several terms as its senior warden, and he belonged for more than fifty years to the Onancock Rotary Club and the local Masonic lodge.

Ayres's most significant achievement may have been his service as legal counsel on a team of attorneys and businessmen that put together the $200 million financial package late in the 1950s that made possible the construction of the Chesapeake Bay Bridge-Tunnel. Until the project was completed on 15 April 1964, he prepared and reviewed contracts and assisted with the state's acquisition of rights-of-way needed for approach roads and buildings.

Ayres married Nellie Marie Bird, of Accomac, on 29 September 1929. They had one son and one daughter. B. Drummond Ayres died of cancer at the Northampton-Accomack Memorial Hospital on 8 January 1984 and was buried in Edgehill Cemetery in Accomac.

Scrapbooks of James E. Mears, Eastern Shore Public Library, Accomac (LVA microfilm); Military Service Records; BVS Marriage Register, Richmond City; *Commonwealth* 19 (Aug. 1952): 21, 22; *A New Era Opens: Chesapeake Bay Bridge-Tunnel* (1964), 35; obituaries in *Richmond News Leader*, 9 Jan. 1984, *Onancock Eastern Shore News*, 12 Jan. 1984 (por.), and *Washington Post*, 13 Jan. 1984.

L. FLOYD NOCK III

B

BABALAS, Peter Kostas (8 July 1922–29 December 1987), attorney and member of the Senate of Virginia, was born in Boston, Massachusetts, the eldest of three children, all sons, of a Greek immigrant restaurant owner, Kostas Babalas, and Catherine Melidone Babalas, who was born in Turkey. He excelled in the local public schools and in 1941 received a full academic scholarship to Harvard University. Babalas interrupted his education to enter the army in 1943. He served as an antiaircraft officer, with the Quartermaster Corps, and later with the 106th Infantry Division in Europe. On 9 December 1945 he was a lieutenant assigned to the military police in Mannheim, Germany, when he was called to the scene of the traffic accident in which General George S. Patton was killed. As Patton lay dying with a broken neck, he gave Babalas his hat. Babalas returned it to Patton's family in 1964 and was quoted in several biographies of Patton about the circumstances of the general's death. Babalas served in the army again during the Korean War.

Babalas returned to Harvard in 1946 and earned a B.S. in economics in 1948. He then entered the law school of the University of Virginia. Following his graduation in 1950 he began the practice of law in Norfolk, specializing in corporate and maritime law. The practice flourished, and by 1960 he was the managing partner of an eight-member firm. He was a shrewd businessman and became a millionaire through investments in shipping, real estate, banks, and insurance companies.

Babalas was active in the Democratic Party and in 1967 was elected to the Senate of Virginia as one of three members from the city of Norfolk. A well-known advocate of civil rights, he was liberal on social issues, conservative on fiscal matters, and firmly opposed to expanding state regulation of businesses and banks. He became chairman of the Committee on Local Government in 1976 and ranked third in Senate seniority in September 1986, when he succeeded to the chairmanship of the powerful Committee on Rules. He was by then also the ranking member of the powerful Committee on Finance. His major accomplishment in the Senate was sponsorship of the act that in 1981 unified all the principal ports in Tidewater Virginia under the Hampton Roads Port Authority.

During his final years in the Senate Babalas was deeply mired in ethical controversy stemming from votes he cast that helped a legal client, the Landbank Equity Corporation, a Virginia Beach second mortgage company that often disguised interest rates as high as 30 percent through hidden charges. In 1984 Babalas received $11,000 in legal fees from the company. On 11 February 1985 he used his vote and the proxy of an absent senator in the Committee on Commerce and Labor to kill by a vote of seven to five a bill that would have made Landbank's lending practices illegal. Six weeks later Landbank began paying Babalas a legal retainer fee of $8,000 a month. Babalas was tried and acquitted in Richmond Circuit Court in August 1986 on two charges of violating the state's Conflict of Interest Act. He consistently denied any wrongdoing and fought an attempt to censure him in the Senate. On 23 January 1987, following emotional deliberation, the Senate of Virginia voted twenty-five to fourteen to censure Babalas for his conduct in the only such censure in modern Virginia history.

Babalas had been suffering from multiple myeloma, or cancer of the bone marrow, since 1979, and a month after the censure vote announced that he would not seek reelection. Babalas had married Lillian Macheras, of Lexington, Virginia, on 27 December 1948, and they had two daughters. Peter Kostas Babalas died in Virginia Beach General Hospital on 29 December 1987 and was buried in Forest Lawn Cemetery in Norfolk.

The author covered Norfolk politics and Babalas's Senate career for the *Norfolk Virginian-Pilot*, the library of which documents his public life; marriage reported in *Rockbridge County News*, 30 Dec. 1948; family history information verified by Lillian Macheras Babalas; censure vote recorded in

JSV, 1987 sess., 156–157; obituaries in *Norfolk Ledger-Star* and *Richmond News Leader*, both 29, 30 Dec. 1987, and *Norfolk Virginian-Pilot* and *Richmond Times-Dispatch* (por.), both 30 Dec. 1987.

WARREN FISKE

BABCOCK, Lemuel E. (17 June 1809–2 March 1897), member of the Convention of 1867–1868, was born in Massachusetts but lived in Cheshire County, New Hampshire, after he married early in the 1830s. He and his wife, Sarah Babcock, had one son and four daughters. Sometime during the 1840s Babcock moved to Virginia. In 1850 the census enumerator in Surry County listed him as a carpenter. By the latter part of 1858 Babcock was residing in the eastern portion of Charles City County, where he acquired a house, owned and operated a lumber business and a sawmill, and with his wife joined the Mount Pleasant Baptist Church.

Babcock acquired four slaves in 1860, when his lumber business was listed as the second largest in the county. In spite of his New England connections and his well-known Union sympathies, he remained in Virginia during the Civil War and tried to live harmoniously with his neighbors, even joining the Home Guard in 1862. Nevertheless, local authorities in 1862 charged him "with reading abolishionary papers to the negroes," but they dismissed the charges for lack of evidence. He did not free his slaves, and in 1862 hired some of them to Robert Douthat, a neighboring planter who was also a major in the Confederate cavalry.

Early in 1864 Virginia authorities arrested Babcock as a "suspicious character" and possible agent for the Union army. He was not, but after that experience he began in May 1864 passing information to the Union army. He was arrested a second time in February 1865 and imprisoned in Castle Thunder in Richmond. One of those arrests, although he probably did not know it at the time, complicated matters for the Richmond espionage ring of Elizabeth Van Lew, because her code name was Babcock. Shortly before the Confederate government evacuated Richmond in April 1865, Babcock was placed on a train for Danville, but he escaped in Amelia County. After the Confederate army surrendered he returned to his home in Charles City County.

Babcock resumed operation of his lumber business and probably expected to remain out of politics. His name did not appear on a list of known and respectable local leaders that an agent for the Freedmen's Bureau compiled in April 1867, and one of the bureau's officers later reported that Babcock was "not remarkable for any particular action as friend of the Freedmen, although he was considered as such and is represented as a good Union Man." His local notoriety as a former prisoner of the Confederate government probably contributed to his election on 22 October 1867 to represent the counties of Charles City and New Kent in the constitutional convention that met in Richmond from 3 December 1867 to 17 April 1868. Babcock received 584 votes from African American voters in Charles City County and only 22 from white voters. His opponent, Edmund Waddill, received overwhelming support from white voters and almost none from blacks. Babcock did not speak during the convention, so far as extant records show. He supported suffrage for African Americans but opposed integrating the new public schools and was against disfranchising the antebellum elite.

Although northerners by birth and Unionists, Babcock and his family were not regarded as carpetbaggers in Charles City County. One of his daughters married into a prominent local family and lived the remainder of her life in Charles City County, as did his only son, Charles Babcock, who served as presiding justice of the county court in 1869 and subsequently for twenty-three years as county treasurer. In 1871 Lemuel Babcock sold his sawmill to his son and his house and land to the local Baptist minister and moved with his wife to Saint Albans, Vermont, where his brother, Elias G. Babcock, resided. He returned to Charles City County on several occasions, and in 1885 his name appears on the list of members of the grand jury. Sarah Babcock died in September 1889, and Lemuel E. Babcock died on 2 March 1897. They are both buried in the cemetery at the site of Manoah Baptist Church in Charles City County.

Birth and death dates from gravestone, Manoah Baptist Church site cemetery; records of Mount Pleasant Baptist Church, VBHS; business affairs documented in Land and

Personal Property Tax Returns, Charles City Co., 1859–1863, RG 48, LVA, in other records in Charles City Co. courthouse, and in Graves family account books, in possession of Charles Graves, of Charles City Co.; Southern Claims Commission; *Richmond Daily Enquirer*, 27 Feb. 1865; *Richmond Daily Dispatch*, 1 Mar. 1865; recollections of Thomas McNiven, Personal Papers Collection, LVA; David D. Ryan, ed., *A Yankee Spy in Richmond: The Civil War Diary of "Crazy Bet" Van Lew* (1996); Report on Prominent Whites and Freedmen by N. M. Brooks, 2 Apr. 1867, and Monthly Narrative Report by Brooks, 25 Nov. 1867, Freedmen's Bureau Records; *Richmond Whig*, 24 Oct. 1867; Election Records, no. 427, RG 13, LVA; Richard L. Hume, "The Membership of the Virginia Constitutional Convention of 1867–1868: A Study of the Beginnings of Congressional Reconstruction in the Upper South," *VMHB* 86 (1978): 479–481; Charles City Co. Will Book, 7:458.

JOHN M. COSKI

BACON, Alice Mabel (26 February 1858–1 May 1918), educator and founder of the Hampton Training School for Nurses (Dixie Hospital), was born in New Haven, Connecticut, the youngest of two sons and three daughters of Leonard Bacon and his second wife, Catherine Elizabeth Terry Bacon. Her remarkable family included nine older half brothers and half sisters. Her father was a well-known Congregational minister who served as pastor of the Center Church in New Haven for more than forty years and subsequently became a professor in the Yale Divinity School. Her aunt Delia Salter Bacon originated the theory that Francis Bacon wrote the plays attributed to William Shakespeare. Her sister-in-law Georgeanna Muirson Woolsey Bacon was a noted Civil War nurse, and her half sister Rebecca Bacon was an assistant principal at Hampton Normal and Agricultural Institute during its early years.

Alice Bacon attended private schools in New Haven until age twelve. During a prolonged illness of her mother, she went to Virginia to live for two years with Rebecca Bacon in Hampton. While there she taught arithmetic and spelling to the younger pupils at Hampton Institute and attended classes with the senior students. She decided to emulate her sister and become a teacher of African American children, but in 1872 her father took in twelve-year-old Stematz Yamakawa, one of several girls the Japanese government had sent to the United States to be educated. Bacon returned to New England, and the two girls lived together as sisters for ten years and became fast friends. Bacon also got to know another Japanese girl, Umé Tsuda. Yamakawa graduated from Vassar College in 1882 and then studied nursing at the Connecticut Training School. Bacon, meanwhile, continued studying at home and in 1880 and 1881 passed college-level examinations for women administered by Harvard University, including tests in philosophy and political economy.

In 1882 Bacon went to Colorado and taught there for one year before returning to Hampton in 1883 to teach for five years in the elementary practice school for student teachers. Her courses included political economy, civics, and geography, and she also acted as librarian. In 1888 she accepted an invitation to teach at the Peeresses' School in Tokyo, a new school for girls of the Japanese nobility. Both Umé Tsuda and Stematz Yamakawa, who had married an influential nobleman, recommended her for the position and welcomed her to Japan. Bacon lived with Tsuda and taught for one year. She reported on her experiences in Japan in a column called "Silhouettes" that she contributed to Hampton's journal, the *Southern Workman*. Two years after she returned to the United States, Bacon published *Japanese Girls and Women* (1891), which described the changes in society and the roles of women since the Japanese feudal system had begun to collapse twenty years earlier. Her second book, *A Japanese Interior* (1893), was an edition of the letters she had written to her family while living with Umé Tsuda in Tokyo.

In the autumn of 1889 Bacon resumed teaching at Hampton, and she also helped establish a small hospital that opened in May 1891. With the support of the institute's principal and with the help of physicians, civic leaders, and ministers, she conducted a campaign to create the hospital and begin a training program for nurses. The Hampton Training School for Nurses, incorporated on 4 March 1892, was commonly called Dixie Hospital after the horse that Bacon used to transport ill patients to the facility. The hospital slowly grew to include a maternity area and a residence for student nurses. She served as secretary of the board from the founding of the hospital through 1897. Bacon was proud that the administration permitted no racial distinctions in admitting patients to the hospital. Later, when contributors demanded racially segregated hospital facilities, she helped draft regulations under which such donors were required to make annual contributions to support separate facilities.

Bacon continued to write "Silhouettes" for the *Southern Workman* to garner public support for the institute and the hospital. Some of the vivid word pictures she drew used dialect to emphasize degrees of ignorance, poverty, and worthiness of the people she sought to help. She also prepared a short report for the John F. Slater Fund in 1896 describing the Cotton States and International Exposition of 1895, which was published as *The Negro and the Atlantic Exposition* in number seven of the fund's *Occasional Papers*.

Bacon went back to Japan in the spring of 1900 and remained through April 1902 to teach at the Tokyo Women's Higher Normal School and at the Girls' English Institute, founded by Umé Tsuda and later popularly known as Tsuda College. The institute was the first nonmission school intended solely for the advanced education of women in Japan. The students were high school graduates who studied to become teachers of English or prepared to continue their higher educations in the English language. Bacon served as assistant to the founder, helped to raise funds, conducted worship services, led discussions on current topics, and taught a heavy load without accepting any payment. The social changes she observed since her previous visit to Japan became the basis of a new chapter in the 1902 revised edition of her *Japanese Girls and Women*. Bacon also published a collection of Japanese folk tales, *In the Land of the Gods: Some Stories of Japan* (1905), and she edited the American edition of Tadayoshi Sakurai's *Human Bullets: A Soldier's Story of Port Arthur* (1907).

Bacon returned to New Haven in 1902 to work on her books and to raise money to support the activities of the civic club she had founded. She also worked to support the foreign mission work of Center Church, and she gave an annual entertainment at Squam Lake Deep Haven Camp, which she conducted in Holderness, New Hampshire, to raise funds for Dixie Hospital. Bacon continued to attend annual meetings of the hospital board and supported improvements in nursing education to meet the requirements for professional registration of nurses. At a special meeting on 5 October 1903, the board adopted her proposal for a new three-year training course. In 1913 a room in Dixie's large new brick hospital building was named for her.

Bacon taught from 1908 to 1910 at Miss Capen's School, a prestigious preparatory school for girls in Northampton, Massachusetts. In her will she bequeathed money to establish a trust fund for the Hampton Training School for Nurses. During her final illness a graduate of Dixie Hospital attended her. Alice Mabel Bacon died in New Haven on 1 May 1918 and was buried there in Grove Street Cemetery.

Bacon's books and approximately eighty "Silhouettes" columns in *Southern Workman* between Feb. 1885 and July 1907 document her life; family history in Thomas M. Baldwin, *Bacon Genealogy: Michael Bacon of Dedham, 1640, and His Descendants* (1915); Alice M. Bacon, "A Child's Impressions of Early Hampton," in Armstrong League of Hampton Workers, Hampton Institute, *Memories of Old Hampton*, 2d ed. (1909), 75–94; Alice Mabel Bacon Papers, Faculty Biographical Files, Samuel Chapman Armstrong Papers, Cora Mae Folsom Papers, Nursing Education Papers, and Dixie Hospital Ledgers, Hampton; Cora Mae Folsom, "The Dixie Hospital in the Beginning," *Southern Workman* 55 (1926): 121–126 (por.); Patricia E. Sloan, "A History of the Establishment and Early Development of Selected Nurse Training Schools for Afro-Americans: 1886–1906" (Ed.D. diss., Teachers College, Columbia University, 1978), 121–158; Cynthia Neverdon-Morton, *Afro-American Women of the South and the Advancement of the Race, 1895–1925* (1989), 21 (por.), 28–31; obituaries in *New Haven Journal Courier* and *New Haven Register*, both 3 May 1918; memorial in *Southern Workman* 47 (1918): 263–264.

PATRICIA E. SLOAN

BACON, Nathaniel (bap. 29 August 1620–16 March 1692), member of the Council, was the only son of James Bacon and Martha Bacon. His father, who also had three daughters by this or another marriage, was rector of Burgate in the county of Suffolk, England. Bacon was probably born at his paternal grandfather's Suffolk seat, Friston Hall, and he was christened on 29 August 1620 in the Parish of Saint Mary's, Bury Saint Edmunds, Suffolk. He was distantly related to the philosopher Francis

Bacon and among later Virginia writers has often been referred to as Nathaniel Bacon Sr., or Nathaniel Bacon the Elder, in order to distinguish him from his namesake cousin, known in Virginia history as Nathaniel Bacon the Rebel.

Little is known about Bacon's youth, but he visited France in 1647 before settling in Virginia by the spring of 1653. He lived first in Isle of Wight County, but by 1656 he had moved to York County. Sometime before March 1655 he married the twice-widowed Ann Bassett Smith Jones. She died shortly thereafter, and he married another widow, Elizabeth Kingsmill Tayloe, about 1656 or 1657. Through his marriages and acquisitions of land in his own right he speedily became a prosperous man of consequence in York County, and he began a long career in politics in March 1656 when he represented the county in the House of Burgesses. By December 1656 he had become a member of the governor's Council, on which he served until sometime in 1659, when he was again elected to the House of Burgesses. On an unrecorded date before 26 August 1660 he was again named to the Council, and he remained a member until his death. By January 1682 he was the senior member, but for reasons that are not clear he yielded seniority to Nicholas Spencer, who served as president and acting governor for nine months beginning in May 1683. Bacon served as president and acting governor on three occasions, during the absences from Virginia of Governor Effingham between June and September 1684 and July and September 1687, and between Effingham's departure from the colony in March 1689 and the beginning of Lieutenant Governor Francis Nicholson's term on 3 June 1690. Bacon was also auditor of the royal revenue in Virginia from May 1675 until he resigned in favor of William Byrd (1652–1704) effective 20 June 1688. The auditor saw that money due to the Crown was collected and sent to London and in return earned a commission that yielded approximately £250 a year.

Bacon's father had an affinity with the Puritans, but if Bacon shared it it did not hinder his rapid rise in Virginia politics and society, nor did he have difficulty adjusting to the transition from the Commonwealth back to royal government in 1660. In spite of being a kinsman of Nathaniel Bacon the Rebel, he remained fiercely loyal to the government of Governor Sir William Berkeley in 1676 and was reported to have offered his relative "a considerable part of his Estate" on the condition that "hee would lay downe his Armes, and become a good subject to his Majestie, that that colony might not be disturbed or destroyed, nor his owne Family stained with soe foule a Blott." The rebels occupied his plantation on King's Creek and caused damage estimated at £1,000.

Nathaniel Bacon had no children, and his principal heir was a niece, Abigail Smith Burwell, who was living in Gloucester County at the time of his death. She and her children inherited Bacon's landholdings consisting of King's Creek plantation of 1,200 acres of land, 1,775 acres in Isle of Wight and Nansemond Counties, 300 acres in New Kent County, 3 acres on Jamestown Island, and a lot in Yorktown. His personal estate was valued after his death at almost £1,200, in addition to £575 in cash legacies specified in his will. Nathaniel Bacon died on 16 March 1692 and was buried at his residence on King's Creek in York County.

Saint Mary's Parish register, Bury Saint Edmunds, Eng.; attendance as burgess recorded in *Journals of House of Burgesses* and in York Co. Deeds, Orders, and Wills, 3:66–67, 96; membership on Council documented in York Co. Deeds, Orders, and Wills, 1:298, 3:125, and Thomas Culpeper's undated memorandum on his copy of his 27 Jan. 1682 royal instructions, PRO CO 1/48, fol. 62; service as acting governor documented in Billings, *Effingham Papers*, 122–124, 310, 313–314, 406–408, 432–434; service as auditor documented in royal warrant of 12 May 1675, PRO CO 1/34, fol. 154, and Marion Tinling, ed., *Correspondence of the Three William Byrds of Westover, Virginia, 1684–1776* (1977), 1:84; quotation and description of losses during Bacon's Rebellion in *VMHB* 5 (1897): 64–65; will in York Co. Deeds, Orders, and Wills, 9:116–117; J. Lesslie Hall, "Ancient Epitaphs and Inscriptions, in York and James City Counties, Virginia," *Collections of the Virginia Historical Society*, new ser., 11 (1892): 104.

PETER V. BERGSTROM

BACON, Nathaniel (2 January 1647–26 October 1676), member of the Council and leader of Bacon's Rebellion, the only son and one of several children of Thomas Bacon and Elizabeth Brooke Bacon, was born at Friston Hall in Suffolk County, England, the seat of his father. His mother died shortly after his birth. Bacon matriculated at Saint Catherine's College, Cambridge University, on 5 May 1661, but two years later his father withdrew him from school, probably due to his inattention to his studies, and hired a tutor to teach him. He made a tour of the Continent in the company of his tutor, was admitted to Gray's Inn on 22 November 1664, and returned to Cambridge, where he received his M.B. in 1667. In May 1670 he married Elizabeth Duke, daughter of Sir Edward Duke, who so disapproved of the match that he disinherited her. Although the couple nonetheless had sufficient property for a comfortable living, Bacon became involved in a fraudulent scheme to sell a parcel of land, which resulted in a lawsuit that persisted for several years after his death. Probably as a consequence, he moved to Virginia in the summer of 1674 with his wife and possibly their two daughters, whose birth dates are unknown. His father sent him off with £1,800 to start his life anew.

In August 1674 Bacon purchased 820 acres of land at Curles Neck in Henrico County from Thomas Ballard (d. 1690) and probably moved into an existing house on the site soon thereafter. He also acquired from Ballard a smaller tract of land near the falls of the James River that became known as Bacon's Quarter. Bacon was related by blood or marriage to several of the most influential people in Virginia, including his cousin Nathaniel Bacon (1620–1692), a member of the governor's Council, Governor Sir William Berkeley, and Frances Culpeper Stephens Berkeley, the governor's wife. Bacon was well connected, well educated, intelligent, tall, and handsome, although somewhat melancholy and, in the view of some Virginians, unpleasantly arrogant. On 3 March 1675, in spite of the brevity of Bacon's residence in Virginia, the governor appointed him one of several new members of the Council.

The rebellion Bacon led against the governor erupted suddenly the next year following a long period of unsettled politics, economic hardship, and, more proximately, a series of genuinely frightening incidents. Skirmishes in 1675 between frontier settlers and Doeg and Susquehannock Indians in the Potomac River valley stimulated a widespread fear of organized Indian raids, fears that were heightened after Virginians learned of the outbreak in New England of what came to be called King Philip's War. By then Bacon had begun participating with William Byrd (1652–1704) in trade with some of the Indians on the southwestern border of the settled parts of Virginia and, as some writers later charged, one result may have been his growing antipathy toward the governor, who was also a significant participant in the Indian trade and therefore a competitor. Bacon's animosity toward the Indians, however, appears to have been the mainspring of his conduct. In September 1675 he seized some friendly Appamattuck Indians whom he accused of stealing corn, for which "rash heady action" the governor rebuked him.

In March 1676 the General Assembly met to prepare for defending the colony and enacted laws to erect forts along the fall line, to try to keep friendly Indians at peace with the colonists, and to cut off the Indian trade temporarily to reduce contacts that might flare into conflicts. By then Indian raids had reached the falls of the James River, and Bacon's own overseer at Bacon's Quarter had been killed in a raid that triggered new alarms. The causes of the rebellion later adduced by royal commissioners included public resentment of the requisite high taxes, which the people believed had bought no real protection. In this charged atmosphere Bacon became the leader of the angry and frightened militiamen in the upper reaches of the James River valley, and he requested permission from the governor to lead an expedition against the hostile Indians. Berkeley's denial of the request increased the resentment of the frontier settlers, augmented Bacon's local popularity, and produced a breach between the governor and the councillor after Bacon went ahead with preparations to attack local, friendly Indians. In May, Berkeley expelled Bacon from the Council and branded him a rebel, at the same time offering to pardon Bacon's followers if they would return to their homes.

Berkeley also called for the election of a new House of Burgesses and convened the new assembly as soon as possible in order to take necessary additional steps to secure the safety of the colony. Bacon, meanwhile, led his men southwest to one of the main Occaneechi villages. He persuaded the Occaneechi to attack a nearby party of hostile Susquehannocks, but the allies soon quarreled and, after a pitched battle, Bacon and his men devastated the Occaneechi village. Berkeley condemned Bacon's actions, but Bacon's men now controlled much of the colony and actually prevented the sheriff of Henrico County from reading the governor's proclamation of condemnation there. Moreover, the Henrico voters elected Bacon and one of his principal lieutenants, James Crews, to the House of Burgesses for the assembly that gathered on 5 June and has historically been referred to as Bacon's Assembly.

On 6 June 1676 Bacon and a company of armed men arrived in Jamestown. Berkeley's agents seized Bacon and carried him before the governor and the assembly, where he apologized on bended knee for his misdeeds and presented a written petition for a pardon. The governor then announced that he was pardoning Bacon and restoring him to his seat on the Council. At this point an assembly member urged that Bacon be made a general to command the campaign against the Indians, and the large crowd of angry men who had descended on Jamestown took up the cry. The governor vacillated, first agreeing to the appointment but then changing his mind, revoking his pardon of Bacon, and again expelling him from the Council.

Bacon left Jamestown, but on 23 June he stormed back into the capital with about 500 men and demanded that the governor commission him as a general to lead the colony against the Indians. A dramatic and dangerous scene ensued, with Bacon's men drawing their arms against the assembled burgesses and the governor literally baring his chest and daring Bacon's men to shoot him. Berkeley nevertheless yielded to the demands of Bacon and his supporters, and the assembly rapidly completed work on the laws of the session. Although later writers referred to these statutes as "Bacon's laws," the extant evidence indicates that he took little or no interest in the proceedings of the assembly.

Bacon withdrew upriver in search of Indians to attack, but late in July the governor again reversed course, once again declared Bacon a rebel, and went to Gloucester County to recruit men to fight him. Bacon and his army marched to Middle Plantation, the site of present-day Williamsburg, while Berkeley retreated to the Eastern Shore. About 30 July Bacon issued the first of a series of declarations of grievance and complaint against Berkeley, together with justifications of his own actions, which he signed as "General, by the consent of the people." Bacon compelled or cajoled many people to subscribe to his declarations accusing the governor of fomenting a civil war and endangering the safety of the colony, and he sent riders into various parts of Virginia to gather signatures to an oath of loyalty to the rebellion and to summon leading men to meet him at Middle Plantation. On 3 August 1676 Bacon obtained the endorsement of seventy of them to his leadership against the Indians, and the next day thirty signatories assented to a more radical declaration that a new assembly was to be chosen under his authority rather than recalling the one that had met in June. Bacon then marched his men into the Dragon Swamp on the lower reaches of the Rappahannock River, where they attacked the friendly Pamunkey Indians.

Early in September the governor returned to Jamestown with a small force and issued another proclamation against Bacon, whereupon Bacon marched there and laid siege to the capital. On 19 September 1676 Berkeley abandoned Jamestown, and Bacon's men occupied and burned it. Bacon's forces in and out of Jamestown were by then beyond control. Many of them apparently spent much of their time ransacking the estates of men identified as loyal to the governor.

By autumn letters from Virginia had arrived in London apprising royal officials of the rebellion. King Charles II formed a three-member commission to assist the governor in suppressing the revolt and to inquire into its causes. On 27 October the king signed a proclamation for putting down the rebellion led by "Nathaniel Bacon the Younger." The king offered to pardon Bacon's lieutenants, whom he characterized as "Persons of mean and desperate Fortunes," if they speedily surrendered. With respect to

Nathaniel Bacon, the proclamation was already a dead letter. On 26 October 1676, the day before the king signed the proclamation, Bacon and the bulk of his following were in Gloucester County where, at the house of Thomas Pate, Nathaniel Bacon died of the "Bloody Flux" (dysentery) and a "Lousey Disease." The place of his burial is not known. Without his impetuous leadership the rebellion soon collapsed, and Berkeley later hanged several of Bacon's most active followers.

Bacon's Rebellion has inspired much writing, including more than a dozen works of fiction, and scholarly interpretations of Nathaniel Bacon's motivations and his significance vary widely. Early in the nineteenth century the Virginia historian John Daly Burk presented Bacon as a patriotic precursor to the American revolutionaries of 1776, an influential interpretation repeated by other writers, most notably Thomas Jefferson Wertenbaker in his *Torchbearer of the Revolution: The Story of Bacon's Rebellion and Its Leader* (1940). Governor Berkeley has had his defenders, too. In *The Governor and the Rebel: A History of Bacon's Rebellion in Virginia* (1957), Wilcomb E. Washburn presented Bacon as the ambitious and impetuous leader of a mob of Indian-hating frontiersmen. However one may interpret him, the rebellion itself preceded significant changes for Virginia. The colonists came under much closer English supervision than before 1676 and, by century's end, they had embraced an economy based on enslaved labor. Bacon's Rebellion is one of the most important and controversial events of Virginia's history, and scholars continue to debate its causes and its significance.

Evidence for birth date discussed in Wertenbaker, *Torchbearer of the Revolution*, 215; scholarly accounts of Bacon's life and the causes, events, and effects of Bacon's Rebellion also include Edmund S. Morgan, *American Slavery, American Freedom: The Ordeal of Colonial Virginia* (1975), 235–292, William L. Shea, *The Virginia Militia in the Seventeenth Century* (1983), 97–121, Stephen Saunders Webb, *1676: The End of American Independence* (1984), 3–245, and Warren M. Billings, John E. Selby, and Thad W. Tate, *Colonial Virginia: A History* (1986), 77–117; full bibliographical essay on primary sources in Washburn, *The Governor and the Rebel*, 167–175; scholarly literature on and fictional accounts of Bacon's Rebellion discussed in Jane Carson, *Bacon's Rebellion, 1676–1976* (1976); John Davenport Neville, ed., *Bacon's Rebellion: Abstracts of Materials in the Colonial Records Project* [1976]; death date in report of royal investigative commission, PRO CO 5/1371, fol. 211.

BRENT TARTER

BADEN, John Alfred (10 May 1913–26 April 1983), suffragan bishop of the Episcopal Diocese of Virginia, was born in Washington, D.C., the only son and eldest of five children of John Alfred Baden and Marion Sturgis Baden. His father worked in the insurance business, and the family moved several times before settling on a farm in Prince Georges County, Maryland, in 1923. Baden spent part of his childhood in Roanoke and in Richmond, where he started elementary school. He graduated from high school in 1930, but the death of his father later that year forced Baden to postpone his plans to attend college. For several years he worked for an insurance company and then began to take classes at the University of Maryland and also at the law school of George Washington University. In 1939 he received both a bachelor of science degree from Maryland and a bachelor of law degree from George Washington.

Baden worked from 1939 until 1942 for Southern States Cooperative Corporation in Frederick, Maryland, where on 11 July 1942 he married Jean Deloris Feaga. They had two sons and one daughter. In February 1942 he enlisted in the United States Navy and spent the war years as a recruitment officer in Bristol, Virginia. Following his discharge from the navy with the rank of chief petty officer in January 1946, he decided to enter the ministry and enrolled in the Virginia Theological Seminary in Alexandria. He graduated with a bachelor of divinity degree and was ordained in 1948.

Baden served as rector of Saint James Church in Monkton and Saint James Mission in Parkton, both in Baltimore County, Maryland, from 1948 to 1958, when he became executive secretary of the Department of Missions of the Diocese of Virginia. In 1959 he became archdeacon of the diocese and held that position for three years. From 1962 until 1973 he was rector of Frederick Parish and minister at Christ Episcopal Church in Winchester, serving as a delegate to the church's general convention from 1964 to 1969 and on the executive council of the diocese from 1968 to 1972. From 1950 to 1973 he served as the founding director of the church's Middle Atlantic Parish Training Program, and he was an early advocate of inexpensive A-frame church buildings for rapidly expanding suburban congregations. Between 1960 and 1980 he was also an adjunct professor at Virginia Theological Seminary, which in 1972 awarded him an honorary doctorate of divinity.

In November 1963 Baden was elected bishop of the Diocese of Northern Michigan, but he declined the post, and he was nominated but not elected suffragan bishop of the Diocese of Virginia in September 1969. Baden was elected to the latter post on 28 April 1973, however, and from then until 1979 he lived in Alexandria, where his duties as assistant to the bishop involved him in all phases of the church's work. His responsibilities included support of missionary work overseas, especially in Tanzania, and mediation of disputes between parish vestries and ministers. He wrote a chapter on the liturgical ministry of bishops for the church's Evangelical Education Society's *Prayer Book Manual* (1981). From 1974 until 1981 he also served on the Virginia State Board of Corrections. In 1979 he contracted cancer and following an operation retired as suffragan bishop and moved to a small farm at Bunker Hill, Berkeley County, West Virginia, where he tended a flock of sheep rather than a congregation. John Alfred Baden died of liver cancer in Alexandria on 26 April 1983 and was buried at the theological seminary there.

Biography and interview in *Virginia Churchman* 81 (15 Apr. 1973): 3; family history information verified by Jean Deloris Feaga Baden and Adelaide Baden Leech; election as suffragan bishop reported in *Virginia Churchman* 82 (May 1973): 1; obituaries in *Alexandria Gazette*, *Richmond Times-Dispatch* (por.), *Washington Post*, and *Winchester Evening Star*, all 27 Apr. 1983, and *Virginia Churchman* 92 (June 1983): 7; memorial in Episcopal Diocese of Virginia, *Journal of the Annual Council* (1984): 53.

ROBERT W. PRICHARD

BAGBY, Bathurst Browne (3 June 1879–6 July 1951), public health official, was born near Stevensville in King and Queen County, the third of four sons and fifth of six children of Alexander Fleet Bagby and Fannie Singleton Walker Bagby. He was educated at local academies and grew up in the Tidewater, moving to Stevensville in 1884 and Tappahannock in 1889. At age seventeen he moved to Washington, D.C., boarded with his brother Edward Benjamin Bagby, and successively attended Columbian Academy and Eastern High School in that city. Awarded a scholarship to Columbian Medical College (now part of George Washington University), he earned an M.D. in 1904. On 28 December 1904 he married Alpha Celeste Johnson, whom he had met in Washington. Their two sons became physicians.

Bagby began his medical practice in Walkerton in King and Queen County. Soon thereafter he earned a reputation as a public health pioneer. At the October 1906 annual meeting of the Medical Society of Virginia, the first such meeting he attended, he delivered a paper that caused a sensation. Although Bailey K. Ashford, a physician working in Puerto Rico, and medical zoologist Charles Wardell Stiles had already focused considerable attention in scientific circles on uncinariasis, or hookworm disease, their findings had little impact on southern physicians. Based on his own clinical experience in Walkerton, Bagby informed his startled audience how extensive the disease was in Virginia and dramatized his point by bringing three hookworm sufferers and sixty vials of hookworms along with him to the meeting. The assembled society members gave him a standing ovation and elected him first vice president. Bagby's presentation soon had important consequences. Two years later, when the General Assembly was debating whether to establish a state health department, his evidence of hookworm infection helped persuade legislators to pass the bill.

In the meantime Bagby, who had suffered from symptoms of tuberculosis, moved to Carrizozo, New Mexico, where he practiced medicine from July 1906 to July 1907. He then returned to Virginia and opened an office in Urbanna in Middlesex County. In May 1908 he moved to West Point, where he practiced medicine for the next fifteen years. He also was elected president of the Public Health Association of Virginia in 1911.

After spending the first half of his professional life in private practice, Bagby began a second career in public health in 1923, when he was appointed the first public health officer of Henrico County. Sanitation was of primary importance. Under his leadership the county installed a sewer system and began a cooperative relationship with the Rockefeller Foundation's International Health Board, which was then promoting the development of modern public health facilities and programs at the county level throughout the South. On 7 May 1924 Bagby joined the Richmond City Health Department, serving simultaneously for five months as acting city health officer while continuing his work for the county. In August 1924 Bagby was appointed chief medical inspector of Richmond's Department of Welfare. He initiated a medical inspection program for the city, conducted a special study of means of typhoid and diphtheria control, and established clinics to fight infant mortality and communicable diseases.

On 1 September 1926 Bagby departed for Georgia to serve as health commissioner for Clarke County and the city of Athens. He found challenging conditions in the county, one of four in the nation and two in the South that were participating in a child health demonstration project financed by the Commonwealth Fund. When the two-year project ended, Bagby returned to Virginia in 1929 to become Southampton County's health officer, a position that he held for two years. In December 1930 he returned to Richmond as director of the Bureau of Child Health of the State Department of Health. During the next decade his duties included the development of medical inspection of schoolchildren and the extension of public health practices in the schools.

Bagby retired in May 1940 when he was sixty-one. He devoted his leisure to hunting and fishing at his 1,500-acre farm near West Point. Although he continued to practice in adjacent counties and agreed to fill a vacancy by serving once again as Richmond's acting health officer and city epidemiologist from 17 December 1940 until 31 May 1941, Bagby spent his last years in Edwardsville in Northumberland County. While there he completed an autobiography that was published in 1950. Bathurst Browne Bagby died at his home in Edwardsville on 6 July 1951 and was buried in Smyrna Christian Church Cemetery in King and Queen County.

Bathurst Browne Bagby, *Recollections* (1950), and "Uncinariasis," *Virginia Medical Semi-Monthly* 11 (1907): 469–471; feature articles in *Richmond News Leader*, 29 May 1940, and *Richmond Times-Dispatch*, 15 Dec. 1940; Child Health Demonstration Series, Commonwealth Fund Records, Rockefeller Archive Center, Sleepy Hollow, N.Y.; *Richmond News Leader*, 8 May 1924, 22, 23 July 1926, 28 Apr. 1927, 26 July 1928, 15 Dec. 1930, 28 May 1940, 12 Mar., 2 June 1941; *Richmond Times-Dispatch*, 29 Aug. 1924; obituaries in *Richmond News Leader* (por.) and *Richmond Times-Dispatch*, both 7 July 1951, and *Virginia Medical Monthly* 78 (1951): 454.

WILLIAM A. LINK

BAGBY, Ellen Matthews (3 April 1879–19 July 1960), preservationist, was born in Richmond, the youngest of four daughters and ninth of ten children of George William Bagby, a noted humorist, and Lucy Parke Chamberlayne Bagby, a civic leader. She attended the exclusive Richmond Female Seminary. Although she made several trips abroad as an adult and spent vacations at Rapidan in Culpeper County, she lived her entire life in Richmond, first in her mother's family home and later, toward the end of her life, in an apartment a few blocks away. She had several beaux, but never married.

Like her mother, Bagby was active in numerous organizations, among them the Episcopal Church, the Association for the Preservation of Virginia Antiquities, the Jamestowne Society, the English Speaking Union, the Colonial Dames, the United Daughters of the Confederacy, the Valentine Museum, the Virginia Historical Society, and the Society for the Prevention of Cruelty to Animals. During World War I she sat on the boards of directors of several community war agencies, and during World War II she belonged to the Richmond Civil Defense Committee. Bagby served on the advisory committee for Saint Margaret's Episcopal School in Tappahannock and on a committee formed to commemorate the centennial of the birth of Virginia writer Thomas Nelson Page. She also edited a new release of her father's writings, *The Old Virginia Gentleman and Other*

Sketches, published in 1938 and reissued in 1943 and 1948.

Diminutive and energetic, Miss Ellen, as she was usually known, had one great passion: Jamestown Island. In 1930 she became chairman of the Jamestown Committee of the Association for the Preservation of Virginia Antiquities, a position once held by her mother and retained by Bagby until her death. Although the organization owned other properties, the profits from admissions and memorabilia sales at Jamestown financed many of its activities, and the work at Jamestown was what most engaged Bagby. The APVA owned twenty-two-and-a-half acres surrounding the church tower ruins at Jamestown, and Bagby supervised the day-to-day operation of the historic site. She hired and fired employees, ordered souvenirs, had booklets and brochures printed, gave talks to visiting groups, worried about lawn mowers, bought supplies, and oversaw construction, painting, and repairs to buildings. No detail was too small for her attention. In 1939, stopping by Jamestown on her way home from a vacation, she learned that one staff member had resigned and another had fallen ill. Bagby abandoned her plans and remained at Jamestown for the rest of the summer, acting as superintendent and hostess.

Bagby also dealt with the National Park Service, which in 1934 acquired the remaining 1,559 acres of Jamestown Island. In 1940 she helped negotiate an agreement between the APVA and the Park Service that provided for the joint administration of the historic site. She delighted in the visits of royalty and entertained the king and queen of Greece in 1953 and the queen mother of the United Kingdom a year later. Bagby was a member of the Jamestown Corporation, which was responsible for two outdoor pageants, *The Common Glory* and *The Founders*, and she was the only woman on the Virginia 350th Anniversary Commission that planned and directed the 1957 commemoration of the first English settlement in Virginia. That year marked the high point of Bagby's administration, with 700,000 visitors, including Queen Elizabeth II, visiting Jamestown.

Colonial Williamsburg and the Jamestown Foundation honored Bagby and her work in a special ceremony on 15 May 1960. On that occasion Carlisle H. Humelsine, the president of Colonial Williamsburg, referred to her as "a kind of historical archangel" of Jamestown. Ellen Matthews Bagby died in her apartment in Richmond on 19 July 1960 and was buried in Hollywood Cemetery.

Lucy Parke Chamberlayne Bagby to Ennion Williams, 6 Jan. 1925, filed in BVS Birth Register, Richmond City; John Marshall Lee, "Miss Ellen M. Bagby and the A.P.V.A.," *Commonwealth* 25 (July 1958): 14–16 (por.); *Newport News Daily Press* and *Richmond Times-Dispatch*, both 16 May 1960; Bagby Family Papers, VHS; W. H. Smith Papers, Williamsburg Historic Records Association, W&M; Association for the Preservation of Virginia Antiquities, *Year Book* (1930–1960); Richard T. Couture, *To Preserve and Protect: A History of the Association for the Preservation of Virginia Antiquities* (1984), 74, 113–128 (por.), 132–134, 160–162; Nancy Elizabeth Packer, *White Gloves & Red Bricks: APVA 1889–1989* (1989), 14–15; obituaries and editorial tributes in *Richmond News Leader* and *Richmond Times-Dispatch* both 20, 21 July 1960.

SUSAN A. RIGGS

BAGBY, Frances Elizabeth Scott (21 March 1853–15 May 1922), civic leader, was born in King and Queen County, the eldest of four sons and three daughters of Azariah Francis Scott, a Baptist minister, and Margaret Elizabeth Holt Scott. Known as Fanny to her family and friends, Scott attended Hollins Institute from 1870 to 1873. She received a departmental diploma in English in 1872, another in Latin a year later, and certificates of proficiency in chemistry and natural philosophy. Her studies also included French, mathematics, and piano/music, and she was awarded a medal for excellence in English composition in 1873.

On 25 April 1876 Scott married a young attorney, Thomas Pollard Bagby, in Essex County. They lived in West Point and had three sons and two daughters between 1877 and 1888. Her husband died of typhoid fever on 8 December 1889. Little is known about her personal finances, but she did not take a job and was able to engage in extensive volunteer work.

Bagby was involved in the mission activities of the Baptist Church on the local and state levels. On 28 April 1884 she hosted the founding meeting of the West Point Baptist Ladies Aid Society, the local branch of the Woman's

Missionary Union of Virginia that was in turn an auxiliary to the Baptist General Association. Later Bagby served as the superintendent of the district WMU and from 1902 to 1905 as an auxiliary delegate to the Dover Baptist Association. She capped her statewide missions activity by serving as president of the Woman's Missionary Union of Virginia from 1905 to 1907.

In March 1896 the West Point Town Council appointed Bagby to King William County's school board. The state superintendent of public instruction, John E. Massey, consulted with the attorney general and informed the county school superintendent that Bagby was ineligible because the law required that school board members be eligible to vote. Nonetheless, her widely reported appointment by the all-male town council attests to her reputation as an intelligent and well-respected community leader. By 1915 Bagby had joined the West Point Equal Suffrage League and served as the group's vice president and legislative chairman.

Bagby was elected the first chairman of the Executive Committee of the Hollins Alumnae Association in 1897, served as the organization's president from 1902 to 1908, and took part in its efforts to raise money for the school's library. Active in the Woman's Christian Temperance Union, she was elected president of the Virginia chapter in 1897. In April 1899 she formed a Young Woman's Branch of the WCTU in King William County. She was also a longtime member of West Point's First Baptist Church and a president of the West Point Community League.

After the turn of the century Bagby began publishing essays, historical fiction, and letters to local and regional newspapers. In her writings she maintained that society could only be saved through missionary work, increased church attendance, and progressive reforms in social and political institutions. Bagby also used her essays to explore her interest in history. In her one book, *Tuckahoe: A Collection of Indian Stories and Legends* (1907), she focused on the lives of the Pamunkey Indians. Other works dealt with the early Baptists and the formation of the American political system. Bagby wrote for a number of newspapers and small journals, such as the short-lived *Southern Magazine*, which published five of her pieces including a 1906 article advancing the novel hypothesis that Pocahontas and Virginia Dare had been one and the same and urging that a monument be erected to her memory. Frances Elizabeth Scott Bagby died suddenly from heart disease on 15 May 1922 while attending a meeting of the West Point post of the American Legion, where reformer Katherine Harwood Waller Barrett was speaking. Bagby was buried in a local cemetery.

BVS Birth Register, King and Queen Co.; BVS Marriage Register, Essex Co.; family history information supplied by Grace N. Dickerson, Richmond, and Elizabeth Cox, Rome, Ga.; Hollins Institute, *Annual Catalogue* (1872/1873): 6–8; *Spinster* (Hollins yearbook) 1 (1898): 113 (por.), 116; John E. Massey to J. H. Gwathmey, 31 Mar. 1896, in *Richmond Dispatch* and *Richmond State*, both 7 Apr. 1896; Woman's Christian Temperance Union of Virginia, *Annual Report* 20 (1902): 40, 44; *Century of Service: A History of Organized Women's Work in First Baptist Church, West Point, Virginia* (1986), 1–3, 14 (por.); Juliette Mather, *Light Three Candles: History of Woman's Missionary Union of Virginia, 1874–1973* [1973], 62, 67; Woman's Missionary Union of Virginia, *Minutes of the Annual Session* 8 (1906): 14–19; 9 (1907): 15–17; Historical Records Survey, West Point, Equal Suffrage League Papers, LVA; Bagby, "Virginia Dare" and "A Memorial to Pocahontas," *Southern Magazine* 1 (Oct. 1906): 13–14 and 1 (Nov. 1906): 13; obituaries in *Richmond Times-Dispatch*, 16 May 1922, and *Religious Herald*, 8 June 1922.

MARY F. BRAME

BAGBY, George William (13 August 1828–29 November 1883), journalist, essayist, and humorist, was born on the Buckingham County plantation of William Evans, his maternal grandfather. He was the only son and elder of two children of George Bagby, owner of a general store in Lynchburg, and Virginia Young Evans Bagby, who were both descended from families that had been in Virginia since before the Revolution. Bagby's mother died when he was about eight years old, and his father sent him and his sister to live on the Cumberland County plantation of their aunt Elizabeth Hobson. Bagby there developed the sensitivity to the minutiae of plantation life that later informed many of his popular essays, including the beautifully crafted 1860 composition, "Fishing on the Appomattox."

When Bagby was ten his father sent him to Edgehill School in Princeton, New Jersey. Two years later he transferred to Hurlbut School in

Philadelphia, and in 1843 he entered Delaware College. He matriculated at the University of Pennsylvania in 1846 and graduated with a degree in medicine in 1849. Bagby may have studied medicine to satisfy his father's wishes, because after he moved back to Lynchburg he made little or no attempt to establish a practice.

In 1853 Bagby and a close friend, George Woodville Latham, began publication of a newspaper, the *Lynchburg Express*, which lasted only three years but launched Bagby on a lifelong career in journalism and writing. In 1857 he moved to Washington, D.C., where he served as correspondent for a number of southern newspapers, started to publish essays in national journals, and began acquiring fame as a writer. His first articles in a journal of wide distribution were "My Wife and My Theory About Wives" and "The Virginia Editor," which appeared in *Harper's New Monthly Magazine* 11 (1855): 779–782 and 14 (1856): 66–69, respectively. In 1858 he published in the *Southern Literary Messenger* the first of his eight "Mozis Addums" letters, addressed to "Billy Ivvins" in "Curdsville, Va." The Addums letters were modeled on the speech of backwoods characters Bagby had known as a boy and were influenced by the well-established tradition of southwest dialect humor, and they were an immediate success. Although Bagby later came to resent the lasting popularity of Mozis Addums, complaining that for many years the name made him "a little sick whenever I heard it," the enormous popularity of the letters was no doubt responsible in part for Bagby's being named successor to John Reuben Thompson in June 1860 as editor of the *Southern Literary Messenger*. In March 1863 he also became associate editor of the *Richmond Whig*.

Relieved to get away from the antislavery fervor of many of Washington's politicians, Bagby enthusiastically supported secession and the Southern cause in his editorials in the *Messenger*, but the war had a disastrous effect on the magazine. After struggling for more than three years to keep the publication alive in the face of dwindling supplies of paper and ink and shrinking subscription rolls, Bagby resigned his position as editor in January 1864, only months before the most-distinguished literary journal in the South ceased publication forever. Bagby joined the Confederate army on 22 April 1861, but the chronic dyspepsia from which he suffered all of his adult life led to his discharge late in September 1861. He tied his fortunes so closely to the Confederate cause that in April 1865 he fled Richmond aboard the same train that carried Jefferson Davis and his entourage to Danville.

Bagby returned to Richmond within a month to join his young wife, Lucy Parke Chamberlayne Bagby, whom he had married on 16 February 1863. They had six sons and four daughters between 1864 and 1882. Faced with the expenses of supporting the growing family, Bagby turned in desperation to the lecture circuit. His humorous writings, especially his "Bacon and Greens" (1866), were ideally suited for public lectures, but he remained in debt. Consequently, from 1867 to 1870 he edited the *Native Virginian*, a new newspaper published first at Orange Court House and later in Gordonsville, Orange County. His efforts to make the newspaper a financial success proved to be vain, however, and in 1870 he returned to Richmond as assistant to the secretary of the commonwealth, who was by law also the state librarian. Until he lost his job when the Readjusters came to power in 1878, Bagby was in charge of the books in the Virginia State Library. He continued to lecture and composed some of his best-known works during those years, including his most famous essay, "The Old Virginia Gentleman," in 1877.

In a series of letters published in the *Richmond State* during the final years of his life, Bagby revealed the abiding tension in his mind and writings between the impulse to describe life in Virginia precisely and accurately and the impulse to sentimentalize the old days in his native commonwealth. At his best, his observations on Southside plantation life are shaped by an admirable blend of accuracy, objectivity, and genuine affection for his subject. Some of the essays, such as "My Uncle Flatback's Plantation," "Fishing on the Appomattox," and "Corn-Field Peas," have held up well. Others more deeply rooted in the ethos of the time have not.

George William Bagby died of the effects of chronic dyspepsia and an ulcer of the tongue at his home in Richmond on 29 November 1883 and was buried in Shockoe Cemetery. Posthumous editions of his essays appeared in 1884–1885, 1910, 1938, 1943, and 1948, the last three edited by his youngest daughter, Ellen Matthews Bagby.

Joseph Leonard King, *Dr. George William Bagby: A Study in Virginia Literature, 1850–1880* (1927); early biographies by Edward S. Gregory in *Selections from the Miscellaneous Writings of Dr. George William Bagby* (1884–1885), 1:xii–xxxvii, and by Churchill Gibson Chamberlayne in *Library of Southern Literature*, ed. Edwin Anderson Alderman et al. (1909–1923), 1:141–146; George William Bagby Papers and Bagby Family Papers, VHS, include several letters relating to birth date: George Bagby to George William Bagby, 24 Aug. 1836, indicates that it was 25 Aug., but George William Bagby always gave his birth date as 13 Aug. 1828, a Wednesday, and George Bagby's undated letter to his sister announced the birth of "a fine boy" on a "Wednesday evening"; Compiled Service Records; marriage reported in *Daily Richmond Enquirer*, 17 Feb. 1863; writings assessed in Thomas Nelson Page, "A Virginia Realist," in *The Old Virginia Gentleman and Other Sketches* (1910), v–xiii (frontispiece por.), Douglas Southall Freeman, "George W. Bagby, Patriot," in *The Old Virginia Gentleman and Other Sketches* (1938), xvii–xxvii, Ritchie Devon Watson Jr., *The Cavalier in Virginia Fiction* (1985), 37–40, and Watson, "George William Bagby," in *Encyclopedia of American Humorists* (1988), 18–21, which contains a bibliography of Bagby's publications; BVS Death Register, Richmond City; obituaries in *Richmond Daily Dispatch* and *Richmond State*, both 30 Nov. 1883.

RITCHIE DEVON WATSON JR.

BAGBY, Lucy Parke Chamberlayne (8 June 1842–15 September 1927), civic leader, was born at Montrose in Henrico County, the sixth of seven daughters and eleventh of fourteen children of Lewis Webb Chamberlayne and Martha Burwell Dabney Chamberlayne. Her mother belonged to a large and prominent network of Virginia families, and her father, a physician and a founder of the Medical College of Virginia, descended from one of the first Jamestown colonists as well as from William Byrd (1674–1744). She was named for Byrd's first wife, Lucy Parke Byrd.

Ten of Chamberlayne's brothers and sisters were deaf, and ten of them died before reaching adulthood. Parke, as she was known, and her brother John Hampden Chamberlayne were the only two hearing children who survived childhood. Her father died in January 1854, after which she left Richmond, where she had been living and attending school, to board at the Episcopal Institute in Staunton. She returned to Richmond later that year and boarded at the Richmond Female Institute, a school respected for its rigorous curriculum. From 1858 to 1860 poor health obliged her to live and study with her mother at Montrose, until indebtedness forced the sale of the family estate, after which she and her mother took rooms in Richmond.

In 1861 Chamberlayne met George William Bagby, a popular young journalist and editor of the *Southern Literary Messenger*, whom she married at Saint Paul's Episcopal Church in Richmond on 16 February 1863. Due to his chronic dyspepsia he could serve only briefly in the Confederate army and spent most of the war as a correspondent for several Southern newspapers and as associate editor of the *Richmond Whig*. Parke Bagby volunteered in the city's military hospitals early in the war, but in 1862 she went to work in a clerical position in the office of the Confederate States Department of the Treasury. Between 1864 and 1882 she also had six sons and four daughters, of whom two sons died young.

The end of the Civil War brought major changes to the Bagby household. The family was poor, frequently going three and four weeks without meat. George Bagby spent most of his time traveling, delivering lectures on topics of political and social interest. Parke Bagby remained in Richmond, taking care of their growing family, housing and feeding boarders to supplement the family income, and revising the editorials that her husband continued to write. In 1870 George Bagby went to work in the Virginia State Library, but he lost his job in 1878 when the Readjuster Party replaced many state employees with its own supporters. He died on 29 November 1883.

Bagby wore mourning for the last half of her life. She arranged for the publication of a two-volume edition of *Selections From the Miscellaneous Writings of Dr. George W. Bagby* (1884–1885) and returned to work outside her home. In January 1884 she became assistant to Virginia's auditor of public accounts. Her responsibilities included managing pension funds and overseeing the distribution of money to the state's colleges and universities. Bagby was the first woman to work as a full-time professional state employee in Virginia. In addition to helping reduce her family's debts, state employment also fed her keen interest in politics, awakened in her a sense of civic responsibility, and brought her lasting friendships with some of the most powerful legislators of the time. She retired in 1905.

In 1889 Bagby helped found the Association for the Preservation of Virginia Antiquities. In 1896 she was named its first recording secretary, and from 1898 until her death she was honorary vice president of the organization. Bagby was also the first chairman of the association's Jamestown Committee and took a leading role in persuading Congress to construct a protective seawall to save the historic settlement site from erosion. As a founder of the APVA, she was at the center of a concerted effort to blot out painful memories of the Civil War by popularizing an interpretation of Virginia's history focused on its English colonial heritage.

Bagby also participated in local charitable work. Early in the 1890s she organized the Ice Mission to enlist prominent Richmonders in collecting and distributing food, ice, milk, and clothing to the city's poor. Throughout the decade she served as president of the Rosemary Library, for many years Richmond's only resource for the borrowing and sharing of books. She also belonged to the Colonial Dames and the United Daughters of the Confederacy and was an honorary member of the Woman's Club of Richmond. Her youngest daughter, Ellen Matthews Bagby, lived with her in Richmond, joined her in her philanthropic and preservation work, and eventually became chairman of the APVA's Jamestown Committee. Although Bagby was politically astute and a skilled advocate, she opposed woman suffrage and refused to endorse proposals to admit women to the University of Virginia or to increase their access to higher education generally.

Bagby had been plagued with poor health in her youth, suffered from puerperal fever following the birth of her third son in 1872, and was treated for diabetes when she was elderly. Despite these problems, she lived a full, long, and active life. Lucy Parke Chamberlayne Bagby died at her home in Richmond on 15 September 1927. In a tribute to her contributions to the city, to the state, and to the mythos of the Confederacy, the flag over the White House of the Confederacy was flown at half-mast on the day of her funeral. She was buried in Shockoe Cemetery in Richmond.

Mary Elizabeth Glade, "Private Lives and Public Myths: The Bagbys of Virginia" (Ph.D. diss., University of Colorado, 1996); Bagby Family Papers, including autobiographical "Chronicles," Richmond Ice and Milk Mission Papers, and Rosemary Public Library Papers, all VHS; marriage reported in *Daily Richmond Enquirer*, 17 Feb. 1863; Churchill G. Chamberlayne, ed., *Ham Chamberlayne—Virginian: Letters and Papers of an Artillery Officer in the War for Southern Independence, 1861–1865* (1932); Richard T. Couture, *To Preserve and Protect: A History of the Association for the Preservation of Virginia Antiquities* (1984), 24, 26–28, 113–114; Nancy Elizabeth Packer, *White Gloves and Red Bricks: APVA, 1889–1989* (1989); James M. Lindgren, *Preserving the Old Dominion: Historic Preservation and Virginia Traditionalism* (1993); obituary and editorial tribute in *Richmond News Leader*, 16 Sept. 1927 (por.); obituary in *Richmond Times-Dispatch*, 16 Sept. 1927.

JOYCE B. MACALLISTER

BAGNALL, Idelia W. M. Johnson (8 September 1872–8 May 1931), civic leader, was born in Norfolk, the only daughter and younger of two children of Mary E. Johnson. She attended local public schools and graduated in 1891 from the Norfolk Mission College, at which she later worked as a teacher and librarian. On 16 September 1897 she married Thomas S. Bagnall, a letter carrier and kinsman of Robert Wellington Bagnall, a Norfolk native who rose to national prominence as an Episcopal minister and leader of chapters of the National Association for the Advancement of Colored People in Detroit and Philadelphia.

Ida W. Bagnall, as she was generally known, emerged early in the twentieth century as a leader in several social service organizations in Norfolk. About 1912 she began working as dock agent for the Colored Women's Protective League. She provided temporary shelter and counseling for women who arrived in Norfolk by train or steamer during the large immigration occasioned by World War I. She worked under the joint sponsorship of the league, the Traveler's Aid Society, and the Young Women's Christian Association. Bagnall eventually became first executive secretary of the Phyllis Wheatley YWCA in Norfolk, held other responsible positions in the YWCA's local and state divisions, and worked with several other charitable and self-help organizations in Tidewater Virginia. She became a founding member of the State Federation of Colored Women's Clubs and formed its junior department.

At one time or another Bagnall held local offices in the Traveler's Aid Society, the White Rose Club, the National Urban League, and the Norfolk branch of the Needlework Guild of America, of which she was president. She helped found the Hamper Basket Exchange, later the Hamper Basket Club, which evolved into Norfolk's Colored United Charities, the most important of all the volunteer agencies serving the African American community in Norfolk during her lifetime, and she was its executive secretary at the time of her death. Bagnall may not have been widely known outside of Norfolk or even among its white citizens, but her long career in public service work attracted attention and was long remembered by Norfolk's black population. In June 1959, twenty-eight years after her death, the Calvert Park Civic League placed a plaque honoring her and her work in Calvert Park, near a public housing development on Bagnall Road, which the Norfolk Housing Authority named in her honor. Bagnall's only child, Wanser Idiliah Bagnall Webb, succeeded her as executive secretary of Colored United Charities. Ida W. Bagnall died in Norfolk on 8 May 1931 from complications resulting from an infected tooth. Most of Norfolk's African American clergymen attended her funeral at the First Baptist Church. She was buried in West Point Cemetery in Norfolk.

BVS Birth and Marriage Registers, Norfolk City; Census, Norfolk City, 1880, 1900 (with variant Dec. 1875 birth date); other family history information provided by grandson John Quincy Adams Webb, Houston, Texas; Norfolk Mission College, *Catalogue* (1894/1895): 6; *Norfolk Journal and Guide*, 20 June 1959, Home Edition; obituary in *Norfolk Journal and Guide*, 16 May 1931.

MARTHA H. BROWN

BAHEN, James (February 1845–11 February 1907), member of the Richmond City Board of Aldermen, was born in County Clare, Ireland, the eldest of four sons and two daughters of Michael Bahen and Margaret Bahen. The family immigrated to Virginia during the 1850s. They moved from Waynesboro to Staunton and by 1860 to Covington, where Michael Bahen worked as a laborer, probably on the railroad projects under construction in that area. After his father died in 1861, James Bahen moved to Richmond. In 1862 he went to Washington, D.C., where he worked as a teamster for the United States government during the Civil War. After the war he returned to Richmond, where his mother operated a series of grocery stores until her death in 1887. On 27 September 1870 he married Margaret Hogan. They had seven sons and four daughters.

Bahen worked for Richmond merchant John Van Lew and several other merchants, grocers, and distillers before opening his own grocery and saloon in Jackson Ward about 1880. His establishment resembled a traditional Irish shebeen such as his mother may have operated, a shop with a drinking room in the back that served as an informal neighborhood gathering place for men. Bahen's shop catered almost exclusively to African Americans because he lived in the center of the principal black neighborhood in Richmond. He became deeply involved in ward politics and, although he was an Irish American, was one of the most influential men in the largely African American Jackson Ward.

Bahen's career in Richmond city politics demonstrates that in practice the politics of the nineteenth-century urban South sometimes resembled that of urban electoral machines in the North. He managed his ward's affairs during the tumultuous 1880s and 1890s, building coalitions with black politicians. In 1887 he was elected to the Richmond Board of Aldermen. A strong ally of John Mitchell Jr., the editor of the *Richmond Planet*, Bahen was a key member of Jackson Ward's Whiskey Ring, a group of independent Republicans, mostly African American, who beat back challenges from the Republican factions that the state party leadership favored. The state party came increasingly under the influence of white men late in the century, and in many areas local black leaders lost influence.

Despite being a white politician in a predominantly black ward, Bahen won reelection to the Board of Aldermen from Jackson Ward through 1901, when Richmond restructured its ward system in anticipation of the elimination of the black vote under the 1902 state constitution. This spelled the end of Bahen's political base, and he retired from politics after completing his term in 1903. His namesake son symbolized the changing times by becoming a Democrat and publicly supporting the disfranchisement of African Americans.

James Bahen died in More's Brook Sanatorium in Charlottesville on 11 February 1907 after having suffered a mental breakdown a few months earlier. He was buried in Mount Calvary Cemetery in Richmond.

Biographies in *Richmond Planet*, 11 June 1892 (por.), and Tyler, *Encyclopedia*, 5:683–684, which contains some incorrect dates; month and year of birth in Census, Richmond City, 1900; variant spellings of surname are common; other family information in obituaries of widow in *Richmond Times-Dispatch*, 22 Feb. 1914, and *Richmond News Leader*, 23 Feb. 1914; Richmond City Marriage Register; Ann Field Alexander, "Black Protest in the New South: John Mitchell, Jr. (1863–1929) and the Richmond *Planet*" (Ph.D. diss., Duke, 1973), esp. 259–263; Michael B. Chesson, "Richmond's Black Councilmen, 1871–96," in *Southern Black Leaders of the Reconstruction Era*, ed. Howard N. Rabinowitz (1982), 191–222; illness described in *Richmond News Leader* and *Richmond Times-Dispatch*, both 27 Nov. 1906; obituary in *Richmond Times-Dispatch*, 12 Feb. 1907 (por.).

GREGG D. KIMBALL

BAILEY, Anne Hennis Trotter (ca. 1742–22 November 1825), legendary frontier character, was said to have been born Anne Hennis in Liverpool, England, and to have been named for Queen Anne, who was on the throne of England when her father, whose name is not recorded, fought at the Battle of Blenheim. When she was about nineteen years old she immigrated to Virginia and settled in Staunton, where in 1765 she married Richard Trotter, a veteran of the French and Indian War who had fought under General Edward Braddock and Colonel George Washington in 1755 and who was later killed at the Battle of Point Pleasant on 10 October 1774. They had one son.

Documented facts about her life during the decade following Trotter's death are scarce, and many legends, some of them very improbable, have developed to fill the void. Several legends persistent enough that they may contain some truth have her leaving her son with friends, dressing in men's clothing, and living a rough frontier life. She may have reported on movements of Indians during and after the Revolutionary War when frontier settlers often feared surprise raids. According to legends that developed about those years she once killed two Native Americans with one well-aimed rifle shot, slept in holes under rocks or in hollow logs, and avoided freezing to death one winter night because her horse breathed warm air into a hollow log. Other legends had her roaming the frontier and killing Indians in many places to avenge the death of Richard Trotter, giving rise later to the sobriquet Mad Anne, or Mad Anne Bailey, her name after she married John Bailey in Greenbrier County on 3 November 1785.

The Baileys lived for nine years at Fort Lee at the site of present-day Charleston, West Virginia. The most famous Anne Bailey legend begins at Fort Lee late in the 1780s or perhaps as late as 1791. A Shawnee party was seen near the fort, and the inhabitants were thrown into panic when they discovered that the fort was out of gunpowder. Braver or more reckless than the men, Anne Bailey mounted her horse and rode all the way to Lewisburg, picked up a supply of powder, and returned to the fort with angry Indians or hungry wolves or both in hot pursuit, just in the nick of time to save all of the settlers. This legend, which did not appear in print until the 1860s, and the other tales have subsequently appeared in many different versions, some of them masquerading as history, many of them transparently fictional, some in song, and one of them in a long poem composed in 1861, but none of them with substantiating documentation.

She was well known in western Virginia, though, probably because some of the legends had some truth in them. One of the first references to carry Bailey's name far beyond her western Virginia home was Anne Newport Royall's *Sketches of History, Life, and Manners, in the United States* (1826), 48–50. Royall introduced "the celebrated heroine, Ann Bailey" to her readers and described her as "a Welch woman," short and stout in her old age, fond of strong drink, and speaking with a pronounced accent. Royall did not include any of the taller tales about Bailey, but she did state that during the Revolutionary War Bailey "would shoulder her rifle, hang her shot-pouch over her shoulder, and lead a horse laden with ammunition to the army, two hundred miles distant, when not a man could be found to undertake the perilous task." That brief account may have referred to her salvation of Fort Lee, but it is also possible that the more colorful and dramatic tale of her rescue of Fort Lee arose out of that brief account.

John Bailey died not long before November 1794. Anne Hennis Trotter Bailey continued to reside in, or wander up and down, the Kanawha River valley for several years until her son, William Trotter, forced the reluctant old woman to move to his farm in Gallia County, Ohio, where she lived alone by choice in a crude log cabin on his property. She died there on 22 November 1825, asleep with her grandchildren before her own fireplace. On 10 October 1901 her remains were reinterred in Tu-Endie-Wei Park in Point Pleasant, West Virginia, near the spot where her first husband had been killed fighting the Shawnee.

Virgil A. Lewis, *Life and Times of Anne Bailey, the Pioneer Heroine of the Great Kanawha Valley* (1891); Livia Simpson-Poffenbarger, ed., *Ann Bailey: Thrilling Adventures of the Heroine of the Kanawha Valley* (1907); facts and legends assessed in Roy Bird Cook, *The Annals of Fort Lee* (1935), 78–96; second marriage recorded in Norman Pontiff Evans, ed., *A Register of the Marriages Celebrated in Greenbrier County, (West) Virginia, 1781–1849* (1983), 3; death notice in *Gallipolis Gallia Gazette*, 3 Dec. 1825.

EDWARD L. HENSON JR.

BAILEY, Etta Rose (19 June 1893–1 November 1971), educator, was born in Sussex County, the third of four children, all daughters, of George Edmund Bailey and Martha Barham Bailey. She grew up in Sussex County and attended the State Normal School for Women (later called Longwood College) in Farmville. She began a career of almost forty years in the Richmond school system with a stint from 1914 to 1924 as a teacher at Fox Elementary School. Bailey twice attended Teachers College, Columbia University, from which she received a B.S. in 1924 and an M.S. in 1929. She taught at Richmond Normal School from 1926 to 1935. In 1932 she studied the German elementary education system at the New York International Institute. She also conducted classes at summer normal institutes at Emory University in Atlanta, Madison College (now James Madison University), the College of William and Mary, and Columbia University.

In September 1935 Bailey became assistant principal of Matthew Fontaine Maury Elementary School in Southside Richmond and in May 1939 became its principal. Possessing imagination and leadership, she enlisted the teachers, parents, and students in successfully applying John Dewey's theories of progressive education to the Maury School. She transformed the old building and molded the curriculum to make the school one of the most innovative in the state. Bailey's peers widely recognized her success, and educators from many other states and several countries visited the Maury School during her years as principal. In October 1950 *Life* magazine featured Maury in a special issue on education, calling it one of the best elementary schools in the United States.

In November 1942 Bailey took a leave of absence to direct a program initiated by the state Department of Education to develop educational child care for women engaged in wartime work. In 1960 she received the Jane Addams Centennial Award from the Virginia Chapter of the National Association of Social Workers for having best exemplified the spirit of Jane Addams in Virginia during the previous five years.

In June 1963 Bailey retired as principal of the Maury School. Shortly afterward she served as interim principal on the integrated faculty of Worsham School in Prince Edward County after the school desegregation crisis had temporarily closed the county's public schools. The Prince Edward Free School Association provided free elementary school classes to African American students at Worsham. Because it had an inadequate library, Bailey gave the school her personal collection of children's books. During her retirement she taught occasionally at Richmond Professional Institute. Etta Rose Bailey died in

Norfolk on 1 November 1971 and was buried in Hollywood Cemetery in Richmond.

Who's Who in American Education 20 (1961–1962): 69; BVS Birth Register, Sussex Co.; Dale Christina Kalkofen, "Matthew F. Maury School, 1934–1970: A Case Study in Educational Innovation" (Ph.D. diss., W&M, 1988); *Richmond News Leader*, 15 Apr. 1937; *Virginia Journal of Education* 36 (1943): 244 (por.); *Life*, 16 Oct. 1950, 124–128; Etta Rose Bailey, "Johnny-Come-Early," *Childhood Education* 33 (1957): 252–256; Bailey's introduction to Marion Nesbitt, *A Public School for Tomorrow: A Description of the Matthew F. Maury School, Richmond, Virginia* (1953; repr. 1957); Neil V. Sullivan, *Bound for Freedom: An Educator's Adventures in Prince Edward County, Virginia* (1965); obituaries in *Richmond News Leader* and *Richmond Times-Dispatch*, both 2 Nov. 1971.

BRENT TARTER

BAILEY, Marjorie Lee (28 May 1923–4 August 1988), Baptist minister, was born in Abingdon and adopted by Ellie Landrum Jones Bailey and Walter Lee Bailey, an executive with a prominent firm of Richmond clothiers. She went to public schools and graduated from John Marshall High School in Richmond in 1940. After one year of prenursing training at Richmond Professional Institute, she attended Blue Mountain College, a Baptist school for women in Mississippi, from 1942 to 1946, but took no degree. Bailey then worked for four years as a home missionary in a riverfront mission in New Orleans. After studying briefly in the summer of 1951 at Southwestern Baptist Theological Seminary in Fort Worth, Texas, she returned to Richmond the same year to care for her widowed mother. Bailey then completed training in clinical pastoral education at the Medical College of Virginia and the Virginia Institute of Pastoral Care.

Bailey became director of the South Richmond Baptist Center shortly after her return to Virginia. On 1 December 1955 she also became acting director of the Hillside Baptist Center and served in that capacity for eighteen months. Bailey remained at the South Richmond center until 1966, when she became director of religious activities and chaplain at the Virginia Correctional Center for Women in Goochland County, serving until 1987. From 1969 to 1977 she also worked with juvenile offenders at Pinecrest Center in South Richmond and during 1973 and 1974 she performed similar duties at the Southampton Correctional Center.

Bailey's study at the Virginia Institute of Pastoral Care coincided with her work with patients at the Medical College of Virginia. While there, a terminally ill patient asked her to administer communion, but because she was not an ordained minister she could not comply with the request. Bailey therefore took the unusual step of preparing for and seeking ordination as a Baptist minister. On 27 February 1972 she was ordained in Bainbridge Baptist Church in Richmond, near the South Richmond Baptist Center of which she had been director. She was the first woman ever ordained by Virginia Baptist General Association and only the third woman to be ordained under the authority of the Southern Baptist Convention.

In August 1977 Bailey became the senior chaplain at the Virginia State Penitentiary. She had been expected to officiate only until the penitentiary hired a permanent chaplain, but Bailey stayed on the job for almost eight years, until June 1985. She always worked a six-day week as she ministered to approximately 1,200 prisoners at both the women's and the men's prisons. Her responsibilities included coordinating religious activities, serving as a religious counselor for the inmates, and conducting worship services. She recognized no barriers of race, creed, or sex, and was said to be always ready to listen, but never to judge. Bailey began a program for mothers in the Goochland County facility that enabled their children to visit and cultivate close relationships, which she regarded as healthy for both the children and their mothers.

Bailey won wide recognition for her ministry to inmates, including an entire chapter devoted to her in a 1978 book on Baptist chaplaincy. She received the 1986 Lewis Hine Award from the National Child Labor Committee. That same year she retired because of illness. Marjorie Lee Bailey died in Richmond on 4 August 1988 after a long bout with cancer and was buried in Forest Lawn Cemetery in Richmond.

Feature articles in *Richmond News Leader*, 6 May 1978, and *Richmond Times-Dispatch*, 17 Nov. 1986; Walker Knight, *Chaplaincy, Love on the Line: The Human Touch in Chaplaincy* (1978), 87–91, 110–113 (por.); *Religious*

Herald, 10, 24 Feb., 9 Mar. 1972 (cover por.); obituaries in *Richmond News Leader* and *Richmond Times-Dispatch*, both 5 Aug. 1988, and *Religious Herald*, 11 Aug. 1988; memorial in *Virginia Baptist Annual* (1988): 169.

HELEN E. FALLS

BAILEY, Odessa Pittard (24 April 1906–8 January 1994), civic leader, was born in Roanoke, the tenth of eleven children of George Nicholas Pittard, a Baptist minister, and Emma C. Board Pittard, a teacher. Odessa Pittard graduated from Roanoke High School in 1923, studied for a year at the National Business College in Roanoke, and from 1924 to 1944 worked in the office of the United States attorney for the western district of Virginia. She studied law in her spare time and was admitted to the bar in 1934. On 3 March 1932 she married Henry Stanley Bailey. They had one daughter.

Odessa Bailey became judge of the Roanoke Juvenile and Domestic Relations Court on 23 September 1944. In spite of privately expressed objections from some city council members to the selection of a woman for the position, by a four to one vote the council appointed Bailey the first woman in Virginia's history to hold a judicial post higher than justice of the peace or county trial justice. She was also the first full-time juvenile court judge in Roanoke and served for one four-year term. Although not a court of record, the Juvenile and Domestic Relations Court was an important branch of the city's judiciary. As its only judge Bailey was brought into frequent contact with troubled children and directed the city's juvenile detention facility. She strengthened enforcement of child-support laws and became one of the state's most vocal advocates for reformed and improved social services for disadvantaged children. A founder of the Virginia Council of Juvenile Court Judges, she served as its president in 1947 and 1948.

Bailey's interest in social work continued after her term on the bench ended in 1948. She served on several state commissions during the 1950s, among them a state commission on sex offenses, another to study problems of juvenile offenders, and the Governor's Advisory Committee on Employment of the Physically Handicapped. In 1950 and 1951 she served as president of the Virginia State Conference of Social Work, and her speech on 20 September 1950 to the New England Conference of State Federations of Women's Clubs on the need for more qualified social workers won a brief mention in the *New York Times*. Bailey later proposed that the money the Virginia General Assembly had appropriated for a memorial to World War II servicemen be spent instead on a facility to help emotionally disturbed children.

Bailey became active in Democratic Party politics as state woman's manager of the unsuccessful gubernatorial campaign of Horace Edwards in 1949. She managed the work of Virginia women on behalf of Adlai Stevenson in the 1952 presidential campaign and attended the Democratic National Convention four years later as a delegate at large. Bailey also served on the board of the General Federation of Women's Clubs and from 1952 to 1954 was president of the Virginia Federation of Women's Clubs. Her agenda focused on the education and health of children, and she lobbied for increased appropriations for the state's mental hospitals. During her presidency the federation helped pay for the mobile art gallery of the Virginia Museum of Fine Arts, reportedly the nation's first traveling artmobile. She was president of the Woman's Club of Roanoke from 1956 to 1958 and also active at one time or another, often simultaneously, as a member or officer of the Roanoke Community Chest and of the city and state units of the Family Service Association, the American Cancer Society, the Virginia Society for Crippled Children and Adults, and the Virginia League for Planned Parenthood.

Following her husband's death in 1957, Bailey founded and for twenty years served as president of a travel agency in Roanoke. In this capacity she traveled widely and often. After she retired she moved to California. She married Milton Schachtebeck in Sacramento on 18 December 1987. He died there in 1992, and she died in or near Davis, California, on 8 January 1994. Odessa Pittard Bailey Schachtebeck was buried in Evergreen Burial Park in Roanoke.

Autobiographical memorandum, 7 Mar. 1957, and biographical newspaper-clipping file, Roanoke City Public Library; family history verified by daughter, Judith Bailey

Gabor, 24 Apr. 1997; Etta Belle Walker Northington, *A History of The Virginia Federation of Women's Clubs, 1907–1957* [1958], 97–101; George Bartlett Curtis, "The Juvenile Court Movement in Virginia: The Child Savers, 1890–1973" (Ph.D. diss., UVA, 1973), 95–98, 141–142; *Richmond News Leader*, 18 Jan. 1945; *New York Times*, 21 Sept. 1950; *Commonwealth* 19 (Nov. 1952): 26 (por.); obituary in *Roanoke Times and World News*, 12 Jan. 1994.

BRENT TARTER

BAILEY, Rufus William (13 April 1793–25 April 1863), educator and author, was born in North Yarmouth, Maine, the second of six sons and second of eight children of Lebbeus Bailey, a respected clockmaker and bell founder, and Sarah Sylvester Myrick Bailey. He graduated from Dartmouth College in 1813 and spent the next year teaching in Salisbury, New Hampshire, and the year after that reading law with Daniel Webster. Having decided that his true vocation was the ministry, he attended Andover Theological Seminary from 1815 to 1816. He served as a tutor at Dartmouth in the academic year 1817–1818 and returned to deliver the annual Phi Beta Kappa lecture there in 1821. Bailey was ordained on 24 November 1819 and began his ministry at the Congregational Church in Norwich, Vermont. He also taught moral philosophy at the American Literary, Scientific and Military Academy in Norwich (now Norwich University). In 1820 he married Lucy C. Hatch. They had three daughters before her death in November 1832.

From 1824 to 1827 Bailey served as pastor to the First Congregational Church in Pittsfield, Massachusetts, and during his tenure there he also founded the Pittsfield Female Academy. Bailey had become a trustee of both Williams College and the University of Vermont before 1827, when for health reasons he left Pittsfield and joined the Presbytery of South Carolina, where he remained for twelve years. He served as pastor of Presbyterian churches in Darlington, Sumter, and Cheraw, and in 1827 he founded Richland Normal School and later served as principal of Rice Spring Military Academy. Bailey moved in 1839 to Fayetteville, North Carolina, where he directed another academy for young women and began acting as an agent for the American Colonization Society.

By 1842 Bailey had married Marietta Perry Lloyd of Waterbury, Connecticut. They had a son and in 1842 moved to Staunton, where Bailey persuaded a number of local Presbyterians to found the Augusta Female Seminary. During his seven years as its principal, Bailey placed the school on a firm foundation. He won the admiration and financial support of the community, designed an academically demanding curriculum, secured a charter from the General Assembly in 1845, and oversaw the construction of and may even have designed the first buildings. Bailey embraced formal education for women and believed them as capable of serious academic study as men. He required his pupils to study philosophy and the natural sciences, but he also insisted that morality and the Bible were the bases of all education. He and his wife, daughters, a niece, and a cousin constituted the faculty. Among his first pupils was Mary Julia Baldwin, who later headed the school for many years and for whom it came to be named. Bailey also occasionally served as supply pastor to the First Presbyterian Church in Staunton, and when he left the city the congregation presented him with an engraved silver coffee service. Hampden-Sydney College awarded him an honorary D.D. in 1859.

In 1849 Bailey resigned from the seminary to become Virginia agent for the American Colonization Society. Although he worked sporadically for years to raise money to send free African Americans to Africa, Bailey did not oppose slavery. His first book, *The Issue: Presented in a Series of Letters on Slavery* (1837), had begun in 1832 as letters in the magazine *Christian Mirror* that were highly critical of northern antislavery writers. *The Family Preacher: or, Domestic Duties Illustrated and Enforced, in Eight Discourses* (1837), contained a discussion of religion and slavery that stood squarely in the center of an emerging body of literature defending the institution of slavery on moral and theological grounds.

Throughout his career in the ministry and in education Bailey wrote industriously. In addition to composing pieces and editing for the magazines *Patriarch* and *Family Library Magazine* in the 1840s, he published some sermons and several other books, including *A Mother's Request Answered in Letters of a Father to his Daughters* (1837); *Daughters at School Instructed in a Series of Letters* (1857); and *Domestic Duties: or, The Family a Nursery for Earth and Heaven* (n.d.). He achieved his greatest success with two works on the English language, *English Grammar: A Simple, Concise, and Comprehensive Manual of the English Language* (1853), a textbook that was reprinted ten times by 1857, and *The Scholar's Companion: or, A Guide to the Orthography, Pronunciation, and Derivation of the English Language*, based on Henry Butter's 1836 book of the same title, which with Bailey's revisions was reprinted more than one hundred times after 1856 and sold more than half a million copies before the end of the century.

Bailey left Virginia for Texas in 1854. He lived in Huntsville, where in 1858 he was appointed professor of languages at Austin College. He remained active in church affairs and served as a commissioner of the First General Assembly of the Southern Presbyterian Church in 1861, and in 1862 he was moderator of the Presbyterian Synod of Texas. In the latter year he was appointed president of Austin College. Rufus William Bailey died of pneumonia in Huntsville on 25 April 1863 and was buried there.

Biography of 1905 by F. B. Bailey in Historical Foundation of the Southern Presbyterian Church, Montreat, N.C., with copy in Mary Baldwin College Library; birth date in George T. Chapman, *Sketches of the Alumni of Dartmouth College* (1867), 163, confirmed in family records of Lebbeus Bailey Sr. and Sarah Sylvester Myrick in Mary Baldwin College Library; *General Catalogue of the Theological Seminary, Andover, Massachusetts, 1808–1908* [1909], 50; great-grandson Edmund D. Campbell supplied additional information; some Bailey letters in LC and in American Colonization Society Papers, LC; Bailey explained his educational theories in *Staunton Spectator*, 20 June 1844; Mary Watters, *The History of Mary Baldwin College, 1842–1942* (1942), 6–50 (por. opp. 48); Patricia H. Menk, *To Live in Time: The Sesquicentennial History of Mary Baldwin College, 1841–1992* (1992), xii (por.), 3–7, 110.

PATRICIA H. MENK

BAKER, Clara Olivia Byrd (22 June 1886–20 October 1979), educator and civic leader, was born in or near Williamsburg, the second of at least five girls and third of eleven children of Charles Byrd and Malvina Carey Braxton Byrd. Her father worked as a farmer, a cook, a drayman, and a woodyard proprietor, and though he could neither read nor write he owned the family's Williamsburg house mortgage-free by 1900 and was one of only thirty-six African Americans in Williamsburg still registered to vote a year after passage of the restrictive Constitution of 1902. Her mother was literate and encouraged her children to obtain all the education they could. Clara Byrd entered Williamsburg's one-room public school for black children at age six in 1892, and after exhausting its limited offerings she studied privately with her instructor, Mary E. Thurston Greenhow, to prepare for the teachers' examination.

In 1902 Clara Byrd earned a certificate to teach in the elementary grades, and she took charge of a one-room school in James City County where her duties included starting a wood fire each morning before classes began and sweeping out the building daily after classes ended. Many of her pupils were both older and larger than she, but she managed them effectively and had few discipline problems.

On 6 July 1905 Byrd married William Hayes Baker, a carpenter who later became sexton and tour guide at Bruton Parish Church. She temporarily left teaching and during the next eleven years had three sons and one daughter. While the children were young she supplemented the family income by working as a seamstress and a cook.

Clara Baker returned to teaching in the James City County public schools in 1920, when the county and the city of Williamsburg were cooperating in the establishment of a public training school for African American children. Baker was assigned first to rented rooms in the Odd Fellows Hall, then to the new James City County Training School in 1924, and ultimately to its replacement, Bruton Heights School, in 1940. While teaching, Baker continued her own education through extension and correspondence courses as well as summer institutes at Hampton Institute and at Virginia State College for Negroes (now Virginia State University), in Ettrick, near Petersburg, from the latter of which she earned a collegiate professional certificate in 1932 and a B.S. in education in 1945. When she retired in June 1952, her salary was $3,000. She was proudest of her success in encouraging many of her students to go on to professional careers. She also took pride in the fact that all of her own children achieved professional success. Her daughter became a schoolteacher, one son became a journalist, and her other two sons became college professors.

For nearly six decades Baker, known as "Smoje" to family and friends, was a leader in the black community of Williamsburg and in efforts to promote interracial cooperation. She was one of the first women to register to vote in Williamsburg after the ratification of the Nineteenth Amendment in 1920, she supported the proposed Equal Rights Amendment, and she remained a staunch advocate of women's involvement in public affairs throughout her life. Her wide-ranging activities included service as a Sunday school teacher and Girl Scout leader and membership in the Virginia Teachers Association, the National Association for the Advancement of Colored People, and the Civic Political League. In 1958 she helped organize a Williamsburg chapter of the National Council of Negro Women, and in 1962 she was a founder of a local chapter of the League of Women Voters. Baker was also instrumental in forming the Williamsburg Area Recreation Association, which built and maintained the city's Quarterpath Park. She was a trustee of the First Baptist Church, treasurer of the local United Council of Church Women, secretary of the Williamsburg Area Interracial Study Group, and board member of the Colonial Youth Center League. When Baker's Williamsburg friends and admirers gathered to pay tribute to her in 1967, the superintendent of schools declared that he could not recall a single worthwhile communitywide effort in which Baker had not participated.

Baker won numerous honors, including the Sojourner Truth Meritorious Service Award from the Tidewater Club of the National Association of Negro Business and Professional Women in 1960 and the Susan B. Anthony Award from the Norfolk and Virginia Beach chapters of the League of Women Voters in 1975.

For seven years following her husband's death on 11 April 1960, Baker continued her volunteer work in Williamsburg and traveled extensively in the United States and abroad. In 1967 she moved in with her daughter's family in Virginia Beach. There she promptly affiliated with the local League of Women Voters, the Retired Teachers Association, and the Woman's Club of Norfolk and plunged into the activities at her daughter's church, Grace Episcopal. Vigorously healthy until the final months of her life, Clara Olivia Byrd Baker died of heart disease in Virginia Beach on 20 October 1979 and was buried beside her husband in Cedar Grove Cemetery in Williamsburg. The Williamsburg–James City County School System paid her a fitting tribute in September 1989 when it opened the Clara Byrd Baker Elementary School near the site where she had begun her teaching career eighty-seven years earlier.

Clara Byrd Baker scrapbooks in possession of daughter Lena B. Bass, Virginia Beach; BVS Marriage Register, Williamsburg City; Williamsburg City Voter Registration Book; *Norfolk Ledger-Star*, 25 Aug. 1971; *Norfolk Journal and Guide*, 15 Feb. 1975 (por.); Rawls Byrd, *History of Public Schools in Williamsburg* (1968), 57–59, 121–122; Charles H. Smith to Clara B. Baker, 2 July 1951, Williamsburg Correspondence, Virginia Teachers Association Papers, Virginia State University Library; League of Women Voters of Williamsburg–James City County, Records, 1962–1974, W&M; obituaries in *Norfolk Virginian-Pilot*, 22 Oct. 1979, *Newport News Daily Press*, 23 Oct. 1979, *Williamsburg Virginia Gazette*, 24 Oct. 1979, and *Norfolk Journal and Guide*, 2 Nov. 1979.

CAM WALKER

BAKER, Elijah (1742–6 November 1798), Baptist minister, was born in Orange County, the second of three sons of Samuel Baker and Margaret Dozier Baker. Samuel Baker moved the family to Lunenburg County some time before 1748, and he died about 1750. Margaret Baker married John Wood by November 1752, and they had one son. Little is known about the youth of Elijah Baker, but he was probably a farmer as a young man.

In 1769 Baker was baptized at a Baptist meeting. Although practically illiterate, he immediately began speaking in church meetings. He joined the Meherrin Baptist Church in Lunenburg County and served as an exhorter and then as a speaker. By 1772 he was minister of Malones Church (also known as Genito

Creek Church) in Lunenburg County, after which he preached as an itinerant minister in many places north of the James River between Richmond and Yorktown, as well as in Gloucester County. Between 1773 and 1775 he helped found five Baptist churches in that area.

On Easter Sunday 1776 Baker began a remarkable ministry on the Eastern Shore with a sermon in Northampton County. He was the first Baptist to preach in either of Virginia's Eastern Shore counties, and he struggled against opposition and persecution. On 1 July 1778 Anglican churchwardens had him jailed in Accomack County for preaching without a license. Fifty-six days later a group of men forcibly removed him from the jail and placed him on board a ship bound for Europe, telling the captain that Baker was a disturber of the peace who should not be set ashore anywhere in the United States. The ship captain decided that Baker was a good man and released him. Baker was the last Baptist minister to be imprisoned for preaching in Virginia.

Baker returned to Northampton County, where he married Sarah Copeland and had one son. After her death he married a widow, Ann Floyd Widgeon, on 5 November 1787. Baker supported himself by farming and eventually accumulated an estate valued at more than £900, but he continued to travel and preach up and down the Delmarva Peninsula. Between the American Revolution and 1798 he helped found six Baptist churches in Virginia, eight in Maryland, and four in Delaware, and in 1782 he took the lead in founding the Salisbury Baptist Association of Eastern Shore churches. Baker became legendary among local Baptists for his dedicated and successful ministry under adverse circumstances. In 1926, the one-hundred-fiftieth anniversary of his first sermon on the Eastern Shore, a monument to him was unveiled at the Accomack County courthouse. Elijah Baker died in Salisbury, Maryland, on 6 November 1798 at the home of his friend Robert Lemmon. He was buried on the Lemmon farm.

John S. Moore, "Elijah Baker (1742–1798): A One-Talent Man Who Succeeded," *Virginia Baptist Register* 30 (1991): 1510–1523; birth and death dates in James B. Taylor, *Lives of Virginia Baptist Ministers*, 1st ser. (1837), 108–113; Woodford B. Hackley, "Genealogical Notes, Elijah Baker," *Virginia Baptist Register* 6 (1967): 286–288; second marriage recorded in Northampton Co. Marriage Register; ministry described in John Asplund, *The Universal Register of the Baptist Denomination* (1794), 23, Robert Baylor Semple, *A History of the Rise and Progress of the Baptists in Virginia* (1810), 392–397, Lewis Peyton Little, *Imprisoned Preachers and Religious Liberty in Virginia* (1938), 469–480, and Morgan Edwards, *Materials Towards a History of the Baptists*, ed. Eve B. Weeks and Mary B. Warren (1984), 2:1–22; will and estate inventory in Northampton Co. Will Book, 31:44–45, 451–464.

JOHN S. MOORE

BAKER, Ernest Ballard (25 November 1917–24 March 1985), attorney and first chief judge of the Virginia Court of Appeals, was born in Richmond, the younger of at least two sons of Samuel Harvey Baker and Jennie Gary Baker. He graduated from Thomas Jefferson High School in Richmond and entered the University of Richmond, but he interrupted his education to serve in the United States Army Corps of Engineers from 1942 to 1945. On his return to the University of Richmond he entered its T. C. Williams School of Law, for admission to which a college degree was not required, and received a law degree in 1947. On 29 October 1949 he married Billy Jane Crosby. They had one son and one daughter.

E. Ballard Baker began his legal career by serving for two years as an assistant attorney general of Virginia. He was an assistant city attorney for the city of Richmond from October 1949 until September 1952, after which he went into private practice. In 1961 he moved to suburban Henrico County and the following year began his judicial career. On 25 April 1962 Baker became a substitute judge of the county and the juvenile and domestic relations courts of Henrico County. He was appointed a full-time judge of the court on 1 July 1963. Three years later he became a judge of the Tenth Judicial Circuit, which encompassed Henrico County and Richmond. When the courts were reorganized in 1973 Henrico County came under the jurisdiction of the new Fourteenth Circuit, and the General Assembly elected Baker one of its judges. He served as chief judge of the circuit from 1 July 1980 until 3 January 1985. While on the bench, Baker served as a member of the Judicial Council of Virginia and from March

1982 until his death was chairman of its Committee on Judicial Administration. He was also a member of the Judicial Conference of Virginia, serving from July 1975 until July 1983 on its Judicial Education Committee, and beginning in January 1977 on its Committee on Model Jury Instructions, including a term as chairman from September 1981 to September 1983. He lectured from time to time on business law and participated in continuing legal education programs at T. C. Williams School of Law.

In 1984 the General Assembly created the Virginia Court of Appeals to relieve some of the burden of the Supreme Court of Virginia. Before that time Virginia had had no intermediate appellate court system, and all appeals competed directly for space on the Supreme Court's docket. The new appellate court consisted of ten judges named by the General Assembly late in November 1984. Baker was the oldest judge elected to the court and also the member with the longest judicial experience. When the Virginia Court of Appeals first convened in Richmond on 4 January 1985, the judges elected Baker to a four-year term as the first chief judge of the new court. He served less than three months. E. Ballard Baker died of a heart attack at his home in Henrico County on 24 March 1985 and was buried in Hollywood Cemetery in Richmond.

Career outlined in resolutions of the court in *Virginia Court of Appeals Reports* 1 (1985): v–viii, and in printed proceedings at presentation of por. in Virginia Court of Appeals on 5 May 1986, copy in Virginia State Law Library; family history information verified by Billy Jane Crosby Baker; obituaries in *Richmond News Leader*, 25 Mar. 1985, and *Richmond Times-Dispatch*, 26 Mar. 1985 (por.); memorial in *University of Richmond Law Review* 19 (1985): 447–449.

ELIZABETH TERRY LONG

BAKER, Helen Ettie (21 February 1885–31 August 1960), educator, was born in Anderson, South Carolina, the youngest of two sons and two daughters of John Joseph Baker and Lucinda Broyles Baker. She attended public schools in Anderson and graduated from Richmond College (now the University of Richmond) with a B.A. in 1907. She then began a lifelong career in education. She taught at Barton Heights High School in Richmond during the 1907–1908 academic year before accepting an appointment as instructor in history and Latin at the Woman's College of Richmond, where she remained until 1915. In 1912 Baker obtained a year's leave of absence to attend Teachers College, Columbia University, from which she received an M.A. in political science in 1913. She returned to the Woman's College and served as dean of the faculty and principal from 1913 through the spring of 1915.

By the summer of 1915 Baker had become convinced that due to the increasing importance of college preparatory education for young women, Richmond needed and could support a new school. With one of her Woman's College colleagues, Mary Carter Anderson, she founded the Collegiate School for Girls. Anderson had previously founded and conducted Buttermilk Academy (or Institute), a one-room school in Hanover County, but neither Baker nor Anderson had independent financial resources or successful experience managing a large educational institution. Nevertheless, they opened the doors of Collegiate School on 23 September 1915 and admitted seventy-five pupils in grades one through twelve. Baker's title was head of the school rather than the conventional one of headmistress. In January 1917 Collegiate merged with the Stratford School to take effect with the autumn 1917 session, thereby increasing the total enrollment to almost three hundred. That spring construction began on a large, new building to which the enlarged school, which retained the name Collegiate, moved that autumn.

During the 1910s Baker served as a vice president of the Virginia Association of Colleges and Secondary Schools (1916–1917) and gained a wide acquaintance among central Virginia educators. In 1914 she supported her friend Orie Latham Hatcher in the creation of the Virginia Bureau of Vocations for Women, which became the Southern Woman's Education Alliance in 1921. Baker was a trustee and secretary when the bureau was incorporated in 1918, and she served on the board of directors of the secretarial school, Smithdeal Business College, that Hatcher helped start. Baker was also a founder in 1920 of the short-lived Columbia School of Music in Richmond, sat on its advisory board, and served as its associate head.

The enlargement of Collegiate and construction of a new building placed a greater financial burden on its resources than Baker, Anderson, and their backers were able to support, and in the summer of 1920 the school was forced into bankruptcy. Within two years, however, other Richmond educators revived Collegiate and, building on the educational foundations that Baker and Anderson had laid, developed it into an academically demanding and prestigious private preparatory school. In the meantime, both founders had left Richmond. Anderson married and went to Kentucky, and Baker moved first to Hendersonville, North Carolina, where she served as principal of Hendersonville High School from 1921 to 1926, and then to Hartsville, South Carolina. She served as dean of girls at Hartsville High School from 1927 until she retired in 1957. Initially she taught American history, but at times she subsequently taught Latin and civics as well. Baker founded the Hartsville Chapter of the National Honor Society, the first NHS chapter in South Carolina, and acted as an advisor for student publications and other extracurricular activities. She served twelve years on the University of South Carolina Board of Women Visitors and wrote on education for various state and national publications. Helen Ettie Baker died of a heart attack in Hartsville on 31 August 1960 and was buried at Silver Brook Cemetery in Anderson, South Carolina.

Biography in *Fifty Years of Collegiate: A History of the Collegiate Schools, 1915–1965* (1967), 16–23 (por.); Richmond College, *Spider* 5 (1905): 17, 58, 95, 161; Columbia University, *Catalogue* (1913–1914): 426; obituaries in *Richmond News Leader* and *Richmond Times-Dispatch*, both 1 Sept. 1960, and *Hartsville Messenger*, 8 Sept. 1960.

EMILY J. SALMON
JOHN S. HOPEWELL

BAKER, Jerman (29 September 1776–28 March 1828), member of the Council and treasurer of Virginia, was born in Chesterfield County, the elder of two children, both sons, of Jerman Baker and Martha Ward Murray Baker. He had one older half sister. His father was a prominent attorney who served in the House of Delegates after the American Revolution. Baker attended the College of William and Mary and on 15 November 1798 married Martha Bolling Eppes. Four of their six sons and three of their four daughters survived childhood.

In 1800 Baker moved his family to Cumberland County after his wife received land there from her father. Baker represented Cumberland in the House of Delegates from December 1803 until January 1807, and he was elected to another one-year term in 1808. Like Congressman John Wayles Eppes, his brother-in-law, Baker was a Jeffersonian Republican, and in 1809 he lost a campaign for the United States House of Representatives against John Randolph of Roanoke. Baker returned to the House of Delegates in 1813 and served until February 1817. By then he was well known, well respected, and experienced, and on 3 January 1818 the House of Delegates elected him to the Council of State. Baker served on this advisory body to the governor until he resigned on 24 January 1820 to become state treasurer in the wake of a defalcation scandal involving John Preston, the office's previous occupant.

Baker had been buying and selling land since not long after his marriage, a practice that eventually led to his downfall. Between 1800 and 1824 he sold all of the land that he and his wife had inherited from their fathers (about 1,300 acres in Chesterfield, Cumberland, and Amelia Counties) and bought about 2,700 acres. Prior to his election as state treasurer, Baker managed to support all of his land transactions without resorting to mortgages. When he sold his land in Cumberland County in 1819 and moved to Richmond, he was clear of debt, had received $2,000 for that sale, and was owed an additional $22,050. A year later, however, he bought a plantation in Amelia County for $13,000 and took out a $10,000 mortgage on it. In 1824 he mortgaged a residence in Richmond, and in November 1825 he paid off one of his mortgages and took out a mortgage on an additional 500 acres in Amelia.

As early as January 1822, when he made his will, Baker knew that he was in financial jeopardy. He named his wife as his executor and authorized her to sell as much of his estate as necessary to pay his debts, "which from misfortune & want of management, & not from gambling, or other dissipation, never having been so addicted, may be numerous." In August 1827 he executed deeds of trust to compensate his wife for the dower rights she had released when he had sold her inheritance and to indemnify the guarantors of a note he had signed at the Bank of the United States. Although getting deeper and deeper into debt, Baker met his mortgage payments and without arousing suspicion continued to maintain his family in a style befitting his status as a well-connected member of the landed gentry and as treasurer of the commonwealth.

Baker did so by embezzling money from the state treasury, eventually taking about $25,000. Late in March 1828 an auditing committee of the Council of State became aware of some irregularities during its quarterly review of the treasurer's accounts. On the day the committee members planned to meet him and seek an explanation, he committed suicide. Jerman Baker contrived a clumsy means of strangling himself and died on 28 March 1828 at his home in Richmond. He was buried in a family cemetery in Chesterfield County. Lawsuits and settlement of the accounts resulting from Baker's embezzlements dragged on for years, but his heirs and sureties eventually repaid most of the money he had stolen.

Baker family Bible records, Misc. Reel 701, LVA; land transactions recorded in deed books of Amelia, Chesterfield, and Cumberland Cos. and of Richmond City Hustings Court; several Baker letters in VHS; Richmond City Hustings Court Will Book, 4:408–409, 423–425, 5:5–7; personal accounts of Baker and records of 1822–1848 concerning his misuse of state funds in General Operational Records, relevant correspondence of 1822–1846 in General Fund records, and Special Funds receipt ledger, 1823–1844, all in Treasury Department Records, RG 12, LVA; *Bullock* v. *Baker et al.*, Ended Cause June 1829, Richmond City Hustings Court Ended Causes; *Wilson et al.* v. *Burfoot* (1845) (2 Grattan) *Virginia Reports*, 43:134; account of money paid to commonwealth by Baker's administrators, 11 Dec. 1845, Nash Family Papers, VHS; *JHD*, 1828–1829 sess., 17, 122, and Doc. no. 3; *Acts of Assembly*, 1828–1829 sess., 147–148; 1829–1830 sess., 120; 1833–1834 sess., 311–312; 1845–1846 sess., 153–155; accounts of death in *Richmond Constitutional Whig*, 29 Mar. 1828, and *Richmond Enquirer*, 1 Apr. 1828.

EMILY J. SALMON

BAKER, John (1769–18 August 1823), attorney and member of the House of Representatives, was the only son among eight children of John Baker and Judith Howard Wood Baker. He was probably born in Frederick County, Maryland. During the Revolutionary War the Bakers moved to the headwaters of Elks Run in the Gap View section of Berkeley County, Virginia. In 1784 they moved within the county to land on Evitts Run adjoining Harewood, the residence of George Washington's brother Samuel Washington.

Baker attended Liberty Hall Academy and then read law. He was admitted to the bar in Berkeley County and by early in the 1790s was practicing in Shepherdstown, a prosperous commercial entrepôt to the Shenandoah Valley. On 4 April 1799 he married Ann Mark, daughter of John Mark, a prominent local Federalist. They had five sons and three daughters. One of the daughters married Thomas Walker Gilmer, a governor of Virginia.

Baker's career in many ways typified that of a successful small-town lawyer of the time. He transacted a wide variety of routine legal business for local residents, but he also acted as counsel and local agent for Baltimore mercantile firms. He later acquired and administered his father-in-law's Traveller's Rest plantation, which had been the home of General Horatio Gates. On one occasion Baker acted to protect the financial interests of one of his sisters and her children from her husband's creditors, which he did by purchasing all their property and arranging for a sale of their slaves. Baker also speculated in property in Shepherdstown, and he and his large extended family eventually moved into the Spangler House, one of the town's finer residences, where he opened a law office.

Baker represented Berkeley County in the House of Delegates for the session of 1798–1799, and he was the first commonwealth's attorney when Jefferson County was created in 1801. He also served four terms as president of the Shepherdstown court of trustees and as the town's attorney. In 1811 a meeting of Federalist politicians at the Globe Tavern in Martinsburg nominated Baker for Congress for the district of Berkeley, Hampshire, and Jefferson Counties. He defeated Daniel Morgan in the election by a margin of almost three to two. As a member of the 12th Congress, Baker voted against declaring war on Great Britain on 4 June 1812, and he criticized President James Madison's conduct of the war. Baker spoke in favor of pensions for Revolutionary War veterans and served on the Committee on the District of Columbia. Otherwise, his service in Congress was unremarkable, and he did not run for reelection. Sixty of his Federalist supporters feted him in Martinsburg on 12 August 1812 at the end of his term. John Baker resumed the practice of law in Shepherdstown and died there on 18 August 1823.

Biographies in F. Vernon Aler, *Aler's History of Martinsburg and Berkeley County, West Virginia* (1888), 188–190 (which gives death date), Alva D. Kenamond, *Prominent Men of Shepherdstown During its First 200 Years* (1963), 23–25 (por.), and Millard Kessler Bushong, *Historic Jefferson County* (1972), 403 (which repeats an unsubstantiated assertion that Baker was one of the defense counsel at Aaron Burr's treason trial in 1807; however, John Baker [d. ca. 1833] of Richmond and Petersburg was almost certainly the young attorney in question); public life and property transactions documented in Jefferson Co. Order and Deed Books and incomplete extant files of *Martinsburgh Gazette*; will, estate inventory, and record of some property sales in Jefferson Co. Will Book, 3:477, 4:168, 176.

JOHN E. STEALEY III

BAKER, Thomas Roberts (30 May 1825–26 November 1906), pharmacist, was born in Richmond, the son of Hilary Baker and Margaret Marshall Roberts Baker. Both of his parents were descended from German immigrants, and his father was an attorney who moved to Richmond from Pennsylvania in 1818 and became treasurer of the Richmond and Fredericksburg Railroad, later the Richmond, Fredericksburg, and Potomac.

T. Roberts Baker, as he was always known, attended Richmond Academy until his father's death in 1840, when he was apprenticed as a pharmacist in the local shop of Alexander Duval. Recognizing the importance of pharmaceutical education, he entered the Philadelphia College of Pharmacy in 1850 and graduated in 1852 with a Ph.G. (graduate in pharmacy) degree after writing his thesis on *Secale corntum*, or ergot of rye, later identified as *Claviceps purpurea*. Baker returned to Richmond, where he was first employed in the shop of Samuel F. Adie and John T. Gray. In 1856 he formed a partnership with Richard H. Meade, advertising their pharmacy as Meade and Baker, "Apothecaries and Chemists at the northeast corner of Main and 10th Streets, just above the New Custom House." The firm pointedly identified Baker as a graduate of the Philadelphia College of Pharmacy to emphasize his professional training and advertised that "Prescriptions will be accurately and promptly dispensed by one of the Partners at all hours of the day or night."

Although Baker could have claimed an exemption from military service during the Civil War, he enlisted in the Richmond Howitzers and served in the Battle of Big Bethel on 10 June 1861. In July the surgeon general ordered Baker to report to the medical department of the army, where he taught hospital stewards for the Army of Northern Virginia. He was appointed a hospital steward himself on 22 March 1862, but the appointment was revoked on 3 February 1863. Evidently he remained active in the war effort thereafter, because he was paroled at Lynchburg on 15 April 1865. Later that year Baker renewed his partnership with Meade. One of their advertisements proclaimed that "if you cannot get a medicine at Meade & Baker's, it cannot be had in the city." Baker retained Meade's name for the firm after his death and operated Meade and Baker until 1891, when he formed the Virginia Pharmacal Company (later Meade and Baker Carbolic Mouth Wash Company) to manufacture Meade and Baker's Carbolic Mouth Wash.

Throughout his career Baker was active in organizations of professional pharmacists. Having graduated from pharmacy school in the same city and in the same year that the American Pharmaceutical Association was founded, Baker became a member in 1856. He chaired the association's reception committee when the organization held its annual national convention in Richmond in September 1873. Two years later he led the Richmond delegation to the meeting in Boston, where he presented a paper "On the Antiseptic Properties of Chloral Hydrate," describing the results of experiments he had conducted jointly with Isaiah H. White of the Medical College of Virginia. At the 1878 meeting in Atlanta, Georgia, Baker presented a comprehensive report on the drug trade in

Virginia, obtaining much of the information from the customs house near his shop. Baker was elected second vice president of the association in 1875 and first vice president in 1879. He also served as temporary chairman of the first meeting of the National Retail Druggists Association in Washington, D.C., on 10 September 1883.

Baker served as the first corresponding secretary of the Richmond Pharmaceutical Association soon after his graduation from pharmacy school, and when the Virginia Pharmaceutical Association was formed at a general meeting in Petersburg on 4 January 1882, Baker was elected its first president. In March 1886 the General Assembly incorporated the association in order "to encourage pharmaceutical talent, to elevate the standard of professional thought, and ultimately restrict the practice of pharmacy to qualified pharmacists and druggists." The law created a five-member Virginia Board of Pharmacy to license and set educational standards for new pharmacists, regulate the practices of druggists, and discipline pharmacists who engaged in unsafe practices. Governor Fitzhugh Lee appointed Baker to a five-year term as a member of the first board. Baker's prominence in state and national pharmacy organizations contributed to the Philadelphia College of Pharmacy's granting him an honorary master of pharmacy degree in 1889.

Baker married Maria Greenhough Burgwyn at the Church of the Advent in Boston, Massachusetts, on 28 October 1868, and they had one son. Baker was a founder of the Young Men's Christian Association of Richmond and served as its president in 1869. He was also a member of Saint Paul's Episcopal Church. T. Roberts Baker died at his home in Richmond on 26 November 1906 and was buried in Hollywood Cemetery there.

Tyler, *Men of Mark*, 4:19–20; Compiled Service Records; marriage reported in *Richmond Daily Enquirer and Examiner* and *Daily Richmond Whig*, both 4 Nov. 1868; Joseph E. England, ed., *The First Century of the Philadelphia College of Pharmacy, 1821–1921* (1922), 466; T. Roberts Baker, "On the Antiseptic Properties of Chloral Hydrate" and "Report on the Drug Trade in Virginia," in American Pharmaceutical Association, *Proceedings of the Annual Meeting* 23 (1875): 710–717, 799–803, and 26 (1878): 646–661; obituaries in *Richmond News Leader* and *Richmond Times-Dispatch*, both 27 Nov. 1906; memorials in *Druggists Circular* 51 (1907): 104 (por.), 134, 148, and Virginia Pharmaceutical Association, *Proceedings of the Annual Meeting* 26 (1907): 31–33.

GEORGE GRIFFENHAGEN

BAKER, William Washington (20 October 1844–21 February 1927), public health advocate and member of the House of Delegates, was born near Hallsboro in northwestern Chesterfield County, the eldest of one son and two daughters known to have been born to John Daniel Baker and Ann Elizabeth Howard Baker. He began school in Chesterfield County, but following his mother's death his father moved the family to Danville. In 1856 Baker became an apprentice in the printing office of the *Danville Register*. After his father moved to Richmond, Baker completed his apprenticeship at the *Richmond Enquirer*, where the editors, John Mitchell and George Stedman, encouraged him to read and study in the library of the editorial room.

In August 1863 Baker enlisted in the Confederate navy and served under the privateer captain John Yates Beall. On 15 November 1863 Union forces captured Beall and his men. Baker was imprisoned in chains at Fort McHenry in Baltimore. He was moved three times before being exchanged in 1864. He returned to Richmond and clerked in the office of the provost marshal, but when the Confederate government abandoned Richmond in April 1865, he went out to join the remnants of the army and was present for the surrender at Appomattox. Baker returned to Chesterfield County after the war and married Sarah Thomas Martin on 25 December 1866. They had three sons and three daughters.

With his brothers-in-law Baker formed the partnership of Martin Brothers and Baker, which manufactured lumber products and ran a tannery in Hallsboro and Manchester. Baker also served as a justice of the peace in Chesterfield County and as a member of the county's board of supervisors, and he published a promotional brochure, *Description of Chesterfield County, Va.* (1888). He was elected to one term in the House of Delegates in 1883 and served again from 1899 through 1916, becoming one of the more influential members of the Democratic Party majority. He chaired the Committee on

Banks, Currency, and Commerce in 1904, the Joint Committee on the Library in 1906, the Committee on Insurance and Banking from 1908 to 1915, and the Committee on Finance during his last year in the House.

Having lost four of his six children to tuberculosis, Baker led the legislative effort to create public sanatoriums for tuberculosis victims, advocated other public health measures, and in 1908 supported reorganizing the State Board of Health and converting it into what became the modern State Department of Health. He served as the first president of the Virginia Tuberculosis Association, and the W. W. Baker Child Welfare Camp in Chesterfield County was named for him. His 1913 address to the graduating class at the Catawba Nurses Training School was published in the state's premier medical journal in the same year, and in 1925 the State Department of Health presented him with an inscribed silver bowl in commemoration of his service to public health in Virginia. A posthumous editorial tribute in the *Richmond News Leader*, probably written by Douglas Southall Freeman, described Baker as "the father of Virginia health work."

While he was serving in the General Assembly, Baker wrote a series of reminiscences of his Civil War experiences and life in Virginia during Reconstruction for the *Richmond Times-Dispatch*, which was republished in one volume in 1910 with an introduction by Freeman stressing the book's great importance. Boasting a long white beard and the nickname of "Captain Billy," Baker was a popular figure who frequented the headquarters of the Department of Health and the Virginia Tuberculosis Association. He also served as one of the Virginia commissioners of the 1907 Jamestown Ter-Centennial Exposition, and in 1915 he was the chairman of the prize-winning Virginia Agricultural Exhibit at the Panama Pacific Exposition in San Francisco. He was also active throughout his adult life in the Middle District Baptist Association, and he was a trustee of Richmond College from 1903 to 1915. William Washington Baker died at Hallsboro on 21 February 1927 and was buried in the cemetery at Bethel Baptist Church in Midlothian.

William Washington Baker, *Memoirs of Service with John Yates Beall, C.S.N.* (1910); *Virginia Medical Semi-Monthly* 40 (1913): 171–175; feature article in *Richmond Times-Dispatch*, 22 Nov. 1936; Chesterfield Co. Marriage Register; obituaries in *Richmond News Leader*, 21 Feb. 1927 (por.), and *Richmond Times-Dispatch*, 22 Feb. 1927; editorial tribute in *Richmond News Leader*, 23 Feb. 1927.

BETTIE WOODSON WEAVER

BALCH, Emily Tapscott Clark. See **CLARK, Emily Tapscott**.

BALDWIN, Briscoe Gerard (18 January 1789–18 May 1852), attorney, member of the Convention of 1829–1830, and judge of the Virginia Court of Appeals, was the eldest of six sons and third of ten children of Winchester physician Cornelius Baldwin and Mary Briscoe Baldwin. He attended Winchester Academy and enrolled in the College of William and Mary in 1806, but shortly thereafter he accepted an offer from his brother-in-law William Daniel to read law in his Cumberland County office. Baldwin was admitted to the bar and established his practice in Staunton in 1809. In 1812 he married Martha Steele Brown, daughter of John Brown, the chancellor of the Staunton district, and they had three sons and three daughters. His eldest son was John Brown Baldwin, a member of the Confederate Congress and Speaker of the House of Delegates.

During the first half of the nineteenth century, Staunton was the most important legal center of western Virginia and boasted a talented bar. Baldwin, Chapman Johnson, Daniel Sheffey, and John Howe Peyton shared the most significant litigation in the courts of Staunton and the neighboring Valley counties. Alexander Hugh Holmes Stuart, himself later a star of the Valley bar, described Baldwin as "not only an able lawyer and skillful special pleader, but one of the most eloquent advocates of his day." Clients, petitioners, investors, and political candidates throughout western Virginia sought Baldwin's aid and advice, and his fame as one of the state's leading advocates spread rapidly. In 1835 he qualified to practice before the Virginia Court of Appeals and thereafter concentrated much of his practice in the appellate courts.

Baldwin served in the Virginia militia and by the 1830s was a brigadier general. He was inclined to stay out of politics, but he did represent Augusta County for three terms in the House of Delegates from 1818 to 1820 and 1822 to 1823. While in the assembly Baldwin supported internal improvements for the western counties and also tried to have the state capital moved to a more central location, preferably Staunton. He also served in the Convention of 1829–1830 and favored western proposals to alter the formula for apportioning seats in the General Assembly that had given an advantage to the small eastern counties at the expense of the large and increasingly populous western counties. Baldwin took the politically dangerous course of urging moderation, which may have alienated some of his more insistent constituents. Widely known as "a bold, and uncompromising man of honor," Baldwin did not display his talents to their best advantage in the convention.

In 1831 Baldwin launched an ambitious new venture. Knowing firsthand the limitations of reading law in an attorney's office, he opened a law school in Staunton, one of the first in the western part of the state. Chancellor Creed Taylor, of Cumberland County, and Judge Henry St. George Tucker, of Winchester, had both conducted law schools, and the College of William and Mary and the University of Virginia also had professors of law on their faculties. Baldwin's innovation was running a law school while still engaged in active practice. He divided his students into two classes, stressing elementary knowledge first, followed by intensive instruction in the practical areas of pleadings, procedure, and the general management of suits both at common law and in equity. The school's moot court program gave students practice in making arguments and being questioned in order to "guard against awkwardness and embarrassment, and fit the student for immediate usefulness." Baldwin conducted his school for approximately eight years.

In 1841 Baldwin was elected to the House of Delegates as a Whig, but he served only a few weeks because on 26 January 1842, after three days of highly partisan balloting, the General Assembly elected him to a seat on the Court of Appeals. Both Democrats and Whigs praised the compromise selection of Baldwin because he was a skilled attorney, and partisan politics had often dictated appointments. While serving on the bench Baldwin began compiling, through a careful reading of previous court decisions, a series of "maxims" (which was incomplete at the time of his death) that would "make surer for himself all the humanities and amenities of judicial and professional conduct." His strong commitment to the ideal of justice and to the elimination of obscurity in the pronouncement of law guided his most important decisions as a judge. In 1844 he clarified the issue of adversary possession of land, that is, under what circumstances a long and public occupation of a property conferred actual ownership of it on the person occupying it. In 1848 he repudiated from the bench the doctrine of fraud per se, which held that if a vendor retained possession of property after selling it, that created a presumption of fraud in the sale. Baldwin stated that application of the broad doctrine in many and varying cases had produced too many "perplexed and conflicting" judgments "abounding in nice disquisitions and subtle distinctions," producing "inextricable confusion" and rendering application of the doctrine "impracticable."

Baldwin served on the court for ten years. The Constitution of 1850 made the office of judge elective, and he declined being a candidate because of ill health. Briscoe Gerard Baldwin died at his residence, Spring Farm, near Staunton on 18 May 1852.

Biographies by Alexander Hugh Holmes Stuart in John Lewis Peyton, *History of Augusta County, Va.* (1882), 375–377, by Seargent S. P. Patteson in *Green Bag* 5 (1893): 364–366, by grandson Thomas D. Ranson, including Baldwin's maxims or rules, in *Virginia Law Register* 1 (1895): 236–237, and by E. Lee Shepard in *Legal Education in Virginia, 1779–1979: A Biographical Approach*, ed. W. Hamilton Bryson (1982), 66–72 (por.); Charles Candee Baldwin, *The Baldwin Genealogy, from 1500 to 1881* (1881); Stuart-Baldwin Papers, UVA; *Introductory Lecture, Delivered by General Briscoe G. Baldwin, Before His Law School in Staunton* [ca. 1831]; election to Court of Appeals reported in *Richmond Whig*, 27, 28, 29, 31 Jan., 2 Feb. 1842; ruling on adversary possession in *Taylor's Devisees* v. *Burnsides* (1844) (1 Grattan), *Virginia Reports*, 42:169, and on fraud per se in *Davis* v. *Turner* (1848) (4 Grattan), *Virginia Reports*, 45:422; obituaries in *Staunton Spectator and General Advertiser*,19, 26 May 1852.

E. LEE SHEPARD

BALDWIN, Dana Olden (20 March 1881–9 November 1972), physician, was born near Belvoir, Chatham County, North Carolina, the eldest of at least three sons and two daughters of James Hayes Baldwin, an African Methodist Episcopal minister, and Mary Crutchfield Baldwin. After graduating at the age of sixteen from the Normal and Collegiate Institute in Apex, Wake County, North Carolina, Baldwin taught school and worked on local farms until his mother persuaded him to become a medical doctor. He attended Leonard Medical College of Shaw University in Raleigh, graduating in 1910.

Baldwin passed the examination of the Virginia State Board of Medical Examiners later in 1910 and began practicing medicine in Martinsville, where he was the only African American doctor for many years, and possibly the first. In Henry County on 24 December 1911 he married a local teacher, Vina A. Flood, a graduate of Hartshorn Memorial College in Richmond. They adopted two girls and raised three boys and a girl as foster children. Later, as Baldwin prospered, he was able to send four young men from the Martinsville area to medical school.

Baldwin's practice was still struggling when the United States entered World War I in the spring of 1917. He volunteered for the Army Medical Corps, received a commission as a lieutenant, and served in Europe with the 92d Division, 317th Sanitary Train. After his discharge from Camp Meade, Maryland, on 2 April 1919, he went to Philadelphia, where he studied and practiced radiology. He also taught ballroom dancing during his time in Pennsylvania, and even when he was in his eighties was said to have been an agile, excellent dancer.

After only a few months in Philadelphia, the Baldwins moved back to Martinsville, where Dana Baldwin resumed his medical practice and Vina Baldwin resumed teaching. He was active in the African Methodist Episcopal Church, belonged to a number of fraternal organizations, founded an annual Martinsville Colored Fair, and served as medical examiner for at least four black insurance companies. Baldwin also bought property. Beginning at the corner of Fayette and Barton Streets, where he had built a house and office in 1914, Baldwin acquired and developed virtually an entire block, starting early in the 1920s and quickly rebuilding after a fire ruined the main building later in the decade. "Baldwin's Block" became the social and commercial center of Martinsville's African American community, housing his medical offices, a brickyard and a textile-manufacturing firm, a candy store, a poolroom, a barber shop, a beauty parlor, a theater, a dentist's office, a drugstore, two restaurants, and his own twenty-seven-bed Saint Mary's Hospital. He later enlarged the hospital, which was renamed Memorial Hospital.

Baldwin practiced medicine until he suffered a stroke in the 1960s. In recognition of his half century as a physician and his long career as a community leader, he received a golden anniversary certificate of honor from Shaw University in 1960. Dana Olden Baldwin died at Memorial Hospital in Martinsville on 9 November 1972 and was buried in the Baldwin Cemetery in Apex, North Carolina. Baldwin's Block has since been razed, but a park in the city of Martinsville is named in his honor.

Caldwell, *History of the American Negro*, 289–291 (por.); interview with Baldwin by John P. Bing, 20 Jan. 1969; BVS Marriage Register, Henry Co.; *Norfolk Journal and Guide*, 17 Aug. 1935 (por.); *Martinsville Tribune*, 21 July 1961; *Martinsville Bulletin*, 4 July 1976, bicentennial edition, and 14 Aug. 1977; obituary in *Martinsville Bulletin*, 10 Nov. 1972.

JUDITH P. JUSTUS
JOHN P. BING

BALDWIN, John Brown (11 January 1820–30 September 1873), attorney, member of the Convention of 1861, member of the Confederate House of Representatives, and Speaker of the House of Delegates, was born in Augusta County, the eldest of three sons and third of six children of Briscoe Gerard Baldwin and Martha Steele Brown Baldwin. He attended local schools and studied at the University of Virginia from 1836 to 1839. In the latter year he returned to Staunton to study law in the office of his father, who was one of the leaders of the bar in the Shenandoah Valley before being elected to the Virginia Court of Appeals early in 1842. Baldwin was admitted to the bar in May 1841, and on 20 September 1842 he married Susan Madison Peyton. They had no children.

Like his father, Baldwin was a Whig and he made his first political speech during the 1844 presidential campaign. He filled in for Alexander Hugh Holmes Stuart, his law partner and brother-in-law, who was the Whig candidate for presidential elector, and he made such an impression debating the Democratic Party representative that local politicians took notice. In 1845 he was elected to represent Augusta County in the House of Delegates. There Baldwin reluctantly sided with those who favored the calling of a state constitutional convention. He supported changes that would allow for partial amendment of the new constitution and link apportionment in the General Assembly directly to population and wealth. His belief that seats in the proposed convention (not actually held for five more years) should be distributed based on the system of representation then in effect, and that the different sections of the state would have to compromise by basing apportionment on the value of taxable property as well as white population, alienated his constituents, many of whom opposed measures that limited their political clout by including the value of slaves in decisions about apportionment. Baldwin accordingly lost his bid for reelection in April 1846.

Baldwin remained active in politics and served on the board of visitors of the University of Virginia from 1856 until 1864. In 1859 he was nominated for the Supreme Court of Appeals, but the General Assembly did not elect him. In 1860 he campaigned for the Constitutional Union Party ticket of John Bell and Edward Everett, which carried Virginia. Baldwin and Stuart were two of Staunton's leading Unionists during the winter of 1860–1861, and on 4 February 1861 they and Unionist Democrat George Baylor were elected to represent Augusta County in the convention called to discuss the possibility of secession. The convention met from 13 February to 1 May 1861, and Baldwin was one of its most emphatic Unionists. He served on the Committee on Federal Relations and, in the longest and most celebrated speech of his life, he spoke for three days, starting 21 March, in favor of preserving the Union.

As the secession crisis neared its climax, Baldwin had a long private meeting with President Abraham Lincoln in Washington on 4 April 1861. Although interpretations of the negotiation later varied, Baldwin tried to persuade Lincoln to take no action that could be deemed hostile to the Southern states, such as reinforcing Fort Sumter in South Carolina, and Lincoln tried to persuade Baldwin to have the Virginia convention adjourn, thus thwarting the secessionists in Virginia. The meeting was inconclusive because Lincoln refused to assure Baldwin that he would not use force to retain control of federal installations in the South, and Baldwin could not assure Lincoln that the Virginia convention would disperse without reconvening in response to future events. Baldwin returned to Richmond to find that while he was meeting with Lincoln the convention had voted 88 to 45 against secession. Baldwin continued to press for reconciliation and compromise, but the Unionist majority in the Virginia convention collapsed two weeks later, and on 17 April 1861 the convention voted 88 to 55 to secede. Baldwin voted against secession but later, as a gesture of support for his native state, signed the Ordinance of Secession.

To the dismay of many old Democrats and advocates of secession, Governor John Letcher appointed Baldwin inspector general of volunteers. On 19 August 1861 Baldwin became colonel of the 52d Virginia Infantry. He served briefly in the mountains of western Virginia but suffered a physical breakdown and resigned on 1 May 1862. Thereafter he was colonel of the Augusta County militia, and although he was called into the field several times, he saw no further action. While still recuperating, Baldwin was elected to the Confederate House of Representatives on 6 November 1861. He defeated Letcher in May 1863 to win reelection and served in Congress for the duration of the war. Baldwin was a member of the Committee on Ways and Means during both Congresses, and during the second he chaired the Special Committee on Impressments. Baldwin was also one of the strongest critics of President Jefferson Davis.

Baldwin returned to Staunton at the end of the Civil War and on 8 May 1865 participated in a meeting of community leaders who urged a speedy restoration of civil government. He swore allegiance to the United States government on 20 May and 5 July, and President Andrew Johnson pardoned Baldwin on 28 September 1865. Baldwin was not in Staunton when news of his pardon was received there, nor was he present on 12 October when he was overwhelmingly elected to one of the three Augusta County seats in the General Assembly without his knowing that he had been nominated. Baldwin was elected Speaker of the House when it convened on 4 December 1865 and presided over three sessions of the assembly between then and the end of April 1867. He became an expert on parliamentary procedure, and the rules of the House that evolved during his speakership were known for many years thereafter as Baldwin's Rules. Baldwin took a cautious and conciliatory middle course between radical reformers and former Confederates. He expressed his beliefs most clearly in Washington on 10 February 1866 in lengthy testimony before the Joint Committee on Reconstruction. He told the congressional leaders that while most Virginians had accepted the verdict handed down on the battlefield and would go along with some civil rights for freedpeople, they were opposed to further extension of the political rights of African Americans. Baldwin quickly became a leader of the Conservative Party in Virginia and was chairman of the party's May 1868 state convention, which almost nominated him for governor in spite of his public announcement that he would decline the nomination. Two months later he headed the Conservative Party's delegation to the Democratic National Convention.

In 1869 Baldwin was a member of the so-called Committee of Nine, led by Alexander Hugh Holmes Stuart, who met with President Ulysses S. Grant to arrange the compromise that brought Reconstruction to an end in Virginia. Its terms permitted the Virginia electorate to vote separately on the ratification of the constitution prepared by the Convention of 1867–1868 and on the clauses of that constitution that would have disfranchised many former Confederate soldiers and government officials. The voters, as predicted, ratified the constitution and defeated the disqualification clauses. This negotiation concluded Baldwin's political career. He returned to the practice of law in Staunton, where he served as counsel for the Chesapeake and Ohio Railroad Company. He also took an interest in local projects. In the General Assembly in 1867 he had pushed through a bill to incorporate the Augusta County Fair, which was later named the Baldwin-Augusta Fair in his honor. In one of his last letters Baldwin requested that the Staunton City Council improve the road leading to the fairgrounds. John Brown Baldwin died at his home in Staunton on 30 September 1873 and was buried in Thornrose Cemetery in Staunton.

Charles Curry, *John Brown Baldwin: Lawyer, Soldier, Statesman* (1928); biography by Joseph Addison Waddell in John Lewis Peyton, *History of Augusta County, Virginia* (1882), 379–385; *Staunton Spectator*, 26 Mar., 30 Apr. 1846, 12 Feb. 1861; Reese and Gaines, *Proceedings of 1861 Convention*, 2:138–146, 166–201, 210–237; divergent views on meeting with Lincoln compiled in *Interview Between President Lincoln and Col. John B. Baldwin, April 4th, 1861: Statements and Evidence* (1866), and assessed in Daniel W. Crofts, *Reluctant Confederates: Upper South Unionists in the Secession Crisis* (1989), 301–307; Compiled Service Records; Robert J. Driver Jr., *52nd Virginia Infantry* (1986), 93; Presidential Pardons; *Staunton Spectator and General Advertiser*, 10, 17 Oct. 1865; *Report of the Joint Committee on Reconstruction*, 39th Cong., 1st sess., 1866, House Rept. 30, serial 1273, appended testimony, pt. 2, 102–109; por. in Augusta Co. Circuit Court, Staunton; obituaries in *Staunton Vindicator*, 3 Oct. 1873, and *Staunton Spectator*, 7 Oct. 1873.

SCOTT HAMPTON HARRIS

BALDWIN, John Thomas (5 September 1910–3 September 1974), botanist, was born in Chase City in Mecklenburg County, the third of five sons and fourth of six children of John Thomas Baldwin and Lona Earle Price Baldwin. He grew up in Keysville in Charlotte County and entered the College of William and Mary intending to study English and Latin and having no interest in or preparation for studying the natural sciences. However, a course in biology from Donald Walton Davis inspired him to change the direction of his life. Continuing his studies in English literature and the Latin language, Baldwin received his A.B. from William and Mary in 1932, but then entered the University of Virginia to study botany. He received his doctorate in biology in 1937.

J. T. Baldwin Jr. taught biology at William and Mary from 1937 until 1939 and at the University of Michigan from 1939 until 1942. His professional specializations were cytogenetics (the branch of molecular pathology concerned with tracing genetic inheritances and relationships), taxonomy (scientific classification), and economic botany. During World War II he left the University of Michigan and traveled to South America for the United States Department of Agriculture to investigate means of improving rubber production. He later accompanied or led a number of important specimen-collecting expeditions to the tropics.

In 1945 and 1946 Baldwin managed the Blandy Experimental Farm, an agricultural research facility near Winchester sponsored by the University of Virginia. In 1946, however, Davis lured him back to William and Mary as heir apparent to the chairmanship of the Department of Biology. Baldwin led an expedition to Liberia in 1947 that resulted in the identification of a species of *Strophanthus*, the plant from which natural cortisone was derived. Although this discovery was Baldwin's major contribution to the study of botany and had great medical significance, he had wide-ranging interests in economic botany and taxonomy and published many scientific papers during his career. He also became known for his plantings of boxwood throughout the campus at William and Mary, reputedly one of the finest such collections in the world.

Baldwin remained at William and Mary until his death, serving as chairman of the biology department from 1952 to 1962. Working with him was not always easy, for he was a brilliant man with a prickly personality and was equally adept at advancing his strongly held opinions and deriding his critics in either English or Latin. J. T. Baldwin Jr. died in Williamsburg on 3 September 1974 and was buried in Ash Camp Cemetery in Keysville.

American Men and Women of Science, 12th ed. (1971), 1:257; typescript of oral history interview with Alfred Ringold Armstrong, 11 Feb. 1976, W&M; Census, Charlotte Co., 1920; obituaries in *Newport News Daily Press*, *New York Times*, and *Richmond News Leader*, all 5 Sept. 1974, and *Williamsburg Virginia Gazette*, 6 Sept. 1974 (por.).

BRENT TARTER

BALDWIN, Mary Julia (4 October 1829–1 July 1897), educator, was born in the Staunton home of her grandparents John Colson Sowers and Mary Heiskell Sowers. She was the only child of a physician, William Daniel Baldwin, and Margaret Sarah Sowers Baldwin, of Winchester, where she spent the first few months of her life. Her father died of consumption in February 1830, and her mother moved back to Staunton, where Mary Julia Baldwin lived, with a few brief interludes, for the remainder of her life. Baldwin's mother died in May 1837, and she grew up in the home of her prosperous grandparents, surrounded by a large and close extended family, of which her uncle Briscoe Gerard Baldwin formed a part.

When she was four years old Baldwin suffered a high and prolonged fever that permanently paralyzed and twisted the left side of her face. Physicians could do nothing to ease the disfigurement, but although she permitted no portraits or photographs to be made of her face, Baldwin was not morbidly sensitive about it and attended school with other children, actively participated in social activities, and attended the local Presbyterian church. In 1842 she enrolled as one of the first pupils in Rufus William Bailey's new Augusta Female Seminary. Frail-looking and somewhat timid, she often assisted her classmates with difficult assignments and graduated first in her class in 1846. Bailey offered his pupils an excellent education much in advance of that available to most young southern women of the time. He stressed high academic standards, encouraged devotion to Christian precepts and community service, and instilled pride and self-reliance in his students. Baldwin's graduation concluded her formal education, but she spent the winter of 1853–1854 in Philadelphia, studying, reading, and attending concerts and art exhibits.

Baldwin lived with her grandmother on the income of her father's estate. She became a regular and eloquent Sunday School teacher for young women, organized a Sunday afternoon class for black children, and taught her grandmother's slaves to read and write. When the Civil War began, she joined with several of her friends to organize and conduct a girls' school that they called Bee Hive Seminary. To that time, nothing in her life or manner suggested that Baldwin would do other than live out her years as an unmarried southern lady, limited and restricted by the conventions of her era.

That traditional pattern changed in 1863 when the Augusta Female Seminary was in danger of being closed and one of the trustees, Joseph Addison Waddell, persuaded Baldwin to take over as principal of the school and convinced the trustees to hire her. Baldwin borrowed furniture, eating utensils, and dictionaries and other books for the pupils and asked the seventy students to pay their tuition and fees with food and fuel. She persuaded William Holmes McGuffey of the University of Virginia to assist her in revamping the curriculum. The seminary had always been more than a finishing school, but Baldwin aspired to advance it to the level of a university and organized it into seven schools patterned on those of the University of Virginia. The course of study included classical and modern languages, rhetoric, grammar, composition, history, higher mathematics, physics and chemistry, and mental and moral philosophy. She developed an outstanding program in music, stressed the visual arts and elocution, and, as new opportunities for women opened up, added such practical subjects as bookkeeping, nutrition, and calisthenics. Like Bailey before her, she required that her students have a "trained intellect and Christian courage."

Baldwin excelled in administration and had a keen business sense, acquiring valuable pieces of real estate and making shrewd investments. She chose her faculty members carefully and attracted their loyalty, so that several of them stayed at the seminary for their entire professional lives. She trained her students with equal care, encouraging them to share her own sense of intellectual curiosity and seeking to stimulate their sense of service and their religious faith. Baldwin remained at the helm of the seminary for thirty-four years, during which the number of students increased from seventy to two hundred fifty and the school came to be considered one of the most distinguished for young women in the southern states. Its alumnae included missionaries, teachers, doctors, lawyers, business leaders, authors, poets, and feminist reformers. In 1895 Baldwin's contributions to all features of the seminary's success prompted its trustees to obtain permission from the General Assembly to rename the school Mary Baldwin Seminary in "acknowledgement of their high appreciation of the valuable service and unparalleled success of the Principal." In 1922 Mary Baldwin College, as it was then styled, became a fully accredited four-year institution of higher learning.

Baldwin's health and vigor deteriorated during the 1890s. She bequeathed her property, which was valued at almost $250,000, to be divided among her family, her church, and the trustees for the benefit of the school, creating the first endowment for the college that bore her name. Mary Julia Baldwin died on 1 July 1897 and was buried in Thornrose Cemetery in Staunton.

Patricia H. Menk, *To Live in Time: The Sesquicentennial History of Mary Baldwin College, 1842–1992* (1992); Mary Watters, *The History of Mary Baldwin College, 1842–1942* (1942); biographies by people who knew her are in Nellie Hotchkiss McCullough, "Miss Mary Julia Baldwin," *Record* 2 (Oct. 1898), the college's alumnae publication, and in Joseph A. Waddell, *History of Mary Baldwin Seminary (Originally Augusta Female Seminary) from 1842 to 1905 Inclusive* (1908), 29–58; Baldwin's application file for admission to Daughters of the American Revolution and other documents and records in Mary Baldwin College Library; obituaries in *Staunton Spectator and Vindicator*, 8 July 1897 (with summary of will), and *Harrisonburg Rockingham Register*, 9 July 1897.

PATRICIA H. MENK

BALDWIN, Noah Calton (30 September 1817–14 January 1903), Baptist minister, was the eldest of three children, all sons, of Enoch W. Baldwin and Esther Baker Baldwin and was born in Ashe County, North Carolina. He attended local schools for a few years but was largely self-educated. During his long life he read widely in theology and philosophy, and he loved poetry and music. At age twenty Baldwin experienced a conversion and thereafter marked the date, 8 May 1838, as his "new birthday." He preached his first sermon on his twenty-first birthday and joined the Methodist Church. He was licensed to preach, but he soon became a Baptist because he believed in baptism by immersion and opposed the baptism of infants. Baldwin was licensed on 1 June 1839 and ordained on 3 October 1840, beginning a peripatetic career as a Baptist minister that lasted until 1895.

In 1840 Baldwin moved to Smyth County and became pastor of both Saint Clair Bottom Church and Middle Fork Church. In 1844 the State Mission Board appointed him to ride as a missionary within the Washington Association in southwestern Virginia. During the ensuing years he preached revival sermons in Grayson, Russell, Scott, Smyth, Tazewell, and Washington Counties in Virginia, and in Hawkins, Sullivan, and Washington Counties in Tennessee. He organized Baptist churches in many places during the next thirty-one years, including the Rye Valley Church and Marion Baptist Church in Smyth County and Friendship Baptist Church, Greenfield Baptist Church, and Glade Spring Baptist Church in Washington County. When the local Baptists split over the issue of missions in 1845, Baldwin sided with the pro-mission faction and helped found the Lebanon Baptist Association. He served as clerk of the association for eleven consecutive years and as moderator at ten annual meetings. In Richmond in 1846 he attended the first annual meeting of the Southern Baptist Convention.

Tall and dignified in appearance, portly in later life, and with snow-white hair and a Vandyke beard, Baldwin was a striking figure in the pulpit. He moved to Washington County in the 1850s and preached in Abingdon until 1856, when he moved to Tennessee. He served as Confederate postmaster of Kingsport, Tennessee, in 1861, but in 1862 moved to nearby Blountville. The following year his house, his store, and a hotel he owned, valued altogether at about $10,000, were destroyed during a Union army raid. Baldwin returned to Virginia after this crushing blow and in 1869 settled in Glade Spring. In 1875 he was the first mayor of the town, but he later purchased a farm near Friendship that he named Whang Doodle Hollow, where he lived for the remainder of his life. He served as pastor of South Fork and Friendship Baptist Churches until 1895. During a period of fifty-five years he became the most prominent Baptist minister in the area of southwestern Virginia of which his churches in Smyth and Washington Counties were the center.

Baldwin married four times but had no children. On 25 December 1838 he married Nancy McMillan, who died of typhoid fever on 26 October 1854. On 17 April 1855 he married Lavenia Murray, who died on 18 October 1867, after which he married Mary Jane Frances Bryan on 20 March 1868. She died on 26 July 1893. He was seventy-six years old on 25 April 1894 when he married Florence S. Harwood, a widow with three young daughters. Often depressed as a result of his domestic afflictions and on many occasions at odds with fellow Baptists and other Protestants, Noah Calton Baldwin died of angina and cancer of the mouth at his home on 14 January 1903. He was buried beside the grave of his second wife in Anderson Cemetery at Adwolf in Smyth County.

Baldwin's diary, 1850–1902, VBHS; biography by stepdaughter Virginia Catherine Harwood in *Bulletin of the Historical Society of Washington County (Va.)* 12 (Sept. 1945): 14–33; por. at South Fork Baptist Church, Smyth County; obituary in *Marion News*, 23 Jan. 1903; memorials in Baptist General Association of Virginia, *Minutes of the Annual Session* 80 (1903): 95–96, and Lebanon Baptist Association, [*Minutes of the Annual Session*] 58 (1903): 24.

MACK H. STURGILL

BALDWIN, William Gibboney (26 May 1860–31 March 1936), cofounder of Baldwin-Felts Detectives, was born in Tazewell County, the eldest of five sons and four daughters of Denison B. Baldwin and Sallie Barns Baldwin. Very little is known about his youth except that he enjoyed reading. He abandoned an early interest in dentistry and turned to detective work about 1884 when he joined the Eureka Detective Agency in Charleston, West Virginia. He married Katherine English, and they had two sons before separating, probably before he moved to Roanoke early in the 1890s.

Baldwin formed his own agency in Roanoke, Baldwin's Railroad Detectives, and took over all of the detective work in the coalfields of western Virginia, West Virginia, and eastern Kentucky for the Norfolk and Western Railway Company, of which his brother-in-law, William Jackson Jenks, was general manager and later vice president. The work consisted of keeping order on trains, preventing or investigating thefts, and controlling the railroad's labor force. Baldwin's agency provided all detective services for the Norfolk and Western until he retired. He took an active role in his company's often violent work. In 1898 Baldwin was acquitted of murder charges in Petersburg after shooting and killing a black man during an arrest. At the trial he claimed to have fired on fourteen men in his capacity as a railroad detective for the Norfolk and Western.

Baldwin was involved in two notorious episodes of racial violence in Roanoke at the turn of the century. After an assault on a white farmer's wife in Roanoke in 1893, he brought in Thomas Smith, an African American, as a suspect. Baldwin then refused to help city officials protect Smith from the violent crowd that had gathered at the jail. A riot broke out and Smith was eventually lynched. In 1904 Baldwin intervened in the case of Henry Williams, an African American man who had been arrested and accused of assaulting and nearly killing a white Roanoke woman. Baldwin extracted a confession from Williams, who later charged that Baldwin had got him drunk in his jail cell and that his confession was both coerced and false. A mob of Roanoke men threatened to lynch Williams after news of the confession was made public, but he survived long enough to be legally hanged later that year.

Baldwin's principal fame came after he formed a partnership with Thomas L. Felts in 1900. Baldwin-Felts Detectives supplied security services to the Norfolk and Western, the Virginian, the Carolina, Clinchfield and Ohio, the Chesapeake and Ohio, the Richmond, Fredericksburg, and Potomac, and the Southern Pacific Railroads, as well as to Morgan's Louisiana and Texas Railroad and Steamship Company. In 1904 Baldwin traveled to Europe on behalf of the National Bureau of Identification, the forerunner of the International Association of Chiefs of Police, to study the emerging science of fingerprinting.

Baldwin-Felts agents took part in the case of Floyd Allen and his Carroll County family. Shortly after Allen and members of his family engaged in a wild shootout in the county courthouse on 14 March 1912, agency detectives left Roanoke to assist in capturing the members of the family who had fled into the rugged mountains. The firm's detectives eventually tracked two of Allen's relatives, Sidna Allen and Wesley Edwards, all the way to Des Moines. The national publicity accorded the manhunt and the many books and legends that grew out of the episode spread the fame of Baldwin-Felts Detectives.

During the 1910s the agency had busy offices in Roanoke and Richmond and in Bluefield and Thurmond in West Virginia. It opened an additional office in Denver after Baldwin-Felts was hired in 1910 to break up a strike of Northern Coal and Coke Company miners. Felts's brother, Albert C. Felts, who directed the Colorado work, designed an armored railroad car mounted with two machine guns that was called the "Death Special," and not without reason, for a number of miners were killed as Baldwin-Felts agents broke up the strike.

Baldwin-Felts became known almost as well as the older Pinkerton Detective Agency, achieving special notoriety in the southern Appalachia coalfields, where it defended the coal companies' interests against miners and the unionization efforts of the United Mine Workers of America. Baldwin-Felts blacklisted union members, intimidated, beat, and even killed union organizers, and worked under cover to identify workers critical of coal-mine owners and operators. Its detectives sometimes hired immigrants or African American miners to spy on their fellow mine workers. Baldwin-Felts even had some of its agents made deputy sheriffs to give legal cover to their work. As permitted by West Virginia law, mine operators employed armed guards who were often Baldwin-Felts agents to serve as private police in many coalfields there.

The agency experienced particularly active and controversial years in 1912 and 1913, when it undertook to break up strikes on Paint and Cabin Creeks near Charleston, West Virginia. At the height of the struggle, Baldwin-Felts had about three hundred agents in the field, and Albert Felts and Lee Felts, another brother of Thomas Felts, took personal control of the mine guards. As in Colorado, Felts used machine guns mounted on a railway car against striking miners. So controversial and violent were the armed mine guards that an investigative commission appointed by William E. Glasscock, the governor of West Virginia, pronounced the mine-guard system "vicious, strike-provoking and un-American" and demanded its termination. Mine guards remained in place until 1934, however, when Congress finally enacted stronger laws to protect the rights of labor union members and organizers.

Baldwin-Felts agents were also involved in the so-called Matewan Massacre of 19 May 1920. After the agency's armed officers evicted striking miners from company housing, Albert Felts, Lee Felts, and five other agents were killed in a shoot-out with Sid Hatfield, the chief of police of Matewan, West Virginia, and his armed supporters. In retaliation, Baldwin-Felts agents shot and killed Hatfield and one other man in August 1921.

Despite the reputation for violence that Baldwin-Felts agents had in the coalfields, William G. Baldwin was a respected Roanoke businessman and local investor who also engaged in a number of small philanthropies. About 1920, after his estranged wife died, he married Jane Dinwiddie, of Roanoke, manager of the W. G. Baldwin Company, the manufacturer of Martha Washington Candy. He retired from Baldwin-Felts in June 1930 to manage his other businesses. William Gibboney Baldwin died in Roanoke on 31 March 1936 and was buried in Evergreen Burial Park in Roanoke.

Brenda McDaniel, "Gun Thugs and Heroes," *Roanoker* 6 (July–Aug. 1979): 54–61, 78–82; Richard M. Hadsell and William E. Coffey, "From Law and Order to Class Warfare: Baldwin-Felts Detectives in the Southern West Virginia Coal Fields," *West Virginia History* 40 (1979): 268–286; Jack M. Jones, *Early Coal Mining in Pocahontas, Virginia* (1983), 118–135; Ann Field Alexander, "'Like an Evil Wind': The Roanoke Riot of 1893 and the Lynching of Thomas Smith," *VMHB* 100 (1992): 185, 188–190, 205; Thomas Felts Papers in Eastern Regional Coal Archives, Craft Memorial Library, Bluefield, W.Va.; Justus Collins Papers, WVU; feature article in *Roanoke World-News*, 13 Mar. 1947; obituaries in *Roanoke Times* (por.) and *Roanoke World-News*, both 1 Apr. 1936.

PAUL SALSTROM

BALL, William (ca. 1615–by 10 November 1680), merchant and planter, was probably born in England, but virtually nothing is known about him before he married Hannah Atherall in London on 2 July 1638. They had at least three sons and at least one daughter. He was almost certainly involved in the tobacco trade between London and Virginia before the 1650s, and he had moved to the colony by 10 December 1653, when he witnessed a Lancaster County deed. Five years later he headed a household in the annual list of tithables in Lancaster County. His appointment to the county court in 1659 indicates that he had by then achieved local prominence.

Ball arrived in Virginia at a propitious time and took advantage of his opportunities. Probably well-capitalized and already knowledgeable in the tobacco trade, he was well placed to profit from the wave of immigration into the fertile lands of the Northern Neck. In the summer of 1659 Ball shipped thirty-one hogsheads of tobacco to England, and in 1660 his payment of taxes on eleven tithables placed him in the top 10 percent of Lancaster County's householders. In January 1664 he purchased 300 acres of land on Narrow Neck Creek and three years later another 240 acres nearby, where he erected his house, later called Millenbeck. In 1667 he and Thomas Chetwood patented 1,600 acres farther up the Rappahannock River. Ball later bought out his partner.

The formation of Middlesex County from Lancaster County about 1669 placed some of the county's old leaders in the new county. With competition thus reduced, Ball became one of Lancaster County's most influential gentlemen. Described as "a greate dealer by the way of merchandize in this County," Ball stepped into all the responsible offices. He became a vestryman, served as presiding judge of the county court by 1670, and represented Lancaster County in the House of Burgesses in 1668 and again between 1670 and 1677. He was sheriff of the county in 1666 and 1678, and he became colonel of the militia in 1672. When he died in the autumn of 1680 he owned six slaves and more than 900 acres of land in Lancaster County and about 1,600 acres in Rappahannock County.

Ball's success as a merchant and planter enabled him to found a notable Northern Neck family. His sons William, Richard, and Joseph all participated in the family business. Although Richard Ball probably died in his thirties, William Ball and Joseph Ball lived long and profitable lives and married, as did their descendants, into some of the most influential families in that part of the colony. The most famous such nuptial came when Mary Ball, Joseph Ball's daughter by his second wife, wed Augustine Washington in 1731, an event through which William Ball became the great-grandfather of George Washington. William Ball dated his will on 15 October 1680 and died before 10 November 1680, when the will was proved in court. He was buried near his home in Lancaster County.

Brief family history, prepared by a descendant in 1789 in part from documents no longer extant, in Horace Edwin Hayden, *Virginia Genealogies* (1891), 47–48; conflicting statements about Bell's background in ibid., 48–81, in Earl L. W. Heck, *Colonel William Ball of Virginia, the Great-Grandfather of Washington* (1928), in Nina Tracy Mann, "William Ball, Merchant," *Northern Neck Historical Magazine* 23 (1973): 2523–2529, and in Margaret Lester Hill, ed., *Ball Families of Virginia's Northern Neck: An Outline* (1990), 1; Lancaster Co. Deed Book, 1:186; public life and landholdings documented in deed and order books of Lancaster Co.; Ball Family Papers, LVA; Joseph Ball letter book, 1743–1749, LC; background information in Robert Anthony Wheeler, "Lancaster County, Virginia, 1650–1750: The Evolution of a Southern Tidewater Community" (Ph.D. diss., Brown University, 1972); Lancaster Co. Will Book, 5:70–71.

James Horn

BALL, William Lee (ca. 2 January 1781–29 February 1824), member of the House of Representatives, was born in Lancaster County, the second of four sons and second of five children of James Ball and Frances Downman Ball. Through his descent from the immigrant merchant, William Ball, he was a distant relative of Mary Ball Washington. He was admitted to the bar in Lancaster County on 18 October 1802, practiced law thereafter, and later served as a justice of the peace. He owned a large plantation in Northumberland County, but he lived on a smaller farm with a large house, called Bewdley, in Lancaster County. An active layman of the Episcopal Church, Ball served as a deputy to the convention of the Diocese of Virginia in 1813. During the War of 1812 he was paymaster for the 92d Regiment Virginia Militia. Ball married Mary Pierce in Fauquier County on 30 April 1804. They had four sons and four daughters.

Ball won election to the House of Delegates in 1805 and served then for one year and again for the years 1810 to 1814. In 1814 he won election to the Senate of Virginia from the district composed of Lancaster, Northumberland, and Richmond Counties and served for three years. In April 1817 Ball was one of three candidates for the United States House of Representatives from the Northern Neck district composed of the counties of King George, Lancaster, Northumberland, Richmond, Stafford, and Westmoreland. He and John P. Hungerford were Republicans, and Henry Lee Jr. was a Federalist. Ball won with a slim margin over Hungerford, while Lee trailed badly. Ball again defeated Hungerford narrowly in an April 1819 rematch, and he was reelected without serious opposition in 1821 and 1823. During his first term in Congress Ball served on a select committee to investigate illegal importations of slaves. He was a member of the Select Committee on Roads and Canals during his second term, and during his third he belonged to the Committee on Elections. Ball seldom spoke during debates, but he went on record against increased pensions for veterans of the War of 1812 unless the House would respond favorably to petitions from Revolutionary War veterans.

William Lee Ball died at his lodgings in Washington on 29 February 1824. An obituary in the *National Intelligencer* characterized Ball in the conventional language of the time as possessing "social and amiable qualities which made him the delight of his friends" and "powers of intellect, which, though seldom called forth, were effective whenever exerted in his public station." After a funeral service in the chamber of the House of Representatives, Ball was buried in the Congressional Cemetery in Washington, D.C.

Margaret Lester Hill, ed., *Ball Families of Virginia's Northern Neck: An Outline* (1990), 12–19; source for traditional birth date of 2 Jan. 1781 no longer known, but obituary gives age at death as about forty-five; Fauquier Co. Marriage Bonds; Horace Edwin Hayden, *Virginia Genealogies* (1891), 128–129; Lancaster Co. Will Book, 28:260–262;

death date in *Niles' Weekly Register* 26 (1824): 12; obituary and description of funeral in *Washington National Intelligencer*, 1, 3 Mar. 1824; obituary reprinted in *Fredericksburg Virginia Herald*, 3 Mar. 1824, and *Richmond Enquirer*, 4 Mar. 1824.

BRUCE A. RAGSDALE

BALLARD, Thomas (d. by 24 March 1690), member of the Council and Speaker of the House of Burgesses, was probably a native of England who immigrated to Virginia as a young man, certainly before the spring of 1651, and lived in either Warwick County or York County. In 1659 his mother Ann (then married to William Thomas) was living in York County, and his two married sisters were also in Virginia. Sometime before April 1652 Ballard was appointed clerk of the York County Court, and he served until 1663 or 1664. In 1660 he was sheriff of York County, although by then he resided at Middle Plantation in James City County.

Ballard acted as an attorney and during the 1650s speculated in land in the new counties of Gloucester and New Kent. He later bought and sold land elsewhere north of the James River. In 1668 he purchased an 820-acre plantation in Henrico County. Six years later he sold it and its buildings, cattle, and "servants" to Nathaniel Bacon (1647–1676), who defaulted after making only the initial down payment. In 1675 Ballard purchased an additional 330 acres at Middle Plantation, which his namesake son and heir sold in 1693 to the trustees of the new College of William and Mary, who in turn erected there the college's first buildings.

In June 1666 the General Assembly called for a cessation of tobacco planting to eliminate a market glut, and Ballard served as one of seven Virginia commissioners who negotiated an agreement with commissioners from Maryland and Carolina to prohibit tobacco planting during 1667. The Privy Council later nullified the agreement. Ballard represented James City County in the House of Burgesses during the brief session of 23 October–9 November 1666. Governor Sir William Berkeley appointed him to the Council in 1670 and he took his seat on 22 June of that year. At the same time he became the naval officer and collector of customs for the upper district of James River.

Ballard and Berkeley were on cordial terms, and in April 1676 the governor identified Ballard as one of only three councillors on whom he believed he could rely. During Bacon's Rebellion in the following months, however, Ballard's loyalties oscillated. In June he urged Berkeley to pardon Nathaniel Bacon for having killed about one hundred fifty Indians, and in July and August Ballard signed three warrants directing Captain Thomas Young to provide foodstuffs for Bacon's followers. (Berkeley later had Young hanged for obeying those instructions.) On 29 July Bacon issued a declaration condemning the governor and identifying Ballard as one of Berkeley's "wicked and pernicious councillors and confederates aiders and assistants against the commonalties in these our cruel commotions." Within a week, however, Ballard joined with several dozen others in signing two declarations in Bacon's support. Ballard also signed Bacon's writs calling for the election of a new assembly to meet in September, and after Berkeley fled to the Eastern Shore, Ballard took one of Bacon's oaths, reportedly after making oral exceptions to certain portions. When Berkeley returned in September to retake Jamestown, Bacon placed a number of women on the ramparts as human shields, and one of them was Thomas Ballard's wife, Anna Ballard.

Ballard and Berkeley remained friends in spite of these apparent changes of heart, and Ballard sat on all of the courts-martial that Berkeley held to try the rebels, except for the trial of Giles Bland. Ballard also witnessed Berkeley's will in March 1677 before the governor returned to England. Ballard's on-again, off-again loyalty then came to the attention of the royal commissioners who were investigating the rebellion. Even though Ballard had stated his willingness to support the administration of the new lieutenant governor, Herbert Jeffreys, the latter suspended Ballard from the Council and from his collectorship in June 1677. Jeffreys distrusted Ballard and characterized him to English officials as "a Fellow of a Turbulent mutinous Spirit, yet one that Knowes how to bee (at every turne) as humble low and penitent as Insolent and Rebellious." The Lords Commissioners of Trade and Plantations agreed that Ballard was too "rash and fiery" and in December suspended him from the Council. In March 1679 the king formally excluded him.

Ballard nevertheless remained one of the most important men in James City County. He served as senior justice of the peace after Bacon's Rebellion, as county lieutenant, and as a vestryman of Bruton Parish. As a leader of the Green Spring faction of former allies of Sir William Berkeley, Ballard was elected to the House of Burgesses in 1680 and on 9 June was chosen Speaker of the House. Although the new governor, Thomas Culpeper, had instructions from London to prevent the election of any of the excluded councillors to the House, he did not attempt to prevent Ballard from taking his seat as a burgess or remove him from the Speaker's chair. During the three sessions of that assembly, from 1680 to 1682, Ballard and the Green Spring faction frequently clashed with Culpeper. Edward Hill defeated Ballard for Speaker in 1684, but Ballard remained in the House through the 1686 session and continued to oppose Culpeper. Shortly before Ballard retired from politics, the General Court assigned him to act as counsel to George Talbot, of Maryland, who was on trial for murdering Christopher Rousby, a royal customs collector. Talbot was convicted and sentenced to hang, but he was later reprieved.

During the final years of his life Ballard made at least two unsuccessful attempts to collect from the estate of Nathaniel Bacon the unpaid balance of the purchase price of the Henrico County plantation. Thomas Ballard and his first wife, Anna Ballard, had four sons and four daughters. She died in September 1678. Thomas Ballard was buried in Bruton Parish on 24 March 1690. His second wife, Alice Ballard, and several of his children survived him.

Kukla, *Speakers and Clerks, 1643–1776*, 74–77; several Thomas Ballards appear in English birth registers during the first three decades of the seventeenth century, with one possibility being the son of William Ballard and Ann Ballard christened at Hartlebury Parish, Worcestershire, on 16 Oct. 1625; first reference to presence in Virginia in Warwick Co. Court Orders (1648–1651), 19; family members identified in York Co. Deeds, Orders, and Wills, 3:124, 171, 5:147, 9:40, 73, and Surry Co. Deeds, Wills, Etc., 1:237, 288; Henrico Co. Order Book (1694–1701), 301; actions during Bacon's Rebellion mentioned in Samuel Wiseman's Book of Record, 1676–1677, Pepysian Library at Magdalene College, Cambridge; Jeffreys quotation in letter of 11 June 1677, PRO CO 1/40, no. 104; exclusion from Council in PRO CO 5/1355; Bruton Parish Register, LVA.

DAPHNE GENTRY

BALLARD, Thomas (d. by 5 October 1710), planter and member of the House of Burgesses, was probably born in James City County, the second of four sons and one of eight children of Thomas Ballard, later a member of the governor's Council, and his first wife, Anna Ballard. He was probably at least twenty-one years old on 24 January 1676, when he qualified as administrator of the estate of Robert Baldry, his wealthy York County godfather. Ballard inherited the bulk of this estate following the death of Baldry's widow about 1684. He remained involved in business and land transactions in James City County as late as the mid-1680s, but he moved to York County by November 1684, when he served on the county grand jury. He became a justice of the peace in York County on 3 June 1691 and remained on the court until his death. Ballard acted as county sheriff from 1693 to 1695, from 1699 to 1700, and again from 1703 to 1705. Six times between 1695 and 1707 he was the tithe-taker for York Parish, he sat on the parish vestry, and he was a founding trustee of Yorktown who served from 24 July 1691 until his death.

His inheritance from Baldry made Ballard one of the wealthiest men in York County. He probably planted tobacco using the labor of some or all of the eighteen slaves on whom he paid taxes in 1700, the same number he owned when he died ten years later. He leased some of his lands to other farmers, and from time to time he was able to lend money to his neighbors. The inventory of his estate taken in the summer of 1711 shows that he owned three substantial tracts of land in York County and personal property worth more than £600, including slaves, livestock, and seventy ounces of silver plate valued at five shillings per ounce, suggesting that he lived in some elegance and comfort. About 1680 he married Katherine Hubbard. Her traditional identification as a daughter of John Hubbard of neighboring Bruton Parish cannot be confirmed from surviving records. They had five sons and four or five daughters.

Ballard represented York County in the House of Burgesses in the assembly of 1691–1693 and from 1696 until his death. When the State House in Jamestown burned on 21 October 1698, Ballard was one of a dozen prominent men then in town whom Governor Francis Nicholson consulted about how to preserve the public records and books of the Council library that were salvaged from the fire. Ballard was also one of the three assembly members designated on 10 April 1703 to oversee the erection of the new capitol in the new city of Williamsburg. Ten years earlier he had sold a tract of land acquired from his father to the trustees of the new College of William and Mary, who erected the schools's first building on the property.

Thomas Ballard attended a meeting of the York County Court on 24 August 1710 but died not long thereafter. His son Matthew Ballard appeared before the county court on 5 October 1710 as his father's executor in a legal matter concerning a runaway servant, and on 27 October 1710 the recently assembled House of Burgesses acted to fill the vacancy created by his death.

Baldry's will (which identifies Ballard's father and his siblings living in 1668) and Ballard's qualification as administrator in York Co. Deeds, Orders, and Wills, 5:147–148; qualification as justice of the peace and service as Yorktown trustee in ibid., 9:27, 42–43; role in advising the governor after 1698 fire and service as overseer for Capitol documented in *Executive Journals of Council* and *Journals of House of Burgesses*; last attendance in court, son's appearance as executor, will, and estate inventory in York Co. Deeds, Orders, and Wills, 14:26, 39, 89–90, 100–101.

PETER V. BERGSTROM

BALLOU, Louis Watkins (12 October 1904–29 April 1979), architect, was born in Halifax County, one of two sons and a daughter of Nathaniel Talley Ballou, a dentist, and Annie J. Ballou, whose maiden name was also Ballou. The family moved to Portsmouth, where Louis Ballou and his brother and sister grew up and attended public schools. Ballou's mother nurtured his artistic inclinations and refined his skills by challenging him every afternoon to draw an apple, insisting that each sketch be better than the previous one. In 1922 Ballou enrolled in the University of Virginia to study architecture. He won awards for his drafting, but he left school in 1926 before graduating, probably to care for his ailing mother who was then in Richmond working for the State Board of Child Welfare.

Ballou worked as a draftsman for the architectural firm of Lee, Smith, and Vandervoort for eight years and enthusiastically entered into Richmond's artistic circles. He joined the Richmond Academy of Arts and participated in many of its programs. A skilled watercolorist, he took top prize in the academy's first annual exhibit in 1931. His early paintings show some of the fluid movement and strength of composition that appeared in the work of contemporary artist Thomas Hart Benton. On 23 June 1931 Ballou married Ellen Frances Patterson, of Danville. They had two sons and one daughter. Their first son, Richard Ballou, became an architect and practiced with his father for twenty years.

While Ballou was at Lee, Smith, and Vandervoort, he directed the renovation of several historic structures. Business was slow during the Great Depression, but Ballou rose to a partnership in the firm, which was renamed Lee, Ballou, and Vandervoort in 1934. In 1938 Ballou opened his own office in Richmond and practiced for five years. From 1943 through the end of World War II he was an executive engineer for the Army Corps of Engineers at the Hampton Roads Port of Embarkation. When he returned to Richmond after the war, Ballou took one of his draftsman, Charles C. Justice, into the firm, and the partnership of Ballou and Justice endured for the remainder of his life. During its early years, Ballou and Justice designed many residences in Richmond. Ballou served as spokesman for the firm and joined and participated in many civic and social organizations, through which he made valuable contacts and obtained new commissions.

A major turning point in Ballou's career took place during the years 1949 to 1951 with the commission to design Mary Washington Hospital in Fredericksburg, which established the ability of Ballou and Justice to design on a large scale and coordinate a complex project. That building led to commissions to design hospitals in Culpeper, Richmond, Warrenton, and Williamsburg. Other lucrative institutional commissions followed and continued through the remainder of Ballou's life, including armories all over Virginia, banks, office buildings, and schools. The firm's best-known and most-successful designs include Saint Mary's Hospital, the Blue Cross–Blue Shield building, the United Daughters of the Confederacy Headquarters, the Theresa Pollak Building at Virginia Commonwealth University, and the state's Monroe Office Building, all in Richmond, and the Jamestown Festival Park complex near the site of the original English settlement.

In one of its most controversial projects, Ballou's firm began designing a new city hall for Richmond in 1958. The firm was already planning the Safety, Health, and Welfare building north of the city hall site. Protracted public debate surrounded the project from its inception because of budget problems, an unworkable civic center plan, and the design that Ballou and his associate, John P. Allen, produced. The city's Planning Commission altered several of the disputed features during a long and antagonistic review process, and the result was a bland, anticlimactic marble tower, completed in 1972, more than twice the height Ballou had specified.

Ballou also directed the architectural work that began in 1962 on the renovation of the Virginia Capitol. Under his design exterior stairs were removed from the hyphens connecting the original building to the wings that had been added during 1904–1906. The new plan added committee rooms and divided the fourth-floor attic into offices and conference rooms. In addition, the whole building was refurbished, rendering the historic structure more efficient for contemporary use.

In 1966, on the strength of the firm's successful modernization of the Capitol as well as Ballou's status as a former president of the University of Virginia's alumni association, Ballou and Justice received the commission to restore the Rotunda on the grounds of the University of Virginia to Thomas Jefferson's original design. After a fire had destroyed the Rotunda in 1895, the renowned architect Stanford White had completely redesigned the building within its shell. Ballou virtually gutted the building, destroying all evidence of both White's and Jefferson's interiors. Many preservationists later criticized the result, which derived from Ballou's preference for adapting historic buildings for modern uses, but he had never received clear guidelines from the university. Even though the project was billed as a restoration, the design team, which included architectural historians, selectively ignored many obvious features of the Rotunda's original appearance and altered the interior with new features such as a ceiling of acoustical panels to deaden the echo in the Dome Room. At its completion in 1976, however, the reconstruction was praised as one of the most appropriate and successful projects of the celebration of the bicentennial of the American Revolution.

Ballou received numerous awards during his five decades of practice in Virginia and was named a life fellow of the American Institute of Architects in 1966. He was a talented painter and architect and the designer of many large, successful institutional projects, but he had neither the genius to make the difficult ideology of modernism truly shine in everyday architecture nor the skill to apply its useful elements as tools in preservation. Moreover, his work was often compromised through the repeated reviews inherent in public projects. Louis Watkins Ballou died of cancer in Richmond on 29 April 1979 and was buried in Hollywood Cemetery in Richmond.

Richard Ballou, John P. Allen, and Elizabeth Landis, office manager for Ballou and Justice, all provided or verified family and professional history information; BVS Marriage Register, Henrico Co.; vertical files at VM; Wells and Dalton, *Virginia Architects*, 17–18; Ballou and Justice described its Jamestown work in "The Jamestown Festival Park: One Part of an Intensive Historical Development," *Virginia Record* 79 (May 1957): 21–26, 45; Warren Strother, "Current Restoration of the State Capitol," *Commonwealth* 30 (Feb. 1963): 21–25; Karen Lang Kummer, "The Evolution of the Virginia State Capitol: 1779–1965" (master's thesis, UVA, 1981); Joseph Lee Vaughan and Omer Allan Gianniny Jr., *Thomas Jefferson's Rotunda Restored, 1973–76* (1981); obituaries in *Richmond News Leader* and *Richmond Times-Dispatch* (por.), both 30 Apr. 1979.

Sarah Shields Driggs

BALZ, Albert George Adam (3 January 1887–1 October 1957), philosopher, was born in Charlottesville, the youngest of three known children, all sons, of Henry Justus Balz and Mary Hartman Balz. His father immigrated from Hesse to the United States in 1864 and became a baker and caterer in Charlottesville after the Civil War. Balz attended public schools and graduated from Charlottesville High School in 1905. He enrolled in the University of Virginia, from which he received an A.B. in 1908 and an A.M. in 1909. Balz taught as an instructor in philosophy at the University of Virginia in the academic year 1910–1911 and as an adjunct professor there the next year. He was a fellow at Columbia University in 1912–1913 while attending graduate school, and received a Ph.D. in philosophy from that institution in 1916.

Balz joined the faculty of the University of Virginia as an assistant professor of philosophy in 1913. He became associate professor in 1916 and full professor in 1920. In addition, he served as chairman of the Department of Philosophy from 1929 to 1955. In 1938 Balz was named Corcoran Professor of Philosophy and retained the chair until his retirement in June 1957. He endowed the Balz Fund for Philosophy to assist departmental graduate students at the University of Virginia, and he presented the university's library with part of his philosophical library before he died and the remainder as a bequest.

Balz published his doctoral dissertation as *Idea and Essence in the Philosophies of Hobbes and Spinoza* (1918), and he saw a one-volume edition of Spinoza's writings on political philosophy into print in 1937. The seventeenth-century rationalist tradition of Hobbes, Descartes, and Spinoza continued to be his primary philosophical interest thereafter. Balz was especially interested in the derivation of Cartesian philosophy from Scholastic and Thomistic thought. During his career he published many scholarly articles and short monographs, culminating in two major volumes, *Cartesian Studies* (1951), and his most important work, *Descartes and the Modern Mind* (1952). In the latter work Balz celebrated Descartes as the thinker who most clearly enunciated the major themes of modernity's development and foresaw modern science and its relationship to theology and faith. *Descartes and the Modern Mind* made its unique and somewhat curious contribution to Cartesian studies by turning back to the thought of Saint Thomas Aquinas as the forerunner for the transition from the medieval to the modern age. Balz viewed Descartes's philosophy not as a revolt, but as a continuation of Thomism, derived from it and wholly intelligible only within it. By affirming the rational pursuit of science, Descartes could be seen as having defined modernity. Balz's reading of Descartes led him to challenge the conventional understanding of the cogito and of Cartesian dualism. Man became not merely a "thinking thing" but a self-conscious spiritual substance. In the twentieth century, Balz suggested, the Thomistic-Cartesian roles of reason and faith persisted in the claims of science (reason) and doctrines of human welfare (moral and political philosophies, theories of human nature, history, and society), which function as a modern substitute for theology (faith). Balz's interpretations of Descartes and Aquinas led him to disagree with his mentor, John Dewey, even before the publication of *Descartes and the Modern Mind*, and in 1949 they exchanged public letters on the subject in the *Journal of Philosophy*.

In 1952 Balz received the Nicholas Murray Butler Medal from Columbia University for his contributions to philosophical scholarship. He served as president of the Eastern Division of the American Philosophical Association, of the Virginia Philosophical Association, of the Southern Society for Philosophy and Psychology, and of the Southern Society for the Philosophy of Religion. He belonged to several other professional societies, and he served on the Charlottesville School Board from 1931 to 1945 and as its chairman from 1939 to 1945. He was a member of Saint Paul's Memorial Episcopal Church in Charlottesville and also an avid gardener. Balz married Dorothy Dean of Utica, New York, on 6 June 1917 and had two sons and one daughter, of whom one son died in infancy. Albert George Adam Balz died in Charlottesville on 1 October 1957 following a stroke and was buried in the University of Virginia Cemetery.

BVS Birth Register, Albemarle Co.; memorials by Frank Geldard, Lewis M. Hammond, and William S. Weedon, 28 Oct. 1957, Minutes of Faculty of Arts and Sciences, and Balz's faculty file, UVA Archives; exchange of letters with Dewey in Jo Ann Boydston et al., eds., *John Dewey, The Later Works, 1925–52* (1981–1990), 16:280–294, 423–442; Balz's other principal publications were "Dualism in Cartesian Psychology and Epistemology," in Columbia University Department of Philosophy, *Studies in the History of Ideas* (1925), 2:83–157, "Evolution and Time," in *Essays in Honor of John Dewey*, ed. Henry Holt (1929), 36–48, "Whitehead, Descartes, and the Bifurcation of Nature," *Journal of Philosophy* 31 (1934): 281–297, "Some Historical Steps toward Parallelism," *Philosophical Review* 44 (1935): 544–566, "The State of Nature and the Social Sciences," *Journal of Philosophy* 34 (1944): 645–664, 673–685, "Man—Thomistic and Cartesian," *Review of Religion* 11 (1947): 339–380, *The Value Doctrine of Karl Marx* (1943), and *Southern Teachers of Philosophy* (1954); Balz collaborated with William S. A. Pott on *The Basis of Social Theory* (1924); obituaries in *Charlottesville Daily Progress*, 2 Oct. 1957 (por.), and *New York Times*, 3 Oct. 1957.

THELMA Z. LAVINE

BANE, Robert Franklin (7 April 1893–23 January 1983), public administrator, was born in Smithfield, the younger of two sons and second of three children of Methodist minister Charles Lee Bane and Carrie Buckner Bane. He attended the local schools and after graduating from high school enrolled in Randolph-Macon College, from which he graduated in 1914. Bane then studied law at Columbia University in New York, but while there he audited courses in general and social work administration.

Frank Bane, as he was generally known, returned to Virginia and spent one year as a teacher and high school principal and two years as superintendent of schools in Nansemond County. He married Lillian Greyson Hoofnagle, of Ashland, on 14 August 1918. They had a son and a daughter. In 1920 the retiring secretary of the Virginia State Board of Charities and Corrections invited Bane to take his place as the board's secretary. Bane and his small staff traveled the state inspecting jails, reformatories, private institutions for the mentally ill, and almshouses. The board was chiefly an inspection agency with little regulatory power, but it reported on conditions to the General Assembly and the governor. After the board was reconstituted in 1922 as the Department of Public Welfare with increased responsibilities for child welfare, Bane acquired additional duties. The board's primary goal was to get children out of jails and into its new system of detention and foster homes where the educational and other needs of children could be better met.

In 1923 Bane left Virginia to become director of the Department of Public Welfare in Knoxville, Tennessee, but in 1926 Governor Harry Flood Byrd lured him back to Virginia as commissioner of public welfare. Under the reorganization of state government that took place during Byrd's administration, the Department of Public Welfare became responsible for all the major state institutions, such as the penitentiary and the state mental health facilities. Bane also became involved in limited state and national efforts to provide relief to unemployed persons at the beginning of the Great Depression. During his work in Virginia and while dealing with the effects of the depression, Bane came to believe that "relief of destitution was a primary responsibility of government at all levels, State, local, and Federal; that all governments should accept that responsibility, appropriate funds for relief and establish adequate public facilities to direct their operation." He broke with past tradition in Virginia and elsewhere by urging governments to administer public welfare programs directly rather than subsidize private relief agencies.

In 1931 Bane moved onto the national stage as the first executive director of the American Public Welfare Association, which he had helped found. During the waning months of Herbert Hoover's presidency, Bane coordinated the establishment of state and local agencies to distribute unemployment relief. Early in the administration of President Franklin D. Roosevelt, Bane joined Harry Hopkins's staff of the Federal Emergency Relief Administration. He continued to press for a coordinated program of direct public assistance, and with a handful of fellow advisors persuaded Hopkins that a federally financed jobs program was needed. Hopkins in turn convinced the president, and Bane then assisted in drafting the plans for the Civil Works Administration, parent organization of the more famous Works Progress Administration. Within its first four months the Civil Works Administration employed four million people at 180,000 sites and spent almost $1 billion.

Bane's greatest accomplishment was the creation of the Social Security Administration. As executive director of the American Public Welfare Association, he had helped draft the legislation that created the Social Security system in 1935. He became the first administrator of the Federal Social Security Board, establishing the administrative structure by which the national program was conducted and acting as spokesman for the new system in countless articles and speeches explaining the philosophy and practical aspects of Social Security to the general public. In later years he was often called the "father of Social Security."

Late in 1938 Bane resigned from the Social Security system to become executive director of the Council of State Governments. At its headquarters in Chicago the council coordinated exchanges of news and ideas among state governments and their agencies and reflected the increasingly professional nature of public administration in state and local government. Bane served as the council's executive director until he retired in 1958, but he was called back into national service several times. During a stint as director of field operations for the Office of Price Administration early in World War II, he used his personal contacts in state government and the nation's schools to create the administrative structure that in three weeks enrolled every person in the United States in programs to ration scarce wartime necessities, a process that had been expected to take six months.

When Bane retired from the Council of State Governments, the normally conservative *Richmond Times-Dispatch* editorially remarked that "Probably no Virginian in this generation, in a non-elected position, has had more influence on national affairs than Frank Bane." He remained active in public administration and spoke out often on questions of federal-state relations. In 1959 President Dwight D. Eisenhower appointed him the first chairman of the U.S. Advisory Council on Intergovernmental Relations. He remained in the post until 1966. Robert Franklin Bane died of cancer in Alexandria on 23 January 1983 and was buried in Arlington National Cemetery.

Frank Bane Papers, UVA; "Frank Bane: Public Administration and Public Welfare," 1965 oral history interview, Regional Oral History Office, General Library, University of California at Berkeley; BVS Marriage Register, Hanover Co.; autobiographical information and personal philosophy in Bane, "Local Government: The Next Half Century," *Virginia Municipal Review* 43 (1966): 97–100; Robert E. Sherwood, *Roosevelt and Hopkins: An Intimate History* (1948), 46, 51–52; *Richmond Times-Dispatch*, 26 May 1958; feature articles in *Richmond Times-Dispatch*, 30 Oct. 1938 (por.), *State Government News* (Dec. 1983), 18, and *Washington Post*, 13 Jan. 1983; obituaries in *Washington Post*, 28 Jan. 1983, and *New York Times* and *Richmond Times-Dispatch*, both 29 Jan. 1983.

RICHARD W. HALL-SIZEMORE

BANISTER, John (ca. 1650–by 16 May 1692), naturalist, was probably born in Twigworth, Gloucestershire, England. His father's name was John Banister, but his mother's name is not known. On 21 June 1667 he matriculated at Magdalen College, Oxford University, and the following year he was one of sixteen choristers admitted on scholarships. He received a B.A. in 1671 and an M.A. in 1674, and he is listed as a chaplain from 1676 to 1678. While Banister was an undergraduate, Robert Morison became Oxford's first professor of botany. Banister probably attended his lectures in the university's Physick Garden and took special interest in the rare North American plants growing there. He prepared a large collection of pressed samples that fills 374 sheets, with as many as nine specimens per sheet. Banister's name is most often associated with original botanical research in North America, but he was one of the first naturalists to describe the internal anatomy of a snail and the first to describe the balancing function of the modified hind wings of true flies.

Under the sponsorship of Morison and Henry Compton, the bishop of London, in 1678 Banister sailed for Barbados and from there to Grenada and then to Virginia, ostensibly as an Anglican minister, but also to study and collect additional specimens of New World plants. He was at the falls of the James River on 6 April 1679, when he wrote Morison of his arrival in Virginia and described some of the plants and animals he had already seen. Banister became friends with William Byrd (1652–1704), who then lived near the falls and was engaged in trading with Indians to the south and west. Banister accompanied Byrd on several trading and exploring expeditions as far as the foothills of the mountains.

At some unrecorded date after his arrival in Virginia, Banister took charge of Bristol Parish, near the mouth of the Appomattox River in that part of Charles City County that eventually became Dinwiddie County. He probably held the position until he died. The death of Morison in 1683 cost Banister one of his principal English patrons, but his marriage not long before the middle of April 1688 to Martha Batte Jones, a young widow, indicates that he intended to remain in Virginia. They had at least one son. Banister was among the clergymen who attended the July 1690 meeting in Jamestown at which plans were laid for the College of William and Mary, and in the same year he obtained a patent for 1,735 acres of land on Hatcher Run near the Appomattox River.

Throughout his years in Virginia, Banister studied the flora and fauna of the colony, made drawings, and greatly enlarged his collection of specimens. He was working toward a comprehensive natural history of Virginia, but he did not live to complete it. Nevertheless, he probably contributed more to science than any other seventeenth-century Virginian. Banister sent many seeds and plants back to Bishop Compton; John Ray published Banister's list of plants and added several new species to his own lists in *Historia Plantarum: Species Hactenus Editas* (1686–1704); and Martin Lister published extracts of four Banister letters in the Royal Society's *Philosophical Transactions* in 1693. After Banister's death his letters, collections, and drawings, most of which found their way to England, made major contributions to the advancement of scientific knowledge. His comments on the plants, animals, agriculture, and native inhabitants of Virginia influenced many other authors, some of whom used his work without attribution. Robert Beverley transcribed portions of Banister's reports without citation in his *History and Present State of Virginia* (1705), as did John Oldmixon in *The British Empire in America* (1708).

Banister's notes and collections were later distributed among several specialists and eventually acquired by some of the most notable collections and libraries in England. His original catalog is now in the British Library, and many of his specimens are in the British Library and in the Sherardian Herbarium at Oxford University. Noted naturalists such as Johann Jacob Dillenius, Martin Lister, James Petiver, and Leonard Plukenet made excellent use of Banister's collections, and some of them credited him with significant discoveries. Petiver employed Banister's notes on fungi in editions of his *Gazophylacii Naturae & Artis* (1702–1709); information on Banister's specimens of insects (a classification that then included mollusks, spiders, and primitive invertebrates) appeared in Lister's *Historia Sive Symposis Methodica Conchyliorum* (1685–1692); and Dillenius included Banister's mosses in his *Historia Muscorum* (1741). Petiver and André Michaux named plants for Banister, and William Houstoun gave the name *Banisteria* to a whole class of tropical and subtropical viny plants, one of which Banister had described as the "Wilde Hop-seed in Barbadoes."

Banister's collections and drawings thus had a lasting influence on biology and in particular on botany. When Carl Linnaeus visited England in 1736 he "beheld with astonishment" the collections of plants and pressed specimens at the Oxford and Chelsea Physick Gardens, both of which contained many of Banister's specimens. In preparing the epic 1753 edition of his *Species Plantarum*, in which he introduced the binomial taxonomy that has ever since governed the classification of all forms of life, Linnaeus frequently cited the works of Morison, Plukenet, and Ray for many of the species and specimens that Banister had procured and described. Linnaeus was well aware of Banister and his work and entered a list of *Banisteria* on the flyleaf of his own copy of Plukenet's *Phytographia* (1691–1705).

On 12 May 1692 Banister wrote his last letter and later that day or the next set out from home on a collecting expedition to the southwest. According to a record entered in the Henrico County Court order book on 16 May 1692, Jacob Colson, an employee of William Byrd who accompanied the expedition, accidentally killed John Banister. According to later, undocumented traditions, Colson shot Banister while the naturalist was collecting plant specimens under a tree or beside a rocky stream. The court's ruling was death by misadventure. Banister was probably buried where he died, thus ending at age forty-two a scientific career of great importance, but also of vast unrealized promise. Byrd became the guardian of Banister's namesake son and obtained his library of eighty or more volumes, some of which are now in Philadelphia libraries. Lieutenant Governor Francis Nicholson directed that Banister's collections of specimens and drawings be assembled and his catalogs copied, and the originals were sent to Bishop Compton in London.

Joseph Ewan and Nesta Dunn Ewan, *John Banister and his Natural History of Virginia, 1678–1692* (1970), prints a number of his letters and catalogs and contains a full list of surviving specimens, papers, and books; age listed as seventeen at matriculation at Magdalen College; marriage mentioned in William Byrd to Jacob Bobart, 16 Apr. 1688, in Marion Tinling, ed., *The Correspondence of the Three William Byrds of Westover, Virginia, 1684–1776* (1977), 1:78; death documented in Henrico Co. Order Book (1678–1693), 418, and in memorandum of bailment by Edward Chilton, 23 June 1692, Colonial Papers, RG 1, LVA.

NESTA DUNN EWAN
JOSEPH EWAN

BANISTER, John (26 December 1734–30 September 1788), member of the Convention of 1776 and member of the Continental Congress, was probably born near the town of Petersburg. His parents were Wilmette Banister and John Banister, a son of noted botanist John Banister and in his own right a prominent planter, business associate of William Byrd (1674–1744), and one of the original trustees of Petersburg. John Banister was educated in England and on 28 September 1753 was admitted to the Middle Temple in London, where he studied law but was not called to the bar. He returned to Virginia and there married Elizabeth Mumford early in 1755. Following her death he married Elizabeth Bland late in the 1750s or early in the 1760s. They had at least one son and probably two daughters before she died in the summer of 1777.

After Banister returned to Virginia he embarked on a long career as a tobacco planter and businessman. He created an industrial complex of sawmills and flour mills along the Appomattox River on the western edge of Petersburg. Banister owned many slaves and probably employed craftsmen such as coopers and millers. Visitors to Petersburg during the 1770s and 1780s often commented on the mills and on his beautiful house, Battersea, which he constructed during the late 1760s or early 1770s. As Banister prospered, he gradually assumed larger and more-important political roles. He became a vestryman of Bristol Parish on 1 December 1764 and a justice of the peace for Dinwiddie County late in 1769. He served in the House of Burgesses with one brief interruption from 1766 until the American Revolution. His first campaign, in 1765, produced an often-quoted reference to the candidate's "swilling the planters with bumbo," or rum punch, in order to win votes. Banister consistently supported protests against British policies during the 1760s and 1770s and attended all five of the Revolutionary Conventions during 1774, 1775, and 1776. In the last convention he voted for independence and served on the committee that prepared the Virginia Declaration of Rights and the first constitution of Virginia. He was also elected to the House of Delegates for the sessions of October 1776 through January 1778 and again from May 1781 through December 1783.

On 17 November 1777 the General Assembly elected Banister to the Continental Congress to succeed Benjamin Harrison, and it reelected him on 29 May 1778. Banister attended Congress at York and at Philadelphia, Pennsylvania, from 16 March to 24 September 1778, though he spent a month from mid-August until mid-September in White Plains, New York, on a committee conferring with General George Washington on the reorganization of the Continental army. Banister signed the Articles of Confederation in Philadelphia on 9 July 1778. Before he resigned his seat in Congress, Banister entered into a commercial arrangement with Robert Morris and Silas Deane, among others, to engage in Franco-American trade. The agreement placed Banister politically at odds with the powerful Lee family, with whom he had never been on good terms anyway, and drew him into the bitter controversy over Deane's conduct as American agent in France.

On 24 September 1778 Banister took a leave of absence from Congress and then resigned shortly after his return to Virginia. He married Ann "Nancy" Blair, of Williamsburg, in February 1779. They had two sons. During participation as a militia colonel in the defense of Petersburg from a British invasion in the spring of 1781, Banister lost some of his valuable property. Thereafter, he lived at the Dinwiddie County plantation, Hatcher's Run, that he had inherited from his father.

On 5 June 1782 the General Assembly elected Banister to the Council of State, but he attended only a few meetings before resigning early in November. He also served in 1784 as the first mayor of Petersburg under its new charter. Banister suffered serious financial losses during and after the Revolutionary War, and his health deteriorated. According to one report, he had become mentally incapacitated by early in 1788. He spent the spring of that year in the West Indies. John Banister returned to Virginia in June and died on 30 September 1788 at Hatcher's Run, where he was buried.

Brief biography in Charles Campbell, *The Bland Papers* (1840), 1:xxvii–xxviii; inaccurate biography in Frederick Horner, *The History of the Blair, Banister, and Braxton Families* (1898), 95–121 (por.); birth recorded in Churchill G. Chamberlayne, ed., *Vestry Book and Register of Bristol Parish, Virginia, 1720–1789* (1898), 287; John Banister Papers, VHS; Smith, *Letters of Delegates*, vols. 9–10; transcript of will in Willie Graham and Mark R. Wenger, "Battersea: A Historical and Architectural Study" (1988 typescript in LVA); death date in Duncan Rose to Thomas Jefferson, 26 Feb. 1789, in *Jefferson Papers*, 14:592; undated death notice in *Richmond Virginia Gazette and Weekly Advertiser*, 16 Oct. 1788.

RICHARD L. JONES

BANISTER, Marion Langhorne Glass (14 December 1868–30 September 1951), Democratic Party leader, was born in Lynchburg, the second of five daughters and fourth of seven children of Robert Henry Glass and his second wife, Margaret Sandford Glass. Her father was a politically prominent newspaper editor, her sister Meta Glass became president of Sweet Briar College, and her four elder half brothers and one half sister included Carter Glass, a United States senator, and Edward Christian Glass, longtime superintendent of public schools in Lynchburg. When she was a girl the family's dinner table conversation frequently turned to political topics, and she naturally developed a keen interest in public affairs. She was educated in the public schools of Lynchburg and taught history at a local high school before her marriage on 2 March 1893 to Blair Banister, an insurance broker who descended from two prominent Virginia families, the Blairs and the Banisters. Their one child, Margaret Sandford Banister, gained some fame for novels about the Civil War.

Mrs. Blair Banister, as she preferred to be known, emerged as a talented journalist by 1910, when she edited the woman's page for the family's *Lynchburg Advance*. Unlike many other editors of women's pages, she emphasized important issues of the day rather than homemaking. While her husband was in France during World War I she accepted a job as one of four publicity writers for the Committee on Public Information in the U.S. Department of Labor. She worked for George Creel in Washington, D.C., and remained in that city and in public life after the war. An independent career woman even before women got the vote, she sought to advance women's interests through the political party system almost immediately after suffrage had been won. From 1921 to 1924 she was assistant to the female vice chairman of the Democratic National Committee and served as publicity director in charge of women's activities. Banister wrote a series of pamphlets designed to persuade newly enfranchised women that a close relationship existed between the interests of the homemaker and the principles of the Democratic Party. The widely circulated booklets were often used in political campaigns. She was a founder of the Woman's National Democratic Club in 1922 and began and edited the *Fortnightly Bulletin*, forerunner of the *Democratic Digest*. In 1924 she compiled and edited the *Women's Campaign Manual* for use by women workers in the presidential campaign. The nationally influential women with whom she worked during those years included Emily Newell Blair, Mary "Molly" Dewson, and Eleanor Roosevelt, who exercised a significant leadership role in the Democratic Party during the 1920s and 1930s.

After the Democratic defeat in the presidential election of 1924 and the closing of the party's national headquarters, Banister became publicity director for the new Mayflower Hotel in Washington, launching and editing its magazine, the *Mayflower's Log*. In 1928 she resigned from the hotel staff to publish the *Washingtonian*, an independent magazine that she put out until the Great Depression forced it to cease production in December 1931. Known for her political and business acumen, she chaired the hospitality committee for Franklin Delano Roosevelt's first inauguration in March 1933. Banister's outstanding success in housing nearly 40,000 people in Washington for the event and her loyalty to the Democratic Party earned her an appointment in July 1933 as the first woman to hold the position of assistant treasurer of the United States.

Aged sixty-five when she obtained her treasury job, Banister was well aware of the importance of her pioneering role. She regarded the appointment as symbolic of the expanding role of women in national politics, and many other women wrote her to express pride in her success and to seek help in securing government jobs. Answering each letter sympathetically, she succeeded in helping many of the aspirants. An ardent New Dealer, in contrast to Senator Carter Glass, and a frequent guest at the White House, Banister agreed completely with the administration's policies. She wrote articles, spoke on the radio, and traveled throughout the country defending Roosevelt's administration.

Marion Langhorne Glass Banister suffered several major illnesses during the last dozen years of her life, but she nevertheless remained in office until she died in Washington, D.C., on 30 September 1951. She was buried in Spring Hill Cemetery in Lynchburg.

Wellington Brink, "Southern Personalities: Mrs. Blair Banister," *Holland's: The Magazine of the South* 53 (Mar. 1934): 11, 15 (por.); Emily Newell Blair, "A Who's Who of Women in Washington," *Good Housekeeping Magazine*, Jan. 1936, 38–39; Marion Langhorne Glass Banister Papers, LC; marriage recorded in parish records of Saint Paul's Episcopal Church, Lynchburg; General Correspondence of George Creel, Chairman, Committee on Public Information, RG 63, NARA; Treasury Department Records, 1933–1956, RG 56, NARA; Banister's pamphlets, a few issues of the *Fortnightly Bulletin*, and an early history of the Woman's National Democratic Club in the club's archives, Washington, D.C.; *Washington Times Herald*, 27 July 1933, 7 May 1934, 23 July 1943; *Washington Star*, 2 Feb., 26 July, 6 Aug. 1933, 24 Mar. 1935; obituaries in *Lynchburg Daily Advance*, *Lynchburg News*, *Washington Post* (por.), and *Washington Star*, all 1 Oct. 1951; editorial tribute in *Lynchburg Daily Advance*, 2 Oct. 1951.

MARY KATE BLACK

BANKS, Linn (23 January 1784–13 January 1842), Speaker of the House of Delegates and member of the House of Representatives, was born in the part of Culpeper County that became Madison County in 1792, one of three sons and seven daughters of Adam Banks and Gracey James Banks. He attended the College of William and Mary and after completing his studies there in 1806 read law. He was admitted to the bar in Madison County on 28 April 1808 and for the remainder of his life practiced in the county courts of Piedmont Virginia. He married Eliza J. H. Sanders, of Raleigh, North Carolina, on 4 April 1811. They had no children.

Banks was a militia captain in the 82d Regiment Virginia Infantry during the War of 1812 and later attained the rank of colonel. Like many of his contemporaries at the bar, Banks sought public office early, winning election to the House of Delegates as a Democratic-Republican in 1812. He speedily became a leader in the assembly, serving on the Committee on Propositions and Grievances and for four years on the powerful Committee on Courts of Justice that virtually controlled the legislative agenda of the House. Banks established himself as a strong defender of states' rights during the wave of reaction in Virginia against postwar Republican nationalism, and he criticized expensive plans for internal improvements to benefit the western portions of the state because he believed that its gains would come at the expense of the eastern population.

On 11 November 1816 Banks was one of three delegates who ran for Speaker of the House of Delegates, but Robert Stanard, of Spotsylvania County, emerged the victor. At the opening of the next assembly, on 1 December 1817, with Stanard no longer in the House, Banks won the post for the first time. He was reelected each of the next twenty-one years and served until 1838, the longest uninterrupted service as Speaker of the House of Delegates to the present. "He held the post so long," noted the editor of the *Richmond Whig* in Banks's obituary, "that he seemed to have a prescriptive right to it, and he maintained it under all mutations of party." Considering the relative weakness of the Senate of Virginia and the limitations on the constitutional powers of the executive, Banks as Speaker was a highly visible and powerful leader both in state government and in the Democratic Party. Acknowledged for his parliamentary skill, impartiality, and urbane manner, he guided the House of Delegates through many debates over complex local and national issues, among them the Missouri Compromise, an embezzlement scandal involving Virginia treasurer Jerman Baker, internal improvements debates, sectional tensions culminating in the Convention of 1829–1830, debates over slavery that took place following a slave insurrection in Southampton County in 1831, and the election and instruction of Virginia's United States senators during the tumultuous years of Andrew Jackson's administration. Only once was Banks seriously challenged in a bid to be reelected Speaker. On 1 December 1834 he defeated Severn E. Parker, of Northampton County, by a vote of sixty-two to sixty.

The resignation of John Mercer Patton from the House of Representatives in 1838 offered Banks the opportunity to stand for higher political office, and he narrowly defeated the Whig Party candidate, Daniel F. Slaughter, in a special election to represent the district composed of the counties of Culpeper, Greene, Madison, Orange, Rappahannock, and Spotsylvania. Banks took his seat on 19 May 1838. He served on the Committee on Claims during his first term and again following his reelection to Congress in 1839. In 1841 he ran for reelection against a fellow Democrat, William "Extra Billy" Smith, who formed a loose alliance with local Whig leaders. When Banks won with a four-vote plurality, Smith challenged the election in the House of Representatives. In an unusual move, Banks resigned on 8 November 1841 so that a second election could be held. On 29 November Smith won a three-way race with Banks and Slaughter, putting Banks out of public office for the first time in almost thirty years.

Banks returned home to his law practice and his farm with its force of between forty-five and fifty slaves. On 13 January 1842 Linn Banks drowned while crossing the Conway River near Wolftown, Madison County, en route to Madison Court House. He was buried at Vale Evergreen, his residence near Graves Mill in Madison County.

Birth and death dates on gravestone, quoted in Jamerson, *Speakers and Clerks, 1776–1996*, 56–57 (por.), 141; Martha W. Hiden, "Adam Banks of Stafford County," *Tyler's Quarterly* 15 (1934): 246–250; *Raleigh Star*, 12 Apr. 1811; political philosophy outlined in letter to Joseph Goode, 26 Feb. 1831, VHS; *Richmond Enquirer*, 8, 11, 15 May 1838, 12 Nov., 3 Dec. 1841; Banks to John Rutherfoord, 8, 10 Nov. 1841, Governor's Office, Letters Received, RG 3, LVA; John W. Bell, *Memoirs of Governor William Smith of Virginia* (1891), 15–17; Madison Co. Will Book, 7:162–163; obituary in *Richmond Whig*, 18 Jan. 1842.

E. LEE SHEPARD

BANKS, Robert Adam (April 1806–28 January 1878), member of the Convention of 1850–1851, was born in Madison County, the only child of Gerard James Banks, a wealthy miller, and Ann Davis Banks. His father died on 15 June 1817, and on 9 December 1818 his mother married William Finks, following which Banks became the ward of his uncle Linn Banks, the Speaker of the House of Delegates.

Banks began working for his stepfather, a local merchant, about 1825. Long before Finks died almost forty years later, their partnership had made Banks wealthy. By 1850 Banks owned eighty-five slaves, the largest number in the county, and at his death he owned more than seven thousand acres of land, again the county's highest total. He became a justice of the peace on 19 August 1834 and served on the Madison County Court until 1860. Banks was commissioned a captain of militia on 24 June 1828 and served until the eve of the Civil War, reaching the rank of major general in 1858.

In 1838 Banks ran for the House of Delegates as a Democrat to succeed Linn Banks, who had been elected to Congress. He lost a close election to the Whig candidate, John Booton, but Banks successfully contested the election and then was reelected for the 1839–1840 session. He lost the 1840 election to Booton by a vote of 378 to 320, but he again successfully challenged the result, resumed his seat in the assembly, and won reelection thereafter through 1846. Banks moved gradually into the ranks of the leadership and became chairman of the important Committee on Propositions and Grievances.

In August 1850 Banks was one of three men elected to represent the district of Culpeper, Greene, Madison, and Orange Counties in the constitutional convention. He served on the committees on elections, on compensation of officers, and on the executive department and ministerial officers, but extant records do not indicate that he played an influential role. Siding with conservative eastern slaveholders, he voted against legislative apportionment based exclusively on the total white population and against unrestricted white manhood suffrage.

Banks remained active in the Democratic Party. He was a delegate to the Democratic National Convention in Cincinnati in 1856, and he was president of the party's state convention that met in Richmond on 16 February 1860. Banks did not join the army during the Civil War but remained at home and served as one of the county commissioners charged with borrowing and allocating money to equip the volunteer companies recruited in the county and provide for the relief of soldiers' families. His friends tried several times to persuade him to reenter elective politics, but he ran for office only once more, winning election to a term in the House of Delegates in 1874.

Banks married Louisa J. Finks, daughter of his stepfather, on 27 April 1847. She died in September 1863. On 25 December 1865 he married Narcissa Thornhill Long, who was thirty-two years his junior. No children were born of either marriage. Robert Adam Banks died at home on 28 January 1878 and was buried in the family graveyard on Linn Banks's estate.

Martha W. Hiden, "Adam Banks of Stafford County," *Tyler's Quarterly* 15 (1934): 246–247, includes month and year of birth from gravestone inscription; Reba Fitzpatrick Lea, *The Lea Family in Nelson County, Virginia: Their History and Genealogy* (1946), 81, 96 (por.), 111, 113; Madison Co. Marriage Bonds and Consents; Contested Election Papers, RG 78, LVA; John Booton correspondence with Belfield Cave, Hill Family Papers, VHS; *JHD*, 1840–1841 sess., Doc. 45; *Richmond Semi-Weekly Examiner*, 6 Aug. 1850; Robert A. Banks to I. L. Twyman, 10 Jan. 1859, Austin-Twyman Papers, W&M; *Daily Richmond Enquirer*, 17 Feb. 1860; Presidential Pardons; obituaries in *Richmond Whig*, 2 Feb. 1878, and *Gordonsville Gazette*, 6 Feb. 1878.

DAPHNE GENTRY

BANKS, Rose Kaufman (8 February 1911–16 December 1981), community theater organizer, was born in Richmond, the only child of Joseph H. Kaufman, a traveling salesman, and Cornelia Miller Kaufman. She attended the local public schools and graduated from John Marshall High School in 1927 and from the Richmond Normal School in 1929. She taught English and drama at Albert Hill Junior High School from 1930 to 1939, and like many other Virginia public schoolteachers she attended summer institutes at Teachers College, Columbia University.

Rose Kaufman became interested in the theater as early as her student days at John Marshall High School. In 1931 she won an award from the Richmond Academy of Arts as the city's best actress for her performance in *The Minuet* by Jack S. Knapp. A commanding woman with a rich, deep contralto voice, she had large impressive eyes and a magnetic personality, but she also suffered from stage fright and preferred directing and producing for local audiences to a stage career that would have required her to leave Richmond. She helped found the Richmond Community Theater, which eventually merged with two other small theater groups into the influential Richmond Theater Guild, and while at Richmond Normal School she was a founder of the Children's Theater and often directed its productions. Kaufman enjoyed taking responsibility and being in charge and realized early that her greatest talents were organizational. As a consequence, she was at the center of Richmond's active theatrical community for fully half a century.

Together with Leslie D. Banks, whom she married in 1938, she was instrumental in keeping local drama alive during the 1930s and 1940s. Leslie Banks started the Richmond Stage Lighting and Scenic Services Company in 1946 and concluded his long professional career as director of Richmond's Mosque from 1969 to 1977. Accompanied by her husband or on her own, Rose Kaufman Banks participated in the formation of the Richmond Symphony, the Richmond Musicians Club, the Richmond Choral Society, the Shakespeare Players, the National Tobacco Festival, the Federated Arts Council of Richmond, and the Richmond Opera Group, for which she directed the early productions.

Rose Kaufman Banks served as drama consultant for the Work Projects Administration in Virginia in 1940, and in 1941 she began her long career with the Richmond City Department of Recreation and Parks. As supervisor of special events and later as superintendent of the central activities division, she began the annual Summer Festival of the Arts at Dogwood Dell in Richmond's Byrd Park and the yearly Christmas Eve nativity pageant. During the Christmas season she also regularly produced *Amahl and the Night Visitors* and *The Nutcracker* at the Mosque. Banks's dream, never fully realized, was to take the performing arts directly to all of the public and to reproduce in all of Richmond's principal neighborhoods the varied cultural enrichment programs that she had created and initially produced in the city's fashionable West End.

Rose Kaufman Banks received almost every honor that civic and arts groups in Richmond could confer, and following her retirement in 1975 she received the Sherwood Reeder Award as the city's outstanding employee. Leslie Banks received the same recognition in 1976, making them the only husband-and-wife team to date to receive the Reeder Award. The Federated Arts Council of Richmond presented her with its seventh annual distinguished service award to the arts in 1977. Both of Banks's children, a son and a daughter, shared their parents' interest in and enthusiasm for the theater. Rose Kaufman Banks died in Richmond on 16 December 1981.

Family and personal history information supplied and verified by Leslie D. Banks; vertical files, Main Branch, Richmond Public Library; feature articles in *Richmond Times-Dispatch*, 6 Dec. 1957, 9 Feb. 1969 (por.), 29 Aug. 1976, 27 Mar. 1977, and *Richmond News Leader*, 4 Aug. 1961, 24 July 1962, 15 Jan. 1963; obituaries in *Richmond News Leader* and *Richmond Times-Dispatch*, both 17 Dec. 1981.

LOIS R. ANGELETTI

BANKS, Walter Scott (13 December 1885–17 October 1970), banker, was born in Goochland County, the elder of two sons and second of three children of Ella Jackson Banks. His ancestors included Goochland natives John Banks and Jacob Banks, free men of color and veterans of military service in the American Revolution. In 1893 his mother sent him to live with an uncle in York, Pennsylvania, where he could obtain a better education than Goochland County offered. The uncle, however, removed him from school in May 1896 and set him to work as a carter hauling dirt at a construction site. A family friend informed his mother of the boy's employment, and she immediately brought him back to Richmond, where she worked as a laundress. There he attended public schools until June 1900, when his formal education ended.

Banks went to work as a porter for a shoe store, delivering shoes to customers. He later recalled that his wages were $3.50 a week, but he told his mother that he earned only $3.00 and used the remainder to purchase texts on bookkeeping, which he studied in the evenings. Banks continued to educate himself in business practices while working as a uniformed elevator operator for a clothing store. He became the manager of the shoe department of the black-owned Saint Luke Emporium on Broad Street in 1905, a post that gave him the security to marry Rebecca Murdaugh in Sussex County on 30 November 1905. After having one son and one daughter, they divorced sometime between 1907, when their daughter was born, and 23 December 1912, when Banks was married in Richmond to Geneva Thornhill, of Lynchburg. They had two sons and two daughters.

Banks became an agent for the Richmond Beneficial Insurance Company in 1906. Organized in 1894 by John Thomas Taylor, the company offered benefits in cases of accident, illness, and death, and grew from its initial capital of $200 into an institution with assets of more than $25,000 in 1906 and agencies across Virginia and the District of Columbia. Banks's work ethic and aptitude for business soon brought him to Taylor's attention, and the older man made Banks his protégé. In 1911, when the company's assets had grown to more than $44,000, Banks became the company's traveling superintendent, supervising agents outside Richmond. By 1920 assets amounted to almost $136,000. Banks meanwhile pursued further education through correspondence courses in accounting.

In 1920 Taylor organized Second Street Savings Bank and named Banks the new institution's cashier, or chief administrative officer. Professing to know nothing of bank operations, Banks quickly researched the subject. The bank opened on 23 October 1920, and its assets grew to almost $39,000 before the end of the year. In 1925 it reported assets of $184,471 and opened a branch office in South Richmond. Growth stalled at that point, and assets fell to $162,000 in 1929. The bank's difficulties mirrored worsening economic conditions in the black community. Assets of the city's other banks owned by blacks, Saint Luke Savings Bank and the Commercial Bank and Trust Company, also declined after 1925.

In the aftermath of the stock market's collapse in October 1929, worried officers of these banks met to discuss merging into a single, more secure institution. On 2 January 1930 Second Street Bank and the larger Saint Luke Savings Bank merged to become Consolidated Bank and Trust Company, with assets of more than $500,000. Maggie Lena Walker, president of the Saint Luke bank, was named chairman of the board of the new bank, Emmett Carroll Burke became president, and Walter S. Banks became secretary-treasurer. In 1931 Consolidated Bank merged with Commercial Bank and Trust.

The merger enabled Consolidated Bank to survive the Great Depression. Because of the poverty of the black community, the lack of support from banks and businesses controlled by whites, and the expense of handling numerous small accounts, successful black-owned banks combined personal service to depositors with very conservative lending practices. African American bankers also believed that bank examiners tended to scrutinize their books especially closely, a perception that reinforced their fiscal conservatism. Banks's careful attention to detail and self-discipline—he strove to be the first to arrive and last to leave each workday—made him an effective manager of Consolidated Bank and Trust.

Burke retired in 1950, and Banks succeeded him as president. That decade's healthy economy enabled him to make Consolidated a "full service" bank. When he retired in 1958 at the age of seventy-three, the bank's assets exceeded $5.1 million, an increase during his presidency of 51 percent. Deposits increased nearly as much, but loans grew by 170 percent. Banks left a secure and modern financial institution to his successors.

In retirement Banks continued to sing in the choir and serve as a deacon at All Souls Presbyterian Church. He also served for several years on the advisory board of the Richmond Redevelopment and Housing Authority and was known in his community for quiet, private philanthropy. Widowed since 1954, Walter Scott Banks died of arteriosclerotic heart disease on 17 October 1970 and was buried at Woodland Cemetery.

Feature article in *Richmond News Leader*, 20 June 1955 (por.); interview with daughter Geraldine D. Foster; MS two-page autobiography in Banks's hand [ca. 1952] in Mrs. Foster's possession (photocopy in DVB files); Luther P. Jackson, *Virginia Negro Soldiers and Seamen in the Revolutionary War* (1944), 25, 29; BVS Marriage Register, Richmond City and Sussex Co.; Commissioner of Insurance of Virginia, *Annual Report*, 1906, 1911, 1920; State Corporation Commission, *Annual Report . . . Showing the Condition of the Incorporated State Banks Operating in Virginia* (1920–1958); Consolidated Bank and Trust Company, *"Let Us Have A Bank That Will Take The Nickels And Turn Them Into Dollars"* [ca. 1991]; *Richmond Afro-American*, 14 Mar. 1981; obituaries in *Richmond Times-Dispatch*, 18 Oct. 1970, *Richmond News Leader*, 19 Oct. 1970, and *Richmond Afro-American*, 24 Oct. 1970 (por.).

JOHN T. KNEEBONE

BANKS, William Lester (2 April 1911–2 November 1986), civil rights leader, was born in Lunenburg County, the son of William Walter Banks and Daisy Hill Banks. He had at least one sister. Banks attended public schools in Alderson in Greenbrier County and in Bluefield, both in West Virginia, and graduated from Bluefield

State College with a major in physical science. From 1935 to 1941 he taught school and served as a principal in Halifax County. Later he became principal of Ruthville High School for African American students in Charles City County. On 23 December 1940 he married Vera Louise Bowman, of Charlotte County. They had one daughter.

W. Lester Banks served as a sergeant in the United States Army during World War II and saw action in the Pacific. He began fighting for civil rights shortly before entering the army. In 1943, when he was a principal in Charles City County, he approached Oliver W. Hill, an attorney working with the National Association for the Advancement of Colored People, about the feasibility of filing suit to require that black and white schools receive equal public support. Banks and Hill were unable to pursue the idea because both men were drafted into the armed services shortly thereafter.

Banks's commitment to the fight for racial justice had impressed Hill and other influential Virginians, and on 1 April 1947 Banks became the first executive secretary of the NAACP's Virginia State Conference. During his tenure of nearly thirty years, Banks challenged segregation and racial discrimination in all spheres of American life and Virginia society. Sometimes he acted with others, but he soon won a well-deserved reputation for bravery because he was not afraid to act alone. On 17 October 1961 Banks was arrested for trespassing after he sought and was refused service in the "Whites Only" section of the privately operated Norfolk and Western Railway Company restaurant in Lynchburg. Two years later a white sawmill worker assaulted him when he staged a sit-in at the section reserved for white patrons in a restaurant in Charlotte County. By persistently refusing to sit apart from white attorneys in Virginia courthouses, an act for which local officials were reluctant to arrest him, Banks helped bring about the desegregation of Virginia's courthouses. He often ventured courageously into hostile territory with "NAACP" emblazoned on the rear window of his car.

Banks devoted most of his efforts to the desegregation of public schools. His work, along with that of attorneys Oliver Hill and Spottswood Robinson, brought the legal resources of the NAACP to bear on the epic thirteen-year struggle to desegregate the public schools in Prince Edward County. The case of *Davis* v. *County School Board of Prince Edward County* was one of those that were considered along with *Brown* v. *Board of Education of Topeka* by the U.S. Supreme Court in its unanimous 1954 ruling that racial segregation of public schools was unconstitutional. Rather than accept desegregation, Prince Edward County officials voted in 1959 to close all public schools in the county, and they remained closed until 1964 when, in part because of the NAACP's efforts, they were finally reopened.

Less conspicuous in public than Robinson, Hill, and some other civil rights activists, Banks worked constantly behind the scenes to advise and support the people who played the public roles. He was highly respected, and as much as almost any other Virginian of his generation he stood up for civil rights and fought for justice for all. In recognition of his pivotal work in the civil rights movement in the mid-twentieth century, the 1985 fiftieth-anniversary convention of the Virginia State Conference of the NAACP was dedicated to Banks, who was by then retired, and in August 1992 the conference posthumously awarded him the Civil Rights Emancipation Emeritus Award. Banks's experiences working behind the scenes and facing hostile crowds, together with his perception that conditions for African Americans in Virginia were gradually improving, persuaded him early in his career that patience, persistence, and nonviolence were his most effective weapons.

On 31 December 1976, when he was sixty-five years old, Banks retired as executive secretary of the Virginia NAACP. He remained a special consultant for several years after he retired, but his health gradually deteriorated. In 1977 he and his wife moved to California, where their daughter lived. W. Lester Banks died of cardiopulmonary arrest as a result of chronic kidney failure on 2 November 1986 in Daniel Freeman Hospital in Inglewood, California, and was buried in Inglewood Cemetery Mortuary.

Biography in *Crisis* 83 (1976): 352; birth and death dates and full name on California Department of Health Services death certificate; Richard Kluger, *Simple Justice: The History of Brown v. Board of Education and Black America's Struggle for Equality* (1975), 472–473, 476, 477–478, 488, 496; Robert Collins Smith, *They Closed Their Schools: Prince Edward County, Virginia, 1951–1964* (1965); *Richmond Times-Dispatch*, 16 July 1976, 28 Oct. 1985, 2 Aug. 1992; *Richmond Afro-American*, 13 Oct. 1951, 29 June (por.), 17 July 1976; obituaries in *Richmond News Leader* and *Richmond Times-Dispatch* (por.), both 3 Nov. 1986, and *Richmond Afro-American*, 8 Nov. 1986; tributes in *Richmond Times-Dispatch*, 5 Nov. 1986, and *Richmond Free Press*, 16/18 Feb. 1995 (por.).

ROBERT A. PRATT

BAPTIST, Edward (12 May 1790–31 March 1863), Baptist minister, educator, and a founder of the University of Richmond, was born in Mecklenburg County, the fourth of five sons and ninth of eleven children of William Glanville Baptist and Margaret Langston Baptist. His father was a successful planter and merchant and a justice of the peace, who educated Baptist in liberal arts and for a business career.

Baptist's mother died sometime before his father's remarriage in January 1806, and the father died in September 1808. In December 1810 Baptist entered Hampden-Sydney College, a Presbyterian school selected perhaps because his mother had raised him in that faith. Baptist experienced a religious conversion about the time he entered college and joined the Baptist Church, but he went on to receive a B.A. from Hampden-Sydney in 1813. Baptist then became a tutor for the James Eastham family in Halifax County. For a short time in 1814 he served with his militia company in the defense of Richmond after the British burned Washington, D.C., during the War of 1812.

After his war service Baptist returned to Hampden-Sydney in 1814 to study theology under Moses Hoge, a distinguished and very orthodox Presbyterian theologian, and completed this work about 1815. In 1820 Baptist received the college's M.A. In 1815 he had been ordained a Baptist minister in a service at the Ash Camp Meeting House in Charlotte County. By August 1816 he had become a pastor at the newly founded Grub Hill Baptist Church in Amelia County. He also preached in neighboring Powhatan County. There on 17 May 1817 he married Judith Elizabeth Eggleston, the niece and adopted daughter of William Hickman and Ann Hickman, with whom Baptist had boarded before his marriage. The Baptists lived at Dunlora, the Hickmans' 900-acre Powhatan County plantation, where they had four daughters and three sons.

Serving local Baptist churches in the area, Baptist was active in denominational affairs and became involved in education. His ministerial work included founding missionary societies, Sunday schools, Bible societies, and temperance organizations in his churches. He also represented Virginia's Baptists at three meetings of the General Missionary Convention, or Triennial Convention. In 1817 he was appointed treasurer by the Powhatan County Board of School Commissioners and became a commissioner himself in 1819. After William Hickman's death in 1820, Baptist assumed the management of the family plantation. In December 1824 he announced that he would open a school on the Dunlora estate, which proved so successful that two years later he hired an assistant.

Baptist helped to found both the Baptist General Association of Virginia in June 1822 and the Virginia Baptist Education Society in June 1830, drafting constitutions for both organizations. He served as first vice president of the education society and at its behest educated some young men the society was sponsoring for the ministry. Baptist offered the students a liberal-arts and theological curriculum, while Ann Hickman provided them with room and board. Baptist taught a second session at Dunlora before the society purchased property near Richmond and moved its seminary there in the summer of 1832. Unwilling to relocate to an urban area because of a bronchial condition, Baptist remained in Powhatan County, where he continued to serve local churches, conduct his school, and manage a growing estate. His two years of educating aspiring Baptist clergymen at his Dunlora school, however, marked the beginning of the University of Richmond.

Despite his renown as an orator, Baptist's work was not widely published, and much of what was printed appeared in the *Religious Herald*, a Baptist journal. He published one series of short essays under the pseudonym

Wickliffe in the *Religious Herald* in reply to a treatise that Presbyterian clergyman John Holt Rice had published with the nom de plume of Pamphleteer. Baptist's response, defending the Baptist Church's doctrine of baptism, was also printed separately as *A Series of Letters Addressed to the Pamphleteer, by Wickliffe, in Reply to an Essay on Baptism* (1830). In 1851 Baptist's sermon on *The Power of Man to Obey the Gospel* was printed, but a collection of sermons that he had prepared for publication in the last years of his life was lost in a fire in Columbia, South Carolina.

By 1835 Baptist and Ann Hickman together owned and managed more than 1,500 acres and one hundred slaves. That year the family moved to Marengo County, Alabama, where Baptist apparently hoped that the milder climate would improve his health. He and Hickman acquired land near Faunsdale and relocated their numerous slaves. Resuming farming and preaching, he was active in the same causes in Alabama as he had been in Virginia, promoting missions, temperance, and education. He served Baptist churches in small towns like Dayton, Demopolis, Spring Hill, and Uniontown, but never accepted city churches that would necessitate leaving his slaves in the hands of a manager who might mistreat them. He was a founding trustee of Howard College in Marion (now Samford University in Birmingham) in 1841, and his address at the opening of its new building in 1846 was published the same year. According to his daughter, he declined the presidency of the college. Baptist was also appointed to the board of trustees of the University of Alabama in Tuscaloosa. Since he had sufficient means to care for himself and his family, he never accepted a salary from any church he served. He later regretted this decision, however, because he believed that he had not sufficiently emphasized the importance of congregational support of ministers.

An invalid the last several years of his life, Edward Baptist died on 31 March 1863 at his plantation, Oakland, in Marengo County, and was buried in the family cemetery there.

Biographies by Charles H. Ryland in *Virginia Baptist Ministers*, ed. George Braxton Taylor, 3d ser. (1912), 28–40, by Frederic W. Boatwright in *Religious Herald*, 27 Nov. 1947, and by Michael P. Gwaltney and W. Harrison Daniel in *Virginia Baptist Register* 30 (1991): 1534–1546 (por.); feature article in *Richmond Times-Dispatch*, 28 July 1935; Baptist's memoirs, identified as diary, VBHS; Powhatan Co. Marriage Register; Land and Personal Property Tax Returns, Powhatan Co., 1835, RG 48, LVA; numerous articles on Baptist in *Religious Herald*, 1828–1831; Reuben E. Alley, *History of the University of Richmond, 1830–1971* (1977), 10–14, 266.

W. Harrison Daniel

BARBEE, Gabriel Thomas (31 July 1814–24 September 1908), first president of the Farmers' Alliance of Virginia, was the second of six sons and third of twelve children of Andrew Russell Barbee and Nancy Britton Barbee. The sculptor William Randolph Barbee was a younger brother. Barbee was born at Hawsbury, in the part of Culpeper County that in 1833 became Rappahannock County. His father, a prosperous farmer, was appointed the first postmaster of Hawsbury in 1832. In the mid-1830s Barbee moved to Petersburg in Hardy County (now in Grant County, West Virginia), where he operated a hotel and, with his elder brother, George B. Barbee, and another partner, ran a general mercantile business. On 10 May 1838 he married Mary E. Burns, of Hardy County. They had three daughters.

In 1847 Barbee won election to the Senate of Virginia, representing Hardy, Page, Shenandoah, and Warren Counties. A Democrat, Barbee served on the influential Committee on Privileges and Elections and on joint committees on the militia, the penitentiary, and the treasurer's accounts. A new state constitution rearranged senatorial districts for the 1852 elections, and he did not return to office.

Not long thereafter Barbee moved to Baltimore, where he was unsuccessful in a wholesale business. He returned to Hardy County and resumed his mercantile pursuits, although he gave his occupation as farmer in 1860. As a Southern sympathizer, Barbee left that Unionist county shortly after the Civil War began, and by 1863 he had settled in Bridgewater. During the war he held several minor positions, including that of purchasing agent for the Confederate government.

In 1867 Barbee purchased a large brick house in Bridgewater and operated it as a hotel.

During the 1870s and 1880s two of his daughters conducted a private school for girls there. The building survives and is known as the Barbee House. Barbee served as mayor of Bridgewater from May 1877 to May 1879, a period when dissident Democrats organized as Readjusters and formed an alliance with reform-minded Republicans. He supported the Readjusters and made the *Bridgewater Journal*, which he purchased in October 1880, an advocate of the cause. As an editor he won a reputation, even with partisan Democrats, for good sense and fair dealing. Barbee sold the newspaper in the aftermath of a statewide Democratic victory in November 1883. Earlier that month Governor William E. Cameron, a Readjuster, had appointed him to the board of visitors of the University of Virginia, a post he held until 1886.

Barbee was a founder of the National Farmers' Alliance in Virginia. Early in 1887 the alliance sent Joseph S. Barbee, Gabriel Barbee's youngest brother, from Texas to establish a presence in Virginia. He stationed himself on his arrival at his brother's home in Bridgewater. Not long thereafter, Gabriel Barbee assumed the role of organizing county alliances in the state. He created the first unit of the alliance at Ottobine in Rockingham County in September 1887, and in November helped to establish there Virginia's first county alliance. Representatives from other counties met at Luray in 1888, set up the Farmers' Alliance of Virginia, and elected Barbee president. Organizing continued, and all but a handful of counties sent representatives to the meeting at Lynchburg in August 1890. Ineligible for reelection as president, Barbee became the organization's treasurer. He also established the West Virginia Farmers' Alliance at Charleston in August 1890.

Leaders of the National Farmers' Alliance met in Ocala, Florida, in December 1890 and drafted political demands, bringing into being the People's, or Populist, Party. Barbee attended the convention and served on its credentials committee. Although political organizing and campaigning reduced Barbee's role somewhat, he continued to contribute to the party's journal, the *Richmond Virginia Sun*, which on 12 October 1892 honored him as "the Father of the Alliance in Virginia." At age eighty Barbee ran for Congress as a Populist candidate in 1894, but he received only twenty-two votes.

Known as Colonel Barbee, he gave many of his friends intricately carved canes that he crafted as a hobby. Gabriel Thomas Barbee had survived his wife and daughters when he died of senile decay on 24 September 1908 at the home of a son-in-law in Romney, West Virginia. He was buried in Greenwood Cemetery in Bridgewater.

Barbee-Summers family Bible record, LVA; Elisabeth B. Johnson and C. E. Johnson Jr., *Rappahannock County, Virginia* (1981), 120–121; Elvin Lycurgus Judy, *History of Grant and Hardy Counties, West Virginia* (1951), 5, 103; *Richmond Enquirer*, 8 May 1847; *Harrisonburg Rockingham Register*, 20 May, 21 Oct. 1880, 6 Dec. 1883, 19 May 1887, 21 Mar. 1889; *Richmond Whig*, 22 Oct. 1883; *Bridgewater Journal*, 30 Nov. 1883; William DuBose Sheldon, *Populism in the Old Dominion: Virginia Farm Politics, 1885–1900* (1935), 16, 29–30, 109; *Richmond Virginia Sun*, 12 Oct. 1892; *Bridgewater Herald*, 12 Oct., 9 Nov. 1894; diary of Henry Smaltz (Smals), 1873–1890, James Madison University Library, Harrisonburg; *Bridgewater Sesquicentennial Edition, 1835–1985* (1985); por. in Bridgewater College Library; obituaries in *Harrisonburg Daily Times* and *Romney Hampshire Review*, both 30 Sept. 1908, and *Staunton Augusta County Argus*, 6 Oct. 1908.

GORDON W. MILLER

BARBEE, Herbert (8 October 1848–22 March 1936), sculptor, was born in Luray, the eldest of four sons and three daughters of William Randolph Barbee and Mary Jane McKay Barbee. Barbee's father, after many years practicing law in order to save enough money, took the family to Florence, Italy, in the mid-1850s to study sculpture in a studio near American sculptors Hiram Powers and Joel Tanner Hart. Herbert Barbee learned the rudiments of sculpture from his father and his father's associates, but little else is known about his education.

The family returned to the United States in 1858 and settled in Washington, D.C. After the Civil War began the Barbees moved to their home in Luray. Following his father's death in 1868, Herbert Barbee worked briefly in partnership with his uncle Gabriel Thomas Barbee, of Bridgewater, and then moved to New York, where he opened his own sculpture studio in 1874. He almost immediately began planning to transfer his father's plaster sculptures, left in the Washington studio during the Civil War, to marble. In 1878 Barbee traveled to Italy, where he made two copies of his father's *Fisher Girl*, as well as a number of bas-reliefs and an original work, *Happy Visions*. Returning to America, Barbee worked in New York, Baltimore, Saint Louis, Cincinnati, and Washington before settling in Hamburg, near Luray, in 1890. He married Blanche E. Stover, of Luray, on 20 February 1895. They had two sons and two daughters.

Much of Barbee's work consisted of portrait bas-reliefs and portrait busts. By 1883 he had completed eight life-size statues, fifteen bas-reliefs, and a number of portrait busts, including one of his father and one of George Washington, both of which George Washington University acquired during the twentieth century. Barbee's reputation rests largely on his marble copies of sculptures that his father had designed: *Coquette*, *Fisher Girl*, *The Lost Pleiad*, and *The Star of the West*, a romanticized image of Pocahontas that won him the first premium at the Louisville Exposition in 1883. He explained the statue as a memorial to the beginning of Virginia and the nation as Pocahontas looks eastward over the Atlantic Ocean for the arrival of the English settlers.

Barbee's original work includes a twenty-eight-foot monument to the rank and file of the Confederate army. Depicting a Confederate soldier on picket duty, the statue was unveiled at Luray in a very elaborate ceremony on 21 July 1898. Barbee also completed sculptural portraits of Confederate commanders Robert E. Lee, Thomas J. "Stonewall" Jackson, and John Singleton Mosby, and *Genius of the Confederacy*, a memorial in Culpeper County that includes a five-foot figure of a woman with a bullet-riddled flag around her shoulders, a saber in her hand, and a wreath of eleven stars representing the Confederate states.

Barbee's work is solid but generally uninspired, extending the classical tradition of mid-nineteenth-century American sculpture, exemplified by Powers and Hart, into the twentieth century. Herbert Barbee died on 22 March 1936 in Centreville, Fairfax County, at the house of one his sons. His body was cremated and the ashes buried in the Stover family cemetery at Luray.

NCAB, 18:424; Jennie Ann Kerkhoff, *Old Homes of Page County, Virginia* (1962), 133–136; *William Randolph Barbee & Herbert Barbee: Two Virginia Sculptors Rediscovered*, exhibition catalog, Dimock Gallery, George Washington University (1977); Barbee-Summers family Bible record, LVA; Barbee Collection, Page Co. Heritage Association, Luray; vertical files, VM; *Richmond Dispatch*, 22 July 1898; feature article in *Richmond Times-Dispatch*, 6 Jan. 1935 (por.); Herbert Barbee, *Retrospection: "The Star of the West," or Princess Pocahontas—Idealized* (n.d.); obituaries in *Richmond Times-Dispatch*, 23 Mar. 1936, and *Luray Page News and Courier*, 24 Mar. 1936.

BARBARA C. BATSON

BARBEE, William Randolph (17 January 1818–16 June 1868), sculptor, was born at Hawsbury in the part of Culpeper County that became Rappahannock County in 1833, the third of six sons and fifth of twelve children of Andrew Russell Barbee and Nancy Britton Barbee. His early attempts at whittling and carving initially served only to convince his parents and teachers that he was just an idle dreamer. When he reached the age of fifteen his parents sent him to the Virginia Baptist Seminary in Richmond. By the time he graduated with honors in 1836, Barbee had decided he wanted to be a professional sculptor. Like most would-be American sculptors of his day, he believed that travel and study in Europe were absolutely essential for the further development of his artistic talent. Faced with the need to earn enough money to pay for his study abroad, Barbee read law in Moorefield, Hardy County, and was admitted to the bar in 1843. After establishing a flourishing practice in Luray, he married Mary Jane McKay in 1847. Two of their four sons and one of their three daughters died young.

By the mid-1850s Barbee had saved enough money to give up his law practice and study sculpture in Europe. With his wife and young children he settled in Florence, Italy, and acquired a studio. He plunged into a period of concentrated study. He apparently worked for a time with fellow American sculptors Hiram Powers and Joel Tanner Hart. While in Florence, Barbee developed the sculptural skills and methods that characterized his subsequent artistic career. He favored an idealized, sentimental classicism that was then popular among American artists and also popular with the public. Barbee produced a number of pieces in marble, among them his principal works, *Coquette* and *Fisher Girl*, both of which were obviously inspired by the creations of Powers and Hart. When exhibited in the United States in 1858 and 1859, they were well received, and both were subsequently sold for substantial sums. Barbee also executed a fine plaster bust of James L. Orr, the Speaker of the United States House of Representatives, which was exhibited at the Pennsylvania Academy of Fine Arts in Philadelphia in 1859.

When Barbee returned to the United States in 1858, he received a great deal of favorable notice in the press. Some of his admirers persuaded the American government to provide him a rent-free studio in the Capitol in Washington. He began work on a frieze in the west wing of the building, but the outbreak of the Civil War abruptly terminated his work, and the government took possession of the studio and its contents, which included more than a dozen finished busts and works of art in addition to models. Barbee valued the items at $39,000.

Barbee regained use of the studio after the war, but his health began to fail. He devoted his final years to work on a life-sized statue of Pocahontas entitled *The Star of the West*. Illness prevented Barbee from completing *The Star of the West* and a number of other works. Among them was one to which he had given long thought and labor, *The Lost Pleiad*, its subject drawn from Greek mythology. Contemporaries recognized Barbee as an artist of talent and promise and ranked him with his fellow Virginian Alexander Galt among the most gifted nineteenth-century American sculptors. Later generations, although not rating Barbee's work as highly as Galt's, appreciated his creativity through the reproductions produced by Barbee's eldest son, Herbert Barbee. William Randolph Barbee died of cancer at the family home near Luray on 16 June 1868. He was buried in Green Hill Cemetery in Luray.

L. Moody Simms Jr., "William Randolph Barbee: Virginia Sculptor," *Virginia Cavalcade* 22 (summer 1972): 40–47 (por.); *NCAB*, 18:423; Barbee-Summers family Bible record, LVA; Barbee Collection, Page Co. Heritage Association, Luray; vertical file, VM; *Richmond Whig and Public Advertiser*, 1, 8 Oct. 1858; *Richmond Daily Dispatch*, 4, 8 Oct. 1858; *New York Times*, 22 Dec. 1859; Charles E. Fairman, *Art and Artists of the Capitol of the United States of America* (1927), 164–165; Albert TenEyck Gardner, *Yankee Stonecutters: The First American School of Sculpture, 1800–1850* (1945), 22; Margaret Farrand Thorp, *The Literary Sculptors* (1965), 78, 187; *William Randolph Barbee & Herbert Barbee: Two Virginia Sculptors Rediscovered*, exhibition catalog, Dimock Gallery, George Washington University (1977); obituaries in *Lynchburg Virginian*, 18 June 1868, *Richmond Enquirer*, 19 June 1868, and *Staunton Spectator*, 23 June 1868; editorial tribute in *Richmond Whig and Advertiser*, semiweekly ed., 23 June 1868.

L. MOODY SIMMS JR.

BARBOUR, Alfred Madison (17 April 1829–4 April 1866), member of the Convention of 1861, was born in Culpeper County, the third of five sons and fourth of seven children of John Strode Barbour (1790–1855) and Eliza A. Byrne Barbour. He attended the University of Virginia from 1847 to 1849, specializing in modern languages and mathematics. In 1853 he moved to Monongalia County, where he studied law and was admitted to the bar two years later. On 5 January 1858 he married Kate A. Daniels. None of their children survived infancy.

Barbour declined an invitation to become secretary to the United States legation in Rio de Janeiro before entering politics in 1857 by winning election to one term in the House of Delegates. In the General Assembly he sponsored a bill to incorporate the Woodburn Female Seminary in Morgantown, supported legislation to stimulate internal improvements in northwestern Virginia, and opposed a bill to merge the counties of Monongalia and Marion.

In the spring of 1858 Barbour was elected a captain in the Monongalia militia, and on 24 December 1858 Secretary of War John B. Floyd appointed him superintendent of the United States armory at Harpers Ferry. Barbour held the politically and militarily sensitive post through the turmoil of the next two and a half years. His first crisis arose when budget cuts forced him to reduce wages and dismiss some of the armory staff. He was in Springfield, Massachusetts, on armory business at the time of the second crisis, when John Brown and a small band of abolitionists seized the arsenal on 16 October 1859. During the third crisis in the winter of 1860–1861, Barbour faced the dilemma of being responsible for protecting the arsenal and the arms while serving in a

Virginia convention some of whose members wanted to acquire the arms for possible use by the state against the federal government.

Barbour was a Democrat who campaigned for Stephen A. Douglas during the 1860 presidential campaign and offered to resign the superintendency because of his partisan political activity. A Unionist during the early months of the secession crisis, Barbour was easily elected on 4 February 1861 to represent Jefferson County in the Virginia Convention that met in Richmond later that month. As the crisis intensified, Barbour supported all proposals that he thought would preserve the Union, but his increasing doubts that compromise would avert war led him to resign the superintendency of the arsenal on 22 March 1861. He was in Harpers Ferry when the convention voted for secession, but he returned to Richmond to sign the Ordinance of Secession and voted for secession in the referendum at the end of April.

On 19 July 1861 Barbour accepted appointment as a major in the Virginia State Quartermaster Corps. He served at the First Battle of Manassas (Bull Run) and became a member of the Confederate army on 24 December 1861. He was assigned to General Joseph E. Johnston as chief quartermaster and served on his staff for the duration of the war except for a brief period on detached duty as quartermaster for General Leonidas L. Polk. Barbour was far from the oversight of the quartermaster general in Richmond, and he routinely ignored official policies, procedures, and regulations. He was lax in keeping and in returning his accounts, and he regularly failed to report to his superiors concerning supplies and funds on hand. In May 1863 the quartermaster general ordered Barbour back to Richmond to account for his actions and on at least one occasion tried to have him cashiered from the service, but Barbour retained Johnston's confidence and his office. Barbour also ran afoul of the Richmond journalist George William Bagby, who accused him of embezzling twenty million dollars. Bagby charged that the army was starving in the field while Major Barbour was living in high style in Montgomery, Alabama, far from the fighting. Bagby and Barbour traded insults but mutual friends arranged apologies before the harsh words brought on a duel.

Barbour surrendered to the Union army in Charlotte, North Carolina, on 26 April 1865 and returned to Richmond, where he signed an amnesty oath in May. By August 1865 he was living in Charles Town, West Virginia, where he applied for and received a pardon from President Andrew Johnson. The following year Alfred Madison Barbour returned to Montgomery, perhaps to start a new life. He died there suddenly on 4 April 1866.

Birth date in matriculation records in UVA archives; information about early life in *Morgantown Virginia Free Press*, 13 Jan. 1859; letters of ordnance officers, RG 156, NARA; Merritt Roe Smith, *Harpers Ferry Armory and the New Technology: The Challenge of Change* (1985), 303–319; Edward H. Phillips, "The Lower Shenandoah Valley during the Civil War: The Impact of War upon the Civilian Population and upon Civil Institutions" (Ph.D. diss., UNC, 1958), 10, 21–22; *Morgantown Virginia Free Press*, 16 Aug., 20 Sept., 18 Oct. 1860, 7 Feb. 1861; Compiled Service Records; Amnesty Papers, Virginia, RG 94, NARA; Presidential Pardons; Jeffrey N. Lash, *Destroyer of the Iron Horse: General Joseph E. Johnston and Confederate Rail Transport, 1861–1865* (1991), esp. 22, 113, 146; obituary, copied from lost issue of *Culpeper Observer*, in *Morgantown Virginia Free Press*, 12 Apr. 1866.

STUART LEE BUTLER

BARBOUR, Benjamin Johnson (14 June 1821–2 December 1894), planter, was born at Barboursville, the large and elegant Orange County estate of his parents, James Barbour (1775–1842) and Lucy Maria Johnson Barbour. He was the last of their four sons and three daughters and was given the same name as their second son, who had died in July 1820. Barbour received his first schooling in England while his father was serving as minister plenipotentiary to Great Britian. He later attended private schools in Virginia and was a student at the University of Virginia from 1837 to 1839, winning the honor of selection as final orator of the Jefferson Literary Society in 1838.

B. Johnson Barbour, as he was always known, spent much of his life out of the public eye as a planter and gentleman scholar. He inherited Barboursville when his father died in 1842, and by 1860 he was the wealthiest man in Orange County, with 7,000 acres of land and

150 slaves. Barbour was active in the Virginia State Agricultural Society from its revival in 1853. Widely known as a student of literature and a scholar of Shakespeare, he befriended such literary figures as John Reuben Thompson and William Gordon McCabe. Barbour was one of the most popular public speakers in Virginia, renowned for long, elaborate orations, replete with literary and classical allusions. He was also an important lay leader in the Episcopal Church, often serving as a delegate to the council of the Diocese of Virginia and in 1880 as an alternate delegate to the national convention.

Barbour was outspoken in his support for the Whig Party and Henry Clay. He delivered the dedicatory address for the statue of Clay that was unveiled in Richmond on 12 April 1860, more than a decade after his mother spearheaded the fund-raising campaign for the monument. Barbour opposed secession until after the firing on Fort Sumter in April 1861, and he took no political or military part in the Civil War. In the first election held after the end of the war in 1865, he ran for the House of Representatives on a platform of sectional reconciliation and states' rights. He overwhelmed his two opponents, former congressman John Strother Pendleton and Richmond political gadfly Martin Meredith Lipscomb, but the House of Representatives refused to seat anyone elected in the southern states in that year, and Barbour never served in Congress.

Barbour's most important public role centered on the University of Virginia. He was prominent in its General Alumni Association, serving four consecutive one-year terms as president starting in 1873. From 1865 to 1873 he sat on the board of visitors, and he was the rector of the university from 1866 to 1872. As rector, he attempted to reduce the university's emphasis on classical studies in favor of a more practical curriculum, including the education of public schoolteachers, and he oversaw the establishment of schools of applied mathematics, civil engineering, and applied chemistry. Barbour often faced opposition from conservative faculty members intent on shifting power over the university's administration from the board to themselves. Combining his interests in education and agriculture, Barbour served from 1879 until his death on the board of the university's Miller Fund, which supported the school's Department of Agriculture, and he served from 1876 to 1878 on the board of the Virginia Agricultural and Mechanical College in Blacksburg.

During Reconstruction Barbour became a Democrat and later opposed the Readjusters, who wished to reduce the taxpayer-funded principal of the state's antebellum public debt and who also courted African American voters. In 1879 he won election to the House of Delegates. During his one term he chaired the Committee on Schools and Colleges and led its investigation into the strife-torn administration of the Agricultural and Mechanical College, which resulted in the appointment of a new board of visitors for the college. In 1885 Barbour unsuccessfully sought the Democratic party nomination for the Senate of Virginia, and four years later Governor Fitzhugh Lee named him one of six delegates to a convention in Saint Louis to promote the inflationary free coinage of silver.

B. Johnson Barbour married Caroline Homassel Watson on 7 November 1844. Of their six sons and five daughters, two sons and three daughters survived childhood. Barbour suffered serious injuries when he fell into a ditch in Charlottesville and died a few weeks later at Barboursville on 2 December 1894. He was buried in the family cemetery at Barboursville.

Barbour family Bible and Barbour Family Papers, UVA; short biography in Paul Brandon Barringer et al., eds., *University of Virginia: Its History, Influence, Equipment and Characteristics* (1904), 2:292; marriage reported in *Richmond Enquirer*, 12 Nov. 1844; many of Barbour's public orations appeared as pamphlets and in newspapers, one of the most important being his Clay statue dedication oration in *Richmond Daily Whig*, 13 Apr. 1860; Alan B. Bromberg, "The Virginia Congressional Elections of 1865: A Test of Southern Loyalty," *VMHB* 84 (1976): 75–98; John S. Patton, *Jefferson, Cabell and the University of Virginia* (1906), 362, 373; Bruce, *University of Virginia*, 4:198–200; obituaries in *Richmond Dispatch* and *Richmond Times*, both 4 Dec. 1894.

ALAN B. BROMBERG

BARBOUR, James (10 June 1775–7 June 1842), Speaker of the House of Delegates, governor of Virginia, and member of the United States Senate, was born in Orange County, the second of four sons and second of eight children of Thomas Barbour and Mary Pendleton Thomas Barbour. His parents both came from prominent landed families, and his father served in the House of Burgesses before the American Revolution and was a justice of the peace for fifty-seven consecutive years. Despite family financial reverses that prevented Barbour from attending college, for his time he still enjoyed considerable privileges. After preparatory study in rhetoric and classical languages at James Waddel's local academy, Barbour read law in Richmond and in 1793, when he was still only eighteen years old, was admitted to the bar and began practicing law in Orange and the neighboring counties.

On 20 October 1795 Barbour married his cousin Lucy Maria Johnson, daughter of another prominent Orange County planter and later a prominent leader of Whig women. They had four sons and three daughters during the ensuing quarter century, the last of whom was Benjamin Johnson Barbour, rector of the University of Virginia. Barbour prospered as a lawyer and in his management of large landholdings in Orange County. In 1817 he began to build an elegant plantation house from a design prepared by his friend Thomas Jefferson. For the rest of his life Barbour resided at Barboursville plantation in Orange County when politics permitted.

Politically ambitious, Barbour used his law practice and family connections, including close ties to James Madison, to win election to the House of Delegates in 1798. He played a leading role in obtaining passage of Madison's Virginia Resolutions against the Alien and Sedition Acts with speeches extolling state sovereignty, strict construction of the Constitution, and limited government. He won reelection in 1799 and served until 1803, sat for another term in 1804, and returned to the House from 1807 through 1812. From December 1809 to January 1812 he served as Speaker of the House of Delegates. Barbour ran for governor of Virginia in 1811 but on 5 December of that year the General Assembly narrowly elected acting governor George William Smith by a vote of 100 to 97. After Smith died on 26 December in the Richmond Theatre fire, on 3 January 1812 the General Assembly elected Barbour governor to succeed him. He was reelected twice and served from 4 January 1812 to 11 December 1814. Barbour's three terms spanned the difficult years of the War of 1812, during which the state was beset by money problems and he struggled to keep militia in the field to protect Virginia from invading British fleets and armies.

Barbour's experiences as governor wrought a major change in his political philosophy. The restrictive political dogma that he and other Republicans had fashioned when they were out of power during the 1790s no longer seemed adequate to him. The nation's society and economy had become much more complex, and he came to value centralized banking and massed capital that could pay for roads and canals to facilitate the movement of people and goods and allow for the support of a stronger military establishment to protect the nation from potential enemies. After three years as one of the best governors the Jeffersonians gave Virginia, Barbour was ineligible for reelection. A coalition of Republicans and Federalists in the General Assembly elected Barbour to the United States Senate on 14 November 1814 by a vote of 107 to 80 over the reluctant candidate of the traditional Republicans, William Wirt.

Along with many other national leaders who emerged from the War of 1812, by the time he entered the Senate Barbour was willing to vote for protective tariffs and other incentives to encourage manufacturing and commerce. He had a major hand in winning Senate approval of the bill to charter the Second Bank of the United States in 1815, and two years later he helped steer through the Senate John C. Calhoun's Bonus Bill to appropriate funds for the construction of internal improvements to stimulate economic development and promote national defense. After President James Madison vetoed the bill on constitutional grounds, Barbour tried unsuccessfully to pass a constitutional amendment to grant Congress the contested power. He ably defended southern interests during the initial debates over the admission of Missouri as a slave state, but unlike his brother Philip Pendleton Barbour, a rising conservative member of the House of Representatives, he subordinated sectional to national considerations and helped enact the compromise that ended the political crisis. Barbour was an able parliamentarian, popular orator, and hard-working committee member. He often worked closely with Madison and with President James Monroe on both domestic and foreign policies. He became chairman of the Senate Committee on Foreign Relations in 1816, and in 1819 he was elected president pro tempore of the Senate.

In March 1825 President John Quincy Adams appointed Barbour secretary of war. Barbour succeeded John C. Calhoun in that office and for the most part continued Calhoun's innovative policies. He accelerated construction of the National Road as a defense measure and pushed other internal improvements projects. As the government official responsible for Indian affairs, Barbour tried to protect the southern Indian tribes, especially the Creeks and Cherokees in Georgia, from encroaching settlers. Governor George Troup, of Georgia, defied Barbour's policy in a challenge to the federal government that was popular among states' rights leaders in Virginia and further alienated Barbour politically from many of his old allies. In May 1828 Adams appointed Barbour minister plenipotentiary to Great Britain. On 1 August he sailed for England, but his career as a diplomat lasted only a year before Adams's successor, Andrew Jackson, recalled and replaced him in May 1829. Before he began his return voyage on 1 October 1829, Barbour received a doctor of civil law degree from Oxford University and visited the Marquis de Lafayette in France.

Barbour returned to Barboursville to manage the 5,000 acres of land he owned there and his labor force of more than 100 slaves. Barbour ran his plantation as a model farm. A student of and vigorous advocate for scientific farming, he conducted many experiments to restore soil fertility, prevent erosion, and increase crop yields. He publicized the results during his presidency of the Albemarle Agricultural Society and with articles in national farm journals and newspapers such as the *Farmer's Register* and the *American Farmer*. Barbour advocated establishing a state board of agriculture to promote scientific farming and a professorship in agriculture and an agricultural experiment station at the University of Virginia. He raised imported Merino sheep and some of the finest thoroughbred horses in Virginia. Although he had broken with many old Jeffersonians over issues of national politics, Barbour shared their devotion to agriculture as the foundation of a republican society and supported Jefferson's proposed system of public education in Virginia.

In December 1830 Barbour returned to the House of Delegates as Orange County's representative but resigned two months later in favor of his opponent, Thomas Davis, who had contested the election. He then served as chairman of the 1831 convention of the National Republican Party that nominated Henry Clay for president and helped organize the Whig Party in Virginia. Barbour also chaired the December 1839 Whig Party convention that nominated William Henry Harrison for president, and he worked for Harrison in the campaign. James Barbour's health began to fail in 1839, and he died of prostate cancer at home on 7 June 1842. He was buried in the family cemetery at Barboursville.

Charles D. Lowery, *James Barbour: A Jeffersonian Republican* (1984), contains full bibliography of primary sources (frontispiece por. by Chester Harding); Barbour family Bible, Barbour Family Papers, and James Barbour Papers, UVA, and smaller collection in New York Public Library; *Richmond Enquirer*, 4 Jan. 1812, 15 Nov. 1814; Hummel and Smith, *Portraits and Statuary*, 5 (por.); contemporary accounts and biographies in John Quincy Adams, *Memoirs*, ed. Charles Francis Adams (1874–1877), Stephen Collins, *Miscellanies* (1845), 209–230, Henry W. Hilliard, *Politics and Pen Pictures at Home and Abroad* (1892), 5, Jeremiah Morton, *Eulogy Upon the Late Governor Barbour* (1842), and [George Watterson], *Letters from Washington, on the Constitution and Laws* (1818), 128, 131.

CHARLES D. LOWERY

BARBOUR, James (26 February 1823–29 October 1895), member of the Convention of 1850–1851 and member of the Convention of 1861, was born in Culpeper County, the second of five sons and third of seven children of John Strode Barbour (1790–1855) and Eliza A. Byrne Barbour. He attended Georgetown College from September to December 1840 and spent the academic year 1841–1842 at the University of Virginia. He then studied law under

John Tayloe Lomax in Fredericksburg and in 1844 was admitted to the bar. On 1 September 1857 he married Fannie T. Beckham, also of Culpeper County, and they had four sons and three daughters.

Barbour entered politics in August 1850 as a successful Democratic Party candidate for one of the three seats in the state constitutional convention from the district comprising Culpeper, Greene, Madison, and Orange Counties. His membership in one of the most prominent political families in Virginia offset his youth and inexperience, and he was appointed to the crucial Committee on the Basis of Apportionment of Representation. Barbour allied himself with delegates from the eastern counties who opposed many of the democratic reforms that western delegates advocated, including apportioning seats in the General Assembly solely on the number of white voters rather than on a mixed basis of white population and the value of taxable property. The reformers prevailed over Barbour and the eastern delegates, with the result that the eastern counties of Virginia lost a measure of their dominance in the General Assembly.

Barbour represented Culpeper County in the House of Delegates in 1852 and 1853 and again from 1857 to 1863. From 1853 to 1855 he served on the board of visitors of the Virginia Military Institute. Barbour was a delegate to the Democratic national convention in 1860 and attended its April and June sessions held respectively in Charleston, South Carolina, and Baltimore, Maryland. During the ensuing presidential campaign he supported John C. Breckinridge, the nominee of the Southern wing of the party.

Barbour helped Governor John Letcher draft a proposal that a national peace conference meet in Washington. On 4 February 1861, the day the conference convened, Barbour easily defeated an avowed secessionist to represent Culpeper County in the convention called to consider Virginia's position during the secession crisis. He served on the important Committee on Federal Relations. Barbour also worked behind the scenes in Washington with Republican senator William H. Seward and Democratic senator Stephen A. Douglas to fashion a compromise to avert civil war. Seward was so impressed that he recommended Barbour for a seat in Abraham Lincoln's cabinet by way of bringing into the new administration a prominent conservative Southern Democrat who might be able to help hold the border states in the Union. Barbour was committed to guarantees of Southerners' unlimited rights to own slaves, rejected all proposals to use coercion to hold seceding states in the Union, and soon realized that no compromise between his position and that of the Republican leaders was possible. Barbour was one of the first and most influential of the Virginia conditional Unionists to pronounce the negotiations a failure, and he voted for secession in the Virginia convention on 4 April, when the motion was defeated, and on 17 April 1861, when it passed.

On 28 April 1862 Barbour entered Confederate service as a major and assistant adjutant general on the staff of General Richard Ewell, but ill health forced him to retire from the service on 30 January 1863. After the war Barbour acquired a controlling interest in the *Richmond Daily Enquirer and Examiner* on 15 July 1867 and owned the influential newspaper until 30 January 1870. He reentered politics after Reconstruction ended in 1870 and came out a year later against Governor Gilbert Carlton Walker and the controversial Funding Act of 1871. Barbour argued that the need to pay for the new system of public schools and to enact debtor relief laws should take precedence over paying off the full principal of the antebellum state debt. He failed in a campaign as an independent against Eppa Hunton for the House of Representatives in November 1874, but he won back his old seat in the House of Delegates in 1877 and served for two years. As chairman of the Committee on Finance he drafted the Barbour Bill, which funded public schools and other government functions, curtailed the use of bond coupons for payment of taxes, and allocated only a small proportion of the state's revenue to debt service. The bill narrowly passed both houses of the General Assembly, only to be vetoed in February 1878 by Governor Frederick William Mackey Holliday, who condemned it as a precursor to debt readjustment.

In 1879 the leading advocates of debt restructuring formed the Readjuster Party under the leadership of William Mahone and won a majority of the General Assembly that sent Mahone to the United States Senate the following year. Despite his previous support for some elements of their platform, Barbour denounced the Readjusters and in 1881 was nominated for lieutenant governor by the opposition Funder Party. He lost in the November election. When the newly constituted Democratic Party swept the remnants of the Readjuster Party from office in 1885, he successfully ran for the House of Delegates once again and served until he retired from politics in 1888. James Barbour died of pneumonia at Beauregard, his house in Culpeper County, on 29 October 1895 and was buried in Citizen's Cemetery (now Fairview Cemetery).

Birth date given by Barbour in Matriculation Book, Registrar's Office, UVA, and repeated on gravestone; family history in Raleigh Travers Green, *Genealogical and Historical Notes on Culpeper County, Virginia* (1900), 140; education described in John Strode Barbour to John C. Calhoun, 30 Nov. 1844, in Robert L. Meriwether et al., eds., *The Papers of John C. Calhoun* (1959–), 20:400; Culpeper Co. Marriage Register; elections to conventions reported in *Richmond Enquirer*, 27 Aug. 1850, *Alexandria Gazette and Virginia Advertiser*, 5, 6 Feb. 1861, and *Richmond Daily Whig*, 5 Feb. 1861; Francis Pendleton Gaines Jr., "The Virginia Constitutional Convention of 1850–51: A Study in Sectionalism" (Ph.D. diss., UVA, 1950), esp. 121–122, 134–135, 142; Henry T. Shanks, *The Secession Movement in Virginia, 1847–1861* (1934); Daniel W. Crofts, *Reluctant Confederates: Upper South Unionists in the Secession Crisis* (1989); speech of 30 Mar. 1861 giving up hope for compromise in *Richmond Enquirer*, 27 Apr. 1861; Complied Service Records; Jack P. Maddex Jr., *The Virginia Conservatives, 1867–1879: A Study in Reconstruction Politics* (1970), 135–136, 261, 264; James Tice Moore, *Two Paths to the New South: The Virginia Debt Controversy, 1870–1883* (1974), 59, 67, 73; obituaries in *Richmond Star* and *Richmond State*, both 30 Oct. 1895, and *Richmond Dispatch*, 31 Oct., 1 Nov. 1895.

DONALD W. GUNTER

BARBOUR, John Strode (8 August 1790–12 January 1855), member of the House of Representatives and member of the Convention of 1829–1830, was born in Culpeper County, the eldest of at least two sons and three daughters of Mordecai Barbour and Elizabeth Strode Barbour. After graduating from the College of William and Mary in 1808, he studied law with his first cousin James Barbour (1775–1842) in Orange County and was admitted to the bar in 1811. Barbour took over his cousin's law practice after James Barbour was elected governor of Virginia in 1812. On 21 November 1815 he married Eliza A. Byrne in Petersburg. Alfred Madison Barbour, James Barbour (1823–1895), and John Strode Barbour (1820–1892), all of whom became politically prominent, were among their five sons and two daughters.

In 1813 Barbour ran successfully for the House of Delegates, serving until 1816 and again from 1820 to 1823. His kinship to the governor probably explains Barbour's choice appointment to the Committee on Courts of Justice during his first year in the assembly. He rose steadily through the ranks in the House of Delegates. During his second year he was also placed on the influential Committee on Finance, and during his third year he advanced to more senior positions in both committees. He also briefly served in the field as aide-de-camp to General William Madison during the War of 1812. When Barbour returned to the General Assembly in 1820, he resumed his seats on the two prestigious committees, and during the session of 1822–1823 he was chairman of the Committee on Courts of Justice.

In the spring of 1823 Barbour ran for the House of Representatives and narrowly defeated Thomas Marshall. He beat Marshall again in 1825 and won easily or without opposition in 1827, 1829, and 1831. During the first half of his decade in Congress Barbour remained politically close to James Barbour and supported appropriations for internal improvements, but in 1828 he joined fellow congressman Philip Pendleton Barbour, James Barbour's brother, in supporting Andrew Jackson against Henry Clay in the presidential campaign. John Strode Barbour increasingly abandoned his old nationalism in favor of states' rights positions, and before the end of Jackson's first term Barbour broke with him, due in part to Jackson's strong exercise of executive power and his removal of federal deposits from the Second Bank of the United States. Barbour allied himself with some of the most conservative Democrats in Virginia and the South, most notably John C. Calhoun, of South Carolina, for whom he named one of his sons. Barbour strenuously opposed the tariff bills of 1828 and 1832 and sided with South Carolina during the Nullification Crisis.

In the spring of 1829 Barbour led the ticket as one of four delegates elected to represent Fauquier and Culpeper Counties at the constitutional convention. He was appointed to the Committee on the Executive Department. In his only set speech at the convention, on 2 November 1829 he opposed all of the demands of western delegates who sought a more democratic government based on universal white male suffrage, the popular election of more public officials, and reapportionment of the General Assembly to reduce the influence of the small eastern counties. Barbour supported the eastern proposition to base assembly representation on a mixture of population and taxable property, not on the number of white voters alone. He eventually backed a compromise that allocated more delegates to the western counties but did not end the dominance of the eastern, slaveholding counties.

Barbour did not seek reelection to Congress in 1833. Instead, he regained his old seat in the House of Delegates and was immediately reappointed chairman of the Committee on Courts of Justice. After the 1833–1834 session he never again sought public office, but he remained active in politics as one of Calhoun's leading supporters in Virginia. In 1844 Barbour took part in an unsuccessful campaign to persuade Calhoun to run for president, and the following year he helped convince Calhoun to return to the Senate and to lead the southern members of Congress. Barbour's last acts of public service came in 1852 as head of the Virginia delegation to the Democratic Party national convention and chairman of the convention committee that traveled to New Hampshire after the assemblage adjourned to notify Franklin Pierce of his nomination for the presidency.

Barbour did not achieve wealth either as a planter or as an attorney. His 380-acre farm in Culpeper County was worth only about $4,000 in 1850, and he owned twelve slaves in 1844. Neither was he among the first rank of Virginia statesmen, but during his forty years in politics he helped lead the state away from the broad nationalism of the early nineteenth century toward the southern nationalism of the 1850s. John Strode Barbour died at his home on 12 January 1855 after a short illness and was buried in the family cemetery on the property.

Letters to, from, and about Barbour in several collections at UVA, including Barbour Family Papers; several Barbour letters in Robert L. Meriwether et al., eds., *The Papers of John C. Calhoun* (1959–), vols. 10, 17–22; incomplete family history in Raleigh Travers Green, *Genealogical and Historical Notes on Culpeper County, Virginia* (1900), 137, 140; marriage reported in *Petersburg Republican*, 24 Nov. 1815; elections reported in *Richmond Enquirer*, 6 May 1823, 26 Apr., 3 May 1825, 4 May 1827, 28 Apr., 15 May, 2 June 1829, 30 Aug. 1831; *Proceedings and Debates of 1829–1830 Convention*, 135–138; Catlin, *Convention of 1829–30* (por.); final illness described in J.Barbour to John S. Barbour, 8 Jan. 1855, in John S. Barbour Papers, LC; obituary in *Daily Richmond Enquirer*, 15 Jan. 1855.

JAMES L. BUGG

BARBOUR, John Strode (29 December 1820–14 May 1892), member of the House of Representatives and member of the United States Senate, was born in Culpeper County, the eldest of five sons and second of seven children of John Strode Barbour (1790–1855) and Eliza A. Byrne Barbour. He was educated in private schools before attending the University of Virginia from 1838 to 1842. He studied law before leaving the university and was a practicing attorney in Culpeper County from 1842 until about 1851.

In 1847 Barbour was elected as a Democrat to the House of Delegates. He served for four years and soon became involved with railroads. The state regularly subsidized railroad construction by purchasing three-fifths of the shares in newly chartered companies, and in 1849 Barbour became the state's representative on the board of directors of the Orange and Alexandria Railroad. In October 1851 the other directors elected him president. He temporarily abandoned his political career and served as president of the railroad from then until he resigned in December 1884. During his long tenure, the railroad, which was renamed the Virginia Midland Railroad in 1881, grew from only a few miles in Fairfax County to about five hundred miles of track between Alexandria and Danville with several branch roads. During the Civil War the railroad was open for only part of its length because of military operations, but Barbour used the road as much as possible to supply the Confederate army. He took no other part in the

Civil War, unlike his brothers James Barbour (1823–1895) and Alfred Madison Barbour, who both served in the Convention of 1861 and held staff positions in the Confederate army.

On 16 October 1865 Barbour married Susan Sewell Daingerfield in Prince Georges County, Maryland. They lived in Alexandria and had no children. Soon after the Civil War the Orange and Alexandria fell under the influence of the Baltimore and Ohio Railroad, which wished to use it to attract central Virginia commerce to Baltimore. At the same time William Mahone was attempting to consolidate three Southside Virginia railroads into the Atlantic, Mississippi, and Ohio Railroad to draw central Virginia commerce to Norfolk. Understandably, Barbour opposed Mahone's plan, and in 1869 he supported Henry Horatio Wells, a radical Republican, for governor of Virginia against the more conservative Gilbert Carlton Walker primarily because Wells opposed Mahone and Walker supported him. In 1871, with Barbour's support, the General Assembly passed a bill to sell the state's interest in the Orange and Alexandria Railroad. The Baltimore and Ohio Railroad purchased this stock and also the shares that the city of Alexandria owned and thereby gained complete control over the Orange and Alexandria. During the following decade Barbour cooperated with the Baltimore and Ohio in its competition with the Richmond and Danville Railroad for business in southern Virginia until the Baltimore and Ohio relinquished control of the new Virginia Midland Railroad to the Richmond and Danville.

Barbour had taken no part in politics while running the Orange and Alexandria Railroad except as necessary to advance its business interests, but his sympathies lay with the conservative Democrats who formed the basis of the Funder Party that opposed William Mahone's Readjusters. In 1880 the Funder convention in the eighth congressional district deadlocked in attempting to nominate a candidate for the House of Representatives and settled on Barbour, who had not been a candidate, as its compromise choice. He easily defeated Republican and Readjuster opponents in the general election and was twice reelected. He became chairman of the Committee on the District of Columbia and also involved himself deeply in Virginia politics.

In 1882 Barbour recruited John E. Massey, a former Readjuster and erstwhile ally of Mahone, to run for Congress against a Readjuster. Massey lost the election, but Barbour gained wide support as a potential state chairman of the Democratic Party. His success as a businessman, his organizational ability, and his ties to wealthy corporations hostile to Mahone and willing to finance expensive campaigns made Barbour a logical choice. In July 1883 the state convention unanimously elected him state party chairman after agreeing to his conditions that the Democrats would fight hard and would accept as final the settlement of the antebellum state debt that had led to Readjuster victories.

Barbour made organization the key to Democratic victory. He carefully and completely restructured the party and maintained close communications with workers at the local level. He recruited prominent speakers to canvass the state, drove party workers to get out the vote, and raised ample funds from wealthy businessmen. Barbour effectively played down the debt question in favor of two other issues—Mahone himself, portrayed by the party as a corrupt political dictator, and racist appeals to white fears of African American domination. The race issue came to the fore following a riot in Danville on 3 November 1883, on the eve of the legislative election, and the Democrats flooded the state with circulars predicting racial violence, miscegenation, and black rule if the Readjusters retained control of the General Assembly. They did not, and Barbour was widely hailed as the architect of the Democratic Party's victory. In 1884 he led the Virginia delegation to the party's national convention and was elected to the Democratic National Committee, a position he retained until his death.

Barbour led the Virginia Democrats to victory again in the 1884 presidential and congressional elections, but his influence in the party he had helped to re-create soon began to decline. Barbour clashed with Representative John Warwick Daniel over control of patronage during the Cleveland administration, and Daniel's young followers often worked to undercut Barbour's leadership. In 1885 Daniel's allies overcame Barbour's opposition and nominated Fitzhugh Lee for governor, but Barbour nonetheless effectively managed Lee's successful campaign against John Sergeant Wise, a Republican and former Readjuster.

As a reward for his effective party leadership, Barbour hoped to be elected to the United States Senate to succeed Mahone, whose term expired in March 1887. However, Daniel defeated Barbour in the party caucus and was subsequently elected in December 1885 by the General Assembly as Mahone's eventual successor. Stung by his defeat and the death of his wife the following February, Barbour retired from Congress and traveled in Europe during the 1886 election campaign. The Democrats missed his leadership and lost five of their eight seats in Congress. In 1887 he was reelected party chairman. The campaign for the General Assembly that year became in part a campaign between Barbour and Mahone to succeed Harrison Holt Riddleberger for Virginia's other U.S. Senate seat in 1889. The Democratic Party easily won the election, the Democratic Party caucus unanimously nominated Barbour for the Senate, and on 20 December 1887 the General Assembly elected him by a strict party vote. Barbour resigned the party chairmanship after he became a senator on 4 March 1889, but when his successor fell ill he resumed the job, and he directed Philip Watkins McKinney's successful gubernatorial campaign against William Mahone that year. Barbour served in the U.S. Senate until his death three years later. A poor orator and by nature more an executive than a legislator, he rarely spoke and was not an influential senator.

Barbour was nominally an Episcopalian. However, his wife was a Catholic and after her death he affiliated with but never converted to the Catholic Church. John Strode Barbour died of heart failure in Washington on 14 May 1892, and two days later a Catholic funeral for him was held in the Senate, apparently the first time a Catholic priest ever officiated in the Senate chamber. Barbour was buried in the Daingerfield-Sewell family cemetery at Poplar Hill in Prince Georges County, Maryland.

Birth date recorded in memorandum in Argosy Collection, UVA; John Strode Barbour Papers, LC; Barbour letters in Basil Brown Gordon Papers, VHS; James Thomas Quinn, "Thomas S. Barbour, Jr., and the Restoration of the Virginia Democracy, 1883–1892" (master's thesis, UVA, 1966); Allen W. Moger, "The Origin of the Democratic Machine in Virginia," *JSH* 8 (1942): 183–209; Charles M. Blackford, *Legal History of the Virginia Midland Railway Co.* (1881); resignation speech of 20 Dec. 1884 in Virginia Midland Railway Company, *Annual Report* 4 (1884): 5–8; obituaries and accounts of funeral in *New York Times*, 15, 17 May 1892, *Richmond Dispatch* and *Richmond Times*, both 15, 17, 18 May 1892, and *Richmond State*, 16 May 1892; *Memorial Addresses on the Life and Character of John S. Barbour (A Senator from Virginia) Delivered in the Senate and House of Representatives, February 3 and 25, 1893*, 52d Cong., 2d sess., 1893, Senate Doc. 64, serial 3068 (frontispiece por.).

ALAN B. BROMBERG

BARBOUR, John Strode (10 August 1866–6 May 1952), member of the Convention of 1901–1902, was born at Beauregard, his family's estate near Brandy Station in Culpeper County, the second of four sons and fourth of seven children of James Barbour (1823–1895) and Fannie T. Beckham Barbour. He was educated at a nearby private school and at William H. Kable's academy in Charles Town, West Virginia. In 1884 he began to read law in the Culpeper office of John Franklin Rixey, and in that town in 1886 he started a weekly newspaper, the *Piedmont Advance*, which operated about two years.

In 1887 Barbour entered the law school at the University of Virginia. After graduating in 1888, he joined Rixey's law practice, where he won a reputation as a skilled attorney. When Rixey was elected to Congress in 1897, Barbour became the small firm's senior partner. On 4 April 1894 he married Mary B. Grimsley, daughter of a local judge. They had no children.

Barbour was a lifelong Democrat. Although he served as mayor of Culpeper from 1897 to 1898, he had taken little part in politics until 23 May 1901, when the voters of Culpeper County elected him without opposition to the constitutional convention scheduled to convene in Richmond on 12 June. As one of the most active of the younger members in attendance, he served on committees on the bill of rights and the government of cities and towns, spoke frequently, and introduced eleven substantive resolutions on varying subjects including local taxes, regulation of liquor licenses, law enforcement, and the suffrage. Barbour was not a member of the committee on the franchise. However, in Democratic Party caucuses on the question he argued for the disfranchisement of all black Virginians and voted against the final text of the restrictive suffrage article that the convention adopted on 4 April 1902, reportedly because it was still too weak, but perhaps because it would also result in the disfranchisement of numerous white Virginians. On 29 May 1902 Barbour joined the majority that voted to proclaim the new constitution in effect without submitting it to the voters for ratification.

In 1907 Barbour moved to Fairfax County and joined with R. Walton Moore and Thomas R. Keith to form a small but distinguished law firm with a general practice and offices in Fairfax County and Washington, D.C. Among Barbour's long-term clients were the Washington Railway and Electric Company and the Potomac Electric and Power Company of the District of Columbia. At his estate in Fairfax County he kept a dairy herd, and he was a founder of, and counsel for, the Maryland and Virginia Milk Producers Association. From 1932 until 1949 he was also a member of the board of the Virginia State Library. John Strode Barbour died at Doctors Hospital in Washington, D.C., on 6 May 1952 after a long illness and was buried two days later in Fairview Cemetery in Culpeper.

Richmond Daily Dispatch, 12 June 1901; Census, Culpeper Co., 1880; *Journal of 1901–1902 Convention*, 49, 50, 487, 504; *Proceedings and Debates of 1901–1902 Convention*, 1:174–183, 364–365, 431–435, 890–891, 898, 1039–1040, 1358, 1419–1421, 2:2137–2139, 2578–2586; *Resolutions of 1901–1902 Convention*, nos. 52, 102, 103, 104, 110, 162, 171, 172, 184, 185, 262; *Convention of 1901–1902 Photographs* (por.); memorial in *Virginia State Bar Association Proceedings* (1953): 155–156 (por.); obituary in *Culpeper Exponent*, 8 May 1952.

Brent Tarter

BARBOUR, Lucy Maria Johnson (29 November 1775–25 November 1860), women's organization leader, was born in Orange County, the only daughter and younger of two children of Benjamin Johnson and Elizabeth Barbour Johnson. As a child she was surrounded by exemplars of public service. Her father was an influential planter and member of the county court, and her uncle Thomas Barbour served Orange County as a burgess and justice of the peace. On 20 October 1795 Lucy Johnson married her first cousin James Barbour (1775–1842), a young lawyer and planter whom she had known since childhood, and the couple lived in Orange County.

Barbour gave birth between 1797 and 1821 to four sons and three daughters. A devoted and exacting mother, she was intimately involved in the details of her children's moral development and education, but her life was marked neither by the domestic isolation nor the spirit of dependence that characterized the lives of many other antebellum plantation mistresses. James Barbour's service as governor of Virginia from 1812 to 1814, United States senator from 1815 to 1825, secretary of war during the administration of John Quincy Adams, and minister plenipotentiary to Great Britain from August 1828 to May 1829 took the family to Richmond, Washington, D.C., and London, where Lucy Barbour earned a reputation as a gracious and popular hostess. She maintained an avid interest in the political issues that occupied her husband. Like him she strongly supported female education, and her friends included Emma Willard, head of the influential Troy Female Seminary in New York.

Lucy Barbour's life stands out as a challenge to the image of antebellum southern ladies as passive and apolitical. While her married life had nurtured her interest in politics, only after her husband's death in 1842 did Barbour translate her political concerns into public action. James Barbour had been instrumental in the creation of the Whig Party in Virginia and was a close friend of party leader Henry Clay. On 17 November 1844 Lucy Barbour wrote to the *Richmond Whig* from Barboursville, the family plantation, urging the "Whig women of Virginia" to give "some token of respect" to Clay, who had just lost his third presidential campaign. A group of Richmond women accordingly met on 9 December 1844 at the First Presbyterian Church, formed the Virginia Association of Ladies for Erecting a Statue to Henry Clay, and elected Barbour president. In the ensuing months auxiliary societies sprang up throughout the state, and membership soon surpassed 2,500.

Barbour's appeal set off a heated debate in the press over the proper bounds of women's involvement in party politics. The Democratic press charged that the partisan activities of Barbour and her supporters were inappropriate for women. In a letter of 4 December 1844 that was also published in the *Richmond Whig*, Barbour countered such attacks, writing boldly that as the "nursing mothers of heroes, statesmen, and divines," women deserved freedom of political thought and expression. In November 1845, having raised nearly $6,000, the association commissioned sculptor Joel Tanner Hart to execute a life-size marble statue of Clay. After years of delay Hart finally finished the statue in 1859. Barbour's failing health had by then compelled her to delegate the management of the association to its vice presidents and directors. The statue was unveiled on the grounds of the Virginia State Capitol in Richmond on 12 April 1860, with Democrats and Whigs, men and women, joining together in a citywide celebration. Her youngest son, Benjamin Johnson Barbour, delivered the dedicatory address extolling Clay's devotion to the preservation of the Union. Lucy Maria Johnson Barbour died shortly thereafter at Barboursville, on 25 November 1860, and was buried in the family cemetery there.

Barbour Family Papers, including Bible records, UVA; Charles D. Lowery, *James Barbour: A Jeffersonian Republican* (1984); *Richmond Whig and Public Advertiser*, 26 Nov., 10, 13 Dec. 1844; Elizabeth R. Varon, "'The Ladies Are Whigs': Lucy Barbour, Henry Clay, and Nineteenth-Century Virginia Politics," *Virginia Cavalcade* 42 (1992): 72–83; Varon, *We Mean to Be Counted: White Women and Politics in Antebellum Virginia* (1998), 88–93, 202–204; Papers of Virginia Association of Ladies for Erecting a Statue to Henry Clay, VHS; *Richmond Daily Whig*, 12–14 Apr. 1860; Orange Co. Will Book, 12:441–442; obituary in *Richmond Daily Whig*, 3 Dec. 1860.

ELIZABETH R. VARON

BARBOUR, Philip Pendleton (25 May 1783–24 or 25 February 1841), Speaker of the House of Representatives, president of the Convention of 1829–1830, and justice of the United States Supreme Court, was born in Orange County, the youngest of four sons and fifth of eight children of Thomas Barbour and Mary Pendleton Thomas Barbour. Barbour's father served in the House of Burgesses from 1769 to 1776 and in the first four Revolutionary Conventions. His mother was closely related to two Caroline County men of note, Edmund Pendleton, after whom he was named, and John Taylor of Caroline, whose political principles he espoused all of his life. In spite of family financial reverses that prevented Philip Pendleton Barbour and his older brother James Barbour (1775–1842) from completing their educations, they were privileged young men by the standards of their day. Philip Pendleton Barbour studied under the local Episcopal minister, Charles O'Niel, and briefly at the College of William and Mary. After lack of money forced him to drop out of school he studied law with St. George Tucker.

Barbour practiced law in Bardstown, Kentucky, for a short time, but in 1802 he moved back to Orange County and opened a law office in Gordonsville. On 4 October 1804 he married Frances Todd Johnson, the sister of James Barbour's wife and also his own first cousin. They had two daughters and five sons. They gave family names to the first four children but named their last three baby boys unconventionally: Quintus, Sextus, and Septimus.

Barbour was elected to the House of Delegates in 1812, only a few months after James Barbour became governor of Virginia. He served two years in the General Assembly and received appointments to two major committees, finance and courts of justice, perhaps because he was the brother of the popular governor. In the spring of 1814 he ran for the House of Representatives to succeed John Dawson, who had died in office. Barbour defeated John Mercer in the special election, defeated him again in the general election in April 1815, and ran unopposed for each of the next four terms, serving in all from 19 September 1814 until 4 March 1825. His decade in the House of Representatives roughly coincided with James Barbour's service in the United States Senate, but the brothers' political views, which had earlier been much the same, diverged radically. Unlike James Barbour, who embraced the postwar nationalism of Henry Clay, John C. Calhoun, and others, and who eventually served as secretary of war in the cabinet of John Quincy Adams, Philip Pendleton Barbour adhered closely to the agrarian, strict construction, states' rights philosophy of what came to be called the Old Republicans in Virginia. He joined Nathaniel Macon from North Carolina and fellow Virginians John Taylor of Caroline, John Randolph of Roanoke, and Judge Spencer Roane in leading opposition to publicly funded internal improvements, the national bank, and the protective tariff. During the debates on the Missouri Compromise, Barbour denounced as unconstitutional every attempt to impose restrictions on the admission of Missouri as a slave state.

Barbour continued to practice law while in Congress, and in 1821 he was among those serving as counsels for the commonwealth when the important case of *Cohens* v. *Virginia* was argued before the United States Supreme Court. Barbour followed his instructions from the state government to argue that the Supreme Court lacked jurisdiction, but Chief Justice John Marshall sweepingly rejected his arguments and asserted that the supremacy clause of the Constitution meant that all congressional statutes took precedence over any laws of a state and that the federal courts could review the rulings of state courts on questions of constitutionality. The decision was a major defeat for strict constructionists such as Barbour. As in all of his political speeches, his argument in *Cohens* v. *Virginia* was a legalistic, forceful, logical call for a strict, almost literal interpretation of the U.S. Constitution that would limit the powers of the national government but not those of the states. Barbour's admirers often complimented his powerful reasoning and uncompromising defense of states' rights, but a Whig newspaper editor pithily summarized opponents' opinions by calling him a "shallow metaphysical hair-splitter."

In December 1821 Barbour was elected Speaker of the House of Representatives, defeating incumbent John W. Taylor, of New York, who had become unpopular with southern members during the Missouri debates due to his opposition to slavery. Barbour served only one two-year term as Speaker because former Speaker Henry Clay was reelected to Congress the following year and in effect reclaimed the office.

Barbour chose not to run for another term in Congress, and on 7 February 1825 the General Assembly elected him one of the judges of the General Court for the eastern district of Virginia. In 1827, however, he consented to run again for the House of Representatives, and he was elected without opposition and reelected for the last time in 1829. Barbour ran again for Speaker when he returned to Congress, but lost to Andrew Stephenson, of Virginia, leaving Barbour free to attack the Adams administration (of which his brother was an important member) unsparingly. Barbour supported Andrew Jackson for president in 1828 and was seriously considered for appointment to Jackson's Cabinet, but he settled for an appointment as judge of the U.S. District Court for Eastern Virginia and on 15 October 1830 resigned from Congress. In spite of his ties with conservative southern Democrats, Barbour stood behind Jackson during the nullification crisis. In 1832 he seemed willing to let southern Democrats try to substitute him for Martin Van Buren for vice president on the Democratic Party ticket, but Barbour withdrew after it became clear that Van Buren would definitely be elected.

In 1829 Barbour ran for a seat in the state constitutional convention. He and former president James Madison received the most votes in the counties of Louisa, Madison, Orange, and Spotsylvania and were two of the four men elected to represent that district in the convention that met from 5 October 1829 through 15 January 1830. Barbour served on the Committee on the Executive Department, frequently acted as chairman of the convention during debates in committee of the whole, and on 9 December was chosen president pro tempore to preside during the absence of President James Monroe, who was ill. After Monroe resigned from the convention, Barbour was unanimously elected president on 12 December 1829. From the beginning Barbour cast his lot with the conservative delegates from the eastern counties in opposition to most of the democratic reforms that the convention was considering. He favored retaining property qualifications for voting and supported allocating representation in the General Assembly on a mixed basis of white population and taxable property that continued the political dominance of the slaveholding counties in eastern Virginia.

Barbour remained a judge of the federal district court for more than five years. In March 1836 Andrew Jackson appointed him to the Supreme Court. The Senate confirmed Barbour by a vote of 30 to 11, and he took his seat at the beginning of the January 1837 term. During service on the Supreme Court of only four years, not long enough to have much impact on its direction or compile a distinctive judicial record, Barbour generally followed the lead of Chief Justice Roger B. Taney in redirecting the Court away from John Marshall's judicial nationalism and broad interpretation of the Constitution. The most important opinion Barbour wrote during his short tenure on the Court was *City of New York* v. *Miln*, decided in 1837, in which he held that the constitutional grant of power to Congress to regulate foreign commerce was not exclusive and that state governments could also regulate aspects of commerce in order to protect public health and safety. The decision complemented Taney's more famous opinion handed down the same year in *Charles River Bridge* v. *Warren Bridge* that laid the constitutional basis for what came to be called the police powers of the states.

Philip Pendleton Barbour died in his sleep during the night of 24–25 February 1841. A physician diagnosed heart disease and surmised that Barbour had probably died early in the morning of 25 February. He was buried near his house, Frascati, in Orange County.

Biographies by Frank Otto Gatell in *The Justices of the United States Supreme Court, 1789–1969*, ed. Leon Friedman and Fred L. Israel (1969), 1:717–727, and by David T. Pride in *The Supreme Court Justices: Illustrated Biographies, 1789–1993*, ed. Clare Cushman (1993), 121–125; eulogistic contemporary evaluations by Joseph Story in (15 Peters), *United States Reports*, 40:v–vii, and by Hugh Blair Grigsby in *The Virginia Convention of 1829–30* (1854), 33–38; marriage and births of children recorded in Barbour family Bible, UVA; some Barbour letters in LC, UVA, VHS, and in the collections of a number of his contemporaries; *Proceedings and Debates of 1829–1830 Convention*, 90–98, 435–438, 507, 608–610, 894–895; Barbour's argument in *Cohens* v. *Virginia* (1821) (6 Wheat.), *United States Reports*, 19:264, at 290–312; opinion in *City of New York* v. *Miln* (1837) (11 Peters), *United States Reports*, 36:102, at 130–143; Hummel and Smith, *Portraits and Statuary*, 6 (por.); death described in Joseph Story to Sarah Wetmore Story, 28 Feb. 1841, in William W. Story, *Life and Letters of Joseph Story* (1851), 2:348–349; obituaries in *Alexandria Gazette* and *Washington National Intelligencer*, both 26 Feb. 1841, *Daily Richmond Whig*, 27 Feb. 1841, and *Richmond Enquirer*, 27 Feb., 2 Mar. 1841.

CHARLES D. LOWERY

BARCO, John William (25 June 1877–2 August 1964), educator, was born in Camden County, North Carolina, the son of Henry L. Barco, a Baptist minister who had been born a slave, and Susan Waters Barco. He grew up near Portsmouth and attended public schools, Hampton Institute, and the Virginia Theological Seminary and College before matriculating at the new Virginia Union University in Richmond in 1899. Barco worked his way through college and also played and coached baseball and football while in school. He received an A.B. with Virginia Union's first graduating class in 1902 and was ordained a minister the same year at Zion Baptist Church in Portsmouth.

Barco briefly served as pastor of First Baptist Church in Salem, Virginia, before returning to Virginia Union in 1903. He headed the Grammar School Department from 1903 to 1907, served as professor of Latin, Hebrew, and history, and directed the summer normal program. He also did graduate work at the University of Chicago and at Andover Theological Seminary.

From 1928 until he retired in 1947, Barco was vice president of Virginia Union. During the 1930s he was intimately involved in setting up his institution's Norfolk branch, which evolved into Norfolk State University. While teaching and serving as an administrator, Barco remained active in college athletics. Early in his career he coached the university football team. His younger brother Henry L. Barco Jr. was a star quarterback on one of his teams and recognized as one of the great players of the era. In 1912 Barco took part in organizing the Colored (now Central) Intercollegiate Athletic Association and served as its vice president during its early years.

Barco devoted most of his life to teaching and to Virginia Union University. He was much less conspicuous than his colleague Gordon Blaine Hancock, who frequently addressed regional and national audiences on questions of race relations. Barco focused his energies largely on his students and the university. As a teacher he demanded the best from his students, at least seven of whom went on to become university presidents. Virginia Union University awarded Barco an honorary doctorate in 1921 and on his retirement in 1947 named him vice president emeritus. In 1948 he came out of retirement to serve as acting dean of the Department of Religion. On 13 February 1959 the new gymnasium of Virginia Union University was named Barco-Stevens Hall, in honor of Barco and Wesley Addison Stevens, a professor of mathematics who began the university's basketball and track programs.

Barco married Lucille Williams, of Norfolk, on 7 June 1905. They had two sons and two daughters. He was an active member of Ebenezer Baptist Church in Richmond, taught in its Sunday school for more than fifty years, and was a member or officer of several community organizations, including the Richmond chapter of the National Association for the Advancement of Colored People, the Young Men's Christian Association, the Virginia State Teachers Association, and the fraternity Alpha Phi Alpha. John William Barco died of prostate cancer at his home in Richmond on 2 August 1964 and was buried at Woodland Cemetery in Richmond.

Biography in Caldwell, *History of the American Negro*, 217–220 (por.); professional career documented in annual catalogs and bulletins in Virginia Union University Archives, especially 1965 bulletin dedicated to Barco's memory; feature articles in *Norfolk Journal and Guide*, 12 June 1948, 30 Mar. 1957; Cecil Raynard Taliaferro, "Virginia Union University: The First One Hundred Years—1864–1964" (Ph.D. diss., University of Pittsburgh, 1975), 43, 99–100; Lyman B. Brooks, *Upward: A History of Norfolk State University* (1973), 27, 39, 46, 90; obituary in *Richmond Afro-American*, 8 Aug. 1964 (por.).

ROBERT M. GOLDMAN

BARGER, Hazel Kathleen Doss (26 March 1911–16 June 1973), Republican Party leader, was born in Botetourt County, the fourth of six daughters and fifth of twelve children of William E. Doss, an insurance salesman, and Delilah Ellen Ruble Doss. She graduated from Jefferson High School in Roanoke and attended and graduated from the Lewis-Gale Hospital School of Nursing in Salem in 1934. She worked as a registered nurse and on 1 September 1934 married Ray Jewell Barger, a Roanoke coal-and-oil dealer and real estate investor. They had one son and one daughter.

After Ray Barger died on 7 November 1951, Hazel K. Barger managed his coal, oil, and real estate business for nearly a decade. She also became interested in politics and took courses in political science at Roanoke College and also attended the University of Virginia Extension Division in Roanoke. In 1952 she participated in the presidential campaign on behalf of Dwight D. Eisenhower and later campaigned with women's groups, serving as a local precinct chairman, president of the Roanoke Republican Woman's Club, and chairman of the Roanoke City Republican Committee from 1954 to 1958. In 1955 she and Abner Linwood Holton Jr. ran as the Republican candidates for the House of Delegates from Roanoke. They opposed a plan by some Democratic Party leaders to withhold state funds from racially desegregated schools. Barger and Holton lost the race by only a few hundred votes, and she also lost a second run for the assembly in 1957.

On 26 April 1958 Barger was elected to the Republican National Committee, a post she held for ten years. She served on the Republican state patronage committee that handled political appointments of the Eisenhower Administration. A delegate and member of the platform committee at Republican national conventions in 1956 and 1960, she also cochaired the unsuccessful campaign of Leigh Hanes, of Roanoke, for a seat in the Senate of Virginia in 1959. Eisenhower appointed Barger to the President's Advisory Committee for the Aging in 1959 and to the Defense Department Advisory Committee in 1960. She made more than a hundred speeches on behalf of the Republicans during the 1960 presidential campaign.

In 1961 Barger became the first woman nominated by a major political party for statewide office in Virginia by seeking and winning the Republican nomination for lieutenant governor. Her opponent was Mills Edwin Godwin Jr., a member of the Senate of Virginia. During her campaign she advocated additional public support for public schools and the creation of a statewide system of community colleges, measures that Godwin supported after he was elected governor four years later. Barger also proposed that Virginia localities be allowed greater control over local public schools and charged that the state exerted too much control over neighborhood schools, a clear criticism of the Democratically controlled General Assembly's program of Massive Resistance to desegregation of the public schools. She also called for the election and appointment of more women to important policy-making positions in government.

Barger and the Republican nominees for governor and attorney general received about 34 percent of the vote. They garnered a larger proportion of the ballots in Northern Virginia, where Massive Resistance had been extremely unpopular, and in traditional Republican strongholds southwest of Roanoke. Eight more years passed before Holton became the first Republican candidate to win a statewide office in Virginia.

Barger had become the most influential Republican woman in Virginia. She served as state campaign manager for Richard May, the Republican candidate for the United States Senate, in 1964. Although she served on the rules committee at the Republican National Convention that year, she refused to endorse the party's presidential candidate, Barry Goldwater. In 1968 Barger directed the Virginia campaign of Nelson A. Rockefeller in his quest for the Republican presidential nomination, sat on the arrangements committee for the national convention, and served as moderator of the GOP Women's Conference. President Richard M. Nixon named her a director of the United Service Organization (USO) in July 1969.

In addition to efforts to get more women interested in politics, Barger played an active role in many civic organizations. She received the Distinguished Service Award of the Virginia Federation of Women's Clubs in 1968 and was a life member of the Virginia Federation of Garden Clubs and of the Valley Junior Woman's Club. She also served as president of the Williamson Road Woman's Club and of the Woman's Missionary Union at Oakland Baptist Church, as vice president of the Roanoke chapter of American Business Women, and as a board member of the Thursday Morning Music Club and the Roanoke chapter of the League of Women Voters.

Hazel Kathleen Doss Barger died of cancer on 16 June 1973 in Lewis-Gale Hospital in Salem and was buried in Fairview Cemetery in Buchanan, Botetourt County.

Family history verified by daughter Bonnie Barger Crockett; BVS Marriage Register, Lynchburg City; other information provided by H. Clyde Pearson and Melville Carico; *Roanoke Times*, 29 Apr. 1958, 14 Sept. 1967 (por.); *Roanoke World-News*, 6 Sept. 1961; campaign statement in *Virginia Journal of Education* 55 (Oct. 1961): 14, 48, 50; *Richmond Times-Dispatch*, 3 Nov. 1961; obituaries in *Roanoke World-News*, 16 June 1973, and *Roanoke Times*, 17 June 1973.

GEORGE A. KEGLEY

BARHAM, Joseph Louis (21 October 1846–20 December 1925), member of the Convention of 1901–1902, was born at Boykins in the southern part of Southampton County, the elder of two sons and third of four children of John Barham, a farmer and hotel keeper, and Louisa Pope Barham. He enrolled in the Virginia Military Institute with the class of 1867 but accumulated too many demerits and departed the school on 15 January 1864. Barham joined the 44th City Battalion of Petersburg, which was composed of boys under the age of eighteen. On reaching army age he entered Confederate service as a private in Company A, 13th Regiment Virginia Cavalry. After the war he went to Colorado and Nebraska, but he returned to Southampton County in 1868, settled at Newsoms, and began a long career as a businessman and gentleman farmer. On 8 December 1875 he married Bettie Patience Langhorne, of Smithfield. They had one son and one daughter.

Barham was a Democrat but seldom sought elective office. He served as sheriff of Southampton County from 1886 to 1887 and on its board of supervisors in May 1901, when he ran unopposed for the county's seat in a state constitutional convention. At the opening of the assemblage on 12 June 1901 Barham stated frankly, "I am a plain business man and farmer. The making of a Constitution is a thing entirely new to me. I have nothing at present to suggest." On 26 June, however, he introduced a resolution to restrict the suffrage to men who had paid taxes on property worth at least $500. Virginia had removed the last property qualifications on voting in 1851, and the resolution died in committee. Barham was appointed to the committee on the executive department. He evidently did not participate in the floor debates, but he voted with the majority on the two most important questions that the convention considered, helping pass a suffrage article designed to disfranchise black voters and voting to put the new constitution into effect without submitting it to a referendum.

Barham was president of the small Meherrin Valley Bank of Boykins from 1906 until about 1924. From 1914 to 1918 he sat on the board of visitors of the Virginia School for the Deaf and the Blind in Staunton. Toward the end of his life he served as commander of the Urquart-Gillett Camp of Confederate Veterans in Portsmouth. On 20 December 1925 Joseph Louis Barham died at his home in Newsoms after a long illness. He was buried in the family cemetery at Newsoms.

Richmond Times, 12 June 1901 (por.); birth date in Joseph Barham File, Alumni Records, VMI; variant birth date of 21 Sept 1846 in Jacob N. Brenaman, *A History of Virginia Conventions* (1902), 96; Census, Southampton Co., 1860; Compiled Service Records; Isle of Wight Co. Marriage Register; *Journal of 1901–1902 Convention*, 49, 83, 487, 504; *Resolutions of 1901–1902 Convention*, no. 82; *Convention of 1901–1902 Photographs* (por.); obituaries in *Norfolk Virginian-Pilot*, 21 Dec. 1925, *Suffolk Herald*, 25 Dec. 1925, and *Confederate Veteran* 34 (1926): 109.

Brent Tarter

BARHAM, Richard Pannell (25 April 1846–23 June 1917), journalist, was born in Southampton County, the only child of Benjamin Barham and Rebecca Biddle Barham. After Barham's father died, his mother remarried and moved with her son to Petersburg, where he grew up and learned the trade of printing. Following a brief interval of service in the Confederate army, he returned to Petersburg, where he worked on the staff of the *Petersburg Appeal*. On 1 May 1870 he purchased the *Petersburg Daily Courier* and served as its editor until he sold it in the summer of 1871. In January 1873 Barham became city editor of the *Appeal*, and after it merged with the *Petersburg Index* in July of that year he served as business manager of the new *Petersburg Index and Appeal*. He became the paper's managing editor in June 1877. In the summer of 1879 he purchased the restyled *Petersburg Index-Appeal* and acted as both editor and publisher from then until he sold the newspaper in November 1910.

The *Petersburg Index-Appeal* was the most important and influential newspaper in the city during Barham's years with it, and he was the most successful editor and publisher in Petersburg at a time when that city was noted for its combative, highly personal journalism. Barham installed the city's first steam press, which helped him get out his newspaper more speedily than his competitors. Somehow he avoided personally alienating some of his influential political opponents, such as William Mahone, whose advocacy of biracial politics contrasted sharply with the strident white supremacy that Barham's newspaper proclaimed. Robert Henry Glass, editor of the *Petersburg Daily Post* from 1876 to 1879, posed the greatest challenge to Barham's journalistic ascendancy, but he also made the most enemies and eventually left Petersburg when he found himself unable to compete successfully with Barham.

In politics Barham sided successively with the Conservatives against the Radical Republicans after the Civil War, with the Funders against the Readjusters, with the Democrats against the Republicans, and in 1896 with the conservative gold Democrats against William Jennings Bryan's free silver Democrats. Barham took one plunge into elective politics. He won election to the House of Delegates as a Conservative in November 1875, following a campaign in which the *Index and Appeal* called for solidarity among conservative, native, white Virginia voters against carpetbaggers, Republicans, Radicals, and African Americans. Barham served only one two-year term, but his continued loyalty to the Democratic Party earned him appointment as postmaster of Petersburg in 1913.

Barham married Ellen M. Perkinson, of Petersburg, on 19 June 1872, and their one child was a son who was stillborn on 12 December 1872. Richard Pannell Barham died of heart and kidney failure at his home in Petersburg on 23 June 1917 and was buried in Blandford Cemetery in that city.

Edward A. Wyatt IV, *Preliminary Checklist for Petersburg, 1786–1876* (1949), 293–294; Census, Petersburg City, 1850; Chesterfield Co. Marriage Register; William D. Henderson, *Gilded Age City: Politics, Life and Labor in Petersburg, Virginia, 1874–1889* (1980), 48–49, 286–287; obituaries in *Petersburg Daily Index–Appeal* and *Richmond Times-Dispatch*, both 24 June 1917.

BRENT TARTER

BARKER, Lillie M. Easterby (4 January 1865– 10 July 1925), Baptist lay leader, was born in Columbia, South Carolina, the eldest of at least five daughters and one son of Samuel R. Easterby and Elizabeth Easterby. She grew up in Charleston, South Carolina, and received her early education at the Menninger School under the tutelage of Lewis Hall Shuck, a Virginia native who was then pastor of Charleston's First Baptist Church.

In the autumn of 1884, possibly at Shuck's suggestion, Easterby enrolled in the Chester Female Institute in Chester, Chesterfield County. On 11 January 1885 she was baptized into the membership of the Second Baptist Church of Richmond, at which time the minister asked her if she "loved the Savior well enough to leave home and work for him among the heathen." The question affected her deeply and brought about her lifelong commitment to the cause of missions. On 6 June 1888 in the First Baptist Church of Charleston, South Carolina, she married John Alexander Barker, a professor at the institute who was also pastor of two Baptist churches in Chesterfield County. They had no children. He had recently volunteered for missionary duty and they sailed on 1 September 1888 for Bahia, Brazil, under the auspices of the Foreign Mission Board of the Southern Baptist Church. Not long after they arrived she developed beriberi, and her physician ordered her back to the United States. The Barkers left Brazil early in 1890 and returned to Virginia.

John A. Barker became minister of the West End Baptist Church in Petersburg in 1891, moved to Clifton Forge in 1897, was pastor at Laurel Hill Baptist Church in Augusta County from 1905 to 1912, and served at two churches in Richmond from 1913 until his death in 1923. As soon as Lillie Barker's health improved she plunged into missionary activities and pursued the work without interruption everywhere her husband's ministry took them. She began as superintendent of the Woman's Missionary Union of the Portsmouth Baptist Association from 1891 to 1896, organizing women in the churches to raise money for the support of foreign missions. During the years 1897 and 1898 she took a leading part in the founding of the Woman's Missionary Union of Virginia. In November 1899 she was elected president, serving until 1901 and again from 1902 to 1905.

At the May 1903 annual national convention of the Woman's Missionary Union of the Southern Baptist Church, Barker was the second Virginian and the first person with actual missionary service to be elected president. She was reelected twice and served until 1906, when she declined to seek a fourth term. During her tenure the union opened the Margaret Home for Missionaries' Children in Greenville, South Carolina, to house children of missionary families while their parents were overseas. The union also finished raising money for its Tichenor Memorial Church Building Loan Fund during Barker's presidency, and it laid plans for a system of missionary societies for young people.

Barker served as the educational secretary of the Woman's Missionary Union of Virginia from 1916 to 1922 and also worked as the organization's college correspondent from 1916 to 1920. Until 1923 she often traveled in Virginia to lead mission study institutes, introduce the study of missions in Sunday school institutes, teach classes in colleges and missionary organizations, and speak to groups about the cause to which she had devoted her life. After John A. Barker died on 22 February 1923, she became executive secretary of the Southern Woman's Education Alliance, of which she had been a board member since 1914. In 1924 she enrolled at Columbia University in order better to equip herself for the new challenge of promoting the education of young women in the South, but she was unable to complete her course work. Lillie M. Easterby Barker died of cancer in a Richmond hospital on 10 July 1925 and was buried in Riverview Cemetery in Richmond.

Biographies in Sally O. Hannah and Wayne D. Hannah, *History of the Laurel Hill Baptist Church, 1851–1976* [ca. 1976], 78–80, and in Henry A. Tupper, *A Decade of Foreign Missions, 1880–1890* (1891), 631, 744–745; marriage reported in *Charleston (S.C.) News and Courier*, 8 June 1888, and *Religious Herald*, 14 June 1888; Lillian E. Barker, "Review of Woman's Work in Virginia," Woman's Missionary Union of Virginia, *Minutes of the Annual Session* 7 (1905): 20–28; Barker's 1905 presidential address, "What Woman Has Done for Missions," *Foreign Mission Journal* 55 (1905): 416–418; 56 (1905): 24–27; Juliette Mather, *Light Three Candles: History of Woman's Missionary Union of Virginia, 1874–1973* [1973], 57–62, 76–78 (por.); some Barker papers and por. at Woman's Missionary Union headquarters, Birmingham, Ala., and other documents at VBHS; death notices in *Richmond News Leader*, 11 July 1925, and *Richmond Times-Dispatch*, 12 July 1925; obituary by O. Latham Hatcher in *Religious Herald*, 30 July 1925; unsigned memorial in *Religious Herald*, 23 July 1925.

REES WATKINS

BARKER, William Horton (23 August 1889–12 August 1973), singer, generally known as Horton Barker or Hortie Barker, was born in Laurel Bloomery, Johnson County, Tennessee. He was the only son and younger of two children of Proctor Barker and Lucy Jane Edwards (or Dickens) Barker, both natives of North Carolina. Shortly after Barker was born, his father, an itinerant lumberman, died or left the family, and his mother married James E. Felts on 24 August 1890. Barker's mother had two daughters with Felts, and Felts had two daughters from his previous marriage. Lucy Felts was listed as a widow in the 1900 census of Washington County, Virginia, but family tradition indicates that she had divorced James Felts. Her children and stepchildren sometimes lived with relatives while she worked as a household servant.

At the age of three Horton Barker fell over a chair and injured his left eye. Eventually, he lost the vision in his right eye as well, and both eyes were removed on 13 November 1910. As a result of his impaired vision he spent much of his youth in institutions, attending the Tennessee School for the Blind in Nashville from the mid-1890s through the 1904–1905 school year. He then transferred to the Virginia School for the Deaf and the Blind in Staunton, which he attended until 1912. Barker learned to read Braille proficiently and enjoyed the Bible and the works of James Fenimore Cooper, Charles Dickens, and William Shakespeare. Music instruction played an important role at the Staunton school, where Barker joined the glee club and was reportedly a fine piano player. He also learned many traditional ballads from his mother and from his schoolmates.

Sometime after he left school Barker and his mother moved in with his sister, her husband, and their children in Saint Clair Bottom near Chilhowie in Smyth County. About 1930 Winston Wilkinson, a collector of traditional music, met Barker and introduced him to other students and collectors. Annabel Morris Buchanan, an organizer of the White Top Mountain Folk Festival, visited Barker in 1931 to collect songs, and he became a regular and highly valued performer at the festival in the 1930s, winning numerous first prizes in the ballad contests. He performed for Eleanor Roosevelt at White Top in 1933 and reprised the performance in a 1937 visit to the White House.

Many folklorists recorded Barker. Virginia collector Arthur Kyle Davis Jr. captured six songs on 15 August 1932 in Chilhowie, and during an April 1939 visit Herbert Halpert recorded seven songs for the Library of Congress's Archive of American Folk-Song. Barker's version of "The Farmer's Curst Wife" appeared on the first set of records issued by the Archive. W. Amos Abrams, a professor and folklorist, taped several Barker performances at Appalachian State Teachers' College in Boone, North Carolina, in 1941 and 1942. At that time Barker and a young folklorist and entrepreneur, Richard Chase, were jointly entertaining audiences at colleges and universities. Barker sang ballads and Chase told Jack tales, a cycle of stories about the adventures of a young trickster-hero named Jack. Barker also appeared in *To Hear Your Banjo Play* (1947), a seminal folklore film narrated by Pete Seeger.

Popular interest in folk music waned, however, and little is known of Barker's life during the remainder of the 1940s and the early part of the 1950s. Field-workers made two recordings of his singing in 1950 and Chase recorded him in 1954. Late in the 1950s Barker tramped throughout Tennessee and North Carolina singing gospel songs with a Bible lecturer. When interest in folk music revived, he thrilled a new generation of music lovers at the University of Chicago Folk Festival in 1961. Sandy Paton, folksinger and collector, saw Barker at the festival and recorded him at Beech Creek, Avery County, North Carolina. These recordings were issued as an album in 1962. Barker also performed at the Newport Folk Festival in Rhode Island and the Festival of American Folklife in Washington, D.C.

Barker sang a cappella in a high, clear voice. The restricted range of his recorded oeuvre, comprised of ballads and hymns, probably reflects not his own interests but those of the collectors who sought him out. Although always in greatest demand for his ballad singing, as a typical folk songster he continually expanded his repertoire with songs that he heard and liked, learning so-called plantation songs, gospel tunes, and popular ditties. He was especially known for his versions of the hymns "Wayfaring Stranger" and "Amazing Grace."

Barker's influence on musical traditions both within and beyond Virginia is difficult to gauge. More significant was his place as a featured performer in an influential movement typified by the White Top Mountain Folk Festival, which promoted the ideal of a pure Anglo-American heritage in Appalachia unspoiled by popular culture, commercial hillbilly music, and other outside influences. Barker met his audience's expectations with a humorous wit and a straightforward delivery of intriguing ballads and moving hymns.

Barker moved to Marion after the death of his sister in 1963. Declining health forced him to give up performing about 1967. He spent several years at a rest home in Marion, and after an operation for a broken hip he was sent to a local nursing home. Horton Barker died in Marion on 12 August 1973 and was buried in Macedonia Cemetery in Smyth County.

W. Amos Abrams, "Horton Barker: Folk Singer Supreme," *North Carolina Folklore Journal* 22 (1974): 141–153; birth date in obituary and other secondary sources; variant birth date of Feb. 1889 in Census, Davidson Co., Tenn., 1900; feature articles with pors. in *Marion Smyth County News*, 11 Oct. 1951, 16 Apr. 1987, and *Washington Post*, 24 Mar. 1963; Sandy Paton, "Horton Barker—An Appreciation," *Sing Out!* 13, no. 2 (1963): 5–8; David E. Whisnant, *All That Is Native and Fine: The Politics of Culture in an American Region* (1983), 193, 197, 233–235 (por.); Arthur Kyle Davis Jr., *Folk-Songs of Virginia* (1949), 343; Barker recordings by Chase, Davis, Halpert, Sam Eskin, and Sidney Robertson Cowell and Maud Karpeles, Archive of Folk Culture, American Folklife Center, LC; LC issued selected songs recorded by Halpert on Alan Lomax, ed., *Anglo-American Ballards* (AFS L1) and Benjamin A. Botkin, ed., *Anglo-American Ballads* (AFS L7); commercial recordings include *Horton Barker: Traditional Singer*, Folkways Records album with liner notes by Paton (1962), and *Virginia Traditions: Ballads from British Tradition*, BRI Recordings album (1976); obituaries in *Bristol Virginia-Tennessean*, 13 Aug. 1973, and *Marion Smyth County News*, 14 Aug. 1973.

GREGG D. KIMBALL
VAUGHAN WEBB

BARKSDALE, Alfred Dickinson (17 July 1892–16 August 1972), United States District Court judge, was born in Houston (now Halifax), the fourth of five sons and eighth of nine children of William Randolph Barksdale, a lawyer, and Hallie Bailey Craddock Barksdale. He was educated in county schools and at Cluster Springs Academy in Halifax County and graduated from the Virginia Military Institute in 1911, ranking eleventh in a class of fifty-two. Barksdale earned a law degree from the University of Virginia in 1915, then settled in Lynchburg. On 15 December 1934 he married Louisa Estill Winfree Phillips, who had one son from her first marriage. They had two daughters.

Dick Barksdale, as he was familiarly known, joined the Musketeers, a volunteer military unit, with which he was stationed in Brownsville, Texas, from June 1916 to February 1917. With America's entry into World War I he enlisted in the regular army in July 1917, serving in France during the summer and autumn of 1918 as a captain in Company M, 116th Infantry, 29th Division. In October 1918 he led a successful attack on a German machine-gun emplacement and a few days later captured another single-handed. Barksdale's bravery earned him the Distinguished Service Cross, the Croix de Guerre with Palm, and the Chevalier of the Legion of Honor.

After the war Barksdale spent a few months in Europe and attended classes in Paris and England before returning to his law practice in Lynchburg. He soon became involved in local Democratic Party politics, serving twice, for a total of ten years, as chairman of the city's Democratic committee. Barksdale won elective office once, serving from 1924 to 1928 in the Senate of Virginia for the district comprising Campbell County and Lynchburg. On 12 July 1938 the governor appointed him judge of the Sixth Judicial Circuit. He served for a year and a half, during part of which he sat on a three-judge panel that heard a controversial annexation suit the city of Richmond brought against Henrico County. Barksdale joined in the court's opinion that granted the city several square miles of county land, but he added an obiter dictum highly critical of the city's cumbersome, bicameral council system.

In December 1939 President Franklin D. Roosevelt named Barksdale federal judge of the Western District of Virginia. He easily won senatorial confirmation and served from February 1940 until his retirement in 1957. Two of the cases Barksdale heard during World War II attracted national attention. He presided over the trial in New York of two dozen members of the German-American Bund charged and convicted of conspiring to counsel resistance to the draft. In October 1942 Barksdale imposed the maximum allowable prison sentence of five years on the convicted men. When handing down the decision he carefully stated that the convictions should cast no doubt on the patriotism of other Americans of German birth or ancestry.

In January 1944 Barksdale ruled in his Lynchburg courtroom on the portal-to-portal pay controversy, a key issue in the 1943 nationwide coal miners' strike. Workers argued that time spent in transit between mine entrances and the underground coal seams constituted part of the workday, but mine operators disagreed. Barksdale issued a declaratory judgment in favor of a southwestern Virginia mining company, Jewel Ridge Coal Corporation, holding that in passing the Fair Labor Standards Act of 1938, Congress had not meant to change the wage structure of the coal-mining industry so radically as to require mine operators to pay portal-to-portal wages. The United Mine Workers of America announced that it would appeal, but the Supreme Court ruled in an unrelated case in March 1944 that the law required portal-to-portal pay for iron miners. Following that controlling precedent, the Fourth Circuit Court of Appeals reversed Barksdale's ruling.

Barksdale retired in the summer of 1957 but still heard cases occasionally for other judges. He served on the boards of visitors of Hollins College for twenty-five years and of the University of Virginia for ten. Virginia Military Institute established a scholarship fund in his name for alumni studying law. A convivial man who enjoyed composing doggerel verse, Alfred Dickinson Barksdale died at his home in Lynchburg on 16 August 1972 and was buried in Spring Hill Cemetery in that city.

Alfred Dickinson Barksdale Papers, UVA; Charles Sterling Hutcheson Papers, LVA; *Richmond News Leader*, 12 July 1919; Glass and Glass, *Virginia Democracy*, 2:73–74; Barksdale's comments on Richmond city government in *Richmond Times-Dispatch*, 23 Jan. 1940; *New York Times*, 22 Oct. 1942, 26 Jan. 1944; *Richmond Times-Dispatch*, 26 Jan. 1944; obituaries in *Lynchburg Daily Advance*, *Lynchburg News*, *Richmond News Leader*, and *Richmond Times-Dispatch*, all 17 Aug. 1972; editorial tribute in *Lynchburg Daily Advance*, 18 Aug. 1972; memorial in *Virginia Bar Association Proceedings* (1973): 306–308 (por.).

Brent Tarter

BARNES, Manly Howell (25 July 1854–13 November 1936), member of the Convention of 1901–1902, was born in James City County, the youngest of six sons and one daughter of William Henry Barnes, a farmer, and Lucy Saunders Williams Barnes. He attended Baltimore City College and graduated in 1880 from Saint John's College in Annapolis. Barnes read law while teaching for two years, then attended a summer session at the University of Virginia's law school. In 1882 he opened a law office in Providence Forge and soon extended his practice to nearby Williamsburg and the adjacent counties. On 7 July 1885 he married Maggie A. Ferrel, of Richmond. They had two sons and one daughter.

Barnes was elected commonwealth's attorney of New Kent County in 1883 and served without interruption until 1922. He was also a member of the Senate of Virginia from 1893 to 1898, representing Charles City, Elizabeth City, James City, King William, New Kent, Warwick, and York Counties. In the spring of 1901 local Democratic Party leaders asked him to be a candidate for a state constitutional convention, other prospective candidates withdrew, and he was elected without opposition from the district that included the counties of Charles City, James City, New Kent, Warwick, and York, and the cities of Newport News and Williamsburg. Barnes served on the Committee on the Organization and Government of Counties and spoke several times on the floor of the convention. He argued for quadrennial sessions of the General Assembly and introduced a resolution "to prevent party legislation" by requiring the assembly to consider public and private bills separately. Probably reflecting his frustrations as a state senator, Barnes asked that the Committee on the Legislative Department find some means to stop "hasty and ill-considered legislation" from being enacted during the final, hurried days of a session. He voted for the suffrage article that was implemented in order to reduce the number of black voters but broke with the Democratic Party majority and unsuccessfully voted to submit the constitution to the voters for ratification.

Barnes was interested in public education. He served on the New Kent County School Board for almost forty years and sat on the board of visitors of the College of William and Mary from 1906 to 1912. His reputation as a fine public speaker was borne out by his remarks at the convention, which marked him as a witty and forceful advocate. Manly Howell Barnes died at his home in Providence Forge on 13 November 1936 and was buried in Hollywood Cemetery in Richmond.

Bruce, Tyler, and Morgan, *History of Virginia*, 4:22–23; BVS Birth Register, James City Co.; Census, James City Co., 1850–1870; BVS Marriage Register, Henrico Co.; Election Records, no. 47, RG 13, LVA; *Richmond Times*, 12 June 1901, 6, 8 (por.); *Journal of 1901–1902 Convention*, 50, 80, 486–487, 504; *Proceedings and Debates of 1901–1902 Convention*, 1:556–559, 877–878, 958–961, 1294; *Resolutions of 1901–1902 Convention*, no. 65; *Convention of 1901–1902 Photographs* (por.); obituaries in *Richmond News Leader* and *Richmond Times-Dispatch*, both 14 Nov. 1936.

BRENT TARTER

BARNES, Thomas H. (28 May 1831–4 June 1913), physician and member of the Convention of 1901–1902, was born in southwest Nansemond County, the youngest of three or four sons and as many as five children of James Barnes, a farmer, and Elizabeth Barnes. He attended the University of Virginia from 1849 to 1852 and graduated from the Medical College of Virginia in 1853. Barnes then returned to Nansemond County and practiced medicine there until he retired about 1888. He frequently attended local fox hunts and was a popular figure known for his long, full beard and for his height, which earned him the nickname "Tall Sycamore of Nansemond." He did not serve in the military during the Civil War and never married.

Barnes was active in local politics for much of his adult life. He served on the Nansemond County Board of Supervisors from early in the 1870s until 1901 and in the House of Delegates from 1874 to 1877. From 1887 to 1894 he represented Isle of Wight, Nansemond, and Southampton Counties in the Senate of Virginia. Barnes was also county chairman of the Democratic Party for many years. In April 1901 he was his party's unanimous choice for Nansemond's seat in a state constitutional convention, and he faced no Republican opposition in the May election. Barnes served on the Committee on the Elective Franchise and chaired the Committee on the Organization and Government of Counties. He took little part in the debates and voted with the majorities that adopted a suffrage article designed to reduce the number of black voters and implemented the constitution without a popular referendum.

Beginning in 1888 and 1889, respectively, Barnes sat for the rest of his life on the boards of visitors of the College of William and Mary and the Medical College of Virginia, serving as president of the latter from 1907 on. Thomas H. Barnes died at his home in Suffolk on 4 June 1913.

Tyler, *Men of Mark*, 4:26–27; Census, Nansemond Co., 1830–1850; *Suffolk Herald*, 5, 12 Apr. 1901; Election Records, no. 47, RG 13, LVA; *Richmond Daily Dispatch*, 12 June 1901; *Journal of 1901–1902 Convention*, 49, 50, 486–487, 504; *Proceedings and Debates of 1901–1902 Convention*, 1:867; *Convention of 1901–1902 Photographs* (por.); two Barnes letters in Lyon G. Tyler Presidential Papers, W&M; obituaries in *Norfolk Virginian-Pilot* (por.) and *Richmond Times-Dispatch*, both 5 June 1913; memorial in *Virginia Medical Semi-Monthly* 18 (1913): 132.

BRENT TARTER

BARNHARDT, James Monroe (16 August 1898–5 July 1975), poultry farmer, was born in Pioneer Mills, Cabarrus County, North Carolina, the fourth of five sons and eleventh of thirteen children of John Addison Barnhardt and Sarah Eliza McClellan Barnhardt. After graduating from North Carolina State College of Agriculture and Engineering in Raleigh in 1918, Barnhardt spent a year in the army and then purchased a 136-acre farm on Urbanna Creek in Middlesex County. On 17 March 1920 he married Margaret Healy, of Urbanna, whom he had met while in college. They had two daughters and one son.

Barnhardt was one of the few farmers to grow cotton as far north as the Rappahannock River following World War I, but after the market declined in the 1920s he turned to poultry raising. His venture was unsuccessful. His chickens contracted coccidiosis, a parasitic disease that killed much of his flock and contaminated the soil. In 1928 he switched to ducks, which were less susceptible to such diseases. Initially he bought fifty White Peking ducklings, a hardy breed with long bodies and deep breasts favored by commercial duck farmers. Lacking a brooder house, he gathered the birds in boxes around the kitchen stove for warmth, a novelty that delighted his small children but proved a distraction to their mother.

A resourceful man, Barnhardt used every available means to improve the operation of his farm and keep down costs, and he enlarged his duck-farming operation rapidly. During the 1930s, when he could not afford the protein-rich foods vital for the health of his flock, he purchased inexpensive, unwanted fish from nearby fisheries, steamed them, and combined them with other foods to provide a nutritious diet for his ducks. He later recycled the nutrients by hosing manure from concrete slabs beneath the duck houses into a cement holding tank and then pumping the liquid into a truck that he equipped with a spreader to apply the rich fertilizer to his grainfields. By 1951 the process was saving him about $2,000 annually. He also built a modern, efficient mill that compressed fish, grain, and other food products into pellets that he fed to the ducks.

Barnhardt's primary domestic market for dressed duck was the corridor encompassing Norfolk, Richmond, Washington, and Baltimore, but he also shipped his product to Chicago and Florida, and overseas to Germany, other countries in Europe, and Saudi Arabia. He exported by-products for use in soups to Hong Kong and through Hong Kong to other destinations in Asia. As his duck production for commercial markets expanded, he also greatly increased his efficiency in shipping duck feathers, a valuable by-product, by using his old cotton baler to increase from 2,500 pounds to 12,000 pounds the quantity of feathers he could pack on each truck. Early in the 1950s the farm's dressing plant was handling about 65,000 ducks a year, packing the fowl in crates and keeping the containers in a freezer plant able to store 40,000 pounds of dressed duck. During the peak season of June and July, the farm's 30,000 birds consumed nearly four tons of food daily. As the number of ducks grew beyond his capacity to feed them from the productions of his own fields, Barnhardt purchased most of his additional foodstuffs from other Middlesex County farms, enriching the local economy and making his duck farm the largest business enterprise in the county.

Barnhardt operated his concern as a sole proprietorship until 9 November 1961, when he incorporated it as Barnhardt Farms, with a capital stock of $200,000. Barnhardt, his wife, and their son, James Monroe Barnhardt Jr., constituted the initial board of directors. In 1963 the company produced 2,287,820 pounds of ready-to-cook duck. By 1975, the peak year of the company's production, Barnhardt Farms, Incorporated, employed 140 people, processed more than a million ducks, and was the largest employer in the county. The firm maintained its own breeder flocks, hatchery, grow-out operation (that is, the raising from chick to full-sized duck), feed-manufacturing mill, processing plant, and cold storage and sales facilities. As the only commercial duck farm in Virginia and the biggest in the South, although not the largest in the United States, its nearly self-sufficient operation made it one of the most successful enterprises of its kind in the country.

James Monroe Barnhardt retired from the presidency of the firm in 1968, but he remained active in its management and served for many years as a member of the National Duckling Council. He died at his home in Middlesex County on 5 July 1975 and was buried in the cemetery at Christ Episcopal Church, of which he had been a vestryman.

Feature article in *Richmond News Leader*, 15 Mar. 1951 (por.); Jessie M. DeBusk et al., eds., *Family Histories of Middlesex County, Virginia* (1982), 238; family and business history information confirmed in interviews with daughter Elizabeth Barnhardt Sanders, grandson James Monroe Barnhardt III, and Taylor L. Grizzard; BVS Marriage Register, Middlesex Co.; annual reports of Virginia Department of Agriculture, Poultry and Egg and Dairy Grading Section, during 1960s and early 1970s; obituary in *Urbanna Southside Sentinel*, 10 July 1975.

DONALD W. GUNTER

BARNUM, Frances Courtenay Baylor. See **BAYLOR, Frances Courtenay**.

BARR, Frank Stringfellow (15 January 1897–3 February 1982), educator, was born in Suffolk, the youngest of two sons and one daughter of William Alexander Barr and Ida Stringfellow Barr. He spent part of his childhood in New Orleans, where his father, a lawyer who became an Episcopal clergyman, was serving as a minister. Known to his friends as "Winkie," Barr never used his first name after he became an adult. He entered Tulane College in 1913, but the following year, with encouragement from the author and essayist Albert Jay Nock, he transferred to the University of Virginia, from which he received a B.A. in philosophy and English literature in 1916 and an M.A. in 1917. He joined the ambulance service of the United States Army in 1917 and served in France until the end of World War I, attaining the rank of sergeant.

Stringfellow Barr began his career in higher education in earnest in the autumn of 1919, when he entered Oxford University's Balliol College as a Rhodes scholar. Although he had not taken a single course in history at the University of Virginia, his fellow Rhodes scholar Scott Buchanan persuaded him to study modern history. Barr received a B.A. with honors in 1921 and an M.A. in 1930. On 13 August 1921 he married Gladys Baldwin, a theology student at King's College, London. They had no children. Barr was awarded a fellowship for postgraduate study at the University of Ghent in Belgium, where he studied in 1922 and 1923. He also received a diploma from the University of Paris, but he never received a doctorate.

Barr returned to the United States in 1923 and spent a year in Asheville, North Carolina, before accepting a position as assistant professor of history at the University of Virginia. He became an associate professor in 1927 and professor of modern European history in 1930. He also served as an advisory editor of the new *Virginia Quarterly Review* from 1926 to 1930 and in the latter year succeeded the founding editor, James Southall Wilson, as the review's editor. Barr's four years as editor were highly successful. He attracted to the journal writers of such high quality and renown as Sherwood Anderson, James Branch Cabell, Aldous Huxley, Howard Mumford Jones, Andrew Lytle, André Maurois, Allen Tate, Robert Penn Warren, and Stark Young.

In 1930 Barr engaged John Crowe Ransom, one of the so-called Southern Agrarians, in a public debate before 3,000 people in Richmond. Ransom opposed industrialization in the South and many of the changes then taking place in the southern states. Barr, on the other hand, urged the South to learn from the experiences of other states so as to benefit from and direct economic and social change. The event was widely covered, discussed in the *New York Times*, and brought Barr national publicity.

Barr relinquished the editorship of the *Virginia Quarterly Review* in 1934 to complete a biography of Giuseppe Mazzini, the first of his eleven books, which he published as *Mazzini: Portrait of an Exile* (1935). Even as he was busily editing and teaching, Barr was developing a new conception of a good liberal arts education. Together with Scott Buchanan, who had joined the University of Virginia's philosophy department, and another Oxonian, political scientist Robert Kent Gooch, he produced a plan for a significant restructuring of the university's academic regime. The reforms probably went beyond what the university's administrators were willing to accept and, as its president, John Lloyd Newcomb, predicted, the changes could not be financed during the Great Depression, but the report attracted the attention of the young president of the University of Chicago, Robert Maynard Hutchens, who invited Barr and Buchanan to his institution. Taking a year's leave of absence in 1936, Barr undertook a comprehensive investigation of the undergraduate curriculum of American higher education.

Before his year at the University of Chicago ended, Barr was offered the presidency of Saint John's College in Annapolis. The small institution, which began as a school late in the seventeenth century and was chartered as a college in 1784, had lost its accreditation and was in financial trouble. Barr accepted and assumed his new duties in July 1937. With Buchanan as one of the deans, he launched an educational revolution. They introduced a radically new four-year curriculum devoted entirely to the study of the world's one hundred greatest books, which the students read and discussed in seminars, tutorials, and laboratories. There were no other required courses, no electives, and no choices. Barr remained at Saint John's for a decade and placed the college and its innovative educational program in the forefront of educational reform.

In 1947 Barr resigned to start a similar college near Pittsfield, Massachusetts, but the institution never opened its doors, and in 1948 he became president of the new Foundation for World Government, an office he held for the next decade. The foundation used its million-dollar endowment to promote research into solutions for world poverty and seek nonviolent answers to international problems. In 1951 Barr moved the foundation's offices from New York City to Charlottesville, and he returned to the University of Virginia for two years as a visiting professor of political science, offering undergraduates an abbreviated version of the great books program. He joined the Rutgers University faculty as a professor of humanities in 1955 and served until he retired from teaching in 1964. From 1966 to 1969 he was a fellow at the Center for the Study of Democratic Institutions in Santa Barbara, California.

Throughout his career Barr advocated numerous reforms. He criticized American foreign policy during the Cold War, denounced persecution of socialists and communists during the 1950s, and condemned Virginia's program of Massive Resistance to the desegregation of public schools. Always an active scholar who contributed to numerous reviews and collections of essays, he spoke and wrote frequently on the benefits of studying the great books of western civilization, and in 1971 he published a book that he had drafted in 1948, *Voices That Endured: The Great Books and the Active Life*. Barr's other principal books included *The Pilgrimage of Western Man: His Search for One World from 1500 to Armistice II* (1949); *Citizens of the World* (1952); a caricature of higher education, *Purely Academic: A Novel* (1958); *The Will of Zeus: A History of Greece from the Origins of Hellenic Culture to the Death of Alexander* (1961); its sequel, *The Mask of Jove: A History of Graeco-Roman Civilization from the Death of Alexander to the Death of Constantine* (1966); and *The Three Worlds of Man* (1963).

Barr retired in 1969 and moved to Kingston, Somerset County, New Jersey, where his wife died in 1974. In May 1979 he returned to Virginia and moved into a nursing home in Alexandria. Stringfellow Barr died there of pneumonia on 3 February 1982, and his body was cremated.

Oral history interview, 12 Sept. 1972, and autobiographical letter to Michael Plunkett, 10 Mar. 1975, UVA Archives; Gladys Baldwin Barr letters in Baldwin Family Papers and Barr letters in various collections, UVA; Census, Richmond City, 1900; Stringfellow Barr, "A College in Session," *Atlantic Monthly* 163 (July 1941): 41–49; obituaries in *New York Times* (por.) and *Richmond Times-Dispatch*, both 5 Feb. 1982, *Newsweek*, 15 Feb. 1982, 92, and *Time*, 15 Feb. 1982, 65.

STAIGE D. BLACKFORD

BARRADALL, Edward (bap. 17 October 1703–19 June 1743), member of the House of Burgesses and attorney general of Virginia, was probably born in London, the eldest of three sons and fourth of nine children of Henry Barradall and Catherine Blumfield Barradall. He was christened on 17 October 1703 in the parish of Saint Paul's, Covent Garden. Both of his brothers and two of his sisters settled in the vicinity of Williamsburg during the 1720s or 1730s, and all four died there unmarried.

Barradall studied law and had moved to Virginia by February 1731. On 14 December 1732 he presented a license to practice law to the Caroline County Court, and his name also appears on documents prepared in Richmond and Westmoreland Counties before the end of that year. He lived initially in Sittenburne Parish in Richmond County but soon moved to Westmoreland County, where he probably acted as a legal agent for Thomas Fairfax, baron Fairfax of Cameron, proprietor of the Northern Neck.

About 1734 Barradall moved to Williamsburg to represent the proprietary in the General Court and before the Council. He probably also expanded his private law practice. Barradall was appointed to the James City County Court on 5 May 1736 and became presiding justice on 15 December 1737. He was elected mayor of Williamsburg at the end of November 1736, and after his one-year term expired he became the city's recorder. On 3 or 4 November 1738 he was elected to the House of Burgesses to represent the College of William and Mary. Barradall chaired the Committee for Courts of Justice and served frequently on drafting committees. He helped prepare legislation to improve the administration of orphans' estates, settle boundary disputes in Northern Neck counties, arbitrate inheritances, and facilitate complicated estate management. He also advocated removal by the Crown of its prohibition against importing foreign salt directly to Virginia, and he drafted bills to tax imported slaves at a prohibitive rate. In 1740 he probably authored the law that denied transported felons accused of committing crimes in Virginia the usual right to a trial by a local jury. The new law allowed "bystanders" who were in Williamsburg during the term of the General Court to serve on the juries. On 11 June 1740 Barradall introduced into the House of Burgesses a bill for the recruitment of soldiers to fight in the war against Spain from among "such able-bodied men as do not follow or exercise any lawful calling or employment, or have not some other lawful and sufficient support and maintenance." The measure became law, helped rid the colony of a number of jobless young men, many of whom died in the Caribbean, and provided a precedent for future colonial impressments of soldiers.

The governor, William Gooch, had named Barradall attorney general of Virginia during the week following incumbent John Clayton's death on 18 November 1737. Gooch also recommended Barradall to the king for a permanent appointment to that office and to the judgeship of the Court of Vice-Admiralty, a position the attorney general customarily held. The royal warrant was duly issued on 7 March 1738, and Barradall took the required oaths before the governor's Council in Williamsburg on 26 October. He served as attorney general until his death, but the fragmentary extant records do not give a clear picture of his performance in office. The Council and the House of Burgesses frequently called on him for legal advice and drafting assistance, but he became best known for his digest of cases heard in the Virginia courts during his time in Williamsburg. Other attorneys and attorneys general also recorded arguments in the General Court, but Barradall's reports are the most numerous and detailed of the few that survive. An eighteenth-century transcript of Barradall's reports, now at the Library of Virginia, provided the copy text for part of Robert Thomas Barton's *Virginia Colonial Decisions* (1909), an important source for the study of colonial legal history. Barton regarded Barradall as "more labored and less interesting" in his recording style than Sir John Randolph, the famous compiler of the next-largest number of known colonial reports, but argued that Barradall showed a "greater display of learning, and more evidence of preparation and research." Barton concluded that Randolph, while perhaps not as good a legal scholar as Barradall, may have been a better advocate.

On 5 January 1736 Barradall married Sarah Fitzhugh, daughter of former councillor William Fitzhugh. They are not known to have had any children. Edward Barradall died in Williamsburg on 19 June 1743 and was buried in the yard of Bruton Parish Church. His unmarried sisters later erected a large monument over the site, where his widow and his two brothers were also buried.

Biographies in Robert T. Barton, ed., *Virginia Colonial Decisions* (1909), 1:243–248, and W. Hamilton Bryson, ed., *The Virginia Law Reporters before 1880* (1977), 71–74; William H. Hunt, ed., *The Registers of St. Paul's Church, Covent Garden, London* (1906–1909), 1:124; Barton and others assert that Barradall was called to the bar from the Inner Temple, but its records provide no confirmation; Patent Book, 14:151, RG 4, LVA; Caroline Co. Order Book (1732–1740), 32, 47; Richmond Co. Account Book (1724–1783), 58; marriage documented in George H. S. King, ed., *Register of Saint Paul's Parish, 1715–1798* (1960), 7; *Williamsburg Virginia Gazette*, 25 Nov. 1737; death recorded in William Gooch to secretary of state, 27 June 1743, PRO CO 5/1337, fols. 279–280; gravestone in Bruton Parish churchyard, Williamsburg.

BRENT TARTER

BARRET, William (29 November 1786–20 January 1871), tobacco manufacturer, was born in Richmond, the fifth of six sons and seventh of eight children of John Barret and Mary Strachan Barret, and lived in the city all his life. His father was a native of Louisa County who became a Richmond merchant during the 1780s and served as mayor in 1791–1792 and again in 1793–1794. Family tradition relates that William Barret became ill while attending the Richmond Theatre with friends on the evening of 26 December 1811 and went home. Shortly thereafter the theater caught fire and seventy-two people died, including several of his friends.

As a young man Barret joined the Richmond Light Infantry Blues, a prestigious militia company. He and his comrades marched to Portsmouth amid rising tensions after the British warship *Leopard* attacked the American frigate *Chesapeake* in 1807, but they saw no action. During the War of 1812 the unit mustered several times in anticipation of British attacks but never engaged in hostilities. Barret rose from private to orderly sergeant during the company's diligent but relatively uneventful service.

Barret's long business career probably began in the family mercantile house and included participation in the 1810s in the tobacco dealership of Higginbotham, Barret, and Company. Sometime during the next decade he opened one of the first large factories in Richmond to manufacture chewing tobacco and quickly amassed what a contemporary called a very large fortune. In 1844 he purchased the sizable brick factory and offices he had rented at Fourteenth and Cary Streets as well as an extensive brick tobacco factory on Main Street between Twenty-Third and Twenty-Fourth Streets. By 1850 his workforce of approximately 100 slaves (about half of whom were probably his own, with the remainder hired from other owners) annually produced 400,000 pounds of chewing tobacco that he sold for about $100,000. By this time one of Barret's slaves had gained considerable notoriety. In 1849 tobacco worker Henry "Box" Brown escaped to Philadelphia in a box shipped from Richmond and became a well-known abolitionist author and speaker.

Early in the 1850s Barret enlarged his factories, and in 1860 he produced 590,000 pounds of tobacco. His firm was one of the ten or twelve largest in the city, which then dominated the chewing tobacco industry in the United States. Barret's best-known brand, called Negro Head, was a rich mixture prepared from carefully chosen strains of tobacco and large quantities of molasses. He marketed it in England and Australia.

Barret was a wealthy bachelor in 1844 when he built a tasteful and elegant house at the corner of Fifth and Cary Streets. The most discerning student of Richmond's residential architecture, Mary Wingfield Scott, stated that Barret's house marked "the high point of Classic Revival architecture in Richmond." On 11 December 1845 he married Margaret Elizabeth Williams Palmer, the widow of James Keith Palmer. They had no children. The Barrets were fond of society, literature, music, and travel. Margaret Barret died on 6 May 1852 in Charleston, South Carolina.

Barret retired about the time the Civil War began. Although never the largest tobacco manufacturer in Richmond, he was one of the wealthiest. He had already invested a large portion of his profits, and he prudently placed the bulk of his wealth in England. His apparent decision to avoid any considerable investment in Confederate bonds enabled him to remain one of the richest men in the city until he died. Barret provided lavishly for his many nieces, nephews, and friends when he composed his last will on 8 April 1869. His estate may have been worth the half-million dollars estimated in a local newspaper. After the business district burned in April 1865, his surviving Richmond real estate alone was still worth more than $34,000. Even after all his generous bequests were doubled and distributed, enough remained to provide $50,000 for each of three Richmond orphanages: the Richmond Male Orphan Society, the Female Humane Orphan Association, and Saint Paul's Church Home.

Barret's life ended tragically. Always fearful of fire following his lucky escape in 1811, he took unusual precautions with his stoves and fireplaces, but after breakfast on 20 January 1871, while lighting his pipe, William Barret set fire to the hem of his dressing gown and was almost immediately engulfed in flames. He died a few hours later and was buried beside his wife in Hollywood Cemetery.

Pendleton family Bible cited in George Warren Chappelear, *Barret* (1934), 12, gives birth date, as does gravestone in Hollywood Cemetery; brief biography in *Richmond Portraits, in an Exhibition of Makers of Richmond, 1737–1860* (1949), 13 (por.); John A. Cutchins, *A Famous Command: The Richmond Light Infantry Blues* (1934), 296, 298, 322; Richmond Light Infantry Blues Minutes (1794–1883), 15–16, LVA; Census, Industrial Schedules, Richmond City, 1850, 1860; Personal Property Tax Returns, Richmond City, 1810–1871, RG 48, LVA; marriage and wife's death reported in *Richmond Semi-Weekly Enquirer*, 6 Jan. 1846, and *Richmond Semi-Weekly Whig*, 14 May 1852; Mary Wingfield Scott, *Houses of Old Richmond* (1941), 220–223, and *Old Richmond Neighborhoods* (1950), 182; Richmond City Hustings Court Will Book, 1:64–67; estate value estimated in *Richmond Daily Dispatch*, 25 Jan. 1871; obituaries in *Richmond Daily Dispatch*, *Richmond Daily Enquirer*, and *Richmond Daily Whig*, all 21 Jan. 1871.

BRENT TARTER

BARRETT, Clifton Waller (1 June 1901–6 November 1991), shipping executive and book collector, was born in Alexandria, the second of four sons and second of five children of Robert South Barrett and Annie Viola Tupper Barrett. Until age six he lived in Mexico City, where his father's business interests had taken him, but he returned to Alexandria and grew up there in the home of his grandmother Katherine Harwood Waller Barrett. He graduated from Alexandria High School in 1917 and attended the University of Virginia from 1917 to 1920, although during World War I he interrupted his university studies for a short period of service with the Student Army Training Corps at Plattsburgh, New York. Barrett served as business manager of the *University of Virginia Magazine* and recorder for the Washington Literary Society, early indications of his interest in literature.

C. Waller Barrett, as he signed most of his publications, left school suddenly in January 1920, for what may have been financial reasons involving a dispute with his father. A month later he found work as a clerk in the New York headquarters of the Munson Steam Ship Line. On 24 April 1924 he married Cornelia Corinne Hughes, the owner's secretary. They had five sons and one daughter. Barrett and Walter Ulsh left Munson in 1932 to start their own shipping firm, the North Atlantic and Gulf Steam Ship Company. Beginning with a single ship that they leased in 1932, they rapidly expanded the company into a major commercial line employing a large fleet. Taking advantage of neglected opportunities and using leased ships and modern navigational techniques, the line prospered, netting a large share of the profitable transportation of sugar from Cuba to the United States.

During World War II Barrett served as director of sugar transportation for the Atlantic Headquarters of the War Shipping Administration. He overcame a shortage of ships by organizing a barge service between Havana and Port Everglades, Florida, in order to move 1.5 millon tons of sugar to the United States. From 1952 to 1954 he served as president of the Cuban Chamber of Commerce in the United States, and he wrote numerous articles for commercial journals on Cuba's economic situation. Barrett increased his wealth with wise investments in diverse stocks. In 1954 he retired as president of North Atlantic and its subsidiary Norgulf so that he could indulge his love of literature and book collecting.

Barrett had been nurtured in an atmosphere of books, and the library was the most important room in his house. By the 1930s he had begun to frequent bookstores in the Wall Street area during his lunch hours. He began serious and systematic collecting in 1939 with a first edition of Booth Tarkington's 1903 novel *Cherry*. Always an ardent reader, Barrett regularly spent the hours commuting by train between Manhattan and his home on Long Island studying American literary history. He began methodically purchasing books and manuscripts, becoming known to members of the book trade in and out of New York, and gaining the acquaintance of well-known bibliophiles and scholars. He was one of the first serious collectors of nineteenth-century American fiction and poetry, a genre that was relatively unexplored at the time. At the suggestion and with the advice of his fellow collector Carroll Atwood Wilson and Professor James Southall Wilson, of the University of Virginia Department of English, Barrett began assembling a comprehensive library of American fiction, poetry, drama, and essays. He also became an active director of the publishing firm of Holt, Rinehart, and Winston, engaging thereby in an area of allied literary interest.

Barrett's growing eminence as a bibliophile of American literature was recognized as early as 1950, when he first addressed the Bibliographical Society of America. During the next four decades he became prominent in American cultural circles and held offices or directorships in many leading library societies, historical foundations, scholarly associations, and academic boards, the most significant being the Bibliographical Society of America; the distinguished Grolier Club in New York, of which he was president from 1957 to 1961; the American Antiquarian Society; and the Columbia University, John Carter Brown, New York Public, Pierpont Morgan, and Princeton University Libraries. He shouldered leadership responsibilities in such Virginia institutions as the James Monroe Memorial Library, Sweet Briar College, the Thomas Jefferson Memorial Foundation, the University of Virginia, the Virginia Historical Society, and the Virginia Museum of Fine Arts. A popular speaker on literary and bibliographical topics, in 1959 he delivered the Regents Lectures at the University of California at Berkeley.

In 1960 Barrett placed his library at the University of Virginia. His aging friend Robert Frost and some four hundred other distinguished guests attended the dedication. Valued then at more than $3 million, the library contained the largest collection of American literature of its kind for the dates 1775 to 1950 and included complete sets of the works of all American writers of note as well as original letters, manuscripts, typescripts, proofsheets, pictures, and other mementos. The Barrett library then comprised more than 30,000 volumes and in excess of 40,000 manuscripts, letters, and other items. He continued to collect and added constantly to the library, which he deeded to the university shortly before his death.

Barrett's numerous honorary degrees included doctorates from Brown and Clark Universities and the College of William and Mary. He also received many awards, including the Sir Thomas More Award from the University of San Francisco, the Donald F. Hyde Award from Princeton University, and the decoration of the Cuban Commander Cross of Céspedes in 1958. At the University of Virginia he was given an honorary membership in Phi Beta Kappa in 1952, the Seven Society Award in 1960, and the Raven Society Award in 1962. Its Department of English established a professorship, lectures, and fellowships bearing his name to honor him for the legacy of national treasures, such as the manuscripts of Stephen Crane's *Red Badge of Courage* and Walt Whitman's *Leaves of Grass,* which are permanently preserved in the Clifton Waller Barrett Library at the University of Virginia.

Travel abroad, including two trips to Europe as guide for Grolier Club literary and cultural tours, became an important part of Barrett's life. While his only daughter attended school in Florence, he resided there for a time and developed an interest in Italian language and literature, especially Dante's *Divine Comedy*, that bore fruit in his creation of an exhibition and keepsake for the Grolier Club on Italian influences on American literature. Barrett also enjoyed golfing, sailing, and gardening. He and his wife were generous hosts and gifted conversationalists who entertained widely, often in private social clubs, while dividing their seasons among residences at Lake Placid, New York, Ocean Ridge, Florida, and Arcadia in Albemarle County.

Cornelia Barrett died in September 1989, and Barrett's own health, weakened by congestive heart failure, deteriorated. Clifton Waller Barrett died at his home in Albemarle County on 6 November 1991 and was buried in the family plot at Aquia Church in Stafford County.

Current Biography Yearbook (1965): 15–18; Clifton Waller Barrett Papers, including bibliography of publications,

UVA; six oral history interviews, 1986–1988, UVA; Barrett's chief articles were "Some Bibliographical Adventures in Americana," *Papers of the Bibliographical Society of America* 44 (1950): 17–28, "Contemporary Collectors X: The Barrett Collection," *Book Collector* 5 (1956): 218–230, "American Fiction: The First Seventy-Five Years" and "John Greenleaf Whittier," *Proceedings of the American Antiquarian Society* 63 (1953): 335–350 and 67 (1957): 125–136; he also edited a collection of lectures by Harold R. Medina, *The Anatomy of Freedom* (1959), and "The Making of a History: Letters of Henry Adams to Henry Vignaud and Charles Scribner, 1879–1913," *Proceedings of the Massachusetts Historical Society* 71 (1957): 204–271; feature article in *New York Times*, 3 Oct. 1954 (por.); Herbert Cahoon, *A Brief Account of the Clifton Waller Barrett Library* (1960); "Barrett Room Dedication," *University of Virginia Alumni News* 48 (May 1960): 12–13; por. by Irene Higgins at UVA; obituaries in *Richmond News Leader*, 7 Nov. 1991 (por.), and *Charlottesville Daily Progress* and *Richmond Times-Dispatch*, both 8 Nov. 1991.

ANNE E. H. FREUDENBERG

BARRETT, James D. (April 1833–1903), member of the Convention of 1867–1868, was born in Louisa County, the son of Wilson Barrett and Lucy Barrett. He and his parents left no traces in the antebellum public records, and an observer just after the Civil War stated that he had been a slave. The historian Luther Porter Jackson later wrote that Barrett was free before emancipation, but his absence from public records makes slave status more likely. Sometime before the war he married Clarissa M. Spotswood, and they had three sons and three daughters, of whom the eldest was born about 1858. As a slave or otherwise, Barrett learned the shoemaker's and carpenter's trades and, in his first appearance in Fluvanna County's records, he was taxed in 1866 as the owner of a horse valued at $50 and other property valued at $40.

Barrett soon became a leader and political activist in Fluvanna County. He was an excellent speaker who participated in the Union League's efforts to educate and organize blacks to seek their rights as citizens. On 17 April 1867 Barrett and two other African Americans represented the county at the Union Republican Convention in Richmond. When an election for delegates to a state constitutional convention was set for 22 October 1867, Barrett made known his candidacy. On 28 September at the courthouse in Palmyra he spoke at a crowded public meeting called to nominate a candidate to be Fluvanna's delegate. The chair selected two whites and two blacks from each of the county's six magisterial districts and, after caucusing, the committee recommended Abraham Shepherd, a white conservative and the clerk of the Fluvanna County Court. The meeting approved the nomination and adjourned, but Barrett immediately announced that he would run anyway. About one hundred more blacks than whites voted in the election, and he carried the county by fifty votes.

Barrett did not play a prominent role at the convention. He served on the Standing Committee on Education and usually voted with the Radical majority but opposed controversial measures designed to disfranchise former Confederates. An observer stated that Barrett was honest and spoke well but could not read or write. His signature on his pay vouchers as a delegate suggests that he had, in fact, acquired at least some level of literacy, and he was described as literate in subsequent censuses.

Barrett evidently did not seek public office again, but he remained prominent in his community near Fork Union. He probably developed his talent as a political orator through preaching. He helped to organize the Thessalonia Baptist Church in 1868 and served as its pastor for many years. In April 1879 he conveyed three-quarters of an acre of his land to the church as a permanent site for its place of worship. In addition Barrett organized a beneficial society through the church. Members made small monetary contributions in return for assistance in time of need, and they named it the Barrett Humane Society in his honor. In the 1890s he also served as pastor at the Byrd Grove Baptist Church.

Clarissa Barrett died of consumption on 30 November 1891, and Barrett married Lizzie Myers on 4 September 1892. They had no children. James D. Barrett died in 1903 and was buried at the Thessalonia Baptist Church's cemetery.

Month and year of birth in Census, Fluvanna Co., 1900, corroborated by ages given in 1870 and 1880 Census and BVS Marriage Register, Fluvanna Co., but tombstone gives birth and death years as 1820 and 1903; Personal Property Tax

Returns, Fluvanna Co., 1866, RG 48, LVA; *Organization, Resolution, and Address of the Union Republican State Convention of Virginia* (1867), 2; Richard G. Lowe, "Virginia's Reconstruction Convention: General Schofield Rates the Delegates," *VMHB* 80 (1972): 351; Jackson, *Negro Office-Holders*, 1–2; *Lynchburg Virginian* and *Richmond Whig*, both 2 Oct. 1867; Election Records, no. 427, RG 13, LVA; *Richmond Dispatch*, 25 Oct. 1867; *Journal of 1867–1868 Convention*, 28; Richard L. Hume, "The Membership of the Virginia Constitutional Convention of 1867–1868: A Study of the Beginnings of Congressional Reconstruction in the Upper South," *VMHB* 86 (1978): 481; Pay Vouchers, Convention of 1867–1868, RG 48, LVA; Jerry L. Holloway, *The Churches of Fluvanna County, Virginia* (1966), 150, 157; Fluvanna Co. Deed Book, 21:496, 22:457–458, 25:288, 28:1–2, 29:277; first wife's death in BVS Death Register, Fluvanna Co.; por. in sanctuary of Thessalonia Baptist Church, Fluvanna Co.

WILLIAM S. HITCHCOCK

BARRETT, Janie Porter (9 August 1865–27 August 1948), educator, was born in Athens, Georgia, the daughter of Julia Porter, an African American domestic servant and seamstress. The name of her father, who may have been white, is unknown. She grew up in Macon, Georgia, where her mother worked for a northern white woman named Skinner who treated the child almost as a member of the family. After Julia Porter married and moved to her own home, Janie Porter remained in the Skinner household. Julia Porter evidently turned down an offer by Skinner to send her daughter north to school, where she might have passed into the white world and left her family forever.

Instead, Janie Porter's mother sent her to Hampton Normal and Agricultural Institute, the first of the self-help, vocational training schools for freedpeople. Porter initially had difficulty adjusting to life in a school whose students largely came from rural backgrounds. In later years she attributed her desire to serve her fellow African Americans to Sir Walter Besant's *All Sorts and Conditions of Men: An Impossible Story*, a utopian novel published in 1882 in which an heiress worked to help the poor of London.

After Porter completed her studies at Hampton in 1884 she taught in a poor rural county in southwestern Georgia. For a year she enjoyed teaching there despite the challenging circumstances, but a chance to return to Hampton to teach in the night school proved irresistible. After the 1887–1888 session she moved on to Lucy Laney's Haines Normal and Industrial Institute in Augusta, Georgia, an academically ambitious high school for black students. Laney, a member of the first graduating class of Atlanta University, was one of many dedicated teachers who sought to give a new generation of African Americans a way to rise in the world by plain living, high thinking, cleanliness, and godliness coupled with academic and vocational training.

Porter returned to Hampton again and on 31 October 1889 married Harris Barrett, a fellow Hampton graduate who worked as a cashier and bookkeeper at the school and became an influential entrepreneur in the town. They lived in Hampton and had one son and three daughters. Rather than becoming another comfortable member of the developing black bourgeoisie, however, Janie Porter Barrett formed a sewing class for neighborhood girls that inspired the formation of other groups. She drew in their mothers, and soon the Locust Street Social Settlement took shape. Just as Jane Addams and Ellen Starr opened the doors of Hull House to their immigrant neighbors in Chicago, Barrett opened hers to her black neighbors. During the next twenty years the settlement reached into every part of the Hampton community. Clubs and classes devoted to mothering, cooking, gardening, poultry raising, quilting, and rug weaving met every afternoon and evening. She encouraged children to play athletic games and worked to improve the community. When the settlement outgrew their own house, the Barretts built a clubhouse on their land.

Locust Street typified the growing number of institutions black people were creating for themselves, paralleling similar developments in white society. Another was the National Association of Colored Women, formed in 1896, which encouraged local clubs to organize state federations. In 1908 Barrett helped found the Virginia State Federation of Colored Women's Clubs, and she served as its president until 1932.

Barrett's concern for young girls may have been inspired by the contrast between the nurturing environment available to her own children and the horrendous conditions in which many black youngsters were struggling to grow up. She often told of finding an eight-year-old girl in jail and becoming convinced of the need for a home for what were then called wayward girls. Barrett challenged the federation she headed to take up the cause and traveled around the state collecting small donations. In 1912 the National Association of Colored Women met in Hampton, which gave her an opportunity to develop wider support and provided an additional source of funds. By 1913 she had enlisted the aid of a small nucleus of white Virginia women, who were perhaps urged on by Mary-Cooke Branch Munford, a prominent white clubwoman from Richmond particularly interested in black education. Barrett always gave due credit to the white women and their clubs, though she recognized the greater constancy of her black supporters.

As money began to come in, Barrett sought advice from the new Russell Sage Foundation, itself an interesting example of the growing influence of women on social reform. The Virginia State Federation of Colored Women's Clubs raised more than $5,000 and bought a farm at Peaks, in Hanover County north of Richmond, to build the school for girls.

White residents near the proposed site of the school objected, but Barrett promised to take charge of the school as its first superintendent and to move it if it proved a nuisance to the neighbors. The objections satisfied, the General Assembly appropriated $3,000 for the Industrial Home School for Colored Girls, later the Virginia Industrial School for Colored Girls, and it opened its doors in January 1915. The Virginia State Federation of Colored Women's Clubs owned and governed the school, which had a large board of visitors composed of whites and blacks. During the campaign to raise money, Harris Barrett died of a stroke on 26 March 1915.

The school embodied nineteenth-century female values. Barrett emphasized that it was a home rather than a prison and instituted a carefully structured system of rewards instead of punishment. Her purpose was to build Christian character. She strictly regulated the behavior of the girls, required them to be clean, and taught them household and agricultural skills so that they could support themselves as domestic servants or farm workers until they established homes of their own. Though Barrett patterned the educational philosophy of the school in some ways on those of Hampton and Tuskegee Institute, she was an unusually gifted and sensitive superintendent who stamped her own personality on the school. She believed in trusting the pupils and ran the school on the honor system. In a typical instance of her methods, when World War I created a shortage of agricultural laborers Barrett offered the services of her girls to help neighboring farmers bring in their harvests in exchange for a share of the crops, thereby creating a body of enthusiastic supporters for the school. She also tried to prevent the exploitation of former students by employers in search of cheap labor. Year after year in carefully worded statements she criticized families, black and white, who failed to offer adequate support and encouragement to the young women who lived and worked in their homes.

Barrett's extraordinary ability to work with white women, facilitated perhaps by her upbringing, probably contributed to the growing support she garnered in the General Assembly and to her ability to raise money from private sources. The cooperation of women like Barrett and Munford enabled Virginia, probably more than any other former Confederate state, to develop strong ties between white and black clubwomen. The African American banker Maggie Lena Walker also gave generously to the school and organized a Council of Colored Women in Richmond, which took responsibility for such activities as an annual Christmas dinner for the girls and staff. Little by little, the successful school received recognition and praise. In the mid-1920s the Russell Sage Foundation identified it as one of the five best such schools in the country.

In 1920 the state took over basic responsibility for the school, though the federation continued to be its mainstay and Barrett continued to manage it until she retired in 1940. She remained bold and innovative. In 1938 she wrote that she stressed training in citizenship and that "voting is a duty as well as a right." At that time it took some courage to tell the government of Virginia that black women were being prepared to be voters.

In the 1920s Barrett took an active part in the Virginia Commission on Interracial Cooperation and in the Richmond Urban League. She served for four years as chairman of the executive board of the National Association of Colored Women, and in 1929 she received the William E. Harmon Award for Distinguished Achievement among Negroes. A year later she was invited to take part in the White House Conference on Child Health and Protection.

Returning to Hampton on her retirement in 1940, Janie Porter Barrett died on 27 August 1948 of diabetes and arteriosclerosis in Hampton Institute's Dixie Hospital and was buried in Elmerton Cemetery in Hampton. Two years after her death the General Assembly renamed the school she had founded the Janie Porter Barrett School for Girls. It was integrated in 1965 and became coeducational in 1972, an appropriate legacy in light of the work of its founding mother to bring about interracial understanding. With a reorganization of the state's correctional system in 1977, the school became the Barrett Learning Center for boys.

Autobiographical statement, ca. 1890, in *Twenty-Two Years' Work of the Hampton Normal and Agricultural Institute* (1893), 208; *The History of Virginia State Federation of Colored Women's Clubs, Inc.* (1996), 20–21, 26–33; Sadie Iola Daniel, *Women Builders* (1931), 53–78; Winona R. Hall, "Janie Porter Barrett: Her Life and Contributions to Social Welfare in Virginia" (master's thesis, Howard University, 1954); Barrett's publications include "Negro Women's Clubs and the Community," *Southern Workman* 39 (1910): 33–34, "Social Work Among Our People," *Proceedings of the Virginia Conference of Charities and Correction* (1912), 14–17, and Barrett, Caroline D. Pratt, and Ida A. Tourtellot, *Community Clubs for Women and Girls* (1912; *Hampton Leaflets*, vol. 6, no. 8); printed annual reports of Virginia Industrial School for Colored Girls, 1916–1939; *Pictorial Record of the Virginia Industrial School* (1932); Cynthia Neverdon-Morton, *Afro-American Women of the South and the Advancement of the Race, 1895–1925* (1989), 105–117, 201, 228 (por., 106); J. E. Davis, "Fertilizing Barren Souls: The Industrial Home School for Delinquent Colored Girls of Virginia," *Southern Workman* 45 (1916): 462–473; Lily Hardy Hammond, *In the Vanguard of a Race* (1922), 78–93; Mary White Ovington, *Portraits in Color* (1927), 181–193; obituary in *Norfolk Journal and Guide*, national ed., 4 Sept. 1948 (por.).

ANNE FIROR SCOTT

BARRETT, Joseph Eagle (24 April 1890–20 October 1971), commissioner of mental hygiene and hospitals, was born in Brookland, near Jonesboro, Arkansas, the only son and eldest of three children of Elmodan Beauregard Barrett and Nevada Gertrude Ware Barrett. He attended the local public schools and took a short course in mechanical engineering at the University of Arkansas during the academic year 1907–1908. He subsequently worked as a bookkeeper, found employment with a druggist, attended medical school for a year, and purchased his own drugstore. During World War I he served in the United States Navy, first as a fireman and then as a pharmacist's mate second class stationed part of the time in the Philippines.

On 22 January 1921 Barrett married Olive Mae Nunn. They had three sons. He completed his studies at the University of Tennessee College of Medicine in 1922 and interned at City Hospital in Saint Louis, where an interest in the relationship between physical illness and psychological disorders led him to choose a career in psychiatry. He worked at the State Hospital for Nervous and Mental Diseases in Little Rock before becoming assistant commissioner of the Massachusetts Department of Mental Hygiene in 1934. From 1937 to 1939 he was the director of the Michigan State Hospital Commission.

In 1937 Barrett served as a consultant for the Virginia Mental Hospital Survey Committee, and his report became the basis for planned improvements in the state's mental health care system. He left Michigan in June 1939 to become supervisor of outpatient clinics and clinical director of the Southwestern State Hospital at Marion. In September 1943 the State Hospital Board named him superintendent of the Eastern State Hospital in Williamsburg. Governor William M. Tuck appointed him commissioner of the State Department of Mental Hygiene and Hospitals on 23 January 1946. Barrett continued to live in Williamsburg and commuted to the commissioner's office in Richmond for the next eleven years. He oversaw the completion of a $23 million building program that had been provided for prior to World War II. Increases in construction costs between the planning and the completion of the work in the mid-1950s were so great, however, that the program fell far short of achieving the goals set for it.

As commissioner, Barrett sought increased appropriations to modernize the hospitals, enlarge the staffs of the mental health facilities, and raise pay to attract and hold competent physicians, nurses, and other professional personnel. He maintained that full funding and full staffing would result in better patient care and significantly lower costs per patient. The standards for facilities, staff, and patient care set by the State Hospital Board were significantly below those recommended by the American Psychiatric Association, but inadequate appropriations from the General Assembly left the department unable to fill many vacant positions or meet even the state's own low standards. Throughout his tenure as commissioner Barrett argued for the stronger commitment to improving mental health care needed to overcome the unfortunate results of decades of neglect to the system.

In 1950 Barrett's department began publishing a journal, *Mental Health in Virginia*, which he used to call for increased funding for medical services. He was a persistent advocate for improved mental health care in Virginia, but even his admirers admitted that he pushed legislators too hard and insistently. In calling for his reappointment, the editorial writers of the *Richmond News Leader* conceded that "when it comes to politicking, Dr. Barrett has all the smoothness of a wood rasp" (20 July 1954). A later editorial acknowledged that he came across as a "stubborn, tenacious fellow, utterly ungifted in the convivial artifices of politics" (14 January 1957). Barrett was also held responsible for funding and management scandals uncovered during the 1950s at several of the state's mental hospitals, although some of the problems probably grew out of longstanding policies and practices. In 1952 the General Assembly divided the department into two administrative sections and established the post of business manager to oversee hospital finances. Two years later Governor Thomas Stanley held up Barrett's reappointment as commissioner for six months because the State Hospital Board had not filled the business manager's post. Still unsatisfied in 1956, the governor obtained passage of a bill placing the commission's business manager in the governor's office. Members of the State Hospital Board angrily interpreted the move as a punishment of Barrett for his outspoken efforts to improve the state's hospitals. Soon after, an investigative committee selected by Stanley criticized Barrett and the board for failing to correct problems at Southwestern State Hospital. Stanley began replacing board members, and in January 1957 Barrett resigned as commissioner to return to the Eastern State Hospital as superintendent.

Barrett's second stint at Eastern State lasted two and a half years. He retired on 15 October 1959, a few months short of his seventieth birthday. He later moved his family to Northport, Alabama, and worked at a mental hospital in nearby Tuscaloosa. Joseph Eagle Barrett died in Northport on 20 October 1971 and was buried in Jonesboro, Arkansas.

Feature articles in *Richmond Times-Dispatch*, 18 Nov. 1956, 23, 24 Aug. 1959 (por.), and *Williamsburg Virginia Gazette*, 28 Aug. 1959; birth and marriage dates in *Who's Who in the South and Southwest* (1950), 1:60; Joseph E. Barrett, "Our Understaffed Mental Hospitals" and "Our Mental Hospitals are Overcrowded," *Commonwealth* 18 (June 1951): 9–11 and (July 1951): 15–17, 40; departmental scandals and Stanley's intervention fully covered in *Richmond News Leader* and *Richmond Times-Dispatch*; obituaries in *Richmond News Leader*, 22 Oct. 1971, and *Williamsburg Virginia Gazette*, 29 Oct. 1971.

DONALD W. GUNTER

BARRETT, Katherine Harwood Waller (24 January 1858–23 February 1925), social reformer, was born in Falmouth in Stafford County, the eldest of ten children, nine of whom were daughters, of Withers Waller and Anna Elizabeth Stribling Waller. During the Civil War she and her mother remained close to the Confederate army, in which her father was a colonel on the staff of General Fitzhugh Lee, and they were present at Appomattox at the end of the war. Waller grew up at Clifton, her father's thousand-acre estate near the Potomac River in Stafford County. She received most of her education at home, but she also attended a local school for one year and the Arlington Institute for Girls in Alexandria for two years more. On 19 July 1876 she married Robert S. Barrett, a twenty-six-year-old Episcopal minister who had recently taken charge of nearby Aquia Church. Between 1877 and 1888 they had four sons and three daughters, of whom one son died young.

Kate Waller Barrett and her husband soon moved to a poor area of Richmond, where she was introduced to the work that occupied most of her adult life. One night a frightened, unmarried girl who had traveled to Richmond with her infant called on the Barretts. As she listened to the young mother's story, Barrett began to question some of her received beliefs. "Where was the terrible degradation, the hopeless depravity" that she had been taught to associate with a "fallen woman?" Upset, Barrett accepted as one of her religious duties the responsibility to assist "this outcast class."

During the 1880s the Barretts moved to Henderson, Kentucky, and then to Atlanta. While her husband was serving as dean of Saint Luke's Cathedral in the latter city, she completed a three-year course of study at the Women's Medical College of Georgia and earned an M.D. in 1892. The valedictorian of her class, she was then thirty-four years old. Two years later, having traveled to Europe with her husband, she completed a nursing course at the Florence Nightingale Training School in London. In 1893 she opened a rescue home in Atlanta where unmarried pregnant girls could find refuge and receive care and education. She successfully sought financial assistance for the enterprise from Charles Nelson Crittenton, a New York millionaire who had already funded other rescue homes in memory of a daughter who had died as a small child.

In 1894 the Barretts moved to Washington, D.C., and two years later the family moved to Alexandria. Following the death of her husband on 12 September 1896, Barrett worked with Crittenton to establish the National Florence Crittenton Mission, the first philanthropic institution to be chartered by Congress. Barrett served as vice president and general superintendent from its incorporation in 1897 until Crittenton's death in 1909, when she became president, a post she held until her death. She wrote several chapters for *Fourteen Years' Work among "Erring Girls," as Conducted by the National Florence Crittenton Mission, with Practical Suggestions for the Same* (1897), contributed numerous articles to the *Florence Crittenton Magazine* between 1898 and 1914, and published *Some Practical Suggestions on the Conduct of a Rescue Home* (1903). Barrett helped establish seventy-eight Florence Crittenton Homes throughout the United States and in Mexico City, Marseilles, Shanghai, and Tokyo. Her missions provided safe shelter and acted as supportive allies for the mothers while encouraging breast-feeding and nurturing of affectionate bonds between mother and child. They also attempted to prepare young women to become competent homemakers and employees, capable of supporting their own children.

Early in 1909 President Theodore Roosevelt invited Barrett to the first White House Conference for Dependent Children. She was a delegate to the international congresses of the World Purity Federation in 1914, 1915, and 1917. During World War I the War Department Commission on Training Camp Activities engaged her to speak to soldiers about venereal disease. In the spring of 1919 she traveled from Paris to Constantinople as a special agent of the United States Immigration Bureau to investigate protective arrangements for women and girls whom the United States intended to deport on moral grounds. President Woodrow Wilson appointed Barrett an observer of the Versailles Peace Conference, and in 1919 he sent her as a delegate to the International Congress of Women in Zurich, where Jane Addams held a reception in her honor.

Barrett also became a leader in the International Council of Women, an organization that Elizabeth Cady Stanton and Susan B. Anthony had founded to promote improvement in the condition of women worldwide. Barrett was a delegate to the world conference in London in 1899 and delivered featured addresses at the conferences in Toronto in 1909 and Rome in 1914. She served as secretary and vice president of the National Council of Women before being elected president in 1911. Barrett's activities in Virginia included two terms as Virginia state regent of the Daughters of the American Revolution, service as honorary vice president of the Equal Suffrage League of Virginia, membership on the board of visitors of the College of William and Mary from 1921 to 1924, and charter membership in the Virginia League of Women Voters. She was elected president of the Women's Auxiliary of the American Legion in 1922 and chosen an honorary member of Phi Beta Kappa in 1924.

Newspaper accounts of Barrett's public addresses regularly noted her power as a speaker. One episode gained fleeting national attention. As a delegate from Virginia to the 1924 Democratic National Convention in New York she delivered a seconding speech for favorite-son candidate Carter Glass. In response to her brief but brilliantly delivered speech, which included high praise for the role of Wall Street in America, a delegate from New Jersey spontaneously placed Barrett's name in nomination for the vice presidency.

Thanks to her wide-ranging social reform interests and influence, Barrett has occasionally been described as a pioneer sociologist. She devoted remarkable physical and intellectual energy to a broad range of concerns that included prostitution, venereal disease, the white slave trade, working conditions for women and children, the welfare of America's returning soldiers and disabled veterans, the education of immigrant families, and woman suffrage. Her travels took her from Alaska to Bangkok, from Mexico to Italy. She spoke to presidents in the White House, to congregations in American churches, and to young girls in saloons. During the latter years of her presidency of the National Florence Crittenton Mission, she drew her son Robert South Barrett into the administration of the agency, and following her death he succeeded her as its president.

Katherine Harwood Waller Barrett died suddenly in her Alexandria home on 23 February 1925 and was buried in the churchyard of Aquia Church in Stafford County. The governor of Virginia ordered the flag to be lowered on the State Capitol in Richmond, the first time that a woman had been so honored.

Several sources give year of birth as 1855 or 1857, but it is 1858 on gravestone; Kate Waller Barrett Papers, including clippings and reminiscences, LC; Barrett scrapbooks, Robert South Barrett Papers, UVA; some Barrett papers in Lloyd House, Alexandria, and other letters and clipping files in Richmond Public Library; National Florence Crittenton Mission Papers, University of Minnesota, Minneapolis; Hugh Milton McIlhany Jr., *Some Virginia Families* (1903), 79–81; family history verified by granddaughter Viola Barrett Pope and great-granddaughter Bruce Greenland Rodenberg; June Peterson, "Dr. Kate Waller Barrett: A Friend of Girls" (master's thesis, Seattle University, 1969); Charles Crittenton, *Brother of Girls* (1910); Otto Wilson and Robert South Barrett, *Fifty Years' Work With Girls, 1883–1933* (1933); Marietta Minnigerode Andrews, *My Studio Window: Sketches of the Pageant of Washington Life* (1928), 239–245; "Kate Waller Barrett, Sociologist," *World's Work* 49 (Nov. 1924): 69–71 (por.); *New York Times*, 23 July 1914, 21 Oct. 1922, 24 May 1924; por. by Eugenie Deland Saugstad at W&M; E. Lee Trinkle to Charles D. Barrett, 25 Feb. 1925, Governor's Office, Letters Received and Sent, RG 3, LVA; obituaries in *Alexandria Gazette*, *Richmond News Leader*, *Richmond Times-Dispatch* (por.), and *Washington Post*, all 24 Feb. 1925.

DIANE MCVITTIE REUKAUF

BARRETT, Robert South (30 March 1877–24 February 1959), business leader and philanthropist, was born Robert Barrett in Richmond, the eldest of four sons and three daughters of Robert S. Barrett and Katherine Harwood Waller Barrett. He grew up in Richmond, in Henderson, Kentucky, and in Atlanta, where his father's service as an Episcopal clergyman took the family. He attended public school in Atlanta and in August 1894 matriculated at the University of the South in Sewanee, Tennessee, where he adopted South as his middle name. He enrolled in Columbian University (now George Washington University) in Washington, D.C., shortly before his father died in 1896, but he never completed his formal higher education.

Barrett moved to New York and by 1898 to Mexico City, where he worked as a freight agent and passenger clerk for the traffic department of the Mexican National Railway Company, and eventually as general agent of the passenger traffic department of a Mexican regional branch of the Southern Railway Company. On 17 November 1898 he married Annie Viola Tupper in Atlanta. They had four sons and one daughter. He and his wife were popular members of the American colony in Mexico City during a time of rapid economic development and the creation of a national railroad network under the aegis of capitalists from Great Britain and the United States. Barrett became manager of the afternoon English-language *Mexico City Daily Record* in 1904, wrote *The Standard Guide to Mexico* (published in 1900, 1901, 1902, 1903, and 1905), and compiled social *Blue Books* for Mexico, Texas, and California.

Leaving Mexico in 1907, Barrett spent two years traveling extensively throughout the Western Hemisphere and Europe. During a stay in London he contemplated establishing a newspaper similar to the European edition of the *New York Herald*, but instead he moved back to Virginia in 1910 and bought a house in Alexandria near that of his mother. There he founded a printing firm and served a term as police commissioner before purchasing one of the nation's oldest newspapers, the *Alexandria Gazette*, in 1911. For six years he edited the paper and used it to promote the Democratic Party. He was elected president of the Virginia Press Association during his final year as editor.

In 1916 Barrett undertook the first of a series of foreign missions on behalf of the United States government, including posts as special agent for the Bureau of Foreign and Domestic Commerce in South America, commercial attaché to the embassy in Argentina, and later as representative there of the War Trade Board and the U.S. Shipping Board. His duties took him throughout all of South America and eventually involved him in the procurement of supplies for American and Allied forces in Europe during World War I. He also wrote several reports for the Department of Commerce on the trade and business of the region, with emphasis on potential markets for American paper and printing machinery. From 1918 to 1922 he resided in Buenos Aires and served as a vice president and general manager of the Paris-based international banking house of Portalis and Company.

Barrett was a wealthy man when he retired in 1922 at the age of forty-five and returned to Alexandria. He devoted himself to a variety of philanthropic, charitable, religious, and literary pursuits, all of which required extensive travel. The strong influence of his distinguished mother, Kate Waller Barrett, who died early in 1925, led naturally to his working under and then succeeding her as president of the National Florence Crittenton Mission, a foundation for the care of unmarried mothers. In that capacity he wrote treatises on *The Care of the Unmarried Mother* (1929) and *Fifty Years' Work with Girls, 1883–1933* (1933), and a series of articles entitled "I Was an Unmarried Mother" for the magazine *True Story*. He sent articles about his travels to the *Alexandria Gazette*, describing in journal form his impressions of life in foreign capitals and countries.

A lifelong interest in fraternal organizations, especially those that encouraged healthy activities for boys, resulted in his election as national grand exalted ruler of the Benevolent and Protective Order of Elks in 1944 and to high offices in the Scottish Rite of Freemasonry in Virginia. He also served as associate secretary of the National Council of the Protestant Episcopal Church and as treasurer of its Commission on Faith and Order. In 1947 he and his wife established the Barrett Foundation for Charitable and Educational Purposes and endowed it with more than $1 million in property. The foundation later divided its resources between the Crittenton Foundation and the Elks National Foundation. The Barretts' patronage assisted in the construction of a hospital for children in Richmond, the Alexandria Boys Club, the Harper Memorial Auditorium at the National Elks Home in Bedford, the Kate Waller Barrett Dormitory at the College of William and Mary, and the Kate Waller Barrett Building for the city library in Alexandria. The University of the South, of which he was a loyal patron, awarded Barrett an honorary doctorate of civil laws in 1930.

Barrett's three sons who lived to adulthood all achieved national prominence. Robert Tullius Tupper Barrett became president of the European branch of Guaranty Trust Company, Clifton Waller Barrett founded a successful shipping company and became a noted collector of American literature, and John Paul Barker Barrett became a rear admiral in the U.S. Navy.

Robert South Barrett spent most of the last year of his life in residence at the National Elks

Home in Bedford, where he died of pneumonia on 24 February 1959. He was buried in the cemetery of Aquia Church in Stafford County.

Biography in Bruce, Tyler, and Morton, *History of Virginia*, 6:130–131; BVS Birth Register, Richmond City, for birth date, given in some obituaries as 20 Mar. 1877; family history information verified by daughter Viola Barrett Pope, son Clifton Waller Barrett, granddaughter Kate Waller Barrett Rennie, and grandson Robert Tullius Tupper Barrett Jr.; Robert South Barrett Papers, including undated copies of *True Story* articles, UVA; obituaries in *Alexandria Gazette*, 24 Feb. 1959, and *New York Times* (por.), *Richmond News Leader*, *Richmond Times-Dispatch*, and *Washington Post*, all 25 Feb. 1959.

ANNE E. H. FREUDENBERG

BARRINGER, Paul Brandon (13 February 1857–9 January 1941), president of Virginia Agricultural and Mechanical College and Polytechnic Institute, was born in Concord, North Carolina, the only son and younger of two children of Rufus Barringer and his first wife, Eugenia Morrison Barringer. His mother died of typhoid fever in June 1858, and in 1859 he was sent to stay at the home of her sister Anna Morrison Jackson, wife of Virginia Military Institute professor Thomas J. Jackson. Barringer returned to North Carolina in 1861 and lived with an uncle during the Civil War while his father rose to the rank of brigadier general in the Confederate army. In the spring of 1865 the eight-year-old Barringer spent a week helping conceal the South Carolina naturalist John Bachman from Union troops, an experience that was pivotal in his life. As Barringer recalled in his memoirs, Bachman spent much of the week demonstrating the wonders of nature to the child and stimulating his interest in nature and science.

Barringer was educated privately until 1871, when he entered Bingham's School in Mebane, North Carolina. The family probably intended to send him to the University of North Carolina, but a visit to Charlottesville one summer proved to be the beginning of a long association with the University of Virginia. He attended the Kenmore University School in Amherst from 1874 to 1875 and the University of Virginia during the academic year 1875–1876. At the June 1876 commencement he received three certificates of graduation in the sciences. Earlier that spring a bout with malarial fever had been the cause of his introduction to another guiding influence in his career, James Lawrence Cabell, the senior professor in the university's medical department. Barringer studied medicine under Cabell the following year and received a medical degree from the University of Virginia in June 1877. A year's postgraduate study at the University of the City of New York earned Barringer a second medical degree in 1878.

Barringer practiced medicine in Dallas, North Carolina, from 1879 to 1881, when he went abroad for a year's study of clinical medicine and hospital administration at medical centers in London, Edinburgh, Dublin, Paris, and Vienna. After his return he established a new practice in Charlotte and gave his first professional paper (on syphilis) to a North Carolina medical convention. On 27 December 1882 he married Nannie Irene Hannah. They had six sons and four daughters. In 1886 Barringer became physician of Davidson College, where he developed a successful preparatory program for students who wanted to enter medical school.

In 1889 Barringer succeeded Cabell as professor of physiology and surgery at the University of Virginia. During the next decade Barringer was instrumental in lengthening the standard medical program from one year to four, and he helped develop public health measures to stem outbreaks of typhoid fever in Charlottesville. In June 1896 he was elected chairman of the faculty, at that time the university's chief executive officer, and held the position until June 1903. In this capacity he directed the rebuilding of the Rotunda after it burned in 1895. Barringer also became a tireless advocate for the creation of a teaching hospital for the university's medical department. In 1899 the board of visitors authorized plans for a hospital and began to raise funds from private sources for its construction.

Barringer's medical writings included *The Venomous Reptiles of the United States, with the Treatment of Wounds Inflicted by Them* (1891), *An Abstract of Physiology for Medical Students and Practitioners* (1894; second edition 1899), and "An Unappreciated Source of Typhoid Infection," *Medical Record* 64 (1903): 971–974.

He served on the Virginia Board of Medical Examiners in 1893 and was elected president of the Medical Society of Virginia in 1906. He also coedited the two-volume *University of Virginia: Its History, Influence, Equipment, and Characteristics* (1904). In 1900 Barringer addressed three medical and educational conventions on the subject of African Americans in the twentieth-century South. Concerned about the effects of crime, poverty, and infant mortality on the population, he called for basic agricultural and industrial education under the strict control of white supervisors. The lectures were published as *The Sacrifice of a Race* (1900), *The American Negro: His Past and Future* (1900), and *Negro Education in the South* (1901).

Barringer was elected president of Virginia Agricultural and Mechanical College and Polytechnic Institute in 1907 and took office on 1 September of that year. During his tenure he raised the entrance requirements, eliminated the preparatory department, and supported programs to strengthen the agricultural curriculum. His unequivocal advocacy of agricultural education with the announced goal of raising it to the level of the engineering program divided the school's teachers. Friction within the faculty, together with such incidents as the loss of the state geological survey to the University of Virginia in 1908, made his presidency a stormy one. The alumni association investigated the college in 1909 and sought Barringer's removal by presenting a variety of charges against him to the board of visitors in January 1910. After a hearing that March, the majority of the board dismissed the charges as unsubstantiated. Barringer's administration continued to be racked by political controversy, however, and he presented his resignation to the board in July 1912. At its request, he stayed on until July 1913.

His presidency concluded, Barringer returned to Charlottesville, where he participated actively in University of Virginia alumni affairs and in historical and genealogical research. At the end of World War I the State Board of Health asked him to help in the effort to halt an outbreak of influenza in the Virginia coalfields and to treat those afflicted by the illness. In his final years Barringer became a popular local personality, recounting tales of his youth to the students who came to visit him, memories presumably stirred by work on his memoirs, which one of his daughters completed and published after his death. Both the University of Virginia and Virginia Polytechnic Institute recognized his contributions to their development by naming campus buildings in his honor.

Paul Brandon Barringer died at his home in Charlottesville on 9 January 1941 and was buried in the University of Virginia Cemetery.

Anna Barringer, ed., *The Natural Bent: The Memoirs of Dr. Paul B. Barringer* (1949); Tyler, *Men of Mark*, 1:158–160 (por.); Bruce, Tyler, and Morton, *History of Virginia*, 4:34–35; feature article in *Virginia Medical Monthly* 85 (1958): 162–163; Barringer Family Papers, including genealogical data, UVA; Paul B. Barringer Presidential Papers, VPI; Bruce, *University of Virginia*, 4:11–15, 195, 237–239, 295–298, 5:178–179, 231, 434; Sarah S. Matthews, *The University of Virginia Hospital (Its First Fifty Years)* [ca. 1961], 13–35, 102–105; Duncan Lyle Kinnear, *The First 100 Years: A History of the Virginia Polytechnic Institute and State University* (1972), 178, 183–217, 222–223, 230; obituaries in *Charlottesville Daily Progress* and *Richmond News Leader*, both 9 Jan. 1941, *Richmond Times-Dispatch*, 10 Jan. 1941 (por.), and *University of Virginia Alumni News* 29 (1941): 69–70, 84; editorial tribute in *Richmond Times-Dispatch*, 10 Jan. 1941; memorial in *Virginia Medical Monthly* 68 (1941): 129–130.

GLENN L. MCMULLEN

BARRON, James (October 1740–14 or 16 May 1787), commodore of the Virginia State Navy, was born at Point Comfort near Hampton, one of six sons and two daughters of Samuel Barron, who moved to Virginia from England sometime during the 1720s or 1730s and commanded a fort at Point Comfort until his death in about 1750. His mother's name is unknown. All but one of Samuel Barron's sons went to sea, with James Barron probably doing so shortly after his father's death. By the 1760s he was in command of a merchant ship that traveled between Great Britain and Virginia transporting tobacco and carrying assorted merchandise, and probably passengers as well. He was noted for quick turnaround times in port and for fast sailing on the high seas, making his voyages profitable ones for his employers. Before he turned twenty-four he married Jane Cowper. Their two children, Samuel Barron

(1765–1810) and James Barron (1768–1851), both served on their father's ships during the American Revolution and became naval officers after the war.

In the autumn of 1775 James Barron and his brother Richard Barron left the merchant service and organized a militia company in Hampton. On 25 December 1775 James Barron took command of the armed pilot boat *Liberty*, which the Virginia Committee of Safety fitted out, while Richard Barron commanded the state's other pilot boat, the *Patriot*. Based at Hampton, *Liberty* and *Patriot* cruised the Chesapeake Bay to warn of large enemy ships and attack weaker ones. With a crew of from twenty to thirty men and armed only with small swivel guns, the *Liberty* was no match for heavily armed ships, but for three years Barron aggressively patrolled the bay, capturing merchant vessels that tried to supply British forces and fighting privateers and the armed tenders of British warships.

Barron was given command of a thirty-six-gun frigate under construction at Gosport in Norfolk County, but he lost the chance to take a large warship to sea when he had to burn the vessel in May 1779 to prevent the British from capturing it. A month later he was appointed to the new Virginia Board of War, the state committee that oversaw all military matters. On 3 May 1780 Governor Thomas Jefferson appointed Barron to the new position of commodore of the Virginia State Navy. Of the fifty warships that the state navy had had in service early in the war, few remained. The British navy had destroyed or captured many and the state had sold others. To increase the number of vessels defending Virginia waters, Barron struggled to repair and arm as many warships as possible. His task became even more difficult when British land and naval forces invaded Virginia early in 1781 and destroyed or captured many of the warships of the Virginia State Navy, while others were sunk by their own crews to keep them out of enemy hands. By the time of the Yorktown campaign, however, Barron had raised several of the sunken vessels and impressed other small craft into service. He employed this makeshift flotilla to collect and deliver supplies to the French and American armies besieging the British force led by General Cornwallis. Barron even lent the state government £10,000 in cash to help rebuild the navy, money that was never repaid.

After the Revolutionary War ended, Barron resumed patrolling the bay in the schooner *Liberty*, the only vessel in the Virginia navy that had served throughout the entire war. Virginia built a new schooner *Patriot* (replacing the one captured by the British in April 1781) to assist *Liberty* in enforcing the state's trade laws, and Barron took command of the small fleet. He cruised aboard *Liberty* for two weeks at a time and then returned to Hampton while someone else took *Patriot* on patrol. James Barron was still on active service when he died at Hampton of unrecorded causes on either 14 or 16 May 1787.

Brief biography giving month and year of birth in *Virginia Historical Register* 1 (1848): 23–27, by son James Barron, whose papers at W&M include family history and a record of his father's Revolutionary War naval service; merchant shipping career documented in *Williamsburg Virginia Gazette* and in *Lloyd's Register of Shipping*, 1768 and 1776; Virginia State Navy Papers, RG 2, LVA, contain Barron correspondence and records of his commands; for dates of service see also Rejected Claims, RG 3, LVA, BW, and LOMC; letter from son James Barron to David Campbell, 18 Oct. 1835, Rejected Claims, indicates that Barron died on 14 May 1787, but obituary in *Richmond Virginia Independent Chronicle*, 23 May 1787, gives 16 May 1787 death date.

JOSEPH GOLDENBERG

BARRON, James (15 September 1768–21 April 1851), naval officer, was born at Little England, the family residence near Hampton, the younger of two children, both sons, of James Barron (1740–1787) and Jane Cowper Barron. He attended local schools until 1780, when he joined the Virginia State Navy, of which his father was then the commodore. He served on his father's ship until the end of the war and afterward patrolled Virginia waters with his father. After his father's death in 1787, he worked as a ship's captain for a Norfolk mercantile firm for more than ten years. In 1790 he married Elizabeth Mosely Armistead. They lived at Little England and had five daughters.

On 9 March 1798 Barron was commissioned a lieutenant in the United States Navy, and on

22 May 1799 he was promoted to captain. After he returned home in April 1801 from duty in the West Indies, Congress directed him to create a signal code for the navy. The signal code he devised was used until 1813, when it fell into British hands. During the Tripolitan War (1801–1805), Barron served as a ship's captain in the Mediterranean, but his ship never saw action. In 1807 he was named commodore of the Mediterranean squadron and on 22 June departed from Norfolk aboard the forty-gun *Chesapeake*, under the command of Charles Gordon. Problems at the naval base caused the *Chesapeake* to leave port unprepared for action, and the ship was still in sight of the Virginia capes when a British man-of-war, the fifty-six-gun *Leopard*, accosted it. The British demanded permission to search the *Chesapeake* for deserters and opened fire when Barron refused, wounding him and nineteen others and killing three crewmen. He was forced to strike his colors and stand by as the British seized four members of the *Chesapeake*'s crew. The American vessel then limped back to Hampton Roads for repairs.

The peacetime attack on the *Chesapeake* created a furor. The public clamored for both retaliation and an explanation, and some of Barron's own officers petitioned for an investigation. A court of inquiry called in turn for a general court-martial. Barron was charged with negligently performing his duties, failing to clear his ship for action, failing to encourage his crew to fight courageously, and failing to do his utmost to take or destroy the *Leopard*. Striking irregularities characterized the court-martial. The officer who acted as judge advocate during the inquiry also served as judge advocate of the court-martial; Barron was brought before junior officers, a departure from usual practice; Commodore John Rogers, who had recently challenged Barron to a duel, presided over the tribunal; Stephen Decatur was named a judge in spite of his protest that he had formed an opinion against Barron during the inquiry; and the findings of the inquiry were incorporated into the minutes of the court-martial. Although the inadequacies of the *Chesapeake*'s preparation for its voyage could hardly be attributed solely to Barron, he was suspended from duty without pay for five years for failing to clear for action on probability of an engagement.

Barron eventually found employment commanding merchant vessels, and when war broke out between the United States and Great Britain in 1812 he became stranded in Copenhagen. On 8 February 1813, with his suspension ended, he wrote to the secretary of the navy requesting a return to duty. No reply was forthcoming. While awaiting a recall to service, Barron indulged his inventive side. A lifelong tinkerer, he hoped to raise money with his inventions of an improved ship's windlass and a rope-making machine.

When Barron arrived at Washington, D.C., in December 1818, he discovered that his status was clouded by allegations of disloyalty during the war. His return inspired criticism from his old enemies, particularly from Stephen Decatur. A prolonged and heated exchange of letters between the two led to a duel on 22 March 1820 in which Barron killed Decatur, an event that further reduced his chances of being recalled to active duty. At Barron's request a court of inquiry met to review charges that he had expressed treasonable sentiments to a British consul regarding the *Chesapeake-Leopard* affair, that he had sailed under a British license during the War of 1812, and that he had deliberately remained in Europe while his country was at war.

On 10 May 1821 the court convened at Brooklyn and after hearing extensive testimony cleared Barron in mid-July 1821 of the more serious charges. However, it ruled that he had not satisfactorily demonstrated that he was unable to come home sooner than he did, and that he therefore had absented himself from his country without permission. He was not reprimanded, but even with assistance from prominent politicians and Virginia's congressional delegation, it took Barron three years to gain reinstatement in the navy. In 1822 Congress printed the records of the courts of inquiry and the general court-martial in which he was the central figure, and he was permitted to write a preface to the records. Finally, on 24 July 1824 Barron received orders to take command of the Philadelphia Navy Yard, and on 2 May

1825 he was transferred to the Gosport Navy Yard in Norfolk.

In November 1828 Barron was offered the command of the Pacific squadron, an offer that he found tempting but felt compelled to decline so that he could continue to press his family's land and financial claims stemming from the Revolutionary War. His first wife having died on 2 July 1823, he married Mary Anne Wilson, of Portsmouth, on 12 November 1829. They had no children. In 1831 Barron returned to the Philadelphia Navy Yard and remained there for six years before requesting to be relieved from duty. For five years he was semiretired, but in 1842, at age seventy-four and as the ranking captain in the navy, he was assigned to the Naval Asylum in Philadelphia, a retirement facility for old sailors and naval officers, for a two-year tour of duty, after which he retired to Norfolk. He had finally achieved a measure of vindication and largely restored his reputation and career. His tinkering also produced some successes, though little profit. Between July 1816 and October 1837 he received fifteen patents, mostly for improvements to devices used on shipboard. One of his unpatented inventions, a ship's ventilator, was widely used throughout the American fleet. Barron also designed a model for an armored steam ram that he called the marine catapulta. The government rejected it as visionary, but his revolutionary concept survived and served as the inspiration for the Confederate ironclad *Virginia*.

Barron tried unsuccessfully for years to obtain the additional bounty lands that he believed his father had earned for his Revolutionary War service. In conjunction with that effort he published short articles on his father, his father's first Revolutionary War ship, the *Liberty*, and his brother, Samuel Barron, who was also a commodore in the United States Navy (*Virginia Historical Register* 1 [1848]: 23–27, 76–80; 3 [1850]: 198–204). James Barron died at his home in Norfolk on 21 April 1851 and was buried in the cemetery at Trinity Church in Portsmouth.

Biography in *Virginia Historical Register* 4 (1851): 161–168; Paul Barron Watson, *The Tragic Career of Commodore James Barron* (1942); William Oliver Stevens, *An Affair of Honor: The Biography of Commodore James Barron, U.S.N.* (1969); James Barron Papers, containing family history documents, W&M; small collection of Barron Family Papers, LVA; service in Virginia State Navy documented in BW and LOMC; documents Barron prepared in seeking additional bounty lands for father's service in Rejected Claims, RG 3, LVA; *Correspondence between the Late Com. Stephen Decatur and Com. James Barron, Which Led to the Fatal Meeting of the 22nd of March, 1820* [ca. 1820]; *Proceedings of the General Court Martial Convened for the Trial of Commodore James Barron* (1822); John C. Emmerson Jr., *The Chesapeake Affair of 1807* (1954); Spencer Tucker, *Injured Honor: The Chesapeake-Leopard Affair, June 22, 1807* (1996); K. Michael Latshaw, "Flawed Judgment: The Court-Martial of Commodore James Barron," *VMHB* 105 (1997): 377–408; obituary and accounts of funeral in *Norfolk Daily Southern Argus*, 22, 24, 26 Apr. 1851.

DONALD W. GUNTER

BARRON, James Smith (3 December 1875–12 January 1941), member of the Senate of Virginia, was born in Warsaw, the second of three sons and fourth of six children of Samuel Barron and Agnes Newton Smith Barron. His father and grandfather, also named Samuel Barron, were officers in the Confederate navy. Until age fourteen he attended the public schools of Richmond County. After working on his family's farm and in sawmills in the area, he moved to Norfolk, where the Virginia-Carolina Chemical Company employed him. Resuming his education, Barron studied first at the College of William and Mary for two years and then at the law school of the University of Virginia, from which he graduated in 1903. He was president of the senior law class and also of the Jefferson Literary Society.

Barron began the practice of law in New York City, but he returned to Norfolk in 1904. He quickly became involved in community civic and political affairs. In 1906 he was elected to the Norfolk Common Council and served until he resigned four years later. On 23 June 1908 Barron married Katherine Massie Ryan at her parents' home in Norfolk. They had one son and one daughter. Thanks to his reputation as an exceptionally able criminal lawyer, a joint session of the city council elected Barron police justice in April 1912, a post he held until October 1914. As police justice he spoke out against vice in the city and corruption in the Norfolk Police Department.

Barron made his most notable public contribution during eight years in the Senate of Virginia. He was elected as a Democrat for the district encompassing the city of Norfolk in 1923 and reelected in 1927. A strong supporter of Governor Harry F. Byrd's reform program, in 1928 Barron sponsored the first antilynching bill ever enacted in any southern state. The passage of the law attracted national attention. Norfolk editor Louis I. Jaffé's condemnation of lynching won a Pulitzer Prize for journalism, and Barron and Byrd received much praise for supporting the bill. Barron also advocated other controversial measures, such as legalized parimutuel betting and termination of state support for Virginia Military Institute. A vocal opponent of Prohibition, he was a founder of the Virginia Association Against the Eighteenth Amendment and in 1933 was vice president of the Virginia convention that ratified the Twenty-first Amendment, which ended Prohibition. Governor John Garland Pollard appointed Barron to the Liquor Control Commission that recommended the creation of the Virginia Alcoholic Beverage Control Board to license the sale of beer and wine and to operate state-owned stores holding a monopoly on sales of all other alcoholic beverages.

A talented orator and loyal Democrat, though never a powerful voice in the Byrd organization, Barron took part in many political campaigns. At the 1928 Democratic National Convention he led the supporters of Governor Alfred E. Smith, of New York, in the Virginia delegation, and during the campaign he spoke on Smith's behalf in Virginia and Maryland. Barron declined to seek reelection to the General Assembly in 1931 and devoted his attention thereafter to his law practice and other interests. An avid golfer, he won the state amateur championship in 1919 and 1920 and assisted in designing the Princess Anne Golf Course. He also served on the board of directors of the Virginia Seashore State Park Commission. James Smith Barron suffered a heart attack late in 1940 and died at his residence, Upper Wolfsnare, near London Bridge in Princess Anne County, on 12 January 1941. An Episcopalian, he was buried in the cemetery of Eastern Shore Chapel in Virginia Beach.

Biography in Bruce, Tyler, and Morton, *History of Virginia*, 4:516–517; genealogical data, which must be used with care, in H. Clarkson Meredith, *Some Old Norfolk Families* [ca. 1976], 31–32; Census, Richmond Co., 1880; marriage reported in *Norfolk Landmark*, 24 June 1908; information provided by nephew S. Barron Segar and cousin Richard S. Barron, both of Norfolk; Barron's papers in possession of grandnephew Samuel B. Segar Jr., of Norfolk; obituaries in *Norfolk Virginian-Pilot* and *Richmond Times-Dispatch*, both 13 Jan. 1941; editorial tribute in *Norfolk Virginian-Pilot*, 14 Jan. 1941; memorial in *Virginia State Bar Association Proceedings* (1941): 128–130 (por.).

JAMES R. SWEENEY

BARRON, Samuel (28 November 1809–26 February 1888), naval officer, was born in Hampton, the son of Samuel Barron (1765–1810) and Jane Sawyer Barron. He had at least one sister. His family had a distinguished naval tradition. His father and his uncle James Barron (1768–1851) were both captains in the United States Navy. They had learned seamanship as young men during the Revolutionary War when their father James Barron (1740–1787), who also had a brother in the navy, was commodore of the Virginia State Navy. Before Barron's first birthday his father died, and as a tribute to the elder Samuel Barron, the Department of the Navy appointed his namesake son a midshipman on 1 January 1812.

When Barron was only six years old the Navy Department ordered him to duty at the Gosport Navy Yard in Portsmouth. He was the youngest person ever to receive a commission and go on active duty in the U.S. Navy. For the first four years he learned his numbers and letters, then before his eleventh birthday he sailed on his first cruise aboard the USS *Columbus*, flagship of the Mediterranean fleet. During his career Barron sailed on thirteen extended cruises, spent more than ten years at sea, and performed shore duty at seven stations. In addition to the Mediterranean, he sailed in the West Indies, off the west coast of Africa, and both coasts of South America. He was aboard the USS *Brandywine* when it returned the Marquis de Lafayette to France in June 1825, and during the Mexican War he commanded the USS *Perry* on the Pacific coast. Barron won promotion to lieutenant at the age of eighteen, was made a commander on 15 July 1847, and in September 1855 rose to the coveted rank of captain.

Barron married Imogen Wright, of Norfolk, on 31 October 1832. They had three sons and three daughters. Barron established a financial arrangement with brokers in New York and Norfolk to provide for his family when he was at sea. As was the custom in Tidewater Virginia, he also supplied his wife with household slaves. Barron was in command of the Navy Station at the Gosport Navy Yard in 1855 when a yellow fever epidemic broke out. He used the navy's resources to help those who were suffering, but his wife and a daughter died as he attended them.

Barron also served during the 1850s as a member of the Lighthouse Board in Washington, where his distinguished bearing and courtly manners won him the nickname of "the Navy diplomat." Tiring of Washington politics and debates on slavery, he requested sea duty and in 1858 received command of the USS *Wabash*, flagship of the Mediterranean squadron. When he returned to the United States in 1860, Barron was assigned once again to the Lighthouse Board, where he shared duties with Raphael Semmes, a future admiral in the Confederate navy.

In the spring of 1861, as the secession crisis grew in intensity, Secretary of the Navy Gideon Welles sent Barron and Senator Stephen R. Mallory, of Florida (the future Confederate secretary of the navy), to mediate between local secessionists and the military personnel at the Pensacola Navy Base. Like Robert E. Lee, Barron strongly opposed secession but decided that he would side with his native state if it left the Union. A few days after Virginia adopted the Ordinance of Secession, Barron tendered his resignation from the U.S. Navy. Welles refused to accept it and on 14 May 1861 dismissed Barron from the service.

On 26 May 1861 Barron received a captain's commission in the Virginia State Navy, and he obtained another in the Confederate States Navy, effective 10 June 1861, after Virginia joined the Confederacy. His first assignment as chief of the Bureau of Orders and Detail was to create a navy. He and his staff managed to acquire ships and arm and man them, although his fleet was never a match for the Union navy. On 20 July 1861 Barron assumed the additional responsibility of defending the North Carolina coast, but he and most of his men were captured on 30 August 1861 when a superior Northern force took Fort Hatteras. He was imprisoned at Fort Columbus in New York Harbor until mid-November 1861, then at Fort Warren in Boston Harbor until his exchange in July 1862.

Following his release Barron spent two months with his children at his sister's home in Warrenton, North Carolina. During that time the Confederate navy ordered him first to take charge of the Navy Ordnance Depot at Charlotte, North Carolina, and then to construct ironclad riverboats at Chattanooga, Tennessee, but he did not report to either place. Finally, he was ordered to take command of all naval forces in Virginia waters and accepted that assignment. As head of the James River Squadron until March 1863, Barron spent most of his time in Richmond serving on various committees rather than aboard his flagship, the *Patrick Henry*. His most difficult duty was restructuring the navy ranks to place them in better alignment with those of the army. He also went on a secret mission to Jackson, Mississippi, with authority to pay $1 million for six Union river gunboats, but Barron found only two gunboats, both in poor condition and under the command of civilian boatmen rather than Union navy officers. Furthermore, the governor of Mississippi and General Joseph E. Johnston had better use for the money, and so Barron arranged to leave the funds in their custody and returned to Richmond.

On 30 August 1863 Barron was ordered to Europe with the rank of commodore. Commander James D. Bulloch at that time had a small fleet of ships under construction and almost ready for action in Great Britain and France. Barron was to serve as the senior Confederate navy officer in Europe and to assume command of the ships. He reached London by 12 October 1863 and arranged for a Liverpool firm to handle Confederate naval funds. He then moved to Paris, where he established his headquarters. Barron made no effort to exercise his higher rank over Bulloch. As senior navy officer he made duty assignments in accordance with Bulloch's wishes, authorized pay vouchers, and played a social role in Paris. By the time Barron settled in Paris, the European nations had discovered alternative sources of cotton and they had decided to remain neutral in the American

Civil War. They accordingly refused to release the warships to the Confederacy.

When Raphael Semmes returned to Europe in 1864 aboard the CSS *Alabama* and entered the harbor of Cherbourg, he wrote Barron requesting relief of his command. Before Barron could act, the USS *Kearsarge* arrived off the harbor and Semmes challenged her to battle. The *Alabama* was sunk, and many of the crew were wounded or killed. Barron saw to the welfare of the wounded, commiserated with Semmes, paid off the officers, and arranged their transportation home. Barron also took control of the CSS *Rappahannock*, a Confederate ship in the harbor of Calais, but French officials detained the ship. Barron's residence in Paris became a well-known center of Southern hospitality, but he achieved little else on behalf of the Confederate States of America.

On 20 January 1865 Barron requested permission to return to Virginia in order to take "a more active part in this war." That permission—indeed, order—arrived in mid-February, and Barron began to arrange the return of most of the officers in Europe. He did not reach home in time to play any other military role, but he found that his family had safely survived, including his namesake son who had also served in the Confederate navy. Barron applied for a presidential pardon in September 1865 but did not receive one until 10 October 1867.

Barron's financial agents had guarded his interests, and he bought a farm called Malvern near Loretto in Essex County. His unmarried daughter Imogen Barron lived with him at Malvern for the remainder of his life in retirement. Samuel Barron died of what was described as old age at his home on 26 February 1888 and was buried in Cedar Grove Cemetery in Norfolk.

Samuel Barron Papers and Barron Family Papers, UVA; Samuel Barron and James Barron Papers, W&M; service records in Naval Historical Center, Wash., D.C.; Warren F. Spencer, *The Confederate Navy in Europe* (1983); John M. Coski, *Capital Navy: The Men, Ships, and Operations of the James River Squadron* (1996), 5–11, 20, 90; Presidential Pardons; Essex Co. Death Register; obituaries in *Norfolk Landmark* and *Richmond Dispatch*, both 28 Feb. 1888, and *Army and Navy Journal* 25 (1888): 627; funeral described in *Norfolk Landmark*, 1 Mar. 1888.

WARREN F. SPENCER

BARROW, David (30 October 1753–14 November 1819), Baptist minister and antislavery leader, was born in Brunswick County, the eldest son and second of at least three children of William Barrow and Amy Lee Barrow. David Barrow had a religious conversion experience at age sixteen and a year later was baptized by Zachariah Thompson and joined the Baptist Church. Between 1771 and 1774 Barrow preached throughout southern Virginia as well as in North Carolina, and about 1772 he was ordained into the ministry. In 1772 he married Sarah Gilliam, of Sussex County. Of their twelve children, five sons and three daughters were alive in 1798. Barrow was essentially a self-taught man who did not study grammar until after he was married. He eventually became well respected for his learning.

From 1774 to 1797 Barrow was minister of the Mill Swamp Baptist Church in Isle of Wight County. While he and another Baptist minister were preaching in neighboring Nansemond County in 1778, a gang of Episcopalians who mocked Baptist beliefs and practices attacked them, twice plunging Barrow into the mud, and dunking the other minister once. Barrow helped organize three churches in the Kehukee Association: Shoulder's Hill and South Quay, both in 1785, and Black Creek in 1786. Barrow preached at South Quay and Black Creek until the mid-1790s. The Kehukee Baptist Association was renamed the Portsmouth Baptist Association in 1791, and Barrow frequently acted as its moderator. He also served briefly on the Southampton County Court in 1792 and 1793.

Barrow freed his two slaves in February 1784 and frequently preached on the immorality of slavery. In 1785 he toured Kentucky, where he preached in Baptist churches and visited his two brothers in Mercer County. The activities of antislavery Baptists in Kentucky in the 1790s drew Barrow westward. In 1797 he made a second trip to Kentucky, where he settled the following year in Montgomery County and founded a school in 1801. When he left Virginia, Barrow published a long *Circular Letter. Southampton County, Virginia. February 14, 1798* [1798] that explained his reasons for emigrating. His move resulted in part from economic necessity. He then had eight children to support but lived on an unproductive farm, had debts, and was under constant pressure from ministerial obligations of hospitality. Without slaves he could not survive economically in Virginia. In his circular letter Barrow explained his socio-political creed, which was Jeffersonian Republican and strongly antislavery.

Shortly after his arrival in Kentucky, Barrow became minister of Mount Sterling Church. He quickly won recognition as a church leader and served on a joint committee that in 1801 negotiated a union between the Elkhorn Association, part of the Regular Baptists to whom Barrow belonged, and the Separate Baptists of the South Kentucky Association, to form the United Baptists. After participating in 1803 in a committee of the Elkhorn Association appointed to quell the doctrinal heresy of unitarianism that had cropped up in some of the churches, Barrow announced publication of *A Letter to a Friend Defending the Important Doctrine of the Trinity*, of which no known copy survives.

Because Barrow openly preached his antislavery views, he was often involved in controversy. A large proportion of the Baptists in Kentucky had abandoned their hostility to slavery by the early years of the nineteenth century. After the Elkhorn Association advised him and other ministers to stop opposing slavery, Barrow left it and joined the neighboring North District Association, only to face charges in that body in 1805 for preaching emancipation. In the following year the North District Baptists expelled him from his seat and appointed a committee to take the ruling against him to his Mount Sterling Church. Many members of Barrow's church supported him and separated from the home church. These events precipitated a general withdrawal of antislavery Baptists from the North District Association.

Although the North District Association late in 1807 reconsidered the case and annulled its expulsion of Barrow, he and Carter Tarrant, another well-known antislavery leader, helped found the independent Baptized Licking-Locust Association, Friends to Humanity, which excluded from communion all slaveholders and people sympathetic to slavery. The following year they organized the secular Kentucky Abolition Society, and Barrow published his most important antislavery tract, *Involuntary, Unmerited, Perpetual, Absolute, Hereditary Slavery, Examined: On the Principles of Nature, Reason, Justice, Policy and Scripture* (1808). Barrow served as president of the Kentucky Abolition Society, which in 1815 unsuccessfully petitioned Congress for a separate territory within the United States to serve as an asylum for emancipated African Americans. As the most prominent and effective antislavery Baptist minister in Kentucky, David Barrow held together the Friends of Humanity association until he died at his home in Montgomery County, Kentucky, on 14 November 1819.

Robert B. Semple, *A History of the Rise and Progress of the Baptists in Virginia* (1810), 343, 352, 357–360; Semple and George W. Beale, *A History of the Rise and Progress of the Baptists in Virginia*, rev. ed. (1894), 460–461; John Henderson Spencer and Burrilla B. Spencer, *A History of Kentucky Baptists, from 1769 to 1885* (1886), 1:192–197, 544–547, 2:17, 118–120; David Benedict, *A General History of the Baptist Denomination in America, and Other Parts of the World* (1813), 2:103, 231–232, 236, 239–240, 245–250; Vivien Sandlund, "'A Devilish and Unnatural Usurpation': Baptist Evangelical Ministers and Antislavery in the Early Nineteenth Century, A Study of the Ideas and Activism of David Barrow," *American Baptist Quarterly* 13 (1994): 262–277; Asa C. Barrow, "David Barrow and His Lulbegrud School, 1801," *Filson Club Historical Quarterly* 7 (1933): 88–93; minute books of Black Creek, Mill Swamp, and South Quay Baptist Churches, LVA photocopies; manumission of Barrow's slaves, 10 Feb. 1784, Southampton Co. Deed Book, 6:208; Richard Furman Papers, South Carolina Baptist Historical Society, Furman University, Greenville, S.C.; copies of Barrow's 1795 journal, Filson Club, Louisville, Ky., and in Draper MSS, 12CC163–184; Barrow's 1797 diary and memoranda and an undated interview of William Barrow by John D. Shane in Draper MSS, 12CC185, 190–191, 210–212.

FREDRIKA J. TEUTE

BARROW, William James (11 December 1904–25 August 1967), paper conservator, was born in Brunswick County, the only son and second of two children of Bernard H. Barrow and Sallie Virginia Archer Barrow. He was educated at Randolph-Macon Academy in Bedford and attended Randolph-Macon College in Ashland from 1923 to 1925, but he did not graduate. He left college to work for his cousin Alfred Barrow, of the Barrow Corporation, a manufacturer of work clothes. Barrow worked in or managed factories in Lynchburg, in Saint Louis, Missouri, in Tacoma, Washington, and in Oakland, California, before the company went bankrupt in 1931 during the Great Depression.

W. J. Barrow, as he was always known as an adult, moved back to Virginia and indulged an interest in historical records. He quickly became convinced that an unmet need existed for skilled people who could restore books and old documents, and he moved to Washington, D.C., to study bookbinding under Marian Lane, a prominent private expert, and observe restoration techniques at the Library of Congress. In 1932 Henry Read McIlwaine, the Virginia state librarian, offered Barrow space in the State Library building to establish the Barrow Restoration Shop in exchange for a library discount on document restoration. He operated his small shop there until 1935. On 6 April 1935 he married Ruth Abbott Gibbs, of Richmond. The eldest of their three sons, Bernard Gibbs Barrow, was appointed one of the original ten members of the Court of Appeals of Virginia in 1985.

In 1935 Barrow moved his shop to the new Mariners' Museum Library in Newport News, where he studied new techniques for strengthening paper with a cellulose acetate lamination process that the National Bureau of Standards had tested and recommended. From 1935 to 1941 Barrow obtained the latest scientific information on cellulose acetate lamination, paper deterioration, permanence, and testing from Bourdon Walter Scribner, head of the bureau's Paper Section, and Morris Samuel Kantrowitz, head of the Technical Division of the United States Government Printing Office. In 1937 Barrow enlisted friends from the Newport News Shipbuilding and Dry Dock Company to design and build laminating equipment that suited the small-scale requirements of his shop. He applied his knowledge of paper chemistry to adapt a process of aqueous alkalization, based on an existing patent, in the restoration of paper. On 7 November 1942 he received patent number 2301996 for his process and marketed it along with his roller-type laminator to large libraries and archives worldwide. Barrow also conducted research with homemade testing equipment on paper permanence, paper splitting, inks, and ink transfer.

After the new Virginia State Library building was completed in 1940, Barrow moved his restoration shop into it and returned to Richmond for good. In 1957 he received the first of several grants for research into paper permanence from the Council of Library Resources, which was then headed by his friend and mentor Verner Warren Clapp, former deputy librarian of Congress. Barrow worked with Clapp to advocate conservation of paper-based documents threatened by chemical decay. Barrow's research predicted that modern papers would deteriorate rapidly and examined the chemical cause. State Librarian Randolph W. Church had the Virginia State Library publish some of Barrow's findings in 1959, 1960, and 1961. In 1960 Barrow helped to develop a production-scale process to manufacture permanent alkaline text-quality wood fiber paper. The council supported this project and also funded the establishment in 1961 of the Barrow Research Laboratory, a fully equipped facility for the study of paper permanence located in the Virginia Historical Society building in Richmond.

Barrow's work sounded an alarm rather than uncovering new facts, since it essentially replicated research done during the 1930s. Beginning in 1939 and extending into the 1970s, Barrow and his associates published more than forty papers on natural and accelerated aging techniques to estimate paper longevity, performance specifications for bookbindings, nonaqueous alkalization methods, synthetic adhesives, strength characteristics of old paper, and nondestructive paper-testing techniques. Barrow convinced restorers and conservators that deterioration was chemically caused and could be slowed by chemical means, which transformed a traditional craft into the scientific profession of paper conservation. His research became known worldwide, and he was the leading expert on the subject. He belonged to many professional organizations, was elected a fellow of the Royal Society of Arts in 1936, and received an honorary doctor of laws degree from Randolph-Macon College in 1966.

W. J. Barrow suffered from heart disease during the final years of his life. He had a heart attack at his home on 25 August 1967 and died that evening at Saint Mary's Hospital in Richmond. He was buried in Lakeview Cemetery in Blackstone. The laboratory remained in operation at the Virginia Historical Society for another decade, and the restoration shop in the Virginia State Library building continued in operation until 1988. Ruth Gibbs Barrow managed the restoration shop until she retired in 1977.

William James Barrow Papers, Ruth G. Barrow Scrapbook, and Barrow Research Laboratory Papers, VHS; family history and professional information supplied or verified by Bernard Gibbs Barrow, James Abbott Barrow, Ruth Gibbs Barrow, William Archer Barrow, Sarah Archer Barrow Davey, Gregory Minnick, Harold S. Sniffen, and William K. Wilson; obituaries of wife and eldest son in *Richmond News Leader*, 2 July 1988, and *Richmond Times-Dispatch*, 31 Mar. 1995; obituaries in *Richmond News Leader*, 26 Aug. 1967, *Richmond Times-Dispatch*, 27 Aug. 1967 (por.), and *American Archivist* 30 (1967): 635–637, which reproduces a biographical press release from the Council on Library Resources.

SALLY CRUZ ROGGIA

BARTON, Mary (1 March 1847–18 June 1901), physician, was born in Alexandria, the eldest of four sons and six daughters of Benjamin Barton and Elizabeth Kennedy Barton. She and two of her sisters were the only children who lived to adulthood. Barton's father was a jeweler and silversmith, active in Alexandria's civic affairs and prosperous enough to maintain a residence in town and another in Fairfax County.

Barton began the study of medicine in 1876 at age twenty-nine, at a time when less than 1 percent of the more than 55,000 trained physicians in the United States were women. Her paternal uncle George Goodall Barton, a medical doctor in New York City, may have influenced her decision to ignore the discouraging odds, and she may have lived with him while she studied medicine. In 1876 she enrolled in the Women's College of the New York Infirmary, which Elizabeth Blackwell had founded eight years previously. Blackwell had been the first woman to earn a medical degree in the United States, and her college provided rigorous medical training for women who were unable to gain admittance in any significant numbers to the established medical colleges. Like all aspiring students, Barton was required to show a diploma from a recognized literary school or to pass a series of entrance examinations that included algebra, geometry, chemistry, botany, and physics. Her ability to do so provides evidence of a thorough early education, which may have begun in her father's extensive library.

To dispel any public doubts about the abilities of the students or the quality of the education, and to prepare graduates to overcome professional resistance from male colleagues, Blackwell and her faculty adopted a curriculum more challenging than that then followed in most men's medical schools. This included three rather than two years of graded study, with eight- instead of six-month sessions, and mandatory clinical training either at the infirmary attached to the school or at one of the hospitals in the city. In addition, each student was required to pass annual exams before advancing, and an independent examining board composed of male and female professors from other medical colleges tested all of the candidates before graduation. Barton was one of seven women who graduated from the Women's College in 1878. The college encouraged postgraduate work, and she may have been one of several graduates who received annual appointments as clinical assistants in the infirmary.

By 1880 Barton had returned to City View, her parents' house in Fairfax County, and was practicing medicine in Alexandria and the surrounding environs. She later moved into Alexandria and is believed to have been the first female doctor in that city to have earned a medical degree. Like most women physicians in the late nineteenth century, Barton probably had a general practice that consisted primarily of women and children, or she may have concentrated on obstetrics and gynecology. Unless she took advantage of Alexandria's proximity to Washington, D.C., and kept in contact with the community of women doctors then practicing in the nation's capital, she would have worked in relative isolation. According to census figures, Barton was one of only twenty-six women practicing medicine in Virginia when she began her medical career. This figure, which remained fairly constant throughout her lifetime and rose to only thirty-two by the time of her death, included all types of physicians. The number of academically trained women doctors in the state was even smaller. These physicians enjoyed little support from their male colleagues, and Barton had been practicing medicine for more than fifteen years before the Medical Society of Virginia began admitting qualified women in 1897.

During part of the time Barton lived in Alexandria, she shared her house with William Barton, who identified himself to the census takers as her stepbrother or brother by adoption. After a twenty-year career in medicine, Mary Barton died in Alexandria on 18 June 1901 from complications resulting from an operation to relieve pleurisy. She was buried in Ivy Hill Cemetery in Alexandria.

Family records in Benjamin Barton Papers, VHS; information on medical education in Annie Sturges Daniel, "'A Cautious Experiment': The History of the New York Infirmary for Women and Children and the Women's Medical College of the New York Infirmary," *Medical Woman's Journal* 47 (1940), esp. 323–325; 48 (1941), esp. 33–36, 76–79, 167–169; obituary in *Alexandria Gazette and Virginia Advertiser*, 19 June 1901.

KELLY HENDERSON HAYES

BARTON, Richard Walker (3 July 1799–15 January 1860), member of the House of Representatives, was one of five sons and three daughters of Richard Peters Barton and Martha Walker Barton. He was probably born at Shady Oak, his father's house in Frederick County about six miles west of Winchester. Barton lived all of his life in Frederick County. In 1802 his father bought 288 acres of land on Opequon Creek, including John Hite's 1753 stone house, a mill, and a distillery. Across the Valley Turnpike from the property was Springdale, which was Barton's residence as an adult. In time the two tracts came to be called Bartonsville. Barton studied law and was admitted to the bar in Winchester. On 14 November 1822 he married Alcinda Winn Gibson, of Culpeper County. They had two sons and one daughter. Alcinda Barton died on 12 December 1829, shortly after giving birth to her third child, and on 30 April 1833 Barton married Caroline Marx, of Richmond. They had two sons and two daughters.

In April 1823 Barton was elected one of Frederick County's two members of the House of Delegates. He served on the Committee for Courts of Justice and the Committee of Roads and Internal Navigation. Barton lost bids for reelection in 1824 and 1825 but in April 1832 won one of the three House seats to which Frederick County was then entitled. He was reelected in 1833 with the largest number of votes in the county and again in 1834 with the second largest number of votes. In December 1834, in the only contested election for Speaker of the House of Delegates during Barton's tenure, he voted for the Whig candidate and as a consequence was appointed ranking member of the Committee on Agriculture and Manufactures.

Barton won election to the House of Delegates once more in April 1838. He returned to the Committee of Roads and Internal Navigation and was appointed chairman of the Committee on Agriculture and Manufactures. By then well known as a local leader of the Whig Party, Barton ran for the United States House of Representatives in 1839, but he lost to Democrat William Lucas by a very narrow margin. In April 1841 he ran again and defeated Lucas. Barton served only one term in Congress and did not seek reelection in 1843. He voted regularly with the Whigs and served on the Committee on Indian Affairs, for which his professional interests in law and business and his past participation in Virginia politics had given him no real preparation.

Barton continued to practice law, and he also speculated in land in Frederick and in nearby Randolph County. By 1850 his real estate alone was worth more than $110,000. Barton enlarged the Springdale property to 610 acres, acquired at least thirty slaves by 1840, and served as the founding president of the Valley Agricultural Society of Frederick County, which began holding its annual cattle show and fair at Winchester in 1856. On 22 April 1858 he conveyed his interest in Springdale to one of his brothers. Richard Walker Barton died on 15 January 1860, the day after he signed a will that was recorded on 6 February 1860. He was buried in the family cemetery at Springdale.

Birth, marriage, and death dates in family Bible records of son Robert T. Barton, made a decade or more after Richard W. Barton's death and printed in *Virginia Genealogist* 8 (1964): 28–30; confused and contradictory family data, including death date of 15 Mar. 1859 on gravestone, printed in Stuart E. Brown Jr., ed., *Rev. Thomas Barton (1728–1780) and Some of His Descendants and Some of Their In-Laws* [ca. 1988], 90–93, 158, 219–223; brief biography, which includes some demonstrable inaccuracies and names thirteen children, in Quarles, *Worthy Lives*, 31–32; election campaigns and failure to run in 1843 reported in *Richmond Enquirer*, 11 Apr. 1823, 16 Apr. 1824, 12 Apr. 1825, 10 Apr. 1832, 9 Apr. 1833, 8 Apr. 1834, 7 Apr. 1835, 1 May 1838, 10 May, 4 June 1839, 28 Apr. 1840, 27, 30 Apr., 11 May 1841, 28 Apr. 1843; Frederick Co. Will Book, 26:228.

DONALD W. GUNTER

BARTON, Robert Thomas (24 November 1842–17 January 1917), attorney and legal scholar, was born in Winchester, the fourth of six sons and eighth of ten children of David Walker Barton and Frances Lucy Jones Barton. He was educated at Winchester Academy and at Bloomfield Academy in Albemarle County, from which he went directly into the Confederate army, serving in the infantry, the Rockbridge Artillery, and on assignment to the Niter and Mining Bureau, which procured niter (saltpeter) for manufacturing gunpowder. Three of his brothers and two of his brothers-in-law died fighting for the Confederacy. After the war Barton returned to Winchester to study law and was admitted to the bar in September 1865. On 19 February 1868 he married Katie K. Knight, of Cecil County, Maryland. They had no children. She died on 11 June 1887. On 10 June 1890 Barton married Gertrude Williamson Baker, who was nearly thirty years his junior. Of their three children, one son and one daughter lived to maturity.

Shortly after the Civil War ended, Barton wrote an extended memoir of his brother-in-law Thomas Marshall, which was published in James B. Avirett, *Memoirs of General Turner Ashby and his Compeers* (1867), 276–317. Barton was later commander of the General Turner Ashby Camp, United Confederate Veterans, in Winchester, and he served on the organization's state committee on the war's history. He was a conservative Democrat who won election in 1883 to the House of Delegates on a platform of opposition to the policies of the Readjusters. As chairman of the Committee on Courts of Justice he took the lead in investigating charges of misbehavior by Readjuster officials, including Attorney General Francis Simpson Blair, whom he unsuccessfully tried to have impeached. Barton was also mayor of Winchester from 1899 to 1902, served on the Board of Visitors of Virginia Military Institute from 1874 to 1876, and also sat on the board of the University College of Medicine in Richmond. In addition to practicing law, he invested in local businesses, including the Winchester Telephone Company and the Farmers and Merchants Bank of Winchester, of which he was president from 1902 until his death.

Although he was a hardworking lawyer with a varied practice, Barton was a scholar at heart. In his most important work, he undertook to replace Conway Robinson's comprehensive but unavailable and outdated three-volume *Practice in the Courts of Law and Equity in Virginia* (1832–1839). Barton's first volume, *Practice in the Courts of Law in Civil Cases, Founded on Robinson's Practice* (1877), familiarly known as *Barton's Practice*, was reissued in a two-volume second edition in 1891–1892. Barton's two-volume continuation, *Pleading and Practice in the Courts of Chancery* (1881–1883), also included information on West Virginia courts and laws. It appeared in revised editions in 1899 and 1926, with the latter, posthumous version prepared by Barton's namesake son, a Richmond attorney.

The usefulness and importance of Barton's publications led to his election in 1892 as the fifth president of the Virginia State Bar Association. His presidential address on "The Punishment of Crime" ruminated at length on the evolution of the British and American systems of criminal law, concluding with a plea for swift, certain, and stiff punishment of persons convicted of crimes. Two years earlier, in an address to the association on "The Romance of the Law," he had argued against needless delays in civil and chancery suits.

In 1891 Barton delivered the annual address to the Virginia Historical Society, speaking on George Washington's introduction to politics. He gave other talks and wrote several short pieces, but his most enduring contribution to historical scholarship was the two-volume *Virginia Colonial Decisions: The Reports by Sir John Randolph and by Edward Barradall of Decisions of the General Court of Virginia, 1728–1741* (1909). The volumes contain transcriptions, made under the personal supervision of William Wallace Scott, the state law librarian, of arguments at the bar in Williamsburg as recorded by two colonial attorneys general of Virginia. Barton's introductory chapters filled most of the first volume and constituted one of the first extended legal histories of the colony. Robert Thomas Barton died at his home on 17 January 1917 and was buried in Mount Hebron Cemetery in Winchester.

Margaretta Barton Colt, *Defend the Valley: A Shenandoah Family in the Civil War* (1994); Tyler, *Men of Mark*, 1:139–142; Glass and Glass, *Virginia Democracy*, 2:357–359; Compiled Service Records; Gertrude Williamson Baker Barton Papers, Duke; Robert T. Barton, "The Romance of the Law" and "The Punishment of Crime," in *Virginia State Bar Association Proceedings* (1891): 173–188 and (1893): 153–181, and "The First Election of Washington to the House of Burgesses," *Collections of the Virginia Historical Society*, new ser., 11 (1892): 113–125; obituaries in *Winchester Evening Star*, 17 Jan. 1917, and *Richmond Times-Dispatch*, 18 Jan. 1917 (por.); memorial in *Virginia State Bar Association Proceedings* (1918): 91–94.

WAVERLEY K. WINFREE

BARTON, Seth Maxwell (8 September 1829–11 April 1900), Confederate army officer, was born in Fredericksburg, one of four sons of Thomas Bowerbank Barton, an attorney, and Susan Stone Barton. He was admitted to the United States Military Academy in 1845 and graduated in 1849, ranked twenty-eighth in a class of forty-three, whereupon he was commissioned a brevet second lieutenant in the 3d Infantry. After service at Fort Columbus, New York, he was promoted to second lieutenant in the 1st Infantry in 1850 and sent to the Southwest for duty on the frontier. He spent most of his time in Texas. On 1 June 1853 he was promoted to first lieutenant. He saw action against the Comanche in February 1857, and on 31 October was promoted to captain. Barton was on leave from late in 1858 to 1860, and he resigned from the U.S. Army effective 11 June 1861 in order to return to Virginia and join the Confederate army.

Barton was commissioned a captain in the regular army of the Confederacy, to rank from 16 March 1861. On 8 July 1861 he was appointed lieutenant colonel of the 3d Arkansas Infantry, with which he served in western Virginia and the Shenandoah Valley, where he was chief engineer for General Thomas J. "Stonewall" Jackson. Barton was promoted to brigadier general on 18 March 1862 and assigned to General Edmund Kirby-Smith's army in eastern Tennessee. In 1863 Barton's brigade fought in the Chickasaw Bayou campaign, at Champion Hill, and at the siege of Vicksburg. Barton was paroled at Vicksburg after its Confederate defenders surrendered on 4 July 1863.

Barton returned to Virginia and married Marianne C. Jenifer in Richmond on 10 August 1863. They had two sons. He was assigned command of the brigade in George E. Pickett's division formerly headed by Lewis A. Armistead, who had been mortally wounded at the Battle of Gettysburg. When Pickett mounted an attack on New Bern, North Carolina, at the beginning of February 1864, Barton was given the task of taking the works in front of the town and preventing enemy reinforcement. He was under orders to combine with Pickett's force for a concerted attack if he was unable to carry out his assignment. His brigade not only failed to reach its objective but also withdrew from the field rather than joining Pickett's command. Rejecting Barton's contention that the terrain around New Bern posed insurmountable obstacles, Picket attributed the failure of the campaign to Barton's lack of aggression. Noting that the press and common rumor were critical of his generalship, Barton argued that his brigade commanders had concurred in his decisions and asked for a court of inquiry to clear his reputation. One was ordered to convene, but it never met. On 11 May 1864 General Robert Ransom relieved Barton of his command for allegedly mishandling his brigade in the fighting south of Richmond on the previous day. Barton's and Ransom's accounts of the episode differ, and subordinates of each supported their commanders. Barton's regimental commanders petitioned for his restoration to command, and at Barton's request a court of inquiry was ordered but it also never met. Barton's field officers unsuccessfully sought his return to the brigade again in August, and he was later given the command of a brigade in the Richmond defenses. On 9 January 1865 he was assigned to a brigade in George Washington Custis Lee's division and served with it until he was captured at Saylers Creek on 6 April. Barton was imprisoned at Fort Warren, Massachusetts, until he took the oath of allegiance to the United States on 16 June 1865.

Barton lived in his hometown of Fredericksburg for the remainder of his life. He worked as a land agent, served on the vestry of Trinity Episcopal Church, was an active Mason, and was said to be a fine chemist. Seth Maxwell Barton died on 11 April 1900 during a visit to Washington, D.C., and was buried in the Fredericksburg City Cemetery.

Brief biographies in Evans, *Confederate Military History,* 4:579–581, in *Thirty-First Annual Reunion of the Association of Graduates of the United States Military Academy* (1900), 138–140 (memoir by Samuel B. Holabird), and in Ezra J. Warner, *Generals in Gray: Lives of the Confederate Commanders* (1959), 18–19 (por.); small collection of Barton-Jenifer Family Papers in LC; George Washington Cullum, *Biographical Register of the Officers and Graduates of the U.S. Military Academy at West Point, N.Y., From its Establishment, in 1802, to 1890,* 3d ed. (1891), 2:391; *OR;* Compiled Service Records; BVS Marriage Register, Richmond City; obituaries in *Fredericksburg Daily Star,* 11 Apr. 1900, and *Fredericksburg Free Lance* and *Richmond Dispatch,* both 12 Apr. 1900.

LEE A. WALLACE JR.

BASKERVILL, Britton (October 1863–25 April 1892), member of the General Assembly, was born a slave in Mecklenburg County. He was the eldest of five children, all sons, of Britton Baskervill, a stonemason, and Sallie Baskervill. Neither of his parents could read or write, but his father's hard work enabled Baskervill to obtain an education, graduating first in 1883 from the Boydton Academic and Bible Institute, in Mecklenburg County, and then in 1885 from the Wayland Institute in Washington, D.C.. He returned to Union Level, in the Flat Creek District of Mecklenburg County, and taught school, farmed, and served as a superintendent of the Sunday school at Bloom Hill Baptist Church.

At its 26 September 1887 convention at Boydton the Mecklenburg County Republican Party nominated Baskervill for the General Assembly. He owed his nomination to factional rivalries at home and to the manipulations of William Mahone, the powerful leader of the state Republican Party. African Americans held a majority among the county's voters and after 1869 had consistently elected black Republicans—Ross Hamilton, Amos A. Dodson, and incumbent Joseph R. Jones—to the General Assembly. In 1887 Hamilton sought Mahone's endorsement, as did William A. Jamieson, the white county clerk. Jones and John M. Sloan, a white native of Ohio whom Jamieson had replaced as county clerk, ensured Mahone's enmity by campaigning against his domination of the party. At the convention Jamieson withdrew, probably at Mahone's orders, and directed his delegates to support Baskervill. Despite Hamilton's assertions to the contrary, Mahone apparently considered him too close to Congressman James Brady, another Mahone enemy, and after several ballots enough of Hamilton's delegates switched to Baskervill to give him the nomination. Jones and Hamilton were said to be contemplating independent campaigns, but they stayed out of the race and Baskervill easily defeated the Democratic candidate.

In the General Assembly, Baskervill voted consistently with the outnumbered Republicans and served on the Committees on Privileges and Elections and on the Chesapeake and its Tributaries. By the time the session ended in March 1888, the congressional campaigns were heating up. Baskervill asked Mahone whether he supported the candidacy of John Mercer Langston in the eleven-county Fourth District. The answer soon was clear: Mahone obtained the Republican nomination for Richard Watson Arnold, a white ally, and prepared to defeat Langston's independent candidacy. His decision further divided the Republicans in Mecklenburg County. Hamilton broke with Mahone to endorse Langston, who received overwhelming support from blacks in the county. Baskervill remained loyal to Mahone, and by the end of the campaign was desperately asking him for cash with which to purchase votes. Despite fraud throughout the district on the part of the Democrats, later documented in a congressional investigation, Langston carried Mecklenburg County by 376 votes and was ultimately seated as Virginia's first African American congressman.

A year later the county's Republicans remained divided and disaffected, but Hamilton managed to repair his relationship with Mahone sufficiently to receive the nomination to the General Assembly, and he subsequently won the election. Baskervill returned to teaching and farming. He probably already had tuberculosis when he contracted influenza in December 1891. Britton Baskervill remained ill until his death on 25 April 1892. He never married but was engaged to an unidentified woman from Richmond when he died. His younger brother William H. Baskervill honored his memory by naming his firstborn son after him.

Census, Mecklenburg Co., 1870, 1880; Jackson, *Negro Office-Holders*, 2; Harold S. Forsythe, "'But My Friends Are Poor': Ross Hamilton and Freedpeople's Politics in Mecklenburg County, Virginia, 1869–1901," *VMHB* 105 (1997): 415, 418–420 (por.), 426, 428; Baskervill to William Mahone, 29 Sept. 1887, 27 Mar., 22 Oct. 1888, Mahone Papers, Duke (all signed B. Baskervill Jr); Election Records, no. 418, RG 13, LVA; *JHD*, 1887–1888 sess., 56, 58; *Richmond Dispatch*, 17 Oct. 1888; Committee on Elections, *John M. Langston* v. *E. C. Venable*, 51st Cong., 1st sess., 1890, House Rept. 2462, serial 2814, 38; BVS Death Register, Mecklenburg Co.; obituary with month and year of birth in *Richmond Planet*, 7 May 1892.

JOHN T. KNEEBONE

BASKERVILL, Henry Eugene (10 March 1867–30 November 1946), architect, was born in Richmond, the only child of Henry Embra Coleman Baskervill and his second wife, Eugenia Jackson Buffington Baskervill. He was educated at Episcopal High School in Alexandria and at Cornell University, where he received a bachelor's degree in electrical engineering in 1889. His course of study for the first three years at Cornell was virtually the same as that for students of mechanical engineering and for students in the College of Architecture, except that engineering students did not study architectural history.

After graduation Baskervill returned to Richmond and took a job as an assistant to the city engineer, Wilford Emory Cutshaw. He helped Cutshaw manage the construction of the new city hall and wrote specifications for the fireproofing of the White House of the Confederacy. In 1902 Baskervill married Ethel Penn-Gaskell Marsh. They had one son.

In 1897 Baskervill and William Churchill Noland formed the architectural firm of Noland and Baskervill, with Noland initially doing most of the design work and Baskervill initially doing the bulk of the engineering work. In the early years their practice succeeded in part because of a lack of serious competition and in part because their family associations and friendships with business and civic leaders helped them to obtain commissions for both residential and commercial work. The variety of their commissions and the varying tastes of their customers led them to work in many idioms, and they excelled in the skillful combination of stylistic elements in one building. The most significant projects credited to the firm include the Virginia State Insurance Company building in Richmond; the 1904 renovation and expansion of the Virginia State Capitol; James H. Dooley's summerhouse, Swannanoa, in Augusta County; the Scott-Bocock House in Richmond; the Scott summer residence, Royal Orchard, in Augusta County; and Baskervill's own Italianate residence of 1913. They also designed buildings in Richmond for the Dooley Hospital and the Young Women's Christian Association.

In 1918 Noland and Baskervill dissolved their partnership, and Baskervill joined with Alfred G. Lambert to form Baskervill and Lambert. In 1932 Baskervill became a member of the Richmond City Planning Commission. Three years earlier his son, Henry Coleman Baskerville (the only family member to add a terminal *e* to the surname), had joined the firm and in 1932 it became Baskervill and Son. Although the firm still designed residences, its focus shifted toward commercial projects. It continued to produce high-quality work, principally in Richmond, including the original building for the Retreat Hospital, the Richmond News Leader Building, the Stuart McGuire residence, and the Crippled Children's Hospital at the Medical College of Virginia. Until his death Baskervill continued to participate in the firm's work, but he gradually relinquished control to his son. Baskervill and Son was one of the most consistently successful central Virginia architectural firms during his lifetime, and at his death Baskervill left an estate valued at more than half a million dollars.

Henry Eugene Baskervill died at his home on 30 November 1946 and was buried in Hollywood Cemetery in Richmond.

Elizabeth Drake Updike, "Henry Eugene Baskervill and William Churchill Noland: Richmond's Response to the American Renaissance" (master's thesis, UVA, 1987); Karen D. Steele, "Henry E. Baskervill: Eclectic Architect," *Richmond Quarterly* 7 (summer 1984): 24–31; Patrick Hamilton Baskervill, *Genealogy of the Baskerville Family and Some Allied Families* (1912), 76–80; Baskervill and Son Papers, including client list, VHS; Wells and Dalton, *Virginia Architects*, 22–24; L. Moody Simms Jr., "William Churchill Noland: Richmond Architect," *Richmond Quarterly* 3 (spring 1981): 43–44; brief history of Baskervill and Son in *Richmond Times-Dispatch*, 18 May 1997; interview with Frances Laws, a retired Noland and Baskervill secretary, 20 Feb. 1987; obituaries in *Richmond News Leader*, 30 Nov. 1946 (por.), and *Richmond Times-Dispatch*, 1 Dec. 1946.

ELIZABETH UPDIKE JIRANEK

BASKERVILLE, Henry Coleman (10 August 1905–28 April 1969), architect, was born in Richmond, the only child of Richmond architect Henry Eugene Baskervill and Ethel Penn-Gaskell Marsh Baskervill. He was educated at the Chamberlayne School in Richmond and graduated from Episcopal High School in Alexandria. He then enrolled in the University of Pennsylvania and received a B.A. in 1926 and an M.A. three years later.

In 1929 he joined his father's architectural firm, Baskervill and Lambert, which in 1932 was reorganized as Baskervill and Son when he became his father's junior partner. He added a final *e* to the family name and as an adult was known as H. Coleman Baskerville. On 3 October 1933 he married Virginia Pegram Morton. They had two daughters and one son.

Baskervill and Son received major commissions in Richmond in the 1930s and early 1940s, weathering poor economic times. These included renovation of the Medical College of Virginia's Egyptian Building (1932) and construction of the MCV Hospital (1936–1941), the combined Virginia State Library and Supreme Court building (1939–1941), the W. T. Grant Company Department Store (1939–1941), and several large private residences. New Deal programs helped fund the state projects, providing the firm with a substantial windfall during the Great Depression.

Baskerville's architectural career was interrupted by World War II when he entered the United States Navy in 1942 as a lieutenant. He served in the Office of the Commander in Chief of the U.S. Fleet before attending several naval schools. In 1945 he was a gunnery officer aboard the USS *Bismarck Sea* when the carrier was sunk by a Japanese warplane during the Battle of Iwo Jima. For his service during this action Baskerville received the Bronze Star for gallantry. Subsequently he was gunnery officer on the USS *Tarawa* until his discharge from active duty later that year with the rank of lieutenant commander. During the Korean War he commanded a naval reserve battalion in Richmond.

With the death of his father in 1946, Baskerville became senior partner in the firm of Baskervill and Son and retained that title for the remainder of his life. Under Baskerville the firm expanded into many different types of architectural projects. It took on several important industrial commissions for large clients during the 1950s, among them a building for the presses of the Richmond Newspapers (1951–1952), the extensive construction of facilities at the Naval Mine Weapons Depot in Yorktown (1952–1957), and several buildings for the Chesapeake and Potomac Telephone Company (1952–1962). The firm also designed new buildings or additions for almost thirty schools during the twenty years after World War II.

The recognition of Baskerville by the American Hospital Association as an approved hospital architect led to at least twenty-one commissions for hospital designs or expansions in Virginia. Among the largest were buildings in Petersburg for Central State Hospital (1951–1952), Richmond's Wood Memorial Dental School (1954), and Richmond Memorial Hospital (1957). Baskerville's interest in health care was reflected in his civic activities. He helped found the Virginia League for Birth Control in 1934 and was its first secretary and treasurer. He served for many years as a director of the league and its successor, the Virginia League for Planned Parenthood, as well as two Richmond hospitals.

Among the fifteen major office buildings Baskerville's firm designed under his leadership, the Seaboard Air Line Railway Company headquarters building (1959) in Richmond was one of the most important. The building is typical of the Modern style employed by the firm in many of its designs for schools, offices, and hospitals in the 1950s and 1960s. These commissions were frequently characterized by heavy framing in metal or stone surrounding large windows. Colored panels or textured brickwork occasionally enlivened the often-sparse facades.

With changes in architectural taste many of the office buildings and schools that Baskerville planned in the Modern style have begun to appear dated, but he and his designers were always sensitive to the traditional decorative requirements of churches and synagogues. In addition to many designs for places of worship that the firm created during its formative years, it received more than twenty important commissions in Virginia between 1946 and Baskerville's death. In Richmond these included the Seventh Street Christian Church (1951), Trinity Methodist Church (1956), and the parish house for Saint Paul's Episcopal Church (1960). In contrast to the commercial buildings in the Modern style, these more traditional designs skillfully combine historic forms with the demands of functionality. With time, these neo-Georgian commissions may be regarded as the most enduring legacy of the firm under H. Coleman Baskerville.

In 1964 Baskerville began a five-year term as a member of the State Board for the Examination and Certification of Architects, but resigned in 1967 due to poor health. He was a member of the American Institute of Architects and received the prestigious William C. Noland Award from its Virginia chapter in 1968. H. Coleman Baskerville died in Richmond on 28 April 1969 and was buried in Hollywood Cemetery in Richmond.

NCAB, 55:20 (por.); Baskervill and Son Papers, VHS; illustrated history of firm in *Richmond Times-Dispatch*, 18 May 1997; Robert P. Winthrop, *Architecture in Downtown Richmond* (1982), 40, 51, 65, 238; Wells and Dalton, *Virginia Architects*, 22–25; obituaries in *Richmond News Leader*, 28 Apr. 1969, and *Richmond Times-Dispatch*, 29 Apr. 1969.

SELDEN RICHARDSON

BASKIN, Joel L. (27 September 1885–27 December 1948), head of the Ku Klux Klan in Virginia, was born in Vaiden, Mississippi, the second of two or three sons and fourth of seven children of Joel Baskin and Clara S. Wise Baskin. His father, a Baptist minister, was a graduate of Mississippi College in Clinton. Little is known about Baskin's early life and education. He later said that he studied law at Mississippi College, but the school has no record of his attendance. By 1917 he was married and living in Birmingham, Alabama, where he worked in the music section of a department store. That same year he joined the Knights of the Ku Klux Klan, Incorporated.

Late in 1925 Baskin moved to Richmond to become the grand dragon, or head, of the Klan in Virginia. Accompanying him was James Esdale, the powerful grand dragon of Alabama and a close associate of Hiram Wesley Evans, the Klan's imperial wizard. Evans probably charged Esdale with the reorganization of the Klan in Virginia, with the latter choosing Baskin to serve as grand dragon.

Klan organizers appeared in the state as early as 1920, but the Klan never became as powerful in Virginia as elsewhere. Opponents—white and black—spoke against the organization from the beginning, and internal disputes slowed recruitment and prevented concerted action. Klansmen joined in the 1925 campaign to block the election of John Michael Purcell, a Catholic, as state treasurer, but Purcell's victory proved the Klan's weakness.

Baskin had taken charge by 26 September 1926, when the Virginia Klan presented a giant American flag and pole to the College of William and Mary. The school's president, Julian Alvin Carroll Chandler, accepted the gift with a speech that emphasized American traditions of liberty and tolerance, thus turning the event into a rebuke of the Klan. Throughout the following eighteen years Baskin effectively supervised the state's local klaverns primarily, it appears, by maintaining a low profile. With its weekly meetings, women's auxiliaries, and brass bands, the Virginia Klan in the 1930s actually resembled other fraternal orders more than it did its own image as a vigilante organization crusading for "100% Americanism." Despite this benign public face Baskin, like other Klan leaders, railed against Communists, blacks, and Catholics in the Klan's national publication and advocated that each Klan district develop a military-style organization.

In September 1937, when United States Supreme Court justice Hugo Black's former Klan membership came to light, Baskin was in New York City. A *New York Times* interviewer described him as "a pleasant-faced, smiling man, with a noticeable Southern accent." Two years later newspapers reported that Baskin was slated to become the Klan's next imperial wizard, replacing Hiram Wesley Evans. As Klan membership had continued to drop, Baskin's official title had expanded to grand dragon for the realm of Virginia, West Virginia, Maryland, and the District of Columbia. The newspapers said that Baskin had broken with Evans when the latter closed the Klan's Washington office to economize during the Great Depression. Although Baskin appeared to be the popular choice for the post, Evans blocked his election.

In the late 1930s some Klan leaders allied with pro-Nazi organizations, which caused the federal government to try to put the Klan out of business during World War II. Baskin viewed these alliances as anti-American and unpatriotic. He banned the grand dragon of New Jersey from meetings within his Klan realm after the latter met with leaders of the German-American Bund in 1940. In April 1944 the Treasury Department sued the Klan for failure to pay its taxes. To settle the case the Klan gave up its charter as a corporation in Georgia and officially disbanded.

On 24 May 1944 a new fraternal order, the American Shores Patrol, applied for a charter in Virginia, which was granted in August. The president of the American Shores Patrol was Joel L. Baskin, now residing in Arlington. The order proclaimed its intention to patrol the shores of the nation to prevent entry of dangerous aliens, but an undercover investigator reported that it was actually a cover for Baskin's old Klan realm.

When living in Richmond, Baskin gave his occupation as lawyer, but he never practiced that profession. In Arlington he called himself an exporter. A devout Baptist, he helped to organize Memorial Baptist Church in Arlington and, after it was formally constituted in 1947, served as a deacon. Joel L. Baskin died at Arlington Hospital on 27 December 1948 of renal failure caused by cancer and was buried in Columbia Gardens Cemetery in Arlington. His wife, Edith May Baskin, and three sons survived him. The State Corporation Commission revoked the charter of the American Shores Patrol in 1951.

Family information provided by son Robert E. Baskin, the Mississippi State Department of Archives and History, the registrar of Mississippi College, and the Southern History Department of the Birmingham Public Library; Baskin's Klan activities and views documented in *Richmond News Leader*, 13 June 1928, 16 Sept. 1937 (por.), 9 June 1939, *New York Times*, 15 Sept. 1937, *Atlanta Constitution*, 28 May, 9 June 1939, *Richmond Times-Dispatch*, 1 Sept. 1940, and articles and reports in *Kourier Magazine*, the Klan's national magazine, to 1936; John M. Craig and Timothy H. Silver, "'Tolerance of the Intolerant': J. A. C. Chandler and the Ku Klux Klan at William and Mary," *South Atlantic Quarterly* 84 (1985): 213–222; David M. Chalmers, *Hooded Americanism: The First Century of the Ku Klux Klan, 1865–1965* (1965), 230–235; American Shores Patrol documented in Charter Book, 205:282–283, and *Baltimore Afro-American*, 28 Sept. 1946, 1 Oct. 1949; obituary in *Richmond Times-Dispatch*, 29 Dec. 1948.

JOHN T. KNEEBONE

BASSE, Nathaniel (bap. 19 December 1589–by 30 August 1654), member of the Council, was the second of twelve sons and second of eighteen children of Humphrey Basse and Mary Buschier Basse. His mother was of Italian descent, and his father was a prosperous London girdler of French ancestry who invested in the Virginia Company of London. Basse was probably born in London and was christened there in the parish of Saint Gabriel Fenchurch on 19 December 1589.

Basse first arrived in Virginia, so far as is known, in March 1619 with Christopher Lawne and other colonists associated in the settlement of Warrosquyoake Plantation in what is now Isle of Wight County. During 1620 Basse returned to England and obtained from the Virginia Company a confirmation of the patent to Warrosquyoake in November of that year. The company reconfirmed this patent in January 1622. In November 1621 Basse received a separate patent in his own name for a 300-acre tract a short distance west of Warrosquyoake on the east side of the Pagan River that has been called Basse's Choice ever since. He returned to Virginia on the *Furtherance* about August or September 1622, after the Powhatan uprising on 22 March 1622 when, according to John Smith's *Generall Historie*, the Indians "had fired Lieutenant Basse his house, with all the rest there about, slaine the people, and so left that Plantation."

Basse represented Warrosquyoake in the General Assembly sessions of February and March 1624, May 1625, March 1628, and October 1629. In June 1625 he signed a petition requesting Charles I to preserve the General Assembly as a fixture of the new royal government of the colony. Soon after arriving in Virginia late in March 1630, Governor Sir John Harvey appointed Basse to the governor's Council. The length of his service is unknown, but he is named as a member on documents dated 20 December 1631 and 21 February 1632. On 6 March 1632 Harvey commissioned Basse "to trade between 34 and 41 degrees North Latitude and to go to New England, Nova Scotia, or the West Indie Islands with instructions to invite the inhabitants hither if any so inclined," and sometime the same month Basse became presiding justice of the court of Warrosquyoake.

Extant records do not indicate whether Basse traveled to the other English colonies as directed, or whether he ever returned to England. He probably either remained in Virginia or returned to the colony following the voyages. The dearth of documentation also obscures much of Basse's personal and family life. Tradition has it that he married Mary Jordan in London on 21 May 1613, that the third son of their ten sons and three daughters married a member of the Nansemond tribe in 1638, and that the Bass family of lower Tidewater Virginia is descended from this son. However, a deposition in England on behalf of his three surviving sisters, identified as his coheirs, asserted that he had died in Virginia without issue, an assertion borne out by a suit brought by Theodorick Bland against William Drummond, attorney of Basse's coheirs, and settled in 1658. Nathaniel Basse died, probably in Virginia, sometime before this 30 August 1654 deposition was taken.

Christening recorded in parish register of St. Gabriel Fenchurch, London; six samples of autograph in PRO CO 1/3 and 1/6 confirm the spelling "Basse," but a decorative device that he attached to the terminal *e* has caused his name to be printed in some sources as "Basses" or "Bassey"; presence in Virginia documented in Kingsbury, *Virginia Company*, in *Minutes of Council and General Court*, and in musters of 1624 and 1625 in PRO CO 1/3; Smith, *Complete Works*, 2:296; Basse is named on a list of councillors Harvey sent to London on 29 May 1630 (PRO CO 1/5, fol. 206); Nansemond connection discussed in Albert D. Bell, *Bass Families of the South* (1961), 5–18; deposition by Edward Basse and Mary Poole on behalf of Basse's three surviving sisters, 30 Aug. 1654, Mayor's Court Depositions, Corporation of London Records Office; sisters identified as coheirs in *Journals of House of Burgesses, 1659/60–1693*, 5.

DAPHNE GENTRY

BASSETT, Burwell (3 March 1734–4 January 1793), member of the Convention of 1788, was born at Eltham, the Bassett family plantation in Blisland Parish, New Kent County. He was the younger of two sons and fourth of six children of William Bassett and Elizabeth Churchill Bassett. His father, the third of that name in a long line of wealthy planters and public servants, died in 1744 while serving in the House of Burgesses, leaving young Burwell Bassett as his principal heir. His older brother, who would ordinarily have inherited the estate, had presumably died young. Bassett's mother subsequently married William Dawson, president of the College of William and Mary and a member of the governor's Council.

Bassett married Ann Kidley Chamberlayne in 1753. She died the next year, and their one daughter did not live to adulthood. Bassett married Anna Maria Dandridge on 7 May 1757. The second marriage added to the already large number of his distinguished relatives, because Anna Bassett was the sister of Martha Dandridge, who married Daniel Parke Custis and then George Washington. The Bassetts had four sons and four daughters, and those who lived to adulthood continued the family tradition of marrying into prominent and well-connected families. Their son Burwell Bassett (1764–1841) also had a long career in politics.

Bassett was one of the wealthiest men in New Kent County. In 1782 he owned four plantations totaling 5,980 acres of land in New Kent and another of more than 1,000 acres in Hanover County. He also offered advice and assistance to George Washington in the management of the enormous Custis estates in and about New Kent County. Bassett held all the public offices appropriate to a gentleman of his standing—justice of the peace almost as soon as he was of age, vestryman by the time he was twenty-four, colonel of the militia even earlier than that, and member of the House of Burgesses from 1762 until 1775. He also served in the first four Revolutionary Conventions.

In the spring of 1777 the voters elected Bassett to the Senate of Virginia from the district composed of the counties of Charles City, James City, and New Kent, and thereafter returned him in each succeeding election. By 1791 he was the senior member of the Senate. Bassett's long legislative career was characterized more by competence and reliability than by brilliance or creativity. In March 1788 Bassett was elected to the convention called to consider the proposed constitution of the United States. Sharing the opinions of his brother-in-law George Washington, he voted for ratification on 25 June 1788. Two days later, however, he voted for an unsuccessful motion to limit the taxing power of the new national government.

During the 1792 session of the Senate, Burwell Bassett was thrown from his horse and seriously injured. He died on 4 January 1793 and was probably buried in the family cemetery at Eltham.

Birth date and family history in Malcolm H. Harris, *Old New Kent County* (1977), 1:42–52; marriages and births of children recorded in Bassett family Bible, VHS photocopy; family financial documents and some letters to Bassett in Burwell Bassett Papers, LC; numerous Bassett letters in George Washington Papers, LC, and various collections in VHS and W&M; *Richmond Virginia Gazette and Weekly Advertiser*, 20 Mar. 1788; Kaminski, *Ratification*, 10:1539–1540, 1557, 1565; por. by Charles Willson Peale owned by Society of the Cincinnati; death documented in Henry Lee to George Washington, 6 Jan. 1793, Washington Papers, LC.

BRENT TARTER

BASSETT, Burwell (18 March 1764–26 February 1841), member of the House of Representatives, was born at Eltham in New Kent County, the second of four sons and fifth of eight children of Burwell Bassett (1734–1793) and Anna Maria Dandridge Bassett. Following a private education, he attended the College of William and Mary. At his father's death he inherited the bulk of the large family estate, which consisted of about 6,000 acres of land in New Kent County and more than 1,000 acres in neighboring Hanover County. On 10 January 1788 Bassett married Elizabeth McCarty, of Westmoreland County, and following her death he married Philadelphia Ann Claiborne, who died in 1834. He had no children. Late in the 1790s Bassett purchased about 350 acres in James City County. He lived in Williamsburg from 1815 until 1837.

Like most public men of his time, Bassett held a commission in the county militia, but his service was largely perfunctory and social except during the British invasion of the Chesapeake in 1814, when he briefly took the field as lieutenant colonel of the 68th Regiment Virginia Militia. Bassett entered politics in 1787 and represented New Kent County in the House of Delegates for three years. His father was then representing the district comprising Charles City, James City, and New Kent Counties in the Senate of Virginia, and following his death Bassett succeeded him in the seat and served from 1793 until 1805.

Bassett ran for the House of Representatives in 1795 but lost a close contest to John Clopton, who served in Congress for many years as a Jeffersonian Republican. In the 1800 presidential election Bassett supported Thomas Jefferson, and four years later he defeated incumbent Federalist congressman Thomas Griffin. Bassett sat in the House of Representatives from 1805 until 1813, when he lost a close election to Federalist Thomas Monteagle Bayly, of Accomack County. In 1815 Bassett returned to Congress and served until he retired in March 1819. The voters of James City County then sent him to the House of Delegates, where he completed two consecutive one-year terms. In 1821 he was elected to Congress again and remained until 1829. Early in that year he announced his second retirement, but friends persuaded him to seek one more term. In the meantime, however, many of the district's leading Democrats had already pledged themselves to the candidacy of Richard Coke, who defeated Bassett in the April 1829 election. Shortly thereafter Bassett came in a poor last in a field of eight candidates for four seats in the Convention of 1829–1830. During his years in Congress he spoke occasionally, taking a special interest in reducing the naval establishment, but served only once on a standing committee, chairing the Committee on Claims during the first session of the 12th Congress. Bassett generally supported states' rights positions advocated by his fellow Virginia Republicans, and during the 1820s he was sharply critical of the administration of John Quincy Adams.

Bassett served on the vestry of Bruton Parish while he resided in Williamsburg and was one of the most prominent and active lay leaders in the Episcopal Church in Virginia. He was a delegate to several state conventions, and in 1827 the convention named him a trustee of the Protestant Episcopal Theological Seminary in Alexandria. Bassett also sponsored a bill in the House of Representatives to incorporate Alexandria's Episcopal Church, but in 1811 President James Madison vetoed the bill, stating that it violated the First Amendment. Bassett also took an interest in public schooling and gave significant support and encouragement to the British educational reformer Joseph Lancaster, who stayed with Bassett in Virginia in 1819.

Bassett remained in many ways a man of the eighteenth century. A grandniece wrote many years later that he had been "perhaps the last man in Virginia who wore small clothes and powdered hair in a queue." He could be condescending toward people he regarded as beneath him in social standing or too obtuse to share his opinions. In 1837 he sold his property in James City County and moved back to Eltham. Burwell Bassett died at Eltham on 26 February 1841 and was probably buried in the family cemetery there.

Birth date in Bassett family Bible, VHS photocopy; first marriage in Westmoreland Co. Marriage Bonds; character sketches in Meade, *Old Churches*, 1:185–187, and in Anna Maria Dandridge Yeatman, "Personal History of the Families Deans and Bassett and of Some of Their Connections," typescript (ca. 1912), 57, VHS; Burwell Bassett Papers, LC; Bassett Family Papers, VHS; Robert A. Brock Collection, Henry E. Huntington Library, San Marino, Calif.; other Bassett letters in collections in LC, UVA, VHS, and W&M; eight letters in Noble E. Cunningham Jr., ed., *Circular Letters of Congressmen to Their Constituents, 1789–1829* (1978); contested elections documented in *Annals of Congress*, 4th Cong., 1st sess., 265–266; 13th Cong., 1st sess., 131–132, 479–481, 486; 1829 electoral defeats reported in *Norfolk and Portsmouth Herald*, 15, 20 Apr., 4, 11 May 1829, and *Richmond Enquirer*, 5 June 1829; public letters to Bassett in Joseph Lancaster, *Letters on National Subjects, auxiliary to Universal Education, and Scientific Knowledge* (1820), 1–16, 45–60, esp. 14; death notice in *Richmond Enquirer*, 4 Mar. 1841; obituary in *Richmond Whig and Public Advertiser*, 5 Mar. 1841.

THOMAS E. BUCKLEY, S.J.
BRENT TARTER

BASSETT, John David (14 July 1866–26 February 1965), furniture manufacturer, was born in Henry County, the fourth of eight sons and fifth of eleven children of John Henry Bassett and Nancy Jane Spencer Bassett. In addition to local schools, he also attended a boarding school at Oak Level. After working on the family farm and as a tobacco buyer, Bassett built a small store on the family's land near the Smith River northwest of Martinsville to take advantage of the construction of the first railroad through that part of the county about 1892. Because it was the only store in the area, a post office was established there with Bassett as the first postmaster. The town that grew up around the store was called Bassett.

On 17 December 1893 Bassett married Nancy Pocahontas Hundley. They had two sons and two daughters. For several years she operated the store while he worked for a Lynchburg mercantile supply company as a traveling salesman in Virginia and North Carolina. Perceiving an unmet market for bark used in tanning hides, Bassett gradually shifted his attention to the operation of a sawmill that produced both bark and lumber. After several years of selling hardwood lumber to furniture manufacturers in other states, in 1902 Bassett, his younger brothers Charles Columbus Bassett and Samuel Henry Bassett, and their brother-in-law Reed L. Stone pooled their resources and established a furniture factory in Bassett. J. D. Bassett became president of the company and initially acted also as its salesman, with the other partners operating the plant. The business achieved success almost immediately, and in 1907 he organized the Bank of Bassett and later created a number of subsidiary companies to produce veneers, glass and mirrors, hardware, and various grades and styles of household furniture. On 4 September 1930 the family consolidated its several furniture companies and formed Bassett Furniture Industries with an initial capitalization of more than $2 million to operate the whole enterprise.

Bassett Furniture Industries grew into the largest complex of furniture factories and one of the largest industries in southern Virginia. Bassett made other investments, including acquisition of a large interest in the Bassett-Walker Knitting Company, but he always devoted himself principally to furniture manufacturing. Except during World War II, when it made wooden bodies and parts for taxicabs and trucks, the firm produced only beds, sofas, chairs, tables, cupboards, and other household items. By the 1950s Bassett Furniture Industries was described as the largest manufacturer of wood furniture in the world. At the time of Bassett's death in 1965, the factories in Bassett and Martinsville covered more than 1.75 million square feet, the company employed about 3,400 people, and its assets of more than $44,400,000 included company housing in Bassett and a showroom in High Point, North Carolina.

With the formation of Bassett Furniture Industries in 1930, Bassett became chairman of the board, but he remained active in the many other affairs of the companies. He was the patriarch of an extended family of furniture manufacturers. His first son, William McKinley Bassett (1894–1960), became president of Bassett Furniture Industries late in 1930 and served until 1956, when he became chairman and J. D. Bassett retired with the title of chairman emeritus. His second son, John Douglas Bassett (1901–1966), succeeded William McKinley Bassett as president and chairman. Their cousin John Edwin Bassett (1901–1988), son of founder C. C. Bassett, followed in his turn. Bassett's daughter Blanche Estelle Bassett married Taylor George Vaughan, who became president of the Vaughan Furniture Company (which Bassett helped organize) in Galax; and his daughter Anne Pocahontas Bassett married Thomas Bahnson Stanley, who was founding president of the Stanley Furniture Company (which Bassett also helped organize) in Stanleytown, Henry County, and who was elected governor of Virginia in 1953. Bassett's commanding position in the furniture-manufacturing industry was exemplified by his election in 1989 as one of the five charter members of the American Furniture Hall of Fame.

Bassett made one brief venture into politics. On 5 September 1925 the state convention of the Republican Party nominated him for treasurer of Virginia. His Democratic opponent was John Michael Purcell, the first Catholic to be nominated for statewide office in Virginia in the twentieth century. Bassett and some of his Republican colleagues must have realized that their only hope for victory lay in defections of Democratic voters resulting in part from religious prejudice. They were somewhat embarrassed, however, by the support they received from such anti-Catholic organizations as the Ku Klux Klan, which subjected Purcell to a semisecret whispering campaign similar to the more famous one conducted against Alfred E. Smith during the 1928 presidential campaign. Shortly before the election, Bassett issued a statement disavowing religious prejudice. Purcell won the election by a margin of about 26,000 votes out of about 139,000 cast. Bassett was mentioned in 1928 as a possible candidate for the United States House of Representatives, but he never again sought elective office.

John David Bassett lived the last five years of his long life in the Martinsville General Hospital. He died there on 26 February 1965 and was buried in a mausoleum in the Bassett family cemetery in Bassett.

The contributor is a granddaughter of Bassett; Milton J. Elliott, "Bassett: Furniture Giant of Virginia," *Common-*

wealth 28 (Dec. 1961): 30–32; Malcolm Donald Coe, ed., *Our Proud Heritage: A Pictorial History of Martinsville and Henry County, Virginia* (1969), 58 (por.), 62; Dorothy Cleal and Hiram H. Herbert, *Foresight, Founders, and Fortitude: The Growth of Industry in Martinsville and Henry County, Virginia* (1970), 25–67, 99–101; Henry Co. Marriage Register; obituaries in *Roanoke Times* and *Roanoke World-News*, both 27 Feb. 1965, *Martinsville Bulletin* (por.), *New York Times*, and *Richmond Times-Dispatch*, all 28 Feb. 1965, and *Bassett Henry County Journal*, 4 Mar. 1965.

MARY ELIZABETH BASSETT MORTEN

BASSETT, William (ca. 1671–11 October 1723), member of the Council, was probably born in New Kent County sometime between late in 1670 and 28 August 1671, the only child of William Bassett and his second wife, Bridget Cary Bassett. His father, who wrote a will on 28 August 1671 and died before the end of the year, had moved to Virginia from England less than a decade earlier and become a wealthy merchant. He was usually identified in contemporary records as Captain William Bassett to distinguish him from a near neighbor of the same name.

At his father's death Bassett inherited almost 5,000 acres of land on the south side of the York River and his father's large brick house just below the present site of the town of West Point. His care was initially entrusted to his mother, but his uncle, Councillor Nathaniel Bacon (1620–1692), subsequently became his guardian. As soon as he came of age Bassett undertook to manage his inherited estate, began adding to it, and by April 1695 had constructed a large new house at Eltham, upstream from that of his father. On 28 November 1693 he married his cousin Joanna Burwell. Of their seven daughters and five sons, the four daughters and one son who reached adulthood all married into prominent Tidewater families. Bassett was one of the wealthiest young gentlemen in Virginia, and he quickly assumed the public offices traditional for a man of his station. He sat on the vestry of Blisland Parish, served as a lieutenant colonel of the New Kent County militia by 1699, and in that year was also a justice of the peace and sheriff. Bassett was elected to the House of Burgesses from New Kent County for the first time in 1693 and was reelected through 1699. In addition he served briefly in the third session of the assembly of 1700–1702, and by 1702 he was a member of the board of visitors of the College of William and Mary.

Between July 1699 and December 1701 Governor Francis Nicholson recommended three times that Bassett be appointed to the governor's Council. On 14 May 1702 Queen Anne finally appointed Bassett a councillor. Bassett agreed to serve only for the duration of Nicholson's administration and attended his first Council meeting on 23 October 1702. Bassett's position soon became awkward. Nicholson's brief and unsuccessful attempt to woo Bassett's sister-in-law Lucy Burwell was only one of several events that created hostility between the governor and several powerful councillors. In 1703 six members of the Council petitioned for Nicholson's recall, leaving Bassett torn between his loyalty toward his friend Nicholson and his family's animosity toward the governor. As Nicholson was preparing to return to England in 1705, Bassett evidently reminded him that he had agreed to serve on the Council only during Nicholson's tenure as governor, but the royal instructions to Nicholson's successor Edward Nott left Bassett on the Council, and he dutifully continued to attend its meetings. Immediately following Nott's sudden death in August 1706, Bassett informed the colony's agent in London, Micajah Perry, that he wished to have his name left off of the next list of councillors. The instructions for Governor Robert Hunter excluded Bassett as requested, but a French warship captured Hunter en route to Virginia, and he and his instructions never reached the colony. The instructions therefore did not take effect. Bassett thus continued to serve until 27 April 1710, after word arrived that the instructions to Hunter's successor, George Hamilton, earl of Orkney, had also omitted Bassett's name.

Although he had once been caught in the middle of unpleasant personal and political arguments among his friends and family members, Bassett retained the respect of all of them. His high standing and great wealth made him a man of consequence in the colony, and Orkney's deputy, Lieutenant Governor Alexander Spotswood, persuaded Bassett during 1711 to accept reappointment to the

Council. Bassett did not take his seat for more than four years, however, because he wanted to be restored to his former position in seniority. Spotswood repeatedly endorsed Bassett's application since he was, as Spotswood put it, "a Gent. of as fine a Character and of as plentiful an Estate as any in this Country." Spotswood's applications on Bassett's behalf having proved unsuccessful, he finally returned to the Council as a junior member on 7 December 1715, only to find that it was again in political turmoil. Spotswood insisted on the right to name men other than councillors to the semiannual courts of oyer and terminer, to which previous governors had always appointed only Council members. Bassett reluctantly sided with his fellow councillors against his friend and patron, and for several years political and personal disagreements made service on the Council distasteful for Bassett. In 1720 Spotswood effected a general reconciliation with his Council at a Williamsburg meeting from which Bassett was absent.

William Bassett continued to serve on the Council until his death on 11 October 1723, which probably occurred at his home. He was buried in the family graveyard at Eltham and reinterred in 1879 at Hollywood Cemetery in Richmond.

Bassett Family Papers and Bassett family Bible records, VHS, contain family history information, including marriage date and birth dates of children; early genealogical and historical references often confuse Bassett and his father with a third William Bassett (ca. 1646–1724), who lived in Saint Peter's Parish, New Kent Co.; some Bassett letters in Ludwell-Lee Papers at VHS, Colonial Papers, RG 1, LVA, and PRO CO 5/1315; letters of Nicholson and Spotswood to Board of Trade (PRO CO 5) document service and seniority on Council, with some published in Robert A. Brock, ed., *The Official Letters of Alexander Spotswood* (1882); birth date estimated in part from will of Capt. William Bassett (copy in VHS), and death date and age at death on long inscription on gravestone at Hollywood Cemetery.

DAPHNE GENTRY

BASSETTE, Andrew William Ernest (November 1857–7 August 1942), attorney and civic leader, was born in Hampton, the youngest of three sons and a daughter of Burrell Bassette and Fannie Bassette. Whether he was born free or a slave is not known. The family was so poor that when Bassette entered Hampton Institute early in the 1870s, the other students laughed at his patched and tattered clothing. Following his graduation in 1876, Bassette taught in schools in Greensville, Sussex, and Surry Counties before returning to Elizabeth City County and teaching there for at least a dozen years. On several occasions he voluntarily took cuts in his small salary to enable the school districts to extend the short school term.

Bassette initially supplemented his income by working a small farm near Hampton. He somehow found time to study law and was admitted to legal practice in Elizabeth City County. He qualified as a notary public on 11 April 1889. His mentor and sponsor may have been local African American attorney James A. Field, commonwealth's attorney of Elizabeth City County from 1887 to 1891, who probably appointed Bassette assistant commonwealth's attorney before the end of the term. Bassette was one of the last African American public officials in the county prior to the conservative-white takeover of local government during the 1890s.

In 1889 "Lawyer Bassette," as he was often called, was one of the dozen founders of the People's Building and Loan Association of Hampton. He wrote its charter and served as its general counsel. The association grew rapidly and by 1904 was capitalized at more than $100,000. Bassette's personal finances improved at the same time. He invested wisely in local real estate and in 1897 reported that he owned property worth $6,200. He joined local fraternal and service organizations, including the Masons, the Odd Fellows, and the Seven Wise Men, and for many years he participated in and several times presided at the annual Emancipation Proclamation Day celebration in Hampton. Bassette also became superintendent of the Sunday school of the First Baptist Church in Hampton and taught there for many years.

Until his death at age eighty-four, Bassette was one of the best-known figures in Hampton's African American community, and the city named one of its schools after him. As impressive as Bassette's own rise from poverty at the end of the Civil War to half a century of distinguished civic leadership had been, his family's subsequent achievements may have been his most significant accomplishment. While still teaching school, on 8 September 1881 Bassette married Louisa P. Boykin, of Surry County. Following her death, on 18 December 1884 he married Ida E. Diggs, of Mathews County. Of their ten children, three sons and three daughters lived to maturity. The sons all attended Howard University and became distinguished professional men and community leaders. Andrew William Ernest Bassette Jr. became an attorney, Burrell Bassette became a physician, and Edward G. Bassette became a dentist. Some of their sons, in their turns, also pursued careers in law and medicine.

In one of his last public appearances, Bassette delivered the principal address at the annual breakfast of Hampton Institute alumni in June 1940. Andrew William Ernest Bassette died at his home in Hampton on 7 August 1942 and was buried in Bassette's Cemetery in Hampton.

A. W. E. Bassette Sr. Papers, including clippings from *Southern Workman* and *Norfolk Journal and Guide*, Hampton; month and year of birth in Census, Elizabeth City Co., 1900; BVS Marriage Register, Elizabeth City Co. and (with names of parents) Matthews Co; brief biography in *Twenty-Two Years' Work of the Hampton Normal and Agricultural Institute* (1893), 65; Robert Francis Engs, *Freedom's First Generation: Black Hampton, Virginia, 1861–1890* (1979), 159, 175, 180; *Southern Workman* 29 (1900): 376; 35 (1906): 412; 58 (1929): 520; obituaries in *Newport News Times-Herald*, 8 Aug. 1942, *Newport News Daily Press*, 9 Aug. 1942, and (with some confusion with namesake son) *Norfolk Journal and Guide*, 15 Aug. 1942.

MICHAEL E. HUCLES

BATES, Fleming (27 February 1779–26 December 1830), member of the Convention of 1829–1830, was born at Belmont in Goochland County, the fourth of seven sons and fifth of twelve children of Thomas Fleming Bates and Caroline Matilda Woodson Bates. Like several of his brothers, Fleming Bates served as an apprentice to the clerk of court in Goochland County. About 1795 he became an assistant in the Hanover County clerk's office, and by 1799 he was also running the local post office. In 1800 he moved to Northumberland County to become deputy to the ailing clerk of court, Catesby Jones. Following Jones's death later that year, Bates assumed the clerkship on 13 October 1800 and held the office for the remainder of his life. Members of the Bates family had been prominent in western Hanover's Cedar Creek Meeting, but Bates's parents were not active Quakers, and he also does not appear to have been a practicing Friend.

On 20 July 1803 Bates married Mary Moss, of Northumberland County. Their only known child died in infancy, and Mary Moss Bates died in 1818. On 6 September 1819 he married Elizabeth Whitehill Moore. They had two sons and two daughters. Following the death of his father in 1805, Bates became guardian of his younger brother Edward Bates, who lived at Bates's residence, Belleville, for two years. Family tradition describes Fleming Bates as a stern disciplinarian, and Edward Bates, subsequently a congressman from Missouri and United States attorney general, later acknowledged that he had benefited from his brother's tutelage. Bates's brothers also included Frederick Bates, governor of Missouri in 1824 and 1825, and James Woodson Bates, the first delegate to Congress from the Arkansas Territory.

Like his father and several of his brothers, Bates was a Jeffersonian Republican. In the mid-1790s, before enthusiasm for the French Revolution waned, family members sometimes addressed each other as "Citizen." Bates took no recorded part in politics before May 1829, when he was one of four delegates elected to represent the district of King George, Lancaster, Northumberland, Prince William, Richmond, Stafford, and Westmoreland Counties in the Virginia constitutional convention that met from October 1829 to January 1830. He made no recorded speeches during the convention sessions, but allied himself with Benjamin Watkins Leigh, Abel Parker Upshur, and other leading eastern conservatives against the reform proposals of the western delegates. Bates voted to retain the property qualification for the franchise and opposed reapportionment of seats in the General Assembly that would reduce the influence of the smaller and less populous eastern counties and augment the influence of the larger and more populous western counties. From the 16 November 1829 vote on the basis of apportionment to the final roll call on

14 January 1830, Bates never swayed from his support of the status quo. The resulting constitution was satisfactory to opponents of reform, and the voters of Northumberland voted 286 to 7 to ratify it.

Fleming Bates died at his home on 26 December 1830 and was buried near Heathsville in a family cemetery at the Handy Gill farm.

Family history documents and list of books in Bates's excellent library in Mrs. W. G. Bates, "Fleming Bates, Clerk of the Court of Northumberland County, 1800–1831," *Bulletin of the Northumberland County Historical Society* 8 (1971): 3–12 (por.); birth and death dates on gravestone; Bates Family Papers, Missouri Historical Society, St. Louis; Edward Bates Papers, VHS; Onward Bates, *Bates et al., of Virginia and Missouri* (1914); Northumberland Co. Marriage Bonds; *Richmond Enquirer*, 29 May, 2 June 1829; will in Northumberland Co. Record Book, 26:463; obituary with death date of 21 Dec. 1830 in *Richmond Daily Whig*, 8 Jan. 1831.

WILLIAM B. OBROCHTA

BATTE, Archibald (d. by 12 April 1830), merchant, was probably born somewhere in Prince George County sometime during the 1780s. His name first appears in the 1809 tax list of that county along with "Milly's children," the residuary legatees of an unmarried white farmer, Robert Batte, who died in 1807. Milly was an unmarried African American woman, and it is possible that Archibald Batte was the son of Milly and of Robert Batte. It is also possible that he was born into slavery and gained his freedom under the provisions of Robert Batte's will. Archibald Batte acquired Robert Batte's fifty-acre farm in Prince George County and also six slaves who had probably belonged to Robert Batte.

Archibald Batte married Nancy Jenkins, of Bermuda Hundred in Chesterfield County, on 2 March 1815. The marriage bond identified them both as free persons of color and bore Batte's signature. They had one son born about 1817 or 1818. In the latter year Batte paid $300 for a half-acre lot in the town of Bermuda Hundred, where for the remainder of his life he operated a grocery store in a building near his house. He was not unique in being an African American slave owner, but he paid taxes on six slaves and named thirteen slaves when he wrote his will in 1830, which was far more slaves than any of the dozen or so other African American slaveholders in Chesterfield County owned at that time, and none of Batte's slaves appears to have been a near relation, which was also unusual among black slave owners in Virginia. Some of Batte's slaves probably worked in his store and others may have worked on his farm. The labor of his slaves helped make Batte almost the only economically independent African American of his time in Chesterfield County. Although he was never wealthy, he owned silverware, mahogany furniture, and china.

In 1818 Batte sued a white man for breaking into his property. Batte lost the suit, but his ability to bring a case and have it seriously considered in court was evidence of how much to his benefit his respectable property ownership was. Nonetheless, as a man of mixed-race ancestry he never enjoyed all the status of a white man of similar achievement. For example, as a "free person of color," in 1822 he had to obtain formal certification from the county court of his "good character," a requirement imposed on no white man, with or without property.

Archibald Batte dated his will on 15 February 1830 and died before 12 April 1830, when the will was proved in court. Nancy Jenkins Batte died less than a year later, and not long thereafter their son moved to Pennsylvania, where he began a new life and passed for a white man, clear evidence of the family's consciousness of the barriers to advancement in the Virginia of the 1830s that no black person, however light skinned and financially successful, could surmount.

Information on Robert Batte and his lost will in Batte and Allied Families Genealogical Notes, LVA; Carter G. Woodson, *Free Negro Owners of Slaves in the United States in 1830* (1924), 34, 41; Jackson, *Free Negro Labor*, 205, 208, 215, 224; Chesterfield Co. Marriage Bonds; other information in Personal Property Tax Returns, Chesterfield Co., RG 48, LVA, and Chesterfield Co. Deed and Order Books; lawsuit of 1818 and certification of good behavior on 13 May 1822 recorded in Chesterfield Co. Order Book, 21:567, 24:6; will and estate records in Chesterfield Co. Will Book, 11:614, 12:26–27, 13:478–479; archaeological excavation of Batte's store site described in Philip J. Schwarz, "Emancipators, Protectors, and Anomalies: Free Black Slaveowners in Virginia," *VMHB* 95 (1987): 317–338.

PHILIP J. SCHWARZ

BATTE, Thomas (fl. 1630s–1690s), explorer, was probably born in Virginia between 1633 and

1638, the second of three sons of John Batte, who arrived in Virginia in 1621, and his wife, whose first name may have been Dorothy. Very few facts of Thomas Batte's life are known. He married a woman named Mary before 1660. They had three daughters and a son, also named Thomas Batte, who was born about 1661 and died early in 1691. On 29 April 1668 Thomas Batte and his younger brother Henry Batte patented 5,878 acres of land on the south side of the James River below the mouth of the Appomattox River, near the property of Abraham Wood, a member of the governor's Council and the leading Indian trader in that part of Virginia.

Many Virginians of Batte's time believed that the Appalachian Mountains lay at the center of a narrow continent. In 1670 Governor Sir William Berkeley dispatched John Lederer into the wilderness to seek "a passage to the further side of the Mountains." Lederer did not reach the "further side," but his expedition prompted Wood to send out his own exploring party headed by Batte and Robert Hallom, or Hallam, about whom even less is known than about Batte. The only two known copies of Hallom's lost journal of the expedition that were evidently taken directly from the original render Batte's surname as Batts and Hallom's as Fallam.

The Batts and Fallam Expedition, as it has thus erroneously come to be known, departed from Fort Henry, near the present site of Petersburg, on 1 September 1671. The party included Thomas Wood, who was probably Abraham Wood's son, one unidentified servant, and Penecute, or Perecute, an Appamattuck guide. Near modern-day Charlotte Courthouse they crossed the Staunton River and picked up additional Appamattuck and Saponi guides. By then Thomas Wood had fallen ill and was left behind. They crossed the Blue Ridge about fifteen miles south of where the city of Roanoke was later founded, left their horses with the Totero Indians on the New River near where Radford now is, picked up another guide, and then traveled westward parallel to the New River to present-day Narrows in Giles County on the Virginia–West Virginia border. The most dangerous leg of the monthlong journey was the steep climb up 1,200-foot-high East River Mountain. While crossing into what is now southern West Virginia, their food ran out and their Totero guide abandoned them. Sustained by haws, grapes, and two turkeys, they reached the Tug Fork near the modern city of Matewan, West Virginia, on the journey's sixteenth day. There, 75 miles west of the crest of the Appalachians and 260 miles west of the frontier settlements of Virginia, they measured for a tidal effect and convinced themselves that the westward-flowing river was "very slowly dropping." Before turning back they marked trees with their initials, "TB" and "RH."

Batte and Hallom, the first Anglo-Virginians to cross the Appalachians, retraced their steps and reached Fort Henry on 1 October 1671. On their way back they learned that Thomas Wood had died. The expedition neither proved nor disproved the theory that the Atlantic and Pacific Oceans were close together. But it established the first solid British and Virginian claims to the Ohio and Mississippi River watersheds, an achievement formally placed on the record when John Clayton presented a transcript of the expedition's journal to the Royal Society in London on 1 August 1688.

Batte was appointed a justice of the peace of Henrico County in April 1683, and the records of the county's orphan's court mentioned his name several times. By August 1689 he had moved out of Henrico County, perhaps back to the land in Bristol Parish he had patented with his brother in 1668. Thomas Batte's name last appears in the public records on 5 August 1695. He probably died not long thereafter.

Batte and his near relatives left no known autographs, and their contemporaries spelled the surname Batt, Batte, Battey, Battes and Batts; by far the most frequently encountered usage is Batte, the spelling used by a clerk in Henrico Co. who evidently attempted to imitate Batte's signature on 9 and 16 May 1692 (Henrico Co. Deeds, Wills, Etc. [1688–1697], 299, 300); previous published identifications of Batte, derived in part from Yorkshire records and from a reference to a man who died near Jamestown in 1674, refer to other people; land patent of 29 Apr. 1668, identifying father and younger brother, in Patent Book, 6:126, RG 4, LVA; Batte was a minor when his elder brother, William Batte, executed an indenture on 3 May 1654, but he was of age by 3 June 1659 (Charles City Co. Order Book [1655–1665], 96, 187); wife's first name and children's names in Henrico Co. Deeds, Wills, Etc. (1677–1692), 290–291, 298–299; Batte's name last appears in Charles City Co. Order Book (1687–1695), 579; Abraham Wood to John Richards, 22 Aug. 1674, identifies the leaders of the expedition as "Thomas Batt and Robert Hallom" (Shaftesbury Papers, PRO 30/24/48); seventeenth-century transcripts of Hallom's journal in PRO CO 1/27, fols. 101–112, and British Library, Add. MSS 4432; nineteenth- and early-twentieth-century printed texts all derive from those two slightly variant manuscripts; expedition discussed thoroughly in Alan Vance Briceland, *Westward from Virginia: The Exploration of the Virginia-Carolina Frontier, 1650–1710* (1987), 124–146.

ALAN VANCE BRICELAND

BATTELLE, Gordon (14 November 1814–7 August 1862), Methodist minister, was born in Newport Township in Washington County, Ohio, the third of four sons and fourth of five children of Ebenezer Battelle and Mary Greene Battelle, who were descended from old New England families. He was educated in the village school and at an academy that an uncle conducted in Brookfield, Massachusetts. He returned to Ohio, worked for a merchant and on flatboats on the Ohio and Mississippi Rivers, and in the summer of 1833 attended Marietta College. Subsequently he entered Allegheny College in Meadville, Pennsylvania, and graduated first in the class of 1840.

On 12 October 1842 Battelle married Mary Louisa Tucker, a native of Windsor, Vermont. They had five daughters and two sons. That same year he entered the Methodist ministry and moved to Virginia as principal of Asbury Seminary in Parkersburg. In December 1843 Battelle took charge of the Methodist-controlled Northwestern Virginia Academy at Clarksburg, where he remained for eight years. He resigned on 4 June 1851 to become minister of the Methodist Church in Charleston and in 1853 was appointed pastor of the Fourth Street Church in Wheeling. He later served as presiding elder of the Clarksburg district and as a delegate to the general conferences of the Methodist Church in 1856 and 1860. Battelle sided with the northern branch of the church when it split over the issue of slavery, and he fought valiantly and successfully to retain the connection between the church and Northwestern Virginia Academy when the divisions within the church jeopardized the link. Battelle was awarded an M.A. from Allegheny College in 1843 and a D.D. from Ohio University in 1860.

Battelle was a staunch Unionist during the secession crisis, and in 1861 his old college messmate, Governor Francis H. Pierpont of the Restored Government at Wheeling, engaged him to visit Union military camps in northwestern Virginia and report on their condition. During that time he was one of four delegates elected to represent Ohio County in the convention that first met in Wheeling on 26 November 1861 to draft a constitution for the proposed new state of West Virginia. Battelle was active and influential at the convention. As chairman of its Committee on Education he was largely responsible for language requiring the legislature to provide a "thorough and efficient" system of free public schools. The provision attracted widespread attention at the time and was one of the most significant differences between prior Virginia constitutions and the new West Virginia constitution. He led an unsuccessful fight for a constitutional mandate for the gradual abolition of slavery, a provision that the United States Senate later insisted be reinstated. Hoping to make a clean break with old Virginia, Battelle suggested naming the new state Kanawha.

In November 1861 Battelle was appointed chaplain of the 1st Regiment Virginia Volunteers in the United States Army. His health began to fail while he was on active duty the next year. He recuperated at home for a brief time early in the summer of 1862 and then returned to service in Washington, D.C. Gordon Battelle died in Washington of typhoid fever on 7 August 1862 and was buried in Newport Township, Ohio.

Oscar D. Lambert, *Pioneer Leaders of Western Virginia* (1935), 143–161; Ethel Clark Lewis, "Gordon Battelle," *West Virginia Review* 13 (1936): 334–335 (por.); George C. Blazier, "The Pioneer Battelles and Their Contributions to the Building of Ohio and West Virginia," *West Virginia History* 15 (1954): 258–268; small collection of family records, including a eulogy by his friend Alexander Martin, in Battelle Memorial Institute, Columbus, Ohio; Richard O. Curry, "A Reappraisal of Statehood Politics in West Virginia," *JSH* 28 (1962): 406; political career documented in *Wheeling Intelligencer*; convention's records and brief biography in Charles H. Ambler, Frances Haney Atwood, and William B. Mathews, eds., *Debates and Proceedings of the First West Virginia Constitutional Convention (1861–1863)* (1942);

Ambler, *A History of Education in West Virginia from Early Colonial Times to the Present* (1951), 61, 83, 99, 109, 134, 136, 138, 188; obituary in *Wheeling Daily Intelligencer*, 8 Aug. 1862.

OTIS K. RICE

BATTLE, John Stewart (11 July 1890–9 April 1972), governor of Virginia, was born in New Bern, North Carolina, the eldest of three sons and two daughters of Henry Wilson Battle, a Baptist minister, and Margaret Stewart Battle. While Battle was young his family moved to Petersburg, where he grew up. The unreconstructed opinions of his paternal grandfather, a former brigadier general in the Confederate army who lived with the family, helped form his political and social beliefs.

After graduating from high school Battle enrolled in Wake Forest College, but he transferred to the University of Virginia after his father became pastor of High Street Baptist Church in Charlottesville. Battle graduated from the University of Virginia and from its law school in 1913. After graduation he went to Texas, but he contracted rheumatic fever and returned to Charlottesville, where he lived for the remainder of his life and practiced law for more than fifty years. On 12 June 1918 he married Mary Jane Lipscomb. Their two children both followed their father into the law. John Stewart Battle (1919–1997) was a founder of the prominent law firm of McGuire Woods Battle and Boothe, and his younger brother William Cullen Battle followed his father into politics and was the unsuccessful Democratic Party candidate for governor of Virginia in 1969.

Battle was elected to the Virginia House of Delegates in 1929. He served two two-year terms and became a friend and supporter of the Democratic Party leader, Harry Flood Byrd. Elected to the Senate of Virginia in 1933, Battle won quick acceptance into the Senate's clublike environment. Dignified yet friendly, he was a great storyteller, enjoyed his whiskey, and became known as one of the Senate's best poker players. He was also an able and intelligent man who took his responsibilities seriously. Like many other Virginia conservatives, Battle had a social conscience that was less sensitive than his personal conscience, and he was comfortable with the conservatism of the Byrd organization. Although he was never one of the small inner circle of party leaders, he was well liked and respected, and by 1946 he had become chairman of the powerful Senate Committee on Finance.

Early in 1947 Battle received Byrd's quiet endorsement to run for governor in 1949. The Democratic Party primary of 1949 was one of the most spirited and exciting in history. Francis Pickens Miller, the leader of the Democratic opposition to Byrd, ran against Battle, as did Horace Edwards, the mayor of Richmond who had served as state party chairman and was popular among party regulars but appeared to be ambitious to supplant Byrd as party leader. Petersburg manufacturer Remmie LeRoy Arnold also entered the race. Battle waged a listless campaign until Byrd organization leaders took control of the campaign. At their urging Battle attacked organized labor, a tactic that won support from crossover Republicans and enabled Battle to win the 2 August 1949 primary with a small plurality. He easily defeated Republican candidate Walter Johnson in the general election in November.

The key to Battle's successes and failures as governor can be found in his personality. He was a born conciliator and harmonizer. An extremely likable man, Battle combined natural dignity with easygoing affability. Even his political opponents rarely wrote unkindly of him in the privacy of their personal correspondence. He was on a first-name basis with nine-tenths of the members of the General Assembly, and his ability to get along with them became the hallmark of his administration. Yet Battle's easygoing nature and desire for harmony also had a negative side. Contented with life, Battle felt no compulsion to seek dragons to slay or wrongs to right. One admirer, Norfolk journalist Guy Friddell, described him as "a big-boned man but his biggest bone was his lazy bone." Nevertheless, when Battle left office in January 1954 the *Washington Post* characterized him as "the most universally popular figure in Virginia public life."

Battle's term as governor was comparatively quiet. Severely handicapped by an ill-advised tax rebate law, he was able to increase public spending only on school construction. State expenditures on other services remained abysmally low. The United States Supreme Court's decision outlawing segregation in public schools was not handed down until after Battle left office, but there were signs of the approaching storm—and the way Virginia would respond—during Battle's term. The increase in school construction and improvements in the quality of schools for African American students was a belated and inadequate attempt to avoid desegregation by making the separate schools for blacks more nearly equal to the schools for whites.

The national spotlight focused on Battle twice during his governorship. Seven African American youths, known as the Martinsville Seven, were convicted and sentenced to death for beating and brutally raping a white woman in January 1947. Civil rights organizations opposed the executions, arguing that no white men had ever been executed in Virginia for raping a white woman and that the death sentences in the Martinsville case resulted from the race of the convicted men. Battle's own racial philosophy either blinded him to the inequity or prevented him from seeing anything unjust in the disparity, and in spite of some misgivings about the sentences imposed on some of the condemned men, he allowed the execution of all seven men in February 1951.

Battle's "finest hour," in the opinions of many Virginia Democrats, took place at the 1952 Democratic national convention. Following southern defections from the party in the preceding presidential election, the convention proposed to require delegates to take what amounted to a loyalty oath promising to have the party's nominees listed on the state ballots. Delegates from Louisiana, South Carolina, and Virginia refused to accede to the proposal, and only Battle's dramatic speech to the convention on 24 July 1952 enabled both sides to agree to a compromise that avoided expulsion of the three delegations from the convention. Battle supported the party's slate in the 1952 general election campaign, even though Byrd and other close political allies and friends of Battle did not.

After retiring at the beginning of 1954, Battle returned to his law practice in Charlottesville. In November 1957 President Dwight David Eisenhower appointed him to the newly formed U.S. Commission on Civil Rights, and until Battle resigned in October 1959 he was the member most inclined to limit the commission's agenda and defend segregationist views. He had been the Virginia Democratic Party's pro-forma favorite son candidate for president at the 1956 convention, and in 1958, when Byrd announced his retirement from the U.S. Senate, Battle and former governor William M. Tuck both desired to succeed Byrd. Fearing a breach in the party, Byrd changed his mind and ran for reelection.

John Stewart Battle suffered a stroke in 1970, and he died in a Charlottesville nursing home on 9 April 1972. He was buried in Monticello Memorial Park in Charlottesville.

Peter R. Henriques, "John S. Battle and Virginia Politics, 1948–1953" (Ph.D. diss., UVA, 1971); John Stewart Battle Papers, UVA; John Stewart Battle Executive Papers, RG 3, LVA; John Stewart Battle Papers, VHS; Henriques, "The Organization Challenged: John S. Battle, Francis P. Miller, and Horace Edwards Run for Governor in 1949," *VMHB* 82 (1974): 372–406; Henriques, "The Byrd Organization Crushes a Liberal Challenge, 1950–1953," *VMHB* 87 (1979): 3–29; Henriques, "John S. Battle, Last Governor of the Quiet Years," in *The Governors of Virginia, 1860–1978*, ed. Edward E. Younger and James T. Moore (1982), 321–332; James R. Sweeney, "A Segregationist on the Civil Rights Commission: John S. Battle, 1957–1959," *VMHB* 105 (1997): 287–316 (por.); Hummel and Smith, *Portraits and Statuary*, 6 (por.); obituaries in *Charlottesville Daily Progress*, *Richmond News Leader*, *Richmond Times-Dispatch*, and *Washington Post*, all 10 Apr. 1972.

PETER R. HENRIQUES

BAUGHMAN, Mary Barney (4 September 1874–30 March 1956), physician, was born in Richmond, the eldest of four sons and four daughters of Emilius Allen Baughman and Mary Nelson Barney Baughman. She spent her childhood in Richmond, where her father and his brothers Greer Baughman and Charles Baughman operated a stationery and printing firm that their father, George Baughman, had established after the Civil War. She entered John Henry Powell's Richmond Female Seminary in 1889 and there developed an interest in the sciences, although she chose an artistic career following her graduation in 1893. Baughman took lessons with noted Virginia artist Lily Logan and with Michel de Tarnowsky, and she also studied in Paris at the Carlo Rossi Studio.

Baughman taught art at the Richmond Art Club in the decade before World War I. She also lectured on anatomy and served as the club's orthopedic gymnast. The athletic, diminutive Baughman opened the first gymnasium for women in Richmond at the All Saints' Parish House, taught classes at the Young Women's Christian Association, and persuaded Richmond's public schools to include gymnastics in the physical education curriculum for girls. She also found time to attend summer sessions in 1901 at the biological laboratory in Cold Springs Harbor, Suffolk County, New York, and in 1904 at the Bureau of University Travel in Boston, Massachusetts.

In the fall of 1917 Baughman entered Westhampton College in Richmond and took courses in the premedical curriculum. A year later the Medical College of Virginia opened its doors to women for the first time as a war expedient. Baughman, aged forty-four, entered along with twenty-two other women, and she graduated in the spring of 1922. While a medical student she continued teaching, serving as lecturer in orthopedics at both Saint Elizabeth's and Sheltering Arms Hospitals. She initially planned to combine her interests in medicine and gymnastics by opening an orthopedic practice, but she ultimately settled on a general practice. Baughman began her internship at Memorial Hospital in Richmond, only the second woman to receive an appointment at MCV's teaching hospital, but she resigned after one month because the hospital refused to pay her. The school paid men who were interns but classified women as volunteers. Baughman was subsequently paid and appointed to the general medical staff in 1923. Shortly thereafter she accepted a position as clinical instructor at MCV, serving in both the Departments of Pediatrics and of Medicine.

Baughman also established a private practice in Richmond and became active in both the Richmond Academy of Medicine and the Medical Society of Virginia. She regularly attended state, regional, and national professional meetings, particularly those relevant to women's health-care issues. In her own practice she took on many gynecological cases. Like other women physicians of her generation, Baughman believed that women were especially well suited for the specialties of obstetrics, gynecology, and pediatrics. In general she was a firm advocate of women's rights, including equal access into the medical profession.

Baughman was reportedly the first person in Richmond to distribute birth control information and the first Richmond physician publicly to advocate scientific birth control. She explained that prevention of unwanted pregnancies was a desirable way to reduce the number of dangerous abortions attempted each year in Virginia. Birth control also won her endorsement as a means of alleviating economic burdens of the poor and controlling the reproduction of people with physical and mental disabilities. She proposed the establishment of birth control clinics to disseminate information on contraception, corresponded with birth control pioneer Margaret Sanger about contraceptive methods, and endorsed the efforts of Sanger's National Committee on Federal Legislation for Birth Control. As chair of the Committee on Public Welfare of the Virginia Federation of Women's Clubs, Baughman helped persuade the federation to endorse family planning in 1935.

Baughman served as president of the Business and Professional Women's Club of Richmond in 1930 and directed the information branch of the Richmond Defense Service Unit during World War II. Mary Barney Baughman retired from the practice of medicine in 1952 and died in Richmond after a long illness on 30 March 1956. She was buried in Hollywood Cemetery in Richmond.

Feature articles in *Richmond News Leader*, 11 Jan. 1937 (por.) and *Richmond Times-Dispatch*, 8 Nov. 1942; BVS Birth Register, Richmond City; Minutes of Executive Committee of Board of Visitors, 27 Sept. 1923, and Mary Baughman to William T. Sanger, 20 Sept. 1925, Faculty File, Sanger Historical Collection, MCV; Baughman to Margaret Sanger, 2 Sept. 1935, Sanger to Baughman, 12 Sept. 1935, and Virginia materials in papers of National Committee on Federal Legislation for Birth Control, Margaret Sanger Papers, LC; Art Club of Richmond, *Catalog School Session* (1911/1912), copy in Adèle Clark Papers, VCU; *Richmond*

Times-Dispatch, 11 Apr. 1930, 18 May 1933, 11 May 1935, 7 Mar. 1937; *Richmond News Leader*, 16 May 1932, 22 June, 13 Nov. 1935, 24 Jan. 1946; Etta Belle Walker Northington, *A History of The Virginia Federation of Women's Clubs, 1907–1957* [1958], 140–144; obituaries in *Richmond News Leader* (por.) and *Richmond Times-Dispatch*, both 31 Mar. 1956, and *Virginia Medical Monthly* 83 (1956): 231.

JODI L. KOSTE

BAUSELL, Lewis Kenneth (17 April 1924–18 September 1944), recipient of the Medal of Honor, was born in Pulaski, the younger of two sons and second of five children of Lawrence Kent Bausell and Margaret Lewis Preston Baugh Bausell. In early childhood he lived in Lebanon in Russell County, before his parents moved to Washington, D.C. When he was fifteen Bausell enlisted in the District of Columbia National Guard, but he was discharged when his age was discovered.

On 15 December 1941 Bausell dropped out of McKinley High School and enlisted in the United States Marines. Following basic training at Parris Island, South Carolina, and advanced training at Camp Lejeune, North Carolina, he was ordered to the Pacific theater of operations in June 1942. He participated in the bloody island-hopping campaigns at Tulagi, Gavutu, Guadalcanal, and Cape Gloucester on New Britain Island, and in 1943 was promoted to corporal in the lst Battalion, 5th Marines, lst Marine Division. On 15 September 1944 the lst Marine Division stormed ashore on the island of Peleliu during the Allied advance on the Philippine Islands. In the first wave of fighting that day to secure a beachhead, Bausell led his men against an enemy pillbox, a reinforced concrete shelter from which the Japanese were directing machine-gun fire on a vital section of the beach. Bausell was the first man to reach the pillbox and fired his weapon directly into the aperture at the Japanese soldiers inside. As his squad closed in on the pillbox, a Japanese defender hurled a grenade into the midst of the American marines. Lewis Kenneth Bausell instantly threw himself on the grenade to shield his men from the blast and was fatally wounded, dying on 18 September 1944 aboard a navy hospital ship. He was buried at sea.

On 11 June 1945 the secretary of the navy presented Bausell's parents a posthumously awarded Medal of Honor in recognition of his heroic sacrifice. Bausell was also awarded the Purple Heart. On 19 November 1945 his parents traveled to Bath, Maine, to christen the navy destroyer USS *Bausell*, named in his honor.

Biography and family information by sister Martha E. Bausell Opperman in *The Heritage of Russell County, Virginia, 1786–1988* (1985–1989), 1:127–128, 2:95–96 (por.); *Commonwealth* 13 (Feb. 1946): 15, 29; W. Edwin Hemphill, *Gold Star Honor Roll of Virginians in the Second World War* (1947), xiii; text of citation in George Lang, Raymond L. Collins, and Gerard F. White, *Medal of Honor Recipients 1863–1994* (1995), 2:2609; award ceremony reported in *New York Times*, 12 June 1945.

DONALD W. GUNTER

BAXTER, George Addison (22 July 1771–24 April 1841), Presbyterian minister and educator, was born in the part of Augusta County that became Rockingham County in 1778, the second son and third of eight children of George Baxter and Mary Love Baxter, both of whom had immigrated to Virginia from Ireland. He entered Liberty Hall Academy (now Washington and Lee University) in 1789 during a student revival, received an A.B. degree in 1796, and studied theology under William Graham, the academy's rector. Baxter received his license to preach from the Lexington Presbytery in April 1797 and traveled as a home missionary that year. He served as principal of New London Academy in Bedford County from 1797 to 1799. On 17 January 1798 Baxter married Annie Christian Fleming. At least four of their nine children were boys, including Sidney Smith Baxter, attorney general of Virginia from 1834 through 1851.

On 19 October 1798 Baxter was elected professor of mathematics, natural philosophy, and astronomy at Washington Academy, as Liberty Hall had been renamed, and duly moved to Lexington in the spring of 1799. In the latter year, after the death of Graham, the trustees selected Baxter to succeed him. Baxter became the first president when the academy was chartered as Washington College in 1813. He taught languages and mathematics for the first three years he was rector and moral philosophy during his entire tenure at Washington College. In addition to a heavy teaching load, he served as pastor of the Lexington Presbyterian Church from 1799 to 1831 and of the nearby New Monmouth Presbyterian Church from 1799 to 1821. Baxter also made annual journeys to ask Presbyterian congregations for money for the struggling school, and he supervised the construction of new buildings in Lexington after the academy building burned in 1803. He persuaded the Virginia branch of the Society of the Cincinnati to donate its funds to the college, but the school received no money from the society until 1848. Baxter relinquished his salary to pay assistant teachers and supported himself on his small salary as a minister and later from the income of his wife's substantial inheritance.

Baxter was a gifted teacher, a master of the Socratic method, and an inspiring classroom and pulpit speaker. The number of his students who became prominent educators, politicians, attorneys, and Presbyterian ministers not only testified to his ability, but also gained Washington College a high reputation for learning. He declined offers of the presidencies of at least two universities, and in 1812 the University of North Carolina awarded him an honorary D.D. Baxter remained as much a minister as an educator, and in 1801 he attended revival meetings in Kentucky and wrote two long and spirited defenses of the controversial and emotional conversion experiences he witnessed there. During his pastorates at Lexington and New Monmouth he participated in revivals in 1802, 1821, 1822, and 1831.

In 1829 Baxter resigned as president of Washington College in order to devote more time to study and pastoral work. In December 1831, however, Baxter became professor of theology at Union Theological Seminary located at Hampden-Sydney College. He served there until his death and was acting president of Hampden-Sydney for one term in 1835. As he had in Lexington, Baxter also officiated at local Presbyterian churches. A traditionalist in many respects, he required ministerial students to spend their first year studying ancient languages, but he also supplemented the traditional theological regimen by assigning legal and scientific treatises.

A learned man and eloquent, albeit theatrical, speaker who often wept while preaching, Baxter was not a prolific writer. He served as an editor of the *Virginia Religious Magazine* that the Synod of Virginia published from 1805 to 1807, and a few of his sermons were printed at the request of those who heard them. His more important publications included his inaugural address as theology professor at Union (1832), which rebuked Presbyterians who deviated from strict Calvinism; his brief *Essay on Baptism* (1833), strongly defending infant baptism and arguing that immersion was not biblically authorized; and *Parity: The Scriptural Order of the Christian Ministry* (1840), a sermon sharply critical of the hierarchical governance of the Episcopal Church.

Baxter played an important role in continuing Presbyterian debates over slavery. At his urging the Lexington Presbytery deposed George Bourne from the ministry for his authorship of a strongly worded 1816 attack on slavery. Though rejecting Bourne's call for immediate abolition, Baxter served in 1818 on a committee of the General Assembly of the Presbyterian Church that advocated gradual emancipation. As northern criticism of southern slaveholders grew stronger, and with many Presbyterians pronouncing slaveholding a sin, Baxter argued in *An Essay on the Abolition of Slavery* (1836) that "certain principles under the influence of Christianity will abolish slavery as soon as the slave is prepared for freedom." Offering no set time for a general emancipation, his qualified defense of slavery on theological grounds stated that people "can possess a slave without moral criminality" so long as "the circumstances of the case makes slavery necessary." Baxter and other southern Presbyterian leaders reacted very strongly to condemnations of slavery, in part on moral and theological grounds but also because the issue widened divisions within the Presbyterian Church.

Even as church debates on slavery intensified, Baxter played a key role in an 1837 schism that arose from other causes. Baxter adhered to the Old School Presbyterians, a wing of the church with strong southern support that defended the strict Calvinism of the Westminster Confession of Faith and rejected the so-called New School theology of modified

Calvinism taught by Nathaniel William Taylor, of New Haven, Connecticut. Baxter and many other Old School leaders deplored the close link they perceived between New School Presbyterians, abolitionists, and followers of evangelist Charles Grandison Finney. Before the national Presbyterian General Assembly of 1837, Baxter and William S. Plumer, of the First Presbyterian Church of Richmond, organized a conference of Old School delegates from the American South and Southwest, at which Baxter presided. The plans laid at this meeting bore fruit at the General Assembly when the Old School Presbyterians "exscinded," or expelled, their New School opponents.

The schism in the Presbyterian Church had serious and unanticipated consequences for Union Theological Seminary. New School faculty members were asked to resign, and some of their supporters accordingly declined to honor pledges they had made to the seminary. The growing spirit of sectionalism and sectarianism reduced the number of nonsouthern seminary students, and enrollment of divinity students dropped from thirty-one to nineteen. Before the long-term consequences of the divisions developed fully, George Addison Baxter died at his home on 24 April 1841 of what was described as apoplexy of the lungs. He was buried in the Union Seminary Cemetery at Hampden-Sydney.

June 1772 birth date on gravestone, but early biographies, including one prepared by daughter, give date as 22 July 1771; collections of Baxter's papers at Union Theological Seminary, Richmond, and W&L; daughter Louisa Baxter's "Reminiscences of Dr. George A. Baxter," W&L; essay on years at Washington College by son Sidney Smith Baxter in *Washington and Lee University Historical Papers* 3 (1892): 45–55; early published biographies in Foote, *Sketches of Virginia*, 2:260–269, 281–294, 556–569, Sprague, *American Pulpit*, 4:192–199, and Henry Alexander White, *Southern Presbyterian Leaders* (1911), 221–231; Botetourt Co. Marriage Register; I. Taylor Sanders II, *Now Let The Gospel Trumpet Blow: A History of New Monmouth Presbyterian Church, 1746–1980* (1986), 38–42, 161; students' notes on his lectures in Lewis R. Willie Notebook, Duke, and John H. Bocock's notes, Union Theological Seminary Library; William Henry Ruffner, "History of Washington College," *Washington and Lee University Historical Papers* 4 (1893): 5–114 (which also contains family history information); Ollinger Crenshaw, *General Lee's College: The Rise and Growth of Washington and Lee University* (1969); Frank Bell Lewis, "Times of Crisis," in *"The Days of Our Years" . . . Sesquicentennial of Union Theological Seminary in Virginia* (1962), 21–31; John Luster Brinkley, *On This Hill: A Narrative History of Hampden-Sydney College 1774–1994* (1994), 143, 162 (por.), 234; Ernest Trice Thompson, *Presbyterians in the South* (1963–1973), vol. 1; Arthur Dicken Thomas Jr., "The Second Great Awakening in Virginia and Slavery Reform, 1785–1837" (Ph.D. diss., Union Theological Seminary, 1981), 404–482; obituary, copied from unlocated issue of *Lynchburg Virginian*, in *Richmond Semi-Weekly Enquirer*, 4 May 1841.

ARTHUR DICKEN THOMAS JR.

BAXTER, John (ca. 1781–1831), member of the Convention of 1829–1830, was probably born in southwestern Augusta County during or not long before 1781. His father was William Baxter, who died before March 1786, and he and a younger sister probably grew up with their paternal grandparents, John Baxter and Mary Baxter, in the section of Augusta County that became Bath County in 1790. Following his grandfather's death in the autumn of 1801, Baxter inherited his father's rifle, his grandfather's farm, cooper's and joiner's tools, and a large collection of books of fiction, history, poetry, and travel.

By 1806 Baxter had married Margaret "Peggy" Moore. They had four sons and three daughters. Baxter added to his landholdings until he owned almost a thousand acres by 1817. He was named a captain in the local militia in 1815, and in 1817 he was elected to the House of Delegates for the first of two consecutive one-year terms. He received appointments to one minor committee and two important ones, those on claims and on roads and internal improvements. Baxter was commissioned to serve on the Bath County Court in May 1820 but never took the qualifying oath. On 30 January 1822, however, Baxter was appointed a justice of the peace for the new county of Pocahontas, which was formed in part from Bath County and included Baxter's residence, and on 6 March 1822 he was commissioned colonel and commandant of the 187th Regiment Virginia Militia, based in Pocahontas County.

In May 1829 Baxter was one of four men elected to the constitutional convention from the large district composed of the counties of Alleghany, Bath, Botetourt, Greenbrier, Monroe, Nicholas, and Pocahontas. He came in fourth in a crowded field but easily outpolled the fifth-place candidate. Baxter attended the convention that met in Richmond from 5 October 1829 through 15 January 1830 and served on the Committee to Consider the Bill of Rights, which promptly reported to the convention that no changes were necessary. As did most of the other delegates from the western counties, Baxter voted to extend the franchise to adult white men who were not freeholders, to abolish the Council of State, to choose the governor by popular election, and to democratize the county court system. Defeated on every important reform, Baxter voted against the constitution that the convention submitted to the voters. After the convention adjourned he lost a bid for a seat on the Council of State. He also considered being a candidate to represent the western counties on the Board of Public Works, but the General Assembly reelected the incumbent board members without opposition.

Later in 1830 Baxter won Pocahontas County's seat in the House of Delegates, and during the session that met from 6 December 1830 to 19 April 1831 he served on the Committee on Privileges and Elections and on the Committee on Militia Laws. John Baxter resigned his colonel's commission by 19 May 1831 and died not long thereafter, probably at home and most likely before the end of the summer of 1831.

Relatives identified in wills of grandfather John Baxter and Margaret Moore, Bath Co. Will Book, 1:192, 2:328, in grandfather's qualification as administrator of estate of William Baxter, Augusta Co. Order Book, 19:290, and in William T. Price, *Historical Sketches of Pocahontas County, West Virginia* (1901), 419–421; Register of Justices and County Officers, Pocahontas Co., RG 13, LVA; Militia Commission Papers, Pocahontas Co., RG 3, LVA; residence shown on 1825 Herman Bőÿe map of Pocahontas Co.; *Richmond Enquirer*, 29 May 1829; *Proceedings and Debates of 1829–1830 Convention*; Bruce, *Rhetoric of Conservatism*, 37; Robert P. Sutton, "The Virginia Constitutional Convention of 1829–30: A Profile Analysis of Late-Jeffersonian Virginia" (Ph.D. diss., UVA, 1967); Catlin, *Convention of 1829–30* (por.); Council election defeat reported in *Richmond Whig*, 21 Jan. 1830; desire for seat on Board of Public Works recorded in Hugh Blair Grigsby's Commonplace Book, VHS, printed in *VMHB* 61 (1953): 328–329.

DAPHNE GENTRY

BAXTER, Sidney Smith (18 November 1802–7 December 1879), attorney general of Virginia, was born in Lexington, one of nine children and probably the third of four boys of George Addison Baxter and Annie Christian Fleming Baxter. In 1821 he graduated from Washington College, of which his father, a Presbyterian minister, was president. Baxter read law in Lexington and was admitted to the bar in Rockbridge County in 1823. His practice was largely confined to the county, district, and circuit courts in Rockbridge and the surrounding counties, but he gained a substantial reputation throughout the region as a talented advocate who worked with a number of prominent fellow attorneys on important local cases.

On 11 December 1834 the General Assembly elected Baxter attorney general of Virginia. Although he lacked political experience, support from a coalition of western Virginia Democrats and Whigs enabled Baxter to defeat Congressman John Mercer Patton by a margin of four votes. At that time the duties of the attorney general were prescribed in only the most limited fashion, but a law enacted in 1835 required the attorney general to issue a formal written opinion whenever the governor or any of the public boards or officers of the commonwealth in Richmond requested legal advice. The statute also required the attorney general to appear as counsel for the state "in all cases in which the commonwealth is interested, depending in the court of appeals, either in the eastern or western district thereof, or in the general court, or in the circuit court of law or chancery for the county of *Henrico*." The attorney general received only a small annual salary in addition to the ordinary attorney's fees for appearances in court, and most attorneys general also continued their private practices, which Baxter did, for a time in association with Richmond attorney Henry Coalter Cabell.

By tradition and by law, the attorney general was an ex officio member of some of the state's governing boards, including the influential Board of Public Works. A consistent and vigorous advocate of internal improvements, Baxter maintained a long involvement with the James River and Kanawha Company and was the proxy for Washington College at the company's shareholder meetings in the 1830s. He was elected to the board in his own right by 1838, although under later rules of legal ethics his simultaneous service as a board member, counsel for the company, and attorney general with responsibility for condemning private property along the intended path of the waterway would have raised questions of conflict of interest.

The attorney general served without any limit on his tenure until the Constitution of 1851 made the office an elective one with a four-year term. The state convention of the Whig Party nominated Baxter for the post in September 1851, but Democrat Willis P. Bocock defeated him in the November general election. After his term of office expired on 1 January 1852, Baxter moved to Washington, D.C., where he practiced in the federal courts and specialized in land claims.

Baxter returned to Richmond early in April 1861. In December of that year the Confederate secretary of war appointed him a special commissioner to investigate cases of political prisoners held by the Confederacy. Baxter feared that unfair or harsh treatment of citizens from the western counties would increase disaffection there, and he accepted the appointment. He examined the charges and evidence against suspected spies or traitors and discharged those against whom he found insufficient evidence. As the war dragged on, Judge Baxter, as he came to be called, was also empowered to investigate exchanges of prisoners of war and conditions in the Confederacy's military prisons in Richmond. At the end of the war Baxter returned to Lexington, where on 12 July 1865 he applied for a presidential pardon. He then moved to southwestern Virginia and reestablished his law practice, first alone and later with Sheldon Langley. He frequently gave legal advice on railroad construction and consolidation in that region. Baxter lived in Wytheville until late in the 1860s and then moved his practice to Marion.

Baxter was active in the Presbyterian Church throughout his life and from 1830 to 1856 served as a trustee of Washington College. He was also active in Masonry and served as grand master of the Grand Lodge of Virginia from 1846 to 1848. A member of Richmond Lodge Number 10 during the Civil War, shortly afterward he published *Free Masonry and the War: Report of the Committee under the Resolutions of 1862, Grand Lodge of Virginia* (1865), a strongly worded but carefully reasoned report defending the Confederacy and southern freemasons from the bitter diatribes leveled at them by the Grand Lodge of America and the grand lodges of several northern states. His essay on the history of Washington College was posthumously published.

Baxter's personal life was haunted by tragedy. On 8 October 1829 he married a Lexington resident, Anna Boucher Nickolls. They had seven children, but two of them died in infancy and his wife and youngest daughter died six days apart in August 1846 while Baxter was in Lewisburg attending a session of the Court of Appeals. His two sons died as a result of service in the Confederate army, with one killed in action in 1862 and the other succumbing in 1867 after contracting jail fever at the notorious prison in Elmira, New York. Another daughter died while visiting Baxter in 1871. As he grew older and his health declined, Baxter retired about 1876 and moved to Tazewell to live with his only surviving child. Sidney Smith Baxter died in Tazewell on 7 December 1879 and was buried with full Masonic honors in a local cemetery.

Baxter customarily signed his name S. S. Baxter but spelled his first name Sidney, although some references give it as Sydney; Baxter letters scattered in Stuart-Baldwin Family Papers, UVA, and Robins Family Papers and Faulkner Family Papers, VHS; *Lynchburg Virginian*, 19 Oct. 1829; *JHD*, 1834–1835 sess., 80–81; *Richmond Semi-Weekly Enquirer*, 13 Dec. 1834; John Mercer Patton to Littleton Waller Tazewell, 18 Dec. 1834, Tazewell Papers, LVA; partly autobiographical pardon application, 12 July 1865, Presidential Pardons; Sidney S. Baxter, "Notes on the History of Washington Academy and College from 1799 to 1829," *Washington and Lee University Historical Papers* 3 (1892): 45–63; framed tintype at VHS; obituaries in *Richmond Dispatch*, 11 Dec. 1879, and *Lynchburg Virginian*, 12 Dec. 1879; memorial in Grand Lodge of Virginia of Ancient York Masons, *Proceedings of the Annual Communication* 103 (1880): 40–42.

E. LEE SHEPARD

BAYLOR, Frances Courtenay (20 January 1848–15 October 1920), writer, was born Frances Courtenay Dawson in Fayetteville, Arkansas, the youngest of four sons and two daughters of James Lowes Dawson and Sophie E. Baylor Dawson. She spent her childhood in Arkansas, Louisiana, and Texas as her father, a retired army captain, moved from place to place in a futile search of a fortune. Her mother and an aunt educated her at home. Her parents separated, probably before the Civil War, and after her mother resumed her maiden name, Frances Courtenay Dawson became Frances Courtenay Baylor. At the end of the Civil War she and her mother moved to Winchester to live with Frances Baylor's sister, Sophie Baylor Walker, wife of Confederate general John G. Walker.

The Baylor and Walker families spent the years 1865–1867 living in England and traveling in Europe, and Baylor visited Europe again in 1873–1874. By the time of her second trip to Europe, Baylor had decided to become a writer, and some of her later novels reflect her experiences in Europe. Her literary career began in the 1870s with the anonymous publication of a play, *Petruchio Tamed*. Her first prose sketches, published under a pseudonym, appeared in a variety of newspapers, including the *Louisville Courier Journal*, *Boston Globe*, *New Orleans Times-Democrat*, *London Truth*, and *Huddersfield Gazette*, and she later published under her own name in the *Richmond Times*. During the next thirty years Baylor contributed at least two dozen signed stories and poems to popular national magazines such as *Lippincott's*, *Atlantic Monthly*, *Ladies Home Journal*, and the *Princeton Review*. She was a well-established author by 1889, when her best stories were collected in *A Shocking Example and Other Sketches*.

Baylor's first novel, *On Both Sides* (1885), went through eleven editions. Her other novels were *Behind the Blue Ridge* (1887); *Juan and Juanita* (1888), a juvenile classic republished in 1926 and 1930; *Claudia Hyde* (1894); *Miss Nina Barrow* (1897); *The Ladder of Fortune* (1899); and *A Georgian Bungalow* (1900). She published nothing more, although a novel in progress, "The Matrimonial Coolie," was found after her death. Baylor's writings reflected the literary fashions prevalent in popular American fiction at the end of the nineteenth century. Her stories feature rich and genteel characters, and are at once sentimental, melodramatic, didactic, and conservative in tone. Despite the idealized situations and weak plots, her Anglo-American novels of manners are lively revelations of individual characters. *Juan and Juanita* is suspenseful and animated, and *Behind the Blue Ridge*, the only novel set in America, displays a convincing grasp of the local speech, manners, and customs of western Virginia. Her contemporaries praised her work as eminently worth reading and exhibiting "exuberant, genuine humor." According to one critic, she could draw with skill a "delightful portraiture . . . of wayward, lovable humanity." Baylor's poetry was mostly in the popular patriotic style. The best examples are "Kind Words to Virginia" and "The Last Confederate," pieces that may reflect the influence of her mother's family, descendants of the wealthy planters and horse breeders of late colonial Caroline County.

In addition to writing and participating in Olla Podrida, a literary club for women in Winchester, Baylor was a Virginia supervisor of the John F. Slater Fund, established in 1882 to promote the education and welfare of African American children. During the 1890s she helped set up industrial schools in Norfolk and Winchester as well as sewing and cooking schools for shopgirls. Baylor distinguished herself from most other Virginia women of her time by becoming a professional writer and taking an interest in the education of working-class and African American children, but she still remained very much committed to the traditional southern values that her fiction depicted and her poetry extolled. On 16 January 1910 she published an article in the *Richmond Times-Dispatch* opposing woman suffrage.

On 24 August 1896 Baylor married George Sherman Barnum, a Savannah, Georgia, railway official of Canadian birth. They had no children, he died not long after the marriage, and she returned to Virginia, first to Lexington and then to Winchester, where she lived for the remainder of her life. She continued to write and publish under her established professional name, Frances Courtenay Baylor, until she died on 15 October 1920 following a stroke suffered while reading in the Handley Library in Winchester. She was buried the following day in Mount Hebron Cemetery.

Partial and conflicting accounts of parents in Charles C. Dawson, *A Collection of Family Records . . . of Various Families and Individuals Bearing the Name Dawson* (1874), 299, and Orval Walker Baylor and Henry Bedinger Baylor, *Baylor's History of the Baylors* (1914), 30, 38–39; Frances E. Willard and Mary A. Livermore, eds., *A Woman of the Century: Fourteen Hundred-Seventy Biographical Sketches Accompanied by Portraits of Leading American Women in All Walks of Life* (1893), 66 (por.); biography by Henry Clinton Ford in *Library of Southern Literature*, ed. Edwin A. Alderman, Joel Chandler Harris, and Charles William Kent (1909–1923), 1:281–285; Florence Waller, "A Feminine Glimpse of Miss Baylor," *Critic*, new ser., 9 (1888): 163–164; Armistead Churchill Gordon Jr., *Virginia Writers of Fugitive Verse* [ca. 1923], 113–116, 271–272; Winchester City Marriage Register; *Winchester Star*, 25 Aug. 1896; *Winchester Times*, 27 Aug. 1896; obituary and account of funeral in *Winchester Evening Star*, 15, 16 Oct. 1920.

CATHERINE T. MISHLER

BAYLOR, George (12 January 1752–9 November 1784), Continental army officer, was born at Newmarket in Caroline County, the large plantation of his parents, John Baylor (1705–1772) and Frances Walker Baylor. He was the third of six sons and sixth of twelve children, of whom two each of his brothers and sisters died in infancy. George Baylor was educated in England but, unlike his elder brother John Baylor, evidently did not attend university there. He probably returned to Virginia soon after the death of his father in order to manage the plantation he had inherited.

Baylor ran unsuccessfully for the House of Burgesses in the summer of 1774, but on the following 10 November he was elected to the Caroline County Committee that was formed to enforce the terms of the nonimportation agreement that the First Continental Congress had adopted. He also joined the local volunteer company with the rank of lieutenant. In July 1775 he went to Philadelphia and persuaded Edmund Pendleton, Benjamin Harrison, Patrick Henry, and Richard Henry Lee to recommend him for the staff of George Washington, an old friend of Baylor's father. Washington had him appointed a lieutenant colonel in the Continental army, and Baylor served as an aide-de-camp on Washington's staff from 15 August 1775 until January 1777. Washington complained privately that Baylor was inexperienced and "not, in the smallest degree, a Penman, though Spirited and willing." Baylor belonged in the field and took part in the Battle of Trenton late in December 1776, after which Washington chose him to take news of the victory to Congress. In a letter to the legislators, Washington again praised Baylor's spirit and recommended him for promotion. When Baylor reported to Congress in Baltimore on the morning of 1 January 1777, Congress immediately resolved "That a horse, properly caparisoned for service, be presented to Lieutenant Colonel Baylor, and that he be recommended to General Washington to be appointed to the command of a regiment of light horse." On 9 January 1777 Washington gave Baylor command of the 3d Continental Dragoons. Baylor returned to Virginia during the spring of 1778 to obtain horses for the cavalry, and while there he married Lucy Page on 30 May 1778. They subsequently had two sons.

On the night of 27–28 September 1778, Baylor was quartered with his troops at Old Tappan, New York, about two and a half miles from the main army. A British force under Major General Charles Grey surprised Baylor's unit and attacked with fixed bayonets, killing, wounding, and capturing many men in an unusually bloody action. Baylor received a bayonet thrust in his lungs and was taken prisoner. On 19 October, while still in captivity, he defended his actions in a letter to Washington, who never reprimanded him even though other officers questioned whether he had taken proper precautions to protect the camp. Baylor was later exchanged and returned to service as colonel of the 1st Continental Dragoons. His regiment guarded Congress in Philadelphia during October 1779, and the following December he was ordered to the southern states, where he saw action during the final years of the war. Although he still suffered from his wound, he remained an enterprising officer, served through the end of the war, and received a brevet promotion to brigadier general on 30 September 1783.

Early in May 1784 Baylor left Virginia for Bridgetown, Barbados, in hopes of recovering his health. The trip was in vain. George Baylor died there of complications from his old wound on 9 November 1784 and was buried the next day in the churchyard of Saint Michael's Cathedral, Bridgetown.

Thomas Demarest, "The Baylor Massacre—Some Assorted Notes and Information," *Bergen County History* (1971): 29–93 (por., 61); Marshall Wingfield, *A History of Caroline County, Virginia* (1924), 374–375; all published sources agree on birth date, although a family Bible record prepared after 1850 (copies in LVA and VHS) gives variant date of 17 Jan. 1752; undated marriage notice in *Williamsburg Virginia Gazette* (Purdie), 12 June 1778; transcript of will, dated 6 May 1783 with codicils of 26 Jan. and 6 May 1784, and proved in court in Virginia on 14 Apr. 1785, and documents that identify sons in *Baylor* v. *Buckner* suit papers, Spotsylvania Superior Court of Chancery; correspondence with Washington in George Washington Papers, LC; Baylor is mentioned often in letters of Washington, other Continental army officers, and members of Congress.

PAUL DAVID NELSON

BAYLOR, George (ca. 1803–27 October 1871), member of the Convention of 1861, was born in Augusta County, one of three sons and five daughters of George Baylor and Catherine Argenbright Baylor. The father's surname appears in some sources as "Behler" and "Bailer," which may indicate that he was of German extraction. About 1832 or 1833 Baylor married Isabella Koiner, and during the next twenty years they had at least four sons and at least six daughters.

During the 1840s Baylor moved to Staunton, where he prospered as a lawyer and in 1850 helped found the local Lutheran church. Although he described himself in 1861 as "a very obscure individual" who was "not known as a public man," he served as recorder of the Staunton City Council in 1858 and 1859, sat briefly on the council in 1860, and was known to be a Democrat. On 29 January 1861 he announced that he would run for the state convention that was to meet in Richmond the following month. He and the other contenders published a schedule of public meetings in the county to lay their views before the voters. In his public announcement of candidacy, Baylor pledged his loyalty to the Union, advocated compromise of sectional differences, opposed coercion of seceding states, and stated that Virginia should not consider secession unless the Northern states refused all compromise proposals. Baylor and two other Unionists, both of whom were former Whigs, were overwhelmingly elected to the convention from Augusta County.

During the convention Baylor supported both delaying tactics and the work of members trying to arrange a compromise. In his one major speech in the convention, begun on the afternoon of 28 February and completed on 1 March 1861, he refuted allegations that he was a "submissionist" and not a true patriot. Baylor voted with the majority against secession on 4 April. He opposed it again on 17 April, after the surrender of Fort Sumter, but when the convention then approved secession Baylor acquiesced in the result, citing the will of his constituents.

Baylor was appointed to fill a vacancy on the Staunton City Council on 31 August 1861 and served until the end of the year. He was then elected an alderman for a year and remained on the council until at least 1 April 1865. His only other recorded part in the Civil War was service on a local committee that collected flour, bacon, and money to help keep the destitute Confederate army in the field early in 1865. Baylor applied for a pardon from President Andrew Johnson in July 1865. A local citizen endorsed the application with a memorandum stating that Baylor was a "highly respected citizen of undoubted loyalty," and the president issued the pardon on 1 August. In October of that year Baylor was one of three Augusta County men elected to the House of Delegates in the first election held after the end of the war. He served only the one term, during which the assembly met in three sessions from 4 December 1865 to 29 April 1867 and he held senior positions on the Committees on Military Affairs and on Lunatic Asylums. In addition to another short stint on the Staunton City Council in 1870, Baylor also served on the boards of Staunton Female Seminary in 1870 and the Virginia Institute for the Education of the Deaf and Dumb and of the Blind in Staunton. George Baylor died of gravel (kidney stones) at his home in Staunton on 27 October 1871 and was buried in Thornrose Cemetery in that city.

Birth dates ranging from 1802 to 1804 can be inferred from ages given in Census, Augusta Co., 1850–1870, Presidential Pardons, and Staunton City Death Register; father's will in Augusta Co. Will Book, 28:234–236; *Staunton Spectator*,

29 Jan., 12 Feb. 1861; Reese and Gaines, *Proceedings of 1861 Convention*, 1:271–273, 282–292; Staunton City Council Minutes; *Staunton Vindicator*, 31 Mar. 1865; *Staunton Spectator and General Advertiser*, 5 Sept., 17 Oct. 1865; William Edward Eisenberg, *The Lutheran Church in Virginia, 1717–1962* (1967), 201, 304, 362; R. Aumon Bass, *History of the Education of the Deaf in Virginia* (1949), 353; obituaries in *Staunton Spectator*, 31 Oct. 1871, and *Staunton Vindicator*, 3 Nov. 1871.

SCOTT HAMPTON HARRIS

BAYLOR, James Bowen (30 May 1849–23 May 1924), surveyor, was born in Albemarle County, the eldest of two sons and a daughter of John Roy Baylor and Anne Bowen Baylor. His father had trained as a physician but gave up medical practice to devote all of his time to managing plantations and slaves in Albemarle and Caroline Counties. After attending the Dinwiddie School, Baylor enrolled at the Virginia Military Institute in February 1864 as a member of the class of 1867. Three months later, he and other VMI cadets participated on 15 May 1864 in the Battle of New Market, in which a force led by Confederate major general John C. Breckinridge defeated the army of Union major general Franz Sigel. Baylor remained with the corps of cadets until it mustered out at Richmond on 2 April 1865.

In 1870 the VMI Board of Visitors recognized the valor of Baylor and the other New Market participants who had not already graduated with their classes by awarding them diplomas (*honoris causa*). Baylor attended the University of Virginia from 1868 to 1872, earning a degree in civil engineering. In 1903 Baylor University in Waco, Texas, honored him with an LL.D.

With the support of an individual whom he later obliquely described as an "Army friend of Gen. Grant," Baylor obtained a temporary job with the United States Coast and Geodetic Survey in 1873. The following year he secured a permanent appointment in that agency through competitive examination. Baylor's career in federal service took him throughout the country as he compiled field data on the earth's magnetism, took hydrographic and astronomical readings, and surveyed and marked boundaries between various states. Perhaps his most notable activity in this last regard occurred in 1908 when he was appointed by the U.S. Supreme Court as one of three commissioners to establish the long-disputed state line between Virginia and Tennessee. From 1908 to 1914 he surveyed the Maine-Quebec border in accordance with provisions of a treaty between the United States and Canada.

Baylor devoted his greatest energy and enthusiasm, however, to the struggle to conserve and expand Virginia's oyster fishery. Convinced that excessive harvesting would soon deplete this valuable marine resource, the 1891–1892 General Assembly had authorized a survey of the state's natural oyster rocks. As stipulated by the legislature, appointees of county courts in the Tidewater and the Eastern Shore were to certify the location of these natural beds, with precise boundaries then to be determined by the U.S. Coast and Geodetic Survey. When this survey was completed, the areas defined as natural oyster beds would remain open to tonging by watermen who paid a license fee. Estuarine, bay, and seaside bottoms not so defined (areas "outside" the survey) could then be leased to oyster planters who were expected to enhance production—and state revenues—through private investment and improved management of their share of the fishery.

After consultations between state and federal authorities, Baylor was assigned to conduct this survey. Employing U.S. government boats and equipment, he accomplished the bulk of the work in 1892 and 1893, although disputes with watermen necessitated resurveys that continued until 1895. Meanwhile, Baylor did not confine his activities to the technical tasks of recording data and making charts. Instead, he became a crusader for oyster planting, using public addresses, official reports, and letters to Rich mond newspapers to lobby for long-term leases and other conservation measures. As a result of these endeavors, his name became virtually synonymous with the movement for regulatory reform, and the "Baylor Survey," published as *Oyster Records* by the Commission of Fisheries, became an enduring blueprint for Virginia's fishery-management program.

Baylor's zeal for oyster conservation manifested itself in other ways as well. In 1894 he provided expert advice for state officials when they purchased a new police steamer for the commonwealth's "oyster navy," and he assisted in defining and marking the Virginia-Maryland boundary through the Chesapeake Bay oyster grounds in 1897–1898 (a prerequisite for effective law enforcement). He also conducted a survey of Louisiana's natural oyster beds and provided counsel and encouragement for advocates of fishery reform in Maryland.

Because of his peripatetic career, which required frequent and prolonged absences from home, at one time or another Baylor maintained residences in Washington, D.C., in Richmond, and at New Market, the family estate in Caroline County. On 5 January 1881 he married Ellen Carter Bruce, of Staunton Hill in Charlotte County, the sister of William Cabell Bruce, a powerful figure in Maryland politics. The Baylors had a son and two daughters before Ellen Baylor died on 27 October 1899. Baylor was a member of the Society of the Cincinnati, the National Geographic Society, the Washington Philosophical Society, and Richmond's Westmoreland Club.

James Bowen Baylor was not long retired from the U.S. Coast and Geodetic Survey when he died on 23 May 1924 at the home of one of his daughters in Ruxton, Baltimore County, Maryland. Hailed in the press as one of the last of the "New Market cadets," he was buried in Richmond's Hollywood Cemetery.

Brief biographies in William Couper, *The V.M.I. New Market Cadets* (1933), 19–20, *Who's Who in America* 13 (1924/1925): 347, and Marshall Wingfield, *A History of Caroline County* (1924), 377–378; Orval Walker Baylor and Henry Bedinger Baylor, *Baylor's History of the Baylors* (1914); description of Ellen Bruce Baylor in William Cabell Bruce, *Recollections* (1936), 33–34; career as surveyor and conservation advocate documented in Baylor Family Papers, UVA; Baylor's publications include *The Oyster Industry: A Series of Letters Written for the Richmond "Dispatch" and "Times" During the Winter of 1892–'93* (1893), *Report to the Governor of Virginia of J. B. Baylor, in Reference to the Survey of the Oyster Grounds*, Doc. 2 appended to *JSV*, 1893–1894 sess., and *Education of the Masses in Its Relation to Production: Address Delivered at Baylor University, Waco, Texas, April 20, 1903* (1903); James Wharton, "The Turbulent Oyster Trade: Part I, In the Nineteenth Century," *Commonwealth* 15 (Nov. 1948): 9–12; Wharton, "J. B. Baylor and the Virginia Oyster Survey," *Commonwealth* 20 (Oct. 1953): 18–19 (por.), 28–29; Bernice Bryant Zuckerman, "Philip Watkins McKinney, Governor of Virginia, 1890–1894" (master's thesis, UVA, 1967), 44–49; 108 volumes of oyster survey records, including rough sketches of oyster rocks, and 16 maps and charts, Office of Auditor of Public Accounts, RG 48, LVA; obituaries in *Baltimore Sun* and *Norfolk Virginian-Pilot*, both 24 May 1924, and *Accomac Peninsula Enterprise*, 31 May 1924.

JAMES TICE MOORE

BAYLOR, John (ca. 1660–11 September 1720), merchant and planter, was born in Tiverton, Devonshire, England, the son of John Baylor and Frances Baylor. He moved to Virginia, probably in company with his father and perhaps his brother Robert Baylor, sometime before 1692. He lived first in Gloucester County but by 1714 had moved to a site on the Mattaponi River in King and Queen County near the present town of Walkerton, where he lived until his death. In 1698 he married a widow, Lucy Todd O'Brien. Family tradition indicates that they had two sons and one daughter, but so far as is known only John Baylor (1705–1772), who won renown as a horse breeder, lived to maturity.

Baylor acquired a large amount of land and became a large-scale tobacco planter, but he was principally a merchant. In 1720 Robert "King" Carter described him as "the greatest merchant in our country" and as "the great negro seller." As the agent for Isaac Hobhouse and Company, of Bristol, for a number of years during the 1710s, Baylor handled sales of slaves that totaled in excess of £15,000. Details are now very scarce, but he probably was engaged in the slave trade at least as early as 1706, and this earlier activity might have generated a business of as much as another £20,000 to £30,000. In payment for slaves Baylor collected tobacco and bills of exchange. Selling the tobacco and redeeming the bills brought him into frequent contact with such English mercantile houses as Micajah Perry and Company, of London, and Lyonel and Samuel Lyde, of Bristol, in addition to Hobhouse and his associates. Baylor appears to have had business ties with numerous Virginia planters and merchants, including Augustine Moore, who was his brother-in-law and succeeded him as Hobhouse's principal Virginia agent. Baylor had family and business ties to John Cooke and Mordecai Cooke, merchants in Gloucester County, and he also did business with his kinsman Robert Bristow, who lived in England but maintained a plantation in Gloucester County.

Probably to further his activities as a land speculator, Baylor headed a group that in June 1705 obtained Council endorsement and official sanction for a proposed expedition to explore and survey the Blue Ridge Mountains, but he is not known to have made the journey. In 1715 Lieutenant Governor Alexander Spotswood made a point of spending the night at Baylor's house on his famous expedition to the crest of the Blue Ridge. By the time of Baylor's death in 1720, he had been associated in speculative land grants totaling about 30,000 acres, and he had patented more than 7,600 acres in his own name. Although his will and the inventory of his personal property do not survive, his estate was later estimated to be worth about £6,500.

Baylor played only a minor role in Virginia politics. He or his namesake father represented Gloucester County in the House of Burgesses for the session of March and April 1693, and he was a burgess from King and Queen County in the sessions held in the spring and fall of 1718. He was listed as both a justice of the peace and a tobacco agent in King and Queen in the roster of civil officers that Spotswood completed on 27 January 1715, but the destruction of most of the county records makes it impossible to determine how long he served in those posts. John Baylor died in Norfolk on 11 September 1720 and was probably buried there.

Family Bible records of John Roy Baylor transcribing earlier family records at VHS; two extended nineteenth-century family history narratives in Baylor Family Papers, CW; year of birth variously given in those sources as 1650 and 1660, with the latter much likelier; Walter E. Minchinton, ed., "The Virginia Letters of Isaac Hobhouse, Merchant of Bristol," *VMHB* 66 (1958): 279–301; Robert Bristow Letter Book, LVA; Spotswood's list of officers in CO 5/1317, fols. 129–130; *Executive Journals of Council*, 3:16; Edward Porter Alexander, ed., *The Journal of John Fontaine, An Irish Huguenot Son in Spain and Virginia, 1710–1719* (1972), 85; place of death and death date of 11 Sept. 1721 in Bible record, although the correct year is undoubtedly 1720 based on Robert Carter's report of Baylor's death late in Sept. 1720 in Louis B. Wright, ed., *Letters of Robert Carter, 1720–1727: The Commercial Interests of a Virginia Gentleman* (1940), 53–54, 55, and a 20 Feb. 1721 legal document on his estate in York Co. Orders and Wills, 16:8.

PETER V. BERGSTROM

BAYLOR, John (12 May 1705–3 April 1772), planter and horse breeder, was the son of the merchant planter John Baylor (ca. 1660–1720) and Lucy Todd O'Brien Baylor. He was probably born at his father's seat near what is now Walkerton in King and Queen County. Family tradition credits him with a brother and a sister, but so far as is known neither one reached maturity.

Baylor was educated at the Putney Grammar School in England. He inherited most or all of the considerable estate in land and personal property of his father. By shrewd purchases and successful speculative investments he acquired more than 12,000 acres in what became Caroline and Orange Counties and invested in land companies seeking even larger grants farther west. Baylor lived for most of his adult life in Caroline County at the large estate he called Newmarket, after the English racecourse of that name. He built a large house there, and after his marriage to Frances Walker on 2 January 1744 they had six sons and six daughters, of whom two sons and two daughters died young. Baylor sent at least two of his sons to England to be educated, including George Baylor (1752–1784), later a colonel of dragoons in the Continental army.

Baylor undertook all of the public duties expected of a gentleman of his wealth and social standing. He served as a senior warden of Drysdale Parish from 1752 to 1761 and again from 1766 until his death. He was a justice of the peace and militia colonel for Caroline County and he also served as county lieutenant of neighboring Orange County. In May 1757 he marched the Caroline County militia to Winchester to reinforce Colonel George Washington's Virginia Regiment, but he did not remain in the field to command the militia in person. During stints representing Caroline County in the House of Burgesses from 1742 to 1752 and again from 1756 to 1765, Baylor was given choice assignments on the Committees on Propositions and Grievances and on Privileges and Elections.

While he was prominent as a land speculator, tobacco planter, and burgess, Baylor was best known among his contemporaries for his horses. Although fond of racing, he eventually gave up the turf in favor of breeding, and he developed one of the largest and finest stables in colonial Virginia. He invested heavily in imported stock and charged large fees for stud services, especially for his most famous horse, Fearnought, for which he paid a thousand guineas in 1764. Fearnought has been generally regarded as the best breeding stallion ever imported into colonial Virginia and is thought to have been more responsible than any other horse for elevating the quality of Virginia stock. By the 1760s Baylor was operating on a very large scale and may have had more than a hundred blooded horses in his stables. The venture increased Baylor's already substantial wealth. He owned more than 200 slaves by 1770 and lived in some elegance, but the inability of many of his Virginia debtors to pay him jeopardized his financial condition. To clear some of his own debts his executors had to sell fifty prime horses shortly after Baylor's death, and his namesake son and principal heir sold Fearnought about 1774. Even so, litigation tied up his complicated estate for decades and prevented his son from erecting a huge Palladian mansion he had planned to build at Newmarket. John Baylor died at Newmarket on 3 April 1772 and was probably interred in the family burial ground on the plantation.

Family Bible records, some of Baylor's business papers, and a letter book are in VHS; family history, partly documented and partly based on tradition, in Orval Walker Baylor and Henry Bedinger Baylor, *Baylor's History of the Baylors* (1914); Thomas E. Campbell, *Colonial Caroline: A History of Caroline County, Virginia* (1954), combining useful information with myths and errors; Washington, *Colonial Series*, 3:199, 4:242–243; Fairfax Harrison, *The Equine F. F. Vs.* (1928), 98–105 (por.); will printed in *VMHB* 24 (1916): 367–373, with a transcript and other documents in suit papers for *Baylor* v. *Buckner*, *Baylor* v. *Baylor*, and *Daingerfield* v. *Rootes*, all in Spotsylvania Superior Court of Chancery; death notice in *Williamsburg Virginia Gazette* (Purdie), 16 Apr. 1772.

PEGRAM JOHNSON III

BAYLOR, William Smith Hanger (7 April 1831–30 August 1862), Confederate army officer, was born in Augusta County, the only son and youngest of three children of Jacob Baylor and Eveline Evans Hanger Baylor. He attended school in Staunton, and at seventeen entered Washington College. After graduation in 1850, he entered the University of Virginia as a law student and completed his law course there in 1853 after taking off the academic year 1851–1852 to study law in Lexington under John White Brockenbrough. Baylor was admitted to the Augusta County bar in November 1853, and in 1857 he was elected commonwealth's attorney.

In July 1858 Baylor was elected captain of the West Augusta Guard. When the company was ordered to Charles Town following John Brown's raid on Harpers Ferry in 1859, Baylor was absent on his honeymoon, having married Mary Hawes Johnson on 18 October. They had one daughter. On 13 April 1861 the volunteer militia companies of Augusta County were organized into the 5th Regiment Virginia Volunteers, and Baylor was elected colonel. When Virginia seceded, the regiment went into active service in the brigade of Thomas J. "Stonewall" Jackson. As part of the reorganization the governor replaced the field officers, and Baylor was appointed major. He was able and popular, and the other officers drafted resolutions declaring their loyalty to him. He figured prominently in the fighting at Falling Waters and at the First Battle of Manassas (Bull Run). Following the resignation of the 5th Virginia's colonel on 5 September 1861, the officers of the regiment petitioned to have Baylor succeed him. Instead, he was appointed lieutenant colonel on 12 September, after which he became dissatisfied with his position and sought reassignment. In November Jackson accordingly appointed him to his staff as inspector general.

During the Romney campaign Baylor won acclaim by leading a cavalry charge that routed the Union forces from Bath. In the reorganization of the army in the spring of 1862, Baylor was unanimously elected colonel of his old regiment on 21 April. He was commended for his part in the fighting at Winchester on 25 May, and at Gaines's Mill. After Brigadier General John H. Winder's death at Cedar Mountain on 9 August 1862, Baylor assumed command of the Stonewall Brigade. On 15 August the brigade officers petitioned for his promotion to brigadier general. He received the appointment, but before the promotion could be confirmed, William Smith Hanger Baylor was killed on

30 August 1862 at the Second Battle of Manassas. He was leading his men, carrying the 33d Regiment's flag, and cheering them on, when a Union volley brought him down. His men retrieved his body from the battlefield, and he was buried at Hebron Presbyterian Church in Augusta County.

John Lipscomb Johnson, ed., *The University Memorial: Biographical Sketches of Alumni of the University of Virginia Who Fell in the Confederate War* (1871), 222–226; biographical memorandum by daughter Lottie Baylor Landrum, Jedediah Hotchkiss Papers, UVA; marriage date confirmed from family history records by great-grandson Baylor Landrum Jr.; Compiled Service Records; Lee A. Wallace Jr., *5th Virginia Infantry* (1988); Jedediah Hotchkiss, *Make Me a Map of the Valley: The Civil War Journal of Stonewall Jackson's Topographer*, ed. Archie P. McDonald (1973); *OR*; Robert Underwood Johnson and Clarence Clough Buel, eds., *Battles and Leaders of the Civil War* (1887–1888), 2:520 (por.); death described in Ezra Eugene Stickley, "Stonewall Brigade at Second Manassas," *Confederate Veteran* 22 (1914): 231–232.

LEE A. WALLACE JR.

BAYLY, Thomas Henry (11 December 1809–22 June 1856), member of the House of Representatives, was born at his father's Mount Custis plantation in Accomack County, the fourth of five sons and fourth of nine children of Thomas Monteagle Bayly and his first wife, Margaret Pettit Cropper Bayly. Bayly went to private schools and in 1828 and 1829 attended the University of Virginia. Then he studied law and was admitted to the bar in Accomack County on 12 October 1831. In 1836 he won election to the House of Delegates, and in 1837 he was appointed general of the 21st Brigade Virginia Militia. Bayly relinquished both offices in 1842 when he was elected a judge of the circuit court. He served on the bench only two years but was often referred to thereafter as Judge Bayly.

Following the resignation from Congress of his cousin Henry Alexander Wise, Bayly ran for the House of Representatives as a states' rights Democrat and won the special election in the spring of 1844. He served in Congress from 6 May until his death. Bayly's eloquence, tact, and assiduity rapidly won him the favor of the Democratic Party leadership. He became chairman of the Committee on Ways and Means in the 31st Congress (1849–1851) and of the Committee on Foreign Affairs in the 32d and 33d Congresses (1851–1855). Although a states' rights Democrat, Bayly was the son of a former Federalist congressman and manifested his deep devotion to the Union by searching for ways to unite southern and northern Democrats during the debates over slavery in the territories. He led the Virginia delegation in supporting Lewis Cass for president in the Democratic national convention of 1848, and he deftly pulled strings in support of the Compromise of 1850. As a consequence, many so-called southern "fireaters" despised him.

Bayly married Evelyn Harrison May, of Petersburg, on 11 May 1837. They had two daughters. He was an attractive man of impressive physique whose wit, conviviality, and courage made him extremely popular in his district. He was also outspoken and combative. Early in his congressional career he came within minutes of fighting a duel with Kentucky congressman Garrett Davis after their spirited debate in the House of Representatives turned personal and ugly, and in 1847 he reportedly shot and wounded one of his neighbors during a fight at Drummondtown (now Accomac) over a division within the Methodist Church. Thomas Henry Bayly died of consumption at his home on 22 June 1856 and was buried at Mount Custis.

Biography in Samuel T. Ross, "Recollections of Bench and Bar of Accomack: An Address Delivered . . . on June 19, 1900," *Onancock Eastern Shore News*, 25 Jan. 1935; birth date in Bayly family Bible record (LVA photocopy); marriage reported in *Richmond Enquirer*, 19 May 1837, and *Richmond Whig*, 23 May 1837; some Bayly letters in LVA; 3 Feb. 1852 letter from Bayly describing his chairmanship of the Committee on Ways and Means in *Norfolk Landmark*, 3 Mar. 1892; several congressional speeches printed as pamphlets; shooting incident reported in *American Beacon, and Norfolk and Portsmouth Daily Advertiser*, 4 Sept. 1847; por. in Bayly Art Museum, UVA; obituaries in *Richmond Dispatch*, 26, 27 June 1856, and *Richmond Enquirer*, 26, 28 June 1856.

BROOKS MILES BARNES

BAYLY, Thomas Monteagle (26 March 1775–7 January 1834), member of the House of Representatives and of the Convention of 1829–1830, was the youngest of three sons and third of five children of Thomas Bayly and Ann Drummond Bayly. He was born at his father's

Hills Farm plantation in Accomack County, educated at Washington Academy in Somerset County, Maryland, and graduated from the College of New Jersey (now Princeton University) in 1794. He returned to Accomack County, where he farmed his Mount Custis plantation, practiced law, and on 24 February 1802 married Margaret Pettit Cropper. They had four daughters and five sons; the fourth son, Thomas Henry Bayly, served in the House of Representatives from 1844 to 1856. After his wife died on 3 December 1823, Thomas M. Bayly married Jane Addison on 21 December 1826. They had two daughters and a son.

Bayly was elected to the House of Delegates as a Federalist in 1798 and was reelected twice, serving until 1801. In 1801 he was elected to the Senate of Virginia to represent Accomack and Northampton Counties. He was reelected in 1805 and served until the end of his second four-year term in 1809. In April 1813 Bayly ran against Republican Representative Burwell Bassett for the congressional seat for the district composed of the city of Williamsburg and the counties of Accomack, Elizabeth City, Gloucester, James City, Matthews, Middlesex, Northampton, and Warwick. Bayly's well-known opposition to the war with Great Britain aided him in an election characterized by a high voter turnout on the antiwar Eastern Shore and an unusually low level of voting in Bassett's strongholds west of the Chesapeake Bay, occasioned in part by the presence of enemy warships. Bayly won the election by a slim margin of fifty-seven votes. Bassett contested the election with the assertion that the poll had been illegally kept open too long in Accomack County, resulting in a greatly inflated vote total for Bayly. The Republican majority in the House of Representatives ruled that Bayly's margin of victory had been obtained illegally, but it did not unseat him in favor of Bassett.

In spite of his opposition to the War of 1812, Bayly of necessity took part in the defense of Virginia, serving in the field in 1814 as lieutenant colonel of the 2d Regiment Virginia Militia. Bayly did not seek reelection to Congress in 1815, preferring instead to devote his attention to his family, his plantation, and his law practice, but he returned twice more to the House of Delegates, serving from 1819 to 1820 and again from 1828 to 1831. In May 1829 he was one of four candidates elected to a state constitutional convention from the district composed of the counties of Accomack, Gloucester, Matthews, Middlesex, and Northampton. During General Assembly debates in February 1829 on the bill for calling the convention, Bayly had endorsed some of the reforms that members from the western counties advocated, including extension of the suffrage to more adult white men and a reapportionment of the seats in the assembly to reduce the dominance of the small counties in Tidewater Virginia. During the convention he continued to support these changes, although he voted with opponents of most of the other reforms proposed. Bayly voted for adoption of the generally conservative constitution that the convention submitted to the voters early in 1830.

By the time he made his will in 1828, Bayly had debts large enough that he set aside the profits of some of his land for five years to satisfy them and ordered that other properties be sold. He then had extensive holdings on the Eastern Shore and in Ohio and Illinois. Thomas Monteagle Bayly died on 7 January 1834 at Mount Custis and was buried in the family cemetery at Hills Farm.

Bayly family Bible record (LVA photocopy); J. Jefferson Looney and Ruth L. Woodward, *Princetonians, 1791–1794: A Biographical Dictionary* (1991), 330–333; *Richmond Enquirer*, 13 Apr., 7, 14 May 1813, 28 Feb., 5, 9 June 1829; *Annals of Congress*, 13th Cong., 1st sess., 131–132, 479–481, 486; 13th Cong., 3d sess., 438–441; Alton Brooks Parker Barnes, *Pungoteague to Petersburg* (1988), 1:69–107; Bruce, *Rhetoric of Conservatism*, 35–36, 50; Catlin, *Convention of 1829–30* (por.); one letter and copy of will in David Higginbotham Papers, VHS; gravestone inscription printed in *WMQ*, 1st ser., 7 (1898): 107; obituary in *Richmond Enquirer*, 28 Jan. 1834.

BROOKS MILES BARNES

BAYNE, Thomas (ca. 1824–5 July 1888), member of the Convention of 1867–1868, was born in North Carolina. His parents were both probably slaves. As a young man he was known as Samuel Nixon, but there is no certainty that this was his name at birth; he may have acquired it from one of the several masters that he served before becoming a fugitive from slavery in 1844.

After eluding capture for twelve months, Nixon was arrested. When no claim was made on him, he was sold to Charles F. Martin, a dentist with whom he moved to Norfolk from North Carolina. Martin soon discovered that Nixon could read and write. The young slave's education, keen intellect, and exceptional talents persuaded the dentist to teach him the rudiments of his profession. Nixon proved to be an able and trustworthy assistant. Martin sent him out at night to make house calls and permitted him to marry a woman named Edna, with whom he had one daughter.

During the 1850s Nixon was an agent for the Underground Railroad, using his freedom of movement in the port city of Norfolk to assist fugitive slaves fleeing northward. By 1855, however, local authorities had become suspicious of his clandestine activities, and he was forced to leave home. His wife died sometime after he fled to Massachusetts. There he adopted Thomas Bayne as his new name and established his own dental practice in New Bedford. His surviving letters reflect his dedication to his medical studies, but he was also politically outspoken, and in 1860 a coalition of Republicans and temperance advocates elected him to the city council.

By May 1865 Bayne had returned to Norfolk, located his daughter, and sent her to Massachusetts. Realizing that the defeat of the Confederate army would not by itself guarantee equal rights for African Americans, he began organizing the black community, working first as a political activist and later as an itinerant preacher loosely affiliated with the Methodist Church. In June 1865 Bayne chaired a committee that drew up an equal suffrage address on behalf of the black citizens of Norfolk. In January 1866 he was chosen vice president of the Colored National Convention that met in Washington, D.C., and on 3 February he appeared before a subcommittee of the Congressional Joint Committee on Reconstruction and testified about the harsh conditions he had observed in his travels in postwar Virginia. A few days later he was a member of a delegation that petitioned President Andrew Johnson for full suffrage.

On 17 April 1867 Bayne was elected a vice president of the Union Republican State Convention when it met in Richmond. Composed mostly of newly enfranchised freedmen anxious to prepare for the upcoming constitutional convention, the meeting received derisive coverage by the conservative Richmond newspapers. By the time the convention reassembled on 1 August, a rift was widening between the radical and moderate forces. Bayne's parliamentary skills enabled him to become a recognized leader of the radical black wing of the Virginia Republican Party.

Bayne and Henry Moseley Bowden, a white Republican, were elected on 22 October 1867 to represent the city of Norfolk in the constitutional convention that met from 3 December 1867 to 17 April 1868. Bayne served on the Committee on Rules and Regulations and the Committee on the Executive Department of Government. The radical Republicans controlled the convention, and Bayne, their most powerful black leader, argued forcefully for integrated public schools and equal suffrage. Despite the contempt of the white press, the constitution that emerged from the convention contained many beneficial reforms, among them universal manhood suffrage, a statewide but segregated public school system, and additional elective public offices.

In May 1869 Bayne presided over a convention of black delegates that assembled in Richmond to oppose the readmission of Virginia to the Union before suffrage was assured. Meanwhile, Bayne had quarreled with white allies over the Republican Party's candidate from the Second Congressional District. In July 1869 he and a white Republican both ran for the seat, resulting in the success of their Conservative opponent. The Republicans fared badly throughout Virginia, and voters rejected the provision of the new state constitution that would have disfranchised many former Confederates and prohibited them from holding office. Bayne was one of the state party's leaders who petitioned Congress in November to enforce the disfranchisement and disability clause or hold a new election. Congress did not grant their request, and in January 1870 President Ulysses S. Grant signed into law the act restoring Virginia to the Union.

With Reconstruction over, Bayne reduced his role in partisan politics but remained active in local elections as late as 1882. He continued to devote himself to his dental practice and his ministry. In July 1887 he wrote a will leaving all of his property to his daughter and her children. His mental condition soon deteriorated, and he was admitted on 30 May 1888 to Central State Lunatic Asylum in Petersburg. Thomas Bayne, the fiery personality of the Reconstruction era, often a lightning rod for the political passions of his enemies, died there of heart disease on 5 July 1888. The place of his burial is unknown.

William Still, *The Underground Rail Road* (1872; repr. 1970), 260–265 (including three letters by Bayne); Jackson, *Negro Office-Holders*, 2–3, gives year of birth, corroborated in Census, Norfolk City, 1870; *New York Weekly Anglo-African*, 28 Apr. 1860; Richard G. Lowe, *Republicans and Reconstruction in Virginia, 1856–70* (1991), and "Testimony from the Old Dominion before the Joint Committee on Reconstruction," *VMHB* 104 (1996): 378, 387; *Report of the Joint Committee on Reconstruction*, 39th Cong., 1st sess., 1866, House Rept. 30, serial 1273, appended testimony, pt. 2, 58–59; Philip S. Foner and George E. Walker, eds., *Proceedings of the Black National and State Conventions, 1865–1900* (1986–), 1:81, 88, 89, 92, 93, 213; *Debates and Proceedings of 1867–1868 Convention*; *Norfolk Journal*, 25 Apr.–1 May 1868; unflattering caricatures in cartoons in *Richmond Southern Opinion*, 15 Feb., 28 Mar. 1868; Bayne to Chester A. Arthur, William Mahone, James D. Brady, and Edward Spaldon [Spalding], 22 Aug. 1882, Mahone Papers, Duke; Norfolk Corporation Will Book, 10:190; illness and death reported in *Norfolk Landmark*, 4, 18, 31 May 1888, and *Norfolk Virginian*, 4 May, 8 July 1888.

TOMMY L. BOGGER

BAYNHAM, William (7 December 1748–8 December 1814), physician, was the younger of two sons of John Baynham, a Caroline County justice of the peace, vestryman, and physician, but his mother's name is not known. He may have had three or more older half or stepbrothers. Baynham decided while still very young to follow his father into medicine. He spent five years as an apprentice to Dr. Thomas Walker, of Albemarle County, and then went to London at age twenty to study at Saint Thomas's Hospital. There he came under the influence of Joseph Else, a noted anatomist, and he developed remarkable skills in the preparation of anatomical specimens.

In 1772, on the recommendation of Else, Baynham became the prosector for Charles Collignon, the professor of anatomy at Cambridge University. During the summer months Baynham practiced surgery in partnership with a prominent surgeon in Margate, Kent. In 1775 Else called Baynham back to London to assist him at Saint Thomas's Hospital. There Baynham supervised the anatomical theater and dissecting room, prepared specimens for the museum, and instructed students in the art of dissecting, injecting, and making anatomical preparations. Baynham's skills impressed, among others, the famous anatomist, William Hunter, and he soon became recognized as England's finest practical anatomist. Else had selected Baynham to be his successor at Saint Thomas's, but after Else's death Baynham lost the appointment to a rival, reportedly by a single vote. On 7 June 1781 Baynham became a member of the Company of Surgeons of London, and he practiced surgery there for four years.

In 1785 Baynham returned to Virginia and established a medical practice in rural Essex County. Despite living away from population centers where his skill could be observed, he soon came to be regarded as one of the finest surgeons in the United States and was often consulted or called away from Essex County to other parts of the country to perform delicate or unusual operations. Baynham performed every known surgical procedure, including operations for stones and cataracts. He was most noted for his publication, in an 1809 article that reported on cases from 1791 and 1799, of the first successful American surgical treatments of extrauterine pregnancy. Baynham's skill was favorably compared to that of Dr. Philip Syng Physick, of Philadelphia, probably the most famous American surgeon during the early years of the nineteenth century.

Baynham was eccentric and said to be irascible, and he was sometimes gloomy and austere. He was a man of few words, but his patients were loyal to him, and his colleagues held him in high regard. Baynham remained a bachelor until he was more than sixty years old, when he married Virginia Mathews on 26 April 1810. Their one son, William Armistead Baynham, became a physician and a Baptist minister. William Baynham died at his home in Essex County on the day following his sixty-sixth birthday, 8 December 1814.

Anonymous but well-informed biography serialized as "A Biographical Sketch of Doctor William Baynham, Late of Essex County, Virginia," *Daily Compiler and Richmond Commercial Register*, 30, 31 Aug., 1 Sept. 1815, and reprinted in large part in *Philadelphia Journal of Medical and Physical Sciences* 4 (1822): 186–203; James Thacher, *American Medical Biography: or, Memoirs of Eminent Physicians* (1828), 1:168–173; Robert William Baird, *Bynam and Baynham Families of America, 1616–1850* (1983), 11–13; Wyndham B. Blanton, *Medicine in Virginia in the Eighteenth Century* (1931), 12–17 (por.); William Baynham, "Account of Two Cases of Extra-Uterine Conception, in One of Which the Foetus was Extracted by an Operation with Success," *New York Medical and Philosophical Journal and Review* 1 (1809): 161–170.

E. RANDOLPH TRICE

BEALE, Frank Dunnington (4 November 1890–8 April 1968), railroad executive, was born in Fredericksburg, the youngest of two sons and a daughter known to have been born to Samuel H. Beale and Sallie Ann Scott Beale. He attended local public schools and graduated from the University of Virginia in 1915 with a degree in civil engineering. Beale began his railroad career in 1910 as an assistant in the engineering division of the Florida Railway. After graduating from college he became an assistant section foreman with the Chesapeake and Ohio Railway Company, and in 1916 he became division engineer for the Clifton Forge division of that railroad. He remained in the post until 1924, except during World War I, when he served with the 314th Field Artillery. He married Frances R. Casey in Clifton Forge on 6 January 1921. They had three sons and three daughters.

Beale's career followed the traditional twentieth-century American railroad executive's path of success, starting out in the operating department and retiring from the board room. In 1924 he served briefly as trainmaster of the Richmond division of the Chesapeake and Ohio. The trainmaster was responsible for seeing that trains had proper crews and adequate equipment and were dispatched and moved over the line as expeditiously as possible. Later in 1924 Beale became trainmaster for the Clifton Forge division, but in 1926 he returned to Richmond as the division superintendent. He was a skilled administrator, and in 1930 the C&O promoted him to assistant general superintendent of the western division of the railroad. He lived in Huntington, West Virginia, until 1940, when he became an assistant vice president and assistant to the president, George Doswell Brooke. Beale then moved to Cleveland, Ohio, the location of the C&O corporate headquarters. From March 1943 to May 1944 he was vice president for operations of the New York, Chicago, and Saint Louis Railroad (the "Nickel Plate"), which at that time the Chesapeake and Ohio controlled.

Brooke had encouraged Beale's career, and after his election in 1943 as chairman of the Virginian Railway, Brooke dismissed its president and hired Beale to replace him on 15 May 1944. The Virginian Railway, which had its corporate headquarters in Norfolk, had been chartered in 1904 as a coal-hauling competitor of the Norfolk and Western Railway Company. A profitable and regionally important enterprise, the Virginian operated a main line almost six hundred miles long, linking Norfolk with the coalfields in western Virginia and southern West Virginia. Beale served as president of the company for almost fifteen years, until the Norfolk and Western took it over in 1958. He then retired from active railroad management, but he served on the board of the Norfolk and Western until his death in a Norfolk hospital on 8 April 1968. Frank Dunnington Beale was buried in Forest Lawn Cemetery in Norfolk.

Biography in *Commonwealth* 11 (June 1944): 18 (por.); Chesapeake and Ohio Railway Company Archives, Chesapeake and Ohio Historical Society, Clifton Forge; Norfolk and Western Railway Archives, VPI; Beale letters on family history in George Harrison Sanford King Papers, VHS; BVS Marriage Register, Clifton Forge; obituaries in *Norfolk Ledger-Star* and *Norfolk Virginian-Pilot*, both 9 Apr. 1968, and *Washington Post*, 10 Apr. 1968.

JOSEPH S. WHITE III

BEALE, George William (21 August 1842–15 July 1921), Baptist minister and historian, was born in Westmoreland County, the eldest of six sons and two daughters of Lucy Maria Brown Beale and Richard Lee Turberville Beale, a congressman and Confederate general. Beale was educated at Fleetwood Academy, Culpeper Military Institute, and Piedmont Academy. On 30 April 1861 he joined a cavalry company being organized in his home area that became Company C of the 9th Virginia Cavalry on 31 August 1861. He served throughout the war, won promotion to first lieutenant in 1862, and sustained wounds during the fighting at Reams Station in 1864 and more seriously on 5 February 1865 at Hatcher's Run near Petersburg. He was recuperating in a private residence near Bowling Green when the war ended.

After his recovery Beale initially taught near his home, but having decided to become a minister he obtained a license to preach later in 1865 and for the next two years worked among the Baptist churches in the vicinity of Westmoreland County. In August 1867 he matriculated at Southern Baptist Theological Seminary in Greenville, South Carolina, studying systematic theology. After his 2 May 1868 graduation Beale was ordained at Machodoc Baptist Church in Westmoreland County on 18 October 1868 and served from then until 1874 as minister at Machodoc and the nearby church at Popes Creek. In 1873 he baptized his father in the waters at Nomini Ferry in Westmoreland County where he himself had been baptized in 1861.

Beale's ministerial career spanned fifty-four years. After six years in Westmoreland, he became pastor in 1874 of the Gay Street Baptist Church in Georgetown, Washington, D.C., serving there until 1879. On 3 December 1879 he married Mary Anna Bouic, the daughter of W. Viers Bouic, a judge in Rockville, Maryland. Of their six children, three sons and two daughters survived to adulthood. Just before he married, Beale accepted a charge in Halifax County and spent the next four years, 1879–1883, as minister to Beth Car Baptist Church at Halifax Court House and Black Walnut Baptist Church. From 1883 to 1894 he was pastor to a congregation in Enon (near Hollins) in Roanoke County and another in Buchanan in Botetourt County. He served concurrently as chaplain to the students and faculty at Hollins Institute from 1884 to 1894. Beale received a D.D. degree from Washington and Lee University in 1894 and returned the same year to the Northern Neck, where he was minister to Coan and Fairfields Baptist Churches in Northumberland County until 1905, and to the churches at Menokin in Richmond County and Nomini from 1905 until declining health forced him to retire in 1919.

Beale was also active in state Baptist organizations. In 1898 he preached a sermon on "The Organized Work of Virginia Baptists During the Nineteenth Century" for the Baptist General Association of Virginia and served as president of the organization for the sessions of 1901 and 1902. He was a trustee of Richmond College from 1883 until 1918 and of the Baptist Orphanage at Salem from 1911 to 1918. Beale was a longtime member of the Virginia Baptist Historical Society and served as first vice president in 1920.

In 1894 Beale published his first major work, a revision and enlargement of Robert B. Semple's *History of the Rise and Progress of Baptists in Virginia*, inaugurating his second career as a historian and writer. Previously he had contributed articles to the *Religious Herald*, cowritten a history of the Buchanan Baptist Church in 1889, and prepared brief histories of the Valley and Rappahannock Baptist Associations in 1892 and 1893, respectively.

After the death of his father in 1893 Beale edited the former regimental commander's manuscript history of the 9th Virginia Cavalry, adding rosters and notes and publishing it in 1899 as *History of the Ninth Virginia Cavalry, in the War Between the States, by the Late Brig. General R. L. T. Beale*. The Sunday School and Bible Board of the Baptist General Association of Virginia issued several pamphlets by Beale for use in Sunday schools. From his study of family Bible records, tombstones, and early manuscripts came many contributions to the *William and Mary Quarterly*. Beale also wrote a chapter on "Baptist Beginnings in Virginia" for Charles F. James's *Documentary History of the Struggle for Religious Liberty in Virginia* (1900) and delivered an address that in 1912 became part of a volume on the history of Westmoreland County. In 1916 he chaired a committee that prepared the history statement that appeared thereafter on the title page of the Baptist General Association's yearly minutes. Beale's last publication was his own Civil War memoir, *A Lieutenant of Cavalry in Lee's Army* (1918).

George William Beale died at his home in Westmoreland County on 15 July 1921 and was buried in the cemetery at nearby Coan Baptist Church.

George Braxton Taylor, *Virginia Baptist Ministers*, 6th ser. (1935), 91–92; Beale's posthumously published "Annals of the Northern Neck of Virginia," with introductory biography of Beale by J. Motley Booker, *Northern Neck of Virginia Historical Magazine* 17 (1967): 1620–1657; George William Beale Papers and por. in VBHS; Compiled Service Records; Robert K. Krick, *9th Virginia Cavalry* (1982); obituaries in *Fredericksburg Free Lance*, 19, 21 July 1921; memorials in *Religious Herald*, 21 July 1921, and *Virginia Baptist Annual* (1921): 137–138.

W. HARRISON DANIEL

BEALE, James Madison Hite (7 February 1786–2 August 1866), member of the House of Representatives, was born at Mount Airy in Shenandoah County, the youngest of four sons and three daughters of Tavener (Taverner) Beale and Elizabeth Hite Beale. He grew up in Shenandoah County, and on 2 December 1806 he married sixteen-year-old Mary Casey Steenbergen, daughter of another Shenandoah County farmer who was, like Beale's own father, moderately prosperous and a sometime member of the General Assembly. Between 1808 and 1827 the Beales had two sons and four daughters.

In about 1813 Beale moved to Mercers Bottom, a few miles from Point Pleasant in Mason County. He and his brother-in-law Peter H. Steenbergen acquired a tract of 2,040 acres of prime agricultural land in 1815, the first of several profitable land investments that Beale made in the vicinity. Beale did not serve in the field during the War of 1812 but had the courtesy title of colonel in the local militia, and in 1818 he was elected to the House of Delegates. He served on the Committee to Examine the Armory at Harpers Ferry and voted for the establishment of the University of Virginia, but during his one term he did not compile a significant legislative record. Beale moved back to Shenandoah County in about 1826, and in 1833 he won election as a Democrat to the House of Representatives for the district comprising Bath, Hardy, Page, Pendleton, Rockingham, and Shenandoah Counties. He was reelected in 1835 and served during his second term as chairman of the Committee on Invalid Pensions. He withdrew from the campaign prior to the election of 1837.

Beale returned to Mason County in about 1844. In the spring of 1849 he was elected to the House of Representatives from the district composed of the counties of Cabell, Doddridge, Harrison, Jackson, Kanawha, Lewis, Mason, Putnam, Ritchie, Taylor, Wayne, Wirt, and Wood. He served as chairman of the Committee on Expenditures on Public Buildings and voted for three of the bills that made up the Compromise of 1850. In 1851, in a three-way race with a Whig and another Democrat, he won reelection and became chairman of the Committee on Manufactures. On 14 January 1853, describing himself as "an old man," Beale announced that he would not seek another term. In 1855 the American (Know Nothing) Party nominated him for lieutenant governor of Virginia. He did not campaign for the office and was not elected.

Beale lived his final years in Point Pleasant as a merchant and owner of a tavern, the Virginia Hotel. He owned two slaves as late as 1859 and was a Unionist during the secession crisis but sympathetic to Virginia during the Civil War. Because of his age he took no military or political part in the war or in the creation of the new state of West Virginia. After his wife died in February 1863, Beale lived with his daughter Catherine Marie Beale Murdoch. When the Civil War ended, Beale still owned real estate valued for tax purposes at more than $9,000. James Madison Hite Beale died on 2 August 1866 while visiting his daughter Mary Caroline Beale Thompson in Putnam County, West Virginia. He was buried in the Beale Cemetery at Gallipolis Ferry, West Virginia.

Brief biography in John P. Hale, *History of the Great Kanawha Valley* (1891), 2:22–23; birth and death dates in Violette S. Machir, *Mason County, W.Va. Cemetery Inscriptions* (1973), 77–78; genealogical and family history information, including marriage date, in unpublished family history memorandum by Elmine Reebel, "Beale, Madison, Taylor, Jordan, Vanmeter, Reebel, Steenbergen, Gill" (copy in Mason Co. clerk's office, Point Pleasant, W.Va.); business and financial information in Land and Personal Property Tax Returns, Mason Co., RG 48, LVA, and in Mason Co. Deed and Will Books; elections to Congress and decisions not to seek additional terms reported in *Richmond Enquirer*, 7 May 1833, 5 May 1835, 9 May 1837, 8 May 1849, 28 Oct. 1851, 18 Jan. 1853; American Party nomination in *Richmond Whig and Public Advertiser*, 16 Mar. 1855.

STEPHEN W. BROWN

BEALE, Richard Lee Turberville (22 May 1819–17 April 1893), member of the House of

Representatives, member of the Convention of 1850–1851, and Confederate army officer, was born at Hickory Hill in Westmoreland County, the third of four sons and eighth of ten children of Robert Beale and Martha Felicia Turberville Beale. He was educated in local schools before attending Northumberland Academy in Virginia and most of one session at Dickinson College in Carlisle, Pennsylvania, late in 1835. Beale returned to Westmoreland County in January 1836 and read law for a year in the office of Willoughby Newton. He then enrolled at the University of Virginia and earned an LL.B. there in July 1838. Beale opened a law office at Hague in Westmoreland County in the summer of 1839 and on 28 May 1840 married Lucy Maria Brown. They had six sons and two daughters.

In April 1847 Beale was the Democratic Party candidate for the House of Representatives from the district that included the counties of Caroline, Essex, King and Queen, King George, King William, Middlesex, Richmond, and Spotsylvania. He defeated Willoughby Newton, who had first been elected as a Whig in 1845, by a margin of about three to two. As a congressman, Beale served on the Committee on the Militia and made one major speech, an impassioned defense on 29 January 1849 of proslavery members and their attempts to find a compromise on the issue of federal regulation of slavery in the territories and the District of Columbia. Beale did not seek reelection in 1849. In 1850 he was one of three delegates elected to represent the counties of King George, Lancaster, Northumberland, Richmond, and Westmoreland in the constitutional convention that met from 14 October 1850 to 1 August 1851. Beale served on the Committee on the Basis and Apportionment of Representation. He seldom spoke during the debates and usually voted with the opponents of democratic innovations. He missed the final vote on the constitution on 31 July 1851. Beale also represented the district composed of Lancaster, Northumberland, Richmond, and Westmoreland Counties in the Senate of Virginia from 1857 to 1860.

On 25 May 1861 Beale was commissioned a lieutenant in a cavalry company known first as Lee's Legion, or Lee's Light Horse, before it was taken into the 9th Virginia Cavalry. Beale was promoted to colonel in 1862 and fought in most of the major battles of the Army of Northern Virginia, including the Seven Days' Battles, the Second Battle of Manassas (Bull Run), Sharpsburg (Antietam), Fredericksburg, Chancellorsville, and Gettysburg. He was twice involved in famous incidents. In June 1862 a reporter for the *Richmond Dispatch* accompanied Beale when General James Ewell Brown Stuart and elements of the 9th Virginia Cavalry rode around George McClellan's army, one of the most daring episodes of the war in Virginia and made more so by the reporter's dispatches. In 1864 Beale commanded the detachment that killed Ulric Dahlgren during the latter's mission to kidnap or kill Jefferson Davis. In October 1864 Beale took command of a brigade in William Henry Fitzhugh Lee's division, and in February 1865 he was promoted to brigadier general to rank from 6 January. On three occasions in 1862 and 1863 he tried to resign from the army but did not state his reasons, and he was severely wounded in September 1863 and again wounded, but not so seriously, early in 1865. Beale and remnants of the 9th Virginia Cavalry were present at the surrender at Appomattox in April 1865.

After the war Beale returned to Westmoreland County, resumed his law practice, and wrote a *History of the Ninth Virginia Cavalry, in the War Between the States*, which his son George William Beale edited and published in 1899, six years after Beale's death. The same son baptized him into the Baptist Church in 1873, and Beale became an active lay leader who was elected moderator of the Rappahannock Baptist Association in August 1881. In 1878 he won a special election for the House of Representatives and subsequently defeated Republican George C. Round and a third candidate in the general election, serving from 23 January 1879 to 3 March 1881. During this stint in Congress Beale sat on the Committees on Commerce and Manufactures and was thwarted in an attempt to obtain federal funding to complete a monument in Fredericksburg to Mary Ball Washington, George Washington's mother. He did not run for reelection in 1880 but continued to practice law and took part in the parade at the unveiling of the Lee Monument in Richmond on 29 May 1890. Richard Lee Turberville Beale died at his home on 17 April 1893 and was buried in the cemetery at Hickory Hill.

Brief biography in William Cathcart, ed., *The Baptist Encyclopædia* (1881), 91; birth date in autobiographical letter to Charles Lanman, 11 Sept. 1858, Lanman Papers, VHS; other letters in Richard Lee Turberville Beale Papers, Duke, and in Beale and Davis Family Papers, UNC; Westmoreland Co. Marriage Bonds; *Richmond Enquirer*, 27 Apr. 1847; *Congressional Globe*, 30th Cong., 2d sess., 389–391; Beale's *History of the Ninth Virginia Cavalry* (frontispiece por. by C. Conway Baker); *OR*; Compiled Service Records; Robert K. Krick, *9th Virginia Cavalry*, 4th ed. (1982); Election Records, no. 110, RG 13, LVA; *Congressional Record*, 46th Cong., 3d sess., 1994; obituary in *Alexandria Gazette*, 20 Apr. 1893, gives death date as 18 Apr. 1893, and other works use 22 Apr. 1893, but son's introductory note to *History of the Ninth Virginia Cavalry* gives death date as 17 Apr. 1893.

ALAN L. GOLDEN

BEALE, Thomas (ca. 1610–by 3 December 1700), member of the Council, was born in England, most likely into the Beale family of London. By 1643 Beale had settled in York County. He had probably married before arriving in Virginia, and by 1648 he certainly had a wife, whose first name was Alice. They had at least two daughters, whose names the extant records do not disclose, and a son, Thomas Beale, who moved to old Rappahannock County in 1673 and died there in October 1679 aged about thirty.

Beale acted as a factor for English tobacco merchants and Virginia planters. He acquired a three-hundred-acre plantation on what is now called Crab Neck, bounded by Back Creek, Cheesman (or Chisman) Creek, and Chesapeake Bay, and another two hundred acres on nearby Bay Tree Creek. He evidently lived on the bank of Back Creek for more than half a century. He served as sheriff of York County in 1645 and may have been a vestryman of Bruton Parish in 1684.

Beale returned to England at least twice and was probably in London when Charles II was restored to the throne in May 1660. A family tradition held that Beale knew both Charles I and Charles II and remained loyal to the monarchy throughout the English Civil War and Interregnum. Beale's court connections are confirmed by the 30 September 1668 recommendation by Charles II that Governor Sir William Berkeley appoint Beale, "of whose abilities and prudence the King has had long experience," commander of the fort at New Point Comfort or "any other fort or castle that may become void."

Between 25 February and 24 April 1661 Berkeley named Beale to the governor's Council. Details of Council service during the 1660s are scarce because of a lack of records, but Beale attended recorded meetings of the Council frequently from the spring of 1670 until Bacon's Rebellion of 1676. Beale's participation in the uprising is not well documented, but he and three other Council members joined Nathaniel Bacon (1647–1676) in signing a writ on 11 August 1676 calling for the election of a new assembly to meet in September. Beale evidently signed none of the three declarations Bacon issued in July and August 1676. Nonetheless, Berkeley specifically excluded Beale and two other councillors from the pardon he proclaimed on 10 February 1677.

Beale's hot temper frequently involved him in legal disputes with his argumentative neighbors and his indentured servants. He had difficulty keeping a civil tongue, especially, as happened more than once, when his wife was insulted. In May 1667 he allegedly caned a man in a dispute over the price of some sugar. At the age of about ninety, Thomas Beale died between 24 May 1700, when he won a judgment in the York County Court, and 3 December 1700, when Alice Beale signed her will as his widow. He was buried, as he requested, in the orchard of his Back Creek plantation. Alice Beale died during the winter of 1702–1703 and was probably buried in the same place.

Deposition of 3 Aug. 1660 (PRO HCA 13/73) gives age as fifty years; Frances Beale Smith Hodges, *The Genealogy of the Beale Family, 1399–1956* (1956), 12–14, contains some inexact family history, recounts the ill-documented tradition that Beale was a partisan of the king during the English Revolution and, as with some histories of the Northern Neck, confounds Beale with his namesake son; Charles II's 30 Sept. 1668 recommendation of Beale in PRO Domestic Entry Book, Charles II, 31:11; writ of 11 Aug. 1676 in PRO CO 1/37, fol. 133; reference to Beale during Bacon's Rebellion in Ann Cotton, "An Account of our Late Troubles in Virginia," first published in *Richmond Enquirer*, 12 Sept. 1804; pardon proclamation of 1677 in PRO CO 1/39, fol. 64; York Co. records contain numerous references to Beale, including depositions on caning incident, evidence on death, and two unsuccessful efforts to probate now-lost will (York Co. Deeds, Orders, Wills, 4:145, 11:336, 434, 486, 12:85).

DAPHNE GENTRY

BEALL, John Yates (1 January 1835–24 February 1865), Confederate navy officer, was born at Walnut Grove, his family's farm near Charles Town, the second of four sons and fourth of nine children of George Brook Beall and Janet Yates Beall. He was educated at home and in September 1852 began law-oriented studies at the University of Virginia, but he left in June 1855 without taking a degree. That August Beall and his older sister set out for Dubuque, Iowa, to join their older brother, a successful land investor, but turned back on learning of their father's serious illness. After the latter's death on 20 August, Beall took over the management of the farm.

Beall was active in the Zion Episcopal Church and known for his serious nature, cultivated tastes, and abstemious habits. He enrolled as a private in the Botts Greys, the Charles Town militia company, after John Brown's raid on Harpers Ferry. While he was on duty during Brown's trial and execution in Charles Town late in 1859, Beall probably met John Wilkes Booth, then a corporal in the Richmond Grays. Postwar stories that they had been close friends since boyhood and that Booth had assassinated President Abraham Lincoln because he believed Lincoln had broken a promise to pardon Beall are apocryphal.

On 18 April 1861 the Botts Greys became Company G of the 2d Virginia Infantry, one of the five regiments that soon comprised General Thomas J. Jackson's famed Stonewall Brigade. On 16 October, while detailed to take a sick soldier to Jefferson County, Beall learned that Lieutenant Colonel Turner Ashby's troops were under attack at nearby Bolivar Heights. Beall joined Ashby and, despite his low rank, led an impromptu charge in the course of which he suffered a severe chest wound. During his long recuperation from this injury, which never fully healed, he visited a Louisiana plantation and met Martha O'Bryan, a Nashville schoolteacher to whom he became secretly engaged.

After Jackson's victory at Winchester on 25 May 1862, Beall joined elements of the army in nearby Jefferson County. He then became separated from Confederate forces during Jackson's retreat up the Shenandoah Valley. Dispirited and unable to locate his unit, Beall again journeyed to Iowa, settling in Cascade, near Dubuque. There his brother helped him obtain a job operating a gristmill under the name John Yates. In September, warned that his Confederate identity was about to be revealed, he fled north and in November reached Dundas, Canada West, near Toronto. While there Beall attempted to enlist for sea duty on a privateer but was dissuaded by doctors. Undeterred, he left in January 1863 for Richmond where, assisted by Colonel Edwin Gray Lee, formerly of the Stonewall Brigade, he presented two proposals to President Jefferson Davis. Beall's plan to free Confederate prisoners on Johnson's Island off of Lake Erie in Sandusky Bay, Ohio, and form an independent military force was rejected, but his offer to conduct irregular naval operations on the Chesapeake Bay won approval. He received a medical discharge from the army on 18 February 1863 and on 5 March was commissioned an acting master in the Confederate navy. Beall joined with Lee, now a navy captain, to recruit a small band of volunteers and establish clandestine headquarters in Mathews County. Their initial efforts were unsuccessful and Lee resigned, leaving Captain Beall in charge. This title, awarded by his men, increased later confusion about his rank and branch of service.

Beall's command of about twenty men, outfitted with a sail canoe and a yawl, inflicted considerable damage by cutting a submarine cable, destroying a lighthouse, and capturing merchant ships carrying supplies. On 15 November 1863 Federal forces, after months of attempts, finally captured the raiders near Tangier Island. Treated initially as pirates, Beall and his men were taken to Fort McHenry, Baltimore, and placed in irons. After periods of confinement on a ship off of Fort Monroe and in a prisoner-of-war camp at Point Lookout, Maryland, Beall was moved to

Union-occupied City Point. In March 1864 he returned to Richmond in a prisoner exchange.

Beall reunited briefly with his fiancée in Georgia, then applied to authorities in Richmond for new assignments. After refusing a lieutenant's commission in the secret service, he returned to Canada in August 1864 and contacted Lieutenant Colonel Jacob Thompson, in charge of Confederate operations on that border. Thompson asked Beall to lead a raid on Johnson's Island to free about 3,000 imprisoned Confederates, a scheme similar to that which Beall had proposed the year before. On 19 September 1864 Beall and nineteen men disguised as civilian passengers seized the *Philo Parsons*, a ferry en route to Sandusky Bay. The raiders entered the bay at nightfall, but their plan to capture the gunboat *Michigan* and force the release of the prisoners on the island went awry when agents assigned to drug the crew of the *Michigan* were apprehended. When the agents failed to give the prearranged signal, Beall's men refused to proceed and returned to Canada.

Beall then joined a small band that attempted to derail trains carrying Confederate prisoners. On 16 December he was apprehended at Niagara Falls and imprisoned in a New York City jail cell. He was taken to Fort Lafayette on 5 January 1865 to be tried by a military commission for his role in the Lake Erie raid, for spying, and for attempting to wreck trains carrying civilian passengers. Major General John Dix blocked communications between Beall and the outside world and denied him his choice of counsel. Although James T. Brady, a prominent New York City attorney, argued ably that Beall was a Confederate naval officer acting under orders, he was convicted. In mid-February he was transferred to Fort Columbus on Governors Island in New York Bay. Brady and others made extraordinary efforts to obtain a pardon, including visits to President Abraham Lincoln, a petition signed by ninety-two members of Congress, and letters to Lincoln and Secretary of War Edwin M. Stanton.

John Yates Beall was hanged on 24 February 1865. His last words were, "I protest against this execution. It is absolute murder—brutal murder. I die in the service and defence of my country." Beall's body was buried in Green-Wood Cemetery in Brooklyn, New York. On 22 March 1870 it was reinterred in the Zion Episcopal Church graveyard in Charles Town.

Cameron S. Moseley, *John Yates Beall: Confederate Commando* (1998); Daniel Bedinger Lucas, *Memoir of John Yates Beall* (1865); John Lipscomb Johnson, *The University Memorial: Biographical Sketches of Alumni of the University of Virginia Who Fell in the Confederate War* (1871), 1:684–702; Compiled Service Records; James H. McNeilly, "John Yates Beall: Account of His Thrilling Career for the South," *Confederate Veteran* 7 (1899): 66–69 (por.); Isaac Markens, *President Lincoln and the Case of John Y. Beall* (1911) (frontispiece por.); Millard Kessler Bushong, *Historic Jefferson County* (1972), 404–406; defense by Beall of espionage charges, recollections of Beall attributed to George E. Mann, and copies of James T. Brady's letters, all in MOC; Richard Micou Daniel research collection, 1938–1981, in private possession; account of execution in *New York Times*, 25 Feb. 1865.

CAMERON S. MOSELEY

BEAMAN, Nathaniel (10 February 1859–15 June 1921), banker and mayor of Norfolk, was born in Murfreesboro, North Carolina, the only son and elder of two children of William Patrick Beaman and Ann Eliza Beaman. He was educated in the Murfreesboro schools and moved around 1879 to Norfolk, where he became a partner in a wholesale grocery firm. He invested in other businesses, including the forerunner of the Norfolk Storage Company, of which he was president by the end of the century.

In 1892 Beaman was elected president of the Bank of Commerce. The bank had been chartered in 1878 and was rechartered as the National Bank of Commerce in 1901. Beaman served as its president for almost thirty years, during which the bank grew from one of the smallest of seven banks in Norfolk when his presidency began to the largest of thirteen banks in Norfolk in 1905. Its net worth grew from a little more than $400 thousand in 1890 to almost $9.25 million in 1914. At the time of Beaman's death it was one of the largest of eighteen banks in Norfolk and among the largest banks in all of eastern Virginia.

Beaman married Katherine Lewis Prentis on 19 October 1887. She was a sister of Robert R.

Prentis, a prominent attorney and judge. Katherine Beaman became regent in 1928 of the Virginia State Society, Daughters of the American Revolution, and also vice president general of the National Daughters of the American Revolution. She served on the sesquicentennial committee for the 1931 commemoration of the Battle of Yorktown and on the George Washington Bicentennial Commission a year later. The Beamans had one daughter and two sons, including Robert Prentis Beaman, who headed the National Bank of Commerce from 1931 to 1942 and saw it through the worst years of the Great Depression.

In 1898 Beaman won election to the Norfolk City Council. He served as chairman of the finance committee and vice president of the Common Council before being named mayor of Norfolk on 14 May 1901 to succeed C. Brooks Johnston, who had resigned. Beaman's term as mayor expired in July 1902. Thereafter he remained active in civic and business affairs as the treasurer of the Jamestown Ter-Centennial Exposition, a director of the Norfolk Chamber of Commerce, the president of the Norfolk-Portsmouth Clearing House Association, and a member of the board of directors of the Merchants and Planters Bank. Nathaniel Beaman suffered from cardiac illness during the final years of his life and died of a heart attack at his home in Norfolk on 15 June 1921. He was buried in Elmwood Cemetery in Norfolk.

Norfolk Virginian-Pilot, June 1900 Twentieth-Century Edition, 30; William H. Stewart, *History of Norfolk County, Virginia, and Representative Citizens* (1902), 589–590 (por.); family history information verified by Nathaniel Beaman III; Bank of Commerce growth documented in Norfolk city directories; obituaries in *Norfolk Ledger-Dispatch*, 16 June 1921, and *Norfolk Virginian-Pilot*, 16, 17 June 1921.

STEPHEN S. MANSFIELD

BEAMS, Jesse Wakefield (25 December 1898–23 July 1977), physicist, was born in Sumner County, Kansas, the elder of two children, both sons, of Jesse Wakefield Beams, a prosperous farmer, and his second wife, Kathryn Wylie Beams. He had four much older half siblings. Beams attended a local one-room school and then high school in nearby Belle Plaine. His parents encouraged him to continue his education, and he entered Fairmount College in Wichita (now Wichita State University). Beams majored in chemistry and mathematics and thought of becoming a physician, but the college's dean, a mathematician, convinced him to go to graduate school in that field and helped him obtain a fellowship in 1921 to the University of Wisconsin in Madison.

Beams's advisor at Wisconsin suggested that he take courses in physics, too. After receiving his master's degree in mathematics in 1922, Beams was uncertain of his future and in need of money. He took a post teaching mathematics and physics at Alabama Polytechnic Institute in Auburn (now Auburn University). His colleague there, Fred Allison, who had recently received his doctorate from the University of Virginia's physics department, encouraged Beams to pursue the study of physics, recommended that he go on for the doctorate, and in 1923 assisted him in getting a fellowship at the University of Virginia.

Beams's graduate research focused on a problem in the fields of spectroscopy and atomic structure that involved measuring electrical discharge in gases. His experiments revealed unanticipated anomalies in the spark spectra of certain elements and earned him his Ph.D. in 1925 with his dissertation on "The Order of Appearance of Certain Lines in the Spark Spectra of Cadmium and Magnesium." To perform his experiments Beams developed a light shutter and a high-speed rotating mirror that enabled him to observe phenomena occurring in extremely short time-intervals. His research won him a prestigious National Research Council fellowship, but because his apparatus at Virginia was still producing valuable data he remained there for another year.

In 1926 Beams went to Yale University on the fellowship. There he met the brilliant young physicist Ernest Orlando Lawrence. Together they experimented on the photoelectric effect, measuring it to minute fractions of a second. They showed that light quanta had a fixed length and differed from what existing theory predicted, a finding later explained by quantum mechanics. After a sojourn in Europe, where they visited physics laboratories, Lawrence moved to the University of California at Berkeley while Beams returned to the University of Virginia in 1928 and joined the faculty as an associate professor of physics. Two years later he became a full professor. Beams married Maxine Sutherland, a teacher and native of Charlottesville, on 16 June 1931. They had no children.

Beams had become intrigued by the possible applications of the high centrifugal field that his revolving mirror produced, and during the 1930s he worked with his graduate students to devise a seal that would enable a centrifuge to spin in a vacuum. The vacuum ultracentrifuge, eventually engineered to revolve a million times a second and exert pressures a billion times that of gravity, made possible the separation of a molecule's constituent parts by sedimentation. Later in the 1930s Beams and his students adapted the ultracentrifuge to produce the first separation of isotopes by centrifuge. Because Beams had successfully separated the uranium isotopes U-235 and U-238, he was one of the physicists called to government service as war approached. Physicists realized that nuclear fission made possible a bomb of immense destructive power, and they feared that Nazi Germany had already set out to produce such a weapon. Beams worked on the separation of uranium isotopes by ultracentrifuge until the Office of Scientific Research and Development chose the diffusion method of separation. He then conducted classified war research for the navy.

After the war Beams resumed research with the ultracentrifuge at the University of Virginia. With a colleague he developed a way of suspending the ultracentrifuge magnetically, which made possible highly accurate measurements of the molecular weights of substances in solution, such as viruses and proteins. This version of the ultracentrifuge also proved an excellent tool for testing the tensile strengths of metals and other materials. Beams and his students employed it to study the physics of light, but its most important applications were for research in medicine, biology, and chemistry.

In 1948 Beams became chairman of the physics department, serving in that post until 1962. Government funding for scientific research expanded greatly during that period, and the department also benefited from the generosity of John Lee Pratt, a wealthy alumnus who funded graduate fellowships. With this help Beams was able to attract and support talented graduate students and expand and strengthen the physics faculty as well, especially in nuclear and solid-state physics. Pratt also paid for a new building to house the department and endowed a professorship, which Beams was awarded in 1953.

In 1943 Beams had been elected to the National Academy of Sciences, and in 1949 he was elected to the American Academy of Arts and Sciences and became president of the Oak Ridge Institute of Nuclear Physics. He also served as president of the Virginia Academy of Science (1947–1948) and of the American Physical Society (1958–1959) and as vice president of the American Philosophical Society (1960). In 1968 President Lyndon B. Johnson awarded him the National Medal of Science. The Southeastern Section of the American Physical Society began presenting the Jesse Beams Award for Outstanding Research in 1973.

In 1969 Beams retired but continued to work in his laboratory, using the ultracentrifuge to extend the measurement of the gravitational constant. Jesse Wakefield Beams died of cancer in Charlottesville on 23 July 1977 and was buried in the University of Virginia Cemetery.

McGraw-Hill Modern Scientists and Engineers (1980), 1:70–72; Anne Roe Papers, including 1952 and 1963 oral history interviews, American Philosophical Society Library, Philadelphia; Jesse Wakefield Beams Papers, including 1972 oral history interview and bibliography of more than 100 scientific papers, UVA; *Richmond Times-Dispatch*, 4 Jan. 1942 (por.); *Commonwealth* 14 (July 1947): 18; 25 (Dec. 1958): 22–23, 89; *Charlottesville Daily Progress*, 22 Feb. 1962; Virginius Dabney, *Mr. Jefferson's University: A History* (1981), 338, 377, 463; *Virginia Journal of Science* 20 (1969): 89; obituaries in *Charlottesville Daily Progress* and *Richmond Times-Dispatch*, both 24 July 1977, and *New York Times* and *Washington Post*, both 25 July 1977; editorial tribute in *Richmond Times-Dispatch*, 28 July 1977; memorial in *Virginia Journal of Science* 28 (1977): 120–121 (por.).

JOHN T. KNEEBONE

BEAN, Robert Bennett (24 March 1874–27 August 1944), physician, was born in Botetourt County, one of five sons and the third of eight children of William Bennett Bean and Arrianna Williamson Carper Bean. After his early formal education ended when he was thirteen, Bean held jobs working on a farm, laboring in a mine, clerking in a general store, managing the dining room at a summer resort, teaching, guarding convict laborers, selling farm machinery, and writing for a small newspaper. He resumed his education by entering the Virginia Agricultural and Mechanical College and Polytechnic Institute and graduated with a B.S. in 1900.

Bean then entered the Johns Hopkins University Medical School, where he studied with two of the nation's premier medical educators, William Osler and Franklin P. Mall. Following his graduation in 1904, Bean joined the staff as an assistant in anatomy during the 1904–1905 academic year. He worked in Mall's laboratory investigating the subclavian artery and comparing the brains of black and white subjects. Bean studied at the Ecole d'Anthropologie de Paris during the summer of 1906 and served as an assistant professor of anatomy at the University of Michigan from 1905 to 1907.

Bean reported on his comparative study of brains in a major scientific paper, "Some Racial Peculiarities of the Negro Brain," *American Journal of Anatomy* 5 (1906): 353–432, which he popularized for a larger audience in two articles, "The Negro Brain" and "The Training of the Negro," in *Century Magazine* 72 (1906): 778–784 and 947–953. Bean's articles appeared to provide scientific proof of the innate inferiority of people of African descent. He stated that his research substantiated "a difference of 20% in favor of the Caucasian," a chasm that made it "useless to try to elevate the negro by education or otherwise" (*Century Magazine*, 783, 784). Some scientists and eugenicists accepted some of Bean's conclusions, but others were skeptical, including Mall, who repeated Bean's study using the same specimens and found no significant evidence of racial differences. Concluding that Bean's research findings were unsound, Mall refuted them in the *American Journal of Anatomy* 9 (1909): 1–32.

Bean never disavowed his 1906 articles, although he was out of the United States during the controversy over them. He served as director of the anatomical laboratory at the Philippine Medical School in Manila from 1907 to 1910. The extensive studies and measurements of the Philippine population he conducted there resulted in several articles and culminated in his first book, *The Racial Anatomy of the Philippine Islanders* (1910). Unlike his 1906 articles, the book avoided imputing moral characteristics to specific racial types, but Bean continued to comment on how specific racial types clustered in specific occupations. In 1910 he returned to the United States as an associate professor of anatomy at Tulane University. He was promoted to full professor in 1914, served as president of the New Orleans Academy of Sciences, and continued to publish articles derived from his research in the Philippines. He also became interested in the relationship between diseases and body types and began to measure the weights of organs in relation to type, race, sex, stature, and age.

In 1916 Bean joined the faculty at the University of Virginia School of Medicine, where he taught until he retired in June 1942. He continued his research and contributed numerous articles to scientific journals in the fields of anatomy and physical anthropology. His second book, *The Races of Man: Differentiation and Dispersal of Man* (1932), owed much to the work of physical anthropologist Aleš Hrdlička, to whom he dedicated it. Following Hrdlička's division of the species into three great races, Bean used broad, stereotypical images to elaborate the differences between the white, the yellow-brown, and the black races, and to describe and depict their subraces. Bean's last large project, begun in 1930 at Hrdlička's suggestion, was a study of old families in Virginia. A series of articles led up to *The Peopling of Virginia* (1938), a dense statistical portrait of Virginia's white population concentrating on persons of English, Scottish, German, Welsh, Irish, and French descent, analyzing measurements of stature, sitting height and leg length, cephalic index, and hair and eye color.

Bean's 1906 articles were largely forgotten in scientific circles, but the Ku Klux Klan's *Kourier Magazine* for February 1927 favorably cited some of his later publications that appeared to substantiate his earlier conclusions, and Carleton Putnam's *Race and Reality: A Search for Solutions* (1967), 52–53, relied in part on the data from the 1906 study and repeated Bean's original interpretation of it. Some supporters of racial segregation also used Bean's early work in attempting to prove the racial inferiority of African Americans. Wesley C. George, of Alabama, cited Bean's work in his 1961 *Biology of the Race Problem*, which the Alabama state government published and which a Richmond company later reprinted.

On 22 May 1907 Bean married Adelaide Leiper Martin. They had two daughters and two sons, including William Bennett Bean, who also became a medical educator and later edited his father's collection, *Sir William Osler: Aphorisms from his Bedside Teachings and Writings* (1950). Bean was a member of the American Association for the Advancement of Science, the Association of American Anatomists, the American Association of Physical Anthropologists, and the Società Romana di Antropologia, and was founding president of the Virginia chapter of Sigma Xi. Robert Bennett Bean suffered from arteriosclerosis and died in a Staunton hospital on 27 August 1944. He was buried in the University of Virginia Cemetery in Charlottesville.

Biographical obituaries by son in *Science* 101 (1945): 346–348, and by Robert J. Terry, with bibliography of Bean's publications, in *American Anthropologist* 48 (1946): 70–74; oral history interview of William Bennett Bean, UVA; evaluations of effects of 1906 articles in Charles V. Roman, *American Civilization and the Negro* (1916), 172–173, 360–361, Walter White, *Rope & Faggot: A Biography of Judge Lynch* (1929), xi–xii, 118–133, Ashley Montagu, *Man's Most Dangerous Myth: The Fallacy of Race* (1942; 5th ed., 1974), 316–317, Gunnar Myrdal, *An American Dilemma: The Negro Problem and Modern Democracy* (1944), 91, Allan Chase, *The Legacy of Malthus: The Social Costs of the New Scientific Racism* (1977), 179–180, 455–456, and Stephen Jay Gould, *The Mismeasure of Man* (1981), 77–82; Bean refused to disavow his 1906 papers in a letter to Burt Green Wilder, 3 Apr. 1909, Wilder Papers, Cornell University Library, Ithaca, N.Y.; obituaries in *Charlottesville Daily Progress* (por.) and *Richmond Times-Dispatch*, both 28 Aug. 1944, and *New York Times*, 3 Sept. 1944.

KENNETH W. ROSE

BEAR, Harry (20 November 1890–30 July 1950), dentist and educator, was born in Richmond, the second of five sons and second of six children of Philip Bear (originally Berestatski) and Mary Meyer Bear, ethnic Poles who had separately emigrated from Russia during the 1880s and married in Richmond on 17 June 1888. By 1900 they had opened a tailor shop and clothing store in Manchester, now part of Richmond, and both lived to see three of their sons become prominent Richmond physicians or dentists.

Bear graduated as class valedictorian from Manchester High School in 1909 and won a scholarship to Richmond College. In 1910 he transferred to the Medical College of Virginia, from which he graduated in 1913 with a degree in dentistry, specializing in exodontia and dental roentgenology. He later studied anesthesiology as well.

From 1913 until 1945 Bear conducted a private dental practice in downtown Richmond. Throughout his career he was very active in numerous professional organizations, with his most important offices including the presidencies of the Richmond Dental Society in 1917–1918, the Virginia State Dental Association in 1926, the American Society of Oral Surgeons and Exodontists in 1931, and the American Association of Dental Schools in 1940. He served as vice president of the American Dental Association in 1929.

In addition to his private practice, Bear taught metallurgy at the Medical College of Virginia's School of Dentistry from 1913 to 1915 and served as an associate professor of chemistry in 1915 and 1916. From 1916 until 1950 he was professor of exodontia and of dental jurisprudence, ethics, and economics. Bear also served twenty-one years as dean of the School of Dentistry, from 1 July 1929 until his death, the longest tenure of any dean to that time. He gave up his private practice when he became the school's first full-time dean in 1945. By then he was one of the best-known and most respected dental educators in the South. Temple University in Philadelphia awarded him an honorary doctor of dental science degree in 1945. During Bear's tenure at MCV the dental school grew from 20 to almost 200 students. He expanded the curriculum and the graduate education program, enlarged the faculty, and encouraged research. The school lacked adequate funds during the

Great Depression and World War II and was threatened with loss of accreditation during the 1940s, but during those lean years Bear laid the groundwork for the erection of a much-needed new building, which was begun in 1951, and for the later expansion and improvement of the school.

More than just the practical aspects of dentistry interested Bear. He wrote and spoke extensively on ethical standards, determination of fees, and dental education. By 1945 he had given almost one hundred speeches and addresses to lay and professional groups and published about forty papers and articles. A student of dental history, his short essays on the subject appeared in the *Bulletin of the Virginia State Dental Association* and the *Journal of the American Dental Association*. The museum of dentistry at MCV is named for him.

Bear was a member of Congregation Beth Ahabah and served on its board of directors. On 19 June 1917 he had married Betty Gellman, a mezzo-soprano well known to Richmond's music lovers. Their two sons both became dentists, with the younger, Samuel Elmer Bear, eventually becoming professor of surgery and chairman of the Department of Oral Surgery at MCV. Betty Bear died on 30 August 1934, and on 5 April 1941 Bear married Elsa Bluethenthal Strause, a widow. They had no children. Harry Bear died in Richmond on 30 July 1950 and was buried in the city's Hebrew Cemetery.

Memorials by Harry Lyons in *Bulletin of the Virginia State Dental Association* 27 (Oct. 1950): 11–13, and by John Bell Williams in *Bulletin of the Medical College of Virginia* 49 (winter 1952): 16–21; *Richmond Times-Dispatch*, 20 June 1917; *Richmond News Leader*, 30 Aug. 1934; biographical material including 1945 bibliography of publications in Sanger Historical File and Pastore Historical File, Tompkins-McCaw Library, MCV; Harry Bear, "Historical Sketch of the Richmond Dental Society, 1894–1930" and "The History of the Virginia State Dental Association, 1870–1942," *Bulletin of the Virginia State Dental Association* 7 (1931): 47–53 and 19 (1943): 44–49, and "Dental Organizations in the United States: A Century of Achievement," *Journal of the American Dental Association* 27 (1940): 425–434; Hummel and Smith, *Portraits and Statuary*, 7 (por.); obituaries in *Richmond News Leader* and *Richmond Times-Dispatch*, both 31 July 1950, and *Journal of the American Dental Association* 41 (1950): 372a–372b (por.).

Douglas S. Belt
Brent Tarter

BEARD, Belle Boone (18 February 1898–12 October 1984), sociologist and gerontologist, was born at Boones Mill in Franklin County, the younger of two daughters and second of four children of James William Beard and Mary Kleindenst Beard. She began her education in a two-room school and after completing high school attended Averett College during the years 1913 to 1915. She then taught in one-room schools in Franklin County before entering Lynchburg College. She graduated with honors in 1923 and taught for the academic year 1923–1924 at Bluefield High School. The next year she served as a field secretary for Lynchburg College.

In 1925 Beard enrolled in the Graduate Department of Social Economy and Social Research at Bryn Mawr College. She studied under Susan Myra Kingsbury but did not complete her doctorate until 1932 because she had to devote much of her time for two years to the care of her unwell mother. Beard's dissertation, an innovative study of juvenile court operations, was published as *Juvenile Probation: An Analysis of the Case Records of Five Hundred Children Studied at the Judge Baker Guidance Clinic and Placed on Probation in the Juvenile Court of Boston* (1934). While a graduate student she had directed the compilation and publication of *Electricity in the Home: Being a List of Books and Articles with Brief Abstracts Prepared in Connection with a Survey of the Social and Economic Effects of the Wider Use of Electricity in the Home* (1927).

In 1931 Beard joined the faculty of Sweet Briar College. She contributed scholarly papers to the college's *Bulletin*, served as chairman of the Department of Sociology from 1934 to 1963, and chaired the Division of Social Studies from 1946 to 1949. Beard used her vacations as well as her academic sabbaticals for research, and she contributed in many ways to the better understanding of public welfare issues and the better functioning of Virginia's welfare system. Her monograph, *Child Welfare in Virginia*, appeared in 1934, and she served as director of county and city organization within the Virginia Department of Public Welfare's Bureau of Public Assistance while on academic leave from

1938 to 1940, organizing and developing in-service training programs and personnel standards. She served as chairman of the Merit System Council of the Department of Public Welfare, as chairman of the Joint Merit System for the state government, and as a member of the Advisory Council on the Virginia Economy.

Beard was president of the Virginia Conference of Social Work from 1936 to 1937, a member of the executive committee of the Virginia Welfare Council from 1935 to 1941, and vice president of the Virginia Commission on Interracial Cooperation from 1938 to 1941. A member or fellow of many national and international sociological and gerontological societies, she served as president of the Virginia Council of Administrative Women in Education from 1940 to 1942 and of the Virginia Social Science Association from 1942 to 1944. Her residence at Sweet Briar was interrupted by stints as a visiting professor of sociology at Vanderbilt University on a Julius Rosenwald Foundation fellowship in the academic year 1945–1946, as a research professor at New Mexico Highlands University in Las Vegas in 1952–1953, as a May K. Houck Foundation fellow in Sarasota, Florida, in 1959–1960, and as a Fulbright lecturer at Seoul National University in Seoul, South Korea, in 1961. She also lectured in Taiwan and the Philippines. Her many honors included Lynchburg College's T. Gibson Hobbs Memorial Award in 1948 for outstanding accomplishments in education and the American Association of Retired Persons' International Woman's Year Citation in 1975.

During the 1930s and 1940s Beard studied social agencies, court systems, housing and community development, and social conditions and problems in the United States, Canada, Mexico, Latin America, and Europe. She also began a long-term study of centenarians that eventually established her as an internationally recognized expert on human longevity. After retiring from the Sweet Briar faculty in 1963, Beard studied gerontology at the Social Science Institute at Washington University in Saint Louis, Missouri. She was a research professor at the University of Georgia in Athens from 1965 to 1968 and director of centenarian research at Lynchburg College from 1968 to 1970. A delegate to White House conferences on aging in 1961 and 1971, she advised Virginia's public agencies on aging and served on the National Centenarian Fellowship Advisory Board. Her forty-year study of centenarians amassed the most extensive archive ever assembled on the subject. Beard published almost fifty papers on gerontology and one book, *Social Competence of Centenarians* (1967), with a second, nearly completed volume, published posthumously as *Centenarians: The New Generation* (1991). In 1982 she donated $200,000 to Lynchburg College, of which she had been a trustee since 1933, to endow the Belle Boone Beard Gerontology Center.

Belle Boone Beard died following a stroke on 12 October 1984 in Virginia Baptist Hospital in Lynchburg. She donated her body for scientific research.

Biography and bibliography of gerontological publications in Belle Boone Beard, *Centenarians: The New Generation*, ed. Nera K. Wilson and Albert J. E. Wilson III (1991), vii–xxi, 276–278 (frontispiece por.); Belle Boone Beard Personal Papers, Lynchburg College Archives; Belle Boone Beard Papers, Faculty Archives, Sweet Briar College; Belle Boone Beard Collection, University of Georgia Library; Mary Ann Dzuback, "Women and Social Research at Bryn Mawr College," *History of Education Quarterly* 33 (1993): 598–602; interviews with Belle Boone Beard, brother Bryan Beard, and nieces Jeanne Beard Snead and Marie Lane; Belle Boone Beard, "The Merit System Plan of the State Department of Public Welfare" and "Geri-Welfare in Virginia," *Virginia Public Welfare* 18 (July 1940): 1, 3–4, and 24 (Mar. 1946): 1, 2–5; *Amherst New Era–Progress*, 31 May 1945; *New York Times*, 14 Nov. 1947, 1 July 1948; *Lynchburg College Alumni News* (Mar. 1958): 4; obituaries in *Lynchburg News and Daily Advance*, 13 Oct. 1984, *Richmond Times-Dispatch*, 19 Oct. 1984 (por.), and *New York Times*, 23 Oct. 1984; editorial tribute in *Lynchburg News and Daily Advance*, 17 Oct. 1984.

NERA K. WILSON
ALBERT J. E. WILSON III

BEAUCHAMP, William Benjamin (16 March 1869–28 June 1931), Methodist bishop, was born in Farnham, Richmond County, the younger of two sons and fourth of five children of Dandridge Cox Beauchamp, a painter, and Margaret Ann Hyson Beauchamp. He attended Farnham Academy and graduated from Randolph-Macon College in 1890 with an A.B. degree. In 1893 he received master of arts and bachelor of divinity degrees from Vanderbilt University.

Beauchamp joined the Virginia Conference of the Methodist Episcopal Church South in November 1893 and spent a year as a minister on trial at Parkview Methodist Church in Portsmouth and a year at Trinity Methodist Church in Norfolk. On 27 November 1895 he married Blanche Whitehurst, of Norfolk. They had three sons and five daughters. In 1895 Beauchamp was appointed pastor of Saint James Methodist Church in Richmond. In 1899 he was transferred to Broad Street Methodist Church in Richmond, and then from 1903 to 1907 he was pastor of Trinity Methodist Church in Newport News. Beauchamp served the Fourth Avenue Church in Louisville, Kentucky, from 1907 to 1911. He then returned to Virginia, officiating from 1911 to 1915 as pastor of the Main Street Methodist Church in Danville and from 1915 to 1917 at Monumental Church in Portsmouth.

During those years Beauchamp became a prominent supporter of missionary work and the ecumenical movement. He attended the World Missionary Conference in Edinburgh, Scotland, in 1906, and he served as president of the missions board of the Virginia conference after his return from Kentucky. In 1917 Beauchamp moved to Nashville, Tennessee, where for five years he was general secretary of the Laymen's Missionary Movement of the Methodist Episcopal Church South. He displayed his administrative skills in May 1919 by directing an eight-day campaign to raise $35 million for overseas missionary work that exceeded its goal by $15 million, making it the most successful fund-raising event the church had ever held. He served as president of the boards of Scarritt Bible Training School in Nashville and of the Ferrum Training School in Virginia.

Beauchamp continued to live in Nashville after his appointment in May 1922 as bishop of the Twelfth Episcopal District with responsibility for directing Methodist missionary work in Europe. During the next three years the church established new conferences in Belgium, France, and Czechoslovakia. He served on the executive committee of the Federal Council of Churches and in 1925 was elected president of the World Brotherhood Federation. Beauchamp resided in Brussels for more than a year while he directed the federation's work before returning to the United States in 1926 to become superintendent of the conferences of north and south Georgia and to teach theology at Emory University in Atlanta. He was elected president of the Methodist Board of Missions in 1926, and he also oversaw Methodist missionary work in Mexico. From 1923 until his death Beauchamp was a member of the board of Randolph-Macon College, which granted him an honorary D.D. in 1906, and in 1926 Southern College of Lakeland, Florida (now Florida Southern College), awarded him an LL.D.

Beauchamp presided over the annual Virginia conference in Norfolk in October 1930, and after he was appointed head of the district encompassing the Baltimore and Virginia conferences in 1931, he moved to Richmond despite being in poor health. William Benjamin Beauchamp died in Saint Elizabeth's Hospital of pernicious anemia on 28 June 1931. His funeral service was held at Centenary Methodist Church in Richmond, and he was buried in Hollywood Cemetery.

Richmond Co. Birth Register gives birth date of 12 Mar. 1869, but Beauchamp consistently gave his birth date as 16 Mar. 1869, which corresponds with age at death recorded in Hollywood Cemetery Interment Register; Norfolk City Marriage Register; short biographies with some errors in John J. Lafferty, *Sketches and Portraits of the Virginia Conference* (1901), 405 (por.), and Arthur L. Stevenson, "The Methodist Ministry," *Northern Neck of Virginia Historical Magazine* 31 (1981): 3352–3354; Nolan B. Harmon, Albea Godbold, and Louise L. Queen, eds., *Encyclopedia of World Methodism* (1974), 1:242; some Beauchamp letters in Warren Akin Candler Papers, Emory University; obituaries in *New York Times*, 29 June 1931, and *Richmond Times-Dispatch*, 29 (por.), 30 June 1931.

DONALD W. GUNTER

BEAZLEY, Frederick Wharton (25 March 1892–2 October 1974), philanthropist, was born in Portsmouth, the elder of two sons and third of four children of Frederick Tomkin Beazley and Bettie Rebecca Sykes Beazley. At about age seventeen, after attending Saint Paul's Academy in Portsmouth, Beazley went to work selling firewood door-to-door. On 3 November 1911 he married Marie Crooks. They had one son. During the 1910s Beazley firmly established himself in the business world by opening a wood and coal company, creating partnerships, and expanding his commercial interests. By the early 1920s he was part-owner of several businesses, including a hardware store, the Enterprise Fuel Company, and the Portsmouth Ice Company.

During the 1920s Beazley focused his interests on coal distribution and ice manufacturing, and after the Atlantic Ice and Coal Company moved from Portsmouth to Atlanta, Georgia, in 1924, Beazley relocated there, too. The company expanded and later changed its name to the Atlantic Company. Beazley served as its president from 1928 until 1943 and as chairman of the board from the latter year until he retired and moved back to Virginia in 1948. By the time of his retirement the Atlantic Company was a multimillion-dollar business that owned and operated breweries, bottling plants, coal-distribution firms, ice plants, cold-storage facilities, and other properties in forty-nine cities and ten states, with about 3,000 employees.

Beazley retired to Bridgeview Farm in Norfolk County and in 1948 formed the Beazley Foundation to benefit his native city. The foundation's first president was Portsmouth attorney Lawrence W. I'Anson, later chief justice of the Supreme Court of Virginia. During the next twenty-five years Beazley contributed $12 to $15 million to the foundation, which became the most active and influential public-service fund in the city. By the mid-1960s, with assets of more than $25 million, it had created and operated five recreational centers and a dental clinic in Portsmouth. In 1957 Beazley established Frederick Junior College and Military Academy, which he named for his father. The college became a four-year, coeducational school in 1961. On 8 March 1968 Beazley donated the small liberal-arts institution to the state's new community college system. He also contributed $1 million to ease the transition from private to public sponsorship. The school is now the Portsmouth campus of Tidewater Community College. In 1972 Beazley contributed another $1 million to the building fund of Portsmouth General Hospital as a memorial to his wife, who had died on 26 October 1967. The hospital named the obstetrical section of its new wing the Marie C. Beazley Pavilion.

Frederick Wharton Beazley died in Portsmouth on 2 October 1974 and was buried in Oak Grove Cemetery there. By his will he left the bulk of his fortune, reportedly worth something less than $40 million, to the Beazley Foundation.

Business career documented in Portsmouth city directories and industrial and public utilities volumes of Moody's financial reports; birth date in *Who's Who in America* (1942–1947): 287; Beazley Foundation charter in Charter Book, 227:528–531; obituary of wife in *Norfolk Virginian-Pilot*, 27 Oct. 1967; feature articles in *Norfolk Virginian-Pilot*, 11 Jan. 1970, 26 Oct. 1974, and *Norfolk Ledger-Star*, 25 Oct. 1974; obituaries in *Norfolk Ledger-Star* and *Norfolk Virginian-Pilot* (por.), both 3 Oct. 1974; editorial tribute in *Norfolk Ledger-Star*, 4 Oct. 1974.

BRENT TARTER

BEAZLEY, Roy Carpenter (23 November 1902–1 September 1985), nurse and educator, was born at Mountview in Orange County, the third of five children, all daughters, of Edward Stark Beazley and Lora Cornelia Carpenter Beazley. Her name was the cause of frequent misidentifications and much humor throughout her life. Her mother had promised after the birth of two daughters to name the third child for her brother regardless of its sex, and she kept her promise.

Beazley was educated in the Orange County public schools and at the State Normal School for Women at Fredericksburg. While she was a student in Fredericksburg in 1918, she became critically ill and spent several months in the college infirmary. Her devotion to one of the nurses who attended her contributed to her eventual decision to give up teaching and become a nurse. Beazley began her teaching career in the public schools of Orange County in 1920 and moved by 1923 to Albemarle County, where she taught until 1927. In September 1927 she and her younger sister Edith Beazley enrolled in the University of Virginia Hospital School of Nursing. Roy Beazley graduated in September 1930 and planned to enter public health nursing, but the superintendent of nurses at the hospital, Josephine McLeod, persuaded her to become head nurse of one of the hospital's medical and surgical units.

Beazley continued her education and received a B.S. in nursing education from the University of Virginia in 1941. She then became an instructor in the Hospital School of Nursing, but her desire to remain close to patients drew her back into the hospital as assistant director of nursing in 1944. After returning to school yet again, in 1953 she received a B.M.A. in Administration in Schools of Nursing from Teachers College, Columbia University. Beazley was appointed director of the University of Virginia Hospital School of Nursing and director of nursing service in 1946 and worked for twenty-three years to develop nursing services at the growing medical center. She played a major role in the evolution of the nursing education program at the University of Virginia, which reached its maturity in September 1956 when it became the University of Virginia School of Nursing.

In 1951 the governor appointed Beazley to the Virginia State Board of Examiners of Nurses. She served for ten years and was president of the board from 1959 until 1961. An active participant in a number of professional organizations, she held several offices in the Virginia State Nurses Association, presided over numerous committees, and was vice president in 1956. Beazley also had a strong interest in the development of education for licensed practical nurses in Virginia. In 1960 she received the Virginia State Nurses Association's prestigious Nancy Vance Award in recognition of long and distinguished service to the profession.

Beazley retired in 1969 and was the first woman at the University of Virginia to be named professor emerita. Before and after retirement she lived with two of her sisters in Charlottesville. Beazley taught an adult Sunday school class at the First Baptist Church in Charlottesville until shortly before her death. Her hobbies were needlework and tending her large rose garden. Roy Carpenter Beazley died of heart failure at the University of Virginia Hospital on 1 September 1985 and was buried in Monticello Memory Gardens in Charlottesville. That November the School of Nursing Alumnae Association voted her the Distinguished Nursing Alumnae Award posthumously.

Feature article in *Virginia Nurse Quarterly* 28 (winter 1960): 30–33; Beazley family papers in possession of sister Edith Beazley Miller, Charlottesville, 1992; interview with Beazley in "Nursing During the Depression Years," 1979 videotape, UVA Health Science Library; Virginia Nurses' Association Archives, MCV; por. at McLeod Hall, UVA; obituaries in *Charlottesville Daily Progress* (por.) and *Richmond Times-Dispatch*, both 2 Sept. 1985, and *University of Virginia Alumni News* 74 (Nov.–Dec. 1985): 66.

EVELYN CRARY BACON

BECKHAM, Benjamin Moore (17 August 1868–30 September 1957), president of Ferrum College, was born in Nottoway County, the second of three sons and second of five children of Lucy Royall Beckham and a Methodist minister, Thomas Moore Beckham. He was educated at New London Academy and at Randolph-Macon College, from which he graduated with a B.A. in 1891. In November of that year he was admitted to the Virginia Conference of the Methodist Episcopal Church South and spent the next two years preaching on circuit in Southside Virginia. He received an M.A. from Randolph-Macon in 1895 and enrolled for a year at Vanderbilt University, where he won the Owen Medal for his work in practical theology.

Beckham returned to Virginia and served as minister at Asbury Methodist Church in Richmond from 1896 to 1899, at Cabell Street Methodist Church in Danville from 1899 to 1903, at the Methodist church in South Boston from 1903 to 1906, and at Memorial Methodist Church in Lynchburg from 1906 to 1909. While in Danville he married Nannie Sue Barrow on 19 June 1901. They had two sons and one daughter.

In 1909 Beckham was named presiding elder of the Danville district. He served in that capacity until 1913 and during that time worked with the Virginia Women's Missionary Society to establish Ferrum Training School, a small coeducational school at Ferrum in Franklin County intended to serve young people in an area remote from good schools. Beckham was named the first principal of the institution in 1913 and served as president from 1923 until he retired in 1934. With the first board of trustees he raised money, acquired buildings, hired a faculty, and opened the school in September 1914 with ninety pupils. Ferrum offered a secondary school education and occupational training. In the tradition of industrial schools of the time the students did much of the work around the school and on its small farm. The trustees added a year of college courses to the curriculum in 1926 and another a year later, transforming the school into a junior college. The State Board of Education duly accredited Ferrum as a junior college in 1928. During the ensuing five years, however, when contributions to the school fell off with the onset of the Great Depression, Beckham disagreed with the trustees about how best to respond. He submitted his resignation as president on 18 October 1933, and the board accepted it on 19 May 1934.

Beckham resumed his ministerial career and temporarily filled vacant pulpits in Methodist churches in Victoria in Lunenburg County, Clifton Forge, Covington, and Roanoke. About ten months after the death of his first wife, he married Emma Kate Snider on 29 December 1948. Benjamin Moore Beckham died in Roanoke on 30 September 1957 and was buried in Green Hill Cemetery in Danville.

James Madison Beckham, *Genealogy of the Beckham Family in Virginia* (1910), 42–43; ministerial appointments recorded in Virginia Annual Conference of the Methodist Church, *Proceedings*; BVS Marriage Register, Danville City; Frank Benjamin Hurt, *A History of Ferrum College: An Uncommon Challenge, 1914–1974* (1977), 13–75 (por., 28); por. by George Solonovich in Ferrum College Library; obituary in *Roanoke Times*, 1 Oct. 1957; memorial in Virginia Annual Conference of Methodist Church, *Proceedings* (1958): 226–228, which gives incorrect dates of service in various Methodist churches.

FRANK BENJAMIN HURT

BECKHAM, Robert Franklin (6 May 1837–5 December 1864), Confederate army officer, was born in Culpeper County, the second of six sons and second of nine children of John Grigsby Beckham and Mary Campbell Moore Beckham. In 1854 his father's friend Congressman William "Extra Billy" Smith appointed Beckham to the United States Military Academy at West Point, from which he graduated ranked sixth of twenty-two in the class of 1859. From 1 October 1859 to 3 May 1861 Beckham served as assistant topographical engineer with the rank of second lieutenant at Detroit, Michigan, where he assisted in conducting surveys of the Great Lakes.

At the outbreak of the Civil War, Beckham resigned from the United States Army and joined that of the Confederacy as a lieutenant in the artillery. At the First Battle of Manassas (Bull Run), his capable direction of his artillery battery earned him praise from General Joseph E. Johnston. Beckham became an aide-de-camp to Major General Gustavus W. Smith on 14 January 1862, and on 16 August 1862 he was promoted to major and became Smith's ordnance officer. Following the death of Major John Pelham, Major General James Ewell Brown Stuart assigned Beckham on 8 April 1863 to the command of the horse artillery of the Army of Northern Virginia. Three weeks later Beckham accompanied Lieutenant General Thomas J. "Stonewall" Jackson on his famous flanking march around the Union army at Chancellorsville and handled the horse artillery so well that Jackson personally congratulated him.

Stuart and the chief of artillery for the Army of Northern Virginia, General William N. Pendleton, both regarded Beckham as one of the best young artillery commanders in Virginia. Beckham was promoted to colonel on 16 February 1864 and assigned to the Army of Tennessee. He served under John Bell Hood and commanded three artillery battalions. On 25 July 1864 Hood named Beckham chief of artillery for the army and unsuccessfully recommended that he be promoted to brigadier general. On 29 November 1864, during Hood's ill-fated invasion of Tennessee, Beckham brought his batteries into action near the town of Columbia and received a mortal head wound. Robert Franklin Beckham died six days later, on 5 December 1864, and was buried in the churchyard of Saint John's Church, Ashwood, Maury County, Tennessee.

James Madison Beckham, *Genealogy of the Beckham Family in Virginia* (1910), 44–50 (por.); Compiled Service Records; Robert J. Trout, *They Followed the Plume: The*

Story of J. E. B. Stuart and His Staff (1993), 56–62; Larry J. Daniel, *Cannoneers in Gray: The Field Artillery of the Army of Tennessee, 1861–1865* (1984), 135, 139, 148, 150, 160–161, 172.

LARRY J. DANIEL

BECKLEY, Alfred (26 May 1802–26 May 1888), civic leader, was born in Washington, D.C., the youngest of three sons and a daughter of Maria Prince Beckley and John James Beckley, the first clerk of the House of Representatives. The only child who lived to maturity, he and his mother lived in Philadelphia for seven years after his father's death in 1807. In 1814 his mother took him to Frankfort, Kentucky, where he lived for five years. Beckley's early education included tutelage under Kean O'Hara, one of the finest classical teachers in Kentucky, after which he spent several months in the household of William Henry Harrison in Indiana. Harrison arranged for President James Monroe to appoint Beckley to the United States Military Academy at West Point, from which Beckley graduated ranked ninth in a class of thirty-five in 1823.

Beckley spent twelve years on active duty, two at Fort Marion near Saint Augustine, Florida; two at Fort Monroe at Old Point Comfort, Virginia; six at Allegheny Arsenal near Pittsburgh, Pennsylvania; and two at Fort Hamilton in New York. While at Allegheny Arsenal in 1832, Beckley married Amelia Neville Craig. Before her death in March 1845 they had six sons and one daughter. In October 1836 Beckley resigned from the army and moved to Fayette County in what is now West Virginia to make a living for his growing family on the remaining part of the large grants of land that his father had received in the 1780s and 1790s. In 1838 he laid off the town of Beckley, which he named for his father, and he built Wildwood, at which he resided for the remainder of his life. On 16 October 1850 he married Jane B. Rapp. They had two sons and one daughter.

For fifty years Beckley was one of the most active public men in the region. He was a local Methodist lay leader and a leading figure in the Virginia temperance movement. He attended his first state temperance convention in 1839 and in 1860 was elected grand worthy patriarch of the Sons of Temperance of Virginia and attended the national convention in Portland, Maine. In 1844 Beckley was a delegate to the Whig Party's national convention. Four years later he helped organize the Giles, Fayette, and Kanawha Turnpike, and in 1850 he led the movement to create Raleigh County out of the portion of Fayette County where he lived. Beckley served for two years as the first clerk of the Raleigh County Circuit Court of Law and Chancery.

On 18 March 1850 the General Assembly elected Beckley a brigadier general in the state's militia. In the summer of 1861 General Henry Alexander Wise called Beckley's brigade into service to guard Cotton Hill near Gauley Bridge and the ferry landings on the New River, but Beckley's men performed so poorly as to be useless, and they were soon disbanded. The Union army arrested Beckley and detained him in Wheeling, but on 18 June 1862 he was paroled and allowed to return home. Three of his sons fought for the Confederacy.

Beckley became the superintendent of schools of Raleigh County in 1872, was elected to the West Virginia House of Delegates for one two-year term in 1877, and served as a delegate-at-large at the 1876 Democratic Party national convention in Saint Louis. Late in life he prepared several incomplete autobiographical sketches, and he drafted but did not publish a history of Raleigh County. Alfred Beckley died of bronchitis at his home on his birthday, 26 May 1888, and was buried at Wildwood.

MS autobiography in John Paxton Davis Papers, LC, excerpted in part in Cecil D. Eby Jr., "Memoirs of a West Pointer in Saint Augustine, 1824–1826," *Florida Historical Quarterly* 42 (1964): 307–320, and in "Recollections of Fort Monroe, 1826–1828: From Autobiography of Lieutenant Alfred Beckley," *VMHB* 72 (1964): 479–489; diaries and other possessions in Wildwood Museum, Beckley, W.Va., described in *Charleston (W.Va.) Sunday Gazette-Mail*, 19 June 1987; family history information in *Beckley Sunday Register*, 19 June 1938; biography, Beckley's draft history of Raleigh Co., and will printed in Harlow Warren, *Beckley USA* (1955–1968), 1:18–74 (frontispiece por.); Greenbrier Co. Marriage Records; death date on gravestone and in Raleigh Co., W.Va., Death Register.

OTIS K. RICE

BECKLEY, John James (4 August 1757–8 April 1807), first clerk of the House of Representatives and first librarian of Congress, one of at least two sons and one daughter of John Beckley and Elizabeth Withers Beckley, of London, may have been born in Exeter, Devonshire, England. When he was eleven years old his family sent Beckley to Virginia, where he was apprenticed to John Clayton, a noted botanist and clerk of Gloucester County. Beckley completed his education in Clayton's household and worked for him in the county clerk's office.

Following Clayton's death at the end of 1773, Beckley moved to Richmond and went to work for the clerk of Henrico County, Thomas Adams. On 17 November 1774 Beckley was appointed clerk of the Henrico County Committee formed to enforce the nonimportation association that the First Continental Congress had adopted, and late in 1775 or early in 1776 he moved to Williamsburg to work for John Pendleton, another former Adams assistant, who was the clerk of the Virginia Committee of Safety. On 7 February 1776 Beckley was appointed assistant clerk of the committee, and on 4 July 1776 he was charged with arranging and preserving its records. His careful work and the patronage of such prominent men as John Pendleton, Edmund Pendleton, and Edmund Randolph led to a quick succession of clerical appointments of increasing responsibility. In 1776 and 1777 Beckley worked as an assistant to the clerk of the Council of State and served as clerk to a number of legislative committees. He succeeded John Pendleton as clerk of the Senate of Virginia in October 1777 and two years later was elected to the more prestigious post of clerk of the House of Delegates, which he held for ten years.

Beckley also studied law in Williamsburg and took over Edmund Randolph's law practice in 1779, just as Randolph had taken over that of Thomas Jefferson in 1774. On 10 April 1779 Beckley was elected a member of Phi Beta Kappa. He became the first clerk of the Virginia Court of Appeals on 30 August 1779 and served until 29 October 1785. At the time the capital was moved to Richmond in the spring of 1780, Beckley was also acting as clerk of the High Court of Chancery. He was elected one of the first aldermen of the city of Richmond in July 1782 and became the second mayor of the city, serving from 1 July 1783 to 6 July 1784. He won another term as mayor on 21 February 1788 and this time held the office until 9 March 1789. In 1782 Beckley obtained a grant of almost fifty thousand acres of land in Greenbrier County, but he did not succeed in using this property or his law practice either to achieve financial security or to launch a political career of his own. In the spring of 1787 he went to Philadelphia in a fruitless attempt to obtain appointment as secretary to the Constitutional Convention. A year later he unsuccessfully ran for one of Greenbrier County's two seats in the Virginia ratification convention, but after his defeat he became the convention's secretary.

In the spring of 1789 Beckley accompanied several Virginia members of the new Congress to New York, where with their support he was elected the first clerk of the House of Representatives on 1 April 1789. By then he had ceased to use his middle name, and he never again resided in Virginia. On 16 October 1790 he married Maria Prince, the daughter of New York merchant James Prince. They had three sons and a daughter, of whom the only one to live to maturity was Alfred Beckley, an army officer and the founder of the town of Beckley. Following the death of his father-in-law, Beckley also took care of his wife's family.

Beckley's life from 1789 until his death was intertwined with the history of the House of Representatives and with the fortunes of the Jeffersonian Republicans. At first secretly and later openly, Beckley assisted in organizing opposition to the policies of Alexander Hamilton. Beckley's close relationship with the printers enabled him to learn the identities of the authors of anonymous political publications, and he was able to assist his friends in the preparation of effective opposition propaganda. Beckley also wrote articles and pamphlets under the pseudonyms Americanus, Calm Observer, and Senex. In 1796 he operated as the nation's first political party manager, organizing the Pennsylvania campaign effort to elect Thomas Jefferson president of the United States. As a result, Beckley lost his job as clerk of the House of Representatives following the Federalist victories in the elections of 1796.

From 1797 to 1801 Beckley continued to organize the Jeffersonian Republicans, but he had to rely on the generosity of his friends, sell some of his Virginia property, and take jobs as clerks to two Philadelphia courts in order to pay his bills. After the Jeffersonians won the national elections of 1800, Beckley was reelected clerk of the House of Representatives, and in January 1802 Jefferson named him to the new position of librarian of Congress. From then until his death Beckley held both positions and continued his work on behalf of the Republicans. As clerk of the House, Beckley followed the procedures he had learned in Virginia. He read impressively from the floor and put the final texts of the journals and statutes in good order, but his passion for orderliness outweighed his sense of history, and he routinely eliminated office clutter by destroying draft documents and working papers that he believed were no longer useful. Consequently, many of the original documents detailing how the House worked during its formative years are lost to history. Beckley's partisanship during his two terms as clerk firmly established the position as a distinctly political one.

John Beckley died in Washington on 8 April 1807 and was buried in a public cemetery in Georgetown.

Birth date in unpublished autobiography of son Alfred Beckley in John Paxton Davis Papers, LC; Edmund Berkeley and Dorothy Smith Berkeley, *John Beckley: Zealous Partisan in a Nation Divided* (1973), includes full bibliography of primary sources; Noble E. Cunningham Jr., "John Beckley: An Early American Party Manager," *WMQ*, 3d ser., 13 (1956): 40–52, *The Jeffersonian Republicans: The Formation of Party Organization, 1789–1801* (1957), and *The Jeffersonian Republicans in Power: Party Operations, 1801–1809* (1963); Linda Grant De Pauw et al., eds., *Documentary History of the First Federal Congress, 1789–1791* (1977–), 3:x–xiv; obituary in *Washington National Intelligencer*, 10 Apr. 1807.

CHARLENE BANGS BICKFORD

BECKWITH, Sir Marmaduke (ca. 1687–by 2 October 1780), clerk of Richmond County, was probably born in Aldborough, Yorkshire, the younger of two children, both sons, of Sir Roger Beckwith, whom King Charles II had created a baronet on 15 April 1681, and his second wife, Elizabeth Jenings Beckwith. As a younger son of a baronet who possessed little landed wealth, he had to make his way in the world on his own, taking advantage of any influential connections he could exploit after his father's death in December 1700. His uncle Edmund Jenings became secretary of the colony of Virginia in 1701, and in 1705 Beckwith sailed for Virginia. During three years as an apprentice copyist in the secretary's Williamsburg office, the chief clerk, Chicheley Corbin Thacker, trained him for a responsible career in the colony's bureaucracy.

On 25 April 1709 Secretary Jenings appointed Beckwith clerk of Richmond County to succeed James Sherlock, who had died. The county clerkship was not just a clerical post but also a desirable office of prestige, influence, and profit. Beckwith took the oaths of office on 4 May 1709 and served as clerk of the Richmond County Court until his death, an unbroken and unequaled occupation of a single Virginia public office of more than seventy-one years. Beckwith used the fees he earned as clerk to begin acquiring land in 1712, and within a decade he had become a moderately prosperous planter. He invested in land until well past middle age and then began importing and breeding fine race horses. In about 1716 he married Elizabeth Brockenbrough Dickenson, widow of Thomas Dickenson, who had been deputy clerk of the county during Sherlock's tenure. They had at least four sons and four daughters.

Some British peerage records state that the title of Beckwith of Aldborough became extinct following the death of Marmaduke Beckwith's brother, the second Sir Roger Beckwith, in May 1743 and Marmaduke Beckwith's subsequent sale of the family's modest holdings in England. Marmaduke Beckwith assumed the style of a baronet, however, and was known ever after in Virginia as Sir Marmaduke Beckwith. By 1748 he was old enough and financially secure enough that he ceased officiating in person as county clerk and relied on two able deputies, Travers Tarpley until 1760 and Leroy Peachey thereafter, to execute all the duties of the clerk's office under Beckwith's actual or nominal supervision. He paid them out of the fees collected in the office, first deducting a percentage of the total amount, which he paid to the secretary of the colony, by whose authority he held the office.

The Virginia Constitution of 1776 eliminated the secretary's right to appoint the county clerks and to receive a portion of their incomes, vesting their appointment in the county courts instead. Despite what the justices of the peace then gently termed "his great Age" and presumed "Inability to Attend this Court in person," Sir Marmaduke Beckwith took the oath of allegiance to the commonwealth of Virginia on 2 September 1776 "to Qualify himself to Act as Clerk" of the county. By then he had distributed portions of his estate to each of his surviving children, with most of the residue going after his death to his eldest living son, who thereupon assumed the style of Sir Jonathan Beckwith. Beckwith had probably depleted his estate in pursuit of the pleasures of the turf, but to what extent is not entirely clear, since he left no will, the estate inventory that Sir Jonathan Beckwith as his administrator belatedly returned in July 1790 is evidently lost, and Sir Jonathan's own complicated affairs were the subject of lawsuits both before and after his death in 1796. Sir Jonathan Beckwith died possessed of twenty-two "family pictures," probably including portraits of his parents. Sir Marmaduke Beckwith died after the Richmond County Court met on 4 September 1780 and before its next meeting on 2 October 1780, when the justices appointed his deputy of twenty years' standing, Leroy Peachey, to succeed him. Beckwith's grandson Sir Jenings Beckwith, who died in Richmond County in 1835, was the last family member to style himself a baronet.

Fragments of family history in John Bernard Burke, *Genealogical and Heraldic History of the Extinct and Dormant Baronetcies of England, Ireland, and Scotland* (1844), 50–52, in Paul Beckwith, *The Beckwiths* (1891), 55–57, in George H. S. King, *Marriages of Richmond County, Virginia, 1668–1853* (1964), 13–14, and in Fairfax Harrison, *The Equine F. F. Vs.* (1928), 112–113; appointments and qualifications as clerk in Richmond Co. Deed Book, 5:68, and Richmond Co. Order Book, 5:24, 25, 18:2; son's inheritance and estate documented in report of *Beckwith* v. *Butler* (1793) (1 Washington), *Virginia Reports*, 1:224–226, and in voluminous suit papers of *Beckwith* v. *Bramham*, Spotsylvania Superior Court of Chancery; appointments of successor as clerk and of Sir Jonathan Beckwith as estate administrator in Richmond Co. Order Book, 18:155, 157; Richmond Co. Account and Deed Books also document the family property and Beckwith's provisions for his children.

BRENT TARTER

BEDINGER, Henry (3 February 1812–26 November 1858), member of the House of Representatives and diplomat, was born near Shepherdstown in Jefferson County, the fourth of five sons and twelfth of thirteen children of Daniel Bedinger and Sarah Rutherford Bedinger. He was educated in private academies in Shepherdstown and Frederick, Maryland, and worked in the Hampshire County clerk's office. At age twenty he moved to Charles Town to read law in the office of his brother-in-law William Lucas. In 1838 he opened his own law office in Shepherdstown, and on 5 June 1839 he married Margaret Rust. They had one son and two daughters before her death on 21 May 1843.

Running as a Democrat, Bedinger defeated the incumbent, his brother-in-law and former law teacher William Lucas, in the April 1845 campaign for the House of Representatives. In April 1847 Bedinger defeated a Whig candidate to win the second of his two terms. He was actively partisan in Congress and supported Democratic and southern sectional positions. He denounced Whig efforts to restrict voting and officeholding by Irish and German immigrants, endorsed the Walker Tariff of 1846 that reduced duties on some imported goods, and applauded the annexation of Texas as a slave state. Like many other southerners he advised against a direct confrontation with Great Britain over the Oregon territory, but he supported President James K. Polk's expansionist policy in the Pacific Northwest. Bedinger also unconditionally supported Polk's conduct of the war with Mexico and demanded thereafter that southern slave owners have full rights to take slaves into the newly acquired territories in the Southwest.

On 14 October 1847, at Willowbank in Flushing, New York, Bedinger married Caroline Bowne Lawrence, daughter of John Watson Lawrence, a Democratic congressman from

New York. They had one son and two daughters. After leaving Congress, Bedinger briefly practiced law in New York, then returned to Shepherdstown where he resumed his practice without making much money. Bedinger was a loyal and needy Democrat who had accumulated enough political capital that in May 1853 President Franklin Pierce appointed him chargé d'affaires to Denmark. Hoping to earn enough money to provide for his family, Bedinger accepted. In 1854 his rank was raised to minister plenipotentiary, making him the first United States minister to Denmark and giving him an increased salary. A favorite at the court of King Frederick VII, Bedinger ably handled the delicate negotiations for the abolition of the Danish Sound Dues. For centuries Denmark had exacted tolls from all ships passing through the narrow waterway connecting the North and the Baltic Seas. Acting on instructions from the Department of State, Bedinger formally objected to the annual assessment of approximately $100,000 on American ships and gave notice that the United States planned to abrogate its 1826 commercial treaty with Denmark. The action prompted the Danes to call a general European conference at which Denmark agreed to abolish the duty and the other participants agreed to compensate Denmark for marking the channel and keeping lighthouses. The United States was not represented at the conference, but Bedinger worked out a bilateral agreement to give American ships free passage through the waterway in exchange for a small contribution to the Danish fund that the general treaty established.

Bedinger's salary did not even cover his expenses in Denmark, and in 1857 he sent his family to New York and resigned, although he remained in Denmark until his successor was appointed and confirmed in 1858. On his return to Shepherdstown, Bedinger prepared to take up a new government post, superintendent of the United States armory at Harpers Ferry. His neighbors welcomed him home with a bonfire and barbecue on 5 November 1858, but he caught pneumonia after giving a speech on the cold, wet occasion. Henry Bedinger died at his home on 26 November 1858 and was buried in the family cemetery at Bedford, just outside of Shepherdstown.

Alexandra Lee Levin, "Henry Bedinger of Virginia: First United States Minister to Denmark," *Virginia Cavalcade* 29 (1980): 184–191 (por.); Lucy Forney Bittinger, *Bittinger and Bedinger Families: Descendants of Adam Büdinger* (1904), 55–63; Bedinger-Dandridge Family Papers, Duke; Henry Bedinger Papers, VHS; *Richmond Enquirer*, 29 Apr. 1845, 4 May, 26 Oct. 1847; Letters of Application and Recommendation during the Administrations of Franklin Pierce and James Buchanan, RG 59, NARA; Soren J. M. P. Fogdall, *Danish-American Diplomacy, 1776–1920* (1922), 66–85; obituary in *Charles Town Virginia Free Press*, 2 Dec. 1858.

JOSEPH A. FRY

BEIRNE, Andrew (1771–16 March 1845), member of the Convention of 1829–1830 and member of the House of Representatives, was born in County Roscommon, Ireland, a younger son of five sons and a daughter of Andrew O'Beirne and Mary Plunkett O'Beirne. He grew up on the family estate, received a classical education, possibly in anticipation that he would enter the priesthood, and attended and may have graduated from Trinity College, Dublin. In 1793, because opportunities were limited in Ireland, he immigrated to the United States. He settled in Philadelphia, where he invested his capital of about $150 in a local business that soon failed. He worked for a time as a peddler and became a successful salesman thanks to his cultivated manner and amiable disposition.

About 1795, having dropped the *O* from his surname, Beirne moved to Greenbrier County, where he opened a store on the farm of Edward Keenan, a fellow Irish immigrant. Soon afterward he married Keenan's daughter Ellen Keenan. They had ten children, of whom five sons and four daughters lived to maturity. After Monroe County was created from Greenbrier County in 1799, Beirne moved his store to the county seat, Union. Two of Beirne's brothers immigrated to Virginia about that time and joined him in a partnership. They transported merchandise to Virginia from Philadelphia and took payment either in money or in ginseng, pelts, cattle, and other goods in kind. Their business flourished rapidly, and they established other stores in western Virginia and elsewhere in the South. Over time Beirne acquired at least seventy-two tracts of land, some of it presumably in payment of his customers' debts. He resided north of Union at Walnut Grove, his plantation of 2,200 acres of the best land in Monroe County.

From 1806 to 1809 Beirne represented Monroe County in the House of Delegates, where he proved himself a staunch Jeffersonian Republican. He was a captain in the county militia during the War of 1812 and was ordered to Norfolk but saw no action. In the spring of 1829 he was one of four men elected to represent the district comprising Alleghany, Bath, Botetourt, Greenbrier, Monroe, Nicholas, and Pocahontas Counties in the constitutional convention that met from 5 October 1829 to 15 January 1830. He served on the Committee on the Legislative Department and usually voted with the other delegates from the western counties in favor of democratic reforms. Disappointed in the constitution that the convention produced, he voted against submitting it to the voters for ratification.

Beirne was elected to the Senate of Virginia later in 1830. He was reelected once and served until 1836. Perhaps because of his business experience, he sat on the Committee on Internal Improvements, and during his final session he also belonged to the Committee on Claims. Beirne was a presidential elector for Democrat Martin Van Buren in 1836, and in the spring of 1837 he was elected to the House of Representatives. Two years later he easily won reelection over a Whig candidate. Beirne did not seek a third term. During his four years in Congress he served on the Committee on the District of Columbia, but he seldom spoke on the floor and exercised no substantial influence.

Beirne was generally regarded as an open and honest businessman, but his success later led to charges that he had reduced his neighbors to vassalage. He was described as intelligent and amiable but also as ugly and very dour in appearance, perhaps because of continuing pain from a severe shoulder injury and his habit as his hearing failed later in life of contorting his face muscles while attempting to follow a conversation. Andrew Beirne died on 16 March 1845 in Gainesville, Alabama, probably while visiting one of his children, leaving an estate appraised at more than $600,000. He was buried in Green Hill Cemetery in Union.

Edward T. White, "Andrew and Oliver Beirne of Monroe County," *West Virginia History* 20 (1958): 16–23; George Flanagan, "Memoir of Andrew Beirne," in William Echols Spragins, ed., *A Brief History and Brief Genealogy of the Andrew Beirne, William Patton, William Echols V, and Robert E. Spragins Lines*, 2d ed. (1956), 269 (por.), 322–335; Andrew Beirne Papers, UNC; year of birth on gravestone; Anne Newport Royall, *Sketches of History, Life, and Manners in the United States* (1826), 36–38; Ruth Woods Dayton, *Greenbrier Pioneers and Their Homes* (1942), 205–209; Oren F. Morton, *A History of Monroe County, West Virginia* (1916), 308–311; Hugh Blair Grigsby, *The Virginia Convention of 1829–30* (1854), 82, 100, 104; Bruce, *Rhetoric of Conservatism*, 37; *Richmond Enquirer*, 29 May 1829, 9 May 1837, 4 June 1839, 4 May 1841; *Lewisburg Palladium of Virginia*, 6 Sept. 1834; obituary in *Richmond Enquirer*, 28 Mar. 1845.

OTIS K. RICE

BELK, John Blanton (3 July 1893–28 May 1972), Presbyterian minister, was born in Chatham, the eldest of three sons and second of eight children of George Washington Belk, pastor of the Chatham Presbyterian Church, and Mary Thornton Blanton Belk. He grew up in Chatham and in Charlotte, North Carolina, where his father moved the family in 1900. From 1911 to 1913 he attended Davidson College, after which he taught in a one-room school near Mills River, Henderson County, North Carolina, for two years and then matriculated at the University of South Carolina in Columbia in 1915. A member of the National Guard, Belk was called to active duty in 1917 and served in France for fourteen months before being discharged in August 1919.

Belk returned to the University of South Carolina and received a B.A. in 1920 and an M.A. in 1921. He also received a B.D. from Columbia Theological Seminary in 1921 and later studied at Union Theological Seminary in New York. On 30 June 1921 Belk married Jennie Bruce Wannamaker in Saint Matthews, South Carolina. They had two daughters and two sons.

Belk ministered to Presbyterian congregations across the South, serving in Piedmont, Greenville County, South Carolina, from 1921 to 1923, Clover, South Carolina, from 1923 to 1924, Orlando, Florida, from 1924 to 1929, and Huntington, West Virginia, from 1929 to 1933. In 1933 he became pastor of Grace Covenant Presbyterian Church, one of the largest Presbyterian congregations in Richmond. Belk soon became mired in a controversy arising from his participation in the Oxford Group Movement, later known as Moral Re-Armament. He espoused Oxford teachings from the pulpit and in his popular radio sermons. Many members of his congregation preferred a more traditional ministry and criticized his advocacy of the movement's attempts to foster a national spiritual revival and spread democratic values throughout the world.

In 1937 the congregation of Grace Covenant Church split over Belk's continued espousal of Oxford principles. Thirty-one of the church's forty-six officers threatened to resign if he did not dissociate himself from the movement. The controversy ignited intense emotions and was covered in detail in the local newspapers. At the request of the church session, East Hanover Presbytery appointed a special commission to investigate the dispute. Chairman Ernest Trice Thompson, of Union Theological Seminary in Virginia, submitted a report that found fault with both the church's officers and its minister. Reconciliation being deemed impossible, the commission dissolved Belk's relationship with the church. On 19 December 1937 several of the leading members of Grace Covenant, including James Scott Parrish and Charles F. Gillette, organized the new church of Saint Giles' and installed Belk as pastor the next month.

Belk remained a public advocate of Moral Re-Armament. His popular sermons and radio ministry made him one of the best-known clergymen in Richmond, and by the time he retired on his sixty-fifth birthday in 1958, Saint Giles' Church was the third largest in the presbytery. Belk received an honorary D.D. from Rollins College in Winter Park, Florida, in 1937 and was elected moderator of East Hanover Presbytery in 1940. From the latter year through 1958 he frequently offered the invocation at the beginning of sessions of the Virginia House of Delegates. He also wrote two books: *Our Fighting Faith* (1944), based on sermons preached at Saint Giles' Presbyterian Church and broadcast over radio station WRVA, and *A Faith to Move Nations* (1969). John Blanton Belk died at his retirement home in Tucson, Arizona, on 28 May 1972 and was buried in the Presbyterian cemetery in Swannanoa, Buncombe County, North Carolina.

Feature articles in *Richmond News Leader*, 26 Dec. 1932, and *Richmond Times-Dispatch*, 31 Mar. 1958, 7 Apr. 1962 (por.); BVS Birth Register, Pittsylvania Co.; Eugene D. Witherspoon, ed., *Ministerial Directory of the Presbyterian Church, U.S., 1861–1967* (1967), 39; Jack Abernathy, *Living Monument: The Story of Grace Covenant Presbyterian Church, Richmond, Virginia, 1790–1990* (1989), 26–34; congregational dispute covered in *Richmond News Leader* and *Richmond Times-Dispatch*, July 1937–Jan. 1938, and George C. Longest, *Genius in the Garden: Charles F. Gillette & Landscape Architecture in Virginia* (1992), 99–107; obituaries in *Tucson Arizona Daily Star*, 29 May 1972, and *Richmond Times-Dispatch*, 30 May 1972.

ROBERT BENEDETTO

BELL, David (d. 15 December 1799), member of the Convention of 1788, was the second son and fifth and youngest child of David Bell and Judith Cary Bell. The date of his birth is not known, but his elder brother, Henry Bell, was born about 1746, and David Bell was certainly born before July 1758. He may have been born at Warwick in Chesterfield County, where his father was a successful merchant, or at Bellmont, a plantation inherited by his mother, which was located in the southern part of Albemarle County that became Buckingham County in 1761. Bell's father was the first clerk of Buckingham County, and his elder brother inherited the bulk of the family's estate and served in the House of Burgesses from 1772 to 1774 and in the House of Delegates from 1781 to 1782.

David Bell's life is poorly documented, in part because many of the records of Buckingham County are lost and in part because of his limited participation in public affairs. In accounts of the Convention of 1788 that considered the proposed United States constitution, his father, who died in 1770, has been mistakenly identified as the delegate from Buckingham County. Bell was elected to the convention in March 1788 and attended the sessions in Richmond from opening day, 2 June, through adjournment on 27 June 1788. He did not speak, insofar as the published records disclose. Bell opposed the new plan of government. On 25 June he voted in favor of requiring amendments before approving the constitution, and when that motion failed, he voted against ratification. In the following year he won election to the House of Delegates. He was reelected three times and served from October 1789 through December 1792. On 1 March 1790 he was appointed a justice of the peace in Buckingham County.

On 12 June 1789 Bell obtained a grant of more than eleven thousand acres of land on both sides of Slate River Mountain in Buckingham and Campbell Counties. He had large debts, and four years later he sold much of his property and moved with his brother-in-law Nathaniel Gist to Bourbon County, Kentucky. In March 1796 he purchased four hundred acres of land from Gist, but in 1797 the Gists recovered the property to settle some of Bell's debts. He never married and lived the last three or four years of his life with his widowed sister Judith Cary Bell Gist. David Bell died at her house, Canewood, in Clarke County, Kentucky, on 15 December 1799. He was probably buried in the family cemetery on the property.

Family relationships reported in *Richmond Virginia Argus*, 25 Jan. 1799; Land Grants, 20:384–387, RG 4, LVA; financial information in *Spiers, Bowman, and Company* v. *David Bell*, n.d., PRO T 79/81, 116–134, and *Hopkirk* v. *Bell's Executors* (1824), Circuit Court, Ended Cases (unrestored, oversize file 1), Box 195, which includes a copy of Bell's first will; Kaminski, *Ratification*, 1538, 1541, 1557, 1565; *Richmond Virginia Gazette and General Advertiser*, 15 May 1793, 17 Mar., 2 Apr. 1794; Bourbon Co. Deed Book, vols. C–D; Judith C. Gist's power of attorney to William Bernard, 1 June 1800, Bernard Papers, LVA; obituary in *Lexington Kentucky Gazette*, 30 Jan. 1800.

DAPHNE GENTRY

BELL, James Pinkney (18 November 1830–24 July 1911), printer, was born in Caroline County, the eldest child of four sons and two daughters of James Bell and Catherine Pleasant Terrell Bell. He left home at age eighteen and between 1849 and 1859 worked in Fredericksburg, Baltimore, Philadelphia, and in Corinth, Mississippi, where in 1859 he was robbed of almost all of his money. Bell returned to Virginia by train and according to family tradition reached Lynchburg at 10:30 A.M. on 1 August 1859 with only five dollars in his pocket. He had probably worked for one or more newspapers, and within a few weeks he found a job as the Lynchburg agent for the *Richmond Dispatch* and the *Baltimore Sun*. Not long thereafter he opened a newsstand and bookshop in Lynchburg. On 23 May 1860 he married Susan Jane Slagle, of Lynchburg. They had three daughters and two sons.

J. P. Bell attempted to join the Confederate army in 1861 but was rejected because he was underweight. He took a job as express manager for the Virginia and Tennessee Railroad and spent much of the war acting as correspondent for the *Richmond Dispatch*. His articles in that newspaper during the war were usually signed "O.K." or "B." Late in 1861 or early in 1862 he compiled and published the *Confederate Almanac and Register for 1862*. Ten of the almanac's thirty-one pages consisted of Bell's "Condensed history of events since November 6th, A.D., 1860." His friend John E. Browne did the printing, and after the war they formed the printing firm of J. P. Bell, Browne, and Company, with offices at the same address as the J. P. Bell and Company bookstore.

Bell and Browne remained business associates until Browne's death in 1904. Bell also brought his brothers Robert H. Bell and Richard T. Bell into the business after the Civil War, and still later his son Robert Otway Bell and two nephews joined the firm. During the 1870s J. P. Bell and Company installed the first steam-operated printing press in Lynchburg, and in 1875 it acquired the city's first office typewriter. By 1879, when it moved into larger quarters and began publishing and printing the Lynchburg city directory, it was the largest job-printing firm in Piedmont Virginia. In 1877 Bell bought the short-lived *Lynchburg Evening Star* but sold it the following year. In September 1878 he started another newspaper, the *Sunday Times*, but it also did not last long. By 1887 the firm operated seven steam presses and employed more than twenty printers and binders in addition to office and sales staff, and it continued to grow thereafter. When it acquired its first linotype machine at the turn of the century, it was publishing volumes of many kinds, including lawbooks and school textbooks. Bell opened sales offices in Richmond and in Roanoke during the 1880s. He also helped charter Lynchburg's first street railway company in 1880, and in 1886 he was the first president of the Marshall Lodge Hospital, which his Masonic lodge had founded. Bell was elected to the board of the Lynchburg National Bank in 1887 and became a vice president in 1893.

In 1890 the J. P. Bell Company was chartered with Bell as president, one of his brothers as vice president, and Lewis G. Bell, who was both his nephew and son-in-law, as one of the directors. Bell retired in 1897 and turned the management of the firm over to Lewis G. Bell, but he died in 1903, and J. P. Bell resumed direction of the firm until 1910, when he retired again. Bell also compiled and in 1905 published *Our Quaker Friends of Ye Olden Time: Being in Part a Transcript of the Minute Books of Cedar Creek Meeting, Hanover County, and the South River Meeting, Campbell County, Va.* Bell's mother came from a Quaker family, and although she had been disowned for marrying outside the church, he paid tribute to the religious principles and family traditions of the Society of Friends in Virginia. He noted in the preface that his Quaker name would have included his mother's maiden name, making him James Pinkney Pleasant Bell, which is how he is listed in some bibliographical reference works.

Bell's wife died on 25 May 1883, and on 21 January 1885 he married Annie Pope Adams, of Fredericksburg. J. P. Bell died in Lynchburg on 24 July 1911 and was buried in Spring Hill Cemetery in Lynchburg.

Birth date in Bell's *Our Quaker Friends of Ye Olden Time*, 20; Roberta D. Cornelius, *J. P. Bell's of Lynchburg, Virginia, Established in 1859* (1959), 3–32 (por.); Lynchburg City and Fredericksburg City Marriage Registers; obituary in *Lynchburg News*, 25 July 1911.

THOMAS G. LEDFORD
BRENT TARTER

BELL, John Hendren (19 November 1883–9 December 1934), physician and principal in a court case, was born in Augusta County, the second of three sons and second of four children of Samuel Henry Lockridge Bell and Sarah Ellen Cosby Bell. His elder brother, Wilbur Cosby Bell, was on the faculty of Virginia Theological Seminary for many years. John Hendren Bell attended Washington and Lee University from 1901 to 1903 and the University of Virginia from 1904 to 1907. Like his father, a graduate of the University of Chicago, he studied medicine and in 1909 graduated from the medical school of the University of the South in Sewanee, Tennessee. He married Elizabeth Spotts Harlowe on 8 April 1909, and they had one daughter.

Bell worked in Gary, McDowell County, West Virginia, as a physician for the United States Coal and Coke Company from 1909 through 1914 and for the Wright Coal and Coke Company in 1915 and part of 1916. Later in 1916 he opened a private practice in Augusta County and served as an assistant physician at Western State Hospital in Staunton. In 1917 Bell joined the staff of the State Colony for Epileptics and Feeble-Minded near Lynchburg. During World War I he served in the United States Army and afterward briefly in the Balkans, where he assisted in the establishment of a hospital.

Bell returned to Lynchburg after the war and in 1925 was appointed superintendent of the State Colony for Epileptics and Feeble-Minded to succeed Albert Sidney Priddy, who had died. Bell inherited from Priddy an important legal case designed to test the constitutionality of the practice of surgical sterilization of persons believed to be incompetent because of feeblemindedness, insanity, alcoholism, epilepsy, or other traits regarded as defects and assumed to be hereditary in origin and therefore preventable by sterilization. Virginia's 1924 Act to Provide for the Sexual Sterilization of Inmates of State Institutions in Certain Cases authorized the staff of the Virginia Colony to perform the procedures.

Priddy and other advocates of eugenic sterilization arranged for a suit to be brought in order that the law and the practice could be tested in the U.S. Supreme Court. They selected Carrie Elizabeth Buck, a young woman who had been committed to the State Colony. The physicians concluded that she had inherited feeblemindedness from her mother and that her infant child showed signs of slow mental development. On 2 May 1927 the Supreme Court upheld the constitutionality of Virginia's law. In the Court's decision in *Buck* v. *Bell*, Justice Oliver Wendell Holmes wrote that the principle that the federal courts had used to sustain compulsory vaccination was broad enough to cover sterilization. Holmes's immediately famous conclusion was that "Three generations of imbeciles are enough" (*United States Reports*, 274:207).

Bell performed the operation on Buck and during the ensuing years presented several papers at professional meetings defending the practice and the assumptions on which it was grounded. He published the lectures as pamphlets entitled *Eugenic Sterilization* (1929), *Opinions as to the Etiology of Mental Disorders* (1929), *The Biological Relationship of Eugenics to the Development of the Human Race* (1930), *Mental Diseases from the Standpoint of the General Practitioner* (1931), and *Eugenic Control and its Relationship to the Science of Life and Reproduction* (1931). During the next five decades more than 8,300 people underwent involuntary surgical sterilization in Virginia's public institutions, and a total of approximately 50,000 such procedures were performed in the United States.

Bell belonged to the American Medical Association, the American Association for the Advancement of Science, the Virginia Academy of Science, and the Medical Society of Virginia. In the summer of 1933 he developed heart disease and first took a leave of absence and then in October resigned as superintendent of the State Colony for Epileptics and Feeble-Minded. In spite of his poor health, or perhaps because his condition was not widely known, he was elected vice president of the American Psychiatric Association in 1934. John Hendren Bell died in Staunton on 9 December 1934.

NCAB, 25:421–422 (por.); J. David Smith and K. Ray Nelson, *The Sterilization of Carrie Buck* (1989); Paul A. Lombardo, "Three Generations, No Imbeciles: New Light on *Buck* v. *Bell*," *New York University Law Review* 60 (1985): 30–62; obituaries in *Lynchburg Daily Advance*, 10 Dec. 1934, *Lynchburg News* and *Staunton News Leader*, both 11 Dec. 1934, and *Virginia Medical Monthly* 61 (1935): 624.

J. DAVID SMITH

BELL, Wilbur Cosby (1 April 1881–6 April 1933), Episcopal minister and educator, was born in Augusta County, the eldest child of three sons and a daughter of Samuel Henry Lockridge Bell, a physician, and Sarah Ellen Cosby Bell. One of his brothers was John Hendren Bell, a prominent eugenicist. Bell was educated at Bridgewater College, founded by the Church of the Brethren, and at Hampden-Sydney College, founded by the Presbyterian Church. He received an A.B. from Hampden-Sydney in 1900 and enrolled in the Protestant Episcopal Theological Seminary in Alexandria (familiarly known as the Virginia Theological Seminary), from which he graduated with a B.D. in 1905. On 21 June 1905 he married Anne Lee Laird, whose grandfather, father, brother, and several other male relatives were Episcopal clergyman or educators. They had no children.

W. Cosby Bell, as he was always known as an adult, served as rector of Trinity Church in Onancock, Accomack County, in 1905 and 1906 before accepting a call to Robert E. Lee Memorial Church in Lexington, where he remained for five years. He focused his attention on the students at Washington and Lee University and at the Virginia Military Institute and founded Episcopal church clubs at both colleges. During his time in Lexington, Bell presented eighty-five students for confirmation. In 1911 he moved to Saint Andrew's Church in Louisville, Kentucky. A year later he was elected to the chair of systematic divinity at the Virginia Theological Seminary to succeed one of his mentors, Richard W. Micou. Except for service as chaplain of the 117th Engineers during World War I, Bell taught at the seminary until his death.

By the 1920s Bell had acquired a reputation as a teacher and lecturer. In 1925 at Holy Trinity Church in Philadelphia he delivered the John Bohlen Lectures, which he published as his first book, *Sharing in Creation: Studies in the Christian View of the World* (1925). He also lectured at the School of Theology of the University of the South in Sewanee, Tennessee, and at Union

Theological Seminary in New York. In 1929 and 1930 he delivered the Bishop Paddock Lectures at the General Theological Seminary in New York, which he published as his second book, *The Making of Man* (1931). His widow subsequently published his work on death and resurrection, *If a Man Die* (1934), and a collection of his lectures, *The Reasonableness of Faith in God* (1937).

In common with other theologians of his generation, Bell sought to reconcile Christian faith and modern thought. Calling himself a professor of the philosophy of the Christian religion, he devoted particular attention to the issues of freedom and necessity, suffering, and the afterlife. Unlike some modernist theologians, he did not abandon traditional formularies of faith but instead added an emphasis on the positive value of conflict, change, and struggle. In *Sharing in Creation*, for example, he wrote that the world "offers us in storm no less than in sunshine the opportunity for the production of spiritual values." He explained suffering by arguing that the "primary objective of the world process is not happiness but the increase of personal life" achieved through struggle "in the school of life" (198–199). In *The Making of Man* he wrote that Christian faith did not conflict with efforts to improve society because "the service of man in the common things of life is found to be identical with the service of God" (277).

Bell received doctor of divinity degrees in 1914 from Washington and Lee and in 1929 from both Princeton Theological Seminary and the Episcopal Theological School of Cambridge, Massachusetts. W. Cosby Bell died of heart disease on 6 April 1933 in a hospital in Washington, D.C., and was buried in the cemetery at Virginia Theological Seminary.

Brief biography in William A. R. Goodwin, *History of the Theological Seminary in Virginia and Its Historical Background* (1923), 675–676; Bell's papers are at Virginia Theological Seminary; BVS Marriage Register, Fauquier Co.; George M. Brooke Jr., *General Lee's Church: The History of the Protestant Episcopal Church in Lexington, Virginia, 1840–1975* (1984), 43–47 (por.); obituaries in *Alexandria Gazette* and *New York Times*, both 7 Apr. 1933, *Lexington Gazette*, 12 Apr. 1933, and *Southern Churchman*, 15 Apr. 1933.

ROBERT W. PRICHARD

BELLWOOD, James (4 December 1840–2 September 1924), agricultural reformer, was the only son and elder of two children of Charles Bellwood and Jane Wade Bellwood. He was born at Cobourg, Northumberland County, in Upper Canada, which became the province of Ontario in 1867. Both of his parents had been born in England, and he had an older half brother. In 1861 he married Helen Elizabeth Turner, who had also been born in England, and they had three sons and one daughter. Although he received no formal higher education, he constantly read agricultural journals. He raised beef cattle near Cobourg until his physician advised him to move to a milder climate after he had contracted a severe case of bronchitis.

In 1887 Bellwood purchased and moved to Auburn Chase, a Chesterfield County farm containing a large house and 1,277 acres of depleted land. Bellwood lived on the farm for the remainder of his life and became a citizen of the United States. Initially he used his property for a cattle-feeding operation, but he soon switched to dairying and built up a herd of about 150 purebred Holsteins to supply milk to markets in Richmond and Petersburg. His sons managed separate portions of the operation, and approximately forty farmhands lived on the property. Bellwood took the unusual step of increasing his employees' wages in order to improve their productivity, and he was one of the first farm managers in Chesterfield County to replace his mules with tractors. Bellwood tripled the yield of his soil with proven methods of soil restoration such as rotating crops, applying lime and natural fertilizers, and planting legumes. He also increased his holdings to almost 3,000 acres. Bellwood made the property profitable and famous. Photographs of his fields, crops, and farm buildings often appeared in such popular agricultural journals as the *Southern Planter*.

In 1914 Bellwood fitted out an entire railroad car with samples of the products of his farm, and it toured the state as an educational exhibit sponsored by the Virginia State Farmers' Institute. In 1915, at the personal request of Governor Henry Carter Stuart and the Virginia commissioners to the Panama-Pacific International Exposition in San Francisco, Bellwood and his sons assembled the largest single agricultural exhibit shown at that world's fair. Of the more than three hundred items displayed, all were products of Bellwood's farm except for the tobacco, which he did not grow but which the exposition officers insisted be shown. The exhibit included hay, nuts, honey, more than eighty varieties of grain and grass seed, and more than fifteen varieties of corn, but it contained no perishable fruits or green vegetables. Bellwood was a natural showman and always displayed his produce to the best advantage. The exhibit won the medal of honor as the best agricultural exhibit at the fair, as well as a medal of honor for hay, four gold medals, seven silver medals, one honorable mention, and a medal of honor for the tobacco.

Bellwood was active in the Virginia State Farmers' Institute, the Virginia State Dairymen's Association, and other agricultural organizations, and for a decade prior to his death served on the board of the Virginia State Fair Association. He was also a member of the Good Roads Association and a prime mover in the establishment of the first electric trolley line between Richmond and Petersburg and in the extension of rural telephone service into Chesterfield County. He supported the consolidation of the cities of Richmond and Manchester and served on the board of the Virginia State Penitentiary from 1918 to 1920. Bellwood also kept a herd of elk on his property, which in 1942 became the site of the United States Army's Defense General Supply Center. James Bellwood died of kidney failure at his home on 2 September 1924 and was buried in Maury Cemetery in Richmond.

Bettie Woodson Weaver, *History and Geography of Chesterfield County, Virginia* (1981), 236–237 (por.); Jeffrey M. O'Dell, *Chesterfield County: Early Architecture and Historic Sites* (1983), 293–294; family history information furnished and verified by Mabel Anne Bellwood Kramer and George Dellinger; Bellwood account books for 1890–1936 and 1910–1921, Chesterfield Co. Historical Society; histories of property in Defense General Supply Center newsletter, *Elk Horn*, Mar. 1965, May 1989; *Southern Planter* 71 (1910): 654–655; 75 (1914): 234–235; 76 (1915): 303, 402, 475; *Richmond News Leader*, 6 Oct. 1942; obituaries in *Petersburg Progress-Index*, *Richmond News Leader*, and *Richmond Times-Dispatch*, all 3 Sept. 1924.

WAVERLY K. WINFREE

BEMISS, Samuel Merrifield (21 February 1894–7 August 1966), businessman and civic leader, was born in New Orleans, Louisiana, the first of three sons and third of eight children of Eli Lockert Bemiss and Cyane Dandridge Williams Bemiss. His mother was a child of Richmond banker John Langbourne Williams, and in 1899 the Bemiss family moved to Richmond, where Lockert Bemiss supervised the construction of a hydroelectric-generating facility for the Virginia Electric Development Company and later served as president of the Richmond Traction Company. He sat on the boards of a number of Richmond corporations and was founding president of the Title Insurance Company of Richmond and of a private bank, the Richmond Trust Company. Lockert Bemiss also took part in many civic activities and instilled in his son a similar sense of public responsibility.

Sam Bemiss was educated at McGuire's University School in Richmond, at Woodberry Forest near Orange, and at the University of Virginia, where he studied English and law from 1913 to 1916 but did not take a degree. In 1916 he returned to Richmond to assist his father in his several business activities. On 10 May 1917 he joined the army as an infantry officer candidate and won promotion from second lieutenant to first lieutenant on 31 December 1917. Bemiss arrived in France in June 1918 and was subsequently credited with shooting down a German airplane with his infantry rifle. According to him, "I don't know if I did it or not." General George H. Jamerson, to whom Bemiss was aide-de-camp, described him as "capable, reliable, energetic and courageous."

In 1919 Bemiss returned to Richmond and joined his father's Richmond Trust Company, and on 27 January 1921 he married Doreen FitzGerald. They had one daughter and one son. In 1925, following his father's death, Bemiss resigned as vice president of the Richmond Trust Company to manage his father-in-law's FitzGerald and Company, which supplied railway commissaries and operated hotels and concessions in the Blue Ridge Mountains. Bemiss was a successful businessman and served as his father had done on the boards of several

Richmond corporations, including the First and Merchants National Bank and the Larus and Brother Tobacco Company. His estate at the time of his death was estimated to be worth half a million dollars.

Bemiss was an avid reader and book collector whose personal library of more than 2,000 volumes was rich in the classics, Elizabethan literature, and Virginia history. He kept a copy of the Bible and an edition of Shakespeare's works beside his bed. He served on the board of the Virginia Historical Society from 1944 until his death and was president from 1952 to 1958. From 1939 to 1953 he also served on the board of the Virginia State Library, and as chairman for the last five years he helped create the library's *Virginia Cavalcade* magazine in 1951. He was vice president of the United States government's Jamestown-Williamsburg-Yorktown Celebration Commission, which cooperated with the Virginia 350th Anniversary Commission in the 1957 commemoration of the settlement of Jamestown. Bemiss wrote the brief introduction for one of the historical volumes that was published in conjunction with the celebration, *The Three Charters of the Virginia Company of London, With Several Related Documents, 1606–1621* (1957). As a board member of the Jamestown Foundation, he also assisted in the creation of the Virginia Colonial Records Project. Shortly before his death he helped found the University Press of Virginia, and the press's building on the grounds of the University of Virginia was named in his honor. Bemiss collected several of his short historical pieces, which principally celebrated the first English colonists in Virginia, in *Ancient Adventures: A Collection of Essays* (1959), and he published several other papers and addresses in *Causeries* (1962).

Bemiss devoted much of his time and energy to civic causes. During the 1930s he served as president of the Children's Home Society of Virginia and helped rescue it from bankruptcy. He was president of the Atlantic Rural Exposition, the official name for the State Fair of Virginia, from 1954 until 1966, and a member of the board of visitors of the Medical College of Virginia from 1945 to 1953, from 1956 to 1960, and from 1961 to 1965. He was also a special assistant to the governor of Virginia for civil defense from 1949 to 1962. In 1955 the University of Richmond awarded him an honorary doctorate in literature for his contributions to education in Virginia, and in the same year the Virginia State Chamber of Commerce presented him its distinguished service award.

Although a lifelong Democrat, Bemiss served as an officer of the Virginia Democrats for Eisenhower during the 1952 presidential campaign, and in spite of his close association with Harry Flood Byrd, Bemiss opposed Byrd's program of Massive Resistance to school desegregation during the 1950s. Bemiss was also a friend of Connecticut's Republican Senator Prescott Bush, with whom he regularly spent summer vacations in Maine.

Bemiss wrote a short family history and personal reminiscence of his youth in the form of a letter to his children and had it privately printed as *Days Before Yesterday: A Letter* (1961). Samuel Merrifield Bemiss died in Richmond on 7 August 1966 and was buried in Hollywood Cemetery in that city.

Bemiss, *Days Before Yesterday*; Bemiss Family Papers and Samuel Merrifield Bemiss Papers, VHS; feature articles in *Richmond Times-Dispatch*, 11 Aug. 1957, 24 Feb. 1958, *Commonwealth* 20 (Mar. 1953): 20, and 22 (May 1955): 25, 44; Military Service Records; Hall, *Portraits*, 23–24 (por.); obituaries in *Richmond News Leader* and *Richmond Times-Dispatch*, both 8 Aug. 1968; editorial tributes in *Richmond News Leader*, 8 Aug. 1966, and *Richmond Times-Dispatch*, 9 Aug. 1966.

W. TAYLOR REVELEY III

BENEDICT, Mary Kendrick (14 July 1876–10 February 1956), president of Sweet Briar College, was born in Rochester, New York, the eldest of three sons and three daughters of Wayland Richardson Benedict and Anne Elizabeth Kendrick Benedict. Both of her grandfathers had been educators in the Rochester area, her father was a Baptist minister and professor of philosophy at the University of Cincinnati, and her mother was a graduate of Elmira College, an author of poetry and books for children, and a founder of the Cincinnati Kindergarten Association.

Benedict grew up in Cincinnati, where she was educated in a private school, and then attended Vassar, from which she graduated Phi Beta Kappa in 1897. She planned to become a physician, but to help pay some of the costs of educating her brothers and sisters she spent two years as a private tutor in Pittsburgh. During the 1899–1900 academic year she studied philosophy under her father at the University of Cincinnati, after which she entered Yale University and received a doctorate from its School of Philosophy and Psychology in 1903.

Benedict taught from 1903 to 1906 at the State Normal School (now Central Missouri State University) in Warrensburg, Missouri. On 21 May 1906 she was hired as the first president of Sweet Briar College in Amherst County. When Benedict arrived in Virginia, she found a half-finished school with only two faculty members and one registered student. She hired additional faculty members, persuaded the trustees to adopt the demanding admissions and academic standards of Vassar as a model, and recruited students. Sweet Briar opened its doors in the autumn of 1906 with thirty-six students. The trustees shared Benedict's dream of creating a rigorous college for women comparable to the best northern women's colleges and southern colleges for men. Although academically strict, she encouraged a relaxed social atmosphere, allowing student dances and male callers on the weekends, both unprecedented in southern female education. Sweet Briar graduated its first class in 1910. Having assumed an important leadership role in higher education for southern women, Benedict in 1909 contributed a chapter on the subject to a major encyclopedia of southern history and culture.

Benedict was not naturally gregarious, preferring to work behind the scenes and shunning most public roles. Sweet Briar had problems that Benedict could not solve by herself, chief among them an insufficient endowment and an inadequate number of well-prepared students. The trustees eased the entrance requirements in order to attract more paying students, a move that struck at the heart of Benedict's goals for women's higher education. During the 1913–1914 academic year Sweet Briar had almost two hundred fifty students enrolled, but only seventy-four were taking the college course. Benedict offered her resignation in October 1914, but the trustees persuaded her to remain on the job another year. During the 1915–1916 academic year she took a leave of absence and enrolled in the medical school at Johns Hopkins University. She resigned as president of Sweet Briar in the spring of 1916 and completed her medical education and received an M.D. in 1919.

Benedict interned at Bellevue Hospital in New York City and then practiced psychiatry at Ring Sanitorium in Arlington, Massachusetts, until 1924, when she became dean of women and resident physician at the Connecticut College for Women in New London. In 1930 she opened a private medical practice in New Haven, where she remained until she retired in 1951 and moved to Glenside, Pennsylvania, to live with her sister. During the 1930s Benedict renewed her contacts with Sweet Briar and its faculty and alumnae, and in 1945 she was honored with the creation of the Mary Kendrick Benedict Scholarship. During the fiftieth anniversary Charter Day celebration at Sweet Briar on 9 February 1956, her former colleagues and students lauded her in absentia. Mary Kendrick Benedict died of a heart attack the following day, 10 February 1956, in Glenside, and was buried in nearby Huntingdon Valley.

Vassar College, alumnae bulletins, esp. 1898, 1899, 1903, 1922, 1924, and *Alumnae Biographical Register Issue* (1939), 77; Benedict files in archives of Yale University, Johns Hopkins University, and Connecticut College; *Rhetor* (State Normal School yearbook) (1906), 10, copy in Central Missouri State University Archives; Martha Lou Lemmon Stohlman, *The Story of Sweet Briar College* (1956), 68–127, 190, 233 (por. after index); Benedict documents in Sweet Briar College Archives; Mary K. Benedict, "The Higher Education of Women in the Southern States," in *The South in the Building of the Nation* (1909–1913), 10:258–271; obituaries in *Lynchburg News* and *Richmond Times-Dispatch*, both 12 Feb. 1956, and *New York Times*, 13 Feb. 1956 (por.).

CYNTHIA FARR BROWN

BENNETT, Jesse (10 July 1769–13 July 1842), physician, was born in Frankford, Philadelphia County, Pennsylvania, the eldest of two sons and one daughter of William Bennett, a merchant, and his wife, whose name has not been discovered. He was educated in Philadelphia and was later said to have attended the medical school of the University of Pennsylvania and studied medicine with Benjamin Rush, but records do not substantiate either assertion. In 1792 Bennett moved to Virginia and began his practice in Rockingham County. On 8 April 1793 he married Elizabeth Hog.

On 14 January 1794 Elizabeth Hog Bennett went into labor with her first child. When Jesse Bennett and another physician whom he had called in for advice concluded that his wife could not safely deliver the baby, Bennett proposed to perform a cesarean section, an operation that had never been successfully attempted in the United States. The other doctor refused to take part in the procedure and left. Bennett then opened his wife's uterus, extracted a baby girl, and removed his wife's ovaries. He closed the incision with linen thread. Both the baby, Maria Bennett, and the mother survived. Bennett later recorded his wife's recovery on page 71 of his copy of *Two Memoirs of the Cesarean Operation*, an 1801 English translation of Jean-Louis Baudelocque, *Recherches et réflexions sur l'opération césarienne* (1798).

Bennett refused to report the pioneering case in the medical literature. His sister-in-law Nancy Hog Hawkins recalled as his reasons that "no doctor with any feelings of delicacy would report an operation he had done on his own wife," and "no strange doctors would believe that operation could be done in the Virginia backwoods and the mother live, and he'd be damned if he would give them a chance to call him a liar." Because of Bennett's silence, medical historians long credited Ephraim McDowell with performing the first successful ovariectomy in the United States in 1809 and John L. Richmond with the first successful American cesarean section in 1827. In 1892 Aquilla Leighton Knight, who had known Bennett, published an extended essay on Bennett and his operation, which helped establish Bennett's claim to priority. In 1959 the Rockingham County Medical Society placed a plaque in the Rockingham Memorial Hospital in Harrisonburg honoring Bennett and his achievement.

The evidence for Bennett's priority is susceptible to challenge. Knight heard the story directly from Bennett and Nancy Hog Hawkins when he was a young man, but his published account of the operation appeared a half-century after Bennett's death and thus depended on recollections of long-ago conversations. The annotated translation of Baudelocque's volume on cesarean operations could not have come into Bennett's possession until at least several years after the operation, and it resurfaced in the twentieth century only after some historians of medicine had questioned Bennett's priority. The whereabouts of Bennett's journals, from which a historian had quoted in 1950, are unknown at present, making impossible a comparison with the hand that inscribed the Baudelocque volume. We do know that Elizabeth Bennett survived the birth of their daughter, who was, as Jesse Bennett said he intended, their only child.

Bennett served as a surgeon's mate in November 1794 during the suppression of the Whiskey Rebellion. In 1797 he moved west to the part of Kanawha County that in 1804 became Mason County. He served as one of Mason County's first justices of the peace, and he represented the county in the House of Delegates from 1805 to 1807. He refused an invitation to join Aaron Burr in the western adventure that led to Burr's indictment for treason in 1807. Bennett traveled to Richmond to be a witness at Burr's trial, but he was not called to testify.

Bennett served as an army surgeon again during the War of 1812. He practiced medicine into the 1820s and also became well known regionally for his profitable farm and for the high quality livestock and racehorses he bred. On 17 February 1833, three years after his wife's death, Bennett married Harriet Fowler. The marriage resulted in an estrangement from his widowed daughter, who remarried and left his home. Jesse Bennett died at Riverview, his residence in Mason County, on 13 July 1842 and was buried in a mausoleum on his property.

Aquilla L. Knight, "Life and Times of Jesse Bennett, M.D., 1769–1842," *Southern Historical Magazine* 2 (1892): 1–12; Augusta Co. Marriage Register; family history information, including photocopies of two Bennett ledgers, in

Poffenbarger Papers, West Virginia State Archives, Charleston, W.Va.; Bennett's copy of *Two Memoirs* in Joseph Lyon Miller Collection, VHS; Joseph Lyon Miller, "Dr. Jesse Bennett (1769–1842), Pioneer Surgeon. Dr. Aquilla Leighton Knight (1823–1897), Humanist," *Virginia Medical Monthly* 55 (1929): 711–714 (por.); Wyndham B. Blanton, *Medicine in Virginia in the Eighteenth Century* (1931), 17–19; Dorothy Poling, "Jesse Bennet, Pioneer Physician and Surgeon," *West Virginia History* 12 (1950): 103–128; *Harrisonburg Daily News-Record*, 26, 28 Jan. 1959; John M. Grubb, "The First Successful Cesarean Section and the First Oophorectomy in the Americas," *West Virginia Medical Journal* 80 (1984): 221–223; the most skeptical reading of the evidence is Arthur G. King, "The Legend of Jesse Bennett's 1794 Caesarean Section," *Bulletin of the History of Medicine* 50 (1976): 242–250.

E. Randolph Trice

BENNETT, Jonathan McCally (4 October 1814–28 October 1887), auditor of public accounts, was born in Lewis County, the fifth son and twelfth and last child of William Bennett and Rebecca McCally Bennett. He attended local schools and read widely but had no formal higher education. Bennett began his career in public life as a deputy sheriff in March 1836. On 18 September 1838 he qualified as deputy clerk of the Lewis County Superior Court of Law and Chancery. He studied law while working as a clerk and was admitted to the bar in April 1843. In March 1845 he became the first commonwealth's attorney of Gilmer County, and he was elected the first mayor of the town of Weston in May 1852. On 7 April 1846 he married Margaret Elizabeth Jackson. They had two sons and two daughters.

In July 1838 Bennett began buying land, eventually amassing one of the largest private estates in western Virginia. By 1850 he owned about thirty-two thousand acres in Lewis, Gilmer, and Upshur Counties, and he was part owner of another twelve thousand acres. Bennett also invested in several businesses, including the Weston and Gauley Bridge Turnpike Company, the Northwestern Virginia Railroad Corporation, and the Exchange Bank of Weston, of which he became president in 1853. Bennett was elected to the House of Delegates for the 1852–1853 session and served on the Democratic Party's state central committee from 1855 to 1857. In 1855 he contended unsuccessfully for the Democratic Party nomination for lieutenant governor, and in 1858 he narrowly lost the nomination for Congress.

On 27 July 1857 the governor, Henry Alexander Wise, appointed Bennett first auditor of public accounts to succeed George W. Clutter, who had died on 15 July. The General Assembly elected Bennett to a full term in December 1857, and he served until the end of the Civil War in April 1865. As first auditor, Bennett was the state's chief financial officer, responsible for directing the treasurer to receive and disburse all state moneys and making recommendations to the General Assembly about taxes, loans, and expenditures. During the Civil War he drastically reduced payments on the state's various debts, issued paper money, shifted military expenditures to the Confederate government, and carefully husbanded Virginia's remaining resources. In 1862 the state authorized Bennett to issue up to $1.3 million dollars in treasury notes. The five-dollar bills of that emission had Bennett's portrait on them and were known as Bennett notes. He managed Virginia's wartime finances so successfully that the state ran a budget surplus, and the General Assembly discontinued the collection of property and license taxes from March 1864 to February 1865. Bennett was widely regarded as one of the best auditors Virginia ever had.

Bennett had no qualms about taking the Confederate side during the Civil War. In the spring of 1861 he supported the appointment of his wife's cousin Thomas J. "Stonewall" Jackson, as a colonel of Virginia volunteers, and then as a brigadier general in the Confederate army. Jackson, in turn, offered Bennett a position on his staff, but he declined. With the collapse of the Confederacy in April 1865, Bennett ceased to be auditor of public accounts and became a fugitive. In July 1865 he returned to Weston, where he sought and on 11 July received a pardon from President Andrew Johnson. Bennett reclaimed his real estate, which a United States marshal had confiscated in 1863, and resumed his law practice.

In 1871 Governor John J. Jacob appointed Bennett to the West Virginia commission to attempt to resolve a dispute between Virginia and West Virginia over their respective shares of the antebellum public debt. In 1872 Bennett was elected to the Senate of West Virginia. He served as chairman of its Committee on Finance and was one of the most influential members of the legislature. After one term he retired from politics for good. He remained a busy investor and served on the board of the Weston and West Fork Railroad and as president of the Weston and Buckhannon Railroad. Jonathan McCally Bennett died in Weston, West Virginia, on 28 October 1887, and was buried in the Macpelah Cemetery in Weston.

Harvey Mitchell Rice, *The Life of Jonathan M. Bennett: A Study of the Virginias in Transition* (1943; frontispiece por.); gravestone inscription gives erroneous 1816 year of birth; Jonathan McCally Bennett Papers, WVU; Presidential Pardons; obituaries in *Richmond Dispatch*, 1 Nov. 1887, and *Charleston Virginia Free Press*, 3 Nov. 1887.

EMILY J. SALMON

BENNETT, Richard (bap. 6 August 1609–by 12 April 1675), governor of Virginia, was one of the sons of Thomas Bennett, a member of a large family of English merchants who dealt extensively in international trade during the seventeenth century. His mother's name is unknown. Bennett was probably born in or near Wivelscombe, Somersetshire, England, where he was baptized on 6 August 1609. He could scarcely have avoided being involved in the young Virginia colony. His uncle Edward Bennett, one of the great London and Amsterdam merchants, was auditor of the Virginia Company of London and in 1621 patented a large property called Bennett's Welcome near the former Indian village of Warraskoyack in what became Isle of Wight County.

In about 1628 Richard Bennett traveled to Virginia to take over management of Bennett's Welcome. Two of his uncles and a younger brother had perished in the colony, but Richard Bennett thrived and used the transatlantic influence and affluence of his family to achieve almost immediate prominence as a prosperous planter and political leader in Virginia. He lived on another of Edward Bennett's properties, Bennett's Choice, on the Nansemond River, and during the 1630s patented more than 2,000 acres of land at Bennett Point and Parraketo Point. Eventually he amassed more than 7,000 acres in Virginia and Maryland, with much of it obtained through the headright system, which awarded him a right to 50 acres for each colonist he transported to Virginia. Overall his family sponsored the immigration of approximately 600 settlers, many of them Puritans, who were to provide him a base of political influence after 1640.

Bennett's political career began with his election to the House of Burgesses as a representative from Warrosquyoake in 1629, and he became a commissioner for that district two years later. He was appointed to the governor's Council in 1642, the same year that he patented 2,000 acres along the south bank of the Rappahannock River. During the turbulent years of the English Civil Wars and Protectorate, Bennett was the highest-ranking and most active Puritan leader in the Chesapeake. With his brother Philip Bennett he recruited three Puritan ministers from the Massachusetts Bay Colony in 1642 to serve the Calvinists of Upper Norfolk County. Governor Sir William Berkeley and other Anglicans were hostile toward the Puritans, however, and made them unwelcome.

In 1646 Bennett organized a mercenary Puritan army to assist the exiled governor of Maryland, Leonard Calvert, in ousting a gang of brigands from his capital at Saint Marys City. Many of the mercenaries remained in Maryland and became the vanguard of a vast Puritan migration to that colony during the years between 1648 and 1650. Bennett's commercial and political connections by then included William Claiborne, of Virginia, and Maurice Thompson, the most influential of all the Puritan merchants of London. Throughout the period Bennett engaged in profitable commerce with England and the Netherlands.

On 26 September 1651 Oliver Cromwell's Council of State appointed Bennett and Claiborne to a four-man commission to force or negotiate the submission of the Chesapeake Bay colonies to the Commonwealth of England. Supported by a Parliamentary fleet, Bennett, Claiborne, and Edmund Curtis, who succeeded to the commission after the other two original members drowned during the transatlantic voyage, accepted Virginia's bloodless capitulation at Jamestown on 12 March 1652 and obtained the surrender of Maryland's leaders two weeks later.

The General Assembly then elected Bennett to the vacant office of governor of Virginia. He served from 30 April 1652 to 31 March 1655, with Claiborne as secretary of the colony. Their administration represented a spectacular temporary triumph for Maurice Thompson's London-based group of mercantile imperialists, which had significantly influenced the Chesapeake's commercial and political evolution since the 1620s. Hoping to achieve the elusive goal of a united, centrally administered Chesapeake, Bennett and Claiborne sought to abrogate Maryland's charter rights to the land north of the Potomac River. By appointing Protestants friendly to Virginia to offices in Maryland and placing like-minded militia colonels on the Council in Jamestown they brought a measure of stability to the Chesapeake. On 5 July 1652 Bennett and a select group of Virginia Puritan émigrés ended a decade of Indian warfare in Maryland by negotiating a comprehensive peace treaty with the powerful Susquehannocks, Claiborne's longtime business partners in the upper Chesapeake beaver trade.

Bennett's ambitious attempts to expand Virginia's political control throughout the Chesapeake region, with unprecedented authority accorded to the House of Burgesses, was a significant milestone, but such profound and rapid change was destined to be short-lived. Given the prevalent revolutionary turmoil in England, Bennett's government lacked the support it needed to withstand either the growing resentment of Virginia's planters toward the new Navigation Acts, designed as they were to terminate the profitable commerce between the colonies and the Netherlands that had helped make men like Bennett wealthy, or the resistance of Catholics and Anglicans to the ideological rigidity of the Puritan leadership in Maryland. The bloody battle of the Severn on 25 March 1655, fought between pro-Calvert and pro-Puritan forces near Bennetts's own lands at Greenbury Point, Maryland, produced such gruesome atrocities that it probably precipitated Bennett's retirement from the governor's office six days later.

It is to Bennett's credit that no such turmoil occurred in Virginia and that even political rivals with religious differences respected the peaceful succession of power at Jamestown. In December 1656 the General Assembly appointed Bennett one of its lobbyists in London, but instead of acting to increase Virginia's power, at Cromwell's instigation he helped negotiate a treaty of 30 November 1657 with Cecil Calvert, second baron Baltimore, that restored Maryland's charter rights and original boundaries. Bennett served again on the governor's Council from 1658 until his death, much of the time during the second administration of his old adversary, Sir William Berkeley. From 1662 to 1672 he also served as the second major general ever appointed in the Virginia militia and helped defend the colony against invasion during the Second Anglo-Dutch War (1672–1674).

Bennett's political designs for a greater Virginia were thwarted, but in his personal life he achieved linkages across the many divisions that separated the two Chesapeake colonies. Late in the 1630s he married Maryann Utie, widow of Councillor John Utie. Their only son, Richard Bennett, attended Harvard College, married into a prominent Catholic family in Maryland, resided there for most of his life, and had a namesake son who became one of the wealthiest planters in Maryland. Bennett's daughters chose influential husbands from both colonies. Elizabeth Bennett married Charles Scarburgh, a Puritan from the Virginia Eastern Shore, and Anna Bennett first wed Theodorick Bland, of Virginia, and then married St. Leger Codd, of Northumberland County, Virginia, and Cecil County, Maryland.

Bennett bequeathed 5,300 acres of land on Maryland's Eastern Shore to three of his grandchildren and donated 300 acres to his local parish to be applied "towards the relief of four poor, aged, or impotent persons." Richard Bennett died, probably at Bennett's Choice, between 15 March 1675, when he dated his will, and 12 April 1675, when it was proved in court.

Adventurers of Purse and Person, 639–640; William Hand Browne, ed., *Proceedings of the Council of Maryland, 1636–1667* (1885; *Archives of Maryland*, vol. 3), 264–335; Robert Brenner, *Merchants and Revolution: Commercial*

Change, Political Conflict, and London's Overseas Traders, 1550–1653 (1993), 101, 103, 143, 145, 183n, 187, 595–596; J. Frederick Fausz, "Merging and Emerging Worlds: Anglo-Indian Interest Groups and the Development of the Seventeenth-Century Chesapeake," in *Colonial Chesapeake Society*, ed. Lois Green Carr, Philip D. Morgan, and Jean B. Russo (1988), 47–98; Wilcomb E. Washburn, *Virginia Under Charles I and Cromwell, 1625–1660* (1957); at least three other Richard Bennetts lived in the Chesapeake area during his years there, leading to numerous errors in early biographies; will in Bence 99, fols. 6–7, Prerogative Court of Canterbury, Eng., printed in *WMQ*, 1st ser., 7 (1899): 307–309.

J. FREDERICK FAUSZ

BENNETT, William Wallace (24 February 1821–9 June 1887), president of Randolph-Macon College, was born in Richmond, a younger member of the large family of Ely Bennett and Mary C. Warrock Bennett. In 1841 he moved to Mecklenburg County to study for the ministry with his brother John R. Bennett, a Methodist minister. He was admitted as a preacher on trial in 1842 and after serving in rural circuits in Bedford, Louisa, and Powhatan Counties, he was assigned to Charlottesville in 1847.

Bennett entered the University of Virginia in 1849 and took classes in modern languages, moral philosophy, natural philosophy, physiology, anatomy, and surgery. The faculty elected him chaplain in 1851, but he resigned soon afterward as a result of sickness. Bennett served as an itinerant minister for a short time and from 1854 to 1858 was presiding elder of the Washington District. He married Virginia Lee Sangster on 20 December 1855. Their three sons and three daughters included the wife of Methodist clergyman James Cannon Jr., who became the foremost Prohibition leader in Virginia.

During the Civil War Bennett headed the Soldiers' Tract Society and served from 1862 to 1864 as a chaplain in the Confederate army. He ran the blockade in 1864 and went to England to obtain more tracts to distribute to soldiers. He preached in the Nottoway District immediately after the war and then from January 1867 to February 1878 edited and published the Virginia Conference's journal, the *Richmond Christian Advocate*, which he owned entirely. In addition to rescuing the journal from financial jeopardy, Bennett used his editorial position to defend southern Methodism while taking occasional swipes at northern crime, at alcohol, and at the Catholic Church. He urged his readers to give greater financial support to the paper and the Methodist Church. In 1873 he joined several Richmond partners in editing the monthly *Journal of Industry*, devoted, according to its masthead, to agriculture, horticulture, immigration, manufactures, and commerce. The magazine survived for twelve monthly issues.

Bennett also wrote extensively on church history during the 1870s. He published *Memorials of Methodism in Virginia, From its Introduction into the State in the Year 1772 to the Year 1829* (1871), *Narrative of the Great Revival Which Prevailed in the Southern Armies During the Late Civil War Between the States of the Federal Union* (1877), and *A History of Methodism, for Our Young People* (1878), and he wrote an unpublished book on Native Americans, "Our Brother In Red." Bennett also helped found the post–Civil War Prohibition movement in Virginia. During the 1880s he edited and published a Prohibition journal, the *Southern Crusader*, and in 1885 he published a trenchant pamphlet, *The Great Red Dragon: An Appeal to Plain People on the Evils and Dangers of the Liquor Traffic*.

In June 1867 Bennett received an honorary D.D. from Randolph-Macon College in Ashland. He became a trustee the next year and was elected president of the board on 4 October 1877, serving until his resignation in June 1882. On 19 November 1877 the trustees selected Bennett to succeed James A. Duncan as president of the college. Like the Methodist journal he had helped save, this Methodist college was financially imperiled. Its annual income was under $12,000, and its debt exceeded $20,000, mostly financed at 8 or 9 percent annual interest. The student body consisted of a hundred or more students, but many of them were sons of Methodist ministers who attended free of tuition. Only about half of each class typically paid tuition, which was the school's principal source of revenue. Bennett appealed personally and successfully to Methodist congregations for donations. He paid off the debt by 1881, in part through raising funds and in part by using students to assist the five-member faculty, which saved money on salaries but drove some students away.

Unlike some of his predecessors, Bennett preferred that the faculty consist of Methodists, and some faculty members left during his tenure as president. Beginning in 1883 he had several of the old frame buildings of the campus pulled down and replaced with ten cottages that collectively housed up to eighty students. At his request, in 1886 the trustees required physical education for all students. He had failed to gain board approval in 1880 for a preparatory school as part of a plan to increase college enrollment, however, and in 1883 his proposal that the college take a tentative step toward coeducation by giving women examinations, presumably for course credit or some sort of certification, garnered no support from the trustees or faculty. Bennett had a brusque manner, and he may have occasionally displayed more courage than tact. Nevertheless, a college prize in history was named for him, his name is on a dormitory, and his portrait hangs in the trustees' board room.

William Wallace Bennett resigned as president of Randolph-Macon College effective 1 September 1886, because of ill health, and he died on 9 June 1887 at Woodbourne, his house near Trevilians in Louisa County. He was buried in Hollywood Cemetery in Richmond.

W. W. Bennett Papers, including unpublished manuscripts, Blackwell Papers, and Randolph-Macon College Board of Trustees Minutes, all in Randolph-Macon College Library, Ashland; Richard Irby, *History of Randolph-Macon College* (1898), 265–286, 295–303; James Edward Scanlon, *Randolph-Macon College: A Southern History, 1825–1967* (1983), 150, 152, 176–178, 189–190, 213–219 (por.), 230, 259, 381; obituaries in *Richmond State*, 9 June 1887, *Richmond Dispatch* and *Richmond Whig*, both 10 June 1887, and *Richmond Christian Advocate*, 16 June 1887, all with 9 June 1887 death date; memorial by F. J. Boggs in Virginia Annual Conference of Methodist Episcopal Church South, *Minutes* 105 (1887): 100–105, with 7 June 1887 death date.

JAMES EDWARD SCANLON

BERKELEY, Edmund (ca. 1671–by 3 March 1719), member of the Council, was probably born in Gloucester County, the only son and elder of two children of Edmund Berkeley and Mary Kempe Berkeley. He was possibly the same Edmund Berkeley who gave testimony in an English chancery proceeding early in 1697, stating that he was "aged 25, born in Virginia." Berkeley's father, the immigrant and founder of the Virginia Berkeleys, likely came from one of the merchant families of that surname in England. He may have been a son of alderman William Berkeley, of London, the descendant of a Shrewsbury family and himself the son of an Edmund Berkeley. By the time of his death early in the 1670s, the immigrant had purchased a significant amount of land and was probably engaged in commerce. Berkeley's mother married John Mann sometime before 1 May 1674.

Edmund Berkeley and his sister were raised with their younger half sister at the home of their stepfather in Gloucester County. Berkeley presumably received his education there. When he came of age he began acquiring land in Gloucester and Middlesex Counties and elsewhere. In 1702 he purchased land on the Piankatank River in Middlesex County, and his mother left him the remainder of her estate when she died in 1704. On 10 February 1707 he purchased 2,000 acres in King William County, and five years later he added an adjoining tract of 1,632 acres, holdings that remained in the family for several generations.

On 1 December 1703 Berkeley married twenty-year-old Lucy Burwell after she had rejected the proposals of Governor Francis Nicholson, whose intemperate pursuit of her offended many influential Virginians and helped enable the governor's enemies in Virginia and England to have him recalled from office. The Berkeleys had two sons and one daughter and lived in Petsworth Parish in Gloucester County. William Byrd (1674–1744) recorded a number of pleasant visits to the household and described Berkeley in May 1709 as "a very good humored man." In 1712 or early in 1713 Berkeley moved his family to lands on the Piankatank River in Middlesex County that he called Barn Elms. There he prospered financially and became a prominent local citizen. He was appointed county lieutenant late in 1715 and was elected to the vestry of Christ Church Parish in 1717.

Berkeley's influence in England through his family connections and his business partners, perhaps including London merchant Micajah Perry, brought him to the attention of George Hamilton, earl of Orkney, absentee governor of the colony, who recommended him to the Board of Trade on 23 July 1713 for appointment to the governor's Council. Queen Anne issued an order to that effect on 8 August and sent it to Virginia that autumn. Berkeley argued that he should be given seniority on the Council from the date of the queen's letter and warrant, rather than from the date on which he was sworn in. Three other members had joined the Council in the interim, and Berkeley insisted on being ranked ahead of them. The issue was disputed in Virginia and England for more than a year until the Board of Trade issued new instructions to the lieutenant governor, which included a list of councillors and specifically ordered that Berkeley's name be placed last. Berkeley conceded and was finally sworn in as a member of the Council on 7 December 1715. He attended meetings only irregularly.

Edmund Berkeley completed and signed his last will on 14 December 1718. At that time he employed several white servants and owned several slaves, a considerable quantity of silver, "his own and Ladies pictures, Eleven house pictures," and about 100 books. He died before 3 March 1719, when his will was proved in the Middlesex County Court. He was undoubtedly buried at Barn Elms, although no stone survives to mark his grave.

Frances Berkeley Young, *The Berkeleys of Barn Elms* (1964), 1–27; Berkeley Family Papers, UVA; marriage date in Berkeley family Bible record, LVA; variant marriage date of 1 Dec. 1704 can be inferred from wife's epitaph; Francis Lewis Berkeley, "The Berkeleys of Barn Elms, Planters of Colonial Virginia, and A Calendar of the Berkeley Papers, 1653–1767, in the Alderman Library, University of Virginia" (master's thesis, UVA, 1940); 1697 testimony in PRO C 24/1195/32; Fairfax Downey, "The Governor Goes A-Wooing: The Swashbuckling Courtship of Nicholson of Virginia, 1699–1705," *VMHB* 55 (1947): 6–19; Churchill G. Chamberlayne, ed., *The Vestry Book of Christ Church Parish, Middlesex County, Virginia, 1663–1767* (1927), 159; Louis B. Wright and Marion Tinling, eds., *The Secret Diary of William Byrd of Westover, 1709–1712* (1941), 30; PRO CO 391/105–106; PRO Privy Council Office 2/84, fols. 219–220; *Executive Journals of Council*, 3:366, 417–418, 491; Middlesex Co. Will Book, B:112–115, 138–148.

EDMUND BERKELEY JR.

BERKELEY, Edmund (5 December 1730–8 July 1802), planter and member of the Convention of 1776, was a grandson of Councillor Edmund Berkeley and his strong-willed wife, Lucy Burwell Berkeley. He was born at Barn Elms, the family seat in Middlesex County, the elder of two sons and second of five children of Edmund Berkeley and Mary Nelson Berkeley. He was often referred to as Edmund Berkeley of Barn Elms to distinguish him from several contemporary namesake cousins and nephews.

On 6 November 1757 Berkeley married Judith Randolph, of Tuckahoe. They had one son and two daughters before her death in April 1763, of whom the son and one daughter died young. On 23 January 1768 he married Mary Burwell, of Carter's Grove. Three of their five sons and all four of their daughters lived to maturity. Following his father's death in 1767, Berkeley was named to succeed him on the Middlesex County Court. A busy planter and unambitious politician, he delayed taking the oath of office as a justice until 24 September 1770. On 24 June 1771 he was sworn in as a vestryman of Christ Church Parish, and on 26 August 1771 he became a colonel in the county militia.

Berkeley inherited considerable landed wealth and managed it profitably. During his long stewardship of Barn Elms the plantation prospered. When Berkeley's estate was inventoried after his death, it consisted of more than 300 slaves and 6,250 acres of land in five tracts in Middlesex, Caroline, King William, and Prince William Counties. In 1802 his taxable land, slaves, livestock, farm implements, and household goods were valued at approximately $90,000.

Late in July 1771 Berkeley won a special election to succeed Philip Ludwell Grymes in the House of Burgesses, and he attended the assemblies of 1772, 1773, 1774, and 1775 without attracting much notice. In May 1774 he signed the call for the first of five Revolutionary Conventions that met from 1774 to 1776. Berkeley was elected to represent Middlesex County at all of the conventions, but missed the third convention and the all-important fifth, which voted for independence and unanimously adopted the Declaration of Rights and the first constitution of Virginia. His participation in the other three conventions, insofar as the fragmentary surviving journals and papers show, was distinctly limited. By virtue of his election to the last convention, Berkeley was eligible to sit in the first House of Delegates in October 1776, but he may have missed most or all of the session.

Berkeley remained on the county court and eventually became the senior justice. He presided for the last time on 24 October 1797, after which he was excused on account of "age and infirmity." Edmund Berkeley died on 8 July 1802 and was probably buried at Barn Elms.

Berkeley family Bible record, LVA; *The Parish Register of Christ Church, Middlesex County, Va., from 1653 to 1812* (1897), 130, 198; Berkeley Family Papers, UVA; Frances Berkeley Young, *The Berkeleys of Barn Elms* (1964), 40–43, 103–104; Middlesex Co. Will Book, 2:148–149, 167–168, 249–256; death described in letter by Carter B. Berkeley, 11 July 1802, Berkeley Family Papers.

BRENT TARTER

BERKELEY, Frances Culpeper Stephens (bap. 27 May 1634–ca. 1695), best known as Lady Frances Berkeley and leader of the Green Spring faction, was the youngest of two sons and three daughters of Thomas Culpeper and Katherine St. Leger Culpeper. She was born in England and baptized at Hollingbourne Church, Kent, on 27 May 1634. Her parents were related to several families interested in the colony of Virginia, and in 1623 her father had become a member of the Virginia Company of London. In 1649 he was made one of the original patentees of the Northern Neck.

Frances Culpeper accompanied her parents to Virginia about 1650. Sometime early in 1653, at the age of eighteen, she married Captain Samuel Stephens, who in October 1667 became governor of the Albemarle settlements. After Stephens died in December 1669, she petitioned the General Court of Virginia for possession of a 1,350-acre plantation in Warwick County called Bolthrope, or Boldrup. An agreement she made with Stephens before their marriage had stipulated that she inherit the property, and because they had no children, the widow received absolute possession of the estate.

As was typical for a widow in seventeenth-century Virginia, particularly for one who could bring both valuable family connections and substantial property to a prospective husband, Frances Culpeper Stephens did not remain unmarried for long. Sometime between 19 May and 21 June 1670, she wed Sir William Berkeley, a childless widower then serving the second of his two long terms as governor of Virginia. The marriage allied the governor even more closely with his old friends and associates in the Culpeper family, and it increased Lady Berkeley's prestige. The marriage gave her the opportunity to play a greater role in Virginia society and politics. The Berkeleys lived near Jamestown at Green Spring, the governor's manor house, where they entertained members of the Council and House of Burgesses. Among the guests were their distant relations, Nathaniel Bacon (1647–1676) and his wife Elizabeth Duke Bacon, who arrived in Virginia in the summer of 1674.

During Bacon's Rebellion in 1676, certainly the most difficult episode of Sir William Berkeley's administration, Lady Berkeley vigorously supported her husband and his policies, garnering praise from his supporters and bitter opposition from his enemies. In June 1676, at a low point for the governor in his political contest with Bacon, she went to England as his personal emissary to the king. She returned to Virginia early in 1677 with Herbert Jeffreys, one of the royal commissioners sent to investigate the rebellion and succeed her husband as governor, and more than a thousand English troops. After the rebellion Sir Francis Moryson, another of the royal commissioners, asked Lady Berkeley to secure a pardon for a man named Jones whom the governor had condemned. Her success in obtaining it demonstrated the strength of her influence to the commissioners.

The commissioners were exceptionally critical of Governor Berkeley's conduct during and after the rebellion, and Berkeley did not always cooperate with them. When two of the commissioners paid their formal farewell visit to the Berkeleys in May 1677, they found that the colony's hangman had been sent to drive their coach. Noting that Lady Berkeley had "peeped" through a window to "see how the show looked," they concluded that she had planned the insulting trick.

After Sir William Berkeley's return to England and his death on 9 July 1677, Lady Berkeley continued to promote her own political interests. She became a leader of the so-called Green Spring faction that met at the Berkeley mansion and included Thomas Ballard (d. 1690), Robert Beverley (1635–1687), Edward Hill, and Philip Ludwell. For the next two years the faction constituted the most powerful political group in Virginia and was often at odds with Governor Jeffreys. With the arrival of Governor Culpeper in 1680, Lady Berkeley's political influence began to decline, although her interest in politics never waned. She persisted for years in efforts to collect the salary that Berkeley was owed at the time of his death, and she enlisted the assistance of the General Assembly in the effort.

By about 1680 Lady Berkeley had married a third time, to Philip Ludwell, secretary of the colony. He eventually became deputy governor of North Carolina (1689–1693) and South Carolina (1693–1694). Although less involved in Virginia politics, Lady Berkeley, as she continued to be called, occasionally petitioned the House of Burgesses on Ludwell's behalf as he managed legal business begun by Governor Berkeley. The couple spent most of their time in Virginia and had a pew built for themselves in Bruton Parish Church. Other Virginians, such as William Byrd (1652–1704) and William Fitzhugh, commented on Lady Berkeley's influence and entrusted information and documents to her care. Her vigorous convictions, lively temperament, and shrewd mind made her a valuable friend and ally and one of the most influential Virginians of her time.

Lady Berkeley is not known to have had any children, although she may have been pregnant at the time of her marriage to Ludwell, and Ludwell's two children from his first marriage lived with them at Green Spring. On 26 February 1684, when she was almost fifty years old, Byrd wrote that Lady Berkeley was "not yet brought to bed" and questioned whether she was, in fact, with child. Later in the same year Byrd again remarked that she was indisposed because of pregnancy but could not say when she might deliver.

Frances Culpeper Stephens Berkeley Ludwell probably died at Green Spring or Jamestown about 1695. A fragment of her gravestone in the cemetery on Jamestown Island bears a partially legible inscription.

Family history in Fairfax Harrison, "Proprietors of the Northern Neck," *VMHB* 33 (1925): 343–358 (por. opp. 352); *Minutes of Council and General Court*, 211, 219, 514; Hening, *Statutes*, 2:321–325; Warren M. Billings, "Berkeley and Effingham: Who Cares?," *VMHB* 97 (1989): 39–41; Sir William Berkeley to Coventry, 1 July 1676, and Petition of Lady Berkeley, [1676], along with others of her letters in vols. 77–78, Coventry Papers, Longleat House, Wiltshire, Eng., Cunliffe-Lister Muniments, bundle 69, North Yorkshire County Record Office, Northallerton, Eng., and Filmer Manuscripts, Kent Archives, Maidstone, Eng.; PRO CO 5/1371, pt. 2:178–179, 180–181; PRO CO 1/40, fols. 61–63, 130–131; Wilcomb E. Washburn, *The Governor and the Rebel: A History of Bacon's Rebellion in Virginia* (1957), 48, 102, 120, 131, 222; *Journals of House of Burgesses, 1659/60–1693*, 115–116, 123, 125, 134, 344; Marion Tinling, ed., *The Correspondence of the Three William Byrds of Westover, Virginia, 1684–1776* (1977), 1:12–13, 17.

TERRI L. SNYDER

BERKELEY, John (ca. 1560–22 March 1622), member of the Council, the only son and one of four children of Sir John Berkeley and his first wife Frances Poyntz Berkeley, was probably born at the family estate, Beverstone Castle in Gloucestershire, England. The Berkeley family had once owned more than thirty manors in eight shires, but by the time of Berkeley's father's death in October 1582, the family estate had been reduced to the one property of Beverstone Castle and Manor. On 6 November 1582 Berkeley married Mary Snell at Kington Saint Michael in Wiltshire, and by the time he left England for Virginia they had six sons and four daughters. The family fortunes continued to decline until at least 1597, when Berkeley sold Beverstone Castle to a cousin and disappeared from the public record for more than twenty years.

During that time Berkeley may have worked as an iron manufacturer, perhaps in collaboration with his Poyntz relatives. His experience in iron smelting and forging brought him to the attention of the Virginia Company of London in

1621. A major goal for the colony of Virginia had been the establishment of a productive and profitable ironworks. Even after the expenditure of more than £4,000 sterling and the sending of more than 150 workmen to Virginia, that hope had not been realized, and the most recent ironmaster, Benjamin Bluett, had been murdered within months of his arrival. In a May 1621 contract similar to that offered Bluett, Berkeley agreed that he would provide 20 skilled men to serve the company for seven years in exchange for a grant of 800 acres of land, £50 to cover his expenses, and free transportation and support for his team for one year. Berkeley's party, including his eldest son, Maurice Berkeley, and three family servants, sailed from the Isle of Wight for Virginia about 25 June 1621.

On 24 July 1621, even before he reached the colony, Berkeley was appointed to the governor's Council. His overall attendance record is unknown, but he went to at least one meeting. When he arrived in the colony, he went almost immediately to the ironworks at Falling Creek, located in what is now Chesterfield County. He found "wood, water, mynes, and stone" at the site, wrote the company that "a more fit place for Iron-workes . . . was not to be found," and promised that by Easter 1622 he would be producing large quantities of high-quality iron. He did not live to fulfill his promise. John Berkeley and twenty-six other persons at the ironworks died in the Indians' concerted uprising of 22 March 1622. The Powhatans damaged much of the equipment at the ironworks and threw some of it into the James River.

Maurice Berkeley, who had been placed in charge of the colony's saltworks in January 1622, survived because he was not at Falling Creek when the Indians attacked. In August 1622 he took charge of the few remaining ironworkers. In January 1623 the Council was considering reinforcing the defenses of the ironworks, but because of the loss of so many of the principal workmen the plan was not put into effect. Shortly afterward Maurice Berkeley returned to England, where in November 1623 his petition to be released from the remainder of his seven-year term of service to the company was granted. The loss of the ironworks, for which John Berkeley had expressed high hopes and in which as much as £5,000 had by then been invested, was one of the financial disasters that soon thereafter reduced the Virginia Company to bankruptcy.

John Smyth of Nibley, *The Berkeley Manuscripts: The Lives of the Berkeleys, Lords of the Honour, Castle and Manor of Berkeley in the County of Gloucester from 1066 to 1618* (1883), 1:85, 353, 355–356, 2:235, 239, 3:100–110; approximate year of birth inferred from marriage date; Eric Gethyn-Jones, *George Thorpe and The Berkeley Company: A Gloucestershire Enterprise in Virginia* (1982), 136–137; Kingsbury, *Virginia Company*, 1:472, 475, 476, 2:497, 3:483, 4:12; Edward Waterhouse, *A Declaration of the State of the Colony in Virginia* (1622), 9–10, 20, 35; Charles E. Hatch Jr. and Thurlow Gates Gregory, "The First American Blast Furnace, 1619–1622: The Birth of a Mighty Industry on Falling Creek in Virginia," *VMHB* 70 (1962): 258–296.

J. FREDERICK FAUSZ

BERKELEY, Lucy Burwell. See **BURWELL, Lucy**.

BERKELEY, Norborne, baron de Botetourt. See **BOTETOURT, Norborne Berkeley, baron de**.

BERKELEY, Norborne (31 March 1828–12 January 1911), Confederate army officer and member of the Convention of 1867–1868, was born in Aldie in Loudoun County, the third of four sons and third of five children of Lewis Berkeley and Frances Callender Noland Berkeley. After attending Episcopal High School near Alexandria, Berkeley entered the Virginia Military Institute. Shortly after his graduation in 1848, he was appointed brigade inspector and assigned for a year to train and drill the Virginia militia.

On 4 December 1849 Berkeley married his relative Lavinia Hart Berkeley, the eldest daughter of Edmund Berkeley and Mary Randolph Spotswood Berkeley, of Staunton. They raised their four sons at Berkeley's Loudoun County farm. On the eve of the Civil War, Berkeley organized and drilled an infantry company, the Champe Rifles, which later became Company D of the 8th Regiment Virginia Infantry. On 8 May 1861 the regiment was organized and taken into service with Berkeley as major. He took charge of much of the early training of the regiment at Leesburg. On 27 April 1862 he was promoted to lieutenant colonel, and he became a colonel on 9 August 1863.

Berkeley was in action at both Battles of Manassas (Bull Run), Balls Bluff, the Seven Days' Battles, and Antietam, among other engagements. The heavy fighting in which it frequently participated won the regiment the "Bloody Eighth" as its nickname, but because Berkeley and his three brothers all became field officers in the regiment, it was also referred to sometimes as the Berkeley Regiment.

After being shot in the foot and right hip during Pickett's Charge, Berkeley was captured at the Battle of Gettysburg on 3 July 1863. As a prisoner of war, he was taken to the hospital at Point Lookout, Maryland, then to Chester, Pennsylvania, and finally to Johnson's Island, near Sandusky, Ohio. On 18 March 1864 he was exchanged and returned to duty, but he was frequently hospitalized with dysentery and later suffered a severe case of boils. Berkeley resigned on 2 March 1865 because of chronic rheumatism. He applied for a presidential pardon on 10 July 1865 and received it on 16 August after Governor Francis H. Pierpont enthusiastically endorsed the application.

Berkeley returned to his farm. On 22 October 1867 the voters in Loudoun County elected him to the constitutional convention that met in Richmond from 3 December 1867 to 17 April 1868. He served on the Committees on Rules and on Military Affairs but evidently did not play a significant role in the convention's deliberations. On 10 January 1868 he asked Francis Henney Smith, superintendent of the Virginia Military Institute, for a copy of a pamphlet that he could use to help defeat a resolution that would have abolished VMI. Smith appeared before the committee to denounce the resolution, which the committee duly killed. Berkeley often voted against changes sought by the reformers, and on the convention's final day he voted against the new constitution.

In January 1872, when the Virginia militia was reorganized, the General Assembly appointed Berkeley a brigadier general, but he preferred to go by the title of colonel that he had earned at Gettysburg. On 15 February 1876 he joined the faculty of the new Virginia Agricultural and Mechanical College as manager of its farm. He retired from the position in 1879 after the death of his wife. While in Blacksburg, Berkeley served as a lay reader and vestryman of the local Episcopal Church. In 1885 he moved to Pendleton, Oregon, to live with his son Norborne Berkeley. While living in Oregon, Berkeley may have continued his involvement in agriculture. He returned to Virginia ten or fifteen years later, and by 1899 was living with his brother Edmund Berkeley at Evergreen in Prince William County.

Norborne Berkeley lived the life of a retired Virginia gentleman farmer thereafter until his death at Evergreen on 12 January 1911. He was buried in the cemetery of the Episcopal church in Haymarket, Prince William County.

Letters, family history records, por., and unpublished memoir, "The Civil War Reminiscences of Norborne Berkeley," Berkeley Family Papers, UVA; biographical and alumni files, including short autobiographical statement, VMI; Compiled Service Records; Norborne Berkeley, "Eighth Virginia's Part in Second Manassas," *Southern Historical Society Papers* 37 (1909): 313–316; John E. Divine, *The Eighth Virginia Infantry*, 2d ed. (1984); Presidential Pardons; tenure at Virginia Agricultural and Mechanical College documented in various collections at VPI; two 1883 letters in William Mahone Papers, Duke; *Fairfax Herald*, 3 June 1904 (por.); obituary in *Fredericksburg Free Lance*, 17 Jan. 1911; memorials in *Confederate Veteran* 19 (1911): 298, 539.

JOHN B. STRAW

BERKELEY, Randolph Carter (9 January 1875–31 January 1960), recipient of the Medal of Honor, was born in Staunton, the youngest of three sons and a daughter of Carter Berkeley, a physician, and Lovie Jane Gilkeson Berkeley. He attended local schools and studied at the Potomac Academy in Alexandria during the academic year 1890–1891. For seven years he worked in a succession of jobs and was the secretary to the Washington agent of the Richmond and Danville Railroad Company when the Spanish-American War broke out. Berkeley was commissioned a second lieutenant in the United States Marines on 8 August 1898. He was stationed at the Washington Navy Yard during the war and was discharged on 9 January 1899.

Berkeley rejoined the Marine Corps as a first lieutenant in April 1899 and served continuously for almost forty years. Assigned to the USS *Oregon* in October 1899, he was stationed in China during the Boxer Rebellion. He was promoted to captain in July 1900, and from 1901 until August 1902 he commanded a contingent of marines aboard the USS *Helena*, a gunboat that patrolled Chinese rivers and coastal areas. From 1904 to 1906 he was stationed in Panama, the Dominican Republic, and Cuba. After his return to the United States, Berkeley married Carrie Anna Phillips in Shepherdstown, West Virginia, on 12 September 1906. She died in 1907 following the birth of a son, James Phillips Berkeley. On 2 October 1911 Berkeley married Bessye Bancroft Russell in New London, Connecticut. They also had one son, Randolph Carter Berkeley Jr. Both children followed their father into the Marine Corps and attained high rank, with James Phillips Berkeley rising to lieutenant general and Randolph Carter Berkeley Jr. becoming a colonel.

During the 1907–1908 global tour of the so-called Great White Fleet, Berkeley commanded a marine detachment aboard the battleship *Kentucky*. He was stationed in thc Philippines and China between 1908 and 1910, and in October 1910 he was promoted to major. In December 1913 Berkeley took command of the 1st Battalion, 2d Advance Base Regiment at Pensacola, Florida. President Woodrow Wilson ordered Berkeley's regiment and others to Vera Cruz, Mexico, in April 1914 in a show of force following the arrest there of American naval personnel. During two days of street fighting on 21 and 22 April, Berkeley personally led his marines against Mexican positions with such skill that his unit suffered minimal casualties. On 4 December 1915 Berkeley was awarded the Medal of Honor for his "distinguished conduct in battle" at Vera Cruz. The citation credited Berkeley with being "eminent and conspicuous in command" and for exhibiting "cool judgment and courage."

When the United States entered World War I, Berkeley was stationed in Guam. He returned to America in November 1917 and spent the next two years at the marine barracks in New York and at Charleston, South Carolina. Berkeley was promoted to colonel in July 1918 and was stationed in Haiti with the 1st Provisional Marine Brigade from 1919 to 1921. He spent most of the remainder of his career at various East Coast posts. He completed a one-year field officers' course at the Marine Corps Schools at Quantico Marine Corps Base in Quantico in August 1925 and spent the next year at the Army War College in Washington, D.C. Following his promotion to brigadier general in July 1930 he commanded the Marine Corps Schools at Quantico for one year. As the first general to hold that post, he initiated a major overhaul of the teaching of amphibious landing tactics. Berkeley was sent to Nicaragua on several missions between 1927 and 1933, ultimately commanding the 2d Marine Brigade there and overseeing the final withdrawal of marines from that country. For his various tours of duty in Nicaragua he received the Navy Cross, the Navy Distinguished Service Medal, and three Nicaraguan decorations. From January 1933 to May 1936 he commanded the marine barracks at Parris Island, South Carolina, and from 1936 until December 1938 he served as president of the Marinc Corps Examining and Retiring Board in Washington.

Randolph Carter Berkeley retired with the rank of major general in February 1939. He lived in Beaufort and Port Royal, South Carolina, until he died in the navy hospital in Beaufort on 31 January 1960. He was buried in Arlington National Cemetery. The navy commissioned the guided missile destroyer *Berkeley* in his honor in 1961.

Unpublished biography, Feb. 1960, including service history and Medal of Honor citation, U.S. Marine Corps History and Museums Division, Washington, D.C.; *NCAB*, 50:87–88 (por.); Kenneth J. Clifford, *Progress and Purpose: A Developmental History of the United States Marine Corps, 1900–1970* (1973), 43–44; obituaries in *New York Times*, *Richmond Times-Dispatch*, and *Staunton Leader*, all 1 Feb. 1960.

DONALD W. GUNTER

BERKELEY, Sir William (1605–9 July 1677), governor of Virginia, was born at Hanworth Manor, the home of his maternal grandparents, in Middlesex County, England, the fourth of five sons and sixth of seven children of Sir Maurice

Berkeley and Elizabeth Killigrew Berkeley. His father owned large properties near his home in Bruton, Somersetshire, as well as in Gloucestershire and London, and sat in Parliament on several occasions before his death in 1617. William Berkeley rose to maturity secure in every benefit of his privileged station. On 14 February 1623 he enrolled at Oxford University, where he earned an A.B. in 1624 and an A.M. in 1629 and was elected a fellow of Merton College. He completed his schooling with two or three years of legal studies at the Middle Temple and a two-year European tour.

When he returned to England, Berkeley sought a career at the court of Charles I. His elder brother, Sir Charles Berkeley, and his first cousin Henry Jermyn secured his appointment in 1632 as a gentleman of the king's privy chamber. The position afforded entrée to royal service, proximity to the monarch, and chances to forge useful relationships. Berkeley joined a circle of poets and playwrights surrounding Queen Henrietta Maria and wrote at least five plays, including *The Lost Lady* (1638), which was performed for the king and queen.

Berkeley gravitated politically toward the moderate royalists. Charles I bestowed rewards on him, including a monopoly on the sale of ice and snow, a reversion of the post of treasurer of the Court of Common Pleas, and several pensions. Secretary of State Sir John Coke sent Berkeley to the Netherlands to persuade the queen's mother, Marie de Medici, not to visit England for fear that her presence would aggravate the king's mounting political difficulties. Berkeley also took part in the Bishops' Wars, for which he received his knighthood at Berwick-upon-Tweed on 12 July 1639.

With England drifting into civil war, Berkeley found his situation in the spring of 1641 unpromising. His relative Sir Thomas Roe suggested a diplomatic posting to Constantinople. About to leave for Turkey, Berkeley seized another opportunity, the Virginia governorship. He somehow induced Sir Francis Wyatt to sell his office and entreated the king to appoint him in Wyatt's place. Charles complied and on 9 August 1641 named Berkeley governor and captain general of the colony.

Like many other immigrants who prospered, Berkeley had a competitive edge when he arrived in 1642: a labor supply and ready access to land. He shipped a contingent of servants with him, and his office entitled him to lease a large plot in James City County known as the Governor's Land, where he raised his first crop of tobacco. Berkeley quickly began accumulating acreage, including a tract known as Green Spring, five miles west of Jamestown. After he acquired Green Spring as a country retreat in 1643, he conducted numerous agricultural trials there searching for substitutes for tobacco. His experiments yielded swift returns. Within five years Berkeley was exporting rice, spirits, fruit, silk, flax, and potash through an extensive network of English, Dutch, West Indian, and colonial merchants. In 1650 he married, but the identity of his wife has never been determined.

Berkeley immersed himself in real estate development and the Indian trade, which led to an interest in developing Jamestown and exploring land beyond Virginia's frontiers. The king ordered him to build Jamestown into a thriving city, which he attempted with only modest results. He achieved more success by encouraging Edward Bland to scout what is now western North Carolina, and he himself explored the Albemarle Sound region. As governor he could have monopolized the Indian trade, but he preferred to bolster the activities of experienced traders and share in their profits at little expense to himself.

Berkeley inherited a troubled colony in troubled times. His survival depended on his ability to navigate between rival factions of Virginians and at the same time carry out the king's commands. He plotted his course during his first years in office with a deftness that belied his inexperience, and he succeeded in following his instructions from the Crown while keeping it at arm's length and not unduly agitating the Puritans. Sizing up colonial politics, Berkeley determined to win the allegiance of leading planters by making common cause with them in opposition to proposals to revive the Virginia Company. He favored planters with offices and ample lands, even those with Puritan leanings or those who challenged his leadership. His willingness to share power enabled the General Assembly to grow into a miniature parliament, abetted a decentralization of authority from province to county, and all but guaranteed the emerging elite an unlimited right of local rule.

On two occasions Berkeley could have moved from Virginia but chose to stay. He returned to England in June 1644 to buy arms to prosecute the colony's war against the Indians. Like his brother Sir John Berkeley he could have pressed Charles for a field command, but instead he hurried back to America. A second opportunity arose in 1652, when he gave Virginia up to the Parliamentarians. Berkeley staunchly avowed Virginia's loyalty to the Stuarts after Charles I perished on the block. He put on a bold show when Oliver Cromwell's Commonwealth sent a fleet to subdue the colony, but drew back at the prospect of spilling blood and negotiated a conciliatory agreement in the spring of 1652 that left Virginia's social and political establishment intact and largely free of outside meddling. The treaty of surrender called for Berkeley to dispose of his property and leave the colony, but he connived with his Puritan successors, convincing them to ignore the agreement and let him live in retirement at Green Spring.

During the next eight years Berkeley enlarged his house, continued his crop trials, and strengthened his commercial ties abroad. All the while, he remained on good terms with Puritan Virginians while maintaining contact with the exiled Charles II and hoping for the king's restoration. The sudden death of Governor Samuel Mathews in January 1660 opened the door to Berkeley's restoration to the governor's office in March. Berkeley went back to England in 1661 to mount his campaign for royal support. His brothers and friends assured him of a ready hearing at court, as did his seat on the newly created Council for Foreign Plantations. Berkeley lobbied publicly and privately for almost a year, and he wrote and published *Discourse and View of Virginia*, which put forth his prescriptions for improving Virginia. He achieved something less than he intended. The king affirmed the concept of diversification but refused to offer any financial support. Charles also warmed to the possibility of limiting the role of tobacco in Virginia's economy and encouraged the building of towns throughout the colony.

In September 1662 Berkeley returned to Virginia steadfastly determined to implement the king's commandments, though in his own way. In the first of a series of misjudgments and misfortunes that eventually destroyed him, his program of diversification failed. Few Virginians matched Berkeley's wealth, his technical competence, or his depth of commitment, and he could not convince the dubious to follow him. Their doubts intensified as they bore the expense of the increased taxes that underwrote the effort. Diversification was largely abandoned late in the 1660s, although Berkeley held to his convictions. He negotiated a so-called "stint" on tobacco cultivation, but Lord Baltimore vetoed it, and the Crown eventually withdrew its tentative endorsement of the proposal.

Berkeley neither accepted nor acceded to Stuart imperialism, choosing instead to ignore it as much as possible. He appreciated none of the underpinnings of Restoration colonial policy. Meanwhile, his friends at court lost their influence with the king. By the 1670s their departure left him few defenders at Whitehall. Charles II and his younger advisers owed him nothing and thought of him as something of a nuisance, if they thought of him at all. Nevertheless, they chose not to remove him until Bacon's Rebellion gave them a reason.

Events overtook Berkeley. The governor had not foreseen the loss of the Dutch trade, war with the Netherlands, the deterioration of peace with the Indians, or the revival of the Northern Neck proprietary. The loss of foreign markets affected tobacco prices, whereas the Second and Third Anglo-Dutch Wars jeopardized the welfare of Virginia in ways Berkeley was unable to forestall. He could slow, but not stop, the frontier skirmishes that at last broke into open warfare in 1675. The renewed grant to the Arlington-Culpeper interests threw Northern Neck land titles into question and caused Berkeley to mount an expensive effort to buy out the proprietors.

Always a haughty man, Berkeley became more peevish as he aged and as the burdens of government weighed more heavily on him. Poor health dulled his faculties, making him rely on a diminishing circle of intimates, especially his second wife, Frances Culpeper Stephens Berkeley, whom he married sometime between 19 May and 21 June 1670. His method of governance failed to assure political harmony, his favorites did not form a cohesive group, and he was slow to punish their misrule. Virginians who stood outside the reach of his bounty or who experienced his wrath increasingly questioned his leadership, though none dared cross him until disagreements over Indian policy drove young Nathaniel Bacon (1647–1676) into rebellion.

The road to rebellion started in July 1675, when a party of Doeg Indians attacked an outlying plantation in Stafford County. The incursion appeared little different from similar incidents that had been part of frontier existence since the conclusion of the Anglo-Powhatan War of 1644–1646. A quick show of force had quelled past troubles, but in 1675 the retaliation set off a series of strokes and counterstrokes that fanned the fears of frontier colonists. Berkeley failed to discern the gravity of the situation and let control slip from his fingers.

In April 1676 Bacon took command of an illegally assembled force of volunteer Indian fighters and ignored the governor's admonition that leading the volunteers constituted mutiny. Angered by Bacon's indifference to his warning, Berkeley took a force of men and tried to head off Bacon's rebels, but they gave him the slip and the governor returned to Jamestown in a fury. He tried to reclaim his authority, first by proclaiming Bacon a rebel and suspending him from the Council, then by dissolving the General Assembly and calling for the first general election of burgesses in fourteen years. Berkeley also circulated a remonstrance explaining his reasons for his dealings with Bacon and vowing to redress whatever grievances the voters had. Two days before the new assembly convened, he asked his superiors in London to replace him with a "more Vigorous Governor."

The General Assembly opened on 5 June 1676 amid the prospect of civil insurrection, rumors of an Indian attack, and fears of what would happen next between Bacon and Berkeley. Voters in Henrico County sent Bacon as one of their burgesses, although the outlaw's right to take his seat was uncertain. Those doubts were resolved following Bacon's capture, pardon, and subsequent return to his plantation upriver from Jamestown. Bacon was absent for the bulk of the session, during which the burgesses and councillors laid plans for taking the fight to the natives and addressed a variety of grievances. As they were completing their business, Bacon marched into the capital at the head of about 500 armed men, extorted a general's commission from the terrified legislators, and marched off to battle the Indians.

Berkeley sent his wife to London to defend his administration, while he engaged in a contest with Bacon that became a duel to the death over who would control Virginia. With Bacon occupied in the search for someone to fight, Berkeley again proclaimed his enemy a rebel and tried to catch him. The governor got little support and fled to the Eastern Shore when Bacon doubled back on him and tried to establish his own command of the colony. He issued several public pronouncements denouncing Berkeley and playing for popular support. More pointedly, he sent a small fleet across Chesapeake Bay to dislodge Berkeley from his stronghold, while he again went off in search of Indians.

Berkeley captured the men Bacon sent against him and returned to regain control over much of lower Tidewater Virginia, including the capital. Bacon then drove Berkeley from Jamestown and burned the city. The rebellion quickly fell apart after Bacon's sudden death on 26 October 1676. By the first weeks of 1677 Berkeley had suppressed the last of the insurrectionaries. He prosecuted and hanged several of the rebellion's leaders.

News of the revolt did not sit well with Berkeley's superiors in London. The Crown dispatched more than a thousand soldiers, a fleet of ships, and a three-member commission to put down Bacon and to investigate the causes of the disturbance. One of those commissioners, Herbert Jeffreys, carried orders to supplant Berkeley as governor, ending the second of two terms collectively totaling twenty-seven years, still a record for the governance of Virginia. The rebellion ended before the troops arrived, and the commissioners and the governor clashed. Berkeley gave way only when it began to appear likely that Jeffreys would forcibly pack him off to England. In May 1677 he sailed across the ocean for the last time to plead his case with the king.

Sick, and weakened by the crossing, six weeks later Berkeley landed in London a broken man. Gone were his allies at court. The old governor's one desire was to clear himself with the king. There was no opportunity. Sir William Berkeley died at Berkeley House in London on 9 July 1677 and was buried four days later at Twickenham, Middlesex.

Birth year in Herald's Visitation of Somerset, 1623, MS 2C.22264AB, College of Arms, London; numerous Berkeley letters in PRO, British Library, and Virginia county records; Robert Cecil Bald, "Sir William Berkeley's *The Lost Lady*," *Library* 17 (1937): 394–426; Warren M. Billings, "Berkeley and Effingham: Who Cares?" and "Sir William Berkeley and the Diversification of the Virginia Economy," *VMHB* 97 (1989): 33–47 (por.) and 104 (1996): 433–454; Billings, "Imagining Green Spring House" and "The Return of Sir William Berkeley," *Virginia Cavalcade* 44 (1994): 84–95 and 47 (1998): 100–109; Billings, John E. Selby, and Thad W. Tate, *Colonial Virginia: A History* (1986), 47–97; Jon Kukla, *Political Institutions in Virginia, 1619–1660* (1989), 81–158; David Hackett Fischer, *Albion's Seed: Four British Folkways in America* (1989), 207–226; Wilcomb E. Washburn, *The Governor and the Rebel: A History of Bacon's Rebellion in Virginia* (1957); Stephen Saunders Webb, *The Governors-General: The English Army and the Definition of the Empire, 1569–1681* (1979), 329–371, and *1676: The End of American Independence* (1984), 3–221; parish register of Saint Mary the Virgin, Twickenham.

WARREN M. BILLINGS

BERLIN, George William (2 December 1824–13 November 1895), member of the Convention of 1861, was born in Carlisle, Pennsylvania, the second of three sons of George Berlin and Catherine Fulwiler Berlin. He had three or four sisters and one younger half sister. Berlin was christened on 18 April 1825 in the First Evangelical Lutheran Church, Carlisle. His mother died in May 1834 and his father remarried shortly thereafter. During his childhood his family moved through Pennsylvania, Maryland, Virginia, and Ohio. In the mid-1840s Berlin, who described himself as "a poor and friendless youth," moved to Staunton, where he attended Lucas P. Thompson's law school in 1845 and 1846 and taught school at nearby Moscow. Berlin was licensed to practice law on 23 February 1846. On 31 March of that year he married Susan Miranda Holt, of Augusta County. They had six sons and three daughters before her death on 22 April 1867, six days after the birth of their youngest daughter.

Berlin established a law practice at Beverley in Randolph County in May 1846 but moved his office to Buckhannon in 1850. He rode the circuit arguing cases and was a leading member in the Sons of Temperance. In 1849 he went to Alabama to investigate lands held there by his father-in-law. Berlin became the first commonwealth's attorney of Upshur County when that county was formed in 1851 and served until 1856. His surviving papers include several draft speeches on the value of education but do not indicate when or where he delivered them.

On 4 February 1861 Berlin defeated John S. Fisher by a margin of 885 to 293 votes to represent Upshur County in the Virginia convention called to consider the secession crisis. Berlin opposed secession and criticized eastern Virginians for neglecting the interests of the western counties. Before the vote was taken he made only one speech on the floor, a lengthy argument delivered during March 1861 against abandoning the Constitution, the Union, and the rights and protection they guaranteed. He voted against a motion for secession on 4 April, when it failed, and again on 17 April, when it passed. Berlin changed his vote on 23 April and made a short speech of explanation blaming the "corrupt powers at Washington" and acknowledging that "all hopes of re-constructing the Union are now at an end."

Berlin returned to Buckhannon and explained his new stance at a well-attended courthouse meeting in May. His change of heart on the issue of Union had made him enemies, however, and on 11 June 1861 he was forced to leave his home without either his family or personal estate. After traveling with the Confederate army bivouacked in the Cheat and Allegheny Mountains, Berlin returned to Richmond for the second and third sessions of the convention later in the year. Unable to return home for fear of being arrested, he escaped indictment only because he had not taken up arms.

With borrowed funds Berlin began a small mercantile establishment at Middlebrook in Augusta County. In August 1862 he bought the Lebanon White Sulphur Spring Hotel with plans to open it for boarding. Later he returned briefly to Alabama and considered moving to property he owned there or perhaps elsewhere in the West. In October 1862 Upshur County Unionists, who between January and March of that year had plundered and mistreated the family, finally permitted Susan Berlin and her children to cross the lines and rejoin Berlin. For the war's duration Berlin operated his store, acted as a Confederate tax collector and, between 1863 and 1865, served as superintendent of the Staunton and Parkersburg Turnpike. In 1864 he purchased Byerly's Mill and other property near Bridgewater. He operated the mill until a flood destroyed it in October 1870.

Berlin took the oath of allegiance to the United States on 26 May 1865 and the amnesty oath on 21 June. He resumed the practice of law in Harrisonburg in February 1866, specializing in land litigation. He also became prominent in local narrow-gauge railroad projects. In February 1868 Berlin began building a new house, which he called Berlinton, on his property southeast of Bridgewater. He subsequently lived at Berlinton and served as a lay leader in the Bridgewater Presbyterian Church. George William Berlin died at his home on 13 November 1895 and was buried in Woodbine Cemetery in Harrisonburg.

Berlin-Martz Family Papers (LVA microfilm), including draft of undated speech at Convention of 1861 as well as letters exchanged with wife during and after convention (por.); birth date in Berlin family Bible in possession of Carol Berlin, Harlan, Ky., 1998; *Hardesty's Historical and Geographical Encyclopedia, Illustrated: Special Virginia Edition*, Rockingham Co. ed. (1884), 403; Clarence E. May, *Life Under Four Flags in North River Basin of Virginia* (1976), 379–381, 453–454, 458, 459, 461, 495, 549; election to Convention of 1861 documented in Betty Hornbeck, *Upshur Brothers of the Blue and Gray* (1967), 5–7; Reese and Gaines, *Proceedings of 1861 Convention*, 4:403–404; obituaries in *Bridgewater Herald*, with erroneous year of birth, and *Harrisonburg Rockingham Register*, both 15 Nov. 1895.

Daphne Gentry

BERNARD, William (1603–31 March 1665), member of the Council, was born William Barnard in Kingsthorpe, Northamptonshire, England, the third of four sons of Sir Francis Barnard and his second wife, Mary Woolhouse Barnard. The first son, born in 1598, had been christened William, but he died in infancy, and the second son, Robert Barnard, became lord of Brampton Hall, Huntingdonshire. Although early records contain variant spellings of the surname, records in Virginia after 1642 usually use the spelling "Bernard."

William Bernard first traveled to Virginia aboard the *Furtherance* in 1621. He settled at Basse's Choice in Warrosquyoake Plantation in what is now Isle of Wight County. During the next twenty years he traveled back and forth to England at least four times. He was probably both the "Willm Bernard" who set out from Gravesend to Virginia in the *America* in May 1635 and the "Willam Barnett" whom a clerk in 1639 recorded as being appointed tobacco inspector for the district extending from Lawne's Creek to Castle Creek in Isle of Wight County. On 8 March 1642 "William Bernard Esq." took the oaths as a member of the Council in the new administration of Governor Sir William Berkeley. Bernard served as a councillor apparently without interruption until his death twenty-three years later. After Virginia surrendered to Parliament in 1652, the General Assembly elected him to the Council, and when Berkeley returned to the governorship in 1660, Bernard remained on the Council. The loss of most of the Council's records for the period makes an assessment of Bernard's long tenure virtually impossible.

According to family tradition Bernard lived in Nansemond County, but his only known landholding prior to his marriage in 1653 was a 1,200-acre tract in Isle of Wight County for which he received a patent on 10 August 1642. Bernard joined other Virginia planters in experimenting with the cultivation of silkworms. His efforts to produce silk in Virginia were as unsuccessful financially as those of his contemporaries. However, his letters to Virginia Ferrar in England helped inspire the poetic muse of her brother John Ferrar. Lines 130–133 of

Ferrar's "Ryming lines" for Samuel Hartlib, *The Reformed Virginian Silk-worm* (1655), read: "Yea worthy Bernard that stout Colonel / Informs the Lady the work most facile / And of rich Silken stuffs, made shortly there / He hopes that he and others shall soone weare."

Sometime before 2 August 1653 Bernard married Lucy Higginson Burwell, widow of the immigrant Lewis Burwell, who had died in November 1652. Bernard probably moved to his wife's property in Gloucester County, and they had one son and two daughters. William Bernard died, probably in Gloucester County, on 31 March 1665.

Variant spellings of surname, the presence of other Bernards in Virginia, and the loss of many Virginia records have resulted in faulty and contradictory biographies and family histories; *Adventurers of Purse and Person, 1607–1624/5*, 117–118; Lelia Bernard Meredith Manning's 1930 Bernard family genealogical chart, LVA; first trip to Virginia and age documented in muster of 7 Feb. 1625, PRO CO 1/3, no. 35; Council service recorded in *Minutes of Council and General Court*, in vol. 1 of Hening, *Statutes*, in vol. B of Lower Norfolk Co. Records, and in vol. 1 of York Co. Deeds, Orders, Wills; marriage documented in York Co. Deeds, Orders, Wills, 1:182–186; death date in will of brother Robert Barnard, *VMHB* 6 (1899): 408.

DAPHNE GENTRY

BERNHART, Peter (fl. 1789–1818), Fraktur artist, was probably born during the 1760s. His origins are obscure. He was of German descent and was probably born in Pennsylvania, although Germany, Maryland, and northern Virginia cannot be ruled out. Bernhart's name is first recorded in the 24 June 1789 edition of Mathias Bartgis's *Virginia Gazette and Winchester Advertiser* as the agent in Keezletown, Rockingham County, for Bartgis's German-language newspaper, the *Virginische Zeitung*. On 19 August 1789 Bernhart announced in the *Gazette* that on "the first of August he commenced the business of riding as Post from Winchester to Staunton" every second week, carrying the mail and English- and German-language newspapers.

In 1792 the Rockingham County tax lists credited Bernhart with ownership of seventy-eight acres of land that he may have acquired when he married and that he sold in two parcels in 1792 and 1793. The tax records show him owning two tracts of six and seven acres from 1799 through 1805. He and his wife Mary, maiden name and date of marriage unknown, had at least three daughters and one son, all of whom were married between 1808 and 1815.

In addition to delivering newspapers to the communities of German immigrants and their descendants in Virginia, Bernhart peddled the decorated baptismal certificates called *Taufschein* produced by Friedrich Krebs, a Pennsylvania schoolmaster and artist. This form of folk art originated in Germany, and immigrants brought the practice to America from the upper Rhineland. The certificates were all drawn and colored by hand, and each one was unique. The mobility of the settlers in western Virginia provided a steady market for them because migrating young people needed proof of their birth and church affiliations to take to new communities.

During the 1790s Bernhart began to draw and color his own Fraktur, as this type of art was later called. In the beginning he merely copied Krebs's matronly mermaids and huge tulips, but by 1800 he had developed his own distinctive, vividly colored designs possibly inspired by the Shenandoah Valley landscape. For well-to-do families Bernhart drew and painted folio-sized sheets featuring a profusion of multicolored birds in wild forests of flowering growth. Families of lesser means purchased smaller versions featuring the traditional startled parrots, podlike blooms, and stylized tulips. Bernhart's work proved popular even though it differed greatly from European and Pennsylvanian prototypes and despite his lack of skill in calligraphy, particularly in the art of writing German gothic letters, which was the principal element of his art. His handwriting, mostly clear and pedantic, but at times careless and shaky, betrayed the insecure spelling of a person who had grown up in America without much formal education.

Bernhart also served as a scrivener for illiterate neighbors, taught school, and traveled about selling his artwork. Early in the nineteenth century he procured printed forms in German and English from local printers, filled them in, and illustrated them. His orders to printers included broadsides with popular poems or songs that he decorated with his motifs and sold.

His two extant broadsides are *Jesus, wohn in meinem Haus* (1809), a house blessing printed by Ambrose Henkel, of New Market, and *Ein Schönes Liedlein* (1816), a song lyric issued by Laurentz Wartmann, of Harrisonburg.

During the thirty years he is known to have worked in Virginia, Bernhart must have produced many Fraktur, only some of which he signed. More than fifty of his pieces have been identified, including house blessings and other family records as well as *Taufscheins*. Collectors singled him out during the 1960s as the most imaginative creator of Fraktur in the United States during the early years of the nineteenth century, and specimens of his work have been acquired by prestigious museums and galleries, including the Philadelphia Museum of Art and the Abby Aldrich Rockefeller Folk Art Collection in Williamsburg. Collections of family papers in the libraries of the University of Virginia and Eastern Mennonite University also contain Fraktur by Bernhart.

Peter Bernhart's name appears for the last time on the Rockingham County personal property tax list in 1816, but he evidently worked in the county until about 1818, after which he either died or moved elsewhere.

Klaus Wust, *Virginia Fraktur: Penmanship as Folk Art* (1970), 20–23, "Fraktur and the Virginia Germans," *Arts in Virginia* 15 (fall 1974): 2–11, and *American Fraktur—Graphic Folk Art, 1745–1855* (1976); three color reproductions of Bernhart's Fraktur in Cynthia Elyce Rubin, ed., *Southern Folk Art* (1985), 82–83; original artwork in Hench Deposit, Henkel Papers, UVA; Solomon Henkel account book, Winchester–Frederick Co. Historical Society, Winchester.

KLAUS WUST

BERRY, Sir John (bap. 7 January 1636–14 February 1690), royal commissioner for Virginia, was born near South Molton in Devonshire, England, the second of seven sons and one of nine children of Elizabeth Moore Berry and Daniel Berry, the vicar of Molland and Knowstone. He was christened on 7 January 1636 in his father's Knowstone Parish. In 1652, because of Daniel Berry's loyalty to the Crown and devotion to the Church of England, local supporters of the Commonwealth drove him from his church and vicarage. John Berry went to sea on a merchant ship out of Plymouth, but a Spanish vessel captured him, and he did not return to England for several years.

Early in the 1660s Berry's family and friends arranged for him to be appointed boatswain of the naval vessel *Swallow*, which in 1663 sailed to Jamaica. Berry won rapid promotions in the Caribbean during the Second Anglo-Dutch War. As commanding officer of the *Mary* in 1665 he captured thirty-two prizes in four months, and in 1667 he commanded a fleet of ten ships that defeated thirty French and Dutch vessels at Nevis. Berry later commanded English warships in action against the Algerine pirates in the Mediterranean. During the Third Anglo-Dutch War he commanded the *Resolution* at the Battle of Sole Bay and rescued the duke of York, for which Charles II knighted him immediately after the battle and made him governor of Deal Castle. Berry also distinguished himself at the Battle of Dogger Bank in May 1673 and later served again in the Mediterranean. He also investigated conditions in the Newfoundland fisheries in 1675 and submitted to the Admiralty a plan for governing the island.

In October 1676 the king named Berry to a commission that led an armed force of ten naval vessels and more than a thousand soldiers to put down Bacon's Rebellion in Virginia and to investigate its causes. The commissioners were Berry, who commanded the fleet, Colonel Herbert Jeffreys, in charge of the soldiers, and Virginian Francis Moryson. Berry and Jeffreys preceded the main body of the force to Virginia, but by the time Berry's flagship, the *Bristol*, dropped anchor in the James River on 29 January 1677, the rebellion was already over. The commissioners informed Governor Sir William Berkeley that the other ships and the remainder of the armed force were en route to the colony, that he should issue a royal pardon to the participants in the rebellion, and that he should step down as governor. Relations between the governor and the commissioners were marked by hostility, suspicion, and cross purposes as the latter attempted to follow their instructions to impose order on the colony that Berkeley insisted was already pacified. Moryson took office as lieutenant governor when Berkeley left

Virginia for England in the spring, and by June 1677 Berry's crew was so ill that he decided to disregard his additional instructions to go to New England and assist royal officials there in the aftermath of what was called King Philip's War. Instead, Berry sailed for London.

Berry was an able and brave naval officer. He saved the life of the duke of York a second time in 1682, and in 1684 he was named one of the commissioners who discharged the duties of the lord high admiral of England after the duke of York was obliged to surrender the office because of his Catholicism. After the duke succeeded to the throne as James II in 1685, Berry was a royal favorite and was promoted to rear admiral in September 1688 and to vice admiral in December of that year. He nevertheless led the Protestant naval officers during the revolution that replaced James II with William and Mary. Berry remained one of the commissioners of the navy and became close to the new king, who appointed him comptroller of the victualling accounts.

Berry and his wife, Lady Rebecca Berry, had one daughter who was born in 1667 but died young. Sir John Berry died at Portsmouth, England, on 14 February 1690. Physicians who examined his body declared that he had been poisoned, but no one was prosecuted for murder, and he may actually have died of a fever. He was buried on 21 February 1690 in Stepney Church near London.

Christening recorded in Knowstone Parish register, Knowstone, Devonshire; John Prince, *Danmonii Orientales Illustres: or, The Worthies of Devon*, 2d ed., rev. (1810), 68–73; John Campbell, *Lives of the British Admirals*, 2d ed. (1781), 2:524–532; John Charnock, *Biographia Navalis: or, Impartial Memoirs of the Lives and Characters of Officers of the Navy of Great Britain, From the Year 1660 to the Present Time* (1794–1798), 1:143–156; Stephen Saunders Webb, *1676: The End of American Independence* (1984); Virginia commission documented in Pepysian Manuscripts, Magdalene College, Cambridge, vol. 2582, in Coventry Manuscripts, Longleat House, Warminister, vols. 76–78, in PRO Adm 2/1738 and 51/134, pt. 3, and in PRO CO 5/1355 and 5/1371; published biographies mistakenly date death in 1691; will proved on 24 Mar. 1690, Prerogative Court of Canterbury, 1690, fol. 36; burial recorded in Saint Dunstan Parish register, Stepney, Middlesex; carved likeness on burial monument in Stepney Church.

STEPHEN SAUNDERS WEBB

BERRY, Llewellyn Longfellow (26 February 1876–23 November 1954), African Methodist Episcopal minister, was born on Butler's Farm near Hampton, the second of five sons and second of eight children of John Berry and Nancy Jenifer Berry. His parents had both been born into slavery, but his father had escaped from the Maryland plantation on which he was born, changed his name from John Miles to John Berry, and served in the United States Army during the Civil War. Berry grew up near Hampton and was educated in its public schools. He had a religious-conversion experience when he was thirteen years old and, intending to go into the ministry, attended Hampton Institute for one year before enrolling in 1895 at Kittrell College, a school of the African Methodist Episcopal Church in Granville County, North Carolina. After graduating in 1899, he began his ministerial career in Pope, Southampton County.

On 26 September 1900 Berry married Beulah Ann Harris, one of his Kittrell classmates. Some of their four sons and three daughters were born at her family's home in North Carolina, where she sometimes lived while he was ministering to his congregations. During the first six years of Berry's ministry, he served a succession of small churches in Virginia and North Carolina. During the academic year 1903–1904 he temporarily left the ministry to teach in North Carolina, and then returned to the ministry and served from 1905 to 1907 at Saint James Church in Winston-Salem and from 1907 to 1911 at Saint Paul Church in Chapel Hill. He then returned to Virginia as minister at Mount Zion Church in Princess Anne County from 1912 to 1914. In the latter year Berry took charge of the substantial Saint James Church in Norfolk, where he remained until 1917. For the next four years he served as presiding elder of the Portsmouth District. He was minister at Emanuel Church in Portsmouth from 1921 to 1926 and again in 1932 and 1933. During his years in Portsmouth he attracted 1,500 new members to the congregation. Between his two terms there, Berry officiated at the prestigious Saint John's Church in Norfolk.

Berry became a leader among Virginia's AME pastors. In 1920 he began regularly attending the denomination's quadrennial General Conferences as a delegate from Virginia. At the 1932 General Conference, Berry lost a bid for the post of general secretary for home and foreign missions to the incumbent, Edmund Higgins Coit. Following Coit's sudden death in 1933, Berry, as the runner-up in the previous election, was the logical choice as his successor, and the mission board elected him secretary on 11 April 1933. He won reelection at five succeeding General Conferences.

Berry moved to New York City, the site of the mission board's headquarters. His church had begun ministering to slaves and free blacks before the Civil War and afterward expanded its outreach to southern freedpeople and African Americans in the West. It also sent missionaries abroad to Africa, the Caribbean, and South America, where the church not only founded congregations and erected churches but also built and staffed schools, orphanages, and hospitals. As secretary of missions, Berry traveled frequently and extensively overseas. In November 1937, for example, he visited AME congregations in Haiti, the Dominican Republic, Jamaica, Trinidad, Barbados, and the Virgin Islands, and he traveled to British Guiana and Dutch Guiana. In March 1939 he went to Africa and inspected AME work in Sierra Leone, Liberia, and the Gold Coast.

Berry also edited the *Voice of Missions*, his department's quarterly journal, from 1933 until 1954. He frequently reported on his work and travels and periodically printed special issues about AME churches in Africa, Bermuda, the Caribbean, and South America. After the church began missionary work in Cuba in 1938, he paid the salary of the superintendent there and published a booklet in English and Spanish about African Methodism. In 1938 Berry prepared *A Little Missionary Journey to a Great Missionary Area*, which chronicled AME development in the West Indies. He also wrote *A Century of Missions of the African Methodist Episcopal Church, 1840–1940* (1942), a lengthy, heavily illustrated volume containing a full account of the missionary efforts of the church on three continents and detailing the work and contributions of the women who served as teachers and did other missionary work alongside the men.

In 1948 Berry unsuccessfully sought election as a bishop, but when he was not chosen he readily accepted reelection as general secretary. He never retired, continuing to work hard and travel regularly around the United States and Canada. Llewellyn Longfellow Berry died on 23 November 1954 at his home in New York and was buried in Elmwood Cemetery in Detroit, where one of his daughters lived.

Leonidas H. Berry, *I Wouldn't Take Nothin' for My Journey: Two Centuries of an Afro-American Minister's Family* (1981; pors.); Israel L. Butt, *History of African Methodism in Virginia* (1908), 228; Caldwell, *History of the American Negro*, 139–142; Llewellyn Longfellow Berry Papers, Schomberg Center for Research in Black Culture, New York; *Who's Who in the General Conference* (1924): 58; Richard R. Wright Jr., ed., *The Encyclopaedia of the African Methodist Episcopal Church*, 2d ed. (1947), 37; *Norfolk Journal and Guide*, 7 Feb. 1948; obituaries in *New York Times*, 26 Nov. 1954, and *Norfolk Journal and Guide*, 4 Dec. 1954.

DENNIS C. DICKERSON

BETTS, Edwin Morris (2 November 1892–27 September 1958), botanist and historian, was born in Raleigh, North Carolina, the youngest of two sons and one daughter of William Cary Betts and Mary Williams Betts. Orphaned at an early age, he spent part of his youth at an orphanage in Goldsboro, North Carolina. After graduating from Oxford High School in Oxford, North Carolina, he studied at the Southern Conservatory of Music in Durham. In the autumn of 1915 he joined the Elon College faculty as codirector of the music department and also enrolled as an undergraduate. In 1918 he became director of the department and the following year received a bachelor's degree.

Betts resigned from Elon College in 1923 and matriculated at the University of Virginia, where he was awarded an M.S. in biology in 1924 and a Ph.D. in 1927. Hired after graduation as an assistant professor of biology at the university, he was promoted to associate professor in 1946 and to full professor in 1951. His early research interests focused on fungi (or ascomycetes), edible morels, and angiosperms. During the summers early in his career, Betts worked at the university's Blandy Experimental Farm in Clarke County. An increasing interest in local plant life brought him face-to-face with a number of trees that Thomas Jefferson had introduced into Albemarle County, which led in turn to further exploration of Jefferson's horticultural and agricultural pursuits. Thanks to his growing expertise Betts was named to the committee that Fiske Kimball had assembled under the auspices of the Thomas Jefferson Memorial Foundation to oversee the restoration of the Monticello gardens.

Betts's work with the foundation and his collaboration with Hazlehurst Bolton Perkins, an eminent gardener, led to their publication of *Thomas Jefferson's Flower Garden at Monticello* (1941), the first scholarly treatment of Monticello's flower borders. Betts also edited *Thomas Jefferson's Garden Book, 1766–1824* (1944), which included excerpts from hundreds of Jefferson's letters and manuscripts. Named one of the ten best works of nonfiction published in the United States that year, the volume became the primary reference tool for students of Jefferson as a gardener. The University of Virginia chapter of Phi Beta Kappa awarded Betts its prize for the year's best and most scholarly work by a member of the university faculty and elected him an honorary member.

Betts also published *The Correspondence between Constantine Samuel Rafinesque and Thomas Jefferson* (1944) and *Groundplans and Prints of the University of Virginia, 1822–1826* (1946). He received a Guggenheim Fellowship for the academic year 1947–1948 to begin the research that led to his edition of *Thomas Jefferson's Farm Book, with Commentary and Relevant Extracts from Other Writings* (1953). In 1956 he began editing Jefferson's letters to relatives, a project completed by James A. Bear Jr. after Betts's death and published as *Family Letters of Thomas Jefferson* (1966).

On 5 September 1928 Betts married his college sweetheart, Mary Hall Stryker. They had one daughter and one son. In 1959 she became the hostess at the University of Virginia's Rotunda. During her tenure of seventeen years, she molded the struggling, informal group of university guides into an efficient program and became known affectionately as "Momma Rotunda."

In 1951 Betts began the first of five summers as director of the Lydia Hinchman House of the Maria Mitchell Association at the Natural Sciences Center in Nantucket, Massachusetts. He served until 1957 when poor health forced his retirement. Edwin Morris Betts died in Charlottesville on 27 September 1958 after he suffered a cerebral hemorrhage while exiting the Alderman Library, where he had been working on his Jefferson family correspondence project. He was buried in the University of Virginia Cemetery in Charlottesville.

Edwin M. Betts Papers, UVA; Census, Wayne Co., N.C., 1900 (with variant birth date of Jan. 1894); Elon College, *Bulletin* (1915–1922); other information verified by children Edwin M. Betts Jr. and Betty Frances Betts Lang; obituaries in *Charlottesville Daily Progress* (por.) and *Richmond Times-Dispatch*, both 29 Sept. 1958; memorial by Horton H. Hobbs Jr. and B. F. D. Runk in *Virginia Journal of Science* 10 (1959): 1–2.

JAMES A. BEAR JR.

BEVAN, Arthur Charles (8 August 1888–1 May 1968), geologist, was born and grew up on a farm near Delaware, Ohio, the elder of two children, both sons, of David Willard Bevan and Mary Leonora Evans Bevan. He graduated from Delaware High School in 1906 and from Ohio Wesleyan University in Delaware with a B.S. in 1912. After teaching at Ohio Wesleyan as an assistant in geology for the 1912–1913 academic year and then as an instructor in geology until he resigned in November 1913, Bevan pursued graduate studies on a fellowship from 1914 to 1917 at the University of Chicago. On 17 June 1914 he married Mary Edna Arthur. They had one son. Bevan taught geology at Ohio State University in Columbus from 1917 to 1919, and at the State University of Montana in Missoula from 1919 to 1921, spending his summers completing fieldwork for a doctorate in geology at the University of Chicago. He received his Ph.D. in December 1921 after completing a dissertation on the geology of the Beartooth Mountains on the Montana-Wyoming border. Bevan also served as an assistant geologist for the Montana Bureau of Mines from 1919 to 1921. He later listed his specialties as structural geology, Paleozoic stratigraphy, geomorphology, glacial geology, industrial minerals, and educational geology.

From 1921 to 1929 Bevan was an assistant professor of geology at the University of Illinois in Urbana, and he worked at the same time for the Illinois State Geological Survey. In March 1929 the Virginia Commission on Conservation and Development appointed Bevan state geologist of Virginia. Prior to that time the geological survey of the state had been an adjunct of the Department of Geology at the University of Virginia under the part-time direction of faculty members, but in 1928 the commission had created a full-time position of state geologist. Bevan moved to Charlottesville and for the next eighteen years directed more than fifty major field surveys of the geological, mineral, and groundwater resources of Virginia. These surveys and other work undertaken while he was state geologist were published in about forty volumes of the geological survey's *Bulletin* and its occasional circulars. Because of its small staff, Bevan's office often cooperated with the United States Geological Survey to conduct fieldwork and to prepare about forty USGS topographic maps of Virginia.

Bevan published more than two dozen papers during his career. The earliest ones dealt with the Rocky Mountains and Illinois, but many were on Virginia subjects. He also published a brief biography of the pioneering Virginia geologist and founder of the Massachusetts Institute of Technology, William Barton Rogers, in 1940. Bevan was active in scientific organizations while in Virginia and served as secretary of the Association of American State Geologists from 1934 to 1936 and as president in 1937. In 1946–1947 he was simultaneously president of the Virginia Academy of Science, a vice president of the American Association for the Advancement of Science, and chairman of the committee on mining geology and industrial minerals of the American Institute of Mining and Metallurgical Engineers. From 1946 to 1949 he also chaired the geology division of the National Research Council. Ohio Wesleyan awarded him an honorary Sc.D. in 1942.

In July 1947 Bevan resigned and returned to Illinois to work as principal geologist for the Illinois State Geological Survey, which had a more diverse program than Virginia's and a staff about four times the size of the one he had headed in Charlottesville. Inadequate support from the state for scientific work probably contributed to Bevan's decision to leave Virginia, and in October 1947 he argued in *Commonwealth*, the magazine of the Virginia State Chamber of Commerce, for speedier publication of the surveys and a stronger commitment by Virginia to geological surveying in the future. Some of the work undertaken during Bevan's tenure was not published until late in the 1950s and the last report did not appear until 1966. These delays in publication slowed commercial ventures such as mining and other extractive industries that relied on accurate geological data.

Bevan worked in Illinois until he retired in September 1955. He divided his retirement years between Santa Rosa, California, and Churchville in Augusta County. In 1966 the Bevans moved to Staunton. Arthur Charles Bevan died in Staunton on 1 May 1968 and was buried in Green Hill Cemetery in Churchville.

Personal papers, including notebooks of Rocky Mountains fieldwork, brief autobiographical statement of 25 Jan. 1959, and unpublished memoirs entitled "The Trail of a Geologist, 1895–1965," American Heritage Center, University of Wyoming, Laramie; biography in *Commonwealth* 13 (June 1946): 18–19 (por.); Arthur C. Bevan, "Summary of the Geology of the Beartooth Mountains, Montana" (Ph.D. diss., University of Chicago, 1921), published in *Journal of Geology* 31 (1923): 441–465, Bevan, "William Barton Rogers, Pioneer American Scientist," *Scientific Monthly* 50 (1940): 110–124, and "The Virginia Geological Survey," *Commonwealth* 14 (Oct. 1947): 12–13; *American Men of Science*, 11th ed. (1965), 1:398; obituaries in *Richmond News Leader* and *Richmond Times-Dispatch*, both 3 May 1968.

BRENT TARTER

BEVERIDGE, Edyth Carter (ca. 1862–29 August 1927), photographer, was born in Richmond, the only daughter and youngest of three children of John Williams Beveridge and his second wife, Lucinda Carter Beveridge. She also had four elder half brothers and two elder half sisters. Her mother died in July 1864, and after the Civil War her father married Sarah S. Harwood Norvell, a widow. Edy Beveridge, as she was known, grew up in a crowded household in the same building where her father operated a grocery and dealt in grain, hay, feed, and other merchandise. He was a successful and respected businessman who provided Beveridge with a good education and financial security that continued in her adulthood, as she never married. At his death in 1896 he left her a trust fund administered by her brothers.

Beveridge attended a Mrs. Garnett's school and then John Powell's Richmond Female Seminary, the most demanding school for girls in Richmond. Her artistic talent became evident at the seminary. She may have received formal art training at the Virginia Mechanic's Institute, and at some point she took art lessons from Lily Logan in Richmond. In 1891 Beveridge won first prize at the Virginia state fair for the best sketch from nature done in pencil. Three years later she registered for copyright her drawings of Lord Botetourt's three-tiered warming stove and of the Speaker's chair formerly in the Virginia House of Burgesses. By the mid-1890s Beveridge was active in Richmond's art circles, exhibiting in various shows, reviewing the city's art scene for the *Richmond Times*, and serving as a founding member and secretary of the Art Club of Richmond. Other than the two copyrighted drawings, which she had reproduced as postcards, and a few works in a family collection, the whereabouts of Beveridge's portraits, drawings, and paintings are unknown.

Beveridge's accomplishments as a photographer have proved more enduring. At the turn of the century photography was fast becoming a popular national pastime and winning acceptance as a legitimate art form. Experimenting initially with the cyanotype process, Beveridge photographed family members and friends, honing her skills at lighting, timing, and composition and eventually equipping her apartment with a darkroom. She quickly gained recognition. In October 1896 the *Confederate Veteran* published two of her photographs of veterans in Richmond and Powhatan, and the following spring her photo-essay on the Richmond Howitzers appeared in the *Illustrated American*, the nation's first photojournalism magazine. A local review praised the latter work as demonstrating that Beveridge had become "as clever with the pen and camera as . . . with the pencil and brush heretofore."

During the 1890s and early in the 1900s Beveridge photographed much of what she admired about her city, including architectural landmarks such as the Executive Mansion, Pratt's Castle, the State Capitol, and the White House of the Confederacy, as well as local churches, hospitals, and theaters. She also captured views of street vendors, firemen, doctors, nurses, school and church groups, ship launches, and the city's pomp-filled monument unveilings. A new venue for Beveridge's talents emerged in October 1899 with the founding of the *Richmond News*, the first city paper that regularly printed local news photographs. It published many of her images, including views of an operating room with surgery in progress that appeared in the 15 June 1901 issue.

Beveridge's reputation as an expert photographer brought her to the attention of other publishers and authors. James Albert Harrison, a University of Virginia professor, used several of her photographs of Richmond in his 1903 edition of the *Life and Letters of Edgar Allan Poe*. The Century Company, a publishing house, also commissioned work from her. Beveridge probably remains best known for "Where Southern Memories Cluster," her photo-essay in the September 1906 issue of the *Ladies' Home Journal*, which gave a national audience its first glimpse inside the White House of the Confederacy in Richmond. The article featured photographs of the fourteen rooms, each devoted to one of the Confederate and border states, and it earned her $200 as well as praise from her native city.

In May and June 1907 *Collier's* published Beveridge's picture of a parade of children pulling the monument of Jefferson Davis through the streets of Richmond and her personally copyrighted photograph of the 30 May unveiling of the J. E. B. Stuart monument, and on 22 June 1907 *Harper's Weekly* printed a different photograph of the latter statue. Beveridge's photographic career thereafter becomes elusive. By 1907 most local newspapers had their own staff photographers, and she may have found it increasingly difficult to find work in a profession that was staunchly and overwhelmingly male dominated. She may even have abandoned photojournalism altogether. Beveridge was listed in the 1910 census as an "Illustrator & Writer" for magazines. That she did not describe herself as a photographer could suggest that she had retired from the pursuit through which she had left her mark on history. Edyth Carter Beveridge died of pneumonia at Saint Luke's Hospital in Richmond on 29 August 1927 and was buried in Hollywood Cemetery in that city.

Stacy Gibbons Moore, "The Photographer as Documentary Artist: The Work of Edyth Carter Beveridge," *Virginia Cavalcade* 41 (1991): 34–47 (por., 35); widely varying birth dates conjecturable from Census, Richmond City, 1870 (age of eight given), 1880 (age of seventeen), 1900 (birth date of June 1870), 1910 (age of thirty-nine); Edyth Carter Beveridge glass-plate negatives and photograph collection, and vertical files, including postcards of drawings, newspaper clippings, and some business correspondence with Century Company and *Richmond News*, VM; photographs of White House of the Confederacy at MOC; other photographs, art work, and papers in possession of grandniece Lucy Dabney, Richmond, 1991; feature articles in *Richmond Times-Dispatch*, 30 May 1948, 6 Jan. 1991; Beveridge's works include an article on "The Progress of Art," *Richmond Times*, 1 Jan. 1898, photo-essays entitled "The Richmond Howitzers," *Illustrated American* 20 (1897): 462–464, and "Where Southern Memories Cluster," *Ladies' Home Journal* 23 (Sept. 1906): 34–35, and photographs published in *Confederate Veteran* 4 (1896): 333, 341, *Collier's*, 4 May 1907, 17, and 15 June 1907, 18, and *Harper's Weekly* 51 (1907): 913; work reviewed in *Richmond Times*, 2 Apr. 1897; death notices in *Richmond News Leader* (giving age as sixty) and *Richmond Times-Dispatch*, both 30 Aug. 1927.

STACY GIBBONS MOORE

BEVERLEY, Harry (d. by 2 February 1731), surveyor, was born in Middlesex County sometime between 1669 and 1673, the second child and second son of three surviving sons and one daughter of Robert Beverley (1635–1687) and his second wife, Mary Keeble Beverley. From one to three additional brothers died young. He may have been christened Henry, a name that occurred at least once among his father's Yorkshire relatives, but he signed himself Harry and that is how virtually every reference to him gives his name. He and his elder brother Robert and his younger brother John spent part of their childhoods in England and began their educations there, but they all returned to Virginia by or not long after the time their father died in March 1687. In July 1688 Harry Beverley selected as his guardian the minister of Abingdon Parish in Gloucester County, John Gwynn, who was the husband of his elder half sister, Margaret Keeble Gwynn.

Beverley married Elizabeth Smith sometime before the end of 1696. Between November 1697 and July 1720 they had eight daughters and two sons. Her large inheritance of property that her Kemp, Lunsford, and Wormeley relatives had acquired included Brandon plantation in Middlesex County. With his wife's estate and his own large inheritance from his wealthy father, Beverley became a man of consequence. He was appointed to the Middlesex County Court in 1701 and became a vestryman of Christ Church Parish a year later. He also became surveyor of King and Queen and of King William Counties, lucrative posts that he held until his death almost thirty years later. In 1706 he laid out the town site for Delaware Town, later known as West Point, in King William County, and in 1710 and 1711 he and another surveyor settled a Virginia–North Carolina boundary dispute. Beverley's surveys sometimes drew criticism from interested parties. For example, in 1702 he laid out a tract in King William County for the Chickahominy, and the governor and Council rebuked him for favoring the Indians.

Beverley acted as a feoffee, or trustee and agent, for the town of Urbanna in Middlesex County in 1704, and the following year several local leaders accused him of acting improperly in attempting to have a new courthouse erected in the town. In June 1705 outside the courthouse Beverley repeatedly struck and bloodied John Grymes, one of these critics. After the governor intervened to end the dispute, Grymes prosecuted Beverley for assault. Nevertheless, Beverley won election that autumn to the House of Burgesses and represented Middlesex County from 1705 to 1707, but local political bickering was so intense that Beverley resigned from the county court in 1709.

In the summer of 1716 Lieutenant Governor Alexander Spotswood gave Beverley command of the sloop *Virgin*, with instructions to sail to the Bahamas in search of wrecked Spanish treasure ships. Within days a Spanish man-of-war captured the *Virgin*, and Beverley and his men were imprisoned in Santo Domingo and later in Vera Cruz. Beverley escaped after seven months and returned to Virginia.

Following his wife's death in 1720, Beverley moved northwest to his Newlands plantation in the area that became Spotsylvania County. Harry Beverley dated his will there on 30 November 1730 and died between that date and 2 February 1731, when the will was proved in the Spotsylvania County Court.

Brent Tarter, "Major Robert Beverley (1635–1687) and His Immediate Family," *Magazine of Virginia Genealogy* 31 (1993): 172–173, 182–183; Darrett B. Rutman and Anita H. Rutman, *A Place in Time: Middlesex County, Virginia, 1650–1750* (1984), 217–225; public life documented in *Executive Journals of Council*, vols. 2–4, and Sarah S. Hughes, *Surveyors and Statesmen: Land Measuring in Colonial Virginia* (1979); Spotsylvania Co. Will Book, A:117–118.

ANITA H. RUTMAN

BEVERLEY, James Bradshaw (27 July 1861–28 April 1926), Populist Party leader, was born at Avenel, his father's farm in Fauquier County, the youngest of six sons and six daughters of Robert Beverley (1822–1901) and Jane Eliza Carter Beverley. He was actually the third son to be named James Bradshaw, the other two having died young. Beverley attended Episcopal High School near Alexandria and the Virginia Military Institute, from which he graduated third in a class of twenty-two in 1879. On 30 October 1889 he married Annie Maxwell Sloan, but she died shortly after the birth of a son in April 1891. On 9 November 1898 he married Amanda Madison Clark, and they had two daughters.

J. Brad Beverley, as he was known, farmed several tracts of land in Fauquier County and lived at Meadowville near The Plains. With his father and brothers Robert Beverley Jr. and John Hill Carter Beverley, he was deeply involved in the politics of agriculture during the 1880s and 1890s. The Beverleys were leaders of the Farmers' Alliance of Virginia, which in June 1892 launched the People's, or Populist, Party of Virginia. Early in the 1890s Beverley served as state lecturer for the alliance and spoke in virtually every county to promote the organization of county suballiances. During the 1892 presidential campaign Beverley was the vice president of the Farmers' Alliance of Virginia and stumped the state for Populist candidates James B. Weaver and James G. Field.

On 3 August 1893 the convention of the People's Party of Virginia nominated Beverley for lieutenant governor on a ticket that included Edmund Randolph Cocke for governor and William S. Gravely for attorney general. Beverley was the best and most experienced public speaker on the slate, and he shouldered the burden of the canvass. He concentrated on the national Populist Party's advocacy of the free coinage of silver rather than on other agrarian and financial reforms. The Republicans did not nominate any statewide candidates in 1893 in order to avoid splitting the opposition to the Democrats, but despite Beverley's efforts the Democratic ticket headed by Charles T. O'Ferrall easily carried the state in November. Beverley believed that Democratic Party corruption in Virginia and the state election laws impeded improvements in agriculture at least as much as did the national monetary policies that the Populists deplored. With his father and many other Populists he shared a deep disgust for President Grover Cleveland, and he became increasingly critical of the political influence of banks, railroads, and large corporations. In 1896 Beverley attended the national convention of the People's Party and gave a speech seconding the party's presidential nomination of William Jennings Bryan shortly after the Democratic Party had also nominated Bryan for president. With that act Beverley's participation in the People's Party ended.

Beverley joined the army during the Spanish-American War but saw no action in the field. Thereafter he was often referred to as Captain J. Brad Beverley, which nevertheless failed to prevent some journalists and later writers from confusing him with his namesake cousins in Leesburg and Winchester. From his home at Meadowville he continued to engage in commercial orcharding and to farm. Beverley made one other venture into electoral politics. In August 1919 he surprised observers by winning the Democratic Party primary for the seat in the Senate of Virginia representing the counties of Fauquier and Loudoun. He was elected without serious opposition in November and served one four-year term, but he did not seek a second term. James Bradshaw Beverley died at his home in Fauquier County on 28 April 1926 and was buried in the graveyard of the Church of Our Savior Episcopal Church (now Little Georgetown Cemetery), near The Plains.

Makers of America: Biographies of Leading Men of Thought and Action (1915–1922), 1:116–120 (por.); Bruce, Tyler, and Morton, *History of Virginia*, 6:264–265; Beverley Family Papers, VHS; John McGill, *The Beverley Family of Virginia* (1956), 553–554, 565; William DuBose Sheldon, *Populism in the Old Dominion: Virginia Farm Politics, 1885–1900* (1935; frontispiece por.); *Richmond Dispatch*, 4 Aug. 1893; *New York Times*, 4 Aug., 3, 6, 8 Nov. 1893; *JHD*, 1893–1894 sess., 65; *Richmond Times-Dispatch*, 7 Aug. 1919; Nancy Chappelear Baird, *Fauquier County, Virginia, Tombstone Inscriptions* (1970), 65; obituaries in *Winchester Evening Star*, 29 Apr. 1926, and *Loudoun Times-Mirror*, 6 May 1926.

BRENT TARTER

BEVERLEY, Peter (bap. 7 May 1663–by 26 March 1729), Speaker of the House of Burgesses and member of the Council, was probably born in Hull, Yorkshire, England, the only known child of Robert Beverley (1635–1687) and his first wife, Elizabeth Beverley. Peter Beverley was christened in the parish of Saint Mary Lowgate in Hull on 7 May 1663, and his mother was buried there two days later. His father soon moved to Virginia, probably leaving Peter Beverley behind with family members.

Peter Beverley may have joined his father in Virginia soon after his father's second marriage in March 1666 and then been sent back to England for his education. By March 1681 Beverley was living with his father in Middlesex County and acting as his agent in the complex land transactions by which Robert Beverley became extremely wealthy and influential. The father was also involved in numerous public controversies, one of which propelled Peter Beverley into his first public responsibilities. After Robert Beverley was suspended from his offices in 1686, Surveyor General Philip Ludwell slipped Peter Beverley into the job of county surveyor, which Governor Effingham described as the most lucrative post in Middlesex County. In the same year Peter Beverley obtained a law license, and after his father's death in March 1687 he moved to the large estate he had inherited on the bank of the Piankatank River in Ware Parish, Gloucester County. About that same time he married Elizabeth Peyton, and they had three daughters, all of whom later married into prominent Virginia families.

Beverley speedily became a man of importance in the colonial government. On 17 April 1691 the House of Burgesses elected him clerk of the House, a position his father had held. On that same day Lieutenant Governor Francis Nicholson, asserting the right to name the clerk of the House, also appointed him to the position, one of a series of joint appointments by which the executive eventually wrested the selection of the clerk away from the legislators. Beverley served as clerk of the House of Burgesses through the meeting of 1698. In the meantime he also served briefly as chief clerk of the General Court and the secretary's office, a post he relinquished to his next-younger half brother Robert Beverley in October 1693. In 1694 Peter Beverley became clerk of Gloucester County and held that office until 1719 or 1720.

The clerkships were important and profitable posts that Beverley used to advance into even more politically influential positions. From 1695 to 1699 he was a member of the committee to revise the laws of the colony, and from 1699 through the end of the committee's work in 1705 he was its clerk. After the statehouse in Jamestown burned on 20 October 1698, he and Robert Beverley retrieved and organized the surviving public records. In 1700 Beverley won election to the House of Burgesses from Gloucester County and served until 1714. On 7 December 1700 he defeated two candidates to become Speaker, and in March 1702 he was reelected over three candidates. Beverley served as Speaker until October 1705, when Benjamin Harrison was elected, probably by defeating him. On 25 October 1710 Beverley was again elected Speaker and served through the session of 1714. In 1715, for reasons that cannot be determined, Beverley was elected to the House by the president and professors of the College of William and Mary rather than the voters of Gloucester County, but on 13 August the House declared the election improper and unseated him. Beverley also acted as treasurer of Virginia while Speaker and until 1723.

Peter Beverley showed more skill than his father and half brother Robert Beverley at staying in the good graces of influential people. He had been a member of the board of visitors of the college for a decade or more by March 1716, when the board appointed him deputy surveyor general of the colony, a post he retained for the remainder of his life. Beverley also served as auditor general of the royal revenue for about a year beginning in the summer of 1716. In 1718, following protracted and bitter quarrels between Lieutenant Governor Alexander Spotswood and members of the Council, Spotswood undertook to replace four of the councillors with Peter Beverley and three other men whom he trusted. On 9 April 1719 the Board of Trade approved the appointment of Beverley in the place of William Byrd (1674–1744), but Byrd successfully petitioned to retain his seat. On 31 May 1720 the Board of Trade approved Beverley's appointment to succeed Councillor John Smith who had died, and he was sworn in as a member of the Council on 31 October 1720. Peter Beverley served on the Council until his death, which occurred on an unrecorded date between the Council meeting of 11 December 1728 and Governor William Gooch's letter of 26 March 1729 reporting Beverley's death to the Board of Trade.

Parish register of Saint Mary Lowgate, Hull, Humberside Record Office, Beverley, Eng.; Brent Tarter, "Major Robert Beverley (1635–1687) and His Immediate Family," *Magazine of Virginia Genealogy* 31 (1993): 163–170, 178; Kukla, *Speakers and Clerks, 1643–1776*, 103–105; Council appointments in PRO CO 391/112, 391/114; *Executive Journals of Council*, vols. 3–4; William Gooch to Board of Trade, 26 Mar. 1729, PRO CO 5/1321, fols. 110–111.

John M. Hemphill II
Daphne Gentry

BEVERLEY, Robert (bap. 3 January 1635–15 March 1687), clerk of the House of Burgesses, was the eldest of four sons and four daughters of Peter Beverley and Susannah Hollis (or Hollice) Beverley of Hull, Yorkshire, England. He was christened in Hull on 3 January 1635 in the parish of Saint Mary Lowgate. Nothing is known about his youth, but he was reasonably well educated, eventually learned something about the law, acquired the rudiments of surveying, and became well acquainted with commerce. Sometime before 1662 he married a woman named Elizabeth, whose maiden name is not known. Their only known child, Peter Beverley, was christened in Saint Mary Lowgate on 7 May 1663, two days before the burial of Elizabeth Beverley.

Robert Beverley moved to Virginia within a few months to start a new life. He settled in that portion of Lancaster County south of the Rappahannock River that in 1669 became Middlesex County. In March 1666 he married Mary Keeble, widow of a local planter, and he began accumulating land, eventually owning about twenty-eight thousand acres in four counties. He became surveyor of Middlesex County, and during the next twenty years he held other local offices, including justice of the peace, vestryman of Christ Church, and major in the militia. During the General Court session in March 1676 he was acting attorney general of the colony. His annual income from his public offices in 1683 was reportedly about £425.

Beverley's main source of income in the early years was commerce. He exported large quantities of his own and his neighbors' tobacco (more than thirty-five thousand pounds during the 1671–1672 season) and imported soap, nails, wrought iron, shoes, haberdashery, cloth, saddles, and other merchandise. He became one of the wealthiest men in that part of Virginia. After his death his personal property alone was worth £1,591, and the debts due to him were valued at about £2,200.

Robert Beverley has often been referred to as Major Robert Beverley or as Robert Beverley the immigrant, to distinguish him from other Robert Beverleys of later generations. He and Mary Keeble Beverley had from four to six sons, of whom three survived childhood, and one daughter. Mary Keeble Beverley died in June 1678, and he married Katherine Hone on 28 March 1679. They had three sons and one daughter. Beverley sent his sons to England to be educated, and the three eldest among those who lived to adulthood, Peter Beverley, Robert Beverley (often referred to as Robert Beverley the historian), and Harry Beverley, made use of their educations and the advantages conferred by a wealthy and influential father to become important in their own right. They and their children made the Beverley family one of the most prominent in Virginia by the early years of the eighteenth century.

Beverley befriended Governor Sir William Berkeley, who probably assisted him in obtaining many of his large and valuable land grants. When Bacon's Rebellion broke out in 1676, Beverley unhesitatingly supported the governor and commanded one of the mounted units that the governor raised in his attempt to crush the rebellion. The royal commissioners later described Beverley as "a person very active & Serviceable in surprizinge & beatinge up of Quarters & Small guards about the Country." Beverley may have suffered damage to his own property as he claimed, but the commissioners also reported that he was "the only person that gott by those unhappy troubles, in Plunderinge (without distinction of honest mens Estates from others)."

For several years Beverley was a leader of the so-called Green Spring faction, political supporters of Berkeley who took their name from Berkeley's James City County residence. In February 1677 the House of Burgesses elected Robert Beverley clerk of the House. That April, when Berkeley's successor Herbert Jeffreys demanded that Beverley turn over to him the legislative journals in his care, Beverley refused to do so without House authorization. The royal commissioners who had been sent to Virginia to quell the rebellion and inquire into its causes forcibly seized the records, and the Privy Council later barred Beverley from office for his attempt to obstruct the commissioners. Beverley nevertheless continued to serve as clerk of the House of Burgesses, even after Governor Culpeper arrived in Virginia with explicit instructions to displace him.

In May 1682 Beverley was charged with taking a prominent part in the plant-cutting riots in Middlesex and surrounding counties. The plant cutters destroyed portions of their own and their neighbors' tobacco crops in an attempt to create a shortage and raise prices. As a result of legislation he had authored the previous year ordering the creation of a town in each county from which tobacco had to be shipped on penalty of seizure, Beverley had acquired large amounts of tobacco and thus had a strong interest in limiting the amount of tobacco exported. He was arrested and confined until 1684, when he was tried before the General Court and found guilty of "high Misdemeanors" but not of treason. He received a pardon after he supplicated the bench "on his bended Knees." Beverley won election to the House of Burgesses the following year and on 3 November 1685 by a vote of nineteen to seventeen won reelection to the office of clerk.

Beverley and Governor Effingham became embroiled in another controversy over the clerkship, and Beverley was charged with altering a bill that had passed the House. On 1 August 1686 the king issued a command again barring Beverley from all civil offices and granting the governor the power of appointing the clerk of the House of Burgesses. Before another trial could be held on the new charges against him, Robert Beverley died at his home on 15 March 1687. He was buried four days later, on the same day that his last son was christened.

Parish register of Saint Mary Lowgate, Hull, Humberside Record Office, Beverley, Eng.; Brent Tarter, "Major Robert Beverley (1635–1687) and His Immediate Family," *Magazine of Virginia Genealogy* 31 (1993): 163–177; Robert Beverley title book, VHS; Darrett B. Rutman and Anita H. Rutman, *A Place in Time: Middlesex County, Virginia, 1650–1750* (1984); Kukla, *Speakers and Clerks, 1643–1776*, 141–143; commissioners' report in Samuel Wiseman's Book of Record, Pepysian Library 2582, Magdalene College, Cambridge University; Hening, *Statutes at Large*, 3:541–571; *Executive Journals of Council*, vol. 1; Billings, *Effingham Papers*; death and burial in *The Parish Register of Christ Church, Middlesex County, Va., from 1653 to 1812* (1897), 29, 32; will in Middlesex Co. Wills Etc. (1675–ca. 1798), 42–44, printed in *VMHB* 3 (1895): 47–51.

EMORY G. EVANS

BEVERLEY, Robert (d. 21 April 1722), usually referred to as Robert Beverley Jr. or Robert Beverley the historian, was probably born in Middlesex County, the eldest child of from four to six sons, three of whom survived childhood, and one daughter of the immigrant Robert Beverley (1635–1687), usually referred to as Major Robert Beverley, and his second wife, Mary Keeble Beverley. He was most likely born about 1667 or 1668 and was of legal age before 1 September 1690, when he succeeded his elder half brother, Peter Beverley, as legal guardian of their younger brother John Beverley. Robert Beverley was educated in England, possibly at

Beverley Grammar School in Yorkshire. He married Ursula Byrd, the young daughter of William Byrd (1652–1704). She died not long after the birth of their only child, William Beverley, who grew up to become a member of the Council. Beverley evidently never married again.

During the 1690s Beverley lived in Jamestown and became a man of reputation and influence. He used his family connections to obtain prestigious and remunerative clerkships that in turn enabled him to add to his large inherited estate. In the spring of 1688 Beverley was working as a copyist in the Jamestown office of the secretary of the colony and doubling as deputy clerk of James City County, but he probably lost his berth in October 1691 when Lieutenant Governor Francis Nicholson ousted William Edwards, the chief clerk of the General Court and the secretary's office. When Christopher Robinson, the second husband of Beverley's stepmother Katherine Hone Beverley Robinson, became secretary of the colony in the summer of 1692 he appointed Beverley to the lucrative clerkship of the new county of King and Queen. Following Robinson's death the next year, Ralph Wormeley, another Middlesex County gentleman close to the Beverley family, became secretary, and he named Peter Beverley chief clerk of the General Court and the secretary's office. Robert Beverley went to work for his half brother, who by then was also clerk of the House of Burgesses. In March 1693 Robert Beverley became clerk to the Committee of Public Claims, and in May of that year he also filled in temporarily for Peter Beverley as clerk of the General Court.

In October 1693 Robert Beverley succeeded his half brother as chief clerk of the General Court and the secretary's office, and as clerk of James City County. Beverley substituted for James Sherlock as clerk of the Council and as clerk of the General Assembly in 1696, and in June 1697 he became register of the Virginia Court of Vice-Admiralty. Following the fire that destroyed the statehouse in Jamestown on 20 October 1698, Peter Beverley and Robert Beverley salvaged and arranged the valuable surviving public papers. Robert Beverley resigned as chief clerk before the end of the month and was subsequently elected to represent Jamestown in the House of Burgesses in 1699 and 1700, and in 1699 he was also elected to the distinguished committee to revise the laws of the colony. In March 1703 he became, like his father and half brother before him, clerk of the House of Burgesses.

Beverley acquired property in Jamestown and in Elizabeth City County, and he was appointed to the Elizabeth City County Court on 27 December 1700. Litigation over ownership of the Elizabeth City County land resulted in an adverse decision in the General Court, and Beverley appealed the decision to the Privy Council. After he sailed for England in the summer of 1703 to prosecute the case, Francis Nicholson, who had returned to Virginia as governor, deprived him of the clerkship of the House of Burgesses and engineered his dismissal as clerk of King and Queen County.

Beverley lost his case in London, but while there he wrote *The History and Present State of Virginia, In Four Parts* (1705), the first published history of a British colony by a native of North America. Three French-language editions were published between 1707 and 1718, probably as promotional literature to be distributed to Protestants in French-speaking portions of Europe. Beverley produced a work of lasting importance by drawing on his personal knowledge, on his extensive reading, and on official records filed in public offices in London. He also included significant portions from the unpublished writings of several other Virginians. The early section of the history relied heavily on Captain John Smith's writings, but the later sections on politics, Native Americans, and the flora, fauna, and agricultural products of the colony used several sources. Beverley's treatment of Bacon's Rebellion clearly reflected his father's loyalty to Governor Sir William Berkeley. The *History* was also sharply critical of Nicholson. Before leaving London, Beverley participated in the campaign against the governor that led to Nicholson's recall at about the same time that the *History* was printed.

Beverley returned to Virginia and resumed the pursuit of wealth. He also returned briefly to politics and represented James City County in the House of Burgesses in 1705–1706 before retiring to his estate, Beverley Park, in King and Queen County. During the 1710s he established friendly relations with Alexander Spotswood and probably accompanied the lieutenant governor on his exploratory journey to the crest of the Blue Ridge Mountains in 1716. Beverley also prepared *An Abridgement of the Publick Laws of Virginia, In Force and Use, June 10, 1720*, which he dedicated to Spotswood. Before sending it to his London publisher Beverley added abridgements of the acts of the assembly session of November–December 1720, in which he represented King and Queen County. The *Abridgement*, which also contained forms for writs and other legal processes, was issued in 1722. That same year, the publisher brought out a second edition of the *History* in which Beverley removed some of his earlier critical remarks about Virginia customs and Governor Nicholson and added new material to bring the historical section up to the same 10 June 1720 date given on the title page of the *Abridgement*.

Beverley's life during the 1710s is not well documented, but he continued to acquire property, including a large interest in 1719 in an iron foundry. He made successful experiments in viticulture while failing in efforts to obtain salaried clerkships to legislative committees. Beverley probably helped his son obtain the clerkship of Essex County in 1717, and he bequeathed most of his large estate to him. Robert Beverley died at Beverley Park on 21 April 1722, possibly without ever seeing the second edition of his *History* or the first edition of his *Abridgement*.

The leading biographies are in Fairfax Harrison, "Robert Beverley, the Historian of Virginia," *VMHB* 36 (1928): 333–344, Louis B. Wright, *The First Gentlemen of Virginia* (1940), 286–311, Richard Beale Davis, *Intellectual Life in the Colonial South, 1585–1763* (1978), 1:84–91, Kukla, *Speakers and Clerks, 1643–1776*, 144–146, J. A. Leo Lemay, "Robert Beverley's *History and Present State of Virginia* and the Emerging American Political Ideology," in *American Letters and the Historical Consciousness: Essays in Honor of Lewis P. Simpson*, ed. J. Gerald Kennedy and Daniel Mark Fogel (1987), 67–111, and Anne Margaret Daniel and Jon Kukla, "Robert Beverley (1673–1722)," in *Fifty Southern Writers Before 1900*, ed. Robert Bain and Joseph M. Flora (1987), 38–43 (which contains a useful bibliography); the traditional birth date of 1673 cannot be sustained; evidence on birth date and on dates of death of wife and birth of son in Brent Tarter, "Major Robert Beverley (1635–1687) and His Immediate Family," *Magazine of Virginia Genealogy* 31 (1993): esp. 170–172, 178–182; appointment as guardian for John Beverley in Middlesex Co. Order Book, 2:482; Robert Beverley title book, VHS; Beverley described the circumstances that led him to write the *History* in the introduction to the 2d ed.; Jon Kukla, "Robert Beverley Assailed: Appellate Jurisdiction and the Problem of Bicameralism in Seventeenth-Century Virginia," *VMHB* 88 (1980): 415–429; a 2d ed. of the *Abridgement* was published in 1728; Louis Wright speculated, in his introduction to his 1945 reprint edition, that Beverley also wrote *An Essay upon the Government of the English Plantations on the Continent of America* (1701), but for its attribution by other scholars to Ralph Wormeley (1650–1703) or to Benjamin Harrison (1673–1710), see Virginia White Fitz, "Ralph Wormeley: Anonymous Essayist," *WMQ*, 3d ser., 26 (1969): 586–595, and Carole Shammas, "Benjamin Harrison III and the Authorship of *An Essay upon the Government of the English Plantations on the Continent of America*," *VMHB* 84 (1976): 166–173; death date given in will of son William Beverley, printed in *VMHB* 22 (1914): 300.

JOHN M. HEMPHILL II
BRENT TARTER

BEVERLEY, Robert (ca. 1740–12 April 1800), planter, was born at his father's plantation in Essex County, one of two sons and three daughters of William Beverley and Elizabeth Bland Beverley. His brother died young. His father took him to England in 1750 for his education and enrolled him in a school at Wakefield. When Beverley matriculated at Trinity College, Cambridge, on 19 May 1757, he gave his age as seventeen. Earlier that year he was admitted to the Middle Temple to study law, and he was called to the bar on 6 February 1761. Beverley returned to Virginia almost immediately to manage the enormous estate he had inherited when his father died in 1756, and consequently he never practiced law.

At his father's death, the Beverley estate consisted of valuable properties in England, more than three thousand acres in several large plantations in Essex County, and huge holdings in the Shenandoah Valley, which combined to make Robert Beverley one of the wealthiest young men in the colony, with an annual income from rents and tobacco of about £1,800 in 1762. On 3 February 1763 he married Maria Carter, daughter of Landon Carter, of Sabine Hall. They had ten sons and six daughters. In 1769 he began several years of construction on a new residence, which was one of the largest and most elegant of all the Georgian plantation mansions in the Rappahannock River valley. His descendants retained his Blandfield mansion until 1983.

Beverley became a member of the Essex County Court by 1764 and served until the outbreak of the Revolutionary War. He eschewed the world of politics, although he kept himself well informed and once, in 1772, commented that he might like to have a seat on the governor's Council. Early in 1775 he was elected to the College of William and Mary's board of visitors, the only public office outside Essex County he held before the Revolution. In 1774 and 1775 Beverley tried to exert a moderating influence on the local political leaders whom he thought were unwisely rushing toward independence. He deplored every action thereafter that widened the breach between Virginia and Great Britain. Beverley opposed independence and refused to take any part in the government of the county or of his parish during the war. The Essex County authorities accordingly deprived him of his arms. Nonetheless, his standing as one of the best-educated and wealthiest men in the region resulted in his being elected to the House of Delegates in 1780, "without offering himself a candidate or being present," according to an unfriendly neighbor. Beverley probably did not take his seat in the legislature, but since he also refrained from active opposition to Virginia during the contest, he was left in peace at his elegant new house for the duration of the war.

In 1787 the Essex County justices of the peace asked the governor to reappoint Beverley to the county court. Spencer Roane angrily petitioned the governor's Council against the proposal, charging that Beverley's actions during the Revolutionary War should disqualify him, but the governor consented after the justices renewed their request. That episode was only one of several conflicts between Beverley and members of the Roane family, culminating two years later when Thomas Roane assaulted Beverley on a public highway and attempted to beat him with his cane. Roane either knocked Beverley from his horse, or Beverley fell while attempting to avoid the blow, and he was injured. Beverley successfully prosecuted Roane for the assault.

In the 1780s Beverley owned approximately fifty thousand acres in at least eight counties, with his largest holdings being in Culpeper and Caroline Counties. He wrote his will in 1793 and added nine codicils to it between then and 24 January 1800. He owned more than four hundred slaves during the 1790s, and his slaves and personal property listed in his Essex County estate inventory were worth almost £8,500. Robert Beverley died at Blandfield on 12 April 1800 and was probably buried there.

Biography in introduction to Robert M. Calhoon, ed., "'A Sorrowful Spectator of These Tumultuous Times'; Robert Beverley Describes the Coming of the Revolution," *VMHB* 73 (1965): 41–55; Maria Carter Beverley family Bible records, including the dates of his marriage and death, printed in *Virginia Genealogist* 16 (1972): 130–131; Robert Beverley's letter book, 1761–1793, LC; architectural research reports establishing date of erection of Blandfield in library of Virginia Department of Historic Resources; James B. Slaughter, *Settlers, Southerners, Americans: The History of Essex County, Virginia, 1608–1984* (1985), 62–75; 1788 appointment as justice documented in *Journals of Council of State*, 4:224–225, 361–362, and *Calendar of Virginia State Papers*, 4:338–340, 5:228, 319–320; will and estate inventory in Essex Co. Will Book, 15:543–554, 16:15–36.

BRENT TARTER

BEVERLEY, Robert (4 July 1822–31 May 1901), agricultural reformer and Populist Party leader, was the elder of two sons and second of six children of James Bradshaw Beverley and Jane Peter Beverley. He was born at the home of his grandfather Robert Beverley in Georgetown, District of Columbia, where his parents lived from 1819 until about 1823. The family then returned to Fauquier County, where his father built Avenel, located near The Plains. Beverley was educated at the Harwood Seminary in or near Somerville in Fauquier County, then at an academy in Warrenton, and finally at Benjamin Hallowell's school in Alexandria. He inherited Avenel after his father's death in 1853 and also acquired several other tracts of land, eventually amounting to more than 1,500 acres, including the adjoining Pignut farm, as well as the

Chapman farm at The Plains. Beverley spent the rest of his life at Avenel, engaging in diversified commercial farming and cattle raising. On 14 June 1843 he married Jane Eliza Carter. Two of their six sons and one of their six daughters died young.

Beverley could best be described as a gentleman farmer. A descendant of Robert Beverley (ca. 1740–1800), who erected Blandfield in Essex County, he was a conspicuous and well-connected member of Virginia society. During the Civil War he spent most of his time with the Confederate commissary department. Once he was jailed briefly in Alexandria, and on several occasions he and other prominent Confederate sympathizers were forced to ride on trains to keep Southern soldiers from derailing them. In seeking a presidential pardon after the war, Beverley stated that he had lived at home throughout the Civil War, limited his political participation to voting in only one Confederate congressional election, and taken no part in the fighting. Nevertheless, he was often referred to by the courtesy title of colonel.

Beverley joined the Virginia State Agricultural Society in 1856 and served as a judge for the society's fourth annual exhibition in October of that year. After the Virginia State Agricultural Society reorganized in 1869, Beverley again served as a judge for the state fair that the society sponsored each year. By 1871 he had paid the fee to become a life member. In 1874 he served on the society's executive committee and on the advisory board for the animal department as well. Three years later Beverley became one of three vice presidents of the society and chief of the cattle department with overall responsibility for the judging of cattle at the annual state fair. He held those positions until he became president of the society in February 1885, an office he retained until the end of 1887. Under Beverley's leadership the society summoned the 1885 organizational meeting of the Farmers' Assembly of the State of Virginia, of which he was president in 1889. The assembly, a frankly political organization of Virginia's planters, pressed the legislature for the creation of a state board of agriculture and improved funding for agricultural education.

Beverley became well known in national agricultural circles. He had helped to found the Farmers' National Congress of the United States, also called the National Agricultural Congress, in 1875, and eight years later was elected its president. During the four years Beverley held the presidency he lobbied in Washington for the establishment of a cabinet-level department of agriculture, larger appropriations for agricultural experiment stations and agricultural research and education, and improvements in the collection and dissemination of accurate weather information. In 1888, as vice president at large of the Inter-state Farmers' Association, Beverley successfully introduced a resolution at the association's second annual meeting recommending that farmers support candidates attuned to farmers' concerns.

Beverley was a Democrat and served as a delegate to the party's 1884 national convention, where he was named to the committee that notified Grover Cleveland of his nomination for the presidency. Beverley's subsequent disappointment with Cleveland's administration and his own inability to persuade Congress to enact any part of the agenda of the Farmers' National Congress caused him to break with the Democrats and to take a leading role in forming the Farmers' Alliance of Virginia, which became the People's, or Populist, Party of Virginia. Beverley later referred to himself as "the Grandfather of the Farmers' Alliance." He also helped establish the national People's Party, attended several of its conventions, and ran in 1892 as one of its Virginia candidates for presidential elector. He supported the party's ambitious platform of economic reforms; agreed with its criticism of the political influence of banks, monopolies, and railroads; and approved of its inflationary policy of coining silver to raise the prices of agricultural commodities. Beverley gave strong support to the Populist platform, but the Farmers' Alliance of Virginia was politically less radical than many of its counterparts in the West and elsewhere in the South. It was led by comparatively prosperous large-scale planters such as Beverley himself, whose holdings at his death were valued at more than $90,000, and it had no affiliation with the smaller Colored Farmers' Alliance of Virginia.

Three of Beverley's sons also participated in the Farmers' Alliance of Virginia and the People's Party, and two of them, John Hill Carter Beverley (1853–1934), who lived in Essex County, and James Bradshaw Beverley (1861–1926), who resided near his father in Fauquier County, assumed leading roles in their own rights. The August 1893 state convention in Lynchburg nominated J. Brad Beverley for lieutenant governor and elected J. H. C. Beverley chairman of the committee on permanent organization at the recommendation of which Robert Beverley was named permanent chairman of the convention. J. H. C. Beverley had also been a candidate for presidential elector in 1892 and remained active as an advocate of agricultural reforms and education after the demise of the People's Party. He served on the State Board of Agriculture from 1899 to 1908 and as its president from 1902 to 1904. Perhaps because of his prior association with the Populists, he was the only Democratic nominee in all of eastern Virginia not elected to a seat in the Virginia Convention of 1901–1902.

Robert Beverley suffered from cataracts and from a variety of debilitating illnesses during the 1890s, and he speedily disappeared from public view after the middle of the decade. He died at his home on 31 May 1901 and was buried in the graveyard of the Church of Our Savior Episcopal Church (now Little Georgetown Cemetery), near The Plains.

John McGill, *The Beverley Family of Virginia* (1956), 552–565; reminiscences of Beverley's life by grandson Robert Beverley Herbert, *Life on a Virginia Farm: Stories and Recollections of Fauquier County* (1968), esp. 46, 56–57, 59, 81–85; estate valuation and many Beverley letters in Beverley Family Papers, VHS; Presidential Pardons; speeches as president of Farmers' National Congress printed in *Southern Planter* 45 (1884): 63–65, 606–612; 47 (1886): 70–72, 487–492; 48 (1887): 65–68; 49 (1888): 21–26; presidential address of 10 Dec. 1889 to Farmers' Assembly of the State of Virginia in *Southern Planter* 51 (1890): 23–24; public letter of 20 Mar. 1888 "To the Young Men of Virginia" in *Richmond State*, 9 June 1888; William DuBose Sheldon, *Populism in the Old Dominion: Virginia Farm Politics, 1885–1900* (1935); Nancy Chappelear Baird, *Fauquier County, Virginia, Tombstone Inscriptions* (1970), 64; obituary in *Richmond Dispatch*, 2 June 1901.

BRENT TARTER

BEVERLEY, Sarah Archie Swanson (28 May 1881–5 February 1968), educator, was born at Whitmell in Pittsylvania County, the youngest of three sons and four daughters of Frank Archer Swanson and Sarah Payne Swanson. She began her education in the two-room Whitmell School and graduated in 1897 from Reidsville High School in Reidsville, North Carolina. She then enrolled in the Randolph-Macon Institute in Danville and two years later entered Randolph-Macon Woman's College in Lynchburg. With her borrowed funds depleted, she left college in 1901 to begin her teaching career in Big Stone Gap.

In 1904 Swanson moved to Bristol, Tennessee, and in 1906 to Laurel, Mississippi, where she taught for two years before returning to Whitmell to care for her ailing father. On 27 June 1912 she married Frank C. Beverley, an employee of the Norfolk and Western Railway Company and moved with him to Bluefield, West Virginia. Two years later she again returned to Whitmell because of her father's poor health. Following his death in 1916, Beverley and her husband acquired the Swanson family farm, which he managed while she resumed her teaching career at Whitmell School the same year. In 1918 she became the principal, a position she held until her retirement in 1951, and in 1918 the newly named Whitmell Farm-Life School also received state accreditation as a four-year high school, the first rural school in the county so designated.

Archie Swanson Beverley, as she was professionally known, also resumed her education, and in the summer of 1918 she worked with Harold W. Foght, chief of the Rural Division of the United States Bureau of Education. During the ensuing summers she traveled to Aberdeen, South Dakota, where Foght had become president of Aberdeen State Teachers College, and she earned a B.S. in 1923. Beverley received an M.A. from Teachers College, Columbia University, in 1932. She often took summer courses at major universities, among them the University of Virginia, the Virginia Agricultural and Mechanical College and Polytechnic Institute, the College of William and Mary, Michigan State University, Ohio State University, the University of Pittsburgh, Syracuse University, the University of Tennessee, and the University of

Wisconsin. In 1934 she attended a short course at the International People's College in Denmark.

During her time as principal of the Whitmell school Beverley devoted much of her energy to filling a need for higher-quality rural education and for training specifically directed to rural educators. To obtain local support and make schools useful to their communities, Beverley tried to transform the country school into a center of rural life. In doing so she was strongly influenced by Mabel Carney, author of *Country Life and the Country School: A Study of the Agencies of Rural Progress and of the Social Relationship of the School to the Country Community* (1912), and a mentor to Beverley.

An energetic and caring principal, she became a recognized leader in rural education at the local, state, and national levels. Under her leadership Whitmell Farm-Life School was remodeled and additional buildings were constructed. The guidance program, instituted in 1922, along with other improvements drew the attention of school administrators from a wide area. In 1920, at Beverley's invitation, the U.S. Bureau of Education held a National Country Life Conference at Whitmell, attracting thousands of people, including the governor of Virginia, the state superintendent of public instruction, and the U.S. commissioner of education. This was followed by a similar conference three years later. During the 1926–1927 academic year Whitmell received accreditation from the Southern Association of Colleges and Secondary Schools.

The Virginia Agricultural and Mechanical College and Polytechnic Institute awarded Beverley a certificate of merit in 1927 for her contributions to agriculture, one of the few women so honored. She lectured at many rural teachers institutes between 1923 and 1935, and she participated in the White House Conference on Rural Education in 1944. Active in many professional and civic organizations, Beverley helped found the Virginia chapter of Delta Kappa Gamma, an honorary society for women educators, which honored her in 1953 as the outstanding woman citizen of the Danville-Pittsylvania area. She was also active in the Whitmell Methodist Church. When she retired in 1951, the Pittsylvania Education Association honored her with a bronze plaque, and the Whitmell high school class of 1951 donated a portrait of her, both of which were placed in the school corridor. Early in her retirement Beverley wrote *Growing Years: The Development of the Whitmell Farm-Life School* (1955), a book recounting the progress of the Whitmell school and describing her philosophy of public education.

Sarah Archie Swanson Beverley died at Memorial Hospital in Danville on 5 February 1968 and was buried at Highland Burial Park in Danville.

Autobiographical statements in *Growing Years*, 3–14, and in Virginia Iota State Organization of Delta Kappa Gamma, *Adventures in Teaching* (1963), 32–40 (por.); BVS Marriage Register, Pittsylvania Co.; obituaries in *Danville Bee* and *Danville Register*, both 6 Feb. 1968, *Chatham Star-Tribune*, 8 Feb. 1968, and *Virginia Journal of Education* 61 (Mar. 1968): 44.

ELIZABETH COMPTON

BEVERLEY, William (ca. 1696–28 February 1756), member of the Council, was the only child of Robert Beverley (d. 1722) and Ursula Byrd Beverley. He was born late in 1695 or early in 1696, probably in Jamestown where his father then lived and where his mother was buried within two years of his birth. Beverley was educated in England. He probably accompanied his father to England in the summer of 1703 and returned to Virginia in the spring of 1711.

On 19 March 1717 twenty-one-year-old William Beverley took the oaths of office as clerk of Essex County. He held the lucrative clerkship until April 1745, although for much of the time he hired deputies to do the work. For a time after his father's death in April 1722 he resided at his father's Beverley Park in nearby King and Queen County, but after his marriage two or three years later to Elizabeth Bland he took up permanent residence in Essex County. Beverley had at least two sons, one of whom died in infancy, and at least three daughters, and in 1750 he took his son Robert Beverley (ca. 1740–1800) to England to be educated. The four children who lived to adulthood married into wealthy families, and under the terms of his will each of the daughters received marriage settlements and bequests worth about £1,500.

Beverley inherited more than 19,000 acres of land. He was temporarily short of cash in 1722 and disposed of his father's share in an ironworks that required an expenditure of money, but he soon patented another 12,000 acres. Beverley planted tobacco on his eastern plantations, owned a tavern license for a time in Caroline County, and became one of the wealthiest men of his generation through the acquisition of large tracts of western land. He traveled to the Shenandoah Valley as early as 1729, and in 1736 he received a grant of almost 120,000 acres in what became Augusta County. In association with James Patton, of Ulster, he helped bring Irish and Scots-Irish immigrants to Virginia and rented or sold land to them. By 1756 Beverley had sold 80,455 acres to new settlers. In 1743 he requested a grant of 20,000 acres from the Fairfax family, and two years later in partnership with his relatives, the politically powerful Robinson family, of King and Queen County, he became part owner of 100,000 acres on the Greenbrier River. Beverley played a key role in the settlement of the Valley of Virginia, and the portion of Augusta County where his initial grant lay is still known as Beverley Manor. A partial inventory of his property taken in 1745 showed that he then had 119 tenants in at least five counties and sixty-one slaves at four of his plantations.

Beverley represented Orange County in the House of Burgesses from 1736 to 1740 and sat for Essex County from 1742 to 1749. He was a leader in the powerful legislative faction dominated by Speaker John Robinson. As early as 1741 Beverley began seeking appointment to the governor's Council, and he also made it known that he was willing to pay as much as £2,000 to purchase the powerful and profitable office of secretary of the colony. In the spring of 1750 the Privy Council approved his appointment to succeed the deceased John Custis on the governor's Council, but Beverley did not take his seat until 30 April 1752, after he returned from England. He went back to England in the summer of 1753 and stayed for more than a year to recover his health and settle his private affairs.

Beverley resumed his seat on the Council in May 1755. He wrote his will at the beginning of December 1755 and bequeathed the bulk of his huge estate to his only surviving son. William Beverley died, probably at his home in Essex County, on 28 February 1756.

Jane Dennison Carson, "William Beverley and Beverley Manor" (master's thesis, UVA, 1937); Brent Tarter, "Major Robert Beverley (1635–1687) and His Immediate Family," *Magazine of Virginia Genealogy* 31 (1993): 180–182, 183; James B. Slaughter, *Settlers, Southerners, Americans: The History of Essex County, Virginia, 1608–1984* (1985), 29–31; William Beverley letter book, 1737–1748, New York Public Library; William Beverley account book, 1745, VHS; Robert D. Mitchell, *Commercialism and Frontier: Perspectives on the Early Shenandoah Valley* (1977), 31–36, 61–65, 80–81; Robert Beverley and R. Carter Beverley, eds., "Diary of William Beverley of 'Blandfield' during a Visit to England, 1750," *VMHB* 36 (1928): 27–35, 161–169; copies of will in *Beverley* v. *Ricketts* suit papers, Spotsylvania District Court, and in *Beverley* v. *Kinney* suit papers, August a Circuit Court Ended Causes, and printed in *VMHB* 22 (1914): 297–301; age and death date on mourning ring discovered in Urbanna in 1929 (*Richmond News Leader*, 5 June 1929, and *Richmond Times-Dispatch*, 6 June 1929).

EMORY G. EVANS

BEVERLY, Frank Monroe (2 January 1857–1 July 1929), writer and poet, was the eldest of four sons and two daughters of William Walter Beverly and Elizabeth Gentry Beverly and was born on a farm in the portion of Wise County that in 1880 became part of the new county of Dickenson. He was christened Franklin but shortened his first name to Frank. In 1860 the family moved to McDowell County and in 1863 to Wyoming County, in the new state of West Virginia. McDowell and Wyoming Counties were the scenes of frequent lawlessness and violence during the Civil War.

The family moved back to Wise County about 1867. Beverly grew up there and was educated in small private schools and at the new public schools at Bolecamp Creek and Darwin. He did not learn to read until he was eleven, but despite seemingly meager educational opportunities, Beverly developed a curiosity about the world around him and beyond the mountains. He acquired a thirst for books and formed a lifelong attachment to literature and writing. In 1875 he began teaching in a school in the Long Fork district of what soon became Dickenson County and also attended an academy in Whitesburg, Kentucky.

On 7 April 1882 Beverly married Mary Jane Fleming. They lived for a year on her seventy-five-acre farm near Clintwood in Dickenson County and then moved to a neighboring farm where they resided until 1902. Here their five sons and three daughters were born. Beverly retired from teaching after eleven years and instead worked as a farmer and at various other occupations. Between 1902 and 1924 he moved several times. In 1907 he briefly owned and edited the *Clintwood News*. He held the office of postmaster of Clintwood twice and worked for seven years in the clerk's office of the Dickenson County Court.

Beverly also cultivated his talent for composition, particularly in verse. He wrote hundreds of poems, many of which appeared in local and regional newspapers, such as the *Norton Crawford's Weekly*, and in a variety of magazines, including *Lee's Texas Magazine*, the *Farmers' Home Journal*, and the *Gospel Herald*. He also published some short stories and served as local correspondent for the *Richmond Times-Dispatch*, for which he produced a number of sketches and articles about life in southwestern Virginia. Eight of his autobiographical sketches appeared under the title "Life in the Appalachian Regions" in the *Big Stone Gap Post* between 16 June and 22 September 1926, and he published a brief family history, "The Beverly Family of Southwest Virginia," in the same paper on 3 October 1928.

The reputation of Beverly rests principally on his poems, which voice an abiding appreciation for the rugged splendor of the mountains in which he lived. His reflections on the beauties of the region and on the consolation he derived from nature won him fame as a regional writer of the southern Appalachians and earned him the sobriquet Poet of the Cumberlands. Beverly never made much money from his writings. Not until shortly before his death, and then only with financial assistance from friends, did he succeed in publishing his one volume of poetry, *Echoes from the Cumberlands* (1928).

Beverly collected books avidly and accumulated approximately 5,000 volumes. For the last five years of his life he was an invalid. After his vision became partially impaired in 1926, he dispersed much of his book collection to the Virginia State Library, which received several hundred volumes, and to the Clintwood Public Library, the Roanoke Public Library, and the library at Radford State Teachers College. Frank Monroe Beverly died on 1 July 1929 at his house, Bonnywicket, in Dickenson County and was buried on a nearby hilltop that he had named Cumberland Cemetery.

James Taylor Adams, "Beverly of Bonnywicket," *Norton Crawford's Weekly*, 2 July 1927 (por.); Elihu Jasper Sutherland, *Some Sandy Basin Characters* (1962), 17–46; Beverly letters in Joseph Labadie Papers, University of Michigan Library, Ann Arbor; Beverly's scrapbooks in James Taylor Adams Papers, Clinch Valley College Library, Wise; BVS Marriage Register, Dickenson Co.; obituaries and editorial tributes in *Richmond Times-Dispatch*, 4 July 1929, *Norton Crawford's Weekly*, 5 July 1929, and *Big Stone Gap Post*, 10 July 1929.

DONALD W. GUNTER

BEYER, Edward (1820–1865), painter, was probably born in the German Rhineland about 1820, but his background is otherwise obscure. After he completed his studies at the Düsseldorf Academy he worked for a time as an artist in Dresden. An etching and two copperplate engravings produced by him or a different German artist of the same name survive from this period.

About 1848 Beyer and his wife moved to the United States. He established himself first in Newark, New Jersey, and later in Philadelphia. In collaboration with Leo Elliott, a French-born artist living in Philadelphia, he created a panorama depicting the wars in Italy and Hungary, a tour de force touted as containing about 90,000 three-foot figures. Beyer exhibited the work in Philadelphia in 1850, in New York the following year, and in Cincinnati in 1853.

Beyer traveled to Virginia in 1854. Captivated by the beauty of the Valley of Virginia, he remained for two-and-a-half years, sketching its towns, spas, and natural wonders. In his landscapes Beyer conveyed a romantic sense of the boundlessness of the natural world. His views of some of Virginia's western towns and fashionable resorts depicted people living harmoniously within the natural world and, by implication, in harmony with each other.

In May 1856 Beyer was in Richmond taking a subscription to publish a volume of reproductions of some of his Virginia scenes. He returned to the German states shortly thereafter to supervise the translation of the original works into lithographs, the printing being done by presses in Dresden and Berlin. Back in Richmond in May 1857, Beyer distributed some unbound sets of the lithographs and published the remainder in 1858 as the *Album of Virginia: or, Illustration of the Old Dominion*. The folio volume consisted of forty plates and an illustrated title page, accompanied by a small descriptive pamphlet possibly written by Samuel Mordecai. The *Album of Virginia* is one of the great mid-nineteenth-century American viewbooks and remains Beyer's best-known work. The popular lithographs are still used to illustrate numerous books and articles on Virginia, and in 1980 the Virginia State Library reproduced the entire set of prints in a reduced format of unbound color plates.

After the publication of the *Album of Virginia*, Beyer returned again to Germany, settling for a time in Meissen, where he created a cyclorama that included well over 100 American landscapes, many of them based on his Virginia views. He displayed the cyclorama in Meissen, Munich, and Berlin. Approximately thirty-five of Beyer's paintings are known, but none of the originals reproduced in the *Album of Virginia* has been located. His panorama and cyclorama are likewise lost. Edward Beyer died in Munich in 1865.

William L. Whitwell, "Edward Beyer (1820–1865)," in Sotheby's, *Important Americana: The Collection of Dr. and Mrs. Henry P. Deyerle . . . May 26, 1995*, auction catalog (1995), n.p.; R. Lewis Wright, "Edward Beyer and the *Album of Virginia*," *Virginia Cavalcade* 22 (spring 1973): 36–47 (por., 38), and "Edward Beyer in America: A German Painter Looks at Virginia," *Art & Antiques* 3 (Nov.– Dec. 1980): 72–77; years of birth and death in Julius Meyer, Hermann Lücke, and Hugo von Tschudi, *Allgemeines Künstler-Lexicon* (1872–1885), 3:788, 789–790, and Ulrich Thieme et al., *Allgemeines Lexicon der Bildenden Künstler* (1907–1950), 3:565; one Beyer letter in VHS; *Richmond Daily Dispatch*, 19 May 1856, 27 May 1857; *Roanoke City Library and the Roanoke Fine Arts Center Present an Exhibition of the Works of Edward Beyer*, exhibition catalog (1974); Susanne Arnold, *Album of Virginia: Picturesque Views of the Old Dominion*, LVA exhibition catalog (1994); Edward Beyer, *Cyclorama, Malerische Reise von Bremen nach New-York und durch die Vereinigten Staaten von Nordamerika*, 2d ed. [ca. 1860s].

VIRGINIUS C. HALL JR.

BICKFORD, James Van Allen (ca. 31 December 1874–14 April 1947), mayor of Hampton, was born in Hampton, the third of four children, all sons, of Selwyn Eugene Bickford and Caroline Matilda Van Allen Bickford. He attended William and Mary during the 1891–1892 academic year and then entered the Virginia Military Institute, from which he graduated in 1896 with a degree in civil engineering. He worked as a draftsman at the Newport News Ship Building and Dry Dock Company and served in a naval reserve unit during the Spanish-American War. Bickford married Katherine West Tabb on 4 January 1899. They had one son. Following his wife's death on 28 August 1904, he married her cousin Helen West Rutherford in 1906. They had one son and one daughter.

Early in the twentieth century Bickford established a sand and gravel business in Hampton and began to deal in real estate. One of the largest projects in which he was engaged was the construction during the 1910s of Langley Field, one of the first military airfields in Virginia. During the winter of 1915–1916 Bickford was appointed to a vacant seat on the Hampton Common Council. He won a full term in 1916 and was reelected at each succeeding municipal election, serving without interruption for almost thirty-one years. As a strong advocate of the new city manager form of government, he helped transform the city's government into the council-manager form in 1920, thereby replacing political management of city services with professional administration.

The council elected Bickford mayor of Hampton on 29 June 1920 . Routinely reelected thereafter, he served for twenty-six consecutive years, until he resigned due to failing health. He was intensely interested in improving the city's streets and bridges and keeping its harbor dredged. During his years as mayor Hampton also built a new city hall. Although his personal ownership of a business engaged in construction and his official support of public construction projects could have provoked charges of conflict of interest, no one ever hinted at impropriety or corruption. A civic leader with a regional rather than a local outlook, Bickford oversaw an expansion of his city that took place in conjunction with the growth of the manufacturing and transportation industries in the greater Hampton Roads area. In September 1937 he was elected to a one-year term as president of the Virginia League of Municipalities.

James Van Allen Bickford resigned as mayor of Hampton on 10 October 1946 and died in Elizabeth Buxton Hospital in Hampton on 14 April 1947. He was buried in the graveyard of Saint John's Episcopal Church in Hampton.

Birth date of 31 Dec. 1874 in Bickford's 30 Sept. 1912 questionnaire response, Alumni Records, VMI, with month and year corroborated by Census, Elizabeth City Co., 1900; Tyler, *Encyclopedia*, 4:989–990; Bruce, Tyler, and Morton, *History of Virginia*, 4:544–545; Glass and Glass, *Virginia Democracy*, 3:542–547, with variant 31 Dec. 1878 birth date (por.); Rogers Dey Whichard, ed., *The History of Lower Tidewater Virginia* (1959), 3:173; BVS Birth Register, Elizabeth City Co., records birth of unnamed son to Bickford's parents on 25 Oct. 1874; Francis W. Hayes Jr., ed., *Elizabeth City Parish, Hampton, Virginia: 19th Century Parish Registers* (1986), 7, with variant 30 Dec. 1874 birth date; John B. Bentley, ed., *Gravestone Inscriptions from the Cemetery of St. John's Episcopal Church, Hampton, Virginia* (1975), 12, with variant 31 Dec. 1876 birth date repeated in obituaries; family history information verified by daughter-in-law Betty Lee Bickford and grandson Paul Bickford; BVS Marriage Register, Elizabeth City Co.; *Newport News Daily Press*, 30 June 1920, 11 Oct. 1946; obituaries in *Newport News Daily Press*, 14, 15 Apr. 1947, and *Newport News Times-Herald*, 14 Apr. 1947; editorial tributes in *Newport News Daily Press* and *Newport News Times-Herald*, both 15 Apr. 1947.

CHERYL YIELDING FALES

BICKLEY, George Washington Lafayette (18 July 1823–10 August 1867), founder of the Knights of the Golden Circle, was born at Bickley's Mills in Russell County, the elder of two children, both sons, of George Bickley and Martha Lamb Bickley. His father and brother died early in the 1830s, and Lafayette Bickley, as he was then known, moved from place to place in Virginia, usually staying with relatives. In 1835 he ran away and spent twelve years in other southern states. He was with relatives in Milton, Florida, in October 1846, and he engaged in a trading business in nearby Geneva, Alabama. Bickley stated that he had educated himself, but he also claimed, in what was almost certainly a falsehood, that he had studied medicine in England. He possessed a good vocabulary, some literary abilities, and a glib tongue.

Late in April 1847 Bickley returned to Virginia via New Orleans and Greencastle, Indiana. In June of that year he was in Prince George County. He then spent some time in North Carolina, where on 3 February 1848 he married a widow identified only as Mrs. V. F. Bell. Their one son was placed with another family when she died in June 1850. Bickley soon returned to Russell County, where the 1850 census taker listed him as a phrenologist with property worth $400.

Late in 1850 or early in 1851 Bickley moved to Tazewell County, setting himself up as a physician in the Union Hotel in Jeffersonville. He found time to write one of the first histories of southwestern Virginia, *History of the Settlement and Indian Wars of Tazewell County, Virginia* (1852), which contained a wealth of information about the region's geography, climate, economy, educational facilities, and customs. It was one of the first publications to comment on the increase of slavery in the mountain counties of southwestern Virginia. Bickley also produced a short novel, *Adalaska: or, The Strange and Mysterious Family of the Cave of Genreva* (1853). *Adalaska* promoted American expansion and Manifest Destiny as well as the viewpoint of what is commonly referred to as the Young America movement.

In 1851 Bickley moved to Cincinnati and joined the faculty of the Eclectic Medical Institute. He assisted in editing the *Eclectic Medical Journal* and contributed to it frequently. Bickley published *Principles of Scientific Botany* in 1853 and the same work the following year as *Positive Medical Agents*. He married Rachel Kinney Dodson, a well-to-do widow and the sister of a Cincinnati banker, joined the Know Nothings, and gained a semblance of respectability. In April 1853 Bickley founded the *West American Review: A Critical Cyclopedia of Literature, Science, and Art*, which failed within six months. A conservative newspaper that he tried to establish as an antidote to Horace Greeley's *New York Tribune* proved similarly unsuccessful. Bickley also experimented with viticulture on his wife's farm in Scioto County, dabbled in land speculation, and briefly edited the *Portsmouth Ohio Pennant*. Then he characteristically tried to have his wife's property put in his own name, but his brother-in-law foiled the attempt and his wife left him, going to Memphis to stay with a sister. The author of Bickley's obituary for the *Abingdon Virginian* wrote that he "married and ran through the fortunes of three wealthy women," but no other evidence for a third marriage has come to light.

Bickley worked for a time as editor of a new weekly, *The Scientific Artisan*, published by the American Patent Company in Cincinnati, of which he was a director. He was dismissed in the spring of 1859. Bickley then formed the Knights of the Golden Circle and assigned himself the title of president general of the American Legion, K.G.C. He devised a set of rituals, oaths, and passwords, and he began to enroll members and collect membership fees. The vague but avowed goal of the Golden Circle was to colonize northern Mexico and eventually annex it to the United States. Like other southern filibusters, he viewed expansion into Mexico and Central America and the creation of new slave states as a way to tip the sectional balance—politically and economically—in favor of the South. Hounded by creditors, he left Ohio on a midnight train and traveled to Washington, Philadelphia, and New York, where he published *Rules, Regulations, and Principles of the Knights of the Golden Circle* (1859).

During 1860 Bickley traveled in the Southern states seeking members for his organization, making false claims, and fueling rumors about his fantasy. Failures dogged his footsteps. A national convention scheduled for Raleigh, North Carolina, was a farce, and a Golden Circle rendezvous on the banks of the Nueces River in Texas failed to take place.

When the Civil War began Bickley tried to transform his filibustering fancy into a military order to aid the Confederacy. He visited Montgomery, Alabama, and Knoxville, Tennessee, where a nephew lived, taking his broken dreams and the headquarters of the Knights of the Golden Circle with him. After he tried to form a corps of Kentuckians and force the state into secession (and charge a membership fee), the editor of the *Louisville Journal* attacked the Golden Circle in a series of long articles in May and June 1861. Two other writers published books on the fantastic organization: Joseph W. Pomfrey, *A True Disclosure and Exposition of the Knights of the Golden Circle* (1861), and James M. Hiatt, *An Authentic Exposition of the K.G.C., Knights of the Golden Circle: or, A History of Secession From 1834 to 1861* (1861). Although not a single Golden Circle chapter existed north of the Ohio River, Republican newspaper editors claimed that the order was extensive and involved in treasonable plots, a bogeyman that served to discredit the Democratic Party and attract support for the organization of Union Leagues.

Bickley served as a surgeon in the 29th Regiment North Carolina Volunteers in the Confederate Army of Tennessee from 28 January 1863 until the summer of that year. When he found himself within the Union lines, however, he presented himself at an army headquarters seeking a pass for himself, his wife, and his child. Instructed to report to General Ambrose E. Burnside in Cincinnati, Bickley went elsewhere. On 17 July 1863 military authorities arrested him in Albany, Delaware County, Indiana, and confiscated the contents of his trunk. The papers proved that Bickley was a dreamer and pretender. Rather than give him a public trial that would prove that the Golden Circle was a farce, the army imprisoned Bickley, first in the state penitentiary in Columbus, Ohio, then in Fort Lafayette, New York, and finally in Fort Warren, Boston Harbor. He wrote long letters to various officials, all of whom ignored his pleas. After President Abraham Lincoln's assassination, a federal investigator visited Bickley to ask if the Golden Circle was involved in the murder plot. Bickley remained in prison until 14 October 1865, when he was released after signing a pledge not to sue the government for keeping him behind bars for twenty-six months, during which no formal charges had ever been filed against him.

Soon after his release Bickley went to England and unsuccessfully tried to organize a lecture tour. George Washington Lafayette Bickley returned to the United States and died in Baltimore on 10 August 1867.

Gloria Jahoda, "The Bickleys of Virginia," *VMHB* 66 (1958): 478; Ollinger Crenshaw, "The Knights of the Golden Circle: The Career of George Bickley," *AHR* 47 (1941): 23–50; family letters quoted in James William Hagy, "George Washington Lafayette Bickley: The Early Years," in *Historical and Biographical Sketches*, Historical Society of Southwest Virginia, *Publication* 6 (1972): 64–74; Compiled Service Records; Frank L. Klement, *Dark Lanterns: Secret Political Societies, Conspiracies, and Treason Trials in the Civil War* (1984), 7–33; George W. L. Bickley Papers, Records of Office of Judge Advocate General (Army), RG 153, NARA; obituary in *Abingdon Virginian*, 4 Oct. 1867.

FRANK L. KLEMENT

BIGGER, Isaac Alexander (25 June 1893–27 January 1955), physician and educator, was born in Bethel, near Clover, South Carolina, the younger of two sons and second of five children of Isaac Alexander Bigger and Mary Neel Johnston Bigger. He grew up in Bethel and in Rock Hill, South Carolina, where his father, a physician, moved the family about 1906. Bigger received his early education at home under the direction of a governess and a tutor who encouraged his passion for reading. He attended Erskine College in Due West, South Carolina, for one year and Davidson College in Davidson, North Carolina, for two more years before entering the medical school of the University of Virginia in 1914. His education was interrupted several times by attacks of bronchial asthma, a condition that prevented his participation in sports and plagued him throughout his professional life. Bigger became president of Nu Sigma Nu medical fraternity, received his medical degree in 1919, and served his surgical residency at the University of Virginia Hospital from 1919 to 1922.

On 9 September 1922 Bigger married a graduate nurse, Beatrice Emily Haslam. They had three daughters. Bigger was a member of the surgical staff at the University of Virginia until 1927 when he joined the faculty of Vanderbilt University in Nashville, Tennessee, as associate professor of surgery. At Vanderbilt he developed an interest in the emerging field of thoracic surgery.

In 1930 Bigger was appointed the first full-time professor of surgery at the Medical College of Virginia in Richmond. At age thirty-seven he was one of the youngest surgery department chairmen in the United States. Working with the chief of medicine, William B. Porter, and the president of the college, William T. Sanger, Bigger played a vital role in elevating the school's academic standing and reputation. He possessed a remarkable knowledge of anatomy and pathology and an uncanny diagnostic ability. His many surgical innovations and his clear and well-organized lectures combined to make him both a fine surgeon and an effective teacher whose devotion to medicine and to the Medical College of Virginia was legendary. He labored long hours teaching students, training residents, and caring for his many patients. He and Bruce Lehman, professor of surgery at the University of Virginia, developed a mutual admiration and friendship that insured peace between potential rival institutions.

Bigger did pioneering work in thoracic surgery, but he avoided excessive specialization. He was coauthor with J. Shelton Horsley of *Operative Surgery* (1937), a two-volume work describing basic and advanced surgical techniques that served as a textbook for many medical schools and went through six editions during his lifetime. He also wrote more than fifty articles on a wide array of surgical topics and on medical education. His lifelong asthmatic condition disqualified him for military service during World War II, but he prepared two military manuals on thoracic surgery.

In 1938 Bigger was president of the Eastern Surgical Society and of the Southern Society of Clinical Surgeons. He also chaired the medical section of the Virginia Academy of Science and the surgical section of the Southern Medical Association, helped found the American Board of Surgery and the Society for Vascular Surgery, became a fellow of the American College of Surgeons in 1941, and served as an examiner on the American Board of Surgery from 1945 until 1951. He became president of the Richmond Academy of Medicine in 1946, of the American Association for Thoracic Surgery in 1947, and of the Southern Surgical Association in 1953. Honors, material gain, and prestige meant little, however, to a man who gave himself completely to his patients, kept his surgical fees pitifully low, and often charged nothing if patients could not afford to pay. In 1950, on the twentieth anniversary of his appointment to the school, his associates and former students presented a portrait of Bigger to the Medical College of Virginia.

The pulmonary problems that had plagued Bigger for years became increasingly disabling during the last two years of his life, resulting in multiple hospitalizations in Richmond and in New York. Isaac Alexander Bigger died in Richmond on 27 January 1955 of complications resulting from his asthma. He was buried in Hollywood Cemetery in Richmond.

Unpublished 1986 biography by Lewis H. Bosher Jr. with letters and oral history interviews, MCV; BVS Marriage Register, Charlottesville; W. Levi Old Jr., "They Made Surgical History in Virginia," *Virginia Medical* 108 (1981): 275; Virginius Dabney, *Virginia Commonwealth University: A Sesquicentennial History* (1987), 78; Hummel and Smith, *Portraits and Statuary,* 8 (por.); obituaries in *Richmond News Leader* and *Richmond Times-Dispatch* (por.), both 28 Jan. 1955, and *Virginia Medical Monthly* 82 (1955): 166–167, 210–211; editorial tribute in *Richmond News Leader*, 28 Jan. 1955.

E. RANDOLPH TRICE

BIGGER, John Bell (3 March 1829–7 June 1899), clerk of the House of Delegates, was born in Richmond, one of thirteen children of Thomas Bibb Bigger and Elizabeth Meredith Russell Bigger. After attending schools in Richmond he went to Massachusetts hoping to learn enough about cotton manufacturing to return to Richmond and operate a water-powered factory. He abandoned these plans in 1852 and went to sea as secretary to the commanding officer of a United States Navy steamship. After two voyages on different ships he returned again to Richmond, and on 16 August 1853 he married Anna Burnley Muse, of Essex County. They lived thereafter in Richmond and had seven daughters and five sons.

Bigger worked in the Richmond post office for his merchant father, who was postmaster of the city from 1845 to 1865. He also followed his father's example by joining the Richmond Light Infantry Blues, a militia company, early in the 1850s. The elder Bigger was a veteran of the War of 1812, captain of the Blues from 1832 to 1839, and a former commander of the 19th Regiment Virginia Militia. Bigger served in the post office until December 1855, when he became clerk of one of the committees of the House of Delegates. He worked for the clerks of the House for the next decade and during the Civil War was assistant to Clerk William F. Gordon. During the Civil War Bigger's small stature and recurrent asthma kept him from field duty, but for the remainder of his life he was active in the Richmond Light Infantry Blues Association.

On 4 December 1865 Bigger defeated Gordon by four votes in the contest for clerk of the House of Delegates, which carried with it the position of master of the rolls. Except for the sessions of 1879 and 1881 when the Readjusters controlled the assembly, Bigger remained the clerk of the House until his death. A dignified but informal man who loved to talk and joke with the members when the legislature was not meeting, he became a highly respected and influential backroom leader of the Democratic Party who also served as secretary of its Richmond and state central committees and frequently as secretary of Democratic state conventions. His office in the Capitol became a favorite gathering place for influential legislators and one of the centers of gravity of the party. An extremely well known and colorful character, he was a walking encyclopedia of House procedures and legislative history.

On 7 June 1899 John Bell Bigger died, or "answered his final roll call," as an obituary writer put it, at his home in Richmond. His death produced lengthy front-page obituaries with engraved portraits in all three of Richmond's daily newspapers. Bigger's body lay in state in the Capitol and was buried in Shockoe Cemetery two days after his death following a well-attended funeral service at Monumental Episcopal Church.

French Biographies and Jamerson, *Speakers and Clerks, 1776–1996*, 88–89 (por.), both contain unverified claims of Confederate military service and other inaccuracies; father's obituary in *Richmond Daily Dispatch*, 6 May 1880; *Richmond Enquirer*, 2 Sept. 1853; Richmond Light Infantry Blues Records, LVA; feature article in *Richmond Times-Dispatch*, 2 Dec. 1934; obituaries and accounts of funeral in *Richmond Evening Leader*, 7, 9 June 1899, and *Richmond Dispatch* and *Richmond Times*, both 8, 10 June 1899; editorial tribute in *Richmond Dispatch*, 9 June 1899.

BRENT TARTER

BIGGERS, Abram Frederick (14 November 1838–28 March 1879), educator, was born in Lynchburg, the second of five sons and seventh of at least eleven children of Abram F. Biggers, a city constable, and Matilda Lynch Roberts Biggers. After attending local private schools Biggers entered Lynchburg College in 1855 and graduated on 30 June 1859. While he was a student he captained one of the school's two military companies, and at the outset of the Civil War he organized the Lynchburg Rifle Grays. He remained the unit's captain until it was mustered into regular Confederate service, but poor health exempted him from service in the field. During the war years Biggers established a law practice, having apparently studied under a local attorney. On 11 November 1865 he was elected a justice of the peace and on 5 April 1866 he was elected an alderman. He married Sallie Chunn Sowers in Clarke County on 14 July 1868. They had one son and four daughters. By 1870 Biggers owned real property valued at $25,000.

On 22 September 1870 Biggers embarked on a new profession when he was appointed the first superintendent of public schools for Lynchburg and Campbell County. After months of planning and preparation, the Lynchburg schools opened on 5 April 1871 to more than 700 students segregated by race in nine rented buildings. Biggers and his newly created school board had selected the curriculum, the textbooks, and the twenty teachers. He had also procured the temporary classrooms and furnished them. Before the school year ended Biggers toured the public schools in several northern cities at the request of the school board.

That summer the Lynchburg City Council funded the purchase of three lots on Monroe, Jackson, and Court Streets for the construction of permanent school facilities. In January 1871 the school board had requested $60,000 for four buildings and an additional $8,000 for expenses, a figure ultimately reduced to $30,000 that was approved for three new structures. Construction began in September. Biggers closely supervised the planning and erection of the buildings, bringing his talents in freehand drawing and draftsmanship to the task. All three schools were completed the following year. In order to give his full attention to the needs of the city schools Biggers resigned as Campbell County school superintendent on 30 September 1871.

A promoter of secondary education, Biggers had also been quick to establish two high schools in Lynchburg, one each for white boys and girls. With little experience as an educator he had built one of the best school systems in the state. After the high schools began operation on 13 March 1872, however, opposition arose over their cost as well as the overall value of secondary education. The debate, in which Biggers participated through local newspaper editorials, increased after it became necessary to consolidate the high schools in 1874. The Lynchburg City Council eventually withdrew its appropriation for the high school altogether, and it did not open for the session of 1878–1879. The closing pleased those who could afford private schools but enraged supporters of public education, who elected a new city council majority in 1879 that promptly reinstated the high school.

The reversal came too late for Biggers, however. Stung by public criticism of the school system, the council's decision to close the high school, and its earlier reduction of his salary, and with his health failing, he had resigned in December 1878 even though his contract had been renewed. Abram Frederick Biggers died of consumption on 28 March 1879 and was buried in Presbyterian Cemetery in Lynchburg. A school at the corner of Clay and Fifth Streets in Lynchburg was named in his honor when it opened in January 1881 and served the city until it was demolished in 1967.

Birth and death dates and first name from tombstone; first name given as Abraham in some sources; Lynch/Adams Families, Rosa Kent Gregory Genealogical Papers, Jones Memorial Library, Lynchburg; Bertha Adams Jordan, *Public Schools of Lynchburg, 1871–1881*, Lynchburg Historical Society–Museum, [Papers] 8, no. 1 (1971); feature article in *Lynchburg News*, 29 Apr. 1934; Edward C. Glass, "School History," typescript from 1887 Lynchburg City Code, Jones Memorial Library; Frances Adams Deyerle and Janet Shaffer, *A Legacy of Learning: The Lynchburg Public Schools, 1871–1986* (1987), 11–17 (por.); Lynchburg City Will Book, G:176; obituaries and accounts of funeral in *Lynchburg Daily News* and *Lynchburg Daily Virginian*, both 29 Mar., 1 Apr. 1879; memorial in *Educational Journal of Virginia* 10 (1879): 236–237.

Cline E. Hall

BIGGINS, Joseph Charles (21 November 1898–28 January 1978), city manager of Newport News, was born in Pittsburgh, the eldest of two sons and two daughters of Lewis Biggins and Jessie Calderwood Biggins. The family moved in 1907 to Newport News, where Biggins attended the local public schools and graduated from Newport News High School. In July 1920 he completed his studies at the apprentice school at the Newport News Ship Building and Dry Dock Company, then went to work for the city planning department in Newport News. Biggins married Bernice O'Neal Fox on 21 December 1922. They had two sons and one daughter.

Newport News had adopted the city manager form of municipal government in 1920. When the second city manager was dismissed on 15 June 1925, J. C. Biggins, to everyone's surprise including his own, was named acting city manager. On 1 July 1925 the city council appointed him city manager. During his early years on the job he tried to remain personally involved in every aspect of the city's administration, and throughout his long tenure he had such a command of facts about the city's finances, schools, streets, and public works that the city council usually adopted his proposals without significant alteration. Biggins refused to let political considerations influence his decisions and was not forthcoming to journalists or others seeking to become knowledgeable about the professional management of the city. As a result he left himself vulnerable to criticism, but some candidates for the council who began as his critics supported him after they were elected and came to depend on his knowledge and skill.

Biggins directed the city administration during the Great Depression and the confusion of the boom years during World War II, and he helped engineer the merger of the city with Warwick County in 1958. He served as city manager and as director of public safety for the enlarged municipality from 1958 until he retired at the end of August 1965, by which time no other city manager in the United States could boast such a long uninterrupted tenure. When he took office, Newport News was a city of approximately four square miles with some 35,000 inhabitants. By the time he retired it had grown to sixty-nine square miles and had a population of about 120,000. Biggins was president of the League of Virginia Municipalities from September 1950 to September 1951, and he was active in so many regional organizations that his name became synonymous with regional development. On the recommendation of the American Municipal Association, Biggins was appointed to the regional advisory board of the United States Office of Civilian Defense in 1941 for the district composed of Virginia, Maryland, Pennsylvania, and the District of Columbia. He served as director of civil defense for Newport News during World War II. He also chaired the Peninsula Industrial Council from 1946 to 1972, belonged to the Peninsula Ports Authority from its founding in 1959 until 1972 and to the Chesapeake Bay Bridge and Tunnel Commission from 1956 until 1965, and sat on the Newport News Planning Commission in the 1950s and 1960s. In 1971 one of the piers at the Newport News marine terminal was named for him, and in 1973 the Peninsula Industrial Council named him First Citizen of Newport News.

Biggins seldom spoke in public and spent most of his time working, even when at home, but he enjoyed duck hunting and joined several fraternal organizations and the Presbyterian Church. J. C. Biggins died in Riverside Hospital in Newport News on 28 January 1978, ten days after the death of his wife, and was buried in Peninsula Memorial Park in Newport News. The city named the lake in Huntington Park in his memory and dedicated a plaque to him there on 15 April 1980.

Family history information furnished by daughter Jessie Frances Biggins, Newport News, 27 July, 19 Aug. 1992; personal and family papers in possession of Jessie Frances Biggins; editorial tributes in *Newport News Times-Herald*, 28 June 1950, and *Newport News Daily Press*, 29 June 1950; feature articles in *Norfolk Virginian-Pilot*, 10 June 1963, *Newport News Times-Herald*, 31 Aug. 1965 (por.), 14 July 1972, 1 Mar. 1973, 15 Apr. 1980; Joseph C. Biggins, "Preparing the Budget," *Virginia Municipal Review* 8 (1931): 86, 90; Annie Lash Jester, *Newport News, Virginia, 1607–1960* (1961), 4–12, 145–146, 174; obituaries in *Newport News Daily Press* and *Newport News Times-Herald*, both 30 Jan. 1978.

CHERYL YIELDING FALES

BIGGS, Joseph Franklin (9 February 1868–24 February 1932), antiques dealer and furniture manufacturer, was born in New York City, the son of John Alden Biggs, a cabinetmaker, and Mary Garland Biggs. He had at least two sisters. When he was seventeen the family moved to Port Jefferson on Long Island, where on 26 October 1890 he married Jennie Morse Brewster. They had one daughter and one son. At the time of his marriage Biggs was working for an upholsterer who specialized in interiors of yachts owned by wealthy New Yorkers.

J. Franklin Biggs moved to Richmond in 1890 or 1891 and for about a decade sold insurance for a succession of companies. His interest in antique furniture led him to open his own antique store in 1902, which did so well that in 1906 he was able to purchase Pratt's Castle, a unique residence overlooking the James River in Richmond. He stocked the house with antique furniture and made it a showcase for the remainder of his life. Perceiving that the market for early American furniture could not be satisfied with authentic pieces, Biggs formed his own manufacturing business, Biggs Antique Furniture Company, in September 1908 to produce replicas of colonial- and federal-period furniture. His specialty was reproducing pieces belonging to notable Virginia families, but he consulted with the noted furniture historian Wallace Nutting about other styles. By the beginning of the 1930s Biggs's factory in Richmond employed more than forty craftsmen producing select furniture for a regional market.

Biggs also had other business interests. By 1930 he owned the Biggs Music Company, which sold musical instruments, phonographs, and radios, and he had purchased the Chesterfield Hills Country Club. On 1 February 1932, possibly as a result of financial difficulties during the Great Depression, he reorganized his business and took out a new charter as Biggs Antique Company, with Biggs continuing as president, his wife as vice president, and his son, daughter, and son-in-law as principal stockholders and officers. Within weeks, however, J. Franklin Biggs died at Grace Hospital in Richmond on 24 February 1932. He was buried in Hollywood Cemetery.

In November 1932 a group of Richmond businessmen purchased the Biggs Antique Company and reopened the factory, which had stopped production after Biggs's death, though the retail stores remained in operation. The new supervisors of the plant had been employees of the Biggs company for many years and were able to rehire nearly forty former workers. In 1938 the business was sold to Lloyd U. Noland, of Newport News. Preserving and building on the reputation that Biggs had created, the new owner retained the well-known name and expanded its business. In 1947 the company was licensed to manufacture facsimiles of authentic pieces from Monticello, and it retained a large share of the regional market until it finally closed late in the 1980s.

Tyler, *Encyclopedia*, 5:660–661; Allyn B. Tunis, ed., *Press Reference Book of Prominent Virginians, Dedicated to the Fourth Estate* (1916), 59; Mary Wingfield Scott, *Houses of Old Richmond* (1941), 286–287; Charter Book, 67:67–68, 166:93–95; company history in *Richmond News Leader*, 26 Nov. 1932, *Commonwealth* 15 (Jan. 1948): 9–10, and two undated company pamphlets in Biggs Antique Company Papers, VM; obituaries in *Richmond News Leader*, 24 Feb. 1932, and *Richmond Times-Dispatch* (por.) and *New York Times*, both 25 Feb. 1932.

J. CHRISTIAN KOLBE

BIGGS, Walter Joseph (4 June 1886–11 February 1968), artist, was born at Big Spring Depot in Montgomery County, the youngest of three sons and three daughters of Walter Joseph Biggs, a prosperous farmer and businessman, and Annie Southall Biggs. Only he and one of his sisters survived early childhood. When he was twelve years old his family moved to Salem, where he attended public school. Biggs displayed artistic talent and later enrolled in a correspondence course in pen-and-ink drawing. His parents sent him to Virginia Agricultural and Mechanical College and Polytechnic Institute in the fall of 1902 to study engineering, but Biggs was unhappy there. In 1903 he sent a sample of his drawings to Charles Schreyvogel, a well-known artist of the era, who advised him to apply to the National Academy of Design in New York City. Armed with this evidence of his talent, Biggs persuaded his reluctant parents to allow him to enroll that autumn at the New York School of Art.

For more than two years Biggs studied painting under various teachers, including Robert Henri, leader of the Ashcan School.

Several of Biggs's classmates became influential artists, among them Edward Hopper, Rockwell Kent, and George Wesley Bellows, with whom Biggs reportedly shared living quarters and a studio during his early days in New York.

Biggs began achieving commercial success in 1905, when his illustrations appeared on the covers of *Young's Magazine* in January and *Field and Stream* in July. After completing his formal art studies he rented a small studio and worked on a variety of projects. His early assignments included illustrations for a story in the *McClure's Magazine* of October 1908, a color frontispiece for Myrtle Reed's novel *Old Rose and Silver* (1909), and drawings for Belle Bushnell's *John Arrowsmith—Planter* (1910). In May 1912 he illustrated a story in *Harper's Monthly Magazine*, launching a twelve-year relationship as a contributor to that magazine. In 1913 Biggs's illustrations appeared in the January issue of the *Delineator*, in Kate Langley Bosher's novel, *The House of Happiness*, and in *The Land of the Spirit*, a collection of short stories by Thomas Nelson Page. He illustrated a series of stories by Armistead Churchill Gordon that appeared in *Scribner's* from 1914 to 1916 and were also published as *Ommirandy: Plantation Life at Kingsmill* (1917). In 1918 he illustrated a story by Alice Hegan Rice for the *Century*. Many of those illustrations were set in the American South, and Biggs won praise during his career for his sympathetic and dignified portrayals of African American life.

In 1919 Biggs moved to an apartment on the top floor of a building on West Sixty-Seventh Street between Central Park West and Columbus Avenue. By the 1930s that city block had become a haven for writers and artists, and Biggs was among those mentioned by syndicated columnist Oscar Odd McIntyre in a piece that compared the area to Paris's Latin Quarter. In 1921 Biggs had a studio built behind his mother's house so that he could work during his frequent visits to Salem. He filled his notebooks with sketches of the Roanoke Valley's people and places for use in his illustrations. On 4 August 1923 he married one of his models, Mildred Armstrong, but by 1937 the childless marriage had ended in divorce.

During the 1920s and 1930s Biggs acquired a national reputation as a leading illustrator. His romantic, impressionistic style, the beauty and artistic quality of his palette, and his mastery of images of the American South impressed the art editors of major magazines. He also became a popular advertising artist, portraying products of major manufacturers in engaging settings that appealed to readers of mass magazines. Biggs's work appeared in nearly all of them, including *Cosmopolitan Magazine*, *Ladies' Home Journal*, *McCall's*, *Saturday Evening Post*, *Scribner's*, and *Vogue*. He also illustrated an Ellen Glasgow story in the December 1924 issue of *Woman's Home Companion*. By the mid–1940s Biggs had put aside oils in favor of the spontaneity of watercolor, using a minimum of water to work the paint and draw out detail, one of his trademarks. Biggs's illustrations rank with those of Howard Chandler Christy and N. C. Wyeth and have achieved the stature of fine art.

Biggs exhibited paintings in shows in New York, Chicago, and Philadelphia, winning many prizes at competitions. Art museums and private collectors acquired his canvasses. He also taught at the Art Students League, the Grand Central School of Art, and the Phoenix Art Institute, and several of his students went on to distinguished careers. Biggs was honored by many arts organizations and became a member of the National Academy of Design, the American Water Color Society, the Philadelphia Water Color Club, the Society of Illustrators, the Salmagundi Club, and Allied Artists of America. On 20 November 1963 he was inducted into the Society of Illustrators' Hall of Fame.

Biggs retired from illustrating late in the 1950s and returned to Salem to live with his sister Lucy Biggs Langhorne in their mother's house. He closed his studio in New York soon after. With more leisure time he resumed working in oil and produced numerous paintings. On 4 June 1961 Biggs received an honorary degree of doctor of fine arts from Roanoke College. In 1965 he was an artist in residence at the college, but by then he was suffering from cataracts and failing health. Remembered with affection as a courtly, modest man, and one of the Roanoke Valley's most celebrated artists, Walter Joseph

Biggs died at the Roanoke Rehabilitation Center on 11 February 1968. He was buried in Sherwood Memorial Park in Salem.

Interest in Biggs's work did not diminish after his death. At a 1968 estate auction that attracted 1,500 people to the Salem–Roanoke Valley Civic Center, more than 100 of his works were sold. The Roanoke Fine Arts Center mounted a show of his art in February 1969. Roanoke College, which owns a large collection of Biggs's paintings and sketchbooks, hosted an exhibition of his work in May 1980 and sponsored a second show in the centennial year of his birth, when it dedicated the Walter Biggs Studio in the Olin Hall Student Art Center.

Biggs's papers, family Bible records, photographs, and news clippings (including otherwise unidentified McIntire column), Fowler Collection, Roanoke College Library; feature articles and interviews in *Richmond Times-Dispatch*, 29 Nov. 1936 (por.), *Salem Times-Register*, 27 May 1938, and Salem Historical Society, *A Guide to Historic Salem* (spring 1997): 1, 6–7; Ernest William Watson, *Forty Illustrators and How They Work* (1946; 3d ed., 1953), 34–41; Michael Ramsey, "Walter Biggs: Celebrated Artist Never Forgot His Hometown," *Roanoker* 6 (July–August 1979): 76–78 (por.); Walt Reed and Roger Reed, *The Illustrator in America, 1880–1980* (1984), esp. 87, 112; Frederic B. Taraba, "The Poetic Light of Walter Biggs," *Step-By-Step Graphics* 6 (May–June 1990): 124–134; exhibition catalogs include *Walter Biggs 1886–1968: "The First Gentleman of the Arts in Roanoke Valley"* (1969), *Walter Biggs' Southern Vision* (1980), and *Walter Biggs Remembered: A Memorial Exhibition of His Life and Art* (1986); obituaries in *New York Times* and *Roanoke World-News*, both 12 Feb. 1968.

DONALD W. GUNTER

BIGNALL, Ann West (d. 20 January 1805), actress, was born in England sometime in the middle or late 1760s, one of at least two daughters and a son of actors Thomas Wade West and Margaretta Sully West. With her parents and her husband, John Bignall, she arrived in the United States in 1790 and joined the Old American Company, one of the largest and most successful traveling theatrical companies in the country. Apparently finding the financial terms offered them unsatisfactory, the family opted instead to form its own company to tour the southern states. Under the leadership of Thomas West, the troupe established an annual theater circuit that extended from Alexandria to Charleston, South Carolina, and also included the cities of Fredericksburg, Norfolk, Petersburg, and Richmond. Alternately called the Virginia Company or the South Carolina Company depending on where it was playing, the troupe flourished until approximately 1810, when the last surviving founding member, Margaretta West, died.

Bignall developed her acting career under the stewardship of her parents, both of whom had performed in London. She benefited from the extraordinary talent her father displayed as a theater manager while assembling an accomplished troupe of actors that became the Old American Company's chief rival in the South. At its peak the Virginia Company employed a thirteen-member orchestra and thirty-three actors, including Thomas Sully, a young nephew of Margaretta West who later became a prominent portrait painter. Elizabeth Arnold, later the mother of Edgar Allan Poe, also performed briefly with the group. The company's extensive repertoire included tragedies, historical dramas, farces, comic operas, musicals, ballets, pantomimes, acrobatics, and fireworks. It often presented southern audiences with American premieres of the latest English productions. The troupe's success led Thomas West to commission Benjamin Henry Latrobe in 1797 to design a theater in Richmond with almost 900 seats, but it was never built.

Bignall served as the company's leading comedienne for fourteen years. She was best known for such roles as Little Pickle in Isaac Bickerstaffe's farce, *The Spoiled Child*, Moggy M'Gilpin in *The Highland Reel*, a comic opera by John O'Keeffe and William Shield, and Betty Blackberry in O'Keeffe's *The Farmer*. Theater critics and audiences consistently praised her, even when the company's performance or the play itself was considered unsuccessful. She was known for always drawing a sizable audience. No unfavorable reviews of her have been found, which is unusual for the period. Even John Bignall, whose acting ability evidently exceeded hers, received criticism. Reviewers described her as a beautiful woman with a sweet voice and compared her to actresses of New York and Philadelphia. Commentators boasted that Bignall was capable of pleasing the critics of Drury Lane or Covent

Garden in London. Aaron Burr, who visited the Petersburg theater on 30 October 1804, described her as "the best female actress in America," unequaled in comic roles.

While nothing is known of her acting career before she emigrated from England, Bignall's husband had been performing there as a strolling player using the stage name Mr. Moneypenny. A superb actor, he shared management of the Virginia Company with his father-in-law and played leading roles in both comedy and tragedy, often opposite his wife. So valuable was he to the Virginia Company that when his death from a lengthy illness seemed inevitable, Thomas West traveled to New York City and Philadelphia in search of an actor to replace him but reported that he could not find "a Bignall" there. The Bignalls may have had children. As early as 1791 playbills for the company listed Mr. Bignall Jr. and J. Bignall.

After John Bignall's death in Charleston on 11 August 1794, Ann West Bignall took over his responsibilities in the management of the troupe. She married James West in Norfolk on 22 May 1795. An English actor who had belonged to the Theatre-Royal in Bath, he made his American debut with the Old American Company in 1792 and joined the Virginia Company two years later. He specialized in comic opera roles and entr'acte songs. No children from this marriage have been identified, and West left the company after her death.

Ann West Bignall West died in Richmond on 20 January 1805. Her *Richmond Enquirer* obituary called her "the most distinguished ornament of the Virginia stage," and after her death that newspaper still compared actresses to "our old favorite, Mrs. J. West."

Suzanne Ketchum Sherman, *Comedies Useful: A History of the American Theatre in the South, 1775–1812* (1998), 85–102, 117–190; Sherman, "Thomas Wade West, Theatrical Impressario, 1790–1799," *WMQ*, 3d ser., 9 (1952): 10–28; Martin Staples Shockley, *The Richmond Stage, 1784–1812* (1977), 55, 76, 118; James H. Dormon Jr., *Theater in the Ante Bellum South, 1815–1861* (1967), 23–26; second marriage reported in *Virginia Star and Petersburg Weekly Advertiser*, 4 June 1795, and *Gentleman's Magazine* 65 (1795): 701; she is identified in playbills first as "Mrs. Bignall," then as "Mrs. J. West," and finally as "Mrs. West, junior"; reviews in *Richmond Virginia Gazette, and General Advertiser*, 24 Nov. 1790, and *Richmond Enquirer*, 12 Sept. 1809; Matthew L. Davis, ed., *Memoirs of Aaron Burr, with Miscellaneous Selections from his Correspondence* (1836–1837), 2:347–349; comanagership of Virginia Company documented in Petersburg City Hustings Court Deed Book, 2:442–443; obituary in *Richmond Enquirer*, 22 Jan. 1805.

Kelly Henderson Hayes

BILLY (fl. 1770s–1780s), principal in a court case, was an African American slave born possibly about 1754, perhaps in Richmond County. In 1781 he was part of the estate of John Tayloe (1721–1779), a wealthy planter and member of the governor's Council. When Billy first came into Tayloe's possession is not known, and his parents and other relatives have not been identified.

Billy may have been the runaway slave sought in April 1774 by Thomas Lawson, Tayloe's iron agent at the Neabsco Furnace in Prince William County. Lawson placed a detailed newspaper advertisement to try to recover Billy, described as a former waiting boy, a skilled ironworker, a stonemason, and a miller. Lawson further depicted Billy as an ingenious twenty-year-old man who had the ability to gain "the good Graces of almost every Body who will listen." In 1782 Tayloe's estate included several men named Billy, making it impossible to determine whether the earlier runaway was the man tried for treason in 1781.

The Prince William County Court indicted "Billy, alias Will, alias William" for "feloniously and traitorously" waging war on 2 April 1781 from an armed vessel against the new state of Virginia. Many African Americans joined the British forces, who had offered freedom to slaves willing to serve the Crown, although other blacks actively supported the American cause. Billy pleaded not guilty and testified that he had been forced to board the vessel against his will and had never taken up arms on behalf of the British. On 8 May 1781, however, four of six Prince William County oyer and terminer judges convicted Billy of treason and sentenced him to hang. They placed his value at £27,000 current money.

Within a week of the verdict Henry Lee (1729–1787) and William Carr, the two dissenting judges, and Mann Page, one of Tayloe's executors, argued to Governor Thomas Jefferson that a slave, being a noncitizen, could not commit treason. Lee and Carr wrote that a slave "not being Admited to the Priviledges of a Citizen owes the State No Allegiance and that the Act declaring what shall be treason cannot be intended by the Legislature to include slaves who have neither lands or other property to forfiet." Their argument about citizenship was very similar to one made on 19 March 1767 by Arthur Lee in his influential public letter on slavery directed to Virginia's legislators and published in William Rind's *Virginia Gazette*. In Billy's defense Henry Lee and William Carr also contested the evidence used against him. Billy received a gubernatorial reprieve until the end of June, and the legislature pardoned him on 14 June 1781. What happened to him after that is not known.

Billy's treason trial was neither the first nor the last such prosecution of a bondsman during the American Revolution. In Norfolk County in 1778 a slave named Bob faced charges of treason and robbery. Like Billy he pleaded not guilty but received the death sentence, and he may have been hanged. During the same period at least one other slave, a man named Sancho, was found guilty of warlike action against the state and hanged, while still another, Jack, may have escaped execution. Similar judicial actions against supposed treason occurred during times of public peril. In the aftermath of Nat Turner's Rebellion, Southampton County justices in October 1831 heard the charge of treason against Jack and Shadrach, only to dismiss the charge tersely: "a slave cannot be tried in this court for Treason." This exemption of enslaved people from treason prosecutions appears to have prevailed in Virginia during the Civil War as well.

Billy made his mark on history because his trial forced white leaders to confront the logic of the peculiar institution. His case was doubly ironic. A slave, he was nevertheless tried for disobeying one of the laws of the commonwealth. Excluded from the protections conferred by citizenship, he was still shielded from execution because Virginia's law of treason could not logically apply to him.

Official copies of trial record in Governor's Office, Letters Received, RG 3, LVA; *Jefferson Papers*, 5:640–643; Mann Page request for pardon of "Will," 7 June 1781, Legislative Petitions, Prince William Co., RG 78, LVA; Personal Property Tax Returns, Richmond Co., 1782, RG 48, LVA; *Williamsburg Virginia Gazette* (Purdie and Dixon), 11 Apr. 1774; Philip J. Schwarz, *Twice Condemned: Slaves and the Criminal Laws of Virginia, 1705–1865* (1988), 84–88, 188–189; Gerald W. Mullin, *Flight and Rebellion: Slave Resistance in Eighteenth-Century Virginia* (1972), 73, 75, 94, 107, 111.

PHILIP J. SCHWARZ

BILLY or **Blind Billy** (ca. 1805–19 April 1855), fifer, was a Lynchburg musician of unknown parentage who was so renowned with his instrument that his death was noted in Lynchburg and Richmond newspapers. The slave of Howell Davies, he eventually gained his freedom. As with many antebellum black musicians, more can be learned about his artistry than his life.

Blind Billy, as he was named in all known references, was part of a long tradition of black military musicians in England and the Virginia colony. Virginia legislative acts of 1723 and 1776 recognized and attempted to regulate blacks as musicians for militia companies. Fife-and-drum ensembles, often called "drum corps" or "martial bands," were once as common as fiddlers, and march tunes were the specialty of the traditional fifer.

Fifers and drummers played on almost every public occasion. After parades, they would station themselves around town and play all day and into the night. One chronicler described Blind Billy standing on a street corner late into the evening playing "delightful old time music" while those outside stopped to listen and those inside were awakened. Blind Billy and Tom Perkins, a bank clerk and violinist, "would stand in the later hours of the night in front of the bank in which Mr. Perkins was employed, [where] they would send forth melody that would inspire a stoic with cheerfulness."

One of the tunes associated with Blind Billy, "Wandering Willie," was a popular tune with diverse titles, which he reportedly played with much pathos. In recollections of Lynchburg written a few years after his death, an elderly local woman asked "who can now play so sweetly for us those touching old Scotch airs" as Blind Billy did. Many of the songs were from the British tradition, but the fife and flute had African associations as well and the musical influence went in both directions. Most fifers played by ear and developed their own variants of folk tunes, turning dance tunes into marches and marches into dance tunes.

Blind Billy was typical of fifers in that he played at balls and parties as well as on public occasions. Violin and flute or fife duos, popular at Virginia dance parties of the eighteenth and early nineteenth centuries, moved quickly from the minuet to the reel or jig. Blind Billy, like other antebellum black musicians throughout Virginia and the South, drew from British tunes and African melodic traditions to create an American music immensely popular with all its audiences.

Described as a dark mulatto with handsome features and formal manners, Blind Billy was said to recognize the voices of all who spoke to him as he walked the city's streets unaided. No source explains his sightlessness, although one account erroneously asserts that he was mute. His owner, Howell Davies, was a physician and pharmacist who may have treated and then acquired him when he was young. Blind Billy's 1855 obituary noted that he had been "raised and owned" by Davies, but that he had obtained his freedom through a subscription raised among the townspeople a few years earlier. Skilled urban slaves in Virginia sometimes accumulated enough money for self-purchase, and Blind Billy's own efforts may have been a factor in his manumission.

What little is known of Blind Billy's family is inscribed on his tombstone, which reads "Erected by Ann Armistead, in memory of her husband Blind Billy." But Billy's surname remains unknown. Whether slave or free, Ann Armistead might have retained her last name if marrying an enslaved person, and an incorrect death date on the marker suggests that it was placed well after Billy's death. The stone is also adorned with a carving of a broken fife. Blind Billy died of pneumonia on 19 April 1855 and was buried by the overseers of the poor in the Old City Cemetery (also known as the Old Methodist Cemetery) in Lynchburg.

Blind Billy is described in Margaret Couch Anthony Cabell, *Sketches and Recollections of Lynchburg by the Oldest Inhabitant (Mrs. Cabell)* (1858; repr. 1974), 204–205, *Lynchburg News*, 12 Apr. 1896 (with tombstone inscription), and W. Asbury Christian, *Lynchburg and Its People* (1900), 161–162; Evelyn Lee Moore and Lucy Harrison Miller Baber, *Behind the Old Brick Wall: A Cemetery Story* (1968), 42, 87; death date in obituary in *Lynchburg Daily Virginian*, 21 Apr. 1855, and death notice in *Richmond Daily Dispatch*, 23 Apr. 1855; variant death date of 20 Apr. 1856 on tombstone; age at death of about fifty in obituary and on tombstone.

MARIE TYLER-MCGRAW

BINFORD, James Henry (21 August 1832–30 July 1876), superintendent of Richmond city public schools, was born in Richmond, the eldest of six sons and three daughters of Pamelia Lockett Binford and John James Binford, a partner in a cabinetmaking firm and a prominent lay leader of Centenary Methodist Church. Binford attended local schools and then studied at the University of Virginia from 1850 to 1852. On his return to Richmond he worked as a schoolteacher.

When the Civil War began Binford was a private in the Richmond Howitzers, an artillery unit in which he served about eighteen months before being discharged because of impaired eyesight. He spent the remaining war years at Camp Lee, near Richmond's western boundary at the Hermitage fairgrounds, where conscripts trained before entering the Confederate army. He served as adjutant with the rank of captain under Colonel John Camden Shields, his former commanding officer in the Howitzers.

After the war Binford briefly joined his father as a partner of Binford and Son, commission merchants and wholesale grocers. He soon returned to teaching, however, and in September 1869 became principal of the private Saint John's German-English School. During this period also Binford married Eliza Marie Smith, a native of Caroline County, and they resided with his widower father. They had two daughters.

On 18 July 1870 the new Conservative city council reorganized Richmond's public school board and unanimously elected Binford superintendent of schools. With the support of philanthropic northerners led by Andrew Washburne, of Massachusetts, the Radical council had established public schools the previous year. In April 1871 the Richmond schools formally became part of the state's new public school system, and Binford received a commission as superintendent from the State Board of Education.

Although Richmond spent slightly less than half as much per pupil throughout his tenure as did northern cities such as Boston, Binford enjoyed strong support from the city school board, which included his former commander Shields. The city issued $100,000 in bonds to build new schools, three of which were under construction before the end of Binford's first year as superintendent. The new building for the city's white high school opened in October 1873, and Binford conferred diplomas at the first commencement exercises on 30 June 1874. His report for that year stated that Richmond had spent $84,000 on public education, double the appropriation of 1870.

The school board also supported Binford's desire to learn from public school systems elsewhere. In August 1870 he and Mayor Henry Keeling Ellyson visited schools in northern states, and Binford made similar investigative trips in the following years. He also brought prominent educators to Richmond to visit the schools and recommend improvements. Successful innovations included weekly teachers' meetings at which Binford led discussions of pedagogical issues. He explained that the meetings, which included calisthenics, encouraged learning from the experiences of others, uniformity in instruction, and a professional interest in the theory and practice of teaching.

The state's superintendent of public education, William Henry Ruffner, regularly cited the successes of the Richmond school system in his annual reports. He published Binford's new curricula for arithmetic and reading in his 1872–1873 report as an example for the state's other schools. As part of his study of pedagogy Binford became active in the National Educational Association and served on its board of directors in 1872–1873. At the annual meeting in 1873 at Elmira, New York, he delivered an address on "The Relation Between School Boards and Superintendents" and was elected president of the NEA's Department of Superintendence (later called the American Association of School Administrators).

Binford was an effective and innovative administrator, and his achievements gave great promise of further service to public education. Unfortunately, about 1874 he fell ill with what was diagnosed as rheumatism of the heart. His health steadily declined, and after the close of the school year in 1876 he went to Red Sulphur Springs in Monroe County, West Virginia, hoping to improve his condition. James Henry Binford died there on 30 July 1876 and was buried at Hollywood Cemetery in Richmond, where the city's teachers placed a monument at his grave to honor his service to the public schools. In 1915 the city introduced junior high schools and named the newest building, which is still in use, for Binford.

Census, Richmond City, 1850–1870; Richmond city directories; Compiled Service Records; Margaret Meagher, *History of Education in Richmond* (1939), 82, 111–115; Virginia Superintendent of Public Instruction, *Annual Report* (1870/1871): 19–21; (1871/1872): 32, 80, 100; (1872/1873): 4–5, 217–225; National Educational Association, *Addresses and Journal of Proceedings* (1873): 248–254, 270–271; "Relation Between School Boards and Superintendents," *Educational Journal of Virginia* 5 (1873): 63–68; *Virginia Journal of Education* 58 (Sept. 1964): 28 (por.); obituaries and memorials in *Richmond State*, 31 July 1876, *Richmond Whig*, 1 Aug. 1876, *Richmond Dispatch*, 1 Aug., 9 Oct. 1876, and *Educational Journal of Virginia* 7 (1876): 499; 8 (1876): 38–39.

JOHN T. KNEEBONE

BINFORD, Jesse Hinton (23 May 1875–10 June 1952), educator, was born near Mechanicsville, the fourth of five sons and fourth of six children of William James Binford and Virginia Norment Binford. He was educated in the Hanover County public schools and at Richmond High School, from which he graduated in 1892. He attended Richmond College, where he played football, won a medal for debating, and earned a coveted place as final orator at commencement in 1896.

The year that he graduated Binford married Nellie C. Hechler. They had three sons and three daughters. He moved to Arkansas, where he taught at a one-room school, studied law, was admitted to the bar, and practiced law until he returned to Virginia in 1899. Binford then served for two years as principal of Valley Elementary School in Richmond, one of the city's all-black schools, located across the street from the city jail. Two years later he was appointed principal of the white Springfield School on Church Hill.

In 1909 Binford became executive secretary of the Co-Operative Education Association of Virginia, the state's most influential organization of educational reformers. During his four years as secretary, he traveled to every county in Virginia to organize school improvement leagues, which were composed primarily of reform-minded women. Under Binford's leadership, the CEA emphasized a wide range of educational and institutional reforms, including school beautification, and drew on a base of support among CEA-affiliated school improvement associations in rural communities, small towns, and cities. Richmond, for example, had an improvement group attached to every school in the city in 1910.

Binford's years with the CEA marked an important transition period for the organization, which had been created by activist women reformers. Richmond newspaper publisher and civic leader John Stewart Bryan became president in 1909, and Binford's appointment coincided with Bryan's insistence that the group reorganize itself into a male-dominated statewide activist group. Binford replaced Landonia Randolph Dashiell, the woman who had been secretary of the CEA and of its predecessor, the Richmond Education Association, and he promoted a different emphasis in school reform. Early organizations such as the REA and CEA had successfully organized crusading movements to arouse public enthusiasm for change. By Binford's time, the reformers faced the different task of giving permanence to reforms by constructing a new bureaucratic apparatus of school supervision.

In 1914 Binford became the first supervisor of white rural schools for the Virginia Department of Education. Having already been elected in 1908 to a one-year term as president of the Virginia State Teachers Association, Binford achieved national recognition in 1914 when he was elected president of the national association of rural school supervisors. The following year, 1915, he served as editor of the *Virginia State Teachers Quarterly* and received a master's degree from the University of Wisconsin, which he had attended during the summers of 1912 through 1914. Binford subsequently studied school supervision and administration at Teachers College of Columbia University during the summers of 1917, 1918, and 1919. He often attended state and national meetings of professional educational societies and wrote for such journals as the *Virginia School Journal* and the *Virginia Journal of Education* to explain and promote his ideas for change. In 1922 he published a textbook, *The Young American Citizen: Civics for Grammar Grades*, which was reprinted two years later.

Binford was appointed assistant superintendent of the public schools of the city of Richmond in 1916. For the next seventeen years he worked constructively and harmoniously with the administrators and teachers in the city's school system. He was therefore the natural choice in June 1933 for promotion to superintendent following the death of the incumbent. As superintendent, Binford was best known for establishing a junior primary grade classification for use during the first two years of elementary school. He abolished the city's formal, half-day final examinations in favor of a system of monthly tests, and he instituted a rule requiring college degrees for all schoolteachers. Early in his tenure he argued vigorously but unsuccessfully for a year-round public school program. During 1941 and the early months of 1942 he helped negotiate an agreement to phase in a program to equalize the salaries of white and black teachers in the Richmond public school system. The measure was a response to a lawsuit that African American teachers filed shortly after the United States courts ruled in 1940 that unequal salary scales were invalid.

Binford was reelected superintendent of schools in 1937 and 1941. He intended to retire in the summer of 1945 when he turned seventy, but the school board persuaded him to remain on the job until after the end of World War II. By the time he retired at the beginning of 1946, his persistent work to increase the budget had made the system one of the best-financed urban school districts in the South.

Following his retirement Binford joined the Mutual Life Insurance Association as treasurer and supervisor of insurance agencies in five states and the District of Columbia. He had also been a director of the Grace Street Bank and of the Grace Securities Corporation. For thirty years he was a member of the Barton Heights Baptist Church, where he taught its Men's Bible Class, and he also led the Businessmen's Bible Class at the Richmond Young Men's Christian Association. In 1921 he was elected president of the Kiwanis Club of Richmond and in 1930 was a governor of the Capitol District of Kiwanis. Binford also served as executive secretary of the successful fund-raising campaign in 1922 to establish the Richmond Public Library, which opened in 1924, and he was a director of the Richmond Chamber of Commerce from 1925 to 1927.

Jesse Hinton Binford died in a Richmond hospital on 10 June 1952 and was buried in Forest Lawn Cemetery.

Mary L. Bruner, *Binford Family Genealogy* (1925), 109; William A. Link, *A Hard Country and a Lonely Place: Schooling, Society, and Reform in Rural Virginia, 1870–1920* (1986), 121, 135; career in Richmond covered in detail in city newspapers; Jesse H. Binford, "Teaching As A Profession," Virginia State Teachers Association, *Annual Proceedings* (1909/1910): 55–60, "Getting Full Value Out of the School" and "Beautifying Our Schools," *Virginia Journal of Education* 4 (1910): 15–16 and 81–85, "Education: The Task of Helping Others," in Hampton Negro Conference, *Annual Report* 14 (1910): 23–26, "Things to Be Taught Besides the Three R's," *Virginia School Journal* 7 (1917): 289–290, "Standardizing the Small Country School," National Education Association, *Addresses and Proceedings of the Annual Meeting* 56 (1918): 595–598, and "Shall We Have Year-Round Schools?," *Virginia Journal of Education* 28 (1934): 99–100; salary equalization plan described in Superintendent of Public Schools of the City of Richmond, *Annual Report* 73 (1943): 25; feature article in *Richmond Times-Dispatch*, 5 Mar. 1945; obituaries with pors. in *Richmond News Leader*, 10 June 1952, and *Richmond Times-Dispatch*, 11 June 1952.

WILLIAM A. LINK

BINGA, Anthony (1 June 1843–21 January 1919), Baptist minister and educator, was born in Amherstburg, Canada West, where his father and mother had fled from slavery. He was the eldest of two sons and a daughter of Anthony Binga and Rhoda Story Binga. His father was pastor of the black Baptist church in Amherstburg and a leader among fugitives from slavery. Binga attended the local school and, aspiring to become a physician, received private tutoring in Latin and anatomy. His parents could not pay for further education, but he accepted a scholarship covering tuition and gladly subsisted on meager fare while working his way through King's Institute at Buxton, Canada West, a town founded by white abolitionist William King.

Binga completed his studies in 1865 and the following year accepted a call to Atchison, Kansas, as a schoolteacher. He fell ill in Kansas and returned to Canada where, in February 1867, he experienced religious conversion and was baptized in the frigid waters of a nearby river. Eight months later the Canadian Anti-Slavery Baptist Association ordained him, and he was quickly called to the Albany Enterprise Academy in Athens County, Ohio, where he became both a preacher and principal. On 2 December 1869 Binga married Rebecca L. Bush, of Xenia, Ohio, the daughter of a Baptist minister. They had two daughters. Binga discovered that to keep the school in Albany alive he had to solicit donations from white philanthropists, which required him to travel, interfering with what he considered his more important work as a preacher. He resigned about 1871 and brought his family back to Canada, seeking a more suitable field.

In January 1872 Binga and his family moved to Richmond. He was welcomed there by William Troy, a Virginia-born free black abolitionist who had lived in Amherstburg during the 1850s and after the Civil War became pastor of the Second Baptist Church in Richmond. Binga quickly found his place. On 1 May 1872 he accepted a call to become pastor of the First Baptist Church in Manchester (now part of Richmond). Meanwhile, he applied to become a teacher in Manchester's public schools and so impressed Beverly Augustus Hancock, the superintendent, that Hancock made Binga the first African American teacher there and gave him responsibility for the secondary school for blacks. Binga, in effect, oversaw the public education of blacks in Manchester at what grew to be six schools. After sixteen years, however, he decided that his church duties required all of his time and resigned as a teacher, despite the school board's request that he reconsider. By all accounts he was a stern disciplinarian, but his students, some of whom became prominent themselves, always expressed respect and affection for him.

Binga was a man of great dignity, and he brought that quality to his ministry. Although he could lead when necessary, he deferred regular business to the board of deacons because he believed that the congregation should control the church. He also expanded voting rights of women members and pushed for construction of a new, larger building, which was dedicated 12 November 1881. As church membership continued to grow and factories expanded into the neighborhood, Binga proposed moving to the site where the church now stands. The new building was dedicated 10 May 1896, and the mortgage was paid on 7 June 1903. Binga discouraged holiday services that seemed to produce more amusement than spirituality. He never delivered more than two sermons on a Sunday, so that he could give each one his full attention. A number of them were published as pamphlets or in a collection entitled *Sermons on Several Occasions* (1889).

In 1874 Binga was elected recording secretary of the Virginia Baptist State Convention, and he was recording secretary of the Virginia Baptist State Sabbath School Convention when it was incorporated in 1889. He became the first chairman of the Foreign Mission Board of the Baptist Foreign Mission Convention in 1880 and remained active in the organization as it evolved into the National Baptist Convention. Over time Binga concluded that too much of the convention's funds were being spent in the United States rather than on missionary work. When he proposed smaller, more economical district missionary conventions in 1896, Virginians helped form an auxiliary of the Lott Carey Baptist Foreign Mission Convention. Binga served on its board.

Other controversies divided black Baptists in Virginia during the 1890s, in particular the relationship of the new Virginia Seminary in Lynchburg to Virginia Union University in Richmond, formed in 1899 from the merger of two seminaries established by the American Baptist Home Mission Society. Black Baptists disagreed over whether Virginia Seminary should accept aid from white northern Baptist organizations at the cost of control over the institution. As a trustee of Virginia Union and longtime supporter of the American Baptist Home Mission Society, for which his father had worked as an agent before the Civil War, Binga was a "cooperationist." Nonetheless, when the "separatists" gained control of the Virginia Baptist State Convention in 1899, the delegates reelected him recording secretary. He resigned, however, and helped to organize the Baptist General Association of Virginia (Colored), of which he became treasurer.

Binga received an honorary D.D. from Shaw University in Raleigh in 1889, and the Lott Carey Convention sent him to London in 1905 as a delegate to the Baptist Congress there. Rebecca Binga died on 26 October 1907 after many years as an invalid. On 2 December 1909 Binga married Mary Virginia Young, and they had one son. Anthony Binga suffered from arteriosclerosis and died suddenly on 21 January 1919. He was buried in the family plot at Mount Olivet Cemetery in Richmond. His widow lived until 1958 and became a civic leader best known for her advocacy of improved recreational facilities.

"Autobiography of Anthony Binga, Jr.," MS written ca. 1917 in possession of Thomasina Talley Binga; Albert W. Pegues, *Our Baptist Ministers and Schools* (1892), 58–61; Joseph B. Earnest Jr., *The Religious Development of the Negro in Virginia* (1914), 217; Frank Lincoln Mather, ed., *Who's Who of the Colored Race* (1915), 1:27; genealogical chart in Anthony J. Binga Sr., "Jesse Binga," *Journal of the Afro-American Historical and Genealogical Society* 2 (1981): 147; father described in Benjamin Drew, *A North-Side View of Slavery* (1856), 291–294, 353–355, and Jason H. Silverman, *Unwelcome Guests: Canada West's Response to American Fugitive Slaves, 1800–1865* (1985), 91–94; William L. Ransome, *History of the First Baptist Church and Some of Her Pastors, South Richmond, Va.* (1935), 26–27, 36–37, 67–82; *Richmond Planet*, 13 May 1893; C. C. Adams and Marshall A. Talley, *Negro Baptists and Foreign Missions* (1944), 23, 32–34, 37; Lester F. Russell, *Black Baptist Secondary Schools in Virginia, 1887–1957: A Study in Black History* (1981), 50–57, 144–150; Anthony Binga, *Sermon and Address* (1887) and *Sermons on Several Occasions* (1889); obituaries of wives in *Richmond Planet*,

2 Nov. 1907, and *Richmond Afro-American*, 26 Apr. 1958; por. at First Baptist Church, South Richmond; obituary in *Richmond Planet*, 1 Feb. 1919 (por.).

JOHN T. KNEEBONE

BINNS, John Alexander (ca. 1761–by 10 November 1813), agricultural reformer, was the eldest of five sons and four daughters of Charles Binns, the first clerk of Loudoun County, and Ann Alexander Binns, who were married by 7 April 1760. The date of his birth is not known, but he was likely born about 1761. Binns married Dewanna Bennett, probably in the autumn of 1782, when his father gave him a 220-acre farm. The couple had no children. Binns became a lieutenant in the Loudoun County militia in 1781 but is not known to have served on active duty during the Revolutionary War.

In 1784 Binns began experimenting with gypsum on his Loudoun County farm. He had read or been advised that applications of gypsum, a mineral consisting of hydrous calcium sulfate and popularly referred to then as plaster of paris, could increase the yields of a number of crops. When he applied it to one of his wheat fields, he doubled his anticipated yield. Binns conducted further experiments with corn and clover, acquired samples of gypsum from France and Nova Scotia to test their relative qualities, and eventually erected a water-powered mill to grind calcareous manures. He kept meticulous records of his applications of gypsum and animal manures and of the yields from both treated and untreated crops. Two generations before Edmund Ruffin began publicizing the same technique, Binns zealously advocated the use of calcium in agriculture. He was also something of a pioneer in calling for the use of legumes to help restore soil fertility.

Binns detailed his experiments and the conclusions derived from two decades of observant farming in a small book, *A Treatise on Practical Farming: Embracing Particularly the Following Subjects, viz. The Use of Plaister of Paris, with Directions for Using It, And General Observations on the Use of Other Manures, On Deep Ploughing, Thick Sowing of Grain, Method of Preventing Fruit Trees From Decaying, and Farming in General* (1803). He described results so remarkable that some people doubted his veracity. Therefore, when he added some short addenda and had a second edition published in Richmond in 1804, he included seventeen affidavits attesting to the accuracy of his claims and to the productivity of his formerly exhausted fields. Thomas Jefferson praised Binns's *Treatise* to a number of his scientific correspondents, stating that Binns's skillful methods had transformed the author from a poor man into a rich one, restored worn-out land on several farms, and helped revive Loudoun County's agricultural economy. Binns remained relatively unknown, but his techniques of manuring with gypsum, plowing deep, and growing clover became known among scientific agriculturists as the Loudoun system. They often credited its development, however, to members of the Janney family, well-known Loudoun County farmers who prospered later in the nineteenth century.

John Alexander Binns died before 10 November 1813, when his will was proved in court. He had signed and dated the last of his several wills on 11 January of that year. The will freed all but one of his slaves when they turned twenty-five, with the one exception ordered to serve Dewanna Binns for six years from the date of the will. Binns specified that when the date of a slave's freedom arrived, he or she was to be taken outside Virginia to be emancipated. The will also offered $500 to any person who would see to it that those provisions of his will were carried into effect if his family or executors failed to follow his wishes. The justices of the peace required a bond of $30,000 for the administration of the estate which, if custom was followed, was twice their estimate of its value.

Rodney H. True, "John Binns of Loudoun," *WMQ*, 2d ser., 2 (1922): 20–39; Charles Preston Poland Jr., *From Frontier to Suburbia* (1976), 84–96; deeds of property from John Alexander to daughter Ann Binns, wife of Charles Binns, 7 Apr. 1760, and from Charles Binns to John Alexander Binns, 7 Sept. 1782, Loudoun Co. Deed Book, B:49–50, N:367–369; farming career documented in *Treatise* and in plantation records for 1785–1796, LC; Edwin Morris Betts, ed., *Thomas Jefferson's Farm Book* (1953), 195–197; Loudoun Co. Will Book, K:343–344.

BRENT TARTER

BINSWANGER, Samuel Emanuel (26 December 1895–11 February 1960), business executive, was born in Richmond, the only son and elder of two children of Harry S. Binswanger and Rebecca Whitlock Binswanger. When he was two years old, he was stricken with polio, which left him paralyzed in the left leg but determined to overcome the handicap. Binswanger was educated at home until the age of eight, when he entered public schools. After graduating from John Marshall High School in Richmond, he attended the New York State College of Agriculture at Cornell University from 1914 to 1918. World War I interrupted his studies, and although his foot kept him from active service, he took a dollar-a-year position with the United States War Trade Board.

While he was a Cornell student Binswanger spent his summers in Richmond working as a salesman, farm laborer, and building-construction assistant. In 1917 he helped in the planning and construction of Langley Field, an aviation facility in Hampton. After the war he lived briefly in Memphis, Tennessee, where he worked for a manufacturer of prefabricated houses. Returning to Richmond in 1920, Binswanger became an office assistant with Binswanger and Company, which his grandfather had founded in 1872. In 1925 he became secretary of the firm and four years later he was promoted to vice president and general manager. He served as president from 1949 until 1958, when he became chairman of the board of directors.

Binswanger and Company began as a small retail store but grew to be a large regional glass, mirror, and building-supply company. By the time of Binswanger's death it was reportedly the largest southern distributor of Libbey-Owens-Ford glass products and had thirty-four branches in sixteen states, four affiliated companies, more than 1,000 employees, and capitalization in excess of $8 million. In addition to his presidency of the parent company, Binswanger served from 1949 to 1958 as vice president and adviser to Binswanger and Company of Tennessee, and to Binswanger and Company of Texas. From 1939 to 1959 he sat on the board of the Spotless Company, local general retailers. He was also active in trade associations.

Binswanger was a lay reader and teacher at Congregation Beth Ahabah in Richmond before serving as its president in 1947 and 1948. For twenty-five years he sat on the board of managers of the congregation's endowment fund, and he was its secretary for ten years and president for four. Binswanger took an active role not only in his synagogue but also in community affairs, two interests that often coincided. For ten years as a young man he was scoutmaster of a troop of Boy Scouts at an area settlement house for recently arrived immigrants, and in 1928 he served as president of the local Scoutmasters' Club. Binswanger sat from 1939 to 1959 on the board of the National Conference of Christians and Jews. From 1949 to 1957 he chaired the board of directors of the Virginia branch of the Anti-Defamation League of B'nai B'rith, and in the latter year the league established a human relations library in his honor. His many years as a director of the Richmond Jewish Community Council included a term as its president in 1942–1943. In 1958 he received the council's Distinguished Community Service Award. Binswanger was chosen in 1954 to serve on the American Jewish Tercentenary Committee, which planned the national observance of three centuries of Jewish American life. He also served on the national board of delegates of the American Jewish Committee.

On 28 September 1939 Binswanger married Virginia VerVeer. They had two sons. Samuel Emanuel Binswanger died in Richmond on 11 February 1960 and was buried in Hebrew Cemetery in Richmond. In 1971 the Jewish Community Federation of Richmond began conferring the annual Sam E. and Virginia Binswanger Young Leadership Award for notable contributions to the Richmond Jewish community.

NCAB, 45:448–449; Binswanger material in Congregation Beth Ahabah Museum and Archives, Richmond, and archives of Jewish Community Federation, Richmond; feature articles in *Richmond News Leader*, 8 Aug. 1955 (por.), 18 Nov. 1957, and *Richmond Times-Dispatch*, 18 Nov. 1957 (por.), 6 Apr. 1997; Myron Berman, *Richmond's Jewry, 1769–1976: Shabbat in Shockoe* (1979), 323; Melvin I. Urofsky, *Commonwealth and Community: The Jewish Experience in Virginia* (1997), 127–128; obituaries in *Richmond News Leader* and *Richmond Times-Dispatch*, both 12 Feb. 1960.

SAUL VIENER

BIRCH, Thomas Erskine (22 August 1763–3 January 1821), educator, was born on the island of Saint Kitts in the British West Indies, the son of Charles Birch, a physician, and Christina Erskine Birch. He was educated at Christ's Hospital in London. After a British ship on which he was a passenger was captured during the American Revolution, he joined the American navy and served for a time under John Paul Jones. Birch was wounded in the thigh during the war and limped for the remainder of his life.

Details about Birch's life are unavailable for some periods, and the date and place of his ordination as a minister of the Presbyterian Church are not recorded. About 1792 he moved to Virginia and in that year married Elizabeth Bohannon Murray. They had two sons before her death in 1798. On 1 June 1803 Birch married Mary Magdalene Miller in Montgomery County. They had seven daughters and three sons.

From about the time of his first marriage until the early years of the nineteenth century, Birch taught oratory and belles-lettres near Richmond. He then moved to Wythe County, where he offered instruction at Anchor and Hope Academy before moving on to Washington County to join the faculty at Abingdon Academy. In teaching rhetoric Birch employed a variety of techniques to assist pupils in speaking well. He trained them in logic and diction as well as intonation and gesture. His principal achievement was the compilation of *The Virginian Orator: Being a Variety of Original and Selected Poems and Dramatic Scenes to Improve the American Youth in the Ornamental and Useful Art of Eloquence and Gesture* (1808). Birch included examples of eloquent exposition, verse, and other compositions by notable Virginians and other Americans as well as some of his own and of his students' productions in order to illustrate good rhetorical styles.

The subject matter was highly patriotic and republican in tone. An important and influential work in a new genre, Birch's *Virginian Orator* anticipated such later nineteenth-century southern rhetoricians as Jonathan J. Judge and Richard Sterling, who followed Birch in recommending the study of classical exemplars as well as modern writers and in cultivating an ornamented style and a romantic sensibility. In his preface Birch promised to publish a second volume with the patriotic title of *The Republican Speaker*, but he never completed it. A posthumous second edition of *The Virginian Orator* appeared in 1823.

Birch occasionally spoke in public on issues of political interest. On 14 April 1812 he delivered a major address at the Wythe County courthouse on behalf of a proposition to abolish property ownership as a prerequisite to the suffrage in Virginia. His "Appeal for Manhood Suffrage" was direct and unembellished, arguing from first principles to their application. He stated that citizens who were required to pay taxes and shoulder arms for their country could not be denied the right to vote simply because they owned no land without violating the principles of the American Revolution.

Birch moved to Kentucky about 1817, when a record identifies him as a Lutheran minister. He established short-lived Washington College in Cynthiana in Harrison County in that state. Thomas Erskine Birch died in Cynthiana on 3 January 1821 and was probably buried at Battle Grove Cemetery there, where his widow is buried.

Birth date in Mary B. Kegley and Francis B. Kegley, *Early Adventurers on the Western Waters* (1980–), 2:143, 249–250; month and year of death in Erskine Birch Essig, biographical notes on Thomas Erskine Birch, undated typescript in Episcopal Diocese of Virginia Papers, VHS; Montgomery Co. Order Book, 13:199, 201–202; Francis B. Kegley, "The People of the Great Southwest: Their Character and Culture," *Mountain Empire* 1 (Jan. 1933): 13; Jouet McGavock Boyd, *History of St. John's Church, Wytheville, Virginia* (1946), 4–5; Mary B. Kegley, *Wythe County, Virginia: A Bicentennial History* (1989), 137–138, 221, 314; Lula Reed Boss, "Mason County, Kentucky, Court Records: Returns of Ministers' Marriages," *Kentucky Ancestors* 5 (1969): 124; Birch's "Appeal for Manhood Suffrage" reprinted in Slemp and Preston, *Addresses*, 17–28.

CALVIN M. LOGUE
JEAN DEHART

BIRD, Abraham (ca. 1731–by 21 March 1820), member of the Convention of 1776, was born about the time his parents, Andrew Byrd and Magdalene Jones Byrd, moved from Pennsylvania to the Shenandoah Valley. He was their second son and probably the second of about nine children. Unlike some other family members, he spelled his surname Bird. His name first appears in the records of Augusta County in the spring of 1754, when he purchased 174 acres of land from his older brother, Andrew Byrd. Abraham Bird became an ensign in the militia of Augusta County in March 1759 and a captain on 18 November 1762. Sometime before 1763 he married Rachel Zeigler. They had five daughters and four sons.

Bird lived most of his adult life on a farm in the portion of Frederick County that became Dunmore County in 1772. In May 1774 he won a special election to the House of Burgesses. Bird attended the short assembly sessions of May 1774 and June 1775, and although he was eligible to attend the first Virginia convention that met in Williamsburg in August 1774, he probably did not. He was elected to the Dunmore County Committee on 10 February 1775 and to the fifth Virginia convention on 23 April 1776. Bird served on the Committee on Propositions and Grievances and attended nearly every session from 6 May through 5 July. He was almost certainly present on the three most important days, on 15 May when the convention unanimously voted for independence, on 12 June when it unanimously adopted the Declaration of Rights, and on 29 June when it unanimously adopted the Constitution of 1776.

Bird served one-year terms in the House of Delegates from 1776 through 1779 and in 1781, 1783, 1785, and 1786. He probably had a hand in the legislative decision during the October 1777 session to change the name of Dunmore County to Shanando (later spelled Shenandoah) County. He was elected to the House of Delegates in 1787 but refused to serve, citing a law passed in 1785 that allowed anyone who had served seven or more terms to decline. Though he missed that session, Bird was elected again in 1788 and attended the assembly that year, and he served a final term in 1796.

In February 1777 Bird became a justice of the peace, and he remained on the county court, often presiding as senior justice, until 1804. He served as coroner, sheriff, and colonel of the militia, and in 1782 he became county lieutenant and was appointed one of the trustees of the town of Woodstock. Bird had been born into a German Lutheran family and his wife had a Presbyterian upbringing, but he became an Episcopalian and was a churchwarden of Beckford Parish in 1798. At that time Bird owned more than six hundred fifty acres of land in Shenandoah County.

All but one of Bird's nine children moved west after the Revolution, and in August or September of 1804 he moved to Kentucky. Abraham Bird died in Fayette County, Kentucky, by 21 March 1820, when his estate was inventoried.

The simultaneous presence in the Shenandoah Valley of several other men named Abraham Bird or Byrd and of several Andrew Birds and Andrew Byrds as well has produced much historiographical confusion, which the subject's distinctive signature helps untangle; Marilyn K. Byrd Harton, Harold K. Byrd, and Carol J. McKenzie Byrd, *Byrds and Sonners of Shenandoah Valley* (1983), 1, 8, and appendix, 3a; William Bird Wylie, *Bird Genealogy* (1903), 1–2; the name appears frequently in Shenandoah Co. Deed, Minute, and Order Books and in Land and Personal Property Tax Returns, Shenandoah Co., RG 48, LVA; will, estate inventory, and record of estate sale in Fayette Co., Ky., Will Book, E:149–151, 179–182, 201–203, with will also copied in Shenandoah Co. Will Book, P:315–317; age at death of eighty-eight in undated death notice in *Lexington (Ky.) Reporter*, 22 Mar. 1820.

DAPHNE GENTRY

BIRD, Henry Dearborn (30 November 1808–15 March 1881), railroad executive, was born in New Castle, Delaware, the youngest of five sons and a daughter of John Bird and Elizabeth Van Leuvenigh Bird. His father, a prominent business leader and member of the Delaware legislature, died in 1810. Bird grew up in New Castle and in Philadelphia, where he lived with his mother, her second husband, and some of his brothers, among whom was the future novelist, poet, and playwright, Robert Montgomery Bird. On 25 February 1833 Bird married Mary Moylan Fox. They had three sons and four daughters.

Bird was a pioneer in the new steam railway industry. He spent the early months of 1832 in England, where he observed railroad construction and locomotive operations. In the summer of 1832 he moved to Virginia to work with Moncure Robinson on the construction of the railroad between Weldon, North Carolina, and

Petersburg. The Petersburg Railroad was one of the first steam railways to go into operation in the South. Petersburg's business leaders obtained a charter for the railroad in 1830 in hopes of diverting commerce away from Albemarle Sound and its canal link to Norfolk by intercepting river traffic on the Roanoke River at Weldon. Bird helped construct the line, acted as transportation agent in 1834, and from 1835 to 1839 was the railroad's chief engineer.

From 2 September 1839 until March 1855 Bird served as the third president of the Petersburg Railroad. During his tenure he faced many problems common to early railroads. The track was originally laid with wooden rails topped with thin iron bars. The wood rotted and had to be replaced frequently, which added to the expense of operating the line, resulted in delays and lost business, hindered the development of scheduled passenger service, and on several occasions threatened cancellation of the profitable contract to carry the mail. In 1850 Bird directed the replacement of all fifty-nine miles of track with new iron rails, and for the remainder of the antebellum period the Petersburg Railroad operated at a profit. The line became an important link in the passenger and freight rail routes that connected Baltimore and Washington with Richmond, Raleigh, and points farther south, and from it the Atlantic Coast Line later evolved.

During the first few years of Bird's presidency, the Petersburg Railroad competed fiercely with the Portsmouth and Roanoke Railroad, which constructed a line from Portsmouth to Weldon in an attempt to defeat Petersburg's bid for Piedmont traffic. The intense and protracted rivalry drew in other railroads and pitted Bird against Moncure Robinson, who had become president of the Richmond, Fredericksburg, and Potomac Railroad. After the demise of the Portsmouth and Roanoke Railroad, the Petersburg Railroad acquired a new competitor for inland business in the form of the new Richmond and Danville Railroad.

Early in the 1850s Bird borrowed money and built a hotel in Weldon in anticipation of an increase in passenger business, but he overextended himself and improperly drew on the credit of the railroad to the amount of $26,493.87. He also owed the railroad approximately $3,460. On 17 February 1855 Bird deeded virtually all of his real and personal property to the Petersburg Railroad, and at the beginning of March he resigned as its president. By indemnifying the railroad he avoided possible prosecution and expensive lawsuits, but he was financially ruined.

Bird's personal financial problems did not destroy his career in railroading, however. Late in the summer of 1858 he was appointed engineer and chief superintendent of the South Side Railroad that connected Petersburg and Lynchburg. After Virginia seceded from the Union in the spring of 1861, Bird embraced the Confederate cause and worked to keep the South Side Railroad in operation, transporting soldiers and supplies to the front and wounded men to the rear. He represented the line at the 15 December 1862 conference of Confederate railroad executives in Augusta, Georgia, and he continued to try to find locomotives and rolling stock to assist the Confederate army as late as the second week in April 1865.

For about five years late in the 1860s and early in the 1870s Bird worked as superintendent of the Lower Appomattox Company in Petersburg, an enterprise that built bridges and cleared river obstructions. Following his wife's death on 30 November 1875, he retired. Henry Dearborn Bird died at his home in Petersburg on 15 March 1881 and was buried the next day in Blandford Cemetery.

Bird Family Papers, VHS; Bird letters in other collections in VHS, in Samuel F. Morse Papers, Historical Society of Pennsylvania, Philadelphia, and Board of Public Works Papers, RG 57, LVA; Howard D. Dozier, *A History of the Atlantic Coast Line Railroad* (1920), 22–35; Peter C. Stewart, "Railroads and Urban Rivalries in Antebellum Eastern Virginia," *VMHB* 81 (1973): 3–22; deed of trust, 17 Feb. 1855, Petersburg City Hustings Court Deed Book, 21:663–666; *OR*; obituary in *Petersburg Index-Appeal*, 16 Mar. 1881.

R. ALLEN BRAHIN

BIRD, Lloyd Campbell (1 August 1894–20 April 1978), businessman and member of the Senate of Virginia, the only child of George Anson Bird and Mary Susan Campbell Bird, was born on their farm near Valley Center in Highland County. He attended Randolph-Macon Academy in Bedford and then entered the pharmacy school at the Medical College of Virginia, graduating in 1917. On 15 September of that year he entered the United States Army as a private in the Medical Reserve, eventually attaining the rank of sergeant and serving in an army hospital in France from July 1918 until World War I ended. Bird went to work as a bacteriologist in 1919 for the State Board of Health in Richmond. He then took graduate courses in bacteriology at the University of Michigan in Ann Arbor and returned to Richmond to teach the subject at MCV in 1924.

In 1925 Bird and Morris Phipps, his former MCV professor, founded Phipps and Bird, Incorporated, manufacturers and distributors of medical and scientific supplies and instruments. Bird served as president of the company from 1928 until it was sold in 1969, at which time he became chairman of the board. He was also president of the nonprofit Allied Scientific Corporation, which acted as a marketing and promotional agent for a number of small producers of medical and scientific equipment. Active in Virginia's scientific community, Bird chaired the local arrangements committee for the meeting of the American Association for the Advancement of Science in Richmond in December 1938, one of the largest conventions held in the city up to that time, and he was president of the Virginia Academy of Science in 1952–1953. He was also a founder in 1941 of the Southern Association of Science and Industry, serving as president from 1944 to 1946 and as chairman of its board in 1951. He received an honorary doctorate of laws from MCV in 1951. In addition to his Richmond manufacturing interests, Bird inherited and managed a sheep-and-cattle farm consisting of almost a thousand acres in Highland County.

In 1933 Bird moved to Chesterfield County, and in 1943 he won election to the Senate of Virginia from the district that initially included the city of Williamsburg and the counties of Charles City, Chesterfield, Henrico, James City, and New Kent. He became an influential member of the conservative Democratic majority in the Senate and was reelected continuously until he retired from politics in 1971. He served on several commissions that studied public school curricula in the 1940s and 1950s, chaired the Advisory Committee on Community Colleges in the 1960s, and sat on the commission established in 1959 to study the use of educational television in schools. Bird was chairman of the Advisory Council on the Virginia Economy established in 1947 and vice chairman of the Virginia 350th Anniversary Commission.

During the school desegregation crisis Bird served as chairman of the Senate Committee on Public Institutions and Education and was a strong behind-the-scenes ally of fellow senators Mills E. Godwin Jr. and Garland Gray in support of Massive Resistance. The key vote that broke the back of official opposition to desegregation occurred in the Senate on 17 April 1959, when members voted twenty to nineteen to refer House Bill 50, a pupil placement bill, to a committee of the whole rather than send it to almost certain death in Bird's committee. Bird voted against the bill when it passed the Senate six days later by a vote of twenty-one to eighteen.

On 8 April 1933 Bird married Lucille Crutchfield Phinney, of Richmond. She had also been his secretary during the early years at Phipps and Bird. A widow, she had one daughter when she married Bird. The couple had one son and one daughter. Lucille Bird died on 5 October 1970, and after a long period of poor health Lloyd Campbell Bird died on 20 April 1978. They were buried in Hollywood Cemetery in Richmond. In 1978 Chesterfield County opened its new Lloyd C. Bird High School, named in his honor.

Biography by son, George C. Bird, in Highland County Historical Society, *The New History of Highland County, Virginia, 1982* (1983), 258 (por.); Lloyd Campbell Bird Papers, UVA; BVS Birth Register, Highland Co.; Military Service Records; Lloyd C. Bird, "Pharmacy, Old and New in Virginia," *Commonwealth* 7 (Apr. 1940): 7–8; feature article in *Richmond News Leader*, 9 Feb. 1959 (por.); obituaries in *Richmond News Leader*, 20 Apr. 1978, and *Richmond Times-Dispatch*, 21 Apr. 1978; editorial tribute in *Richmond News Leader*, 2 May 1978.

BRENT TARTER

BIRD, Mark (23 December 1810–2 January 1883), member of the Convention of 1850–

1851, was born in Woodstock, the youngest of five sons and one of six children of George Bird and Hannah Allen Bird. His grandfather Abraham Bird served in the Convention of 1776. On 18 October 1834 Bird married Sarah Clarke Macon Hite in Frederick County, and they had six sons and four daughters. In 1840 Bird bought property in Woodstock, where he lived for the remainder of his life in a house he called the Bird's Nest.

Bird began practicing law in Woodstock by the middle of the 1830s. On 12 October 1846 the Shenandoah County Court elected him commonwealth's attorney. He held the office without apparent interruption until the 1870s. In March 1847 Bird was appointed one of the trustees for the Woodstock Female Seminary, and he was also a charter member of the Shenandoah Lodge No. 32 of the Independent Order of Odd Fellows. He took little or no recorded part in partisan politics, but early in January 1851 he was elected to the Virginia constitutional convention to succeed Green Berry Samuels, who had resigned. On 18 January 1851 Bird took his seat as the fourth representative of the district composed of the counties of Hardy, Shenandoah, and Warren. He was appointed to the Committee on the Legislative Department of the Government, but the records of the convention contain almost nothing about his participation or his views on the most important subjects being debated. Bird was frequently absent from the convention and did not vote on the key question of the basis of representation either in the committee of the whole or when the final vote was taken. He was present on 31 July 1851 to vote in favor of adoption of the constitution.

Bird's only recorded participation in the Civil War was as chairman of his county's board of commissioners that paid out the money the county court appropriated for arming and equipping the local volunteers. On 25 March 1875 the General Assembly passed an act dividing the Twelfth Judicial Circuit and forming a new Eighteenth Circuit encompassing the counties of Page, Rockingham, and Shenandoah. Two days later the legislators elected Bird judge of the new circuit court by a vote of 114 to 6. Mark Bird served as judge until his death at his residence on 2 January 1883. He was buried in Massanutten Cemetery in Woodstock, as was his widow, who died 5 July 1896. Bird's gravestone has the simple inscription, "An upright Judge and gentleman."

Birth and death dates from gravestone, Massanutten Cemetery, Woodstock; John W. Wayland, *A History of Shenandoah County, Virginia* (1927), 584–585, 692–693; family relationships in mother's will, Shenandoah Co. Will Book, S:127–128, and Census, Shenandoah Co., 1850–1880; Frederick Co. Marriage Bonds; service as commonwealth's attorney documented in Shenandoah Co. Minute Book; obituaries in *Richmond Whig*, 5 Jan. 1883, and *Winchester Times*, 10 Jan. 1883.

DAPHNE GENTRY

BIRD, Robert Montgomery (13 June 1867–4 June 1938), chemist, was born in Petersburg, the eldest of nine children of Henry Van Leuvenigh Bird, a Confederate veteran and railroad agent, and Margaret Randolph Bird. He was a grandnephew of Robert Montgomery Bird, an eminent playwright and novelist. Bird attended local schools and then joined his father at the Norfolk and Western Railroad as a clerk in 1885. Ten years later he entered Hampden-Sydney College as a sophomore and received B.A. and B.S. degrees in 1897. Bird then attended Johns Hopkins University in Baltimore, which had pioneered in the laboratory method of teaching sciences, and earned a Ph.D. in 1901. While at Johns Hopkins he also taught at Frederick College in Maryland for a year and met Caroline Reid, of Baltimore, whom he married on 11 June 1902 in Mount Washington, Baltimore County, Maryland. They had one son and one daughter. After a year on the faculty at Mississippi Agricultural and Mechanical College (now Mississippi State University), in 1902 Bird went to the University of Missouri in Columbia as professor of chemistry.

In 1907 Bird accepted an appointment as professor of chemistry at the University of Virginia. John William Mallet, the founder and chairman of the modern chemistry program at the university, and Francis Perry Dunnington, who taught analytical chemistry, had determined in 1906 to expand the department. They separated organic and physical chemistry from the general chemistry course, made them independent courses, arranged for a former dining hall to be converted into a laboratory for undergraduates, and hired Bird to supervise the general chemistry program. Mallet emphasized laboratory instruction over lectures and provided engineering students with different course work from that assigned to the other undergraduates in his classes. When ill health required Mallet to retire in 1908, his successor organized organic and physical chemistry into a separate school, akin to Dunnington's school of analytical chemistry. Bird thus found himself in charge of a school of chemistry that, despite its name, was actually one of three chemistry programs conducted at different locations.

As the faculty grew in size and the curriculum expanded, student enrollment in chemistry courses rose. As early as 1908 Bird's annual report to the university president proposed construction of a new, two-story chemistry building. In 1915 two donors finally provided the funds needed to erect and equip a new building, which all three schools of chemistry would occupy. As chairman of the Building Committee, Bird supervised the furnishing of the structure's interior. The new building opened in the autumn of 1917, and by the mid-1920s chemistry instruction had been consolidated into a single school under one chairman. With the hiring of additional faculty members, Bird gave up the general chemistry course in 1919 to teach organic chemistry, an assignment that he retained until his death.

Bird also made contributions outside the university. He edited a collection of readings designed for students, *Modern Science Reader: With Special Reference to Chemistry* (1911), which proved popular enough to go through six editions by 1928. Bird published numerous scientific papers on topics including wood extracts and the use of toxic agents to protect orchards against insect pests. During World War I he served as an expert for the United States Army Chemical Warfare Service. He was a fellow of the American Association for the Advancement of Science and of the American Institute of Chemistry as well as a vestryman at Saint Paul's Memorial Church in Charlottesville. Robert Montgomery Bird died on 4 June 1938 and was buried in the University of Virginia Cemetery.

NCAB, 38:576; *Charlottesville Daily Progress*, 24 Feb. 1938 (por.); Bruce, *University of Virginia*, 5:144; Hugh Miller Spencer, *A History of the School of Chemistry at the University of Virginia, 1825–1943* (1983), 61–75; correspondence concerning construction of Cobb Chemistry Laboratory, UVA Archives; obituaries in *Charlottesville Daily Progress*, 4 June 1938, and *University of Virginia Alumni News* 26 (1938): 195, 211.

JOHN T. KNEEBONE

BIRDSONG, McLemore (11 December 1911–3 June 1977), pediatrician and medical educator, was born in Suffolk, the youngest of five sons and three daughters of Thomas Henry Birdsong and Martha Lewis McLemore Birdsong. His father owned much land and marketed agricultural products on a large scale in a family business that later became the Birdsong Corporation. His mother's prominent Suffolk family included her brothers James L. McLemore, a lawyer and circuit court judge, and Thomas McLemore, a physician credited by Birdsong with inspiring his own career choice.

Birdsong graduated from Suffolk High School in 1930 and entered Randolph-Macon College. He had qualified for medical school by the end of his third year of college and, after the death of his father on 5 October 1933, his elder brothers recommended that he go directly to medical school. Birdsong reluctantly complied and entered the University of Virginia Medical School during the 1933–1934 academic year. He studied under Lawrence Thomas Royster, the school's first teacher of pediatrics, and graduated in June 1937. On 18 October 1941 he married Charlotte Clarke Spain, a 1938 nursing graduate, and they had three sons.

Birdsong stayed on at the University of Virginia after graduation, serving an internship in pediatrics. He spent two years as an instructor, obtaining experience that confirmed him in his choice of medical specialty. Royster arranged for Birdsong to spend the 1940–1941 school year in Boston as a resident in pediatrics at Children's Hospital, which was affiliated with the Harvard Medical School. He returned to the University of Virginia in July 1941 as an assistant professor. Ill health forced Royster to retire in January 1942, leaving his colleague William Wirt Waddell and Birdsong as the entire Department of Pediatrics. The pair shared a medical practice as well as teaching responsibilities. The war years were strenuous, as the understaffed medical school instituted an accelerated training program to produce the physicians needed for the military. Birdsong taught, conducted research, and maintained his practice, which, because of the dearth of physicians in the state, required house calls across a wide section of Virginia. He wanted to enter the military service himself, but working in Charlottesville had the advantage of keeping him close to his wife and his first child, who was born in 1943.

Birdsong viewed himself as a clinician and teacher, not as a researcher, although he published several scientific papers reporting on clinical tests of new medicines and medical procedures. In 1948 income from his family's corporation enabled him to decline a job offer in Roanoke that would have tripled his salary. He served one-year terms as president of the Virginia Pediatric Society (now the Virginia chapter of the American Academy of Pediatrics) in 1949–1950, the Albemarle County Medical Society in 1952–1953, and the Medical Society of Virginia in 1964–1965, chaired the Pediatric Section of the Southern Medical Association in 1959, and helped to found the Southern Society for Pediatric Research in 1960. Birdsong also took part in community affairs. In 1946 he was president of the local Rotary Club and beginning in 1949 he served for fourteen years on the Albemarle County Planning Commission. For many of those years he unsuccessfully advocated annexation to unify the governments of Charlottesville and Albemarle County.

Birdsong's most important service was to the University of Virginia and its medical school. He became a leader and faculty coordinator of the Medical Alumni Association after 1949 and, coming from a political family, knew how to organize the successful lobbying campaign that financed construction of a new, eight-story, 419-bed hospital dedicated on 14 April 1961. He succeeded Waddell in 1960 as chairman of the pediatrics department and recruited his own successor in 1964. Birdsong was one of six faculty members appointed in 1967 to a special committee to study whether the university should become coeducational. He concluded that the school could no longer exclude women legally and that it should therefore accept the change gracefully. On 15 December 1968 the committee called for the university to rescind existing restrictions on the admission of women students.

In 1974 Birdsong received the first McLemore Birdsong Award for Outstanding Teaching in the Department of Pediatrics, and a year later he won the Alumni Distinguished Service Award. He retired and became professor emeritus of pediatrics on 30 June 1975. In 1977 the University of Virginia established the McLemore Birdsong Chair of Pediatrics in his honor. McLemore Birdsong died of myocardial failure at home on 3 June 1977 and was buried at Monticello Memorial Park in Charlottesville.

James L. McLemore III, *B. F. McLemore: His Ancestors and Descendants* (1991), 361–384; oral history interview with McLemore Birdsong, 21 Jan. 1976, UVA; feature articles in *Virginia Medical Monthly* 91 (1964): 523–524 (por.), and *Richmond Times-Dispatch*, 29 June 1975 (por.); obituaries in *Charlottesville Daily Progress*, 5 June 1977, and *Virginia Medical* 104 (1977): 583; memorial in *Virginia Medical* 105 (1978): 23–24.

JOHN T. KNEEBONE

BISHOP, Carter Richard (22 May 1849–21 August 1941), civil engineer and preservationist, was born in Petersburg, the second of four sons and second of five children of Carter Richard Bishop and Mary Elizabeth Head Bishop. He received some schooling before being admitted to the Virginia Military Institute in 1864, when it was situated in the almshouse in Richmond. The cadets moved into the trenches outside of Richmond a few days before the evacuation of the city, and on 3 April 1865, the day that Richmond fell, Bishop was captured.

Bishop attended McCabe's University School in Petersburg after the war and then entered Hampden-Sydney College. He graduated in 1870 and in July 1871 was appointed superintendent of the high school in Owensboro, Kentucky, where he taught until 1876. He then returned to Petersburg and worked under the direction of his father, who was the cashier of the Commercial National Bank. After his father died in 1877, Bishop succeeded him as cashier. In 1886 he became cashier of the new National Bank of Petersburg, a position he held for twenty years. He married Catharine Kirk in Petersburg on 8 November 1881. Their one son died at the age of twenty.

Bishop served on the Petersburg City Council from 1894 to 1910 and invested in the local electric power company. He also acted as a civil engineer on several major local projects, including the electrical development of Petersburg, Richmond, and Hopewell. Bishop's greatest engineering feat was his plan for diverting the main stream of the Appomattox River, which flooded the lower portions of Petersburg after heavy rains. His plan called for construction of a two-mile canal to carry off floodwater. At the groundbreaking ceremony in September 1904 the United States Army Corps of Engineers presented Bishop with a silver spade to move the first shovel of earth.

Captain Bishop, as he was known locally, looked and acted the part of the quintessential Confederate veteran. Wearing his gray uniform and sporting a silver goatee, he became a widely recognized figure. He served as adjutant of the A. P. Hill Camp of the United Confederate Veterans for twenty-five years and later became the judge advocate general of the Virginia Division of the UCV. Bishop regularly took part in reunions and established cordial relationships with northern veterans' groups. His pamphlet, *The Cockade City of the Union* (1907), summarized the siege of Petersburg for educational use and to promote local tourism. Bishop also actively promoted the establishment of a national battlefield park at Petersburg, working in close cooperation with Massachusetts siege veterans to win it congressional and presidential authorization. He persuaded local landowners to donate or sell their property to the park and surveyed the land included within its boundaries. Named by the Secretary of War to the three-man commission authorized by Congress to study the feasibility of a park, he later chaired the commission that oversaw the site. On 20 June 1932 Bishop played a prominent part in the dedication of the Petersburg National Military Park. He often led tours of the battlefields around Petersburg and was recognized as an authority on the subject. Also in June 1932 he received an honorary Sc.D. from Hampden-Sydney College.

Carter Richard Bishop died in Petersburg on 21 August 1941 after a long illness and was buried in Blandford Cemetery in Petersburg.

Biographies in Evans, *Confederate Military History*, 4:729–730, Tyler, *Men of Mark*, 5:32–34, and Bruce, Tyler, and Morton, *History of Virginia*, 4:66; some Bishop letters in VHS; *Petersburg Daily Courier*, 7 June 1870; *Petersburg Daily Sun*, 14 Nov. 1877; *Petersburg Daily Post* and *Petersburg Index and Appeal*, both 15 Nov. 1877; *Petersburg Rural Messenger*, 12 Nov. 1881; *Petersburg Progress-Index*, 20 June 1932 (por.); Historian's Files, Petersburg National Battlefield; Lee A. Wallace Jr. and Martin R. Conway, *A History of Petersburg National Battlefield* (1983), 55–62; obituary in *Petersburg Progress-Index*, 21 Aug. 1941 (por.).

JAMES H. BLANKENSHIP JR.

BISHOP, Curtis Vance (8 July 1894–19 February 1966), president of Averett College, was born in Inman, Spartanburg County, South Carolina, the second of three sons and third of six children of Albert Palmer Bishop and Nannie Evelyn Thompson Bishop. He was raised on a cotton farm, educated at a local academy, and served in the navy during World War I. Bishop studied at the University of Richmond for two years after leaving the military. He then taught at Spartan Academy in Spartanburg County and attended Furman University in neighboring Greenville County, South Carolina, graduating in 1924. Bishop taught at Furman after his graduation. During the summers he took graduate courses in English at the University of Texas and received an A.M. in 1928. Bishop married Helen Butler McDowell on 31 July 1924, and they had two sons.

In 1930 Bishop accepted the vice presidency of Averett College, a small Baptist school for women in Danville that combined a college preparatory department with a two-year college curriculum. Bishop also taught English, served as acting president of the college in 1934, and was vice president and business manager from 1935 to 1936, when he was appointed president. Until his death thirty years later he strove as president to make Averett one of the best junior colleges in the East. During his long tenure he abolished the preparatory department, improved the quality and tripled the size of the faculty, added preprofessional programs, and saw Averett begin awarding associate degrees in 1957. During Bishop's presidency student enrollment rose from about 220 to more than 600, and the college constructed four new buildings and modernized and enlarged others, more than doubling the size of the campus.

Bishop became a national leader among junior college administrators. He believed that junior colleges were important components of the nation's system of higher education, and in 1939 he became secretary-treasurer of the new Junior College Division of the Southern Association of Colleges and Secondary Schools. In 1940 he helped organize the Southern Association of Junior Colleges and served as its president in 1942. He became a member of the board of the American Association of Junior Colleges in 1946, was elected vice president in 1948, and served as president in 1949. Bishop was also elected vice president of the Virginia Association of Colleges in February 1955. His involvement in the Southern Association of Baptist Colleges and Schools included a term as its president in 1965. While Bishop believed that private and church-supported schools had important roles to play in society, he also supported a statewide system of public junior colleges. The Virginia community college system was created the year he died.

Bishop also took leadership roles in the civic life of Danville. He was active in the Young Men's Christian Association and the Boy Scouts of America. He joined the Danville Rotary Club, was elected its president in 1931, and in 1945–1946 served as district governor of Rotary International. Elected vice president of the Danville Chamber of Commerce in 1945 and president in 1946, he also sat on the boards of trustees of the Memorial Hospital and of the Community Chest. He served as a deacon and taught in the Sunday school at Danville's First Baptist Church.

Bishop won election to the Danville City Council in 1950 and served as mayor from 1950 to 1957, during which time he supported bond issues to finance improvements in the public schools and helped transform Danville's municipal government to the council-manager form. Following a heart attack in 1957 Bishop resigned as mayor but completed his term on the council. He was also influential in the conservative Democratic Party organization in Danville, but along with many other conservative Democrats he supported Republican presidential candidates during the 1950s and 1960s.

In December 1951 the Kiwanis Club presented Bishop its Outstanding Citizen of Danville Award, and he received honorary doctorates from Furman University in 1943 and the University of Richmond in 1957. Early in 1966 Curtis Vance Bishop developed pneumonia followed by a stroke and died at Danville Memorial Hospital on 19 February 1966. He was buried in Mountain View Cemetery in Danville.

James Arnold Davis, "Dr. Curtis V. Bishop: Focus on a Junior College Career, 1930–1966" (Ph.D. diss., University of Florida, 1973); Jack Irby Hayes Jr., *A History of Averett College* (1984), 95–144 (pors., 96, 115); Curtis Vance Bishop, "Recent Trends in Junior College Education," in Association of Virginia Colleges, *Proceedings of the Annual Meeting* 35 (1949): 57–60, and "Mutual Responsibilities of the Local Church and the Christian School," *Religious Herald*, 28 Jan. 1965, 9, 21; obituary and editorial tribute in *Danville Register*, 20 Feb. 1966; memorial in *Virginia Baptist Annual* (1966): 102.

EMILY J. SALMON

BITTING, Charles Carroll (March 1830–24 December 1898), Baptist minister, was born in Philadelphia, the eldest of at least three sons and one daughter of Jordan Dodge Bitting and Sarah Walker Bucknell Bitting. At the age of seventeen he was baptized and joined the Broad Street Baptist Church. He graduated from Philadelphia Central High School and attended the University at Lewisburg (now Bucknell University) in Lewisburg, Pennsylvania, from 1849 to 1851 and Madison University (now Colgate University) in Hamilton, New York, from 1851 to 1852. He taught at Tennessee Baptist Female College in Nashville and moved to Murfreesboro when the school was relocated there. He was ordained into the Baptist ministry on 23 April 1854 against the wishes of his father, who disliked the dependence of ministers on the donations of church members.

In December 1855 Bitting became pastor of the Mount Olivet Baptist Church in Hanover County and married Caroline S. Shaddinger, of Philadelphia. They had three sons and three daughters. Bitting moved to Louisa County in 1856 and added Hopeful Baptist Church to his responsibilities. He served the two churches until 1859, when he became pastor of the First Baptist Church in Alexandria. During the Civil War, the Union army arrested Bitting twice after he refused to swear allegiance to the United States. On several occasions he and other prisoners were placed on Union troop and supply trains in hopes of preventing the Confederates under John Singleton Mosby from attacking. Nevertheless, he continued to preach and minister to his congregation until the end of the war.

In 1866 Bitting was appointed secretary of the Sunday School Board of the Southern Baptist Convention and moved to Greenville, South Carolina. When the board moved its headquarters to Memphis in 1868, Bitting resigned and returned to Virginia to become pastor of the First Baptist Church in Lynchburg. During his three years there the church increased its membership from 209 to 430 and established a mission that soon evolved into College Hill Baptist Church. As a member of Lynchburg's first school board in 1871 he helped to launch the city's public school system.

Bitting moved to Richmond later in 1871 to become the southern secretary of the American Baptist Publication Society. His main tasks were to promote Sunday schools and Bible societies in the region, work that involved extensive travel in Virginia, Tennessee, and the Carolinas. At the same time he also became interim pastor of Richmond's Second Baptist Church. After one year with the society he resigned to become the full-time pastor of Second Baptist. During his four years at that church, he added 150 people to its regular membership.

In 1871 Bitting was elected both statistical secretary of the Baptist General Association of Virginia and a member of the board of trustees of Richmond College. He served in the latter capacity for ten years and chaired the Memorial Committee for Richmond College, which raised $300,000 during the mid-1870s in honor of eighteenth-century Virginia Baptists who had been persecuted for their beliefs and practices. Furman University, a Baptist institution in South Carolina, awarded him an honorary D.D. in 1872. Bitting took a six-month leave of absence from Second Baptist in 1875 and, thanks to the liberality of his uncle William Bucknell, traveled in Europe, Egypt, and Palestine.

Bitting resigned his Richmond pastorate in 1876 to become minister of the Franklin Square Baptist Church in Baltimore. He presided over the renovation of the church and more than doubled its membership. After seven years in Baltimore, Bitting was appointed Bible secretary for the American Baptist Publication Society and moved to Philadelphia in 1883. From October 1884 he was also the society's missionary secretary, and he served as a trustee of Bucknell University from 1889 until his death.

Bitting was an effective preacher, an able administrator of denominational agencies, and the author of several books and sermons. His first publication, a pamphlet on *Modern Dancing* (1858), denounced dancing as unscriptural, destructive to piety, and injurious to health. In Alexandria he issued a *Memento of Mrs. Marian Speiden* (1867) in honor of a woman who had been a devoted member and Sunday school worker in his church. In Lynchburg Bitting published *Religious Liberty and the Baptists* (1869) and began research for *Notes on the History of the Strawberry Baptist Association of Virginia, For One Hundred Years, From 1776 to 1876* (1879). His last major publication was *Bible Societies and the Baptists* (1883), which described the formation of Bible societies in Germany, France, England, and the United States and emphasized the close association of Baptists with those organizations.

Poor health forced Bitting to retire from his posts at the American Baptist Publication Society in 1895, but he remained active in the society until his death. Charles Carroll Bitting died in Philadelphia on 24 December 1898 and was buried in Laurel Hill Cemetery in that city.

George Braxton Taylor, *Virginia Baptist Ministers*, 4th ser. (1913), 328–338; anecdotes by son William C. Bitting in

Baptist 6 (1926): 1576; *Religious Herald*, 20 Dec. 1855, 8 June, 21 Dec. 1871, 24 Aug. 1916; Herman A. Norton, *Religion in Tennessee, 1777–1945* (1981), 54; Blanche Sydnor White, *First Baptist Church, Lynchburg, 1815–1965* (n.d.), 47–48; William Cathcart, *The Baptist Encyclopædia* (1881), 1:103 (por.); Belle Gayle Ellyson, *The History of Second Baptist Church, Richmond, Virginia 1820–1970* (1970), 34; S. B. Cousins et al., *Historical Sketch of Second Baptist Church, Richmond, Virginia* (1964), 26; John F. Weishampel, ed., *History of Baptist Churches in Maryland* (1885), 140; Franklin Wilson, *Historical Sketch of the Franklin Square Baptist Church, Baltimore* (1880), 14; Christopher R. Blackall, *A Story of Six Decades* (1885), 90 (por.); Lemuel C. Barnes et al., *Pioneers of Light: The First Century of the American Baptist Publication Society, 1824–1924* (1924), 322; obituaries in *Philadelphia Inquirer*, 25 Dec. 1898, and *Baltimore Sun*, 26 Dec. 1898; memorials in *Religious Herald*, 29 Dec. 1898, and 5, 12, 19 Jan. 1899, and Pennsylvania Baptist State Mission Society, *Anniversary* 72 (1899): 8.

W. HARRISON DANIEL

BITTLE, David Frederick (19 November 1811–25 September 1876), president of Roanoke College, was born in Frederick County, Maryland, the eldest of two sons and three daughters of Thomas Bittle and Mary Baer Bittle. He grew up on his father's farm and as a boy spoke only German. He attended local schools and began studying English in his teens. In 1830 Bittle's Lutheran pastor arranged for him to attend the gymnasium that in 1832 was chartered as Pennsylvania College and later became Gettysburg College. He graduated in 1835 and entered the theological seminary in Gettysburg. Bittle received his license to preach in 1837. On 13 November of that year he married Louisa Catherine Krauth, a Virginian then living with her brother, the president of Pennsylvania College. They had three sons and three daughters.

Bittle and his wife moved to Virginia, and he began his ministry in Augusta County, where he served churches in Churchville, Middlebrook, and Mount Tabor. He also took an interest in education and was elected president of the Education Society, which had as its goal the encouragement of young men to go into the ministry. In the autumn of 1842 at his house in Augusta County, Bittle started the Virginia Institute, an academy for young boys. The school became popular and won endorsements from the Lutheran Synods of Virginia and Western Virginia in May and June 1843. Christopher C. Baughman, a former classmate of Bittle at Gettysburg, acted as the principal and instructor of ancient languages, while Bittle taught mathematics. On 30 January 1845 the General Assembly chartered the school as the Virginia Collegiate Institute.

In August 1845 Bittle moved to Middletown, Frederick County, Maryland, where he served as pastor of the Lutheran Church for six years before moving to Hagerstown for two years more. He organized academies for young women in Hagerstown and in Lutherville, Baltimore County, Maryland, and published a short book entitled *A Plea for Female Education: Comprising Documents and Facts Illustrative of the Importance of the Subject* (1852). Unlike many other nineteenth-century men, Bittle believed that women could profit from academically rigorous higher education. In the meantime Baughman had moved the Virginia Collegiate Institute to Salem and, with the support of Lutherans from several synods in Virginia, Maryland, and North Carolina, reconstituted it as Roanoke College in 1853.

The board of trustees elected Bittle the first president of Roanoke College on 3 June 1853, and he moved to Salem later that year. He served not only as the president of the college and as one of its instructors but also as its chaplain and as minister to two congregations in the area. While raising funds for Roanoke College, Bittle publicized throughout Virginia, North Carolina, and Tennessee its mission of preparing young men to enter the Lutheran ministry and giving them a broad-based education to serve society. He published several of his speeches on education as part of his promotional work for the college.

During Bittle's tenure as president the size of Roanoke's student body grew from 38 in 1853 to 177 during the 1876–1877 session. During the latter year students from fifteen states and from Mexico attended the college. Besides working to increase enrollment, erect new buildings, and raise funds, Bittle took special pride in the development of the library, which grew during his administration from about 2,000 volumes in 1857 to 4,000 by 1861 and 14,000 by the middle of the 1870s. The college had the good fortune to avoid any closings or destruction of its facilities during the Civil War.

After twenty-three years as president of Roanoke College, David Frederick Bittle died in Salem on 25 September 1876 and was buried in East Hill Cemetery in that city.

William Henry Ruffner, *Dr. Bittle and Roanoke College* (1876); George Diehl, *Sketch of the Life and Labors of Rev. David F. Bittle, D.D.* (1877); early census records give the surname as Biddle; Simon C. Wells, *Memorial Address: Delivered at the Opening of the Bittle Memorial Hall, Roanoke College* (1880); William McCauley, ed., *History of Roanoke County, Salem, Roanoke City, Virginia, and Representative Citizens* (1902), 307–312; Bittle's MS sermon notes, Lutheran Theological Seminary Library, Gettysburg, Pa.; Charles W. Cassell, William J. Finck, and Elon O. Henkel, eds., *History of the Lutheran Church in Virginia and East Tennessee* (1930), 108–109, 205, 209, 291–293, 343, 348, 359; William Edward Eisenberg, *The First Hundred Years, Roanoke College, 1842–1942* (1942), 12–142, 362, 425; Mark F. Miller, *"Dear Old Roanoke": A Sesquicentennial Portrait, 1842–1992* (1992), 1–59, 62–64, 241 (pors., 2, 6, 30, 45, 56); *Roanoke Collegian* 1 (1875): 1–2; obituaries in *Staunton Spectator and General Advertiser*, 3 Oct. 1876, and *Roanoke Collegian* 3 (1876): 12–13.

SARAH SIMMONS

BLACK, Aline Elizabeth (23 March 1906–22 August 1974), principal in a court case, was born in Norfolk, the only daughter and third of four children of Charles Black and Ida Black. She attended the local public schools and graduated from Booker T. Washington High School. In 1924, with a temporary teaching certificate, she began working in the Norfolk public school system as a science instructor. Black graduated from Virginia Normal and Industrial Institute (now Virginia State University) in 1926 and continued her education at the University of Pennsylvania in Philadelphia, enrolling in 1931 and receiving an M.S. in 1935.

As an African American, Black received a substantially smaller salary than a comparably qualified white teacher. Racial disparity in salaries had been a long-standing grievance of the Norfolk Teachers Association and the Virginia State Teachers Association, which together enlisted the cooperation of the National Association for the Advancement of Colored People to challenge the double standard as a violation of the Fourteenth Amendment to the United States Constitution. Black volunteered to be the plaintiff in the suit, which was filed in the state circuit court in Norfolk in March 1939. The local court dismissed the case, and Black's attorneys, chief among whom was Thurgood Marshall, filed an appeal with the Virginia Supreme Court of Appeals. In June 1939 the Norfolk School Board declined to renew Black's contract in retaliation for her having sued the school system. The Supreme Court of Appeals then denied the appeal on the grounds that Black was no longer an employee and therefore lacked the standing to sue.

Black's dismissal outraged Norfolk's African American community and embarrassed many of the city's white leaders. Another Norfolk teacher, Melvin O. Alston, took Black's place as plaintiff and a new suit was filed to reopen the issue. In November 1940 the United States Supreme Court upheld an appellate court's ruling that teacher salaries fell under the protection of the Fourteenth Amendment. The Norfolk School Board then promised to raise the salaries of black teachers. The case Black helped initiate enjoyed partial success in establishing the principal of equal pay, but it did not establish a binding precedent in future legal battles against racial discrimination in public education and employment.

Black completed part of the requirements for a doctorate in chemistry at New York University after losing her job, but she returned to Norfolk in 1941 when the school board rehired her. She resumed teaching science at Booker T. Washington High School and remained there until 1970, when she became an instructional development specialist at Jacox Junior High School. Active in the local chapter of the NAACP and in the Education Association of Norfolk, she received the latter's Backbone Award in 1971 in recognition of her important contribution to educational and professional equality. She retired in 1973.

Black had married Frank A. Hicks during World War II, and they had one daughter. Aline Elizabeth Black Hicks died in Norfolk on 22 August 1974 and was buried in Calvary Cemetery in Norfolk.

Mark V. Tushnet, *The NAACP's Legal Strategy Against Segregated Education, 1925–1950* (1987), 77–81; Earl Lewis,

In Their Own Interests: Race, Class, and Power in Twentieth-Century Norfolk (1991), 155–165; legal documents and some Black correspondence in Equalization Cases, Legal Files, NAACP Papers, LC; *Norfolk Journal and Guide*, 5 Nov. 1938, 21 June 1941 (por.), 18 Dec. 1971; obituaries in *Norfolk Journal and Guide* and *Norfolk Virginian-Pilot*, both 24 Aug. 1974.

BRENT TARTER

BLACK, Barron Foster (ca. November 1894–1 March 1974), attorney, was the elder of two children, both sons, of Foster Black and Jennie M. Tilley Black. He was born in Berkley in Norfolk County. His father, who died in 1903, was the proprietor of two Norfolk knitting mills, a bank president, and a director of the Chesapeake Land Company, a local real estate development corporation. Black was educated in the public schools of Norfolk, graduated from Maury High School in 1913, and attended the University of Virginia, from which he graduated in 1917. When the United States entered World War I he was rejected for American military service because he was underweight. He then sailed to France at his own expense, joined the French army as a private in its ambulance service on 2 September 1917, and served until his discharge as a sergeant on 2 March 1919.

Black returned to the University of Virginia after the war and in 1920 earned a law degree, specializing in admiralty and maritime law. He moved back to Norfolk and in 1921 opened a law office. In 1925 he joined the local firm of Hughes, Vandeventer, and Eggleston. Black became one of Norfolk's leading authorities on admiralty and maritime law, legal specialties foreign to most other Virginia attorneys and to all but about 10 percent of Norfolk law firms. He practiced principally in the United States courts in Norfolk, and he eventually became the senior partner of what at the time of his death was Vandeventer, Black, Meredith, and Martin. He served as president of the Norfolk-Portsmouth Bar Association in 1940–1941 and until his death remained one of the leaders of the maritime bar in Tidewater Virginia.

As a maritime lawyer, Black developed an early and continuing interest in shipping and the Hampton Roads regional economy. He served on the board of the James River Bridge Corporation from 1938 until the state took it over in 1949 and was president of the Hampton Roads Maritime Association from 1952 to 1959, during which time the ports of Hampton Roads underwent substantial expansion and the channels of Norfolk harbor and Thimble Shoals were improved. In 1961 Black received the Commerce Builder Award from the Virginia World Trade Conference, and in 1962 the Hampton Roads Maritime Association named him "Mr. Hampton Roads."

In 1945 Governor Colgate Whitehead Darden Jr., a friend and college classmate, appointed Black to the board of visitors of the University of Virginia. Black served on the board until 1967, and he was rector of the university from 1949 to 1956 while Darden was president of the university. During Black's tenure as rector, the university faced crises over such controversial issues as the alleged presence of Communists on the campus, payments to university athletes, and the admission of the first African American students. In 1989 the law school of the University of Virginia established the Barron F. Black Research Fellowship in the fields of admiralty and corporate law. He also served on the board of visitors for Sweet Briar College.

On 24 November 1925 Black married Aileen Pettit Taylor, and they had three daughters. Black played a prominent role in Norfolk's civic life. During World War II he served as vice president of the Norfolk Community Fund and as a director of the United War Fund. He acted as legal advisor to the Children's Hospital of the King's Daughters in Norfolk and was a member of the city's Council on Higher Education. In the 1940s Black established the Norfolk Foundation, a trust fund dedicated to advancing Norfolk's cultural life, and he served on the board of the Norfolk Public Library for many years beginning in the 1930s. He found the city council's failure to support the library frustrating. Therefore, in his capacity as chairman of the foundation's disbursement committee Black offered $100,000 in 1957 from the estate of his deceased brother, Munro Black, to help erect a new public library building in downtown Norfolk. That and a contribution of $500,000 from

Bessie Kirn in memory of her parents made possible the construction of the Kirn Memorial Library, which was dedicated in 1962. In 1977 the Norfolk Public Library system named one of its new branch libraries after Barron F. Black.

Barron Foster Black suffered from heart disease during the last years of his life and died of a heart attack on 1 March 1974. He was buried in Cedar Grove Cemetery in Norfolk.

Military Service Records (with 27 Nov. 1894 birth date); biographies in *Commonwealth* 16 (June 1949): 45–46 (with 25 Nov. 1894 birth date) and 27 (Apr. 1960): 25–26 (with 26 Nov. 1894 birth date); family history information supplied by widow Aileen Pettit Taylor Black and daughter Jane Black Clark (giving 27 Nov. 1893 birth date); Census, Norfolk Co., 1900 (with Nov. 1893 birth date); records at Alumni Office, UVA (with 20 Nov. 1894 birth date); obituary and editorial tribute in *Norfolk Ledger-Dispatch*, 2 Mar. 1974 (por.).

THOMAS M. COSTA

BLACK, Harvey (27 August 1827–19 October 1888), physician, was born in Blacksburg, the eldest of six sons and second of twelve children of Alexander Black and Elizabeth McDonald Black. According to family tradition he did not use the *e* in his given name, and Black's signature on his marriage bond is "Harvy," but as an adult he regularly signed his name as H. Black, and he was almost always identified publicly as Harvey Black. He attended nearby schools, and when he was about eighteen years old he began to study medicine under two local doctors. In January 1847, early in the war with Mexico, he enlisted in the 1st Regiment Virginia Volunteers. After three months he was made a hospital steward, and following his discharge from the army in July 1848 he entered medical school at the University of Virginia, from which he graduated on 29 June 1849.

Black embarked on a long trip to the Northwest, hoping to find a suitable place to set up his practice. During a four-month trip, largely on horseback, he traveled as far west as Iowa and bought land in Wisconsin before he decided to return to his native Blacksburg and begin a medical practice there. On 15 September 1852 he married Mary Irby Kent. They had three sons and one daughter. Black practiced medicine in Blacksburg until the Civil War broke out. He enlisted in the 4th Regiment Virginia Infantry on 4 May 1861. Transferred briefly to the 5th Regiment, he returned to the 4th as regimental surgeon on 2 August 1861. In December 1862 Black was named surgeon in charge of the newly formed field hospital of the Second Corps, Army of Northern Virginia, a position he held until the end of the war. The field hospital was larger and better equipped than regimental hospitals, but unlike general hospitals it was mobile. It followed the Second Corps during its bloody campaigns, serving between engagements as a receiving hospital to care for soldiers referred by the regimental surgeons. On 2 May 1863 General Thomas J. "Stonewall" Jackson was brought to Black's field hospital after being wounded at the Battle of Chancellorsville, and Black assisted Hunter Holmes McGuire in amputating Jackson's left arm early the next morning.

After Black was paroled at Appomattox Court House on 9 April 1865, he resumed his private medical practice in Blacksburg. In 1871 he was elected one of the vice presidents of the Medical Society of Virginia, and a year later he became the society's third president. Black delivered his presidential address in 1873 on the need to regulate unqualified medical practitioners and adulterated medicines. When he relinquished the presidency he was chosen an honorary fellow of the society.

Black was also active in 1872 in the political negotiations that led to the founding of the Virginia Agricultural and Mechanical College in Blacksburg. He and Peter Henry Whisner, president of the struggling Preston and Olin Institute, suggested to John E. Penn, a member of the Senate of Virginia, that the institute's property could be given to the state if Blacksburg were chosen as the location of a proposed land-grant college. Black was also instrumental in securing a bond issue by the citizens of Montgomery County that resulted in a $20,000 grant to the state to assist the new college. On 19 March 1872 the bill that established the college in Blacksburg became law. Black served on the new school's board of visitors, which elected him the first rector of the college at its inaugural meeting in Richmond on 25 and 26 March 1872.

In November 1875 Black's medical career took a new and unexpected turn when the board of the state's Eastern Lunatic Asylum in Williamsburg selected him, apparently without his prior knowledge, as the new superintendent. Although he lacked experience and training in psychiatry he accepted the position and served two three-year terms as superintendent beginning 1 January 1876. Under his leadership the asylum experimented with allowing some recuperating patients periods of reentry in the outside world as a means of preparing them for living apart from the institution. Black's tenure at Eastern Lunatic Asylum ended in March 1882 when, partly due to philosophical differences and partly because of a quarrel over bookkeeping practices, the asylum's board chose not to reappoint him.

Black returned to Blacksburg and his private practice as a physician, only to be called again into the public sphere three years later. In November 1885 he ran as a Democrat and won Montgomery County's seat in the House of Delegates, serving in sessions that sat from December 1885 to March 1886 and from March to May 1887. In the assembly Black played a central role in the selection of Marion as the site for a mental hospital authorized for construction in the southwestern part of the state. He had already been appointed to the board of the new institution when it was founded in 1884, before a site had been selected. On 1 March 1887 the directors unanimously chose Black as the first superintendent.

For several years Black had suffered from an enlarged prostate and vesical calculus. In October 1887, when Black was in Richmond, Hunter Holmes McGuire operated on him in an attempt to relieve the condition. Early in October 1888 McGuire performed a second operation, but Harvey Black did not recover, and he died in Saint Luke's Home in Richmond on 19 October 1888. He was buried in Westview Cemetery in Blacksburg.

Unsigned memoir by John S. Apperson in Southwestern Lunatic Asylum, *Annual Report* (1888): 35–41; diaries, letters, and Apperson's draft of memoir in Black-Kent-Apperson Family Papers, VPI; Harvey Black Ledgers, 1865–1893, Duke; Montgomery Co. Marriage Bonds and Ministers Returns; Compiled Service Records; Glenn L. McMullen, "Tending the Wounded: Two Virginians in the Confederate Medical Corps," *Virginia Cavalcade* 40 (1991): 172–183; McMullen, ed., *The Civil War Letters of Dr. Harvey Black* (1995; frontispiece por.); Duncan Lyle Kinnear, *The First 100 Years: A History of Virginia Polytechnic Institute and State University* (1972), 12, 14, 36, 43–45; Harvey Black, "The Duties of the Society and the State Regarding Irregular Practitioners and Adulterated Medicines," *Transactions of the Medical Society of Virginia* 4 (1873): 41–53; Black's terminal illness chronicled in Hunter Holmes McGuire, "Operative Treatment in Cases of Enlarged Prostate," *Virginia Medical Monthly* 15 (1888): 445–456; obituary in *Richmond Dispatch*, 20 Oct. 1888; memorials in *Transactions of the Medical Society of Virginia* 19 (1888): 261–262, and *Virginia Medical Monthly* 15 (1888): 604–605.

GLENN L. MCMULLEN

BLACK, Leonard A. (8 March 1820–28 April 1883), Baptist minister, was born a slave in Anne Arundel County, Maryland. His 1847 autobiography and an 1882 biography based on interviews with him differ materially, and corroborating evidence for either is scant. The names of his parents and siblings are unknown. Black stated in his autobiography that his mother and sister were sold away from the plantation when he was about six years old and that he had four elder brothers, of whom three escaped to the North before he, too, made his way there. In contrast to that harrowing account of his overland escape to New England about 1837, the later biography indicates merely that an uncle took him from Maryland to Portland, Maine, about 1828.

Regardless of how Black got to New England, his association there with George H. Black, a native of the West Indies and Baptist minister, was a turning point. In November 1838 George Black moved to Boston to become pastor of the Independent Baptist Church, the city's oldest African American Baptist congregation. Leonard Black also moved to Boston, because he had fallen in love with George Black's daughter, Mary A. (or Maya) Black, whom he married. They had at least four sons in addition to a child who died young.

Following his father-in-law's death in 1842, Black moved to Providence, Rhode Island, where he joined Jeremiah Asher's African American Baptist congregation and occasionally preached. Despite the warnings of others that he lacked sufficient education, Black believed that he had been called to the ministry. After traveling and preaching on his own, he finally received an invitation from a congregation on Nantucket Island. There, with editorial help from a friend, he completed a narrative of his life. Published in Boston in 1847, *The Life and Sufferings of Leonard Black, a Fugitive from Slavery*, is an account of Black's spiritual development as well as an indictment of slavery. It is still read today as a minor example of the literary genre known as the slave narrative.

Black attended theological school for a few years, funded with assistance that he said he received from Francis Wayland, president of Brown University, and possibly also with proceeds from the sale of his book. In 1850 Black was serving as pastor of the Third Baptist Church in Stonington, Connecticut. A year or so later he moved to the Concord Street Baptist Church in Brooklyn, New York, then in 1855 to the new Third Baptist Church in nearby East Brooklyn. His first wife died sometime after 1850, and about 1859 he married Mary Anne Wheeden, a member of his East Brooklyn church. They had two daughters who lived to adulthood. Black later stated that he served as a chaplain to troops from New York during the Civil War, but no record of his service has been located. In 1867 he traveled in Europe and then accepted a call to a church in New Haven, Connecticut.

Black moved to Virginia about 1871 to become the second black pastor of the First Baptist Church in Norfolk. He stayed there for only two years, but his congregation valued his integrity and services so highly that on his departure its leaders published resolutions of gratitude in the newspapers. On 19 November 1873 Black was installed as the new pastor of the First Baptist Church, also known as the Harrison Street Church, in Petersburg. The church was one of the oldest and largest in the state. He spent the rest of his life there, baptizing more than 2,200 persons and nearly doubling the church's membership. Black also served as treasurer of the Shiloh Baptist Association and became known for his particular concern for the spiritual condition of the young men in his congregation, perhaps a reflection of his own hard and sometimes lonely struggle to manhood. His two daughters married men from Norfolk, and by 1880 Black and his wife had four grandchildren.

Black developed Bright's disease, a kidney malfunction, and by October 1882 he was too ill to preach regularly. He recovered sufficient strength to be elected chairman of the State Mission Board of the Virginia Baptist State Convention in February 1883, but soon relapsed. Leonard A. Black died in Petersburg on 28 April 1883. His funeral was reportedly one of the largest ever held in the city. A crowd estimated at 5,000 persons overflowed the church, where more than a dozen clergymen from around the state participated in the service. Forty-two carriages followed the hearse to Providence Cemetery, and workaday activity came to a halt in Petersburg as thousands more people lined the way to his grave. Friends raised funds for a stone monument with a bas-relief portrait of Black that was dedicated on 1 October 1883 at the cemetery, since renamed People's Memorial Cemetery.

The Life and Sufferings of Leonard Black, a Fugitive from Slavery (1847); biography in *Petersburg Lancet*, 15 July 1882, reprinted in George Freeman Bragg Jr., ed., *Men of Maryland* (1925), 53–54; George A. Levesque, "Inherent Reformers—Inherited Orthodoxy: Black Baptists in Boston, 1800–1873," *Journal of Negro History* 60 (1975): 509–512; James Oliver Horton and Lois E. Horton, *Black Bostonians* (1979), 41; William L. Andrews, *To Tell a Free Story: The First Century of Afro-American Autobiography, 1760–1865* (1986), 14, 140; Marion Wilson Starling, *The Slave Narrative: Its Place in American History* (1988), 132–133; Census, New London Co., Ct., 1850, and Petersburg City, 1880 (with erroneous birthplace of Lowell, Mass.); Mechal Sobel, *Trabelin' On: The Slave Journey to an Afro-Baptist Faith* (1979), 263; James Melvin Washington, *Frustrated Fellowship: The Black Baptist Quest for Social Power* (1986), 215; *Washington New National Era and Citizen*, 11 Dec. 1873; *Petersburg Lancet*, 17 Feb., 19 May, 11 Aug., 6 Oct. 1883 (with 28 Apr. 1883 death date); Anne Arundel Co. birthplace and variant death date of 29 Apr. 1883 in BVS Death Register, Petersburg City; William D. Henderson, *Gilded Age City: Politics, Life, and Labor in Petersburg, Virginia, 1874–1889* (1980), 315–316; obituaries and accounts of funeral in *Petersburg Index-Appeal*, 30 Apr. (with 28 Apr. 1883 death date), 2 May 1883, *Petersburg Lancet*, 5 May 1883, and *New York Globe*, 12, 19 May 1883.

JOHN T. KNEEBONE

BLACK, Samuel (3 March 1813–12 or 13 July 1899), Methodist minister, was born on a farm in Greenbrier County, one of four sons and four daughters of Joseph Black and Abigail Black. Like his father he became a farmer, but he may also have taught school. In 1832 he heard a sermon that led him to join the Methodist Episcopal Church, and in 1840 he began his ministerial career by preaching at a camp meeting in neighboring Nicholas County. Black was soon recommended for admission to the Ohio Conference, which had jurisdiction over many of the western counties of Virginia, and later in 1840 he received his first appointment, as junior preacher to the Methodist church in Sutton. He was ordained a deacon in 1842 and an elder two years later.

During the 1840s the Methodist Episcopal Church split into northern and southern branches, chiefly over the issue of slavery. On 28 March 1846 Black sided with the new Methodist Episcopal Church South by joining its Kentucky Conference, which included many western Virginia counties. He served the new conference until 1850, proselytizing so successfully that he converted virtually every Methodist in the district to his point of view. At a meeting in Parkersburg in September 1850 he helped organize the new Western Virginia Conference of the Methodist Episcopal Church South. Black married Mary Elizabeth Gibson in Lewis County on 23 August 1854. They had two sons and three daughters.

Black was one of the most influential Methodist ministers in the area that in 1863 became West Virginia. At least two churches were named for him. He continued to travel and preach until 1890 when, at the end of fifty years of ministry, he asked to be placed on superannuated status. In many ways he was typical of the plain, earnest, undereducated circuit riders of the nineteenth century. Although he lacked the eloquence of some of his contemporaries, he had a reputation as a spirited debater. Following his retirement from the ministry he returned to his farm in Greenbrier County. Samuel Black broke a hip in 1897 while tending his cattle and was probably bedridden much of the time from then until he died at his home on 12 or 13 July 1899.

Brief biographies in Otis K. Rice, *A History of Greenbrier County* (1986), 217, and clipping from unidentified newspaper (por.), Methodist Collection, West Virginia Wesleyan College Library, Buckhannon; father's will in Greenbrier Co. Will Book, 2:122–123, abstracted in *Journal of the Greenbrier Historical Society* 4, no. 3 (1983): 39; some Black letters in George W. Smith Papers, WVU; death date of 12 July 1899 in obituary in *Greenbrier Independent*, 20 July 1899; birth date and death date of 13 July 1899 in memorial in Western Virginia Conference of Methodist Episcopal Church South, *Journal of the Annual Session* 46 (1899): 31–37.

Brent Tarter

BLACK, William Marshall (29 August 1869–15 July 1950), educator and librarian, was born in Lynchburg, the youngest of two sons and a daughter of William Marshall Black, an express agent, and Mildred Black Black. His father died in 1871, and Black was raised by his mother. He graduated from Lynchburg High School in 1886, attended the University of Virginia for two years, and was hired in 1888 as an instructor of German and Latin in Staunton High School. Black taught at Western Maryland College in Westminster from 1891 to 1901, receiving its A.M. in 1893 and rising to associate professor of Latin and Greek and dean of the faculty. He took a one-year leave of absence during the academic year 1894–1895 to study classical philosophy at the Harvard University Graduate School, at the conclusion of which he was awarded a Harvard A.B.

Black returned to Lynchburg in 1901 to teach German at Lynchburg High School. On 2 December 1903 he married Lucile Watkins, of Lynchburg. They had two sons and one daughter. In 1905 Black was appointed acting principal of the high school, and from 1906 until 1918 he served as principal. He revamped the curriculum, expanded the athletics program, and improved the library and science laboratories, laying foundations that made Lynchburg High School one of the best and most innovative public schools in Virginia. Black took a keen interest in libraries. In 1908 he became librarian of the new, privately funded George M. Jones Memorial Library, the only lending library available to white residents of the city until the tax-supported Lynchburg Public Library, which was open to all citizens, was established in 1966.

At an educational conference in 1908 Black participated in the reorganization of the Virginia

Library Association, which had been established three years earlier under the auspices of the Virginia State Library. He served two years as secretary of the association and was elected president in 1910. In his presidential address on "The Value of a Library Commission," delivered in Richmond in November 1910, Black advocated expanding the Virginia State Library's traveling-library program and hiring an organizer to help communities and schools establish and improve their libraries. He urged a statewide expansion of library resources linked to the movement to improve public schools that was then producing major changes in Virginia's educational system. Black's call for action did not bear immediate fruit. As late as 1922 Virginia still had only six libraries supported by public funds. His speech, however, added momentum to the outreach program at the Virginia State Library, leading in time to the creation of more public libraries and the expansion of library facilities in the public schools.

In 1918 Black resigned from the Lynchburg school system to manage the business affairs of his widowed mother-in-law, Jimmie Lelin Watts Watkins, whose husband, George Putnam Watkins, had been a prominent shoe distributor, banker, and coal producer. In 1920 Black returned to teaching as an instructor of German at Randolph-Macon Woman's College in Lynchburg. In 1923 he became assistant to the president, and a year later he was appointed registrar and director of public relations. Black retired with a change of college administrations in 1933 and devoted the remainder of his life to chess, golf, the Lions Club, and the Court Street Methodist Church, to which he belonged for forty-five years. He also composed poetry during his retirement and worked occasionally as a translator. William Marshall Black died at his home in Lynchburg on 15 July 1950 and was buried in Spring Hill Cemetery.

Birth date verified from family records in possession of grandson Wilmer H. Paine Jr.; *Harvard University Catalogue* (1894/1895): 294; *Lynchburg News*, 3 Dec. 1903; presidential address published in *Public Libraries* 16 (1911): 53–56 and *Virginia Journal of Education* 4 (1911): 276–279, and reported at length in *Richmond Times-Dispatch*, 26 Nov. 1910; obituary in *Lynchburg News*, 16 July 1950 (por.).

THOMAS J. HEHMAN

BLACKAMORE, Arthur (bap. 12 August 1679–after 1723), writer, was probably born in London. He was the elder of two sons and fourth of seven children of Arthur Blackamore and Ann (or Anne) Hathern Blackamore and was christened on 12 August 1679 in the parish of Saint-Gregory-by-Saint-Paul in London. He matriculated at Christ Church College, Oxford University, on 7 May 1695 but took no degree. On 3 October 1707 he received the queen's bounty of £20 to finance his trip to Virginia as a chaplain, and shortly after he arrived he became the master of the grammar school of the College of William and Mary.

Blackamore presided over the small grammar school until 1717. He was a good linguist and apparently a skilled classicist, but he became an alcoholic and between 1709 and 1716 the board of visitors threatened him several times with dismissal if he did not mend his ways. His attempts to reform were never successful.

During his sober periods Blackamore did well, and he became friendly with Lieutenant Governor Alexander Spotswood. From 1693 the College of William and Mary had been permitted to submit a sample of Latin verse to the governor annually in lieu of a quitrent, and on 5 November 1716 Blackamore delivered a poem entitled "Expeditio Ultramontana," celebrating Spotswood's recent exploratory expedition to the crest of the Blue Ridge Mountains. The poem helped spread the fame of the expedition and also began the romantic treatment of it that subsequent writers and poets continued and enhanced. Manuscript copies of Blackamore's poem circulated in Virginia for years, and George Seagood published an English translation in the *Annapolis Maryland Gazette* of 24 June 1729.

In the spring of 1717 Blackamore applied for a letter of recommendation from the college authorities in order to return to England to continue his education and be ordained into the ministry. The college's president, James Blair, wrote a detailed letter about Blackamore to the bishop of London, explaining how his drinking was so scandalous that the grammar school had deteriorated to only a few students. Blair thereby ended Blackamore's career in Virginia and also his chance of ever entering the ministry.

After Blackamore returned to England he wrote several pieces of fiction that were precursors of the modern novel. Some of them contained thinly veiled references to Virginia. *The Perfidious Brethren, or the Religious Triumvirate: Displayed in Three Ecclesiastical Novels* (1720), which he dedicated to Spotswood, portrayed rapacious, conniving clergymen who were probably modeled on James Blair. Blackamore also published a condensed edition of Joseph Bingham's ten-volume *Origines Ecclesiasticæ: or, The Antiquities of the Christian Church* (1708–1722), under the title *Ecclesiæ Primitivæ Notitia: or, A Summary of Christian Antiquities* (1722). His last-known publication, *Luck at Last: or, the Happy Unfortunate* (1723), dedicated to his former Virginia student David Bray, was reissued as *The Distress'd Fair, or Happy Unfortunate* (1737). It echoed Aphra Behn's *The Wandering Beauty: A Novel* (1698) and anticipated Samuel Richardson's *The History of Pamela; or, Virtue Rewarded* (1740).

It is not known if Arthur Blackamore married or had children, or when or where he died.

Baptism recorded in register of Parish of Saint-Gregory-by-Saint-Paul, London, Eng.; Richard Beale Davis, "Arthur Blackamore: The Virginia Colony and the Early English Novel," *VMHB* 75 (1967): 22–34, and *Intellectual Life in the Colonial South* (1978), 3:1458–1459, 1487–1488; Susan H. Godson et al., *The College of William and Mary: A History* (1993), 1:51–52; James Blair to bishop of London, 14 May 1717, Fulham Palace Papers, Lambeth Palace Library, Eng.; Seagood's translation reprinted in *Mr. Blackamore's Expeditio Ultramontana*, ed. Earl Gregg Swem (1960); *Luck at Last* reprinted in *Four Before Richardson: Selected English Novels, 1720–1727*, ed. William H. McBurney (1963).

KEVIN J. HAYES

BLACKBURN, Richard (ca. 1706–15 July 1757), builder and planter, was born in Ripon in Yorkshire, England. He and a brother immigrated to Virginia sometime in the 1720s. Blackburn lived for several years in Gloucester County, where he married a widow named Mrs. Elliott whose other names are not recorded. They had a son who was born in October 1731. After his first wife died, about 1733 Blackburn married Mary Watts Ashton, of Westmoreland County. They had two sons and four daughters.

Blackburn got his start as a builder and rose quickly into the ranks of the landed elite. On 9 June 1733 he contracted with the vestry of Truro Parish in Fairfax County to erect a church. A deed the same year described him as a carpenter, and at the time of his death several carpenters were working for him. Blackburn had moved about 1732 to the new county of Prince William, where he became a local leader. He served as a justice of the peace during the 1740s and 1750s, was sheriff in 1741, and in 1749 was a founding trustee of the town of Dumfries. Blackburn rose to the rank of colonel in the militia and became both a vestryman and churchwarden for Dettingen Parish after it was founded in 1745. He also served in the House of Burgesses during the spring 1746 assembly session. Soon after moving to Prince William County he built a house near the mouth of Neabsco Creek that he called Rippon Lodge. The commodious frame house, one of the oldest and best-preserved early-eighteenth-century houses in the northern part of Virginia, is of sufficient architectural interest that it was placed on the Virginia Register of Historic Sites in 1971.

Blackburn's extended family consisted of his own children, a nephew, two stepsons and a stepdaughter from his second wife's first marriage, and one other child who may have been a stepson from his first marriage. He supported this large family with income from more than 21,000 acres of land that he divided into several working plantations in Prince William and the neighboring counties. He also owned and operated a gristmill and invested in a variety of other local economic enterprises. For more than a quarter of a century Blackburn associated closely with members of the Fairfax, Lee, Washington, and other prominent families on the south side of the Potomac River. His only surviving son, Thomas Blackburn, was a member of the House of Burgesses from Prince William County when the American Revolution began.

Richard Blackburn died at Rippon Lodge on 15 July 1757 and was buried in the family graveyard there.

Biography in *Tyler's Quarterly Historical and Genealogical Magazine* 31 (1949): 38–43, 107–113; one Richard Blackburne, son of William Blackburne, was christened not far from Ripon at Saint Michael-le-Belfry, city of York, on 2 Dec. 1705; family history documents in George Harrison Sanford King Papers, VHS; Truro Parish Vestry Book, 9 June, 12 Oct. 1733, 11 Oct. 1734, LC; occupation given in first dated record of Prince William Co. residence, Prince William Co. Deed Book, B:66–67; Blackburn to William Fairfax, 22 Aug. 1735, Robert A. Brock Collection, Henry E. Huntington Library, San Marino, Calif.; many other references to Blackburn and family in Prince William Co. Deed and Order Books and in records of Dettingen Parish; Virginia Writers' Project, *Prince William: The Story of Its People and Its Places* (1941), esp. 84–85; Calder Loth, ed., *The Virginia Landmarks Register*, 3d ed. (1986), 351; will transcribed in Prince William Co. Land Causes (1805–1816), 360–365; death date and age at death on gravestone inscription in *WMQ*, 1st ser., 4 (1896): 267.

RAYMOND C. BAILEY

BLACKBURN, Samuel (ca. May 1761–2 March 1835), attorney, was born in Frederick County, the youngest of nine sons and two daughters of Benjamin Blackburn and Mary Blackburn. The family moved to Virginia from Pennsylvania well before Blackburn's birth, migrated to Augusta County in 1774, and subsequently moved to western North Carolina. Blackburn probably intended to go into the Presbyterian ministry when he entered Liberty Hall Academy (now Washington and Lee University). A brief interval of service in the army during the closing months of the Revolutionary War interrupted his education, but he received an A.B. from Liberty Hall in 1785. On 18 August of that year Blackburn married Ann Mathews, a daughter of George Mathews. Apparently accompanied by the newlyweds, Mathews soon moved from Staunton to Georgia, where he had begun acquiring land in Wilkes County in March 1784. Blackburn and his wife had no children of their own but adopted a son who died young.

In Georgia Blackburn became rector of an academy at Washington in Wilkes County and prepared himself for the legal profession. Aided no doubt by the political eminence of his father-in-law, who served as governor of Georgia from 1787 to 1788 and 1793 to 1796, Blackburn became a general in the militia and won election to the Georgia State Senate, representing Elbert County from 1791 to 1795. During the 1794–1795 session Blackburn was accused of helping to gain legislative passage of the infamous Yazoo land bill, which granted approximately 50 million acres west of the Chattahoochee River to four companies for $500,000. His father-in-law, then serving his second term as governor, had been granting land liberally in order to settle Georgia's undeveloped frontier. Unlike some of his predecessors, however, Mathews had awarded vast tracts to a few speculators and corrupt politicians and signed the bill. No wrongdoing was proved on the part of either the governor or Blackburn, but the widely circulated accusations made Blackburn very unpopular.

In disgust Blackburn returned to Virginia by May 1796, bringing nineteen slaves with him. He immediately purchased a tract of land in Bath County, part of an estate named Cloverdale. Blackburn built a house there that became known as the Wilderness Farm. On 8 and 15 November 1796 Blackford qualified to practice law in Bath and Augusta Counties. He lived in Bath County for the rest of his life. In 1805 Blackburn contracted to purchase another 1,734 acres of the original 2,080-acre Cloverdale tract but did not take legal possession until 1815 after litigation settled ownership of the property. With these purchases Blackburn brought his total landholdings to 2,173 acres.

General Blackburn, as he was usually called, became an extremely successful attorney at a time when the bar in that part of Virginia was one of the most distinguished and competitive in the state. His speeches in court, sometimes eloquent, sometimes humorous, and sometimes bitterly sarcastic, became legendary. Blackburn became one of the wealthiest men in Bath County. At the time of his death the value of his total estate in Bath and Augusta Counties probably exceeded $140,000.

In politics Blackburn was a Federalist, and he may have continued to regard himself as one even after the party ceased to exist. He represented Bath County in the House of Delegates during the assemblies of 1799–1801, 1809–1811, 1812–1813, 1816–1818, 1820–1822, 1823–1824, and 1825–1826. In 1811 and 1813 he lost congressional elections to William McCoy, a Republican, and he also ran unsuccessfully for the Virginia Convention of 1829–1830. As competitive and vocally opinionated in politics as in court, Blackburn became notorious for what one acquaintance described as his "strong abusive denunciations of the Republicans." His speeches as printed in pamphlets and extracted in newspapers employed a debating style that was vigorous, partisan, learned, and often eloquent. One nineteenth-century writer credited Blackburn with drafting the first antidueling law in Virginia, adopted in January 1810, although the legislative records contain no corroborative evidence. In 1819 he served as a commissioner from Virginia to consult with representatives of other states interested in opening transportation links between the East Coast and the Ohio River and in removing obstructions to the navigation of the Ohio. Blackburn submitted a long report on the subject to the General Assembly in December of that year.

Blackburn served as a trustee of his alma mater, which became known as Washington Academy, then Washington College, from 31 January 1797 until 19 July 1830. At the time of his death he owned forty-six slaves and stipulated in his will that if they would agree to immigrate to Liberia, he would manumit them and pay their travel expenses. All but two took advantage of the opportunity to gain freedom. Samuel Blackburn died at his Wilderness plantation on 2 March 1835. His widow had his body buried in the churchyard of Trinity Episcopal Church in Staunton and erected a monument over his grave.

Biographies in George R. Gilmer, *Sketches of Some of the First Settlers of Upper Georgia* (1855; repr. 1965), 68–70, in Joseph Addison Waddell, *Annals of Augusta County, Virginia, from 1726 to 1871* (1886), 247–249, in Oren F. Morton, *Annals of Bath County, Virginia* (1917), 166, and in *Washington and Lee University Historical Papers* 4 (1893): 167–172; gravestone gives age at death of seventy-three years, nine months; Vinnetta Wells Ranke, *The Blackburn Genealogy* (1939), 93–96; Frances Blackburn Hilliard, *Blackburns Today and Yesterday* (1978), 292–315; Augusta Co. Marriage Bonds; Augusta Co. Circuit Court Deed Book, 1A:215–220; Bath Co. Deed Book, 4:527–530, 5:78–80; partly autobiographical public letter in *Richmond Enquirer*, 28 Apr. 1829; report on Ohio River commerce in *JHD*, 1819–1820 sess., 19–23; will and records of estate and immigration of former slaves in Bath Co. Will Book, 4:304–309, 310, 311–315, 326–329, 428–431; obituaries in *Richmond Whig and Public Advertiser*, 10 Mar. 1835, and *Richmond Enquirer*, 20 Mar. 1835, copying from lost issue of *Staunton Spectator*.

BRENT TARTER

BLACKFORD, Benjamin (31 October 1767–20 August 1855), iron manufacturer, was born in either New Jersey or Pennsylvania. His mother was Mary De Hart Blackford and conflicting family traditions and records identify his father as either Martin Blackford or Jacob Blackford. Family tradition, rendered doubtful by his age, also held that he joined the Continental army and was present at Cornwallis's surrender at Yorktown in October 1781. As a young man Blackford worked as a clerk at Thomas Thornberg's Pine Grove iron furnace near Carlisle, Pennsylvania. By 1800 Blackford had become one of Thornberg's partners in leasing and operating the Catoctin Furnace in Frederick County, Maryland. They manufactured stoves and other commercial iron products and during the War of 1812 cast ordnance for the army.

Blackford married Isabella Arthur in 1792. They had four sons and two daughters. In 1808 Blackford and several partners, including some of his wife's close relatives, purchased the Redwell and Columbia iron furnaces in Shenandoah County. Blackford renamed one of them Isabella Furnace in honor of his wife. By 1813, shortly after Blackford moved to the part of Shenandoah County that in 1831 became Page County, the partnership was known as Blackford, Arthur, and Company. During the next two decades Blackford and his partners created an important refining and manufacturing complex that included Isabella, Caroline, and Elizabeth Furnaces as well as Speedwell and Union Forges. He employed skilled laborers, many of whom had worked for him in Pennsylvania and Maryland, as well as slaves, some of whom he hired from nearby neighbors and some of whom he or his partnerships owned. He also employed a few free blacks. The community that grew up around Isabella Furnace consisted of twenty-two families in 1820, and of the eighty-two people then working at the furnace, almost one-third were slaves. Ten years later Blackford had more than seventy slaves working at his forges and furnaces.

Blackford entered the iron industry at an opportune time, was fortunate in his choice of partners, was a skillful manager, and later boasted that by the time he was twenty-one he had made a thousand dollars for each of his years. In the spring of 1833 he bought out his remaining partners and formed a new partnership with his oldest son, Thomas Thornberg Blackford. Benjamin Blackford and Son owned more than three thousand acres of land in Page County. The company manufactured iron products, including cooking utensils, plowshares, stoves, and bells, the casting of which posed special technical problems. By 1835 its business amounted to about $50,000 annually. The company's wagon trains carried Blackford's ironwork to Fredericksburg for shipment by water to markets in Tidewater Virginia, Alexandria, Baltimore, and Washington.

The panic of 1837 eventually brought ruin to Blackford. He had lent money to other businessmen or endorsed their notes, and when they began to fail he refused to evade his responsibility to them and began to sell property to cover the obligations. By January 1840 Blackford was in debt for more than $61,600 in notes and accounts. He signed a deed of trust on Isabella Furnace and Speedwell Forge that included his company's raw materials and finished ironwork, slaves, and other property, but he was unable to settle his debts within the three years specified. During the following three years he sold the remainder of his interests in the ironworks and in 1846 moved to Lynchburg to live with Thomas Thornberg Blackford and later with his younger son William Mathews Blackford.

Benjamin Blackford had been an active Federalist when he lived in Maryland. During the 1830s he supported the Whig Party. He was also a local lay leader in the Episcopal Church and represented his parish as a lay delegate to the annual meetings of the diocesan council before he retired to Lynchburg. On 20 August 1855 Benjamin Blackford died in Lynchburg and was buried in the Presbyterian cemetery there. On 5 May 1863 his remains were moved to Spring Hill Cemetery in Lynchburg.

Conflicting biographical and family history information in Blackford Family Papers, UNC, in William Willis Blackford, MS family history, VHS, and in William Mathews Blackford diary, UVA, extracted in part in Susan Leigh Colston Blackford, *Memoirs of Life In and Out of the Army in Virginia during the War Between the States* (1894–1896; repr. 1996 and in abridgement in 1947 as *Letters from Lee's Army*); ironworks documented in Land and Personal Property Tax Returns, Shenandoah and Page Cos., RG 48, LVA, in deed books of Shenandoah and Page Cos., and in reminiscences of Mann Almond printed in *Luray Page Courier*, 27 Sept., 18 Oct. 1877; Blackford and Son partnership agreement and Blackford's 1840 deed of trust in Page Co. Deed Book, A:337, D:88–97, 264–265; obituary in *Lynchburg Daily Virginian*, 21 Aug. 1855.

DAPHNE GENTRY

BLACKFORD, Charles Minor (17 October 1833–10 March 1903), attorney, was born in Fredericksburg, the third of six sons and fourth of eight children of William Mathews Blackford and Mary Berkeley Minor Blackford. Plagued by a weak constitution and poor eyesight, he had a difficult childhood and did not begin school until age eleven.

Blackford attended school in Fredericksburg until the family moved to Lynchburg in 1846, where he continued his education under several tutors. He matriculated at the University of Virginia in October 1850, entered its law school three years later, and received his law degree on 29 June 1855. Shortly after graduation Blackford opened a Lynchburg law office with William Tudor Yancey on 1 August 1855. After they dissolved their partnership in 1857, Blackford practiced alone until 1861. On 19 February 1856 he married Susan Leigh Colston, of Albemarle County. They had four sons and two daughters.

Although his family opposed secession during the winter of 1860–1861, Charles Blackford and his four surviving brothers served in the Confederate army. He volunteered on 13 May 1861 and became a lieutenant in Company B of the 2d Regiment Virginia Cavalry. Elected captain of his company on 27 August 1861 and reelected in April 1862, Blackford served in many of the major engagements of the war, including the First Battle of Manassas (Bull Run), the 1862 Shenandoah Valley campaign, and the fighting around Fredericksburg later that year. In December 1862 his legal experience led to his appointment as a judge advocate. In 1863 he was appointed judge advocate general of the First Corps, Army of Northern Virginia, and served in that capacity until late in 1864, when he was assigned to duties in Richmond.

Blackford was the first lawyer to reopen his office in Lynchburg after the war. A firm that he started with Thomas J. Kirkpatrick in 1866 endured until 1895. Blackford was a highly respected and successful corporate lawyer who represented railroads throughout the state. He served as a counsel and board member of the Virginia Midland Railroad and personally crafted the legal documents that led to its reconstitution as part of the Southern Railway in 1895. His arguments on appeal were credited with the development of several important precedents in Virginia corporate law. Blackford was a founder of the Virginia State Bar Association, served on its first executive committee, and was elected president in 1894. In his presidential address he called for the better education of attorneys and for all attorneys and judges to keep up their interests in literature and history, which he believed would make them better practitioners, better advocates, and better civic leaders.

Blackford was a leading citizen in postwar Lynchburg. He became president of the Peoples Savings Bank in 1874 and continued as president when it became the Peoples National Bank, serving from 1882 until his death. He also served a term as president of the Lynchburg Bankers' Association. From 1869 until 1881 he was city attorney for Lynchburg and published two compilations of city ordinances. A member of the Episcopal Church, Blackford was vestryman of Saint Paul's Church in Lynchburg and for many years regularly attended church conferences as a parish delegate. A research and writing project in which he took special pride was his forty-page *Historical Sketch of the Book of Common Prayer* (1893).

A popular public speaker, Blackford talked often on religious topics, the law, and the Civil War. After he lost most of his hair he delivered a humorous oration on baldness that a friend described as "a conglomeration of all that is grotesque, clever and witty" on that subject. The Civil War was his recurring theme. One of Blackford's longest public addresses became a short book, *Campaign and Battle of Lynchburg* (1901). His most enduring work was an edition of his wartime letters and other family material that his wife had printed in a very limited edition as *Memoirs of Life In and Out of the Army in Virginia During the War Between the States* (1894–1896; reprinted 1996) and that their grandson reissued in a 1947 abridgement as *Letters from Lee's Army*.

Blackford never entered electoral politics. Like his father he was a Whig as a young man. He became a Democrat after the Civil War, but during the 1896 presidential campaign he split from the party because of its endorsement of the free coinage of silver. In 1895 Blackford formed a new law partnership with his son Raleigh Colston Blackford and John D. Horsley. After the turn of the century his eyesight again deteriorated, and he was nearly blind at the time of his death. Charles Minor Blackford died of pneumonia at his house in Lynchburg on 10 March 1903 and was buried in the family plot at Spring Hill Cemetery in Lynchburg.

Blackford Family Collection, including Blackford's Civil War letters, Jones Memorial Library, Lynchburg; Charles Minor Blackford Sr. and Thomas Jellis Kirkpatrick Papers, Duke; Compiled Service Records; Robert J. Driver, *2nd Virginia Cavalry* (1995), esp. 196; Presidential Pardons; Blackford's presidential address and his "The Trials and Trial of Jefferson Davis" in *Virginia State Bar Association Proceedings* (1895): 145–173 and 13 (1900): 231–274; obituaries and editorial tributes in *Richmond News Leader*, 10, 12 Mar. 1903, and *Richmond Times-Dispatch*, 11 Mar. 1903; memorial in *Virginia State Bar Association Proceedings* (1903): 67–74 (por. opp. 67), reprinted in Pecquet du Bellet, *Virginia Families*, 1:189–194.

KEVIN CONLEY RUFFNER

BLACKFORD, Launcelot Minor (23 February 1837–23 May 1914), educator, was born in Fredericksburg, the fifth of six sons and sixth of eight children of William Mathews Blackford and Mary Berkeley Minor Blackford. His parents were deeply religious and active in various reform movements and the Episcopal Church. In 1846 the family moved to Lynchburg, where Blackford was educated privately before entering the University of Virginia in 1855. He began a lifelong career as an educator during his years at the university, augmenting his income by teaching part time at a military school in Charlottesville. In 1860 he received an M.A. and began teaching at the Virginia Female Institute in Staunton.

Despite the family's Unionist sympathies, Blackford and his four surviving brothers all entered Confederate service during the Civil War. On 2 September 1861 Blackford enlisted as a private in the Rockbridge Artillery. The battery was attached to Thomas J. "Stonewall" Jackson's division during the Shenandoah Valley campaign of 1862, and Blackford fought in numerous battles, including engagements at Kernstown, Winchester, Cross Keys, and Port Republic. After a brief illness he returned to duty and participated in fighting at Cedar Run and the Second Battle of Manassas (Bull Run) in August 1862. Late in September he was detailed for hospital duty, probably a stint as secretary to a surgeon in Lynchburg. On 20 March 1863 Blackford was appointed clerk to the military court of the First Army Corps, where he worked for his brother Charles Minor Blackford, the judge advocate. Family connections also played a role in his next assignment as adjutant to his cousin Lieutenant Colonel Richard L. Maury, commander of the 24th Regiment Virginia Infantry, late in 1864. After service in the trenches of Petersburg and in defense of Richmond, Blackford was captured at Saylers Creek on 6 April 1865.

In the fall of 1865 Blackford returned to teaching at the Norwood School in Nelson County. He taught languages his first year and then served as associate principal for the next four sessions. In the summer of 1870 he became principal at Episcopal High School, founded by the Diocese of Virginia in 1839 to satisfy the need for a secondary school serving Episcopal boys, especially those preparing for the ministry. Located about three miles west of Alexandria near the Episcopal Theological Seminary, the school had been disrupted by the Civil War and stood on a somewhat tenuous footing when Blackford arrived.

Beyond boosting enrollment and correcting deficiencies in school buildings and grounds, Blackford changed the school's operations in ways that reflected his admiration of the English public school system. He traveled to Europe often in the 1870s and 1880s and visited several English schools. Blackford established a monitor system, whereby older students assisted in the teaching and governance of younger boys. Inspired by the examples of Eton and Rugby, he encouraged athletics as an important part of his pupils' development.

Despite these English influences, the moral education given the students had a distinctly southern cast. Committed to producing Christian gentlemen, Blackford held up as the embodiment of this ideal such Confederate heroes as Robert E. Lee, Jefferson Davis, and Stonewall Jackson. Like Blackford, many of the instructors had served the South as soldiers or officers. Lectures, memorial ceremonies, and other events confirmed the holiness of the Lost Cause for the largely southern student body. When students formed a literary society in 1870, they named it the Fairfax Literary Society after Randolph Fairfax, an alumnus of Episcopal High School and Civil War messmate of Blackford who was killed in the Battle of Fredericksburg. In 1874 students formed the Blackford Literary Society, honoring their principal.

Religion played an important role in student life. Scripture readings and prayers occurred every morning and night, and students attended two services and Bible classes each Sunday. Blackford also enriched the development of his charges by direct mentoring and held informal readings at night, often of English literature, which many boys devotedly attended. These activities went beyond the initial intent of the institution—novels had originally been banned—and demonstrated Blackford's commitment to his students. In the first school catalog he issued, that of 1870–1871, he gave as his goal inspiring such "sentiments of honour and moral responsibility as will lead the pupil to govern himself." Blackford instituted an honor code similar to the one in force at the University of Virginia and usually relied on appeals to a student's inner moral compass rather than on corporal punishment to correct transgressions. Not surprisingly, Blackford's "old boys," as alumni were called in another imitation of English custom, were extremely loyal to him and to the school.

Although never a large institution, Episcopal High School grew steadily from 35 students in the 1870–1871 school year to 133 students in 1909–1910. Its emphasis on rigorous academics, character building, and physical activity made it an excellent training ground for the service academies and military careers. Blackford's emphasis on classics and the school's religious basis attracted many future seminarians. The thorough training in English exposition and rhetoric, combined with the extensive social and family connections of most graduates, produced numerous political and social leaders.

In 1866 Blackford was elected a member of the Virginia Educational Association. He frequently attended its annual convention and on 15 July 1874 was elected to a one-year term as president. Blackford received an LL.D. from Washington and Lee University in 1904 and was elected to Phi Beta Kappa by both the College of William and Mary and the University of Virginia. He served twenty-three years on the standing committee of the Diocese of Virginia and regularly attended the annual meetings of its council.

Blackford married Elizabeth Chew Ambler on 5 August 1884. They had five sons and one daughter. Two sons entered the ministry and the other three became physicians, among them Staige Davis Blackford, who achieved fame as a military surgeon in World War II. With his health declining after a minor stroke suffered in 1909, Blackford became principal emeritus and gave up active control of the school in the 1913–1914 school year. Launcelot Minor Blackford died on 23 May 1914 at Greenwood, his country house near Episcopal High School, and was buried in Ivy Hill Cemetery in Alexandria.

Tyler, *Men of Mark*, 3:34–35; Blackford's diaries for 1847–1855 and 1873–1913, UNC; Blackford Family Papers, UVA; Patricia M. Gantt, "Emblem of an Age: The Rich Legacy of L. M. Blackford's 'Intellectual Pantry,'" *Southern Quarterly* 30 (winter–spring 1992): 123–130; Compiled Service Records; Robert J. Driver Jr., *The 1st and 2nd Rockbridge Artillery* (1987); Susan Leigh Blackford, comp., *Memoirs of Life In and Out of the Army in Virginia During the War Between the States* (1894–1896; repr. 1996); Arthur Barksdale Kinsolving, *The Story of a Southern School: The Episcopal High School of Virginia* (1922); Richard Pardee Williams Jr., *The High School: A History of the Episcopal High School in Virginia at Alexandria* (1964), 114–127 (por.); Episcopal High School catalogs; obituaries and account of funeral in *Alexandria Gazette*, 23, 25, 26 May 1914, and *Southern Churchman*, 30 May, 6 June 1914.

GREGG D. KIMBALL

BLACKFORD, Mary Berkeley Minor (2 December 1802–15 September 1896), antislavery leader, was born in Fredericksburg, the only daughter and second or third of eight children of John Minor and his second wife, Lucy Landon Carter Minor. John Minor died when his daughter was thirteen, and she remained very close to her mother for the rest of her mother's long life. Mary Minor received an unusually fine education for a girl of her generation, though whether at home, from private tutors, or at a local school for girls is not known. She matured into an eloquent, determined, and formidable woman who exerted a powerful influence within her large circle of family and friends.

On 12 October 1825 Minor married William Mathews Blackford, a Fredericksburg attorney, in Caroline County. She suffered for virtually her entire adult life from a debilitating back problem and often spent long intervals in bed. Nonetheless, during her first fifteen years of marriage she had six sons and two daughters, all but one of whom lived to maturity under her watchful eye. Although she descended from prominent Virginia landed families and married the son of a prosperous iron manufacturer, Blackford was never wealthy. She inherited relatively little from her father, and her husband, an able, hard-working man, never made much money. Until 1846 they lived in Fredericksburg, where William Blackford edited and published a Whig newspaper, although he spent the period from 1842 to 1845 in Bogotá as chargé d'affaires to New Granada, leaving her to care for the children and supervise the household. After his return to the United States they moved to Lynchburg, where he edited another Whig newspaper for several years and then served as cashier of the Exchange Bank of Lynchburg.

Blackford and her husband were both deeply religious people determined to translate their beliefs into social reform. They belonged to the Episcopal Church and she was a lifelong temperance advocate, but she felt constrained by the conventions of the time from playing a public role too prominent for a lady of her social standing. She wielded influence principally through her personal example and her ever-active pen. Blackford was profoundly affected by the tragedies she saw every day as a member of a slaveholding society, and like several of her close relatives she developed antislavery opinions. William Blackford shared his wife's enthusiasm for the colonization cause, but not her antislavery views. For Mary Blackford colonization paved the way for emancipation, but her husband saw it only as a means to rid the state of its free black population.

Blackford became the most prominent female colonizationist in Virginia. She participated in the American Colonization Society from early adulthood until the outbreak of the Civil War and corresponded with its national officers for thirty years. During her years in Fredericksburg she raised funds and assisted both free blacks and recently freed slaves in immigrating to Liberia. In 1829 she founded the Fredericksburg and Falmouth Female Auxiliary to the American Colonization Society. The auxiliary distributed tracts and by May 1830 had raised $500 and recruited eighteen women as ACS life members, including Dolley Payne Todd Madison. The Fredericksburg society was the best-publicized female auxiliary in Virginia. Its first annual "Report of the Board of Managers," written by Blackford, was published as a broadside and in the Methodist *Christian Sentinel*. In the fall of 1832 she began a journal, "Notes Illustrative of the Wrongs of Slavery," in which she cataloged the horrors of slavery, recorded her personal feelings, and detailed her activities.

Blackford's brother Launcelot Byrd Minor became a missionary in Liberia, and Blackford corresponded with him and with several of her family's former slaves and others whom she had assisted in emigrating there from Virginia. She never retreated from her moral position. In 1834, however, frustrated with the "unaccountable apathy . . . benumbing the public mind," she announced that the auxiliary was reinventing itself as the Ladies' Society of Fredericksburg and Falmouth, for the Promotion of Female Education in Africa. By 1837 it was helping to fund a girls' academy in Liberia run by Presbyterian missionaries. When Blackford and her family moved to Lynchburg in 1846, her public work for the ACS ended.

Despite Blackford's antipathy to slavery, the family owned a few household slaves purchased by William Blackford to assist his wife, who grew increasingly infirm with each succeeding pregnancy. As sectional tensions worsened Blackford felt increasingly alienated from her family. Her husband, who had stressed the degradation of the free black population instead of the possibility of ending slavery, grew more sectional in his attitude after 1850. Mary Blackford lamented that secessionism was unpatriotic. "To see my sons arrayed against one part of their country, our own 'Star Spangled Banner,' and in such a cause," she wrote to her brother in January 1861, "is a sorrow that makes me feel the grave is the only place for me." After her husband's death on 14 or 15 April 1864, she spent most of the remainder of her long life living quietly in the Alexandria home of her son Launcelot Minor Blackford. Mary Berkeley Minor Blackford died there on 15 September 1896 and was buried in Spring Hill Cemetery in Lynchburg.

L. Minor Blackford, *Mine Eyes Have Seen the Glory: The Story of a Virginia Lady, Mary Berkeley Minor Blackford, 1802–1896* (1954; frontispiece por.); Blackford letters in family papers at UNC, UVA, VHS, and American Colonization Society Papers, LC; *Fredericksburg Virginia Herald*, 15 Oct. 1825; Elizabeth R. Varon, *We Mean to Be Counted: White Women and Politics in Antebellum Virginia* (1998), 45–46, 53–56, 59–60, 65–66, 151–152, 167; Patricia P. Hickin, "Antislavery in Virginia, 1831–1861" (Ph.D. diss., UVA, 1968); *Christian Sentinel*, 22 June 1832; *African Repository and Colonial Journal* 10 (1834): 252–253; 13 (1837): 311–313; obituaries in *Alexandria Gazette*, 15 Sept. 1896, and *Fredericksburg Free Lance*, 17 Sept. 1896; obituary and account of funeral in *Lynchburg Daily News*, 16, 17 Sept. 1896.

BRENT TARTER

BLACKFORD, Staige Davis (28 December 1898–17 July 1949), physician and medical educator, was born in Alexandria, the youngest of five sons and one daughter (of whom the daughter died young) of Launcelot Minor Blackford and Elizabeth Chew Ambler Blackford. He was educated at Episcopal High School near Alexandria, of which his father was principal until just before his death in 1914. After a short interval as secretary to his father's successor, Blackford enlisted on 29 May 1917 as a private in one of two University of Virginia sections of the United States Army Ambulance Service. He arrived in France on 10 January 1918, was awarded the Croix de Guerre with silver star for his service in action later that year, and was discharged on 23 April 1919.

Possibly inspired by his elder brother John Minor Blackford, a University of Virginia alumnus and successful physician, Blackford embarked on the study of medicine. He entered the University of Virginia in 1919 and graduated in 1923 after serving as captain of the football team and joining Alpha Omega Alpha, Delta Kappa Epsilon, the Raven Society, and the Z Society. He completed his medical degree at the University of Virginia two years later, interned at Massachusetts General Hospital, and then joined the faculty of the University of Virginia in the autumn of 1927 as students' physician, becoming an instructor the next year, assistant professor of medicine in 1937, and associate professor in 1942. On 20 August 1927 he married Lydia Harper Fishburne, of Charlottesville, in New York City. They had one son and one daughter.

Blackford published papers on tularemia, spontaneous pneumothorax, subarachnoid hemorrhage, and gastrointestinal diseases. Shortly after joining the faculty of the University of Virginia he reorganized the Medical School's outpatient department and transformed it into an integral part of the teaching hospital. It cared for more than 100,000 indigent patients during Blackford's years in Charlottesville. He also reorganized the clinical staff of the Medical School's teaching hospital, developed a postgraduate medical education program, designed a series of refresher courses for practicing physicians, and served as the first editor of the school's *Medical Alumni Bulletin*.

Early in 1942 Blackford organized and became the medical director of the university-sponsored 8th Evacuation Hospital, a 750-bed military facility. With the rank of lieutenant colonel, Blackford served as the mobile unit's chief of medicine from 1 July 1942 until April 1945. The hospital staff consisted of nearly 50 commissioned officers, more than 50 commissioned nurses, and more than 300 noncommissioned officers and privates. It was the first hospital group to land at Casablanca in November 1942 during the North African campaign. Transferred to Oran in the summer of 1943, the unit landed in Italy with American invasion forces in the Gulf of Salerno in September 1943. Blackford and his command served behind advancing troops at Salerno, Naples, Cassino, Florence, and Verona. The 8th became a model for combat medical hospitals of the time, treating more than 48,000 admitted patients and another 45,000 outpatients. For his World War II service Blackford received the Legion of Merit from the United States and the Medal of French Morocco.

Immediately after the war Blackford chaired the university's Committee on Postgraduate Medical Education. He became professor of the practice of medicine in 1946 and served as head of the Gastroenterology Division of the Internal Medicine Department. In 1949, as a consultant to the army, he toured military hospitals in Germany and Austria. An active member of the Medical Society of Virginia, Blackford was also a fellow of the American College of Physicians, a member of the American Clinical and Climatological Association, an examiner for the American Board of Internal Medicine, and a trustee of Episcopal High School.

Staige Davis Blackford suffered a heart attack on 3 July 1949 while visiting friends in Lynchburg and died in Charlottesville on 17 July 1949. He was buried in the University of Virginia Cemetery, and the university honored him by establishing the annual Staige Davis Blackford Memorial Lecture series.

Biography in Sarah S. Matthews, *The University of Virginia Hospital (Its First Fifty Years)* [ca. 1961], 114–116; Military Service Records; *Charlottesville Daily Progress*, 22 Aug. 1927; Byrd Stuart Leavell, *The 8th Evac.: A History of the University of Virginia Hospital Unit in World War II* (1970) (pors., frontispiece and opp. 100); obituaries in *Charlottesville Daily Progress* (por.) and *New York Times*, both 18 July 1949; memorials in *University of Virginia Alumni News Letter* 2 (Sept. 1949): 5, *University of Virginia Alumni News* 38 (Oct. 1949): 16, 19, and *Virginia Medical Monthly* 76 (1949): 497, 556.

ROBERT J. BRUGGER

BLACKFORD, William Mathews (19 August 1801–14 or 15 April 1864), journalist, was born at Catoctin Furnace in Frederick County, Maryland, the third of four sons and fourth of six children of Benjamin Blackford and Isabella Arthur Blackford. He grew up there and in Shenandoah County, where his father owned and operated a large and profitable ironworks. By 1824 Blackford had qualified as an attorney, and in January 1825 he moved to Fredericksburg and began to practice law. On 12 October 1825 he married Mary Berkeley Minor in Caroline County. They had two daughters and six sons.

In addition to his law practice, Blackford acted as an agent for several years for the Mutual Assurance Society of Virginia. In 1828 he bought the *Fredericksburg Political Arena and Literary Messenger* from his brother-in-law and plunged into the presidential campaign on behalf of President John Quincy Adams. Blackford owned and edited the *Political Arena* until October 1841 and consistently and vigorously supported the Whig Party. Blackford and his wife were both active in the Episcopal Church, in the temperance movement, and in Fredericksburg auxiliaries of the American Colonization Society, which they were instrumental in founding and running.

On 10 February 1842 President John Tyler appointed Blackford chargé d'affaires to New Granada. Blackford and his son William Willis Blackford lived in Bogotá for almost three years while he tried to settle the long-standing American claims against New Granada resulting from seizures of ships and cargoes during the South American wars for independence. Blackford soon concluded that he would have as little success as his predecessors unless the United States imposed a naval blockade. He turned his attention to negotiating a postal convention, which was signed on 6 March 1844 and ratified on 20 December. Blackford also negotiated a commercial treaty between New Granada and the United States, but because the treaty did not end discriminatory duties, the United States Senate never ratified it. While in New Granada Blackford also kept a watchful eye on French and British attempts to secure exclusive rights to construct a railroad or a canal across the Isthmus of Panama.

Blackford returned to the United States on 12 February 1845 after the Democratic Party won the presidential election of 1844, and he resigned as chargé d'affaires effective 13 May 1845. In March 1846 he bought a controlling interest in, and became the editor of, the *Lynchburg Virginian*, the most influential Whig newspaper in Piedmont Virginia. Blackford sold his interest in the *Virginian* in 1850 when he was appointed postmaster of Lynchburg. After the Democratic Party took over the presidency in 1853, Blackford lost his job as postmaster, and on 4 May 1853 he became cashier of the new Exchange Bank of Lynchburg. He remained cashier until his death.

Blackford opposed secession in 1861 but after the fact became a firm supporter of the Confederacy. Five of his sons fought in the Confederate army, he opened his home to sick and wounded Confederate soldiers, and after the Battle of Fredericksburg he raised $4,000 for the citizens of his old hometown. Blackford was an early admirer of Thomas J. "Stonewall" Jackson and served as an escort when his body passed through Lynchburg. In June 1863 Blackford accepted the position of Confederate States Treasury agent in Lynchburg. William Mathews Blackford died at his Lynchburg home during the night of 14–15 April 1864 and was buried in Spring Hill Cemetery there.

William Mathews Blackford Diaries, 1849– 1864, UVA; family history in Susan Leigh Colston Blackford, *Memoirs of Life In and Out of the Army in Virginia During the War Between the States* (1894–1896; repr. 1996 and in abridgement in 1947 as *Letters from Lee's Army*), and in Blackford Family Papers and William Willis Blackford's MS family history, VHS; other Blackford family papers at UVA and Duke; 1863–1864 account books in Maryland Historical Society, Baltimore; *Fredericksburg Virginia Herald*, 15 Oct. 1825; speech on colonization excerpted in *African Repository and Colonial Journal* 4 (1828): 73–76; editorials in *Fredericksburg Political Arena*, 12 Oct. 1841, and *Lynchburg Virginian*, 23 Mar. 1846; L. Minor Blackford, *Mine Eyes Have Seen the Glory: The Story of a Virginia Lady, Mary Berkeley Minor Blackford, 1802–1896* (1954; por. opp. 154); E. Taylor Parks, *Colombia and the United States, 1765–1934* (1935), 165–177; Diplomatic Dispatches, Colombia, vol. 10, RG 59, NARA, printed in part in Robert L. Meriwether et al., eds., *Papers of John C. Calhoun* (1959–), vols. 19–21; obituaries in *Richmond Daily Whig*, 16 Apr. 1864, and *Lynchburg Virginian*, 18 Apr. 1864.

DONALD W. GUNTER

BLACKFORD, William Willis (23 March 1831–1 May 1905), Confederate army officer and civil engineer, was born in Fredericksburg, the second of six sons and third of eight children of William Mathews Blackford and Mary Berkeley Minor Blackford. At age eleven he accompanied his father to Bogotá, New Granada, where his father served for three years as chargé d'affaires. Blackford learned Spanish in Bogotá and excelled in horsemanship. The year after he and his father returned to Virginia in 1845, the family moved to Lynchburg. Blackford continued his education and then worked on railroad construction survey crews for three years, saving enough money to study engineering at the University of Virginia for the academic year 1849–1850.

Blackford worked as a civil engineer during the construction of the Virginia and Tennessee Railroad and was acting chief engineer when the road was completed. On 10 January 1856 he married Mary Trigg Robertson, of Richmond. Of their four daughters and three sons, two daughters and one son died in infancy. Between his marriage and the outbreak of the Civil War, Blackford and his wife moved to Washington County, where he became a partner with his father-in-law, former governor Wyndham Robertson, in a gypsum-mining operation near Abingdon.

Following John Brown's raid on Harpers Ferry in October 1859, Blackford organized the Washington Mounted Rifles as part of the county militia and was elected lieutenant. Although opposed to secession, he led his company into Confederate service in July 1861 as part of the 1st Virginia Cavalry, under the command of Lieutenant Colonel James Ewell Brown Stuart. Blackford served as Stuart's aide-de-camp and on 3 October 1861 was promoted to captain. In May and June 1862 Blackford was detached to supervise construction of pontoon bridges across the James River, but he rejoined the cavalry before the Seven Days' Battles and rode with Stuart's cavalry in every major engagement of the war except Chancellorsville. One of Stuart's best officers, he was wounded twice and had at least three horses killed under him. On 19 January 1864 Blackford was promoted to major of engineers, and on 1 April he was promoted to lieutenant colonel and sent to Petersburg, where he supervised the digging of shafts and tunnels to detect Union attempts to place subterranean mines under Confederate emplacements. Blackford surrendered at Appomattox Court House on 9 April 1865.

After the Civil War ended Blackford worked as chief engineer for the Lynchburg and Danville Railroad. His wife died in 1866, after which he and his children moved to Terrebonne Parish, Louisiana, where he operated a sugar plantation that his father-in-law had given him. A flood in 1874 destroyed much of the property, and Blackford returned to Virginia. From 1880 to 1882 he was professor of mechanics and drawing at the Virginia Agricultural and Mechanical College at Blacksburg, and he also served as superintendent of grounds and buildings and landscaped the campus. Between 1882 and 1890 Blackford worked as a construction engineer for the Baltimore and Ohio Railroad on its line between Baltimore and Philadelphia and on the construction of a railroad between Lynchburg and Durham, North Carolina. Blackford then retired and moved to Princess Anne County.

A number of Blackford's Civil War letters appeared in Susan Leigh Colston Blackford's *Memoirs of Life In and Out of the Army in Virginia During the War Between the States* (1894–1896; reprinted 1996 and in abridgement as *Letters from Lee's Army*, 1947). Douglas Southall Freeman and other historians have found the volume useful. Blackford also composed an account of his Civil War experiences early in the 1890s. It was published as *War Years with Jeb Stuart* (1946), with an introduction by Freeman. The direct and unembellished style, interesting anecdotes, and vivid descriptions of battlefield scenes make it an outstanding memoir of a Confederate cavalry officer.

During his last two years Blackford worked with the United States Department of Fisheries unsuccessfully experimenting with means of artificially fattening oysters. William Willis Blackford died of apoplexy at his home in Princess Anne County on 1 May 1905 and was buried in Sinking Spring Cemetery in Abingdon.

Robert J. Trout, *They Followed the Plume: The Story of J.E.B. Stuart and His Staff* (1993), 63–67 (por.); chapter one of Blackford's *War Years with Jeb Stuart* is autobiographical; letters and short autobiography in Blackford's MS family history and Blackford Family Papers, VHS; evidently Blackford was named at his baptism for William Wilberforce, the great English opponent of the slave trade, with the subsequent substitution of "Willis" for "Wilberforce" coming at an unspecified later date (Pecquet du Bellet, *Virginia Families*, 2:211); BVS Marriage Register, Richmond City; Compiled Service Records; obituaries in *Norfolk Landmark* and *Richmond News Leader*, both 3 May 1905.

DONALD W. GUNTER

BLACKWELL, James Heyward (ca. 5 February 1864–14 October 1931), educator, was the eldest of two sons and two daughters of James W. (probably William) Blackwell and Charlotte Chatman (or Chatham) Blackwell. He was probably born a slave in Marion. By 1870 the family had moved to Manchester, across the James River from Richmond, where his father was a stonemason. Although Blackwell's parents could not read or write, they encouraged him to obtain an education. In or after 1872 he came under the tutelage of Anthony Binga, the only African American teacher in Manchester's public schools and pastor of the First Baptist Church, to which Blackwell belonged. Blackwell went on to graduate in 1880 from the Richmond Theological Institute (now Virginia Union University).

On 5 September 1880 Blackwell began his career as a teacher in New Kent County. After two terms he returned to Manchester, where blacks had successfully lobbied for the employment of African American teachers. The city's school for blacks opened in 1882 with Binga as principal and Blackwell as one of the three teachers. He succeeded Binga as principal in 1888. On 29 May 1891 the school graduated its first students from a three-year high school curriculum that Blackwell had initiated.

On 8 July 1885 Blackwell married Annie Estelle Jordan, a Petersburg teacher and sister of William H. Jordan, a member of the General Assembly. They had two sons and one daughter. Considered one of the area's rising young men, Blackwell became a speaker and organizer for the United Order of True Reformers. In 1891 he helped found the Virginia Industrial Mercantile and Building and Loan Association. He served as secretary and general manager of the ambitious enterprise, which according to its state charter proposed to operate general mercantile stores, to hold yearly fairs showing the "industrial and material advancement of our race," and through loans to enable "persons of limited means to secure comfortable houses for their families."

The association did not survive the economic depression of the 1890s. As conditions improved, however, Blackwell and eleven others chartered the Benevolent Investment and Relief Association on 19 February 1898. Blackwell again served as secretary and manager. He reported on 2 April 1902 that the company employed eighty-two people and had issued more than 12,000 insurance policies. Despite initial success the company dissolved about 1906. It faced stiff competition from several other Richmond insurance companies operated by African Americans, and the expense of handling numerous small policies made it difficult to build the cash reserves necessary for survival.

In 1910 the cities of Manchester and Richmond consolidated, and Blackwell's school was named the Maury School. Because Richmond did not permit blacks to serve as principals of public schools, he was demoted to a teacher after twenty-two years in his post. Even more disheartening, the high school students were sent to the larger Armstrong High School. Blackwell remained de facto chief administrator of the Maury School until 1916 when, with completion of a new annex, it was renamed the Dunbar School and a white man became principal.

Blackwell developed still more outlets for his talents. For twenty years he was treasurer of the Virginia Baptist State Sabbath School Convention. He aided in the survival of the Smallwood Institute, located at Claremont in Surry County, after the death in 1912 of its founder, John J. Smallwood. In addition to serving as the school's secretary, he was its president in 1915 and 1916. In partnership with his elder son, James H. Blackwell Jr., he organized the Southside Realty Company. Blackwell also served as an officer of the Hawkins Company and the World's Wonder Chemical Company, both manufacturers of beauty products, and for a time he was president of the Loprice Land Corporation. His two sons enjoyed successful professional careers. James H. Blackwell Jr. was a Richmond physician and longtime secretary of the Old Dominion Medical Society, and George W. Blackwell became a lawyer and politician in Chicago.

After more than forty years in public education, Blackwell retired in 1922. During the remainder of his life he managed two employment agencies, the Interstate Colored Teachers Agency and the Better Service Bureau. James Heyward Blackwell died in Richmond on 14 October 1931 and was buried in the family plot at Mount Olivet Cemetery in that city. In 1951 the Dunbar School became a combined elementary and junior high school, and the following year the Richmond School Board renamed it the James H. Blackwell School. An elementary school alone since 1970, it has given its name to the surrounding neighborhood.

Birth date of 5 Feb. 1864 in Caldwell, *History of the American Negro*, 13–14, 478–481 (por.); *Richmond Planet*, 22 Aug. 1891 (gives 5 Feb. 1862 birth date), 19 Feb. 1898, 5 Apr. 1902 (por.); Census, Chesterfield Co., 1870, 1880, and Manchester City, 1900 (gives Feb. 1865 birth date); information provided by granddaughter Grace Blackwell Perkins; BVS Marriage Register, Petersburg City, with age at marriage of twenty-four; *Richmond Virginia Star*, 30 Apr. 1881; *Petersburg Lancet*, 28 Oct. 1882, 11 July 1885; *Richmond Southern News*, 15 Oct. 1892; *Acts of Assembly*, 1897–1898 sess., 440–441; Charter Book, 18:308–311; *Richmond Afro-American*, 17 Dec. 1938; obituaries of sons in *Richmond Afro-American*, 11 Feb. 1950, 13 Feb. 1960; death notice in *Richmond News Leader*, 15 Oct. 1931; obituary in *Norfolk Journal and Guide*, 24 Oct. 1931 (por.), with age at death of "about sixty."

John T. Kneebone

BLACKWELL, John Chapman (31 August 1812–21 February 1885), educator, was born in Lunenburg County, the third of four sons and seventh of eight children of John Blackwell and Mary Dunn Edmondson Blackwell. He converted to Methodism at the age of fourteen while a student at Ebenezer Academy in Brunswick County. In 1831 he entered Washington College in Lexington, remaining there until a new Methodist institution, Randolph-Macon College, opened eighteen months later in Boydton. Blackwell was Randolph-Macon's first graduate, receiving a B.A. with honors in 1835. He stayed on as a tutor at the college until his marriage on 14 July 1836 to Mary Bertonia Letcher, of Lexington, whom he had met while a student at Washington College. They had six sons and six daughters.

Blackwell returned to Lunenburg County and with his brother Thomas Blackwell opened Hinton Hill Academy for boys in 1839. He received an M.A. from Randolph-Macon College in 1840 and served as headmaster and teacher of classics at Hinton Hill Academy for nine years. Because of chronic health problems he chose teaching as his profession rather than the Methodist ministry, which would have meant moving to a new church every few years. However, he preached at local churches on request and performed marriage and funeral ceremonies to supplement his teaching income.

In 1848 Blackwell became president of the Female Collegiate Institute in Buckingham County. Established in 1837 as the first chartered college for women in Virginia, the institute had been forced to close in 1843 because of heavy debts. When it reopened five years later with Blackwell in charge, it was operated under the auspices of the Methodist Episcopal Church South. The college prospered for the first several years of Blackwell's administration. "Old Master," as he was affectionately known to his students, taught mathematics, natural sciences, and ethics, and he eased the institute's strict code of conduct, which had forbidden students to talk or laugh during meals or recess. By 1861, however, the Female Collegiate Institute had fallen into debt again, and the disruptions of the Civil War added to the school's problems and led to its final closure two years later.

In 1863 Blackwell accepted a post as president of the Female College of Petersburg, but it, too, could not survive the war and closed in 1864. In 1865 Blackwell returned as professor of chemistry to his alma mater, from which he had received an honorary D.D. in 1861. He was one of only four faculty members at the struggling college at the end of the war. During his three-year tenure at Randolph-Macon, Blackwell was active both as a professor and as a member of the board of trustees, to which he had been elected in 1858. He served as temporary president of the college from August to

October 1866, and later that year he and the newly elected president traveled to Baltimore to request aid to revive the college from the Baltimore Conference of the Methodist Episcopal Church South. Two years later he was one of three trustees appointed to offer the presidency of Randolph-Macon to Jefferson Davis, who declined. Blackwell was also one of six trustees who in 1864 had studied the feasibility of relocating Randolph-Macon to another site in Virginia. Blackwell voted with the majority of the board on 24 June 1868 to move the college to Ashland, but he resigned his teaching position immediately thereafter because he was unwilling to move his own family to Ashland.

In 1868 Blackwell became president of the Danville Female College, another Methodist institution struggling with debt. The Virginia Annual Conference credited Blackwell with keeping the school open during the next two years, but he resigned after the 1869–1870 term, pleading failing health. The college was sold a year later to pay its debts. Blackwell then attempted to buy the properties of the Buckingham Female Collegiate Institute, which were also being auctioned off to pay its debts. He may have had plans to revive the school, but he could simply have been attempting to recover a portion of the $8,212 lien he had filed against the institute's shareholders in 1866. His bid was rejected, and the vacant school remained entangled for years in legal battles.

Blackwell never taught again. He and his wife lived with their eldest daughter, Mary Elizabeth Blackwell Hanes, in Buckingham County. John Chapman Blackwell died at his daughter's house, Humanity Hall, on 21 February 1885, and was buried in a cemetery adjoining the old grounds of the Buckingham Female Collegiate Institute.

Paul R. White Sr., *Taproots: A Virginia & Carolina Legacy*, 2d ed. (1986), 146–168, 173–178, 363–364; William M. E. Rachal, "Virginia's First College for Women: The Female Collegiate Institute in Buckingham County," *Virginia Cavalcade* 2 (summer 1952): 44–47 (por.); Sue Roberson West, *Buckingham Female Collegiate Institute, First Chartered College for Women in Virginia, 1837–1843, 1848–1863: A Documentary History* (1990), 23, 32–54; Richard Irby, *History of Randolph-Macon College, Virginia* (1898), 57 (por.), 85–86, 145, 150–158, 168–173; James Edward Scanlon, *Randolph-Macon College: A Southern History, 1825–1967* (1983), 96–97, 119, 123, 145; Alvin L. Hall, *The History of Stratford College* (1974), 13–15; obituary in *Richmond Christian Advocate*, 2 Apr. 1885.

KELLY HENDERSON HAYES

BLACKWELL, John Davenport (17 June 1822–26 June 1887), Methodist minister, was born in Fauquier County, the second of four sons and third of seven children of John Blackwell and Rebecca Davenport Blackwell, affluent farmers and active Methodists. His mother died in 1831 and his father remarried a year later. The new couple had no children. Blackwell began his education under a local tutor, then went to a boarding school in Warrenton, and ultimately attended Dickinson College in Carlisle, Pennsylvania, from which he received an A.B. in 1846.

Blackwell experienced a religious conversion at age fourteen and entered the ministry in 1846, about the same time that the Baltimore Conference, within whose territory he had grown up, split into southern and northern branches. His first charge was as an assistant with a church in the Bedford Circuit, which was part of the new Virginia Conference. For fifteen years Blackwell served successively as minister at Methodist churches in Hampton and Farmville, as chaplain of Randolph-Macon College in Boydton, and again as minister in Fairfax, Washington, D.C., Warrenton, Richmond at Union Methodist Church, the Nottoway Circuit, and Richmond at Trinity Methodist Church. On 8 November 1853 he married Julia Anna Butts in Southampton County. Before her death on 18 August 1866 they had three sons and three daughters, including Robert Emory Blackwell, later president of Randolph-Macon College.

During the Civil War Blackwell was pastor of the Granby Street Methodist Church in Norfolk when the United States Army occupied the city in May 1862. He refused to take a loyalty oath and managed to cross through the lines. On 1 March 1864 he became chaplain to the 18th Regiment Virginia Infantry. He served for a time in North Carolina, then participated in the siege of Petersburg, and retreated with the Confederate army to Appomattox Court House, where he was present on 9 April 1865 at the surrender of the Army of Northern Virginia.

Blackwell resumed his ministry after the war and held pastorates in Warrenton and Amherst and at Cumberland Street Methodist Church in Norfolk and Washington Street Methodist Church in Petersburg. He served as presiding elder, or overseer, of pastors in the Murfreesboro Conference in North Carolina and in the Lynchburg and Charlottesville Districts in Virginia. In 1883 he became pastor of Monumental Methodist Church in Portsmouth. Blackwell had married again, to Frances Grayson Smith, in Fauquier County on 16 December 1869. They had four sons and two daughters.

During his postwar career Blackwell became prominent among Virginia Methodists. He received an honorary D.D. from Randolph-Macon College in 1873, served as one of three Virginia delegates to the Methodist Centennial Conference in 1884, and was a delegate to the General Conference of the Methodist Episcopal Church South for almost two decades before his death. No one could lure him away from the pulpit. He twice refused appointments to the presidency of Wesleyan Female College in Murfreesboro, North Carolina, declined an invitation to become president of Martha Washington College in Abingdon, and in June 1876 turned down an offer to lead Randolph-Macon College.

Between July and October 1873, during Blackwell's pastorate at Cumberland Street Church in Norfolk, he and Father Matthew O'Keefe of that city's Saint Mary's Catholic Church exchanged a series of sharp public letters in the local newspaper, the *Norfolk Virginian*, and in the state's Methodist newspaper, the *Richmond Christian Advocate*, concerning topics on which Methodists and Catholics disagreed, including the scriptural authority of Catholic doctrine and the concept of papal infallibility. O'Keefe published his end of the exchange in *The Key to True Christianity* (1874). Blackwell responded with his own letters and some additional essays in *God's Word Our Guide: or, Scriptural Christianity Vindicated, in a Series of Letters Addressed to Rev. M. O'Keefe* (1874). O'Keefe had the final word with *Noctes Sepianæ; or, An Exposé of the Cuttle-Fish Tactics; False Allegations; Misstatements, Scriptural and Historical; of the Work of Rev. J. D. Blackwell, A.M., D.D., Entitled "God's Word our Guide"* (1875).

John Davenport Blackwell died at the parsonage in Portsmouth early on 26 June 1887, three days after developing peritonitis. More than a thousand people attended his funeral at Monumental Church, and more than fifty clergymen, including twenty-five Methodist pastors, participated in the service. He was buried in the Warrenton Cemetery in Warrenton.

John J. Lafferty, *Sketches of the Virginia Conference, Methodist Episcopal Church, South* (1880), 49–50, and *Sketches and Portraits of the General Conference of the Methodist Episcopal Church, South* (1886), 77 (por. opp. 73); BVS Marriage Register, Southampton and Fauquier Cos.; Compiled Service Records; James I. Robertson Jr., *18th Virginia Infantry*, 2d ed. (1984), 26, 41; obituaries and accounts of funeral in *Norfolk Public Ledger*, 27, 28 June 1887, *Norfolk Virginian*, 28–30 June, 2 July 1887, *Richmond Dispatch*, 28 June 1887, and *Richmond Christian Advocate*, 30 June, 7 July 1887; memoirs and tributes in Register, Monumental Methodist Church, Portsmouth (LVA microfilm), by Alexander G. Brown in *Richmond Christian Advocate*, 14 July 1887, and by William E. Judkins in Virginia Annual Conference of Methodist Episcopal Church South, *Minutes* (1887): 106–110.

BETH BARTON SCHWEIGER

BLACKWELL, Robert Emory (14 November 1854–7 July 1938), president of Randolph-Macon College, was born in Warrenton, the eldest of three sons and three daughters of John Davenport Blackwell, a prominent Methodist minister, and his first wife, Julia Anna Butts Blackwell. He attended Bethel Academy in Fauquier County and entered Randolph-Macon College in 1868 when he was only thirteen years old, during the school's first year at Ashland. With only one year excepted, Blackwell was to be connected with the college until his death seventy years later.

Blackwell earned an M.A. in 1874. He spent the academic year 1874–1875 as an assistant at the college and then attended lectures at the University of Leipzig for one year. In 1876 he returned to Randolph-Macon to succeed Thomas R. Price as professor of English. Blackwell always described himself as a teacher rather than a professor, or later president, and believed that his principal mission was to educate his students and help them think for themselves. He was a popular and respected teacher but not at heart a scholar. He found writing difficult and produced only one book, collaborating with James Albert Harrison on *Harrison and Blackwell's Easy Lessons in French* (1887). On 28 August 1877 he married Theela Epia Duncan, a daughter of James Armstrong Duncan, the president of Randolph-Macon. They had one daughter.

In 1902 a divided board of trustees elected Blackwell president of Randolph-Macon College. He did not initially have strong support from all of the members, and the manner of his election suggests that he was thought of as a stopgap or compromise, perhaps to prevent the election of the Reverend James Cannon Jr. Ironically, Blackwell remained in the post for the next thirty-six years and became the senior college president in Virginia. He received honorary degrees from Duke, Wesleyan, and Washington and Lee Universities and from Wofford College. From 1909 to 1911 he served as president of the Association of Colleges and Preparatory Schools of the Southern States. During many years as a lay leader of the Methodist Episcopal Church South he worked for its reunification with the church's northern branch.

Between 1907 and 1914 an acrimonious struggle took place between Cannon and Blackwell's cousin William Waugh Smith, president of Randolph-Macon Woman's College, over the ownership of the Randolph-Macon system of schools. The conflict ended with a court decision giving legal ownership to the board of trustees rather than the Virginia and Baltimore Conferences of the Methodist Church. Blackwell managed to avoid becoming a principal figure in the controversy, which left the college's natural constituency bitter and divided.

In the 1920s Randolph-Macon raised $600,000 for the endowment (a third of which came from the Rockefeller General Education Board), built Alumni Gymnasium, and received $60,000 from the Carnegie Foundation for a new library. The college refused an offer of $1 million and 100 acres of land from citizens of Norfolk on condition that the college move to that city. Blackwell was determined to keep the college small so that it could "hand-cultivate" students, as he put it. By the force of his personality rather than through generous salaries, he attracted and retained a small but dedicated group of teachers. Blackwell was firm in defending his faculty against the fundamentalists of the 1920s. In the next decade the college added no new buildings in spite of an increase in the student body from fewer than 200 to nearly 300. By the time of his death the Great Depression had severely reduced the value of the endowment, and the college's physical facilities had deteriorated badly.

A man who lived his faith, Blackwell was more important for what he was and represented than for what he did. One important exception was his role as a founder and the first president of the Virginia Commission on Interracial Cooperation in 1919, a time when such a step was far from popular. Blackwell's leadership of the organization, which continued until his death, eased the way for other influential men to join it. John Manuel Gandy, president of Virginia State College for Negroes in Ettrick, near Petersburg, maintained that Blackwell "sought to find out what was possible to do rather than trying to locate the idealistic thing to do." By attacking individual cases of injustice rather than the system of segregation, Blackwell therefore gained the respect of many African Americans in Virginia without losing the trust of those white Virginians who had no desire to end segregation.

An imposing man, at the peak of his career Blackwell was five feet ten inches tall with blue eyes, a beard, and gray hair. He was often said to look like Robert E. Lee, to which he characteristically responded that their only common trait was working for small salaries. On his eightieth birthday he took up golf as his new hobby.

In the spring of 1938 Blackwell became ill while attending a conference of the Methodist Episcopal Church South in Birmingham, Alabama. Robert Emory Blackwell died in Emory University Hospital in Atlanta on 7 July 1938 and was buried in Woodland Cemetery in Ashland. An endowed chair in the humanities and an auditorium at Randolph-Macon College were later named for him.

Biographies in Bruce, Tyler, and Morton, *History of Virginia*, 4:276, *NCAB*, 33:309, and *Madison Quarterly* 7 (1947): 49–60; Robert Emory Blackwell Papers, Board of Trustees Papers, and Faculty Minutes, Randolph-Macon College Library, Ashland; James Edward Scanlon, *Randolph-Macon College: A Southern History, 1825–1967* (1983); additional information provided by Hugh Scott, Caroline Ellis Simpson, Grellett Collins Simpson, and George Spotswood Tarry; Virginia Commission on Interracial Cooperation Papers, including pamphlet entitled *Virginia's Goodwill Ambassador: Dr. Robert Emory Blackwell, Chairman Virginia Commission on Interracial Cooperation* (1935), Clark Atlanta University Library; por. by Annie W. R. Mahood in Peele Hall, Randolph-Macon College; obituary in *Richmond Times-Dispatch*, 8 July 1938 (por.).

JAMES EDWARD SCANLON

BLAETTERMANN, George Wilhelm (4 April 1782–1 January 1850), educator, was born in the town of Langensalza, Saxony, the second of three sons and third of four children of Johann Wilhelm Blättermann and Barbara Elisabeth Bürkin Blättermann. As a young man he exhibited a remarkable aptitude for languages. During studies at the universities in Leipzig, Heidelberg, and Göttingen he mastered English, French, Italian, and Latin and acquired the ability to teach Anglo-Saxon, Danish, Dutch, Portuguese, Spanish, and Swedish. Deeply impressed with the emerging German romantic tradition, he also became an admirer of Napoleon Bonaparte and served in the commissary corps during the French emperor's unsuccessful invasion of Russia. Blättermann lived in France and Italy before moving to London, where he taught, anglicized the spelling of his surname to Blaettermann, and married Elizabeth Charlotte Dean, who was also a teacher. About 1820 they adopted two of her grandnephews.

While living in London during the 1810s Blaettermann met many Americans and through them learned about the creation of the University of Virginia. In April 1819 he offered to join the faculty as professor of modern languages. The university's founder, Thomas Jefferson, was enthusiastic about Anglo-Saxon history, law, and language, and when the university's buildings were almost ready to receive students, he arranged for Blaettermann to be hired. Late in 1824 Blaettermann arrived in Charlottesville, where Jefferson described him as "rather a rough looking German, speaking English roughly, but of an excellent mind and high qualifications."

Despite his skills as a linguist Blaettermann failed as a teacher. He alienated his fellow professors, insulted and bored his students, marked up the books in the library, and displayed crude, insensitive, and ungentlemanly behavior that swiftly made him the most unpopular member of the original faculty. Enrollment in his classes fell so far that in 1830 the university reduced his salary in order to hire a tutor to assist the students. As the years passed Blaettermann became ever more obnoxious as a colleague and ineffective as a teacher. During a period of student unruliness late in the 1830s he was mobbed in the classroom, and when he retreated to his residence at Pavilion IV, the irate students besieged him there. One of the few students to profit from Blaettermann's pedagogy was Edgar Allan Poe, who attended the university in 1826.

The Blaettermanns had a stormy marriage that concluded on 8 September 1840 with an agreement for a legal separation. George Blaettermann gave up an improved lot of about three-and-a-half acres located between the town and the university for Elizabeth Blaettermann's separate maintenance and relinquished his legal rights over her and her property, leaving her "as if she were unmarried." The separation was far from amiable. Either just before or just after the conclusion of the legal arrangements, he publicly beat her twice in the street. Rumors of domestic violence had already aroused the suspicions of other faculty members, and the chairman of the faculty immediately notified the board of visitors. On 14 September 1840 the board examined the evidence, heard Blaettermann's defense of his conduct, and then unanimously dismissed him from the faculty.

Blaettermann retired to his 700-acre farm in Albemarle County. In 1843 he considered opening an agricultural college in Charlottesville. Elizabeth Blaettermann lived in the town, where she operated a seminary for young ladies and survived her estranged husband by almost fifteen years. George Wilhelm Blaettermann died suddenly on 1 January 1850. The faculty consented to his burial in the University of Virginia Cemetery, but he was probably buried on his farm in an unmarked grave.

Ronald B. Head, "The Declension of George W. Blaettermann: First Professor of Modern Languages at the University of Virginia," *Virginia Cavalcade* 31 (1982): 182–191, based in part on reminiscences of grandnephew George Walter Clements Blatterman, ca. 1902, with later annotations by his daughter Katherine M. Blatterman, UVA; birth recorded in Evangelische Kirche, Bad Langensalza, Germany; Blaettermann letters in Thomas Jefferson Papers, UVA; Richard Beale Davis, ed., *Correspondence of Thomas Jefferson and Francis Walker Gilmer, 1814–1826* (1946), 19, 22, 86–88, 108, 114–116, 121–124; George Ticknor to Thomas Jefferson, 27 May 1819, and Thomas Jefferson to James Madison, 26 Dec. 1824, Thomas Jefferson Papers, LC; Albemarle Co. Order Book (1830–1831), 133; dismissal in Visitors Minutes, 14 Sept. 1840, UVA; Blaettermann's publications include contributions to John Lewis, *Tables of Comparative Etymology and Analogous Formations* (1828), "Arabic Work on Agriculture" and "On Manures from Coal, and Dutch Ashes," *Farmers' Register* 1 (1834): 515–518, 540–541, and *A Discourse on the Use of Lime in Agriculture* (1846); Census, Albemarle Co., 1840; separate maintenance agreement in Albemarle Co. Deed Book, 38:179–182; estate inventory and sales in Albemarle Co. Will Book, 19:461–465, 20:10–19; obituary from *Charlottesville Jeffersonian Republican* reprinted in *Richmond Whig and Public Advertiser*, 5 Jan. 1850, and *Richmond Enquirer*, 8 Jan. 1850.

BRENT TARTER

BLAIKLEY, Catherine Kaidyee (ca. 1695–by 25 October 1771), midwife, was probably born in York County, the only daughter and one of two children of William Kaidyee and Martha Kaidyee. She married William Blaikley, a James City County watchmaker, on 11 September 1718. The couple had at least three daughters, one of whom is known to have reached adulthood, and two sons who died young. Another child may have been William Blaikley's son by a previous marriage. The Blaikleys enjoyed a comfortable standard of living at the time of William Blaikley's death. He was buried on 30 May 1736, and his will was proved on 21 June 1736. An estate inventory taken then includes several slaves, japanned tea tables, looking glasses, pictures, a silver cup, teaspoons, and tea tongs.

Catherine Blaikley had a long and active widowhood. She inherited her husband's entire estate, including fifty acres of land in Henrico County, a mill in Brunswick County, and a town lot in Williamsburg, where she resided. As the capital of colonial Virginia, Williamsburg provided Blaikley with the opportunity to lease rooms and supply board to men who were attending to legal and political business in town. Providing lodging was an acceptable economic pursuit for a widow in eighteenth-century Virginia, and she seems to have prospered. Maintaining her own account with a Yorktown merchant, she purchased goods and paid in cash. In August 1769 she advertised for a lost red morocco pocketbook, the contents of which (seven or eight pounds in paper money, some bills, some silver, business receipts, and other papers, including one about some drugs) suggest that she had maintained her standard of living.

The reference to drugs highlights Blaikley's fame as a midwife in Williamsburg and its vicinity. She had probably begun her career as a midwife by 1739. While Blaikley was no ordinary woman, her prominence was based on socially accepted pursuits for self-supporting women. In the seventeenth and eighteenth centuries, offering lodging and midwifery were means by which a woman could support herself in an economy based largely on credit and barter. At the time of her death the *Virginia Gazette* praised her as "an eminent Midwife" who brought "upwards of three Thousand Children into the World." The population of the capital consisted then of about 2,000 people, so she had delivered the equivalent of one-and-a-half times the entire population of the city.

Blaikley's life reveals the options and the limits on the options that were available to able and ambitious women in urban areas in eighteenth-century Virginia. By the time of her death male midwives were appearing on the scene, and in November 1771 another Virginia midwife announced that she had studied and practiced midwifery with the local male doctors. During the remaining years of the eighteenth century and into the nineteenth, physicians gradually displaced female midwives in the traditional role of assistants at childbirth.

An undated notice in a 24 October 1771 Williamsburg newspaper announced the death of Catherine Kaidyee Blaikley. Her tombstone in the cemetery at Bruton Parish Church gave her date of death as 25 October 1771, however, and as newspapers at this time were occasionally published a day or two after the date on their mastheads, the latter date cannot be ruled out.

Age at death of seventy-six in undated death notice in *Williamsburg Virginia Gazette* (Purdie and Dixon), 24 Oct. 1771; different readings of gravestone inscription give variant ages at death of seventy-three (J. Lesslie Hall, "Ancient Epitaphs and Inscriptions of York and James City Counties, Virginia," *Collections of the Virginia Historical Society*, new ser., 11 [1892]: 70–71) and seventy-five (*Bruton Parish Churchyard and Church: A Guide to the Tombstones, Monuments, and Mural Tablets* [1976], 10); family relationships and economic status documented in York Co. Wills and Inventories, 18:297, 312–316, 329, 19:168; genealogy given in *WMQ*, 1st ser., 21 (1913): 189; transcription of sampler giving marriage date and birth dates of children in *WMQ*, 1st ser., 2 (1894): 212; financial transactions recorded in Burwell Account Book (1738–1765), 101, CW, in John Mercer Ledger (1741–1750), 1:148, Bucks County Historical Society, Doylestown, Pa., microfilm at CW; and in Mordecai Booth Ledger (1746–1752), 203, Baylor Family Papers, VHS; *Williamsburg Virginia Gazette* (Rind), 10 Aug. 1769.

LINDA L. STURTZ

BLAIN, Daniel (ca. 1773–19 March 1814), Presbyterian minister and educator, was born in Abbeville County, South Carolina, probably the eldest son and second child of the three sons and three daughters of Michael Blain, a farmer, and Helena Owens Blain. During his formative years in a frontier environment seething with political and military strife, he attended a classical school run by Francis Cummins, a Presbyterian clergyman who probably influenced Blain in his decision to embark on a career as a clergyman and educator.

When Blain was about twenty years old he traveled to Virginia and enrolled in Liberty Hall Academy (now Washington and Lee University) in Rockbridge County, where he acquired the academic and theological training needed to enter the Presbyterian ministry. Under the tutelage of William Graham he studied the Greek New Testament, classical literature, mathematics, covenant theology, and Scottish common sense philosophy. After receiving an A.B. in 1796, he became an instructor at the New London Academy in neighboring Bedford County, which was operated by fellow Liberty Hall alumnus George Addison Baxter.

In 1797 the Presbytery of Lexington received Blain as a ministerial candidate, and it licensed him to preach on 13 April 1798. He served as a supply pastor for several churches during the following year and on 19 November 1800 was ordained and installed as pastor of Oxford and Timber Ridge Presbyterian Churches, both in Rockbridge County. He ministered to both congregations until his death. Blain married Mary Hanna on 3 June 1799. They had five daughters and one son.

In the spring of 1799 Blain and Baxter both returned from the New London Academy to their alma mater, which had been renamed Washington Academy. Baxter became rector and, after three years of teaching without a formal title, Blain became professor of languages and mathematics in 1802. They were the only two regular professors until 1813. During Blain's tenure the course of study at the Lexington institution was nearly identical to that at the Presbyterian-dominated College of New Jersey (now Princeton University). As a preacher, teacher, and writer, Blain helped to advance the causes of Presbyterianism, evangelical Protestantism, and higher education in the Valley of Virginia. He was a founder of and frequent contributor to the *Virginia Religious Magazine*, a Presbyterian monthly published in Lexington between 1804 and 1807. His articles included several polemics against deism, which many Presbyterian clergymen regarded as a grave threat to evangelicalism.

Known throughout Rockbridge County as the "amiable Mr. Blain," he was a popular clergyman and teacher. Daniel Blain died of pneumonia on 19 March 1814 and was buried in Lexington in what became Jackson Memorial Cemetery.

Biographies in Foote, *Sketches of Virginia*, 2:294–301, William Henry Ruffner, "The History of Washington College, Now Washington and Lee University, During the First Half of the Nineteenth Century," *Washington and Lee Historical Papers* 4 (1893): 44–46, and George West Diehl, *Old Oxford and Her Families* (1971), 37–40; Ollinger Crenshaw, *General Lee's College: The Rise and Growth of Washington and Lee University* (1969), 35–40; Dorthie Kirkpatrick and Edwin C. Kirkpatrick, *Rockbridge County Marriages, 1778–1850* (1985), 37–41; Rockbridge Co. Will Book, 2:45–46; death date in Lexington Presbytery Minutes, 21 Apr. 1814, Union Theological Seminary Library, Richmond, and in all secondary sources; variant death date of 13 Mar. 1814 and age at death of forty-one in William Couper, ed., *Jackson Memorial Cemetery Survey, Complete to 1960* (1968), 48.

RONALD W. LONG

BLAIR, Archibald (by 1665–4 March 1733), physician and merchant, was probably born in the county of Roxburgh, Scotland, the youngest of three sons and one of seven children of Peter Blair, the rector of Jedburgh Parish, and Mary Hamilton Blair. He graduated from the University of Edinburgh in 1685, studied medicine, was married by 1686 to a woman whose name is not known, and had a son, John Blair, born sometime in 1687. Blair's wife probably died during the 1690s, and before 1700 he and his young son moved to Virginia, where his eldest brother, James Blair, had become one of the leading clergymen and educators in the colony.

Archibald Blair practiced medicine in the new city of Williamsburg for the remainder of his life. Soon after his arrival in Virginia he also joined his brother and Philip Ludwell in the joint ownership of a retail store in Williamsburg. Archibald Blair owned half the stock and was in charge of operating what came to be known as Dr. Blair's Store. The store probably offered a wide variety of locally made and imported goods for sale, and given Blair's medical training, probably stocked patent medicines, too. With the assistance of William Prentis, who eventually became one of Williamsburg's most successful merchants, and of his own son, Blair made his store into an important financial center. It provided credit and banking arrangements in an economy that lacked formal financial services. Blair reportedly accepted only cash in payment for the merchandise he sold, but planters strapped for money could expect him in turn to pay hard currency for their tobacco. Collectors sometimes deposited their tax receipts at Blair's store, and Prentis often acted as an agent or paymaster on behalf of the colonial government. At the time of Blair's death his half-interest in the store was worth about £3,500.

In 1716 Blair purchased four lots in Williamsburg and built one of the first houses on Market Square. His public career was overshadowed by the greater roles his brother and son played, but Archibald Blair was a man of importance in Williamsburg for more than thirty years. The incomplete surviving records disclose that he served as a justice of the peace for James City County as early as 1710 and for York County from 1722 to 1733, as a major in the York County militia from 1724 until his death, as a Bruton Parish vestryman from 1718 until at least 1721 and perhaps until his death, as a collector of tithes for the parish between 1722 and 1732, as a director of the city of Williamsburg shortly after its founding, and as one of the original aldermen of the city in 1722. In addition, Blair was a member of the House of Burgesses representing Jamestown in 1718 and from 1728 until 1733 and representing James City County from 1720 to 1726. Lieutenant Governor Alexander Spotswood recommended that Blair be placed on the governor's Council in 1713, but Blair was not appointed.

Before 25 February 1703 Blair married Sarah Archer Fowler, widow of the colony's former attorney general Bartholomew Fowler. She probably bore at least some of Blair's four daughters. He later married Mary Wilson Roscow Cary. Blair's daughters married into influential Virginia families, and his son's political career culminated in four stints as acting governor of the colony. Archibald Blair died in Williamsburg on 4 March 1733 and was probably buried there.

Daphne Gentry and Brent Tarter, "The Blair Family of Colonial Williamsburg: A Research Note," *Magazine of Virginia Genealogy* 32 (1994): 103–112; University of Edinburgh, *Catalogue of Graduates* (1858), 127; public service documented in York Co. records; William G. Keener, "Blair-Prentis-Cary Partnership: The Store and Its Operation" (unpublished research report, CW, 1957); store records in Webb-Prentis Family Papers, UVA, including death date in 4 Oct. 1733 annual audit of Prentis's store.

LINDA H. ROWE

BLAIR, Archibald (ca. 1753–7 October 1824), clerk of the Council, was the younger of two sons and one of at least seven children of James Blair and Anne Hardyman Blair. His birthplace was probably either the family's plantation in Prince George County or nearby Williamsburg, where his father served as clerk to the deputy auditor of the revenue, John Blair (ca. 1687–1771), who was also the senior member of the governor's Council. Blair was most likely educated by tutors or members of his well-educated family. As a young man he probably worked as an assistant to his cousin John Blair (1731–1800), the last clerk of the Council before the American Revolution.

In July 1776, after John Blair had been elected to the new Council of State, the Council named Archibald Blair its clerk, enabling him, in effect, to succeed his cousin. Blair served as clerk for almost twenty-five years. Governor Thomas Jefferson entrusted him with transporting the public records from Williamsburg to Richmond when the capital was moved in the spring of 1780, and from April 1781 to April 1783 Blair acted as keeper of the remnants of the Council's library. As clerk of the Council, Blair was the one servant of the new commonwealth who was always present at the seat of government. He copied, oversaw the copying of, or authenticated most of the documents and letters that passed through the executive offices between the first administration of Patrick Henry and that of James Monroe, and he dealt with all or most of the consequential public men of his time in his capacity as clerk to the executive branch of the state government. His autograph appears on many varied and significant public records, and he may have known as much as anyone about the state's government and officers.

For some unspecified reason Blair fell out of favor with the members of the Council in the spring or early in the summer of 1800. During the remainder of the year he sought to retain his job or at least to have the causes of his impending dismissal recorded. After repeated delays, the Council voted on 16 January 1801 to elect Daniel L. Hylton to the position of clerk of the Council.

Blair retired to his house and gardens, which occupied an entire city block near the State Capitol in Richmond. In October 1786 he had married Mary "Molly" Whiting, of Gloucester County, and they had three sons and one daughter. He owned several small tracts of land in the vicinity of Richmond. Perhaps in part as a result of opportunities about which he had learned while serving as clerk, Blair also acquired title to more than 130,000 acres of land in the West, much of it in Kentucky and Ohio. He owned shares in several internal improvements companies as well, and served as a director of the James River Canal Company. In 1819 he identified himself as a merchant with a store at F and Eighth Streets, which he probably operated with his son Beverley Blair. Following a long period of poor health, Archibald Blair died in Richmond on 7 October 1824.

Daphne Gentry and Brent Tarter, "The Blair Family of Colonial Williamsburg: A Research Note," *Magazine of Virginia Genealogy* 32 (1994): 103–112; government service documented in journals of Council of State, RG 75, LVA; Blair to James Monroe, 7 June 1800, Governor's Office, Letters Received, RG 3, LVA; undated marriage notice in *Richmond Virginia Independent Chronicle*, 18 Oct. 1786; Richmond City Hustings Court Will Book, 4:106–109; obituary with age at death of seventy in *Richmond Enquirer*, 8 Oct. 1824.

DAPHNE GENTRY

BLAIR, Francis Simpson (6 November 1839–14 January 1899), attorney general of Virginia, was born in Jonesboro, Tennessee, the youngest of at least five sons and one daughter of Mary Chester Blair and John Blair, a former Democratic member of the House of Representatives. He attended Emory and Henry College and the University of Tennessee in Knoxville, from which he graduated in 1860. Blair had begun to study law when the Civil War broke out. He joined the Confederate army in 1861, fought at Shiloh and many other engagements in the western theater, and was a captain in the 60th Regiment Tennessee Infantry when he was captured at Vicksburg in July 1863. During his internment in the prison camp at Johnson's Island, Blair resumed reading law. He completed his studies after his release and settled in Wytheville, where he lived for the remainder of his life. On 16 November 1865 he married Sallie K. Pierce, of Wythe County. They had five sons and one daughter.

Blair, who used the first name Frank, initially won recognition in southwestern Virginia as a criminal defense attorney, but he later moved into more lucrative civil litigation and served as counsel for a number of corporations. He also took a keen interest in politics. During the 1870s Blair's endorsement of the inflationary policies of the Greenback Party put him at odds with much of Virginia's political establishment. He frequently criticized the state's Conservative Party, which he charged with prolonging divisions left over from the Civil War, and he opposed the Conservatives' apparent design to drive African Americans out of politics through the poll tax and complicated election laws. Blair also denounced the Conservative Party for its support of the Funding Act of 1871, which when implemented threatened to impoverish the state's new public school system and overtax the public in order to pay off the state debt at face value. State politics polarized between Funders, who supported the Funding Act, and Readjusters, who proposed to reduce the amount of debt to be honored. On 25 February 1879 Blair served as temporary chairman of the convention in Mozart Hall in Richmond at which the Readjuster Party was formed. The party ultimately succeeded by appealing to reformers, Republicans, disaffected Conservatives, and black voters, although Blair was one of many prominent Readjusters who announced in 1880 that they would vote Democratic in that year's presidential election.

Blair never backed down from his support for full legal rights for blacks, and he was a witty and powerful public speaker who delighted in denouncing the Funders. As a result Conservative newspaper editors frequently attacked him and often misrepresented his comments. In June 1881 the Readjuster Party nominated a full ticket of candidates for statewide office, including William Evelyn Cameron, a former Conservative, for governor; John Francis Lewis, a Republican, for lieutenant governor; and Blair, who was usually described as a Greenbacker, for attorney general. Blair stumped the state speaking colorfully and effectively, and in November the Readjusters swept to victory. He led the ticket, defeating his Conservative opponent Philip Watkins McKinney by more than 12,000 votes out of about 220,000 cast.

Blair served as attorney general of Virginia from 1 January 1882 to 1 January 1886. He played an influential role in the early months of the Cameron administration and helped the Readjusters oust many Funders from influential state offices. They replaced all of the members of the boards of visitors of the Virginia Agricultural and Mechanical College, the Virginia Military Institute, and the University of Virginia, with Blair serving on the new board of the latter institution from 1882 until 1886.

Blair also defended the new Readjuster laws in state and federal courts. He was successful so often that after the Readjusters lost control of the General Assembly in the election of 1883, he faced retaliation from the Conservatives, who had begun calling themselves Democrats. In November 1884 Democrats investigated Blair's expense accounts with a view to impeaching him, but the impeachment attempt failed. They then passed a law that enabled the auditor of public accounts to deny him his salary but were again thwarted in the spring of 1885 when the Supreme Court of Appeals ruled in Blair's favor after he sued for his pay.

Having achieved its main purpose of debt adjustment in 1882 and 1883, the Readjuster Party quickly disintegrated. Some of its leaders joined William Mahone and most of the African American members in moving to the Republican Party, while many white adherents returned to the Democratic Party. Blair joined the Republicans and served as a delegate to the Republican National Convention in 1884. A year later he ran for the gubernatorial nomination, but he lost to John Sergeant Wise and was instead nominated for reelection as the Republican candidate for attorney general. The Democrats carried the state in November 1885. After leading the Readjuster ticket in 1881, Blair trailed the Republican ticket in 1885 by a small fraction and lost to Rufus Adolphus Ayers by a margin of more than 16,000 votes out of more than 288,000 cast.

Blair returned to Wytheville and resumed the practice of law, with his son Robert William Blair becoming his partner in 1895. He remained active in the Republican Party and in 1888 was a candidate for presidential elector. Frank Simpson Blair died of complications of bronchitis at his home on 14 January 1899 and was buried in East End Cemetery in Wytheville.

Birth date in W. R. Chitwood, *Tombstone Inscriptions, East End Cemetery and St. Mary's Catholic Church Cemetery, Wytheville, Va.* (1977), 5; brief biographies in *Richmond Daily Whig*, 21 July 1885 (with 1843 year of birth), and Slemp and Preston, *Addresses*, 374; some letters in Leonidas Campbell Houk Papers, McClurg Historical Collection, Knox County Public Library, Knoxville, Tenn.; many letters in William Mahone Papers, Duke; Wythe Co. Marriage Register; election returns, 1881, 1885, Election Records, vol. 52, RG 13, LVA; *Reports of the Majority and Minority of the Special Committee of the House Appointed to Inquire What Sums Have Been Drawn From the Treasury by Attorney-General Blair* and *Report of the Special Committee of the House Appointed to Inquire What Sums Have Been Illegally Drawn From the Treasury*, Docs. 5 and 8 appended to *JHD*, 1884 sess.; salary dispute resolved in *Blair* v. *Marye* (1885), *Virginia Reports*, 80:485; obituaries in *Lynchburg News*, *Richmond Dispatch*, and *Richmond Times*, all 15 Jan. 1899 (with variant birth date of 16 Nov. 1839 in latter two), and *Norfolk Virginian-Pilot*, 15, 17 Jan. 1899; memorial in *Virginia State Bar Association Proceedings* (1899): 100–102 (with 6 Nov. 1839 birth date).

BRENT TARTER

BLAIR, Jacob Beeson (11 April 1821–12 February 1901), member of the House of Representatives, was born in Parkersburg, the second of three sons and second of four children of David Blair and Elizabeth Beeson Blair. His parents died in 1835, and Blair, who had attended the common schools of Parkersburg and worked as a carpenter's apprentice, completed his education by reading law in the Parkersburg office of his uncle John Jay Jackson. Blair practiced law from 1844 to 1856 in Ritchie County. He married Josephine A. Jackson on 21 November 1850, and they had two daughters before her death in 1856. He then moved back to Parkersburg, where his in-laws could supervise the care and education of his daughters and where with his brother-in-law William L. Jackson he practiced law.

Blair was a Unionist during the secession crisis, and following the resignation of Representative John J. Carlisle to become a member of the United States Senate, the voters elected Blair to the House of Representatives. Blair completed Carlisle's unexpired term, was reelected after West Virginia was admitted to the Union, and served in Congress from 2 December 1861 to 3 March 1865. He was best known for advocating the admission to the Union of the new state of West Virginia. He reportedly spent three hours with President Abraham Lincoln on 31 December 1862 attempting to persuade Lincoln to sign the West Virginia statehood bill. Blair returned to the White House early in the morning of 1 January 1863, and Lincoln informed him then that he had already signed the bill.

Blair did not run for reelection to Congress in 1864, but he won election in 1868 to the West Virginia House of Delegates for the district comprising Pleasants and Wood Counties. President Andrew Johnson appointed him U.S. minister to Costa Rica in 1868. Blair served in Costa Rica from October 1868 until the summer of 1873. Diplomatic service in Costa Rica was not arduous, but Blair maintained cordial relations with a succession of Costa Rican presidents who appeared to be plunging the nation into bankruptcy with railroad and canal construction schemes, some of which involved American promoters. Two years after Blair returned to the United States, President Ulysses S. Grant appointed him an associate justice of the supreme court of the territory of Wyoming. Blair moved to Laramie and lived there and served on the court from 14 February 1876 to 23 April 1888, when he retired to Salt Lake City, Utah. There he speculated in real estate, served from 1892 to 1895 as a probate judge for Salt Lake County, and from 1897 until his death was surveyor general of Utah. Jacob Beeson Blair died of a heart attack on 12 February 1901 and was buried in Mount Olivet Cemetery in Salt Lake City, Utah.

Family history in Stephen C. Shaw, *Historical Sketches of the Life and Character of the Hon. Jacob Beeson, an Early Pioneer of Wood County, Virginia (Now) West Virginia, and His Descendants* (1881), 8–9; George W. Atkinson and Alvarro F. Gibbens, *Prominent Men of West Virginia* (1890), 278–280 (por.); Wes Cochran, *Ritchie County, West Virginia, Marriages, 1843–1915* (1985), 5; manuscripts in Archibald W. Campbell Papers and John J. Davis Papers, WVU; diplomatic correspondence in *Papers Relating to the Foreign Relations of the United States* (1868–1873), with tenure summarized in 1873 vol., 1:210–212; A. C. Campbell, "Fading Memories," *Annals of Wyoming* 15 (1943): 39–45; obituaries in *Parkersburg Daily Morning News* and *Parkersburg Sentinel*, both 13 Feb. 1901, and *Parkersburg Daily State Journal* and *Salt Lake City Daily Tribune*, both 14 Feb. 1901.

GARY J. TUCKER

BLAIR, James (ca. 1655–18 April 1743), Anglican minister and member of the Council, was probably born in Edinburgh, Scotland, the eldest of three sons and four daughters of Peter Blair, a clergyman, and Mary Hamilton Blair. After beginning his formal education at Marischal College, Aberdeen, Blair studied at the University of Edinburgh from 1669 to 1673, when he received the degree of master of arts. He remained at Edinburgh for several additional years studying theology. In the summer of 1679 he was ordained by John Paterson, bishop of Edinburgh.

That same summer Blair was appointed minister at Cranstoun Parish, a few miles outside Edinburgh. He remained two and a half years, serving, according to the bishop, "with exemplary diligence, care and gravity," although a dispute with parish landowners over his reimbursement for repairs to the manse suggests that the combative nature that he later exhibited in Virginia was already well developed. In December 1681 Blair was removed from his parish after he refused to subscribe to a test oath that the Scottish Parliament imposed because it would have required him to accept the Roman Catholic duke of York as head of the Scottish church when he became king. Blair left for England, where he gained the support of Gilbert Burnet, a fellow Scottish cleric who later became bishop of Salisbury. Burnet secured Blair a clerkship in the Rolls Office and provided him an opportunity to meet other influential Anglican clerics, including Henry Compton, who as bishop of London had jurisdiction over the Anglican church in the American colonies. Compton persuaded Blair to accept an appointment in Virginia as rector of Henrico Parish (then frequently referred to as Varina Parish).

Blair's career advanced rapidly after his arrival in Virginia late in 1685. Preaching at other parish churches as well as at his own, he came to know and be known to members of the colony's most important families. Within two years he made the first of many land purchases, and on 2 June 1687 he married seventeen-year-old Sarah Harrison, of Surry County. The marriage was unhappy. At the wedding she adamantly refused to assent to the portion of the ceremony obliging her to obey her husband. They apparently had no children, and she may have become an alcoholic. Sarah Harrison Blair died on 5 May 1713, and James Blair lived another thirty years as a widower.

Blair's marriage brought him into the inner circle of the colony's leading families, and his relatives often dominated the influential governor's Council. His ecclesiastical career prospered. In mid-May 1690 a new lieutenant governor, Francis Nicholson, arrived in Virginia, bringing a commission of 15 December 1689 from Bishop Compton naming Blair commissary, or the bishop's representative with authority to preside over the Anglican clergy of the colony in administrative matters. Often thought to have been the first to hold that office in Virginia, Blair had in fact been preceded in the post by John Clayton.

Blair moved without delay to establish his authority by calling a convocation of the clergy for 23 July 1690. Neither his Scottish origins nor his tendency to side with the Virginia laity in religious affairs endeared him to the larger number of his fellow clerics, who often opposed him vigorously, especially in the infrequent convocations that he called. The convocations held in August 1705 and April 1719 proved particularly rancorous. In the latter meeting his fellow clergymen unsuccessfully challenged the validity of his ordination in Scotland, a move that could have lost him his influential positions as rector and commissary. Blair's initial convocation was more auspicious, however, for he there first advanced "Several Propositions" for the founding of a college in the colony and won enthusiastic support. In cooperation with Nicholson, who deserves to rank with Blair as a cofounder, he cultivated the support of Virginia's political leaders. By June 1691 Blair left for England to seek the backing of King William, Queen Mary, and others. His mission required almost two years and resulted in the grant of a royal charter for the College of William and Mary on 8 February 1693 as well as substantial public and private financial support.

Blair returned to Virginia in triumph. Named president for life in the charter, he launched the new college on land acquired at the crossroads settlement of Middle Plantation a few miles from the capital at Jamestown. His task was not easy. In his absence enthusiasm for the project had declined, and Sir Edmund Andros, the new governor, was openly hostile. Blair nonetheless managed to inaugurate one branch of the institution, its grammar school, and to commence construction of a building. Over Andros's objections Blair also secured a place on the Council, taking his seat for the first time on 18 July 1694. The next year he consolidated his position when he became rector of James City Parish, close to the seat of government as well as the new college. Blair's relations with the governor soon worsened, and following his public criticism of Andros and the other councillors, they suspended him on 26 April 1695. He was reinstated on 25 September 1696 but suspended again on 20 April 1697.

The infighting between Blair and Andros culminated in the summer of 1697 when, with financial and political backing from Francis Nicholson, Blair returned to England to present his grievances to ecclesiastical and political authorities. A key hearing before the archbishop of Canterbury and bishop of London was a one-sided affair with Blair able to speak in person to the sympathetic panel. The absent Andros was primarily represented by the young William Byrd (1674–1744), who was never allowed to deliver the lengthy brief he had prepared. On 31 May 1698 Andros was granted permission to resign and return to England on personal business.

During his English sojourn Blair collaborated with two other men experienced in the government of Virginia, Henry Hartwell and Edward Chilton, in preparing a long report for the newly created Board of Trade on the state of affairs of the colony and how to improve it. Published nearly thirty years later as *The Present State of Virginia, and the College* (1727), it quickly became one of the more influential contemporary books about the condition of Virginia and the lives of Virginians at the end of the seventeenth century.

Nicholson succeeded Andros as governor in December 1698 shortly after Blair's return to Virginia. Blair was eventually reappointed to the Council, taking his seat on 9 June 1701 and serving for the remainder of his life. Although he cooperated with Nicholson in 1699 in a successful effort to move the capital from Jamestown to Middle Plantation, which was renamed Williamsburg, the two equally imperious men came into conflict during the next few years. The ill will culminated in Blair's second trip to England to lobby for the removal of a governor. He left in 1703, bearing a petition that he and five other Council members had signed. Nicholson was at a distinct disadvantage due to his inability to appear in person, the death early in the hearings of his principal defender, and the capture by the French of the vessel carrying his supporting documentation. On 5 April 1705 the Board of Trade removed Nicholson as governor of Virginia.

Blair's success was, however, hardly complete. Nicholson remained a trustee of the college and continued with the support of most of Virginia's Anglican clergy to oppose Blair's direction of the college and his attempts to govern the colonial church. Then on 29 October 1705 the main college building caught fire and burned to its exterior walls. The resultant inquiry stirred further animosity between Blair and his opponents. In 1710 the death of one of his most outspoken clerical opponents, Solomon Whateley, afforded Blair the opportunity to become rector of Bruton Parish Church in Williamsburg, and for more than a decade he had no serious difficulty with Governor Edward Nott or his successor, Lieutenant Governor Alexander Spotswood. Blair used the time to solidify his position with Virginia political leaders. By that time, too, his brother Archibald Blair (by 1665–1733), a physician who had also immigrated to Virginia, had established himself as a successful Williamsburg merchant in a firm in which James Blair, to his considerable profit, became a silent partner.

Rebuilding the college was a more serious challenge, but Blair made the first of two rescues of William and Mary from the brink of failure. With the help of Spotswood and others, he found new money in England and America, began reconstruction of the college building that was first occupied by 1716 and largely completed by 1721, and for the first time expanded instruction beyond the grammar school by appointing a master of the Indian School and the first professor of natural philosophy and mathematics, Hugh Jones. As early as 1718 or 1719, however, Blair became embroiled in a controversy with Spotswood. The issues at stake had more to do with religious and political matters than with the college, and they again brought Blair into conflict with his fellow clerics, including the faculty. In 1721 he set off for England again. On this occasion, however, Spotswood was already in difficulty with his superiors on other grounds, and thus the commissary's role in his dismissal has often been overemphasized, adding to Blair's not entirely deserved reputation as a breaker of governors.

The trip afforded Blair an opportunity to arrange for publication in London of *Our Saviour's Divine Sermon on the Mount* (1722), a five-volume collection of 117 sermons he had delivered between 1707 and 1721. True to character, Blair was dissatisfied with sales, but the sermons were reprinted in four volumes in 1740 and in Danish in 1761. The sermons dealt more with matters of morality and personal conduct than with doctrine, a reminder that, despite his other concerns and interests, Blair was an active parish minister throughout his long career.

Blair was in his late sixties when he returned from England on the same ship with the new lieutenant governor, Hugh Drysdale. Blair appeared to be at the height of his power in the political establishment of Virginia. Yet despite its new building the college that he had founded and headed for more than three decades was once again on the verge of extinction, with a dearth of funds and students and a curriculum confined to precollegiate instruction in the grammar and Indian schools. Blair set to work and by the end of the 1720s had achieved nothing less than a second founding of the institution, helped again by a period in which few political issues diverted him from the task. A round of new construction added the Brafferton (1723) to house the Indian school and the library, a chapel wing on the main building (1732), and a president's house (1733). The crowning achievements, however, were the preparation of the first college statutes in 1727; the hiring for the first time of the full complement of six masters, including professors of moral and natural philosophy and divinity; and with those preconditions met, the transfer of the original charter of 1693 into the hands of the president and masters on 15 August 1729.

Blair was able to use his secure position in the social and political elite of Virginia to contribute significantly to the evolution of autonomous institutions in the colony. Rather than an outpost of imperial culture controlled by a largely English clerical faculty, under Blair's guidance William and Mary became a college governed primarily by prominent colonists who sat on its board of visitors and shaped it to serve their educational goals. Likewise, Blair's actions as commissary aided the development of an established Anglican church dominated by laymen who ran its parish vestries, a model that more closely resembled the operations of the church in Scotland during Blair's youth and ministry in that country than it did the functioning of the parent Church of England during the eighteenth century.

Blair's relations with Lieutenant Governor William Gooch, the last chief executive on whose Council he served, were amicable. Gooch's private opinion of Blair was negative, but he resolved to "kill him with kindness." By then Blair was declining in health and vigor. In his last years he retained all of his official positions as president of the college, commissary, parish rector, and councillor, although he was not always able to perform all of his duties. The senior member of the Council, Blair served as president (in effect, acting governor) from 15 October 1740 to July 1741 while Gooch was away on a military expedition to the West Indies.

The childless Blair had a sizable estate to dispose of when he composed his will in 1743. He made several charitable bequests, including £100 for teaching poor children and £500 for the education of a clergyman. He left his books to the library of the College of William and Mary and the remainder of his estate, estimated at £10,000, to his favorite nephew John Blair (ca. 1687–1771), whose education he had overseen. James Blair died in Williamsburg of a gangrenous rupture on 18 April 1743. He was buried beside his wife in the Jamestown churchyard.

Parke Rouse Jr., *James Blair of Virginia* (1971); Samuel R. Mohler, "Commissary James Blair, Churchman, Educator, and Politician of Colonial Virginia" (Ph.D. diss., Univ. of Chicago, 1940); parentage established and birth date conjectured in Daphne Gentry and Brent Tarter, "The Blair Family of Colonial Williamsburg: A Research Note," *Magazine of Virginia Genealogy* 32 (1994): 103–112; P. G. Scott,

"James Blair and the Scottish Church: A New Source," *WMQ*, 3d ser., 33 (1976): 300–308; Blair letters in Fulham Palace Papers, Lambeth Palace Library, Eng.; Edward L. Bond, "Anglican Theology and Devotion in James Blair's Virginia, 1685–1743: Private Piety in the Public Church," *VMHB* 104 (1996): 313–340; John C. Van Horne, ed., "The Correspondence of James Blair as Acting Governor of Virginia, 1740–1741," *VMHB* 84 (1976): 19–48; Susan H. Godson et al., *The College of William and Mary: A History* (1993), 1:3–80 (frontispiece por.); J. E. Morpurgo, *Their Majesties' Royall Colledge: William and Mary in the Seventeenth and Eighteenth Centuries* (1976), 22–110; terms of lost will described in 24 Feb. 1748 annual audit of William Prentis's Williamsburg store, Webb-Prentis Family Papers, UVA; death described in William Gooch to bishop of London, 10 May 1743, in William Stevens Perry, *Papers Relating to the History of the Church in Virginia, A.D. 1650–1776* (1870), 367.

THAD W. TATE

BLAIR, John (ca. 1687–5 November 1771), president of the Council, was the only recorded son of Archibald Blair and his first wife, whose name is not known. He was born in Scotland before his father immigrated to Virginia in the 1690s. He was educated at the College of William and Mary and lived virtually all of his life in Williamsburg.

Blair was a manager of the mercantile house in Williamsburg known as Dr. Blair's Store, of which his father was the largest shareholder, until Archibald Blair died in 1733. For about fourteen years during the 1740s and 1750s Blair was a partner of John Blair Jr., the son of a cousin, in another Williamsburg store. The names of John Blair and John Blair Jr. often appear together in the records of York County. Blair also owned several valuable properties in Williamsburg, including the Raleigh Tavern, which he rented to a succession of tavern keepers and sold in 1742, and the Chowning Tavern, which he owned from 1726 to sometime before 1739. In 1745 Blair and seventeen other men received a grant for one hundred thousand acres of land on the Potomac and Youghiogheny Rivers.

Blair's long and distinguished public career may have begun as early as 1715, when he or a namesake cousin was named keeper of the royal storehouse in Williamsburg. Blair took the oaths of office as a justice of the peace for York County on 17 August 1724 and served until he was sworn in as a member of the governor's Council more than two decades later. He was appointed naval officer for the upper district of the James River on 5 February 1727 and held that post until he became deputy auditor general on 15 August 1728. Blair remained deputy auditor until his death. He succeeded his father as burgess for Jamestown in 1734, and he represented Williamsburg from 1736 to 1740. He was probably the John Blair who served as mayor of Williamsburg in 1751. He also served as a vestryman of Bruton Parish beginning at least as early as 1744, was a churchwarden about 1749, and was a visitor of the College of William and Mary in 1758. Blair served as clerk of the governor's Council from 22 April 1741 until 15 October 1741, during part of which his uncle James Blair was acting governor.

In February 1745 Governor William Gooch recommended that John Blair be appointed to a vacant seat on the Council. Gooch had not recommended him earlier because Blair "was in narrow Circumstances," but with his inheritance of approximately £10,000 from James Blair, he had become "a proper Person to have a Seat at that Board." Unknown to Gooch, on 15 November 1744 the king had already named Blair to the Council to fill a different vacancy. Blair took his seat on 6 August 1745 and served until 15 October 1770. In August 1757 he became the senior member, or president, of the Council and as such served as acting governor on four occasions: from the departure of Robert Dinwiddie on 12 January 1758 to the arrival of Francis Fauquier on 5 June 1758; in September and October 1761 while Fauquier was in New York to consult with General Jeffery Amherst; from late in September until early in December 1763 during Fauquier's absence in Georgia; and from the death of Fauquier on 4 March 1768 to the arrival of Norborne Berkeley, baron de Botetourt, on 26 October 1768. When Botetourt died on 15 October 1770, Blair would have become acting governor a fifth time, but because of his old age and ill health he resigned from the Council that day. The Council later petitioned the king to grant Blair a pension, citing his long service and the "moderate Estate" from which he had to support his large family, but the king and Privy Council took no action before Blair's death.

During his first term as acting governor, Blair called the General Assembly into session.

In response to his address to the assembly on 31 March 1758 relaying the ministry's request that Virginia raise an additional force for offensive operations against the French in the Ohio Valley, the assembly voted to create a second regiment. In March 1768, during his last term as acting governor, Blair again called the General Assembly into session, as Fauquier had intended to do. After the session closed in April, Blair transmitted to London the assembly's addresses to the king and Parliament challenging the asserted right of Parliament to tax the colonies. The addresses so offended the ministry that Botetourt was speedily appointed governor of Virginia and sent to Williamsburg with instructions to put a stop to such protests. During his last term as acting governor Blair also learned that a fire had destroyed a convent and eighty-eight houses in Montreal, and at his urging the clergymen of Virginia raised £360 sterling in a special collection to aid the victims.

The post that Blair held the longest was deputy auditor general. During forty-three years in this office he was responsible for examining and certifying the accuracy of the accounts of the royal revenues, which included quitrents and the tax of two shillings per hogshead on exported tobacco. Blair reformed the procedures and improved the record keeping in the auditor's office in order to thwart the schemes some Virginians had used to avoid paying quitrents. Probably because of his poor health and the death of his assistant, Blair did not manage his office well during the last two years of his life, and when his namesake son became deputy auditor in 1771 the accounts were in chaos.

Blair served on the committee of three councillors and six burgesses appointed in 1745 to revise the laws of Virginia. He also belonged to a committee that oversaw the rebuilding of the Capitol after it burned in 1747, to another appointed in 1763 to correspond with Virginia's London agent, and to the board of trustees of the public hospital for lunatics established in 1769. Blair had the unique distinction of participating in bricklaying ceremonies for both of the Capitol buildings erected in Williamsburg.

Blair's only known marriage was to his first cousin Mary Munro about 1726. They had at least eight daughters and four sons. Their fourth child, also named John Blair, became an associate justice of the United States Supreme Court. John Blair died in Williamsburg on 5 November 1771 and was buried in Bruton Parish churchyard.

Daphne Gentry and Brent Tarter, "The Blair Family of Colonial Williamsburg: A Research Note," *Magazine of Virginia Genealogy* 32 (1994): 103–112; extensive documentation on family and business affairs and public service in research files of CW; inheritance mentioned in William Gooch to Board of Trade, PRO CO 5/1326, fol. 140; 1751 diary, in VHS, printed in *WMQ*, 1st ser., 7 (1899): 134–153; 8 (1899): 1–17; letters as acting governor in PRO CO 5/18, 5/70, 5/1329, 5/1346, 5/1372, in PRO War Office 34/37, and in Washington, *Colonial Series*, vol. 5; York Co. Wills, 22:44–47; age at death in obituary in *Williamsburg Virginia Gazette* (Purdie and Dixon), 7 Nov. 1771.

JOHN C. VAN HORNE

BLAIR, John (November 1731–31 August 1800), member of the Convention of 1776, member of the Federal Convention of 1787, and associate justice of the United States Supreme Court, was the second of four sons and fourth of at least twelve children of John Blair (ca. 1687–1771) and Mary Munro Blair. He was born in Williamsburg, where his father served for more than twenty-five years as a member of the governor's Council and was four times acting governor of the colony. He attended the College of William and Mary and on 2 June 1753 was admitted to the Middle Temple in London, where he studied law and from which he was called to the bar on 20 May 1757. On 26 December 1756 in Edinburgh, Scotland, he married his cousin Jean Blair. They had at least one son and at least four daughters.

John Blair practiced law as a member of the bar of the General Court in Williamsburg from 1757 to 1770 and represented the College of William and Mary in the House of Burgesses from 1766 to 1770. He served on the House committee that in April 1768 produced strongly worded resolutions questioning the asserted right of Parliament to tax the colonies, and in May 1769 he presided over the burgesses during the sessions of the committee of the whole house that prepared an address to the king that condemned parliamentary policies with such force that Governor Botetourt dissolved the assembly. Botetourt appointed Blair clerk of the governor's Council in August 1770, and after the death of Blair's father in 1771, he succeeded him as deputy auditor of the royal revenue in Virginia. Blair gave up his law practice after he became clerk of the Council, and he held the clerk's and deputy auditor's offices until the royal government collapsed in 1775.

On 20 January 1776 the Virginia Convention of 1775–1776 named Blair one of three commissioners of admiralty to enforce the trade regulations that the Virginia convention had adopted. The two or three remaining faculty members of the College of William and Mary chose him on 8 April 1776 to represent them in the Convention of 1776, at which he served on the committee that prepared the Virginia Declaration of Rights and the Virginia Constitution of 1776. The convention elected him to the Council of State, on which he served for a year and a half.

In October 1777 the General Assembly appointed Blair to the General Court. He served on the court for three years, and in 1779 and 1780 was its senior member. On 23 November 1780 the assembly elected him to the High Court of Chancery. During the years 1783–1785 Blair and his fellow chancellors Edmund Pendleton and George Wythe prepared an edition of the Virginia statutes that became known as the Chancellors' Revisal, although it was a compilation, not a revision, of the laws. As a member of the General Court and of the High Court of Chancery, Blair belonged ex officio to the Virginia Court of Appeals. One of the most influential decisions that court rendered during Blair's tenure was in *Commonwealth* v. *Posey* (1787) (4 Call), *Virginia Reports*, 8:109, in which Blair joined a majority of the judges in ruling that established precedents of the English common law, handed down before the American Revolution, should be accepted in the courts of Virginia.

An earlier but equally important case heard by Blair as a member of the Court of Appeals was *Commonwealth* v. *Caton* (1782) (4 Call), *Virginia Reports*, 8:5, which raised the issue of judicial review, asking whether the court's power extended to striking down legislative acts that it deemed unconstitutional. The published report of the case indicates that Blair concurred in Wythe's assertion of the right of judicial review, but according to Pendleton's notes Blair took no position on the issue. In May 1788, however, Blair implicitly endorsed judicial review when he joined the other judges of the Court of Appeals in a remonstrance to the General Assembly and declared that a statute that had increased the duties and responsibilities of the judges without a corresponding increase in their salaries infringed unconstitutionally on the independence of the judiciary. The judges requested that the assembly revise the law, and in December 1788, following a reorganization of the state's judiciary, the assembly appointed Blair one of the first judges of the new Court of Appeals.

Blair was one of the Virginia delegates to the constitutional convention that met in Philadelphia in 1787. He did not speak on the floor of the convention insofar as the extant records disclose. He signed the Constitution of the United States and in 1788 represented York County in the Virginia ratification convention. He made no recorded speeches and voted for unconditional ratification, although he served on the committee that recommended amendments to the Constitution.

In the summer of 1789 President George Washington appointed Blair to the new United States Supreme Court. He was sworn in on 30 September 1789 as one of the first associate justices, but his frequent illnesses and the sickness of his wife, who died on 22 November 1792, caused him to miss many of the sessions of the Supreme Court during the early years, which fortunately were not busy ones. Blair presided at trials as a circuit court judge, holding court between 1789 and 1795 in twelve states. In an important Pennsylvania case, *Collet* v. *Collet* (1792) (2 Dallas), *United States Reports*, 2:294, Blair concurred in the opinions of the other circuit court judges that the state was free to enact a naturalization law even though the Constitution also granted Congress that power. In Essex, New Hampshire, Blair made his most important ruling as a circuit judge in *Penhallow et al.* v. *Doane's Administrators* (1795) (3 Dallas),

United States Reports, 3:54, a decision subsequently appealed to the Supreme Court. At the trial and in his opinion on appeal, Blair ruled that by investing Congress with the power to make war, the states had also given it the authority to create a court of admiralty that could overturn decisions of the state admiralty courts. On appeal Blair agreed to reduce the damages he had awarded at the trial, but the Supreme Court affirmed his opinion about the power of Congress.

The most controversial case in which Blair participated while on the Supreme Court was *Chisholm* v. *Georgia* (1793) (2 Dallas), *United States Reports*, 2:419. He and the other justices ruled that the Constitution allowed a citizen of one state to bring suit in federal court against the government of another state. Blair based his opinion entirely on the wording of the Constitution and dismissed as irrelevant the political theories and legal history that some other judges used in reaching the same conclusion. The outcome of the case was so unpopular that in order to overturn it Congress proposed and the state legislatures quickly ratified the Eleventh Amendment to the Constitution.

John Blair resigned from the Supreme Court on 25 October 1795 because of his poor health. Although he took little part in partisan politics, he was recognized as a Federalist. In May 1797 he served as foreman of a federal grand jury that met in Richmond and at the prompting of Justice James Iredell declared that the circular letters of Virginia congressman Samuel Jordan Cabell, which had denounced the election of John Adams to the presidency and deplored the possibility of war with France, were "a real evil" that tended "to encrease or produce a foreign influence ruinous to the peace, happiness and independence of the United States." The declaration outraged many prominent Virginia Republicans. John Blair died at his home in Williamsburg on 31 August 1800 and was buried in the churchyard of Bruton Parish church.

Biography and family letters in Frederick Horner, *The History of the Blair, Banister, and Braxton Families* (1898), 64–79 (por.); other biographies in Hugh Blair Grigsby, *The Virginia Convention of 1776* (1855), 70–75, and J. Elliott Drinard, "John Blair, Jr., 1732–1800," *Virginia State Bar Association Proceedings* (1927): 436–449; Daphne Gentry and Brent Tarter, "The Blair Family of Colonial Williamsburg: A Research Note," *Magazine of Virginia Genealogy* 32 (1994): 103–112; Francis J. Grant, ed., *Register of Marriages of the City of Edinburgh, 1751–1800* (1922), 65; David John Mays, ed., *The Letters and Papers of Edmund Pendleton, 1734–1803* (1967), 2:416–427, 504–509; Kaminski, *Ratification*, 10:1539–1540, 1565; Supreme Court service, official letters, and 1797 grand jury episode in Maeva Marcus et al., eds., *Documentary History of the Supreme Court of the United States, 1789–1800* (1985–); por. by Charles Willson Peale in LC; will in *Peachy* v. *Henderson* (1821) case file, Superior Court of Chancery, Staunton; date of death and age at death from gravestone inscription, *Bruton Parish Churchyard and Church: A Guide to the Tombstones, Monuments, and Mural Tablets* (1976), 52; obituary in *Norfolk Herald*, 4 Sept. 1800, reprinted in *Richmond Virginia Gazette, and General Advertiser*, 5 Sept. 1800, and *Richmond Virginia Argus*, 9 Sept. 1800.

MARK F. FERNANDEZ

BLAIR, John Durburrow (15 October 1759–10 January 1823), Presbyterian minister, was born at Fagg's Manor, Chester County, Pennsylvania, one of twelve children, of whom four sons and three daughters reached adulthood, of John Blair, a Presbyterian minister and teacher, and Elizabeth Durburrow Blair. He was probably educated in his father's academy at Fagg's Manor, after which he entered the College of New Jersey (now Princeton University), where his father had been a professor of divinity from 1769 to 1771. Blair graduated from the college in 1775 and for the next five years taught school in New Jersey or New York. He may also have served briefly in the Revolutionary War.

Blair became a teacher at Washington-Henry Academy in Hanover County in 1780. He taught there for ten years and served as president from 14 January 1782 to 3 December 1790. He also studied theology, and on 28 October 1784 the Hanover Presbytery licensed him to preach. He served as minister of Pole Green Church in Hanover County from sometime in 1785 until 1821. After he moved to Richmond about the end of 1790 he conducted services at Pole Green Church only once or twice a month. The Presbyterians of Richmond were not organized as a church, and Blair required them to attend services at Pole Green for the performance of the sacraments.

On 4 March 1785 Blair married Mary Winston, a daughter of Geddes Winston, one of the wealthiest men in Richmond. They had two daughters and six sons. Blair enjoyed the social pleasures and comforts to which his marriage introduced him. A jovial and fun-loving man, he took a lively and conspicuous part in Richmond's social life. He also conducted small academies for boys and for girls in Richmond, but in 1796 he declined an invitation to become president of Hampden-Sydney College. He was a founder of the Bible Society of Virginia in 1813 and served as its second president. Blair was elected president of the Richmond Library Society in 1814.

Blair was an urbane rationalist and a popular minister who often departed from his prepared texts and spoke informally and wittily from the pulpit. On 2 December 1799 the House of Delegates elected him its chaplain and reelected him in 1800 and 1801, but a Baptist minister, John Courtney, was elected chaplain in 1802. Blair's sermon, "On the Death of Washington," preached at the request of the House of Delegates in January 1800, was one of the few of his sermons published during his life. After his death his widow arranged for the publication of a substantial volume, *Sermons Collected from the Manuscripts of the Late Rev. John D. Blair* (1825).

For many of his years in Richmond, Blair preached to the Presbyterians of the city in the Henrico Parish Church or in the Virginia Capitol, alternating Sunday services with John Buchanan, the Episcopal pastor of the parish. Blair and Buchanan became fast friends, and the unmarried Buchanan spent much time as a guest in Blair's household. They shared a taste for puns and for writing doggerel verse, and they did not let their differences over forms of church governance disturb their friendship. Both men preached religious tolerance and advocated the use of music in church services, which placed them at odds with some of the Baptists and Methodists of the city. They were the only clergymen who belonged to the Richmond Quoit Club, which met for drink and games and fellowship at Buchanan's farm.

Following the fire in the Richmond Theatre on 26 December 1811 that killed seventy-six people, Blair and Buchanan led the movement to construct Monumental Church on the site of the disaster, probably with the hope that they and their congregations would share the church. The more numerous Episcopalians eventually appropriated the building for themselves, an action that finally led the Presbyterians to erect the first Presbyterian church in Richmond, which was completed in 1821.

The reputation of Blair and Buchanan as friends and as joint representatives of an era of genial tolerance in ecclesiastical matters was well known to their contemporaries and was embellished many years later in George Wythe Munford's *The Two Parsons* (1884). Because of the winning personalities of the two principals and Munford's nostalgic prose style, the book's interpretation of Richmond's early history became popular. John Durburrow Blair died at his home in Richmond on 10 January 1823, about three weeks after Buchanan had died, and was buried in Shockoe Cemetery.

Richard A. Harrison, *Princetonians, 1769–1775: A Biographical Dictionary* (1980), 452–456 (por.); Sprague, *American Pulpit*, 3:459–462; Louisa Coleman Gordon Blair, *Blairs of Richmond, Virginia: The Descendants of Reverend John Durburrow Blair and Mary Winston Blair, His Wife* (1933); Blair letters in Munford-Ellis Family Papers, Duke, and Robert A. Brock Collection, Henry E. Huntington Library, San Marino, Calif.; Washington-Henry Academy Trustees' Minutes, 14 Jan. 1782–3 Dec. 1790, 14 May 1802, LVA; Hall, *Portraits*, 27–28 (por.); obituaries in *Richmond Compiler* and *Richmond Enquirer*, both 11, 14 Jan. 1823, and *Evangelical and Literary Magazine* 4 (1823): 51–54.

MAURICE DUKE

BLAIR, Lewis Harvie (21 June 1834–26 November 1916), author, was born in Richmond, the sixth of eight sons and eleventh of thirteen children of John Geddes Blair and Sara Ann Eyre Heron Blair. His paternal grandfather was the eminent Presbyterian clergyman John Durburrow Blair, and his maternal grandfather, James Heron, was a prosperous merchant engaged in trade with the West Indies. His father, a loyal Whig and veteran of the War of 1812, was a longtime cashier at the Farmers Bank of Virginia.

Blair attended several private schools in the Richmond area, but his education was somewhat indifferent, and when he left school after his father's death in 1851 he had not gone beyond trigonometry, Cicero, and the rudiments of Greek. A lifetime of reading provided his real education. Blair went to Texas, where his elder brother William Blair, an army captain, had obtained a position for him as a civilian clerk with the army. After four years Blair returned to Richmond to work for another brother, John Blair, in a dry goods firm. In 1857 he went to Detroit, Michigan, where he again worked as an army clerk until 1860.

After the Civil War began Blair bided his time until, threatened by the Conscription Act of 1862, he enlisted on 22 March of that year so that he could select his branch of service. He chose the artillery and in spite of his family connections declined to seek a commission. Entering Company A, 13th Battalion Virginia Light Artillery as a private, he was slightly wounded later in 1862 but spent much of the war detailed as a clerk. He emerged from the military at war's end still a private and with a record of challenging authority, engaging in fistfights, and spending time in stockade confinement. He later pronounced his years in the Confederate army a waste of time "in the vain effort to maintain that most monstrous institution, African slavery."

Back in Richmond, Blair used a $20 greenback from his mother to start a wholesale auction business. For three years he ran a retail store in Amelia County, and in 1868, $7,000 richer, he returned to Richmond and entered the wholesale grocery business. On 5 August 1867 he married Alice Wayles Harrison in Amelia County. They had six sons and one daughter.

Success followed with a Midas-like touch, in Blair's grocery business, as treasurer of the Stephen Putney Shoe Company, and as owner of one of the largest real-estate businesses in Richmond. Always independent, outspoken, and opinionated, he maintained views on politics, social questions, and the economy that almost always differed from those of Virginia's established families and dominant leaders. Although a grandson of one of Richmond's most distinguished clergyman, Blair had no interest in religion and belonged to no church. He frequently contributed letters to the Richmond newspapers, mostly on economic subjects. An advocate of free trade, unlike many other businessmen, he deplored the high tariffs of the late nineteenth century. In 1886 he published *Unwise Laws: A Consideration of the Operations of a Protective Tariff upon Industry, Commerce, and Society*. The book received mixed, but generally good, reviews in several minor newspapers.

Blair also wrote to the newspapers about the New South, a South of industry, banking, mining, and business, as opposed to the Old South of slavery, cotton, and tobacco. In a series of articles for the *New York Independent* in 1887, Blair declared that the New South was a mere figment of the imagination of such promoters as Atlanta's Henry W. Grady. He conceded that much progress toward an industrial South had been made since 1865, but only in a few places, such as Birmingham and Chattanooga. Elsewhere lay only squalor, poverty, and rural hopelessness. Northern industry, meanwhile, had grown by leaps and bounds and spread into the rural Midwest, leaving the South in about the same position in riches that it had been in with regard to the North in 1860.

Blair asked why this was so. Arguing that the South surely did not lack natural resources or intellectual ingenuity, he concluded that the region lagged behind because it persisted in treating African Americans, one-third of its population, as second-class citizens and virtual serfs on the land, with poor and racially segregated schools that could not prepare them for productive contributions to southern life. Blair marshaled and polished his arguments, added to them, and published *The Prosperity of the South Dependent upon the Elevation of the Negro* (1889). The heart of his argument was that it made good business sense for the South to treat African Americans decently and to educate all of its citizens well.

The volume was well received nationally, with highly favorable reviews in newspapers from New York to San Francisco. The *Chicago Tribune* called it "the most remarkable contribution from the South upon the race problem which has yet appeared," and the *New York Tribune* declared that "if there were more Blairs in the South," a truly "New South" might come about. He accepted an invitation to speak to the African Congress held in Chicago in 1893 in connection with the World's Columbian Exposition but was unable to attend, and his address on "The Southern Problem and its Solution" was read to the gathering on his behalf. Blair continued to speak out on public issues. His pamphlet on monetary policy, *A Standard of Value, Considered in its Relation to the Currency* (1893), dealt with one of the most-debated political topics of the decade.

Many white Richmonders were appalled at the heretical *Prosperity of the South*. Newspapers refused to review it, and Blair experienced social ostracism. Such isolation scarcely bothered him, however, since he had no social interests, was affiliated with no church, and neither smoked nor drank, either privately or in any of Richmond's clubs. His business, his family, his constant reading, and his writing were his only true interests.

Blair's wife died on 5 February 1894, and during the next four years he concentrated on his business affairs and wrote an autobiography that he never attempted to publish. On 27 October 1898 he married a widow, Martha Ruffin Feild, of Mecklenburg County. They had four daughters.

Sometime between 1898 and 1915 Blair completely reversed himself on the race question. He remained progressive in thought otherwise and supported the reforms undertaken by President Woodrow Wilson, but like many of his progressive contemporaries in the North, he turned against African Americans. In an unpublished manuscript that repudiated just about everything he had written in *Prosperity of the South*, Blair proclaimed "the humblest Caucasian" to be "the superior of the highest African or half-breed." The black, he declared, was a "very different being," the product of his "African nature and antecedents." What, then, was the place of blacks in the South? "Absolute subordination to the whites," he wrote.

The only explanation Blair offered for this complete reversal of the views he had boldly expressed only a few years before was his simple statement in a letter to a New York friend that "I think I reasoned logically from my premises, but since then, experience and observation have convinced me of the fallacy of my premises." He also revised the autobiography he had written earlier, turning it into the harmless, antiquarian musings of an old man, devoid of insights into his radical change of mind on the most important public issue of his time.

Wealthy, worshiped by his second wife, Blair lived out his remaining years among the choice oil paintings and fine eighteenth-century Chinese porcelain that he had collected for his plush residence on Richmond's fashionable Monument Avenue. Lewis Harvie Blair died of a heart attack at his home in Richmond on 26 November 1916 and was buried in that city's Hollywood Cemetery.

Charles E. Wynes, "Lewis Harvie Blair, Virginia Reformer: The Uplift of the Negro and Southern Prosperity," *VMHB* 72 (1964): 3–18 (por. opp. 3); two unpublished autobiographies in possession of Blair family; Louisa Coleman Gordon Blair, *Blairs of Richmond, Virginia: The Descendants of Reverend John Durburrow Blair and Mary Winston Blair, His Wife* (1933), 10–11, 21–22; Tyler, *Men of Mark*, 4:32–34 (por.); Compiled Service Records; BVS Marriage Register, Amelia Co.; C. Vann Woodward, *A Southern Prophecy: The Prosperity of the South Dependent upon the Elevation of the Negro* (1964), esp. xi–xlvi; Lewis Harvie Blair, "The Southern Problem and Its Solution," *Our Day* 12 (1893): 361–376; obituaries in *Richmond News Leader* and *Richmond Times-Dispatch*, both 27 Nov. 1916.

CHARLES E. WYNES

BLAIR, Maria (August 1841–1 April 1924), educator and civic leader, was born in Richmond, the younger of two children, both daughters, of Thomas Rutherfoord Blair and Margaret Edmundson Blair. Her mother died in 1842, and after the death of her father in 1846, Blair went to live with her uncle and guardian Walter Dabney Blair, a successful wholesale grocer, in a house on East Leigh Street that had been built by Maria Blair's grandfather John Durburrow Blair, a prominent Presbyterian minister. She lived there with members of her extended family for nearly sixty years.

Blair received her education at the Southern Female Institute, one of Richmond's most distinguished private schools for girls, graduating in 1858 with a specialty in literature. During the next fifteen years she probably assisted at home with the care of her aging uncle and aunt and took part in the activities of Richmond's growing Presbyterian women's organizations, such as the Ladies' Society of the Second Presbyterian

Church or the Circle of Industry, later the Ladies' Industrial Society, within her own United (later Grace Street) Presbyterian Church.

Sometime in the mid-1870s Blair opened a school for girls in her Leigh Street residence, moving it in 1882 to a location nearby on North Seventh Street. She closed this school in 1884 and sometime in the next few years joined the faculty of the prestigious Richmond Female Seminary, where she taught literature and the history of art until 1897, with the exception of the 1894–1895 school year, when she taught at Mary Johnson's private school on West Grace Street. For the twenty-seven years from 1897 until her death, Blair gave private classes on art, literature, and European culture in her home to young women studying for college entrance examinations or interested in continuing education. Many of her classes prepared young women and men for travel abroad. In the 1890s and early in the 1900s, Blair often accompanied groups of Richmonders making their grand tour of Europe, serving as a guide to the major cultural and historic points of interest. Between 1903 and 1906 she supplemented her income by teaching part time in a school founded by one of her former students, Virginia Randolph Ellett, which later became Saint Catherine's School.

Blair became increasingly active in Richmond's Presbyterian community in the 1880s and 1890s. In 1885 she volunteered to assist Moses Drury Hoge, pastor of the Second Presbyterian Church, with a mission church that he had established in a working-class neighborhood centered on Seventeenth and Main Streets. For years Blair taught Bible classes for women there, taking a particular interest in young girls who worked in local factories, and she spent many hours a week visiting the homes of needy families in the area surrounding the Old Market Mission. In 1890 the mission was organized into an independent church, eventually known as Hoge Memorial Church, and Blair transferred her membership to the new congregation. She took a strong interest in the movement to tie together the many local women's missionary societies in eastern Virginia into what became in 1888 the Woman's Foreign Missionary Union of East Hanover Presbytery. In 1894 she spoke at numerous churches in the presbytery encouraging other churchwomen to organize and affiliate with the new union.

Perhaps encouraged by the success of the church groups to which she belonged, Blair helped create several women's cultural clubs in Richmond. In March 1894 she became a charter member of the Saturday Afternoon Club, a literary discussion group for women that included many notable Richmond writers, educators, and community leaders. Later that same year she joined Mary-Cooke Branch Munford, Jane Crawford Looney Lewis, and eleven other prominent Richmonders in founding the Woman's Club, which quickly became one of the largest and most influential women's organizations in the state. Blair served as vice president of the club from its founding until March 1897. In 1906 the club established an honorary membership category for "distinguished literary women" and selected Blair along with novelists Ellen Glasgow and Mary Johnston. Blair also claimed to have been instrumental, behind the scenes, in encouraging Richmond women to start the Every Monday Club and other cultural and voluntary associations.

Despite her public accomplishments in literary and educational circles, Blair remained a staunch traditionalist regarding the role of women in political life. She steadfastly opposed extending the right to vote to women, serving about 1917 as a vice president of the Virginia Association Opposed to Woman Suffrage.

During a thirty-five-year career teaching middle- and upper-class Richmonders, Blair earned a reputation as one of the city's premier educators and intellectuals. A petite woman with a gentle and charming manner, she was a gifted lecturer who could hold an audience spellbound. Blair was in great demand as a public speaker and traveled throughout eastern Virginia addressing women's clubs, church groups, patriotic societies, and community organizations. She continued to lecture until a few years before her death and collected and published several of her favorite lectures as *Art and Historical Lectures Given by Miss Maria Blair* (1921). Maria Blair died of apoplexy in her apartment in Richmond on 1 April 1924 and was buried in Shockoe Cemetery.

Edward Alvey Jr., "Maria Blair: 'A Gentlewoman of Another School,'" *Richmond Quarterly* 5 (fall 1982): 42–45; Louisa Coleman Gordon Blair, *Blairs of Richmond, Virginia: The Descendants of Reverend John Durburrow Blair and Mary Winston Blair, His Wife* (1933), 49, 122; Wyndham B. Blanton, *The Making of a Downtown Church: The History of the Second Presbyterian Church, Richmond, Virginia, 1845–1945* (1945), 146, 165–166, 171, 192, 386, 413–414; Lucy C. Cole, *History of Woman's Work in the East Hanover Presbytery* (1938), 84; Margaret Meagher, *History of Education in Richmond* (1939), 83, 85; records of Woman's Club (por.), Every Monday Club, and Saturday Afternoon Club, all in VHS; Sandra Gioia Treadway, *Women of Mark: A History of The Woman's Club of Richmond, Virginia, 1894–1994* (1995); several Blair letters in Bagby Family Papers and Ellett–Saint Catherine's Alumnae Association Papers, VHS; age at death of eighty-two years, seven months, in Shockoe Cemetery Interment Register; year of birth on tombstone; variant birth date of Aug. 1843 in Census, Richmond City, 1900; obituary in *Richmond News Leader*, 1 Apr. 1924 (por.); obituary and editorial tribute in *Richmond Times-Dispatch*, 2 Apr. 1924.

SANDRA GIOIA TREADWAY

BLAIR, Robert William (22 January 1873–8 June 1924), member of the Convention of 1901–1902, was born in Wytheville, the fourth of five sons and fourth of six children of Francis Simpson Blair and Sallie K. Pierce Blair. His father was a prominent attorney who later became attorney general of Virginia and a leader of the Republican Party. Blair attended the University of Virginia and graduated from its law school in 1895. He returned to Wytheville, joined his father's law practice, and soon became chairman of the Wythe County Republican Party.

On 8 April 1901 the Republicans nominated Blair for the county's seat in that year's constitutional convention and adopted forceful resolutions opposing most of the stated reasons for holding the convention, specifically proposals to disfranchise black Virginians. In the 23 May election Blair narrowly defeated the Democratic candidate, county judge John Hall Fulton, 1,492 to 1,469. Blair was one of only a dozen Republicans in the hundred-member convention, and one of the youngest members as well. He therefore had scant opportunity to influence the outcome. Though Blair seldom spoke except on the most important issues, he made a strong speech on 13 February 1902 condemning most of the work of the convention, and he argued for several hours on 4 April against the restrictive suffrage provisions that the convention adopted later that day. He voted against adoption of the constitution on 6 June 1902. Blair's most prominent moment occurred on 19 September 1901 when, on behalf of the Republican members, he eulogized William McKinley during the convention's memorial service for the assassinated president.

In the meantime the Republican state convention meeting in Roanoke had nominated Blair for lieutenant governor of Virginia on 21 August 1901. He was under the thirty-year age limit for the office, and after enduring tongue-in-cheek Democratic remarks that he would indeed be of an age to serve before a Republican could ever be elected, Blair withdrew on 3 September. In about 1907 Blair took a job with the United States Bureau of Internal Revenue and moved to Richmond, where he lived for a year and joined the Richmond Light Infantry Blues. He was then transferred to Cincinnati, where he continued to participate in the National Guard. During World War I he served as a captain in the 85th Division's motor transportation corps.

Following his discharge in 1919, Blair moved to Detroit, Michigan, where he resumed the practice of law and continued to serve in the army reserves, reaching the rank of lieutenant colonel. Early in the 1920s he and his wife, Eva Blair, bought a house in Windsor, Ontario. While boarding a yacht that was to take him to the Republican National Convention in Cleveland, Robert William Blair fell into the Detroit River and drowned on 8 June 1924. His body was recovered two days later and buried in East End Cemetery in Wytheville.

Brief biographies in *Richmond Dispatch*, 12 June 1901, and Slemp and Preston, *Addresses*, 433; *Marion News*, 12 Apr. 1901; *Roanoke Times*, 25 May 1901; Election Records, vol. 47, RG 13, LVA; *Proceedings and Debates of 1901–1902 Convention*, 1:485–486, 2:2405–2406, 3116–3139; *Convention of 1901–1902 Photographs* (por.); McKinley eulogy in *Richmond Dispatch* and *Richmond Times*, both 20 Sept. 1901, and reprinted in Slemp and Preston, *Addresses*, 434–437; nomination for lieutenant governor and withdrawal reported in *Richmond Dispatch*, 22 Aug. 1901, and *Richmond Times*, 22 Aug., 4 Sept. 1901; obituaries and reports on death in *Detroit News*, 9, 10 June 1924; *Windsor (Ont.) Border Cities Star*, 9 June 1924, *Detroit Free Press*, 10 (por.), 11 June 1924, and *Richmond Times-Dispatch* and *Roanoke Times*, both 10 June 1924.

BRENT TARTER

BLAIR, Walter (10 November 1835–12 September 1909), educator and classical scholar, was born in Richmond, the elder of two sons and second of three children of Walter Dabney Blair and his second wife, Louisa Edmonia Wills Blair. By his father's first marriage he had two half brothers and a half sister. His paternal grandfather was Richmond's most famous early Presbyterian minister, John Durburrow Blair, and his father was a prosperous merchant and social leader.

Blair was a precocious student who went at age fifteen to the school conducted by his father's cousin Robert Lewis Dabney at Tinkling Spring in Augusta County. After three years there he entered the junior class at Hampden-Sydney College in 1853 and graduated second in his class with a B.A. in 1855. The faculty immediately engaged him as an instructor in the college's preparatory department. In 1857 he became adjunct professor of languages and taught Latin and Greek. He became professor of Latin two years later. In 1860 he took a leave of absence to study at the Universities of Berlin and Leipzig, but he abandoned plans to take a German doctorate and returned to Virginia in 1862. There he enlisted in the Richmond Howitzers, an artillery unit in the Confederate army. He became a sergeant major and served until the end of the war, seeing considerable action but escaping injury.

After the war Blair resumed teaching at Hampden-Sydney. In 1871 he took on the additional responsibility of teaching German. Pupils remembered him affectionately and gratefully as an exacting and well-respected teacher. Those who went on to graduate study in the classics enhanced his and the college's reputation by their thorough preparation. Prodigiously learned, Blair sought to inculcate in his pupils some of his own elegance and finesse in the use of language. Despite a crushing teaching load and the lack of a nearby research library, he succeeded in publishing a few reviews and one seminally important book. *Latin Pronunciation: An Inquiry into the Proper Sounds of the Latin Language during the Classical Period* (1874), with its exhaustive and judicious treatment of the sources, established him as a scholar of the first rank. Along with the work of the eminent Basil Lanneau Gildersleeve at the University of Virginia, Blair's book settled the still-standard conventions of the "European method" for the pronunciation of nonecclesiastical Latin in America. He received an honorary Litt.D. from Washington and Lee University in 1883.

Blair turned down several invitations to take the chair of Latin at larger, better-equipped institutions. When Johns Hopkins University was organized in 1875, Gildersleeve moved there from Charlottesville as the founding professor of Greek and approved the president's suggestion that Blair join the faculty as Gildersleeve's Latin "yoke-fellow." Blair declined the offer. His devotion to Hampden-Sydney also showed in his substantial generosity to the school. He gave the college a collection of photographs of classical sites, purchased on a visit to Europe in the 1890s, and he took the extraordinary step of personally paying an assistant (the college being unable to afford one) when his eyesight began to deteriorate. Most of the other faculty members were close friends, his former teachers, or his former pupils. This congenial society provided the perfect milieu for the retiring and affable Blair, who was regarded by acquaintances as the archetypal Virginia gentleman. Having inherited considerable wealth, he dispensed hospitality at his home to colleagues, campus visitors, and students alike.

Blair taught without interruption until 1896, when he retired because of irreversibly failing vision and was elected professor emeritus. He served as clerk of the faculty during the 1889–1890 academic year. When he retired, his friends and pupils presented an oil portrait of him to the college, where it still hangs. Blair moved his family to Richmond in 1899 to live closer to the medical specialists he needed for treatment of his eyes.

On 27 April 1874 Blair had married Ellen Donnell Smith, of Baltimore. Their one child, Ellen Donnell Codrington Blair, became prominent in Richmond society and championed several social causes during the early years of the twentieth century. In 1931 Blair's daughter endowed the Walter Blair Professorship of Latin at Hampden-Sydney College. Walter Blair died of uremia in Atlantic City, New Jersey, on 12 September 1909 and was buried in Hollywood Cemetery in Richmond.

Tyler, *Encyclopedia*, Special Limited Supplement (1929), 55–57; *NCAB*, 16:142; Louisa Coleman Gordon Blair, *Blairs of Richmond, Virginia: The Descendants of Reverend John Durburrow Blair and Mary Winston Blair, His Wife* (1933), 46–47, 121–122 (por.); Blair family Bible records, VHS; Ward W. Briggs Jr., ed., *The Letters of Basil Lanneau Gildersleeve* (1987), 68; William H. Whiting Jr., *The Professors at Hampden-Sydney College, 1877–1880: The Recollections of One of Their Students* [ca. 1934], 14–19; John Luster Brinkley, *On This Hill: A Narrative History of Hampden-Sydney College 1774–1994* (1994), esp. 333, 347, 412, 413, 416, 429, 432 (por., 408); Walter Blair, "Instruction, Higher and Lower, in Latin: Translation," *Educational Journal of Virginia* 5 (1873): 49–54; obituary in *Richmond Times-Dispatch*, 14 Sept. 1909; memoir by Richard McIlwaine in *Hampden-Sidney Magazine* 27 (1909): 44–46.

JOHN LUSTER BRINKLEY

BLAKELY, Francis Joseph (3 June 1902–17 October 1956), Catholic priest, was born in Philadelphia, the son of James Drexel Blakely and Mary Kelly Blakely. He attended Ascension Parochial School and Saint Joseph's Preparatory School in Philadelphia and in 1921 graduated from Saint Joseph's College. In 1926 Blakely graduated from Saint Vincent's Seminary in Philadelphia, and on 11 June 1926 he was ordained a priest. He also became an accomplished musician skilled on the organ, piano, and violin. Blakely began his musical studies at the Combs Conservatory and Curtis Institute of Music in Philadelphia and continued them in France at the Conservatoire Nationale de Musique et de Déclamation in Paris and the Benedictine Abbey of Saint Pierre in Solesmes. One of his two sisters also entered the church and became a nun.

Blakely taught at Saint Joseph's College in 1926 and 1927 and at Niagara University in New York beginning in 1928. On 20 December 1938 he became assistant pastor at Sacred Heart Cathedral in Richmond, where he also served as director of music for the Diocese of Richmond and as moderator of the Council of Catholic Women. In July 1944 he was appointed administrator of the Catholic Church of the Holy Comforter in Charlottesville and in 1945 became pastor of the parish. He established the Newman Club at the University of Virginia and taught a course in music, perhaps the first Catholic priest to teach at the university.

Blakely became pastor of Saint Mary's Church in Norfolk in June 1949, and for the next seven years contributed materially to the high quality of the city's church music. In 1952 he was transferred to Blessed Sacrament Catholic Church in Norfolk. The parish had no school, and Blakely initiated a fund-raising campaign to construct a school and parish house. He successfully appealed to members of Norfolk's Protestant and Jewish congregations for funds, to building-supply firms for materials, and to members of Norfolk's labor unions, who provided many free hours of construction work. Such donations accounted for more than half of the $175,000 cost of the school. The two-story school was erected in less than four months, and when it opened in September 1953 it was referred to as "Father Blakely's Miracle School."

The parochial schools of the Diocese of Richmond then enrolled more than 21,000 students. The Catholic school system in Virginia was racially segregated, with separate parochial schools for African American parishes, a parallel to the legally segregated public school system. The same arrangement prevailed in many other southern states, although several southern dioceses desegregated their parochial schools early in the 1950s. In the first part of May 1954, a few days before the United States Supreme Court ruled in *Brown* v. *Board of Education of Topeka, Kansas*, that racial segregation in public school systems was unconstitutional, the Diocese of Richmond announced that African American pupils would be admitted to previously all-white Catholic high schools. The policy applied not only to cities like Roanoke, where there had been no Catholic high school for African Americans, but also to cities like Norfolk, where the church had sponsored one or more black high schools.

Blakely had already quietly begun the desegregation of one of Norfolk's parochial elementary schools. He had admitted an African American student to the new Blessed Sacrament School in November 1953, even though the student was too young to attend classes when first enrolled. When Blakely's action attracted public notice in July 1954, he explained that the "policy of making Catholic education available to all Catholics is as old as the Catholic Church itself. I couldn't imagine myself rejecting any Catholic who applied for such education, whether he were a Negro, an Oriental or an Indian." The desegregation of the Catholic schools that Blakely began and that the Diocese of Richmond encouraged could have served as a model for the state's political leaders had they chosen to desegregate the public schools of Virginia rather than resist enforcement of the Supreme Court's ruling.

Francis Joseph Blakely died of complications resulting from cirrhosis of the liver in De Paul Hospital in Norfolk on 17 October 1956. He was buried in Holy Sepulcher Cemetery in Philadelphia.

Career documented in files of Diocese of Richmond; "Miracle School" described in *Norfolk Virginian-Pilot*, 18 Oct. 1953 (por.), and *Catholic Virginian*, 30 Oct. 1953; desegregation covered in *Catholic Virginian*, 21 May, 16 July, 24 Sept. 1954, *Norfolk Ledger-Dispatch*, 15 July 1954, *Norfolk Virginian-Pilot*, 16 July 1954, and *Norfolk Journal and Guide*, 24 July 1954; obituaries in *Norfolk Ledger-Dispatch*, 17 Oct. 1956, *Norfolk Virginian-Pilot*, 18 Oct. 1956, and *Catholic Virginian*, 26 Oct. 1956; editorial tribute stressing church music in *Norfolk Virginian-Pilot*, 19 Oct. 1956.

STEPHEN S. MANSFIELD

BLAKEY, Angus Rucker (3 September 1816–3 February 1896), member of the Convention of 1861, was born in Madison County, the eldest of two sons and two daughters of James D. Blakey, a farmer, and Margaret Rucker Blakey. He attended the University of Virginia for the 1834–1835 school year and then read law under Judge Philip Pendleton Barbour.

After his studies A. R. Blakey, as he was known throughout his professional life, practiced law in Greene, Madison, and Orange Counties. He served as commonwealth's attorney of Greene County from 1838 to 1850 and of Madison County from 1843 to 1864. On 12 December 1844 he married Jane Eliza Johnston. They had four sons and two daughters.

Blakey had joined the Order of the Sons of Temperance by 1847 and promoted the temperance cause by giving speeches and distributing literature. In the early 1850s he contributed money and land toward the construction of Orange and Madison Church, the first Presbyterian Church in Madison County. On 1 April 1854 Blakey and his wife deeded the lot to the church's board of trustees, on which Blakey served.

By 1860 Blakey was a successful attorney with considerable wealth. That year he valued his real estate holdings at close to $19,000 and his personal estate, which included four slaves, at nearly $25,000. Madison County voters elected Blakey as their delegate to the secession convention that assembled in Richmond on 13 February 1861.

Blakey played a small but consequential role at the convention, where he voted in favor of secession. He spoke on state sovereignty, the election of representatives to the Confederate Congress, the issuance of treasury notes by the commonwealth, and the removal of the seal of secrecy from the convention's proceedings. In March he twice chastised the chairman of the Committee on Federal Relations for attempting to limit discussion by the delegates. Declaring that his constituents rejected "a Black Republican Union," on 1 April 1861 Blakey presented several resolutions in favor of separation. On 24 April he offered two successful amendments to the election schedule for ratification of the secession ordinance, providing for absentee voting by members of the military, and he also carried a motion suspending the upcoming election for Virginia's representatives to the United States Congress.

During the early years of the Civil War Blakey remained in Madison County, where chronic diseases of the throat and liver kept him out of military service. At the convention he had proposed an ordinance, eventually tabled, that would have regulated the salt trade to prevent extortionate pricing, but he apparently speculated in that and other commodities himself and encouraged a nephew to do the same. In January 1864 Blakey moved his family to Rockbridge County, and on 16 April he enrolled in

Lexington in Company B, Rockbridge County Reserves. In that capacity he helped collect the tobacco tithe in neighboring Nelson County. In December Blakey became a clerk in the Enrolling Office in Rockbridge County, a position which he held until the end of the war. In August 1865 he received a presidential pardon.

Later in 1865 Blakey and his family settled in Charlottesville, where he practiced law and championed the University of Virginia. In 1872 he and several other men successfully called for the incorporation of the Society of the Alumni of the University of Virginia, and Blakey was a charter member of its executive committee.

Beginning with the inaugural issue of 10 April 1873, Blakey helped revive the moribund *Charlottesville Jeffersonian Republican*, serving as associate publisher and senior editor. Although he emphasized that the weekly was not a party organ, during the next ten years he filled the editorial page with appeals on behalf of the Conservatives, Funders, and Democrats and with denunciations of the Republicans and Readjusters that were sometimes accompanied by race-baiting imagery typical of the period. Reflecting the paper's efforts to succeed as a family publication, it featured a column of poetry on the front page, provided detailed coverage of the university in particular and education in general, and once encouraged its female readers to shun suitors who neglected to vote.

Eventually Blakey handed over control of the *Jeffersonian Republican* to his son James Blakey. On 14 May 1884 Blakey and his partners leased the paper to the younger Blakey and William H. Prout, and James Blakey became publisher in his own right in April 1886. A. R. Blakey initially offered editorial guidance, but father and son soon fell out over the issue of alcohol consumption. James Blakey's zeal to prohibit the liquor trade surpassed his father's more moderate temperance views, and the son attacked his father as only a "theoretical" temperance supporter in a 26 April 1886 extra sponsored by the Charlottesville Local-Option Alliance. In August 1886 the elder Blakey and the Grape and Fruit Growers' Association took up the gauntlet by launching a new monthly, the *Charlottesville Grape and Fruit Growers Advocate*. As editor-in-chief Blakey defended the use of fruit to make alcoholic beverages. Not only did Prohibition invade privacy and threaten Virginia's economy, Blakey argued, it was also immoral and "subversive of the doctrines of Jesus Christ." The *Grape and Fruit Growers Advocate* also contained gardening and farming advice columns, recipes, and other items typical of agricultural journals of the day.

Blakey and his son appear to have reconciled by the end of the decade. On 27 November 1889 James Blakey announced a merger between the *Jeffersonian Republican* and the *Fruit and Grape Grower*, the later name of his father's monthly. Angus Rucker Blakey died in Charlottesville on 3 February 1896 and was buried in Maplewood Cemetery there.

Birth date in French Biographies; Angus R. Blakey Papers, Duke; Census, Madison Co., 1850, 1860 (Lists of Inhabitants and Slave Schedules), and Albemarle Co., 1870; Bernard Buckner Blakey, *A Blakey Book* (1977), 137–138; Rockbridge Co. Marriage Register; Margaret G. Davis, *Madison County, Virginia: A Revised History* (1977), 280; Reese and Gaines, *Proceedings of 1861 Convention*, 2:544–547, 653–655, 744–751, 3:652–658, 4:415–418, 642–643, 650–656, 717–719, 765–766, 772; Reese, *Journals and Papers of 1861 Convention*, vol. 2, n.p., 23 Nov. 1861 Ordinance Concerning Salt; Compiled Service Records; Presidential Pardons; Bruce, *University of Virginia*, 4:202; *Charlottesville Jeffersonian Republican*, 8 Oct. 1873, 14 May 1884, 26 Apr. 1886, 27 Nov. 1889; *Grape and Fruit Growers Advocate*, Aug. 1886; obituary in *Richmond Dispatch*, 4 Feb. 1896.

ANTOINETTE G. VAN ZELM

BLANCHFIELD, Florence Aby (1 April 1882–12 May 1971), superintendent of the Army Nurse Corps, was born in Riverton, Warren County, to Joseph Plunkett Blanchfield, a stonemason and railroad worker, and Mary Louvenia Anderson Blanchfield, a practical nurse. Blanchfield was the second of three daughters, all of whom became nurses, and fifth of nine children. The family moved frequently but resided in the village of Oranda in Shenandoah County long enough for Blanchfield to attend local schools and the private Oranda Institute in 1898–1899.

Motivated to pursue a career in nursing by the death of one of her brothers, Blanchfield enrolled in the South Side Hospital Training School for Nurses in Pittsburgh. After graduating in 1906, she worked in Baltimore as a private-duty nurse and studied at the sanatorium of Howard Atwood Kelly, a key figure in the development of the field of gynecology and a professor of medicine at Johns Hopkins University. Blanchfield entered medical administration, serving from 1909 to 1913 as director of the nursing school and superintendent of the fifty-six-bed Suburban General Hospital in Allegheny County, Pennsylvania. She left that hospital to broaden her knowledge of nursing, working for a year in the Panama Canal Zone and then attending business school for two years while employed as emergency surgical nurse for a large plant of the United States Steel Corporation near Pittsburgh. She returned to Suburban General in 1916.

When the United States entered World War I in 1917, Blanchfield volunteered for the Army Nurse Corps and served in France as acting chief nurse at American Expeditionary Force Camp Hospital 15 from December 1917 to January 1919. With the war's end she returned temporarily to her former post at Suburban General but rejoined the ANC in January 1920 and became a first lieutenant in June when ANC officers achieved ranks similar to army officers but without the same authority, pay, or privileges. Her career in the small, peacetime military took her to hospitals in Michigan, Indiana, California, the Philippines, Washington, D.C., Georgia, Missouri, and China before she was assigned in 1935 to the surgeon general's staff in Washington. Four years later, as the United States prepared for war, she was promoted to the rank of captain and made the assistant to the superintendent of the ANC.

After the United States entered World War II, Blanchfield received a temporary army commission as lieutenant colonel on 13 March 1942. Although she and the superintendent, a colonel, wore the insignia of their ranks, they were denied the pay of that grade, a decision that exacerbated the long-standing anger of ANC members with the army's refusal to grant nurses full military status. The number of nurses on active duty nearly doubled in the first six months after Pearl Harbor, and the ANC hurried to establish training programs for the newcomers. Meanwhile the superintendent fell ill late in January 1943, and Blanchfield became acting superintendent. On 1 June 1943, following her predecessor's retirement, Colonel Florence Blanchfield took the oath as the seventh superintendent of the Army Nurse Corps.

Blanchfield's most important task was to oversee efficiently the vast increase in the ANC's numbers necessitated by a burgeoning military. Rather than create a new Army School of Nursing, civilian nursing schools were authorized to prepare cadet nurses, who then entered active service via new basic-training schools proposed by Blanchfield, where they learned military regulations. She assigned surgical nurses to hospitals near the front lines for the first time. When the war ended in 1945, more than 57,000 army nurses were serving in domestic and overseas hospitals.

Blanchfield campaigned for permanent rank and status in the army for the ANC. Without rank, she argued, nurses had no clearly defined role, and the ANC might be supplanted by the new Women's Army Corps, whose officers did receive permanent commissions. Through articles, interviews, and effective lobbying, she pressed her case. On 22 June 1944 Congress granted army nurses temporary army commissions with full pay and privileges of their ranks, but only for the duration of the war plus six months. After the war they were also made eligible for all veterans' benefits, but not until 16 April 1947, with passage of the Army-Navy Nurse Act, did nurses gain permanent commissioned-officer status. Blanchfield received army serial number N-1 and thus became the first woman to hold a permanent commission in the U.S. Army, which was presented to her by General Dwight D. Eisenhower on 18 July 1947.

On 30 September 1947 Blanchfield retired after nearly three decades of active duty. The army had awarded her the Distinguished Service Medal on 14 June 1945 for her leadership during the war, and the International Red Cross recognized her in 1951 with the Florence Nightingale Medal, nursing's highest honor. Her longtime advocacy of sports for women was honored in 1956 when the all-army women's tennis singles championship trophy was named for her. In retirement she lived in Arlington with a sister and brother-in-law and collaborated with Mary W. Standlee on an unpublished history of the Army Nurse Corps. Florence Aby Blanchfield died of heart disease on 12 May 1971 at Walter Reed General Hospital in Washington, D.C., and was buried with full military honors in Arlington National Cemetery. A military hospital named after her was dedicated in September 1982 at Fort Campbell, Kentucky, the first such facility named for a woman.

Records of Army Nurse Corps, U.S. Army Military History Institute, Carlisle, Pa.; Records of Surgeon General's Office, RG 112, NARA; Florence Aby Blanchfield Collection, Nursing Archives, Boston University Library; BVS Birth Register, Warren Co.; *Current Biography* (1943): 53–55 (por.); Vern L. Bullough, Olga Maranjian Church, and Alice P. Stein, eds., *American Nursing: A Biographical Dictionary* (1988), 36–41; Robert V. Piemonte and Cindy Gurney, eds., *Highlights in the History of the Army Nurse Corps* (1987), 13–15, 20–21; Elizabeth A. Shields, "A History of the United States Army Nurse Corps (Female): 1901–1937" (Ed.D. diss., Columbia University Teachers College, 1980), 111; Susanne Teepe Gaskins, "G.I. Nurses at War: Gender and Professionalization in the Army Nurse Corps during World War II" (Ph.D. diss., University of California at Riverside, 1994), 106–121, 311–314; Barbara Brooks Tomblin, *G.I. Nightingales: The Army Nurse Corps in World War II* (1996), 187–189, 202, 207; *New York Times*, 16 Mar. 1942, 11 Feb., 2 June 1943, 15 June 1945, 19 July 1947; Florence A. Blanchfield, "New Status in Military Nursing: Peacetime Opportunities in the Army Nurse Corps," *American Journal of Nursing* 47 (1947): 603–605; obituaries in *New York Times*, 13 May 1971, and *Washington Post*, 14 May 1971 (por.).

D'ANN CAMPBELL

Library of Congress Cataloging-in-Publication Data

Dictionary of Virginia biography / editors, John T. Kneebone . . . [et al.].
p. cm.
Includes bibliographical references and index.
Contents: v. 1. Aaroe–Blanchfield
ISBN 0-88490-189-0
1. Virginia—Biography—Dictionaries. I. Kneebone, John T.
F225.D54 1998 98-39746
920.0755—dc21 CIP

Dictionary of Virginia Biography, Volume One: Aaroe–Blanchfield was designed by Sara Daniels Bowersox of the Library of Virginia. Page layout was produced by Paris Ashton-Bressler and Frances James of the Virginia Department of General Services, Office of Graphic Communications, using Apple Power Macintosh 7600/120 and QuarkXPress 3.32. Text was composed in Times Roman and Italic. Printed on acid-free, Glatfelter Natural, 60-lb. text, by Braun-Brumfield, Inc., Ann Arbor, Michigan.